Consumer Litigation

and Insurance Defense

Second Revised Edition

Willy E. Rice

cognella
San Diego, CA

First published in the United States of America in 2011 by Cognella, a division of University Readers, Inc.

Front Cover:
Cover design by Monica Hui Hekman

13 12 11 10 09   1 2 3 4 5

Printed in the United States of America

ISBN: 978-160927-274-6

cognella

www.cognella.com 800.200.3908

Contents

PART II
CONSUMER LITIGATION AND INSURANCE DEFENSE UNDER UNIFORM INSURANCE ACTS AND COMMON LAW

Introduction

Teaching Torts Without Insurance: A Second-Best Solution
45 St. Louis U. L.J. 857 (2001)
David A. Fischer and Robert H. Jerry, II

Teachers, scholars and practitioners have long appreciated the symbiotic relationship of torts and insurance. Indeed, the assertion that tort law and insurance law are intertwined is utterly unremarkable; many commentators have observed that tort law cannot be understood if the business of insurance and the law regulating it is ignored, and that insurance law cannot be understood if tort law is ignored. Several generations of law students have read casebooks, which in varying degrees pay homage to the connections between torts and insurance. Many law review articles and noteworthy books (or portions thereof) have plumbed the tort-insurance relationship.

Although one of us has taught Torts for many years but has never taught Insurance, and the other of us has taught Insurance for many years but has never taught Torts, both of us have both long believed that each of our respective principal subjects is diminished if it is studied without the rich context provided by the other's primary field. Neither of us would operate a motor vehicle, set up a business, or venture very far from home without insurance; we suggest that it is just as unwise to teach torts without insurance.

We do not dwell, however, on what is lost in torts if insurance is ignored. Rather, we examine how the study of torts is enriched when insurance concepts play a role in students' analysis. Our discussion is divided into two parts. Part I offers a "macro" perspective on the connections between tort and insurance. . . . Although many interesting points are embedded in the voluminous array of teaching materials and scholarship on the torts-insurance intersection, we underscore two particularly important ones. First, whether tort law's substantive doctrines successfully implement tort law's underlying policies cannot be assessed without considering the influence of insurance. Second, the impact of insurance on the tort litigation process is so profound as to make it impossible to understand tort litigation without understanding the structure of the liability insurance contract.

* * *

The conclusion that insurance has had — and will continue to have —a profound influence on tort theory and process seems, at least to us, beyond serious dispute. Moreover, that insurance can either further or frustrate tort law's underlying objectives is equally apparent. Sometimes the impact of insurance on tort theory or process is obvious, and at other times the impact is subtle and indirect. Sometimes, insurance takes a prominent and explicit role in a court's formulation of a substantive rule. At other times insurance considerations lurk in the background, providing the unspoken motives for many of the parties' tactical decisions, including who to sue, what claims to assert, and what strategies to employ in the litigation.

* * *

In a broader context, tort law works with a wide variety of private and public insurance mechanisms — including health, disability, and life insurance; first-party automobile insurance coverages; Medicare; Medicaid; the Social Security Disability and Social Security Income programs; Workers Compensation systems in the fifty states; and a number of federal programs, ranging from the Veterans' benefits programs, the Black Lung Benefits Program, and more — to compensate victims of loss. When the boundaries of the inquiry are defined as "loss compensation," tort law's compensatory scheme is dwarfed many times over by these other compensation mechanisms. . . .

It is, of course, naive to think that any first-year law school course can even begin to approach a meaningful study of these diverse systems of loss compensation. We suggest, however, that at some point in the torts course students should at least be alerted to the general contours of the big picture. And it is here that exploration of the tort-insurance intersection may have some of its greatest value: by insisting that first-year law students reflect upon the impact of insurance law on tort doctrine and practice, one demonstrates that acquiring an understanding of the substantive principles in a first-year course is only a first step in a life-long effort to appreciate the rich doctrinal relationships that permeate the entirety of the American legal system.

Professors Fischer and Jerry's observations are sound and their concern and interests are clear. But, a stronger statement is warranted. Simply put, too much segregation or "ghettoization" appears among law courses. However, to be fair and in light of modern necessity, law schools must segregate courses into large categories. Traditionally, "civil" and "criminal" courses comprise the two largest, primary categories. Second, within those primary categories, there are two larger subcategories — "procedural" and "substantive" courses. Third, among the "substantive civil courses," one finds more division. Law curricula contain tort-based and contract-based offerings. And, among these latter civil-law courses, one discovers large bodies of both common-law and statutory rules.

Of course, one could argue that the alleged "ghettoization" of law courses is not as pronounced as this author or Professors Fischer and Jerry suggest. Many law professors' interests, research and writings center on legal issues and conflicts that cut across all bodies of law. And, those academicians certainly construct and offer "hybrid," "advanced" or "specialty courses. "Consumer Law" and "Insurance Law" are excellent examples of such hybrid courses.

This casebook falls into this latter category. And it has two parts and multiple chapters. Part I presents cases and materials that highlight consumers' litigation under Texas Deceptive Trade Practices Act (DTPA). And Part II covers consumers' litigation under the Texas Insurance Code. However, at best, these general descriptions of the cases and materials in Parts I and II are superficial. And the reason is not complicated.

Some consumers purchase billions of dollars worth of insurance annually under a variety of contracts. And when insurers breach those contracts, the resulting causes of action may sound in contract or in tort. For example, a tort-based cause of action is likely to occur if the insurer breaches its common-law duty of good faith and faith dealings — which is associated with "special contractual relationships." Conversely, many other consumers and sellers form trillions of transactions involving the sale of goods and services. And when conflicts arise between those buyers and sellers, consumers may commence actions sounding in tort, sounding in contract as well as actions under the DTPA and Insurance Code.

Therefore, although the materials in this text carefully review the DTPA and Texas Insurance Code, this casebook also presents even broader discussions of numerous procedural and substantive issues as well as common-law rules that appear in DTPA and insurance litigation nationwide.

One final point must be stressed. Undeniably, teaching torts, contracts or any law course without a healthy measure of insurance law is problematic and nonsensical. But consider this. The DTPA is clearly a statute; and, the causes of action that consumers may commence under the DTPA sound in tort. Therefore, teaching insurance law or the DTPA without encouraging students to understand and appreciate the extremely important interrelationship between these two bodies of laws is *prima facie* evidence of gross negligence. This text has been constructed, therefore, to prevent such negligence.

PART I

Consumer Litigation Under Uniform Deceptive Trade Practices Acts and the Common Law

Chapter One: Proof of a Person's Standing to Sue as a Consumer

Before a plaintiff can secure damages or any other remedy under various theories of recovery, a plaintiff must establish a *prima facie case*. For example, to establish a breach-of-contract action, a plaintiff must prove 1) the existence of a valid contract; 2) consideration; 3) a material breach; and 4) proof that the breach was the cause in fact and proximate cause of an injury and damages. *Burns v. American National Ins. Co*., 280 S.W. 762, 765 (Tex. Com. App. 1926). Similarly, "a plaintiff has the burden [to prove] all elements of his cause of action under the DTPA." *Farmers & Merchants State Bank v. Ferguson,* 617 S.W.2d 918, 920 (Tex. 1981).

Section 17.50(a)(1) of the DTPA provides that a consumer may maintain an action against a defendant for the latter's violating §17.46. Section 17.46(a) outlaws any "[f]alse, misleading, or deceptive acts or practices in the conduct of any trade or commerce." Section 17.46(b) lists significantly more unlawfully false, misleading, or deceptive violations. However, Section 17.45 (4) defines a consumer this way:

[A]n individual, partnership, corporation, this state, or a subdivision or agency of this state who seeks or acquires by purchase or lease, any goods or services, except that the term does not include a business consumer that has assets of $25 million or more, or that is owned or controlled by a corporation or entity with assets of $25 million or more.

This chapter explores the various interpretations of the phrases in Section 17.45(4). To be sure, the rulings of the courts of Texas and the Court of Appeals for the Fifth Circuit's rulings are not harmonious vis-à-vis identifying the probative evidence required to prove one's "consumer" status under the DTPA.

A. *Proof of the Element — An "Intent to Seek or Acquire"*

Melody Home Manufacturing Company v. Barnes
741 S.W.2d 349 (Tex. 1987)

The court's opinion of June 17, 1987 is withdrawn and the following is substituted therefor.

This is a Deceptive Trade Practices-Consumer Protection Act (DTPA) implied warranty case. Lonnie and Donna Barnes sued Melody Home Manufacturing Company under the DTPA for breach of an implied warranty that repairs would be done in a good and workmanlike manner and for other DTPA violations. The jury found that Melody Home knowingly breached this implied warranty and awarded discretionary damages. The trial court rendered judgment for the Barneses and the court of appeals affirmed the judgment of the trial court. We affirm the judgment of the court of appeals.

In 1979, the Barneses ordered a modular pre-fabricated home from Melody Home. Their home was delivered in May 1980. After the Barneses moved in, they continually experienced puddles and dampness inside the house. Over two years after moving in, they discovered that a sink was not connected to the drain in one of the interior walls.

The continual leak caused severe damage to the home's sheetrock, insulation, and flooring. The Barneses told Melody Home about the problem. Workmen from Melody Home came out twice, but their efforts were unsatisfactory, and additional damages were caused by the repair. The workmen cut and tore linoleum while attempting to repair the home. Moreover, they failed to reconnect the washing machine drain, causing the house to flood with resulting damage to the floors, cabinets, and carpeting.

The Barneses then filed this DTPA implied warranty suit against Melody Home. The jury found that Melody Home failed to construct the home in a good and workmanlike manner. The jury further found that Melody Home breached its implied warranty to repair in a good and workmanlike manner and that this breach was knowing. Based on its finding that Melody Home knowingly breached the implied warranty, the jury awarded $5,000 in discretionary damages under Tex.Bus. & Com.Code Ann. § 17.50(b)(1).

Melody Home appealed the award of DTPA discretionary damages. The court of appeals held that the sale of a service carries with it the implied warranty that the service will be performed in a skillful and workmanlike manner and affirmed the judgment of the trial court.

Melody Home first challenges the Barneses' status as consumers with regard to the repairs. DTPA plaintiffs must qualify as consumers, as that term is defined in Tex.Bus. & Com.Code Ann. § 17.45(4) to maintain a private cause of action under section 17.50 of the Act. *Flenniken v. Longview Bank & Trust Co.,* 661 S.W.2d 705, 706 (Tex.1983). We have recognized at least two requirements to establish DTPA consumer status. First, the plaintiffs must have sought or acquired goods or services by purchase or lease. *Sherman Simon Enter., Inc. v. Lorac Service Corp.,* 724 S.W.2d 13,

15 (Tex. 1987); *Cameron v. Terrell & Garrett, Inc.,* 618 S.W.2d 535, 539 (Tex.1981). Second, the goods or services purchased or leased must form the basis of the complaint.

It is uncontroverted that the Barneses purchased goods and thus were "consumers" when they originally bought the home. Melody Home's attempts to repair the defects in the home were, by definition, "services" under the DTPA. Section 17.45(2) defines "services" as "work, labor or service purchased ... for use including services furnished in connection with the sale or *repair* of goods." (emphasis added). Melody Home argues that the Barneses were not "consumers" with regard to the repair services because they did not purchase them with cash. The absence of a cash transfer is not determinative because DTPA plaintiffs establish their standing as consumers in terms of their relationship to a transaction, not by their contractual relationship with the defendant. *Flenniken,* 661 S.W.2d at 707. The question then is whether the Barneses "purchased" the repair services within the meaning of the Act.

In *Humber v. Morton,* 426 S.W.2d 554 (Tex.1968), this court held that a builder/vendor impliedly warrants to a purchaser that a building constructed for residential use has been constructed in a good and workmanlike manner and is suitable for human habitation. *Evans v. J. Stiles, Inc.,* 689 S.W.2d 399, 400 (Tex.1985). When the Barneses discovered the defect in their home, they had the option to immediately sue for money damages or give Melody Home the opportunity to cure the problem. The parties' choices to allow and make repairs relate back to the original purchase and were a continuation of that transaction.

The Barneses did not lose their consumer status by allowing Melody Home to attempt to correct the problem and by deferring their lawsuit. Under Melody Home's argument the Barneses would be penalized by losing their consumer status because they allowed repairs. The law encourages dispute resolution prior to litigation. *See* Tex.Bus. & Com. Code Ann. § 17.50A . Accordingly we hold that the Barneses "purchased" the repair services.

Houston Livestock Show and Rodeo, Inc. v. Hamrick
125 S.W.3d 555
(Tex. App.-Austin 2003)

Appellant Houston Livestock Show and Rodeo, Inc. (Livestock Show) appeals from a judgment awarding appellees — Leslie Hamrick and her parents, T.L. Hamrick and Connie Hamrick, Jimmy Barton and his parents, Craig Barton and Jacque Barton, and Kevin Copeland — damages . . . Appellees sued the Livestock Show and the Texas Veterinary Medical Diagnostic Laboratory (Lab) alleging breach of contract, conversion, negligence, gross negligence, defamation, intentional or reckless infliction of emotional distress, and [for violations under] the Texas Deceptive Trade Practices Act (DTPA), Tex. Bus. & Com. Code Ann. §§ 17.41-.63]

The jury returned a favorable verdict for appellees against the Livestock Show for the DTPA violations and defamation, as well as negligence and gross negligence against the Lab. The jury, however, found absence of malice as to the Livestock Show's defamatory statements. . . .The

Livestock Show brings this appeal .... challenging the... consumer status of the parents... We will reform the district-court judgment and, as reformed, affirm.

Factual and Procedural Background

In 1991 Leslie Hamrick, Jimmy Barton, and Kevin Copeland, all high-school students, entered farm animals they had raised in the Junior Livestock Show competition at the Livestock Show. They vied with other competitors in various animal classes for a chance at winning the contest and auction proceeds from the sale of their animals. As prescribed by Livestock Show rules, the Exhibitors were members of their schools' FFA or 4-H programs, operating under the guidance of the Texas Education Agency (the "TEA"). Their FFA and 4-H programs, and to a certain extent their parents, supervised the Exhibitors' raising of their animals. Hamrick and Barton entered lambs, and Copeland entered a steer in the Junior Livestock Show. Each won their respective class, entitling them to participate in the Livestock Show's junior auction. The competition's rules required the animals to undergo drug testing for illegal substances, commonly used to improve an animal's appearance. The drug tests revealed illegal substances in all three animals, and the Livestock Show disqualified the Exhibitors. This action arises from the drug testing procedures and the Livestock Show's actions toward appellees.

Junior Livestock Show rule 16 states that "unethically fitted livestock" are prohibited, and exhibitors showing such animals would be disqualified and "barred from future competition" at the Livestock Show. The Livestock Show instituted animal drug testing to "teach and reward 4-H and FFA students for good animal husbandry," while "endeavor[ing] to protect the public from consuming tainted meat." Moreover, the rule warned exhibitors that the Livestock Show's drug test results were final and without recourse.

Livestock Show applications and entry fees submitted by Agricultural Science Teachers and County Extension Agents included the signature of both instructor and exhibitor. The reverse side of each application included a waiver of liability and a statement notifying the signatories that the Livestock Show had the right to test the animals for medication or drugs. Below this statement, the application contained lines on which the exhibitor and the exhibitor's parent or guardian signed. The exhibitors and their parents or guardians also signed and returned a notarized form stating that they would abide by the rules, and that no unauthorized substances had been given to the animals. In the event an animal required testing, the exhibitor and his or her parent or guardian would witness the collection of a urine specimen from the animal and sign another form acknowledging that they were present for the collection. Pending a successful drug test, the prizes and auction proceeds, less the Livestock Show's commission, would be disbursed.

Appellees paid the appropriate entry fees and submitted their applications. Each won ribbons in their respective class, entitling them to participate in the auction. At auction, Hamrick's lamb brought $12,020, Barton's lamb brought $1520, and Copeland's steer brought $5060. Pursuant to its drug testing rules, the Livestock Show obtained a urine sample from Barton's lamb on February 27. The next day, the Livestock Show collected urine samples from Hamrick's lamb and Copeland's steer. The Livestock Show split the samples into two parts, with the Lab testing one half, while the Livestock Show retained and froze the remainder. The Lab tested the specimens following the auction, and the Livestock Show retained the auction proceeds pending review of the results.

The Livestock Show selected the Lab, located at Texas A & M University, to test the urine samples. The testing procedures involved two different sets of tests: one set to detect lasix or furosemide, and another to detect clenbuterol.[FN8] Two sections of the Lab were involved in the animals' drug testing. To detect lasix, the drug testing section conducted an enzyme-linked immunosorbent assay ("ELISA") screening test, after which the toxicology section conducted a high-performance liquid chromatography ("HPLC") confirmatory test. The Lab used the ELISA test to screen a large number of samples, narrowing the field by indicating which samples required a more detailed analysis. In 1991 the Lab selected a then-existing ELISA test to screen animal urine for lasix. The ELISA tests conducted on Hamrick's and Barton's samples indicated the likely presence of lasix, which triggered the need for a confirmatory test. The toxicology section then conducted the HPLC with fluorescence. The HPLC indicated the presence of lasix in both samples.

The Lab employed a different test to screen the urine samples for clenbuterol. This test was specifically designed by the Lab and used only that year. In 1991 clenbuterol was first making an appearance in livestock show animals as a way to improve their appearance. Accordingly, the Livestock Show allocated funds to the Lab for development of a screening test capable of detecting clenbuterol. The Lab's head of toxicology, Dr. John Reagor, along with a "Dr. Spainhauer," developed a procedure utilizing the Lab's gas chromatograph with flame ionization detection to detect the presence of clenbuterol in animal urine. The procedure was represented to have been adapted from current scientific literature. This test confirmed the presence of clenbuterol in Copeland's steer.

Following the confirmatory testing, the Lab, on March 10, reported to the Livestock Show that Hamrick's lamb had tested positive. Nine days later, the Lab reported that Barton's lamb and Copeland's steer had both tested positive as well. Thereafter, the Livestock Show notified the Exhibitors and their schools that they had been disqualified because of the positive drug tests. Additionally, the Livestock Show informed appellees that they were barred from participating in Houston Livestock Shows for the remainder of their lives. . . .

The procedural history of the case spans more than ten years and the record is extensive. [But ultimately, a] jury found the following in favor of appellees: 1) $300,000 in mental anguish damages; 2) $115,000 in injury-to-reputation damages; 3) $12,020 for Leslie Hamrick's loss of prize money; 4) $190,000 in attorney's fees for trial and appeal; and 5) $630,000 in additional DTPA damages. [Defendants appealed]. . . .

The Parents as Consumers Under the DTPA

[T]he Livestock Show argues that the appellee parents are not consumers for purposes of the DTPA and that there is no evidence or factually insufficient evidence to support their status as consumers. The Livestock Show contends that "[t]he basis of [appellee parents'] complaint is the drug testing performed by the Diagnostic Lab, [and] [t]hat is not a valid basis for a claim against the [Livestock Show] under the DTPA." The Livestock Show argues that the parents sought, acquired, or purchased nothing from the Livestock Show that could form the basis of the complaint and that they were not exhibitors in the show. This Court has previously held that all appellees were consumers under the DTPA . . . .The Livestock Show, however, argues that under the "law of the case" doctrine, this Court could not have rendered judgment on the issue as a matter of law, as appellees assert, because appellees filed no cross-motion for summary judgment on the issue.

The DTPA mandates liberal construction to promote the underlying purpose of the act. Tex. Bus. & Com.Code Ann. § 17.44 (West 2002). A "consumer" under the DTPA is defined as "an individual, partnership, corporation, this state, or a subdivision or agency of this state who seeks or acquires, by purchase or lease, any goods or services." *Id.* § 17.45(4). To qualify as a consumer, the plaintiff must meet two requirements: (1) the person must seek or acquire goods or services by purchase or lease and (2) the goods or services purchased or leased must form the basis of the complaint. *Sherman Simon Enters., Inc. v. Lorac Serv. Corp.,* 724 S.W.2d 13, 14 (Tex.1987); *see also* Tex. Bus. & Com.Code Ann. § 17.45(2) (West 2002) ("'Services' means work, labor, or service purchased or leased for use...."). The word "purchase," in the context of the DTPA, has been defined as the actual transmission of services from one person to another by voluntary act or agreement, founded on valuable consideration. *Hall v. Bean,* 582 S.W.2d 263, 265 (Tex.Civ.App.-Beaumont 1979, no writ). A plaintiff's standing as a consumer is established by its relationship to the transaction, not by a contractual relationship with the defendant. *Flenniken v. Longview Bank & Trust Co.,* 661 S.W.2d 705, 707 (Tex.1983). Whether a plaintiff is a consumer under the DTPA is a question of law for the trial court).

We need not decide whether the law-of-the-case doctrine applies because the district court determined as a matter of law that the parents were consumers, and the evidence adduced at trial supports such holding. The parents were involved in the entire animal-showing process. The parents signed waivers of liability, which approved the Livestock Show's right to test the animals for unauthorized drugs. They also signed a notarized form stating that they would abide by the Livestock Show rules and that no illegal substances had been administered to the animals.

Additionally, when an Exhibitor's animal was subjected to drug testing, an Exhibitor's parent witnessed the taking of the sample, after which the parent signed another form acknowledging that the parents witnessed the event. The parents, as well as the Exhibitors, were subject to the threat of a lifetime banishment from future shows in the event of a disqualification resulting from illegal drug use. The myriad of services that the Livestock Show provided to the Exhibitors and their parents included the use of the facilities for their children, animal judging, drug testing, and the auction. Simply stated, the Exhibitors could not have entered the competition without their parents' express joinder and participation.

We hold that the district court was correct in concluding the parties were consumers because (1) the parents did seek or acquire the services of the Livestock Show, indicated by their authorization, participation, and potential exclusion from all future shows; and (2) the services provided by the Livestock Show form the basis of the complaint. We overrule the Livestock Show's third issue. . . .

Conclusion

We reform the district court's judgment to provide that the court's award of attorney's fees on appeal is made expressly contingent upon the ultimate success of appellees. In all other respects, we affirm the district-court judgment as reformed.

B. *Proof of the Element — An "Intent to Purchase or Lease"*

Kennedy v. Sale
689 S.W.2d 890
(Tex. 1985)

This cause involves the definition of "consumer" under the Texas Deceptive Trade Practice-Consumer Protection Act ("DTPA"). Tex. Bus. & Com. Code Ann. § 17.45(4). The question presented is whether an employee complaining of misrepresentations of the provisions of a group insurance policy is a "consumer," though the employer alone purchased the policy. The court of appeals held that the employee was not a consumer. We reverse the judgment of the court of appeals and affirm that of the trial court.

Francis Kennedy was an employee of the Martin County Hospital District. The Board of Managers of the hospital district decided to change group insurance carriers, from Blue Cross/Blue Shield to Southwest Medical Corporation Trust. J. Woodford Sale was the insurance agent.

After the policy was accepted, but before it went into effect, Sale met with hospital employees to explain the new provisions and benefits, as well as to collect signed enrollment cards from each employee. Kennedy and other employees testified that at this meeting Sale misrepresented the preexisting condition coverage, claiming that the policy offered full coverage without qualification, when in fact the policy provided only $4000 maximum coverage during the first year. Kennedy also testified that had he been correctly informed, he would have enrolled under his wife's group plan, which provided full coverage.

Shortly thereafter, Kennedy underwent surgery for a preexisting condition. The policy paid $4,000; Kennedy brought suit against Sale for the balance of $11,338.21, alleging a violation of the DTPA and common law fraud. The jury found that Sale had misrepresented preexisting condition coverage to Kennedy, but not to the Board of Managers. The trial court rendered judgment for Kennedy on his DTPA cause of action. The court of appeals, with one justice dissenting, reversed this judgment but remanded for a new trial on the common law fraud theory.

The court of appeals held that because Kennedy did not purchase the policy benefits directly from Sale, he was not a "consumer" as defined by the DTPA. In reaching this conclusion, the court of appeals placed substantial reliance on *Delaney Realty, Inc. v. Ozuna,* 593 S.W.2d 797 (Tex.Civ. App.-El Paso), *writ ref'd n.r.e. per curiam,* 600 S.W.2d 780 (Tex.1980). This court, while refusing writ, did not endorse the *Delaney Realty* court's reasoning. 600 S.W.2d 780 (Tex. 1980). Less than one year later, we expressly disapproved the result in *Cameron v. Terrell & Garrett, Inc.*, 618 S.W.2d 535, 539-40 (Tex.1981).

While *Cameron v. Terrell & Garrett, Inc.* is not conclusive on the question here presented, the decision is nonetheless highly instructive. The question presented in *Cameron* was whether a real estate agent could be held in violation of the DTPA where he was neither the buyer nor the seller of the property. In a unanimous opinion, we stated:

> We find no indication in the definition of consumer in section 17.45(4), or any other provision of the Act, that the legislature intended to restrict its application only to deceptive trade practices committed by persons who furnish the goods or services on which the complaint is based. *Nor do we find any indication that the legislature intended to restrict its application by any other similar privity requirement.*" 618 S.W.2d at 540-41 (emphasis added).

This court further stated:

> "The Act is designed to protect consumers from any deceptive trade practice made in connection with the purchase or lease of any goods or services.... To this end, we must give the Act, under the rule of liberal construction, its most comprehensive application possible without doing any violence to its terms."
> *Id.* at 541.

Keeping these principles in mind, we turn to an examination of the instant cause. The DTPA defines "consumer" as "an individual ... who *seeks or acquires by purchase or lease,* any goods or services." Tex.Bus. & Comm. Code Ann. § 17.45(4) (Vernon Supp.1985) (emphasis added). The court of appeals gave two reasons why Kennedy did not qualify as a consumer. First, it was suggested that Kennedy did not "seek or acquire" the policy benefits. While Kennedy did not "seek" the benefits (since the new policy was negotiated by the hospital district's Board of Managers without his input), he most assuredly did "acquire" those benefits when he was covered by the policy's provisions.

The second rationale advanced by the court of appeals is that Kennedy did not "purchase" the policy from Sale, because he paid no consideration to Sale. While the Act's definition of "consumer" includes one who "acquires by purchase or lease," it does not necessarily follow from that language that the consumer must himself be the one who purchases or leases. For example, it could reasonably be said that Kennedy did "acquire" the policy benefits "by purchase," albeit a purchase consummated for his benefit by the hospital district's Board of Managers.

To accept the construction favored by Sale, that only direct purchasers can be consumers, would be to read additional or different language into the DTPA, in contravention of the Act's mandate of liberal construction. The legislature could easily have drafted such a restriction into the definition of "consumer," for example, by use of the words "purchaser or lessee," but did not do so. As this court stated in *Cameron:*

> "[W]e believe every word excluded from a statute must . . . be presumed to have been excluded for a reason. Only when it is necessary to give effect to the clear legislative intent can we insert additional words or requirements into a statutory provision." 618 S.W.2d at 540.

We therefore hold that, under the facts of this case, Francis Kennedy was a consumer and thus entitled to maintain a cause of action under the DTPA. As this court recently stated in *Flenniken v. Longview Bank & Trust Co.,* 661 S.W.2d 705, 707 (Tex. 1983):

> "Privity between the plaintiff and defendant is not a consideration in deciding the plaintiff's status as a consumer under the DTPA.... A plaintiff establishes his standing as a consumer in terms of his relationship to a transaction, not by a contractual relationship with the defendant. The only requirement is that the goods or services sought or acquired by the consumer form the basis of his complaint."

For the foregoing reasons, we reverse the judgment of the court of appeals and affirm the judgment of the trial court.

NOTES & QUESTIONS

1) Citing Texas common law, the Texas Supreme Court has issued a variety of rulings about privity of contract: In *Natividad v. Alexsis, Inc.,* 875 S.W.2d 695, 698 (Tex.1994), the Texas Supreme Court held: If privity of contract does not exist between a plaintiff and an insurer, a special relationship does not exist as a matter of law. Without a special relationship, the insurance company does not owe a duty of good faith and fair dealing.

2) What are the elements of a "special relationship?" In *American Centennial Ins. Co. v. Canal Ins. Co*., 843 S.W.2d 480, 484 (Tex. 1992), the Supreme Court declared: "Under Texas law, attorneys are not ordinarily liable for damages to a nonclient, because privity of contract is absent."

3) In *Garcia v. Texas Instruments, Inc.,* 610 S.W.2d 456, 465 (Tex.1980), the Supreme court held that "privity of contract is not a requirement for a Uniform Commercial Code implied warranty action involving personal injury." *McKisson v. Sales Affiliates, Inc*., 416 S.W.2d 787, 791 (Tex.1967) (citing Texas law and concluding that privity of contract is not required when a cause of action is based upon principles of strict liability in tort).

4) In *Garcia v. Texas Instruments, Inc.***,** 610 S.W.2d 456, 463-464 (Tex. 1980), the Texas Supreme Court discussed the difference between horizontal and vertical privity. One of the problems traditionally involved in products liability litigation has been of privity of contract—i.e., whether there could be recovery against a supplier for injuries caused by a defective product when the person who suffered the injury was not a direct party to the sale, and hence was not in privity of contract with the manufacturer or seller of a defective product. There are two types of

privity of contract. "Vertical privity" includes all parties in the distribution chain from the initial supplier of the product to the ultimate purchaser. "Horizontal privity" describes the relationship between the original supplier and any non-purchasing party who uses or is affected by the product, such as the family of the ultimate purchaser or a bystander.

Wellborn v. Sears, Roebuck & Company
970 F.2d 1420
(5th Cir. 1991)

This diversity case is a products liability action involving an automatic garage door opener manufactured by the Chamberlain Group, Inc. (Chamberlain) and distributed by Sears, Roebuck & Co. (Sears). Marilyn Wellborn (Wellborn) brought this action against Sears and Chamberlain after her son was killed as a result of the garage door opener malfunctioning. We affirm in part and certify the question—Does a decedent's cause of action under the Texas Deceptive Trade Practices — Consumer Protection Act survive under the Texas Survival Statute—to the Texas Supreme Court.

I.

In late 1986, Wellborn bought a Chamberlain automatic garage door opener from Sears. Wellborn's friend, Jerome Smith (Smith), installed it in Wellborn's garage in April or May of 1987. While installing the opener, Wellborn and Smith studied the owners' manual, and then they performed the test outlined in that manual. Testing the garage door opener, however, Wellborn and Smith used a "two by four" instead of the one-inch obstacle described in the owners' manual.

Moreover, subsequent to installing the opener in 1987, Wellborn did not perform the annual test to determine whether any further adjustments to the opener were necessary. Wellborn often worked the night shift and, on those evenings, she left her fourteen-year-old son, Bobby, at home without supervision. During the evening of November 2, 1988, Wellborn telephoned Bobby at home but he did not answer. She then telephoned Smith and, at her request, Smith went to the Wellborns' home. There, Smith found Bobby pinned underneath the garage door with his skateboard next to his feet. Smith activated the automatic garage door opener, and the garage door rose.

Investigating officers subsequently arrived at the Wellborns' and tested the garage door and the opener: They placed their hands under the door about two feet from the ground, and found that the garage door worked properly. When the officers tested the garage door in the same manner from about eight inches, however, the garage door did not reverse. An expert later determined that the garage door did not reverse because of faulty installation. The force adjustments had been set to maximum and the length of the door arm was too short.

In November of 1989, Wellborn brought this suit against Sears and Chamberlain. At trial, the parties offered evidence as to how the accident occurred. Wellborn testified that Bobby was aware of the dangers of getting beneath garage doors and that Bobby knew that the garage door opener was a piece of machinery designed to raise and lower the garage door. One of the Wellborns' older neighbors testified that she had observed Bobby playing a "game" where he raced under the closing garage door. The investigating officer and another expert agreed that the accident's probable cause was Bobby's attempt to race the closing door on his skateboard. The defendants' experts testified that the blunt trauma to Bobby's forehead probably meant that Bobby hit his forehead on the concrete driveway and was knocked unconscious and that the garage door then struck Bobby's back, which restricted his ability to breathe. According to Wellborn's experts, Bobby struggled to free himself, and remained conscious for a minimum of three to five minutes—possibly as long as several hours. Bobby eventually lost consciousness and died.

* * *

The defendants contend that, because Bobby neither sought nor acquired the garage door opener for purchase or lease, Bobby does not meet the DTPA's definition of "consumer." Instead, the defendants argue, Bobby was a "mere incidental user of the garage door opener—he was not even licensed to drive [and therefore] he could not use the garage door opener for its primary purpose." We disagree.

The DTPA provides that a consumer is entitled to recover both actual and additional damages plus attorney fees. A "consumer" is defined as one "who seeks or acquires by purchase or lease . . . any goods or services. . . ." The Texas Supreme Court has liberally construed terms of the DTPA in order to effectuate the Act's comprehensive application. Direct contractual privity between an individual and the defendant is not a consideration in determining an individual's status as a consumer under the DTPA. Standing as a consumer is established in terms of the individual's "relationship to the transaction, not by a contractual relationship with the defendant." *Birchfield v. Texarkana Mem. Hosp.*, 747 S.W.2d 361, 368 (Tex. 1987). Thus, one may acquire goods or services that have been purchased by another for the plaintiff's benefit.

In *Kennedy*, the Texas Supreme Court expressly held that one need not have been a purchaser in order to qualify for consumer status under the DTPA. *Kennedy* held that an employee covered by group insurance purchased by his employer was a consumer in that he acquired the benefits of the services of the policy due to the coverage of the policy provisions, irrespective of the fact that he did not actually purchase the policy benefits from the agent. Subsequently, the Texas Supreme Court extended consumer status to a minor who, through the efforts of her parents, acquired goods and services from the defendants. *Birchfield* held that the minor acquired goods and services, "regardless of the fact that she obviously did not contract for them."

Although Bobby did not enter into a contractual relationship with the defendants, he acquired the garage door opener and the benefits it provided. Wellborn did not purchase the garage door opener specifically for Bobby's benefit[.] [N]evertheless, Bobby lived with Wellborn and regularly used the garage door opener until . . . death. Wellborn testified that one of the reasons that she bought the garage door opener was to provide additional security for Bobby on the nights that Bobby was home by himself. Indeed, Wellborn had instructed Bobby to lock the house up at night. Because Bobby acquired the garage door opener when it was purchased for his benefit, installed in his home, and used by him, we hold that, under the facts of this case, Bobby is a consumer.

* * *

For the foregoing reasons, we AFFIRM the district court's judgment in its entirety except that we CERTIFY the following question to the Texas Supreme Court: Does a decedent's cause of action under the Texas Deceptive Trade Practices—Consumer Protection Act survives under the Texas Survival Statute?

C. *Proof of the Element — "Goods or Services"*

Chamrad v. Volvo Cars of North America
145 F.3d 671
(5th Cir. 1998)

James Chamrad appeals an adverse summary judgment in favor of Volvo Cars of North America which was based on the conclusion that Chamrad lacks standing as a "consumer" under the Texas Deceptive Trade Practices-Consumer Protection Act (DTPA). Finding no error, we affirm.

BACKGROUND

In 1989, Chamrad and Nancy O'Connor, Chamrad's girlfriend, began shopping for a car for O'Connor. They made three trips to the Royal Motors Volvo dealership in San Francisco, where they then were living. They were informed that the air bags would deploy in collisions at 15 miles per hour and up, protecting the driver and passenger.

O'Connor subsequently purchased a 1989 Volvo station wagon from a Texas dealer. On December 18, 1994, Chamrad had an accident while driving O'Connor's vehicle. The airbag did not deploy and Chamrad suffered serious injuries in the accident.

Chamrad and O'Connor were married in June 1995 and in October 1995 they filed suit against the defendant in state court alleging breach of express warranties and violation of the DTPA. Volvo removed the action to federal court and was granted summary judgment as to all of the plaintiffs' claims. Chamrad appeals the district court's dismissal of his claim under the DTPA.

* * *

ANALYSIS

Under the DTPA, only a consumer may allege deceptive trade practices... Tex. Bus. & Com.Code. Ann. § 17.50. The elements of a DTPA cause of action are: 1) The plaintiff is a consumer; 2) the defendant engaged in false, misleading, or deceptive acts; and 3) these acts constituted a producing cause of the consumer's damages. Tex. Bus. & Com.Code.Ann § 17.41 *et seq.; Doe v. Boys Clubs of Greater Dallas, Inc.,* 907 S.W.2d 472 (Tex.1995). We agree with the district court's conclusion that Chamrad failed to qualify as a "consumer," which is defined as an individual "who seeks or acquires by purchase or lease, any goods or services." Tex.Bus. & Com. Code Ann. § 17.45(4).

Chamrad claims that he is a consumer under the Act. He contends that direct contractual privity between an individual and the defendant is not a factor in determining an individual's status as a consumer, and that the appropriate focus is the individual's relationship to the transaction. Prior to the purchase of the car Chamrad and O'Connor, who were engaged to be married, shopped for a vehicle with the intentions of purchasing a safe, family car. Chamrad maintains that his relationship to the purchase of the vehicle qualifies him as a consumer. We are not persuaded. Based on the facts presented in this case, Chamrad's relationship to the transaction was tenuous and he was no more than an incidental beneficiary.

Chamrad has not established that his relationship to the transaction was significant. In *Rodriguez v. Ed Hicks Imports,* 767 S.W.2d 187 (Tex.App.-Corpus Christi 1989), the plaintiff suffered injuries when the radiator on his girlfriend's automobile exploded, spraying him with scalding liquid. Rodriguez brought a personal injury action against the seller of the automobile alleging several causes of action, including a claim under the DTPA. The Texas Court of Appeals affirmed summary judgment for the defendant on the DTPA claim, concluding that Rodriguez was not a consumer. He was not involved in the purchase of the car and therefore he did not acquire by purchase or lease any goods or services that formed the basis of the complaint. *Rodriguez,* 767 S.W.2d at 191

Although he visited several Volvo dealerships in San Francisco, Chamrad never visited the Advantage Leasing dealership in Victoria, Texas, where the subject vehicle was purchased, nor did he make logistical or financial arrangements for the purchase. O'Connor paid for the car and placed the title in her name. Chamrad had no relationship whatsoever to that transaction. Chamrad was no more than an incidental beneficiary of the purchase. In order to claim "consumer" status, the underlying transaction must be consummated with intent to benefit the claimant.

In *Arthur Andersen & Co. v. Perry Equip. Corp.,* 945 S.W.2d 812 (Tex.1997) *citing Kennedy v. Sale,* 689 S.W.2d 890 (Tex.1985), Perry Equipment sued Arthur Andersen for making a faulty audit, which Perry relied on in deciding to purchase Maloney Pipeline Systems. Arthur Andersen contended that Perry was not a consumer under the DTPA because it did not purchase the services which were the basis of the DTPA claim. The Texas Supreme Court, however, held that "the DTPA does not require the consumer to be an actual purchaser or lessor of the goods or services as long as the consumer is the beneficiary of those goods or services."

[I]n *Arthur Andersen . . .* not only was there an underlying relationship [but] the audit at issue was for the benefit of both Perry and Maloney. Arthur Andersen was aware that Perry had required the audit as a condition of sale and would rely on the accuracy of its work. In *Wellborn v. Sears Roebuck & Co.,* 970 F.2d 1420 (5th Cir.1992), we concluded that a young boy, killed when he was pinned underneath a garage door when the automatic door opener failed to reverse, was a consumer under the DTPA because he was a beneficiary of his mother's purchase of the door opener. We found that because the door was purchased for his benefit, installed in his home, and used by him; he was a consumer. *See Also, Kennedy v. Sale,* 689 S.W.2d 890, 892 (Tex.1985) (an employee covered by group insurance, purchased by his employer, was a consumer because he acquired benefits of the services of the policy).

In this case, unlike in *Arthur Andersen* and *Wellborn,* there is no evidence to support the proposition that O'Connor, in seeking to acquire or purchase a good or service, bought the vehicle with the intent to benefit Chamrad. Neither at the time of the purchase nor the accident were Chamrad and O'Connor married. At all relevant times Chamrad owned his own vehicle. The Volvo belonged to O'Connor and was for her use. Finally, the record reflects that over approximately a five-year period Chamrad drove the vehicle on only one occasion, the night of the accident.

We are persuaded that the record does not support the claim that Chamrad had a relationship to the transaction or that he was more than an incidental beneficiary of the purchase of the car. He therefore was not a consumer under the Act and lacks standing to invoke the DTPA. The judgment appealed is AFFIRMED.

Frizzell v. Cook
790 S.W.2d 41
(Tex. App. -San Antonio 1990)

This is an appeal by Mrs. Norris N. Frizzell [appellant] . . . from an order granting . . . M.E. "Doc" Cook, Harvie D. Lindeman, E.F. Hutton & Company, Inc., and Shearson Lehman Hutton, Inc.'s [appellees'] motion for partial summary judgment. At issue . . . is whether the trial court properly rendered partial summary judgment based on appellant's pleading, and . . . whether the Texas Securities Act (TSA), Tex. Rev. Civ. Stat. Ann. art. 581-33"preempted" appellant's cause of action under the Deceptive Trade Practices Act (DTPA) Tex. Bus. & Com. Code Ann. §§ 17.41-.63

Appellant filed her original petition . . . and alleged that appellees, a national brokerage firm and its employees, engaged in tortious conduct in the course of providing her with investment and counseling services relating to the investment of the life insurance proceeds provided by her deceased husband. The unlawful acts of appellees . . . include alleged violations of 1) the DTPA, 2) Tex. Bus. & Com. Code § 27.01, 3) [Federal Securities Act of 1933, 15 U.S.C. § 77a], and 4) the common law duty of good faith and fair dealing.

II

The basis for the motion is that the DTPA does not apply to claims of misrepresentation in connection with securities actions such as alleged by the Plaintiff. The Texas Legislature has enacted The Texas Security [sic] Act which specifically affords a cause of action for alleged misrepresentations in connection with securities transactions, and this statute preempts the DTPA in this area.

Appellant, in her response to appellees' motion for summary judgment, among other statements, stated:

> As is obvious from reading of Plaintiff's Original Petition, Plaintiff's allegations of wrongs covered under the Deceptive Trade Practices Act are not limited to misrepresentations related only to specific purchases or sales of securities, as described in Art. 581-33.... Plaintiff has complained not just about such misrepresentations but about "churning" of her account and unauthorized purchases and sales, as well as an unconscionable failure of Defendants to take action after Plaintiff complained of the individual Defendants' unauthorized and wrongful conduct ... that Defendants intentionally did not provide the services advertised....

The trial court, in granting the partial summary judgment to appellees, decreed that "Plaintiff should take nothing by her cause of action under the Texas Deceptive Trade Practices Act." Thereafter, the trial court severed appellant's claims under the DTPA from her remaining claims, including claims under the TSA. The severed DTPA claims were assigned a separate number (88-CI-08905-A), and the partial summary judgment then became a final judgment, which appellant has appealed.

Appellant claims in her first point of error that "[t]he Trial Court erred in granting partial summary judgment against Appellant because the Texas Securities Act does not 'preempt' an action under the Texas Deceptive Trade Practices-Consumer Protection Act as a matter of law." We sustain the point, which makes it unnecessary for us to consider appellant's remaining points of error.

In the instant case, the trial court found . . . that the cause of action pleaded by appellant was . . . inconsistent and inapposite to the TSA. It was this finding that caused the trial court to render judgment that appellant did not have a cause of action under the DTPA.

Appellees contend that the judgment of the trial court was mandated by the holding of the Texas Supreme Court in *E.F. Hutton & Co. v. Youngblood,* 30 Tex. Sup. Ct. J. 508 (June 24, 1987), *withdrawn,* 741 S.W.2d 363 (Tex.1987) (the withdrawn opinion), and is fully supported by the holding in *Allais v. Donaldson, Lufkin & Jenrette,* 532 F.Supp. 749 (S. D. Tex.1982).

It is well settled under Texas law that an unpublished opinion of an appellate court is of no precedential value. *Berry v. Berry,* 647 S.W.2d 945, 947 (Tex.1983); *Merrill Lynch, Pierce, Fenner & Smith, Inc. v. McCollum,* 666 S.W.2d 604, 610 (Tex.App.-Houston [14th Dist.] 1984, writ ref'd n.r.e.), *cert. denied,* 469 U.S. 1127 (1985) .

We apply that rule to the case at bar and hold that the withdrawn opinion of the Supreme Court in *Youngblood* has "no precedential value." The effect of the withdrawn opinion is to leave intact the holding of the Corpus Christi Court of Appeals in all matters relevant to the DTPA action before the court of appeals. *See E.F. Hutton & Co. v. Youngblood,* 708 S.W.2d 865 (Tex.App.-Corpus Christi 1986), *modified,* 741 S.W.2d 363 (Tex.1987) (judgment of court of appeals modified "so as to disallow recovery of attorney's fees by the Youngbloods. As modified, the judgment of the court of appeals is affirmed." We do not consider the withdrawn opinion in disposing of the appeal in the case at bar.

Hutton argued before the Corpus Christi Court of Appeals that Youngblood was not a consumer because "[a]s the investment advice was a service neither purchased or leased, that is, without consideration. . . it was beyond the coverage of the DTPA." *E.F. Hutton & Co. v. Youngblood,* 708 S.W.2d at 868. The court of appeals rejected that argument noting:

> Appellant's branch manager testified that, as a 'full-service brokerage house,' Hutton received higher commissions than would a 'discount brokerage house,' because more *services* were provided for their customers. In the transaction sued upon, appellant was to be paid a 4% commission for assisting appellees in obtaining their securities which would accomplish a tax free rollover. The services of tax and investment counseling and assisting in the purchase of securities were inextricably intertwined. *See Knight v. International Harvester Credit Corp.,* 627 S.W.2d 382 (Tex.1982). Appellees sought and received from appellant expert tax and investment counseling as to the taxable consequences of the transaction, without which the sale of securities would not have been made. We find that the appellees were consumers of a service purchased from appellant, E.F. Hutton. *Id.* at 868-69

For summary judgment purposes, appellant . . . alleged . . . that appellant sought appellees' investment and counseling services.

* * *

The provision of the TSA at issue in the instant case was enacted in 1977. Article 581-33A(2) was then amended, effective May 25, 1979. . . . After these changes to the TSA, the DTPA was substantially amended in 1979 . . . to include, *inter alia,* the language in section 17.43 expressly stating that a violation of another statute (like the TSA) may also be a violation of the DTPA. The Legislature also reenacted the affirmative relief provisions of section 17.50, which give rise to the claim *sub judice* in this case. These amendments became effective August 27, 1979, which was after the effective date of the TSA amendments. Consequently, the later enacted DTPA provisions control.

* * *

Since the Legislature is never presumed to have done a useless act, *Cameron v. Terrell & Garrett, Inc.,* 618 S.W.2d 535, 540 (Tex.1981), the Legislature is presumed to have intended, by making both the TSA and DTPA cumulative of each other and by amending section 17.43 of the DTPA after the enactment of article 581-33 A(2) (the "due diligence defense" of the TSA), it is apparent that actions could be brought under both acts. However, a double recovery for the same act is precluded. There is nothing in either the TSA [or] the DTPA that expressly exempts securities transactions from the scope of the DTPA. The "exemption" that appellees rely on, therefore, is an implied exemption, and the Texas Supreme Court has refused to imply exemptions or exceptions not mandated by the Legislature. *See Chastain v. Koonce,* 700 S.W.2d 579, 583 (Tex.1985) (refusing to imply intent requirement for unconscionability); *Weitzel v. Barnes,* 691 S.W.2d 598, 600 (Tex.1985) (refusing to imply reliance requirement for misrepresentation); *Smith v. Baldwin,* 611 S.W.2d 611, 616-17 (Tex.1980) (refusing to imply an intent requirement).

The Supreme Court of Texas, in *Melody Home Mfg. Co. v. Barnes,* 741 S.W.2d 349, 354 (Tex.1987), stated: The legislative history of the DTPA indicates that the Act was intended to apply to all service providers. In the case presented by this appeal, appellant . . . alleged that she contracted to "acquire" the "services" of defendants (appellees).

This Court has previously held that both the DTPA and TSA apply to securities transactions. In *Vick v. George,* 671 S.W.2d 541 (Tex.App.-San Antonio 1983), *rev'd on other grounds,* 686 S.W.2d 99 (Tex. 1984). . . . The appellant in *Vick* argued that recovery could not be had under both the TSA and the DTPA. This Court agreed, noting that while *double recovery* was precluded by the 1979 amendments to the DTPA the appellees had the right to elect whether damages would be imposed under the DTPA or the TSA based on the jury's findings. The Court held:

> Plaintiffs correctly state that recovery under either the TSA or the DTPA is not exclusive of any other rights or remedies that may exist. Article 581-33(A), and § 17.43 (amended 1979). It is axiomatic, however, that an aggrieved party is entitled to but one recovery for the same loss. *American Transfer and Storage Co. v. Brown,* 584 S.W.2d 284, 293 (Tex.Civ.App.-Dallas 1979), *rev'd on other grounds,* 601 S.W.2d 931 (Tex.1980). *Id.* at 551

* * *

In *Nottingham v. General American Communications Corp.,* 811 F.2d 873 (5th Cir.1987), *cert. denied,* 484 U.S. 854 (1987), the defendant argued that it was error for the district court to submit claims under both the DTPA and securities statutes. The court held: "It was not error to submit both claims to the jury," and further stated:

> As we recently explained in *Federal Deposit Insurance Corporation v. Munn,* 804 F.2d 860, 865 (5th Cir. 1986), *services related to the sale of a security may be services covered by the DTPA when they also are objectives of the transaction.* The contract for legal services, the Production Facilities Agreement, and the Distribution Agreement, among others, were plainly for services that were objectives of the transaction in this case. *Id.* at 878 (emphasis added).

The holding in *Nottingham* parallels the decision by this Court in *Vick,* and the holding by the Corpus Christi Court of Appeals in *Youngblood.* We hold that appellant was a consumer under the DTPA and the trial court erred in granting partial summary judgment that plaintiff (appellant) take nothing by her cause of action under the Texas Deceptive Trade Practices Act. Since both the TSA and the DTPA have cumulative remedies provisions, in our opinion the Legislature intended neither Act to "preempt" or replace the other. Therefore, we hold that the TSA does not "preempt" a cause of action under the DTPA as a matter of law, as contended by appellees. Appellant's first point of error is sustained.

The judgment of the trial court is reversed and the cause is remanded to the trial court for a trial on the merits.

Riverside National Bank v. Lewis
603 S.W.2d 169 (Tex. 1980)

This case primarily involves the question whether one who seeks a loan from a bank in order to refinance a car qualifies as a "consumer" under the Deceptive Trade Practices Act (DTPA). The trial court disallowed recovery under the DTPA, but the court of civil appeals reformed the judgment to hold the bank liable under the DTPA. Since we believe that Mr. Lewis was not a "consumer" in the instant transaction, we hold that the trial court correctly denied recovery under the DTPA. We also hold that under this record, Lewis is entitled to recover from Riverside Bank upon his cause of action for common law fraud. Further, we hold that there is some evidence to support recovery of exemplary damages for fraud. We remand the cause to the court of civil appeals to pass upon the sufficiency of the evidence as to exemplary damages.

The relevant facts are as follows: In February, 1975, Lewis purchased a new Cadillac El Dorado. Allied Bank provided almost $10,500.00 in financing. To secure the loan, Allied Bank took a security interest in the car and kept a $6,000.00 certificate of deposit as security. Lewis failed to make the first payment due on April 10, and a check that he gave a few days later was returned for insufficient funds. After these occurrences, Mr. Little, Lewis' loan officer at Allied Bank, asked Lewis to move the loan to another bank.

After two unsuccessful attempts to refinance the loan, Lewis went to Riverside Bank on May 2. Arthur Carroll, a junior loan officer, helped Lewis complete a loan application, and told Lewis that the application would have to be approved by his superiors at the Bank. At that time, Carroll called the Allied Bank loan officer, Mr. Little, and told him that Lewis had applied for the loan at Riverside Bank.

On May 6, 1975, Carroll called Little once again. During this phone conversation, Carroll informed Little that the loan had been approved, and requested Little to have Allied Bank forward a draft, the title, and the certificate of deposit to Riverside Bank. After forwarding these items, there was no communication between Little and Carroll until May 14, 1975.

On May 14, Little called Carroll in order to determine why the draft had not been paid. Carroll told Little that the draft had been held up due to a senior loan officer's questions, but that it would be paid on the next day. On May 15, Little informed Carroll that he wanted the draft paid immediately, or returned. Carroll replied that the draft had been paid, and the cashier's check was in the mail. The next day, May 16, Carroll told Little that the draft would not be paid.

During the course of these communications between Little, at Allied Bank, and Carroll, at Riverside Bank, James Means, executive vice-president at Riverside National Bank, did some investigation of Lewis' loan application. Upon calling Allied Bank, Means discovered that Lewis' application misrepresented his net income and did not disclose the fact that he had already failed to make his first, and only, payment. Thus, on May 14, Means decided that Riverside would not make the loan to Lewis.

On May 15, however, Carroll called Lewis, told him that the loan had been approved, and asked him to come to the bank to sign the necessary papers. Lewis complied with the request, signing a promissory note in the amount of $12,871.80 on May 15. This note was kept by Riverside until the time of trial, although it was never sought to be collected. As previously stated, on May 15, Carroll was also representing to Allied Bank that the loan would be taken by Riverside Bank.

After being told on May 16 that Riverside would not take the loan, Allied Bank repossessed the car and sold it at auction. The sale failed to generate sufficient money to cover the full loan at Allied, and a deficiency of $3,177.50 was deducted from Lewis' certificate of deposit, with the balance being returned to him.

Lewis sued Riverside for the losses he suffered in this transaction, claiming that Riverside, through Carroll, had (1) engaged in fraud, (2) breached its contract to loan money, (3) engaged in deceptive trade practices against him, and (4) converted his property by retaining the promissory note, yet refusing to lend him money.

After trial to a jury, the jury found that Riverside had (1) wrongfully dishonored the draft sent by Allied to Riverside, (2) committed fraud on Lewis by refusing to make the loan, and (3) violated the Deceptive Trade Practices Act by refusing to lend the money. The jury found that Lewis had suffered actual damages in the amount of $3,277.50. As a consequence of finding that Riverside had acted with malice in refusing this loan, the jury also found that $10,000.00 should be awarded as exemplary damages. The jury also found that reasonable attorney's fees would be $6,700.00.

The trial court entered judgment for Lewis in the amount of $13,277.50, representing the actual and exemplary damages under the fraud theory of action. The court also held that the DTPA was not applicable to the instant transaction, and declined to enter judgment under the theory of recovery for treble damages and attorney's fees.

* * *

RIVERSIDE'S LIABILITY UNDER THE DECEPTIVE TRADE PRACTICES ACT

The alleged deceptive acts in this case occurred during May, 1975. Accordingly, the statutory provisions that govern this case are those that were in effect at the time that the alleged deceptive acts occurred.

* * *

The Act thus differentiates between the remedies available to correct violations of the Act. A "person" may have engaged in a deceptive act by presenting any misleading information concerning any item of value. See sections 17.46(a), 17.45(6). Any person engaging in such deceptive practices may be subjected to a suit by the Consumer Protection Division of the Attorney General's Office, under section 17.47. But, one who engages in deceptive acts may not be subjected to a private suit for damages under the Act unless the aggrieved party is a consumer. Section 17.50 expressly declares, in its caption: Relief for Consumers. Furthermore, section 17.50 provides that a consumer may maintain a cause of action if aggrieved by deceptive practices. The Legislature granted no such remedy by means of a private cause of action for any person; one must be a consumer.

It has been argued that any person ought to be permitted to sue if aggrieved by a deceptive act. This contention relies on the broad definition of "trade" and "commerce" and the liberal interpretation of the DTPA that is promoted by section 17.44. We disagree with this position for two reasons. First, the scope of "trade" and "commerce" defines the acts that are illegal ; it does not purport to say who may maintain a private cause of action. Rather, it is the definition of consumer that delineates the class of persons that may maintain a private cause of action. Second, the rule of liberal interpretation should not be applied in a manner that negates the statutory definition of the word "consumer." To ignore the Legislature's definition of "consumer," and permit any aggrieved person to maintain a private cause of action under the DTPA, ignores the well established presumption that legislative choice of words is such that every word has meaning. *See Jessen Associates, Inc. v. Bullock,* 531 S.W.2d 593 (Tex.1975).

To read the Act in such a manner that "trade" and "commerce" define the class of persons who are consumers would constitute a judicial deletion of section 17.45(4), which defines consumer in terms of a purchaser of "goods" and "services," and not in connection with "trade" and "commerce." This we cannot do. Thus, we hold that a person who brings a private lawsuit under section 17.50 must be a consumer, as defined in section 17.45(4). The other courts that have considered this issue have been in accord. *See, e. g., Hi-Line Electric Co. v. Travelers Insurance* Co., 587 S.W.2d 488 (Tex.Civ.App. Dallas 1979), writ ref'd n. r. e., 593 S.W.2d 953 (1980) (per curiam); *Russell v. Hartford Casualty Insurance Co.,* 548 S.W.2d 737 (Tex.Civ.App. Austin 1977, writ ref'd n. r. e.).

In his transaction with Riverside Bank, Lewis sought only to borrow money in an effort to avoid repossession of his car. He sought to pay for the use of money over a period of time. Other than Lewis' payment for the use of money, there was nothing else for which he paid, or which he sought to acquire. In order to determine whether Lewis was a "consumer" entitled to maintain a private cause of action under section 17.50 of the DTPA, we must determine whether, in this transaction, Lewis sought or acquired "by purchase or lease, any goods or services."

1. Lewis did not seek or acquire any "goods" in his transaction with Riverside Bank.

Section 17.45(1) of the DTPA defines goods as "tangible chattels bought for use." Since Lewis sought nothing other than the use of money from Riverside Bank, it is necessary to determine whether money was a "tangible chattel" that could be classified as a good. After examination of the appropriate statutes, we conclude that money is not such a "good."

Nowhere in the DTPA is "chattel" defined so as to specifically include or exclude "money" from the definition of "goods." A cursory examination of analogous statutes, however, demonstrates that money has not yet been included in the category of "goods" or "chattels."

The DTPA is a part of the Texas Business and Commerce Code. Accordingly, it is appropriate to look to other sections of the Code to determine the proper characterization of money. Section 1.201

of the Texas Business and Commerce Code, which sets forth the general definitions of the terms used in the Code, provides: (24) "Money " means a medium of exchange authorized or adopted by a domestic or foreign government as a part of its currency.

A specific definition of "goods" is found in section 2.105, which provides: (a) "Goods" means all things . . . which are movable at the time of identification to the contract for sale other than the money in which the price is to be paid . . . .

Section 9.105(a)(8) similarly provides: (8) "Goods" includes all things which are movable at the time the security interest attaches or which are fixtures . . . but does not include money . . . .

Thus, consistent with these analogous statutory provisions, we hold that money is not a "tangible chattel," or "goods" as defined by the DTPA. Rather, money is properly characterized as a currency of exchange that enables the holder to acquire goods. Thus, Lewis, in arranging for the instant loan, did not seek to acquire, through purchase or lease, any "goods" as defined by the DTPA.

2. LEWIS DID NOT SEEK OR ACQUIRE ANY "SERVICES" IN HIS TRANSACTION WITH RIVERSIDE BANK.

Section 17.45(2) of the DTPA defines services as "work, labor, and services for other than commercial or business use, including services furnished in connection with the sale or repair of goods." Lewis contends that, in the instant transaction, he sought an "extension of credit." This extension of credit, he claims, is a service as defined by the DTPA. We disagree.

In this case, Lewis sought to borrow money : he sought nothing else. Money, as money, is quite obviously neither work nor labor. Seeking to acquire the use of money likewise is not a seeking of work or labor. Rather, it is an attempt to acquire an item of value. We hold that an attempt to borrow money is not an attempt to acquire either work or labor as contemplated in the DTPA.

"Services" was defined by this Court in *Van Zandt v. Fort Worth Press*, 359 S.W.2d 893, 895 (Tex. 1962). We defined services as: "action or use that furthers some end or purpose: conduct or performance that assists or benefits someone or something: deeds useful or instrumental toward some object." This definition described "services" in terms of "action," "conduct," performance" and "deeds." All of these synonyms demonstrate that services [include] an activity on behalf of one party by another. This characterization indicates that "services" is similar in nature to work or labor.

Accordingly, we hold that Lewis' attempt to acquire money, or the use of money, was not an attempt to acquire services.

We find support for our conclusion that the DTPA's use of the word "services" did not include the extension of credit, or the borrowing of money, in another statute: the Home Solicitations Transactions chapter of the Interest-Consumer Credit-Consumer Protection Title. In the Home Solicitations Transactions Act, the Legislature gave to "consumers," as defined in that act, certain rights with respect to contracts that had been signed as a result of a home solicitation. In that act, the

Legislature defined "consumer" as "an individual who seeks or acquires real or personal property, services, money, or credit for personal, family, or household purposes." Article 5069-13.01(2).

Interestingly enough, the Legislature enacted this statute during the same session in which the DTPA was originally enacted. The presence of the words "money or credit" within the definition of "consumer" in the Home Solicitations Act, and their corresponding absence from the analogous provision in the DTPA, indicates that the seeking of an "extension of credit" is not the seeking of a "service" as defined in the DTPA.

Obviously, the Legislature knew how to include the extension of credit and borrowing of money within the scope of coverage of protective legislation, when it intended to cover such transactions. The simple addition of the words "money or credit" within the definition of "consumer" in the DTPA would have accomplished such a purpose in the DTPA. The Legislature's exclusion of these terms from the DTPA, in light of its contemporaneous inclusion of the same terms in the Home Solicitations Transactions Act, evidences a clear legislative intent that the extension of credit was not to be covered under the DTPA.

It has also been argued that in the course of extending credit, Riverside Bank necessarily provided other services to Lewis. These services could have included such things as help in filling out his loan application, financial counseling, and the processing of his loan. It has been contended that these activities constituted "services" as defined by the DTPA, and thus made Lewis a "consumer" who could maintain a private cause of action under section 17.50. We disagree.

The evidence in this case establishes that Lewis approached Riverside Bank with one objective; he sought to acquire money. He attempted to obtain this money by promising to repay the indebtedness in the future, with interest. Put simply, he sought to exchange future amounts of money for that amount which he desired to have in the present. There is no evidence that he sought to acquire anything other than this use of money.

The argument that services existed in the lending of money, and in the process of determining whether to lend money, and were necessarily a part of the interest rate or purchase price of the loan, is not supported by the evidence adduced at trial. This argument, contained in the briefs, is merely hypothetical. There is nothing to support it in the Statement of Facts.

Additionally, Lewis' sole complaint about the transaction concerned the Bank's failure to make him the loan. He has made no complaint concerning the quality of these collateral activities that he now claims constitute a service. In the absence of a claim concerning these collateral activities, we hold that Lewis did not seek either "goods or services" as defined under the DTPA.

Accordingly, Lewis was not a "consumer" who could bring suit under section 17.50 of the DTPA.

Flenniken v. Longview Bank & Trust Company
661 S.W.2d 705
(Tex.1983)

Mr. and Mrs. James Flenniken instituted this suit against the Longview Bank & Trust Co. seeking damages for wrongful foreclosure and violation of the Deceptive Trade Practices Act, Tex. Bus. & Com.Code Ann. § 17.41 *et seq.* Based on the jury's finding that the Bank engaged in an unconscionable course of action in causing the sale of the Flennikens' property, the trial court rendered judgment that the Flennikens recover $25,974 treble damages, attorney's fees, and court costs. The court of appeals reversed the trial court's judgment in part, holding that the Flennikens were not "consumers" and were not entitled to recover treble damages or attorney's fees under the DTPA. We reverse the judgment of the court of appeals and affirm the judgment of the trial court.

On October 28, 1976, the Flennikens and Charles Easterwood entered into a mechanic's and materialman's lien contract, whereby Easterwood agreed to construct a residence on the Flennikens' property. In exchange for Easterwood's services, the Flennikens paid Easterwood $5,010 and executed a $42,500 mechanic's lien note, naming Easterwood as payee. This note was further secured by a deed of trust to the Flennikens' property, in which the Bank's vice-president, J.M. Bell, was named as trustee. On this same date, Easterwood assigned the Flennikens' note and his contract lien to the Bank in return for the Bank's commitment to provide interim construction financing.

Under the terms of the lien contract, Easterwood was to complete the Flennikens' residence by April 28, 1977. Between November 2, 1976, and January 7, 1977, the Bank made four disbursements of construction funds to Easterwood, totalling $32,000. Easterwood, however, later abandoned the contract after completing only 20 percent of the work. On December 6, 1977, after the Flennikens and the Bank failed to agree on what to do with the unfinished house, the Bank foreclosed on the property under the terms of the deed of trust.

The Bank does not challenge the jury's finding that foreclosure was an unconscionable course of action. Instead, the Bank argues that the Flennikens are not "consumers" as that term is defined in section 17.45(4) of the DTPA. We disagree.

It is clear that only a "consumer" has standing to maintain a private cause of action for treble damages and attorney's fees under section 17.50(a) of the DTPA. *Knight v. International Harvester Credit Corp.,* 627 S.W.2d 382, 388 (Tex.1982); *Cameron v. Terrell & Garrett, Inc.,* 618 S.W.2d 535, 538 (Tex.1981); *Riverside National Bank v. Lewis,* 603 S.W.2d 169, 173 (Tex.1980). Section 17.45(4) defines a consumer as "an individual ... who seeks or acquires by purchase or lease, any goods or services." Under the DTPA, goods include "real property purchased ... for use," Tex.Bus. & Com.Code Ann. § 17.45(1), and services include "services furnished in connection with the sale ... of goods." *Id.* § 17.45(2).

Section 17.45(4), however, only describes the class of persons entitled to bring suit under section 17.50; it does not define the class of persons subject to liability under the DTPA. The range of possible defendants is limited only by the exemptions provided in section 17.49. Section 17.50(a)

(3), for example, allows a consumer to "maintain an action if he has been adversely affected by ... any unconscionable action or course of action by *any person.*"

In the instant case, the court of appeals recognized that the Flennikens were consumers to the extent they sought to acquire a house from Easterwood, as well as his services. The court of appeals, however, treated Easterwood's assignment of their note to the Bank as a separate transaction in which the Flennikens did not seek or acquire any goods or services. According to the court of appeals, the Bank's unconscionable course of action did not occur in connection with the Flennikens' transaction with Easterwood, but in connection with Easterwood's transaction with the Bank. Thus, the court of appeals held that the Flennikens were not consumers as to the Bank because the purchase of the house and Easterwood's services did not form the basis of their complaint.

This holding erroneously suggests that the Flennikens were required to seek or acquire goods or services *from the Bank* in order to meet the statutory definition of consumer, a contention we rejected in *Cameron v. Terrell & Garrett, Inc., supra.* Privity between the plaintiff and defendant is not a consideration in deciding the plaintiff's status as a consumer under the DTPA. *Cameron v. Terrell & Garrett, Inc.,* 618 S.W.2d at 541; *accord Gupta v. Ritter Homes, Inc.,* 646 S.W.2d 168 (Tex.1983); *Stagner v. Friendswood Development Co.,* 620 S.W.2d 103 (Tex.1981) (per curiam). A plaintiff establishes his standing as a consumer in terms of his relationship to a transaction, not by a contractual relationship with the defendant. The only requirement is that the goods or services sought or acquired by the consumer form the basis of his complaint. *Cameron v. Terrell & Garrett, Inc.,* 618 S.W.2d at 539.

Similarly, the fact that the Bank's unconscionable course of action occurred after the Flennikens and Easterwood entered into the contract for the sale of the house does not exempt the Bank from liability under the DTPA. Under section 17.50(a)(3) there is no requirement that the defendant's unconscionable act occur simultaneously with the sale or lease of the goods or services that form the basis of the consumer's complaint. *Cf. Leal v. Furniture Barn, Inc.,* 571 S.W.2d 864, 865 (Tex.1978). If, in the context of a transaction in goods or services, any person engages in an unconscionable course of action which adversely affects a consumer, that person is subject to liability under the DTPA. Tex.Bus. & Com.Code Ann. § 17.50(a)(3); *see* D. Bragg, P. Maxwell & J. Longley, *Texas Consumer Litigation* 21 (2d ed. 1983).

The court of appeals erred in holding that the basis of the Flennikens' complaint was Easterwood's transaction with the Bank, rather than their transaction with Easterwood. From the Flennikens' perspective, there was only one transaction: the purchase of a house. The financing scheme Easterwood arranged with the Bank was merely his means of making a sale. The Bank's unconscionable act in causing the sale of the Flennikens' property and the partially built house arose out of the Flennikens' transaction with Easterwood.

The Flennikens, therefore, were consumers as to all parties who sought to enjoy the benefits of that transaction, including the Bank. *Knight v. International Harvester Credit Corp.,* 627 S.W.2d at 389. Clearly, the Bank had no greater right to foreclose on the Flennikens' property than did Easterwood. If Easterwood had foreclosed his lien under these circumstances, and if a jury had found his actions to be unconscionable, there is no question that he would be subject to liability under the DTPA. The Bank-which wrongfully exercised a power it derived from Easterwood's transaction with the Flennikens-is subject to the same liability.

The Bank, however, also argues that the Flennikens are not consumers under our holding in *Riverside National Bank v. Lewis, supra.* Again, we disagree.

In *Riverside,* we held that money is not a good or service under the DTPA, and that one who seeks only money in a transaction is not a consumer under section 17.45(4). In *Riverside,* however, the *sole* basis of Lewis' complaint was the Bank's failure to lend him money as it had promised it would. The limited nature of his complaint was reiterated throughout our opinion:

> In his transaction with Riverside Bank, Lewis sought *only* to borrow money in an effort to avoid repossession of his car.... Other than Lewis' payment for the use of money, there was *nothing else* for which he paid or which he sought to acquire.603 S.W.2d at 173 (emphasis added). In this case, Lewis sought to borrow money: he sought *nothing else. Id.* at 174 (emphasis added). There is no evidence that he sought to acquire *anything other* than this use of money. . . . Lewis' *sole* complaint about the transaction concerned the Bank's failure to make him the loan. *Id.* at 175 (emphasis added).

In this case, the Flennikens make no complaint as to the Bank's lending activities. Unlike Lewis, the Flennikens did not seek to borrow money; they sought to acquire a house. The house thus forms the basis of their complaint.

The judgment of the court of appeals is reversed. The judgment of the trial court awarding the Flennikens treble damages and attorney's fees under the DTPA is affirmed.

Chapter Two: Proof that An Alleged Violator May Be Sued

After a person establishes that it has standing under the DTPA to sue as a consumer, the person must overcome an equally challenging hurdle. Put simply, an aggrieving consumer may not be able to sue every individual, social, political, or business entity or institution that might have had some association with a particular transaction in goods or services. Therefore, it is important to ask: Does privity of contract place a limitation on who qualifies as a DTPA defendant? Does a person's legal status determine whether the person must defend itself against a DTPA action?

As you read the cases appearing in this chapter, try to isolate the theories that courts employ to determine who or which entity "qualifies" as a DTPA defendant. As you will discover, there is no bright-line or universal test. And the primary explanation is not terribly difficult. The DTPA does not clearly list the entities that qualify as defendants. Of course, the Texas Legislature amended the DTPA in 1995 and exempted certain activities and created statutory, qualified immunity for certain entities. Consider Section 17.49 which reads:

§ 17.49. Exemptions.

(a) Nothing in this subchapter shall apply to the owner or employees of a regularly published newspaper, magazine, or telephone directory, or broadcast station, or billboard, wherein any advertisement in violation of this subchapter is published or disseminated, unless it is established that the owner or employees of the advertising medium have knowledge of the false, deceptive, or misleading acts or practices declared to be unlawful by this subchapter, or had a direct or substantial financial interest in the sale or distribution of the unlawfully advertised good or service. Financial interest as used in this section relates to an expectation which would be the direct result of such advertisement.

(b) Nothing in this subchapter shall apply to acts or practices authorized under specific rules or regulations promulgated by the Federal Trade Commission under Section 5(a)(1) of the Federal Trade Commission Act [15 U.S.C.A. 45(a)(1)]. The provisions of this subchapter do apply to any act or practice prohibited or not specifically authorized by a rule or regulation of the Federal Trade Commission. An act or practice is not specifically authorized if no rule or regulation has been issued on the act or practice.

(c) Nothing in this subchapter shall apply to a claim for damages based on the rendering of a professional service, the essence of which is the providing of advice, judgment, opinion, or similar professional skill. This exemption does not apply to:

(1) an express misrepresentation of a material fact that cannot be characterized as advice, judgment, or opinion;

(2) a failure to disclose information in violation of Section 17.46(b)(24);

(3) an unconscionable action or course of action that cannot be characterized as advice, judgment, or opinion;

(4) breach of an express warranty that cannot be characterized as advice, judgment, or opinion; or.

(5) a violation of Section 17.46(b)(26).

(d) Subsection (c) applies to a cause of action brought against the person who provided the professional service and a cause of action brought against any entity that could be found to be vicariously liable for the person's conduct.

(e) Except as specifically provided by Subsections (b) and (h), Section 17.50, nothing in this subchapter shall apply to a cause of action for bodily injury or death or for the infliction of mental anguish.

(f) Nothing in the subchapter shall apply to a claim arising out of a written contract if:

(1) the contract relates to a transaction, a project, or a set of transactions related to the same project involving total consideration by the consumer of more than $100,000;

(2) in negotiating the contract the consumer is represented by legal counsel who is not directly or indirectly identified, suggested, or selected by the defendant or an agent of the defendant; and

(3) the contract does not involve the consumer's residence.

(g) Nothing in this subchapter shall apply to a cause of action arising from a transaction, a project, or a set of transactions relating to the same project, involving total consideration by the consumer of more than $500,000, other than a cause of action involving a consumer's residence.

A. *Principals and Agents as DTPA Defendants*

Cameron v. Terrell & Garrett, Inc.
618 S.W.2d 535
(Tex. 1981)

This is a deceptive trade practice case. Jerry D. Cameron and Jo Ann Cameron, purchasers of a house, brought this suit for treble damages against the seller's real estate agent, Terrell & Garrett, Inc., for a misrepresentation of the square footage in the house. The primary question presented is whether the Camerons are consumers within the meaning of the Deceptive Trade Practices-Consumer Protection Act (DTPA). The trial court rendered a take-nothing judgment *non obstante veredicto* for Terrell & Garrett. The court of civil appeals affirmed but on different grounds. The court of civil appeals held that the Camerons were not consumers and, therefore, could not bring a private lawsuit against Terrell & Garrett for a deceptive trade practice violation. We hold the Camerons are consumers. We also hold that there is some evidence to support the jury verdict for the Camerons. Accordingly, we reverse the judgment of the court of civil appeals and render judgment for the Camerons in accordance with the verdict.

In October 1975 the Camerons purchased a house in Arlington, Texas. The sellers, who are not parties to this lawsuit, had listed the house for sale with Terrell & Garrett, a real estate brokerage and agency firm. In listing the house for sale, the sellers were required to execute a listing agreement whereby they were to pay Terrell & Garrett a commission of six percent of the purchase price if Terrell & Garrett obtained a sale within a certain period. As part of its normal business practice, Terrell & Garrett then listed the house in the Multiple Listing Service (MLS) guide of the Arlington Board of Realtors. In doing so, Terrell & Garrett submitted some general information about the house for publication in the MLS guide. Included in this information was a statement that the house contained 2400 square feet. There is testimony that this statement was made to represent the number of square feet of heated and air conditioned space in the house.

On September 6, 1975, the Camerons were driving with their own real estate agent and looking for a house when they found the house in question. While stopped in front of the house, their realtor showed them the statement in the MLS guide that it contained 2400 square feet. The Camerons testified that they relied on the statement to mean that the house had 2400 square feet of heated and air conditioned space. Also, the Camerons testified that they agreed to purchase the house for $52,957.04 in reliance on this statement because they thought they were purchasing a house with 2400 square feet of heated and air conditioned space for $22.06 per square foot.

After purchasing and moving into the house, the Camerons had it measured and found out it actually contained only 2245 square feet of heated and air conditioned space 155 feet less than represented by Terrell & Garrett. However, they also discovered that if the garage, porch, and wall space were included, the house would have had a total of 2400 square feet of space.

The Camerons sued Terrell & Garrett for damages, alleging a cause of action under the DTPA for a misrepresentation made in a real estate transaction. The basis of the Camerons' deceptive trade practice claim is that Terrell & Garrett falsely represented in the MLS guide the number of square feet in the house. They alleged actual damages of $3,419.30, which they computed by multiplying the cost of the house per square foot as represented ($22.06) times the square footage deficiency (155 feet). The Camerons sought treble damages, reasonable attorney's fees and court costs under section 17.50(b) of the Act.

The case was submitted on special issues to the jury for a violation of the general prohibition in section 17.46(a) as authorized by section 17.50(a)(1). The jury returned a verdict for the Camerons. Terrell & Garrett then filed motions to disregard jury findings and for judgment notwithstanding the verdict, challenging in part the legal sufficiency of the evidence to support the jury's answers to special issues. The trial court sustained Terrell & Garrett's motions on the basis there was no evidence to support the jury's answers to the following special issues:

> "SPECIAL ISSUE NO. 2 ....
>
> "Do you find from a preponderance of the evidence that the Defendant's representation that the house in question contained two thousand four hundred square feet was false, misleading or deceptive act or practice? ....
>
> "Answer 'We do' or 'We do not.'
>
> "ANSWER: 'We do.'
>
> "SPECIAL ISSUE NO. 3 ....
>
> "Do you find from a preponderance of the evidence that the Defendant's representation of the quantity of square feet in the house in question was a producing cause of actual damages sustained by the Plaintiffs? ....
>
> "Answer 'We do' or 'We do not.'
>
> "ANSWER: 'We do' "; and
>
> "SPECIAL ISSUE NO. 4 ....
>
> "What sum of money, if any, if paid now in cash, do you find from a preponderance of the evidence would fairly and reasonably compensate the Plaintiffs for their actual damages, if any?
>
> "Answer in dollars and cents, if any.
>
> "ANSWER: $3,419.30."

The trial court rendered a take-nothing judgment against the Camerons notwithstanding the verdict.

On appeal, the Camerons contended that the trial court erred in setting aside the jury verdict because there was some evidence to support the jury's answers to special issues number 2, 3, and 4. However, to vitiate the verdict, Terrell & Garrett contended by crosspoint that the Camerons could not bring a private lawsuit under the DTPA because the Camerons were not consumers, as defined in section 17.45(4), as to them. The court of civil appeals sustained the contentions of both parties and, as a result, affirmed the trial court's take-nothing judgment. In this case, the Camerons' sole contention is that the court of civil appeals erred in holding they were not consumers as defined in section 17.45(4).

In *Riverside National Bank v. Lewis*, 603 S.W.2d 169, 173 (Tex.1980), we recognized that a person must qualify as a consumer as that term is defined in section 17.45(4) to maintain a private cause of action for treble damages under section 17.50 of the Act. To the same effect are Section 17.45(4) defines consumer as "an individual, partnership, or corporation who seeks or acquires by purchase or lease, any goods or services."

We have also recognized at least two requirements that must be established for a person to qualify as a consumer under the DTPA. One requirement is that the person must have sought or acquired goods or services by purchase or lease. *Riverside National Bank v. Lewis, supra* at 174; see *Woods v. Littleton*, 554 S.W.2d 662, 666 (Tex.1977). Another requirement recognized by this Court is that the goods or services purchased or leased must form the basis of the complaint. *Riverside National Bank v. Lewis, supra* at 175; *Woods v. Littleton, supra* at 666; see also *Rutherford v. Whataburger, Inc., supra* at 444; *Delaney Realty, Inc. v. Ozuna*, 593 S.W.2d 797, 800 (Tex.Civ. App. El Paso), writ ref'd n.r.e. per curiam, 600 S.W.2d 780 (1980); and *Ferguson v. Beal, supra* at 653. If either requirement is lacking, the person aggrieved by a deceptive act or practice must look to the common law or some other statutory provision for redress.

The Camerons satisfy both of these requirements in the case at hand. Although the Camerons alleged that they "sought or acquired the services" of Terrell & Garrett, it is clear that their complaint is not based on any alleged misrepresentation of the quality or quantity of services rendered by Terrell & Garrett. Instead, the Camerons' complaint is based solely on an alleged misrepresentation of the quantity of square feet in the house. At the time of this alleged deceptive trade practice, section 17.45(1) defined goods to include "... real property purchased ... for use."

Terrell & Garrett seeks to have this Court impose a type of privity requirement into the definition of consumer. It contends that a person must seek or acquire goods or services furnished by the person he is suing to qualify as a consumer under the DTPA. To be a consumer, it is submitted that if this requirement were imposed, a defendant would have to be in the same chain of title with the good or service on which the complaint is based. It argues that under this requirement the Camerons could not be consumers as to Terrell & Garrett because it was the seller's agent and did not furnish any goods or services that were sought or acquired by the Camerons. As authority for the imposition of this additional requirement to the qualifications of a consumer, Terrell & Garrett cites *Hi-Line Electric Co. v. Travelers Insurance Co.*, 587 S.W.2d 488 (Tex.Civ.App. Dallas 1979), writ ref'd n.r.e. per curiam, 593 S.W.2d 953 (1980), and *Barthlow v. Metcalf*, 594 S.W.2d 143 (Tex. Civ.App. Houston (1st dist.) 1979, writ dism'd), where it was held that a consumer is one who seeks or acquires goods or services furnished by the defendant.

In the case of *Delaney Realty Co. v. Ozuna,* 593 S.W.2d 797 (Tex. Civ. App.- El Paso), writ ref'd n.r.e. per curiam, 600 S.W.2d 780 (1980), a seller of a house represented to the purchaser that the house was not subject to flooding. The seller's real estate agent, however, made no representation about the tendency of the house to flood. The house did flood. The purchaser sued the seller and seller's agent under the DTPA, alleging that the seller misrepresented that the house was not susceptible to flooding and the seller's agent should have ascertained this condition of the house, and should have warned them about the susceptibility of the house to flooding. The court of civil appeals held that since the purchaser did not purchase any goods or services from the seller's agent, the purchaser did not fall within the definition of consumer and thus could not bring suit under the DTPA. In a per curiam opinion, we agreed with the judgment of the court of civil appeals stating there was no evidence that the seller's agent made any misrepresentation about flooding. However, we refused the purchasers' application for writ of error, no reversible error, stating:

> "This action should not be interpreted as an implied approval of the lower court's discussion concerning the (purchasers') failure to qualify as 'consumers' under the DTPA with respect to (the seller's agent) .... We reserve this question of statutory construction for the future." 600 S.W.2d at 782.

We are now called upon to answer this question of statutory construction expressly reserved in *Delaney*. In all interpretations of the Act, our primary objective is to ascertain the legislature's intent. *Woods v. Littleton, supra* at 665. To do that, we must look to the Act as a whole, and not [to] its isolated provisions, keeping in mind at all times "the old law, the evil, and the remedy." *Id.* The legislature itself directed that the Act "shall be liberally construed to promote its underlying purposes which are to protect consumers against false, misleading, and deceptive acts or practices, unconscionable actions and breaches of warranty and to provide efficient and economical procedures to secure such protection." Section 17.44.

The breadth of the Act is evidenced by section 17.49 which sets out the exemptions to the DTPA. That section does not provide an exemption for deceptive trade practices by persons who do not furnish the goods or services on which the complaint is based. Rather, it only exempts from the Act certain media owners and employees who publish and disseminate deceptive advertisements of goods and services for third parties. That same exemption, however, does not extend immunity from the Act where the media defendants (1) knew of the deception in the advertisement or (2) had a direct or substantial financial interest in the unlawfully advertised good or service. These media defendants, of course, do not furnish the goods or services that they advertise for third parties. Consequently, if the Act already excluded defendants who do not furnish the goods or services, as argued by Terrell & Garrett, there would have been no need for the legislature to exempt media defendants from liability or to have provided that media defendants could be sued in the two situations mentioned above. The legislature is never presumed to have done a useless act. *Red River National Bank v. Ferguson*, 206 S.W.2d 923 (Tex. 1918)

Similarly, if the legislature had intended to place such a restriction on the class of persons who could be sued under the Act for deceptive trade practices, it could easily have done so by simply drafting the restriction into the definition of consumer or some other provision of the Act. . . . It is a rule of statutory construction that every word of a statute must be presumed to have been used for a purpose. *Eddins-Walcher Butane Co. v. Calvert*, 298 S.W.2d 93, 96 (Tex. 1957). Likewise, we believe every word excluded from a statute must also be presumed to have been excluded for a purpose. Only when it is necessary to give effect to the clear legislative intent can we insert additional words or requirements into a statutory provision.

We find no indication in the definition of consumer in section 17.45(4), or any other provision of the Act, that the legislature intended to restrict its application only to deceptive trade practices committed by persons who furnish the goods or services on which the complaint is based. Nor do we find any indication that the legislature intended to restrict its application by any other similar privity requirement. In contrast, privity requirements have been dispensed with altogether in negligence suits, in implied warranty suits for economic loss, and, for the most part, privity requirements have also been abolished in strict liability suits. *See Nobility Homes of Texas, Inc. v. Shivers,* 557 S.W.2d 77 (Tex. 1977). The Act is designed to protect consumers from any deceptive trade practice made in connection with the purchase or lease of any goods or services. *Hi-Line Electric Co. v. Travelers Insurance Co., supra* at 490. To this end, we must give the Act, under the rule of liberal construction, its most comprehensive application possible without doing any violence to its terms.

Consumer is defined in section 17.45(4) only in terms of a person's relationship to a transaction in goods or services. It does not purport to define a consumer in terms of a person's relationship to the party he is suing. Section 17.45(4) does nothing more than describe the class of persons who can bring a suit for treble damages under section 17.50. *Riverside National Bank v. Lewis, supra* at 173. It does not say who a consumer can sue under section 17.50 for a deceptive trade practice violation. With respect to whom a consumer can sue, section 17.50(a)(1), the subsection under which this suit was tried, expressly states that a consumer can bring a suit if he has been adversely affected by "the use or employment by any person of an act or practice declared to be unlawful in section 17.46." Terrell & Garrett is a person under the Act. We, therefore, hold that a person need not seek or acquire goods or services furnished by the defendant to be a consumer as defined in the DTPA.

To the extent that language in *Hi-Line Electric Co. v. Travelers Insurance Co., supra,* and *Barthlow v. Metcalf*, supra, is inconsistent with this opinion, it is disapproved. We have considered both cases and find their respective holdings to be supported on other grounds announced therein. Whether the Act should be so restricted is a matter for the legislature and not this Court. Accordingly, we hold the Camerons are consumers because they purchased the goods on which their complaint is based.

Because we have held that the court of civil appeals erred on the grounds on which it affirmed the judgment of the trial court, we must consider Terrell & Garrett's crosspoints before this Court to see if there are any grounds presented therein to affirm the court of civil appeals' judgment. In doing so, we find three crosspoints challenging the court of civil appeals' ruling there is some evidence to support the jury findings to special issue numbers 2, 3, and 4, which are set out above. The jury answered each special issue in favor of the Camerons. For that reason, we are required to consider only the evidence and the reasonable inferences that can be drawn therefrom, in their most favorable light, to support these jury findings. We have considered each of these crosspoints and we agree with the ruling of the court of civil appeals on the legal sufficiency of the evidence to support these jury findings.

We, therefore, reverse the judgments below and render judgment for the Camerons in accordance with the jury verdict. The Camerons are also entitled to treble damages, reasonable attorney's fees, and costs as authorized by the DTPA.

Miller v. Keyser
90 S.W.3d 712
(Tex. 2002)

Under the Deceptive Trade Practices Consumer Protection Act (DTPA), we are asked whether an agent for a disclosed principal may be held liable for passing along false representations made in the course and scope of his employment. The court of appeals answered that question no. To the contrary, we hold that because the DTPA allows a consumer to bring suit against "any person," Tex. Bus. & Com.Code § 17.50(a)(1), an agent may be held personally liable for the misrepresentations he makes when acting within the scope of his employment. As a result, we reverse the court of appeals' judgment, and remand this cause to the court of appeals for proceedings consistent with this opinion.

I. Background

Barry Keyser worked as a sales agent for D.B. Interests, Inc., a Texas corporation doing business as The Homemaker. In 1992 and 1993, Keyser sold Homemaker homes built in Oakbrook, a new subdivision located in Pearland, Texas. Keyser showed prospective purchasers the different lots available, as well as how each home would fit on the lots. The lots were subject to a drainage easement held by the Brazoria County Drainage District on the back twenty-feet of each lot. Each purchaser knew about the drainage easement on his or her lot.

David and Lynette Miller and several other homeowners (the "homeowners") bought Homemaker homes from Keyser in the Oakbrook subdivision. The homeowners informed Keyser that they were interested in larger backyards, many wanting extra space for their children and pets. Keyser represented to the homeowners that The Homemaker lots were oversized and that they were in fact larger than the lots of a competing builder in the subdivision. Keyser told the homeowners that even with the existence of the easement, the lots could be fenced along the back of the property line. The homeowners paid a premium for these "oversized" lots.

In 1994, after the homeowners built their homes, some received a letter from the Brazoria County Drainage District telling them that all fences in the easement must be removed at the owners' expense. As a result, the homeowners sued the owner of The Homemaker, Dennis Bailey, and sales agent, Barry Keyser, for common-law fraud and misrepresentations in violation of the DTPA. The homeowners claim that Keyser misrepresented the size of the lots and where the fencing could be placed at the back of the lots. The homeowners sought to recover damages for the fence and landscaping repairs and a return of the excess charges paid for the lots.

The homeowners also joined The Homemaker, but all claims against the corporation were dismissed as untimely. At trial, the trial court granted a directed verdict in favor of Dennis Bailey. The trial court found that Bailey had no direct communication with the homeowners, and he therefore made no misrepresentations about the lots. After the jury answered seven questions in favor of the homeowners, the trial court rendered judgment against Keyser.

Keyser appealed, arguing that as a matter of law, under the DTPA, a corporate agent cannot be held personally liable for company misrepresentations. In reversing the trial court's judgment, the court of appeals relied on our decision in *Karl & Kelly Co., Inc. v. McLerran,* 646 S.W.2d 174 (Tex.1983) to support its conclusion that an agent acting within the scope of his employment cannot be held personally liable under the DTPA. The court of appeals reasoned that, in light of the jury findings that Keyser did not act fraudulently and acted only in the scope of his employment, the trial court erred in rendering a judgment against him. We granted the homeowners' petition for review to consider this question.

II. Agent Liability Under the DTPA

Under the DTPA, a consumer may bring suit against *any person* whose false, misleading, or deceptive acts, or other practices enumerated in the Act are the producing cause of the consumer's harm. A consumer may also bring suit for "any unconscionable action or course of action by *any person.*" The DTPA broadly defines "person" as "an individual, partnership, corporation, association, or other group, however organized." The DTPA is a consumer protection statute, and according to the Legislature, is to be construed liberally to promote its central purpose.

Keyser personally participated in the sale of every home sold to the homeowners. He personally made the representations about the size of the lot and the location of the fence. He is the only person with whom the homeowners had any contact. Based on the plain language of the statute, Keyser is liable for his own DTPA violations.

Keyser argues that he should not be held liable because he did not, in fact, know that his representations were false. But a DTPA claim does not require that the consumer prove the employee acted knowingly or intentionally. The DTPA requires that the consumer show that the misrepresentation was false and that the false misrepresentation was the producing cause of the consumer's damages. A consumer is not required to prove intent to make a misrepresentation to recover under the DTPA. The DTPA was enacted to "protect consumers against false, misleading, and deceptive business practices, unconscionable actions, and breaches of warranty" and to provide consumers with a means to redress deceptive practices "without the burden of proof and numerous defenses encountered in a common law fraud or breach of warranty suit." Misrepresentations that may not be actionable under common law fraud may be actionable under the DTPA. Thus, Keyser may be held liable under the DTPA even if he did not know that his representations were false or even if he did not intend to deceive anyone.

Keyser further argues that he is not a "person" subject to the DTPA because at all times, he was acting solely on behalf of The Homemaker. He contends that the statute should not be read to allow a consumer to sue any individual person absent a showing that this individual acted outside the scope of his employment or that this individual acted knowingly. For support, Keyser points to our *per curiam* opinion in *Karl & Kelly Co., Inc. v. McLerran.* 646 S.W.2d at 175.

The issues in *McLerran* arose in the context of a post-answer default judgment. The defendants, an architect and a real-estate agent involved in the construction of a home, were sued under the DTPA based on their representations about the workmanlike quality of the home. The default judgment happened because the defendants answered but failed to appear at trial. To support the default judgment, the McLerrans had the burden to prove that the defendants were liable. In reversing the court of appeals' judgment, we noted that the McLerrans produced no evidence that the defendants acted in their individual capacities. And we held that agents of a corporation are not liable for the company's misrepresentations unless there is a finding that the agents acted as the alter ego of the corporation.

Ten months after our decision in *McLerran,* this Court decided *Light v. Wilson,* 663 S.W.2d 813 (Tex. 1983). In *Light,* the owner of a construction company was sued individually for unconscionable acts and breaches of implied and express warranties in violation of the DTPA. *Id.* at 814.We declined to hold this corporate agent individually liable because there was no finding that the agent individually violated the DTPA. This conclusion necessarily implied that individual liability could attach if it was found that the agent *personally* violated the DTPA.

Justice Spears,in his concurring opinion, asserted that *Light* implicitly overruled the decision in *McLerran.* As stated by Justice Spears, "[l]iability in these cases is based on the agent's own actions, not his status as agent." We agree with this statement. Thus, if there is evidence that the agent personally made misrepresentations, then that agent can be held personally liable.

We recognized our implicit holding in *Light* less than two years later in *Weitzel v. Barnes.* 691 S.W.2d 598 (Tex.1985). In *Weitzel,* we concluded that when corporate officers make affirmative misrepresentations in connection with the sale of a home, the agents are personally liable under the DTPA even though they were acting on behalf of the corporation. *Id.* at 601.Liability attaches because the officers *themselves* made the misrepresentations. Our holdings in *Light* and *Weitzel* comport with Texas' longstanding rule that a corporate agent is personally liable for his own fraudulent or tortious acts. *See Leyendecker & Assocs., Inc. v. Wechter,* 683 S.W.2d 369, 375 (Tex.1984); *Light,* 663 S.W.2d at 815. The plain language of the DTPA is in harmony with this rule.

Here, the jury expressly found that Keyser personally violated the DTPA and that his false, misleading, and deceptive actions were the producing cause of the homeowners' harm. The evidence supports that finding. Keyser showed the homeowners the plats of land, he showed them the size of the lots, he told them where their fences could be located, and he was paid $40,000 in commission as a result of his sales. The plain language of the DTPA grants the homeowners a cause of action against "any person" who violates the Act. Even though the jury found that Keyser acted "solely within the course and scope of his employment ... as an agent for [T]he Homemaker," this finding does not excuse Keyser from DTPA liability.

Our analysis on agent liability is not affected by the agent's or the employee's position in the company. The court of appeals distinguished *Weitzel* from this case based on the fact that the corporate agents were officers of the corporation. But the definition of "person" under the DTPA makes no such distinction, and other provision implies that one's status in the corporation determines liability. Agents are personally liable for their own torts. There is no basis for concluding differently based on the claims brought under the DTPA. Accordingly, we hold that an agent may be held personally liable for his own violations of the DTPA.

Keyser points to the language of the DTPA indemnity provision to purportedly advance his theory that an agent acting for a corporation cannot be held individually liable. Section 17.555 states: "[a] person against whom an action has been brought under this subchapter may seek contribution or indemnity from one who, under the statute law or at common law, may have liability for the damaging event of which the consumer complains." Keyser says that because Section 17.555 includes the common law, the DTPA recognizes the common law doctrine of *respondeat superior.* Thus, if the agent or employee is acting on behalf of the corporation and in the scope of his employment, the corporation alone is the responsible party. The agent is only liable under the DTPA when he acts knowingly or outside the scope of his employment.

We think this indemnification provision supports a contrary inference. The statute actually contemplates that an agent may be innocent of any knowing misrepresentation by merely passing along information of the company. The language of Section 17.555 does not excuse an agent from being a party to a suit. Rather, the indemnification provision provides a means for an agent to recoup his loss from the employer if the employer is responsible for the consumer's harm. The DTPA permits "consumers to seek DTPA recourse against those with whom they have engaged in a consumer transaction." Then, if another causes the agent's liability, the agent may seek statutory contribution or indemnity against that entity.

Here, The Homemaker is an entity that may have liability for the homeowners' harm. If Keyser was truly just passing along company information, then he has a right to seek indemnity against The Homemaker. Even though the DTPA subjects an agent or employee acting within the scope of employment to DTPA liability, the DTPA also offers protection. Agents and employees receive protection through the indemnification provision.

Finally, the DTPA identifies a wide range of persons who may be sued, but also identifies an exemption in Section 17.49. Section 17.49(a) exempts from DTPA liability "the owner or employees" of certain advertising media. But a media employee may still be sued if the employee acts with "knowledge of the false, deceptive, or misleading acts or practices. . ." or has a "substantial financial interest in the sale or distribution of the unlawfully advertised good or service." The homeowners argue, and we agree, that the exemption of Section 17.49 only excuses from DTPA liability advertising media employees.

Further, Section 17.49 demonstrates that the Legislature knew how to exempt employees from liability for innocent misrepresentations. And it chose to only exempt media employees. If all employees of any enterprise were meant to be excluded from the DTPA because they were acting on behalf of their employers, then Section 17.49 would be unnecessary. As we stated in *Cameron v. Terrell & Garrett, Inc.*, 618 S.W.2d 535, 540 (Tex. 1981) if the [L]egislature had intended to place such a restriction on the class of persons who could be sued under the Act for deceptive trade practices, it could easily have done so by simply drafting the restriction into the definition of *consumer* or some other provision of the Act.

The Legislature did not do so, and we presume the Legislature did not perform a needless act by enacting Section 17.49. The Legislature created a limited exemption for advertising media employees, and it drafted the statute to allow a consumer to bring suit against "any person" who causes the consumer's harm. Thus, as the statute is written, "any person" who makes a representation is liable under the Act if that representation is false, misleading, or deceptive. Any other reading of the DTPA renders Section 17.49's language useless.

The court of appeals states that, even if one interprets the statute to excuse from DTPA liability those employees acting innocently on behalf of their employers, Section 17.49 still serves a purpose. Section 17.49 "protects media employees (and their employers) from liability based on another's false advertising." But the court of appeals expands the limited exemption in Section 17.49 beyond its own terms. It ignores the plain language of the DTPA to create an additional exemption for employees who pass along company information. The court of appeals interpreted the "any person" language of the DTPA to excuse all employees or agents for their innocent misrepresentations made while on the job, and it distinguished between employees who act on their own and employees who act on behalf of their employers. Under this interpretation, no express employee exemption provision would be required, and as a result, the language of Section 17.49 would be superfluous.

The purpose of the DTPA is not only to deter the conduct the DTPA forbids but also to provide consumers with an efficient means to redress deceptive business practices. Creating an exemption for corporate agents and employees would do little to further that purpose.

In the event an employee is held liable for unknowingly passing along false company information, that employee can seek statutory contribution or indemnification from the employer. The provision works to ensure that the responsible party is the one that actually pays, even if that party is not the one actually sued. If the indemnification proves to be not enough protection for agents, the Legislature can amend the statute to prevent further mischief. We decline to judicially create an exemption that does not exist in the statute for agents acting solely on behalf of their employers. In doing so, we also acknowledge the amicus brief received from the Attorney General, in which the General asserts that judicially creating such an exemption would adversely affect the General's ability to enforce the statute, which ultimately will affect the protections afforded to consumers. *See* Tex. Bus. & Com.Code § 17.47(a).

III. Conclusion

Keyser is a "person" under the language of the DTPA. Because the plain language of the DTPA provides for agent liability when that agent personally violates the DTPA, we reverse the judgment of the court of appeals. Keyser raised additional issues in the court of appeals that were not presented to this Court. Pursuant to Rule 53.4 of the Texas Rules of Appellate Procedure, we remand this case to the court of appeals for further proceedings.

NOTES & QUESTIONS

1) Under Texas common law, a principal is not liable for an agent's intentional acts if the latter are not closely connected with the employee's authorized duties. See *GTE Southwest, Inc. v. Bruce,* 998 S.W.2d 605, 617-618 (Tex. 1999). And in *Qantel Business Systems, Inc. v. Custom Controls Co.*, 761 S.W.2d 302, 305 (Tex. 1988), the Texas Supreme Court stated: The traditional common law theories of vicarious liability, such as agency or *respondeat superior,* provide an adequate basis for creating vicarious liability under the DTPA. The DTPA does not recognize or envision the expansion of common law theories of vicarious liability to include "inextricably intertwined," or the mere existence of a "relationship" between parties. Therefore, is it reasonable to conclude that a principal will be vicariously liable under the DTPA whenever an agent harms a consumer, within the scope of his employment or agency?

2) Consider the court's decision in *Broussard v. San Juan Products, Inc.*, 273 S.W.3d 400, (Tex.App.-Beaumont 2008):

> This appeal concerns whether a manufacturer may be held liable as principal when an authorized dealer for the manufacturer's product sells another company's product, using a similar product name, to a consumer. We affirm the summary judgment granted to the defendants by the trial court.
>
> Robin Broussard purchased what she believed was a San Juan Capistrano fiberglass swimming pool from Hamilton Pools, Inc. Defects appeared after installation, and Broussard determined that the product she purchased was a "knock-off" manufactured by San Juan Pools of Texas, Inc. Broussard initially sued Howard S. "Buddy" Hamilton, Stacy Jo Hamilton-Long, Hamilton Pools, Inc. d/b/a San Juan Pools of Beaumont, and San Juan Pools of Texas, Inc., the alleged sellers and manufacturer of the defective pool, for deceptive trade practices, fraud, breach of warranty, and breach of contract.
>
> Broussard amended her petition, adding as defendants the manufacturer of genuine San Juan Capistrano swimming pools, American Environmental Container Corporation (AECC), and its licensor, San Juan Products, Inc. (SJP). Broussard alleges that Hamilton Pools and Buddy Hamilton as agents of AECC, breached the contract and warranty and engaged in deceptive trade practices and fraud. The trial court granted the traditional and no-evidence motions for summary judgment filed by SJP and AECC and severed those claims into the separate suit from which Broussard appeals.
>
> Broussard argues that when an innocent third party suffers a loss from misconduct of an agent acting within the scope of his apparent authority, the principal is responsible. *See W.C. Biggers & Co. v. First Nat'l Bank,* 29 S.W.2d 841, 842 (Tex.

Civ.App.-Texarkana 1930, writ dism'd w.o.j.). While true, a dealer is not *per se* an agent of the manufacturer and the terms of the dealership agreement determine the nature of the relationship. *Gabaldon v. Gen. Motors Corp.,* 876 S.W.2d 367, 369 (Tex.App.-El Paso 1993, no writ).

The appellees argue there is no summary judgment evidence that they authorized Buddy Hamilton and/or Hamilton Pools to transact business on behalf of SJP or AECC. The . . . dealer agreement between Hamilton Pools and AECC states that Hamilton Pools is an independent company engaged in the retail sales of pools, that AECC's relationship to Hamilton Pools shall be that of independent supplier, and expressly disclaims that Hamilton Pools would be an agent or employee of AECC. . . . Broussard contends that the apparent agency doctrine applies here.

Apparent agency arises solely from conduct of the principal communicated to a third party. *Gaines v. Kelly,* 235 S.W.3d 179, 182 (Tex.2007). The alleged principal must either knowingly permits the purported agent to hold himself out as having authority, or the alleged principal must exercise such lack of ordinary care as to clothe the purported agent with indicia of authority, leading a reasonably prudent person to believe the agent has authority to bind the principal. *Id.* "Because an agent's authority is presumed to be co-extensive with the business entrusted to his care, it includes only those contracts and acts incidental to the management of the particular business with which he is entrusted." *Id.* at 185. The relevant issue is not merely the existence of an agency relationship, but also the scope of that agency. *Id.* at 184. We may consider only the principal's conduct leading a third party to believe that the agent has authority. *NationsBank, N.A. v. Dilling,* 922 S.W.2d 950, 953 (Tex.1996). We must look beyond permission given to sell its products, which is in itself insufficient to bestow apparent authority for other purposes. *See Ins. Co. of N. Am. v. Morris,* 981 S.W.2d 667, 672 (Tex.1998).

The dealer agreement in this case allowed Hamilton Pools to use the trade names "San Juan" only in connection with the sale of pools supplied by AECC. AECC did not grant Hamilton Pools the right to use the name "San Juan" in the dealer's trade name. The issue, then, is whether some other conduct on the part of AECC and SJP clothed Hamilton Pools or Buddy Hamilton with the authority to transact business for AECC and SJP.

The appellees argue there is no summary judgment evidence that they vested Buddy Hamilton or Hamilton Pools with the apparent authority to act in their behalf. Broussard had no contact with AECC or SJP prior to the sale and there is no summary judgment evidence that Buddy Hamilton or Hamilton Pools ever represented to Broussard that either Hamilton or his company were representatives of SJP or AECC or claimed that they were acting on behalf of SJP or AECC. What Buddy Hamilton and Hamilton Pools allegedly represented to Broussard was only that Hamilton Pools was selling Broussard a San Juan pool. In other words, Broussard thought Hamilton was selling her a San Juan pool, but did not believe that San Juan was selling her a pool directly.

Broussard contends the appellees had knowledge that Hamilton Pools and Buddy Hamilton were selling non-AECC manufactured pools as pools manufactured by the appellees, but did not terminate the dealer agreement and failed to take action against Hamilton Pools and Buddy Hamilton. She also contends the summary judgment evidence shows the appellees provided sales and promotional material to Hamilton Pools. She argues that the appellees' lack of action created an apparent agency relationship whereby the appellees are vicariously liable for the acts of Hamilton Pools and Buddy Hamilton. "[T]he principal's full knowledge of all material facts is essential to establish a claim of apparent authority based on estoppel." *Gaines,* 235 S.W.3d at 182.

The summary judgment evidence regarding the appellees' knowledge that Hamilton Pools and Buddy Hamilton were selling "knock-offs" comes from two sources: Henry Eads and Kyle Mehl. Henry Eads bought a pool from Hamilton Pools in 1995. Buddy Hamilton told Eads it was a San Juan pool. When defects appeared in the product, Eads looked up "sanjuanpools.com" on the internet and obtained the company's telephone number. Eads called San Juan, and the woman who spoke to Eads told him he would need to talk to his dealer about his problem with his pool. . . . [Ultimately, Eads replied that they could do anything to him absent his serial number appearing on the pool]. There is no evidence that Eads communicated to the appellees that Hamilton Pools or Buddy Hamilton had falsely represented to Eads that the pool had been manufactured by the appellees.

* * *

The appellees argue that use of a manufacturer's logo in a dealer's promotional material does not create apparent authority for the dealer to act for the manufacturer. . . .Hamilton Pools was an authorized dealer for AECC in 1994, but the marketing material provided to Broussard was distributed by the pool's manufacturer, San Juan Pools of Texas, Inc., not AECC or SJP. . . .

Broussard argues that the Supreme Court applies a "more liberal standard" for apparent agency for DTPA causes of action than that which applies to claims at common law. The case on which she relies held that lack of actual authority is not a defense to a DTPA cause of action if the defendant's agent is acting within the scope of his apparent authority. *See Royal Globe Ins. Co. v. Bar Consultants, Inc.,* 577 S.W.2d 688, 694 (Tex.1979). . . .

Broussard alleges that AECC and SJP are vicariously liable for the deceptive and fraudulent acts of Buddy Hamilton and Hamilton Pools but she does not allege that AECC or SJP committed a deceptive trade practice or fraud other than through Buddy Hamilton and Hamilton Pools as the alleged agents of AECC and SJP. We hold [that] the trial court did not err in granting summary judgment on the grounds that AECC and SJP are not vicariously liable. Accordingly, the judgment is affirmed.

B. Third-Party Manufacturers, Producers and Suppliers as DTPA Defendants

Amstadt v. United States Brass Corporation
919 S.W.2d 644
(Tex. 1996)

In these three cases, homeowners have sued the manufacturers of a polybutylene plumbing system for negligence and violations of the Deceptive Trade Practices-Consumer Protection Act. TEX. BUS. & COM. CODE §§ 17.41-17.63 (DTPA). The common issue is whether the Legislature intended that upstream suppliers of raw materials and component parts be liable under the DTPA when none of their misrepresentations reached the consumers. This precise issue, which to our knowledge has never before been raised in the twenty-three-year history of the DTPA, animates the appeals in *Barrett v. United States Brass Corp.*, *United States Brass Corp. v. Knowlton/ Kochie*, and *United States Brass Corp. v. Andraus*.

* * *

We hold that, although the homeowners who obtained a jury finding of negligence may recover on that theory, no homeowner may recover from Celanese, Shell, or U.S. Brass under the DTPA because these manufacturers' alleged DTPA violations did not occur in connection with the homeowners' purchase of their homes. We accordingly reverse the judgments of the courts of appeals with regard to DTPA liability in all three causes.

* * *

I. FACTS

U.S. Brass, Shell, and Celanese v. Andraus

In *Andraus*, the owners of approximately 95 homes in the Fairmont Park West subdivision in La Porte, Texas, sued General Homes Corporation (the developer and homebuilder), U.S. Brass, Shell Oil Company, and Hoechst Celanese Corporation after experiencing problems with their plumbing. U.S. Brass designed and manufactured the plumbing system.

The plumbing system used flexible plastic pipes made of polybutylene resin connected by fittings made of a plastic compound called Celcon. The pipes and fittings were joined together by a copper or aluminum crimp ring placed around the outside of the pipe at the point where the pipe and fitting were connected. The ring, fitting, and pipe were then compressed using a large wrench-like tool designed by U.S. Brass. The pressure from the crimp ring deformed the pipe and fitting, creating a water-tight seal.

Celanese manufactured Celcon and supplied Celcon pellets to U.S. Brass to be molded into fittings. Celanese promoted the use of Celcon in plumbing applications to U.S. Brass and other manufacturers, and knew that U.S. Brass used Celcon to make the fittings. Shell produced the polybutylene resin and provided it in raw form to U.S. Brass. U.S. Brass formed the resin into the pipe used in the plumbing system.

In the early 1980s, U.S. Brass and Shell promoted the plumbing system to municipal officials in La Porte in order to obtain building code approval of the system for residential use. U.S. Brass and Shell also marketed the system to homebuilders, including General Homes. General Homes installed U.S. Brass' plumbing system in homes it built in 1980, 1981, and 1982. In 1982, some of these systems began to fail. Cracks developed in the Celcon fittings that eventually caused leaks. At trial, the parties vigorously disputed what caused the fittings to fail. Some of the experts testified that degradation of the Celcon from exposure to the households' chlorinated water caused the cracks in the fittings. Others testified that inadequate design, defective manufacture, and improper installation, or a combination of these problems along with chemical degradation created excessive stress, which caused the fittings to crack.

The homeowners sued General Homes, U.S. Brass, Shell, Celanese, and Vanguard Plastics, Inc. (a competitor of U.S. Brass, later dismissed from the suit). General Homes is not a party to this appeal. The homeowners alleged that the plumbing system's failure caused property damage and mental anguish. They sought damages based on negligence, fraud, and violations of the DTPA.

A jury found that U.S. Brass, Shell, and Celanese had made misrepresentations under the DTPA and were negligent. The jury also found that U.S. Brass had acted unconscionably and was grossly negligent. The trial court ruled that the statute of limitations barred the negligence claims of fifty-six households, and rendered a take-nothing judgment against five households for unspecified reasons. Three households elected to recover on the negligence findings, and the trial court rendered judgment accordingly. The trial court also rendered judgment for the eighty-six households that elected recovery under the DTPA.

Celanese, Shell, and U.S. Brass appealed. The court of appeals reversed the trial court's judgment in part and affirmed it in part. Specifically, the court of appeals affirmed DTPA liability because it concluded that "there was a link between the representations made and the use of the plumbing system in the plaintiffs' homes, which ultimately caused damage."

Kochie v. U.S. Brass

In *Knowlton/Kochie*, homeowners sued General Homes, Buckner Boulevard Plumbing Company (a plumbing contractor), Celanese, Shell, U.S. Brass, and Vanguard. They asserted claims for negligence, strict liability, and misrepresentation and unconscionability under the DTPA based on the defendants' representations about the characteristics of the plumbing systems to homebuilders. They claimed that absent such representations, General Homes would not have installed the defective systems.

Celanese, Shell, U.S. Brass, and General Homes moved for summary judgment based on *res judicata* and the statute of limitations. The trial court granted the motion with respect to five households, led by the Knowltons, without specifying the grounds. The Knowlton households had bought their homes from people who had previously sued and recovered damages caused by the plumbing systems.

The remaining households, led by the Kochies, dismissed their claims against General Homes, Buckner, Celanese, and Shell, and proceeded to trial against U.S. Brass and Vanguard. After closing argument but before the jury returned a verdict, they also settled with Vanguard. The jury returned a verdict in favor of sixty-nine households. Forty-eight households elected recovery under the DTPA and twenty-one elected recovery for negligence. The trial court rendered judgment accordingly against U.S. Brass.

U.S. Brass appealed, complaining that the Kochie homeowners were not consumers under the DTPA. The court of appeals rejected that complaint. The Knowlton homeowners also appealed. The court of appeals reversed the summary judgment rendered against them, holding that neither res judicata nor the statute of limitations barred their actions.

Barrett v. U.S. Brass

In *Barrett*, several hundred homeowners sued nine companies, including U.S. Brass, alleging negligence, strict liability, and violations of the DTPA. The trial court put thirty-six homeowners to trial as a test group. The group settled with all defendants except U.S. Brass.

The trial proceeded against U.S. Brass. The trial court directed a verdict against nine households because U.S. Brass' products were not used in their homes. These nine did not appeal. The jury found in favor of twenty-three households for negligence and DTPA violations, but found against four households. The trial court rendered judgment against the four latter households, who were also unsuccessful at the court of appeals. The twenty-three households that obtained favorable jury findings elected to recover under the DTPA. The trial court, however, granted U.S. Brass' motion to disregard the jury's answers under the DTPA and rendered judgment based solely on negligence.

The court of appeals reversed the judgment in part, holding that all the homeowners were consumers under the DTPA, but that only seven of the twenty-three homeowners had produced sufficient evidence that U.S. Brass' misrepresentations were a producing cause of their injuries. The court also held that there was no evidence of producing cause with regard to the sixteen other households.

II. DECEPTIVE TRADE PRACTICES ACT

A.

The DTPA grants consumers a cause of action for false, misleading, or deceptive acts or practices. Tex. Bus. & Com. Code § 17.50(a)(1); §, 603 S.W.2d 169, 173 (Tex. 1980). The DTPA defines a "consumer" as "an individual . . . who seeks or acquires by purchase or lease, any goods or services." Tex. Bus. & Com. Code § 17.45(4). Privity of contract with a defendant is not required for the plaintiff to be a consumer. *E.g., Home Sav. Ass'n v. Guerra*, 733 S.W.2d 134, 136 (Tex. 1987); *Kennedy v. Sale*, 689 S.W.2d 890, 892-93 (Tex. 1985); *Flenniken v. Longview Bank & Trust*

Co., 661 S.W.2d 705, 707 (Tex. 1983); *Cameron v. Terrell & Garrett, Inc.*, 618 S.W.2d 535, 540-41 (Tex. 1981).

A consumer must, in order to prevail on a DTPA claim, also establish that each defendant violated a specific provision of the Act, and that the violation was a producing cause of the claimant's injury.

The manufacturers argue that DTPA liability, while not limited to those in contractual privity with the consumer, cannot extend to all entities in the chain of production or distribution when none of those entities' alleged misrepresentations ever reached the consumer. The homeowners, on the other hand, argue that a misrepresentation by any entity in the chain of distribution that is the cause-in-fact of actual damages entitles them to recover under the DTPA. We do not agree with the homeowners' contention. To accept the homeowners' argument would extend DTPA liability to upstream manufacturers or suppliers to an extent not intended by the Legislature when it enacted the DTPA.

The purpose of the DTPA is to "protect consumers against false, misleading, and deceptive business practices, unconscionable actions, and breaches of warranty and to provide efficient and economical procedures to secure such protection." TEX. BUS. & COM. CODE § 17.44. As we have explained, that purpose is, in part, to encourage consumers to litigate claims that would not otherwise be economically feasible and to deter the conduct the DTPA forbids.

Although the DTPA was designed to supplement common-law causes of action, we are not persuaded that the Legislature intended the DTPA to reach upstream manufacturers and suppliers when their misrepresentations are not communicated to the consumer. Despite its broad, overlapping prohibitions, we must keep in mind why the Legislature created this simple, nontechnical cause of action: to protect consumers in consumer transactions. Consistent with that intent, we hold that the defendant's deceptive conduct must occur in connection with a consumer transaction, as we explain below.

In *Cameron v. Terrell & Garrett, Inc.*, we said: "The Act is designed to protect consumers from any deceptive trade practices made in connection with the purchase or lease of any goods or services." 618 S.W.2d 535, 541 (Tex. 1981). The in-connection-with requirement imposes a limitation on liability that is consistent with the underlying purposes of the DTPA. Without this limitation, we would merely substitute the defendant's introduction of a particular product into the stream of commerce for the conduct that was found to have violated the DTPA. We find no authority for shifting the focus of a DTPA claim from whether the defendant committed a deceptive act to whether a product that was sold caused an injury. Requiring a connection between the plaintiffs, their transactions, and the defendants' conduct enunciates a limitation we have alluded to, but not fully articulated, in prior cases.

While our words have varied, the concept has been consistent: the defendant's deceptive trade act or practice is not actionable under the DTPA unless it was committed in connection with the plaintiff's transaction in goods or services.

In the three cases before us today, the homeowners purchased homes equipped with polybutylene plumbing systems. These systems are goods, and they form the basis of the homeowners' complaints. The homeowners are, therefore, consumers under the DTPA. TEX. BUS. & COM. CODE § 17.45(4). To determine whether the defendants may be liable under the DTPA, we must examine whether their conduct occurred in connection with the plaintiffs' purchase of their homes.

B. Celanese

Celanese manufactured the polybutylene compound, Celcon, and supplied Celcon pellets to U.S. Brass for its use in molding the plumbing system fittings. Celanese promoted the use of Celcon in plumbing applications to U.S. Brass and other manufacturers, and knew that U.S. Brass used Celcon to make fittings for its plumbing systems. Celanese did not control U.S. Brass' selection of raw materials, did not design the parts or tools, and did not instruct or train the homebuilders' plumbers. Celanese told U.S. Brass that it should mold prototype components from Celcon and subject them to the most severe anticipated end-use conditions. Celanese also informed U.S. Brass of Celcon's potential limitations in high-chlorine conditions. Celanese's marketing efforts were limited to promoting its material to the manufacturers of the plumbing systems. It did not market the systems to homebuilders or building code officials, or market the finished homes to the consumers. The manufacturers of the plumbing systems and the building code officials, and to a lesser degree the homebuilders, were intermediaries capable of assessing the suitability of Celcon for use in the systems.

None of these facts supports the conclusion that Celanese's misrepresentations were made in connection with the plaintiffs' purchase of their homes. Celanese exercised little or no control over the manufacture and installation of the finished plumbing systems, much less the manufacture and sale of the homes. Celanese had no influence over the terms of the sales to the homeowners. At most, Celanese enjoyed the benefit of selling a raw material to a downstream manufacturer.

We hold that, under these circumstances, Celanese's conduct did not occur in connection with the plaintiffs' purchase of their homes; consequently, that conduct cannot support DTPA liability. Therefore, we reverse the court of appeals' judgment in Andraus permitting recovery under the DTPA against Celanese.

C. Shell

Shell produced the polybutylene resin from which U.S. Brass manufactured the pipes used in the plumbing system. As with Celanese, Shell did not control U.S. Brass' selection of raw materials, did not design the parts or tools, and did not instruct or train the homebuilders' plumbers. However, Shell played a substantial role in marketing U.S. Brass' entire system for new homes in the early 1980s. It undertook a marketing campaign and directly contacted homebuilders to promote the system and increase the market for polybutylene resin. Several homebuilders testified that they learned about U.S. Brass' plumbing system from Shell at trade shows and from Shell salespeople who visited them. The record contains some evidence that La Porte building officials would not have approved the plumbing system for residential use absent Shell's representations about its quality, reliability, and longevity. Finally, there is some evidence that the homebuilders installed the systems in reliance on the same representations.

As was the case with Celanese, these facts do not support the conclusion that Shell's misrepresentations were made in connection with the relevant consumer transactions, the purchase of the homes. Shell had no control over the manufacture or installation of the plumbing systems, or of the homes ultimately purchased by the consumers. Shell had no influence over the terms of the consumers' purchases. Although Shell actively promoted use of the plumbing systems in residential homes, there is no evidence that the information provided to homebuilders or building code officials was intended to be or actually was passed on to consumers. Importantly, Shell's marketing efforts were not incorporated into the efforts to market homes to the plaintiffs in this case. Also, any information provided by Shell was subject to independent evaluation by building code officials and by homebuilders.

We therefore conclude that Shell's conduct was not sufficiently connected with the plaintiffs' purchase of their homes to support DTPA liability. We therefore render judgment in *Andraus* that plaintiffs take nothing from Shell on their DTPA claims. (No judgment was rendered against Shell in *Knowlton/Kochie* or *Barrett.*)

D. U.S. Brass

U.S. Brass designed and manufactured the plumbing system at issue. It selected the raw materials, designed and manufactured the parts and tools, and trained the homebuilders' plumbers. In the late 1970s and early 1980s, U.S. Brass sought approval of the system for residential use from building code officials. Together with Shell it conducted a sales campaign aimed at the new home market and targeted individual builders. U.S. Brass represented to builders that the polybutylene plumbing system was durable and would last twenty-five years, was easy to install, required fewer joints, and was a quality product with characteristics superior to copper, galvanized steel, and PVC plumbing systems. U.S. Brass' and Shell's representatives met with homebuilders many times. U.S. Brass also provided homebuilders with a catalog on the plumbing system representing that the pipes and fittings would not corrode and that the pipes would not freeze or experience mineral build-up.

Although the conduct of U.S. Brass comes closer to being in connection with the plaintiffs' purchase of their homes than the conduct of Shell or Celanese, it also falls short of meeting the nexus required for DTPA liability. U.S. Brass exercised significant control over the design and installation of the plumbing systems, but as with Shell and Celanese, U.S. Brass had no role in the sale of the homes to the plaintiffs. As with Shell, U.S. Brass' marketing efforts were not intended to, nor were they, incorporated into the marketing of the homes to the plaintiffs. Finally, U.S. Brass' products were subject to independent evaluation by building code officials, homebuilders, and the plumbing contractors who installed the materials. Viewed in this context, we conclude that U.S. Brass' actions were not connected with the plaintiffs' transactions, that is, the sale of the homes, in a way that justifies liability under the DTPA.

Our analysis of U.S. Brass' connection with the consumer transactions applies with equal force to allegations based on misrepresentations and unconscionable acts. The subject matter of the misrepresentations and the conduct found to be unconscionable is virtually identical. Because we conclude that the totality of U.S. Brass' involvement in the consumer transaction is insufficient to support DTPA liability, we reverse the judgments against U.S. Brass under both theories of DTPA liability.

Although we have concluded that the homeowners have no DTPA cause of action against Celanese, Shell, and U.S. Brass, no one disputes that they have a DTPA cause of action against General Homes, their seller. Given this recourse under the DTPA against the seller, and the contribution and indemnity provision of the DTPA, *see* TEX. BUS. & COM. CODE § 17.555, we think that rather than permit limitless upstream DTPA liability under these circumstances, the Legislature more likely intended for consumers to seek DTPA recourse against those with whom they have engaged in a consumer transaction. Then, to the extent that the seller's DTPA liability is caused or contributed to by the otherwise actionable misconduct of upstream manufacturers or suppliers, the seller may seek contribution or indemnity against them. Additionally, homeowners may obtain direct relief for foreseeable injuries due to the negligence of these parties.

* * *

NOTES & QUESTIONS

1) In *Amstadt*, the Supreme Court of Texas was clear: "[A third-party] defendant's deceptive trade act or practice is not actionable under the DTPA unless it was committed *in connection with* the plaintiff's transaction in goods or services." But this rule appears to focus on what a defendant *communicates* to a consumer rather than on what a defendant allows a consumer to think or believe about a defective product or service. Consider the in-connection-with rule. Is a defendant only liable for express misrepresentations or defective practices—using words, models, or samples?

2) Assume a third-party defendant promises to deliver a certain product or perform a service of a particular standard, quality, or grade and performs without disclosing to the ultimate user that the service or product deviates considerably from what was promised. Does the in-connection-with rule apply? Does it shield the third-party defendant from DTPA liability? May the disgruntled consumer employ the "inextricably intertwined" rule to circumvent the application of the *in-connection-with* rule? Consider the court's summary-judgment ruling in the next case.

Hou-Tex, Inc. v. Landmark Graphics
26 S.W.3d 103
(Tex.App.-Houston [14 Dist.] 2000)

Hou-Tex signed an oil, gas, and mineral lease to develop a prospective oil and gas field under land owned by the Angerstein family in Victoria County, Texas. To help choose the best site for an oil well on the land, Hou-Tex hired a geological contractor named Saguaro Seismic Surveys, L.C. Saguaro conducted a geophysical survey and interpreted its seismic data with a computer software program called SeisVision to help choose the best location for the oil well. SeisVision helped to select a site called Angerstein No. 1 . . . [which was] was a dry hole. Saguaro either used a beta, or test, version of SeisVision or a commercial version licensed to Anasazi Explorations, a consultant company hired by Saguaro to provide software support.

The well was 1,150 feet east and 650 feet north of the site where it should have been drilled. This deviation was the result of a defect in SeisVision — a "bug" in computer parlance — that miscalculated data from plots of land with irregular boundaries. In March 1996, Saguaro reported this bug to SeisVision's developer at Landmark. The developer told Saguaro that Landmark had known about the bug since August 1995. Landmark had corrected the problem in an updated version of SeisVision, which it had sent to only some of its clients. Neither Saguaro nor its consultant, Anasazi, had been told about the bug or sent the updated version.

Hou-Tex filed suit against Landmark for the costs of drilling Angerstein No. 1, alleging that Landmark . . . violated the Deceptive Trade Practices Act. Landmark filed for summary judgment, arguing that it. . . could not be sued under the DTPA because it was not connected to the services provided by Saguaro. The trial court granted Landmark a general summary judgment.

* * *

Deceptive Trade Practices Act

In point of error five, Hou-Tex contends that the trial court erred in granting summary judgment on its DTPA claim. Specifically, Hou-Tex argues that Landmark's disclaimers do not comply with section 17.42 of the DTPA to constitute a valid waiver and disclaimer of the act's protections. Tex. Bus. & Com.Code Ann. § 17.42. Landmark replies that it is not liable under the DTPA because the DTPA does not impose derivative liability on a defendant based on an innocent involvement in a business transaction.

The purpose of the DTPA is to "protect consumers against false, misleading, and deceptive business practices, unconscionable actions, and breaches of warranty and to provide efficient and economical procedures to secure such protection." Tex. Bus. & Com.Code Ann. § 17.44. A consumer suing under the DTPA need not establish contractual privity of contract with the defendant. *Home Sav. Ass'n v. Guerra,* 733 S.W.2d 134, 136 (Tex.1987).

However, the DTPA is not without limitation, and liability will not be imposed merely because a defendant introduced a particular product into the stream of commerce. *See Amstadt v. U.S. Brass Corp.,* 919 S.W.2d 644, 650 (Tex.1996). The DTPA is not intended to reach upstream manufacturers when their misrepresentations are not communicated to the consumer. *See id.* at 649. Hou-Tex argues that deceptive conduct may nonetheless be actionable under the DTPA if it is "inextricably intertwined" with a consumer transaction, citing *Knight v. International Harvester Credit Corp.,* 627 S.W.2d 382, 389 (Tex.1982). *Knight* is distinguishable from this case.

In *Knight,* there was one transaction —the sale of a truck on an installment basis— and two defendants who worked together to make the transaction. *See id.* Here, Landmark did not work with Saguaro to secure Hou-Tex's purchase of geological services. Further, the Texas Supreme Court has since cautioned that "inextricably intertwined" is not an additional theory of vicarious liability under the DTPA. *See Qantel Bus. Sys., Inc. v. Custom Controls Co.,* 761 S.W.2d 302, 305 (Tex.1988). Instead, for DTPA liability, the defendant's deceptive conduct must occur in connection with the consumer's transaction in goods or services. *See Amstadt,* 919 S.W.2d at 649-50.

Thus, we search the summary judgment record for evidence of Landmark's deceptive conduct and for evidence that such deceptive conduct occurred in connection with Hou-Tex's transaction with Saguaro for its services. The evidence shows that in 1994, Saguaro was a beta tester of the newly developed SeisVision software. By February 1995, Saguaro had in its possession a licensed version of the software, which was operated by and may have been licensed to Saguaro's consultant, a company called Anasazi Explorations.

In July 1995, Saguaro contracted with Hou-Tex to provide it geophysical and geographical expertise. Apparently throughout this time, Saguaro's consultant, Anasazi, was in weekly telephone contact with the software developer. Landmark was thus aware that Anasazi was using the software in its work for Saguaro's customers. During these telephone conversations, Landmark's employee and Anasazi's principal discussed limitations of and bugs in the software.

At no time did Landmark tell Anasazi, or Saguaro, about the particular bug that plagued the Angerstein No. 1 well. When Anasazi informed Landmark about this bug after Hou-Tex drilled the dry well in January 1996, Landmark's employee told them that he had learned about the bug in August 1995 from another user. He had even corrected the bug and sent an updated version of the software to some clients.

Even if we construe this evidence as a deceptive act on the part of Landmark, there must still be evidence that someone communicated the deception to Hou-Tex in connection with its acquisition of Saguaro's services. Landmark's summary judgment evidence shows that it had no communication with Hou-Tex and made no representations to it. Having established this, the burden shifts to Hou-Tex to offer controverting evidence that creates a fact issue. *See Centeq Realty,* 899 S.W.2d at 197.

Although Hou-Tex argues that Landmark's misrepresentations were communicated by Saguaro, it provides no supporting evidence. There is no evidence that Hou-Tex even knew about the software until after it failed.

Accordingly, there is no fact issue that Landmark's conduct was not communicated to Hou-Tex in connection with Hou-Tex's transaction for services from Saguaro. Consequently, Landmark's conduct cannot support DTPA liability, and we overrule point of error five.

C. *Family Members and Relatives as DTPA Defendants*

McDuffie v. Blassingame
883 S.W.2d 329
(Tex.App.-Amarillo 1994)

Appellant, Ronald McDuffie, filed suit against appellees, Carol McDuffie, Kenneth E. Blassingame, *Blassingame and Osburn, P.C.* (the firm), and Robert O'Donnell (collectively referred to as the appellees), for violation of the Texas Deceptive Trade Practices and Consumer Protection Act (DTPA). Tex. Bus. & Com.Code Ann. § 17.01 *et seq.*. In three partial summary judgments, the trial court ruled in favor of the appellees that Ronald take nothing on his action. Later, the court rendered judgment for attorney's fees in favor of Carol, Blassingame, and the firm based on their counterclaims alleging that Ronald's action was groundless, brought in bad faith, and brought for the purpose of harassment. We affirm.

* * *

Carol and Ronald were divorced in 1982. Carol was appointed managing conservator of their two minor children, and Ronald was appointed possessory conservator with visitation rights. In June 1989, Carol filed a motion to modify in a suit affecting the parent-child relationship, seeking to modify visitation rights and medical insurance coverage (the prior suit). Blassingame was Carol's attorney in the prior suit and a partner in the firm. O'Donnell is judge of the 301st District Court of Dallas County and presided over the prior suit.

On September 10, 1991, Ronald filed this cause of action under the [DTPA], alleging that the appellees forced him into the expense and emotional distress of a trial. The appellees answered and all parties filed motions for summary judgment on Ronald's action. In addition, Carol, Blassingame, and the firm filed counterclaims, alleging that Ronald's action was groundless, brought in bad faith, and brought for the purpose of harassment. In three partial summary judgments, the trial court denied Ronald's motion and granted the appellees' motions. Then, after an evidentiary hearing on the counterclaims, the trial court rendered judgment in favor of Carol, Blassingame, and the firm for reasonable attorney's fees.

By his first and third points of error, Ronald contends the trial court erred in granting Carol's, Blassingame's, and the firm's motions for summary judgment on his action, and denying his motion for summary judgment and motion for reconsideration because he established every element of his deceptive trade practice claim as a matter of law. These contentions are without merit.

In order to recover on a deceptive trade practice claim, the plaintiff must show 1) he is a consumer, 2) the defendant committed a false, misleading, or deceptive act or practice, and 3) such false, misleading, or deceptive act or practice constituted a producing cause of the plaintiff's actual damages. *Miller v. Soliz,* 648 S.W.2d 734, 739 (Tex.App.-Corpus Christi 1983, no writ). The issue that was properly before the trial court and . . . now [before] this Court is whether Ronald was a consumer as defined in the [DTPA].

Consumer status under the [DTPA] is a question of law to be determined by the court. *Hedley Feedlot, Inc. v. Weatherly Trust,* 855 S.W.2d 826, 831 (Tex.App.-Amarillo 1993, writ denied). The [DTPA] defines consumer as an individual "of this state who seeks or acquires by purchase or lease, any goods or services." Tex.Bus. and Comm.Code § 17.45(4) (Vernon 1987). Thus, in order for the party bringing an action under the [DTPA] to establish consumer status, the individual (1) must have sought or acquired services or goods by purchase or lease, and (2) the goods or services purchased or leased must be the basis of the complaint. *Melody Home Mfg. Co. v. Barnes,* 741 S.W.2d 349, 351-352 (Tex.1987).

There is no requirement of privity between a plaintiff and defendant in order to establish a cause of action under the [DTPA]. *Cameron v. Terrell & Garrett, Inc.,* 618 S.W.2d 535, 540-41 (Tex.1981). Nevertheless, the consumer must be involved in the transaction at least to the extent that he seeks to enjoy benefits as a third party of the transaction involving the purchase or lease of a good or service. *Flenniken v. Longview Bank and Trust Co.,* 661 S.W.2d 705, 707-08 (Tex.1983).

Here, Carol swore by affidavit that she never provided or promised services to Ronald, and that he was not a consumer as to her. In his affidavit, Blassingame averred that he represented Carol against Ronald in the prior suit. He claimed that he never represented Ronald or received any benefit from him for advice given. He also stated that Ronald was not a consumer as to him. Hence, Carol, Blassingame, and the firm did not provide any goods or services to Ronald. Neither did Ronald seek or acquire any goods or services by purchase or lease from Carol, Blassingame, or the firm.

Ronald contends he was forced to acquire the services of all the appellees by being cited to appear in the prior suit. This argument, however, is inconsequential because Ronald simply acquired no services, voluntarily or involuntarily, and entered into no transaction by purchase or lease with any appellee. Additionally, Ronald was not involved in any purchase or lease transaction to the extent that he sought to enjoy benefits from the contractual relationship between Carol, Blassingame, and the firm. Consequently, Ronald failed to establish an essential element of his cause of action because the record discloses that he was not a consumer as a matter of law. Points one and three are overruled.

NOTES & QUESTIONS

1) Under Texas law, proof of a contractual relationship is not a requirement under the DTPA. Yet, in *McDuffie*, the appellate court decided that an adverse summary judgment was proper because the plaintiff was "not involved in any purchase or lease transaction to the extent that he sought to enjoy benefits from the contractual relationship." Is this a sound ruling?

2) Under Texas law and in many respects, marriage is a contractual relationship. See, *Hilley v. Hilley*, 342 S.W.2d 565, 573 (Tex. 1961). Therefore, one would expect spouses to "acquire" goods

and services from each other, and to misrepresent their intentions. Does the DTPA cover those deceptive, familial transactions in goods and services?

Mosk v. Thomas
183 S.W.3d 691
(Tex. App. -Houston [14 Dist.] 2003)

Milton Mosk (Mosk) and Cheryl Thomas (Thomas) were first married on November 9, 1992. The marriage was terminated by divorce in November 1997. As part of the property settlement agreement, Mosk gave Thomas a promissory note in the amount of $37,200.

Mosk and Thomas were remarried in February 1999. Thomas sold her residence and the couple purchased a house in Sugar Land located at 31 Pembroke. The second marriage also ended in divorce on March 23, 2000. The property division in the second divorce was facilitated by a mediated property settlement agreement. Under the terms of the Rule 11 agreement, Mosk was to get the Pembroke property. To assure recovery of her half of the marital estate, the parties agreed that Thomas would take a promissory note for $47,500. The pertinent handwritten provisions of the agreement are as follows:

> (g) Agreements regarding property (division of community estate, confirmation of separate property and allocation of debts): 1) House to H; W to vacate by 4/15/00. H to be responsible for mortgage & SW note; 2) H to execute a real property lien note in principal amount of $47,500 — with payments to commence October 1, 2000, [at] $800/month ($400 on 1st & $400 on the 15th of each month). This note will replace the promissory note in the original amount of $37,200 executed by H on 11/18/97 & which note will be considered null & void no interest shall accrue unless note becomes delinquent, then interest at rate of 10% per annum.

Pursuant to the Rule 11 agreement, Thomas executed a special warranty deed conveying her interest in the Pembroke property to Mosk. Mosk, in turn, executed a real property lien note in the amount of $47,500. The real property lien note, however, contained the following proviso that was not in the handwritten Rule 11 agreement:

> In the event the property securing this Note is sold or transferred, Payee [Thomas] shall release any lien created by this note upon written demand by the Grantor [Mosk] herein. Grantor shall replace the collateral with a lien of equal stature on replacement property acquired by him.

The real property lien note was secured by a third lien deed of trust containing similar terms regarding the sale of the property:

> (11) If all or any part of the Property is sold or transferred, Beneficiary [Thomas] agrees that Grantor [Mosk] will be entitled to a release of the lien created herein

> upon written demand by Grantor. Further, in the event that all or any part of the above described property is sold or transferred, Grantor shall replace the collateral with a lien of equal stature to the lien herein created on a replacement Property acquired by Grantor. In the event Beneficiary fails to tender the required release within five (5) business days of demand therefore, Beneficiary grants to Grantor a power of attorney coupled with an interest to execute said release.

Although both the real property lien note and the third lien deed of trust purport to bind Thomas, the documents were executed solely by Mosk.

Thereafter, Mosk married Denise Jucker in June 2000. . . . [A]nd he moved out of the Pembroke property. Mosk put the property up for sale . . . . [S]hortly thereafter, Samy Rehem agreed to buy the property for $285,000. Mosk executed a sales agreement with Rehem in which both parties agreed to close on the sale by July 11, 2000.

On June 19, 2000, Mosk's attorney sent a letter to Thomas's attorney making the following demand:

> Pursuant to the terms of Paragraph 11 of the [Third Lien Deed of Trust], please be advised that Milton Mosk has an Earnest Money Contract for the sale of the above described real property. Mr. Mosk is prepared to replace the lien granted upon the referenced real property with a first and superior security interest in and to his 1995 Toyota 4 door automobile. All things considered, a security interest in the Toyota probably constitutes a superior lien position than that created by the Third Lien Deed of Trust. As you are aware, Ms. Mosk [Thomas] has 5 days to tender a release of the Third Lien Deed of Trust document.

Thomas refused to tender a release of her lien. Thus, on June 27, 2000, Mosk's attorney sent another [demand] letter directly to Thomas in which he threatened to sue her if she did not execute a release:

> Your refusal to release the subject real property from operation of the Lien is clearly A BREACH OF YOUR CONTRACT with my client. In addition, since my client is a CONSUMER as that term is defined by the TEXAS BUSINESS AND COMMERCE CODE, your actions probably constitute a violation of the TEXAS DECEPTIVE TRADE PRACTICES Act (DTPA). Since the transaction in question involves the acquisition of real property, your actions further constitute a violation of Article 27.01 (Fraud in a Real Estate Transaction) of the TEXAS BUSINESS AND COMMERCE CODE. I bring these matters to your attention because I am recommending to my client that he file a civil lawsuit against you for the recovery of his damages. In addition, as you may be aware, both the [DTPA] and the [Fraud in a Real Estate Transaction] statute allow for recovery of exemplary damages and attorney's fees by a successful Plaintiff.

The threats proved unsuccessful and Thomas refused to release her deed of trust. Mosk could not, therefore, complete the sale of the Pembroke property.

On July 28, 2000, Rehem's attorney sent a demand letter to Mosk seeking recovery of $3,198.01 in damages stemming from Mosk's breach of the sales agreement. When Mosk refused to pay, Rehem sued to recover his damages.

Mosk, in turn, sued Thomas for breach of contract, fraud in a real estate transaction, indemnification for claims asserted against him by Rehem, DTPA violations, and a declaratory judgment. Mosk also sought punitive damages of at least $250,000.

Thomas responded with a general denial— her ANSWER.

[But Thomas also filed] a countersuit common-law fraud, fraudulent misrepresentation, intentional infliction of emotional distress, breach of contract, and violations of the DTPA.

To facilitate a resolution of all the claims, *Rehem's suit against Mosk* was consolidated with *Mosk's suit against Thomas*, and *Thomas's [suit] against Mosk.*

Both Thomas and Mosk filed motions for summary judgment. The trial court granted Mosk an interlocutory summary judgment on all of Thomas's claims except her DTPA cause of action. Thomas's motion for summary judgment was denied.

Accordingly, the trial court ordered that Thomas take nothing as to all of her claims save her DTPA cause of action.

Thereafter, the parties proceeded to trial before the court. After considering the evidence adduced by the parties, the trial court rendered a final judgment. It ordered: Mosk [should] take nothing on his claims against his ex-wife, Thomas, Thomas [could] recover ATTORNEY FEES from Mosk in the amount of $17,500; and, Rehem [could] recover from Mosk $5,554.21 in damages and attorney fees.

NOTES & QUESTIONS

1) Under Texas law, a contractual relationship, per se, is not mandatory to form a mutually binding obligation involving goods and services. A promise for a promise may bind parties who sell, buy, deliver or "transact at" in goods and services. See, *Ft. Worth & R.G. Ry. Co. v. Lindsey* 32 S.W. 714, 716 Tex. Civ. App. 1895) (reiterating that a promisee's promise is sufficient to bind him, and once the promisor makes a promise he is also bound, because a promise for a promise creates a mutuality of obligation.)

2) Now consider the promise-for-a-promise rule. May parents, children and grandparents commence successful DTPA actions against each other if they promise to deliver services and goods and decide not to honor their mutual obligations?

3) Section 17.46(b) presents a long "laundry list" of DTPA violations. Should one's intentional violation of a mutually binding obligation —based on a promise — be included in the DTPA list? Is it already included under one of the current deceptive practices?

D. Assignees and "Holders in Due Course" as DTPA Defendants

The survivability of a cause of action depends on whether common-law principles or a statute allow the action to survive. Generally, common-law rules are the default rules unless survival statutes state otherwise. *United States Casualty v. Rice,* 18 S.W.2d 760, 761 (Tex.Civ.App.-Dallas 1929, writ ref'd). In addition, under the common law, actions involving primarily property and property rights survive, but those involving a purely personal right terminated with the death of the aggrieved party. *Johnson v. Rolls,* 97 Tex. 453, 79 S.W. 513, 514 (1904)

The DTPA does not directly provide for the survival of an action brought under its terms. See *Harding v. State Nat'l Bank of El Paso*, 387 S.W.2d 768, 769 (Tex. Civ. App.-El Paso 1965, no writ), and *Texas & N.O.R.R. v. Smith,* 35 Tex. Civ. App. 351, 353 (1904, no writ). In Texas, an action will survive if it is assignable, but it will not survive if it is not assignable. *Harding*, 387 S.W.2d at 769 and *Smith,* 35 Tex. Civ. App. at 353. Also, "the general rule in Texas has been that causes of action are assignable absent a statutory bar." *Vinson & Elkins v. Moran*, 946 S.W.2d 381, 390 (Tex. App. - Houston [14th Dist.] 1997, writ dism'd by agr.)

The DTPA does not explicitly bar the assignment of a DTPA claim. In fact, the act is silent regarding this issue. Therefore, in light of Texas's general rule, may a DTPA claimant assign her cause of action? Conversely, may an aggrieved consumer bring a successful DTPA action against an assignee?

PPG Industries, Inc. v. JMB/Houston Centers Partners Ltd. Partnership
146 S.W.3d 79
(Tex. 2004)

I. Background

One Houston Center, a forty-six-story skyscraper in downtown Houston, was completed in April 1978 and originally owned by Houston Center Corporation (HCC). The exterior included more than 12,000 Twindows, a dual-pane glass window unit manufactured and installed by PPG. Twindows were chosen for their insulating ability and color, which blended with other buildings in the Houston Center complex.

By July of 1982, a large number of the Twindows showed fogging and discoloration. At HCC's request, PPG manufactured and installed replacements for one-fourth of the building's windows pursuant to a contractual warranty. The replacement project took more than two years.

Several years later, HCC entered negotiations to sell One Houston Center to JMB. During its due diligence, JMB learned of the earlier window problems and that to a limited extent they continued. When JMB inquired whether any warranties still applied, PPG replied that all had expired.

JMB bought the building "as is" in December 1989 as part of a $375 million purchase. HCC assigned to JMB all warranties relating to the building, and JMB waived all DTPA claims against HCC.

When extensive Twindows problems appeared in 1991, JMB sued PPG for violating the DTPA and breaching warranties issued to HCC. A jury found for JMB on all claims, assessing the cost to replace every Twindow in the building with comparable but nondefective window units at $4,745,037. The trial court trebled the award under the mandatory provisions of the 1973 DTPA, and after a bench trial awarded another $1,716,181 in attorney fees.

II. Assignment of DTPA Claims

A

PPG first attacks the DTPA award, asserting that DTPA claims cannot be assigned. To determine whether DTPA claims are assignable, we look first to the words of the statute.

The sale of Twindows was a sale of goods, and thus subject to the warranty provisions of Chapter 2 of the Texas Business and Commerce Code (the UCC).Chapter 17 of the same Code (the DTPA) allows consumers to bring breach of warranty claims under that chapter as well. Thus, a consumer may choose to bring warranty claims under either chapter, or both as JMB did here.

The purposes and provisions of the UCC and the DTPA are, of course, not the same; otherwise, there would have been no need for both. The primary difference relevant here is that the UCC expressly provides that warranty claims are assignable, while the DTPA says nothing about assignment.

A statute's silence can be significant. When the Legislature includes a right or remedy in one part of a code but omits it in another, which may be precisely what the Legislature intended. If so, we must honor that difference.

Of course, legislatures do not always mean to say something by silence. Legislative silence may be due to mistake, oversight, lack of consensus, implied delegation to courts or agencies, or an intent to avoid unnecessary repetition. But we must at least begin our analysis by noting that the Legislature clearly knew how to indicate that warranty claims were assignable, but did not do so in the DTPA.

B

In some cases of statutory silence, we have looked to the statute's purpose for guidance. Accordingly, we next look to the purposes of the DTPA to determine whether assignment of claims is consistent with its goals.

The DTPA's primary goal was to protect consumers by encouraging them to bring consumer complaints:

> This subchapter shall be liberally construed and applied to promote its underlying purposes, which are to protect consumers against false, misleading, and deceptive business practices, unconscionable actions, and breaches of warranty and to provide efficient and economical procedures to secure such protection. Tex. Bus. & Com. Code § 17.44(a).

While the DTPA allows the attorney general to bring consumer protection actions, one of the statute's primary purposes is to encourage *consumers themselves* to file their *own* complaints: [The Legislature] provided for the recovery of attorney's fees under the Deceptive Trade Practices Act, as encouragement to *those abused* by certain proscribed conduct to avail *themselves* of the remedies of the Act. See, *First City Bank-Farmers Branch, Tex. v. Guex,* 677 S.W.2d 25, 30 (Tex.1984) (emphasis added) and §§ 17.46(a) and 17.47.

* * *

[O]ne purpose of the DTPA's treble damages provisions is to encourage *privately initiated* consumer litigation, reducing the need for public enforcement. *See*, *Pennington v. Singleton,* 606 S.W.2d 682, 690 (Tex.1980) (emphasis added).

* * *

[T]he legislative intent [was] to encourage *aggrieved consumers* to seek redress and to deter unscrupulous sellers who engage in deceptive trade practices.

Making DTPA claims assignable would have just the opposite effect: instead of swindled consumers bringing their own DTPA claims, they will be brought by someone else.

The Legislature did not intend the DTPA for everybody. It limited DTPA complaints to "consumers," and excluded a number of parties and transactions from the DTPA, including claims by businesses with more than $25 million in assets, and certain claims in which consumers were represented by legal counsel. If DTPA claims can be assigned, a party excluded by the statute (such as JMB here) could nevertheless assert DTPA claims by stepping into the shoes of a qualifying assignor. This would frustrate the clear intent of the Legislature.

The court of appeals reasoned that assignment would accord with one of the DTPA's other purposes-discouraging consumer fraud. But this proves too much; commercial trading in almost any kind of claim would likely encourage its proliferation, but raises a host of other concerns.

First, the DTPA's treble-damage provisions were intended to motivate affected consumers; they may provide a different motivation for those who might traffic in such claims. It is one thing to place the power of treble damages in the hands of aggrieved parties or the attorney general; it is quite another to place it in the hands of those considering litigation for commercial profit. Second, appraising the value of a chose in action is never easy, due to the absence of objective measures or markets. Consumers are likely to be at a severe negotiating disadvantage with the kinds of entrepreneurs willing to buy DTPA claims cheap and settle them dear. The result of making DTPA claims assignable is likely to be that some consumers will be deceived twice.

Third, in many cases consumers may not even know they have DTPA claims when they sign a general assignment included in contractual boilerplate. If such assignments are valid, the claims meant to protect consumers will quite literally be gone before they know it. In this case for example, both JMB and HCC were wealthy and sophisticated corporations, yet both denied any knowledge of a potential DTPA claim against PPG at the time of the 1989 building sale.

There was no assignment of claims generally, and no mention specifically of DTPA claims against PPG; instead, JMB relies solely on a general assignment of the building's warranties. If this is enough, then HCC assigned away its DTPA rights against PPG without knowing it and without receiving anything for it; the $10 million in incentive damages left over after every Twindow is replaced will serve as a pure windfall for JMB. Every conceivable purpose of the statute is defeated if consumers may lose their claims by accident.

JMB makes no attempt to defend commercial marketing of DTPA claims, arguing only for assignment in cases like this-in which it bought the underlying building and will bear the costs of repairing it. But allowing DTPA claims by those who purchase defective goods from a consumer shifts the focus of the DTPA from deceptive *practices* to defective *products.* If DTPA claims may be assigned to subsequent buyers like JMB, treble damages will often go to wealthy entrepreneurs rather than the consumers who were actually defrauded.

Moreover, JMB's only claim here is based on the written assignment. JMB acquired no DTPA claims merely by becoming a subsequent owner of One Houston Center, and asserts none in its own right. As JMB's only basis for DTPA claims is the written assignment, it is hard to see how its claims are different from those that might be obtained by arbitrageurs.

In sum, allowing assignment of DTPA claims would ensure that aggrieved consumers do not file them, that some consumers receive nothing in compensation, and others are deceived a second time. All would defeat the very purposes for which the DTPA was enacted.

C

In some cases of statutory silence, we have also looked to related common-law principles. With respect to the assignment of claims, we have recognized the collapse of the common-law rule that generally prohibited such assignments. But the assignability of *most* claims does not mean *all* are assignable; exceptions may be required due to equity and public policy.

Courts addressing assignability have often distinguished between claims that are property-based and remedial and claims that are personal and punitive, holding that the former are assignable and the latter are not. The DTPA claims here (unlike the warranty claims under the UCC) clearly fall in the latter category.

Unlike most other states, Texas adopted the UCC without choosing any of its three options concerning who may sue on warranties; instead, the Legislature expressly delegated that choice to the courts. Pursuant to that mandate, in *Nobility Homes of Texas, Inc. v. Shivers,* we held a downstream purchaser of a mobile home could bring implied warranty claims directly against a remote manufacturer, even though there was no privity of contract between them. While it appears we have never addressed the same issue regarding express warranties, several lower courts have applied the same rule in that context-express warranties pass with the goods.

But in *Amstadt v. U.S. Brass Corp.,* we held downstream purchasers of non-mobile homes could *not* bring DTPA claims against remote manufacturers and suppliers of a defective plumbing system, because the deceptive acts alleged were not committed against or communicated to them in connection with their own purchases. Recognizing the similarity to this case, JMB asserted no DTPA claims in its own right, as it had no connection with PPG's original Twindows sale, and never saw any PPG advertisements or warranties before it bought the building.

Thus, we have established a clear distinction between DTPA and warranty claims: a downstream buyer *can* sue a remote seller for breach of an implied warranty, but *cannot* sue under the DTPA. Clearly, if warranty claims are assignable because they are "property-based," DTPA claims must be something else; there must be a "personal" aspect in being "duped" that does not pass to subsequent buyers the way a warranty does.

DTPA claims generally are also punitive rather than remedial. In this respect, it is important to remember that the DTPA overlaps many common-law causes of action, including breach of contract, warranty, fraud, misrepresentation, and negligence. Frequently, the DTPA is pleaded not because it is the *only* remedy, but because it is the most *favorable* remedy. In this case, for example, JMB pleaded one set of factual allegations that was then incorporated wholesale into claims for breach of contract, warranty, and the DTPA. The contract and warranty claims offered a remedy, but only the DTPA offered treble damages.

In such cases, the most important role of the DTPA is the remedies it *adds,* not the ones it *duplicates.* Economic damages and attorney's fees are certainly remedial, but they were recoverable in contract and warranty long before the DTPA was passed. The DTPA adds mental anguish and punitive damages —damages that could hardly be more personal.

JMB never asserted a claim for mental anguish, but many DTPA claimants do and will. If consumers can assign their DTPA claims, they may still have to testify at trial about the nature, duration, and severity of their mental anguish, but someone else will keep the money.

JMB argues the DTPA's treble damages are remedial rather than punitive because they address individual rather than public injuries. Our dissenting colleagues would also find DTPA damages remedial, but overlook the fact that twenty years ago we held exactly the opposite. In *Pace v. State,* we held a DTPA treble-damage award could not be recovered from the Real Estate Recovery Fund (a fund set up for " *reimbursing* aggrieved persons") because "treble damages under the DTPA are punitive damages." 650 S.W.2d 64, 65 (Tex.1983) (emphasis in original); JMB also points to cases in which federal statutory penalties have been held assignable. Statutes that create a remedy where none previously existed may be remedial; for example, there was no remedy at common law for being driven out of business by a monopolist. But that cannot be said of JMB's warranty claims here.

Of course, if manufacturers make representations or warranties directly to consumers, the latter may sue directly (despite the absence of privity) for breach of express warranty *U.S. Pipe & Foundry Co. v. City of Waco,* 108 S.W.2d 432, 434-435 (Tex.1937), or violation of the DTPA. But JMB neither alleged nor proved that was the case here. As DTPA claims are too "personal" and "punitive" to pass with goods from one owner to the next, it is hard to see why they should pass with the same goods by assignment.

D

Finally, we must consider whether assignment of DTPA claims may increase or distort litigation. "We have never upheld assignments in the face of those concerns." We have prohibited assignments that may skew the trial process, confuse or mislead the jury, promote collusion among nominal adversaries, or misdirect damages from more culpable to less culpable defendants

First, as noted above, DTPA claims are unlike most contract-related claims in providing for mental anguish and punitive damages. Jurors are bound to experience some confusion in assessing mental anguish of a consumer, or punitive damages based on "the situation and sensibilities of the parties," *Transp. Ins. Co. v. Moriel,* 879 S.W.2d 10, 35 (Tex.1994), when the affected consumer is not a party. The Legislature intended DTPA lawsuits to be "efficient and economical" Tex. Bus. & Com. Code § 17.44(a) ; assessing personal and punitive damages in these circumstances is likely to make that goal difficult.

But more important, there is a serious risk here of skewing the adversarial process. When A sells goods to B who sells them to C, if the goods prove defective and there were no dealings between A and C (as is often the case in the stream of commerce), C will naturally look to B for a breach-of-contract remedy. But if DTPA claims are assignable, B and C both have a strong incentive to direct the suit elsewhere for relief. If B settles with C for a small amount and assigns any DTPA claims it may have against A, C now has a case with potential punitive damages, and B has avoided potential liability. Thus the litigation will continue with the parties in different roles-precisely the results that have led us to prohibit assignments in other contexts.

In this case JMB made no complaints against HCC, even though the window problems JMB discovered were very similar to the ones HCC encountered a few years before. Further, to avoid any discovery rule problems, HCC joined JMB in downplaying the earlier problems that must have seemed disastrous to HCC at the time. We cast no aspersions on the litigants here; we only note that assignability of DTPA claims may encourage some buyers to cooperate-if not collude-with a seller who may have been the one that actually misled them.

E

The DTPA is primarily concerned with people-both the deceivers and the deceived. This gives the entire act a personal aspect that cannot be squared with a rule that allows assignment of DTPA claims as if they were merely another piece of property.

Our dissenting colleagues assert we should skip over the question of DTPA assignability (which they proceed to address in detail) to address the "threshold" question whether HCC had a valid DTPA claim to assign. In reviewing this DTPA judgment in favor of an assignee, an appellate court could first ask whether the assignment, if proper, concerned a valid DTPA claim (as our colleagues do), or whether the DTPA claim, if proper, could be assigned (as do we). Clearly, the more important question to the jurisprudence of the state is whether DTPA claims can be transferred (a matter of conflict in the courts of appeals), not whether pre-1983 DTPA claims survived the 1983 amendments (a matter as to which there has been neither case nor conflict in the twenty years since).

Our dissenting colleagues suggest in a hypothetical that under our decision today, if A tampers with a car's odometer before selling it to B who sells it to C, C has no DTPA remedy against A. Of course, that is already the case under *Amstadt* if there is no assignment. Moreover, C can also sue B under the DTPA (perhaps for representing the car had lower mileage than it really had), and B can bring an indemnity and contribution claim under the DTPA against A. If we assume (as their hypothetical does) that A did the tampering, the effect is likely to be the same-A pays DTPA damages, and C receives them. *But if B did the tampering* (and given the severe federal penalties, no one is likely to admit it), the assignment of DTPA claims skews the normal litigation process by encouraging C to combine with B against A.

Because only an assignment is before us, we do not decide whether DTPA claims survive to a consumer's heirs, a related but sometimes distinct inquiry. For the same reason, we also reserve for another day the assignment of claims that were created within and could not be brought without the DTPA, such as false going-out-of-business sales or price-gouging during a disaster. Finally, our holding does not prohibit equitable assignments, such as a contingent-fee interest assigned to a consumer's attorney.

But because of the statutory differences between the UCC and the DTPA, the personal litigation by consumers that was the DTPA's primary purpose, the personal and punitive nature of both DTPA claims and DTPA damages, and the risks to the adversarial process, we hold that DTPA claims generally cannot be assigned by an aggrieved consumer to someone else.

Home Savings Association v. Guerra
733 S.W.2d 134
(Tex. 1987)

This is an action brought by Louis Guerra against Modern Builders and Supply and Home Savings Association to recover damages as a result of a home solicitation transaction. On appeal, the issue is whether an assignee of a retail installment contract can be held deriva tively liable for the seller's misconduct in excess of the amount paid by the buyer under the contract.

In 1984, Guerra and Modern Builders entered into a retail installment contract which contained a notice provision required by the Federal Trade Commission (discussed below). Under the contract, Modern Builders agreed to add rock siding to Guerra's home and make repairs to the existing structure for $7,700.00. Guerra executed a ten-year promissory note which included a time-price differential payable in monthly installments of $125.69. Modern Builders assigned the note and the retail installment contract to Home Savings in exchange for $7,700.00. Thereafter, the rock siding crumbled, and Guerra brought suit against Modern Builders and Home Savings, as assignee, alleging violations of the Deceptive Trade Practices Act (DTPA) and the Home Solicitation Act. At that time, Guerra had made installment payments totaling $1,256.90. Pursuant to a jury verdict, the trial court rendered judgment for Guerra against Modern Builders and Home Savings, jointly and severally, for $25,000.00 plus attorney's fees of $10,000.00. In addition, the trial court declared the promissory note void.

On appeal by Home Savings, the court of appeals affirmed the trial court judgment and held that an assignee of commercial paper could be held liable for seller misconduct, in excess of the amount paid under the contract, under the Federal Trade Commission rule, 16 C.F.R. § 433.2 (1976). We disagree and therefore reverse the judgment of the court of appeals.

The FTC rule provides:

> In connection with any sale or lease of goods or services to consumers, in or effecting commerce as "commerce" is defined in the Federal Trade Commission Act, it is an unfair or deceptive act or practice within the meaning of Section 5 of that Act for a seller, directly or indirectly to:
>
> (a) Take or receive a consumer credit contract which fails to contain the following provision in at least ten point, bold face, type:
>
> **NOTICE**
>
> **ANY HOLDER OF THIS CONSUMER CREDIT CONTRACT IS SUBJECT TO ALL CLAIMS AND DEFENSES WHICH THE DEBTOR COULD ASSERT AGAINST THE SELLER OF GOODS OR SERVICES OBTAINED PURSUANT HERETO OR WITH THE PROCEEDS HEREOF. RECOVERY HEREUNDER BY THE DEBTOR SHALL NOT EXCEED AMOUNTS PAID BY THE DEBTOR HEREUNDER.**

16 C.F.R. § 433.2 (1976)

In adopting this rule, the FTC determined that a consumer credit transaction, which separated the consumer's duty to pay from the seller's duty to fulfill his obligations, constituted an unfair and deceptive practice. *Statement of Basis and Purpose,* 40 FED. REG. 53,506, 53,522 (1975). The rule was aimed primarily at situations in which a seller executed a credit contract and then assigned the contract to a credit company which took it free and clear of any claims and defenses the buyer had against the seller. *Guidelines on Trade Regulation Rule Concerning Preservation of Consumers' Claims and Defenses,* 41 FED. REG. 20,022, 20,023 (1976). The creditor's status as a holder in due course operated to cut off claims and defenses such as breach of contract, breach of warranty, misrepresentation, or fraud on the part of the seller. 40 FED. REG. at 53,522.

The reciprocal duties of the buyer and seller which were mutually dependent under ordinary contract law became independent of one another. Thus, the buyer's duty to pay the creditor was not excused upon the seller's failure to perform. In abrogating the holder in due course rule in consumer credit transactions, the FTC preserved the consumer's claims and defenses against the creditor-assignee. The FTC rule was therefore designed to reallocate the cost of seller misconduct to the creditor. The commission felt the creditor was in a better position to absorb the loss or recover the cost from the guilty party-the seller.

We must determine the extent to which the buyer's claim for seller misconduct is preserved against the creditor. Home Savings contends its liability to Guerra is limited to the amount paid by Guerra under the contract, $1,256.90. We agree. The notice provision required by the FTC rule includes the sentence, "Recovery hereunder by the debtor shall not exceed amounts paid by the debtor hereunder." In explaining the mechanics of the rule, the FTC's Bureau of Consumer Protection stated:

> This limits the consumer to a refund of monies paid under the contract, in the event that an affirmative money recovery is sought. In other words, the consumer may assert, by way of claim or defense, a right not to pay all or part of the outstanding balance owed the creditor under the contract; but the consumer will not be entitled to receive from the creditor an affirmative recovery which exceeds the amounts of money the consumer has paid in.
>
> * * *
>
> The limitation on affirmative recovery does not eliminate any other rights the consumer may have as a matter of local, state, or federal statute. The words "recovery hereunder" which appear in the text of the Notice refer specifically to a recovery under the Notice. If a larger affirmative recovery is available against a creditor as a matter of state law, the consumer would retain this right.
>
> * * *

> The Rule does apply to all claims or defenses connected with the transaction, whether in tort or contract. When, under state law, a consumer would have a tort claim against the seller that would defeat a seller's right to further payments or allow the consumer to recover affirmatively, this claim is preserved against the holder. This is, of course, subject to the limitation of recovery under this Rule to the amounts paid in.

41 Fed. Reg. at 20,023-24

These guidelines limit the creditor's derivative liability to the amount paid under the contract. A rule of unlimited liability would place the creditor in the position of an absolute insurer or guarantor of the seller's performance. We do not construe this to be the purpose of the FTC rule. We hold that a creditor's derivative liability for seller misconduct under the FTC rule is limited to the amount paid by the consumer under the credit contract. Our holding is supported by several commercial law commentators. We disapprove of the language in *De La Fuenta v. Home Savings Association,* 669 S.W.2d 137 (Tex.App.-Corpus Christi 1984, no writ), to the extent that it is inconsistent with this opinion.

We realize the limitation provision does not limit or foreclose a consumer's right of recovery against the creditor based on independent state law grounds. 41 FED. REG. at 20,023. However, Guerra has not pleaded or proven an independent cause of action against Home Savings under either the DTPA or the Home Solicitation Act. Moreover, Guerra obtained no jury findings that Home Savings participated in any of the wrongful acts of which he complains. All of the jury findings pertained to wrongful acts committed solely by Modern Builders. Guerra premised Home Savings's liability strictly on its admission that it was the holder of the note.

In the absence of evidence and jury findings that Guerra was adversely affected by a false, misleading or deceptive act or unconscionable action on the part of Home Savings, Home Savings has no liability under the DTPA. Although a consumer suing under the DTPA need not establish contractual privity with the defendant, he must show that the defendant has committed a deceptive act which is the producing cause of the consumer's damages. *Weitzel v. Barnes,* 691 S.W.2d 598, 600 (Tex.1985); *Cameron v. Terrell & Garrett,* 618 S.W.2d 535, 541 (Tex. 1982). The DTPA does not attach derivative liability to a defendant based on an innocent involvement in a business transaction. *See, e.g., Light v. Wilson,* 663 S.W.2d 813, 814 (Tex.1983); *Cameron,* 618 S.W.2d at 541; *Building Concepts, Inc. v. Duncan,* 667 S.W.2d 897, 901 (Tex.App.-Houston [14th Dist.] 1984, writ ref'd n.r.e.). To hold a creditor liable in a consumer credit transaction, the creditor must be shown to have some connection either with the actual sales transaction or with a deceptive act related to financing the transaction. *Flenniken v. Longview Bank & Trust Co.,* 661 S.W.2d 705, 707 (Tex.1983); *Knight v. International Harvester Credit Corp.,* 627 S.W.2d 382, 389 (Tex.1982).

In *Knight v. International Harvester Credit Corp.,* we held that the seller and creditor-assignee "were so *inextricably intertwined* in the transaction as to be equally responsible for the conduct of the sale." 627 S.W.2d at 389 (emphasis added). In that case, International Harvester had drafted and supplied the seller with the retail installment contract which prominently bore the insignia of International Harvester at the top of the first page. The contract provided both for the sale of the good and the payment over time with interest. Most of the contracts used by the seller were provided by International Harvester. We concluded that, because of this close connection, International Harvester was involved in more than a mere extension of credit. We held the buyer was a consumer with respect to International Harvester as well as the seller. 627 S.W.2d at 388-89.

Conversely, although Home Savings supplied Modern Builders with the installment contract used in this transaction, the contract was a standard FHA form. There was no indication that Home Savings drafted the contract nor any other evidence that Home Savings was "inextricably intertwined" with Modern Builders. Furthermore, there were no pleadings nor jury findings to support a holding that the two defendants were inextricably intertwined. Guerra simply never advanced this theory of recovery.

Because there is no evidence or findings supporting an independent ground of recovery against Home Savings based on state law, we hold Home Savings's liability is limited to the amount paid under the contract, $1,256.90. This holding is in harmony with our decision in *Kish v. Van Note,* 692 S.W.2d 463 (Tex.1985). In that case, we examined the liability of an assignee-bank under an installment contract containing the FTC notice provision. Although we did not discuss the purpose or intent of the FTC rule, we held that, because the bank had not violated the DTPA, its joint and several liability was limited to the amount paid under the contract plus attorneys fees. 692 S.W.2d at 468.

The trial court also rendered judgment against Modern Builders and Home Savings, jointly and severally, for $10,000 in attorney's fees. Home Savings claims the trial court erred in holding it jointly and severally liable for attorney's fees because its liability is limited to $1,256.90, rather than the full $25,000. However, the special issue on attorney's fees requested the jury to find Guerra's attorneys fees for the entire case, rather than separately allocating the fees to each claim. Therefore, because Home Savings did not object to this broad attorney's fees issue, any complaint that the trial court failed to segregate the fees as to each claim has been waived. *Matthews v. Candlewood Builders,* 685 S.W.2d 649, 650 (Tex. 1985). Accordingly, we hold Home Savings jointly and severally liable for attorney's fees of $10,000.

We affirm the trial court's judgment awarding Guerra $10,000 attorney's fees. We also affirm that part of the judgment declaring the note void. We reverse the judgment of the court of appeals holding Home Savings jointly and severally liable for $25,000 and render judgment against Home Savings for $1,256.90.

NOTES & QUESTIONS

1) Reported cases are also replete with rules regarding the rights and obligations of third-party plaintiffs: assignees, third-party victims, third-party beneficiaries, bystanders, subrogees and others. Do all third-party plaintiffs have standing to sue under the DTPA? Do they all qualify as consumers?

2) Consider the court's analysis in *Service Corp. Intern. v. Aragon,* 268 S.W.3d 112, 117 (Tex. App.-Eastland 2008) about the rights of third-party plaintiffs under the DTPA:

> Only a "consumer" has standing to sue under the DTPA. *See* Section 17.50. The DTPA defines consumer as one "who seeks or acquires by purchase or lease, any goods or services." Section 17.45(4). A plaintiff need not establish privity of contract to be a consumer. *Amstadt v. U.S. Brass Corp.,* 919 S.W.2d 644, 649 (Tex.1996). Instead a plaintiff's standing as a consumer is established by her relationship to the transaction. *Lukasik v. San Antonio Blue Haven Pools, Inc.,* 21 S.W.3d 394, 401 (Tex.App.-San Antonio 2000, no pet.).
>
> A third-party beneficiary may qualify as a consumer as long as the transaction was specifically required by or intended to benefit the third party and the good or service was rendered to benefit the third party. *Arthur Andersen & Co. v. Perry Equip. Corp.,* 945 S.W.2d 812, 815 (Tex.1997). When determining whether a third-party beneficiary qualifies as a consumer, courts have considered whether the third party was the primary intended beneficiary or if it derived only an incidental benefit.
>
> For example, in *Kennedy v. Sale,* 689 S.W.2d 890, 892 (Tex.1985), employees were the primary intended beneficiary of an insurance policy purchased by their employer and, therefore, were consumers.
>
> Conversely, in *Vinson & Elkins v. Moran,* 946 S.W.2d 381, 408 (Tex.App.-Houston [14th Dist.] 1997, writ dism'd by agr.) (will beneficiaries injured by estate counsel's legal malpractice), and *Brandon v. American Sterilizer Co.,* 880 S.W.2d 488, 492 (Tex.App.-Austin 1994, no writ) (hospital employee injured by defectively repaired gas sterilizer), the third parties were only incidental beneficiaries and, therefore, were not consumers.
>
> No Texas decision directly addresses who the intended beneficiaries are when a cemetery plot or funeral services are purchased, but Texas courts have allowed immediate family members to bring common-law actions for mishandling a corpse. *See, e.g., Clark v. Smith,* 494 S.W.2d 192 (Tex.Civ.App.-Dallas 1973, writ ref'd n.r.e.).
>
> In this case, a son contracted with the defendant to take his mother's body from a hospital to the defendant's place of business and to maintain the body in suitable condition for decent burial. The defendant took possession of the decedent's body but allowed it to decompose. *Id.* at 194-95. The jury awarded mental anguish damages to each of the decedent's four children. The court suggested a remittitur but affirmed their right to recover. *Id.* at 198.
>
> Thus, even though only one of the decedent's children dealt with the defendant, because each was allowed to recover, the defendant's duty ran to all four. If a company taking possession of a body has a duty to the decedent's children, it is

reasonable to conclude as the trial court did that SCI's interment services were intended for the benefit of Obie's immediate family and that each was a consumer.

Issue No. One is overruled.

E. Physicians and Healthcare Professionals as DTPA Defendants

Sorokolit, M.D. v. Rhodes
889 S.W.2d 239
(Tex. 1994)

This case requires that we determine whether section 12.01(a) of the Medical Liability and Insurance Improvement Act precludes an action for knowing misrepresentation or breach of an express warranty under the Deceptive Trade Practices Act (DTPA). Janice Rhodes (Rhodes) sued Bob Sorokolit, M.D. ("Dr. Sorokolit") for medical malpractice, breach of implied and express warranties, and knowing misrepresentation. Rhodes subsequently dropped all allegations of negligence and proceeded solely on the warranty and misrepresentation claims under the DTPA.

Dr. Sorokolit filed special exceptions, arguing that Rhodes' DTPA claims are precluded under section 12.01(a). The trial court sustained the special exceptions and dismissed the case. The court of appeals reversed in part and remanded. For the reasons explained herein, we affirm the judgment of the court of appeals.

I

For the purpose of reviewing the dismissal, because it is based on special exceptions, we accept as true all material factual allegations and all factual statements reasonably inferred from the allegations set forth in Rhodes' pleadings. When Rhodes first saw Dr. Sorokolit for a proposed breast augmentation surgery, he guaranteed and warranted the results of the surgery. Dr. Sorokolit instructed Rhodes and her husband to select a picture of a nude model from a magazine, promising that, following surgery, her breasts would look just like those in the picture she selected.

The result was not as guaranteed. Rhodes sued Dr. Sorokolit for medical malpractice, breach of implied and express warranties under the DTPA, and knowing misrepresentation under the DTPA, but later dropped the malpractice claims. In her DTPA allegations, Rhodes contends that Dr. Sorokolit's conduct amounted to false, misleading, and deceptive acts and practices for the following reasons:

1) [Dr. Sorokolit] represented to [Rhodes] that his services had characteristics, uses and benefits which [they] did not have;
2) [Dr. Sorokolit] represented to [Rhodes] that his services were of a particular standard, quality and grade when they were another;

3) [Dr. Sorokolit] represented to [Rhodes] that his warranty involved rights which he did not have or involve; [and]
4) [Dr. Sorokolit] breached his express and implied warranty to perform his services in a good and workmanlike manner.

Finally, Rhodes alleges that Dr. Sorokolit knowingly committed the described acts and practices. Sustaining Dr. Sorokolit's special exceptions, the trial court ruled that a physician cannot be sued under the DTPA for conduct arising from the provision of professional medical services. The court of appeals reversed in part and remanded, holding that section 12.01(a) bars DTPA claims for breach of implied warranty but that section 12.01(a) does not bar DTPA claims based on knowing misrepresentation or breach of express warranty.

II

In his sole point of error, Dr. Sorokolit argues that section 12.01(a) of the Medical Liability and Insurance Improvement Act precludes an action for knowing misrepresentation or breach of an express warranty under the DTPA. We disagree.

The goal of statutory construction is to give effect to the intent of the legislature. If language in a statute is unambiguous, this court must seek the intent of the legislature as found in the plain and common meaning of the words and terms used. In applying the plain and common meaning of the language in a statute, courts may not by implication enlarge the meaning of any word in the statute beyond its ordinary meaning; such implication is inappropriate when legislative intent may be gathered from a reasonable interpretation of the statute as it is written.

The language of section 12.01(a) is clear, unambiguous, and, when construed as written, not devoid of meaning. Section 12.01(a) states that there can be no DTPA claim against a physician or health care provider for damages for personal injury or death if the damages result, or are alleged to result, from the physician's negligence. Because the legislature has not defined "negligence" as it is used in section 12.01(a), we apply its common law meaning. Tex. Rev. Civ. Stat. Ann. art. 4590i, § 1.03(b) (Vernon Supp.1994) (requiring that any legal term not defined in the statute be given its common law meaning); treating it as a breach of the accepted standard of medical care that proximately causes damages. Although the DTPA does not create a cause of action for negligence . . . plaintiffs at times attempt to bring what might otherwise be negligence claims as DTPA suits.

Because section 12.01(a) operates to bar characterization of medical negligence claims against physicians and health care providers as DTPA claims, we conclude that section 12.01(a) is not meaningless as written. Consequently, it is our duty to construe the statute as written by the legislature. If the legislature had intended otherwise, it could have expressed its intent in plain and specific language. *Id.* at 528-529. Accordingly, we conclude that section 12.01(a) only precludes a DTPA suit against a physician for negligence—that is, a suit founded on a breach of the accepted standard of medical care.

III

There can be no DTPA claim against a physician for damages for personal injury or death if the damages result, or are alleged to result, from the physician's negligence; however, if the alleged DTPA claim is not based on the physician's breach of the accepted standard of medical care, section 12.01(a) does not preclude suit for violation of the DTPA. Thus, the underlying nature of the claim determines whether section 12.01(a) prevents suit for violation of the DTPA. Claims that a physician or health care provider was negligent may not be recast as DTPA actions to avoid the standards set forth in the Medical Liability and Insurance Improvement Act.

Rhodes does not allege that Dr. Sorokolit deviated from the accepted standard of care in performing the surgery, nor is it evident that her DTPA suit for knowing misrepresentation and breach of express warranty is merely the recharacterization of a negligence suit. Her claim is that Dr. Sorokolit guaranteed the results of his surgery and that the doctor knowingly breached his express warranty of a particular result and knowingly misrepresented his skills and the results he could achieve. The DTPA defines "knowingly" as meaning "actual awareness of the falsity, deception, or unfairness of the act or practice giving rise to the consumer's claim or . . . actual awareness of the act or practice constituting the breach of warranty. . . ." Tex. Bus. & Com. Code Ann. § 17.45(9) . Neither DTPA claim involves negligence — neither requires a determination of whether a physician failed to meet the standard of medical care; each claim, by its nature, concerns intentional deception and intentional breach of express guarantees.

Accordingly, we hold that section 12.01(a), which does preclude DTPA suits founded on a breach of the accepted standard of medical care, does not preclude suits under the DTPA for knowing misrepresentation or breach of express warranty in cases in which a physician or health care provider warrants a particular result. For the reasons explained herein, we affirm the judgment of the court of appeals.

Murphy v. Russell
167 S.W.3d 835
(Tex. 2005)

PER CURIAM

Johnette Russell sued an anesthesiologist, Mark Murphy, after he allegedly administered a general anesthetic without her consent during a biopsy. The trial court dismissed Russell's suit because she failed to provide an expert report in accordance with section 13.01 of former Texas Revised Civil Statutes article 4590i.[1]

---

1 Act of May 5, 1995, 74th Leg., R.S., ch. 140, § 1, 1995 Tex. Gen. Laws 985, 985-87 (adding expert report requirement, at former Tex. Rev. Civ. Stat. art. 4590i, § 13.01(d)), *repealed and recodified as amended by* Act of June 2, 2003, 78th Leg., R.S., ch. 204, §§ 10.01, 10.09, and 23.02(a), (d), 2003 Tex. Gen. Laws 847, 864, 884, 898-899 ("House Bill 4") (adopting chapter 74 of the Texas Civil Practice and Remedies Code, applicable only to actions filed on or after September 1, 2003, and continuing prior law in effect for actions filed before that date) (current version at Tex. Civ. Prac. & Rem. Code § 74.351 ("Expert Report")).

The court of appeals reversed, holding that Russell's claims are not "health care liability claims." We reverse the court of appeals' judgment and dismiss this suit.

Russell's petition in the trial court alleges the following facts. In September 1998, Russell went to the Zale Lipshy Hospital in Dallas for a biopsy. She told a nurse, who had approached her to insert an intravenous line, that she would only permit the administration of a local anesthetic. She asked to discuss the matter with the anesthesiologist, Dr. Mark Murphy, and told him she did not want to be sedated or to lose consciousness. Murphy assured her that he would not sedate her but told her he still wanted to insert an IV line to administer a saline solution and perhaps antibiotics. Once she was in the operating room, the hospital staff inserted an air tube in her nose, and she lost consciousness. When she awoke in the recovery room, Murphy admitted he had sedated her contrary to her instructions.

Russell sued Murphy, asserting battery, breach of contract, and violations of the Deceptive Trade Practices Act (DTPA), seeking actual, exemplary, and additional DTPA damages. Tex. Bus. & Com.Code §§ 17.46, 17.50. Russell did not file an expert report within 180 days of filing suit or at any time thereafter, and Murphy moved to dismiss her lawsuit, arguing that the claims are "health care liability claims" subject to the requirements of former article 4590i. The trial court granted the motion and dismissed the case. The court of appeals reversed the trial court's judgment, reasoning that "Russell does not allege and need not prove that Murphy deviated from any standard of medical care, health care, or safety", and therefore no expert medical report was required. This was incorrect.

Former article 4590i and its expert report requirements apply to a patient's claims, regardless of whether they are tort or contract claims, when those claims come within the statutory definition of a "health care liability claim." That definition is:

"Health care liability claim" means a cause of action against a health care provider or physician for treatment, lack of treatment, or other claimed departure from accepted standards of medical care or health care or safety which proximately results in injury to or death of the patient, whether the patient's claim or cause of action sounds in tort or contract.

"Health care" is also a defined term:

> "Health care" means any act or treatment performed or furnished, or which should have been performed or furnished, by any health care provider for, to, or on behalf of a patient during the patient's medical care, treatment, or confinement. Act of May 30, 1977, at § 1.03(a)(2) (current version at Tex. Civ. Prac. & Rem. Code § 74.001(a)(10)).

"Medical care" is defined:

> "Medical care" means any act defined as practicing medicine in Article 4510, Revised Civil Statutes of Texas, 1925, as amended, performed or furnished, or which should have been performed, by one licensed to practice medicine in Texas for, to, or on behalf of a patient during the patient's care, treatment, or confinement.

Former article 4590i provides that in every suit in which a health care liability claim is asserted, an expert report must be filed within 180 days after suit was filed, subject to certain extensions not relevant here. The requirements for an expert report are specified:

> "Expert report" means a written report by an expert that provides a fair summary of the expert's opinions as of the date of the report regarding applicable standards of care, the manner in which the care rendered by the physician or health care provider failed to meet the standards, and the causal relationship between that failure and the injury, harm, or damages claimed.

Russell's battery claim arises from treatment rendered by Murphy. Medical treatment will not constitute a battery unless it is provided without the patient's consent. *Miller ex rel. Miller v. HCA, Inc.*, 118 S.W.3d 758, 767 (Tex. 2003). But failure to obtain consent does not automatically result in liability. There may be reasons for providing treatment without specific consent that do not breach any applicable standard of care. The existence or nonexistence of such reasons is necessarily the subject of expert testimony. In enacting former article 4590i, the Legislature intended health care liability claims to be scrutinized by an expert or experts before the suit can proceed. Russell cannot avoid the requirements of former article 4590i, including its expert report requirement and caps on damages, by filing a bare-bones pleading that asserts battery based on lack of consent.

We reaffirm that a claimant cannot escape the Legislature's statutory scheme by artful pleading. *See Garland Cmty. Hosp. v. Rose,* 156 S.W.3d 541, 543 (Tex.2004); *MacGregor Med. Ass'n v. Campbell,* 985 S.W.2d 38, 40 (Tex.1998).

It must also be borne in mind that article 4590i's expert report requirement establishes a threshold over which a claimant must proceed to continue a lawsuit. It does not establish a requirement for recovery. It may be that once discovery is complete and the case is tried, there is no need for expert testimony. In a case alleging lack of consent, a factfinder might reasonably conclude that there was a battery and that some damages were sustained without the need for expert testimony. But the Legislature envisioned that discovery and the ultimate determination of what issues are submitted to the factfinder should not go forward unless at least one expert has examined the case and opined as to the applicable standard of care, that it was breached, and that there is a causal relationship between the failure to meet the standard of care and the injury, harm, or damages claimed. The fact that in the final analysis, expert testimony may not be necessary to support a verdict does not mean the claim is not a health care liability claim. A claim may be a health care liability claim to which the damage caps and expert report requirements are applicable and yet not require expert testimony to prevail at trial.

Russell cannot circumvent an expert examination of her claims simply by asserting that she did not consent to a general anesthetic and that the physician admitted he failed to follow her wishes regarding anesthesia, because there may be reasons why the administration of a general anesthetic did not breach any applicable standard of care. It might be that there were emergency circumstances that arguably warranted general anesthesia without Russell's consent, or that a general anesthetic was administered without Murphy's actual knowledge at the time it was done. Under such circumstances, expert testimony about the standard of care and breach of that standard might be necessary at trial, yet if we were to accept Russell's cribbed interpretation of the term "health care liability claim," her suit would proceed without the threshold expert report contemplated by former article 4590i.

With regard to Russell's DTPA claims, she alleges that Dr. Murphy sedated her after he expressly represented and warranted that he would not. In the procedural posture of this case, we are not called upon to determine whether section 12.01 of former article 4590i bars the applicability of the DTPA to these claims. Former section 12.01(a) provided:

> "Notwithstanding any other law, no provisions of Sections 17.41-17.63, Business & Commerce Code, shall apply to physicians or health care providers as defined in Section 1.03(3) of this Act, with respect to claims for damages for personal injury or death resulting, or alleged to have resulted, from negligence on the part of any physician or health care provider." *See* former Tex. Rev. Civ. Stat. art. 4590i, § 12.01, *repealed and recodified as amended by* Act of June 2, 2003, 78th Leg., R.S., ch. 204, § 10.09, 2003 Tex. Gen. Laws 847, 884 (current version at Tex. Civ. Prac. & Rem. Code § 74.004).

The only question before us is whether Russell was required to file an expert report in order to proceed with her suit. We have held that representations like those Russell has alleged "are nothing more than an attempt to recast [a] malpractice claim as a DTPA action." *See*, *Gormley v. Stover,* 907 S.W.2d 448, 450 (Tex.1995) and *Earle v. Ratliff,* 998 S.W.2d 882, 892-893 (Tex.1999).

In *Gormley v. Stover,* the claimant alleged that a dentist represented he could perform a bone graft with no problems, represented that a skin graft would work as well as a bone graft, and made other representations regarding her prognosis. We held that these allegations "all have to do with whether [the dentist's] selection of the surgical procedure and performance of it met the standard of care for dentists in such circumstances." *Id.* at 450

Similarly, Russell's allegations "all have to do with" whether the administration of a general anesthetic under all the circumstances met the standard of care for anesthesiologists. Accordingly, all of her claims, including her DTPA claims, are "health care liability claims."

Because Russell's suit asserted health care liability claims, she was required to provide Murphy with an expert report in order to proceed with those claims. Because Russell failed to do so within the statutory period, we reverse the court of appeals' judgment without hearing oral argument and dismiss Russell's suit.

NOTES & QUESTIONS

1) Once more, Tex. Bus. & Com. Code Ann. § 17.44 requires courts to construe and apply the DTPA liberally to promote its underlying purposes, which are: 1) to protect consumers against false, misleading and deceptive business practices, unconscionable actions, and breach of warranties, and 2) to provide efficient and economical procedures to secure such protection.

2) But again, Tex. Civ. Prac. & Rem. Code § 74.004(a) is clear: "Notwithstanding any other law, Sections 17.41-17.63 [of the] Business & Commerce Code . . . do not apply to physicians or health care providers with respect to claims for damages for personal injury or death resulting, or alleged to have resulted, from negligence on the part of any physician or health care provider."

3) The DTPA does not list the professional defendants who may sue or be sued. Therefore, one should ask: May a consumer commence a successful DTPA "personal injury" lawsuit against all other professionals? See *White Budd Van Ness P'ship v. Major-Gladys Drive Joint Venture*, 798 S.W.2d 805, 807 (Tex. App.-Beaumont 1990, writ dism'd) (affirming that a client may bring a DTPA action against an architect who allegedly committed malpractice). But see Tex. Civ. Prac. & Rem. Code § 74.004(b). It does not prevent consumers from filing DTPA causes against pharmacists. What is the test for allowing disgruntled consumers to sue some but not all professionals?

F. *Lawyers and Law Firms as DTPA Defendants*

Latham v. Castillo
972 S.W.2d 66
(Tex. 1998)

On January 3, 1986, Audona Castillo prematurely gave birth to twin daughters, Kay and Sara, at Taft Hospital. Born with birth defects, the girls were immediately transferred to Driscoll Foundation Children's Hospital where both underwent surgery. Sara died approximately one week later.

The Castillos then filed a medical malpractice suit against Driscoll Hospital on Sara's behalf and received a $6,000,000 default judgment. Later, their attorney, Rene Rodriguez, settled the case for $70,000.

Kay Castillo, the surviving twin, died on February 14, 1988. In December 1989, the Castillos hired B. Mills Latham to file a legal malpractice claim against Rodriguez for settling the default judgment and to pursue a medical malpractice claim against Driscoll Hospital for Kay's death.

While Latham settled the legal malpractice claim against Rodriguez for $400,000, the statute of limitations ran on the Castillos' medical malpractice claim on February 14, 1990 without suit being filed.

The Castillos then sued Latham for legal malpractice because Latham failed to file the medical malpractice action for Kay's death within the two-year statute of limitations.

The Castillos also sued Latham for unconscionable action under the DTPA because Latham affirmatively represented to them that he had filed and was actively prosecuting the medical malpractice claim.

Finally, the Castillos alleged that Latham wrongfully misrepresented himself, breached the contract of employment, and was negligent.

After the Castillos presented their case to a jury, the trial court granted a directed verdict for Latham that the Castillos take nothing. The court of appeals reversed and remanded, holding that the Castillos had presented some evidence to prevent a directed verdict on their DTPA claim.

The court of appeals also remanded the "remaining theories of recovery"—fraudulent misrepresentation and breach of contract—without discussion. The court of appeals affirmed the directed verdict on the negligence claim, however, because the Castillos did not present evidence that "but for" Latham's negligence, the medical malpractice suit would have been successful.

The central question before us is whether the Castillos have presented some evidence to support each element of their DTPA cause of action. We hold that they have done so.

The Legislature amended the DTPA in 1995. Act of May 19, 1995, 74th Leg., R.S., ch. 414, 1995 Tex. Gen. Laws 2988. Unless otherwise noted, all DTPA references will be to the pre-amendment provisions applicable when this suit was filed. Under the amendments effective September 1, 1995, lawyers may not be sued under the DTPA unless they engage in one of the following acts:

1) an express misrepresentation of a material fact that cannot be characterized as advice, judgment, or opinion;
2) a failure to disclose;
3) an unconscionable action or course of action that cannot be characterized as advice, judgment, or opinion; or,
4) an express warranty that cannot be characterized as advice, judgment, or opinion. Tex. Bus. & Com. Code § 17.49(c)

The Castillos alleged Latham's conduct constituted an "unconscionable action or course of action" that violated the DTPA. Tex. Bus. & Com. Code § 17.50(a)(3)

Under section 17.45, "unconscionable action or course of action" means "an act or practice which, to a person's detriment: (A) takes advantage of the lack of knowledge, ability, experience, or capacity of a person to a grossly unfair degree; or (B) results in a gross disparity between the value received and consideration paid, in a transaction involving transfer of consideration." *Id.* § 17.45(5)

The Castillos have relied only on subsection (A) in asserting that Latham's actions were unconscionable. To be actionable under subsection (A), the resulting unfairness must be "glaringly noticeable, flagrant, complete and unmitigated." *See, Chastain v. Koonce,* 700 S.W.2d 579, 584 (Tex. 1985)

Attorneys can be found to have engaged in unconscionable conduct by the way they represent their clients. *See, e.g., DeBakey v. Staggs,* 605 S.W.2d 631, 633 (Tex. Civ. App.—Houston [1st Dist.] 1980), *writ ref'd n.r.e. per curiam,* 612 S.W.2d 924 (Tex. 1981) (finding an attorney unconscionably took advantage of a client to a grossly unfair degree when the attorney knowingly failed to obtain in a timely manner a name change for the client's minor child).

The Castillos assert that Latham acted unconscionably in representing that he was actively prosecuting their medical malpractice claim for Kay's death when in fact he was not. The Castillos depended on Latham to file suit against the hospital for Kay's death. As Mrs. Castillo testified, "You trust in a professional because they know more than you." The record reveals, and Latham's attorney conceded at oral argument before this Court, that there is some evidence that Latham told the Castillos he had filed the medical malpractice claim when in fact he had not.

Although he affirmatively represented to them that he was actively pursuing the claim, Latham never did file the suit and limitations ran. As a result, the Castillos lost the opportunity to prosecute their claim against the hospital for Kay's death.

Viewing Latham's actions in the light we must, his actions are similar to the attorney's conduct in *DeBakey.* Latham took advantage of the trust the Castillos placed in him as an attorney. Therefore, the Castillos have presented some evidence that they were taken advantage of to a grossly unfair degree.

Latham argues, however, that the Castillos' DTPA claim is essentially a dressed-up legal malpractice claim. Therefore, he asserts, the Castillos must prove that they would have won the medical malpractice case for Kay's death in order to recover. Because they did not present any evidence on this, Latham argues, the Castillos cannot recover. We disagree.

The legislative intent in enacting the DTPA was to provide plaintiffs a remedy where the common law fails. *See, Woo v. Great Southwestern Acceptance Corp.,* 565 S.W.2d 290, 298 (Tex. Civ. App. ¾Waco 1978, writ ref'd n.r.e.). Section 17.43 states that the remedies provided by the Act "are *in addition* to any other procedures or remedies provided for in any other law." Tex. Bus. & Com. Code § 17.43 (emphasis added)

Moreover, the Legislature mandates that the DTPA is to be "liberally construed and applied to promote its underlying purposes." *Id.* § 17.44 Recasting the Castillos' DTPA claim — as merely a legal malpractice claim would subvert the Legislature's clear purpose in enacting the DTPA¾ to deter deceptive business practices.

If the Castillos had only alleged that Latham negligently failed to timely file their claim, their claim would properly be one for legal malpractice. However, the Castillos alleged and presented some evidence that Latham affirmatively misrepresented to them that he had filed and was actively prosecuting their claim. It is the difference between negligent conduct and deceptive conduct. To recast this claim as one for legal malpractice is to ignore this distinction.

The Legislature enacted the DTPA to curtail this type of deceptive conduct. Thus, the DTPA does not require and the Castillos need not prove the "suit within a suit" element when suing an attorney under the DTPA. The Castillos have presented some evidence of unconscionable action.

It is not enough that the Castillos merely prove an unconscionable action or course of action by Latham, however. Latham's unconscionable action must have been the producing cause of actual damages. TEX. BUS. & COM. CODE § 17.50(a). Latham argues that the Castillos cannot recover mental anguish damages under the DTPA without first proving an economic injury. We disagree.

Section 17.50(a) of the DTPA ¾ as it appeared when this suit was filed ¾ [stated that a] "consumer may maintain an action where any of the following constitute a producing cause of *actual damages.*"(emphasis added). In 1995, the Legislature amended section 17.50(a) to provide that "[a] consumer may maintain an action where any of the following constitute a producing cause of economic damages *or damages for mental anguish:...* (3) any unconscionable action or course of action by any person."

We have stated that the term "actual damages," as used in the DTPA, means those recoverable at common law. *See, Brown v. American Transfer & Storage Co.,* 601 S.W.2d 931, 939 (Tex. 1980) It is axiomatic that mental anguish damages *are* actual damages recoverable at common law for "some common law torts ¾and by analogy for knowing violations of certain statutes such as the DECEPTIVE TRADE PRACTICES ACT." *See, City of Tyler v. Likes,* 962 S.W.2d 489, 495 (Tex. 1997)

Therefore, the Castillos do not have to first prove that they have suffered economic damages in order to recover mental anguish damages. The Castillos have satisfied their burden on the damages element of a DTPA cause of action if they have presented some evidence of mental anguish. . . . We hold that the Castillos have presented some evidence to support each element of their DTPA cause of action. Therefore, we affirm the court of appeals' remand of the DTPA cause of action.

NOTES & QUESTIONS

Unresolved Problems In Texas Legal Malpractice Law
36 St. Mary's L.J. 989 (2005)
Stephen E. McConnico

As a general rule, Texas law does not allow the "fracturing" of legal malpractice claims into multiple causes of action. Courts have struggled with this fracturing principle over the last several years, in an effort to determine whether all claims clients bring against their attorneys should be treated only as legal malpractice claims based on negligence or can be brought as distinct causes of action in certain circumstances.

The emerging principle is that claims brought against attorneys based on the quality of their representation should be brought only as traditional legal malpractice claims based on professional negligence. *Barcelo v. Elliot*, 923 S.W.2d 575, 580 (Tex. 1996) (citing *Cosgrove v. Grimes,* 774 S.W.2d 662, 665 (Tex. 1989)); *Cosgrove v. Grimes,* 774 S.W.2d 662, 665 (Tex. 1989) (holding that a legal malpractice action in Texas is traditionally based on professional negligence). The plaintiff must prove: 1) there is a duty owed by the attorney to the client, 2) that duty was breached, 3) the breach proximately caused the client's injury, and 4) damages resulted. *Cosgrove,* 774 S.W.2d at 665. Claims based on truly distinct allegations, however, may be brought as separate causes of action. . .

Clients may not sue their attorneys for breach of contract based on allegations that the legal services performed were inadequate or otherwise failed to comply with the contract for services between the attorney and client. . . Similar to breach of contract claims, claims for breach of express or implied warranty are not proper if they are based on allegations that an attorney failed to provide good or competent legal services. *Greathouse v. McConnell*, 982 S.W.2d 165, 172 (Tex. App.-- Houston [1st Dist.] 1998, pet. denied). In fact, Texas law does not even recognize an implied warranty of good and workmanlike performance of professional services, such as legal services. *Parkway Co. v. Woodruff*, 901 S.W.2d 434, 438-439 (Tex. 1994). Thus, plaintiffs may not complain that an attorney expressly or impliedly warranted to provide legal services of a particular quality. These types of allegations may only be brought as claims of legal malpractice.

Violations of the Deceptive Trade Practices Act

As with breach of contract and breach of warranty claims, claims brought under the DTPA are subject to the fracturing rule if they are based on the attorney's failure to comply with the standard of care in representing the client. If the claims are based on affirmative misrepresentations of material fact, however, they may be outside the scope of the fracturing rule.

Some early fracturing cases had suggested that all claims against attorneys arising out of their legal representation, including claims brought under the DTPA, were subject to the fracturing rule[.] [Therefore, they should proceed] only as legal malpractice claims. But in 1998 the Texas Supreme Court issued *Latham v. Castillo*, which clarified that attorneys are still subject to DTPA liability, despite the fracturing rule, so long as the claims are based on affirmative misrepresentations of material fact (i.e., deceptive conduct) and not on mere allegations of inadequate legal representation or negligence.

Guest v. Cochran
993 S.W.2d 397
(Tex. App.-Houston [14th Dist.] 1999)

I. Background

Henry G. Guest, Sr. and Ada Madrid C. Guest, now deceased, were the parents of [Henry G. Guest, Jr.,] and his sisters — Mary Guest Kaeppel (Kaeppel) and Gloria Guest Reynolds. In 1993, Cochran — an attorney and long-time friend of Kaeppel and her husband, Dr. Christopher Kaeppel, was hired to perform estate planning services for Mr. and Mrs. Guest. [Henry Junior] alleges that Cochran conspired with Kaeppel so that she would obtain a disproportionate share of their parents' estates. In support of this contention, [Henry Junior] claims that all correspondence was between Cochran and Kaeppel, not Mr. and Mrs. Guest. Moreover, Mr. Guest was ill, weak, and in need of a blood transfusion.

On May 5, 1993, Mr. and Mrs. Guest met with Cochran for the first time. Cochran drafted several documents for Mr. and Mrs. Guest, including an irrevocable trust, a deed of gift, a power of attorney, and new wills. Subsequently, on May 17, 1993, Mr. and Mrs. Guest signed the new wills that Cochran had drafted. The new wills, which named each of the Guests' children independent co-executors of the estates, provided that the surviving spouse would receive the other spouse's estate in its entirety, free of trust. If there was no surviving spouse, the Guests' three children would receive equal shares of the estate. The wills did not contain a bypass trust, which. . . [Henry Junior believed] would have minimized the estate taxes.

The irrevocable trust named Kaeppel as trustee. [Henry Junior] claims that this would have given Kaeppel a disproportionate share of the Guests' estates. Mr. and Mrs. Guest, however, did not sign the irrevocable trust or deed of gift because, according to Guest, they did not want to favor Kaeppel over their other children.

On June 14, 1993, Mr. Guest passed away. As provided in the wills, the Guests' three children were independent co-executors of Mr. Guest's estate. Cochran continued as attorney for Mr. Guest's estate. Mrs. Guest passed away on May 17, 1995. [Henry Junior] and his sisters were independent co-executors of Mrs. Guest's estate. Mr. and Mrs. Guest had combined estates of $800,000.00. Mrs. Guest's estate paid $60,000.00 in estate taxes.

[Henry Junior] sued Cochran on June 13, 1995. [Henry Junior] filed his first amended petition on September 28, 1995, seeking damages for excess federal estate taxes paid out of Mrs. Guest's estate. [Henry Junior], individually and as independent co-executor of his parents' estates, sued Cochran for claims of attorney malpractice, conspiracy to breach fiduciary duty, fraud, constructive fraud, negligence, gross negligence, and violations of the Texas Deceptive Trade Practices Act (DTPA).

With respect to his malpractice and DTPA claims, [Henry Junior] asserted that Cochran failed: 1) to include a bypass trust or other estate planning mechanism in the will which would have allowed the estates to avoid paying any taxes; and 2) to advise either Mrs. Guest or the executors of Mr. Guest's estate that Mrs. Guest could execute a valid disclaimer of a portion of her "inheritance" from Mr. Guest so that her estate would not have to pay any taxes. Guest based his fraud and conspiracy claims on Cochran's activities and dealings with the Kaeppels and the way in which Cochran dealt with the Guests while he was performing estate planning services for them.

Cochran moved for summary judgment on [Henry Junior]'s first amended petition based on lack of privity or lack of an attorney-client relationship between [Henry Junior] and Cochran. [Henry Junior] responded that Cochran's motion failed to address the claims he brought in his representative capacity on behalf of the estates as independent co-executor. . . .

In a single point of error, with five subparts, [Henry Junior] claims the trial court erred in granting summary judgment in favor of Cochran because () the summary judgment motion did not acknowledge that [Henry Junior], as independent co-executor, sued Cochran on behalf of the estates; b) [Henry Junior] has standing as independent co-executor to bring attorney malpractice claims on behalf of the estates; c) [Henry Junior] has standing as independent co-executor to bring claims for breach of fiduciary duty, fraud, and constructive fraud on behalf of the estates; (d) Cochran failed to establish that [Henry Junior], individually, or as independent co-executor, did not have standing to bring DTPA claims on behalf of the estates; and e) the motion for summary judgment failed to address the additional claim [Henry Junior] raised in the second amended petition.

IV. [Henry Junior]'s Individual Claims

C. DTPA

[Henry Junior] contends the trial court erred in dismissing his DTPA claims. In his summary judgment motion, Cochran argued [Henry Junior] was not a "consumer" for purposes of the DTPA because [Henry Junior] did not "seek or acquire" any "goods or services' " from Cochran.
The DTPA provides: "False, misleading, or deceptive acts or practices in the conduct of any trade or commerce are hereby declared unlawful...." Tex. Bus. & Com. Code Ann. § 17.46(a) (Vernon 1987).

To recover under the DTPA, the plaintiff must establish that (1) he was a consumer of the defendant's goods or services; (2) the defendant committed false, misleading, or deceptive acts in connection with the lease or sale of goods or services; and (3) such acts were a producing cause of actual damages to the plaintiff. *See Brown v. Bank of Galveston, N.A.,* 963 S.W.2d 511, 513 (Tex.1998). At the time [Henry Junior] filed this lawsuit, legal services were "services" under the DTPA. *See DeBakey v. Staggs,* 612 S.W.2d 924, 925 (Tex.1981); *Wright,* 956 S.W.2d at 47.

> Effective September 1, 1995, the DTPA was amended to exempt from application of the act claims for damages based on the rendering of legal services. *See* Tex. Bus. & Com. Code Ann. § 17.49. The 1995 amendment applies to claims upon which suit is filed on or after September 1, 1996. Guest filed this lawsuit on June 13, 1995, thus falling under the law in effect prior to the effective date of the amended statute.

A consumer is someone who seeks to purchase or lease goods or services. *See* Tex. Bus. & Com. Code Ann. § 17.45(4); *Arthur Andersen & Co. v. Perry Equip. Corp.,* 945 S.W.2d 812, 815 (Tex. 1997). To qualify as a consumer, the plaintiff must satisfy two requirements: (1) he must have sought or acquired the goods or services by purchase or lease, and (2) the goods or services must form the basis of the complaint. *See Vinson & Elkins v. Moran,* 946 S.W.2d 381, 406-07 (Tex. App.-Houston [14th Dist.] 1997, writ dism'd by agr.); *Hand v. Dean Witter Reynolds, Inc.,* 889 S.W.2d 483, 496 (Tex. App.-Houston [14th Dist.] 1994, writ denied), citing *Cameron v. Terrell & Garrett, Inc.,* 618 S.W.2d 535, 539 (Tex.1981)

The plaintiff, however, need not establish contractual privity with the defendant in a DTPA claim. *See Amstadt v. United States Brass Corp.,* 919 S.W.2d 644, 649 (Tex.1996). This includes a cause of action under the DTPA against an attorney. *See Thompson v. Vinson & Elkins,* 859 S.W.2d 617, 625 (Tex.App.-Houston [1st Dist.] 1993, writ denied). A party's consumer status does not turn on whether there is a contractual relationship with the defendant, but rather, it is determined by the parties' relationship to the transaction. *See Arthur Andersen & Co.,* 945 S.W.2d at 815. A plaintiff may be a consumer of the legal services he acquires, if a third party actually purchases the services for the plaintiff's benefit. *See Wright,* 956 S.W.2d at 47; *Perez v. Kirk & Carrigan,* 822 S.W.2d 261, 268 (Tex.App.-Corpus Christi 1991, writ denied). Whether the plaintiff is a consumer is a question of law. *See Moran,* 946 S.W.2d at 406; *Hand,* 889 S.W.2d at 496.

Citing to this court's decision in *Vinson & Elkins v. Moran,* [Henry Junior] argues a third-party may be a consumer under the DTPA when the goods or services are purchased for the benefit of a third-party. In *Moran,* the executors of an estate hired Vinson & Elkins to assist with the administration of the estate. 946 S.W.2d at 386. Later, the beneficiaries of the estate sued Vinson & Elkins for legal malpractice. With respect to their DTPA claim, the beneficiaries argued that although the executors of the estate hired Vinson & Elkins, the beneficiaries were "consumers" for purposes of the DTPA. *See id.* at 407. The *Moran* court observed the executor's purpose in hiring the law firm was for the orderly administration of the estate, which in turn, would extend to the beneficiaries in the form of a more orderly administration. *See id.* at 408.

[Henry Junior]'s reliance on *Moran,* however, is misplaced. The court went on to conclude that while any benefit derived by the beneficiaries from the "purchase" of Vinson & Elkins's legal services "was merely incidental to the main purpose, *i.e.,* legal assistance to the executors," the executors did not hire the law firm for the principal purpose of providing a benefit to the beneficiaries. *See id.* The court explained:

> The mere fact that these third parties are benefitted, or damaged, by the attorney's performance does not make the third parties consumers with rights to an action under the DTPA. These third parties are "incidental beneficiaries," and we do not believe the legislature intended to confer consumer status on them. Beneficiaries of a will or trust are, in this respect, no different; they may incidentally benefit or be damaged by the attorney hired to represent the executor. This does not give them consumer status under the DTPA. *Id.*

We find the reasoning in *Moran* equally applicable to the facts at hand. Any benefit derived by the beneficiaries of a will from the estate work provided by an attorney is purely incidental. It is the testator, not the beneficiaries, who hires an attorney to draft the testamentary documents which will carry out his intent.

Furthermore, this court has addressed a situation in which the plaintiff, who was both a beneficiary and an executrix under a will, claimed consumer status under the DTPA. *See Wright,* 956 S.W.2d at 47-48. The court found that because the plaintiff's "relationship to the will was primarily one of beneficiary and executrix, her acquisition of legal services from [the defendant], if any, was gratuitous and incidental to the terms of the will or the durable power of attorney, and not because [the testator] intended to purchase legal services for [the plaintiff's] benefit." *Id.* at 48. The *Wright* court held that the plaintiff was not a consumer under the DTPA. *See id.*

Here, also, [Henry Junior]'s relationship to the will was primarily that of beneficiary, and any acquisition of legal services from Cochran was gratuitous and incidental to the terms of his parents' wills. We conclude, therefore, that [Henry Junior] was not a consumer under the DTPA and the trial court did not err in granting summary judgment on this claim. We, therefore, overrule subpart (d) of [Henry Junior]'s sole point of error.

V. Conclusion

We sustain [Henry Junior]'s point of error and reverse the judgment of the trial court as to a) [Henry Junior]'s claims brought in his *representative capacity on behalf of the estates*: legal malpractice, negligence, gross negligence, breach of fiduciary duty, fraud, constructive fraud, and DTPA violations; and b) the claim for negligent misrepresentation raised in [Henry Junior]'s second amended petition.

Those unaddressed claims are remanded to the trial court. We affirm the judgment of the trial court as to [Henry Junior]'s *individual claims* for legal malpractice, negligence, gross negligence, breach of fiduciary duty, fraud, and constructive fraud, and DTPA violations.

NOTES & QUESTIONS

1) Again, Texas law does not recognize an implied warranty of good and workmanlike performance of professional legal services. But, where there is a "special relationship" (say between an insurer and an insured), the law creates a common-law duty of good faith and fair dealing. See *Subaru of Am. v. David McDavid Nissan, Inc.*, 84 S.W.3d 212, 225 (Tex. 2002) and *Arnold v. National County Mut. Fire Ins. Co.*, 725 S.W.2d 165, 167 (Tex.1987)

2) Assume there is a "special relationship" between an attorney and a client. May a client commence an action against an attorney for allegedly breaching the common law duty of good faith and fair dealing?

3) If the answer is yes, what would be the cause of action — DTPA, breach-of-contract, negligence, — or a combination?

G. Lenders and Creditors as DTPA Defendants

Lenders and the Texas DTPA: A Step Back From The Brink
48 SMU L. Rev. 487 (1995)
James W. Paulsen

In 1980, in *Riverside National Bank v. Lewis*, 603 S.W.2d 169 (Tex. 1980), the Texas Supreme Court decided that the borrowing of money was neither a "good" nor a "service," and that an aggrieved debtor therefore lacked standing to bring a consumer claim under the Texas DTPA. Id. at 175 -176. *The decision initially was interpreted as precluding lender liability under the DTPA.* In the years that immediately followed, however, a succession of further decisions created significant exceptions to this rule, culminating in the Texas Supreme Court's observation that *Riverside* has been "limited . . to its facts." *La Sara Grain Co. v. First Nat'l Bank of Mercedes,* 673 S.W.2d 558, 566 (Tex. 1984). Many DTPA claims against lenders now are based on "collateral services" provided to a borrower in the course of a lending relationship ., *Herndon v. First Nat'l Bank of Tulia*, 802 S.W.2d 396, 399 (Tex. App. -- Amarillo 1991, writ denied), or on the theory that a loan is "inextricably intertwined" with a consumer transaction. *Knight v. Int'l Harvester Credit Corp*., 627 S.W.2d 382, 389 (Tex. 1982)

As these judicially-developed exceptions have begun to swallow up the seemingly clear rule of *Riverside*, commentators have criticized the *Riverside* court's rationale as "superficial" or simply "incorrect," and the *Riverside* rule as "continually limited and narrowed" to the point that it is "almost extinct." Lower courts, emboldened by an apparent Texas Supreme Court trend to read *Riverside* more and more strictly, now issue opinions plainly inconsistent with its holding.

* * *

[While] the author would readily concede to critics of the decision that the Texas Supreme Court's holding in *Riverside* is "limited," that limitation is simply a demarcation of legal territory that has not yet been explored fully in a judicial opinion or otherwise.

Perhaps the best proof that a few new things remain to be said about lender liability under the Texas DTPA is the fact that . . . the *Riverside* court [never examined] the legislative debate leading up to enactment of the DTPA, despite the fact that the decision is grounded entirely on statutory construction. In addition, to the author's knowledge, no DTPA lender decision has looked for guidance to "relevant and pertinent decisions of courts in other jurisdictions," despite the fact that a 1979 amendment to the DTPA now permits such inquiries. . . . [The] current Texas DTPA, by its own language and under settled rules of statutory construction, does not apply, and was never intended to apply, to loan transactions.

* * *

C. Whittling Away At *Riverside*

After *Riverside,* courts often have found particular lending transactions to fall within one of the three possible exceptions to the Riverside rule just discussed. The principal exceptions are situations in which the lender offers "collateral services," not simply a loan, or in which the lender is "inextricably intertwined" with the underlying consumer transaction. A substantial body of authority has grown up around each. While there has been comparatively less discussion of the third, or "loans as services" exception, such exception merits examination because adoption of the doctrine would mean the practical reversal of *Riverside.*

1. The "Collateral Services" Doctrine

In *Riverside*, . . . the Texas Supreme Court noted the borrower's argument that "services" exist in the process of determining whether to loan money, but rejected the argument as "merely hypothetical" because no evidence was presented on the point at trial. In a footnote, however, the court carefully reserved the point for a possible further decision[:]

> Accordingly, we do not pass upon the question whether a bank's misrepresentation concerning its activities, such as the availability of financial counseling, the cost of processing a loan or the ability to pay a customer's monthly bills, could constitute a deceptive act in connection with a sale of "services." We only hold that where those activities are not the subject of the complaint, then the presence of such collateral activities in a transaction otherwise not covered by the DTPA does not subject the parties to liability under the DTPA.

* * *

2. The Inexplicably Inconsistent "Inextricably Intertwined" Standard

Borrowers' attempts to hold their lenders liable under the Texas DTPA on a "collateral services" theory have not been the only — or even the principal — avenue of attack on the *Riverside* doctrine. Since *Riverside*, on at least a half-dozen occasions, the Texas Supreme Court has tried to explain, expand upon or limit what now is known as the "inextricably intertwined" doctrine. The difficulty of the issue is apparent from the sheer number and procedural convolution of the cases. In the three years immediately following the doctrine's modest debut in *Knight v. International Harvester Credit Corporation*, 627 S.W.2d 382, 389 (Tex. 1982), the Texas Supreme Court issued four decisions on the subject. . . . The language of these decisions sometimes is vague, confusing, or inconsistent with other decisions. Nonetheless, since this dubious line of authority represents virtually all the Texas Supreme Court's post- *Riverside* DTPA jurisprudence, the cases must be studied closely for what little light they can shed upon the subject. . . .To a good number of later courts and commentators, the . . . language has come to mean that whenever loan proceeds are used to buy a good or service, the lender automatically is subject to possible DTPA liability.

Chapter Three: Establishing DTPA Causes of Action

Under the DTPA, a consumer may commence five independent causes of action against any person who engages in false, misleading, or deceptive practices. Section 17.50(a)(1) creates a "pure-DTPA" cause of action. A consumer may base the cause of action on any one of several violations appearing on the DTPA's "laundry list" of violations in Section 17.46(b).

Even more important, the DTPA itself does not create a statutory right to initiate a breach-of-warranty action. However, under § 17.50(a)(2), a consumer may file either an action for breach of an express warranty, breach of an implied warranty or both. See *Southwestern Bell Telephone Co. v. FDP Corp.*, 811 S.W.2d 572, 576 (Tex. 1991).

Under § 17.50(a)(3), an aggrieved consumer may also commence an action against any person whose "unconscionable action or course of action" injures the consumer. And § 17.50(a)(4) permits a consumer to initiate an action against insurers as well as against the agents of those persons who violate Art. § 541 of the Texas Insurance Code.

Finally, under § 17.50(h), a consumer may commence a DTPA cause of action if another statute grants that right. Currently, there are nearly thirty "tie-in statutes" that expressly identify and outlaw "false, misleading or deceptive acts or practices" in Texas. (See APPENDIX). And those statutes permit consumers to secure remedies under the DTPA — Subchapter E, Chapter 17, Business & Commerce Code.

For sure, all five causes of action may proceed individually in a Texas or a federal district court. But disgruntled consumers may also file a mixed-actions or mixed-claims lawsuit, listing any combination of the five causes of action. Along with other pertinent information, this chapter outlines the respective elements that a plaintiff must establish to prevail under each DTPA-related cause of action.

A. *DTPA's Laundry List of Prohibited Violations*

Section 17.46(b) reads:

Except as provided in Subsection (d) of this section, the term "false, misleading, or deceptive acts or practices" includes, but is not limited to, the following acts:

1) passing off goods or services as those of another;
2) causing confusion or misunderstanding as to the source, sponsorship, approval, or certification of goods or services;
3) causing confusion or misunderstanding as to affiliation, connection, or association with, or certification by, another;
4) using deceptive representations or designations of geographic origin in connection with goods or services;
5) representing that goods or services have sponsorship, approval, characteristics, ingredients, uses, benefits, or quantities which they do not have or that a person has a sponsorship, approval, status, affiliation, or connection which he does not;
6) representing that goods are original or new if they are deteriorated, reconditioned, reclaimed, used, or secondhand;
7) representing that goods or services are of a particular standard, quality, or grade, or that goods are of a particular style or model, if they are of another;
8) disparaging the goods, services, or business of another by false or misleading representation of facts;
9) advertising goods or services with intent not to sell them as advertised;
10) advertising goods or services with intent not to supply a reasonable expectable public demand, unless the advertisements disclosed a limitation of quantity;
11) making false or misleading statements of fact concerning the reasons for, existence of, or amount of price reductions;
12) representing that an agreement confers or involves rights, remedies, or obligations which it does not have or involve, or which are prohibited by law;
13) knowingly making false or misleading statements of fact concerning the need for parts, replacement, or repair service;
14) misrepresenting the authority of a salesman, representative or agent to negotiate the final terms of a consumer transaction;
15) basing a charge for the repair of any item in whole or in part on a guaranty or warranty instead of on the value of the actual repairs made or work to be performed on the item without stating separately the charges for the work and the charge for the warranty or guaranty, if any;
16) disconnecting, turning back, or resetting the odometer of any motor vehicle so as to reduce the number of miles indicated on the odometer gauge;

17) advertising of any sale by fraudulently representing that a person is going out of business;

18) advertising, selling, or distributing a card which purports to be a prescription drug identification card issued under Section 4151.152, Insurance Code, in accordance with rules adopted by the commissioner of insurance, which offers a discount on the purchase of health care goods or services from a third party provider, and which is not evidence of insurance coverage, unless:

    (A) the discount is authorized under an agreement between the seller of the card and the provider of those goods and services or the discount or card is offered to members of the seller;

    (B) the seller does not represent that the card provides insurance coverage of any kind; and

    (C) the discount is not false, misleading, or deceptive;

19) using or employing a chain referral sales plan in connection with the sale or offer to sell of goods, merchandise, or anything of value, which uses the sales technique, plan, arrangement, or agreement in which the buyer or prospective buyer is offered the opportunity to purchase merchandise or goods and in connection with the purchase receives the seller's promise or representation that the buyer shall have the right to receive compensation or consideration in any form for furnishing to the seller the names of other prospective buyers if receipt of the compensation or consideration is contingent upon the occurrence of an event subsequent to the time the buyer purchases the merchandise or goods;

20) representing that a guarantee or warranty confers or involves rights or remedies which it does not have or involve, provided, however, that nothing in this subchapter shall be construed to expand the implied warranty of merchantability as defined in Sections 2.314 through 2.318 and Sections 2A.212 through 2A.216 to involve obligations in excess of those which are appropriate to the goods;

21) promoting a pyramid promotional scheme, as defined by Section 17.461;

22) representing that work or services have been performed on, or parts replaced in, goods when the work or services were not performed or the parts replaced;

23) filing suit founded upon a written contractual obligation of and signed by the defendant to pay money arising out of or based on a consumer transaction for goods, services, loans, or extensions of credit intended primarily for personal, family, household, or agricultural use in any county other than in the county in which the defendant resides at the time of the commencement of the action or in the county in which the defendant in fact signed the contract; provided, however, that a violation of this subsection shall not occur where it is shown by the person filing such suit he neither knew or had reason to know that the county in which such suit was filed was neither the county in which the defendant resides at the commencement of the suit nor the county in which the defendant in fact signed the contract;

24) failing to disclose information concerning goods or services which was known at the time of the transaction if such failure to disclose such information was intended to induce the consumer into a transaction into which the consumer would not have entered had the information been disclosed;

25) using the term "corporation," "incorporated," or an abbreviation of either of those terms in the name of a business entity that is not incorporated under the laws of this state or another jurisdiction

26) selling, offering to sell, or illegally promoting an annuity contract under Chapter 22, Acts of the 57th Legislature, 3rd Called Session, 1962 (Article 6228a-5, Vernon's Texas Civil Statutes), with the intent that the annuity contract will be the subject of a salary reduction agreement, as defined by that Act, if the annuity contract is not an eligible qualified investment under that Act or is not registered with the Teacher Retirement System of Texas as required by Section 8A of that Act; or

27) taking advantage of a disaster declared by the governor under Chapter 418, Government Code, by:

    (A) selling or leasing fuel, food, medicine, or another necessity at an exorbitant or excessive price; or

    (B) demanding an exorbitant or excessive price in connection with the sale or lease of fuel, food, medicine, or another necessity.

Section 17.46(c) reads:

1) It is the intent of the legislature that in construing Subsection (a) of this section in suits brought under Section 17.47 of this subchapter the courts to the extent possible will be guided by Subsection (b) of this section and the interpretations given by the Federal Trade Commission and federal courts to Section 5(a)(1) of the Federal Trade Commission Act [15 U.S.C.A. § 45(a)(1)].

2) In construing this subchapter the court shall not be prohibited from considering relevant and pertinent decisions of courts in other jurisdictions.

Section 17.46(d) states: For the purposes of the relief authorized in Subdivision (1) of Subsection (a) of Section 17.50 of this subchapter, the term "false, misleading, or deceptive acts or practices" is limited to the acts enumerated in specific subdivisions of Subsection (b) of this section.

B. *Proving a "Pure-DTPA" Cause of Action*

Pennington v. Singleton
606 S.W.2d 682
(Tex.1980)

This suit was brought by the purchaser of a boat for damages for misrepresentations made by the seller to induce the sale. The trial court rendered judgment for the plaintiff. The court of civil appeals, on motion for rehearing, reversed and rendered judgment that the plaintiff take nothing. We reverse the judgment of the court of civil appeals and affirm that of the trial court.

The facts, as found by the trial court, are as follows: In May of 1975 J. W. Singleton sold his used boat, motor, and trailer to Charles Pennington. Singleton had never sold a boat before and was not in the business of selling boats. Singleton made oral statements to Pennington to the effect that the boat, motor, and trailer had just had $500 worth of work done, making the boat and motor in "excellent condition," "perfect condition," and "just like new." These statements were made as statements of material fact, and not as merely opinion or puffing. The statements were false because the gear housing of the motor had been cracked and inadequately repaired. Singleton did not know the statements were false, nor did he make the statements recklessly because he had not experienced any difficulty with the boat after it was repaired. Pennington relied on the statements and would not have purchased the boat without them.

In July of 1975 the gear housing required repairs costing $481.68 because at the time of the sale to Pennington, the gear housing was not in adequate condition for its intended use. The statements made by Singleton were found to have caused an unconscionable result.

The trial court's conclusions of law were that 1) Pennington had not proved the elements of common law fraud, and 2) that he had proved a cause of action under the Texas Deceptive Trade Practices-Consumer Protection Act. Accordingly, the trial court found that Pennington was entitled to an amount equal to three times his actual damages of $481.68. Before trial, however, the parties had agreed to a $500 limit on exemplary damages, if such damages were recoverable. Because of this stipulation the trial court's judgment was reduced to $981.68.

On appeal to the court of civil appeals, Singleton contended that the Deceptive Trade Practices-Consumer Protection Act (DTPA) is inapplicable when the person misrepresenting goods or services is not in the business of selling or leasing those goods or services. The court of civil appeals, with one judge dissenting, disagreed and affirmed the trial court's judgment. In his motion for rehearing, Singleton contended that the treble damages provision of the DTPA could not be constitutionally applied.

The court of civil appeals agreed, holding that none of the subdivisions of § 17.46(b) were applicable, and that Singleton could not be held liable for treble damages under § 17.46(a) or § 17.50(a)(3) without a showing that his misrepresentations were made knowingly or with wrongful intent. Accordingly, the court of civil appeals reversed the judgment of the trial court and rendered judgment that Pennington take nothing.

Pennington's application for writ of error to this court was granted to consider whether the court of civil appeals correctly construed the DTPA as applied to a private cause of action.

In *Woods v. Littleton*, 554 S.W.2d 662 (Tex. 1977), the principles applicable in construing the DTPA were set out. The primary emphasis is on the intention of the legislature, keeping in view "the old law, the evil and the remedy." Legislative intent should be determined from the language of the entire Act and not isolated portions. The court is not necessarily confined to the literal meaning of the words used, and the legislative intent rather than the strict letter of the Act will control. The Act itself provides in § 17.44 that it "shall be liberally construed and applied to promote its underlying purposes, which are to protect consumers against false, misleading, and deceptive business practices, unconscionable actions, and breaches of warranty and to provide efficient and economical procedures to secure such protection." *Id.* at 665.

To provide individual consumers with a method and incentive to discourage deceptive trade practices, the legislature included § 17.50, thereby creating a private cause of action for mandatory treble damages. *Woods v. Littleton, supra* at 670. Section 17.50(a) has four subdivisions, which list categories of prohibited conduct. A finding that the defendant's acts fall within one of these subdivisions may entitle the plaintiff to the remedies allowed by § 17.50(b). Sections 17.50(a) and (b) provide in pertinent part:

* * *

With these considerations in mind, we will determine whether Pennington has proved one or more causes of action under § 17.50(a), and if so, whether Singleton is liable for treble damages as provided in § 17.50(b).

CONSUMER CAUSES OF ACTION UNDER § 17.50(a)

Section 17.50(a)(1) provides that a consumer may maintain an action for violations of § 17.46. Section 17.46(a) declares unlawful any "(f)alse, misleading, or deceptive acts or practices in the conduct of any trade or commerce." Section 17.46(b) lists a number of more specifically defined acts that are prohibited as being unlawfully false, misleading, or deceptive. Section 17.46(a) and the relevant subdivisions of § 17.46(b) provide:

> Sec. 17.46. Deceptive Trade Practices Unlawful
>
> (a) False, misleading, or deceptive acts or practices in the conduct of any trade or commerce are hereby declared unlawful.
>
> (b) The term 'false, misleading, or deceptive acts or practices' includes, but is not limited to, the following acts:
>
> (5) representing that goods or services have sponsorship, approval, characteristics, ingredients, uses, benefits, or quantities which they do not have or that a person has a sponsorship, approval, status, affiliation, or connection which he does not;

(7) representing that goods or services are of a particular standard, quality, or grade, or that goods are of a particular style or model, if they are of another; . . ."

Pennington contends that subdivisions (5) and (7) of § 17.46(b) are applicable to the misrepresentations made about the boat.

Subdivision (5) prohibits representing that a good has characteristics, uses, or benefits that it does not have. The boat sold to Pennington was represented to have the characteristics of a "new" boat or a boat in "excellent" or "perfect" condition. The boat did not have these characteristics because of the cracked gear housing. The boat was also represented to produce the uses and benefits of a "new" boat or a boat in "excellent" or "perfect" condition. Because of the cracked gear housing, the boat could not produce those benefits. A good may lack its claimed characteristics or fail to bring about its claimed uses or benefits because it is not in good mechanical condition, or for other reasons such as its design or manufacture.

In *United Postage Corp. v. Kammeyer*, 581 S.W.2d 716 (Tex.Civ.App.-Dallas 1979, no writ), a vending machine was represented to have a certain selling capacity. Because it lacked that capacity, it was held to lack its claimed characteristics, uses, or benefits. *Id.* at 721. We do not agree with Singleton's argument that false statements about the boat's mechanical condition did not relate to its characteristics, uses, or benefits. Regardless of the reason, when a good does not have the characteristics it is represented to have, or perform as represented, the injury to the consumer is the same. There is no justification for excluding some misrepresentations and including others on the basis of the reason for their falsity.

Subdivision (7) prohibits representing that a good is of a particular standard, quality, grade, style, or model if it is of another. Quality is a measure of degree; as to particular goods quality may be calibrated by standard or grade, as with eggs or meat, or specified by style or model, as with machinery. Even when specific categories are not devised, the good may still be described with more general words of quality. Words like "excellent" and "perfect" are words indicating a high degree of quality. Because the boat was in poor mechanical condition, its condition was of poor quality and the representations were false.

The terms used in §§ 17.46(b)(5) and (7) such as "characteristics" or "quality" are not defined in the DTPA. Therefore, they must be given their ordinary meanings. The general objective of subdivisions (5) and (7) is to ensure that descriptions of goods or services offered for sale are accurate. Misrepresentations, so long as they are of a material fact and not merely "puffing" or opinion, are nevertheless actionable even though they are broad descriptions such as were made to Pennington. The DTPA prohibits false general descriptions about the good, as well as misrepresentations pertaining to more specific information. Sometimes language only generally related to a product or its attributes will convey definite implications.

Some overlap may occur as a result of broadly interpreting the listed violations in § 17.46(b). A broad interpretation is warranted, however, due to human inventiveness in engaging in deceptive or misleading conduct. The legislature did not intend its express purpose of protecting consumers from false trade practices to be circumvented by those who would seek out loopholes in the Act's provisions. For this reason, the legislature initially provided consumers with an action under the "catch-all" provisions of § 17.46(a), as well as for the violations listed in § 17.46(b).

According to Pennington, apart from a cause of action under § 17.46(b), he has alternative causes of action under § 17.50(a). Before the 1979 amendments to the DTPA, misrepresentations not falling within any subdivision of § 17.46(b) could give rise to a cause of action under § 17.46(a). Pennington argues that by its literal terms, § 17.46(a) is applicable, the trial court having found that Singleton's statements were false and misleading. The trial court also found that the misrepresentations caused an unconscionable result. Section 17.50(a)(3) gives rise to a private cause of action for "any unconscionable action," and, according to Pennington, is also applicable to the facts as found by the trial court. The court of civil appeals, however, denied recovery under § 17.46(a) and § 17.50(a)(3), reasoning that treble damages could not be constitutionally imposed without proof that Singleton intended to deceive Pennington or knew the falsity of his statements. This brings us to the decisive issue in this case: whether treble damages may be constitutionally imposed as a remedy for any of the causes of action allowed by § 17.50(a).

[The Texas Supreme Court concluded that the treble damages provisions under § 17.50(b) was constitutional.]

APPLICABILITY OF THE DTPA TO NONMERCHANTS

By cross-point Singleton urges that the DTPA does not apply to an isolated sale of a good by one who is not engaged in the business of selling that good. We agree with the court of civil appeals' first opinion, which held that the Act cannot reasonably be construed as so restricted. Section 17.46 prohibits false, misleading, or deceptive acts in "trade or commerce." "Trade" and "commerce" are broadly defined in § 17.45(6) as "the advertising, offering for sale, sale, lease, or distribution of any good or service, of any property, tangible or intangible, real, personal, or mixed, and any other article, commodity, or thing of value, wherever situated, and shall include any trade or commerce directly or indirectly affecting the people of this state." Section 17.50(a)(1) allows a private cause of action for "any person's" unlawful trade practice. "Person" is defined in § 17.45(3) as "an individual, partnership, corporation, association, or other group, however organized." No exception is provided for persons engaged in trade or commerce who are not in the business of selling; other exemptions are allowed in § 17.49.

The legislature explicitly defined the type of transactions included within the DTPA and the persons against whom a private action may be brought. No indication is made that persons not in the business of selling are to be excluded. Furthermore, it is reasonable to assume that the private action was included in the DTPA to provide a remedy for one-time abuses that could not be adequately handled by state enforcement. For these reasons, we hold that a private cause of action is available against nonmerchants as well as merchants.

CONCLUSION

For the reasons stated above, we conclude that the misrepresentations made by Singleton give rise to a cause of action under § 17.46(b) and that treble damage liability does not make § 17.46(b) unconstitutionally vague or unconstitutional as an excessive fine. Accordingly, we hold that Pennington is entitled to the relief granted under the DTPA by the trial court. The judgment of the court of civil appeals is reversed and that of the trial court is affirmed.

Robinson v. Preston Chrysler-Plymouth, Inc.
633 S.W.2d 500
(Tex. 1982)

Weldon and Lurlene Robinson sued Preston Chrysler-Plymouth, Inc. for violations of the Texas Deceptive Trade Practices-Consumer Protection Act, (DTPA), Tex. Bus. & Com.Code Ann. §§ 17.46(a) and (b)(5), (6), and (7). The Robinsons alleged that they purchased a car from Preston in 1975, but that the car had been damaged, repaired and used as a lease car prior to the sale. Based upon the jury's verdict, the trial court rendered judgment for the Robinsons for $800, trebled, plus attorney's fees. The court of civil appeals reversed the judgment of the trial court and rendered judgment holding that failure to disclose facts without knowledge of those facts is not a deceptive trade practice. While we agree with this holding, we reverse the judgment of the court of civil appeals and remand the case to the trial court for a new trial on the Robinsons' misrepresentation claim.

The Robinsons testified that in January, 1975, they saw a Preston Chrysler-Plymouth advertisement in the newspaper. The ad announced, "SPECIAL SHIPMENT OF LEFTOVER '74 CHRYSLERS & PLYMOUTHS! JUST ARRIVED! Factory Special Purchase Direct from Chrysler!" Under this heading were pictured '74 Plymouth Furys, '74 Chrysler station wagons, '74 Plymouth Satellites and Sebrings, and '75 Chrysler Cordobas.

The Robinsons went to Preston and asked to see the cars in the advertisement. The salesman showed them a '74 Chrysler four-door sedan, and told them that it was from the shipment in the ad. Although they noticed that the car had 1,800 miles on the odometer, the Robinsons testified that a salesman told them not to worry about the mileage because the car was new. The Robinsons subsequently bought the car.

About two months later the car was wrecked. During repairs the Robinsons learned for the first time that their car had been wrecked previously, and they later learned that it had been leased. At trial, Preston's vice president admitted that he knew that the car had been leased prior to the sale, but stated that he had no knowledge that the car had been wrecked and repaired. He testified that the car the Robinsons purchased was not from the shipment in the newspaper ad.

The jury found that the car had been damaged and repaired, that it had been used as a lease car, that Preston had failed to disclose these facts, that the failure to disclose these facts adversely affected the Robinsons, and that the fair market value of the car at the time of sale was $4,000. Since the Robinsons paid $4,800 for the car, judgment was rendered for the difference, $800, trebled, and attorney's fees.

The court of civil appeals reversed the judgment of the trial court and rendered judgment that the Robinsons take nothing. The court found no evidence that Preston knew the car had been wrecked and repaired, and thus, Preston had no duty to disclose such facts. In the opinion of the court of civil appeals, failure to disclose facts by one who has no knowledge of those facts is not a false, misleading, or deceptive act or practice. The court further held that, although Preston had knowledge that the car was used as a lease car prior to the purchase, the Robinsons could not recover under that finding because there was no evidence of damages due to the fact that the car had been leased.

The Robinsons' primary argument is that the court of civil appeals erred in holding that Preston's failure to disclose that the car had been wrecked was not a deceptive trade practice. They contend that one may commit a deceptive trade practice if he fails to disclose material facts to a buyer even if he has no knowledge of those facts. We do not agree with the Robinsons' argument.

At the time the Robinsons brought this action, failure to disclose material facts was not listed as one of the violations of the "laundry list" of section 17.46(b) of the DTPA. Thus, this failure to disclose claim must come within section 17.46(a), which prohibits all "false, misleading, or deceptive acts or practices in the conduct of any trade or commerce." The question is whether failure to disclose facts, in an action brought under section 17.46(a), prior to the 1979 amendments, is a deceptive trade practice if the speaker has no knowledge of those facts. In 1979, section 17.46(b)(23) was added to the list of deceptive trade practices. Under subsection (23) one commits a deceptive trade practice if he fails to "disclose information concerning goods or services which was known at the time of transaction" if the failure to disclose was intended to induce the buyer into a transaction he would not have otherwise entered. Thus, the legislature has incorporated a knowledge requirement in this new example of a violation of the DTPA. Although section 17.46(b) is only a list of deceptive trade practices, and is not all inclusive, an addition to section 17.46(b) is some indication of the legislative intent regarding the coverage of section 17.46(a). See generally, Stanford v. Butler, 181 S.W.2d 269 (Tex. 1944).

The Robinsons rely on *Pennington v. Singleton,* 606 S.W.2d 682 (Tex.1980). In *Pennington,* we held that prior to the 1979 amendments treble damages could be recovered without proof of knowledge or intent under those subdivisions of the "laundry list" of section 17.46(b) that do not expressly require knowledge or intent. Since their claim does not come within the laundry list of section 17.46(b), the Robinsons urge that under Pennington, knowledge is not required. Pennington did not discuss whether knowledge or intent was required to prove a cause of action under section 17.46(a). Also, *Pennington* was a misrepresentation case.

We recognize a distinction between misrepresentations and failure to disclose information, and agree with the court of civil appeals that one cannot be held liable under the DTPA for failure to disclose facts about which he does not know. When a seller makes representations to the buyer, he is under a duty to know if his statements are true. No such duty to know the facts are true arises when the seller does not make representations, but merely fails to reveal information which he does not know.

In most consumer transactions, however, more than mere failure to disclose the facts is involved because the seller normally makes some representation about the goods. In this case, there is evidence not only of Preston's failure to disclose facts, but that Preston made misrepresentations to the Robinsons. Preston advertised in the local newspaper that it was selling '74 Chryslers and Plymouths "direct from Chrysler." The Robinsons asked to see cars from the shipment in the ad and were told the car that they purchased was from that shipment.

Although this case went to the jury only on the failure to disclose issue, the Robinsons pleaded violations of sections 17.46(a) and 17.46(b)(5), (6), and (7). As stated before, section 17.46(a) prohibits all "false misleading, or deceptive acts or practices in the conduct of any trade or commerce." Subsections (5), (6), and (7) concern misrepresentations. Subsection (b)(5) prohibits representing that a good has "sponsorship, approval, characteristics, ingredients, uses, benefits, or quantities" that it does not have, and subsection (6) prohibits representing goods are new if they are "deteriorated, reconditioned, reclaimed, used, or secondhand." Subsection (7) prohibits representing that a good is "of a particular standard, quality, or grade," "style, or model," if it is not.

The Robinsons also argue that the court of civil appeals erred in rendering judgment and not remanding the case for new trial because they requested several misrepresentation issues which were refused by the trial court. One issue would have inquired whether Preston represented to the Robinsons that the car was "of a particular standard or quality when it was of another." Other issues inquired whether Preston represented that the car had sponsorship or ingredients it did not have, and whether Preston represented that the Robinsons were original owners of the car when it was previously owned.

We agree that the trial court should have submitted misrepresentation issues to the jury. Consequently, we reverse the judgment of the court of civil appeals and remand the case to the trial court for a new trial.

C. DTPA Action for Breach of an Express Warranty

Consumer Protection - Breach of Warranty - Merger Doctrine No Defense to Deceptive Trade Practices Suit for Breach of Express Warranty —
***Alvarado v. Bolton*, 749 S.W. 2d47 (Tex. 1988)**
20 St. Mary's L.J. 689 (1989)
Robert Carl Jones

Under the DTPA, a consumer [who complains about a breach of warranty may bring a] suit against the breaching party without confronting common-law defenses which would bar the suit. However, because the DTPA does not contain specific warranties, DTPA suits seeking damages for a breach of warranty must allege the existence of an independently created warranty. These independent warranties are generally created under statutes enacted by the legislature, and from implied or express warranties provided by contract or the common law. However, prior to enforcement of any warranty, the courts look to both the source of the warranty's creation as well as the parties' subsequent agreement to limit, modify, or exclude the warranty.

La Sara Grain Company v. First National Bank of Mercedes
673 S.W.2d 558
(Tex. 1984)

This action concerns a bank's liability for honoring checks with fewer than the required number of signatures, failing to follow a restrictive endorsement, and other alleged wrongful acts and deceptive trade practices which allowed an employee to embezzle funds from his employer. After a nonjury trial, the district court rendered judgment against the bank for $911,329.66; that figure included actual damages, additional damages under the Deceptive Trade Practices Act (DTPA), interest, and attorney's fees. The court of appeals reversed the judgment of the trial court and rendered judgment that plaintiff La Sara take nothing. We affirm that portion of the judgment of the court of appeals that removed the award of DTPA additional damages. We reverse the judgment of the court of appeals in all other regards, and affirm the trial court judgment for actual damages. We remand the cause for the consideration of a factual insufficiency point and for the recalculation of prejudgment interest.

La Sara Grain Company, a corporation, hired Harold Jones as general manager and opened a checking account with First National Bank of Mercedes in 1975. La Sara filed with the bank a corporate resolution naming the four officers of the corporation as authorized signatories and providing that any two of them could sign checks for the corporation. Jones was one of the officers named in this resolution. The bank also provided La Sara with a signature card; however, during its circulation among the four officers, the card was altered to require only one signature rather than two. From the spring of 1975 to the fall of 1978, the bank honored checks drawn on La Sara's account bearing the signature of only one officer, ordinarily Jones, the officer in charge of La Sara's day-to-day affairs. During this period, La Sara received monthly statements of its account with the bank.

In the fall of 1978, La Sara fired Jones. An audit subsequently revealed that Jones had embezzled over $300,000. In July of 1979, La Sara filed suit against Jones to recover the amounts embezzled. La Sara thereafter amended its petition to join as defendants Fidelity & Deposit Company of Maryland and the First National Bank of Mercedes. Prior to trial, La Sara settled its claims against Jones and Fidelity. Jones agreed to make restitution; Fidelity paid $90,000 to settle La Sara's claim on a fidelity bond and then intervened in La Sara's suit against the bank, claiming a right to subrogation.

* * *

II. La Sara's DTPA Claim

La Sara also contends that the bank has violated the Deceptive Trade Practices-Consumer Protection Act. Tex. Bus. & Com. Code Ann. §§ 17.41-.63. La Sara claims that as part of the depository contract the bank impliedly warranted the dual-signature requirement adopted in La Sara's corporate resolution. La Sara alleges that the bank breached this warranty when it paid checks signed only by Jones and is therefore liable for treble damages under section 17.50(a)(2). In addition to the checks, La Sara contends that the bank's practice of splitting items payable to La Sara between the accounts of Jones and La Sara, of making loans in La Sara's name without proper authorization, and of allowing Jones to orally withdraw money from La Sara's account violated the general prohibition against "(f)alse, misleading or deceptive acts or practices in the conduct of any trade or commerce" contained in the 1977 act. The trial court agreed.

The court of appeals reversed the judgment of the trial court and rendered judgment that La Sara take nothing on its DTPA claim. The court of appeals found no evidence of a false, misleading, or deceptive act or practice in violation of sections 17.46(a) and 17.50(a)(1). The court did agree that the bank had breached an implied warranty in paying La Sara's checks on only one signature, but held that La Sara's cause of action for breach of warranty accrued in 1975 when the checking account was first opened. The court of appeals reasoned that La Sara was not a consumer then because the 1975 version of the DTPA defined services as "work, labor, or services purchased or leased for use for other than commercial or business use." *See Farmers & Merchants State Bank v. Ferguson,* 617 S.W.2d 918, 920 (Tex.1981).

A. DTPA § 17.50(a)(2) — Breach of Warranty

Section 17.50(a)(2) provides that a consumer may maintain an action if he has been adversely affected by the breach of an express or implied warranty. A consumer is defined as an "individual, partnership or corporation, or governmental entity who seeks or acquires by purchase or lease any goods or services." Tex. Bus. & Com. Code Ann. § 17.45(4). The services provided by a bank in connection with a checking account are within the scope of the DTPA. *Farmer's & Merchants State Bank v. Ferguson,* 605 S.W.2d 320, 324 (Tex.Civ.App.-Fort Worth 1980), *aff'd on other grounds,* 617 S.W.2d 918 (Tex.1981).

The court of appeals erred in applying the 1975 act to all of La Sara's checks. The applicable version of the DTPA is determined by the date the deceptive act or practice occurs. *Woods v. Littleton,* 554 S.W.2d 662, 666 (Tex.1977). If the bank breached a warranty by honoring La Sara's checks on an unauthorized signature, La Sara's cause of action accrued under the version of the DTPA in force at the time the checks were paid. The 1977 Act would therefore apply to those checks paid after May 23, 1977, the effective date of the amendment which deleted the phrase "for other than commercial or business use" from the definition of services. Because La Sara qualifies as a consumer under the 1977 act, we must determine whether the bank breached an implied warranty by paying checks contrary to La Sara's instructions.

The DTPA does not define the term "warranty." Furthermore, the act does not create any warranties; therefore any warranty must be established independently of the act. *Cheney v. Parks,* 605 S.W.2d 640, 642 (Tex. Civ. App.-Houston [1st Dist.] 1980, writ ref'd n.r.e.) While express warranties are imposed by agreement of the parties to the contract, *Rinehart v. Sonitrol of Dallas, Inc.,* 620 S.W.2d 660, 662-663 (Tex.Civ.App.-Dallas 1981, writ ref'd n.r.e.); Tex.Bus. & Com.Code Ann. § 2.313 (Tex. UCC) (Vernon 1968), implied warranties are created by operation of law and are grounded more in tort than in contract. *Humber v. Morton,* 426 S.W.2d 554 (Tex. 1968). Implied warranties are derived primarily from statute, although some have their origin at common law. *See Kamarath v. Bennett,* 568 S.W.2d 658 (Tex.1978); *Jacob E. Decker & Sons, Inc. v. Capps,* 164 S.W.2d 828 (Tex.1942).

One statutory source of implied warranties is the Uniform Commercial Code. *See, e.g.,* Tex. Bus. & Com. Code Ann. §§ 2.314, 2.315 (Tex.UCC) (Vernon 1968). Although the UCC imposes a number of warranties on customers and collecting banks in the payment process, *see id.* § 4.207, there is no mention of a warranty by a payor bank in favor of its customer. All of the warranties created in section 4.207 concern either the item itself (for instance, that it has not been materially altered) or the holder's relationship to it (that he has good title, for example). Each of these warranties goes to a present fact. On the other hand, when section 4.207 speaks of a promise to accept the return of a dishonored item, it speaks of an "engagement." Generally, courts are to construe statutes so as to harmonize with other relevant laws, if possible. *State v. Standard Oil Co.,* 107 S.W.2d 550 (Tex. 1937). We hold that the bank's implied promise that it will not pay checks on an unauthorized signature is not a warranty, but only an implied term of the contract. A mere breach of contract is not a violation of the DTPA. *Ashford Development, Inc. v. USLife Real Estate Services Corp.,* 661 S.W.2d 933, 935 (Tex. 1983).

B. DTPA §§ 17.46(a) & 17.50(a)(1) — Deceptive Trade Practice

La Sara next contends that the bank's practice of paying its checks on an unauthorized signature violated the 1977 act's general prohibition against "(f)alse, misleading or deceptive acts or practices in the conduct of any trade or commerce." Tex.Bus. & Com.Code Ann. §§ 17.46(a), 17.50(a)(1). We, however, like the court of appeals find no evidence that the bank's payment of La Sara's checks on only one signature was a deceptive trade practice. La Sara was fully informed of the bank's practice; each month the bank returned La Sara's cancelled checks with a statement of its account. Before 1979, it was an open question whether the failure to disclose material facts was a violation of 17.46(a). *See Robinson v. Preston Chrysler-Plymouth,* 633 S.W.2d 500 (Tex.1982) (failure to disclose an unknown material fact not a deceptive trade practice). This case, however, does not even involve a failure to disclose; the bank sent La Sara notice of all transactions. Although the bank's conduct may have been in bad faith under the UCC, it was not false, misleading, or deceptive.

In addition to the checks, the trial court found the $14,000 oral withdrawal and the two unauthorized loans to be deceptive trade practices. La Sara argues the court of appeals has erred in failing to address and affirm these findings. The first loan and the oral withdrawal, however, provide no basis for a DTPA claim because both occurred during the period governed by the 1975 act when La Sara did not qualify as a consumer of services. Only the second loan originated after the

1977 amendment to the DTPA which expanded the definition of services to include business and commercial uses. La Sara maintains that this loan was a deceptive trade practice under sections 17.46(a) and 17.50(a)(1) because it was made without proper authorization and the proceeds were split between the accounts of La Sara and Jones.

We first considered whether a loan might provide the basis for a DTPA claim in *Riverside National Bank v. Lewis,* 603 S.W.2d 169 (Tex.1980). In *Riverside* the plaintiff Lewis sought to refinance the loan on his automobile through Riverside Bank. Riverside advised Lewis that the loan had been approved, but subsequently refused to lend the money. After his car was repossessed and sold, Lewis sued Riverside Bank alleging that the Bank's conduct violated the DTPA. We held that Lewis was not a consumer and therefore had no claim under the DTPA. We said that a person who seeks only to borrow money is not a consumer because the lending of money involves neither a good nor a service.

Since the holding in *Riverside,* we have twice limited the case to its facts, emphasizing that Lewis sought only the extension of credit from Riverside, and nothing more. In *Knight v. International Harvester Credit Corp.,* 627 S.W.2d 382, 389 (Tex.1982), we held a lender subject to a DTPA claim because the lender and seller "were so inextricably intertwined in the transaction as to be equally responsible for the conduct of the sale." In determining that the borrower was a consumer, we considered the borrower's purpose for the loan. We distinguished *Riverside* because the borrower there sought only the extension of credit, whereas "Knight's objective in the transaction was the purchase of a dump truck." 627 S.W.2d at 389. In *Flenniken v. Longview Bank & Trust Co.,* 661 S.W.2d 705 (Tex.1983), we held the purchaser of a home could sue the bank under the DTPA for an unconscionable course of conduct in foreclosing on his partially constructed home. The bank had agreed to provide the interim financing to the builder in return for an assignment of the purchaser's note and mechanic's lien contract. Again we viewed the transaction from the purchasers' perspective and concluded "the Flennikens did not seek to borrow money; they sought to acquire a house." 661 S.W.2d at 708.

The rule of law that *Knight* and *Flenniken* announced is not restricted to cases involving financial institutions. In *Cameron v. Terrell and Garrett Co.,* 618 S.W.2d 535 (Tex.1981) we held that a buyer of a house could bring a DTPA action against a realtor from whom he had purchased nothing. In *Cameron,* the realtor, who was the seller's agent, represented to the buyer that the house in question was larger than it actually was. We held that the buyer was a DTPA consumer because of the purchase of the house; therefore, he could bring a DTPA action against anyone in the transaction who violated the act.

Under *Knight* and *Flenniken,* a lender may be subject to a DTPA claim if the borrower's "objective" is the purchase or lease of a good or service thereby qualifying the borrower as a consumer. Obviously, we cannot determine La Sara's objective concerning this loan, because La Sara's complaint is that it did not authorize the transaction. There is no evidence, however, that Jones represented to the bank that the loan was to purchase or lease goods or services that the bank thought the loan was for that purpose, or that the loan was one of a series with which La Sara obtained goods or services. In fact, there is no evidence that La Sara ever borrowed money from the bank for goods or services. Because the loan involves only the extension of credit, La Sara has not shown itself to be a consumer and therefore has no DTPA claim.

Southwestern Bell Telephone Company v. FDP Corporation
811 S.W.2d 572
(Tex. 1991)

Respondent's motion for rehearing is granted. Our opinion of March 6, 1991 is withdrawn, and the following is substituted in its place.

The issue in this case is whether a seller's partial failure to perform under a sales agreement may serve as the basis for a breach of warranty claim under the Texas Deceptive Trade Practice-Consumer Protection Act, Tex.Bus. & Com. Code §§ 17.41-17.63 (DTPA). The court of appeals held that certain oral statements made by the seller to induce a sale constituted an express warranty, and that the seller's failure to perform one of the items in the contract was a breach of that warranty. 749 S.W.2d 569. The court further held that a contractual limitation of damages clause could not limit the buyer's recovery under the DTPA for the breach of warranty. We disagree with the latter conclusion. We hold that the limitation clause was part of the warranty upon which the buyer's claim is based and it therefore limits his recovery. We reverse the judgment of the court of appeals and render judgment that FDP Corporation take nothing.

Frank Prasek, the president of FDP Corporation, met with Max Williams, a Southwestern Bell representative, in early 1980 to discuss advertising in the next edition of the Houston Yellow Pages. During this meeting, Prasek complained that a previous Yellow Pages advertisement for FDP had contained an error in its text. Williams assured Prasek that the new advertisement would be published correctly. Bell and FDP then executed a written advertising contract calling for a boldface listing of FDP's hair design business under "BARBERS," a boldface listing under "BEAUTY SALONS," a double quarter column display under "BARBERS," and a cross reference under "BEAUTY SALONS" to that display.

When the Yellow Pages was published in June, 1980, the boldface listings and the cross reference appeared without error, but the display was not included. Bell nevertheless billed FDP for all the items. Under protest, FDP made several installment payments. In January 1981, Bell finally realized its mistake and returned the sums previously paid by FDP for the omitted display. Thereafter, FDP's attorney made a written demand that Bell reimburse FDP for lost profits allegedly caused by Bell's failure to publish the advertisement. When Bell did not meet this demand, FDP filed suit, alleging negligence and violation of the DTPA.

FDP's claims were tried to a jury, which returned a verdict generally favorable to Bell. The jury failed to find that the omission of the advertisement was caused by Bell's negligence, that Bell committed any "laundry list" violations under the DTPA, or that Bell was responsible for any unconscionable action or course of action under the DTPA. *See* Tex. Bus. & Com. Code §§ 17.46(b), 17.50(a)(3). The jury did find, however, that Bell expressly warranted that it would publish FDP's advertisement, that Bell breached the warranty, and that the breach was a producing cause of damages to FDP. Nevertheless, the jury found that FDP incurred no lost profits, which was the only element of damages submitted. Based on this verdict, the trial court rendered judgment that FDP take nothing, and FDP appealed.

The court of appeals reversed the judgment of the trial court. The court found sufficient evidence to support the jury's findings of breach of warranty and producing cause, and held that the jury's failure to find damages was against the great weight and preponderance of the evidence. The court of appeals therefore remanded the cause for a new trial, and Bell appealed to this court. Bell argues that FDP's only claim is for breach of contract, not breach of warranty. It asserts that a warranty is a guarantee to accomplish a result or a guarantee of the truth of an assertion. According to Bell, Williams' statements at most constitute a promise to perform in the future, not a guarantee of performance. Thus, Bell concludes, no express warranty was made. If a warranty was created, Bell asserts that its liability for breach is limited under the advertising contract to return of the money FDP paid for the display.

FDP argues that a warranty need not be an absolute guarantee and the seller need not intend to create a warranty. According to FDP, a promise to perform an act in the future can be a warranty just like any other promise or affirmation. FDP further argues that it relied on Williams' statements and it would be unfair not to enforce them. Finally, FDP asserts that the contractual liability limitation is unenforceable either because it is an invalid liquidated damages provision or because such a waiver violates the policy of the DTPA. Tex.Bus. & Com.Code § 17.42.

Our first inquiry is whether FDP's allegations state a claim for breach of warranty, which is actionable under the DTPA, or merely a claim for breach of contract. Because Bell's sale of advertising is predominantly a service transaction, not a sale of goods, the warranty provisions of Article Two of the Uniform Commercial Code (UCC) do not explicitly govern this case. *See* Tex. Bus. & Com. Code § 2.102 (Tex. UCC). Therefore, we begin this inquiry by examining the common law of warranty.

Although it is well-established that express warranties are enforced in service transactions, *see Hawkins v. McGee,* 84 N. H. 114, 146 A. 641 (1929), warranty law has primarily developed in the context of the sale of goods. Scholars have traced its historical roots back to 13th and 14th century England. *See, e.g.,* B. Clark & C. Smith, The Law of Product Warranties 1-1 to 1-13 (1984); Sullivan, *Innovation in the Law of Warranty: The Burden of Reform,* 32 Hastings L.J. 341, 343-351 (1980). Early English courts, established specifically to resolve disputes among traders, required sellers to rectify any defect in the goods they sold, even if the sellers were unaware of the defect when they sold them. Hamilton, *The Ancient Maxim Caveat Emptor,* 40 Yale L.J. 1133, 1158-59 (1931). By the middle of the nineteenth century, however, most courts embraced a doctrine more conducive to an expanding market economy. As William Wetmore Story wrote in 1844, "The general rule of law, applicable to all sales, is, that the buyer buys at his own risk; *caveat emptor.* " W. Story, 2A Treatise on the Law of Contracts 333 (4th ed. 1856).

During this period, a seller could still be held liable for a defect inconsistent with an express warranty, but such warranties were created only if the seller used the particular words warrant or guarantee. As one commentator noted, "mere affirmations or general expressions of quality would not suffice." Sullivan, *supra,* at 347. Moreover, even when a seller gave an explicit express warranty, such a warranty was viewed as collateral to the main contract. Indeed, Story introduced his chapter on warranties by stating: "The question which comes naturally next in order, *after the contract of sale is completed, and the goods are reduced to the possession of the vendee,* is, whether the goods are the quality and nature which the vendee intended to buy." Story, *supra,* at 333 (emphasis added).

As the twentieth century approached, the doctrine of caveat emptor no longer seemed to fit the changing American commercial setting. *Sullivan, supra,* at 355-58. Mass production and transactions between distant parties limited buyers' opportunities to inspect. "The law responded to these changes by a gradual recession of the doctrine of caveat emptor and expansion of implied warranties." *Id.* at 356. Along with the adoption of implied warranties came a relaxation of the requirements for creating express warranties.

Just after the turn of the century, the Uniform Sales Act (USA) codified the trend toward increased warranty liability. The USA, which was never adopted in Texas, provided for the implied warranties of merchantability and fitness for a particular purpose. USA § 15 (1906). It also codified the concept that no particular words are necessary to create an express warranty. *Id.* at § 12. Nearly fifty years later, the UCC carried forward the USA's codification of warranty law. Article Two of the Code has been adopted by every state except Louisiana, and it is the primary influence on modern warranty law. *Sullivan, supra,* at 389.

This historical review illustrates that, although they may have helped accelerate emerging, pro-consumer trends, the two uniform acts upon which most twentieth century warranty cases are based essentially codified the common law of warranty. *See also* Tex. Bus. & Com. Code § 1.103. This observation is especially true with respect to express warranties, which never faced the degree of judicial antipathy with which implied warranties were viewed in the nineteenth century. Thus, although the case at bar involves a service transaction, reference to the Code is instructive. *See also* Tex.Bus. & Com.Code § 2.313 (Comment 2).

The UCC recognizes that breach of contract and breach of warranty are not the same cause of action. The remedies for breach of contract are set forth in section 2.711, and are available to a buyer "[w]here the seller fails to make delivery." Tex. Bus. & Com. Code § 2.711(a). The remedies for breach of warranty, however, are set forth in section 2.714, and are available to a buyer who has finally accepted goods, but discovers that the goods are defective in some manner. Tex.Bus. & Com.Code § 2.714, § 2.711 (Comment 1) Indeed, "the whole purpose of the law of warranty is to determine what it is that the seller has in essence agreed to sell." Tex.Bus. & Com.Code § 2.313 (Comment 4). No sound reason exists to apply a different standard when the contract is for services instead of goods. In light of the forgoing discussion of the purpose and rationale for warranty liability, we reject Bell's argument that its failure to publish the double quarter column display was exclusively a breach of contract.

We hold that Bell's omission of the display was a defect in the performance of its advertising contract. FDP purchased a package of advertising service; Bell delivered most of the services it agreed to provide, but by omitting a critical item, it delivered an incomplete package. As the directory was published only once per year, FDP had no alternative but to accept the advertising package Bell delivered, even though it was different from and less desirable than what Bell had in essence agreed to sell. Thus, there is some evidence to support the jury's finding that the defect in Bell's performance constituted a breach of its warranty to publish FDP's advertising correctly.

Having concluded that Bell made and breached an express warranty, the next issue is whether its liability for that breach can be limited by the written advertising contract, which provides in part:

> The applicant agrees that the Telephone Company shall not be liable for errors in or omissions of the directory advertising beyond the amount paid for the directory advertising omitted, or in which errors occur, for the issue life of the directory involved.

The court of appeals held this provision invalid under the DTPA's policy against waiver of consumers' statutory rights. Tex. Bus. & Com. Code § 17.42. The court based this holding on *Martin v. Lou Poliquin Enterprises, Inc.,* 696 S.W.2d 180 (Tex.App.-Houston [14th Dist.] 1985, writ ref'd n.r.e.), and *Hycel, Inc. v. Wittstruck,* 690 S.W.2d 914 (Tex.App.-Waco 1985, writ dism'd). *Hycel* held that a seller may not use a contractual liquidated damages provision to limit a consumer's recovery for the commission of a deceptive trade practice specifically described and prohibited under the DTPA "laundry list." Tex. Bus. & Com. Code § 17.46(b). *Martin* held that a liability limitation clause could not limit recovery under the DTPA, but it did not describe which provision of the DTPA gave rise to the liability.

We agree that a liability limitation would be invalid under § 17.42 insofar as it purported to waive liability for an act defined as deceptive under § 17.46(b). Unlike a "laundry list" claim, however, an action for breach of warranty is not a creation of the Act. *La Sara Grain v. First Nat'l Bank of Mercedes,* 673 S.W.2d 558, 565 (Tex. 1984). Because claims for breach of warranty derive from common-law principles or other statutory provisions, we must consult these sources in determining the nature and extent of warranties. *Id.* For example, the UCC creates an implied warranty of merchantability, and it also allows sellers to disclaim the warranty if certain specific prerequisites are met. Tex.Bus. & Com.Code § 2.316; *see also Cate v. Dover Corp.,* 790 S.W.2d 559 (Tex.1990). Such a disclaimer does not offend the "no waiver" provision in a suit for breach of warranty under the DTPA. *See Singleton v. LaCoure,* 712 S.W.2d 757, 760 (Tex.App.-Houston [14th Dist.] 1986, writ ref'd n.r.e.).

Pursuant to the UCC's definition of express warranty, the jury found that Bell's promise to publish the advertising accurately became "a part of the basis of the bargain." Another part of the basis of the bargain was FDP's agreement to limit Bell's liability to the return of the amount paid for the omitted or erroneous items. Thus, Bell gave a limited warranty. The jury failed to find that the limitation of Bell's liability was unconscionable or that Bell violated the DTPA. Under these circumstances, the court of appeals erred in failing to enforce the parties' agreement to limit Bell's liability.

The court of appeals also held that the jury's finding that FDP should recover no lost profits damages from Bell was against the great weight and preponderance of the evidence. Because we have held that the liability limit was part of the warranty, however, any jury finding regarding lost profits is irrelevant. When Bell omitted FDP's display from the 1980 Yellow Pages, Bell's contractual obligation to FDP was to return the money FDP paid for that display.

FDP also argued in the court of appeals that the jury's failure to find Bell negligent was against the great weight and preponderance of the evidence. The court of appeals did not reach this issue because it concluded that a remand was necessary for other reasons. Because the basis for the court's remand is erroneous and because FDP's alternative argument for a remand challenges the factual sufficiency of the evidence, we would normally remand this cause to the court of appeals. *Stanglin v. Keda Development Corp.,* 713 S.W.2d 94, 95 (Tex. 1986). We have recently concluded, however, that a claim of lost profits for failure to publish an advertisement in the Yellow Pages is cognizable in contract, but not in tort. *Southwestern Bell Telephone Co. v. DeLanney,* 809 S.W.2d 493 (Tex. 1991). Under *DeLanney,* FDP states no cause of action for negligence; therefore, FDP's factual sufficiency point is moot.

The judgment of the court of appeals is reversed and judgment is rendered that FDP take nothing.

NOTES & QUESTIONS

1) Again, to file a DTPA-related cause of action for a breach of warranty, a complainant must prove her right to proceed under the common law or a statute. Assume that she overcomes that burden. What must she prove to prevail in a breach-of-warranty lawsuit? What are the elements?

2) Under the Texas Uniform Commercial Code (UCC), a plaintiff must prove the following elements to prevail in an action for breach of an express warranty involving the sale of goods: a) a sale of goods; b) a representation about the quality of goods; c) evidence that the representation became the basis of the bargain regarding their title, quality or characteristics; d) failure of the goods to comply with the representation; e) notification of the breach; f) causation, g) injury and h) damages. *Crosbyton Seed Co. v. Menchura Farms,* 875 S.W.2d 353, 361 (Tex. App.-Corpus Christi 1994, no writ).

3) The elements associated with a common-law action for breach of an express warranty for services are the following: a) sale of services; b) evidence of a representation that served as the basis of the bargain regarding their title, quality or characteristics; c) failure of the services to comply with the representation; d) notification of the breach; e) causation; f) injury to the buyer and g) damages. *Southwestern Bell Tel. Co. v. FDP,* 811 S.W.2d 575, 576 (Tex. 1991).

4) *See also, Head v. U.S. Inspect DFW, Inc.,* 159 S.W.3d 731 (Tex.App.-Fort Worth 2005):

Jacqueline Head appeals from the trial court's grant of summary judgment in favor of. . . Affordable Inspections, Inc. (Affordable) and John Fox. Head argues at the trial court erred in 1) holding that the professional services exemption barred her claims under the Deceptive Trade Practices Act

(DTPA), 2) holding that a limitation of liability clause in Head's contract with Affordable applied to her breach of contract and negligence claims, and 3) awarding attorneys' fees to Appellees. We affirm in part and reverse and remand in part.

* * *

Breach of Express Warranty

Lastly, Head states that she pleaded that Affordable and Fox breached an express warranty that did not constitute advice, opinion, or judgment and that her claim therefore fit within the fourth exception to the professional services bar in the DTPA. Tex. Bus. & Com. Code Ann. § 17.49(c)(4). Appellees contend that Head failed to plead breach of express warranty as a violation of the DTPA. We disagree. Head expressly pleaded DTPA violations by breach of both express and implied warranty in her First Amended Original Petition. And, in her response to the motion for summary judgment, Head asserted that Affordable and Fox breached express warranties set forth in the inspection agreement that (1) "a licensed professional real estate inspector would perform the inspection" and (2) "that the inspection would be conducted in accordance with the standards of the Texas Real Estate Commission."

In an excerpt from Fox's deposition attached to Head's response, Fox acknowledged that he would have fallen below his own standard of care by allowing Blaeser to inspect the roof unsupervised. This is some evidence that Affordable and Fox breached these warranties by delegating the attic and roof inspection to Blaeser. Additionally, expert reports attached to Head's affidavit provide some evidence that some, if not all, of the problematic conditions involving leakage and deterioration of the roof were revealed through old patches that pre-existed the inspection by Appellees and that those conditions should have been visible on the date of the inspection.

Generally, in order to recover for breach of an express warranty under the DTPA, a plaintiff must prove that (1) he or she is a consumer, (2) a warranty was made, (3) the warranty was breached, and (4) as a result of the breach, an injury resulted. *U.S. Tire-Tech, Inc. v. Boeran, B.V.,* 110 S.W.3d 194, 197 (Tex.App.-Houston [1st Dist.] 2003, pet. denied). The DTPA does not define or create any warranties. *Parkway Co.,* 901 S.W.2d at 438. Warranties actionable under the DTPA, both express and implied, must first be recognized by common law or created by statute. *Id.* Therefore, we must first determine whether an express warranty was created.

An express warranty is created when a seller makes an affirmation of fact or a promise to the purchaser that relates to the sale and warrants a conformity to the affirmation as promised. *Humble Nat'l Bank v. DCV, Inc.,* 933 S.W.2d 224, 233 (Tex.App.-Houston [14th Dist.] 1996, writ denied). Because warranty law has developed mainly in transactions involving goods, we may look to the Texas Business and Commerce Code, which concerns express warranties and the sale of goods, for guidance. *Southwestern Bell Tel. Co. v. FDP Corp.,* 811 S.W.2d 572, 575 (Tex.1991) (holding that reference to the Texas Business and Commerce Code is instructive in service transactions); *Humble Nat'l Bank,* 933 S.W.2d at 233 (holding that in determining when a fact or promise becomes part of the basis of the bargain, a court may look to section 2.313 of the Texas Business and Commerce Code, which concerns express warranties and the sale of goods). As the supreme court recognized in *FDP*:

The UCC recognizes that breach of contract and breach of warranty are not the same cause of action. The remedies for breach of contract are set forth in section 2.711, and are available to a buyer "[w]here the seller fails to make delivery." Tex. Bus. & Com.Code Ann. § 2.711(a). The remedies for breach of warranty, however, are set forth in section 2.714, and are available to a buyer who has finally accepted goods, but discovers that the goods are defective in some manner. Tex. Bus. & Com.Code Ann. § 2.714, § 2.711 (Comment 1). 811 S.W.2d at 576.

D. DTPA Action for Breach of an Implied Warranty

Under English and early Texas common law, courts found implied warranties when sellers' knowledge about goods or services greatly exceeded the knowledge of consumers or buyers. *Jacob E. Decker & Sons, Inc. v. Capps*, 164 S.W.2d 828, 829 (Tex.1942) (finding that the consumer was unable to inspect food for purity prior to consumption); *Jones v. George*, 56 Tex. 149, 152-53 (1882) (finding an implied warranty where a buyer was unable to inspect goods).

Currently, under Texas law, service providers are liable for breaching an implied warranty of good and workmanlike performance of services. See, e.g., *Bachynski v. Fox and Co.*, 662 S.W.2d 771, 773 (Tex. App.-Houston [14th Dist.] 1983, no writ) (finding the untimely preparation of a tax return was a breach of duty to perform in good and workmanlike manner); *Clark v. Smith*, 494 S.W.2d 192, 196-97 (Tex. Civ. App.-Dallas 1973, writ ref'd n.r.e.) (concluding that the improper disposal of a corpse was a breach of duty to perform in workmanlike manner); and, *Moody v. Messer*, 489 S.W.2d 319, 321 (Tex. Civ. App. -Corpus Christi 1972, no writ) (concluding that every professional service contract implies duty of good and workmanlike performance of work).

In *Humber v. Morton*, 426 S.W.2d 554, 556 (Tex. 1968), the Texas Supreme Court concluded that the doctrine of *caveat emptor* was severe and unjust. As a consequence, the court declared: Every residential construction contract contains an implied warranty that the home will be constructed in a good and workmanlike manner. The DTPA allows a consumer to commence an action for breach of an implied warranty. What must a DTPA plaintiff prove?

Melody Home Manufacturing Company v. Barnes
741 S.W.2d 349
(Tex. 1987)

The court's opinion of June 17, 1987 is withdrawn and the following is substituted[.]

This is a Deceptive Trade Practices-Consumer Protection Act (DTPA) implied warranty case. Lonnie and Donna Barnes sued Melody Home Manufacturing Company under the DTPA for breach of an implied warranty that repairs would be done in a good and workmanlike manner and for other DTPA violations. The jury found that Melody Home knowingly breached this implied warranty and awarded discretionary damages. The trial court rendered judgment for the Barneses and the court of appeals affirmed the judgment of the trial court. We affirm the judgment of the court of appeals.

In 1979, the Barneses ordered a modular pre-fabricated home from Melody Home. Their home was delivered in May 1980. After the Barneses moved in, they continually experienced puddles and dampness inside the house. Over two years after moving in, they discovered that a sink was not connected to the drain in one of the interior walls.

The continual leak caused severe damage to the home's sheetrock, insulation, and flooring. The Barneses told Melody Home about the problem. Workmen from Melody Home came out twice, but their efforts were unsatisfactory, and additional damages were caused by the repair. The workmen cut and tore linoleum while attempting to repair the home. Moreover, they failed to reconnect the washing machine drain, causing the house to flood with resulting damage to the floors, cabinets, and carpeting.

The Barneses then filed this DTPA implied warranty suit against Melody Home. The jury found that Melody Home failed to construct the home in a good and workmanlike manner. The jury further found that Melody Home breached its implied warranty to repair in a good and workmanlike manner and that this breach was knowing. Based on its finding that Melody Home knowingly breached the implied warranty, the jury awarded $5,000 in discretionary damages under Tex.Bus. & Com.Code Ann. § 17.50(b)(1).

Melody Home appealed the award of DTPA discretionary damages. The court of appeals held that the sale of a service carries with it the implied warranty that the service will be performed in a skillful and workmanlike manner and affirmed the judgment of the trial court.

Melody Home first challenges the Barneses' status as consumers with regard to the repairs. DTPA plaintiffs must qualify as consumers, as that term is defined in Tex.Bus. & Com.Code Ann. § 17.45(4) (Vernon Supp.1987), to maintain a private cause of action under section 17.50 of the Act. *Flenniken v. Longview Bank & Trust Co.,* 661 S.W.2d 705, 706 (Tex.1983). We have recognized at least two requirements to establish DTPA consumer status. First, the plaintiffs must have sought or acquired goods or services by purchase or lease. *Sherman Simon Enter., Inc. v. Lorac Service Corp.,* 724 S.W.2d 13, 15 (Tex. 1987); *Cameron v. Terrell & Garrett, Inc.,* 618 S.W.2d 535, 539 (Tex.1981). Second, the goods or services purchased or leased must form the basis of the complaint. *Sherman Simon Enter., Inc.,* 724 S.W.2d at 15; *Cameron,* 618 S.W.2d at 539.

It is uncontroverted that the Barneses purchased goods and thus were "consumers" when they originally bought the home. Melody Home's attempts to repair the defects in the home were, by definition, "services" under the DTPA. Section 17.45(2) defines "services" as "work, labor or service purchased ... for use including services furnished in connection with the sale or *repair* of goods." (emphasis added). Melody Home argues that the Barneses were not "consumers" with regard to the repair services because they did not purchase them with cash. *See, e.g., Exxon Corp. v. Dunn,* 581 S.W.2d 500 (Tex.Civ.App.-Dallas 1979, no writ). The absence of a cash transfer is not determinative because DTPA plaintiffs establish their standing as consumers in terms of their relationship to a transaction, not by their contractual relationship with the defendant. *Flenniken,* 661 S.W.2d at 707. The question then is whether the Barneses "purchased" the repair services within the meaning of the Act.

In *Humber v. Morton,* 426 S.W.2d 554 (Tex.1968), this court held that a builder/vendor impliedly warrants to a purchaser that a building constructed for residential use has been constructed in a good and workmanlike manner and is suitable for human habitation. *Evans v. J. Stiles, Inc.,* 689 S.W.2d 399, 400 (Tex.1985). When the Barneses discovered the defect in their home, they had the option to immediately sue for money damages or give Melody Home the opportunity to cure the problem. The parties' choices to allow and make repairs relate back to the original purchase and were a continuation of that transaction.

The Barneses did not lose their consumer status by allowing Melody Home to attempt to correct the problem and by deferring their lawsuit. Under Melody Home's argument the Barneses would be penalized by losing their consumer status because they allowed repairs. The law encourages dispute resolution prior to litigation. *See* Tex.Bus. & Com.Code Ann. § 17.50A (Vernon Supp.1987). Accordingly we hold that the Barneses "purchased" the repair services.

Melody Home next contends that repair services do not carry with them an implied warranty that they will be performed in a good and workmanlike manner. Implied warranties are created by operation of law and are grounded more in tort than in contract. *La Sara Grain v. First Nat'l Bank of Mercedes,* 673 S.W.2d 558, 565 (Tex.1984); *Humber,* 426 S.W.2d at 556. A number of courts of appeals decisions have expressly or impliedly recognized such an implied warranty. In addition, several articles, comments, and notes have concluded that the doctrine of implied warranty should apply to services. Despite its importance, this court has never ruled on this issue. *But see Dennis v. Allison,* 698 S.W.2d 94, 96 (Tex.1985)

An implied warranty arises by operation of law when public policy so mandates. *Dennis v. Allison,* 698 S.W.2d at 95; *Jacob E. Decker & Sons, Inc. v. Capps,* 139 Tex. 609, 164 S.W.2d 828, 829 (1942). Unlike the situations in *Nobility Homes of Texas, Inc. v. Shivers,* 557 S.W.2d 77, 78 (1977) and *La Sara Grain,* 673 S.W.2d at 565, consumers of services do not have the protection of a statutory or common law implied warranty scheme. The issue presented in this case is whether the protection of Texas consumers requires the utilization of an implied warranty that repair services of existing tangible goods or property will be performed in a good and workmanlike manner as a matter of public policy. *Nobility Homes of Texas, Inc.,* 557 S.W.2d at 78.

During the last thirty-five years, the United States has shifted from a goods to a services oriented economy. With this change has come a marked decrease in the quality of services. Similar quality control problems and consumer protection interests led this court and the legislature to apply the theory of implied warranty to products, goods, and new houses. *See Humber,* 426 S.W.2d at 562; *McKisson v. Sales Affiliates, Inc.,* 416 S.W.2d 787, 789 (Tex.1967); *Jacob E. Decker & Sons,* 164 S.W.2d at 832; *see also* Tex.Bus. & Com.Code Ann. § 2.314

Just as with products, an examination of several strict liability policies favors the extension of the theory of implied warranty to service transactions. First, the public interest in protecting consumers from inferior services is paramount to any monetary damages imposed upon sellers who breach an implied warranty. Second, a service provider is in a much better position to prevent loss than is the consumer of the service. Many services are so complicated and individually tailored that a consumer is unable to independently determine quality and must depend on the experience, skill, and expertise of the service provider. Third, a consumer should be able to rely upon the expertise of the service provider. The application of implied warranty to services would encourage justifiable reliance on the service providers who would have more incentive to increase and maintain the quality of the services they provide. Fourth, a service provider is better able to absorb the cost of damages associated with inferior services through insurance and price manipulation than is the individual consumer.

As Justice Norvell wrote in *Humber:*

> That Court best serves the law which recognizes that the rules of law which grew up in a remote generation may, in the fullness of experience, be found to serve another generation badly, and which discards the old rule when it finds that another rule of law represents what should be according to the established and settled judgment of society, and no considerable property rights have become vested in reliance on the old rule.426 S.W.2d at 561-62,

The caveat emptor rule as applied to services such as repairs is an anachronism patently out of harmony with modern service buying practices. It does a disservice not only to the ordinary prudent purchaser but to the industry itself by encouraging the purveyor of shoddy workmanship. *Id.* at 562.

We hold that an implied warranty to repair or modify existing tangible goods or property in a good and workmanlike manner is available to consumers suing under the DTPA. The legislative history of the DTPA indicates that the Act was intended to apply to all service providers.

This case does not involve the laundry list of false misleading or deceptive acts or practices made actionable by section 17.50(a)(1) of the DTPA. Instead, this case presents the question whether an implied warranty applies to repair or modification services of existing tangible goods or property. The question whether an implied warranty applies to services in which the essence of the transaction is the exercise of professional judgment by the service provider is not before us. *Cf. DeBakey v. Staggs,* 612 S.W.2d 924 (Tex.1981) (attorney's clients suing under the DTPA for attorney's "unconscionable" actions are "consumers"). *But see Dennis v. Allison,* 698 S.W.2d 94 (Tex.1985) (implied warranty not available to doctor's patient injured by improper treatment).

We define good and workmanlike as that quality of work performed by one who has the knowledge, training, or experience necessary for the successful practice of a trade or occupation and performed in a manner generally considered proficient by those capable of judging such work. *See Griffin v. Eakin,* 656 S.W.2d 187, 190-91 (Tex.App.-Austin 1983, writ ref'd n.r.e.); *Burnett & Bean v. Miller,* 205 Ala. 606, 88 So. 871, 872 (1921). *Cf. Garcia v. Color Tile Distrib. Co.,* 75 N.M. 570, 408 P.2d 145, 148 (1965); *Fairbanks, Morse & Co. v. Miller,* 80 Okl. 265, 195 P. 1083, 1090 (1921). We do not require repairmen to guarantee the *results* of their work; we only require those who repair or modify existing tangible goods or property to *perform* those services in a good and workmanlike manner.

In this case, the breach of the implied warranty was plainly within the common knowledge of laymen and did not require expert testimony. The jurors had sufficient knowledge to find that the failure to connect a washing machine drain would not be considered good and workmanlike by those capable of judging repair work.

Consistent with the trend in recent consumer protection legislation and sound public policy, we further hold that the implied warranty that repair or modification services of existing tangible goods or property will be performed in a good and workmanlike manner may not be waived or disclaimed. *See e.g.* Tex.Bus. & Com. Code Ann. § 17.42 (Vernon Supp.1987) (DTPA waiver unenforceable and void); Tex.Rev.Civ.Stat.Ann. art. 5221f, § 18 (Vernon Supp.1987) (waiver of the provisions of the Manufactured Housing Standards Act unenforceable and void). It would be incongruous if public policy required the creation of an implied warranty, yet allowed the warranty to be disclaimed and its protection eliminated merely by a pre-printed standard form disclaimer or an unintelligible merger clause. *See G-W-L, Inc. v. Robichaux,* 643 S.W.2d 392, 394-95 (Tex.1982) (Spears, J., dissenting).

When disclaimers are permitted, adhesion contracts-standardized contract forms offered to consumers of goods and services on an essentially "take it or leave it" basis which limit the duties and liabilities of the stronger party-become commonplace. *See, e.g., King v. Larsen Realty, Inc.,* 121 Cal.App.3d 349, 175 Cal.Rptr. 226, 231 (1981); *Wheeler v. St. Joseph Hosp.,* 63 Cal.App.3d 345, 133 Cal.Rptr. 775, 783 (1976); *Star Finance Corp. v. McGee,* 27 Ill.App.3d 421, 326 N.E.2d 518, 522 (1975); *Cushman v. Frankel,* 111 Mich.App. 604, 314 N.W.2d 705, 707 (1981); *Guthmann v. La Vida Llena,* 103 N.M. 506, 709 P.2d 675, 678 (1985). The consumer continues to expect that the service will be performed in a good and workmanlike manner regardless of the small print in the contract. A disclaimer allows the service provider to circumvent this expectation and encourages shoddy workmanship. To the extent that it conflicts with this opinion, we overrule *G-W-L, Inc. v. Robichaux,* 643 S.W.2d 392.

The final issue is whether the jury's finding that Melody Home committed a *knowing* breach of this implied warranty justifies the award of discretionary damages under the DTPA. Section 17.50(a) of the DTPA provides that: "A consumer may maintain an action where any of the following constitute a producing cause of actual damages: ... (2) breach of an express or implied warranty." The DTPA does not define the term "warranty" nor does it create any warranties. *La Sara Grain,* 673 S.W.2d at 565.

The DTPA should be liberally construed and applied to promote its underlying purposes-protecting consumers against breaches of warranty and providing efficient economical procedures to secure such protection. Tex.Bus. & Com. Code Ann. § 17.44 (Vernon Supp.1987). As mentioned earlier, section 17.45(2) expresses the legislative intent that providers of services should not escape the requirements of the Act. Allowing consumers to sue under section 17.50(a) for breach of an implied warranty that repair services will be done in a good and workmanlike manner is a logical, consistent, and intended interpretation of the Act. Therefore it follows that the breach of an implied warranty to repair or modify existing tangible goods or property in a good and workmanlike manner is actionable under section 17.50(a)(2) of the DTPA.

We overrule all of Melody Home's points of error and affirm the judgment of the court of appeals.

* * *

CONCURRING OPINION OF JUSTICE GONZALEZ

My concurring opinion of June 17, 1987 is withdrawn and the following is substituted.

I concur with the court's judgment, but the creation of a new implied warranty is unnecessary, confusing and ill advised. I agree with the court's conclusion that Melody breached an implied warranty actionable under the Deceptive Trade Practices Act. Tex.Bus. & Com. Code Ann. §§ 17.41-17.63. However, I would hold that the warranty arises only as a limited extension of the *Humber* warranty that a builder/vendor will construct a home in a good and workmanlike manner. *Humber v. Morton,* 426 S.W.2d 554 (Tex.1968).

Who would have thought when writ was granted that the court would use this cause to create a new warranty and to overrule *G-W-L, Inc. v. Robichaux,* 643 S.W.2d 392 (Tex.1982). I did not and neither did the Barneses, who asked us only to hold that the *Humber* warranty applied to the repair efforts of a builder/vendor such as Melody. The majority opinion is unrecognizable from the case that was argued and briefed.

The court does not write on a clean slate when it creates an implied warranty, applicable to providers of repair services of tangible goods or property actionable under the DTPA. We are not free to create substantive rights by rewriting a statute under the guise of interpretation. Yet, the court's uninvited imposition of an implied warranty upon all repair service transactions does just that by extending the scope of the DTPA far beyond its intended bounds. The majority's action constitutes an improper excursion into the legislative arena. *See Seay v. Hall,* 677 S.W.2d 19, 25 (Tex.1984); *Ex Parte Salter,* 452 S.W.2d 711 (Tex.Civ.App.-Houston [1st Dist.] 1970, writ ref'd).

* * *

EXISTING REMEDIES

The tenor of the court's policy discussion, is that the purchaser of services lacks a remedy for substandard performance. Such a suggestion is unfounded because the service consumer has a choice of remedies for substandard performance under both contract and tort. *Montgomery Ward & Co. v. Scharrenbeck,* 146 Tex. 153, 204 S.W.2d 508 (1947). The implied duty of good and workmanlike performance has been applied under contract principles as an affirmative defense (failure of consideration) or offensively under negligence principles to collect damages proximately caused by unskillful and deficient work. *See Compton v. Polonski,* 567 S.W.2d 835 (Tex.Civ.App.-Corpus Christi 1978, no writ); *New Trends, Inc. v. Stafford-Lowdon Co.,* 537 S.W.2d 778 (Tex.Civ.

App.-Fort Worth 1976, writ ref'd n.r.e.); *Westbrook v. Watts,* 268 S.W.2d 694 (Tex.Civ.App.-Waco 1954, writ ref'd n.r.e.).

Moreover, providers of services are already subject to suit under the "laundry list" of deceptive acts contained in section 17.46 of the DTPA. *See, e.g.,* Tex.Bus. & Com.Code Ann. § 17.46(b)(5) (Vernon Supp. 1987) (representing that services have characteristics or benefits which they do not have); § 17.46(b)(7) (representing that services are of a particular standard, quality or grade, if they are of another); § 17.46(b)(21) (representing that services have been performed that have not been performed). In a contract action, the consumer can recover attorney fees under Chapter 38 of the Civil Practice and Remedies Code. Tex.Civ.Prac. & Rem.Code Ann. §§ 38.001-38.006 (Vernon 1987). Before the court concludes the additional remedies provided by an implied warranty under the DTPA are necessary to protect any Texas consumer, more evidence of such need should be forthcoming than is presented here.

The question posed by the court is who should bear the loss. This question answers itself. Obviously, if the service provider has negligently performed his job, he should respond in damages. The real question is not should we compensate the injured plaintiff, but how much should we punish the service provider. In egregious cases, exemplary damages are already available for grossly negligent conduct. I see no compelling policy reason based in this record for subjecting negligent providers of service who do not engage in deception to the statutory penalties prescribed by the DTPA as a matter of law.

* * *

If my interpretation is in error and it is the court's intention to dispense with proof of negligence and extend the strict liability in tort to certain service providers, we are adopting a decidedly minority view. Virtually all efforts to extend strict liability in tort to pure service transactions have been rebuffed. The Restatement also recommends that the conduct of service providers be judged by a negligence standard. *Restatement (2d) of Torts,* § 404 (1965).

Our court has adopted the rule of strict liability in tort as set forth in Section 402A of the *Restatement (2d) of Torts.* The Restatement deals specifically and only with the sale of a product. This is not by accident because strict tort liability policy considerations are not easily translated to the sale of services. In fact, there exist a number of countervailing policy considerations against extending strict tort liability to the service provider. The service provider cannot effectively distribute the risk of loss to consumers. Unlike the mass production of products for distribution to the consuming public, there exists no mass production of services. Services are custom tailored to meet the particular needs of the individual consumer. Consequently, there exists no vast body of distant consumers who are confronted with the difficult burden of tracing and proving unreliable and incompetent workmanship by the service performer. The service transaction emanates from a face to face contractual relationship in which the service consumer seeks a skilled, knowledgeable, and experienced service provider.

The service provider sells skill and time. Time limits the number of consumers that may be serviced. It is unrealistic to suggest that a service provider has the ability to effectively spread the risk among his limited number of customers.

Centex Homes v. Buecher
95 S.W.3d 266
(Tex. 2003)

The issue in this case is whether a homebuilder may disclaim the implied warranties of habitability and good and workmanlike construction that accompany a new home sale. The sales contract here provided that the builder's express limited warranty replaced all other warranties, including these two implied warranties. Holding that the implied warranties of habitability and good and workmanlike construction could not be waived, the court of appeals reversed the trial court's judgment and remanded the homeowners' claims for further proceedings.

We agree with the court of appeals that the implied warranty of habitability cannot be waived except under limited circumstances not implicated here. We disagree, however, that the implied warranty of good and workmanlike construction cannot be disclaimed. When the parties' agreement sufficiently describes the manner, performance or quality of construction, the express agreement may supersede the implied warranty of good workmanship. Although we do not agree in all respects with the court of appeals' reasoning, we affirm its judgment remanding this cause to the trial court.

I.

Michael Buecher and other homeowners purchased new homes built by Centex Homes or Centex Real Estate Corporation doing business as Centex Homes. Each homeowner signed a standard form sales agreement prepared by Centex. The homeowners allege that the agreement contained a one-year limited express warranty in lieu of and waiving the implied warranties of habitability and good and workmanlike construction. Specifically, the disclaimer provision provided:

> At closing Seller will deliver to Purchaser, Seller's standard form of homeowner's Limited Home Warranty against defects in workmanship and materials, a copy of which is available to Purchaser. PURCHASER AGREES TO ACCEPT SAID HOMEOWNER'S WARRANTY AT CLOSING IN LIEU OF ALL OTHER WARRANTIES, WHATSOEVER, WHETHER EXPRESSED OR IMPLIED BY LAW, AND INCLUDING BUT NOT LIMITED TO THE IMPLIED WARRANTIES OF GOOD WORKMANLIKE CONSTRUCTION AND HABITABILITY. PURCHASER ACKNOWLEDGES AND AGREES THAT SELLER IS RELYING ON THIS WAIVER AND WOULD NOT SELL THE PROPERTY TO PURCHASER WITHOUT THIS WAIVER. Purchaser's initials in the margin indicate their approval of this section 8. (Emphasis in original.)

After Buecher and the other plaintiffs purchased their homes, they sued Centex alleging fraud, misrepresentation, negligence, and violation of the Texas Deceptive Trade Practices-Consumer Protection Act (DTPA) in connection with the construction and sale of their new homes. The homeowners also sought to certify a class action against Centex, seeking (1) an injunction to prevent Centex from asserting that the implied warranties of habitability and good and workmanlike construction had been waived by the provisions in its sales contracts; (2) an injunction prohibiting Centex from asserting to any homeowner or subsequent purchaser that it had no liability for construction defects beyond the period set forth in the express warranty it gave in lieu of implied warranties; (3) a declaration that the disclaimer provision is unenforceable as a matter of law; and (4) notification to all purchasers and subsequent purchasers within the putative class that Centex's waiver of implied warranties is void and unenforceable.

Centex filed a special exception and motion to dismiss the proposed class action. Relying on *G-W-L, Inc. v. Robichaux,* 643 S.W.2d 392 (Tex.1982), it argued that a purchaser of a new home can waive the implied warranties of good and workmanlike construction and habitability if the language waiving those warranties is clear and free from doubt. Centex asserted that the waiver at issue in this case was clear and free from doubt. Centex also argued that its waiver provision did not violate the DTPA's anti-waiver provision because the DTPA does not create any implied warranty of good and workmanlike construction or habitability, but only provides an additional remedy for breach of implied warranties.

The homeowners announced in open court that they could not amend their petition to meet Centex's special exception. The trial court (1) granted the special exception; (2) struck all the class action allegations based on the contention that the disclaimer provision is illegal, void, or unenforceable; (3) severed those claims from the homeowners' individual claims; and (4) dismissed the proposed class action. The homeowners appealed. A divided court of appeals, sitting en banc, reversed the trial court's judgment and remanded the cause for further proceedings. 18 S.W.3d 807, 811. The court of appeals held that a homebuilder may not disclaim or cause a homeowner to waive the implied warranties of habitability and good and workmanlike construction. *Id.* at 808.

II.

In *Humber v. Morton,* 426 S.W.2d 554, 555 (Tex.1968), this Court recognized that a builder of a new home impliedly warrants that the residence is constructed in a good and workmanlike manner and is suitable for human habitation. In replacing caveat emptor with these two implied warranties, we noted the significance of a new home purchase for most buyers and the difficulty of discovering or guarding against latent defects in construction:

> The old rule of caveat emptor does not satisfy the demands of justice in [the sale of new homes]. The purchase of a home is not an everyday transaction for the average family, and in many instances is the most important transaction of a lifetime. To apply the rule of caveat emptor to an inexperienced buyer, and in favor of a builder who is daily engaged in the business of building and selling houses, is manifestly a denial of justice.

Humber, 426 S.W.2d at 561. Subsequently, in *G-W-L, Inc. v. Robichaux,* we conflated the *Humber* warranties of good workmanship and habitability, concluding that the "Humber warranty" could be disclaimed or waived if that intent were clearly expressed in the parties' agreement. *Robichaux,*

643 S.W.2d at 393. Centex therefore argues that the court of appeals' holding that the implied warranties of good and workmanlike construction and habitability cannot be waived conflicts with *Robichaux.*

The homeowners respond that *Robichaux* is no longer the law in Texas because it was overruled in *Melody Home Manufacturing Co. v. Barnes,* 741 S.W.2d 349, 355 (Tex.1987). *Melody Home* recognized for the first time an implied warranty of good workmanship in the repair or modification of tangible goods or property. *Id.* at 354. The Court further announced as a matter of public policy that this implied warranty for repair services could not be waived or disclaimed. *Id.* at 355. Referencing the dissent in *Robichaux,* the Court noted the incongruity of requiring the creation of an implied warranty and yet permitting its elimination "by a pre-printed standard form disclaimer or an unintelligible merger clause." *Id.* The Court suggested that such disclaimers should not be allowed because they encouraged shoddy workmanship, thus circumventing the consumer's reasonable expectations that the job would be performed with reasonable skill. *Id.* At the end of this discussion, the Court purported to overrule *Robichaux* "[t]o the extent that it conflicts with this opinion." *Id.* The meaning and scope of this statement have proven elusive because it is unclear to what extent *Robichaux* and *Melody Home* actually conflict.

Factually, the two cases do not conflict at all. *Melody Home* does not apply the *Humber* warranties at issue in *Robichaux.* But the implied warranty of good and workmanlike construction in *Humber* and the implied warranty of good and workmanlike repair services in *Melody Home* are very similar, and yet the two cases diverge drastically on appropriate public policy in this area. *Melody Home* rejects *Robichaux's* notion that the implied warranty of good workmanship may freely be disclaimed as long as that intention is clearly expressed. *Id.* Because the two cases are factually distinguishable, yet legally antithetical, other authorities have had trouble determining how much of *Robichaux* survives *Melody Home.*

Some have concluded that after *Melody Home* the *Humber* warranties could no longer be waived or disclaimed. *See Haney v. Purcell Co.,* 796 S.W.2d 782, 786 n. 3 (Tex.App.-Houston [1st Dist.] 1990, writ denied) (*Melody Home* overruled *Robichaux* "with regard to the issue of waiver of warranty"). But because *Melody Home* and *Robichaux* involve different implied warranties, an argument can be made that the two opinions do not actually conflict, and thus *Robichaux's* waiver of the *Humber* warranties survives. Because *Melody Home* has cast doubt on the validity of *Robichaux's* waiver holding, we re-examine our holding in that case.

III.

In *Robichaux,* the alleged defect in the buyers' new home was a sagging roof. The trial court rendered judgment for the buyers on jury findings that the builder "had failed to construct the roof in a good workmanlike manner and that the house was not merchantable at the time of completion." *Robichaux,* 643 S.W.2d at 392. The court of appeals affirmed.

We disagreed and rendered judgment for the builder. *Id.* We held that the implied "warranty of merchantability" was a sales warranty under the Texas Uniform Commercial Code, which did not apply to the sale of a house. *Id.* at 394. Then, in reviewing the jury finding that the roof was not constructed in a good and workmanlike manner, the Court conflated the *Humber* warranties of good workmanship and habitability, referring to the warranty at issue as both the "implied warranty of fitness" and the "implied warranty of habitability." *Id.* at 393. In fact, the implied warranty of habitability was not at issue in the case because the jury had only found a breach of the implied warranty of good and workmanlike performance. *See id.* at 392. The Court nevertheless concluded that language in the sales documents that there were no "warranties, express or implied, in addition to said written instruments" was sufficiently clear to effectively disclaim the implied warranty of habitability. *Id.* at 393.

A

Centex argues that we should adhere to *Robichaux* because it is consistent with decisions from other states allowing parties to expressly disclaim the implied warranties that ordinarily arise with new home sales. (citations omitted)

* * *

[W]e have defined a breach of this implied warranty in Texas to be a defect "of a nature which will render the premises unsafe, or unsanitary, or otherwise unfit for living therein." *Kamarath v. Bennett,* 568 S.W.2d 658, 661 (Tex.1978).

* * *

[Other state-court] cases either ignore the implied warranty of habitability or treat it as part of the implied warranty of good workmanship. In Texas, however, the two warranties provide separate and distinct protection for the new home buyer. *See Evans v. J. Stiles, Inc.,* 689 S.W.2d 399, 400 (Tex.1985) (possible to breach warranty of good workmanship without breaching warranty of habitability); *accord Chandler v. Madsen,* 197 Mont. 234, 642 P.2d 1028, 1031 (1982) (distinguishing between the two implied warranties). Unfortunately, as in *Robichaux,* we have not always been careful to distinguish between the two. *See Robichaux,* 643 S.W.2d at 393. But because they are distinct and different warranties, it is important to consider the particular purpose of each when considering issues of waiver or disclaimer.

B

The implied warranty of good workmanship focuses on the builder's conduct, while the implied warranty of habitability focuses on the state of the completed structure. Through the implied warranty of good workmanship, the common law recognizes that a new home builder should perform with at least a minimal standard of care. This implied warranty requires the builder to construct the home in the same manner as would a generally proficient builder engaged in similar work and performing under similar circumstances. *See Melody Home Mfg. Co. v. Barnes,* 741 S.W.2d 349, 354-55 (Tex.1987). The implied warranty of good workmanship serves as a "gap-filler" or "default warranty"; it applies unless and until the parties express a contrary intention. *See* Thus, the implied warranty of good workmanship attaches to a new home sale if the parties' agreement does not provide how the builder or the structure is to perform.

The implied warranty of habitability, on the other hand, looks only to the finished product:

> [T]he implied warranty of habitability is a result oriented concept based upon specific public policy considerations. These include the propriety of shifting the costs of defective construction from consumers to builders who are presumed better able to absorb such costs; the nature of the transaction which involves the purchase of a manufactured product, a house; the buyer's inferior bargaining position; the foreseeable risk of harm resulting from defects to consumers; consumer difficulty in ascertaining defective conditions; and justifiable reliance by consumers on a builder's expertise and implied representations.

This implied warranty is more limited in scope, protecting the purchaser only from those defects that undermine the very basis of the bargain. *Id.* at 1015. It requires the builder to provide a house that is safe, sanitary, and otherwise fit for human habitation. *Kamarath,* 568 S.W.2d at 660. In other words, this implied warranty only protects new home buyers from conditions that are so defective that the property is unsuitable for its intended use as a home. As compared to the warranty of good workmanship, "the warranty of habitability represents a form of strict liability since the adequacy of the completed structure and not the manner of performance by the builder governs liability."

These two implied warranties parallel one another, and they may overlap. For example, a builder's inferior workmanship could compromise the structure and cause the home to be unsafe. But a builder's failure to perform good workmanship is actionable even when the outcome does not impair habitability. *Evans,* 689 S.W.2d at 400. Similarly, a home could be well constructed and yet unfit for human habitation if, for example, a builder constructed a home with good workmanship but on a toxic waste site. Unfortunately, many courts, including this one, have not consistently recognized these distinctions.

C

In *Robichaux,* we failed to distinguish between habitability and good workmanship, conflating the two implied warranties and concluding that they could be disclaimed with clear language. *Robichaux,* 643 S.W.2d at 393. And although habitability was not at issue, we indiscriminately swept it into our analysis. That analysis further omitted any discussion of the public policy considerations that prompted the creation of the *Humber* warranties in the first place. *See Humber,* 426 S.W.2d at 561 (rejecting rule of caveat emptor in new home sales); *see also* 17 Richard A. Lord, Williston On Contracts § 50:30(4th ed.2000) (noting that the modern trend rejects rule of caveat emptor in new home sales).

We created the *Humber* implied warranties to protect the average home buyer who lacks the ability and expertise to discover defects in a new house. *Humber,* 426 S.W.2d at 561. Such buyer generally expects to receive a house that is structurally sound, habitable and free of hidden defects, and these implied warranties serve to protect the buyer's reasonable expectations. While the parties are free to define for themselves the quality of workmanship, there is generally no substitute for habitability. The implied warranty of habitability is thus an essential part of a new home sale.

The Supreme Court of Missouri has stated that while it does not "reject outright the possibility of a valid disclaimer or modification [of the implied warranty of habitability] under any set of facts," a valid waiver requires more than clear and unambiguous language. *Crowder v. Vandendeale,* 564 S.W.2d 879, 881 (Mo.1978) (en banc). Under *Crowder,* the builder is required to prove that the buyer actually understood what he or she was waiving:

> [One's] seeking the benefit of such a disclaimer must not only show a conspicuous provision which fully discloses the consequences of its inclusion but also that such was *in fact* the agreement reached. The heavy burden thus placed upon the builder is completely justified, for by his assertion of the disclaimer he is seeking to show that the buyer has relinquished protection afforded him by public policy. A knowing waiver of this protection will not be readily implied." *Id.* at 881 n. 4.

We agree with the Missouri Supreme Court that the warranty of habitability can be waived only to the extent that defects are adequately disclosed. Thus only in unique circumstances, such as when a purchaser buys a problem house with express and full knowledge of the defects that affect its habitability, should a waiver of this warranty be recognized.

The implied warranty of good workmanship, however, defines the level of performance expected when the parties fail to make express provision in their contract. It functions as a gap-filler whose purpose is to supply terms that are omitted from but necessary to the contract's performance. *See* Restatement (Second) Contracts § 204 (1981)(*Supplying an Omitted Essential Term*). As a gap-filler, the parties' agreement may supersede the implied standard for workmanship, but the agreement cannot simply disclaim it. *See generally Lenape Res. Corp. v. Tenn. Gas Pipeline Co.,* 925 S.W.2d 565, 570 (Tex.1996) (interpreting UCC gap-filler).

IV.

In conclusion, we hold that the implied warranty of good workmanship may be disclaimed by the parties when their agreement provides for the manner, performance or quality of the desired construction. We further hold that the warranty of habitability may not be disclaimed generally. This latter implied warranty, however, only extends to defects that render the property so defective that it is unsuitable for its intended use as a home. Further, the implied warranty of habitability extends only to latent defects. It does not include defects, even substantial ones, that are known by or expressly disclosed to the buyer.

In the trial court, the homeowners, who had purchased homes from Centex under standardized contracts disclaiming the implied warranty of habitability and the implied warranty of good and workmanlike construction, sought a judicial declaration as a class that the disclaimer was unenforceable. The trial court concluded that the disclaimer provision validly waived both implied warranties and dismissed the class claims. Without deciding whether a class action is appropriate in this case, we remand the class claims for consideration in light of our clarification of the purpose and protection afforded by these implied warranties.

The court of appeals' judgment is affirmed.

Gym-N-I Playgrounds, Inc. v. Snider
220 S.W.3d 905
(Tex. 2007)

Commercial real estate landlords impliedly warrant that their premises are suitable for the tenants' intended commercial purposes. In this case, however, the tenants expressly disclaimed that warranty. We must decide whether the disclaimer precludes the tenants' suit against the landlord for breach of the warranty. We also decide whether the tenants' agreement to lease the commercial building "as is" prevents them from suing the landlord for other claims based on the property's condition. We answer both questions "yes" and affirm the court of appeals' judgment.

I. Background

In 1981, Ron Snider founded Gym-N-I Playgrounds, Inc., a playground equipment manufacturing company. The business grew rapidly. In 1983, Snider purchased six acres of land in New Braunfels and subsequently constructed a 20,075 square foot building for the business. By the late 1980s, Gym-N-I employed about twenty people, including Bonnie Caddell and Patrick Finn, to whom Snider later sold the business. Caddell was Gym-N-I's bookkeeper; Finn performed miscellaneous jobs including assembling and installing playgrounds, maintaining machinery, purchasing supplies, and managing human resources.

The City of New Braunfels' fire code requires owners to install sprinkler systems for any building exceeding 20,000 square feet if the building contains certain combustible materials. Gym-N-I's building exceeded that threshold, and the fire marshal recommended, but did not require, that the building have a sprinkler system. Both Caddell and Finn knew that the fire marshal's recommendation was never implemented.

Eventually, Finn and Caddell purchased the business, and Snider leased them the building. Each party was represented by counsel during the lease negotiations. Finn and Caddell decided not to inspect the premises before leasing because, as Caddell testified, they "knew more about the building" than anyone else.

The lease provided that Gym-N-I would: 1) accept the building "as is," expressly waiving all warranties; 2) obtain insurance on the building to cover fire-related loss; and 3) perform maintenance and repairs. The lease also contained a holdover provision.

The lease was signed on September 30, 1993, and the original term expired in September of 1996. The parties did not execute a new instrument, but Gym-N-I continued to pay and Snider continued to accept monthly rent checks. On August 10, 2000, a fire destroyed the building.

II. Procedural History

Snider's insurer, American Economy Insurance Company, paid him approximately $400,000 for the loss of the building. Gym-N-I received nearly $1,000,000 under its insurance policy covering the building's contents and business interruption. Thereafter, American Economy brought a subrogation suit against Gym-N-I, which filed cross-claims against American Economy and third-party claims against Snider. Ultimately, all parties other than Gym-N-I and Snider were dismissed prior to this appeal.

Gym-N-I's suit against Snider alleged that defective electrical wiring and the lack of a sprinkler system caused the fire. Gym-N-I sued for negligence, negligence per se, gross negligence, Deceptive Trade Practices-Consumer Protection Act violations, breach of the implied warranty of suitability for commercial purposes, fraud, premises liability, res ipsa loquitur, and breach of contract.

Snider's summary judgment motion argued that all of Gym-N-I's claims, except the breach of contract claim, were barred by the "as is" clause and warranty disclaimer, or were alternatively precluded by the lease's waiver of subrogation clause. The parties settled the contract claim, and the trial court granted Snider a final summary judgment. In the court of appeals, Gym-N-I argued that the "as is" clause was no longer in effect after the original lease term ended in 1996, and that even if it was, the clause was unenforceable.

The court of appeals affirmed the trial court's judgment. We granted Gym-N-I's petition for review.

III. Issues Presented

Gym-N-I argues that: (1) the "as is" clause lapsed when the original lease term expired; (2) the clause does not waive claims for breach of the implied warranty of suitability, negligence per se, gross negligence, and fraud; (3) the absence of a sprinkler system constitutes a latent premises defect; and (4) the waiver of subrogation clause is not valid. We hold that the "as is" clause was in effect at the time of the fire, the implied warranty of suitability disclaimer expressly and effectively disclaimed that warranty, and the "as is" clause negated the causation element of Gym-N-I's other claims against Snider. Consequently, we do not reach Gym-N-I's remaining issues.

IV. Discussion

A. Enforceability of the "As Is" Clause

Gym-N-I argues that the "as is" provision did not survive when lease's original term expired. Gym-N-I contends that because it never exercised the lease's renewal options, and the lease expired almost four years before the fire, the parties "shared a simple month-to-month, landlord-tenant relationship under the 'holding over' clause of the original lease" when the fire occurred. Citing *Bockelmann v. Marynick*, 788 S.W.2d 569 (Tex.1990), Gym-N-I argues that the holdover tenancy is a "new tenancy" to which the terms of the original lease do not apply.

Snider responds that, under the written lease, the "as is" clause, along with all other terms of the lease, governs during any holdover month-to-month tenancy. The court of appeals held that the "as is" clause survived the original lease term's expiration. We agree.

Gym-N-I and Snider allowed the original lease agreement to expire without executing a new instrument. Because Gym-N-I continued to occupy the premises, it was a holdover tenant. The parties agree that their relationship was best characterized as a month-to-month tenancy as contemplated by the holdover clause in the lease. That clause provides that "[a]ny holding over without written consent of Landlord shall constitute a lease from month-to-month, under the terms and provisions of this Lease to the extent applicable to a tenancy from month-to-month." (Emphasis added.) Although Gym-N-I argues that the tenancy is not governed by the lease's terms, we cannot ignore the plain and ordinary meaning of the phrase "under the terms and provisions of this Lease." We hold that "under the terms and provisions of this Lease" means just that: the lease governed the month-to-month tenancy. Thus, the "as is" clause was in effect when the fire occurred.

Furthermore, Gym-N-I's reliance on Bockelmann is misplaced. . . . *Bockelmann* stands for the proposition that a cotenant who does not holdover is not liable for unpaid rent incurred when the other cotenant holds over; thus, it does not support Gym-N-I's argument that the original lease terms did not apply to the holdover tenancy.

Having concluded that the "as is" provision was still in effect when the fire occurred, we next address whether it waives some or all of Gym-N-I's claims.

B. Effect of the Implied Warranty of Suitability Disclaimer

Gym-N-I argues that the "as is" provision cannot nullify the implied warranty of suitability as to the defects at issue in this case. Gym-N-I contends that our Davidow opinion authorized a waiver of the implied warranty of suitability only when the lease makes the tenant responsible for certain specifically enumerated defects. Davidow v. Inwood North Professional Group-Phase I, 747 S.W.2d 373, 377 (Tex.1988). Consequently, the general "as is" provision in this lease could not waive the warranty.

Snider answers that Gym-N-I's claim for breach of the implied warranty of suitability is waived because the lease's "as is" clause expressly disclaimed that warranty. *See Prudential Ins. Co. Of Am. v. Jefferson Assocs., Ltd.*, 896 S.W.2d 156, 161 (Tex.1995). We agree with Snider.

We first recognized the implied warranty of suitability for intended commercial purposes in *Davidow.* 747 S.W.2d at 377. The warranty means "that at the inception of the lease there are no latent defects in the facilities that are vital to the use of the premises for their intended commercial purpose and that these essential facilities will remain in a suitable condition." Id. Davidow illustrates the purpose of the implied warranty of suitability. Dr. Davidow leased office space from Inwood for his medical practice and began experiencing problems soon after moving into the building. *Davidow*, 747 S.W.2d at 374. The problems were extensive: inadequate air conditioning, a leaky roof, pest and rodent infestations, inadequate lighting, periods of no electricity, a filthy parking lot, and repeated vandalization. *Id.* at 374- 75. Davidow eventually vacated the premises and ceased paying rent before the lease expired. *Id.* at 375. Inwood sued Davidow for the unpaid rent. *Id.* Davidow raised the affirmative defenses of material breach of contract and breach of the implied warranty that the premises were suitable for use as a medical office. Id. We agreed with Davidow's argument that "commercial tenants generally rely on their landlords' greater abilities to inspect and repair the premises." *Id.* at 376. Davidow merely expanded the application of the implied warranty of habitability already recognized in residential leases in *Kamarath v. Bennett,* 568 S.W.2d 658, 660-61 (Tex.1978).

While Davidow did not address whether or how the implied warranty of suitability may be waived, we did say that if "the parties to a lease expressly agree that the tenant will repair certain defects, then the provisions of the lease will control." *Davidow,* 747 S.W.2d at 377. We also listed several factors to consider when determining a breach of the warranty, including: the nature of the defect; its effect on the tenant's use of the premises; the length of time the defect persisted; the age of the structure; the amount of the rent; the area in which the premises are located; whether the tenant waived the defects; and whether the defect resulted from any unusual or abnormal use by the tenant. Thus, *Davidow* both recognized the implied warranty of suitability and noted that the agreement's terms could alter that warranty. We had no occasion to decide the manner in which the warranty could be waived.

* * *

In *Prudential,* we were asked to determine the effect of an "as is" clause on a buyer's claim for damages against the seller based on the condition of the commercial property. In that case, Goldman bought an office building from Prudential Insurance Company. The contract's "as is" clause provided:

> Seller and Purchaser agree that Purchaser is taking the Property "AS IS" with any and all latent and patent defects and that there is no warranty by Seller that the Property is fit for a particular purpose. Purchaser acknowledges that it is not relying upon any representation, statement or other assertion with respect to the Property condition, but is relying upon its examination of the Property. Purchaser takes the Property under the express understanding there are no express or implied warranties (except for limited warranties of title set forth in the closing documents). *Id.* at 160.

Goldman, a knowledgeable real estate investor, had the property inspected by his maintenance supervisor, his property manager, and an independent professional engineering firm; none of the inspectors discovered the asbestos that would later become the basis of the lawsuit. In addition, there was no evidence that Prudential knew--before the parties completed the sale--that the building contained asbestos. Goldman later discovered that the building contained asbestos fireproofing when he tried to refinance the building. He sued Prudential, alleging violations of the Texas Deceptive Trade Practices — Consumer Protection Act, negligence, fraud, and breach of the duty of good faith and fair dealing. We held that the "as is" provision negated the causation element necessary for Goldman to recover on each asserted cause of action:

> The sole cause of a buyer's injury [when he agrees to purchase something "as is"], by his own admission, is the buyer himself. He has agreed to take the full risk of determining the value of the purchase. He is not obliged to do so; he could insist instead that the seller assume part or all of that risk by obtaining warranties to the desired effect. If the seller is willing to give such assurances, however, he will ordinarily insist upon additional compensation. Rather than pay more, a buyer may choose to rely entirely upon his own determination of the condition and value of his purchase. In making this choice, he removes the possibility that the seller's conduct will cause him damage. *Id.* at 161.

Thus, by agreeing to purchase the property "as is," Goldman agreed to rely on his own appraisal of the bargain, and he accepted the risk that he may err. Id. We did not address what effect, if any, an "as is" provision would have on a claim for breach of the implied warranty of suitability, as this warranty applies only to commercial leases and Prudential involved a sale of commercial property.

Today, we squarely address whether an express disclaimer may waive the implied warranty of suitability in a commercial lease. Davidow noted that the provisions of the lease would control if the parties expressly agreed that the tenant would repair certain defects. *Prudential* stands for the proposition that — absent fraud in the inducement — an "as is" provision can waive claims based on a condition of the property. Taken together, these cases lead to one logical conclusion: the implied warranty of suitability is waived when, as here, the lease expressly disclaims that warranty. We hold, therefore, that as a matter of law, Gym-N-I waived the implied warranty of suitability.

Our conclusion that the implied warranty of suitability may be contractually waived is also supported by public policy. Texas strongly favors parties' freedom of contract. *BMG Direct Mktg., Inc. v. Peake*, 178 S.W.3d 763, 767 (Tex. 2005); *In re Prudential Ins. Co. of Am.,* 148 S.W.3d 124, 129 (Tex. 2004) ("As a rule, parties have the right to contract as they see fit as long as their agreement does not violate the law or public policy."). We recently reaffirmed this policy, stating that:

> [P]ublic policy requires ... that men of full age and competent understanding shall have the utmost liberty of contracting, and that their contracts when entered into freely and voluntarily shall be held sacred and shall be enforced by Courts of justice. Therefore, you have this paramount public policy to consider--that you are not lightly to interfere with this freedom of contract.

Freedom of contract allows parties to bargain for mutually agreeable terms and allocate risks as they see fit. A lessee may wish to make her own determination of the commercial suitability of premises for her intended purposes. By assuming the risk that the premises may be unsuitable, she may negotiate a lower lease price that reflects that risk allocation. Alternatively, the lessee is free to rely on the lessor's assurances and negotiate a contract that leaves the implied warranty of suitability intact.

We recognize that our holding today stands in contrast to the implied warranty of habitability, which "can be waived only to the extent that defects are adequately disclosed." *Centex Homes v. Buecher*, 95 S.W.3d 266, 274 (Tex. 2002). The implied warranty of habitability "applies in almost all jurisdictions only to residential tenancies" while commercial tenancies are "excluded primarily on the rationale that the feature of unequal bargaining power justifying the imposition of the warranty in residential leases is not present in commercial transactions." While most states recognize the implied warranty of habitability, four of the six state high courts to consider the implied warranty of suitability in commercial leases have declined to adopt it. The fact that the lessor impliedly warrants suitability in Texas ensures that, when the warranty is waived, the parties focus their attention on who is responsible for discovering and repairing latent defects, and they may allocate the risk accordingly. We see no compelling reason to disturb that market transaction here.

NOTES & QUESTIONS

---

1) Does a suit for breach of an implied warranty sound in contract or in tort? See *Humber v. Morton*, 426 S.W.2d 554, 556 (Tex. 1968) ("It might further be pointed out that generally in Texas, the notion of implied warranty arising from sales is considered to be a tort rather than a contract concept.").

2) See also *Smith v. Reid*, 658 S.W.2d 800, 801-802 (Tex. App. Ct. — Dallas, 1983):

> The underlying question, then, is: Does a suit for breach of an implied warranty sound in contract or in tort? The answer to that question is found in studying the historical development of the doctrine of implied warranty. A careful analysis of the development of the doctrine of implied warranty reveals that it grew out of the general form of action known as "trespass on the case" and was a species of such action known as "trespass on the case for deceit." The doctrine first arose in cases dealing with the sale of food. There the implied warranty had no basis in contract but was based squarely upon the public policy of protecting public health. The doctrine preceded by a century the action of special assumpsit, the forebearer of modern contract law. "It had no necessary contractual underpinnings and was based solely on an obligation imposed by law rather than by the express language of this contract between the parties. In short, the basis and genesis of the doctrine of implied warranty was grounded in tort and not in contract.

E. DTPA Action for Unconscionable Conduct

Section 17.45(5) of the DTPA reads: "An 'unconscionable action or course of action" means an act or practice which, to a consumer's detriment, takes advantage of the lack of knowledge, ability, experience, or capacity of the consumer to a grossly unfair degree." And in *Bradford v. Vento,* 48 S.W.3d 749, 760 (Tex. 2001), the Texas Supreme Court declared: "To prove an unconscionable action or course of action, a plaintiff must show that the defendant took advantage of his lack of knowledge and that the resulting unfairness was glaringly noticeable, flagrant, complete and unmitigated." But there are several common-law rules regarding unconscionable conduct. This section will review those rules.

Chastain v. Koonce
700 S.W.2d 579
(Tex. 1985)

Our opinion of June 19, 1985 is withdrawn and this opinion is substituted.

This deceptive trade practices case requires us to first determine if petitioners are consumers under the Deceptive Trade Practices-Consumer Protection Act. If so, we must examine whether the evidence supports a finding that respondents committed an unconscionable action or course of action. The Chastains and three other couples who purchased property from Charles Koonce and J.P. Stroud, recovered judgment against Koonce and Stroud based on jury findings of unconscionable actions or an unconscionable course of action. The court of appeals reversed the trial court judgment, finding no evidence of unconscionability and refusing to consider whether the purchasers were consumers within the meaning of the DTPA. The Chastains and other purchasers petition this court to address the consumer question and to restore the jury finding of unconscionability based on the evidence. Finding no reversible error in the court of appeals' judgment, we affirm that judgment.

In 1979, Charles Koonce and J.P. Stroud began to sell five-acre tracts on the northern boundary of their 320 acre farm. At trial, there was ample testimony that Koonce and Stroud told the purchasers that lot 1 at the northeastern corner would be commercial but that lots 2 through 15 would be restricted for residential use only. Claiming they relied on these representations, the Chastains and the other three couples independently purchased lots 4, 5, 6 and 9 by warranty deed. The deeds contained restrictions concerning pets, maintenance and square footage of improvements. In addition, the deed restrictions mandated that the respective lots be used only for single family residential purposes. No subdivision map or plat was ever filed.

In January 1981, Koonce and Stroud sold lot 2 to David Metts. About seven months later, after the Chastains and other residential purchasers had constructed houses on their lots, Metts built an oilfield pipe storage yard on his property. All four residential couples testified that this commercial use of lot 2 was contrary to the sellers' representations of the restrictions on lots 2 through 15. Gary Chastain, who purchased lot 4, then began to make arrangements to acquire lot 3, to ensure that it remained residential. He testified that during these arrangements, Stroud threatened him. Specifically, Chastain stated that Stroud threatened to put a rubber plant up behind lots 2 through 15 and burn rubber all day, if Chastain did not stop complaining. Chastain also testified that Stroud sarcastically threatened to reacquire lot 3, and to put something "real nice" next door. Finally, Stroud threatened to knock Chastain's head off and his teeth out.

The jury found that Koonce and Stroud had made express warranties, misrepresentations, and had committed an unconscionable action or course of action in regards to the use of lot 2. The trial court disregarded the express warranty findings but rendered judgment for the purchasers based on the misrepresentations as unconscionable actions. The court of appeals determined that even if the purchasers did qualify as consumers, they could not recover because the jury finding of unconscionability was without support in the evidence.

Although we agree with the court of appeals' result, we must examine the question of the purchasers as consumers, before we can examine the unconscionability question. If the purchasers are not consumers, then they have no standing under the act. Only consumers may recover under Tex. Bus. & Com.Code § 17.50(a). *Flenniken v. Longview Bank and Trust Co.,* 661 S.W.2d 705, 706 (Tex.1983). The statute itself defines a consumer to be an "individual ... who seeks or acquires by purchase or lease, any goods or services." Tex. Bus. & Com.Code § 17.45(4).

In addition, in *Cameron v. Terrell & Garrett, Inc.,* 618 S.W.2d 535, 539 (Tex.1981), this court also determined that the goods or services sought or acquired by lease or purchase must form the basis of the complaint. Koonce and Stroud contend that the purchasers do not meet this second part of the test because they are complaining about lot number 2, a piece of property which none of the couples sought or acquired. Additionally, the sellers argue that the lots purchased by the four couples are not the basis of their complaint. The purchasers argue that the DTPA was specifically amended to cover real estate and that the act should be construed liberally to protect consumers. Tex. Bus. & Com.Code § 17.44. Further, the Chastains and other purchasers argue that the purchase of a home is the ultimate consumer purchase and thus is in need of the specific protections which the DTPA provides.

The arguments made in this case relative to whether the purchasers are consumers under the DTPA are extremely similar to arguments made in *Parks v. U.S. Homes Corporation, Inc.,* 652 S.W.2d 479, 484 (Tex.Civ.App.-Houston [1st Dist.] 1983, writ dism'd). In *Parks,* the purchasers bought homes in a subdivision after relying on representations of the seller's agent that the subdivision would be restricted to homes of a particular style and price range. After the three complainants purchased their houses by deeds lacking deed restrictions, the developer altered its plan and the purchasers brought suit under the DTPA. In that case, the court of appeals determined that under the two-prong test ([1] acquiring or seeking to acquire goods or services by purchase or lease and [2] those goods or services must be the basis of the complaint), the purchasers of those homes were consumers. Similarly, we find the four couples who purchased land from Koonce and Stroud to be consumers within the meaning of the DTPA.

Recognizing that consumers have to meet both parts of the two-part definition, the *Parks* court first pointed out that real property is a good under the act. Tex.Bus. & Com.Code § 17.45(1). The act was specifically amended in 1975 to clarify the legislature's intent to insure that real property purchases could support individual causes of action. Because the four couples purchased land from the seller, they qualify as consumers under the first part of the definition.

Koonce and Stroud contest the purchasers' standing under the second prong of the test. This prong was first enunciated in *Riverside National Bank v. Lewis,* 603 S.W.2d 169 (Tex.1980), and in

Cameron. The DTPA is to be construed liberally to promote its underlying purposes "which are to protect consumers against false, misleading, and deceptive business practices, unconscionable actions, and breaches of warranty." Tex.Bus. & Com.Code § 17.44. In addition, this court has determined that the act "clearly declares deceptive trade practices in the conduct of a real estate sale to be unlawful." *Woods v. Littleton,* 554 S.W.2d 662, 667 (Tex.1977).

The purchasers here are complaining of conduct occurring during the transaction which resulted in the purchase of these lots. Koonce and Stroud made representations calculated to induce these purchasers to buy the lots and which enhanced the desirability of the property. Thus, the purchasers are complaining about an aspect of the lots purchased and the transaction involved. Finally, we note that the legislature contemplated this type of situation as exhibited by the floor debate in the Texas Senate discussing sellers' promises which would not be fulfilled. The specific example used in the debate was promising the erection of a shopping center with no intent to follow through on the promise. Debate on Tex. S. B. 48 on the floor of the Senate, 64th Leg. 3 (Feb. 10, 1975) (transcript available). Thus, we conclude that the purchasers in this suit qualify as consumers and have standing to sue under the DTPA.

Having decided that the purchasers are covered by the DTPA, we now may consider the second point of error, which complains that there was evidence to support the jury finding of unconscionability. The jury found that Koonce and Stroud had engaged in an unconscionable action or course of action with regard to the purchasers. Unconscionable action or course of action is defined by statute to describe an act which:

A. Takes advantage of the lack of knowledge, ability, or capacity of a person to a grossly unfair degree; or

B. Results in a gross disparity between the value received and the consideration paid in a transaction involving the transfer of consideration. Tex. Bus. & Com. Code § 17.45(5).

The purchasers did not specify whether they sought to show unconscionability under part A or B of the definition, so we must examine the facts to see if they support a finding of unconscionability under either definition.

Under the facts of our case, the purchasers failed to show any disparity between the value received and the consideration paid in the transaction. The record is devoid of any expert testimony relating to the value of the property at the time of the purchase. In addition, among the purchasers only Gary Chastain testified as to the consideration paid for the property. The only relevant testimony concerning land values in the record is expert testimony which explains the value at the time of trial and the value the land would have attained had the pipeyard not been placed on lot 2. These values were far in excess of the amount which Gary and Georgia Chastain paid for their lot.

The only other way in which the purchasers can recover is to show that Koonce and Stroud took advantage of the purchasers' lack of knowledge, ability, or capacity to a *grossly* unfair degree. We must assume that every word of a statute was used for a purpose and every word in that statute must be given effect if possible. *Eddins-Walcher Butane Co. v. Calvert,* 156 Tex. 587, 298 S.W.2d 93, 96 (1957). Thus we must find evidence not simply that Koonce and Stroud took unfair advantage of the purchasers but that the advantage was grossly unfair. *See also Valley Datsun v. Martinez,* 578 S.W.2d 485 (Tex.Civ.App.-Corpus Christi 1979, no writ). We are unable to find any Texas case which defines this distinction.

In *Hurst v. Sears, Roebuck & Co.,* 647 S.W.2d 249 (Tex.1983), we explained that impossibility of performance did not preclude a representation from being unconscionable. In addition, in that case we pointed out that a failure to do the impossible could be unconscionable if the promisor knew of the impossibility of the task when he promised to undertake it. *Id.* at 251. Knowledge or intent alone cannot, however, be the distinguishing factor of unconscionability, because the DTPA specifically provides for special damages if a consumer can show that the deceptive or misleading act was committed knowingly. *See* Tex.Bus. & Com.Code § 17.50(b)(1). Although knowledge and intent may make an act unconscionable, there must be some other means of distinction as well.

Koonce and Stroud contend that defining the difference between gross unfairness and mere unfairness is analogous to defining the difference between gross negligence and negligence. The comparison and analogy to this case are inappropriate. In *Burk Royalty Co. v. Walls,* 616 S.W.2d 911, 920 (Tex. 1981), this court defined gross negligence as: [T]hat entire want of care which would raise the belief that the act or omission complained of was the result of a conscious indifference to the right or welfare of the person or persons to be affected by it.

We also wrote:

> What lifts *ordinary* negligence into *gross* negligence is the mental attitude of the defendant; that is what justifies the penal nature of the imposition of exemplary damages. The plaintiff must show that the defendant was consciously, i.e., knowingly, indifferent to his rights, welfare and safety. In other words, the plaintiff must show that the defendant knew about the peril, but his acts or omissions demonstrated that he didn't care. *Burk Royalty Co.,* 616 S.W.2d at 922.

Section 17.45(5) does not expressly require a consumer prove the mental attitude of the defendant in order to recover actual damages. The legislative history of the 1979 amendments to the DTPA supports the conclusion that the legislature did not intend to require proof of intent, knowledge or conscious indifference to support recovery. As originally filed in the Senate, section 17.45(5)(A) would have been amended to read: Unconscionable action or course of action" means an act or practice which, to a person's detriment . . . *was intended to and did take* [takes] advantage of the lack of knowledge, ability, experience, or capacity of a person to a grossly unfair degree.

The intent language was deleted prior to the legislature's passage of the DTPA amendments. This deletion discloses a legislative intent to reject a scienter requirement. *Weitzel v. Barnes,* 691 S.W.2d 598, 600 (Tex. 1985); *Big H Auto Auction, Inc. v. Saenz,* 665 S.W.2d 756, 758 (Tex. 1984).

Section 17.45(5) is intended to be an objective standard. As the laundry list provisions of section 17.46(b) demonstrate, the legislature knows how to include a scienter requirement when it so chooses. In six of the twenty-three prohibitions listed in section 17.46(b), the legislature incorporated scienter requirements. *See* Tex.Bus. & Com.Code § 17.46(b), (9), (10), (13), (17), (22), (23). The remaining seventeen prohibitions are objective. For example, it is not necessary to show under section 17.46(b)(7) that the defendant intended to mislead or deceive the consumer-only that the defendant represented goods or services to be of a particular standard when they were of another. *Smith v. Baldwin,* 611 S.W.2d 611 (Tex.1980). By this analysis, under section 17.45(5)(A), a consumer need only prove that he was taken advantage of to a grossly unfair degree. This should be determined by examining the entire transaction and not by inquiring whether the defendant intended to take advantage of the consumer or acted with knowledge or conscious indifference.

It is a traditional rule of statutory construction that a word used in different parts of a statute will generally be given the same meaning throughout. The legislature used forms of the word "gross" in both subdivisions A and B of section 17.45(5). In subdivision B, an unconscionable action is defined as one which results in a *gross* disparity between the value received and the consideration paid. Subdivision A defines an unconscionable action as one which takes advantage of a person to a *grossly* unfair degree.

A consumer's proof of gross disparity under subdivision B does not require proof that the defendant acted intentionally, knowingly or with conscious indifference. Likewise, a consumer's proof of gross unfairness does not require proof that the defendant acted intentionally or knowingly to bring about the result.

The term "gross" should be given its ordinary meaning of glaringly noticeable, flagrant, complete and unmitigated. *Webster's Third New International Dictionary* 1002 (1976). The courts have had no problem determining what constitutes a gross disparity under subdivision B of section 17.45(5). A slight disparity between the consideration paid and the value received is not unconscionable; a glaring and flagrant disparity is. Unfairness is perhaps a more nebulous term than disparity, but this is not a reason to create a new definition for "gross."

Taking advantage of a consumer's lack of knowledge to a grossly unfair degree thus requires a showing that the resulting unfairness was glaringly noticeable, flagrant, complete and unmitigated. Based on the record as a whole, we find no evidence that the Chastains and the other three couples were taken advantage of to a grossly unfair degree.

The purchasers emphasize the telephone conversation between Gary Chastain and J.P. Stroud, in which Stroud threatened physical violence and to place a rubber burning plant in the vicinity of Gary Chastain's land. We find this unpersuasive. The phone conversation occurred approximately *one year* after the alleged misrepresentations occurred and do not reflect on the unfairness of the original transaction between the purchasers and Koonce and Stroud. As a result, we find no evidence of unconscionability.

Although we find that the purchasers have standing to sue under the DTPA, we affirm the court of appeals' judgment that there is no evidence of unconscionability. Accordingly, the judgment of the court of appeals is affirmed. Petitioners' motion for rehearing is overruled.

NOTES & QUESTIONS

1) There are two forms of unconscionability: procedural and substantive. Consider the following discussion, which appears in 8 WILLISTON ON CONTRACTS § 18:10 (4th ed.):

> The concept of unconscionability was meant to counteract two generic forms of abuses . . . [T]he first . . . relates to procedural deficiencies in the contract formation process, such as deception or a refusal to bargain over contract terms. . . [T]he second . . . relates to the substantive contract terms themselves and whether those terms are unreasonably favorable to the more powerful party. . . .
>
> [T]his formulation requires a showing that the contract was both procedurally and substantively unconscionable when made. . . . [A] finding of a procedural abuse, inherent in the formation process, must be coupled as well with a substantive abuse, such as an unfair or unreasonably harsh contractual term which benefits the drafting party at the other party's expense. . . .The distinction between procedural and substantive abuses, however, may become quite blurred. . . . [O]verwhelming bargaining strength or use of fine print or incomprehensible legalese may reflect procedural unfairness [because] it takes advantage of or surprises the victim of the clause[.] [On the other hand], the terms contained in the resulting contract—whether in fine print or legal "gobbledygook" — would hardly be of concern unless they were substantively harmful to the nondrafting party as well.]

2) Must a plaintiff be concerned about the distinctions between procedural and substantive unconscionability before commencing a DTPA-unconscionability cause of action? What is the difference between "substantive unconscionability" and "an unconscionable course of action?"

Bennett v. Bailey
597 S.W.2d 532
(Tex. Civ. App. 1980)

Plaintiff, Lenore Bailey, sued defendants, M. L. Bennett, individually and d/b/a Fiesta Dance Clubs, M. L. B. Properties, Inc., and Clark Sesler, manager of Fiesta Dance Clubs, seeking damages for alleged violations of the Deceptive Trade Practices-Consumer Protection Act, Tex. Bus. & Com. Code Ann. § 17.41 et seq. The trial court rendered judgment, based on jury findings, against the defendants for treble damages of $78,001.00 plus attorney's fees. Defendants appeal. We affirm.

Plaintiff, a widow, paid Fiesta $29,669.45 within approximately two months for dance lessons. She was offered an additional dance contract costing $49,000.00. She refused the offer. Upon her refusal, she was offered a new $9,000.00 contract. Again, she refused. Shortly thereafter, she was injured by a Fiesta dance instructor while dancing.

The jury found in Special Issues 1, 2 and 3 that Bennett, Sesler and Simmons, a Fiesta dance instructor, engaged in an "unconscionable act or course of action" in their dealings with plaintiff concerning dancing instructions. Tex.Bus. & Com.Code Ann. § 17.50(a)(3).

The trial court defined "unconscionable act or course of action" as the term is presently defined in Section 17.45(5) of the Deceptive Trade Practices Act. The instruction stated:

> In answering Questions 1, 2 and 3, you are instructed that the term "unconscionable act or course of action" means an act or practice which, to a person's detriment: (a) takes advantage of the lack of knowledge, ability, experience or capacity of a person to a grossly unfair degree; or (b) results in a gross disparity between the value received and consideration paid, in a transaction involving transfer of consideration.

Defendants did not object to the court's definition. Defendants now argue the court committed "fundamental" error in applying the statutory definition because the term had not been statutorily defined at the time of the transactions made the basis of plaintiff's suit. We disagree. Our Supreme Court in McCauley v. Consolidated Underwriters, 157 Tex. 475, 304 S.W.2d 265 (1957) held that fundamental error is an error which directly and adversely affects the interest of the public generally, as that interest is declared by our statutes or Constitution. The trial court did not commit fundamental error.

Defendants next contend the trial court erred in the submission of the "unconscionable act or course of action" issues because, as submitted, the issues fail to identify or be conditioned upon a specific act or course of action.

Plaintiff alleged generally in her petition that the defendants committed "deceptive trade practices," and she sought recovery under the "Deceptive Trade Practices-Consumer Protection Act." She made no specific allegations. Defendants did not except to the general allegations. We hold that under the general pleading the court did not err in submitting the issues broadly. *Mobil Chemical Company v. Bell*, 517 S.W.2d 245 (Tex.1974). Defendants cite *Scott v. Atchison, Topeka and Santa Fe Railway Company*, 572 S.W.2d 273 (Tex.1978) and *American Transfer and Storage Company v. Brown,* 584 S.W.2d 284 (Tex.Civ.App. Dallas 1979, writ granted). They are not controlling. In those cases, the plaintiffs alleged specific acts. A global submission, without proper limitation, may be improper when there is a variance between the pleadings and the evidence. There is no variance in the instant case. *Siebenlist v. Harville,* 596 S.W.2d 113 (Tex. 1980).

Defendants further assert that there is no evidence, or alternatively, factually insufficient evidence to support the jury's answers to Special Issues 1, 2 and 3. We disagree. In considering defendants' no evidence points, we must review the evidence in its most favorable light, considering only the evidence and inferences supporting the findings, and reject the evidence and inferences contrary to the findings. Martinez v. Delta Brands, Inc., 515 S.W.2d 263 (Tex.1974). We consider and weigh all the evidence when passing upon defendants' factually insufficient evidence points. *In re King's Estate,* 244 S.W.2d 660 (Tex. 1951).

Plaintiff first learned of the Fiesta Dance Club in January 1976 when she read an advertisement offering a $60.00 membership for $5.00. She took the introductory lessons. Her instructor, Barrera, told her that she danced "rather well" and that she should take the "Fun and Confidence" dance course that consisted of 32 lessons. Plaintiff signed her first contract and paid Fiesta $616.00. Shortly thereafter, her new instructor, Maldonado, told plaintiff that he had been working most of the night on a new plan for her. She told Maldonado she could not afford the new course. Maldonado told her that he wanted her to do it, and took her to Sesler's office. After talking with Sesler and Bennett, she signed her second contract on March 5, 1976, and paid Fiesta $10,153.46 after withdrawing $9,000.00 from her savings account. Sesler told plaintiff they would always pick her up for the night parties since she suffered night blindness. She testified that Bennett told her they would "throw in" a trip to Las Vegas if she signed the contract.

The second contract, called the Bronze and Silver Dance Programs, provided for 550 additional lessons. After signing the second contract, a new instructor, Simmons, was assigned to plaintiff. Simmons told plaintiff that he was asked by Sesler to come to Fiesta and teach her. Seven lessons later, Simmons told plaintiff that he had worked all day Sunday on a new plan for her. Plaintiff testified she told Simmons she could not take the new course. She stated that Simmons physically "dragged" her into Sesler's office. Simmons, Sesler and Bennett told plaintiff she should take the "Gold and Supreme Gold" course, and that she should join the "Tiffany Club," which consisted of five ladies. Plaintiff was told that before she could become a member of the club she would have to go to Dallas and pass a dance test.

The new Tiffany contract would cost $18,900.00. There is evidence that before going to Dallas, plaintiff paid Fiesta $5,900.00 on the new $18,900.00 contract. Plaintiff, Bennett, Sesler and Simmons flew to Dallas. The dance test took about 15 minutes. Plaintiff passed. That evening, Bennett, Sesler and Simmons took plaintiff out for dining and dancing. Plaintiff signed the new $18,900.00 contract on March 29, 1976. Bennett stated they would "throw in" a trip to Hawaii. At the time plaintiff paid the $18,900.00, she had only taken 22 hours of the second contract which provided for 550 lessons. Shortly thereafter, Simmons left and Mitchell became plaintiff's new dance instructor.

After dancing with Mitchell on "video," plaintiff was invited back to Sesler's office and given a "corsage." Plaintiff testified the videotape was shown in color on a television screen. She stated it was "very pretty." She said that at this time, Bennett and Sesler proposed a new $49,000.00 contract. Plaintiff refused the proposal. Bennett and Sesler counterposed a new $9,000.00 contract. Plaintiff again refused. The discussion covering the $49,000.00 contract occurred in June or July, 1976. Plaintiff testified that after she refused to sign the $49,000.00 contract, she no longer received compliments and attention from the Fiesta staff. She was told that they would no longer pick her up at night for the night parties.

Shortly thereafter, while dancing at the studio, an instructor stepped on her foot. It was approximately 11 weeks before she could wear a shoe on the injured foot. When the foot healed, she returned to the studio and the same instructor, while dancing with plaintiff, picked her up and spun her in the air. Plaintiff sustained two broken ribs. Plaintiff decided she would not return for additional lessons. At that time, she had 1,027 units remaining on the three contracts. The trip to Las Vegas was cancelled and the date for the Hawaii trip was never set.

From the evidence, the jury could reasonably conclude that, prior to signing each contract, plaintiff was subjected to a calculated treatment of flattery and that her better judgment was diminished by excessive compliments. Bennett, Sesler, and the individual dance instructors were to receive a percentage of money paid by plaintiff on the various contracts. The jury could evaluate defendants' motives by their conduct. As soon as plaintiff commenced a particular program, a new instructor would appear, and a new, more expensive contract would be offered.

When plaintiff finally refused to sign further contracts, defendants' attitude toward plaintiff altered radically. The jury could properly infer from the evidence that plaintiff was a lonely widow who lacked the knowledge, ability, experience, or capacity to withstand the premeditated attention lavished upon her by defendants, who purposely took advantage of her vulnerability to a grossly unfair degree. We hold there is some evidence to support the jury's answers to Special Issues 1, 2 and 3, and after reviewing all the evidence, we hold the evidence is factually sufficient to support the findings by the jury.

No producing cause issues were submitted. There was no objection to the omission. We hold there is some evidence to support the trial court's implied finding that the producing cause of plaintiff's actual damages was the "unconscionable act or course of action" of each defendant. Tex. R. Civ. P. 279.

We overrule defendants' attack upon the award of attorney's fees. We think the stipulation of counsel is adequate to support the award. Defendants' reliance on Bray v. Curtis, 544 S.W.2d 816 (Tex.Civ.App. Corpus Christi 1976, writ ref'd n. r. e.) is misplaced. In that case, the complaining party properly objected to the submission of the attorney's fee issue.

The jury also found that defendants made certain misrepresentations to plaintiff and that the specific misrepresentations constituted a "deceptive trade practice." Tex.Bus. & Com.Code Ann. § 17.46(a); *Spradling v. Williams,* 566 S.W.2d 561 (Tex.1978). Defendants attack these findings. We will not pass on or discuss defendants' points of error pertaining to the specific acts found by the jury to constitute deceptive trade practices. The jury's finding that defendants engaged in an unconscionable act or course of action is sufficient to uphold the award of treble damages and attorney's fees. The judgment of the trial court is affirmed

NOTES & QUESTIONS

1) In *Brittan Communications Intern. Corp. v. Southwestern Bell Telephone Co.* 313 F.3d 899, 907 (5th Cir. 2002) and citing Texas law, the Fifth Circuit outlined the elements that a plaintiff must prove to prevail in a DTPA-unconscionability cause of action. The plaintiff must establish that: 1) plaintiff is a consumer under the DTPA; 2) a defendant engaged in an unconscionable action or course of action; and 3) the acts were the producing cause of plaintiff's damages *Brown v. Bank of Galveston, N.A.,* 963 S.W.2d 511, 513 (Tex. 1998).

2) During their first year in law school, students learn that unconscionable acts preclude the formation of valid contracts. In that context, unconscionability is an affirmative defense that bars the enforcement of invalid contracts. Is unconscionability an affirmative defense against a DTPA-unconscionability cause of action?

DeBakey v. Staggs
605 S.W.2d 631(Tex. Civ. App. 1980),
***aff'd,* 612 S.W.2d 924 (Tex. 1981)**

This is an appeal from a judgment rendered after a nonjury trial wherein appellees were awarded damages of $420, trebled, and attorney's fees of. $1000.

The principal questions are 1) whether legal services are incorporated under § 17.45(2) of the Deceptive Trade Practices Act (Act) (2) whether a client is a consumer as defined in § 17.45(4) of the Act and (3) whether the evidence supported the conclusions and findings of the court that the appellant's conduct constituted an "unconscionable action or course of action" prohibited by § 17.45(5) of the Act.

We answer all of these questions in the affirmative and, as modified, affirm the judgment of the trial court.

In April of 1977, appellant was retained by appellees Marilyn and Donny Staggs to perform the legal services necessary to change the name of Rhonda Kay McWhorter to Rhonda Kay Staggs. Rhonda Kay, a minor, was the daughter of Mrs. Staggs by a prior marriage and the step-daughter of Mr. Staggs. A retainer of $120 was paid by the appellees to appellant, on an agreed total fee of $250.00

The petition was filed in May of 1977, and after citation by publication was obtained on the natural father, the cause was heard on October 14, 1977. Because of numerous defects and insufficiencies in the handling of the cause, the order changing the name of Rhonda Kay was not signed and appellees eventually hired other counsel and paid him $300.00 to complete the proceeding.

Thereafter, this suit was filed alleging, among other things, a cause of action under Sec. 17.41 of the Deceptive Trade Practices Act. Appellees alleged they sustained damages because of the necessity of hiring other counsel to complete the procedure and for mental anguish occasioned by the delay.

Appellant is challenging the evidentiary basis supporting the trial court's findings that:

1) he did not secure the appointment of an attorney ad litem;
2) he knew the petition was defective at the time it was filed;
3) he was advised by the court that an attorney ad litem, as well as a statement of the evidence were required because service of citation had been obtained by publication;
4) he did not return the fee of $120.00; and
5) his services were of no value to the appellees.

The appellant is also challenging the trial court's conclusions of law that:

1) appellant's failure to timely obtain the change of name was detrimental to appellees;
2) appellant's failure to timely obtain the change of name took advantage of the appellees' lack of knowledge, ability, experience and capability to a grossly unfair degree;
3) appellant's knowing failure to properly and timely obtain the change of name resulted in a gross disparity between the value received and the consideration paid;
4) the appellees sustained actual damages in the amount of $420; and
5) the appellees were entitled to treble damages and attorney's fees in the amount of $1,000.

Appellant in eight points of error, attacks the first four findings listed above. However, appellant admitted these facts at trial, therefore these points of error are overruled.

Appellant's 11th and 12th points of error allege that the trial court's conclusion of law that the failure of the appellant to timely obtain the change of name was detrimental to the appellees was not supported by the evidence, or alternatively, was against the great weight and preponderance of the evidence. These points are overruled. After approximately 18 months had passed and this relatively simple procedure had not been completed, appellees were justified in retaining other counsel, which cost them extra money. This testimony is sufficient to support these findings.

Appellant's 13th and 14th points of error attack the sufficiency of the evidence supporting the trial court's conclusion that the failure of the appellant to timely obtain the change of name took advantage of the lack of knowledge, ability, experience and capacity of appellees to a grossly unfair degree.

It is undisputed that appellant was retained to change the name of Rhonda Kay McWhorter and that appellees, who were not lawyers, were depending on him to effect this. It is also undisputed that although appellant knew it was required by law, he failed to file a verified petition, he failed to file the written consent of the minor, and he failed to file a statement of the evidence, any of which failures would legally justify the court's refusal to grant the change of name in this case.

Appellant's own testimony revealed that he was contacted by a clerk of the court seven months after presenting the matter for hearing, and informed of four errors which needed to be corrected before the court would sign the order changing the name of Rhonda Kay. During this seven month period appellant did not make inquiry of the court pertaining to the delay in signing the proposed order nor did appellant correct or complete these matters prior to the retention of substituted counsel. This evidence is sufficient to warrant the conclusion by the trial court that appellant's conduct took advantage of the appellees' lack of knowledge, experience and capacity to an unfair degree.

Appellant's points of error 17 and 18 complain that there was no evidence or, alternatively, insufficient evidence supporting the conclusion of law that appellees were damaged in the amount of $420.

Appellant agreed to handle the change of name for $250.00. The appellees testified that they paid appellant $120.00 and, because appellant failed to complete the task, they were required to pay an additional $300 to the successor lawyer. The total cash outlay was $420.00. Deducting the amount $250 which they initially promised to pay appellant, leaves an excess of $170.00 which they were required to pay by reason of appellant's conduct. The correct damages should be treble the sum of $170.00, which is $510.

Under these points of error appellant further urges that appellees do not qualify as "consumers" within the purview of Sec. 17.41 et seq. of the DTPA, Bus. & Com.Code, reasoning that appellees were purchasing services of an intangible nature. Appellant cites *Snyder's Smart Shop Inc. v. Santi*, 590 S.W.2d 167 (Tex.Civ.App.-Corpus Christi 1979 no writ) which held that the sale of accounts receivable, an intangible, was not subject to the Act. The basis for the court's holding in Santi was that accounts receivable were neither goods nor services as defined by the Act. In the instant case the issue is whether legal services are covered by the Act. We hold that the act applied to the purchase or acquisition of legal services.

The legislature has directed the courts to liberally construe the act in order to effectuate its broad purposes. DTPA § 17.44. The act defines "services" as work, labor or services purchased or leased for use, including services furnished in connection with the sale or repair of goods. DTPA § 17.45(2). A "consumer" is defined as an individual, partnership, corporation, association, or governmental entity who seeks or acquires by purchase or lease any goods or services. DTPA § 17.45(4). The attorney sells legal services and the client purchases them. Unless exempted elsewhere in the statutes, the attorney as well as other professionals are subject to the provisions of the Act. Physicians and health care providers have been specifically exempted from the provisions of DTPA where the litigation is based on a claim of negligence. Tex. Rev. Civ. Stat. Ann. art. 4590i, § 12.01(a). However, an amendment to the Act, which would have exempted all professional services, was tabled. Therefore, it is reasonable to conclude that the legislature intended legal services to be covered by the Act.

In points of error 19 and 20 appellant argues that the court erred in trebling the damage award and in awarding attorneys fees.

Briefly, the appellant contends that attorney's fees should not have been allowed nor the damages trebled because appellees did not give 30 days notice prior to filing suit. On May 10, 1978, which was more than 30 days before suit was filed, a letter was written by the successor attorney to the appellant which clearly set forth the wrongs alleged and the damages claimed and notifying him of their intention to file suit under the DTPA if the damages were not paid. At trial, appellant acknowledged timely receipt of the letter. These points are overruled.

Appellant's points of error nine, ten, fifteen and sixteen, although considered by the court, need not be discussed because the trial court's judgment can be, and is, affirmed upon the basis that the appellant committed an unconscionable act by taking advantage of the appellees lack of knowledge, ability, experience, and capacity to a grossly unfair degree.

F. Proving a DTPA Action—Violations Under the Texas Insurance Code

Once more, under § 17.50(a)(4) of the DTPA, a consumer of insurance and insurance services may initiate a cause action against insurers as well as against insurance agents. But, the language in the DTPA is specific: It gives plaintiffs the right to bring a DTPA action if there is evidence of some violation under Art. § 541 of the Texas Insurance Code. However, whether consumers may file a DTPA action against any person who engages in the "business of insurance" and violates any section in the Texas Insurance Code or insurance-related common-law principles also has generated a considerable amount of litigation.

Part II of this text presents a thorough review of insurance law and numerous procedural and substantive issues. But this section also covers some of the DTPA-specific issues and controversies involving insurance consumers, insurers and their various insurance agents.

TEXAS INSURANCE CODE
SUBCHAPTER B. DECEPTIVE, UNFAIR, AND PROHIBITED PRACTICES
CHAPTER 541. UNFAIR METHODS OF COMPETITION AND UNFAIR OR DECEPTIVE ACTS OR PRACTICES

[FORMERLY ART. 21.21, § 4(10) REPEALED]

Section 541.060 — Unfair Settlement Practices.

(a) It is an unfair method of competition or an unfair or deceptive act or practice in the business of insurance to engage in the following unfair settlement practices with respect to a claim by an insured or beneficiary:

(1) misrepresenting to a claimant a material fact or policy provision relating to coverage at issue;

(2) failing to attempt in good faith to effectuate a prompt, fair, and equitable settlement of:

  (A) a claim with respect to which the insurer's liability has become reasonably clear; or

  (B) a claim under one portion of a policy with respect to which the insurer's liability has become reasonably clear to influence the claimant to settle another claim under another portion of the coverage unless payment under one portion of the coverage constitutes evidence of liability under another portion;

(3) failing to promptly provide to a policyholder a reasonable explanation of the basis in the policy, in relation to the facts or applicable law, for the insurer's denial of a claim or offer of a compromise settlement of a claim;

(4) failing within a reasonable time to:
  (A) affirm or deny coverage of a claim to a policyholder; or
  (B) submit a reservation of rights to a policyholder;

(5) refusing, failing, or unreasonably delaying a settlement offer under applicable first-party coverage on the basis that other coverage may be available or that third parties are responsible for the damages suffered, except as may be specifically provided in the policy;

(6) undertaking to enforce a full and final release of a claim from a policyholder when only a partial payment has been made, unless the payment is a compromise settle-ment of a doubtful or disputed claim;

(7) refusing to pay a claim without conducting a reasonable investigation with respect to the claim;

(8) with respect to a Texas personal automobile insurance policy, delaying or refusing settlement of a claim solely because there is other insurance of a different kind available to satisfy all or part of the loss forming the basis of that claim; or

(9) requiring a claimant as a condition of settling a claim to produce the claimant's federal income tax returns for examination or investigation by the person unless:
  (A) a court orders the claimant to produce those tax returns;
  (B) the claim involves a fire loss; or
  (C) the claim involves lost profits or income.

(b) Subsection (a) does not provide a cause of action to a third party asserting one or more claims against an insured covered under a liability insurance policy.

Added by Acts 2003, 78th Leg., ch. 1274, Sec. 2, eff. April 1, 2005

— 0 —

Texas Insurance Code
Subchapter D. Private Action For Damages
Chapter 541. Unfair Methods Of Competition And Unfair Or Deceptive Acts Or Practices

[Art. 21.21, § 16(a), repealed]

Section 541.151 — Private Action For Damages Authorized

A person who sustains actual damages may bring an action against another person for those damages caused by the other person engaging in an act or practice:

(1) defined by Subchapter B to be an unfair method of competition or an unfair or deceptive act or practice in the business of insurance; or

(2) specifically enumerated in Section 17.46(b), Business & Commerce Code (DTPA), as an unlawful deceptive trade practice if the person bringing the action shows that the person relied on the act or practice to the person's detriment.

Added by Acts 2003, 78th Leg., ch. 1274, § 2, eff. April 1, 2005.

— 0 —

Texas Insurance Code
Chapter 542. Processing And Settlement Of Claims
Subchapter A. Unfair Claim Settlement Practices

[Formerly Art. 21.21-2, repealed]

Sec. § 542.003 — Unfair Claim Settlement Practices Prohibited.

(a) An insurer engaging in business in this state may not engage in an unfair claim settlement practice.

(b) Any of the following acts by an insurer constitutes unfair claim settlement practices:

(1) knowingly misrepresenting to a claimant pertinent facts or policy provisions relating to coverage at issue;

(2) failing to acknowledge with reasonable promptness pertinent communications relating to a claim arising under the insurer's policy;

(3) failing to adopt and implement reasonable standards for the prompt investigation of claims arising under the insurer's policies;

(4) not attempting in good faith to effect a prompt, fair, and equitable settlement of a claim submitted in which liability has become reasonably clear;

(5) compelling a policyholder to institute a suit to recover an amount due under a policy by offering substantially less than the amount ultimately recovered in a suit brought by the policyholder;

(6) failing to maintain the information required by Section 542.005; or

(7) committing another act the commissioner determines by rule constitutes an unfair claim settlement practice.

Added by Acts 2003, 78th Leg., ch. 1274, § 2, eff. April 1, 2005.

— 0 —

TEXAS INSURANCE CODE
CHAPTER 542. PROCESSING AND SETTLEMENT OF CLAIMS
SUBCHAPTER A. UNFAIR CLAIM SETTLEMENT PRACTICES

Sec. § 542.004 — Examination of Tax Returns Prohibited.

(a) An insurer regulated under this code may not require a claimant, as a condition of settling a claim, to produce the claimant's federal income tax returns for examination or investigation by the insurer unless:
  (1) the claimant is ordered to produce the tax returns by a court; or
  (2) the claim involves:
    (A) a fire loss; or
    (B) a loss of profits or income.

(b) An insurer that violates this section commits:
  (1) a prohibited practice under this subchapter; and
  (2) a deceptive trade practice under Subchapter E, Chapter 17, and Business & Commerce Code (DTPA) — [Formerly Art. 21.21-2, § 2(c), repealed]

(c) A claimant affected by a violation of this section is entitled to remedies under Subchapter E, Chapter 17, Business & Commerce Code (DTPA) — [Formerly Art. 21.21-2, § 2(c), repealed]

Added by Acts 2003, 78th Leg., ch. 1274, § 2, eff. April 1, 2005

1st Party ins dispute

Vail v. Texas Farm Bureau Mutual Insurance Company
754 S.W.2d 129
(Tex. 1988)

This case presents the question of whether an insured has a cause of action against an insurer for unfair claims settlement practices under the Deceptive Trade Practices Act or the Texas Insurance Code. Petitioners Melvin and Maryanne Vail insured their home under a policy issued by respondent Texas Farm Bureau Mutual Insurance Company. The home was destroyed by fire during the policy period, and Texas Farm refused to pay the Vails' claim. The Vails sued Texas Farm for the full amount of the policy and for damages under the Deceptive Trade Practices Act (DTPA), Tex.Bus.

& Com. Code Ann. § 17.41 et seq. and the Texas Insurance Code, Tex. Ins. Code Ann. art. 21.21, alleging a bad faith failure to pay the claim.

Based on a jury verdict, the trial court rendered judgment for the Vails for treble the amount of the policy, prejudgment interest on the trebled amount, and attorney's fees. The court of appeals reversed that part of the trial court's judgment that trebled the actual damages and permitted the Vails to recover only the policy limit as actual damages, prejudgment interest on that amount, and attorney's fees. We reverse the judgment of the court of appeals in part and render judgment that the Vails recover treble the amount of the policy, prejudgment interest on the amount of the policy only, and attorney's fees.

The Vails purchased a fire insurance policy from Texas Farm in 1978. Under the policy, the home was insured for $25,000, and the contents were insured for $10,000. The Vails' home burned on July 18, 1979 during the term of the policy. The agent for Texas Farm informed the Vails that the company would not "willingly" pay the claim, allegedly because the Vails had not provided an adequate list of the contents destroyed in the fire. The adequacy of the contents list had no bearing, however, on Texas Farm's duty to pay under the policy on the home itself. Texas Farm notified the Vails on August 15, 1979 that it had denied the claims for both the home and the contents based on the inadequate contents list.

Texas Farm then hired an engineering firm to conduct an arson investigation. The engineering firm concluded that no fire-setting materials were present on the Vails' site. After receiving the engineering firm's report, Texas Farm engaged the State Fire Marshal's office to conduct a second arson investigation. An investigator for the Fire Marshal's office tested four samples of fire debris. One sample showed no fire-setting materials were present. The other three samples indicated the presence of fire-setting materials. Expert testimony at trial, however, indicated that the three samples were tested under conditions that raised questions as to validity of the results. Based on the Fire Marshal's report, Texas Farm changed its basis for denying the claim from an inadequate contents list to arson.

The Vails sued Texas Farm, seeking recovery on the policy, treble damages, and attorney's fees based on unfair claims settlement practices. The Vails alleged violations of the DTPA and the Insurance Code. Texas Farm lodged special exceptions to the Vails' pleadings, complaining of lack of notice. The trial court struck all of the DTPA and Insurance Code allegations with the exception of the following:

> In the alternative, Defendant violated the Tex.Bus. and Com. Code, § 17.50(a)(4) by employing or using acts which violate art. 21.21 of the Texas Insurance Code, or rules and regulations issued by the State Board of Insurance under said art. 21.21, as follows:(b) By engaging in the practices contrary to Sec. 4 of Insurance Board Order 18663, Sec. (a), which acts were unfair or deceptive as defined by art. 21.21-2, Sec. 2(d) by not attempting in good faith to effectuate prompt, fair, and equitable settlements on claims submitted in which liability had become reasonably clear.

The case proceeded on the basis of these statutory allegations and the Vails' claim that Texas Farm had breached the common-law duty of good faith and fair dealing. The jury found that Texas Farm had intentionally failed to exercise good faith in the processing of the Vails' claim by refusing to settle the claim promptly, fairly, and equitably after Texas Farm's liability had become reasonably clear. Based on the jury findings, the trial court awarded the Vails the full policy limit of $35,000, trebled that amount, and awarded attorney's fees and prejudgment interest on the trebled figure.

The court of appeals reversed that part of the trial court's judgment that trebled the actual damages awarded the Vails. The court of appeals held that there is no private cause of action for unfair claims settlement practices under the DTPA or Insurance Code. The court of appeals modified the trial court's judgment to permit the Vails to recover only the combined policy limit of $35,000 on the home and contents, prejudgment interest on that amount, and attorney's fees.

The Vails contend that they properly pleaded, proved, and obtained jury findings under the DTPA and the Insurance Code so as to entitle them to recover treble damages. Texas Farm responds with two arguments. First, Texas Farm asserts that the Vails failed to adequately plead violations of the DTPA and the Insurance Code. Second, Texas Farm argues that even if the pleadings provided adequate notice of the DTPA and Insurance Code claims, the Vails failed to state a cause of action under Texas law.

The Vails' pleadings allege that Texas Farm violated section 17.50(a)(4) of the DTPA by engaging in acts that violate article 21.21 of the Texas Insurance Code or rules or regulations promulgated pursuant to that article. Section 17.50(a)(4) of the DTPA provides:

> A consumer may maintain an action where any of the following constitutes a producing cause of actual damages: . . . (4) The use or employment by any person of an act or practice in violation of Art. 21.21, Texas Insurance Code, as amended, or rules and regulations issued by the State Board of Insurance under Art. 21.21, Texas Insurance Code, as amended. Tex. Bus. & Com. Code Ann. § 17.50(a)(4).

Texas Farm contends that section 17.50(a)(4) of the DTPA does not incorporate section 16 of article 21.21, the "remedies" provision that defines the types of unfair or deceptive acts or practices for which article 21.21 relief may be granted. The language of section 17.50(a)(4) of the DTPA, however, by its terms, incorporates article 21.21 of the Insurance Code in its entirety. *See Mobile County Mutual Ins. Co. v. Jewell,* 555 S.W.2d 903, 910 (Tex.Civ.App.-El Paso 1977, writ ref'd n.r.e.). Texas Farm was given adequate notice that the Vails were seeking relief under section 17.50(a)(4) of the DTPA for conduct proscribed by section 16 of article 21.21 of the Insurance Code. Tex. R. Civ. P. 47; *Stone v. Lawyers Title Ins. Co.,* 554 S.W.2d 183, 187 (Tex.1977).

Texas Farm maintains that even if the Vails' pleadings provide adequate notice of their claims under section 17.50(a)(4) of the DTPA and article 21.21, § 16 of the Insurance Code, the Vails nevertheless failed to state a cause of action under Texas law. Texas Farm argues that the Texas legislature has limited the remedy for unfair claims settlement practices to that contained in article 21.21-2 of the Insurance Code. Article 21.21-2 authorizes the State Board of Insurance to issue cease and desist orders upon finding that an insurer has engaged in unfair claims settlement practices. Tex.

Ins. Code Ann. art. 21.21-2 (Vernon 1981). It has been held, however, that article 21.21-2 does not confer a private cause of action upon individuals injured by unfair claims settlement practices. *Lone Star Life Ins. Co. v. Griffin,* 574 S.W.2d 576, 580 (Tex.Civ.App.-Beaumont 1978, writ ref'd n.r.e.). Texas Farm concludes that the legislature, by enacting article 21.21-2, "sealed off" any private cause of action for unfair claims settlement practices under the DTPA or Insurance Code.

The DTPA and the Insurance Code each grant relief for unfair or deceptive acts or practices in the business of insurance. Tex.Bus. & Com.Code Ann. § 17.50(a)(4) (Vernon 1987); Tex. Ins. Code Ann. art. 21.21 §§ 3, 16 (Vernon Supp. 1988). The business of insurance includes the investigation and adjustment of claims and losses. *Aetna Casualty & Surety Co. v. Marshall,* 724 S.W.2d 770, 771-72 (Tex.1987); Tex. Ins. Code Ann. art. 1.14-1, § 2(a) (Vernon Supp.1988). There is no provision in the DTPA or the Insurance Code that exempts insurers from liability for conduct relating to the handling of insurance claims. *See Melody Home Manufacturing Co. v. Barnes,* 741 S.W.2d 349, 354 n. 7 (Tex.1987) . . . .

The legislature has mandated that the DTPA and the Insurance Code are to be liberally construed to promote the remedial purposes of those statutes. Tex. Bus. & Com.Code Ann. § 17.44. Tex. Ins. Code Ann. art. 21.21, § 1(b). Section 17.50(a)(4) of the DTPA incorporates section 16 of article 21.21 of the Insurance Code. Section 16 permits recovery by any person who has been injured by another's engaging in:

> [1] any of the practices declared to be unfair or deceptive by Section 4 of article 21.21;
>
> [2] conduct defined in rules or regulations lawfully adopted by the Board under article 21.21 as unfair methods of competition and unfair or deceptive acts or practices in the business of insurance; or
>
> [3] any practice defined by Section 17.46 of the Business & Commerce Code, as amended, as an unlawful deceptive trade practice. Tex. Ins. Code Ann. art. 21.21, § 16(a)

The Vails contend that Texas Farm engaged in the second and third types of conduct prohibited by section 16 by engaging in practices declared by a rule or regulation of the State Board of Insurance to be unfair or deceptive; and by engaging in acts that constitute an unlisted deceptive trade practice under section 17.46 of the DTPA. We will address each of the separate theories advanced by the Vails to support their recovery of treble damages under section 17.50(a)(4) of the DTPA and section 16 of article 21.21 of the Insurance Code.

* * *

In *Arnold v. National County Mutual Fire Ins. Co.,* 725 S.W.2d 165, 167 (Tex.1987), we held that as between an insurer and the insured, there is a duty on the part of the insurer to deal fairly and in good faith in the processing of claims. In *Aranda v. Insurance Co. of North America,* 748 S.W.2d 210, 212-13 (1988), we held that an insurer breaches the duty of good faith and fair dealing by failing to promptly and equitably pay an insured's claim when liability becomes reasonably clear. Our holdings in *Arnold* and *Aranda* are determinations pursuant to law that an insurer's lack of good faith in processing a claim is an unfair or deceptive act. The Vails therefore stated a cause of action for unfair claims settlement practices under section 17.50(a)(4) of the DTPA and article 21.21, § 16 of the Insurance Code through the incorporation of Board Order 18663, § 4(b) and the holdings of this court in *Arnold* and *Aranda.*

The Vails pleaded and proved that Texas Farm failed to exercise good faith in the processing of their claims. The Vails are thus entitled to recover under section 17.50(a)(4) of the DTPA.

Unfair Claims Settlement Practices Under Section 17.46 of the DTPA

Section 16 of article 21.21 also prohibits an insurer from engaging in any practice defined by section 17.46 of the DTPA. Section 17.46 of the DTPA enumerates specific acts as "false, misleading, or deceptive acts or practices," but this enumeration does not constitute an exclusive list of acts that violate the prohibition against deceptive trade practices. *Spradling v. Williams,* 566 S.W.2d 561, 564 (Tex.1978). Section 17.46 encompasses *any* type of business activity that deceives consumers. *Id.* at 563. When an unlisted practice is alleged, the plaintiff must obtain a finding that the act or practice occurred and that it was deceptive. *Id.* at 564.

Article 21.21, § 16 of the Insurance Code makes actionable *any* violation of section 17.46 of the DTPA. *Aetna Casualty & Surety Co. v. Marshall,* 724 S.W.2d 770, 772 (Tex.1987). Thus, section 16 of article 21.21 incorporates any unlisted practice that is determined to be false, misleading, or deceptive. *Allstate Ins. Co. v. Kelly,* 680 S.W.2d 595, 605 (Tex.App.-Tyler 1984, writ ref'd n.r.e.).

The Vails assert that the failure to attempt to settle a claim promptly, fairly, and equitably when liability becomes reasonably clear is an unlisted deceptive trade practice under section 17.46 of the DTPA. The Vails further contend that they obtained a jury finding that Texas Farm had engaged in a deceptive act because the jury answered Special Issue No. 4 as follows:

> Do you find from a preponderance of the evidence that the defendant intentionally failed to exercise good faith in the investigation, processing, and denial of the claim made the basis of this lawsuit?
>
> Answer: "We do."

The jury made the requisite determination that Texas Farm had engaged in a deceptive act or practice when it found that Texas Farm had failed to exercise good faith in the handling of the Vails' claim. The jury also found that Texas Farm's failure was intentional, although no such finding is expressly required by the pre-1985 Insurance Code.

The Vails stated and proved a cause of action under section 17.50(a)(4) of the DTPA and article 21.21, § 16 of the Insurance Code by pleading and proving that Texas Farm had committed an unlisted deceptive trade practice under section 17.46 of the DTPA.

We hold that the Vails stated and proved a cause of action for unfair claims settlement practices under section 17.50(a)(4) of the DTPA on any one of three alternative grounds: (1) by incorporating article 21.21, § 16 of the Insurance Code, section 4(a) of Board Order 18663, and the definition of an unfair claims settlement practice in article 21.21-2, § 2(d) of the Insurance Code; (2) by incorporating article 21.21, § 16 of the Insurance Code, section 4(b) of Board Order 18663, and the determinations made by this court in *Arnold* and *Aranda* ; and (3) by incorporating article 21.21, § 16 of the Insurance Code and section 17.46 of the DTPA.

NOTES & QUESTIONS

1) In *Vail*, the plaintiffs alleged that the insurer's failure to pay the claim was "bad faith." Does "bad faith" appear among the various violations outlined in the DTPA "laundry list?" Does a cause of action for "bad faith" sound in contract or tort? DTPA actions sound in tort and not in contract. See *PPG Industries, Inc. v. JMB/Houston Centers Partners Ltd. Partnership,* 146 S.W.3d 79 (Tex. 2004).

2) Consider the facts in *Vail*. May a "first-party" insurance consumer commence an Independent Tort of Bad Faith action as well as a breach-of-contract action against the insurer? May a third-party victim of an insurance accident commence a "direct" DTPA or breach-of-contract action against an insured's liability insurer? May the insured assign a first-party DTPA action? Consider the next case.

Allstate Insurance Company v. Watson
876 S.W.2d 145
(Tex. 1994)

Respondent's motion for rehearing is overruled. We withdraw our opinion of November 24, 1993 and substitute the following opinion in its place.

The issue in this case is whether the legislature has conferred upon a third party claimant a direct cause of action against an insurer for unfair claim settlement practices under section 16 of art. 21.21 of the Texas Insurance Code. We hold that a third party claimant has no such direct cause of action under art. 21.21 and therefore, we reverse in part and affirm in part the judgment of the court of appeals.

Kathleen Watson was injured in a car accident on March 31, 1989. The driver of the other car was M.D. Townley, an insured under an automobile liability policy issued by Allstate Insurance Company. Watson filed suit on June 28, 1989 against Townley alleging that Townley was negligent and that his negligence was a proximate cause of the accident and her injuries. In the same action, Watson also sued Allstate under art. 21.21, section 16, for alleged unfair claim settlement practices in failing to attempt in good faith to effectuate prompt settlement of her claims where liability had become reasonably clear and in denying or unreasonably delaying payment of her claim. Watson alleged that Allstate's conduct violated 28 Tex. Admin. Code § 21.3 (Board Order 18663) and section 17.46 of the Texas Deceptive Trade Practices-Consumer Protection Act (DTPA), thereby giving rise to her cause of action under art. 21.21, section 16.

In addition to her claim under art. 21.21, Watson alleged violations of the DTPA, breach of contract, breach of the duty of good faith and fair dealing, and sought a declaratory judgment that Watson was an intended third party beneficiary of the Allstate liability policy.

On Allstate's motion, the trial court severed the claims against Allstate, struck Watson's pleadings as to Allstate for failure to state a claim, and granted Allstate's motion for summary judgment. The court of appeals affirmed the judgment of the trial court, 828 S.W.2d 423, except as to Watson's claim under art. 21.21 of the Texas Insurance Code. 828 S.W.2d at 425. The court of appeals reversed and remanded Watson's art. 21.21 claim, holding that Watson, as a third party beneficiary of an automobile liability policy, could bring an action under art. 21.21 without first proceeding directly against the named insured of the policy. For the reasons stated below, we reverse the judgment of the court of appeals concerning Watson's art. 21.21 claim.

I.

In this case, we are asked to expand our holding in *Vail v. Texas Farm Bureau Mutual Ins. Co.,* 754 S.W.2d 129 (Tex.1988) and conclude that section 16 of art. 21.21 confers upon third party claimants a direct cause of action against an insurer for unfair claim settlement practices. In essence, we are asked to extend to a party adverse to the insured, the same duties and obligations insurers owe to their insureds under *Vail.* For the reasons stated below, we decline to do so.

To have a private cause of action for alleged unfair claim settlement practices under art. 21.21, section 16, such practices must be declared unfair or deceptive acts or practices in the business of insurance in section 4 of art. 21.21, the rules and regulations of the State Board of Insurance adopted under art. 21.21, or be defined unlawful deceptive trade practices in section 17.46 of the DTPA. Tex. Ins. Code Ann. art. 21.21, § 16. The full text of art. 21.21, section 16(a) reads:

> Any person who has sustained actual damages as a result of another's engaging in an act or practice declared in Section 4 of this Article or in rules or regulations lawfully adopted by the Board under this Article to be unfair methods of competition or unfair or deceptive acts or practices in the business of insurance or in any practice defined by section 17.46 of the Business & Commerce Code, as amended, as an unlawful deceptive trade practice may maintain an action against the person or persons engaging in such acts or practices.

We address each basis for art. 21.21 liability separately.

A. Section 4 of Art. 21.21

The express purpose of art. 21.21 is to regulate trade practices in the business of insurance by defining or providing for determination of "*all such practices in this state which constitute unfair methods of competition or unfair or deceptive acts or practices* and prohibiting such practices. Tex.Ins.Code Ann. art. 21.21, § 1 (emphasis added). Section 4 of art. 21.21 defines those practices that constitute unfair methods of competition or unfair or deceptive acts or practices. *Id.* at § 4. We note that unlike section 17.46 of the DTPA, discussed below, section 4 of art. 21.21 does not use the phrase "includes, but is not limited to" when defining prohibited acts. As written, art. 21.21, section 4, is an exclusive list of statutory unfair or deceptive acts or practices in the business of insurance. Within this list, section 4 does *not* define unfair claim settlement practices as an unfair or deceptive act or practice. Unfair claim settlement practices are not actionable under art. 21.21, section 16, by virtue of art. 21.21, section 4.

B. Rules and Regulations Adopted Under Art. 21.21

Board Order 18663 was adopted by the State Board of Insurance pursuant to art. 21.21. Through that order, Watson claims she is entitled to sue Allstate for unfair claim settlement practices. Board Order 18663 *does not* declare unfair claim settlement practices to be an unfair or deceptive act or practice. Rather, like art. 21.21 of the Insurance Code, this regulation prohibits insurers from engaging in unfair or deceptive acts or practices as *defined elsewhere.* The relevant portion of Board Order 18663 provides:

> (a) Misrepresentation of insurance policies, unfair competition, and unfair practices by insurers, agents and other connected persons are prohibited by Article 21.20 and Article 21.21 or by other provisions of the Insurance Code. No person shall engage in this state in any trade practice that is a misrepresentation of an insurance policy, that is an unfair method of competition, or that is an *unfair or deceptive act or practice as defined by* the provisions of the Insurance Code or as defined by these sections and other rules and regulations of the State Board of Insurance authorized by the Code.
>
> (b) Irrespective of the fact that the improper trade practice is not defined in any other section of these rules and regulations, no person shall engage in this state in any trade practice which is determined pursuant by law to be an unfair method of competition or an unfair or deceptive act or practice in the business of insurance.

Because Board Order 18663 does not declare unfair claim settlement practices to be an unfair or deceptive act or practice, such practices are not actionable under art. 21.21 by reference to Board Order 18663 alone. Tex.Ins.Code Ann. art. 21.21, § 16.

Watson argues, however, that through Board Order 18663, Board Order 41454 is implicated. This Court held in *Vail* that an insured could not rely on Board Order 41454 because the definition of unfair or deceptive acts or practices required that such acts be committed with "such frequency as to indicate a general business practice." *Vail,* 754 S.W.2d at 135. Thus, *Vail* precludes Watson's claims under Board Order 41454. While Board Order 41454 was amended effective August 19, 1992 to delete any frequency requirement, because of its effective date, this amendment does not apply to this case. In any event, Board Order 41454 was adopted pursuant to art. 21.21-2, not art.

21.21 and, thus, cannot form the basis of a claim under art. 21.21, section 16. Tex.Ins.Code Ann. art. 21.21, § 16.

Watson also argues that art. 21.21-2, which defines and prohibits unfair claim settlement practices, is made available as a private cause of action through Board Order 18663. To the contrary, art. 21.21-2 does not create a private cause of action for violations of that statute. . . .

C. Section 17.46 of the DTPA

Art. 21.21, section 16 provides a private cause of action for any practice *defined by* section 17.46 of the DTPA as an unlawful deceptive trade practice. Tex.Ins.Code Ann. art. 21.21, § 16. "Unfair claim settlement practices" is not among the enumerated items defined by section 17.46 as an unlawful deceptive trade practice. While section 17.46 may not be a complete list of unlawful deceptive trade practices for purposes of asserting claims under the DTPA, art. 21.21 expressly makes actionable those acts or practices that, in fact, are defined in section 17.46 as unlawful deceptive trade practices. Unfair claim settlement practices are not listed and, therefore, they are not actionable under art. 21.21, section 16 of the Insurance Code.

II.

To be sure, art. 21.21, section 16 is worded as providing a cause of action to "any person." However, for Watson to assert her cause of action against Allstate for unfair claim settlement practices, she must do so through the reasoning of *Vail. Vail,* an opinion delivered in 1988, followed closely after our decision in *Arnold v. National County Mutual Ins. Co.,* 725 S.W.2d 165 (Tex.1987). *Vail* thus presented the question of construction of art. 21.21, section 16 in the context of an insured-insurer relationship and in light of the preexisting common law duty of good faith and fair dealing recognized in *Arnold.* In reaching our decision today, we are particularly mindful of the duties imposed on insurers as to their insureds. *See Vail,* 754 S.W.2d at 136; *Arnold,* 725 S.W.2d at 167. *Vail* is predicated upon this Court's expressed belief that a special relationship exists between an insured and the insurer. *See Arnold,* 725 S.W.2d at 167. *Vail* remains the law as to claims for alleged unfair claim settlement practices brought by insureds against their insurers.

Watson, however, is not an insured. Rather, she asserts her claims against Allstate as a third party to the contract between Allstate and its insured. The obligations imposed by art. 21.21 of the Insurance Code and *Vail* are engrafted onto the contract between the insurer and insured and are extra-contractual in nature. A third party claimant has no contract with the insurer or the insured, has not paid any premiums, has no legal relationship to the insurer or special relationship of trust with the insurer, and in short, has no basis upon which to expect or demand the benefit of the extra-contractual obligations imposed on insurers under art. 21.21 with regard to their insureds. Nothing in *Vail* suggests that the extra-contractual obligations, rights, and remedies of art. 21.21, section 16 extend to third party claimants.

More to the point, in construing art. 21.21, section 16 as Watson would have us construe it to give her standing in this case, we would undermine the duties insurers owe to their insureds under *Vail* and *Arnold.* In construing art. 21.21 in *Vail,* we were not faced with potentially conflicting duties.

There is nothing inconsistent between the common law duty of good faith and fair dealing owed by an insurer to its insured and a duty imposed under *Vail* and art. 21.21, section 16 on an insurer as to its insured prohibiting unfair claim settlement practices. Were we to extend to third party claimants the same duties insurers owe to their insureds, insurers would be faced with owing coextensive and conflicting duties.

An insurer owes to its insured a duty to defend the insured *against* the claims asserted by a third party. Recognizing concomitant and coextensive duties under art. 21.21 to third party claimants, parties adverse to the insured, necessarily compromises the duties the insurer owes to its insured. In fact, the logical result of permitting a separate and direct cause of action in favor of third party claimants allows third parties to sue for unfair claim settlement practices *even though the insured has no claim for an unfair claim settlement practice.* As troublesome, it is conceivable that in attempting to settle claims pursuant to the demands of a third party claimant, insurers may be liable to the insured for settling too quickly. *See Texas Farmers Insurance Co. v. Soriano,* 844 S.W.2d 808 (Tex.App.-San Antonio 1993, writ granted) (affirming a judgment for actual and punitive damages against an insurer and in favor of the insured for breach of the common law duty of good faith and fair dealing where the insurer attempted to settle multiple claims for its underinsured by offering the full policy limits against the insured's wishes). In refusing to provide a direct cause of action for third party claimants, the legislature may well have been aware of this potential for conflicting duties. We will not construe art. 21.21 or *Vail,* absent explicit directive from the legislature, so as to compromise the insurer's loyalties and obligations owed to the insured.

We hold that Watson, as a third party claimant, lacks standing under section 16 of art. 21.21 to sue Allstate directly for unfair claim settlement practices.

III.

In coming to our conclusion, we also note that the court of appeals incorrectly determined that Watson had standing to sue under art. 21.21 as a third party beneficiary of the automobile liability policy. 828 S.W.2d at 428. In *Dairyland County Mutual Ins. Co. v. Childress,* 650 S.W.2d 770 (Tex.1983), this Court held that for purposes of recovering attorney's fees under an insurance contract, a third party who has obtained a judgment against an insured is an intended third party beneficiary of the insurance contract and is entitled to enforce the contract. *Dairyland* does not give third party claimants standing to sue to enforce the extra-contractual obligations under art. 21.21, section 16. Therefore, *Dairyland* is not applicable to this case.

The court of appeals erred in reversing the trial court's judgment as to Watson's art. 21.21 claim. We reverse in part the judgment of the court of appeals as to Watson's art. 21.21 claim and affirm the remainder of the judgment of the court of appeals.

Perez ex rel. Perez v. Blue Cross Blue Shield of Texas, Inc.
127 S.W.3d 826
(Tex. App.-Austin 2003)

In this insurance case, we must decide whether articles 21.21-6 and 21.21-8 of the insurance code allow a cause of action for denial of health insurance coverage to an individual with Down Syndrome. Appellant Brandon Perez, by and through his next friend, Debra Perez, individually and on behalf of similarly situated individuals, appeals the district court's grant of summary judgment in favor of appellee Blue Cross Blue Shield of Texas (BCBSTX or Blue Cross). . . . For the reasons set forth below, we affirm the order of the district court granting Blue Cross's motion for summary judgment and denying Perez's motions for summary judgment.

FACTUAL AND PROCEDURAL BACKGROUND

The pertinent facts of this case are not in dispute. In August 2000, Debra Perez applied for an individual Blue Cross health insurance policy for herself and her twelve-year-old son, Brandon Perez. She stated on the application that Brandon has Down Syndrome but is "very, very healthy." Blue Cross provided coverage for Debra but excluded Brandon from the policy because of his diagnosis of Down Syndrome. Debra requested reconsideration of the decision, asking why Blue Cross never requested copies of Brandon's medical records or interviewed his doctor. She enclosed with her request a letter from Miguel Ibarra, M.D., Brandon's doctor for ten years, who stated that Brandon did not require any more medical care than any other healthy boy his age. Blue Cross did not reconsider the application. In an internal e-mail some months later, a Blue Cross representative wrote that "[w]e did not request any medical information on Brandon because Down's Syndrome is an automatic decline in our Underwriting Guidelines."

Brandon, through his mother, filed suit in Travis County on behalf of himself and a putative class of all persons denied health insurance "based on a Down Syndrome diagnosis." Perez sought a declaratory judgment that Blue Cross's practice of denying coverage to "healthy persons with Down Syndrome" violates, among other statutes, articles 21.21-6 and 21.21-8 of the insurance code and section 17.46(b)(12) of the deceptive trade practices act (DTPA). *See* Tex. Ins. Code Ann. arts. 21.21-6, 8); Tex. Bus. & Com. Code Ann. § 17.46(b)(12). Perez further sought to enjoin Blue Cross from denying health insurance coverage to "individuals diagnosed with Down Syndrome."

Both Perez and Blue Cross filed traditional motions for summary judgment. Perez contended that he was entitled to summary judgment because Blue Cross did not raise the affirmative defense that its decision to deny coverage was based on "sound underwriting or actuarial principles reasonably related to actual or anticipated loss experience." Tex. Ins. Code Ann. art. 21.21-6, § 4(a). Blue Cross raised the affirmative defense in an amended answer and asserted that it was entitled to summary judgment because: Perez's claims were moot because he obtained health insurance through another insurance company; Perez did not have valid causes of action under articles 21.21-6 and 21.21-8 of the insurance code; and the denial of health insurance coverage was justified because it was based on sound underwriting or actuarial principles reasonably related to actual or anticipated loss experience.

Perez then filed a no-evidence motion for summary judgment on the ground that Blue Cross presented no evidence of its affirmative defense, in part because Blue Cross's actuarial expert, Jay Ripps, did not support his conclusions in his affidavit with actuarial data and based his conclusions on "additional materials provided to me by counsel." The district court granted Blue Cross's motion for summary judgment, denied Perez's motions for summary judgment, and overruled Perez's objection to the Ripps affidavit. Perez appeals the grant of summary judgment in favor of Blue Cross, the failure to exclude the Ripps affidavit, and the denial of his own motions for summary judgment.

ANALYSIS

Whether Perez's Claims are Moot

In his first issue, Perez contends that the district court erred in granting summary judgment because his claims are not moot. Blue Cross argues that this case is moot because Perez has obtained health insurance through another insurer. We disagree with Blue Cross. Under the mootness doctrine, appellate courts may only determine cases in which an actual controversy exists. *See Camarena v. Texas Employment Comm'n,* 754 S.W.2d 149, 151 (Tex.1988); *University Interscholastic League v. Buchanan,* 848 S.W.2d 298, 304 (Tex.App.-Austin 1993, no writ). In general, a case becomes moot when the issues presented are no longer "live" or the parties lack a legally cognizable interest in the outcome. *See United States Parole Comm'n v. Geraghty,* 445 U.S. 388, 396 (1980). Here, Perez retains a legally cognizable interest in the outcome were a court to issue an injunction that Blue Cross discontinue its practice of denying health insurance coverage to people with Down Syndrome. Furthermore, Perez has a live claim for actual damages. Because his causes of action are not moot, we sustain Perez's first issue.

* * *

Cause of Action under Article 21.21-6 of the Insurance Code

In his third issue, Perez asserts that he has a valid cause of action under article 21.21-6 of the insurance code. Tex. Ins. Code Ann. art. 21.21-6. Although Perez agrees with Blue Cross that article 21.21-6 does not provide for a private right of action because only the insurance commissioner may assess penalties under this provision, *see id.* § 5(a), he nevertheless contends that he may assert a claim under article 21.21-6 by way of insurance code article 21.21-8 and the DTPA "laundry list." *See id.* art. 21.21-8; Tex. Bus. & Com.Code Ann. § 17.46(b). This requires us to apply principles of statutory construction.

Statutory construction is a question of law, which we review *de novo. Texas Dep't of Transp. v. Needham,* 82 S.W.3d 314, 318 (Tex. 2002). We must ascertain and give effect to the legislature's intent for the provision we are construing. *See Fleming Foods v. Rylander,* 6 S.W.3d 278, 284 (Tex.1999); *Union Bankers Ins. Co. v. Shelton,* 889 S.W.2d 278, 280 (Tex.1994); *Calvert v. Texas Pipe Line Co.,* 517 S.W.2d 777, 780 (Tex.1974). The legislature's intent should be determined by reading the language used in the particular statute and construing the statute in its entirety. *See In re Bay Area Citizens Against Lawsuit Abuse,* 982 S.W.2d 371, 380 (Tex.1998); *Taylor v. Firemen's*

& Policemen's Civil Serv. Comm'n, 616 S.W.2d 187, 190 (Tex.1981). Further, we should read every word, phrase, and expression in a statute as if it were deliberately chosen, and presume the words excluded from the statute are done so purposefully. *See Gables Realty Ltd. P'ship v. Travis Cent. Appraisal Dist.,* 81 S.W.3d 869, 873 (Tex.App.-Austin 2002, pet. denied); *City of Austin v. Quick,* 930 S.W.2d 678, 687 (Tex.App.-Austin 1996) (citing *Cameron v. Terrell & Garrett, Inc.,* 618 S.W.2d 535, 540 (Tex.1981)), *aff'd,* 7 S.W.3d 109 (Tex.1999); *see also* 2A Norman J. Singer, *Sutherland Statutory Construction* § 47.25 (6th ed.2000) (stating that there is generally an inference that omissions from a statute are intentional).

Article 21.21-6 does not on its face provide a private cause of action. *See* Tex. Ins.Code. Ann. art. 21.21-6. Unlike article 21.21-8, article 21.21-6 is silent on the availability of a private civil remedy for an alleged violation. *Compare id. with id.* art. 21.21-8. Section five of article 21.21-6 addresses remedies for its violation, speaking only to administrative remedies that the insurance commissioner may pursue: "any legal entity ... found to be in violation ... is subject to the sanctions authorized by Chapter 82 of this code or administrative penalties authorized by Chapter 84 of this code. The commissioner may also utilize the cease and desist procedures authorized by Chapter 83 of this code." *Id.* art. 21.21-6, § 5.

By analogy, article 21.21-2 of the insurance code, prohibiting unfair claim settlement practices, also does not explicitly provide for a private cause of action; instead, it outlines detailed administrative remedies that the commissioner may pursue. *See id.* art. 21.21-2 (West Supp.2004). The supreme court has held that article 21.21-2 does not create a private cause of action for violations of that article. *Allstate Ins. Co. v. Watson,* 876 S.W.2d 145, 148-49 (Tex.1994); *see also American Physicians Ins. Exch. v. Garcia,* 876 S.W.2d 842, 847 n. 11 (Tex.1994) (Article 21.21-2 is "subject to enforcement only by the State Board of Insurance."). The reasoning of *Allstate* applies because article 21.21-6, while not spelling out specific administrative remedies, incorporates remedies set forth in chapters 82, 83, and 84 of the insurance code. Tex. Ins. Code Ann. art. 21.21-6, § 5(a). Thus, we rely on *Allstate* to hold that there is no private cause of action available under article 21.21-6.

We now turn to our examination of article 21.21-6 and its relationship with article 21.21-8. Under article 21.21-6, entitled "Unfair Discrimination," "[n]o person shall engage in any practice of unfair discrimination which is defined in this article or is determined pursuant to this article to be a practice of unfair discrimination in the business of insurance." *Id.* § 1. Unfair discrimination includes "refusing to insure ... because of disability or partial disability." *Id.* § 3(c). Article 21.21-8 provides that "[n]o person shall engage in any unfair discrimination by making or permitting any unfair discrimination between individuals of the same class and of essentially the same hazard." *Id.* art. 21.21-8, § 2.

Perez contends that a violation of article 21.21-6 is a violation of article 21.21-8 because (i) both provisions were enacted in the same legislative session and refer to each other; (ii) 21.21-8, being more general, encompasses the more specific article 21.21-6; and (iii) the legislature intended both statutes to address the same types of problems by entitling them both "Unfair Discrimination" and applying both to insurers. Blue Cross disputes that Perez may bring a cause of action under article 21.21-6 and counters that even if Perez may bring a claim under this provision, Blue Cross's decision not to insure was not a violation because it was "based upon sound underwriting or actuarial principles reasonably related to actual or anticipated loss experience." *Id.* art. 21.21-6, § 4(a) (affirmative defense to allegation of unfair discrimination).

As to Perez's first argument, the provisions do not refer to each other. Without such a cross-reference or some demonstration in the legislative history of an interrelationship, we cannot say that the remedy in article 21.21-8 encompasses that in article 21.21-6 simply because the provisions were enacted in the same legislative session. If anything, the opposite is true because, as discussed below, the statutes offer different remedies. Concerning Perez's second argument, assuming without deciding that article 21.21-8 is more general than article 21.21-6, it is a well-settled principle of statutory construction that a more specific statute controls over a more general one. *See, e.g., Columbia Hosp. Corp. of Houston v. Moore,* 92 S.W.3d 470, 473 & n. 19 (Tex. 2002).

As to Perez's third argument, our examination of the statutes and their legislative history does not lead us to conclude that one may bring a private cause of action through article 21.21-6 by way of article 21.21-8. The fact that article 21.21-8 provides for a private cause of action, *see id.* art. 21.21-8, § 3, whereas article 21.21-6 allows only a public remedy, *see id.* art. 21.21-6, § 5, belies the suggestion that one provision encompasses the other. This distinction is borne out by the legislative history. The caption for article 21.21-6, enacted as part of a bill providing public remedies, reads that the act relates "to certain acts of unfair discrimination in the business of insurance ... providing *administrative remedies.*" Act of June 8, 1995, 74th Leg., R.S., ch. 415, § 1, 1995 Tex. Gen. Laws 3005, 3005 (emphasis added).

Article 21.21-8 was enacted in a separate chapter containing consumer protection provisions. The caption reads that the act relates "to *civil remedies* for deceptive, unfair, or discriminatory practices." Act of June 8, 1995, 74th Leg., ch. 414, § 18, 1995 Tex. Gen. Laws 2988, 3003 (emphasis added). We are also mindful of our holding that the definitions of "unfair discrimination" in the two provisions are not interchangeable. *See Cortez v. Progressive County Mut. Ins. Co.,* 61 S.W.3d 68, 73 (Tex.App.-Austin 2001) ("[W]hile article 21.21-6 prohibits discrimination based on differential treatment of members of *different classes,* article 21.21-8 prohibits discrimination based on differential treatment between individual members *within the same class.*"). Accordingly, we hold that Perez may not bring a private cause of action under article 21.21-6 by way of article 21.21-8.

Perez also asserts that he may bring a cause of action under article 21.21-6 through the DTPA laundry list. Blue Cross does not contend that the DTPA has no application, only that Perez has no claim under the DTPA because he is not a consumer. A consumer under the DTPA is a person who seeks or acquires goods or services by purchase or lease. *See* Tex. Bus. & Com.Code Ann. § 17.45(4) (West 2002). However, because the record does not demonstrate that Blue Cross presented this argument to the trial court, it is waived for purposes of appeal.

Assuming without deciding that the DTPA does apply, there was no evidence of a DTPA violation: Perez argues that Blue Cross's discrimination violated an "unlisted practice" in the DTPA laundry list. The supreme court has held, however, that although the laundry list is not exclusive for DTPA purposes, it is exclusive for deceptive trade practices claims through article 21.21 of the insurance code. *Watson,* 876 S.W.2d at 149. More importantly, Perez's petition referred specifically and only to section 17.46(b)(12) of the laundry list, which requires evidence of "representing that an agreement confers or involves rights, remedies, or obligations which it does not have or involve, or which are prohibited by law." Tex. Bus. & Com.Code Ann. § 17.46(b)(12).

There is no evidence that Blue Cross made any such representations. In the application for health insurance, Blue Cross made no promise that it would provide coverage. It instead declared that "This application does not provide coverage of any kind unless approval is provided by Blue Cross and Blue Shield of Texas, Inc." Having found that Perez cannot bring a private cause of action under article 21.21-6 by way of article 21.21-8 and did not present evidence of a DTPA violation, we need not address Blue Cross's contention that it established its affirmative defense as to Perez's article 21.21-6 claim. We overrule Perez's third issue.

Cause of Action under Article 21.21-8 of the Insurance Code

In his second issue, Perez contends he has a valid cause of action under article 21.21-8. This provision states that "[n]o person shall engage in any unfair discrimination by making or permitting any unfair discrimination between individuals of the same class and of essentially the same hazard." Tex. Ins. Code Ann. art. 21.21-8, § 2. Perez argues that because the relevant class is either "the average person" or "all twelve-year-old boys," Blue Cross engaged in unfair discrimination by refusing to insure someone within the class who has Down Syndrome. Blue Cross counters that Perez may not maintain an action under article 21.21-8 because he did not satisfy the statutory requirement of sustaining economic damages. *See id.* § 3(a). Blue Cross, however, did not raise this argument in the trial court; therefore, we may not consider it.

Blue Cross further contends that refusal to insure does not constitute unfair discrimination under article 21.21-8 because section two of the provision does not include the phrase "refusing to insure." *See id.* § 2. However, under section four, entitled "Affirmative Defenses," an insurance company is not in violation of section two if a "refusal to insure," among other actions, "is based upon sound actuarial principles." *Id.* § 4. Thus, reading sections two and four together, as we must, article 21.21-8 prohibits an insurance company's refusal to insure one person of the "same class and of essentially the same hazard" as another person who receives coverage.

Blue Cross next contends that, because only persons with Down Syndrome constitute "individuals of the same class and of essentially the same hazard," it did not unfairly discriminate in declining to insure all persons within that class. Blue Cross argues in the alternative that it proved as a matter of law that its refusal to insure was based on "sound actuarial principles," an affirmative defense to a claim under article 21.21-8. *Id.* Even assuming that the relevant class is either "the average person" or "all twelve-year-old boys," as Perez proposes, Blue Cross's conduct did not constitute unfair discrimination under article 21.21-8. Unfair discrimination occurs when an insurance company treats a person differently, without justification, than another person not only of the same class but also "*of essentially the same hazard.*" *Id.* § 2 (emphasis added).

Here, both sides presented evidence that a person with Down Syndrome is not of essentially the same hazard as a person without the disability. The affidavit of Golder Wilson, M.D., Perez's medical expert, alone establishes that persons with Down Syndrome have up to a fifty percent incidence of heart problems, seventy percent incidence of vision and hearing deficits, and ninety percent incidence of periodontal disease. He further stated that "over 50 percent of individuals with Down Syndrome have medically uneventful lives," which implies that a large percentage has increased medical risks. The affidavit of Benjamin Carnovale, M.D., Blue Cross's medical expert, establishes that people with Down Syndrome "frequently have a lowered resistance to infection," "are at greater risk from autoimmune diseases," and are more likely to suffer seizures than people without Down Syndrome. With those statistics, we cannot say that a person with Down Syndrome is of essentially the same hazard as a person without the disability.

Therefore, we conclude that Blue Cross's refusal to insure Perez because he has Down Syndrome did not constitute unfair discrimination under article 21.21-8 between individuals of the same class and essentially the same hazard. If the relevant class is all persons, both parties presented sufficient proof that persons with Down Syndrome have greater medical risks than the average person and therefore are not of the same hazard as the average person. If the relevant class is all persons with Down Syndrome, then Blue Cross did not unfairly discriminate because it treated all persons within that class and hazard in the same manner.

We overrule Perez's second issue. In light of our disposition of Perez's second and third issues concerning his causes of action under articles 21.21-6 and 21.21-8, we need not address whether Blue Cross's denial of coverage was based on sound actuarial principles. We affirm the order of the district court granting Blue Cross's motion for summary judgment and denying Perez's motions for summary judgment.

CONCLUSION

Perez's claims are not moot simply because he has since obtained health insurance from another insurance company. He retains a legally cognizable interest, at the least, in his claim for injunctive relief that Blue Cross discontinue the practice of declining to insure people with Down Syndrome. Further, we do not find that the district court abused its discretion in admitting the affidavit of Blue Cross's actuarial expert witness. Although the expert relied generally, in part, on "additional materials provided to me by counsel," he tied each of his opinions to specific documents. We cannot say that the specific documents on which he relied were not of the type reasonably relied upon by experts in his field.

Perez may not maintain a cause of action under article 21.21-6 of the insurance code because (i) the statute provides only for a public remedy; (ii) the statute does not tie in with article 21.21-8 to create a private right of action; and (iii) Perez did not present sufficient proof of a cause of action under the DTPA laundry list by way of article 21.21-6. *See* Tex. Ins. Code Ann. arts. 21.21-6, 8; Tex. Bus. & Com.Code Ann. § 17.46(b).

Perez additionally may not maintain a cause of action under article 21.21-8 because Blue Cross's policy of declining to insure all persons with Down Syndrome does not unfairly discriminate between persons of the same class and of essentially the same hazard. *See* Tex. Ins. Code Ann. art. 21.21-8, § 2. For these reasons, we affirm the order of the district court granting Blue Cross's motion for summary judgment and denying Perez's motions for summary judgment.

NOTES & QUESTIONS

1) In *Perez*, the Court of Appeals ruled against the child, concluding that the "denial of health insurance coverage was justified because it was based on sound underwriting or actuarial principles reasonably related to actual or anticipated loss experience." Is this convincing? May the same insurer discriminate against racial minorities—who are more likely to have severe hypertension—and escape liability under the DTPA's "laundry list" and Texas Insurance Code?

2) Even more significant, the court concluded that "Perez did not present sufficient proof of a cause of action under the DTPA laundry list by way of article 21.21-6." The child's mother asked the insurer to insure Perez under "an individual Blue Cross health insurance policy." Would the outcome in *Perez* be different if Perez had sought insurance coverage under a "group policy?"

3) Does the DTPA prevent insurers from discriminating against members of a group who apply for or have medical benefits under a group health insurance contract? See *Forbau v. Aetna Life Ins. Co.* 876 S.W.2d 132, 134 (Tex. 1994) (concluding that a DTPA violation occurred under a group health insurance contract).

Chapter Four:
Establishing DTPA Causes of Action Under Other Tie-In Statutes

Very often, a legislature enacts a statute and gives only the attorney general of the state or a commissioner the right to enforce the statute. However, as we have discovered, the Texas attorney general as well as consumers, has a right to enforce the DTPA.

But the DTPA has an added feature. To repeat, § 17.50(h) gives consumers the right to commence a DTPA-related cause of action if another statute creates a private right of action for those same consumers. Both the DTPA and "tie-in statutes" expressly identify and prohibit "false, misleading or deceptive acts or practices." In many instances, when one compares the list of prohibitive acts in the § 17.46(b) "laundry list" with the "laundry lists" appearing in several tie-in statutes, one finds that the lists are fairly similar. Actually, barring a few instances, the words and phrases in the tie-in statues and in § 17.46(b) are somewhat redundant.

Given the large number of tie-in statutes and cases, a thorough discussion of each will not appear in this chapter. Instead, only three cases are discussed. However, those cases illustrate some of the major procedural and substantive questions that have evolved when consumers file mixed-claims and mixed-causes lawsuits involving the DTPA and one or several tie-in statutes.

A. DTPA Action and Texas Debt Collection Act

GreenPoint Credit Corporation v. Perez
75 S.W.3d 40
(Tex. App.-San Antonio. 2002)

This unfair debt collections act case involves an illegal threat by a finance company to put an elderly woman in jail for a debt that she did not owe, on a mobile home she did not own. A jury awarded substantial actual and punitive damages. The case comes to this court principally on the excessiveness of actual damages, and the absence of the predicate requirements necessary to impose damages against the corporation, as opposed to the overzealous employee.

The case began when an employee of the finance company, GreenPoint Credit Corp. (GreenPoint), made a demanding phone call to Ninfa Perez (Mrs. Perez). The substance of the phone call was that Mrs. Perez was woefully behind on her mobile home payments and that she must pay up or face the consequences. The call was not only disturbing to Mrs. Perez, it was also mystifying. She owned no mobile home and had no idea what the representative was talking about. Her attempts to explain this to the representative fell on deaf ears. He gave her the company's phone number and told her to pay the bill. Mrs. Perez was at a substantial disadvantage in this and subsequent dealings with GreenPoint. She was 72 years old, did not speak or understand English, and had a medical history of anxiety disorders. She had lived in the same house all her life, and her sole source of income was a modest monthly Social Security check. She had a daughter, Zulema Torres (Torres), who lived across the street and cared for her mother. Mrs. Perez did not own a mobile home, and there was no evidence she had ever owned one.

GreenPoint's records, however, indicated Mrs. Perez was the buyer and borrower on a mobile home in which GreenPoint provided financing. Much later it became clear what the problem was. It turned out that Mrs. Perez's granddaughter, Melissa Perez, negotiated the purchase of the mobile home by fraudulently providing the seller with her grandmother's financial information and forging her signature. This was unknown to either party at the time, and is not critical to the appeal. All parties now agree that Mrs. Perez did not purchase the mobile home.

The day after Mrs. Perez received the initial mystifying call, the GreenPoint representative again telephoned Mrs. Perez and demanded payment on the mobile home. Mrs. Perez again denied having purchased the mobile home and informed the representative that she had not sent in any payments. Mrs. Perez testified that the representative then became rude and began using obscene language. She said that the representative then told her that if she did not send in a payment that day, a sheriff's deputy was going to come and put her in jail that afternoon, at 2 p.m. This about did Mrs. Perez in. When Torres went to see her mother later that day, she found her distraught and crying. Mrs. Perez asked Torres to take her to see the Duval County Sheriff, Santiago Barrera, Jr. ("Barrera"), because she was going to be put in jail, and apparently was ready to turn herself in.

Torres then drove her mother to the Sheriff's office. Mrs. Perez told Barrera about the call from GreenPoint and their threat to put her in jail. Barrera testified that Mrs. Perez was crying and extremely upset. He tried to calm her down and assured her that he was not going to put her in jail. The Sheriff then called GreenPoint himself and told them that they had the wrong person. He informed GreenPoint that Mrs. Perez owned no mobile home and that Mrs. Perez's signature did not match the one on the document. The Sheriff's words also fell on deaf ears. GreenPoint's representative continued to insist that Mrs. Perez owed the money.

Approximately two weeks later, GreenPoint sent a field representative to Mrs. Perez's home to investigate the case. The representative completed a Field Contact Form in which he stated that Mrs. Perez continued to deny having signed any contract and that Mrs. Perez provided him with an ID and a social security card. The representative also obtained a handwritten affidavit from Mrs.

Perez, signed and notarized, in which she swore that she had never signed any documents for the purchase of a mobile home, and never consented for anyone else to provide her personal information for such. Despite the evidence that they had the wrong person, GreenPoint sued anyway.

GreenPoint filed suit against Mrs. Perez and her granddaughter, Melissa Perez, asserting causes of action for conversion, judicial foreclosure, payment of indebtedness, and attorney's fees. Melissa Perez never answered, and the trial court rendered a default judgment against her. Mrs. Perez generally denied GreenPoint's allegations and filed a counterclaim against GreenPoint. She asserted causes of action for violations of the Texas Debt Collection Act, [Tex. Fin.Code Ann. §§ 392.001-.404] and the Deceptive Trade Practices Act, intentional infliction of emotional distress, and negligence. She also alleged that GreenPoint acted with malice entitling her to exemplary damages.

The case was bifurcated and tried to a jury. GreenPoint eventually abandoned its claims against Mrs. Perez, and the case was submitted to the jury on Mrs. Perez's counterclaims under the Debt Collection Act. After the first phase of the trial, the jury found the following: (1) GreenPoint's unreasonable collection efforts were a producing cause of injury to Mrs. Perez; (2) GreenPoint engaged in such unreasonable collection efforts knowingly and intentionally; (3) Mrs. Perez sustained $3,000,000 in damages in the past and would sustain $2,000,000 in damages in the future; (4) the injury to Mrs. Perez resulted from malice by GreenPoint; (5) a vice-principal of GreenPoint intentionally or knowingly caused serious mental deficiency, impairment, or injury to an elderly person; and (6) the actions of GreenPoint did not result from a bona fide error that occurred notwithstanding the use of reasonable procedures adopted to avoid such error.

After the second phase of the trial, the jury assessed $10,000,000 in exemplary damages against GreenPoint for the injuries caused to Perez. The trial court rendered judgment on the verdict over GreenPoint's motion for judgment notwithstanding the verdict. GreenPoint filed a motion for new trial based on juror disqualification / misconduct and improper arguments of opposing counsel. The trial court held an evidentiary hearing on the motion. The trial court never ruled on the motion, and it was overruled by operation of law.

GreenPoint raises four issues on appeal, arguing: (1) the jury's award of actual damages is excessive; (2) the evidence is legally and factually insufficient to support the jury's award of exemplary damages; (3) the trial court erred in not granting a new trial based on juror disqualification and/or juror misconduct; and (4) the trial court erred in not granting a new trial based on improper and incurable comments made by Perez's counsel regarding GreenPoint's net worth. We affirm in part and reverse in part the trial court's judgment.

Discussion

A. Actual Damages

"A claim that damages are excessive is reviewed under a factual sufficiency analysis." *Southwest Tex. Coors, Inc. v. Morales,* 948 S.W.2d 948, 951 (Tex.App.-San Antonio 1997, no writ). "We examine all the evidence to determine whether the award is supported by sufficient evidence and order remittitur only if the award is so against the great weight and preponderance of the evidence as to be manifestly unjust." *Id.* If sufficient probative evidence exists supporting the jury's verdict, the reviewing court is not entitled to substitute its judgment for that of the jury. *J. Wigglesworth Co. v. Peeples,* 985 S.W.2d 659, 666 (Tex. App.-Fort Worth 1999, pet. denied). It is particularly within the province of the jury to resolve matters which are necessarily speculative and not subject to precise mathematical calculations such as physical pain and mental anguish. *Morales,* 948 S.W.2d at 952. "Because personal injury damages are unliquidated and incapable of measurement by any certain standard, the jury has broad discretion in fixing the amount of the award." *Peeples,* 985 S.W.2d at 665.

"When a damage issue is submitted in broad form, ascertaining the amount the jury awarded for each element of damages is difficult, if not impossible." *Wal-Mart Stores, Inc. v. Garcia* 30 S.W.3d 19, 24 (Tex. App.-San Antonio 2000, no pet.). "An appellant who seeks to challenge a multi-element damage award on appeal must address each element and show the evidence is insufficient to support the entire award." *Id.* "If there is just one element that is supported by the evidence, the damages award will be affirmed if it is supported by the evidence." *Greater Houston Trans. Co. v. Zrubeck,* 850 S.W.2d 579, 589 (Tex.App.-Corpus Christi 1993, writ denied).

GreenPoint challenges the compensatory damages as being excessive, with no or insufficient evidence to support them. The compensatory damage issue was asked in the broad form, with the elements of physical pain, mental anguish, medical care and disfigurement listed. The only separation of the damages was as to past and future. The jury awarded $3,000,000 for past damages and $2,000,000 for future damages.

As any element submitted to the jury could support the verdict if there was sufficient evidence underpinning it, the appellant's burden of overturning the verdict has been termed "extremely difficult." *See id.* The evidence supporting the damages, and their reasonable inferences, are as follows:

1. This was an extraordinarily traumatic event for Mrs. Perez. Handicapped by advancing age, a demonstrated history of anxiety and nervousness, inability to understand the language, culturally insulated, and uneducated, she had few protection mechanisms available to counter the unexpected threats.

2. The threat of being put in jail is calculated to put fear and anxiety into every citizen's heart. It is the very tool used by our justice system to control bad behavior in our society. Even a hardened criminal may think twice before doing something that will cause him to be locked away from society. If a criminal may be frightened by jail, how much more mental and physical anguish would be suffered by a woman in the position of Mrs. Perez? Compound this with the uncontradicted testimony that she did not even understand what fault she had committed. Mrs. Perez found herself in a truly kafkaesque world, where her reputation and peaceful old age were in immediate jeopardy.

3. The evidence showed that Mrs. Perez was so distraught that she sought out Sheriff Barrera, who testified she was crying and extremely upset. An old woman, with a good reputation, might well prefer a voluntary surrender to a peace officer in preference to being arrested in her own neighborhood, with the attendant disgrace to herself and her family that also lives in the neighborhood.

4. Physical evidence of Mrs. Perez's injuries were also before the jury. Graphic photographs of eruptions of her skin and disfiguring, angry running sores were evidence of the turmoil within. There was also evidence of heart palpitations, shortness of breath, nausea, sleeplessness, panic attacks, difficulty in concentrating, irritability, reclusiveness and elevated blood pressure which caused the doctor to prescribe various medications.

5. Her physician, Dr. Reynolds, said that these medical problems resulted from her "problems and hassles" with GreenPoint.

6. As the problems were still continuing at the time of the trial, the jury could have reasonably inferred that they would extend into the future.

Dr. Reynold's testified that he treated Mrs. Perez for a number of ailments including the shingles and a stress related psychological condition. He testified that both her physical and emotional problems were caused by stress resulting from Mrs. Perez's problems with GreenPoint. In addition, he corroborated Mrs. Perez's testimony that the sores and blisters on her body were extremely painful. Through an interpreter, Mrs. Perez testified as to the painful sores on her body, her embarrassment, anxiety, and emotional pain resulting from GreenPoint's threat to put her in jail. Torres, Mrs. Perez's daughter, also testified about her mother's mental anguish. She testified that Mrs. Perez now has trouble sleeping at night. On several occasions, Torres has had to spend the night with her mother. She testified that she never had to do this before the threatening call from GreenPoint. Torres also testified that her mother is reluctant to leave the house and is embarrassed to be seen by her neighbors.

The evidence regarding damages is not so against the great weight and preponderance of the evidence to be manifestly unjust. *See Morales,* 948 S.W.2d at 951. Enough probative evidence exists supporting the jury's award that we will not substitute our judgment for that of the jury. *See Peeples,* 985 S.W.2d at 666. It is impossible to put an exact dollar amount on the amount of damages GreenPoint's threat caused Mrs. Perez. As such, it was within the province of the jury to resolve this matter. *See Morales,* 948 S.W.2d at 952. The jury had the broad discretion to determine the proper amount of compensation. *See Peeples,* 985 S.W.2d at 665. Because we find there is evidence to support the jury's damage award, we overrule GreenPoint's first point of error. *See Zrubeck,* 850 S.W.2d at 589.

B. Exemplary Damages

As with actual damages, an appellate court may reverse an exemplary damage award only if the evidence supporting the award is so against the great weight and preponderance of the evidence as to be manifestly unjust. *Lubbock County v. Strube,* 953 S.W.2d 847, 860 (Tex.App.-Austin 1997, pet. denied). An award of exemplary damages is governed by Chapter 41 of the Texas Civil Practice and Remedies Code. Tex. Civ. Prac. & Rem. Code Ann. § 41.002(a) (Vernon 1997). Accordingly, a claimant seeking exemplary damages must prove by clear and convincing evidence that the harm from which the claimant seeks exemplary damages resulted from fraud or malice on the part of the defendant. *Id.* § 41.003(a). The Chapter provides for a bifurcated trial upon the motion of a defendant. *Id.* § 41.0009(a).

With respect to a corporation, exemplary damages "are warranted only when the act is that of the corporation rather than the act of its 'ordinary servants or agents.' " *Hammerly Oaks, Inc. v. Edwards,* 958 S.W.2d 387, 391 (Tex.1997). "Thus, a corporation's liability for punitive damages is placed on very different grounds than respondeat superior." *Id.* Exemplary damages can properly be awarded against a corporation because of an act by an agent only if the court finds one of the following: (1) the principal authorized the doing and the manner of the act; (2) the agent was unfit and the principal was reckless in employing him; (3) the agent was employed in a managerial capacity and was acting in the scope of employment; or (4) the employer or a manager of the employer ratified or approved the act. *Id.*

GreenPoint asserts that Mrs. Perez failed to present evidence demonstrating that the conduct complained of was attributable to the corporation. Mrs. Perez contends that the evidence supports the jury's award of exemplary damages. She argues that because a violation of the Texas Debt Collection Act is also actionable as a DTPA violation, the jury's award is proper under the DTPA's provision for discretionary trebling of actual damages.

Mrs. Perez presented no evidence with respect to any of the four bases for imposing exemplary damages against a corporation. The record contains no evidence that GreenPoint authorized the representative who called Mrs. Perez to threaten her with jail. Mrs. Perez did not present any evidence that the representative was unfit and that GreenPoint was reckless in employing the representative. No evidence exists that GreenPoint's representative was employed in a managerial capacity. Finally, Mrs. Perez presented no evidence that GreenPoint ratified or approved the representative's threat of jail. The only evidence with respect to any of these factors was presented by GreenPoint. Kelly Sanchez testified on behalf of GreenPoint and stated that company policy forbids threatening a person with jail, and that doing so would be grounds for immediate termination of that employee. As a result, exemplary damages were not warranted against GreenPoint because the wrongful act was that of its agent and not the corporation itself. *See id.*

Mrs. Perez's argument that the exemplary damage award is proper as additional damages under the DTPA lacks merit. Although a violation of the Texas Debt Collection Act is a deceptive trade practice actionable under the DTPA, neither the evidence presented at trial nor the two jury charges indicate that Mrs. Perez sought recovery under that statute. *See* Tex. Fin. Code Ann. § 392.404(a). Furthermore, it is clear from the jury charge at both stages of the trial that the jury was to consider exemplary damages, not additional damages under the DTPA. Neither charge includes any questions relating to additional damages under the DTPA. We sustain GreenPoint's second point of error and reverse the award of exemplary damages.

* * *

Conclusion

The portion of the trial court's judgment awarding $10,000,000 in exemplary damages is reversed, and judgment is rendered that Mrs. Perez is not entitled to recover any exemplary damages. In all other respects, the judgment of the trial court is affirmed.

NOTES & QUESTIONS

1) The Texas Debt Collection Act—Tex. Fin. Code Ann. §§ 392.404(a)(b) read:

(a) A violation of this chapter is a deceptive trade practice under Subchapter E, Chapter 17, Business & Commerce Code, and is actionable under that subchapter.

(b) This chapter does not affect or alter a remedy at law or in equity otherwise available to a debtor, creditor, governmental entity, or other legal entity.

2) In *GreenPoint*, the court concluded: "Although a violation of the Texas Debt Collection Act is a deceptive trade practice actionable under the DTPA, neither the evidence presented at trial nor the two jury charges indicate that Mrs. Perez sought recovery under that statute." In light of the language in Tex. Fin. Code Ann. § 392.404(a), must an aggrieved debtor/borrower actually plead that a creditor violated the Texas Debt Collection Act? Or is it sufficient to plead that the creditor's debt-collection activities violated the DTPA?

3) Proof of actual damages is a burden that plaintiff must overcome to prevail under the DTPA—Tex. Bus. & Com. Code § 17.50(a); Texas Debt Collection Act—Tex. Fin. Code § 392.403(a)(2) ; and the Federal Fair Debt Collection Act—15 U.S.C. § 1692 *k* (a)(1).

4) Courts have declared that DTPA and Debt Collection Act causes of action fall within the scope of arbitration agreements. See *Jack B. Anglin Co., Inc. v. Tipps,* 842 S.W.2d 266, 270-71 (Tex.1992) (concluding that a DTPA claim was subject to arbitration, since the Federal Arbitration Act preempts DTPA's non-waiver provisions), and *In re Conseco Finance Servicing Corp.,* 19 S.W.3d 562, 570-71 (Tex. App.-Waco 2000, orig. proceeding) (concluding that the Debt Collection Act and DTPA claims were subject to arbitration, as they arose from or related to the contract).

5) Which act is superior? Do provisions under the DTPA preempt provisions under the "tie-in statutes?" Or does the latter preempt DTPA provisions? The next case should provide some insight and answers.

B. DTPA Action and Texas Residential Construction Liability Act

Gentry v. Squires Construction, Inc.
188 S.W.3d 396
(Tex. App.--Dallas 2006)

Randy and Barbara Gentry appeal the trial court's judgment in favor of Squires Construction, Inc. and against the Gentrys on their counter-claims against Squires Construction and third-party claims against Lewis Almon Squires. The trial court awarded Squires Construction its reasonable costs for labor and materials under the theory of *quantum meruit* in the amount of $16,134 and ordered each party to bear its own costs and attorneys' fees.

The Gentrys raise [these] . . . points: 1) the trial court erred when it concluded Squires Construction was entitled to be paid for work done under the theory of *quantum merit*, . . 2) the Gentrys claims were preempted by the Texas Residential Construction Liability Act (RCLA), and the Gentrys were not entitled to attorneys' fees. . . . Squires Construction cross-appealed. In Squires Construction's sole issue, it argues the trial court erred when it concluded that it was not entitled to attorneys' fees.

We conclude the trial court did not err when it concluded Squires Construction was entitled to be paid for work done under the theory of quantum meruit and the Gentrys were not entitled to attorneys' fees. However, the trial court erred when it concluded the Gentrys' claims were preempted by the RCLA and Squires Construction was not entitled to attorneys' fees . . .

FACTUAL AND PROCEDURAL BACKGROUND

The Gentrys contacted Squires Construction about building a house. The Gentrys showed Squires Construction a photograph of what they wanted their new home to look like, but they did not have any blueprints. Squires Construction told the Gentrys it could build the home based on its own drawings because the Gentrys wanted to save money. Then, the Gentrys entered into a written contract with Squires Construction. Under the contract, the Gentrys were going to purchase several items and do some of the work themselves. The parties agreed that Squires Construction would be paid through the lender by submitting draw requests.

When Squires Construction made its final draw request to the lender, the Gentrys refused the payment. The Gentrys complained of numerous construction defects, including the first floor of their home was built with eight foot ceilings instead of ten foot ceilings as called for by the building plans, problems with the front porch, and leaking windows that were not caulked.

Squires Construction sued the Gentrys for breach of contract and foreclosure of the lien, or in the alternative quantum meruit. The Gentrys filed counter-claims against Squires Construction and third-party claims against Squires alleging breach of contract, breach of implied warranty, violations of the DTPA, and fraud, or in the alternative seeking rescission of the contract. After the Gentrys filed their counter- and third-party claims, Squires Construction inspected the property and made a settlement offer, which was rejected.

The case was tried before the court. After the trial, the trial court rendered judgment in favor of Squires Construction under the alternative theory of quantum meruit in the amount of $16,134. All relief requested by the Gentrys was denied. Squires Construction requested findings of fact and conclusions of law and both Squires Construction and the Gentrys filed motions for new trial. The trial court issued findings of fact and conclusions of law and the motions for new trial were overruled by operation of law.

II. CONCLUSIONS OF LAW

[T]he Gentrys argue the trial court erred when it concluded: 1) Squires Construction was entitled to be paid for work done under the theory of quantum merit after finding it did not substantially comply with the contract; 2) their claims against Squires Construction and Squires were preempted by the RCLA; and 3) they were not entitled to attorneys' fees on their breach of contract and fraud claims. In Squires Construction's cross-appeal, it argues the trial court erred when it concluded they were not entitled to attorneys' fees.

* * *

B. Conclusion that Squire Construction Entitled to Recover Under *Quantum Meruit*

In their first and second issues, the Gentrys argue the trial court erred when it concluded Squires Construction was entitled to be paid for work done under the theory of quantum meruit after finding it did not substantially comply with the contract. Squires Construction responds that quantum meruit is a viable cause of action for a construction contractor who has not substantially performed the underlying contract.

1. Applicable Law

Quantum meruit is an equitable theory of recovery based on an implied agreement to pay for benefits received. *Heldenfels Bros., Inc. v. City of Corpus Christi,* 832 S.W.2d 39, 41 (Tex. 1992). Recovery under the theory of *quantum meruit* is prohibited if an express contract covers the services or materials for which the claimant seeks recovery. *Truly v. Austin,* 744 S.W.2d 934, 936 (Tex.1988). However, there is an exception with respect to construction contracts. *See id.* at 937. A contractor may recover the reasonable value of the services rendered and accepted or the materials supplied under the theory of quantum meruit if: 1) the services rendered and accepted are not covered by the contract; 2) the contractor partially performed under the terms of an express contract, but was prohibited from completing the contract because of the owner's breach; or 3) the contractor breached but the owner accepted and retained the benefits of the contractor's partial performance. *See Truly,* 744 S.W.2d at 936-937

2. Application of the Law to the Facts

The Gentrys challenge the trial court's third conclusion of law, which states: [Squires Construction] is entitled to be paid for work done on a quantum meruit basis.

The Gentrys contend the trial court's findings of fact do not support the third conclusion of law. They point to the following findings:

2) [Squires Construction's] proposal to build [the Gentrys'] house (Plaintiff's Exhibit # 1), which was accepted by [the Gentrys], specified "The first floor will have 10′ walls ..."

3) The undisputed testimony is that the first floor has 8 ft [sic] walls.

5) Although the testimony varies as to whether there was an agreement to change to 8 foot walls on the first floor, there is no dispute that no written alteration of the plans was ever executed.

6) [The Gentrys] did not waive the requirement of having 10 foot walls on the first floor.

7) [Squires Construction] did not substantially comply with the contract.

The Gentrys and Squires Construction confuse the application of the doctrine of substantial compliance. It will not normally prohibit the implementation of the theory of *quantum meruit.*[1] Nevertheless we review the trial court's conclusions of law de novo.

---

1 The doctrine of substantial performance is a separate form of equitable relief from quantum meruit. The doctrine of substantial performance allows a contractor who has performed under the contract to sue on the contract. *Dobbins v. Redden,* 785 S.W.2d 377, 378 (Tex.1990) (op. on reh'g, per curiam). A contractor may also assert the doctrine of substantial performance as an affirmative defense to a breach of contract claim. *See Smith v. Smith,* 112 S.W.3d 275, 279 (Tex.App.-Corpus Christi 2003, pet. denied).Substantial performance is a condition precedent to a contractor's right to bring a lawsuit on the contract. *Atkinson v. Jackson Bros.,* 270 S.W. 848, 850 (Tex. Comm'n App.1925, holding appr'd); *TA Operating Corp. v. Solar Applications Eng'g, Inc.,* 191 S.W.3d 173, 2005 WL 2401879, at *3 (Tex.App.-San Antonio Sept.28, 2005, no pet.). The doctrine of substantial performance recognizes the contractor has not completed construction and is in breach of the contract. *See Dobbins,* 785 S.W.2d at 378; *Vance v. My Apartment Steak House of San Antonio, Inc.,* 677 S.W.2d 480, 482 (Tex.1984); *Solar Applications,* at ----, 2005 WL 2401879, at *3; *Patel v. Ambassador Drycleaning Co.,* 86 S.W.3d 304, 306-07 (Tex.App.-Eastland 2002, no pet.). However, the doctrine assumes, if there is substantial performance, the breach is immaterial. *See Atkinson,* 270 S.W. at 851; *Solar Applications,* at ----, 2005 WL 2401879, at *3; *Patel,* 86 S.W.3d at 306-07. Under the doctrine of substantial performance, a contractor may recover the full contract price less the cost of remedying those defects that are remediable. *Vance,* 677 S.W.2d at 481. If the owner counterclaims alleging the contractor is in breach of the construction contract, the owner's measure of damages is the cost of completing the job or of remedying those defects that are remediable. *Weitzul Constr., Inc. v. Outdoor Environs,* 849 S.W.2d 359, 363 (Tex.App.-Dallas 1993, writ denied). However, if the owner has paid only part of the contract price to the contractor, then the amount of the owner's damages is credited against the balance of his payments owed on the contract. *Id.* The contractor bears the burden of proof under the doctrine of substantial performance. *See Vance,* 677 S.W.2d at 482; *Weitzul,* 849 S.W.2d at 363; *Interfirst Bank Dallas, N.A. v. U.S. Fidelity & Guar. Co.,* 774 S.W.2d 391, 402 (Tex.App.-Dallas 1989, writ denied). The contractor must prove: (1) he substantially performed in accordance with the contract; (2) the consideration owed to him under the contract; and (3) the cost of remedying the defects due to his errors or omissions. *See Vance,* 677 S.W.2d at 483; *Weitzul,* 849 S.W.2d at 363.

Although the trial court found that Squires Construction failed to substantially comply with the contract, there was evidence that it partially performed under the contract and the Gentrys accepted and retained the benefits of Squires Construction's partial performance. Accordingly, we conclude the trial court did not err when it concluded Squires Construction was entitled to be paid its costs for labor and materials under the theory of *quantum meruit*.

The Gentrys' first and second issues are decided against them. The trial court's judgment is affirmed, in part, with respect to its third conclusion of law determining that Squires Construction is entitled to be paid for work done on a *quantum meruit* basis.

C. Preemption Under the RCLA

[T]he Gentrys argue the trial court erred when it concluded their claims were preempted by the RCLA. Squires Construction and Squires respond that the trial court did not abuse its discretion because it found they complied with the "reasonable offer" provisions of the RCLA.

1. Applicable Law

The RCLA does not create a cause of action because it does not: 1) provide a complete structure for liability or 2) contain a description of what conduct will result in liability or an express statement of the elements of a cause of action. *See* Tex. Prop.Code Ann. § 27.005 ; *Sanders v. Construction Equity, Inc.,* 42 S.W.3d 364, 370 (Tex.App.-Beaumont 2001, pet. denied). Instead, the RCLA modifies causes of action for damages resulting from construction defects in residences by limiting and controlling causes of action that otherwise exist. *See Sanders,* 42 S.W.3d at 370.

The RCLA provides defenses, limitations on damages, and determines the standard of causation. *See* Tex. Prop.Code Ann. §§ 27.003, 27.004, 27.006 ; *Sanders,* 42 S.W.3d at 370. Also, the RCLA sets forth notice provisions and encourages settlement through its procedures. *See* Tex. Prop.Code Ann. § 27.004; *Sanders,* 42 S.W.3d at 370. However, the RCLA does prevail over any conflict between it and any other law, including the DTPA or a common law cause of action. *See* Tex. Prop.Code Ann. § 27.002; *Sanders,* 42 S.W.3d at 370.The RCLA does not preempt the DTPA. *See Sanders,* 42 S.W.3d at 371; *see also In re Kimball Hill Homes Texas, Inc.,* 969 S.W.2d 522, 526 (Tex.App.-Houston [14th Dist.] 1998, orig. proceeding).

The DTPA is the only cause of action mentioned in the application section of the RCLA. *See* Tex. Prop.Code Ann. § 27.002; *Sanders,* 42 S.W.3d at 371. The DTPA is also mentioned in section 27.004(m), which provides that "[t]he inspection and repair provisions of the RCLA are in addition to any rights of inspection and settlement provided by common law or by another statute, including Section 17.505 [of the DTPA]." *See* Tex. Prop.Code Ann. § 27.004(m); *Sanders,* 42 S.W.3d at 371.

Further, the DTPA provides that the RCLA "prevails over this subchapter to the extent of any conflict." Tex. Bus. & Com. Code Ann. § 17.44(b). *Sanders,* 42 S.W.3d at 371. It is unreasonable to assume the Texas Legislature retained the rights of inspection and settlement under the DTPA, but preempted the liability structure under the DTPA that gives rise to those rights. *Sanders,* 42 S.W.3d at 371.

The RCLA does not preempt and clearly authorizes suits for breach of contract or breach of warranty after the presuit requirements have been completed. *Sanders,* 42 S.W.3d at 372; *see also Kimball,* 969 S.W.2d at 526. The RCLA provides that a residential sales contract must include language that references the RCLA and its notice provisions, inspection and cure requirements, and damage limitations. *See* Tex. Prop. Code Ann. § 27.007. It would be an anomaly for a statute to anticipate that a written contract and warranty would be given to a purchaser, but preempt a claim for breach of contract or breach of warranty. *See Sanders,* 42 S.W.3d at 372.

The RCLA does not preempt a fraud claim. *See Bruce v. Jim Walters Homes,* 943 S.W.2d 121, 123 (Tex. App.-San Antonio 1997, writ denied); *see also Kimball,* 969 S.W.2d at 526. Although the misrepresentations alleged in an action for fraud may be in regard to construction or a construction defect, the wrong sought to be redressed is not the subject of the misrepresentation, but the act of misrepresentation. *See Bruce,* 943 S.W.2d at 123. It is unreasonable to conclude the Texas Legislature denied homeowners the opportunity to seek damages for fraud because it entitled them to recover actual damages for construction defects under the RCLA.

2. Application of the Law to the Facts

The Gentrys' assertion that the trial court erred when it concluded their claims were preempted by the RCLA appears to challenge the trial court's . . . conclusions of law, which state: 1) [The Gentrys] claims under the Deceptive Trade Practices Act are preempted by the Residential Construction Liability Act; [and] 2) Since [the Gentrys] are not entitled to damages other than the cost of repairs, they are not entitled to retain other monies held as a result of the last construction draw.

First, we must determine whether the trial court's conclusions of law are correct as a matter of law. The RCLA does not preempt the DTPA. *See Sanders,* 42 S.W.3d at 371. Therefore, the trial court's first conclusion is incorrect. However, the Gentrys claim the trial court concluded that all of their causes of action were preempted. The trial court's conclusion of law states only that their DTPA claims were preempted. Nevertheless, to the extent the trial court's second conclusion purports to preempt the Gentrys' remaining claims for breach of contract, breach of warranty, and fraud, the RCLA does not preempt those causes of action. *See Sanders,* 42 S.W.3d at 372 (breach of contract and warranty); *Bruce,* 943 S.W.2d at 123 (fraud).

Second, we must determine whether the trial court's findings of fact support the judgment under a different legal theory. Because the trial court determined the DTPA was preempted by the RCLA, it did not try the claims so there are no findings of fact that may support the judgment against the Gentrys as to that cause of action. Accordingly, we conclude the trial court erred when it determined the Gentrys' DTPA claims were preempted.

The Gentrys' third issue is decided in their favor. The trial court's judgment is reversed, in part, as to its conclusion that the Gentrys' counter-and third-party DTPA claims are preempted and the case is remanded for a new trial on the Gentrys' counter- and third-party DTPA claims. Based on our resolution of the Gentrys' third issue, we need not address their seventh and eighth issues that claim the trial court erred when it failed to award them recovery under the DTPA or their fourteenth issue that claims the trial court erred when it failed to award them attorneys' fees based on their DTPA claims.

* * *

V. CONCLUSION

The trial court did not err when it concluded Squires Construction was entitled to be paid for work done under the theory of *quantum meruit* . . . but erred when it concluded the Gentrys' claims were preempted by the RCLA . . . . The evidence is legally and factually sufficient to support the trial court's findings of fact. . . . The trial court's judgment is affirmed, in part, and reversed and remanded, in part, for a trial on the Gentrys' DTPA claims . . . .

NOTES & QUESTIONS

---

1) For obvious reasons, the Texas Residential Construction Liability Act (RCLA)—Tex. Prop. Code Ann. § 27.001 *et seq.*—is a major DTPA "tie-in statute." The RCLA applies to "any action to recover damages or other relief arising from a construction defect, except a claim for personal injury, survival, or wrongful death or for damage to goods." Tex. Prop.Code Ann. § 27.002(a)(1).

2) The RCLA contains various notice and settlement-offer requirements that must precede such actions. *Id.* § 27.004. The substance of these requirements varies depending on whether the particular residential construction dispute involves state-sponsored inspection issues and whether there is a dispute-resolution process under the Residential Construction Commission Act (RCCA) —Title 16 of the Texas Property Code. Tex. Prop. Code Ann. §§ 401.001-430.011. State-sponsored inspection and dispute resolution procedures may be found under Subtitle D of the RCCA. *Id.* §§ 426.001-430.011.

C. *DTPA Action and Texas Health Spa Act*

DiGangi v. 24 Hour Fitness USA, Inc.
2005 WL 1367945
(Tex. App. — Dallas, 2005)

Jeffrey Michael DiGangi was injured while using a fitness machine manufactured by Bodymaster's at 24 Hour Fitness USA, Inc. According to DiGangi, he was using the machine correctly when the cable broke, allowing a bar to hit him in the head and mouth. DiGangi brought suit against 24 Hour, claiming negligence as well as breach of warranty and misrepresentation under the Deceptive Trade Practices-Consumer Protection Act (DTPA) and the Health Spa Act. The trial court granted summary judgment for 24 Hour. On appeal, DiGangi only asserts that the trial court erred in entering summary judgment based on his claim under the DTPA and Health Spa Act. We affirm the trial court's judgment.

BACKGROUND

In his original petition, DiGangi alleged that 24 Hour had violated the DTPA by committing the following misleading acts:

(1) causing confusion or misunderstanding as to the source, sponsorship, approval, or certification of goods or services;
(2) causing confusion or misunderstanding as to affiliation, connection, or association with, or certification by, another;
(3) representing that goods or services have sponsorship, approval, characteristics, ingredients, uses, benefits, or quantities, which they do not have, or that a person has sponsorship, approval, status, affiliation, or connection, which he or she does not;
(4) advertising goods or services with intent not to sell them as advertised;
(5) representing that an agreement confers or involves rights, remedies, or obligations, which it does not have or involve, or which are prohibited by law;
(6) representing that work or services have been performed on, or parts replaced in, goods when the work or services were not performed or the parts replaced; and
(7) failing to disclose information concerning goods or services which was known at the time of the transaction with the intention to induce the consumer into a transaction into which the consumer would not have entered had the information been disclosed. Tex. Bus. & Com. Code Ann. § 17.46

DiGangi likewise alleged violations of the Health Spa Act — Tex. Occ. Code Ann. § 702. He specifically alleged that 24 Hour had made material misrepresentations regarding the availability, quality, or extent of the facilities or services of the health spa. *See* Tex. Occ. Code A nn. § 702.402 (Vernon 2004). DiGangi asked for damages for medical care and expenses, physical pain and suffering, physical impairment, loss of earnings, loss of earning capacity, disfigurement, mental anguish, and cost of medical monitoring and prevention.

In its motion for summary judgment, 24 Hour argued that DiGangi had no viable cause of action. Specifically, 24 Hour asserted that DiGangi's personal injury claims are not within the purview of the current provisions of the DTPA.

In his response, DiGangi argued that the DTPA is applicable in his case. According to DiGangi, the DTPA allows consumers to recover their economic damages resulting from a bodily injury when those damages are based upon a breach of warranty or a misrepresentation. His sworn affidavit stated that he had joined 24 Hour before it opened for business and before much of the equipment had been delivered based on the representations that 24 Hour would have "top of the line" and "state of the art" exercise equipment and that the facility would provide "excellent, prompt, and complete customer service."

Because this equipment was in the care, custody, and control of 24 Hour, DiGangi argued that there is a compelling need for the imposition of an implied warranty that the services provided by 24 Hour are safe for the club member. He attached the club membership agreement, which reflects DiGangi (1) voluntarily accepted risk of injury, (2) agreed that 24 Hour would not be liable for any injury, including bodily injury or economic loss, as a result of negligence on 24 Hour's part, (3) acknowledged that 24 Hour did not manufacture any of its equipment and that 24 Hour leased or purchased its equipment from third parties, (4) acknowledged that 24 Hour provides recreational services, and (5) acknowledged that 24 Hour could not be held liable for defective products.

DiGangi further argued that the Health Spa Act, which prohibits a material misrepresentation to a member regarding the quality or extent of the facilities, constitutes a DTPA "tie-in" statute that allows recovery of all actual damages. Each party basically reiterates its summary judgment argument on appeal. Because we agree that DiGangi had no viable cause of action under the DTPA, we conclude that the trial court was correct in granting summary judgment in favor of 24 Hour.

* * *

DISCUSSION

The Exceptions

In 1995, the 74th Texas Legislature revised the DTPA to include the following provision: "Except as specifically provided by Subsections (b) and (h), Section 17.50, nothing in this subchapter shall apply to a cause of action for bodily injury or death or for the infliction of mental anguish." Tex. Bus. & Com. Code Ann. § 17.49(e). DiGangi urges that he may rely on these exceptions to proceed on his claim for bodily injury. The plain meaning of the statute is clearly contrary to his argument. *See Fitzgerald v. Advanced Spine Fixation Sys., Inc.*, 996 S.W.2d 864, 865 (Tex. 1999) (if the statute's language is clear and unambiguous, the Courts adopt the interpretation that the statute's words support).

Economic damages normally include compensatory damages for pecuniary loss, including costs of repair and replacement but not exemplary damages or damages for physical pain and mental anguish, loss of consortium, disfigurement, physical impairment, or loss of companionship and society. Tex. Bus. & Com. Code Ann. § 17.45(11). Section 17.50(b) allows a consumer to recover any economic damages to which he is entitled under the DTPA, plus damages for mental anguish if the violation of the DTPA was committed knowingly or intentionally. Tex. Bus. & Com. Code Ann. § 17.50(b). Thus, a consumer may add on mental anguish damages if he is first entitled to economic damages under the DTPA. As we discuss below, DiGangi is not entitled to any damages under the DTPA.

Section 17.50(h) allows a consumer to bring a cause of action under the DTPA if he is granted that right by another law. Tex. Bus. & Com. Code Ann. § 17.50(h). DiGangi asserts that the Health Spa Act grants him that right. The Health Spa Act is designed to protect the public against unfair practices involving health spa contracts and the marketing of health spa services. Tex. Occ. Code Ann. § 702.002(a). There is nothing within the language of the statute affording a right of action for bodily injury. We cannot conclude that the Health Spa Act is a tie-in statute allowing DiGangi to recover damages for personal injury under the DTPA.

Warranty

DiGangi cites the provision allowing a consumer to recover under the DTPA for a breach of an implied warranty that is a producing cause of economic damages or mental anguish. Tex. Bus. & Com. Code Ann. § 17.50(a). So that he can apply this provision to his case, he argues for the imposition of an implied service warranty that the equipment had been inspected, had been maintained, and was safe for spa members.

Although the DTPA prohibits the breach of an implied warranty, it does not create an implied warranty. Tex. Bus. & Com.Code Ann. § 17.50(a). Unlike the implied warranties imposed on certain sales transactions under the Uniform Commercial Code, an implied service warranty arises under the common law when public policy mandates. *Melody Home Mfg. Co. v. Barnes,* 741 S.W.2d 349, 353 (Tex.1987). An implied warranty will not be judicially imposed unless there is a compelling need; that is, there are no other adequate remedies available to the consumer. *Parkway Co. v. Woodruff,* 901 S.W.2d 434, 438-39 (Tex.1995).

In this case, even if we assume that all allegations and facts in DiGangi's pleadings are true and indulge all inferences in his pleadings in the light most favorable to him, there is nothing to indicate that poor maintenance caused DiGangi's accident or that 24 Hour was responsible for that maintenance. And DiGangi has not show a compelling need for the judicial imposition of such an implied warranty. We overrule this issue.

CONCLUSION

Having overruled DiGangi's sole issue, we affirm the judgment of the trial court.

Chapter Five: DTPA Violations and Proof of Causation

Proof of causation is essential for recovery under all causes of action. For example, to establish a *prima facie* case of negligence, one must prove cause in fact and proximate cause if one expects to win. *See, Brown v. Edwards Transfer Co.,* 764 S.W.2d 220, 223 (Tex. 1988).

To prevail under a DTPA cause of action, a plaintiff must also prove causation. But there is a different rule: A plaintiff must prove that the defendant's misrepresentation, unconscionable action or another violation was the producing cause of the plaintiff's injuries and damages. TEX. BUS. & COM. CODE ANN. § 17.50(a). See also *Alexander v. Turtur & Assocs., Inc.,* 146 S.W.3d 113, 117 (Tex. 2004)

But what is a "producing cause?" Does it embrace both cause in fact and proximate cause? Does it require an act to be a "substantial factor" in causing the injuries? Is a producing cause the same as an "efficient cause?" Is it a contributing cause? Or is a producing cause the same as a substantial factor, which produces an injury and damages?

To be sure, these are hard questions. And although the Texas Supreme Court has tried to give definitive answers, there is still much confusion about a "producing cause." The cases and discussion in this chapter highlight the questions and confusion.

A. Common-Law Causation Rules —Proximate Cause and Cause in Fact

Doe v. Boys Clubs of Greater Dallas, Inc.
907 S.W.2d 472
(Tex. 1995)

This is a suit against a boys club for damages arising from the sexual molestation of boys by a volunteer worker. The plaintiffs brought a cause of action primarily based on negligence and the Texas Deceptive Trade Practices-Consumer Protection Act (DTPA). Tex. Bus. & Com. Code § 17.46(b)(5), § 17.46(b)(23) and §17.50(a). The trial court granted summary judgment for the Boys Clubs of Greater Dallas, Inc., and the court of appeals affirmed. Because we hold that the plaintiffs failed to raise fact issues on key elements of each of their claims against the Boys Club, particularly on the elements of proximate and producing cause, we affirm the judgment of the court of appeals.

* * *

The plaintiffs brought this negligence and DTPA action against the Boys Club and Mullens in June 1990. Among other claims, they alleged that the Boys Club negligently accepted Mullens as a volunteer without investigation or screening, negligently failed to supervise him, failed to disclose material information about Mullens, misrepresented that the club thoroughly investigated its volunteers, and misrepresented that the club and its workers had characteristics they did not have. The trial court granted the Boys Club's motion for summary judgment and severed the action against the club from the action against Mullens.

The court of appeals affirmed summary judgment for the Boys Club. On the negligence claims, it ruled that the Boys Club owed a duty to exercise reasonable care in selecting its workers, including volunteers such as Mullens, and that the Boys Club breached this duty. However, the court of appeals held as a matter of law that the Boys Club could not reasonably foresee Mullens's assaults on the boys; in the absence of an element of proximate cause, therefore, summary judgment on the plaintiffs' negligence actions was proper. *Id.* at 952.

* * *

The plaintiffs appeal the holdings that there was no proximate cause and no producing cause as a matter of law to support the negligence and DTPA claims, respectively. A defendant is entitled to summary judgment if it disproves an essential element of the plaintiff's causes of action as a matter of law. *Lear Siegler, Inc. v. Perez,* 819 S.W.2d 470, 471 (Tex.1991) (a negligence case); *Anderson v. Snider,* 808 S.W.2d 54, 55 (Tex.1991) (a DTPA case). In reviewing a summary judgment, we consider the evidence in the light most favorable to the non-movant and resolve any doubt in the non-movant's favor. *Nixon v. Mr. Property Management Co.,* 690 S.W.2d 546, 548-49 (Tex.1985).

* * *

II.

The elements of a negligence cause of action are a duty, a breach of that duty, and damages proximately caused by the breach of duty. *Greater Houston Transp. Co. v. Phillips,* 801 S.W.2d 523, 525 (Tex.1990); *El Chico Corp. v. Poole,* 732 S.W.2d 306, 311 (Tex.1987). Assuming without deciding that the Boys Club owed the plaintiffs the duty to exercise reasonable care in investigating its personnel and that it breached that duty, we focus on the issue whether the Boys Club's failure to investigate, screen, or supervise its volunteers proximately caused the injuries the plaintiffs allege.

The components of proximate cause are cause in fact and foreseeability. *Travis v. City of Mesquite,* 830 S.W.2d 94, 98 (Tex. 1992). These elements cannot be established by mere conjecture, guess, or speculation. *McClure v. Allied Stores of Tex., Inc.,* 608 S.W.2d 901, 903 (Tex.1980); *Farley v. MM Cattle Co.,* 529 S.W.2d 751, 755 (Tex.1 975). The test for cause in fact is whether the negligent "act or omission was a substantial factor in bringing about injury," without which the harm would not have occurred. *Prudential,* 896 S.W.2d at 161 (citing *McClure,* 608 S.W.2d at 903). *See Havner v. E-Z Mart Stores, Inc.,* 825 S.W.2d 456, 458-59 (Tex.1992); *Brown v. Edwards Transfer Co.,* 764 S.W.2d 220, 223 (Tex. 1988).

Cause in fact is not shown if the defendant's negligence did no more than furnish a condition which made the injury possible. *See Bell v. Campbell,* 434 S.W.2d 117, 120 (Tex.1968). As we stated in *Carey v. Pure Distrib. Corp.,* 124 S.W.2d 847, 849 (Tex.1939), "The evidence must go further, and show that such negligence was the proximate, and not the remote, cause of resulting injuries.... [and] justify the conclusion that such injury was the natural and probable result thereof." *See, e.g., Boyd v. Fuel Distribs., Inc.,* 795 S.W.2d 266, 272 (Tex.App.-Austin 1990, writ denied) (holding that a convenience store's sale of beer to an eighteen-year-old was not the cause in fact of a drunk driver's fatal car accident because the sale was to the passenger and not to the driver); *Texas Am. Bank v. Boggess,* 673 S.W.2d 398, 402 (Tex.App.-Fort Worth 1984, writ dism'd by agr.) (ruling that a bank's employment of a repossessor was not the cause in fact of the car owner's injuries since the owner was injured by a person that the repossessor had hired without the bank's knowledge).

In other words, even if the injury would not have happened but for the defendant's conduct, the connection between the defendant and the plaintiff's injuries simply may be too attenuated to constitute legal cause. *See Union Pump Co. v. Allbritton,* 898 S.W.2d 773, 776 (Tex.1995); *Lear Siegler,* 819 S.W.2d at 472.

We conclude that if the Boys Club breached a duty to investigate, screen, or supervise volunteers, this breach was not the cause in fact of the plaintiffs' injuries. Assuming the Boys Club had investigated Mullens's criminal record, revelation of the two misdemeanor DWI convictions would not have precluded Mullens's presence at the club. The club knew that Mullens was a probationer under court order to perform community service; further investigation would only have provided details about the nature of his offenses. There is no evidence that the Boys Club would not have taken Mullens as a volunteer if it had known he had been convicted for driving while intoxicated.

We conclude that Mullens's presence at the club was not due to breach of any duty to screen or to investigate. *See East Tex. Theatres, Inc. v. Rutledge,* 453 S.W.2d 466, 468-69 (Tex.1970) (finding no cause in fact because no evidence established that, had a theater operator removed "rowdy persons" from a balcony, the person who injured the plaintiff would have been removed). Moreover, Mullens' presence at the club was but a preliminary condition in the course of events which made possible his assaults on A.C. and R.M. Coe and on C.G. Doe. Lastly, since there is no evidence that Mullens molested or assaulted any boys at the club's premises, there is no evidence the Boys Club's alleged failure to supervise was a producing cause of the injuries to A.C. and R.M. Coe or to C.G. Doe. We hold as a matter of law that the Boys Club's failure to investigate, screen, or supervise its workers was not the cause in fact of the plaintiffs' injuries.

Foreseeability, the other aspect of proximate cause, requires that a person of ordinary intelligence should have anticipated the danger created by a negligent act or omission. *Nixon,* 690 S.W.2d at 549-50. The danger of injury is foreseeable if its "general character ... might reasonably have been anticipated." *Id.* at 551 (quoting *Carey,* 124 S.W.2d at 849) (emphasis omitted). The question of foreseeability, and proximate cause generally, involves a practical inquiry based on "common experience applied to human conduct." *City of Gladewater v. Pike,* 727 S.W.2d 514, 518 (Tex.1987) (quoting *Cook Consultants, Inc. v. Larson,* 700 S.W.2d 231, 236 (Tex.App.-Dallas 1985, writ ref'd n.r.e.)). It asks whether the injury "might reasonably have been contemplated" as a result of the defendant's conduct. *McClure,* 608 S.W.2d at 903. Foreseeability requires more than someone, viewing the facts in retrospect, theorizing an extraordinary sequence of events whereby the defendant's conduct brings about the injury. *See* Restatement (Second) of Torts § 435(2) (1965).

In this case, we agree with the court of appeals that if the Boys Club had investigated Mullens's criminal record, the resulting information would not have caused the club reasonably to anticipate his subsequent sexual assaults on the minor plaintiffs. 868 S.W.2d at 952. The prior DWI convictions did not indicate criminal conduct in any way akin to sexual assault of young boys. The course of events was such that Mullens's assaults of A.C. and R.M. Coe and C.G. Doe was so remotely related to the Boys Club's failure to investigate, screen, or supervise volunteers that no reasonable mind could anticipate the result. Mullens's prior record could not have caused the Boys Club reasonably to anticipate the danger he presented to the plaintiffs.

Because the plaintiffs' evidence did not raise a fact question concerning cause in fact or foreseeability, there was no evidence that the Boys Club's failure to investigate, screen, or supervise Mullens was the proximate cause of the boys' injuries. *See Schneider v. Esperanza Transmission Co.,* 744 S.W.2d 595, 596-97 (Tex.1987) (in a negligent entrustment case, finding no proximate cause because the defendant's entrustment of a truck to a driver did not cause the accident, and the defendant's knowledge about the driver did not lead it to foresee the danger resulting in injury). Therefore, we affirm the judgment of the court of appeals on the negligence claims in favor of the Boys Club.

NOTES & QUESTIONS

1) An extremely interesting statement appears in *Doe v. Boys Clubs of Greater Dallas, Inc.*, 907 S.W.2d 472, 481 (Tex. 1995):

> Raising a fact question of producing cause, as with proximate cause, requires some evidence that the defendant's act or omission was the cause in fact of the plaintiff's injury. *Prudential,* 896 S.W.2d at 161. . . . In short, the plaintiffs here had to raise a fact issue of an "unbroken causal connection" between the misrepresentation to Mrs. Coe and her grandsons' injuries. *See Texas Indem. Ins. Co. v. Staggs,* 134 S.W.2d 1026, 1030 (Tex. 1940).

2) The "unbroken causal connection" rule is clear enough. But one should also ask: Does the concurrent causation doctrine apply to DTPA actions?

3) Consider what the court of appeals wrote in *Allison v. Fire Insurance Exchange*, 98 S.W.3d 227, 258 (Tex. App. -Austin 2002) about the doctrine of concurrent causation:

> Ballard brought actions for negligence, negligence per se, breach of contract, deceptive trade practices, and breach of good faith and fair dealing in insurance claims handling, all of which allegedly caused damages to the Ballard house.
>
> * * *
>
> FIE contends in its second issue that the evidence is legally and factually insufficient to support the jury's findings that FIE engaged in deceptive trade practices, unconscionable conduct, and fraudulent conduct. Ballard counters that FIE waived this argument because it did not properly brief this issue. *See* Tex. R. App. P. 38.1(h). Because FIE's argument on this issue is grounded in its lengthy discussion that it did not breach its duty of good faith and fair dealing, we find that FIE sufficiently briefed this issue for the Court.
>
> The jury found that FIE violated the DTPA by engaging in a false, misleading, or deceptive act or practice by 1) representing that services had or would have characteristics or benefits that they did not have, 2) representing that services are or will be of a particular standard or quality when they were of another, 3) representing that an agreement confers or involves rights, remedies, or obligations that it did not have or involve, or 4) representing that work or services have been performed, when the work or services were not performed. *See* Tex. Bus. & Com.Code Ann. §§ 17.46(b)(5), (7), (12) and (22).
>
> * * *

FIE asserted in its second amended answer that Ballard had the burden of segregating damages among covered and non-covered losses, under the doctrine of concurrent causation. Under this doctrine, when covered and non-covered perils combine to create a loss, the insured is entitled to recover only that portion of the damage caused solely by the covered peril. *Travelers Indem. Co. v. McKillip,* 469 S.W.2d 160, 162 (Tex.1971); *Wallis v. United Servs. Auto. Ass'n,* 2 S.W.3d 300, 302-03 (Tex. App. -San Antonio 1999, pet. denied).

The doctrine of concurrent causation is not an affirmative defense or an avoidance issue; rather, it is a rule embodying the basic principle that insureds are not entitled to recover under their insurance policies unless they prove that their damage is covered by the policy. *Wallis,* 2 S.W.3d at 303. Thus, an insured may only recover for the amount of damage caused solely by the covered peril. *Id.* The burden is on the insured to prove coverage. *Id.* The insured must therefore present some evidence upon which the jury can allocate the damages attributable to the covered peril. *Id.* Because allocation is central to the claim for coverage, an insured's failure to carry the burden of proof on allocation is fatal to the claim. *Id.* The insured must attempt to segregate the loss caused by the covered peril from the loss caused by the excluded peril. *Id.*

The doctrine of concurrent causation is inapplicable in this case for two reasons. First, FIE never denied any claim at issue in this appeal on the ground that the claim was a non-covered peril. Second, FIE asserted the doctrine of concurrent causation pursuant to Article 21.58(b) of the Insurance Code, which states that "[i] n any suit to recover under a contract of insurance, the insurer has the burden of proof as to any avoidance or affirmative defense that must be affirmatively pleaded under the Texas Rules of Civil Procedure." Tex. Ins. Code Ann. art. 21.58(b). All of Ballard's claims presented to the jury were extra-contractual, beyond recovery under the contract of insurance.

Therefore, we overrule FIE's sixth point of error and affirm the district court's ruling granting Ballard's no-evidence summary judgment on concurrent causation.

B. DTPA Causation Rules—Producing Cause, But For and Substantial Factor Tests

In *General Motors Corp. v. Saenz,* 873 S.W.2d 353, 357 (Tex. 1993), the Texas Supreme Court stated:

We next consider whether GM's failure to provide warnings and instructions concerning the maximum loading of the Model C-50, different from those contained on the doorplate and in the owner's manual, caused the accident in this

> case. Plaintiffs must show that GM's failure was a proximate cause of the accident to recover on their negligence claim, and a producing cause to recover on their strict liability claim — the difference being that proof of proximate cause entails a showing that the accident was foreseeable, while proof of producing cause does not. The element common to both proximate cause and producing cause is actual causation in fact. Thus, to recover on either of their claims plaintiffs must show that *but for* GM's omission the accident would not have occurred.

However, lower courts allow plaintiffs to use several tests to establish cause in fact—the *but for* test, the *substantial factor* test, and the *greatly multiplies* test.

Under the DTPA, may a plaintiff also use the latter two standards to establish that a violation was the producing cause of the injury and damages? May a plaintiff use any combination of the three standards? The next two cases provide less-than-stellar answers to these questions.

Ford Motor Company v. Ledesma
242 S.W.3d 32
(Tex. 2007)

In this products liability case, Ford Motor Co. argues that the trial court reversibly erred in charging the jury by giving an incomplete definition of "manufacturing defect." We agree. Additionally, we hold that a frequently submitted definition of "producing cause" should no longer be used. We remand the case for a new trial under a jury charge that reflects our applicable case law, including our decision today.

I. Background

In March 1999, Tiburicio Ledesma, Jr. purchased a new Ford F-350 Super Duty pickup truck for his construction business. The truck had four rear tires, two on each side, surrounded by fiberglass fenders extending beyond the sides of the truck.

On June 5, 1999, Ledesma turned onto a two-lane street in Austin and began to accelerate. He testified that after shifting gears the truck suddenly began to lurch, and he lost control, striking two parked cars, a Firebird and a Civic, on the side of the street. The truck then hit the street curb and came to rest. At the time of the accident, the truck's odometer read about 4,100 miles.

Power from the truck engine is conveyed to the rear axle by the drive shaft, which connects the transmission in the front of the truck with the differential/rear axle assembly in the rear. As seen in the trial exhibit reproduced below, the rear-axle housing is attached to two sets of rear leaf springs by u-bolts, which wrap around the axle housing and are bolted to a rear spring plate that sits on top of the leaf-spring assembly. On each side of the truck, two u-bolts attach the rear-axle housing to a spring plate and set of leaf springs.

Both parties agree that the truck's rear leaf spring and axle assembly came apart and that this separation caused the drive shaft to dislodge from the transmission. The core dispute centers on *when* and *why* this malfunction occurred and whether it *caused* the collision or *resulted* from it. That is, did a manufacturing defect trigger the right rear-axle displacement and cause Ledesma to lose control of the truck and strike the parked cars (as Ledesma claims), or did the right rear axle detach when Ledesma struck the parked cars and curb (as Ford claims)?

At trial, Ledesma claimed that he lost control of the truck when its drive shaft separated from the transmission and "pronged" on the pavement, causing him to hit the parked cars. A police officer testified that he investigated the accident scene and prepared a report based on Ledesma's description of the accident. The report makes no mention of any other witnesses. Ledesma also presented two expert witnesses in support of his manufacturing defect claim, as discussed below.

Ford presented an expert, Dan May, in support of its theory that the axle-to-spring attachment failed, not because of a manufacturing defect, but because of the forces exerted on it when Ledesma struck the parked vehicles and curb. Among other efforts to discredit May, Ledesma emphasized to the jury that May was a long-time Ford employee and had never found a defect in a Ford product.

Ford also called the owner of the Firebird, Edward Plyant, who testified by deposition that he witnessed the accident from a driveway. Plyant testified that Ledesma was speeding and inattentive and struck the Firebird at a high rate of speed. Ledesma testified that Plyant did not see the accident, but came outside after hearing the ensuing commotion, and that Plyant had unsuccessfully sued Ledesma.

The jury sided 11-1 with Ledesma, finding that a manufacturing defect caused the accident and that Ledesma was not contributorily negligent, and awarding economic damages of $215,380. The court of appeals affirmed.

II. Discussion

* * *

B. Jury Charge

Ford complains that, over its objection, the trial court improperly instructed the jury on the definitions of manufacturing defect and producing cause. The jury affirmatively answered Question No. 1 of the jury charge, which asked: Was there a manufacturing defect in the 1999 Ford F-350 pickup truck at the time it left Ford's possession that was a producing cause of the June 5, 1999 incident in question?

A "defect" means a condition of the product that renders it unreasonably dangerous. An "unreasonably dangerous" product is one that is dangerous to an extent beyond that which would be contemplated by the ordinary user of the product, with the ordinary knowledge common to the community as to the product's characteristics.

"Producing cause" means an efficient, exciting, or contributing cause that, in a natural sequence, produces the incident in question. There may be more than one producing cause.

In defining defect, the trial court followed Texas Pattern Jury Charge (PJC) 71.3. — COMM. ON PATTERN JURY CHARGES, STATE BAR OF TEX., TEXAS PATTERN JURY CHARGES — MALPRACTICE, PREMISES & PRODUCTS PJC 71.3 (2d ed.2002).

As specified in the comment to PJC 71.3, the trial court included in the question the definition of producing cause found in PJC 70.1. Ford objected that both PJC 71.3 and PJC 70.1 were "not accurate under the law" and failed to track this Court's precedent. We agree.

* * *

3. Producing Cause

Ford separately complains that the trial court improperly instructed the jury on producing cause. The trial court, following PJC 70.1, instructed the jury: " 'Producing cause' means an efficient, exciting, or contributing cause that, in a natural sequence, produces the incident in question. There may be more than one producing cause."

Ford contends that this definition is an incorrect statement of Texas law, and that a valid definition would state that producing cause "means that cause which, in a natural sequence, was a substantial factor in bringing about an event, and without which the event would not have occurred. There may be more than one producing cause." Ford requested the trial court to use this definition.

We agree with Ledesma that the second part of the court's definition, recognizing that there may be more than one producing cause of an event, is correct. And we have seemed to sanction the first part, employing it ourselves several times in describing producing cause. *See Brown v. Bank of Galveston, Nat'l Ass'n,* 963 S.W.2d 511, 514 (Tex. 1998) ("A producing cause is an efficient, exciting, or contributing cause, which in the natural sequence of events, produces injuries or damages."); *Union Pump Co. v. Allbritton,* 898 S.W.2d 773, 775 (Tex. 1995) ("A producing cause is 'an efficient, exciting, or contributing cause,' which in a natural sequence, produced injuries or damages complained of, if any."), quoting *Haynes & Boone v. Bowser Bouldin, Ltd.,* 896 S.W.2d 179, 182 (Tex. 1995) and *Rourke v. Garza,* 530 S.W.2d 794, 801 (Tex. 1975).

But we have also described a producing cause as one "that is a substantial factor that brings about injury and without which the injury would not have occurred," the definition Ford asks us to adopt. See, *Trinity Universal Ins. Co. v. Bleeker,* 966 S.W.2d 489, 491 (Tex.1998); *see also Doe v. Boys Clubs of Greater Dallas, Inc.,* 907 S.W.2d 472, 481 (Tex. 1995) ("A producing cause is a substantial factor which brings about the injury and without which the injury would not have occurred."); *Union Pump,* 898 S.W.2d at 775 (noting that causation in fact is common to both proximate and producing cause, and that "[c]ause in fact means that the defendant's act or omission was a substantial factor in bringing about the injury which would not otherwise have occurred"); *Prudential Ins. Co. of Am. v. Jefferson Assocs., Ltd.,* 896 S.W.2d 156, 161 (Tex. 1995) (holding that the element of actual causation in fact common to both proximate and producing cause "requires proof that an act or omission was a substantial factor in bringing about injury which would not otherwise have occurred").

To say that a producing cause is "an efficient, exciting, or contributing cause that, in a natural sequence, produces the incident in question" is incomplete and, more importantly, provides little concrete guidance to the jury. Juries must ponder the meaning of "efficient" and "exciting" in this context. These adjectives are foreign to modern English language as a means to describe a cause, and offer little practical help to a jury striving to make the often difficult causation determination in a products case.

Defining producing cause as being a substantial factor in bringing about an injury, and without which the injury would not have occurred, is easily understood and conveys the essential components of producing cause that 1) the cause must be a substantial cause of the event in issue and 2) it must be a but-for cause, namely one without which the event would not have occurred.
This is the definition that should be given in the jury charge.

We reverse the court of appeals' judgment and remand this case to the trial court for further proceedings.

NOTES & QUESTIONS

1) In *Ledesma*, the Texas Supreme Court reaffirmed its ruling in *Haynes & Boone v. Bowser Bouldin, Ltd.*, 896 S.W.2d 179, 182 (Tex. 1995): There may be more than one producing cause. In light of this rule, must DTPA plaintiffs prove each?

2) To prove a negligence or a breach-of-contract cause of action, plaintiff must prove one cause in fact and one proximate cause. Defendant's negligence must be the cause in fact and proximate cause of an injury and damages. Additionally defendant's breach of contract must be the cause in fact and proximate cause of an injury and damages.

3) However, under the rule in *Ledesma,* a defendant's DTPA violation is a "producing cause" if a) the violation is "a substantial cause" of injury/damages, *and* 2) defendant's DTPA violation must be a "but for cause," one without which the plaintiff's injury/damages would not have occurred. Is this clear? Has the court created a greater burden for DTPA plaintiffs?

4) Why does *Ledesma* require a DTPA plaintiff to prove both a "substantial cause" and "but for" causation? Isn't that redundant?

Chapter Six:
Remedies Under DTPA

This chapter covers DTPA remedies. At the outset, it is important to stress: under the DTPA, aggrieved consumers may receive a wide variety of equitable and common-law remedies if they prevail. First, the current version of § 17.50(b) reads:

> In a suit filed under this section, each consumer who prevails may obtain:
>
> (1) the amount of economic damages found by the trier of fact. If the trier of fact finds that the conduct of the defendant was committed knowingly, the consumer may also recover damages for mental anguish, as found by the trier of fact, and the trier of fact may award not more than three times the amount of economic damages; or if the trier of fact finds the conduct was committed intentionally, the consumer may recover damages for mental anguish, as found by the trier of fact, and the trier of fact may award not more than three times the amount of damages for mental anguish and economic damages;
>
> (2) an order enjoining such acts or failure to act;
>
> (3) orders necessary to restore to any party to the suit any money or property, real or personal, which may have been acquired in violation of this subchapter; and
>
> (4) any other relief which the court deems proper, including the appointment of a receiver or the revocation of a license or certificate authorizing a person to engage in business in this state if the judgment has not been satisfied within three months of the date of the final judgment. The court may not revoke or suspend a license to do business in this state or appoint a receiver to take over the affairs of a person who has failed to satisfy a judgment if the person is a licensee of or regulated by a state agency which has statutory authority to revoke or suspend a license or to appoint a receiver or trustee. Costs and fees of such receivership or other relief shall be assessed against the defendant.

But there is more. Under §§ 17.50(d) and (e), a successful consumer may collect attorneys' fees and funds to pay court costs. Those sections state:

> (d) Each consumer who prevails shall be awarded court costs and reasonable and necessary attorneys' fees; and.
>
> (e) In computing additional damages under Subsection (b), attorneys' fees, costs, and prejudgment interest may not be considered.

Arguably, § 17.50(b) allows a consumer to receive conjunctive remedies: actual damages, treble damages, penalty damages, "additional" damages, attorneys' fees, temporary and permanent injunctions as well as "any other relief" such as declaratory judgments and various restoration orders — rescission, restitution and revocation However, § 17.43 leaves little doubt regarding whether the enumerated remedies are cumulative or exhaustive. That section reads in relevant part:

> The provisions of this subchapter are not exclusive. The remedies provided in this subchapter are in addition to any other procedures or remedies provided for in any other law; provided, however, that no recovery shall be permitted under both this subchapter and another law of both damages and penalties for the same act or practice.

Discussions of some of these remedies and related issues appear below.

A. *Equitable Relief — Declaratory Judgments and Injunctions*

Parks v. U.S. Home Corporation
652 S.W.2d 479
(Tex. App. – Hous.[1st Dist.] 1983)

This is an appeal from the denial of an application for a temporary injunction.

Steven Parks and twenty-four other homeowners (Parks et.al.) filed their original petition alleging that they had purchased homes in Westbranch Village from U.S. Home Corporation. Parks et.al. alleged that U.S. Home's sales agent, Wilmeth, had represented to them that all remaining homes in Westbranch Village would be of the same price range ($89,950 to $100,950) and Victorian style, and that they had relied on such representations.

Parks et.al. further alleged that after they had purchased their homes U.S. Home's agent informed them that U.S. Home did not intend to construct homes of the same price range and Victorian style on the remaining lots in Westbranch Village. Parks et.al. complained that the lower priced homes would seriously diminish or destroy the market value of their homes.

Parks et.al. contended that all property is unique, and that "one of the characteristics of the uniqueness of each piece of property is the nature and use of adjacent and nearby property and the value of the improvements thereon." They alleged that part of the consideration for which they paid the purchase price was the "representation, affirmation, and guarantee" by U.S. Home, through its agent, that Westbranch Village would be completed with homes of the same style and price range as those they had purchased.

Parks et.al. alleged that the U.S. Homes had violated § 17.46(b)(23) of the Deceptive Trade Practices Act, in that at the time of closing the sale to Parks et.al., U.S. Home knew that it did not intend to comply with its representations. They further alleged that failure to disclose this information induced Parks et.al. to purchase their homes and, thus, constituted a false, misleading, or deceptive act or practice under the DTPA.

They alleged that U.S. Home had also violated § 17.46(b)(5) of the Deceptive Trade Practices Act, in that U.S. Home clearly and unequivocally represented and guaranteed that the homes purchased by Parks et.al. would be located in a subdivision made up of homes of the same style and price range. They alleged that the U.S. Homes had, therefore, represented that the homes purchased by Parks et.al. had characteristics, benefits, or qualities which they did not, in fact, have.

Parks et.al. further contended that U.S. Home had violated § 17.50(a)(3) by following an unconscionable action or course of action (the proposed building of lower priced homes in Westbranch Village) which would cause the value of Parks et.al.' homes to be seriously diminished or destroyed, and which would result in a gross disparity between the value of their homes and the consideration paid.

Parks et.al. alleged that they had no adequate remedy at law for the damage done or threatened by U.S. Home, because the real property involved was unique. They alleged that monetary damages were therefore wholly inadequate, and prayed for both temporary and permanent injunctions enjoining U.S. Home from constructing homes in Westbranch Village selling for less than $89,000.

U.S. Home answered by way of general denial. The temporary injunction hearing was held on October 13, 1982, at which the following evidence was introduced:

> Parks et.al. were led to U.S. Home's subdivision by billboard advertisements stating "Westbranch Village-Victorian Homes, from the '80's." Parks et.al. dealt solely with U.S. Home's sales agent, Ms. Rosie Wilmeth, whose business card was entitled, "Westbranch Village-Home of the Victorian." Three models of Victorian homes were available, ranging in price from $89,950 to $100,950.
>
> Ms. Wilmeth told Parks et.al. that on each lot in the area designated on her sales map as "Westbranch Village" there would be constructed one of the three Victorian models. She stated that no lesser-priced home, or style other than the three Victorian models, would be constructed in Westbranch Village. Ms. Wilmeth admitted that she had made such representations, but denied that she had made any "guarantees."

> Parks et.al. testified that they would not have purchased their homes but for the representations.
>
> Ms. Wilmeth admitted that she had been informed of U.S. Home's change of plans as of August 31, 1982, prior to several closings, but failed to inform Parks et.al. of this fact because she "didn't think it was important." Although she asserted that she would have informed Parks et.al., had they asked, Parks et.al. offered testimony that on at least one occasion she failed to disclose such information after direct inquiry.
>
> Parks et.al. testified that they were concerned that their property values would decline and that the character of the neighborhood would change, should lesser priced homes of another style be built around their homes. However, U.S. Home's representatives testified that there was nothing unique about the lots located in Westbranch Village, and no one passing from the other section of the subdivision into Westbranch Village would be aware of any differentiation. The discontinuation of the construction of the Victorian models had not diminished the asking price for those Victorian homes not yet sold, nor had it caused a change in the character of the subdivision. U.S. Home's representatives further testified that Westbranch Village had not been planned as a Victorian home community in order to create or enhance property values, but that, in fact, the only reason Westbranch Village had been designated as the location for the Victorian models had been to avoid confusion among U.S. Home's sales people at its two sales offices.
>
> U.S. Home's representative Dennis Bailey, Division President, testified that continuing to build the Victorian home product line would result in monthly losses of $30,000.00 over a four year period. Total cessation of construction in Westbranch Village would result in yearly losses of $250,000.00 in interest payments. Mr. Bailey testified that only residences selling for at least $70,000.00 would be built in Westbranch Village.

At the close of the evidence, the trial court entered its order denying the application for temporary injunction. The order contained the following findings of fact and conclusions of law:

> (1) Defendant erected a billboard which stated that homes in the Westbranch Village would consist of homes from the $80's.
>
> (2) Oral statements were made by defendant or its representative to the plaintiffs that homes within Westbranch Village would consist of homes with a sales price of at least $80,000 and be constructed only with a Victorian front elevation.
>
> (3) Plaintiffs relied on such statements when they purchased their homes.
>
> (4) Defendant has since changed its position and now intends to build homes in the subject area with a sales price of less than $80,000 but not less than $70,000 and with a front elevation consisting of styles in addition and different than Victorian.

(5) There exist no deed restrictions pertaining to the subject property at all relevant times which required defendant to build only homes (i) at sales price of not less than $80,000 and (ii) with Victorian style front elevations.

(6) Plaintiffs failed to meet their burden of proof that irreparable harm will be caused by defendant's action if not abated by a temporary injunction, or that plaintiffs were entitled to a temporary injunction as a matter of law.

(7) Any harm or damage, if any, caused by defendant to plaintiff could be compensable in damages, if any, because the defendant was financially solvent and one of the largest home builders in the nation.

Parks et.al. requested the following additional findings of fact:

(1) Each of the plaintiffs purchased one of three (3) models shown to them by the defendant's representative.

(2) As of July 19, 1982, the sales price of the smallest of the three (3) models shown to plaintiffs was $89,950.

(3) Defendant or its representative made oral statements to the plaintiffs that all of the homes to be built in Westbranch Village would be of the same price and style as the three (3) models shown to plaintiffs.

(4) Plaintiffs would not have purchased their homes from the defendant had the defendant or its representative disclosed that lesser priced homes than the three (3) models shown to plaintiffs would be built throughout the remainder of Westbranch Village.

(5) One characteristic or quality of a home is the size, price, and style of other homes built nearby in the same subdivision.

(6) If the defendant constructs homes throughout the remainder of Westbranch Village of a lower price and of a different style than the models shown to plaintiffs, the homes purchased by plaintiffs would not have a characteristic or quality as represented by the defendant.

The court refused all requested findings except numbers one and four.

Parks et.al. assert three points of error on appeal, and consolidate them in their argument:

(1) The trial court abused its discretion as a matter of law in denying the temporary injunction because Parks et.al. showed a probable right to injunctive relief and a probable injury.

(2) The trial court abused its discretion as a matter of law because it failed to apply the law correctly to the undisputed facts.

(3) The trial court abused its discretion in apparently basing the denial of the temporary injunction on the fact that Parks et.al. have an adequate remedy at law in damages.

Parks et.al. contend, as an initial matter, that they have standing as "consumers" to sue under the Texas Deceptive Trade Practices Act (DTPA), because the Act applies to consumers of new homes, citing *Norwood Builders, Inc. v. Toler,* 609 S.W.2d 861 (Tex. Civ. App.-Houston [14th Dist] 1981, writ ref'd n.r.e.), as authority. U.S. Home disputes this assertion. It contends that Parks et.al. have no standing complain of the use to be made of property which they have not purchased.

It seems clear that Parks et.al. have standing to bring suit under the DTPA as "consumers" of "goods," as they complain specifically that misrepresentations were made to them which induced them to purchase their homes and lots. The Supreme Court stated, in *Cameron v. Terrell & Garrett, Inc.,* 618 S.W.2d 535 (Tex.1981), that to qualify as a consumer under the Act, the person must have sought or acquired goods by purchase or lease, and the goods purchased or leased must form the *basis* of the complaint. Real property was included in the definition of "goods" in § 17.45(1) Tex. Bus. & Com.Code Ann. (Vernon 1982), by amendment effective as of September 1, 1975.

While U.S. Home strenuously asserts that the *basis* of Parks et.al.' complaint is not the homes and lots actually purchased, it appears that the DTPA was intended to reach Parks et.al.' complaints. The Supreme Court, in *Woods v. Littleton,* 554 S.W.2d 662 (Tex.1977), stated that the Act "clearly declares deceptive practices in the *conduct* of a real estate sale to be unlawful" (emphasis added). Moreover, § 17.44 Tex. Bus. & Com. Code Ann. states that the DTPA shall be liberally construed and applied to promote its underlying purposes, which are to protect consumers against false, misleading, and deceptive business practices, unconscionable actions, and breaches of warranty, and to provide efficient and economical procedures to secure such protection. See also *Rinehart v. Sonitrol of Dallas, Inc.,* 620 S.W.2d 660 (Tex.Civ.App.-Dallas 1981, writ ref'd n.r.e.).

Parks et.al. specifically contend that they have proved a probable right to recovery under both § 17.46(b)(5) and (23) Tex. Bus. & Com.Code Ann. and that under § 17.50(b)(2) they are entitled to injunctive relief. They contend that the trial court's findings of fact support their right to recovery as a matter of law.

Section 17.46(b)(5) makes it a deceptive trade practice to represent that goods have sponsorship, approval, characteristics, ingredients, uses, benefits, or qualities which they do not have. *Intentional* misrepresentation is not required to show a violation of this subdivision, so long as the misrepresentation is not mere "puffing." See *Pennington v. Singleton,* 606 S.W.2d 682 (Tex.1980), and *Smith v. Baldwin,* 611 S.W.2d 611 (Tex.1980). It is not at all clear, however, that the use to be put to contiguous or surrounding property is a "characteristic or quality" of Parks et.al.' home and lot. No cases have addressed misrepresentations regarding use of surrounding property in a cause of action based on § 17.46(b)(5) of the DTPA since real estate purchases have come within its purview. Contrary to Parks et.al.' assertion, the court in *Ratcliff v. Trenholm,* 596 S.W.2d 645

(Tex. Civ. App. Tyler 1980, writ ref'd n.r.e.), did not address the issue or provide any guidance for this court.

The trial court in the case at bar specifically refused to adopt Parks et.al.' requested finding of fact that "one characteristic or quality of a home is the size, price, and style of other homes built nearby in the same subdivision." It did, however, find that no deed restrictions exist pertaining to price and style of homes in the subdivision.

In view of the case law interpreting "characteristic" or "benefit," we hold that Parks et.al.' particular complaint is not within the purview of § 17.46(b)(5). To date, "characteristic" or "benefit" has only been interpreted to refer to attributes of the goods actually purchased. See, e.g., *Pennington, supra.*

Parks et.al.' contention that they are entitled to relief under § 17.46(b)(23) is likewise ill-founded. They assert that U.S. Home's sales agent intentionally failed to disclose U.S. Home's change in development plans, and that this nondisclosure induced Parks et.al. to purchase their homes.

However, as U.S. Home points out, § 17.46(b)(23) prohibits: The failure to disclose information concerning goods or services which was known at the time of the transaction if such failure to disclose such information was intended to induce the consumer into a transaction into which the consumer would not have entered had the information been disclosed.

U.S. Home stresses that the undisclosed information must be *known* to the participant withholding such information, and that the failure to disclose must be *intended* to induce the purchase.

In this case the evidence as to the reason for the failure to disclose was sharply disputed. The trial court, as trier of fact, was the judge of the credibility of the witnesses and the weight to be given their testimony. This court, in reviewing the evidence, is required not only to give effect to the findings as made, but also to presume omitted findings in support of the judgment, if such findings are supported by the evidence. *Kroger Co. v. Warren,* 420 S.W.2d 218 (Tex. Civ. App.-Houston [1st Dist.] 1967, no writ). There was evidence from which the trial court could have found that the nondisclosure was not motivated by intent to induce the purchase, and, thus, that Parks et.al. did not sustain their burden of proof under § 17.46(b)(23).

The grant or denial of a temporary injunction is within the sound discretion of the trial court. This court, in reviewing the trial court's decision, is limited to consideration of whether or not the trial court clearly abused its discretion. *Western Hills Theaters v. Motion Picture Machine Operators Local § 330,* 495 S.W.2d 39 (Tex. Civ. App.-Fort Worth 1973, no writ). "Abuse of discretion" implies more than an error of judgment; it must amount to "arbitrary and unreasonable" action by the trial court. *Bennett v. Northcutt,* 544 S.W.2d 703 (Tex.Civ.App.-Dallas 1976, no writ). In determining whether there has been an abuse of discretion, the Court of Appeals is required to view the evidence in the light most favorable to the action of the trial court, and indulge every legal presumption in favor of the judgment.

In order to obtain injunctive relief, the applicant must show a substantial likelihood of success on the merits, a substantial threat of irreparable injury, that the threatened injury to the applicant outweighs the threatened harm the injunction may cause to the defendants, and that the granting of the injunction will serve the public interest. *Bean v. Southwestern Waste Management Corp.,* 482 F. Supp. 673 (1979); *Arkansas Louisiana Gas Co. v. Fender,* 593 S.W.2d 122 (Tex. Civ. App.-Tyler 1979, no writ). These factors must also be established in order to obtain injunctive relief under § 17.50(b)(2) Tex.Bus. & Com.Code Ann. (Vernon 1982). See *Woods v. Littleton, supra; Wesware, Inc. v. State of Texas,* 488 S.W.2d 844 (Tex.Civ.App.-Austin 1972, no writ).

The trial court found that Parks et.al. failed to meet their burden of proof that they were entitled to a temporary injunction as a matter of law. Implied in that finding was the determination that Parks et.al. had not shown a substantial likelihood of success on the merits. Because there was evidence upon which the trial court could have based such a finding, it did not abuse its discretion in denying the application for a temporary injunction.

With regard to Parks et.al.' contention that the trial court abused its discretion in finding that Parks et.al. could be adequately compensated in damages, Parks et.al. urge that where real property is concerned, an action for damages is not an adequate remedy. They further assert that the representations constituted oral deed restrictions which may be enforced by means of injunction without the necessity of proving amount of damages or irreparable injury. They rely upon *Protestant Episcopal Church Council v. McKinney,* 339 S.W.2d 400 (Tex.Civ.App.-Eastland 1960, writ ref'd), and *North Texas Trust Co. v. Brittson,* 279 S.W. 892 (Tex.Civ.App.-Dallas 1926, writ dism'd), as authority.

Parks et.al. err in claiming that the simple fact that real property is involved mandates injunctive relief. As the court held *Crestview Ltd. v. Foremost Ins. Co.,* 621 S.W.2d 816 (Tex.Civ.App.-Austin 1981, writ ref'd n.r.e.), the applicant must show a probable right and a probable injury before injunctive relief will be available.

Parks et.al. also err in asserting that the oral representations made in this case constitute deed restrictions which must be enforced by injunction. The court in *North Texas Trust Co., supra,* stated that where the owner of land, by a map or by other unequivocal acts or declarations, indicates that a particular lot or plot is to be dedicated or reserved to or for a particular use *of a public or quasi public character,* those who are thus induced to purchase lots in an addition take, as appurtenant, every advantage, privilege, and *easement* which was represented as belonging to or as a part of the same (emphasis added).

The critical fact in that case was the public or quasi-public nature of the dedication, a block to be used as the site of a community or civic center. The dedication created an easement, which irrevocably vested rights in the lot purchasers and, through them, in the public. The purported oral deed restrictions in the instant case do not vest any rights in Parks et.al. by virtue of a public or quasi-public use.

In light of the evidence adduced at the hearing, the trial court did not abuse its discretion in determining that damages would adequately compensate Parks et.al., should they prevail on the merits. Parks et.al. stressed their concern about diminished market value of their homes due to U.S. Home's threatened conduct. Parks et.al. introduced no evidence of demonstrated or potential loss on their part. They simply testified that they feared decline in the market value of their homes. Evidence introduced at trial tended to refute the likelihood of diminished value or change in the character of the neighborhood.

Furthermore, in balancing the harm which would ensue to Parks et.al. should an injunction not be granted, with the harm which would ensue to U.S. Home should an injunction be granted, the trial court had evidence before it from which it could have concluded that harm to U.S. Home outweighed any harm Parks et.al. might suffer. U.S. Home demonstrated potential loss of at least $30,000 per month during cessation of construction, while, as stated above, Parks et.al. failed to introduce any evidence of potential loss.

The trial court did not abuse its discretion in denying the temporary injunction. Appellant's three points of error are overruled. The judgment of the trial court is affirmed.

NOTES & QUESTIONS

1) Section § 17.50(b)(2) of the DTPA allows a prevailing party to obtain "an order enjoining [false, deceptive, misleading or unconscionable] acts or failure to act." However, Texas's settled common-law and equitable principles govern whether and how temporary or permanent DTPA injunctions will be issued.

2) What are the legal and equitable standards that courts employ to decide whether to issue temporary and permanent injunctions?

3) "A temporary injunction is an extraordinary remedy and does not issue as a matter of right." *Butnaru v. Ford Motor Co.,* 84 S.W.3d 198, 204 (Tex. 2002). The purpose of a temporary injunction is to preserve the status quo until a trial on the merits. *Walling v. Metcalfe,* 863 S.W.2d 56, 58 (Tex. 1993). "Status quo is defined as 'the last, actual, peaceable, noncontested status which preceded the pending controversy.'" *Universal Health Servs., Inc. v. Thompson,* 24 S.W.3d 570, 577 (Tex. App.-Austin 2000, no pet.), quoting *Transp. Co. v. Robertson Transps., Inc.,* 261 S.W.2d 549, 553-54 (Tex. 1953)

4) When issuing temporary and permanent injunctions, a court may not abuse its discretion. A trial court abuses its discretion when it acts arbitrarily and unreasonably or when it misapplies the law to the established facts of the case. *Downer v. Aquamarine Operators, Inc.,* 701 S.W.2d 238, 241-42 (Tex.1985); *State v. Sw. Bell Tel. Co.,* 526 S.W.2d 526, 528 (Tex.1975). *See also, CA Partners v. Spears,* 274 S.W.3d 51, 80 (Tex.App.-Houston [14th Dist.] 2008) (regarding the issuance of a permanent injunction), and *Jim Rutherford Invs., Inc. v. Terramar Beach Cmty. Ass'n,* 25 S.W.3d 845, 848 (Tex.App.-Houston [14th Dist.] 2000, pet. denied) (stressing a court may not abuse its discretion when awarding permanent injunctive relief).

Dairyland County Mutual Insurance Company of Texas v. Childress
650 S.W.2d 770
(Tex. 1983)

This is a dispute as to liability insurance coverage provided by a family automobile insurance policy containing a non-owner's endorsement. Harry Childress and the passengers in his automobile at the time of the collision along with the owner of a private residence damaged as a result of the collision (Childress) sued Frederick Booth (Booth), the insured, for damages arising out of the collision. While this suit was pending, Dairyland County Mutual Insurance Company of Texas (Dairyland), the insuror, sued Booth seeking a declaratory judgment that the non-owner's policy did not cover an automobile furnished to the insured for his regular use. An agreed judgment was rendered declaring that no coverage was provided. Childress were not made a party to the declaratory judgment action.

After securing a judgment against Booth, Childress sued Dairyland for the amount of the judgment, for attorney's fees and for recovery under the Deceptive Trade Practices Act — Tex. Bus. & Com. Code Ann. § 17.50(c). Dairyland filed a cross action for attorney's fees alleging the DTPA suit was not filed in good faith. The trial court rendered judgment that both parties take nothing. The court of appeals affirmed the take nothing judgment against Dairyland but reversed and rendered judgment for Childress for the policy limits of $11,000 personal injury and $5,000 property damage, for attorney's fees in the amount of $6,400 and for interest on the judgment against Booth. We affirm the judgment of the court of appeals.

The issues presented are: 1) whether a non-owner's policy provides coverage for an automobile not owned by the named insured but furnished for his regular use; 2) whether the Childress plaintiffs were bound by a declaratory judgment action between the insurer and the insured, to which the plaintiffs were not made parties; 3) what evidence is necessary to sustain attorney's fees for a defendant alleging a bad faith suit under the DTPA; and 4) whether a judgment creditor of an insured covered by an automobile liability insurance policy is entitled to attorney's fees under Tex. Rev. Civ. Stat. Ann. Art. 2226 in a suit against the insured based on the judgment.

COVERAGE UNDER NON-OWNER'S ENDORSEMENT

Booth was the named insured under two separate automobile liability insurance policies issued by Dairyland. Policy No. 41-0349565 was an owner's policy written on a 1971 Dodge automobile. Policy No. 41-0350933 was a non-owner's policy. These policies consist of the following: 1) each contains the same basic policy outlining the type of coverage provided and the rights and duties of the insured and the insuror; 2) each contains a policy declaration sheet setting out the vehicle covered by the basic policy. The owners policy enumerated a 1971 Dodge as insured and the non-owners policy listed "non-owners" in the place for description of the insured vehicle; and 3) the non-owners policy also contains a non-owners endorsement explaining what vehicles are covered under the policy.

There is no contention before us that the owner's policy provided coverage for the accident in this case.

At the time of the collision Booth was driving a Chevrolet automobile owned by Para Gowens. The jury found in response to a special issue that the Chevrolet was furnished to Booth for his regular use. Dairyland contends that the finding precludes coverage. The basis for that contention is a definition of "non-owned automobile" contained in the basic policy. "Non-owned automobile" means an automobile ... not owned by or furnished for the regular use of either the named insured or any relative, other than a temporary substitute automobile.

However, the non-owner's endorsement attached to the policy in question states that it becomes a part of the policy to which it is attached, that the insurance afforded by the policy for bodily injury liability and property damage liability applies with respect to the use of *any* automobile by or in behalf of the named insured subject to the following [condition]: "The insurance does not apply . . . to any automobile owned by the named insured."

The other listed exclusions are not pertinent to this case. We interpret the endorsement according to its plain language. That interpretation compels us to hold that the policy provided bodily injury liability and property damage liability coverage for Booth while he was driving the Chevrolet automobile which was furnished for his regular use. We find that this definition comports with the purpose of the non-owner's endorsement as is explained in *Fire, Casualty and Surety Bulletin,* Personal Auto En-1, (January, 1982), an insurance industry publication:

> *The most usual need for the Extended Nonowned* [sic] *endorsement, perhaps, is to delete the exclusions of nonowned* [sic] *auto 'furnished or available for the regular use' of the named insured or any family member.* If, for an obvious example, the named insured is allowed to drive a work car home on a regular basis and use it for personal use, a regular Personal Auto policy does not provide coverage as to that car-while it is being used by anyone. Likewise, a car *furnished to a family member* of the named insured is not covered, except with respect to the *named insured's* use of the car. The Extended Nonowned [sic] endorsement deletes both exclusions as they would otherwise apply to the individual named in the endorsement. (Emphasis added).

EFFECT OF THE DECLARATORY JUDGMENT

Childress filed suit against Booth on May 17, 1976. Dairyland hired attorney Mark T. Davenport to defend Booth and paid him for his services. Davenport filed an answer for Booth on June 4, 1976. On June 15, 1976, Dairyland filed suit for declaratory judgment that the non-owner's policy did not provide Booth coverage for the collision with Childress. On January 17, 1977, an agreed judgment was rendered that Dairyland had no duty to defend Booth and that the non-owner's policy provided no coverage for Booth respecting the collision with Childress. On July 18, 1978, judgment was rendered for Childress in this suit against Booth.

Dairyland relies upon the doctrines of res judicata and collateral estoppel to support its contention that Childress is bound by the declaratory judgment. Their argument is that Childress' suit is derivative of Booth's coverage and therefore they are in privity with Booth, citing *Benson v. Wanda Petroleum Co.,* 468 S.W.2d 361 (Tex. 1971); *Kirby Lumber Co. v. Southern Lumber Co.,* 145 Tex.

151, 196 S.W.2d 387, 388 (1946); *Cain v. Balcom,* 130 Tex. 497, 109 S.W.2d 1044 (1937); and *Davis v. Dairyland County Mutual Insurance Co. of Texas,* 582 S.W.2d 591 (Tex.Civ.App.-Dallas 1979, writ ref'd n.r.e.). Our examination of the cases cited by Dairyland reveals that they are all distinguishable from the instant case on their facts.

* * *

In the present action, Childress could exercise no control over the declaratory judgment suit. Their interests were not represented by a party to the action nor were they successors in interest to a party. In fact the purpose of the suit was to work against their interest.

The Uniform Declaratory Judgment Act was adopted by Texas in the enactment of Art. 2524-1, Tex. Rev. Civ. Stat. Ann. Section 11 of that statute states in pertinent part: When declaratory relief is sought, all persons shall be made parties who have or claim any interest which would be affected by the declaration, and no declaration shall prejudice the rights of persons not parties to the proceeding.

No Texas appellate courts have considered the application of that statute to a fact situation such as the one before us. Those states which have addressed the precise question before us have unanimously held that a party in Childress' position is not barred by res judicata or collateral estoppel from pursuing a suit against the insuror to recover under the terms of the policy. *Southern Farm Bureau Casualty Insurance Co. v. Robinson,* 236 Ark. 268, 365 S.W.2d 454, 457 (1963); *Shapiro v. Republic Indemnity Co.,* 52 Cal.2d 437, 341 P.2d 289, 291 (1959); *Pharr v. Canal Insurance Co.,* 233 S.C. 266, 104 S.E.2d 394 (1958).

We hold that Childress and Booth were not in privity respecting the declaratory judgment suit and the doctrine of *res judicata* and collateral estoppel is not applicable to Childress' suit against Dairyland. . . . The judgment of the court of appeals is affirmed.

NOTES & QUESTIONS

1) Texas Uniform Declaratory Judgments Act—Tex. Civ. Prac. & Rem. Code § 37.004(a) reads:

> "A *person interested* under a deed, will, written contract, or other writings constituting a contract or whose rights, status, or other legal relations are affected by a statute, municipal ordinance, contract, or franchise may have determined any question of construction or validity arising under the instrument, statute, ordinance, contract, or franchise and obtain a declaration of rights, status, or other legal relations there under."

2) Assume that an interested person or party has not received notice of an impending declaratory-judgment trial. Will the interested party be prejudiced, given that the court will only interpret, say, an insurance contract and declare rights and obligations under that contract?

3) What is the distinction between an *ex parte* proceeding and a declaratory judgment trial?

4) Is it possible for an absent party to "defend" himself in a declaratory judgment trial?

Lozano v. Ocwen Federal Bank, FSB
489 F.3d 636
(5th Cir. 2007)

John and Susie Lozano appeal the district court's order granting summary judgment in favor of Ocwen Federal Bank on the Lozanos' claims related to Ocwen's foreclosure of their home in Houston, Texas. The Lozanos sought a declaratory judgment to void the foreclosure and remove the cloud of title on the property. They also sought damages for alleged violations of Texas and federal law governing foreclosures. The district court granted Ocwen's motion for summary judgment and purported to dismiss the entire case. For the reasons stated below, we affirm in part and reverse in part.

I.

On April 15, 1980, the Lozanos executed a promissory note for $76,500, payable to University Savings over a thirty year term at 12% interest, for the purchase of a home. They also executed a deed of trust granting University Savings a lien on their homestead. The Lozanos submitted cancelled checks showing that they thereafter made two unscheduled payments to University Savings on the note: a $12,000 payment on September 30, 1980, and an $11,000 payment on June 1, 1981. The parties agree that University Savings never credited these payments to the balance owed on the note.

University Savings subsequently transferred the note and deed of trust to Federal Home Loan Bank of Dallas in 1989. Between 1989 and 1997, when Ocwen purchased the note and deed of trust, they changed hands several times. According to the district court, the note and deed of trust were subject to the following transfers: first, on May 9, 1990 the note was assigned from Federal Home Loan Bank of Dallas to the Resolution Trust Company ("RTC") as receiver for University Federal Savings Association; second, on November 15, 1990 the note was assigned from RTC as receiver for University Savings Association to RTC as receiver for University Federal Savings Association; and third, in an undated assignment, the note was assigned from RTC as receiver for University Federal Savings Association to Ryland Mortgage Company. Following the transfer to Ryland there is a gap in the chain of title. Ocwen purchased the note, by that time apparently in default, from Credit Suisse First Boston Mortgage Capital LLC on May 31, 1997. On December 17, 1997, the deed of trust was also transferred to Ocwen. Thereafter, Ocwen sold the note to LaSalle National Bank in 1998, but has remained the servicer of the note.

The Lozanos filed for bankruptcy in 1996, 1998, and 2000. During these bankruptcies the Lozanos asserted, and the bankruptcy court accepted, that the Lozanos owed a substantial sum on the note at issue. Additionally, the Lozanos entered into two forbearance agreements with Ocwen, one in 1999 and one in 2001, where they acknowledged default on the note and agreed to modify the note's terms in exchange for Ocwen's promise not to foreclose at that time. As part of the 2001 forbearance agreement, the Lozanos also represented that they had no defenses or setoffs with respect to their obligation to pay the note.

In 2002, the Lozanos again defaulted on the note and Ocwen foreclosed and purchased the property at a foreclosure sale on March 3, 2003. The Lozanos responded by bringing suit in Texas state court seeking declaratory relief and damages based on their 1980 and 1981 prepayments and Ocwen's alleged violations of notice and verification requirements under state and federal law. Ocwen removed to federal court on the basis of diversity jurisdiction.

After fairly extensive discovery, the parties filed cross motions for summary judgment. The main thrust of the Lozanos' argument was that the foreclosure was void because, considering the prepayments they made in 1980 and 1981, they had paid the note in full by 1990. Ocwen argued it was entitled to summary judgment based on, *inter alia,* the affirmative defenses of judicial estoppel (based on assertions made in the prior bankruptcy proceedings) and "estoppel" (based on the forbearance agreements). The district court granted Ocwen's motion and denied the Lozanos' motions for summary judgment and for leave to amend their complaint, and it entered a take nothing judgment against the Lozanos. The Lozanos timely appealed.

II.

* * *

The Lozanos brought claims for (A) a declaratory judgment to set aside the deed executed on the foreclosure sale, and (B) damages for alleged violations of the Texas Deceptive Trade Practices Act (DTPA), Tex. Bus. & Com.Code § 17.46(b)(12) , and the Fair Debt Collection Practices Act (FDCPA), 15 U.S.C. § 1692. The district court purported to dispose of each claim in its Opinion and Order on Summary Judgment.

A. Declaratory Judgment

The Lozanos sought a declaratory judgment to set aside the foreclosure on three grounds: 1) they had previously paid the entire the balance of the note, 2) Ocwen allegedly failed to comply with the Texas Property Code's foreclosure notice provisions, and 3) Ocwen allegedly violated the FDCPA.

1. Pre-payment of the Note

The district court held that judicial estoppel, promissory estoppel, and the statute of limitations barred the Lozanos from asserting that, by virtue of their prepayments to University Savings in 1980 and 1981, they had fully paid the note by 1990. Because we affirm on quasi estoppel grounds, we need not decide whether judicial estoppel or the statute of limitations also bar this claim.

In the 1999 and 2001 forbearance agreements, the Lozanos made several promises in exchange for Ocwen's promise not to foreclose based on the pending delinquencies. The 1999 agreement provided that Ocwen would modify the note to reflect an unpaid balance of $90,148, and the Lozanos promised to pay that balance at 12% interest over twenty-seven years by monthly payments of $938.85. In the 2001 agreement, the Lozanos acknowledged another default and affirmed their obligation to pay the balance of the note, which they stated was $85,295.40. In that agreement, the Lozanos further conceded that "by their execution and delivery hereof, that they have no defense, set off or counterclaim with respect to the default or their obligation under the Note and Mortgage."

Citing the Lozanos' representations and promises in the forbearance agreements, the district court held the doctrine of promissory estoppel prevented the Lozanos from asserting that they fully paid the mortgage in 1990. The court agreed with Ocwen that 1) the Lozanos made representations, 2) the Lozanos could foresee that those representations would be relied upon by Ocwen, and 3) Ocwen substantially relied upon the representations to its detriment by not foreclosing on the property. *Moore" Burger, Inc. v. Phillips Petroleum Co.,* 492 S.W.2d 934, 937 (Tex. 1972) (discussing the elements of promissory estoppel).

The Lozanos argue on appeal that promissory estoppel is inapplicable here because the forbearance agreements constitute valid contracts, and Texas courts have held that promissory estoppel may only be applied when no valid contract exists. *See Doctors Hosp. 1997, L.P. v. Sambuca Houston, L.P.,* 154 S.W.3d 634, 636-37 (Tex. App.- Houston [14th Dist.] 2004, pet. abated). We agree the district court may have erred in styling this ground for relief as promissory estoppel. Nonetheless, the Lozanos made representations in a binding contract, and now seek to take a position inconsistent with those representations. Prudence and case law dictate that this cannot be allowed.

Estoppel by contract, also known as "quasi estoppel," forbids a party to a contract from taking a position inconsistent with the terms of the contract when that position prejudices another. *Johnson v. Structured Asset Servs., LLC,* 148 S.W.3d 711, 721-22 (Tex.App.-Dallas 2004, no pet.). "The doctrine applies when it would be unconscionable to allow a person to maintain a position inconsistent with one to which ... he accepted a benefit." *Lopez v. Munoz, Hockema & Reed, L.L.P.,* 22 S.W.3d 857, 864 (Tex. 2000). In other words, the doctrine forbids a party from accepting the benefits of a transaction and then subsequently taking an inconsistent position to avoid corresponding obligations or effects. *Atkinson Gas Co. v. Albrecht,* 878 S.W.2d 236, 240 (Tex.App.-Corpus Christi 1994, writ denied).

In the 1999 forbearance agreement, the Lozanos agreed to pay more than $90,000 over the following twenty-seven years. In the 2001 forbearance agreement, they reaffirmed their obligations under the note and acknowledged that they had no defenses to their obligation to pay. But now they claim they do have a defense: that they have previously paid the note in full in 1990. That claim is patently inconsistent with the representations the Lozanos made in the forbearance agreements. Further, Ocwen, who agreed not to foreclose in 1999 and 2001 despite the Lozanos' default, would be prejudiced by the Lozanos' new position. In sum, it would be unconscionable to allow the Lozanos to accept the benefit of the forbearance agreements and then allow them to take an inconsistent position to avoid its obligations.

The Lozanos argue that Ocwen did not raise the quasi estoppel argument until appeal and thus waived it. However, Ocwen pleaded "estoppel" generally as an affirmative defense and moved for summary judgment on "estoppel" grounds. This Court has referred to quasi estoppel as simply "estoppel." *See, e.g., Bott v. J.F. Shea Co.,* 299 F.3d 508, 512 (5th Cir.2002) ("[W]e [have] noted that a precise description of the core basis of *estoppel* is that one who retains benefits under a transaction cannot avoid its obligations and is estopped to take an inconsistent position." (internal quotation marks omitted) (emphasis added)). This position is in accord with the view of Texas courts, whose interpretation of the law of "estoppel" we apply. *See Eckland Consultants, Inc. v. Ryder, Stilwell Inc.,* 176 S.W.3d 80, 88 n. 5 (Tex.App.-Houston [1st Dist.] 2004, no pet.) ("A general plea of estoppel is sufficient to raise the affirmative defense of quasi-estoppel.").

Under the facts of this case, and given the similarity of the doctrines of promissory estoppel and quasi estoppel, we find that Ocwen's styling of its argument as "estoppel" instead of "quasi estoppel" does not prohibit our consideration of that argument here. In reaching that conclusion we are influenced by the fact that Ocwen pled and consistently argued that the Lozanos were estopped from asserting that the note was fully paid in 1990 when they acknowledged and affirmed the debt in the forbearance agreements in 1999 and 2001. Further, Ocwen submitted the forbearance agreements into evidence in support of this argument. As a result, the Lozanos have been on notice of this argument since Ocwen first raised it in their answer as an affirmative defense.

Lastly, we acknowledge that the district court, after discussion of the applicable facts, found the elements for promissory estoppel satisfied. "We may affirm a summary judgment on any ground supported by the record, even if it is different from that relied on by the district court." *Holtzclaw v. DSC Commc'ns Corp.,* 255 F.3d 254, 258 (5th Cir.2001). The record indicates the Lozanos took a position in the forbearance agreements and accepted the benefits of that position and now seek to take an inconsistent position that would prejudice Ocwen. Thus, the record fully supports the application of quasi estoppel, see *Lopez,* 22 S.W.3d at 864, and we may affirm on that basis. *See Holtzclaw,* 255 F.3d at 258.

Because we agree with the district court that the Lozanos are estopped from taking a position contrary to the position they took in the forbearance agreements, we affirm the dismissal of the prepayment claim.

2. Alleged Violations of the Texas Property Code

In addition to arguing the foreclosure was void because they had already paid the mortgage in full, the Lozanos also sought to void the foreclosure on the basis that Ocwen violated the notice requirements in the Texas Property Code. *See* Tex. Prop.Code Ann. § 51.002(d) (requiring mortgage servicers to serve debtors in default with written notice of default and give the debtor at least twenty days to cure the default before foreclosing); *see also Mitchell v. Texas Commerce Bank-Irving,* 680 S.W.2d 681, 682 (Tex.App.-Fort Worth 1984, writ ref'd n.r.e.) (holding that failure to comply with section 51.002 invalidates the foreclosure).

Ocwen did not move for summary judgment on this claim, and although the district court granted summary judgment and purportedly dismissed the entire case, it did not address this claim in its

Opinion and Order on Summary Judgment. Generally, "a district court may not grant summary judgment *sua sponte* on grounds not requested by the moving party." *Baker v. Metro. Life Ins. Co.,* 364 F.3d 624, 632 (5th Cir.2004) (quoting *John Deere Co.* v. *Am. Nat'l Bank,* 809 F.2d 1190, 1192 (5th Cir.1987)). An exception exists when the district court gives a party ten days notice; in those situations a court may grant summary judgment *sua sponte* on grounds not urged in a pending motion. *See Judwin Properties, Inc. v. U.S. Fire Ins. Co.,* 973 F.2d 432, 436-37 (5th Cir.1992).

Here the record does not indicate the district court gave any notice to the Lozanos before dismissing this claim *sua sponte.* Consequently, the Lozanos were not on notice to present arguments on this claim in their response to Ocwen's summary judgment motion, and the court did not have the benefit of the parties' arguments.

Ocwen argues that this claim is dependent on the Lozanos' prepayments claim; that is, if we do not recognize the prepayments this claim must fail as a matter of law. This argument is unpersuasive. Section 51.002(d) contains a notice requirement that may be violated even if the debt is valid. *See* Tex. Prop.Code Ann. § 51.002(d). Further, the statute of limitations does not bar this claim. It is undisputed the foreclosure occurred in March 2003 and the Lozanos filed this suit two months later in May 2003, well within the allowed period. Consequently, we reverse and remand for consideration of the Lozanos' Texas Property Code claim.

3. Alleged Violation of the Fair Debt Collection Practices Act

The third ground for a declaratory judgment was a claim under the FDCPA, and the Lozanos also sought damages for the alleged violation this statute. The FDCPA provides in pertinent part:

> If the consumer notifies the debt collector in writing within . . . [thirty days] that the debt, or any portion thereof, is disputed, or that the consumer requests the name and address of the original creditor, the debt collector shall cease collection of the debt, or any disputed portion thereof, until the debt collector obtains verification of the debt or a copy of a judgment, or the name and address of the original creditor, and a copy of such verification or judgment, or name and address of the original creditor, is mailed to the consumer by the debt collector. 15 U.S.C. § 1692g(b).

The Lozanos alleged that they timely requested proof of the validity of the debt from Ocwen and that Ocwen failed to provide that information before foreclosing. However, Ocwen did not mention the FDCPA claim in its motion for summary judgment. The district court dismissed the claim *sua sponte* finding that, to the extent the Lozanos based this claim on their prepayments, it was barred. Alternatively, the court found this claim was not accurately pled to allow the court to analyze it. In particular, the court noted the Lozanos did not allege that Ocwen was a "debt collector" as required by § 1692g(b).

The Lozanos argue that the court erred in dismissing this claim *sua sponte* because the court did not give prior notice. *See Baker,* 364 F.3d at 632; *see also Washington v. Resolution Trust Corp.,* 68 F.3d 935, 939 (5th Cir.1995) (allowing a district court to grant summary judgment *sua sponte,* but only after giving ten days notice). For the same reasons we reversed the *sua sponte* dismissal of the Texas Property Code claim, *see supra* Part II(A)(2), we reverse the dismissal of the FDCPA claim.

Even if we characterized this action as a *sua sponte* dismissal for failure to state a claim under Rule 12(b)(6), as Ocwen argues, we would reach the same result. We have held that a district court is "authorized to consider the sufficiency of the complaint on its own initiative." *Guthrie v. Tifco Indus.*, 941 F.2d 374, 379 (5th Cir.1991). And if the court finds the complaint fails to state a claim, it may dismiss " 'as long as the procedure employed is fair.' " *Bazrowx v. Scott,* 136 F.3d 1053, 1054 (5th Cir.1998). We have recently held that a district court's failure to give notice prior to *sua sponte* dismissal for failure to state a claim was unfair under the circumstances. *See Carroll v. Fort James Corp.,* 470 F.3d 1171, 1177 (5th Cir. 2006).

* * *

We do not always require notice prior to *sua sponte* dismissal for failure to state a claim, as long as the plaintiff has alleged his "best case." *See Bazrowx,* 136 F.3d at 1054 (citing *Jacquez v. Procunier,* 801 F.2d 789, 792-93 (5th Cir.1986)). In *Jacquez* we held, in the context of a § 1983 action, that "[a]t some point a court must decide that a plaintiff has had fair opportunity to make his case; if, after that time, a cause of action has not been established, the court should finally dismiss the suit." *Jacquez,* 801 F.2d at 792. The Court in *Jacquez* dismissed a claim after the plaintiff filed a deficient complaint and repeatedly declared the adequacy of that complaint in a lengthy response to defendant's motion to dismiss. *Id.* Thus, *Jacquez* is readily distinguishable because there the plaintiff repeatedly represented that his complaint adequately stated the cause of action and refused to file a supplemental complaint even in the face of a motion to dismiss. *See id.*

In the case at bar, the Lozanos had no notice that their complaint was deficient. Notice would have allowed the Lozanos an opportunity to seek leave to amend their complaint to allege that cause of action properly. Based on our *de novo* review, we hold that the district court erred in dismissing the FDCPA claim *sua sponte* without notice. *See Carroll,* 470 F.3d at 1177.

* * *

III.

For the foregoing reasons we affirm the district court's order denying the Lozanos leave to amend their complaint. Further, we affirm the court's order of September 29, 2005, to the extent it dismisses the Lozanos' prepayment claim, and we vacate that order to the extent it dismisses the Lozanos' Texas Property Code claim, their FDCPA claim, and their DTPA claim. We remand for consideration of the Texas Property Code Claim, the FDCPA claim, and the DTPA claim.

NOTES

Declaratory Judgment Act, 28 U.S.C. § 2201(a) is a federal statute. It reads in pertinent part:

> In a case of actual controversy within its jurisdiction, . . . any court of the United States . . .may declare the rights and other legal relations of any interested party seeking such declaration, whether or not further relief is or could be sought. Any such declaration shall have the force and effect of a final judgment or decree and shall be reviewable as such.

B. *Proof of Damages*

1. "Actual Damages" or "Economic Damages"

The following insightful information appears in *Matheus v. Sasser,* 164 S.W.3d 453, 458-459 (Tex. App.-Fort Worth 2005):

> **PROPER MEASURE OF DAMAGES**
>
> In response to Matheus's argument that his damages are appropriately measured by the number of square feet by which the property was short times the price he paid per square foot, Appellees argue that there are only two measures of damages for misrepresentation, "benefit of bargain" and "out of pocket," and that Matheus's testimony based solely on those calculations is no evidence under either measure of damages. Although we agree that Matheus's evidence does not satisfy either of those measures of damages, we disagree that those are the only measures of damages available for misrepresentation under the DTPA.
>
> The applicable version of the DTPA provides that a consumer may recover "economic damages," defined as "compensatory damages for pecuniary loss, including costs of repair or replacement." Tex. Bus. & Com.Code Ann. §§ 17.45(11), 17.50(b)(1) (Vernon 2002). We have found no case suggesting that the term "economic damages" carries any different meaning than "actual damages" as allowed under the prior version of the DTPA.
>
>> In 1995, the legislature amended section 17.50(b)(1) to permit recovery of "economic damages" instead of "actual damages." Act of May 29, 1989, 71st Leg., R.S., ch. 380, § 2, 1989 Tex. Gen. Laws 1490, 1491, *amended by* Act of May 19, 1995, 74th Leg., R.S., ch. 414, § 5, 1995 Tex. Gen. Laws

> 2988, 2992 (current version at Tex. Bus. & Com. Code Ann. § 17.50(b)(1). After the amendment, appellate courts have used the terms "actual damages" and "economic damages" interchangeably and cited as authority Texas Supreme Court cases applying the statute prior to the amendment. *See Ford Motor Co. v. Cooper,* 125 S.W.3d 794, 798-99 (Tex. App.-Texarkana 2004, no pet.) (citing *W.O. Bankston Nissan, Inc. v. Walters,* 754 S.W.2d 127, 128 (Tex.1988) and *Leyendecker & Assocs., Inc. v. Wechter,* 683 S.W.2d 369, 373 (Tex.1984)); *Valley Nissan, Inc. v. Davila,* 133 S.W.3d 702, 713 (Tex. App.-Corpus Christi 2003, no pet.) (citing *Farrell v. Hunt,* 714 S.W.2d 298, 300 (Tex.1986).

Therefore, we may appropriately apply the case law decided under the prior and current versions of the Act. Actual damages for misrepresentation under the DTPA are those recoverable at common law. *Arthur Andersen & Co. v. Perry Equip. Corp.,* 945 S.W.2d 812, 816 (Tex.1997). *Brown v. American Transfer & Storage Co.,* 601 S.W.2d 931, 939 (Tex.1980). [Under the] common law, actual damages are either "direct" or "consequential." *Id.* (citing *Henry S. Miller Co. v. Bynum,* 836 S.W.2d 160, 163 (Tex. 1992) (Phillips, C.J., concurring).

Direct damages are the necessary and usual result of the defendant's wrongful act; they flow naturally and necessarily from the wrong. *Arthur Andersen,* 945 S.W.2d at 816. Direct damages are those that are conclusively presumed to have been foreseen or contemplated by the party as the result of his wrongful act. *Henry S. Miller Co.,* 836 S.W.2d at 163. Consequential damages, on the other hand, are those that result naturally, but not necessarily, from the acts complained of.

2. Measuring "Actual Economic Damages" — Using the "Benefit of the Bargain" and "Out of Pocket" Rules

W.O. Bankston Nissan, Inc. v. Walters
754 S.W.2d 127
(Tex. 1988)

This is a Deceptive Trade Practices Act case arising out of the purchase of a pickup truck by Kelly Joe Walters from W.O. Bankston Nissan, Inc. The trial court entered judgment n.o.v. that Walters take nothing. The court of appeals, in an unpublished opinion, reversed the trial court's judgment and rendered judgment on the jury verdict. We reverse the judgment of the court of appeals and affirm the judgment of the trial court.

Walters contacted his friend Buddy Wood, who was a salesman for Bankston, to discuss trading in his 280-ZX for a pickup truck. Walters test drove the pickup in question and agreed to purchase it. He and Wood agreed upon a trade-in value of $7,700 for the 280-ZX. Wood prepared a Workup

Sheet which showed the pickup to be a 1982 model. He also prepared an Odometer Statement and a Warranty Sheet, both of which showed the pickup to be a 1981 model. Walters took possession of the pickup and Bankston took possession of the 280-ZX and sold it for $7,700, the value agreed upon by Wood and Walters. Bankston then paid off the $5,832.01 balance owed by Walters on the 280-ZX.

Several days later, Walters experienced mechanical difficulty with the pickup and returned it to Bankston, who repaired the problem at no cost. Walters subsequently experienced additional problems with the pickup. During this time, Walters' Credit Union notified him that the truck was a 1981 model, not a 1982 model, and that it would not finance the truck. Walters then demanded that Bankston take back the pickup and return his 280-ZX. He was informed that the 280-ZX had been sold and was offered the difference between the $7,700 agreed value and the loan balance Bankston had paid. Walters refused and filed suit.

The jury found that Bankston represented that the pickup was a 1982 model; that the misrepresentation was a producing cause of actual damages; that the actual damages included loss of the 280-ZX; and that the 280-ZX had a fair market value of $9,800 on the date of the sale. No other damage issues were submitted. Bankston objected to the submission of the above issues, asserting that the issues did not present a proper measure of damages.

The dispositive issue in this case is the correct measure of damages. In a DTPA case, the plaintiff is entitled to actual damages. Tex. Bus. & Comm.Code § 17.50(b)(1). This court has defined actual damages as those recoverable at common law. *Farrell v. Hunt,* 714 S.W.2d 298, 300 (Tex. 1986); *Brown v. American Transfer & Storage Co.,* 601 S.W.2d 931, 939 (Tex. 1980). Under common law, there are two measures of damages for misrepresentation: 1) the "out of pocket" measure, which is the "difference between the value of that which was parted with and the value of that which was received"; and 2) the "benefit of the bargain" measure, which is the difference between the value as represented and the value actually received. The DTPA permits a plaintiff to recover either the "out of pocket" or the "benefit of the bargain" damages, whichever is greater. *Leyendecker & Associates, Inc. v. Wechter,* 683 S.W.2d 369, 373 (Tex.1984) and *Vista Chevrolet, Inc. v. Lewis,* 709 S.W.2d 176 (Tex.1986).

Walters' burden of proof in this case was to show either the difference between the fair market value of the pickup as delivered and the value of the truck as it was represented; or the difference in value between that with which he parted and that which he received. He did neither. Walters had the burden of requesting jury issues on the proper measure of damages. Having failed to do so, his cause of action must fail.

The judgment of the court of appeals is reversed and the judgment of the trial court is affirmed.

Justice Mauzy concurring on Motion For Rehearing

I concur in the result reached by the majority. I would however like to add that in cases brought under the Deceptive Trade Practices-Consumer Protection Act, Tex.Bus. & Com.Code Ann. § 17.41 et seq. damages are recoverable "to compensate for the actual loss sustained as a result of the defendant's conduct." *Kish v. Van Note,* 692 S.W.2d 463, 466 (Tex. 1985). I would further note that under the facts of this case, either an "out of pocket" or "benefit of the bargain" measure of damages was appropriate. Nevertheless, as this court held in *Kish,* the "out of pocket" and "benefit of the bargain" rules are not the exclusive means of measuring damages in a DTPA action. 692 S.W.2d at 466. The allowable measure of damages may appropriately include related and necessary expenses that are incurred after the deceptive act or practice has become apparent and the measure of damages under either the "out of pocket" or "benefit of the bargain" theory should in no way be read as exclusive.

3. Cumulative and "Other" Damages

Mayo v. John Hancock Mutual Life Insurance Company
711 S.W.2d 5
(Tex. 1986)

This is an appeal from a summary judgment against Steve and Diane Mayo in their suit against John Hancock Mutual Life Insurance Company of Boston, Massachusetts. The court of appeals affirmed the summary judgment. We reverse the judgment of the court of appeals and remand the cause for trial.

Steve Mayo was employed by Hutron Aerospace Company and was covered by a group insurance policy issued by John Hancock Mutual Life Insurance Company. The policy provided maternity benefits. It further provided that coverage would end upon termination of employment. However, the policy also contained an exception allowing the coverage of a totally disabled dependent to continue until the disability ended. Steve was terminated on December 19, 1980. His wife, Diane, gave birth on January 27, 1981. John Hancock denied the Mayos' claim for maternity benefits.

The Mayos sued John Hancock for breach of contract; violation of Art. 3.62 of the Tex. Ins. Code ; violation of Art. 21.21 § 16 of the Tex. Ins. Code; and for breach of the Tex. Bus. & Comm. Code § 17.46 (Deceptive Trade Practices Act). The trial court, on motion by John Hancock and over the Mayos' objection, severed the breach of contract and Art. 3.62 causes of action from the Art. 21.21 § 16 and DTPA causes of action. Article 3.62 provides recovery for the amount of the loss, 12% damages, and reasonable attorney's fees when the insurance company liable for the loss fails to pay the claim within 30 days after demand. Article 21.21 § 16 and the DTPA provide for recovery of actual damages for unfair or deceptive trade practices with the possibility of recovering treble damages. The Mayos tried the breach of contract and Art. 3.62 causes of action first. The jury found that Diane was totally disabled as of December 19, 1980, and awarded actual damages equal to the Mayos' medical expenses plus 12% penalty and attorney's fees.

John Hancock filed a motion for summary judgment alleging only that the Art. 21.21 § 16 and DTPA claims were barred because of recovery of actual damages in the contract and Art. 3.62 claims. In affirming that judgment, the court of appeals relied solely on the grounds stated in the

Motion for Summary Judgment and *Connecticut General v. Stice,* 640 S.W.2d 955 (Tex.App.-Dallas 1982, writ ref'd n.r.e.). The summary judgment was proper only if the motion for summary judgment and the supporting affidavits showed that John Hancock was entitled to judgment as a matter of law. *Teer v. Duddlesten,* 664 S.W.2d 702 (Tex. 1984).

The dispositive issue in this case is whether the recovery of actual damages equal to the amount of medical expense payable under the policy plus 12% penalty, for failure to timely pay the policy benefits, barred treble damages under Art. 21.21 § 16 or the DTPA. In *Connecticut General v. Stice,* the plaintiff brought an action to recover the proceeds of an insurance policy on the life of her deceased husband and treble damages based on deceptive and misleading practices under the Tex. Ins. Code and the DTPA. The court of appeals held that because Stice was entitled to recover the proceeds, she had thus not suffered any actual damages.

However, the court in *Stice* did not address two points which could have been dispositive of that case. Those points were: (1) there was no evidence of a misrepresentation, and (2) any claim for misrepresentation was barred by the statute of limitations. Thus our refusing error in *Stice* was not an indication that we approved the language of that case relied upon here by the court of appeals that recovery under Art. 3.62 barred recovery under Art. 21.21 § 16 or the DTPA. The court of appeals in this case held that § 17.43 of the DTPA precluded the Mayos' causes of action in the present case by the following language:

> The provisions of this subchapter are not exclusive. The remedies provided in this subchapter are in addition to any other procedures or remedies provided for in any other law; provided, however, that no recovery shall be permitted under *both* this subchapter and another law of *both actual damages and penalties for the same act or practice.*

We hold that the court of appeals misinterpreted the clear and unambiguous language of that statutory provision. The statute merely limits a plaintiff from recovering actual and punitive damages for a specific act under one law and then recovering actual and punitive damages for the very same act under the provisions of the DTPA. In the prior trial, the Mayos recovered their actual damages plus 12% penalties for John Hancock's violation of Art. 3.62 of the Tex. Ins. Code In the present case, they seek to recover actual damages plus punitive damages for a violation of Art. 21.21 § 16 of the Tex. Ins. Code and Section 17.46 of the DTPA. The violation of Art. 3.62 is based on failure to pay under the policy within 30 days. The violation of Art. 21.21 § 16 and the DTPA is based on false, misleading or deceptive trade practices. Recovery of the 12% penalty under Art. 3.62 plus recovery of treble damages under Art. 21.21 § 16 and the DTPA would not constitute recovery "for the same act or practice." The question of whether the Mayos could prove their causes of action under Art. 21.21 § 16 and the DTPA is not before us because it was not raised in the motion for summary judgment.

The Mayos' pleadings in this case stated a cause of action. The motion for summary judgment did not set out a legal bar to that cause of action. Therefore the trial court and the court of appeals erred in sustaining the motion for summary judgment. In the event the Mayos prevail at trial of this cause, their judgment should be offset by the amount of actual damages recovered in the prior trial.

We reverse the judgment of the court of appeals and remand to the trial court for trial on the Art. 21.21 § 16 and DTPA causes of action.

Henry S. Miller Company v. Bynum
836 S.W .2d 160
(Tex. 1992)

This case presents two questions: (1) whether there was good cause to permit a named individual party to testify at trial when the party was not listed in response to a discovery request for disclosure of witnesses; and (2) whether the evidence supported the damages awarded. We hold that the trial judge did not abuse his discretion in finding there was good cause — [one] sufficient to require admission and that there was some evidence to support the award of damages.

Douglas Bynum, Jr. and Starfire Engineering, Inc. d/b/a Tiffany's Hair Styles leased space in the Wood Winds Shopping Center for a hair-styling salon. Henry S. Miller Co., was a leasing agent for the shopping center and handled Bynum's lease. After Bynum moved into the shopping center, the leased space did not conform to Bynum's expectations so he brought this action against Henry S. Miller Company, alleging violations of the Deceptive Trade Practices Act (DTPA). Tex. Bus. & Com. Code §§ 17.41-.63. After a trial to the court, the court rendered judgment in favor of Bynum for $60,426 actual damages and $120,852 additional damages. The court of appeals affirmed.

* * *

II.

Miller argues that Bynum offered no evidence to support an out-of-pocket or benefit-of-the-bargain measure of damages. *See W.O. Bankston Nissan, Inc. v. Walters,* 754 S.W.2d 127, 128 (Tex. 1988) (out-of-pocket and benefit-of-the-bargain are two measures of damages under the DTPA). However, the DTPA allows recovery for actual damages. Tex. Bus & Com. Code § 17. 50(b)(1). This court has defined actual damages under the DTPA as "the total loss sustained [by the consumer] as a result of the deceptive trade practice." *Kish v. Van Note,* 692 S.W.2d 463, 466 (Tex. 1985); *Smith v. Baldwin,* 611 S.W.2d 611, 617 (Tex. 1981).

Actual damages "includ[e] related and reasonably necessary expenses." *Kish,* 692 S.W.2d at 466; Therefore, such direct measures as "benefit-of-the-bargain" and "out-of-pocket" are not exclusive. We have permitted other damages to ensure that the plaintiff is made whole. *See Kish,* 692 S.W.2d at 466-68 (damages for removing defective product); *White v. Southwestern Bell Telephone Co.,* 651 S.W.2d 260 (Tex.1983) (lost profits); *Smith v. Baldwin,* 611 S.W.2d 611, 617 (Tex. 1981) (interest on indebtedness); *see also Mead v. Johnson Group, Inc.,* 615 S.W.2d 685, 687 (Tex. 1981) (loss of credit); *Village Mobile Homes, Inc. v. Porter,* 716 S.W.2d 543 (Tex. App.-Austin 1986, writ ref'd n.r.e.) (loss for improvements made).

One element of the damages Bynum pleaded for was $60,426.00 in lost capital investment. The trial court awarded $60,426.00 in actual damages. Miller's no evidence point challenging these damages contended that the exclusive measures of actual damages under the DTPA are the out-of-pocket and benefit-of-the-bargain measures. Miller's no evidence challenge fails because these measures are not exclusive. Further, even if Miller raised a general no evidence challenge to the damages award, the record contains some evidence to support the trial court's award of these damages to Bynum as part of the actual loss he sustained.

The judgment of the court of appeals is affirmed.

4. Damages for "Mental Anguish"

Parkway Company v. Woodruff
901 S.W.2d 434
(Tex. 1995)

I. Facts

The Sugar Creek Corporation and its successor-in-interest, the Parkway Company (collectively, Parkway), created a real estate development known as Sugar Creek on the south side of Houston. Parkway prepared the land for homebuilding by platting, surveying, regrading, building roads, and dealing with local regulatory and utility authorities. The Sugar Creek community was developed over a period of years, and included plans for retail and recreational areas.

In 1977 Harrington Homes purchased the lot at issue, in section 24 of the development, and built a house on it. After Harrington Homes sold it to the original occupants, the house was resold and occupied by another homeowner before Ray and Constance Woodruff bought it and moved in during April 1981.

In 1983 Parkway began to develop Sugar Creek section 34, which lies immediately to the east of the Woodruffs' lot and the Kaneb tract, a large commercial tract that lies to the north of the Woodruffs' lot and the rest of section 24. During the course of its work in early 1983, Parkway began constructing a wall along the line dividing section 34 from the Kaneb tract and section 24.

Ray Woodruff, who holds an engineering degree, advised Parkway by letter on February 3, 1983, that the wall might alter drainage patterns on his lot. Six days later, during a heavy rainstorm, the Woodruffs observed that regrading activities on section 34 had diverted runoff from the Kaneb tract onto their land.

* * *

When Hurricane Alicia struck the Texas coast on August 18, 1983, run-off from the Kaneb tract flooded the Woodruffs' sun room. The house flooded again in 1986, 1987, and 1989. As a result, the house suffered a cracked foundation and other structural damage.

The Woodruffs filed suit . . . [alleging] that Parkway was liable under the DTPA for: (1) unconscionable conduct; (2) false, misleading, or deceptive acts or practices; and (3) the knowing breach of an implied warranty to perform "development services" in "a good and workmanlike manner." Parkway, in turn, filed third-party claims against its engineers, the owners of the Kaneb tract, and Harrington Homes. The Woodruffs later amended their petition to sue directly these additional parties.

At trial, the district court granted a directed verdict in favor of Harrington Homes and Parkway's engineers. . . . The jury also found that Parkway violated the Water Code, that it knowingly breached an implied warranty, and that it acted unconscionably. The jury declined, however, to find that Parkway . . . engaged in any false, misleading, or deceptive acts or practices . . . . The court rendered judgment for actual damages of $220,000, including $120,000 for diminution in value and $100,000 for repairs to the Woodruffs' house. Based on the DTPA findings, the trial court also rendered judgment for the Woodruffs for "additional" damages, a percentage-based award of attorney's fees, and mental anguish damages.

The court of appeals affirmed most of the trial court's judgment, but deleted any damages for mental anguish, and added $14,000 in out-of-pocket expenses claimed by the Woodruffs.

II. DTPA Violations

The Woodruffs allege that Parkway violated the DTPA by breaching an implied warranty to perform future development services in a good and workmanlike manner, or alternatively, by committing an unconscionable act.

* * *

IV. Mental Anguish

The Woodruffs challenge the court of appeals' deletion of their award for mental anguish based on legal insufficiency. The court of appeals concluded that "the evidence simply does not demonstrate mental anguish as that term is defined by law." 857 S.W.2d at 916. We agree with the court of appeals.

At the outset, we emphasize the limited nature of our present inquiry: we are focusing only on the type of evidence required to support an award of mental anguish damages in cases in which recovery is allowed. Nonetheless, we find it helpful to begin with a historical overview of mental anguish damages before addressing the legal sufficiency of the Woodruffs' evidence of their mental anguish.

The history of mental anguish damages in Anglo-American jurisprudence is convoluted and complex. Mental anguish claims have long been distrusted by the common law, and an early general rule developed that mental anguish damages were not recoverable. *See Lynch v. Knight,* 11 Eng. Rep. 854, 863 (H.L.1961). The inherently subjective nature of mental anguish and the concomitant potential for false claims were two of the most commonly cited reasons for skepticism about such claims. *See, e.g., Battalla v. State,* 176 N.E.2d 729, 731-32 (N.Y. 1961); *Knaub v. Gotwalt,* 220 A.2d 646, 647 (Pa. 1966). Exceptions to the general rule gradually emerged, falling into roughly two categories. Recovery for mental anguish was permitted when the mental suffering was: 1) accompanied by a physical injury resulting from a physical impact, or 2) produced by a particularly upsetting or disturbing event.

Once the threshold requirements of physical injury and impact or of particularly disturbing events were met, recovery of mental anguish damages was not hard to justify. Mental suffering could be inferred from the fact of physical injury. The Missouri Supreme Court, for example, justified this inference by reasoning that "the mind is as much a part of the body as the bones and muscles, and an injury to the body included the whole, and its effects were not separable." *Connell v. Western Union Tel. Co.,* 116 Mo. 34, 22 S.W. 345, 349 (1893).

Similarly, once particularly disturbing events were proved by reference to objective phenomena or conditions, the law generally allowed the claimant's mental suffering to be presumed to flow from such events. The oldest examples of this category of cases are those involving assault, slander, and other intentional torts. *See, e.g., I. de S. v. W. de S.,* Y.B. 22 Edw. III, fo. 99, pl. 60 (1348) (allowing tavern-keeper to recover when the defendant threw a hatchet at the tavern-keeper's wife).

Although limiting mental anguish damages to cases with either physical impact or disturbing events avoided many evidentiary problems, the limitations were admittedly arbitrary: some claimants with relatively minor mental anguish recovered, while others who might have suffered significant anguish were precluded from any recovery. As a result, many of these limitations were first relaxed and later abandoned. The requirement of a physical impact was relaxed, and recovery for mental anguish was permitted so long as the anguish manifested itself physically. Abandonment of the physical impact requirement led the way to recovery for mental injuries suffered by bystanders in the "zone of danger," *see id.* (noting that 14 states have expanded recovery for mental anguish to this point and no further); and even to specified parties beyond this zone. *See, e.g., Dillon v. Legg,* 441 P.2d 912, 920 (Cal. 1968) (allowing recovery for mental anguish by a witness to the injury of a close relative). In recent years, several states have eliminated the physical manifestation requirement altogether.

Over time, the disturbing events exception also yielded to pressure to provide compensation in more routine cases. Courts took cognizance of mental anguish injuries not only in cases of malicious intentional wrongs, but also in cases involving violations of statutes. Some jurisdictions came to recognize a distinct legal duty to avoid even the negligent infliction of emotional harm itself.

Texas law has generally followed the same ad hoc pattern of development. We initially allowed mental anguish damages only in cases in which there was a physical injury. *See Hill v. Kimball,* 76 Tex. 210, 13 S.W. 59, 59 (1890) ("Probably an action will not lie when there is no injury except the suffering of the fright itself....”). At the turn of the century, we allowed recovery for mental anguish unaccompanied by physical impact injury, provided the mental anguish had a physical manifestation. *See Hill,* 13 S.W. at 59; *Gulf, C. & S.F. Ry. Co. v. Hayter,* 93 Tex. 239, 54 S.W. 944, 945 (1900). We eased the physical impact rule even further when we adopted the bystander rule from *Dillon v. Legg* in *Freeman v. City of Pasadena,* 744 S.W.2d 923, 923-24 (Tex. 1988).

Texas courts have also struggled to distinguish between the disturbing events that justify mental anguish damages and those that do not. Unwilling to confine mental anguish damages to intentional torts, our courts have allowed mental anguish damages for such things as failing to deliver a telegraph relating to death or last illness, *see Stuart v. Western Union Tel. Co.,* 66 Tex. 580, 18 S.W. 351, 353 (1885); sending a passenger to the wrong destination, *see Texas & Pac. Ry. Co. v. Armstrong,* 51 S.W. 835, 836 (Tex. 1899); and mishandling a corpse. *See Pat H. Foley & Co. v. Wyatt,* 442 S.W.2d 904, 907 (Tex.Civ.App.-Houston [14th Dist.] 1969, writ ref'd n.r.e.).

The physical manifestation requirement was first excused under exceptional circumstances, and then abandoned completely in 1987. *See St. Elizabeth Hosp. v. Garrard,* 730 S.W.2d 649, 654 (Tex. 1987), *overruled on other grounds, Boyles v. Kerr,* 855 S.W.2d 593 (Tex. 1993). Similarly, the types of culpable conduct for which mental anguish damages were allowed expanded to include more commonplace misconduct, such as knowing misrepresentations in a consumer transaction. *See Luna v. North Star Dodge Sales, Inc.,* 667 S.W.2d 115 (Tex.1984).

As mental anguish damages have became more readily available, members of this Court have voiced concerns about the potential for over-compensation and even double recovery. *See Moore v. Lillebo,* 722 S.W.2d 683, 688-692 (Tex.1986) (Spears, J., joined by Gonzalez, J., dissenting) (arguing that elimination of physical manifestation requirement for recovery of mental anguish damages would allow damages for non-compensable sorrow, anger, worry, and fear, and in a wrongful death case, would duplicate those damages already allowed for loss of companionship and society). *See also Birchfield v. Texarkana Memorial Hosp.,* 747 S.W.2d 361, 368-69 (Tex. 1987) (disallowing recovery for “shock and emotional trauma” as duplicative of award for mental anguish). Genuineness of a claim of mental anguish has never been the solitary basis for judicial concerns about this species of recovery. Rather, the variability and thus unpredictability of such awards, due to the broad discretion routinely afforded juries when awarding mental anguish damages, helps to explain some of the artificial constraints historically placed on the recovery of such damages.

The early requirements for establishing the recoverability of mental anguish damages served primarily as proxies for direct evidence of mental injury. When, for example, evidence of a physical manifestation of a mental injury was required, evidence tended to be directed at proving the manifestation, rather than proving the amount of actual anguish. Similarly, when recovery of mental anguish damages was limited to cases of especially culpable conduct, the focus of the evidence tended to be on the nature of the malfeasance, rather than on the extent of anguish. *See, e.g., Texas & Pac. Ry. Co. v. Armstrong,* 93 Tex. 31, 51 S.W. 835 (1899) (devoting a significant portion of the opinion to the details of the railroad's mistaken issuance of a ticket to the wrong destination, but only a single sentence to the passenger's reaction).

The erosion of these proxies as a substitute for proof of mental anguish has created a vacuum of sorts, in which the only guidance given by trial courts to juries is a confounding definition of mental anguish, of which the following is typical: The term "mental anguish" implies a relatively high degree of mental pain and distress. It is more than mere disappointment, anger, resentment or embarrassment, although it may include all of these. It includes a mental sensation of pain resulting from such painful emotions as grief, severe disappointment, indignation, wounded pride, shame, despair and/or public humiliation. *Trevino v. Southwestern Bell Tel. Co.,* 582 S.W.2d 582, 584 (Tex.Civ.App.-Corpus Christi 1979, no writ). This definition requires a jury to distinguish between disappointment and severe disappointment, between embarrassment and wounded pride, between anger and indignation. It is little wonder that courts and juries have found this and similar definitions of mental anguish "somewhat unwieldy." *Sanchez v. Guerrero,* 885 S.W.2d 487, 494 (Tex.Civ.App.-El Paso 1994, no writ).

When a challenge is made to the sufficiency of the evidence to go to the jury or to support the jury's finding, the same type of problem persists. The reviewing court must distinguish between shades and degrees of emotion. These distinctions are critical under our substantive law because evidence of lesser reactions cannot support an award of mental anguish damages.

Under this admittedly nebulous definition and the traditional standard of review, it is nevertheless clear that an award of mental anguish damages will survive a legal sufficiency challenge when the plaintiffs have introduced direct evidence of the nature, duration, and severity of their mental anguish, thus establishing a substantial disruption in the plaintiffs' daily routine. Such evidence, whether in the form of the claimants' own testimony, that of third parties, or that of experts, is more likely to provide the fact finder with adequate details to assess mental anguish claims. Although we stop short of requiring this type of evidence in all cases in which mental anguish damages are sought, the absence of this type of evidence, particularly when it can be readily supplied or procured by the plaintiff, justifies close judicial scrutiny of other evidence offered on this element of damages.

When claimants fail to present direct evidence of the nature, duration, or severity of their anguish, we apply traditional "no evidence" standards to determine whether the record reveals any evidence of "a high degree of mental pain and distress" that is "more than mere worry, anxiety, vexation, embarrassment, or anger" to support any award of damages. *See J.B. Custom Design & Bldg. v. Clawson,* 794 S.W.2d 38, 43 (Tex.App.-Houston [1st Dist.] 1990, no writ). In applying this standard to the record before us, we conclude that the jurors here were left to speculate about the existence of compensable mental anguish in this case.

Only two passages of the testimony directly addressed the Woodruffs' mental state. Ray Woodruff testified: I was hot. I was very disturbed about that, and called him and said, "I would like to sell you a house. I think you have just flooded my property, I think you have messed up my house." I begged the guy not to. Constance Woodruff made the following statements in one passage of her testimony (which is reprinted in full in the court of appeals' opinion): [I]t's just not pleasant walking around on cement floors. . . . . Well, [our life] changed. It just — I don't know, it's a hard feeling to describe, unless you go through it. It was just upsetting, Ray would come home and he would become very quiet. He was — I guess we both were. It caused some friction between us because I wanted to just get it done and get over with and things couldn't move as quickly as I wanted them to. . . . Afraid? I wasn't afraid. I guess I was-I was just upset that it changed our life style. We were all very happy, and since I lived at home quite-well, most of the time, it meant a lot to me. I'm a very private person, and I really maybe depended upon my house a little more than other people.

These statements show that the Woodruffs felt anger, frustration, or vexation, but they do not support the conclusion that these emotions rose to a compensable level. For the most part, the quoted testimony does nothing but cite the existence of "mere emotions": "I was hot," "It was just upsetting," and "I was just upset." It does not support the conclusion that the Woodruffs suffered compensable mental anguish.

Not only is the record devoid of direct evidence of the nature, duration, or severity of the Woodruffs' mental anguish, there is also no circumstantial evidence other than the fact of the flooding itself to support any award of mental anguish. As we have noted, historically, some types of disturbing or shocking injuries have been found sufficient to support an inference that the injury was accompanied by mental anguish. As a general matter, though, qualifying events have demonstrated a threat to one's physical safety or reputation or involved the death of, or serious injury to, a family member. While the flooding of the Woodruffs' home certainly disrupted their lives temporarily, under our substantive law this type of disruption will not support an inference that compensable mental anguish occurred. Evidence of Parkway's negligence and the resulting property damage cannot alone support the mental anguish damages.

We therefore affirm the court of appeals' holding that the evidence of mental anguish damages was legally insufficient.

5. "Exemplary Damages"

Tony Gullo Motors I, L.P. v. Chapa
212 S.W.3d 299
(Tex. 2006)

Nury Chapa bought a Toyota Highlander from Tony Gullo Motors for $30,207.38; they disagree what model of the car was involved. After a two-day trial, the six jurors answered 15 questions concerning breach of contract, fraud, and under the Texas Deceptive Trade Practices—Consumer Protection Act, Tex. Bus. & Com. Code §§ 17.41-.63 (DTPA) in Chapa's favor. They also found a difference in value of the two models of $7,213, mental anguish damages of $21,639, exemplary damages of $250,000, and attorney's fees of $20,000.

The trial court disregarded the mental anguish and exemplary awards on the ground that Chapa's only claim was for breach of contract, and the fee award because Chapa had not segregated fees attributable to that claim alone. In a *per curiam* memorandum opinion, the Ninth Court of Appeals disagreed with both conclusions, reinstating all the awards but reducing exemplary damages to $125,000.

We agree that Chapa could assert her claim in several forms, but disagree that she could recover in all of them. Further, the court of appeals' judgment included exemplary damages exceeding the bounds of constitutional law and attorney's fees exceeding the bounds of Texas law. Accordingly, we reverse and remand for further proceedings.

I. Election of Remedies

In entering judgment for Chapa on all her contract, fraud, and DTPA claims, the court of appeals violated the one-satisfaction rule. "There can be but one recovery for one injury, and the fact that . . . there may be more than one theory of liability[ ] does not modify this rule. *Stewart Title Guar. Co. v. Sterling,* 822 S.W.2d 1, 8 (Tex. 1991)

Chapa alleged only one injury — delivery of a base-model Highlander rather than a Highlander Limited. While she could certainly plead more than one theory of liability, she could not recover on more than one.

For breach of contract, Chapa could recover economic damages and attorney's fees, but not mental anguish or exemplary damages. The court of appeals erred by simply awarding them all. *See Stewart Title Guar. Co. v. Aiello,* 941 S.W.2d 68, 72 (Tex.1997) (holding mental anguish and exemplary damages unavailable for breach of contract).

For fraud, she could recover economic damages, mental anguish, and exemplary damages, but not attorney's fees. *See New Amsterdam Cas. Co. v. Texas Indus.,* 414 S.W.2d 914, 915 (Tex.1967) (stating that "attorney's fees are not recoverable either in an action in tort or a suit upon a contract unless provided by statute or by contract between the parties"); *see also Neeley v. Bankers Trust Co. of Texas,* 757 F.2d 621, 633 (5th Cir.1985).

For a DTPA violation, she could recover economic damages, mental anguish, and attorney's fees, but not additional damages beyond $21,639 (three times her economic damages). *See* Tex. Bus. & Com. Code § 17.50(b)(1). For acts committed intentionally, a consumer may recover additional damages up to three times the amount of economic and mental anguish damages combined, *see id.;* with regard to the DTPA, Chapa only requested and obtained a jury finding that Gullo Motor's violations were committed knowingly.

But as Chapa was the prevailing party, she is still entitled to judgment on the most favorable theory supported by the pleadings, evidence, and verdict. *See Gulf States Utils. Co. v. Low,* 79 S.W.3d 561, 566 (Tex.2002); *Boyce Iron Works,* 747 S.W.2d at 787 (Tex.1988). Gullo Motors does not challenge the jury's breach of contract or economic damages findings in this Court. Accordingly, the only question before us is whether Chapa is entitled to anything more.

* * *

III. Exemplary Damages

The jury found Gullo Motors had committed deceptive acts knowingly and found clear and convincing evidence that it had committed fraud. Beyond arguing that Chapa can only sue in contract, Gullo Motors does not challenge either finding. As we have rejected that argument, Chapa is entitled under the verdict to exemplary damages for either fraud or violation of the DTPA.

But both parties challenge the court of appeals' judgment reinstating exemplary damages but reducing them to $125,000 —Gullo Motors because the reinstatement went too far, and Chapa because it did not go far enough. Although the jury assessed exemplary damages for both fraud and deceptive acts at $250,000, the DTPA caps those damages at $21,639 (three times Chapa's economic loss of $7,213). . . *See,* Tex. Bus. & Com. Code § 17.50(b)(1). The same statutory provision limits additional damages to three times economic and mental anguish damages if conduct is committed *intentionally*; but Chapa only requested a jury finding whether Gullo Motors' committed deceptive acts *knowingly.*

[T]he fraud award is capped at $200,000. *See* Tex. Civ. Prac. & Rem. Code § 41.008(b) (capping exemplary damages at the greater of (1) noneconomic damages plus two times economic damages, or (2) $200,000). Accordingly, the court of appeals' opinion and the parties' briefs address only whether the exemplary damages were properly awarded based on fraud.

* * *

B

We review not whether the exemplary damage award is exorbitant (as the dissent says), but whether it is constitutional. In reviewing the amount of an exemplary damage award for constitutionality, we have been directed to consider three "guideposts": (1) the nature of the defendant's conduct, (2) the ratio between exemplary and compensatory damages, and (3) the size of civil penalties in comparable cases. *BMW of N. Am. v. Gore,* 517 U.S. 559, 575, (1996)

The reprehensibility of Gullo Motors' conduct (the most important of the guideposts) depends in turn on five more factors, all but one of which weigh against exemplary damages here. Gullo Motors' actions did not cause physical rather than economic harm, did not threaten the health or safety of others, and did not involve repeated acts rather than an isolated incident. Chapa claims she was financially vulnerable, but the only harm she alleged (that her SUV did not have Michelin tires and lumbar-support seats) did not threaten financial ruin. Only the last factor, that the conduct at issue was deceitful rather than accidental, points in Chapa's favor. The existence of a single factor "may not be sufficient to sustain a punitive damages award."

Touching the second guidepost, the Supreme Court has declined to adopt a bright-line ratio between actual and exemplary damages, but has stated that "few awards exceeding a single-digit ratio ... will satisfy due process." Further, the Court has pointed to early statutes authorizing awards of double, treble, or quadruple damages as support for the conclusion that "four times the amount of compensatory damages might be close to the line of constitutional impropriety." Here, the court of appeals' award exceeds four times Chapa's total compensatory award, and is more than 17 times her economic damages. Further, the jury's award of precisely $21,639 for mental anguish-exactly three times her economic damages of $7,213-supports the Supreme Court's observation that emotional damages themselves often include a punitive element. The court of appeals' judgment at least pushes against, if not exceeds, the constitutional limits.

Finally, we must compare the exemplary damages awarded here to civil penalties authorized in comparable cases. The Texas Occupations Code provides for a maximum civil penalty of $ 10,000 for statutory or regulatory violations by motor vehicle dealers. Similarly, the attorney general could collect not more than $20,000 as a civil penalty under the DTPA in a case like this. These are precisely the kinds of penalties for comparable misconduct the Supreme Court has used-and says we must use-in our constitutional analysis.

Chapa argues we should consider the possibility that Gullo Motors might be found criminally liable or lose its license for what happened here. But she provides no proof that such a sanction has ever been awarded in a case like this. "[T]he remote possibility of a criminal sanction does not automatically sustain a punitive damages award."

The dissent reaches a different conclusion only by changing the constitutional standards. The Supreme Court says "repeated conduct" refers to recidivism; the dissent says it means reiterating a single misrepresentation to a single consumer. The Supreme Court says $1,000,000 in emotional anguish does not mean there are "physical injuries"; the dissent says $21,000 in emotional anguish is enough to conclude otherwise. The Supreme Court says multiplying damages by a factor of 4 is "close to the line of constitutional impropriety"; the dissent says using a factor of 4.33 is unworthy of our review. The Supreme Court says we must look to the civil penalties "imposed in *comparable* cases"; the dissent says we should look to the general $200,000 cap applicable to *all* exemplary cases regardless of their nature. The Supreme Court says exemplary damages "pose an acute danger of arbitrary deprivation of property"; the dissent perceives no danger in pushing against the constitutional limits in all fraud cases, as the only factor present here (deceitful conduct) is present in every one.

While finding the jury verdict of $250,000 constitutionally excessive, the court of appeals gave no explanation for its award of half that amount. Exemplary damages are not susceptible to precise calculation, but this is still five to ten times more than comparable civil penalties, or what Chapa could recover under the consumer-friendly DTPA. *Cf. PPG Indus., Inc. v. JMB/Houston Ctrs. Partners Ltd. P'ship,* 146 S.W.3d 79, 89 (Tex.2004) ("Frequently, the DTPA is pleaded not because it is the *only* remedy, but because it is the most *favorable* remedy.") (italics in original).

Pushing exemplary damages to the absolute constitutional limit in a case like this leaves no room for greater punishment in cases involving death, grievous physical injury, financial ruin, or actions that endanger a large segment of the public. *See Transp. Ins. Co. v. Moriel,* 879 S.W.2d 10, 24 (Tex.1994). 1 On this record, Gullo Motors' conduct merited exemplary damages, but the amount assessed by the court of appeals exceeds constitutional limits.

* * *

V. Conclusion

Because the jury found in Chapa's favor on all her claims, she is entitled to recover on the most favorable theory the verdict would support. But she is not required to make that election until she knows her choices.

Under either fraud or the DTPA, Chapa is entitled to $7,213 in economic damages and $21,639, in mental anguish. The court of appeals must reassess her exemplary damages, and a jury must reassess her attorney's fees. There is no rule establishing which should go first, but for practical reasons we remand first to the court of appeals. At the trial level, the most Chapa could recover under the DTPA would be additional damages of $21,639 (three times her economic damages) plus attorney's fees of something less than $20,000 (depending on the new verdict). If the court of appeals' reassessment of exemplary damages for fraud exceeds this amount, Chapa would obviously be better off electing that recovery; if not, then the court of appeals should thereafter remand to the trial court for a new trial on attorney's fees. Accordingly, we remand to the court of appeals for further proceedings consistent with this opinion.

6. "Additional Damages"

Again, when a jury finds a "knowing" violation, it may award additional damages under the DTPA. *See* Tex.Bus. & Com.Code Ann. § 17.50 . But how should a consumer measure or prove "additional damages"? The next two cases outline the consumer's burden and identify the requirements that one must satisfy before securing "additional damages under the DTPA.

Alamo National l Bank v. Kraus
616 S.W.2d 908
(Tex.1981)

This is a personal injury and wrongful death case. A jury found that Defendants Alamo National Bank and Kelly Salvage Company acted with negligence and gross negligence which proximately caused the death of Nancy Marie Kraus and the injury of her son, John L. Kraus. The trial court disregarded a jury finding and denied recovery against the Bank. Judgment was rendered against Kelly Salvage Company for actual and exemplary damages. The Court of Civil Appeals reformed the trial court's judgment and decreed that plaintiffs recover actual and exemplary damages from Alamo National Bank and affirmed the judgment against Kelly Salvage Company. We affirm the judgment of the Court of Civil Appeals.

Alamo National Bank owned the Old Household Furniture Store building. The building was a three-story masonry structure located across St. Mary's Street from the Bank in downtown San Antonio. The west wall of the building faced St. Mary's Street and the Bank.

In April 1976, the Bank contracted with Kelly Salvage Company to demolish the building. Demolition began on April 23 under a demolition permit issued by the City. Rather than demolish the building one story at a time, Kelly Salvage demolished the building in vertical sections beginning with the east wall. Two interior limestone walls, which ran parallel to the east and west walls, divided the building into thirds. First, the roof on the east one-third was removed and that section was demolished. Second, the roof on the middle one-third was removed and that section was demolished. The last section to be demolished was the west one-third which faced St. Mary's Street.

About 5 p. m. on September 14, the west wall of the building fell across St. Mary's Street and on a car driven by Nancy Marie Kraus. Mrs. Kraus was killed and her minor son, John L. Kraus, was injured. The wall was supported by five three-quarter inch steel cables. However, the steel support to the wall had been removed, the load support members had been cut, and the wall was not laterally braced.

John W. Kraus, Jr., individually and as next friend of his minor son, John L. Kraus, and Fred and Letty Petty, the surviving heirs of Nancy Marie Kraus, sued Alamo National Bank and Kelly Salvage, for the death of Mrs. Kraus and personal injuries to her son, John L. Kraus. A jury found: (1) Kelly Salvage was negligent and acted with gross negligence in its demolition of the Old Household Furniture Store building and such negligence and gross negligence proximately caused the occurrence in question; (2) the demolition of the Old Household Furniture Store building was inherently dangerous work and Alamo National Bank knew, contemplated, had reason to know, or had reason to contemplate that the demolition of the building was inherently dangerous work when it hired Kelly Salvage Company; and (3) Alamo National Bank was negligent and acted with gross negligence in connection with the demolition of the Old Household Furniture Store building and such negligence and gross negligence proximately caused the occurrence in question.

The jury awarded the following damages:

1) $20,000 actual damages to John W. Kraus, Jr.;
2) $226,000 actual damages to John L. Kraus;
3) $5,000 actual damages to Fred Petty;
4) $5,000 actual damages to Letty Petty;
5) $500,000 exemplary damages to John W. Kraus, Jr. against Alamo National Bank;
6) $500,000 exemplary damages to John L. Kraus against Alamo National Bank;
7) $500,000 exemplary damages to John W. Kraus, Jr. against Kelly Salvage; and
8) $500,000 exemplary damages to John L. Kraus against Kelly Salvage.

The trial court disregarded the jury's finding of inherently dangerous work and rendered judgment that plaintiffs take nothing against Alamo National Bank. The trial court rendered judgment on the verdict against Kelly Salvage.

The Court of Civil Appeals reformed and affirmed the judgment of the trial court. It rendered judgment that John W. Kraus, Jr. recover the following damages: $25,803.46 in actual damages against Alamo National Bank and Kelly Salvage; $500,000 in exemplary damages against Alamo

National Bank; and $500,000 in exemplary damages against Kelly Salvage. Alamo National Bank argues that the award of exemplary damages to John W. Kraus, Jr. is excessive and disproportionate to the actual damages awarded.

Exemplary damages must be reasonably proportioned to actual damages. *Southwestern Investment Company v. Neeley*, 452 S.W.2d 705 (Tex. 1970); *Fort Worth Elevators Company v. Russell*, 123 Tex. 128, 70 S.W.2d 397 (1934). There can be no set rule or ratio between the amount of actual and exemplary damages which will be considered reasonable. This determination must depend upon the facts of each particular case. *First Security Bank & Trust Company v. Roach*, 493 S.W.2d 612 (Tex. Civ. App. Dallas 1973, writ ref'd n. r. e.); *Cain v. Fontana*, 423 S.W.2d 134 (Tex. Civ. App. San Antonio 1967, writ ref'd n. r. e.).

Factors to consider in determining whether an award of exemplary damages is reasonable include (1) the nature of the wrong, (2) the character of the conduct involved, (3) the degree of culpability of the wrongdoer, (4) the situation and sensibilities of the parties concerned, and (5) the extent to which such conduct offends a public sense of justice and propriety.

Whether the amount of damages awarded by the jury is excessive is a question of fact over which this Court has no jurisdiction. *Southwestern Investment Company v. Neeley*, supra; *Flanigan v. Carswell*, 324 S.W.2d 835 (Tex. 1959). Whether the Court of Civil Appeals applied an erroneous standard in determining the excessiveness of damages presents a question of law within the jurisdiction of this Court. *Flanigan v. Carswell*, supra; *Dallas Railway & Terminal Company v. Farnsworth,* 148 Tex. 584, 227 S.W.2d 1017 (1950). The Court of Civil Appeals applied the proper standards for reviewing an award of exemplary damages for excessiveness. 586 S.W.2d at 207-08.

The Old Household Furniture Store building demolition site was located directly across St. Mary's Street from the Alamo National Bank. The officers and directors of the Bank had regular visual contact with the deteriorating condition of the building as Kelly Salvage removed the support from the three-story walls. Several witnesses testified that the west wall was leaning toward St. Mary's Street up to two weeks before it collapsed. A local television station broadcast an interview with a safety engineer about the wall and the potentially dangerous condition it created.

About noon the day the wall fell, Benton Davies notified Mary Frances Keller, an Assistant Vice President of the Bank, that the west wall was leaning toward St. Mary's Street and constituted a dangerous condition. Ms. Keller immediately told Bradford Breuer, a Vice President, who was in charge of the demolition project. Mr. Breuer took no action. Throughout the demolition project, the Bank and its officers and directors did nothing to protect the safety of pedestrians and motorists who passed beneath the west wall.

The jury found that Alamo National Bank was negligent and acted with gross negligence in the demolition of the Old Household Furniture Store building and the negligence and gross negligence proximately caused the occurrence in question. The owner or occupant of premises abutting a highway has a duty to exercise reasonable care not to jeopardize or endanger the safety of persons using the highway as a means of passage or travel. The owner or occupant is liable for any injury that proximately results from his negligence. *Atchison v. Texas & P. Ry. Co.*, 143 Tex. 466, 186 S.W.2d 228 (1945.

The trial court submitted a definition of inherently dangerous work which Alamo National Bank contends is incorrect because it does not limit inherently dangerous work to that work which creates a peril no matter how skillfully performed. We do not reach this question because the Court of Civil Appeals reformed the judgment of the trial court and properly rendered judgment against Alamo National Bank upon the negligence findings by the jury. Error, if any, in submitting this definition of inherently dangerous work was harmless because it was not reasonably calculated to cause nor did it probably cause the rendition of an improper judgment. Rule 434, Tex. R. Civ. Pro.

The judgment of the Court of Civil Appeals is affirmed.

Jim Walter Homes, Inc. v. Valencia
690 S.W.2d 239
(Tex. 1985)

The questions considered are whether the trial court properly calculated damages resulting from a knowing violation of the Texas Deceptive Trade Practices-Consumer Protection Act (DTPA), Tex. Bus. & Com.Code Ann. §§ 17.41-. 63 ; whether there is some evidence to support the jury's finding that Jim Walter Homes, Inc. and Mid-State Homes, Inc. (Jim Walter Homes) knowingly violated the DTPA; and whether the Valencias gave Jim Walter Homes sufficient notice of their DTPA claim. Jim Walter Homes was found to have violated both the DTPA and the Texas Consumer Credit Code (Credit Code), Tex. Rev. Civ. Stat. Ann. art. 5069-6.01 to 6.09 (Vernon Supp.1985). Judgment was rendered that the Valencias recover $49,728 based upon the DTPA violation and that Jim Walter Homes forfeit all amounts owing on the construction of the house based upon the Credit Code violation. The court of appeals affirmed. 679 S.W.2d 29. We modify the judgment of the court of appeals and affirm that judgment as modified.

Jose and Elodia Valencia entered into a contract with Jim Walter Homes for the construction of a house on the Valencias' property. Under the terms of the contract, the Valencias were to pay the total price of the house in 180 monthly installments after "release" of the house to them. Jim Walter Homes secured payment of the debt by executing a Mechanics Lien Contract with Power of Sale.

Jim Walter Homes "released" the house to the Valencias and awaited payment. The Valencias did not make payment and after the third monthly payment had accrued, Jim Walter Homes accelerated the note and attempted foreclosure. The Valencias then sought to enjoin the foreclosure and to recover damages under the DTPA and the Credit Code. Jim Walter Homes counterclaimed for the amounts due under the contract. The alleged Credit Code violations and Jim Walter Homes's counterclaim were tried to the court. The alleged DTPA violations were tried to a jury.

The jury found that Jim Walter Homes had represented that the house was constructed in a good, substantial, and workmanlike manner but that it was not so constructed; that this act was a producing cause of the Valencias' damages; and that the Valencias had sustained actual damages of $12,682. The jury further found that Jim Walter Homes "knowingly" made the misrepresentations to the Valencias and the jury awarded the Valencias the sum of $38,046 in discretionary additional damages based on the knowing violation. Based on these jury findings and after a remittitur of $3000, the trial court rendered judgment for the Valencias on their DTPA claim for $49,728.

We first consider the method used to calculate the Valencias' damages. Section 17.50(b)(1) of the DTPA provides that a consumer who prevails may obtain:

> the amount of actual damages found by the trier of fact. In addition the court shall award two times that portion of the actual damages that does not exceed $1000. If the trier of fact finds that the conduct of the defendant was committed knowingly, the trier of fact may award not more than three times the amount of actual damages in excess of $1000.

The trial court arrived at the $49,728 figure by first awarding the Valencias $12,682 in actual damages under sentence number one of section 17.50(b)(1). Next, the court awarded them $2000 under the second sentence. To these amounts, the trial court added three times the amount of their actual damages in excess of $1000. This method of calculation resulted in quadrupling actual damages less $1000. Relying on what it believed to be the plain meaning of the statute and the apparent legislative intent in amending section 17.50(b)(1), the court of appeals affirmed this method of calculation.

The court of appeals holding conflicts with another recent court of appeals decision. In *Jasso v. Duran,* 681 S.W.2d 279 (Tex.App.-Houston [14th Dist.] 1984, writ pending), the court modified the trial court's judgment to award the prevailing consumer who received the maximum award on his claim an amount equal to three times actual damages. The court reasoned that section 17.50(b)(1) clearly disallowed a quadrupling of damages and that the legislature never intended to authorize quadrupling under any circumstances.

The present case is governed by the 1979 amendments to the DTPA. This is the first time this court has been presented with the issue of how damages should be calculated under section 17.50(b)(1) as it was amended. We noted in *Martin v. McKee,* 663 S.W.2d 446, 447 (Tex.1984), that there are three types of damages described by the section; however, the only issue we considered in that case was whether the plaintiff waived recovery of discretionary damages under sentence three of the section by failing to request a special issue on these damages. In *Luna v. North Star Dodge Sales, Inc.,* 667 S.W.2d 115, 116 (Tex.1984), we recited the trial court's calculation of damages but we did not decide whether the trial court applied the correct method of calculation.

Prior to enactment of the 1979 amendments to the DTPA, trebling of any actual damages was mandatory. *Woods v. Littleton,* 554 S.W.2d 662, 669 (Tex.1977). A seller could be held liable for treble damages even for innocent misrepresentations. We find that the legislature sought to mitigate the harsh effects of this rule without leaving consumers unprotected from deceptive practices. We further find that the legislature sought to achieve three things by amending section 17.50(b)(1): (1) to preserve mandatory treble damages for consumers with small claims causes of action; (2)

to eliminate automatic treble damages against sellers who make innocent misrepresentations; and (3) to allow consumers to recover treble damages at the discretion of the trier of fact in cases of knowing violations of the DTPA. The legislature implemented its goals by providing in the first two sentences of section 17.50(b)(1) for the mandatory trebling of that portion of actual damages that does not exceed $1000 in all DTPA cases. In the third sentence of section 17.50(b)(1), the legislature allowed the trier of fact to award in its discretion " *not more than* three times the amount of actual damages in excess of $1000" in cases in which the deceptive act or practice is found to have been committed knowingly.

We find no legislative intent to provide for a quadrupling of damages in any case. Consistent with the legislative purpose, we hold that under section 17.50(b)(1), the maximum amount of damages recoverable in a suit in which actual damages resulting from a knowing violation of the DTPA exceed $1000 is three times the first $1000 of actual damages plus three times the actual damages in excess of $1000. That amount is equal to a trebling of actual damages.

In the present case, the Valencias should have recovered the following damages: (1) three times the first $1000 of actual damages $3,000 . . . [and] (2) not more than three times the amount of actual damages in excess of $1000 — ($11,682 X 3) = $35,046.

Accordingly, we modify the judgment of the court of appeals by reducing the total amount of damages awarded the Valencias to $38,046 as required by section 17.50(b)(1).

The Valencias argue that disallowing a recovery of quadruple their actual damages less $1000 violates section 17.44 of the DTPA. We disagree. Section 17.44 calls for a liberal construction of the DTPA in furtherance of its purpose "to protect consumers against false, misleading, and deceptive business practices, unconscionable actions, and breaches of warranty and to provide efficient and economical procedures to secure such protection." The purpose of allowing multiple recoveries is two-fold: to encourage consumers to initiate litigation and to deter sellers from violating the DTPA. *See Singleton v. Pennington,* 606 S.W.2d 682, 690 (Tex.1980).

Our interpretation of section 17.50(b)(1) does not frustrate that purpose. Section 17.50(b)(1) as we have construed it to allow a maximum award of an amount equal to treble actual damages against knowing DTPA violators retains the incentive for consumers to go to court to pursue their claims. The provision so construed still serves to thwart the efforts of unscrupulous sellers who make knowing misrepresentations. Upon proof of a knowingly deceptive act, a consumer may obtain the same effective relief under the 1979 amendment to section 17.50(b)(1) as he could under the pre-1979 provision.

We next consider Jim Walter Homes's contention that there is no evidence to support the jury's finding that Jim Walter Homes "knowingly" violated the DTPA. Section 17.45(9) of the DTPA defines "knowingly" as "actual awareness of the falsity, deception, or unfairness of the act or practice giving rise to the consumer's claim . . . ., but actual awareness may be inferred where objective manifestations indicate that a person acted with actual awareness." Jim Walter Homes argues that the alleged misrepresentations were made to the Valencias at the time they entered the contract and that in order for Jim Walter Homes to have violated the DTPA "knowingly," the Valencias would have to show that Jim Walter Homes did not intend to build the house in compliance with the contract from the outset. This argument is without merit.

The act or practice giving rise to the Valencias' cause of action was not the misrepresentations made to them at the time they entered into the contract; it was the act of building the house defectively after representing that the house would be built in a good and workmanlike manner. The jury was instructed in accordance with the definition contained in section 17.45(9). The record contains evidence from which the jury could have inferred that Jim Walter Homes knew that the house was defective at the time of construction. For example, two building inspectors testified that the piers supporting the house were improperly poured and that Jim Walter Homes attempted to cover up these defects with plaster. From this and other evidence in the record the jury could have inferred that Jim Walter Homes committed a knowing violation of the DTPA.

Finally, Jim Walter Homes argues that the Valencias should not recover under the DTPA because they failed to comply with the notice requirement of DTPA section 17.50A(a). That section requires the consumer to give written notice advising the person against whom the consumer seeks damages of the consumer's specific complaint and the amount of damages sought at least 30 days before filing suit. The purpose of the notice requirement is to discourage litigation and encourage settlements of consumer complaints. *North American Van Lines v. Bauerle,* 678 S.W.2d 229, 235 (Tex. App.-Fort Worth 1984, writ ref'd n.r.e.); *Barnard v. Mecom,* 650 S.W.2d 123, 127 (Tex. App.-Corpus Christi 1983, writ ref'd n.r.e.). The letter sent by the Valencias' attorney effectuated that purpose and complied with section 17.50A(a).

We have fully considered all of Jim Walter Homes's remaining points and have determined these points to be without merit. We therefore modify the judgment of the court of appeals by reducing the amount of damages awarded to the Valencias to $38,046 and we affirm the court of appeals' judgment as modified.

Haynes & Boone v. Bowser Boudlin, Ltd.,
896 S.W.2d 179
(Tex. 1995)

Bowser Bouldin, Ltd. (Bouldin) recovered judgment for malpractice and violation of the Deceptive Trades Practices — Consumer Protection Act (DTPA), Tex. Bus. & Com. Code §§ 17.41-.63, against its law firm Haynes & Boone for the firm's handling of Bouldin's suit with Blockbuster, Inc. Bouldin elected DTPA damages. The trial court awarded Bouldin damages for the loss of investment in a shopping center in which Blockbuster was a tenant, the deficiency balance Bouldin was obligated to pay when the center was foreclosed upon by its creditor, the cost of settlement of the Blockbuster litigation, lost rents from Blockbuster, and money paid to Haynes & Boone to conduct the Blockbuster litigation.

Haynes & Boone objected to the submission of the loss of investment and deficiency damages to the jury. On appeal, the court of appeals suggested remittitur as to the lost rents and the amounts paid to settle the Blockbuster suit, which Bouldin satisfied, and then affirmed. We reverse the judgment of the court of appeals and remand the case to the court of appeals for reconsideration of the punitive damages.

I.

Bouldin is a strip shopping center developer. It completed the Highland View shopping center in Dallas in 1987 with Blockbuster as the "anchor" tenant.

To build the center, Bouldin obtained a construction loan. The construction loan had a short maturity that required Bouldin to either refinance or sell the property shortly after completion of construction. Bouldin's theory of damage is premised on the generally accepted business consideration by developers that a certain type of tenant, or "anchor tenant," is required to make a shopping center successful. These tenants are required because they are helpful in attracting financial backing to the project due to their own financial and commercial stability, and because their established record of attracting commercial traffic will attract other tenants. Blockbuster, Inc. is considered an "anchor" tenant, and Bouldin pre-leased space to Blockbuster in the shopping center.

After completion of the shopping center and three months into the lease, Blockbuster became dissatisfied with the location. Bouldin had leased the space above Blockbuster to Sparx, a nightclub, and early on, water leaked into Blockbuster causing a loss of $25,000 in videotapes. Additionally, customers of Sparx began causing parking congestion and various other problems for Blockbuster.

Although Blockbuster was successful in obtaining a temporary restraining order enjoining the use of valet parking by Sparx and reserving parking spaces for Blockbuster, it also initiated a suit against Bouldin seeking rescission of its lease. In support of its suit Blockbuster claimed that Bouldin breached the lease, breached the covenant of quiet enjoyment, and made fraudulent representations. At this point, Bouldin retained Richard Capshaw of Haynes & Boone to defend it. An early settlement attempt was unsuccessful.

Haynes & Boone does not contest that its associate Richard Capshaw mishandled the Blockbuster litigation. During the litigation, Capshaw failed to timely respond to certain discovery requests from Blockbuster. As a result the trial court sanctioned Bouldin by striking all of its pleadings. Capshaw, although bringing a successful motion to reconsider, thereafter failed to follow through with the trial court's reconsidered sanctions order that required Bouldin to pay $1,500 in attorney's fees to Blockbuster by July 19, 1988. Consequently, Bouldin's pleadings were again struck and a default judgment was rendered in favor of Blockbuster. Bouldin settled with Blockbuster on terms which permitted Blockbuster to cancel its lease on ninety days notice. According to Bouldin, this was an unfavorable settlement resulting from the procedural posture of the case.

During the period of litigation with Blockbuster, Bouldin received two offers to buy the shopping center. Bouldin also made efforts to obtain permanent financing for the shopping center in order to pay off the construction loans. In June of 1987, Bouldin was provided a $5.35 million earnest money contract for the sale of the shopping center. That deal fell through in January 1988. In April

1988, Bouldin was offered a second earnest money contract for $4.4 million, but this was cancelled by the offeror in May 1988. The default judgment was entered in July 1988. Bouldin was unable to sell or to obtain refinancing and consequently, it defaulted on the construction note and lost the shopping center through foreclosure.

* * *

III.

In addition to actual damages, the jury found that Haynes & Boone acted knowingly and awarded $1.5 million in punitive damages. Because nearly all of the actual damages awarded have been reversed on appeal, we remand to the court of appeals for reconsideration of the punitive damage award in light of this opinion and *Alamo Nat'l Bank v. Kraus,* 616 S.W.2d 908, 910 (Tex.1981). Consequently, we do not reach the issue of whether the court of appeals performed a proper factual sufficiency review regarding the award of punitive damages.

C. *Attorney's Fees*

1. Which Party Pays Attorney's Fees?

Tony Gullo Motors I, L.P. v. Chapa
212 S.W.3d 299
(Tex. 2006)

IV. Attorney's Fees

The jury found a reasonable and necessary attorney's fee "in this case" was $20,000. During and after trial, Gullo Motors objected that fees were not recoverable for Chapa's fraud claim, and thus had to be excluded. We agree, and thus reverse and remand the fee issue for a new trial.

For more than a century, Texas law has not allowed recovery of attorney's fees unless authorized by statute or contract. *See, e.g., Buckhannon Bd. and Care Home, Inc. v. West Virginia Dept. of Health and Human Res.,* 532 U.S. 598, 602, (2001) ("In the United States, parties are ordinarily required to bear their own attorney's fees-the prevailing party is not entitled to collect from the loser. Under this 'American Rule, " we follow "a general practice of not awarding fees to a prevailing party absent explicit statutory authority.").This rule is so venerable and ubiquitous in American courts it is known as "the American Rule." Absent a contract or statute, trial courts do not have inherent authority to require a losing party to pay the prevailing party's fees. *Travelers Indem. Co. of Connecticut v. Mayfield,* 923 S.W.2d 590, 594 (Tex.1996).

As a result, fee claimants have always been required to segregate fees between claims for which they are recoverable and claims for which they are not. *See Stewart Title Guar. Co. v. Aiello,*

941 S.W.2d 68, 73 (Tex.1997); *Stewart Title Guar. Co. v. Sterling,* 822 S.W.2d 1, 10 (Tex.1991); *Matthews v. Candlewood Builders, Inc.,* 685 S.W.2d 649, 650 (Tex.1985); *Int'l Sec. Life Ins. Co. v. Finck,* 496 S.W.2d 544, 547 (Tex.1973).

We recognized an exception to this historical practice in 1991 that has since threatened to swallow the rule. In *Stewart Title Guaranty Co. v. Sterling,* we affirmed the general rule: "the plaintiff is required to show that [attorney's] fees were incurred while suing the defendant sought to be charged with the fees on a claim which allows recovery of such fees." 822 S.W.2d at 10. But we then added:

> A recognized exception to this duty to segregate arises when the attorney's fees rendered are in connection with claims arising out of the same transaction and are so interrelated that their "prosecution or defense entails proof or denial of essentially the same facts." *Flint & Assoc. v. Intercontinental Pipe & Steel, Inc.,* 739 S.W.2d 622, 624-25 (Tex.App.-Dallas 1987, writ denied). Therefore, when the causes of action involved in the suit are dependent upon the same set of facts or circumstances and thus are "interwined to the point of being inseparable," the party suing for attorney's fees may recover the entire amount covering all claims. *Gill Sav. Ass'n v. Chair King, Inc.,* 783 S.W.2d 674, 680 (Tex.App.-Houston [14th Dist.] 1989), *modified,* 797 S.W.2d 31 (Tex.1990) (remanded to the trial court for reexamination of attorney's fee award). *Id.* at 11-12.

As the only two authorities cited in this passage suggest, this exception had not been recognized by this Court before, but only by a few courts of appeals beginning about ten years earlier. In fact, we did not even apply the exception in *Sterling* (as the fees there could be segregated), and appear to have applied it only once since.

But the courts of appeals have been flooded with claims that recoverable and unrecoverable fees are inextricably intertwined. As the exception can make all fees recoverable (even if Texas law has long said they are not), it is no surprise that more and more claimants have sought to invoke it. Moreover, as the details of an attorney's work are shrouded in the attorney-client privilege, it may be hard for anyone else to tell whether the work on several claims truly was inextricably intertwined.

The exception has also been hard to apply consistently. The courts of appeals have disagreed about what makes two claims inextricably intertwined-some focusing on the underlying facts, others on the elements that must be proved, and others on some combination of the two. Some do not require testimony that claims are intertwined, while others do. When faced with fraud and breach of contract claims like those here, some have held the claims inextricably intertwined, and others just the opposite.

As *Sterling* suggests the need to segregate fees is a question of law, the courts of appeals have generally (though not always) applied a *de novo* standard of review. That standard, of course, gives no deference to the factual determinations of the trial judge or the jury. But the fees necessary to prove particular claims often turn on such facts-how hard something was to discover and prove, how strongly it supported particular inferences or conclusions, how much difference it might make to the verdict, and a host of other details that include judgment and credibility questions about who had to do what and what it was worth. Given all these details, it may often be impossible to state as a matter of law the extent to which certain claims can or cannot be segregated; the issue is more a mixed question of law and fact for the jury.

This case illustrates several of these difficulties. The court of appeals held that Chapa was not required to segregate fees (and thus could recover 100 percent of them) because she "was required to prove essentially the same facts in pursuing each of her three causes of action." But when Chapa's attorneys were drafting her pleadings or the jury charge relating to fraud, there is no question those fees were not recoverable. Nor does Texas law permit them to be compensated for preparing and presenting evidence regarding the defendant's net worth.

Further, the effort to recover 100 percent of their fees has required Chapa's attorneys to take a position inconsistent with her underlying claims. As noted above, Chapa has insisted (and we have agreed) that her claims were more than a mere breach of contract-they could be asserted in fraud. But when it came time to segregate fees, her attorneys testified that their work on the fraud claim could not possibly be distinguished from that on the contract and DTPA claims. Having prevailed in her argument that the claims are distinct, it is hard to see how she can also claim they are inextricably intertwined.

It is certainly true that Chapa's fraud, contract, and DTPA claims were all "dependent upon the same set of facts or circumstances," but that does not mean they all required the same research, discovery, proof, or legal expertise. Nor are unrecoverable fees rendered recoverable merely because they are nominal; there is no such exception in any contract, statute, or "the American Rule." To the extent *Sterling* suggested that a common set of underlying facts necessarily made all claims arising therefrom "inseparable" and all legal fees recoverable, it went too far.

But *Sterling* was certainly correct that many if not most legal fees in such cases cannot and need not be precisely allocated to one claim or the other. Many of the services involved in preparing a contract or DTPA claim for trial must still be incurred if tort claims are appended to it; adding the latter claims does not render the former services unrecoverable. Requests for standard disclosures, proof of background facts, depositions of the primary actors, discovery motions and hearings, *voir dire* of the jury, and a host of other services may be necessary whether a claim is filed alone or with others. To the extent such services would have been incurred on a recoverable claim alone, they are not disallowed simply because they do double service.

Accordingly, we reaffirm the rule that if any attorney's fees relate solely to a claim for which such fees are unrecoverable, a claimant must segregate recoverable from unrecoverable fees. Intertwined facts do not make tort fees recoverable; it is only when discrete legal services advance both a recoverable and unrecoverable claim that they are so intertwined that they need not be segregated. We modify *Sterling* to that extent.

This standard does not require more precise proof for attorney's fees than for any other claims or expenses. Here, Chapa's attorneys did not have to keep separate time records when they drafted the fraud, contract, or DTPA paragraphs of her petition; an opinion would have sufficed stating that, for example, 95 percent of their drafting time would have been necessary even if there had been no fraud claim. The court of appeals could then have applied standard factual and legal sufficiency review to the jury's verdict based on that evidence.

There may, of course, be some disputes about fees that a trial or appellate court should decide as a matter of law. For example, to prevail on a contract claim a party must overcome any and all affirmative defenses (such as limitations, *res judicata,* or prior material breach), and the opposing party who raises them should not be allowed to suggest to the jury that overcoming those defenses was unnecessary. But when, as here, it cannot be denied that at least some of the attorney's fees are attributable only to claims for which fees are not recoverable, segregation of fees ought to be required and the jury ought to decide the rest. Chapa's failure to segregate her attorney's fees does not mean she cannot recover any. Unsegregated attorney's fees for the entire case are some evidence of what the segregated amount should be. We have applied this same rule for lost profits, medical expenses, and attorney's fees — an unsegregated damages award requires a remand. Accordingly, remand is required.

2. Measuring Attorney's Fees

Arthur Anderson & Company v. Perry Equipment Corporation
945 S.W.2d 812
(Tex. 1997)

We withdraw our opinion of January 10, 1997, and substitute the following in its place. The parties' motions for rehearing are overruled.

In this accounting malpractice case, Perry Equipment Corporation (PECO) sued the accounting firm of Arthur Andersen for a faulty audit, which PECO relied on to purchase another company, Maloney Pipeline Systems. The audit favorably reported Maloney's financial condition when, in fact, the company was suffering substantial losses. Fourteen months after the sale, Maloney filed for bankruptcy. PECO sued for violations of the Deceptive Trade Practice Act, fraud, negligence, negligent misrepresentation, gross negligence, and breach of implied warranty. Based on the jury's verdict, the trial court rendered judgment for PECO. The court of appeals affirmed. 898 S.W.2d 914.

We address three issues presented by Arthur Anderson's application for writ of error. First, Arthur Andersen challenges PECO's consumer status because Maloney, rather than PECO, actually paid for the audit. Second, Arthur Andersen claims that the trial court failed to instruct the jury on the correct measure of damages. Third, Arthur Andersen contests the attorney's fees award, arguing that the percentage of recovery method is not a proper measure of attorney's fees under the DTPA, and that even if such fees were recoverable, no evidence supports the award. For the reasons discussed below, we reverse the judgment of the court of appeals and remand this case to the trial court for further proceedings.

* * *

I

Because we are remanding the case for a new trial, we turn now to Arthur Andersen's complaint that the trial court improperly awarded attorney's fees calculated as a percentage of recovery. Attorney contingency fee contracts serve two main purposes. First, they allow plaintiffs who cannot afford to pay a lawyer up-front to pay the lawyer out of any recovery. Second, such contracts, because they offer the potential of a greater fee than might be earned under an hourly billing method, compensate the attorney for the risk that the attorney will receive no fee whatsoever if the case is lost. *Id.* The lawyer in effect lends the value of his services, which is secured by a share in the client's potential recovery. Under some contingency fee contracts, the attorney also agrees to advance the out-of-pocket costs of the litigation. In such cases, the attorney not only risks loss of the fee, but also risks loss of actual expenditures.

Arthur Andersen complains that an award of contingency fees under a fee-shifting statute like the DTPA forces defendants to pay fees unrelated to the amount of work performed. While this is not always true, shifting these fees to the defendant presents two problems.

First, a contingent fee award based solely on evidence of a percentage fee agreement between a lawyer and client may be determined without regard to many of the factors that should be considered when determining reasonableness. The DTPA allows recovery of "reasonable and necessary attorneys' fees." Tex. Bus. & Com. Code § 17.50(d). Factors that a factfinder should consider when determining the reasonableness of a fee include:

1) the time and labor required, the novelty and difficulty of the questions involved, and the skill required to perform the legal service properly;
2) the likelihood . . . that the acceptance of the particular employment will preclude other employment by the lawyer;
3) the fee customarily charged in the locality for similar legal services;
4) the amount involved and the results obtained;
5) the time limitations imposed by the client or by the circumstances;
6) the nature and length of the professional relationship with the client;
7) the experience, reputation, and ability of the lawyer or lawyers performing the services; and
8) whether the fee is fixed or contingent on results obtained or uncertainty of collection before the legal services have been rendered.

TEX. DISCIPLINARY R. PROF. CONDUCT 1.04, reprinted in TEX. GOV'T CODE, tit. 2, subtit. G app. (STATE BAR RULES, art. X, § 9); *see also Ragsdale v. Progressive Voters League*, 801 S.W.2d 880, 881 (Tex. 1990); *cf. General Motors Corp. v. Bloyed*, 916 S.W.2d 949, 960-961 (Tex. 1996) (discussing the relative strengths and weaknesses of the contingent fee and lodestar methods of awarding attorneys fees in the context of a court-approved class action settlement). While we do not doubt that many plaintiffs must contract for a contingent fee to secure the services of a lawyer, we do not believe that the DTPA authorizes the shifting of the plaintiff's entire contingent fee to the defendant without consideration of the factors required by the Rules of Professional Conduct. A contingent fee may indeed be a reasonable fee from the standpoint of the parties to the contract. But, we cannot agree that the mere fact that a party and a lawyer have agreed to a contingent fee means that the fee arrangement is in and of itself reasonable for purposes of shifting that fee to the defendant.

A party's contingent fee agreement should be considered by the factfinder, *see* TEX. DISCIPLINARY R. PROF. CONDUCT 1.04 (8), and is therefore admissible in evidence, but that agreement cannot alone support an award of attorney's fees under Texas Business and Commerce Code section 17.50(d). . In other words, the plaintiff cannot simply ask the jury to award a percentage of the recovery as a fee because without evidence of the factors identified in Disciplinary Rule 1.04, the jury has no meaningful way to determine if the fees were in fact reasonable and necessary.

Second, because the jury is not informed what the total amount of the judgment will be, the jury can only speculate about whether a percentage of that unknown recovery will represent a reasonable and necessary fee in that particular case. Rather than leave this question to speculation, the jury must decide the question of attorney's fees specifically in light of the work performed in the very case for which the fee is sought.

In light of these concerns, we hold that to recover attorney's fees under the DTPA, the plaintiff must prove that the amount of fees was both reasonably incurred and necessary to the prosecution of the case at bar, not as a percentage of the judgment.

For the foregoing reasons, we reverse the judgment of the court of appeals and remand this cause to the trial court for further proceedings consistent with this opinion.

3. Off-Setting, Net Recovery and Attorney's Fees

McKinley v. Drozd
685 S.W.2d 7
(Tex. 1985)

The issue in this case is whether a party claiming damages under the Texas Deceptive Trade Practices Act (DTPA), Tex. Bus. & Com. Code Ann. §§ 17.41-.63, and under Tex. Rev. Civ. Stat. Ann. article 2226 must receive a net recovery in the entire lawsuit to recover attorney's fees, or whether any recovery, even though entirely offset by an opposing claim, is sufficient to sustain an award of attorney's fees. The trial court awarded attorney's fees to the petitioners, Dr. and Mrs. McKinley. The court of appeals disallowed the award because the petitioners did not obtain a net recovery. 670 S.W.2d 405. We reverse the judgment of the court of appeals and affirm the trial court.

Drozd, a general contractor, brought suit against the McKinleys to recover the balance due on a construction contract on the McKinleys' new home, and to recover attorney's fees under Tex.Rev. Civ.Stat.Ann. article 2226 (Vernon Supp.1984). The McKinleys counterclaimed against Drozd alleging conversion, breach of contract, and several violations of the DTPA. The McKinleys also sought attorney's fees under the DTPA and under article 2226 in connection with their contractual claim.

The case was tried before a jury, which found that the McKinleys owed Drozd $24,836.71 under the construction contract, that Drozd owed the McKinleys $4150.05 for breach of contract in failing to deliver two rugs, and that Drozd owed the McKinleys $7500.00 in damages for a DTPA violation. Based on this verdict the trial court awarded Drozd a net recovery of $13,186.66 and awarded each party attorney's fees of $30,000.00 for the trial, $8000.00 for a successful appeal to the court of appeals, and $5000.00 for a successful appeal to this court. Finally, the court ordered all costs of court to be divided equally between the parties.

The court of appeals held that the McKinleys were not entitled to any attorney's fees because they did not receive a net recovery. The trial court judgment as modified was affirmed, including the equal division of court costs between the parties.

The McKinleys bring to this court the sole issue of whether the court of appeals was correct in eliminating their attorney's fees award because they did not obtain a net recovery in the lawsuit. We will address separately the claim under section 17.50(d) of the DTPA and the claim under article 2226.

Attorneys Fees Under the DTPA

Section 17.50(d) of the Business and Commerce Code provides that "[e]ach consumer who prevails shall be awarded court costs and reasonable and necessary attorney's fees." This language is not entirely helpful as it does not answer the question of whether one must prevail only under his DTPA claim or must obtain a net recovery in the entire lawsuit.

The McKinleys' primary argument in support of allowing the award of attorney's fees is that to disallow the award would disrupt the legislative intent behind the DTPA to protect consumers, recognized by this court in *Woods v. Littleton,* 554 S.W.2d 662 (Tex.1977). Drozd primarily argues that a DTPA consumer whose recovery is entirely offset cannot be said to have prevailed, because the final judgment provides no relief to the consumer. Both sides cite decisions of the courts of appeals which they contend support their respective positions. This issue is one of first impression for this court, and several of the cases briefed by the parties are distinguishable; however, the following opinions have squarely addressed this issue.

In *Guerra v. Brumlow,* 630 S.W.2d 425, 430-31 (Tex.App.-San Antonio 1982, no writ), the San Antonio court of appeals, without elaboration, held that any recovery under the DTPA, even though entirely offset by a counterclaim, was sufficient to entitle a consumer to attorney's fees. The Fourteenth court of appeals reached the opposite result in *Widmer v. Stamps,* 663 S.W.2d 875, 882-83 (Tex.App.-Houston [14th Dist.] 1983, no writ). That court specifically rejected the view of the *Guerra* court primarily on the grounds that the wording between the DTPA and Tex. Rev. Civ. Stat. Ann. article 2226 is so "strikingly similar" that the same result should be reached under each statute, and the parties in that case agreed that courts have declined to award attorney's fees under article 2226 in the absence of a net recovery. The *Widmer* court acknowledged the argument that section 17.44 of the DTPA calls for liberal construction to protect consumers and to provide economical procedures to secure this protection, but held that the consumers in that case did not "prevail" because they did not obtain a net recovery.

In a more recent opinion, a different panel of the Fourteenth court of appeals rejected the requirement of a "net recovery" to obtain attorney's fees under the DTPA. *Building Concepts, Inc. v. Duncan,* 667 S.W.2d 897, 904-05 (Tex.App.-Houston [14th Dist.] 1984, writ ref'd n.r.e.). The *Building Concepts* court based its decision on the legislature's mandate in section 17.44 to liberally construe the act to protect consumers. The court, while recognizing its disagreement with *Widmer,* declared that the legislature could not have intended that a successful claimant under the DTPA be denied attorney's fees because the claim is offset by a claim of the other party.

The Corpus Christi court of appeals has twice expressed that attorney's fees are not recoverable in the absence of a net recovery. In *Birds Construction, Inc. v. McKay,* 657 S.W.2d 514, 516 (Tex. App.- Corpus Christi 1983, no writ), the court stated in dicta the requirement of a net recovery to obtain attorney's fees, and in the present case, the Corpus Christi court has reversed an award of attorney's fees on that basis.

We hold the better view is to allow consumers to recover attorney's fees under section 17.50(d) of the DTPA incurred in the successful prosecution of a claim for damages under the Act, even though the claim might be entirely offset by a claim of an opposing party. This is consistent with the legislative mandate to liberally construe the act to protect consumers from deceptive practices, and the legislative intent to provide consumers with an efficient and economical means to seek redress for those deceptive practices. Tex. Bus. & Com. Code Ann. § 17.44. In construing the language of the DTPA, the more sensible meaning of the word "prevail" is to prevail in a claim under the Act, rather than to obtain a net recovery on all claims joined in one lawsuit. As the *Building Concepts* opinion pointed out, suits against a general contractor over the construction of a home often involve large counterclaims. 667 S.W.2d at 905. We do not believe that the legislature intended to deprive these consumers of their attorney's fees.

Drozd contends that because the net recovery rule has been followed in applying article 2226, the same rule should apply under the DTPA; however, the issue of DTPA attorney's fees is not controlled by the construction of article 2226. Although there are similarities in the policy and intent behind these statutes, the wording of the statutes is different, and the statutes were enacted for different reasons, thus prompting our separate analysis of each.

Finally, Drozd points out that this court has decided that in calculating treble damages, offsets against DTPA recoveries should be deducted before trebling. *See Durham v. St. John,* 645 S.W.2d 261, 262 (Tex.1983); *Smith v. Baldwin,* 611 S.W.2d 611, 617 (Tex.1980). Therefore, Drozd argues that since a net recovery is required for treble damages, by analogy, it should be required for an award of attorney's fees. The issue of calculating treble damages has not been preserved for our review, and whether to award attorney's fees is a separate question. Our decision in *Smith v. Baldwin* rested upon the meaning of "actual damages" in section 17.50(b)(1), an expression which is not included in the attorney's fees provision. Also, the policy behind granting the punitive award of treble damages is different than granting attorney's fees, and this is particularly clear under the current version of the statute. The treble damage award is called for under certain states of culpability of the DTPA defendant, but the attorney's fee award is given to all prevailing consumers and is not based on the culpability of the DTPA defendant, but on the need to provide an economical remedy for victims of the specified types of deceptive activities.

For the foregoing reasons, we hold that a consumer who is awarded actual damages under the DTPA should also be awarded attorney's fees, even though the damage award is entirely offset by an opposing claim and the DTPA consumer receives no net recovery.

Attorney's Fees Under Article 2226

The next question in this case is to determine whether a net recovery is needed to support an attorney's fee award under article 2226. As Drozd demonstrates in his reply brief, the courts of appeals have uniformly denied attorney's fees under this article in the absence of a net recovery. The earlier cases merely held that it was within the province of the trial court to deny attorney's fees under the article. *See Latham v. Dement,* 409 S.W.2d 429, 434 (Tex.Civ.App.-Dallas 1966, writ ref'd n.r.e.); *Johnny Morrow's Wrecking Crew v. Slate,* 368 S.W.2d 32, 33 (Tex.Civ.App.-Fort Worth 1963, writ ref'd n.r.e.); *Paddock Engineering Co. v. Rife,* 310 S.W.2d 594, 597 (Tex.Civ. App.-Fort Worth 1958, writ ref'd n.r.e.).

The rule was extended in *L Q Motor Inns v. Boysen,* 503 S.W.2d 411, 412 (Tex.Civ.App.-Houston [14th Dist.] 1973, writ ref'd n.r.e.) to hold a trial court in error for allowing attorney's fees under article 2226 in the absence of a net recovery. The *L Q Motor Inns* court stated that the purpose of article 2226 is to encourage the settlement of out-of-court claims, and without elaboration, announced the net recovery requirement.

During the time span of these decisions, article 2226 was amended several times. The most important change which seems to have gone unnoticed occurred in the 1977 amendment. Prior to that time, the statute, in pertinent part, provided that "if, at the expiration of 30 days [after presenting claim], the claim has not been paid or satisfied, and [the claimant] should finally obtain judgment for any amount thereof as presented for payment ..., he may, if represented by an attorney, also recover, in addition to his claim and costs, a reasonable amount as attorney's fees." Act of May 17, 1971, ch. 225, § 1, 1971 Tex. Gen. Laws 1073. In 1977, the statute was amended to its present wording that "if, at the expiration of 30 days [after presenting claim], payment for the just amount owing has not been tendered, the claimant may ... recover in addition to his claim and costs, a reasonable amount as attorney's fees." Tex.Rev.Civ.Stat.Ann. article 2226 . . ..

The earlier decisions, and *L Q Motor Inns* in particular, were decided under the language requiring the claimant to "finally obtain judgment" for some amount. While this wording was not totally clear, it could easily be construed to require a net recovery in the judgment resolving all claims and counterclaims. Under the present wording, however, all that is required to obtain attorney's fees is a "just amount owing" not tendered within thirty days. While a favorable trial court judgment on the article 2226 claim is needed to establish that the claim is "just," the amended language*11 (Cite as: 685 S.W.2d 7, *11)does not impose the requirement of a net recovery, because the justness of a claim within article 2226 is not dependent upon the outcome of other claims or counterclaims joined in the lawsuit.

We hold that the proper construction of article 2226 is to allow recovery of attorney's fees incurred in prosecuting a just claim under the article, even if the amount of the claim is entirely offset by an opposing party's claim. This is more consistent with the legislative intent to discourage a party from unnecessarily litigating and defending a just claim within article 2226. *Tenneco Oil Co. v. Padre Drilling Co.,* 453 S.W.2d 814, 819 (Tex.1970). In addition, the statute was formerly strictly construed; however, the legislature amended article 2226 to mandate that "[t]his Act shall be liberally construed to promote its underlying purposes."

Accordingly, we disapprove of the language in the previously cited cases requiring a net recovery in order to obtain attorney's fees under article 2226 or under the DTPA. The judgment of the court of appeals is reversed, and the trial court judgment is affirmed.

Chapter Seven:
DTPA Defendants' Common-Law and Statutory Defenses

A primary purpose of the DTPA is to allow injured consumers to commence several causes of action without having to confront and overcome various common-law defenses. *Smith v. Baldwin*, 611 S.W.2d 611, 616 (Tex. 1980). To help achieve that end, the Supreme Court of Texas has held: 1) Waivers of consumers' protection and rights violate Texas's public policy. Therefore, such waivers are void and unenforceable. *First Title Co. of Waco v. Garrett,* 860 S.W.2d 74, 77-78 (Tex. 1993); 2) The doctrine of merger does not defeat a DTPA cause of action. *Alvarado v. Bolton*, 749 S.W.2d 47, 48 (Tex. 1988); and 3) Oral representations are admissible and may serve as the basis of a DTPA cause of action without violating the parol evidence rule. *Weitzel v. Barnes*, 691 S.W.2d 598, 599-600 (Tex. 1985).

Also, lower courts in Texas have prohibited certain affirmative defenses in DTPA-related trials. For example, one court held that estoppel is not a defense and does not bar a DTPA action. *Kuehnhoefer v. Welch,* 893 S.W.2d 689, 692 (Tex.App-Texarkana 1995, writ denied). And another tribunal declared that principles of ratification do not apply to DTPA claims. *Shenandoah Assoc. v. J & K Prop., Inc.,* 741 S.W.2d 470, 496 (Tex.App.-Dallas 1987, writ denied).

Nevertheless, DTPA defendants may raise many statutory and common-law defenses. To illustrate, one court declared: The doctrines of accord and satisfaction may bar a DTPA cause of action that arises out of a contract-based claim. *Ostrow v. United Bus. Machs., Inc.,* 982 S.W.2d 101, 105 (Tex. App.-Houston [1st Dist.] 1998, no pet.). Another court concluded that illegality and a violation of public policy bar plaintiffs' DTPA actions. *Johnson v. McLeaish*, 1995 WL 500308, *10 (Tex. App.—Dallas, writ denied). Still, other courts have held that the statute of frauds prevents a plaintiff from commencing a DTPA cause of action. *Keriotis v. Lombardo Rental Trust*, 607 S.W.2d 44, 46 (Tex. App.-Beaumont 1980, writ ref'd n.r.e)

There is more. Federal preemption doctrine bars some DTPA actions. Also, the DTPA itself exempts certain claims and persons from its reach. For example, absent a misrepresentation or fraud, a mere breach of contract is not a false, misleading or deceptive act; thus, it does not violate the DTPA. See, e.g., *Dev., Inc. v. USLife Real Estate Serv. Corp.*, 661 S.W.2d 933, 935 (Tex. 1983). And plaintiffs may not divide or fracture, say, a legal malpractice claim and commence both a DTPA action and a legal malpractice cause of action. *Latham v. Castillo*, 972 S.W.2d 66, 68 (Tex. 1998).

This chapter discusses various defenses that DTPA defendants may raise, focusing primarily on some of the most litigated affirmative defenses and statutory exemptions that appear in DTPA lawsuits.

A. *Statutes-of-Limitations Defense*

When the DTPA was enacted in 1973, it did not have a statute-of-limitations provision. So there was confusion regarding the maximum amount of time a plaintiff had to commence a pure-DTPA, a DTPA-unconscionability or a DTPA-related, breach-of-warranty action. To illustrate, courts generally required the consumer to commence a breach-of-warranty action "within four years after the cause of action shall have accrued." See, e.g., *Holifield v. Coronado Building, Inc.* 594 S.W.2d 214, 216 (Tex. Civ. App.- Houston [14th Dist.] 1980). The prevailing view was that breach-of-warranty actions evolved out of contractual agreements. Therefore, the four-year limitations period was correct. See *W. R. Weaver Co. v. Burroughs Corp.,* 580 S.W.2d 76, 80 (Tex. Civ. App.- El Paso, 1979). On the other hand, consumers had two years to commence a pure-DTPA or a DTPA-unconscionability cause of action. See *Marcotte v. American Motorists Insurance Co.* 709 F.2d 378, 380 (5th Cir. 1983) (concluding that a two-year statute of limitations applied to a DTPA suit involving misrepresentations).

In 1979, the Texas Legislature amended the DTPA and inserted § 17.565. That statute-of-limitations provision reads:

> All actions brought under this subchapter must be commenced within two years after the date on which the false, misleading, or deceptive act or practice occurred or within two years after the consumer discovered or in the exercise of reasonable diligence should have discovered the occurrence of the false, misleading, or deceptive act or practice. The period of limitation provided in this section may be extended for a period of 180 days if the plaintiff proves that failure timely to commence the action was caused by the defendant's knowingly engaging in conduct solely calculated to induce the plaintiff to refrain from or postpone the commencement of the action.

The limitations period for a DTPA action is two years. Tex. Bus. & Comm. Code Ann. § 17.565. The limitations period for fraud is four years. Tex. Civ. Prac. & Rem. Code Ann. § 16.004(a)(4).

However, determining which rule of accrual applies is a question of law. *Moreno v. Sterling Drug, Inc.,* 787 S.W.2d 348, 351 (Tex.1990). Therefore, statutes-of-limitations rulings are varied.

Ordinarily, the statute of limitations begins to run when a particular cause of action accrues. *S. V. v. R. V.,* 933 S.W.2d 1, 4 (Tex.1996). But what is the meaning of "accrues?" Without defining the term, one rule states that a cause of action accrues when facts come into existence authorizing one to seek a judicial remedy. Another rule states that the statute of limitations does not toll even if a consumer has not determined her total damages. Still another states: The discovery of the injury and its general cause—rather than the discovery of all elements of a cause of action—starts the running of the statute. And the Texas Supreme Court has reaffirmed its position: The limitations clock starts running, even if a consumer does not know the specific cause of his injury, the responsible party, or the full extent of the injury.

KPMG Peat Marwick v. Harrison County Housing Finance Corporation
988 S.W.2d 746
(Tex. 1999)

We are asked to decide whether Harrison County Housing Finance Corporation's (HCH) claims against KPMG Peat Marwick, LLP for violations of the Deceptive Trade Practices Act and negligence are barred by the two-year statute of limitations. The trial court granted summary judgment for Peat Marwick on all of HCH's claims. But the court of appeals reversed the trial court's summary judgment on the DTPA and negligence claims and remanded these for trial.

Applying the discovery rule, the court of appeals held that neither claim was time-barred. It reasoned that Peat Marwick had not presented conclusive evidence that HCH discovered or in the exercise of reasonable diligence should have discovered the wrongful act which allegedly caused its injury more than two years before HCH filed suit.

To the contrary, we conclude that Peat Marwick has conclusively established that HCH's claims against Peat Marwick accrued more than two years before suit was filed. Accordingly, we reverse the court of appeals' judgment on both the DTPA and negligence claims and render judgment that HCH take nothing.

From 1980 to 1990, Peat Marwick provided accounting and auditing services to HCH for a series of bonds HCH had issued. In addition, Peat Marwick was to ensure that the trustee for the bonds, First Interstate Bank of California, complied with the trust indenture.

Under the trust indenture, one of First Interstate's duties as trustee was overseeing a capital reserve fund established to pay principal or to redeem bonds. And during the period of the auditing services, specifically in 1985, First Interstate hired, on its own behalf, a partner from Peat Marwick to prepare a special procedures report about the trust assets. But Peat Marwick did not tell HCH about this dual representation.

On February 1, 1993, HCH filed suit against First Interstate and one of its shareholders, alleging breach of fiduciary duty, breach of contract, negligence, and gross negligence. HCH alleged that in February 1989, First Interstate prematurely sold assets in the capital reserve fund, resulting in a loss in excess of $621,000 when the bonds were refunded in December 1991. First Interstate and its shareholder moved for summary judgment on several grounds, including that the bank had not mismanaged the trust funds, that HCH was well informed of the bank's actions through monthly reports, and that HCH's claims were barred by the applicable statutes of limitations. Without specifying the grounds, the trial court granted First Interstate's motion for summary judgment. HCH did not appeal.

On October 1, 1993, while the First Interstate lawsuit was still pending, HCH learned about Peat Marwick's 1985 agreement with First Interstate and that Peat Marwick's 1985 audit of First Interstate's records had revealed irregularities in First Interstate's accounting of the trust assets. According to HCH, Peat Marwick informed First Interstate but not HCH of the irregularities. HCH further claims it then discovered that Peat Marwick had advised First Interstate that the capital reserve fund could be set at an amount lower than what the trust indenture required. And HCH asserts that Peat Marwick did not report that advice to HCH.

HCH sued Peat Marwick in federal court on July 14, 1995, but the case was dismissed for lack of subject matter jurisdiction. HCH then filed suit in state court. For this appeal, Peat Marwick concedes that July 14, 1995, is the applicable date to determine whether HCH's claims were barred when filed. Tex. Civ. Prac. & Rem. Code § 16.064(a).

In this case, HCH alleged that Peat Marwick, as the trust's auditor, either negligently or intentionally failed to disclose First Interstate's mismanagement of the trust. HCH further alleged causes of action for breach of warranty (which is not part of this appeal) and violations of the DTPA.

In support of its motion for summary judgment on limitations grounds, Peat Marwick attached HCH's original petition in the suit against First Interstate. That petition sought recovery for the same injury-the premature selling of the fund assets in 1989 resulting in a loss in excess of $621,000-that HCH alleges in this suit was caused by Peat Marwick's wrongful conduct. Peat Marwick contends that the petition against First Interstate demonstrates that HCH knew of its claim no later than February 1, 1993. Apparently in response, HCH amended its petition to allege that not until October 1, 1993, did it learn of Peat Marwick's role in the disputed financial irregularities. But it does not appear that HCH filed a formal response to Peat Marwick's motion for summary judgment or produced any evidence to defeat the motion. As mentioned, the trial court granted summary judgment.

* * *

A DTPA claim is subject to a two-year statute of limitations. The claim accrues when "the consumer discovered or in the exercise of reasonable diligence should have discovered the occurrence of the false, misleading, or deceptive act or practice." Tex. Bus. & Com.Code § 17.565. Thus, the discovery rule applies to HCH's DTPA claim. *Murphy v. Campbell,* 964 S.W.2d 265, 271 (Tex.1997) We note that effective September 1, 1995, the Legislature amended the DTPA to exempt professional services with some exceptions. But because this suit was originally filed before that date, the 1995 amendments do not apply. Tex. Bus. & Com. Code § 17.49(c).

Contending that during the relevant time period Peat Marwick had worked for First Interstate independently as well as for HCH, HCH argues that its claims against Peat Marwick did not accrue until October 1, 1993, when it learned through discovery in the First Interstate suit that Peat Marwick knew of financial irregularities in the bond issue but failed to report them to HCH. In agreeing with HCH, the court of appeals erroneously concluded that in recent decisions this Court employed a "new formulation" of the discovery rule. *Diaz v. Westphal,* 941 S.W.2d 96, 99 (Tex.1997); *S.V. v. R.V.,* 933 S.W.2d 1, 4 (Tex.1996).

The court of appeals held that under this "new formulation," a claim does not accrue until plaintiff knows not only of the injury, but the specific nature of each wrongful act that may have caused the injury. This is incorrect. The rule in those cases was, as it is in this one, that accrual occurs when the plaintiff knew or should have known of the wrongfully caused injury. *See Murphy,* 964 S.W.2d at 271; *Diaz,* 941 S.W.2d at 99; *S.V.,* 933 S.W.2d at 4. *See also Childs v. Haussecker,* 974 S.W.2d 31, 40 (Tex.1998); *Russell v. Ingersoll-Rand Co.,* 841 S.W.2d 343, 344 n. 3 (Tex. 1992); *Moreno v. Sterling Drug, Inc.,* 787 S.W.2d 348, 351 (Tex. 1990).

The summary judgment evidence established that the wrongful injury HCH alleges it suffered is the loss of over $621,000 in December 1991 when it refunded the bonds following the premature sale in 1989 of the reserve fund assets. Significantly, HCH sued First Interstate over this precise injury in early 1993, less than two years later. Indisputably, HCH was aware by then of its injury and that its injury was caused by the wrongful conduct of another.

The loss from the premature sale of the fund assets should have caused HCH to investigate not only the possibility that First Interstate had mismanaged the fund assets, as HCH apparently did because it sued First Interstate, but also Peat Marwick's possible involvement in the mismanagement and loss. HCH had hired Peat Marwick to do annual trust asset audits, including the reserve fund, to ensure compliance with the trust indenture. Therefore, the loss should have caused HCH to also investigate why its auditor, Peat Marwick, did not discover or report the mismanagement.

As an independent ground to defeat summary judgment, HCH asserts that Peat Marwick fraudulently concealed its wrongful conduct, and limitations did not begin to run until HCH knew or should have known of its injury. HCH also asserts that its pleading is sufficient summary judgment evidence of the affirmative defense of fraudulent concealment to defeat Peat Marwick's summary judgment motion. In both respects, HCH is incorrect.

First, a party asserting fraudulent concealment as an affirmative defense to the statute of limitations has the burden to raise it in response to the summary judgment motion *See* Tex. R. Civ. P. 166a(c); *Hudson v. Wakefield,* 711 S.W.2d 628, 630 n. 1 (Tex.1986) . . . and to come forward with summary judgment evidence raising a fact issue on each element of the fraudulent concealment defense. *American Petrofina, Inc. v. Allen* 887 S.W.2d 829, 830 (Tex.1994); *Nichols v. Smith,* 507 S.W.2d 518, 521 (Tex. 1974).A mere pleading does not satisfy either burden. Thus, even assuming that HCH pled fraudulent concealment as an affirmative defense to Peat Marwick's answer pleading limitations, HCH still had to respond to Peat Marwick's summary judgment motion. There is no such response in the record. Therefore, HCH did not carry its burden to both plead the defense and support it with summary judgment evidence.

Second, when a defendant has fraudulently concealed the facts forming the basis of the plaintiff's claim, limitations does not begin to run until the claimant, using reasonable diligence, discovered or should have discovered the injury. *See Computer Assocs. Int'l, Inc. v. Altai, Inc.,* 918 S.W.2d 453, 455 (Tex.1994); *Estate of Stonecipher v. Estate of Butts,* 591 S.W.2d 806, 809 (Tex.1979).

Because Peat Marwick's summary judgment evidence conclusively established that HCH discovered its injury more than two years before it sued Peat Marwick, Peat Marwick is entitled to summary judgment. As with the discovery rule, once HCH knew that it had been injured by fund mismanagement, it should have investigated why its auditor, Peat Marwick, had failed to discover or report the mismanagement to HCH. Accordingly, fraudulent concealment pleadings do not rescue HCH's DTPA claim.

III. Accrual of HCH's Negligence Claim

Under Section 16.003 of the Civil Practice and Remedies Code, negligence claims, including accounting malpractice, must be brought "not later than two years after the day the cause of action accrues." Tex. Civ. Prac. & Rem.Code § 16.003(a); *see also Murphy,* 964 S.W.2d at 270. Because the statute does not define or specify when accrual occurs, we look to the common law to determine when a cause of action accrues. *See Childs,* 974 S.W.2d at 36; *Murphy,* 964 S.W.2d at 270.

HCH argues that its negligence claim against Peat Marwick did not accrue until it learned through discovery in the First Interstate suit of Peat Marwick's wrongful conduct. We disagree. This Court has never considered whether the discovery rule applies to auditing malpractice claims. Assuming without deciding that it does, however, the summary judgment evidence establishes that HCH knew or should have known of its negligence claim more than two years before it filed suit.

HCH relies on the same wrongfully caused injury asserted in the DTPA cause of action to claim that Peat Marwick was negligent. And as we have mentioned, the evidence conclusively establishes that HCH knew of the reserve fund's mismanagement, at least, no later than when it filed the first suit against First Interstate, February 1, 1993. Consequently, HCH's negligence claim is also time-barred. Furthermore, as with HCH's DTPA claims, its fraudulent concealment pleadings do not rescue the negligence claim.

Peat Marwick has established the affirmative defense of limitations by conclusively showing that HCH's causes of action accrued more than two years before HCH filed suit. As a result, limitations bars HCH's claims for DTPA violations and negligence and Peat Marwick is entitled to summary judgment. Therefore, we reverse the court of appeals' judgment and render judgment that HCH take nothing.

Underkofler v. Vanasek
53 S.W.3d 343
(Tex. 2001)

In this legal-malpractice case we answer two statute-of-limitation questions: First, whether the statute of limitations has run on the client's common-law claims; second, whether the statute has run on the client's Deceptive Trade Practices Consumer Protection Act claims. The trial court granted summary judgment for the attorneys on all claims. The court of appeals reversed and remanded as to all claims except breach of implied warranty under the DTPA. 50 S.W.3d 1. In accord with our decision announced today in *Apex Towing Co. v. Tolin,* 41 S.W.3d 118 (Tex. 2001), we affirm the court of appeals' judgment that the client's common-law claims in this case were timely filed under the tolling rule of *Hughes v. Mahaney & Higgins,* 821 S.W.2d 154 (Tex. 1991).

We also affirm its judgment that the attorneys were not entitled to summary judgment on the basis that the client's settlement of the underlying case eliminated any claim for damages. However, we reverse the court of appeals' judgment remanding the DTPA claims, and hold that the *Hughes* rule does not toll the statute of limitations incorporated into the DTPA. Accordingly, we affirm the court of appeals' judgment in part and reverse and render judgment in part that Respondent take nothing on his DTPA claims.

Respondent Hugh Vanasek hired petitioners Paul Underkofler and his law firm, Goins, Underkofler, Crawford & Langdon (collectively, "Underkofler"), to pursue recovery on a note against the maker, a limited partnership, and against its partners as guarantors. A nonjury trial began on June 6, 1991. That same day, the trial court ordered the parties to mediation, which was ultimately unsuccessful. The record indicates that throughout the spring and fall of 1991, Vanasek had concerns about Underkofler's representation and ability to handle the lawsuit. Two of the defendants filed for bankruptcy in late 1991. Vanasek wrote a letter to one of Underkofler's partners on April 7, 1992, outlining his complaints about Underkofler. Underkofler then filed a motion to withdraw from the case, which the trial court granted on May 22, 1992. After Underkofler withdrew, Vanasek hired another attorney to represent him in that lawsuit. After an almost three-year recess, trial resumed on April 29, 1994. Trial was again recessed and reset several times. Vanasek eventually settled with some of the defendants. The trial court finally rendered judgment on the settlement agreement and against the several remaining defendants, who did not appear for trial, on September 23, 1994.

Before the parties reached the settlement agreement, on April 6, 1994, Vanasek sued Underkofler for malpractice, alleging negligence, gross negligence, breach of contract, breach of implied and express warranties, and DTPA violations. Underkofler moved for summary judgment on a number of grounds, including that limitations barred all of Vanasek's claims and that Vanasek's settlement of the underlying case eliminated any claim for damages. The trial court granted Underkofler's motion. The court of appeals affirmed the summary judgment for Underkofler regarding Vanasek's breach of implied warranty claim under the DTPA, but reversed and remanded as to all the remaining claims. 50 S.W.3d at 15.

On the common-law claims, the court held, among other things, that *Hughes* tolled limitations "until there was a final judgment or other resolution in the underlying litigation." 50 S.W.3d at 14.

It further determined, with one justice dissenting, that limitations on the remaining DTPA claims should also be tolled because the policy reasons behind *Hughes* likewise applied to those claims. 50 S.W.3d at 14. The court also determined that Underkofler had not conclusively proved that Vanasek's settlement of the underlying suit had eliminated any claim for damages. Underkofler filed this petition for review, challenging the court of appeals' application of the *Hughes* tolling rule to the claims in this case and the court's ruling on the effect of the settlement.

With regard to Vanasek's common-law malpractice claims, for the reasons we explain today in *Apex Towing Co. v. Tolin,* 41 S.W.3d 118 (Tex.2001), the court of appeals in this case correctly held that *Hughes* applies to this case. As we further explain in *Apex,* 41 S.W.3d at 121, and the court of appeals also correctly noted in this case, continued representation by the malpractice defendant is not a requirement under *Hughes.* 50 S.W.3d at 13-14. Vanasek's malpractice claims arise out of the underlying litigation on the note. Under *Hughes,* limitations were therefore tolled until the underlying litigation was concluded by the trial court's rendition of a final judgment, which was not appealed, on September 23, 1994. Vanasek's April 6, 1994 malpractice suit was thus timely filed.

We also agree with the court of appeals that Underkofler was not entitled to summary judgment on the basis that Vanasek's settlement of the underlying case eliminated any claim for damages. The settlement did not include all the defendants, and part of Vanasek's malpractice claim is that the delay occasioned by the adjournment of the trial permitted two defendants to file for bankruptcy, which contributed to his agreeing to a less favorable settlement. As the court of appeals explained, these facts do not support Underkofler's position that he conclusively established that all of Vanasek's damages were speculative as a matter of law or that as a matter of law Vanasek has conclusively received full satisfaction for his injury by settling the underlying case.

We cannot agree with the court of appeals, however, that the common-law rule we adopted in *Hughes* also applies to Vanasek's DTPA claims.[1] The Legislature has adopted a specific statute of limitations for DTPA claims, and has included only two exceptions to the general rule that [the] limitation begins to run on the date the wrongful act occurred, a discovery rule and a fraudulent concealment rule:

> All actions brought under this subchapter must be commenced within two years after the date on which the false, misleading, or deceptive act or practice occurred or within two years after the consumer discovered or in the exercise of reasonable diligence should have discovered the occurrence of the false, misleading, or deceptive act or practice. The period of limitation provided in this section may be extended for a period of 180 days if the plaintiff proves that failure timely to commence the action was caused by the defendant's knowingly engaging in

---

1 We note that in 1995 the Legislature amended the DTPA to exclude from its purview claims for damages based on "the rendering of a professional service, the essence of which is the providing of advice, judgment, opinion, or similar professional skill." Tex. Bus. & Com.Code § 17.49(c). Because Vanasek's claims accrued before September 1, 1995, the effective date of the amendment, and he filed his claims before September 1, 1996, the amendment does not apply to those claims. *See* Act of May 19, 1995, 74th Leg., R.S., ch. 414, § 20(b), 1995 Tex. Gen. Laws 3004.

> conduct solely calculated to induce the plaintiff to refrain from or postpone the commencement of the action. Tex. Bus. & Com. Code § 17.565.

We defer to the Legislature's explicit policy determination that only two exceptions apply to the statute of limitations for these statutory claims, and we will not rewrite the statute to add the *Hughes* tolling rule as a third.

We must also address *Aduddell v. Parkhill,* 821 S.W.2d 158 (Tex.1991), issued the same day we issued *Hughes.* In *Aduddell,* we did apply *Hughes* to a legal-malpractice case alleging common-law negligence and DTPA claims. (In fact, in *Hughes* the client also alleged DTPA violations, but did not challenge on appeal the trial court's summary judgment for the attorneys on those claims. 821 S.W.2d at 156 n. 3.) The extent of our analysis in *Aduddell* was:

> Today, in *Hughes v. Mahaney,* 821 S.W.2d 154 (Tex.1991), we announce a new rule tolling limitations until all appeals of the underlying claim are exhausted when an attorney allegedly commits malpractice while providing legal services in the prosecution or defense of a claim which results in litigation. Because that tolling provision also applies to the facts of this case, we reverse the judgment of the court of appeals and remand this cause to the trial court for further proceedings consistent with this opinion.

In light of the brevity of our analysis in *Aduddell,* and our conclusion today that the Legislature has circumscribed the exceptions to limitations for DTPA claims, we overrule *Aduddell* to the extent it applied *Hughes* to DTPA claims.

As we have concluded that the *Hughes* tolling rule does not apply to Vanasek's DTPA claims, we must apply the limitations section of the DTPA to determine if those claims were timely filed. *See* Tex. Bus. & Com. Code § 17.565. Underkofler is entitled to summary judgment on proof that Vanasek did not file his lawsuit within the statutory limitations period. *See KPMG Peat Marwick v. Harrison County Hous. Fin. Corp.,* 988 S.W.2d 746, 748-49 (Tex.1999); *Burns v. Thomas,* 786 S.W.2d 266, 267 (Tex.1990). Underkofler's summary judgment evidence establishes that throughout the spring and fall of 1991, Vanasek was aware of and expressed his specific complaints about Underkofler's representation, which complaints form the basis of his DTPA claims. Vanasek did not file his malpractice claims until April 6, 1994. Summary judgment in favor of Underkofler and his firm on these claims was therefore proper.

Accordingly, we affirm the court of appeals' judgment remanding Vanasek's common-law claims, but reverse the court of appeals' judgment on his DTPA claims and render judgment that he take nothing on those claims.

B. Pre-Suit Notice Defense

Section 17.505 of the DTPA has pre-suit notice requirements. It reads:

> (a) As a prerequisite to filing a suit seeking damages under Subdivision (1) of Subsection (b) of Section 17.50 of this subchapter against any person, a consumer shall give written notice to the person at least 60 days before filing the suit advising the person in reasonable detail of the consumer's specific complaint and the amount of economic damages, damages for mental anguish, and expenses, including attorneys' fees, if any, reasonably incurred by the consumer in asserting the claim against the defendant. During the 60-day period a written request to inspect, in a reasonable manner and at a reasonable time and place, the goods that are the subject of the consumer's action or claim may be presented to the consumer.
>
> (b) If the giving of 60 days' written notice is rendered impracticable by reason of the necessity of filing suit in order to prevent the expiration of the statute of limitations or if the consumer's claim is asserted by way of counterclaim, the notice provided for in Subsection (a) of this section is not required, but the tender provided for by Subsection (d), Section 17.506 of this subchapter may be made within 60 days after service of the suit or counterclaim.
>
> (c) A person against whom a suit is pending who does not receive written notice, as required by Subsection (a), may file a plea in abatement not later than the 30th day after the date the person files an original answer in the court in which the suit is pending. This subsection does not apply if Subsection (b) applies.
>
> (d) The court shall abate the suit if the court, after a hearing, finds that the person is entitled to an abatement because notice was not provided as required by this section. A suit is automatically abated without the order of the court beginning on the 11th day after the date a plea in abatement is filed under Subsection (c) if the plea in abatement:
>
> (1) is verified and alleges that the person against whom the suit is pending did not receive the written notice as required by Subsection (a); and
>
> (2) is not controverted by an affidavit filed by the consumer before the 11th day after the date on which the plea in abatement is filed.
>
> (e) An abatement under Subsection (d) continues until the 60th day after the date that written notice is served in compliance with Subsection (a).

Clearly, before a consumer files a DTPA lawsuit, the consumer must notify the defendant. But there are questions which are not addressed in § 17.505. May a consumer give notice "as soon as practicable" or within a "reasonable amount of time?" Who has the burden of proving that the notice requirement was satisfied? May a consumer substitute actual and oral notices for written notices? And assuming that a consumer does not give a timely notice, may a DTPA action still go to trial under some other theory? Do pre-suit notice requirements under "tie-in statutes" preempt the DTPA's notice requirements or are they compatible? This section addresses some of these questions.

Hines v. Hash
843 S.W.2d 464
(Tex. 1992)

The Texas Deceptive Trade Practices—Consumer Protection Act provides that "[a]s a prerequisite to filing a suit seeking damages" under the Act, "a consumer shall give written notice" to the defendant of his complaint. Tex. Bus. & Com. Code § 17.505(a). We granted writ of error in this case to consider the proper application of this provision.

Dutch Hines sued C.W. Hash, Jr. for damages under the DTPA, complaining that the roof Hash had installed on his home leaked. In his original petition Hines alleged that notice of his claim had been sent to Hash by certified mail, return receipt requested, and had been returned unclaimed. In his original answer, Hash asserted as an affirmative defense that he had never received any notice of Hines' complaint until he was served with suit papers, and therefore had not been able to tender Hines a settlement offer. However, Hash never requested the trial court to abate the suit so that he could make such an offer, nor does it appear that he was prevented from making a settlement offer even without the abatement.

The evidence at trial concerning notice was undisputed. The notice letter to Hash and the envelope in which it was sent were admitted into evidence, showing three unsuccessful attempts at delivery before it was returned to Hines. Hash did not dispute that the envelope was accurately addressed to him. In fact, he testified he knew at the time that he had a certified letter at the post office but did not pick it up because he was leaving town each morning before the post office opened to work in another city and was not returning home until after the post office closed. He also testified that it was not convenient for him to arrange to have someone else pick up the letter.

Hines did not challenge Hash's explanation for not having received the letter. Hash moved for an instructed verdict after Hines rested and again at the close of all the evidence, urging lack of notice as a complete bar to Hines' claim. The trial court denied Hash's motions and refused Hash's requested jury question on the issue of notice. The jury found that Hash knowingly violated the DTPA in several particulars and assessed Hines' actual damages at $9,249.00. The trial court rendered judgment on the verdict for a total of $35,822.67, which included actual damages, twice that sum in statutory damages, prejudgment interest of $4,225.67, and attorney fees of $3,850.00.

The court of appeals, noting a lack of uniformity in the cases applying the notice requirement in the DTPA, held that the DTPA mandates actual delivery of notice. The court reasoned that the purpose of the notice requirement, "to afford the opportunity for presuit negotiations and settlement in avoidance of lengthy and costly litigation", could be preserved only if notice is actually received by the defendant, either by certified mail as prescribed in the statute, or "by other means readily available." *Id.* at 315. The court also cited our decision in *Cail v. Service Motors, Inc.,* 660 S.W.2d 814, 815 (Tex.1983), where we stated that "[a] prerequisite to recovery [of damages under the DTPA] is delivery of written notice...." The court concluded that Hines' failure to deliver notice to Hash was reversible error, and that the case should be remanded for a new trial with instructions to the trial court to abate proceedings for not more than 60 days to allow Hines to comply with the notice requirement. To Hash's argument that this result allowed Hines to disregard the statutory notice requirement without penalty, the court answered that a new trial was penalty enough.

Hines argues that the notice required by the DTPA is given when it is mailed to the defendant at the correct address, regardless of whether it is actually received. Thus, Hines contends that he fully complied with the DTPA. He also argues that even if actual delivery is required, his failure to give notice should not result in reversal of the trial court's judgment and remand for proper notice and a new trial. We find it necessary to address only the latter argument. Before we do, we examine the history of the statutory provision and the cases applying it.

There was no notice provision in the DTPA as originally enacted in 1973. Deceptive Trade Practices-Consumer Protection Act (approved May 21, 1973), 63rd Leg., R.S., ch. 143, § 1, 1973 Tex. Gen. Laws 322. It was added in 1977 by the following provision:

§ 17.50A. Damages: Defenses

> In an action brought under Section 17.50 of this subchapter, actual damages only and attorney's fees reasonable in relation to the amount of work expended and court costs may be awarded where the defendant:
>
> * * *
>
> (2) proves that he had no written notice of the consumer's complaint before suit was filed, or that within 30 days after he was given written notice he tendered to the consumer (a) the cash value of the consideration received from the consumer or the cash value of the benefit promised, whichever is greater, and (b) the expenses, including attorney's fees, if any, reasonably incurred by the consumer in asserting his claim against the defendant. . . . [Act approved May 23, 1977, 65th Leg., R.S., ch. 216, § 6, 1977 Tex. Gen. Laws 600, 604].

The 1977 version of the statute placed the burden on defendant to plead and prove lack of notice. If defendant met this burden, the statute expressly provided that plaintiff could recover only actual damages and not additional statutory damages. One court suggested that if plaintiff did not give notice as required before filing suit, he could nonsuit, give notice, and then refile the identical suit. *See Chrysler Corp. v. McMorries,* 657 S.W.2d 858, 867-868 (Tex.App.-Amarillo 1983, no writ). Two others held that defendant's failure to plead and prove that he did not receive notice waived any defense. *Bolton v. Alvarado,* 762 S.W.2d 215, 216-217 (Tex.App.-Houston [1st Dist.]

1988, writ denied) (trial court did not err in overruling defendants' objection to the submission of DTPA issues to the jury because defendants neither pleaded nor proved lack of notice); *Chrysler-Plymouth City, Inc. v. Guerrero,* 620 S.W.2d 700, 706 (Tex.Civ.App.-San Antonio 1981, no writ).

In 1979, the statutory provision was amended as follows:

§ 17.50A NOTICE: OFFER OF SETTLEMENT

> (a) As a prerequisite to filing a suit seeking damages under Subdivision (1) of Subsection (b) of Section 17.50 of this subchapter against any person, a consumer shall give written notice to the person at least 30 days before filing the suit advising the person of the consumer's specific complaint and the amount of actual damages and expenses, including attorneys' fees, if any, reasonably incurred by the consumer in asserting the claim against the defendant. [ACT APPROVED JUNE 13, 1979, 66TH LEG., R.S., CH. 603, § 5, 1979 TEX. GEN. LAWS 1327, 1330].

This provision was in effect when the events of this case occurred and suit was filed, and it therefore governs this case. *See Winkle Chevy-Olds-Pontiac, Inc. v. Condon,* 830 S.W.2d 740, 745 n. 4 (Tex.App.-Corpus Christi 1992, writ dism'd); *Schenck v. Ebby Halliday Real Estate, Inc.,* 803 S.W.2d 361, 373 (Tex.App.-Fort Worth 1990, no writ); *see also Wolfe,* 664 S.W.2d at 103-104.[2]

Within 30 days of receiving the required notice, a person may tender a written offer to settle, and if the consumer rejects the offer and does not recover substantially different damages at trial, recovery is limited to the amount of the offer. Tex. Bus. & Com. Code § 17.505(b)-(e). A person may also within the same period tender payment of the actual damages and expenses claimed, and then may assert that tender in complete defense to an action for damages under the DTPA. *Id.* § 17.506(d).

Unlike the 1977 provision, the 1979 version places the burden on plaintiff to plead that he gave notice. However, defendant must raise a timely objection to plaintiff's failure to plead. *See Star-Tel v. Nacogdoches Telecommunications Inc.,* 755 S.W.2d 146, 149 (Tex.App.-Houston [1st Dist.] 1988, no writ) (special exception filed during trial but before the charge to the jury was not timely). If a defendant specifically denies receiving notice, plaintiff must prove either that he provided it, or that he was excused from providing it . . . [under] section 17.505(b)[3]. . . . If a defendant does not

2 The statute has since been amended further, but the differences between the 1979 version and the current notice provision are not significant to our analysis. One change was in 1987, when section 17.50A was renumbered section 17.505. Act approved May 25, 1987, 70th Leg., R.S., ch. 167, § 5.02(4), 1987 Tex. Gen. & Spec. Laws 1338, 1361. The only other changes were in 1989, when the provision was amended to increase the notice required from 30 days to 60 days, and to add after the words, "advising the person", the words, "in reasonable detail". Act approved June 14, 1989, 71st Leg., R.S., ch. 380, § 3(a), 1989 Tex. Gen. Laws 1490, 1491-92.

3 Notice is excused if it "is rendered impracticable by reason of the necessity of filing suit in order to prevent the expiration of the statute of limitations or if the consumer's claims is asserted by way of counterclaim". Tex. Bus. & Com. Code § 17.505(b).

specifically deny receiving notice, then plaintiff is excused from proof by Rule 54, Tex. R. Civ. P. Defendant must object to plaintiff's failure to meet his burden of proof in order to preserve error.

The notice requirement of the DTPA is clearly mandatory, but that feature alone does not determine the consequences for failure to comply with it. The Legislature may prescribe the consequences for failure to comply with statutory requirements, as it did in 1977 by providing that a failure to give notice limited plaintiff to recovery of actual damages, attorney fees and court costs. Hines argues that it has also done so in the 1979 provision by making notice "a prerequisite to filing a suit." Hines cites three cases in support of his argument. All three cases merely recite the statutory language. The issue is not whether notice is a prerequisite to a DTPA action for damages —clearly, it is— but what the effect of lack of notice is. As we read the 1979 provision, it does not specify the consequences for noncompliance.

When the statute is silent, we have looked to its purpose for guidance. Thus, in *State v. $435,000,* 842 S.W.2d 642 (Tex.1992) (per curiam), we recently held that the statutory requirement that a hearing be set within 30 days of the filing of an action for forfeiture of property used in drug trafficking was mandatory, but that the failure to comply does not necessitate dismissal of the action. In a case more directly related to the one before us, we held that the notice of a health care liability claim required by the Medical Liability and Insurance Improvement Act, Tex. Rev. Civ. Stat. art. 4590i, § 4.01 is mandatory, but that the failure to give notice does not require dismissal of the action. *Schepps v. Presbyterian Hosp.,* 652 S.W.2d 934, 938 (Tex.1983). We concluded that the purpose of the notice requirement, to encourage pre-suit negotiations so as to avoid the expense of litigation, is better served by abating an action filed without notice for the duration of the statutory notice period to allow the parties to negotiate, than by dismissing the action altogether. *Hutchinson v. Wood,* 657 S.W.2d 782 (Tex.1983).

Three courts have concluded that if notice is not given under the DTPA, plaintiff is limited to recovering actual damages and cannot obtain additional damages allowed by the Act. *Hollingsworth Roofing Co. v. Morrison,* 668 S.W.2d 872, 875 (Tex. App.-Fort Worth 1984, no writ) (citing *Schepps* and *Hutchison*); *Blumenthal,* 646 S.W.2d at 286-287); *Boyd Int'l, Ltd. v. Honeywell, Inc.,* 837 F.2d 1312, 1316 (5th Cir.1988). Although this was the result expressly prescribed by the 1977 notice provision, it was removed from the 1979 version. We presume the Legislature intended by its 1979 amendment that the failure to give notice should no longer result in a limitation of damages. Since the provision is now silent on the effect of noncompliance, we must consider the purpose of the statute as we would in other cases.[4]

---

4 Many other statutes require notice before actions or claims can be filed. *E.g.,* Tex. Rev.Civ.Stat.Ann. art. 1524(h) (Vernon 1980) (appeal to district court by low income housing corporations); *id.* art. 5221k, § 6.01 (Vernon 1987) (suits for violations of the Commission on Human Rights Act); Art. 8308-5.01 (Vernon Supp.1992) (claims under the Workers' Compensation Act); Tex. Civ. Prac. & Rem.Code § 30.004 (suits involving the state, state agencies or parties represented by the Attorney General); *id.* § 38.002 (claims for attorney fees); *id.* § 101.101 (suits against governmental units under the Tort Claims Act); Tex. Fam. Code § 36.07 (suits for violation of possessory interests in children); Tex. Ins. Code art. 21.21, § 16(e) (suits for statutory violations); Tex. Loc. Gov't Code § 54.017 (enforcement of health and safety ordinances); *id.* § 81.041 (suits against counties); Tex. Prop. Code § 24.005 (eviction suits); *id.* § 27.004 (suits against contractors for construction defects); *id.* § 53.056 (mechanic's liens); Tex. Tax Code § 321.309 (suits by municipalities for delinquent taxes). The purposes of

The purpose of the DTPA notice provision is the same as that of the Medical Liability and Insurance Improvement Act: "to discourage litigation and encourage settlements of consumer complaints." *Jim Walter Homes, Inc. v. Valencia,* 690 S.W.2d 239, 242 (Tex.1985). When a plaintiff fails to comply with the requirement, abatement of the action for the statutory notice period is more consistent with the purpose of notice than dismissal. While the action is abated, the parties may discuss their positions as they would have done during the period for pre-suit notice. Hash argues that this result allows a plaintiff to ignore the notice requirement with virtual impunity, the only penalty being a slight delay in the litigation.

But the consequence of noncompliance is not necessarily punishment. It may be limited, as we think it is here, to enforcement of the purpose of notice. The initiation of litigation without notice may have effects other than denying the parties a pre-suit opportunity to negotiate. It may polarize the parties and prejudice their discussions. It may also result in expense to the defendant in filing an answer, requesting abatement, and otherwise responding to the litigation. If such effects actually occur, the trial court is empowered to remedy them by appropriate sanctions under Rule 13, Tex. R.Civ.P. But it is not necessary to the purpose of notice in these circumstances to dismiss plaintiff's action if notice is not given.

We therefore conclude that if a plaintiff files an action for damages under the DTPA without first giving the required notice, and a defendant timely requests an abatement, the trial court must abate the proceedings for 60 days. Tex. Bus. & Com. Code art. 17.505(a). To be timely, the request for an abatement must be made while the purpose of notice — settlement and avoidance of litigation expense — remains viable. Thus, defendant must request an abatement with the filing of an answer or very soon thereafter. If the trial court determines that plaintiff has failed to give notice as required by the statute, the action must be abated. Defendant is entitled, but not obliged, to seek review of a denial of abatement by mandamus. Defendant may wait until appeal from the final judgment to seek review of a denial of abatement, but the trial court's error must be shown to have been harmful to obtain reversal. Tex. R. App. P. 81(b)(1). Ordinarily, this would require a showing that defendant was unable to limit his damages under the statute by tendering a settlement offer.

During the abatement the notice required by statute must be given, "advising the person in reasonable detail of the consumer's specific complaint and the amount of actual damages and expenses, including attorneys' fees, if any, reasonably incurred by the consumer in asserting the claim against the defendant." Tex. Bus. & Com. Code § 17.505(a). Other notice, such as actual or oral notice, is insufficient because it does not comply with the statutory insistence upon reasonably certain specificity. Because defendant's response to notice may limit or preclude damages, it is necessary for notice to have some formality to it. If a plaintiff fails to give notice while the action is abated for that purpose, it should be dismissed. *See Miller v. Kossey,* 802 S.W.2d 873, 876-77 (Tex. App.-Amarillo 1991, writ denied) (no notice for more than six months after abatement granted

---

these various notice requirements vary, as do the consequences for noncompliance. Hash contends that *Weirich v. Weirich,* 833 S.W.2d 942 (Tex.1992), holds that a cause of action under Tex. Fam. Code § 36.07(a) is not allowed if the notice required by that provision is not given. *Weirich* did not specifically address this issue, although it did disallow recovery because of the lack of notice. In any event, we express no opinion whether the purpose of that provision would warrant a different consequence for noncompliance than failure to give notice under the DTPA.

until date set for trial). A defendant who fails to make a timely request for abatement must be considered to have waived his objection to the lack of notice. *See Miller v. Presswood,* 743 S.W.2d 275, 281 (Tex.App.-Beaumont 1987, writ denied); *Pool Co.,* 681 S.W.2d at 219.

In this case, Hash waived notice under the DTPA by failing to request abatement. Therefore, the court of appeals erred in holding that the trial court committed reversible error and that the case must be remanded to allow plaintiff to give notice. Other courts of appeals have reached similar results, and to that extent we disapprove those decisions. Accordingly, the judgment of the court of appeals is reversed and the judgment of the trial court is affirmed.

NOTES & QUESTIONS

1) Consider the Fifth Circuit's pre-suit, notice-requirement ruling in *Wellborn v. Sears, Roebuck & Co.,* 970 F.2d 1420 (5th Cir. 1991):

> This diversity case is a products liability action involving an automatic garage door opener manufactured by the Chamberlain Group, Inc. (Chamberlain) and distributed by Sears, Roebuck & Co. (Sears). Marilyn Wellborn (Wellborn) brought this action against Sears and Chamberlain after her son was killed as a result of the garage door opener malfunctioning. We affirm in part and certify the question—Does a decedent's cause of action under the Texas Deceptive Trade Practices — Consumer Protection Act survive under the Texas Survival Statute—to the Texas Supreme Court.
>
> * * *
>
> Following trial, the jury, finding that Wellborn and Bobby were not contributorily negligent, returned a verdict in favor of Wellborn. The district court accepted the verdict and entered judgment. Sears and Chamberlain then moved for judgment notwithstanding the verdict, for a new trial, for remittitur, and to alter or am the judgment. The district court denied the motion for judgment n.o.v., for a new trial, and to alter or am the judgment. However, because Wellborn did not provide Chamberlain with proper statutory notice, the district court granted the defendants' motion for remittitur in part, thereby deleting the additional DTPA damages awarded against Chamberlain.
>
> * * *
>
> This appeal [concerns] . . . whether the DTPA's notice requirement requires actual notice to the defendant.
>
> * * *

In her cross-appeal, Wellborn challenges the district court's conclusion that she is not entitled to the additional damages the jury awarded against Chamberlain because she did not give Chamberlain proper pre-suit notice.

The DTPA requires that a plaintiff serve the defendant with a demand letter as a prerequisite to filing suit. *See* Tex. Bus. & Com. Code Ann. § 17.505(a) (West 1987 and Supp.1992); *see also Automobile Ins. Co. of Hartford v. Davila,* 805 S.W.2d 897, 901-02 (Tex.App.-Corpus Christi 1991, writ denied). "This notice must advise the person of the consumer's specific complaint and the amount of actual damages and expenses, including attorney's fees, if any, reasonably incurred by the consumer in asserting the claim against the defendant." *Davila,* 805 S.W.2d at 901-02, *citing* Tex. Bus. & Com. Code Ann. § 17.505(a). It was therefore Wellborn's burden to provide Chamberlain with proper written notice as a prerequisite to recovering additional damages against Chamberlain.

On August 2, 1989, Wellborn forwarded a notice letter to Sears. Approximately two weeks later, Wellborn's counsel received a copy of a Sears' letter to Chamberlain. In this letter, Sears forwarded Wellborn's claim to Chamberlain and requested that Chamberlain advise Wellborn of its position regarding the claim. Counsel for both defendants subsequently informed Wellborn's counsel that he was representing both defendants on Wellborn's claim and that all correspondence should be sent to him. Wellborn's notice letter to Sears did not inform Chamberlain of any complaint that Wellborn had against Chamberlain. It was addressed to and made complaints against "Sears Roebuck & Co."

Wellborn complained of alleged "false, misleading and deceptive acts and a course of conduct by Sears in violation of the DTPA." Supplemental Record Excerpts, tab 3. Wellborn complained that Sears represented and warranted that the garage door opener was safe and efficient, and that Sears was aware of the defect but failed to correct it or warn consumers about the product. Wellborn's DTPA notice letter to Sears did not mention Chamberlain or any conduct by Chamberlain. We find that Wellborn failed to provide Chamberlain the statutorily prescribed written notice. *See Davila,* 805 S.W.2d at 901-02. Therefore, we affirm the district court's deletion of additional damages against Chamberlain.

2) In *Wellborn*, the Fifth Circuit concluded that a consumer cannot recover additional damages under the DTPA without giving a pre-suit notice to the defendant. Does the DTPA § 17.505 support the Fifth Circuit's conclusion?

3) Is *Wellborn* a correct interpretation or statement of Texas law? Does the Texas Supreme Court's pre-suit notice ruling in *Hines v. Hash* support the Fifth Circuit's conclusion in *Wellborn*?

Richardson v. Foster & Sear, L.L.P.
257 S.W.3d 782
(Tex. App. -Fort Worth 2008)

Appellant LaShun Richardson, a pro se inmate, appeals from the trial court's order dismissing his claims against Appellees Foster & Sear, L.L.P. and Scott W. Wert (Foster & Sear) for failing to serve them with notice of suit under the Texas Deceptive Trade Practices Act ("DTPA"). We reverse and remand.

Background

Richardson's father, Willie Richardson, hired Foster & Sear to represent him for a personal injury claim resulting from asbestos exposure. Willie died before resolution of the claim. Richardson and his sister —Willie's only heirs — agreed to allow Foster & Sear to represent their interests as Willie's heirs in the asbestos litigation.

Richardson sued Foster & Sear on May 22, 2006, for "negligence, professional negligence, breach of warranty, breach of contract and gross negligence" and DTPA violations. He alleged that Foster & Sear settled the asbestos claim without his approval and withheld settlement proceeds from him.

Foster & Sear filed an original answer and verified plea in abatement, asserting that Richardson had failed to serve presuit notice of his claim under the DTPA. Foster & Sear later filed a motion to abate, and the trial court abated the suit on August 22, 2006, "until written notice is tendered to Defendants in accordance with the Texas Business and Commerce Code."

On August 30, 2006, Richardson served a one-page letter on Foster & Sear, stating that he would "submit a claim of professional liability against you in reference to the underlying asbestos litigation" for "misrepresentation . . . and fraudulent misrepresentation . . . that has formed the basis of my claim in connection with negligence . . . and professional negligence." Richardson did not state an amount of actual damages, but he stated that he sought exemplary damages of $1.5 million.

Richardson filed a motion to lift the abatement on November 15, 2006. The trial court denied his motion on February 20, 2007.

On March 5, 2007, Richardson served a second DTPA notice letter on Foster & Sear through their attorney. This second letter is six pages long and alleges that Foster & Sear settled the underlying asbestos claim with various defendants but failed to forward Richardson's share of the settlement proceeds to him. Richardson demanded a total of $500,000 to settle the various claims asserted in the letter.

On April 17, 2007, Foster & Sear filed a motion to dismiss Richardson's suit, arguing in a single sentence that Richardson's March 5, 2007 letter did not meet the requirements of the DTPA. The motion did not explain in what way the letter was deficient or cite any authority other than the

DTPA. Richardson filed an "objection" to the motion to dismiss, asserting that his March 5 letter fulfilled the DTPA's notice requirements.

On May 22, 2007, the trial court signed an order dismissing Richardson's entire suit against Foster & Sear, including his non-DTPA causes of action. This appeal followed. In a single issue, Richardson argues that the trial court abused its discretion by dismissing his claims.

Standard of Review

To determine whether a trial court abused its discretion, we must decide whether the trial court acted without reference to any guiding rules or principles; in other words, we must decide whether the act was arbitrary or unreasonable. *Downer v. Aquamarine Operators, Inc.*, 701 S.W.2d 238, 241-242 (Tex. 1985). Merely because a trial court may decide a matter within its discretion in a different manner than an appellate court would in a similar circumstance does not demonstrate that an abuse of discretion has occurred. *Id.*

DTPA's Notice Requirement

Under DTPA section 17.505(a), a plaintiff must give notice of a DTPA claim to a defendant sixty days before filing suit:

> As a prerequisite to filing a suit seeking damages under Subdivision (1) of Subsection (b) of Section 17.50 of this subchapter against any person, a consumer shall give written notice to the person at least 60 days before filing the suit advising the person in reasonable detail of the consumer's specific complaint and the amount of economic damages, damages for mental anguish, and expenses, including attorneys' fees, if any, reasonably incurred by the consumer in asserting the claim against the defendant. During the 60-day period a written request to inspect, in a reasonable manner and at a reasonable time and place, the goods that are the subject of the consumer's action or claim may be presented to the consumer.

The purpose of the notice provision is to discourage litigation and encourage settlement of consumer complaints. *Hines v. Hash,* 843 S.W.2d 464, 468 (Tex.1992). When the supreme court decided *Hines* in 1992, the Legislature had not specified a consequence for noncompliance with the DTPA's notice requirement. After analyzing the purpose of the requirement and the consequences for noncompliance imposed by the lower courts, the supreme court held that "[w]hen a plaintiff fails to comply with the requirement, abatement of the action for the statutory notice period is more consistent with the purpose of notice than dismissal." *Id.* at 468-69.

Three years later, the Legislature amended the DTPA to conform the notice provision to the *Hines* opinion and provide for abatement when a DTPA plaintiff fails to give presuit notice. The current version of the statute — Tex. Bus. & Com.Code Ann. §§ 17.505(d), (e) —continue[] to specify that abatement is the appropriate remedy when a plaintiff fails to provide presuit notice:

(d) The court shall abate the suit if the court, after a hearing, finds that the person is entitled to an abatement because notice was not provided as required by this section. A suit is automatically abated without the order of the court beginning on the 11th day after the date a plea in abatement is filed under Subsection (c) if the plea in abatement:

(1) is verified and alleges that the person against whom the suit is pending did not receive the written notice as required by Subsection (a); and

(2) is not controverted by an affidavit filed by the consumer before the 11th day after the date on which the plea in abatement is filed.

(e) An abatement under Subsection (d) continues until the 60th day after the date that written notice is served in compliance with Subsection (a).

Thus, when a plaintiff fails to provide presuit notice under subsection (a), the trial court must abate the suit until the plaintiff serves notice that complies with subsection (a).

Although the Legislature has specified abatement as the remedy when a plaintiff fails to serve presuit notice, it has not specified a consequence when a plaintiff fails to serve notice, or serves an inadequate notice, while the suit is abated for that purpose. But the *Hines* opinion does address this scenario, albeit in dicta: "If a plaintiff fails to give notice while the action is abated for that purpose, it should be dismissed." *Hines,* 843 S.W.2d at 469 (citing *Miller v. Kossey,* 802 S.W.2d 873, 876-77 (Tex.App.-Amarillo 1991, writ denied)). In *Miller,* a DTPA plaintiff gave presuit notice under the applicable version of the DTPA, but later conceded in open court that the notice was inadequate. *Miller,* 802 S.W.2d at 874-75.

The trial court ordered the plaintiff to serve a new notice within seven days of the order, but the plaintiff did not serve a new notice until some six months later and on the eve of trial. The trial court found that the new notice was untimely under the court's prior order and did not comply with the DTPA's notice requirements, and it dismissed the plaintiff's claims. The court of appeals held that the trial court was authorized to dismiss the claims because the plaintiff failed to comply with the court's order. Thus, although the DTPA does not expressly provide for dismissal when a plaintiff fails to serve the defendant with postsuit notice when the suit is abated for that purpose, dismissal is appropriate in some circumstances.

Richardson's DTPA Claims

Richardson argues that the trial court abused its discretion by dismissing his claims because his March 5, 2007 letter complied with section 17.505(a). In reply, Foster & Sear contends that because Richardson cites no case law to support his argument that his letter gave adequate notice, "his only argument is 'yes, I did!' " We note that Foster & Sear cite no authority in this court or the trial court to show that Richardson's notice was inadequate; thus, in the spirit of fairness, we may characterize their only argument as "no, he didn't!"

To elevate the discourse to an appropriate legal level and determine whether Richardson's notice was adequate, we look to the requirements expressly set forth in section 17.505(a). The requirements establish a fairly low threshold for a notice letter. A DTPA notice must advise the defendant in reasonable detail of (1) the consumer's specific complaint and (2) the amount of economic damages, damages for mental anguish, and expenses, including attorneys' fees, if any, reasonably incurred by the consumer in asserting the claim against the defendant.

Richardson's March 5 letter, while not a model of clarity and eloquence, states in enough detail for this court-knowing nothing of his claims and allegations except what he asserted in his letter-to grasp the basis of his complaints against Foster & Sear, namely, that after agreeing to represent his interests in whatever claims his deceased father had for asbestos exposure, they settled those claims without his permission and refused to divulge his share of the settlement proceeds. As for damages, Richardson specifically states that he seeks $50,000 in settlement of his claim that Foster & Sear deprived him of $89,800 in settlement proceeds and his associated mental anguish.

He further states that $250,000 "would be considered fair and reasonable" compensation for his claims for "negligence, professional negligence, . . . misrepresentation, breach of warranty, breach of fiduciary duty, breach of contract," and his DTPA claims and associated mental anguish. He also asserts that Foster & Sear failed to advise him "of the limitations on representation of the client, i.e., that attorney's undertaking the case did not ext to representing the client, survivor, [and] beneficiary," for which Richardson seeks $200,000. He summarized his claims with a demand for "[a] total of $500,000 for all combined legal injuries sustained, that constituted Deceptive Trade Practices."

Thus, Richardson's six-page letter set out the basis of his complaints against Foster & Sear and the amount of economic and mental anguish damages he seeks as required by section 17.505(a). The letter is sufficiently specific to allow Foster & Sear to determine whether to settle with Richardson or undertake the cost and risk of litigation. Thus, it states Richardson's claims and damages "in reasonable detail" as required by section 17.505(a) and fulfils the purpose of the notice requirement, to discourage litigation and encourage settlement of consumer complaints. *See Hines,* 843 S.W.2d at 468.

We hold that Richardson's March 5 letter complied with the minimal requirements of section 17.505(a) by providing in reasonable detail his specific complaints and the damages he sought sufficient to fulfill the purpose of the DTPA's notice requirement. We therefore sustain his sole issue as it pertains to his DTPA causes of action.

Conclusion

Having sustained Richardson's sole issue, we vacate the trial court's order of dismissal and remand the case for further proceedings.

Hernandez v. Lautensack
201 S.W.3d 771
(Tex.App.-Fort Worth, 2006)

Roy Hernandez, individually and d/b/a/ Hernandez Roofing and Philip Lautensack filed cross appeals from a judgment in favor of Lautensack concerning the roof Hernandez put on Lautensack's house. In three issues, Hernandez argues that Lautensack's presuit notice under the Residential Construction Liability Act was untimely, that there was no evidence that Lautensack's alleged damages were reasonable, and that the trial court erred in awarding attorney's fees to Lautensack because his presuit demand was excessive. In two issues, Lautensack argues that the evidence conclusively proved his attorney's fees in an amount double what the jury awarded to him and that the trial court erred by refusing to reopen testimony so that Lautensack's counsel could testify about appellate attorney's fees. We modify the trial court's judgment and affirm it as modified.

II. Factual and Procedural Background

In 1999, Lautensack hired Hernandez to replace the slate tile roof on Lautensack's residence at a cost of $20,000. The new roof had many leaks that Hernandez was unable to stop. In 2002, Hernandez told Lautensack that the leaks were the result of hail damage and offered to replace the roof for $9,100 in labor charges if Lautensack provided new slate tiles at a cost of $25,000. Unhappy with Hernandez's prior work, Lautensack hired another roofer, Kip Petty, to install a new cement tile roof for $32,300. Petty documented several defects in Hernandez's previous roofing job, including lack of proper underlayment, lack of metal flashing, and improper tile spacing. Petty replaced the roof in September 2002.

Lautensack sent Hernandez a claim notice letter on February 12, 2003, by certified and regular mail. The letter described various problems with the roof, alleged breaches of express warranties and DTPA violations, and threatened litigation unless Hernandez paid Lautensack $41,880. The certified letter was returned unclaimed; the regular letter was not returned. Hernandez did not reply.

Lautensack sued Hernandez on April 17, 2003, for breach of contract, misrepresentation, fraud, and deceptive trade practices and sought actual damages, attorney's fees, and exemplary damages. Hernandez responded with a plea in abatement claiming that Lautensack had failed to serve the requisite presuit notice under the Residential Construction Liability Act (RCLA). *See* Tex. Prop. Code Ann. §§ 27.001-.003, .0031, .004, .0041, .0042, .005-.006, and .007. Though Lautensack contended that his first letter was sufficient notice under the RCLA, he eventually sent a second notice letter in response to Hernandez's plea in abatement.

The case was ultimately tried to a jury. The jury returned a verdict in favor of Lautensack on all causes of action and awarded him $24,750 in actual damages plus $10,680 in attorney's fees. The jury also found that Lautensack's RCLA notice was untimely because it did not give Hernandez the opportunity to inspect the alleged roof defects and offer to repair them. For reasons not relevant to this appeal, the trial court disregarded the jury's answers to the breach of warranty and DTPA issues. The trial court then signed a judgment in favor of Lautensack for the amounts awarded by the jury. Both parties appealed.

III. Discussion

A. Hernandez's Issues

1. Timeliness of RCLA Notice

In his first issue, Hernandez argues that the trial court erred by rendering judgment for Lautensack because the jury found that Lautensack's presuit notice failed to meet the requirements of the RCLA. We disagree.

Section 27.004 of the RCLA provides that a claimant seeking damages arising from a contractor's construction defect must give the contractor written notice of the alleged defect more than sixty days before filing suit. Tex. Prop.Code Ann. § 27.004(a). After receiving notice, the contractor has thirty-five days to inspect the property and forty-five days to make a written offer of settlement. *Id.* § 27.004(a)-(b). Under the RCLA as amended in 2003, failure of the claimant to give the requisite presuit notice results in dismissal of the suit. *Id.* § 27.004(d).

But as Hernandez concedes in his brief, the prior version of the RCLA applicable to this suit contained no dismissal provision; instead, it provided for abatement of a suit where the claimant failed to provide the requisite presuit notice. *See* Act of May 17, 1995, 74th Leg., R.S., ch. 414, § 10, 1995 Tex. Gen. Laws 2988, 2996 (amended 2003) (current version at Tex. Prop. Code Ann. § 27.004(d)).

The trial court submitted the following question to the jury as part of the charge:

Do you find that, 60 days preceding the filing of this suit by Philip Lautensack against Roy Hernandez, Philip Lautensack gave written notice by Certified Mail/Return Receipt Requested to Roy Hernandez specifying, in reasonable detail, the construction defects that are the subject of the complaint at a time when Roy Hernandez could have performed any of the following:

> a) Within 35 days of receipt of the written notice, Roy Hernandez had a reasonable opportunity to inspect the property, to determine the nature and cause of the construction defect and the nature and extent of repairs necessary to remedy the construction defect?
>
> b) Within 45 days of receipt of the written notice, make an offer to repair, or to have repaired by an independent contractor at Roy Hernandez's expense, the construction defect described in the notice?

The jury answered "no" to both parts of the question.

Hernandez argues that the jury's answers to this question compel a judgment in his favor. Hernandez does not argue that the content of Lautensack's notice was deficient; rather, he argues that by replacing the roof before he sent his notice letter, Lautensack deprived Hernandez of the opportunity to inspect the property and offer to repair the alleged defects under RCLA section 27.004.

We reject Hernandez's argument for several reasons. First, the practical effect of Hernandez's argument is to engraft the dismissal provision of the current RCLA onto the prior version that controls this case. This we cannot do. We must apply the law as the legislature wrote it. Second, the RCLA's intent to give a contractor a reasonable opportunity to inspect the property upon request was effectuated under the facts of this case. The undisputed evidence at trial proved that Hernandez did in fact inspect the roof many times when he attempted to repair leaks before it was replaced and submitted a bid to replace the roof in September 2002. Lautensack rejected Hernandez's bid and chose to have his roof replaced by another contractor. Third, the RCLA expressly provides that a contractor may make a monetary settlement offer, not just an offer to repair the defects. Tex. Prop. Code Ann. § 27.004(b), (n). The fact that Lautensack had the defective roof replaced before he sent his notice letter did not deprive Hernandez of the opportunity to inspect the roof, make an offer to repair or replace the roof, or make a timely, monetary settlement offer.

The version of the RCLA that governs this suit simply does not provide for the result that Hernandez seeks. We overrule his first issue.

NOTES & QUESTIONS

1) What is the distinction between an "abatement of action" and a "plea in abatement?"

2) Abatement of Action: In *Hollingsworth v. Bagley,* 1872 WL 7390, *1 (Tex.), the Texas Supreme Court wrote:

> The appellant brought suit in the district court against Cameron and Scott. No cost bond was required from the plaintiff. Pending the suit, both the defendants died, and the suit abated, and was never revived against the representatives of either of them. But the court permitted the officers of the court to have judgment against the plaintiff for the sum of twenty-two dollars and fifteen cents, on which execution issued on the twenty-eighth day of July, 1869; was levied on the land described in the petition; and it was sold to N. G. Bagley, the appellee, on the first Tuesday in August, 1869. . . There can be no valid judgment where there are no proper parties to the record; and after the death of the defendants, the officers of the court could not, as such, be substituted in a manner to entitle them to judgment in the original action against the plaintiff, for costs, although the plaintiff is undoubtedly liable to the officers of court for costs which he himself made in the action.

3) Plea in Abatement: In *Lipinski v. Lipinski,* 1995 WL 517333, *1 [Tex. App.-Hous. [14 Dist.) 1995], the appellate court wrote the following:

The essence of appellant's argument is that the trial court mischaracterized the plea in abatement as a plea to the jurisdiction. As such, the pleading was an ineffective substitute for challenging jurisdiction and should be disregarded. We disagree. Appellant's argument misconstrues the purpose behind a plea in abatement, which is utilized as a means of suspending further action in a lawsuit until the reason for the abatement has been removed. It is a not a plea in bar, such as a plea to the jurisdiction.

4) Now, assume a litigant employs the doctrine of reliance to prove a cause of action or an affirmative defense. Must the litigant prove "reliance" or "detrimental reliance?"

5) DTPA § 17.50(a)(1)(B) reads: A consumer may maintain an action where any of the following constitutes a producing cause of economic damages or damages for mental anguish: The use or employment by any person of a false, misleading, or deceptive act or practice that is ... relied on by a consumer to the consumer's detriment.

C. Defenses — "No Reliance" and "Disclaimer of Reliance"

Henry Schein, Inc. v. Stromboe
102 S.W.3d 675
(Tex. 2002)

Under Rule 42(b)(4) of the Texas Rules of Civil Procedure, the district court certified a nationwide class of some 20,000 purchasers of three dental practice management software products. There are members of this class in all fifty states. The five named plaintiffs and their counsel allege that the software was defective and was sold under false pretenses on which buyers relied. Some of the causes of action they assert are breach of contract, breach of express and implied warranties, fraudulent and negligent misrepresentations, and violations of the Texas Deceptive Trade Practices-Consumer Protection Act, Tex. Bus. & Com. Code §§ 17.41-.63. They claim[ed] actual, special, consequential, exemplary, and statutory damages, as well as restitution of all amounts paid-up to $74,000 per purchaser, or $1.48 billion overall.

The district court determined to adjudicate all of these claims, including those of out-of-state purchasers, under Texas law. On interlocutory appeal, the court of appeals affirmed. We conclude that the representative plaintiffs have failed to demonstrate, as Rule 42(b)(4) requires they must, "that the questions of law or fact common to the members of the class predominate over any questions affecting only individual members, and that a class action is superior to other available methods for the fair and efficient adjudication of the controversy." Tex. R. Civ. P. 42(b)(4). Accordingly, we decertify the class and remand the case to the district court for further proceedings.

I

Henry Schein, Inc. and two subsidiaries, Easy Dental Systems, Inc. and Dentisoft, Inc. (Schein), produced and marketed three office management software applications for dental practices, one DOS-based, "Easy Dental," and two Windows-based, "Easy Dental for Windows" and "Easy Dental Lite." Shelly E. Stromboe, D.D.S., a purchaser of the Windows software, and Jeanne N. Taylor, D.D.S., a purchaser of the DOS software, sued Schein on behalf of themselves and a class of all purchasers of the software in the nation (Taylor). Stromboe and Taylor have filed separate petitions in the trial court.

Stromboe's petition alleges that in the process of opening her own dental office, she contacted Schein for advice about what management software program would be best for her. "In reliance on Schein's recommendation," Stromboe alleges, she selected "Easy Dental Lite". When she tried to use the software, she says, she found that [t]he program had numerous defects, some of which included: a) inability to add a new insurance carrier; b) inability to properly print a fee list; c) inability to delete accounts; () inability to activate or inactivate a patient account; e) continual operating errors; f) inability to completely delete an appointment, replacing an appointment with another patient's; h) [sic] inability to add emergency information on a new patient; i) inability to properly credit accounts on the accounting software; j) inadequate space to fill in a treatment plan; (k) Electronic Claims processing problems; *l)* production of error messages on the computer; m) inability to save patient notes; n) multiple inconveniences; *o*) inability to properly age accounts receivable; and p) a total lack of multi-tasking capabilities.

Stromboe contends that she complained to Schein, who admitted that the software was defective but "steered" her to its more expensive product, "Easy Dental for Windows," which she purchased. Stromboe alleges that she was required to have all of her data converted for the new program. In doing so, she lost time, records and production. Easy Dental for Windows also had bugs and defects which corrupted Plaintiff's data and made the system inoperable.
Stromboe's petition asserts the following causes of action:

- breach of contract;
- breach of express warranties-specifically, that "[d]efendants represented to Plaintiff Stromboe that its practice management software systems and products would satisfy Plaintiff's computer system and software needs to effectively manage and run a dental practice";
- breach of implied warranties-specifically, merchantability —Tex. Bus. & Com. Code § 2.314
- fraudulent misrepresentations which "Plaintiff Stromboe and the Windows Class have relied on . . . to their damage, unaware of the false and misleading nature of the information provided to them by Defendants . . . ;
- negligent misrepresentations on which "Plaintiff Stromboe and the Windows Class relied ... and have been damaged as a result"-specifically including all of the misrepresentations alleged to have been fraudulent;
- promissory estoppel —that "(a) Defendants made promises; (b) it was foreseeable that Plaintiff Stromboe and the Windows Class would rely on

Defendants' promises; and (c) Plaintiff Stromboe and the Windows Class substantially relied on these promises to their detriment";

- DTPA violations — specifically, by:

  (a) causing confusion or misunderstanding as to the source, sponsorship, approval, or certification of goods or services;
  (b) causing confusion or misunderstanding as to affiliation, connection, or association with or certification by another;
  (c) representing that goods or services have sponsorship, approval, characteristics, uses, and benefits that they do not have;
  (d) representing the goods or services or of a particular standard quality or grade when they were of another;
  (e) advertising goods or services with intent not to sell them as advertised;
  (g) [sic] making false and misleading statements of fact concerning the reason for existence of or amount of price reductions;
  (h) representing that services had been performed when services were not performed;
  (i) failing to disclose information concerning goods or services that was known at the time of the transaction and with the intent to induce a consumer into a transaction which the consumer would not have entered into had the information been disclosed; and
  (j) representing an agreement confers or involves rights, remedies or obligations which it does not have or involve, or which are prohibited by law" — §§ 17.46(b)(2), (3), (5), (7), (9), (11), (12), (22), (24) and, § 17.50(a)(1).

- engaging in an unconscionable action or course of action — § 17.50(a)(3) — defined . . . as "an act or practice which, to a consumer's detriment, takes advantage of the lack of knowledge, ability, experience, or capacity of the consumer to a grossly unfair degree" — § 17.45(5); and
- breaching express and implied warranties — § 17.50(a)(2); and
- unjust enrichment.

* * *

In the prayer of the petition, Stromboe requests for herself and all class members "actual, special and consequential damages, including attorney's fees", "exemplary damages", "actual damages" caused by the DTPA violations, "additional damages" under the DTPA, and "restitution of all money or property that Defendants have collected from Plaintiff Stromboe and the Windows Class."

Finally, Stromboe's petition alleges that [a] class action is an appropriate vehicle for relief in this case [because] . . . there is a well-defined community of interest in the questions of law or fact affecting the Class that predominates over any questions affecting only individual members, including:

i) whether Defendants engaged in deceptive acts and practices in selling and guaranteeing software products and support services to Plaintiff Stromboe and members of the Windows Class through misrepresentations and deceit;

ii) whether Defendants caused Plaintiff Stromboe and members of the Windows Class to rely upon false or misleading information and enter into contracts with Defendants;

iii) whether Defendants breached the contracts entered into with Plaintiff Stromboe and members of the Windows Class;

iv) whether Plaintiff Stromboe and members of the Windows Class have sustained damages, and the proper measure of any damages;

v) whether Defendants' products have defects common to all users of said products; and

vi) whether Defendants' common marketing strategy has perpetuated a fraud on the public.

* * *

In *Bernal,* we held that it is improper to certify a class without knowing how the claims can and will likely be tried. A trial court's certification order must indicate how the claims will likely be tried so that conformance with Rule 42 may be meaningfully evaluated. "Given the plaintiffs' burden, a court cannot rely on [mere] assurances of counsel that any problems with predominance or superiority can be overcome." 22 S.W.3d at 435 (citing and quoting *Castano v. American Tobacco Co.,* 84 F.3d 734, 742, 744 (5th Cir.1996)

Schein argues that the court of appeals failed to hold the trial court's certification order to this standard. We agree.

* * *

The plaintiffs argue correctly that *Bernal* should not be read to require a "trial plan" by that name, set out in a separate document. Rule 42 does not require adoption of a trial plan as a mere formality; rather, according to *Bernal,* the rule requires a rigorous analysis and a specific explanation of how class claims are to proceed to trial. Here, the trial court concluded only:

There are no insurmountable difficulties likely to be encountered in the management of this case, including the management of damage issues. It may be possible to determine damages on a class wide basis from Defendants' records, but if that cannot be done, the Court finds nothing to indicate that damages could not be efficiently determined through proof of claim forms, individual damage hearings, or other manageable means.

* * *

Schein argues that the court of appeals' standard of review, both as stated and as applied, conflicts with the highlighted language in *Bernal.* We agree.

* * *

Similarly, the court of appeals brushed aside arguments that the trial court had not explained how other individual issues, like reliance, and other claims, like fraud, would be tried. *Bernal* does not permit these issues to be a matter of an appellate court's confidence in a trial court's rulings. . . .

IV

Rule 42(a) prescribes the following prerequisites for a class action:

> One or more members of a class may sue or be sued as representative parties on behalf of all only if (1) the class is so numerous that joinder of all members is impracticable, (2) there are questions of law, or fact common to the class, (3) the claims or defenses of the representative parties are typical of the claims or defenses of the class, and (4) the representative parties will fairly and adequately protect the interests of the class. Tex.R. Civ. P. 42(a)

Rule 42(b)(4) provides that:

> An action may be maintained as a class action if the prerequisites of subdivision (a) are satisfied, and in addition:
>
> * * *
>
> (4) the court finds that the questions of law or fact common to the members of the class predominate over any questions affecting only individual members, and that a class action is superior to other available methods for the fair and efficient adjudication of the controversy. The matters pertinent to the findings include: (A) the interest of members of the class in individually controlling the prosecution or defense of separate actions; (B) the extent and nature of any litigation concerning the controversy already commenced by or against members of the class; (C) the desirability or undesirability of concentrating the litigation of the claims in the particular forum; (D) the difficulties likely to be encountered in the management of a class action.

Schein argues that the plaintiffs have failed to show that "the questions of law or fact common to the members of the class predominate over any questions affecting only individual members," as the rule requires.

Specifically, Schein argues that individual questions regarding reliance, damages, and the applicable law predominate. We examine each of these categories separately and then consider whether, on the whole, the plaintiffs have met their burden under the rule. "The test for predominance is not whether common issues outnumber uncommon issues but ... 'whether common or individual issues will be the object of most of the efforts of the litigants and the court.'" *Bernal,* 22 S.W.3d at 434, quoting *Central Power & Light Co. v. City of San Juan,* 962 S.W.2d 602, 610 (Tex.App.-Corpus Christi 1998, writ dism'd w.o.j.).

A

As we have noted, reliance is an element of five of the plaintiffs' causes of action: fraud, breach of express warranty (to a certain extent), negligent misrepresentation, promissory estoppel, and DTPA "laundry list violations." The burden on plaintiffs to prove reliance in order to recover on any of these theories is in no way altered by the assertion of claims on behalf of a class. As we stressed in *Bernal:*

> The class action is a procedural device intended to advance judicial economy by trying claims together that lend themselves to collective treatment. It is not meant to alter the parties' burdens of proof, right to a jury trial, or the substantive prerequisites to recovery under a given tort. Procedural devices may "not be construed to enlarge or diminish any substantive rights or obligations of any parties to any civil action." Tex.R. Civ. P. 815; *see also* Tex. Gov't Code § 22.004(a); *In re Ethyl Corp.,* 975 S.W.2d 606, 613 (Tex.1998) ("The systemic urge to aggregate litigation must not be allowed to trump our dedication to justice, and we must take care that each individual plaintiff's— and defendant's —cause not be lost in the shadow of a towering mass litigation.") (quoting *In re Brooklyn Navy Yard Asbestos Litig.,* 971 F.2d 831, 853 (2d Cir.1992)). Although a goal of our system is to resolve lawsuits with "great expedition and dispatch and at the least expense," the supreme objective of the courts is "to obtain a just, fair, equitable and impartial adjudication of the rights of litigants under established principles of substantive law." Tex.R. Civ. P. 1. This means that "convenience and economy must yield to a paramount concern for a fair and impartial trial." *In re Ethyl Corp.,* 975 S.W.2d at 613. And basic to the right to a fair trial-indeed, basic to the very essence of the adversarial process-is that each party have the opportunity to adequately and vigorously present any material claims and defenses. 22 S.W.3d at 437.

Thus, the 20,000 class members in the present case are held to the same standards of proof of reliance — and for that matter all the other elements of their claims — that they would be required to meet if each sued individually. This does not mean, of course, that reliance or other elements of their causes of action cannot be proved class-wide with evidence generally applicable to all class members; class-wide proof is possible when class-wide evidence exists. But evidence insufficient to prove reliance in a suit by an individual does not become sufficient in a class action simply because there are more plaintiffs.

Inescapably individual differences cannot be concealed in a throng. The procedural device of a class action eliminates the necessity of adducing the same evidence over and over again in a multitude of individual actions; it does not lessen the quality of evidence required in an individual action or relax substantive burdens of proof. If a plaintiff could prove reliance in an individual action with the same evidence offered to show class-wide reliance, then the issue is one of law and fact common to the class. The question the court must decide before certifying a class, after rigorous analysis and not merely a lick and a prayer, is whether the plaintiffs have demonstrated that they can meet their burden of proof in such a way that common issues predominate over individual ones.

The plaintiffs contend that they have established "class-wide reliance" on misrepresentations made by Schein, but this is not supported by the record. It is true, as the plaintiffs say, that there is evidence that Schein *wanted* purchasers to rely on its advertisements and other representations about its software products, as most marketers of any product would, but there is no evidence that purchasers *actually did* rely on Schein's statements so uniformly that common issues of reliance predominate over individual issues. To the contrary, there is, for example, significant evidence that purchasers relied on recommendations from colleagues and others rather than any statements made directly or indirectly by Schein.

The trial court did not explain in its certification order how the plaintiffs can avoid individual proof of reliance or why the necessity for such proof would not defeat the predominance requirement for certification. Such an explanation would be an important part of the trial plan required by *Bernal.* The court of appeals premised affirmance of the order on the mistaken belief that reliance was not an element of the plaintiffs' principal causes of action.

The Fifth Circuit has recently observed that if "individual reliance is necessary to prove actual damages, a class action may not be certified on this issue." *Perrone v. General Motors Acceptance Corp.,* 232 F.3d 433, 440 (5th Cir. 2000). We need not and do not decide whether a class asserting a cause of action requiring proof of reliance, like the class alleged here, can ever be certified. We hold only that the plaintiffs in this case have failed to show that individual issues of reliance do not preclude the necessary finding of predominance under Rule 42(b)(4).

* * *

The judgment of the court of appeals must be reversed. We cannot say, of course, that no class can be certified in this case; that matter must be decided by the trial court in the first instance. We conclude only that the certification order before us is improper. The case is therefore remanded to the trial court for further proceedings.

* * *

Ford Motor Company v. Ocanas
138 S.W.3d 447
(Tex. App. -Corpus Christi 2004)

This opinion addresses two interlocutory appeals challenging the certification of a Texas class and nationwide class. The two class actions arise from the same underlying facts and involve the same causes of action.

In cause number 13-02-015-CV, appellant, Ford Motor Company ("Ford"), challenges the class certification of consumers in Texas who purchased Ford F-150s in 2000 or 2001 with an optional towing package that was marketed to have a larger radiator than F-150s without the towing package. By four issues, it argues the trial court abused its discretion when it: (1, 3) determined the requirements of rule 42(b)(4) were met; (2) allowed plaintiff's class action to proceed without a trial plan; and (4) determined that the named plaintiff could adequately represent the class. We reverse and remand cause number 13-02-015-CV.

In cause number 13-02-215-CV, Ford appeals the certification of a nationwide class for individuals, other than Texas consumers, who purchased new model year 2000 or 2001 F-150s with the optional "Class III Towing Group" or the "Heavy Duty Electrical/Cooling Group." By five issues, appellant alleges the trial court abused its discretion when it: 1) determined that the nationwide class met the predominance and superiority requirements of Rule 42(b)(4); 2) shifted the burden of persuasion to appellant on how the claims will likely be tried; 3) improperly certified a nationwide class because it disturbs an order on appeal; 4) named appellee, as a class representative; and 5) compounded the fatal defects in the statewide class by certifying the nationwide class action. We reverse and remand cause number 13-02-215-CV.

I. Facts and Procedural History

Appellee, filed suit and sought class certification against appellant on April 3, 2001 alleging: (1) breach of express warranties; (2) breach of the implied warranties of merchantability; and (3) violations of the Deceptive Trade Practices—Consumer Protection Act (DTPA). He also sought the following damages on behalf of the class: (1) cost of replacing the existing radiator with the upgraded radiator; (2) loss of use of the vehicle during the time of replacement; and (3) additional damages, attorney's fees, and costs under the DTPA. Tex. Bus. & Com. Code Ann. § 17.50

According to appellee, appellant represented to consumers that F-150s with the Class III towing package would come with a larger radiator than F-150s without the Class III towing package. However, appellee purchased an F-150 with the optional Class III towing package that lacked the larger radiator. Evidence at the certification hearing indicated F-150s with the towing package were inted to have a larger radiator, but an error during assembly equipped them with a base radiator. The trial court certified the class under Rule 42(b)(4) and named appellee class representative for individuals "who purchased in Texas new model year 2000-2001 F-150 vehicles manufactured or sold by [appellant], which vehicles included either the Class III towing group or the Heavy-Duty Electrical/Cooling Group (the class)."

While the Texas class certification order was on appeal, appellee moved for a nationwide class certification. On March 25, 2002, the trial court granted the nationwide class certification under Rule 42(b)(4) for "[a]ll persons who purchased in any State of the United States of America, other than Texas, new model year 2000-2001 F-150 vehicles included in either the Class III Towing Group or the Heavy-Duty Electrical/Cooling Group. (the Class)." In the certification order, the trial court stated the predominance requirement was met "because the two overwhelming predominant questions are: 1) Did Ford describe the affected vehicles as having upgraded radiators?; and 2) Did Ford deliver the trucks as represented?"

The trial court rejected appellant's argument that a state-by-state choice-of-law analysis must be done for each of the fifty states before a nationwide class could be certified "because a class certification order need not address choice of law." Further, the trial court stated that it would follow the In re Bridgestone/Firestone products liability litigation as a model for handling a nationwide class and resolving choice-of-law issues.

II. Discussion

In both appeals, appellant contends the trial court abused its discretion in determining the plaintiff met his burden in establishing the predominance and superiority requirements of rule 42(b)(4). In particular, appellant argues individualized evidence from each class member will be necessary to prove appellee's claims for breach of express and implied warranties, and for violations of the DTPA. Appellant also contends the trial court failed to consider which substantive state laws apply to appellee's claims and how variations in state substantive laws would be managed in the nationwide class action. "We examine each of these categories separately and then consider whether, on the whole, [appellee has] met [his] burden under the rule." *Henry Schein, Inc. v. Stromboe*, 102 S.W.3d 675, 693 (Tex. 2002)

A. Standard of Review

We review a trial court's ruling certifying a class for an abuse of discretion. *Century Power & Light v. City of San Juan,* 962 S.W.2d 602, 607 (Tex.App.-Corpus Christi 1998, pet. denied). However, a reviewing court will not indulge every presumption in favor of the trial court's ruling on certification issues. *Henry Schein, Inc.,* 102 S.W.3d at 691. Actual compliance "with [Texas Rule of Civil Procedure] 42 must be demonstrated; it cannot be presumed." *Southwestern Ref. Co. v. Bernal,* 22 S.W.3d 425, 435 (Tex. 2000) and Tex. R. Civ. P. 42. A court makes a meaningful determination of certification issues by going beyond the pleadings to understand the claims, defenses, relevant facts, and substantive law. A court must perform a rigorous analysis to determine whether all prerequisites to class certification have been met and how the claims will be tried. Finally, the burden is on the party seeking class certification to prove the rule 42 requirements are met.

Rule 42 provides a two-step process for class certifications. See Tex.R. Civ. P. 42. First, all class actions must meet the four prerequisites of rule 42(a): 1) numerosity; 2) commonality; 3) typicality; and 4) adequacy of representation. Tex.R. Civ. P. 42(a); *Henry Schein, Inc.*, 102 S.W.3d at 692; *Bernal,* 22 S.W.3d at 433. Second, the class action must meet one of four subdivisions under rule 42(b). Rule 42(b)(4) requires a trial court to make two additional findings in order to certify a class action: predominance and superiority. Tex. R. Civ. P. 42(b)(4). Both the Texas and nationwide class certification orders stated appellee satisfied Rule 42(b)(4)'s requirements. Therefore, we consider whether this class certification satisfies rule 42(b)(4).

B. Rule 42(b)(4)

Rule 42(b)(4)'s purpose is to provide for economy of effort and uniformity of result without unduly diluting the procedural safeguards for members of the class or the opposing party. *See Gen. Motors Corp. v. Bloyed*, 916 S.W.2d 949, 952-53 (Tex.1996) (discussing objectives of rule 42. Rule 42(b)(4) allows a class action to proceed if:

> the court finds that the questions of law or fact common to the members of the class predominate over any questions affecting only individual members, and that a class action is superior to other available methods for the fair and efficient adjudication of the controversy. The matters pertinent to the findings include: (A) the interest of members of the class in individually controlling the prosecution or defense of separate actions; (B) the extent and nature of any litigation concerning the controversy already commenced by or against members of the class; (C) the desirability or undesirability of concentrating the litigation of the claims in the particular forum; (D) the difficulties likely to be encountered in the management of a class action.

We first consider rule 42(b)(4)'s predominance requirement because "it is one of the most stringent prerequisites to class certification." Bernal, 22 S.W.3d at 433

1. Predominance

The purpose of the predominance requirement is to "prevent class action litigation when the sheer complexity and diversity of the individual issues would overwhelm or confuse the jury or severely compromise a party's ability to present viable claims or defenses." *Id.* at 434. "The test for predominance is not whether common issues outnumber uncommon issues, but ... 'whether common or individual issues will be the object of most of the efforts of the litigants and the court.'" Common issues will not predominate "[i]f, after common issues are resolved, presenting and resolving individual issues is likely to be an overwhelming or unmanageable task for a single jury." We consider appellee's claims for breach of express warranties and violations of the DTPA to determine whether appellee demonstrated that common issues of law or fact predominate. *Henry Schein, Inc.*, 102 S.W.3d at 693.

a. Express Warranties and DTPA Violations

Appellant directs our attention to Henry Schein, Inc. in support of its position that individual issues predominate over common questions of law and fact. See id. at 678. In Henry Schein, Inc., five plaintiffs filed suit against a manufacturer of dental management software programs for DOS and Windows based software. Id. They alleged various causes of action including breach of implied and express warranties and violations of the DTPA. Id. The trial court certified a nationwide class of 20,000 purchasers under rule 42(b)(4). The supreme court reversed because the certification order did not comply with rule 42(b)(4). *Id.* at 694.

The supreme court stated "the court of appeals premised affirmance of the order on the mistaken belief that was not an element of the plaintiff's principal causes of action." Id. The court held that reliance was a required element of proof for breach of express warranties and DTPA "laundry list violations." Id. at 693; see Tex. Bus. & Com. Code Ann. § 2.313(a)(1) (defining an express warranty as "[a]ny affirmation of fact or promise made by the seller to the buyer which relates to the goods and becomes part of the basis of the bargain " (emphasis added)); Tex. Bus. & Com. Code Ann. § 17.50(a)(1) ("A consumer may maintain an action where any of the following constitute a producing cause of economic damages or damages for mental anguish: (1) the use or employment by any person of a false, misleading, or deceptive act or practice that is: (A) [a laundry list violation]; and (B) relied on by a consumer to a consumer's detriment."

Therefore, the court held that to recover for breach of express warranties and violations of the DTPA, each class member was required to prove reliance on misrepresentations made by the defendant. *Henry Schein, Inc.,* 102 S.W.3d at 693. This is because class actions are a procedural device intended to try like claims together, but "not meant to alter the parties' burdens of proof, right to a jury trial, or the substantive prerequisites to recovery under a given tort."

The court then determined that although there was "evidence that Schein wanted [plaintiffs] to rely on its advertisements ... there [was] no evidence that [plaintiffs] actually did rely Schein's statements so uniformly that common issues of reliance predominate over individual issues." Therefore, the supreme court held that "the plaintiffs in this case have failed to show that individual issues of reliance do not preclude the necessary finding of predominance under rule 42(b)(4)."

Like the plaintiffs in Henry Schein, Inc., appellees pleaded breach of express and warranties and DTPA "laundry list" violations which require each class member to prove reliance as a prerequisite to recovery. Further, although there is evidence that appellant intended for customers to rely on representations that F-150s with a Class III towing package would come with larger radiators, "there is no evidence that purchasers actually did rely "on appellant's statements "so uniformly that common issues of reliance predominate over individual issues. The supreme court noted that it is possible to certify a class where reliance is a required element of proof if the plaintiffs can "prove reliance in an individual action with the same proof offered to show class-wide reliance." However, appellee did not meet this burden.

b. Choice-of-law issues

The nationwide class certification compounds the defects of the statewide class action because it improperly applied Michigan law to the nationwide class action since that is where appellant is headquartered. At the certification hearing, appellee relied on *In re Bridgestone/Firestone, Inc. Tires Products Liability Litigation*, 155 F.Supp.2d 1069, 1076 (S.D.Ind.2001), rev'd, 288 F.3d 1012 (7th Cir.2002), as a model for resolving choice-of-law issues for the nationwide class. In that case, the court resolved choice-of-law issues by concluding the laws of the defendants' headquarters applied to the entire class. *Id.* at 1015.

However, Texas "does not apply the law of the state where a defendant is headquartered to every claim for economic damages that can be alleged against the defendant." *Henry Schein, Inc.* 102 S.W.3d at 698. Instead, Texas follows the Restatement's "substantial relationship" test to resolve choice-of-law issues. *Hughes Wood Prod., Inc. v. Wagner,* 18 S.W.3d 202, 205 (Tex. 2000). Under this approach, courts consider "the qualitative nature of the particular contacts" with a state, and the "state policies underlying the particular substantive issue[s]" before deciding which state's law to apply. *Duncan v. Cessna Aircraft, Co.*, 665 S.W.2d 414, 421 (Tex.1984).

Appellee failed to properly address choice-of-law issues in seeking class certification including how variances among states' consumer protection laws could or would be handled. Thus, appellee failed to demonstrate that common legal issues predominate over individual ones.

2. Superiority

Rule 42(b)(4) also requires a class action to be "superior to other available methods for the fair and efficient adjudication of the controversy." Tex.R. Civ. P. 42(b)(4); *Henry Schein Inc.*, 102 S.W.3d at 699. Efficiency, however, should not be had at the expense of a fair adjudication. That is, the right to a fair trial requires "that each party have the opportunity to adequately and vigorously present any material claims and defenses."

Here, the certification order states that "[a] class action is superior to other available methods for the fair and efficient adjudication of this controversy." The certification order does not discuss how individual issues, such as reliance, will be addressed to fairly allow appellant to present viable claims or defenses. We find that appellee failed to establish that this class action is more efficient than other methods of adjudicating the class members' claims given the necessity of individual determinations regarding reliance and choice-of-law analysis. We hold that the appellee failed to satisfy the superiority requirement of rule 42(b)(4). See Tex.R. Civ. P. 42(b)(4).

III. Conclusion

We do not say "that no class can be certified in this case; that matter must be decided by the trial court in the first instance." *Henry Schein, Inc.*, 102 S.W.3d at 701. We find only that appellee failed to show that individualized determinations will not predominate over common questions of law or fact, and that this class action is more efficient than other methods of adjudicating the class members' claims. We recognize that the trial court did not have the benefit of *Henry Schein, Inc.* when it certified this class. However, following *Henry Schein, Inc.*, as we must, we reverse the judgment of the trial court and remand for further proceedings.

NOTES & QUESTIONS

1) The term "reliance" or "rely" appears frequently in the DTPA, in "tie-in" statutes as well as among common-law and equitable principles. Certainly, the term may be an element of various causes of action. May it be an element of a common-law or statutory defense? Is there a definitive standard of proof to determine "reliance" or the "absence of reliance?

2) What is the major distinction between the assertion "no reliance" and "disclaimer of reliance?"

Schlumberger Technology Corporation v. Swanson
959 S.W.2d 171
(Tex. 1997)

This is a commercial dispute. In settling this dispute, the Swansons signed a release that disclaimed reliance on the representations of Schlumberger. The question is whether this disclaimer precludes, as a matter of law, the Swansons from recovering damages against Schlumberger for fraudulently inducing them to settle. The trial court granted a judgment for Schlumberger notwithstanding the jury's verdict for the Swansons. The court of appeals reversed, holding that the disclaimer of reliance did not preclude the Swansons' fraudulent inducement claim. We agree with the trial court. Accordingly, we reverse the court of appeals' judgment and render judgment for Schlumberger.

I. FACTS

In the 1970s, John Swanson and his brother George Swanson approached SEDCO, Inc. about a proposal to mine diamonds from the ocean floor in deep waters off the South African coast. SEDCO had expertise in offshore oil and gas drilling and had mined manganese nodules off the ocean floor. The Swansons, whose family had been in the mining industry in South Africa for several decades, had contacts with the South African government. By letter dated October 17, 1978, SEDCO agreed to a three-phase project. In Phase I, SEDCO would study the feasibility of the sea-diamond project. In Phase II, a lease was to be acquired and prospecting was to begin. Phase III was to be commercial mining. The agreement provided that SEDCO had exclusive authority to determine whether to proceed with Phases II and III.

* * *

The Swansons were to use their goodwill and contacts to obtain concession rights and any licenses or permits the South African government required. They also were to provide SEDCO with information on diamond mining generally and offshore mining specifically. For their part, the Swansons would be paid a consulting fee through Phases I and II and a royalty, if any, on any diamonds mined during Phases II and III. Should the project ever become commercially productive, the Swansons had the right to purchase five percent of the shares in the company contemplated to be formed to mine the diamonds.

* * *

Almost immediately after receiving the leases, SEDCO, DeBeers, and Seltrust began negotiating a joint venture agreement to jointly develop the mining project. . . . In early January 1987, the Swansons became concerned about rumors that Schlumberger was going to stop funding its share or withdraw from the joint venture.

* * *

Instead, in February 1988, a little more than a year after Schlumberger gave notice of its withdrawal from the joint venture, the Swansons agreed that Schlumberger would buy their interest for two million South African rand (about $814,000). In exchange, the Swansons relinquished all rights, claims, and interests in the offshore diamond project and Lease 3C and released all causes of action against Schlumberger, known or unknown. In the release, the Swansons specifically agreed that they were not relying on any statement or representation of Schlumberger, SEDCO, or Sedswan, that they were relying on their own judgment, and that they had been represented by counsel who had explained the entire contents and legal consequences of the release.

Schlumberger thereafter sold Sedswan's interest to DeBeers and Seltrust for 10 million rand (about $4,100,000). After recouping its investment in the project of 6.8 million rand (about $2,767,000), buying out the Swansons' interests for two million rand (about $814,000) and paying them an additional $200,000 in consulting fees, Schlumberger netted 778,000 rand (about $319,000) from the offshore diamond project.

Asserting that Schlumberger had misrepresented the project's viability and value, the Swansons then sued Schlumberger and its parent corporation, Schlumberger Limited, Inc., for fraudulently inducing them to sell their interest at an undervalued price. The Swansons also alleged breach of fiduciary duty.

The jury found for the Swansons and against Schlumberger on all issues. The jury awarded the Swansons fifteen million dollars in actual damages, thirty-five million dollars in exemplary damages on a statutory fraud claim under section 27.01 of the Texas Business and Commerce Code, ten million dollars in exemplary damages on the common law claims, and attorney's fees. As already mentioned, the trial court rendered a judgment notwithstanding the verdict, but the court of appeals reversed and rendered judgment in accordance with the jury's findings.

Here, Schlumberger contends that the release precludes all of the Swansons' claims as a matter of law; that there is no evidence of common law fraud, statutory fraud under section 27.01 of the Texas Business and Commerce Code, or breach of fiduciary duty; and that the court of appeals erred in awarding prejudgment interest on future damages. We agree that the release precludes all of the Swansons' claims as a matter of law. Accordingly, we reverse the court of appeals' judgment and render judgment for Schlumberger. Because of our disposition, we need not reach the prejudgment interest issue.

* * *

III. DISCLAIMER OF RELIANCE

Given that Schlumberger and the Swansons were dealing with each other at arm's length, we now turn to Schlumberger's contention that the disclaimer of reliance clause in the release precludes the Swansons' fraudulent inducement claim. It does.

To support their fraudulent inducement claim, the Swansons alleged that Schlumberger made several affirmative misrepresentations during their negotiations over the withdrawal of Sedswan from the joint venture. The Swansons had seen an April 1986 Schlumberger evaluation that described the project as "economical," but noted that the "commerciality" of the project would not be determined until 1988 or 1989. Despite the 1986 evaluation, and without having undertaken any later studies, Schlumberger represented to the Swansons that the project was neither technologically feasible nor commercially viable. In addition, Schlumberger represented that the project had a negative value and that Sedswan would be lucky to get out with its costs.

At trial, the evidence was undisputed that there are diamonds on the ocean floor off South Africa. It was further undisputed that, as of the time of trial in 1993, no one had begun mining diamonds. Also, it was undisputed that Seltrust's successor sold its interest to DeBeers in 1992 for only slightly more than its project costs. On the other hand, there was substantial dispute about whether the project was technologically feasible or commercially viable. Schlumberger brings a point of error asserting that there is legally insufficient evidence of fraud, but it does not argue in its briefing in this Court that its representations about the project's technological or commercial infeasibility were immaterial, were merely opinion, or were either not knowingly made or not made without knowledge of the truth. *See Prudential Ins. Co. v. Jefferson Assocs.,* 896 S.W.2d 156, 163 (Tex.1995). Accordingly, we assume, as we must, that Schlumberger misrepresented the project's technological feasibility and commercial viability and that such misrepresentations are actionable as fraudulent inducement.

In this light, Schlumberger asks us to adopt a *per se* rule that the presence of independent legal counsel always precludes a claim that a party fraudulently induced a release. Texas law does not support such a rule.

Texas law favors and encourages voluntary settlements and orderly dispute resolution. However, a release is a contract, and like any other contract, is subject to avoidance on grounds such as fraud or mistake. *See Williams v. Glash,* 789 S.W.2d 261, 264 (Tex.1990); *Dallas Farm Mach. Co. v. Reaves,* 158 Tex. 1, 307 S.W.2d 233, 236-37 (1957). Yet our early decisions are not entirely consistent. Several of our opinions conclude that a release could be set aside if it was induced by a fraudulent representation or promise-even if the release contained language disclaiming that any such representation had been made. Other cases hold to the contrary.

In *Texas & Pacific Railway Co. v. Presley,* 137 Tex. 232, 152 S.W.2d 1105 (Tex.1941), an injured worker settled his claim against his employer for $50, executing a release providing that he relied upon his own judgment as to the extent and duration of his injuries and that no promise of employment or other agreement not mentioned in the release had been made to him. *Id.* at 1106. The worker later sued to set aside the release, contending that his employer's doctor had misrepresented the extent of his injuries and that the employer had promised him permanent employment for executing the release, with no intention of fulfilling that promise. *See id.* We held that proof of these contentions would be sufficient to set aside the release. *Id.* at 1108. This could be done, we decided, even though the plaintiff may have read and understood the release. *Id.* at 1107.

Similarly, in *Edward Thompson Co. v. Sawyers,* 111 Tex. 374, 234 S.W. 873 (1921), a buyer purchased a set of legal encyclopedias based on the seller's oral promise that it would continue to publish and deliver annual supplements for at least fifteen years. The buyer proved that the seller made this promise with no intention of fulfilling it. We held that this constituted fraud sufficient to set aside the agreement, even though the written contract provided that no representations or guaranties had been made by the seller that were not expressed therein. "Promises made without intention of fulfillment, in order to induce others to make contracts, are as culpable and as harmful as are willful misrepresentations of existing facts. Hence contracts may be avoided alike for such fraudulent promises and for such misrepresentations." *Id.* at 874. We explained that, where a contract is induced by fraud, there is in reality no contract because there is no "real assent" to the agreement. *Id.* Thus, the defrauded party is not bound by any of the contractual provisions, "including those relating to representations or guaranties which induced its execution." *Id.* at 874-75.

There are other early cases, however, that reach the opposite result. For example, in *Distributors Investment Co. v. Patton,* 130 Tex. 449, 110 S.W.2d 47 (Tex.1937), the seller of a tractor sued the buyer on his promissory note. In defense, the buyer contended that the seller had fraudulently induced the transaction by orally misrepresenting the tractor's capabilities. The contract provided that the tractor was sold "as is," and further provided that no other representations had been made. *Id.* at 48. We held that, in light of these contract provisions, an action for rescission could not be maintained on account of oral representations. Although recognizing that "fraud vitiates a contract," we concluded that the fraud must be something more than merely oral representations that conflict with the terms of the written contract. *Id.* Instead, to vitiate the contract, the fraud must be such that it "prevents the coming into existence of any valid contract at all." *Id.*; *see also Avery Co. v. Harrison Co.,* 267 S.W. 254, 256 (Tex. Com. App.1924, judgm't adopted); *J.I. Case Threshing Mach. Co. v. Manes,* 254 S.W. 929, 931 (Tex. Com. App.1923, judgm't adopted); *Wright v. Couch,* 54 S.W.2d 207, 209 (Tex.Civ.App.-Eastland 1932, no writ).

In *Dallas Farm Machinery Co. v. Reaves,* 158 Tex. 1, 307 S.W.2d 233 (1957), we considered whether parol evidence was admissible, despite a merger clause in a written contract, to establish that a contract was induced by fraud. The seller brought suit against the purchaser of a tractor and loader for the balance due on the purchase contract. The buyer counterclaimed for rescission, claiming that he was fraudulently induced to contract by false representations about the work capacities of the tractor and loader. The seller argued that a merger clause providing that the contract was "the entire contract relating to the sale and warranty" of the equipment and that "no warranty is made or authorized to be made other than herein set forth" precluded the buyer's fraudulent inducement claim. *Id.* at 234. In resolving the parties' dispute, we considered the two lines of cases discussed previously and concluded that they represented conflicting lines of authority that could not be distinguished on any principled ground. *See id.* at 238-39. We resolved the conflict by holding, as a matter of policy, that a merger clause can be avoided based on fraud in the inducement and that the parol evidence rule does not bar proof of such fraud. *See id.* at 239. In doing so, we brought the law on the subject "into harmony with the great weight of authority, with the rule of the Restatement of the Law of Contracts, and with the views of eminent textwriters." *Id.* (citations omitted).

Juxtaposed to this authority, we have a competing concern-the ability of parties to fully and finally resolve disputes between them. Parties should be able to bargain for and execute a release barring all further dispute. This principle necessarily contemplates that parties may disclaim reliance on representations. And such a disclaimer, where the parties' intent is clear and specific, should be effective to negate a fraudulent inducement claim. As an example, a disclaimer of reliance may conclusively negate the element of reliance, which is essential to a fraudulent inducement claim. *See Prudential,* 896 S.W.2d at 161-62 (holding that agreement to buy property "as is," in which buyer included "voluntary, freely negotiated affirmation that he was depending on his own assessment of the building," precluded claim for damages when building was found to contain asbestos); *Estes v. Hartford Accident & Indem. Co.,* 46 S.W.2d 413, 417-18 (Tex.Civ.App.-El Paso 1932, writ ref'd) (affirming directed verdict upholding release where evidence conclusively negated reliance on alleged misrepresentations). The question is under which circumstances such disclaimers are binding.

In this case, the Swansons contend that they agreed to Schlumberger's low-price buyout offer only after they were induced by misrepresentations about the value and feasibility of the sea-diamond project. We conclude that our well-established rules of contract interpretation govern whether the Swansons gave the requisite clear and unequivocal expression of intent necessary to disclaim reliance on these specific representations by Schlumberger. The contract and the circumstances surrounding its formation determine whether the disclaimer of reliance is binding. *See Columbia Gas Transmission Corp. v. New Ulm Gas, Ltd.,* 940 S.W.2d 587, 591 (Tex.1996); *National Union Fire Ins. Co. v. CBI Indus., Inc.,* 907 S.W.2d 517, 520 (Tex.1995); *Prudential,* 896 S.W.2d at 162. Because the parties were attempting to put an end to their deal, and had become embroiled in a dispute over the feasibility and value of the project, we conclude that the disclaimer of reliance the Swansons gave conclusively negates the element of reliance.

In negotiating the release, highly competent and able legal counsel represented both parties and, as we have said above, the parties were dealing at arm's length. Further, both Schlumberger and the Swansons are knowledgeable and sophisticated business players. The Swansons have been involved in traditional diamond mining in South Africa for several decades. They and Schlumberger, a multinational corporation, were engaged in a business venture involving tens of millions of dollars and in negotiations to sell their interests ultimately for several million dollars.

Significantly, throughout the parties' negotiations, the Swansons disagreed with Schlumberger about the feasibility and value of the sea-diamond project. Schlumberger never convinced the Swansons that DeBeers' offer was a good deal; four days before he signed the release, John Swanson wrote to his attorney that the Swansons' lease interest was "worth billions." The Swansons seriously considered suing Schlumberger even *before* the sale to DeBeers and Seltrust. Indeed, the release states that the Swansons claimed that they had an interest in the mining consortium and in Schlumberger's prospecting lease, and that Schlumberger was "liable to the Swansons in connection with the prospecting or exploration of diamonds or other precious stones or minerals in South Africa." In this connection, the release recites thatthere is considerable doubt, disagreement, dispute and controversy with reference to the validity of the Swansons' claim against [Schlumberger] and as to the legal or moral liability of [Schlumberger] for any amount of damages or justification for legal relief, and there is further doubt, disagreement, uncertainty and confusion as to the amount of said liability, if any.

Further, the Swansons released all "causes of action of whatsoever nature, or any other legal theory arising out of the circumstances described above, from any and all liability damages of any kind known or unknown, whether in contract or tort." The sole purpose of the release was to end the dispute about the value of this commercial project between Schlumberger and the Swansons once and for all.

In this context and in clear language, the Swansons unequivocally disclaimed reliance upon representations by Schlumberger about the project's feasibility and value. They said:

> [E]ach of us [the Swansons] expressly warrants and represents and does hereby state ... and represent ... that no promise or agreement which is not herein expressed has been made to him or her in executing this release, and that none of us is relying upon any statement or representation of any agent of the parties being released hereby. Each of us is relying on his or her own judgment and each has been represented by Hubert Johnson as legal counsel in this matter. The aforesaid legal counsel has read and explained to each of us the entire contents of this Release in Full, as well as the legal consequences of this Release .... (emphasis added)

Because courts are to assume that the parties intended every contractual provision to have some meaning, *see Columbia Gas,* 940 S.W.2d at 591; *Lenape Resources Corp. v. Tennessee Gas Pipeline Co.,* 925 S.W.2d 565, 574 (Tex.1996), we must presume that the parties contemplated, by the inclusion of this clause, that the Swansons would not rely on any representations of Schlumberger about the commercial feasibility and value of this project, which, after all, was the very dispute that the release was supposed to resolve. Therefore, we conclude that the disclaimer of reliance is binding and, as a matter of law, precludes the Swansons' claim that they were fraudulently induced to sell their interest in the sea-diamond project.

In sum, we hold that a release that clearly expresses the parties' intent to waive fraudulent inducement claims, or one that disclaims reliance on representations about specific matters in dispute, can preclude a claim of fraudulent inducement. We emphasize that a disclaimer of reliance or merger clause will not always bar a fraudulent inducement claim. *See Prudential,* 896 S.W.2d at 162 (identifying some circumstances in which "as is" clause would not preclude fraudulent inducement claim). We conclude only that on this record, the disclaimer of reliance conclusively negates as a matter of law the element of reliance on representations about the feasibility and value of the sea-diamond mining project needed to support the Swansons' claim of fraudulent inducement. As there is no evidence of a fiduciary or confidential relationship, the trial court correctly rendered a judgment notwithstanding the verdict against the Swansons on their claims of breach of fiduciary duty and fraudulent inducement.

* * *

V. SECTION 27.01 OF THE TEXAS BUSINESS & COMMERCE CODE

In addition to finding breach of fiduciary duty and common-law fraud, the jury found that Schlumberger committed fraud in connection with a real estate transaction in violation of section 27.01 of the Texas Business and Commerce Code. Tex. Bus. & Com. Code § 27.01. Schlumberger contends that section 27.01 does not apply to the Swansons' interest in the sea-diamond project. Schlumberger argues that the Swansons' interest at most was an interest in a prospecting lease off the South African coast, which under both South African and Texas law is a personal property interest, and not an interest in real estate.

We need not consider the choice-of-law and applicability issues Schlumberger raises. Nor do we approve or disapprove of the court of appeals' discussion on the application and construction of section 27.01 in this case. For our purposes, we assume, without deciding, that section 27.01 applies to Schlumberger's purchase of the Swansons' interest. Given that assumption, we hold that the disclaimer of reliance precludes the Swansons' statutory fraud claim.

As with the common law, reliance is a necessary element of a statutory fraud claim under section 27.01. Tex. Bus. & Com.Code § 27.01(a)(1)(B). As is clear from our previous discussion, the disclaimer of reliance in this case conclusively negates the Swansons' allegation that they relied on misrepresentations about commercial feasibility and value by Schlumberger in selling their interest in the sea-diamond project. The trial court's judgment notwithstanding the verdict was in all respects proper.

* * *

We reverse the judgment of the court of appeals and render judgment that the Swansons take nothing.

1. Consider the language in Tex. Bus. & Com. Code § 27.01.

FRAUD IN REAL ESTATE AND STOCK TRANSACTIONS ACT

(a) Fraud in a transaction involving real estate or stock in a corporation or joint stock company consists of a
  (1) false representation of a past or existing material fact, when the false representation is(A) made to a person for the purpose of inducing that person to enter into a contract; and (B) relied on by that person in entering into that contract; or
  (2) false promise to do an act, when the false promise is
    (A) material;
    (B) made with the intention of not fulfilling it;
    (C) made to a person for the purpose of inducing that person to enter into a contract; and
    (D) relied on by that person in entering into that contract.

(b) A person who makes a false representation or false promise commits the fraud described in Subsection (a) of this section and is liable to the person defrauded for actual damages.

(c) A person who makes a false representation or false promise with actual awareness of the falsity thereof commits the fraud described in Subsection (a) of this section and is liable to the person defrauded for exemplary damages. Actual awareness may be inferred where objective manifestations indicate that a person acted with actual awareness.

(d) A person who (1) has actual awareness of the falsity of a representation or promise made by another person and (2) fails to disclose the falsity of the representation or promise to the person defrauded, and (3) benefits from the false representation or promise commits the fraud described in Subsection (a) of this section and is liable to the person defrauded for exemplary damages. Actual awareness may be inferred where objective manifestations indicate that a person acted with actual awareness.

(e) Any person who violates the provisions of this section shall be liable to the person defrauded for reasonable and necessary attorney's fees, expert witness fees, costs for copies of depositions, and costs of court.

2. In Schlumberger, rules about merger clauses appear frequently. If you read Texas's and other jurisdictions' case law, you will discover that the purpose of a merger or integration clause is to prevent the parties to a contract from claiming — after the contract's formation — that the contract does not reflect their intent or understanding. In addition, a merger clause prevents either party from asserting that a subsequent oral agreement or writing is not consistent with their prior agreement. A properly constructed merger or integration clause might read:

> This Agreement and the attached exhibits contain the parties' entire agreement about the subject matter of this Agreement. In addition, this Agreement supersedes all of the parties' prior negotiations, agreements and understandings. This Agreement may only be amended by a written document which all parties have voluntarily executed.

All parties to a contract should ensure that all of their promises, expectations, understanding, obligations and conditions appear in the written contract. Otherwise, one might not be able to enforce oral or unwritten promises.

D. Waiver and "As Is" Defenses

As discussed in the preceding section, waivers are generally unenforceable under the DTPA. Moreover, waivers in otherwise bargained-for-exchange, negotiated or standardized contracts are void under the DTPA — unless they are carefully designed according to a set of strict instructions. But arguably, waivers and "as is" clauses are fairly similar. Both effectively prevent plaintiffs from asserting either common-law or statutory rights. Texas common law is clear: A court may find an implied waiver if "surrounding facts and circumstances" clearly demonstrate that a consumer had an intent to waive a right. *Jernigan v. Langley,* 111 S.W.3d 153, 156 (Tex. 2003). Therefore, one's acknowledging and embracing the terms of an "as is" clause is arguably evidence of one's impliedly waiving a right to complain later.

There is, however, a significant difference between waiver and "as is" clauses. Again, before an agreement is consummated, an "as is" clause notifies the consumer that he has no legal or equitable right to complain about the condition or quality of goods or services after the formation of the agreement. Also, under the DTPA, an "as is" provision is a supervening act that breaks the causal link between a DTPA defendant's alleged violation and a consumer's alleged injury and damages. This section explores these two latter points more thoroughly.

DTPA § 17.42 — Waivers: Public Policy

(a) Any waiver by a consumer of the provisions of this subchapter is contrary to public policy and is unenforceable and void; provided, however, that a waiver is valid and enforceable if:

(1) the waiver is in writing and is signed by the consumer;

(2) the consumer is not in a significantly disparate bargaining position; and

(3) the consumer is represented by legal counsel in seeking or acquiring the goods or services.

(b) A waiver under Subsection (a) is not effective if the consumer's legal counsel was directly or indirectly identified, suggested, or selected by a defendant or an agent of the defendant.

(c) A waiver under this section must be:
   (1) conspicuous and in bold-face type of at least 10 points in size;
   (2) identified by the heading "Waiver of Consumer Rights," or words of similar meaning; and
   (3) in substantially the following form:

   "I waive my rights under the Deceptive Trade Practices-Consumer Protection Act, Section 17.41 et seq., Business & Commerce Code, a law that gives consumers special rights and protections. After consultation with an attorney of my own selection, I voluntarily consent to this waiver."

(d) The waiver required by Subsection (c) may be modified to waive only specified rights under this subchapter.

(e) The fact that a consumer has signed a waiver under this section is not a defense to an action brought by the attorney general under Section 17.47.

Prudential Insurance Company of America v. Jefferson Associates, Ltd.
896 S.W.2d 156
(Tex. 1995)

We granted writ of error in this case to decide whether a buyer who agrees, freely and without fraudulent inducement, to purchase commercial real estate "as is" can recover damages from the seller when the property is later discovered not to be in as good a condition as the buyer believed it was when he inspected it before the sale. We hold he cannot.

I

F.B. Goldman bought the Jefferson Building, a four-story office building in Austin, from The Prudential Insurance Company of America in 1984. Over two years later Goldman discovered that the building contained asbestos fireproofing. He then filed this suit against Prudential. (Four months after he bought the building, Goldman conveyed it to Jefferson Associates, Ltd., a limited partnership which he formed with other investors for the purpose of owning the building, and which is a plaintiff with Goldman in this suit. Because their interests are aligned, we refer to Goldman only.) The gist of Goldman's complaints is that Prudential misrepresented the condition of the building to him and failed to disclose that it contained asbestos which impaired its value. Prudential vigorously disputes Goldman's allegations, but since Goldman prevailed at trial, we must view the evidence in the light most favorable to him. Prudential's central argument here is a legal one, namely, that Goldman is not entitled to damages because he bought the building "as is."

Prudential provided the original permanent financing for construction of the Jefferson Building in 1972 and acquired the building four years later through foreclosure. In 1983, Prudential offered the building for sale by a closed bidding process in which offers were submitted in the form of proposed contracts. Prudential invited bidders to review financial records pertaining to the building and to inspect the premises. Goldman had tried to buy the building from Prudential before, and he submitted a bid. Goldman was a knowledgeable real estate investor who owned an interest in at least thirty commercial buildings. He was president of Transland Management Company, a commercial property management firm in Dallas that had developed, built, rehabilitated, owned or managed properties valued altogether at about $100 million. He had bought and sold several large investment properties on an "as is" basis.

Before bidding on the building, Goldman had it inspected by his maintenance supervisor, Timmy Don Kirk, and also by his property manager and an independent professional engineering firm. Kirk testified that Donna Buchanan, Prudential's on-site property manager, told him that the building was "superb", "super fine", and "one of the finest little properties in the City of Austin". Kirk also testified that Buchanan told him that the building had no defects except for a mechanical room foundation problem. These are the statements Goldman claims misrepresented the condition of the building, and we assume they were made.

Kirk asked Buchanan for the building plans and specifications, but she mistakenly told him she had only the "as-built" drawings, which she gave him. She referred him to the architects for additional information. Neither Goldman nor anyone on his behalf contacted the architects or made any further effort to obtain the plans and specifications. In fact, Prudential had the plans and specifications Kirk requested but did not make them available to Goldman during their negotiations. Prudential contends it could not locate the plans and specifications at the time; Goldman contends Prudential concealed them. Again, we assume Goldman is correct. Those specifications called for use of a fireproofing material called Monokote®, or an approved substitute. Information published by the manufacturer of Monokote® about the time the building was built stated that the product contained asbestos; but information published several years later stated that the product did not contain asbestos. Kirk was not aware of any of this information and stated that had he seen plans calling for Monokote®, he would not have known that the product might have contained asbestos. Even someone aware of the information published by the manufacturer could not be certain whether any Monokote® used in the Jefferson Building contained asbestos. Nor could anyone be certain from the specifications alone whether Monokote®, or an approved substitute, was actually used in the building. Thus, when the original architects reviewed the specifications in 1987, some three years after the sale, they saw nothing to indicate that the building contained asbestos.

Throughout the 1970s, there was a growing public concern that asbestos in a building could pose a health hazard. By 1983, before the sale to Goldman, Prudential knew of this concern and feared that it could adversely affect a building's marketability. Prudential also knew that buildings built about the same time as the Jefferson Building often contained asbestos fireproofing, and that there was thus a good chance that asbestos was used in the Jefferson Building. However, there is no evidence that Prudential actually knew before Goldman filed this lawsuit that the Jefferson Building contained asbestos. Goldman and Kirk testified that they were unaware of the public concern over asbestos and thus did not raise the issue during negotiations with Prudential.

Goldman bought the Jefferson Building for $7,150,000 cash. The contract he submitted contained the following provision:

> As a material part of the consideration for this Agreement, Seller and Purchaser agree that Purchaser is taking the Property "AS IS" with any and all latent and patent defects and that there is no warranty by Seller that the Property is fit for a particular purpose. Purchaser acknowledges that it is not relying upon any representation, statement or other assertion with respect to the Property condition, but is relying upon its examination of the Property. Purchaser takes the Property under the express understanding there are no express or implied warranties (except for limited warranties of title set forth in the closing documents). Provisions of this Section 15 shall survive the Closing.

The contract also provided: "In no event shall a Purchaser have the right to recover consequential damages. Purchaser hereby waives any action under the Texas Deceptive Trade Practices Act."

Three years later, when Goldman tried to refinance the building, a potential lender required evidence that the building did not contain asbestos. Goldman obtained a letter to that effect from the two original architects, which was based on their review of the construction specifications. When the building was inspected, however, the asbestos fireproofing was discovered. Goldman then sued Prudential alleging violations of the Texas Deceptive Trade Practices-Consumer Protection Act, Tex. Bus. & Com.Code §§ 17.41-.63 [DTPA], fraud, negligence, and breach of the duty of good faith and fair dealing.

At trial, the parties agreed to submit a single question to the jury concerning liability: "Do you find from a preponderance of the evidence that the Plaintiffs should be entitled to recover damages from the Defendant as the result of any wrongful conduct by the Defendant?" The jury answered this question affirmatively. While there was evidence at trial that the asbestos in the building did not pose a health hazard, did not need to be removed, and could be managed in place at a cost of $61,000, the jury found that the difference between the consideration Goldman paid and the value received was $6,023,993.03. The jury also found that punitive damages should be awarded against Prudential in the amount of $14,300,000.00. In accordance with the verdict, the trial court rendered judgment which, including interest, costs and attorney fees, totaled $25,692,571.58. The court of appeals affirmed. 839 S.W.2d 866.

II

A

The effect of the jury's affirmative answer to the question quoted above is to establish Prudential's liability for actual damages on any cause of action pleaded by Goldman that is supported by some evidence. However, combining all liability theories in a single question does not obviate the necessity for proof of all elements of at least one cause of action. Stated another way, Goldman is entitled to recover damages if, but only if, some evidence supports each element of one pleaded cause of action. Neither Goldman nor Prudential disputes that this is the proper method of analyzing this case.

Proof of causation is essential for recovery on all of Goldman's causes of action. Negligence, for example, requires proof of proximate cause. *Brown v. Edwards Transfer Co.,* 764 S.W.2d 220, 223 (Tex. 1988). For DTPA violations, only producing cause must be shown. Tex.Bus. & Com.Code § 17.50(a). The element common to both proximate cause and producing cause is actual causation in fact. *General Motors Corp. v. Saenz,* 873 S.W.2d 353, 357 (Tex.1993). This requires proof that an act or omission was a substantial factor in bringing about injury which would not otherwise have occurred. *McClure v. Allied Stores of Texas, Inc.,* 608 S.W.2d 901, 903 (Tex. 1980). Unless there is some evidence that Prudential caused Goldman damages, and this evidence satisfies the requirement of actual causation in fact, Goldman is not entitled to recover on any of his claims.

We think Goldman's agreement to buy the Jefferson Building "as is" precludes him from proving that Prudential's conduct caused him any harm. By agreeing to purchase something "as is", a buyer agrees to make his own appraisal of the bargain and to accept the risk that he may be wrong. *Mid Continent Aircraft Corp. v. Curry County Spraying Serv. Inc.,* 572 S.W.2d 308, 313 (Tex.1978).

The seller gives no assurances, express or implied, concerning the value or condition of the thing sold. *See* Tex.Bus. & Com.Code § 2.316(c)(1) ("as is" agreement excludes implied warranties in contract covered by UCC). Goldman agreed to take the property "with any and all latent and patent defects" "under the express understanding that there are no express or implied warranties" (except those related to title), including specifically, "that there is no warranty by Seller that the Property is fit for a particular purpose." Goldman acknowledged that he was not "relying upon any representation, statement or other assertion with respect to the Property condition" and was instead relying upon his own "examination of the Property." While it should not be necessary in every "as is" provision to go into this much detail, Goldman's contract leaves no doubt exactly what he agreed to.

Goldman's "as is" agreement negates his claim that any action by Prudential caused his injury. His contractual disavowal of reliance upon any representation by Prudential was an important element of their arm's-length transaction and is binding on Goldman unless set aside. The "as is" agreement negates causation essential to recovery on all the theories Goldman asserts-DTPA violations, fraud (excluding, of course, fraud in the inducement of the "as is" agreement, which Goldman does not assert), negligence, and breach of the duty of good faith and fair dealing. Thus, Goldman's injury could not have been caused by Prudential.

A valid "as is" agreement, like the one in this case, prevents a buyer from holding a seller liable if the thing sold turns out to be worth less than the price paid because it is impossible for the buyer's injury on account of this disparity to have been caused by the seller. *See Mid Continent,* 572 S.W.2d at 313 (the buyer "has taken the entire risk as to the quality of the [property] and the resulting loss"); *see also Dubow v. Dragon,* 746 S.W.2d 857, 860 (Tex.App.-Dallas 1988, no writ) ("as a matter of law, [buyers'] 'careful' inspection of the house's condition constituted a new and independent basis for the purchase which intervened and superseded [sellers'] wrongful act"); *Camden Machine & Tool, Inc. v. Cascade Co.,* 870 S.W.2d 304, 312 (Tex.App.-Fort Worth 1993, no writ) (characterizing *Dubow* as holding that "the producing cause was [buyer's] reliance on the inspection and professional opinions which constituted a new and independent basis for the purchase").

The sole cause of a buyer's injury in such circumstances, by his own admission, is the buyer himself. He has agreed to take the full risk of determining the value of the purchase. He is not obliged to do so; he could insist instead that the seller assume part or all of that risk by obtaining warranties to the desired effect. If the seller is willing to give such assurances, however, he will ordinarily insist upon additional compensation. Rather than pay more, a buyer may choose to rely entirely upon his own determination of the condition and value of his purchase. In making this choice, he removes the possibility that the seller's conduct will cause him damage.

Justice Cornyn's concurring opinion argues that Goldman's "as is" agreement relevant to whether Prudential caused him harm, but not controlling. If Goldman's position at trial were the same as the position he took in the "as is" agreement, he could not recover on any of the theories he asserts. Unable to show any reason why the agreement should not be enforced, such as fraudulent inducement, Goldman ought to be held to his voluntary, freely negotiated affirmation that he was depending on his own assessment of the building. Justice Cornyn's concurring opinion suggests that Prudential should prevail if this was an arm's-length transaction. Goldman does not dispute that it was.

By our holding today we do not suggest that an "as is" agreement can have this determinative effect in every circumstance. A buyer is not bound by an agreement to purchase something "as is" that he is induced to make because of a fraudulent representation or concealment of information by the seller. *Weitzel v. Barnes,* 691 S.W.2d 598, 601 (Tex. 1985); *Dallas Farm Mach. Co. v. Reaves,* 307 S.W.2d 233, 240 (Tex. 1957); *see Cockburn v. Mercantile Petroleum, Inc.,* 296 S.W.2d 316, 326 (Tex. Civ. App.-Dallas 1956, writ ref'd n.r.e.). A seller cannot have it both ways: he cannot assure the buyer of the condition of a thing to obtain the buyer's agreement to purchase "as is", and then disavow the assurance which procured the "as is" agreement. Also, a buyer is not bound by an "as is" agreement if he is entitled to inspect the condition of what is being sold but is impaired by the seller's conduct. A seller cannot obstruct an inspection for defects in his property and still insist that the buyer take it "as is". In circumstances such as these an "as is" agreement does not bar recovery against the seller.

We also recognize that other aspects of a transaction may make an "as is" agreement unenforceable. The nature of the transaction and the totality of the circumstances surrounding the agreement must be considered. Where the "as is" clause is an important part of the basis of the bargain, not an incidental or "boiler-plate" provision, and is entered into by parties of relatively equal bargaining position, a buyer's affirmation and agreement that he is not relying on representations by the seller should be given effect. Justice Cornyn's concurring opinion argues that such factors are generally not important, and that "as is" agreements must be given the same effect in every transaction absent fraud or adhesion. We simply disagree. We think it too obvious for argument that an "as is" agreement freely negotiated by similarly sophisticated parties as part of the bargain in an arm's-length transaction has a different effect than a provision in a standard form contract which cannot be negotiated and cannot serve as the basis of the parties' bargain.

* * *

III

While the "as is" agreement in this case negates the element of causation essential to all of Goldman's claims, two problems under the DTPA remain to be addressed.

A

Section 17.42 of the DTPA states that a "waiver by a consumer of the provisions of [the DTPA] is contrary to public policy and is unenforceable and void . . . ." Tex.Bus. & Com.Code § 17.42. The provision in Goldman's contract expressly waiving any action under the DTPA violates this prohibition and is therefore void. The "as is" provision, however, does not violate the prohibition.

Goldman's "as is" agreement is not a waiver of DTPA rights; it is a statement that no basis exists for the assertion of such rights. Goldman agreed in the "as is" provision, not that he would never sue Prudential for breach of express and implied warranties in violation of the DTPA, but that no warranties were made. The agreement states: "Purchaser takes the Property under the express understanding there are no express or implied warranties...." Goldman's agreement was not that he would never claim that Prudential's conduct caused him harm, but that in fact Prudential did not harm him and could not have done so, since he was relying entirely upon his own examination of the property. The agreement states: "Purchaser acknowledges that it is not relying upon any representation, statement or other assertion with respect to the Property condition, but is relying upon its examination of the Property." Having made these admissions freely in a negotiated agreement, Goldman is bound by them. Goldman's agreement does not say he cannot sue Prudential for violating the DTPA; it says he cannot win the suit. He cannot win because he has asserted facts which negate proof of causation required for recovery.

Justice Cornyn's concurring opinion charges that the Court has rewritten the DTPA, substituting its will for the Legislature's. Our decision does no violence to the DTPA. A buyer like Goldman simply confirms by his agreement precisely what was and was not the producing cause of the agreement, and accordingly what could and could not be the producing cause of any injury the buyer might suffer.

B

Our decision in this case does not conflict with our opinion in *Weitzel v. Barnes,* 691 S.W.2d 598 (Tex.1985), a case on which Goldman and Prudential both rely. To the contrary, *Weitzel* provides support for the conclusion we reach here.

The Weitzels bought a remodeled home under a contract which gave them the right to inspect the home and provided that if they failed to do so they agreed to accept it in the condition received. The Weitzels' agreement did not state, as Goldman's did, that they were relying entirely on their own inspection of the property and not on any statement made by their seller. Unlike Goldman, the Weitzels did not inspect the property, and when they found that the plumbing and air conditioning systems did not function properly, they sued the seller for representing to them that those systems complied with city code specifications. The Weitzels alleged that the seller made this representation to induce them to buy the home, and that based upon this representation they did not inspect the home before closing. The court of appeals held that admission of evidence of the representation violated the parol evidence rule, but in dicta stated that proof of reliance was required to show a DTPA violation. *Barnes v. Weitzel,* 678 S.W.2d 747, 750 (Tex.App.-Fort Worth 1984). This Court held that evidence of the representation was not parol, and in its own admitted dicta, stated that proof of reliance was not required by the DTPA.

The issue which is dispositive in Goldman's case-whether his "as is" agreement establishes that Prudential could not have been a producing cause of his harm-was not raised in *Weitzel.* The Court indicated that if the Weitzels' seller had not represented the condition of the property, the "as is" agreement might have protected him from liability. But the seller did not argue, and the Court did not consider, whether an "as is" agreement is enforceable unless fraudulently induced, or how it would affect proof of causation.

Weitzel does confirm, however, that proof of producing cause is required to establish liability under the DTPA. 691 S.W.2d at 600. That requirement is the focus of our decision in the present case. Thus, we view today's decision as consistent with *Weitzel.*

* * *

For the reasons explained, we conclude that Goldman's agreement to buy the Jefferson Building "as is", in these circumstances, conclusively shows that nothing Prudential did caused Goldman damages. Accordingly, we reverse the judgment of the court of appeals and render judgment that Goldman take nothing.

Bynum v. Prudential Residential Services, Ltd. Partnership
129 S.W.3d 781
(Tex. App.-Houston [1 Dist.] 2004)

On this day, . . . we withdraw our previous opinion of November 10, 2003, and issue this opinion in its stead. Our judgment of November 10, 2003, remains unchanged.

Appellants, Jimmy and Hillary Bynum, individually and as next friends of their minor children, Thomas and Clark Bynum, sued various Prudential entities (Prudential), R & R Inspection Service, Peverely Engineering Inc., Ray Kindsfather, and John and Susan McNamara, appellees, asserting claims of breach of contract, breach of express and implied warranties, violation of deed restrictions, violations of the DTPA, fraud, violations of section 27.01 of the Texas Business and Commerce Code, negligence, negligence *per se,* negligent misrepresentation, failure to provide disclosures required by section 5.008 of the Texas Property Code, and strict products liability. Additionally, the Bynums sought the equitable relief of rescission, and a constructive trust.

Prudential and the McNamaras filed both no-evidence and traditional motions for summary judgment that were granted by the trial court as to all of the claims raised by the Bynums against them. The Bynums' claims against Prudential and the McNamaras were then severed by the trial court from the Bynums' claims against remaining defendants so that the judgment disposing of the Bynums' claims against Prudential and McNamara would become final.

The Bynums assert nine issues on appeal, which we reduce to seven issues for the disposition of the case, contending that summary judgment against them was improper because 1) the "as is" clause in the purchase agreement cannot be enforced against the Bynums; 2) there is an issue of material fact as to whether there was a breach of express and implied warranties; 3) there is an issue of material fact as to whether, under section 5.008 of the Texas Property Code, they were entitled to terminate)the purchase of their home and recover monies paid; 4) there is an issue of material fact as to whether the Bynums are entitled to the equitable relief of recission under the doctrine of mistake; and 5) there is an issue of material fact as to where Prudential or the McNamaras engaged in statutory fraud or negligent misrepresentation. Additionally, the Bynums argue that the trial court erred in refusing to grant their motion for partial summary judgment against the McNamaras on their claim of negligence *per se,* and erred in denying the Bynums' motion for continuance. We affirm.

Facts

We review the facts of this case taking all evidence in favor of the Bynums as true. *Nixon v. Mr. Prop. Mgmt. Co.,* 690 S.W.2d 546, 548-549 (Tex.1985).

In 1999, the McNamaras hired Ray Kindsfather to remodel their home over a period of several months. Most of the work involved remodeling two bathrooms in the house. The hall bath was enlarged by the removal of a wall, and a shower, commode, and sink were added to it. Significant electrical and plumbing work was done in both of the bathrooms, and new sewer lines were added to connect with previously existing ones.

In early 2000, the McNamaras decided to sell their home. In April of 2000, the McNamaras' employer hired Prudential to help the McNamaras sell their home and relocate to a new city. The McNamaras separately hired a third-party agent with Martha Turner Properties to list the home for sale and represent their interests. The McNamaras filled out and faxed to Prudential a "Homeowners Disclosure Statement," (HDS) provided by Prudential, for the purpose of aiding Prudential in the appraisal and purchase process. In the HDS, one of the questions was as follows: "were any structural additions, changes, or repairs made to the property by former owners without obtaining all necessary permits and government approvals?" To that question, the McNamaras answered "no." The following question in the HDS asked "have you made any structural additions, changes, or repairs to the property?" The McNamaras answered "yes," and next to the "yes" box wrote "remodeled bathrooms." The third question asked "have you obtained all necessary permits and government approvals?" To this question, the McNamaras wrote "N/A."

The Bynums, who purchased the home from Prudential, received two section 5.008 disclosure statements on the home. *See* Tex. Prop.Code Ann. § 5.008. One was from the McNamaras, and the other was from Prudential. On the McNamaras' disclosure form, the McNamaras checked "no" to the question of whether they were aware of any "room additions, structural modifications, or other alterations or repairs made without necessary permits or not in compliance with building codes in effect at that time." The disclosure form from Prudential was signed and dated by Prudential, but on each of the pages, the sections with questions regarding the condition of the property was marked out with an "X."

On May 4, 2000, the Bynums signed an earnest money contract offer to purchase the home for $341,000. The Bynums also signed and initialed a five-page rider that was incorporated as part of the offer. The rider contained the following statement: "Buyer understands that Seller is a relocation management company and has never lived in or on the Property. The Property, including the contents, being sold and purchased are not new, and are being sold 'as is'-in their present condition." The rider also contained an option period under which the Bynums, after paying $500.00, could terminate the contract for any reason within five days after the contract was signed. The rider provided that if the Bynums did not terminate the contract during the option period, then they were "deemed to have accepted the Property in its current condition." With regard to the section 5.008 disclosure statements from the McNamaras and Prudential, the rider provided "BUYER AGREES THAT BUYER IS NOT RELYING ON THE ACCURACY OF THESE DOCUMENTS." Finally, the rider contained a provision stating the following:

> Buyer's (a) failure to notify Seller in writing of any defects within the time limits provided in this Rider, or (b) acceptance of the Deed at settlement shall constitute Buyer's full acceptance of the condition of the Property and a waiver of Buyer's right to object to its condition or assert any claim related to the Property at any time in the future. This provision shall survive delivery of the Deed and the closing.

Prudential accepted the Bynums' earnest money contract offer on May 8, 2000. On May 20, 2000, the contract was amended to allow for a few additional terms, among which was the term that "Buyer accepts the Property in its present condition; provided Seller, at Seller's expense, shall complete the following repairs and treatment: ..." The parties are not in dispute as to whether Prudential made the repairs.

Prior to closing, the Bynums had the home inspected by professional inspectors. The electrical work, plumbing, and structural modifications performed during the remodeling, however, were, according to the Bynums, either behind walls, covered with insulation, or buried in the concrete slab, and, thus, were not readily subject to inspection. On November 11, 2000, after the closing, and several months after the Bynums moved into the house, Jimmy Bynum noticed that sewer water was leaking into the backyard as a shower inside of the house was being run. This problem was the first of many that were eventually discovered. Upon further investigation, the Bynums discovered that, because of the absence of a vent pipe, sewer water was collecting under the master bath and was spilling over the side of the house into the backyard.

The Bynums also found that the areas outside of the hall bath were "soggy," which was being caused by a problem with the sewer drainage from the hall bathroom. In the attic of the home, it was discovered that prohibited PVC plastic pipe had been used, and that, as a result, a leak had developed, allowing, what the Bynums contend, is toxic Stachybotrys mold to grow. Additionally, the electrical connections in the bathrooms were not grounded, which created an electrocution hazard, and the new framing, done after the remodeling, was not adequately supporting the attic, which caused a crack to appear in a bedroom ceiling.

The Bynums contend that much of the work performed was in violation of the codes of the City of Houston, and would have failed inspection by City of Houston building inspectors. Some of the violations that are alleged by the Bynums to have occurred in the remodeling of the home include (1) failure to obtain the necessary plumbing, electrical, and building permits; (2) failure to have licensed electricians and licensed plumbers do the electrical and plumbing work; (3) prohibited use of PVC pipe within the home; and (4) prohibited use of an open sewer vent line.
As a result of the violations and subsequent mold problem, the Bynums vacated the home, leaving their possessions behind to be treated for mold. The Bynums claim that the mold caused Clarke and Thomas Bynum to suffer respiratory problems, and that they are financially unable to repair the defective remodeling performed on the house.

Standard of Review

The standard for reviewing a motion for summary judgment is as follows: 1) the movant for summary judgment has the burden of showing that there is no genuine issue of material fact and that the movant is entitled to judgment as a matter of law; 2) in deciding whether there is a disputed material fact issue precluding summary judgment, evidence favorable to the nonmovant will be taken as true; and 3) every reasonable inference must be indulged in favor of the nonmovant and any doubts resolved in the nonmovant's favor. *Nixon,* 690 S.W.2d at 548-49. A defendant is entitled to summary judgment if at least one element of each of the plaintiff's causes of action is negated as a matter of law. *Doe v. Boys Clubs of Greater Dallas, Inc.,* 907 S.W.2d 472, 476-77 (Tex.1995).

A no-evidence motion for summary judgment is proper when, after adequate time for discovery, the respondent produces no evidence to support one or more essential elements on the cause of action specified in the motion. *Howell v. Hilton Hotels Corp.,* 84 S.W.3d 708, 715 (Tex.App.-Houston [1st Dist.] 2002, no pet.)

The Validity of the "As Is" Clause

In issue one, the Bynums argue that the "as is" clause, and the other like clauses in the Prudential rider or earnest money contract that purport to disclaim warranties cannot be used to bar their claims against Prudential and the McNamaras because the clauses (1) are inconspicuous boiler-plate terms entered into by parties of greatly disproportionate sophistication; (2) are the product of fraudulent misrepresentation or concealment of information; (3) cannot be used to release a party from intentional wrongful future conduct; (4) cannot be used to waive DTPA claims; and (5) cannot be enforced against the Bynum's minor children.

The Texas Supreme Court has held that, generally, an "as is" clause will defeat the element of causation in DTPA, fraud, and negligence claims. *Prudential Ins. Co. of Am. v. Jefferson Assocs., Ltd.,* 896 S.W.2d 156, 161 (Tex.1995). When an agreement to purchase something "as is" is executed, a buyer agrees to make his own appraisal of the bargain and accept the risk that he may be wrong. *Id.* The seller gives no assurances, express or implied, concerning the value or condition of the thing sold, and the buyer chooses to rely completely on his own determination of the condition and value of the purchase, removing the possibility that the seller's conduct will cause him damage. *Id.*

There are, however, exceptions to the general rule. A buyer is not bound by an "as is" clause that is the product of fraudulent representation or concealment of information by the seller. *Smith v. Levine,* 911 S.W.2d 427, 431-32 (Tex.App.-San Antonio 1995, writ denied) (holding that "as is" clause in contract for purchase of house did not negate element of causation when there was evidence of affirmative misrepresentations by seller). As the court in the *Prudential* decision noted,

> A seller cannot have it both ways: he cannot assure the buyer of the condition of a thing to obtain the buyer's agreement to purchase "as is", and then disavow the assurance which procured the "as is" agreement. Also, a buyer is not bound by an "as is" agreement if he is entitled to inspect the condition of what is being sold but is impaired by the seller's conduct. A seller cannot obstruct an inspection for defects in his property and still insist that the buyer take it "as is." In circumstances such as these an "as is" agreement does not bar recovery against the seller. *Prudential,* 896 S.W.2d at 162.

In determining whether an "as is" clause is enforceable, we must also review the totality of the circumstances surrounding the agreement. Whether the "as is" clause is an important part of the basis of the bargain, rather than an incidental "boiler-plate" provision, and whether the parties have relatively equal bargaining positions, are factors to consider.

Surrounding Circumstances and Sophistication of the Parties

The Bynums contend that the "as is" clause and other like disclaimers in the Prudential Rider and earnest money contract are not binding on them because the Bynums were "lacking any sophistication in purchasing property or reviewing contracts," and because the disclaimers were inconspicuous boiler-plate provisions.

We will not dispute the Bynums' contention that the "as is" clause in the Prudential rider agreement was a standard boiler-plate provision, but we are not convinced that the Bynums were so unsophisticated that enforcing the provisions would be unfair. We agree with the Bynums that Prudential, a large company that specializes in real estate transactions, has a great amount of sophistication, but the Bynums did not face Prudential alone. During the Bynums' dealings with Prudential, the Bynums were represented by Joan Bynum, a licensed real estate broker with

Greenwood King Properties. Additionally, the Bynums were not strangers to "as is" contracts. Mr. Bynum testified in his deposition that he had purchased and sold other properties before buying the home in this case, including property that was purchased "as is." Mr. Bynum also testified that he was a manager for Salvage Sale, which was a company that sold salvaged goods "as is." Finally, the Bynums, before closing on the house, had the home inspected by professional inspectors.

We do not believe that, under these circumstances, the Bynums are entitled to have the "as is" clause set aside on the grounds that they were unsophisticated purchasers agreeing to boiler-plate provisions. *See id.* As for the Bynums' argument that the agreement was inconspicuous, there is no dispute that the Bynums were aware that they were purchasing the house "as is." Mr. Bynum testified in his deposition that he read the "as is" clause at the time that he signed the agreement. A party who, before entering into a contract, has actual knowledge of terms that he later complains of, is not entitled to escape enforcement of those terms on the ground that the terms are inconspicuous. *See Cate v. Dover Corp.,* 790 S.W.2d 559, 562 (Tex.1990).

Accordingly, we hold that the Bynums are not entitled to have the "as is" clause and like disclaimers set aside on the grounds that the terms were inconspicuous boiler-plate provisions that were agreed to by unsophisticated purchasers.

Fraudulent Representation and Concealment

The Bynums also allege that the "as is" clause is not enforceable because Prudential and the McNamaras fraudulently misrepresented and concealed material facts. The Bynums contend that the McNamaras and Prudential knew that the remodeling was done without the proper permits, but that they purposefully withheld the information from the Bynums.

In order to set aside the "as is" clause on the basis of fraudulent misrepresentation, the Bynums must show actual knowledge of the misrepresentation. *Prudential,* 896 S.W.2d at 162 ("as is" clause could not be set aside on basis of fraudulent misrepresentation because, while there may have been evidence that Prudential should have known of property condition, there was no evidence that they actually knew of condition).

The Bynums contend that the HDS sent by the McNamaras to Prudential is some evidence that the McNamaras and Prudential knew that remodeling work had been done without the necessary permits. We disagree. In the HDS, question 7(a) was as follows: "were any structural additions, changes, or repairs made to the property by former owners without obtaining all necessary permits and government approvals?" The McNamaras answered "no." Question 7(b) asked "have you made any structural additions, changes, or repairs to the property?" The McNamaras answered "yes," and next to the "yes" box wrote "remodeled bathrooms." Question 7(c) asked "have you obtained all necessary permits and government approvals?" To this question, the McNamaras wrote "N/A."

We do not see an inconsistency in the answers given by the McNamaras on the HDS. The only reasonable interpretation to be given the McNamara's "N/A" response to question 7(c) is that they believed that the question was "not applicable" because no permits were necessary for the remodeling that they admitted having done. As such, the HDS that the McNamaras provided to Prudential is consistent with the McNamaras' representation to the Bynum's in the § 5.008 disclosure that they were "not aware" of modifications made without necessary permits. Put simply, the McNamara's "N/A" answer does not create a reasonable inference that the McNamaras knew that permits were necessary, but not obtained.

Having determined that there is no evidence that Prudential had actual knowledge that the McNamaras remodeled their home without the required permits, we now determine if there was any other evidence that the McNamaras had actual knowledge that the remodeling was performed without necessary permits.

In the McNamaras' section 5.008 disclosure form provided to the Bynums, the McNamaras answered "no" to the question of whether they had knowledge of any "room additions, structural modifications, or other alterations or repairs made without necessary permits or not in compliance with building codes in effect at that time." The Bynums argue that the McNamaras made the disclosure with actual knowledge of its falsity, and cite the following as factors in support of such a finding: (1) the HDS form submitted to Prudential by the McNamaras shows that the McNamaras knew that they should have had permits; (2) Mrs. McNamara's deposition indicates that she intentionally did not obtain approval for the remodeling from the Civic Association, which was required under the deed restrictions; (3) the McNamaras failed to inquire as to the qualifications of Mr. Kindsfather; (4) the McNamaras had heard of building permits; (5) the McNamaras' neighbors remodeled their homes with building permits, and the permits are required to be posted in a window and visible from the street; and (6) Mr. Kindsfather, who performed the work, allegedly stated to Mr. Bynum that his standard policy was to tell homeowners about the options of proceeding either with or without building permits, and the consequences of either action.

As an initial matter, we will discuss factors (1) and (6) listed above. As we have already discussed, the McNamara's "N/A" response on the HDS does not create any inference that the McNamaras knew that permits were required, but did not obtain them. As such, (1) above provides no evidentiary support for the Bynums.

Similarly, (6) above cannot be considered as evidentiary support for the Bynums because issue of Kindsfather's statement was not raised in response to the motion for summary judgment. Instead, Kindsfather's alleged statement was offered to the court in connection with the Bynums' motion for continuance. When there is a no-evidence motion for summary judgment, as was the case here, the trial court must grant the motion unless the respondent produces summary judgment evidence raising a genuine issue of material fact. Tex.R. Civ. P. 166a(i). In this case, the Bynums did not produce the affidavit as evidence to support their causes of action; rather, the affidavit was executed by Mr. Bynum in support of the Bynums' motion for continuance.

Further, the Bynums, in their written responses to the motions for summary judgment from Prudential and the McNamaras, never argued that the alleged statement from Kindsfather was evidence that supported their causes of action. Accordingly, we will not consider the evidentiary value of the affidavit on appeal. *See State Bd. of Ins. v. Westland Film Indus.,* 705 S.W.2d 695, 696 (Tex.1986) (holding that, on appeal, non-movant may not raise grounds that it did not raise in trial court in opposition to motion for summary judgment); *City of Houston v. Clear Creek Basin Auth.*, 589 S.W.2d 671, 674-75 (Tex.1979).

Having determined that numbers (1) and (6) do not provide any evidentiary support for the Bynums, we review the Bynums' remaining evidence to determine whether they sufficiently raise a fact question about whether the McNamara's had actual knowledge that permits were required, but not obtained. If we consider as true the Bynums' evidence that the McNamaras had intentionally declined to obtain approval from the Civic Association, had failed to inquire as to Kindsfather's qualifications, had heard of building permits, and had neighbors that had obtained building permits, we conclude there is still insufficient evidence to raise a fact issue about the McNamara's actual knowledge that their remodeling was done without the necessary permits.

In *Prudential,* the court held that, even though there was evidence that Prudential knew that most buildings built in the same era as the building in question contained asbestos, and even though there was evidence that Prudential should have suspected the use of asbestos in the building, that evidence was not evidence that Prudential "actually knew" of the asbestos. *Prudential,* 896 S.W.2d at 160, 162.

In this case, the evidence produced by the Bynums is no more compelling than the evidence produced by the plaintiff in *Prudential.* While the evidence might support the proposition that the McNamaras were careless in remodeling their home and were aware that building permits existed and were sometimes required for building projects, there is no evidence that the McNamaras actually knew that they had remodeled without the necessary permits. *See id.* Accordingly, we hold that, because there is no evidence of intentional misrepresentation or concealment by the McNamaras or Prudential, the Bynums are not entitled to have the "as is" clause set aside on those grounds.

Intentional Wrongful Future Conduct

The Bynums argue that the "as is" clause cannot release Prudential or the McNamaras from liability for their intentional wrongful future conduct. The intentional wrongful future conduct complained of by the Bynums is the violation of Prudential and the McNamaras' continuing obligation to disclose material information to the Bynums, namely, the HDS furnished by the McNamaras to Prudential.

A cause of action exists under the DTPA if a seller fails to disclose information concerning goods or services which was known at the time of the transaction if such failure to disclose such information was intended to induce the consumer into a transaction that the consumer would not have entered into had the information been disclosed. Tex. Bus. & Com.Code Ann. § 17.46(b)(24). We have already determined that the Bynums produced no evidence showing that either the McNamaras or Prudential had actual knowledge that the remodeling was done without necessary permits. Accordingly, there being no evidence of intentional wrongful conduct, we need not further discuss the Bynums' contention.

Waiver of DTPA Claims

The Bynums argue that, even if the "as is" clause is enforceable, it cannot be used to waive their claims under the DTPA because the "as is" clause does not comply with the waiver requirements of the DTPA. Tex. Bus. & Com. Code Ann. § 17.42(a)-(d)

A similar argument was made by the appellant in the *Prudential* decision. The *Prudential* court resolved the issue by stating that the "as is" clause is not a waiver of DTPA rights, such that the waiver provisions of the DTPA need be complied with; rather, it is a statement that no basis exists for the assertion of such rights. *Prudential,* 896 S.W.2d at 163-64. The court further held that the "as is" clause indicates the agreement of the buyer that there were no express or implied warranties, and that the seller's conduct did not harm, and would not harm him because the buyer was relying entirely upon his own examination of the property. *Id.* at 164. Accordingly, we hold that, here, as in *Prudential,* the "as is" clause can be used as a basis for summary judgment against the buyer as to his DTPA claims, and the seller need not comply with the waiver requirements of the DTPA.

Applicability of "As Is" Clause to the Bynums' Minor Children

The Bynums contend that, because their minor children do not have capacity to contract and were not parties to the agreement, they should not be bound by the "as is" clause.

Under the DTPA, a plaintiff must have standing as a consumer in order to assert rights. . . . Tex. Bus. & Com. Code Ann. § 17.50 and *Flenniken v. Longview Bank & Trust Co.,* 661 S.W.2d 705, 706 (Tex.1983). A plaintiff's standing as a consumer is established by his relationship with the transaction, not by a contractual relationship with the seller. *Kennedy v. Sale,* 689 S.W.2d 890, 892-93 (Tex. 1985), and *Flenniken,* 661 S.W.2d at 707. A third-party beneficiary can have standing to assert a cause of action under the DTPA if the transaction was intended to benefit the third party. *See Wellborn v. Sears, Roebuck & Co.,* 970 F.2d 1420, 1426-27 (5th Cir.1992) (son of woman who purchased garage door opener had standing to sue under the DTPA because the purpose of the purchase was to benefit the son).

In this case, even if the Bynum children are intended beneficiaries of the contract to purchase the home, such that they have standing to sue under the DTPA, there is no authority cited by the Bynums, or any authority that we could find, that would support the proposition that the Bynum children, as intended beneficiaries, would not be bound by the terms to the contract, such that the "as is" clause would not apply to them.

Generally, a third-party beneficiary will not have greater rights under a contract than the party who bargained for their benefit. Accordingly, because third-party beneficiaries are not entitled to greater contractual rights than were bargained for by the original parties to the contract, we hold that the Bynum children are not entitled to have the "as is" clause set aside on the ground that they were not parties to the contract.

NOTES & QUESTIONS

1) What is the test to determine whether an "as is" clause was the "basis of the bargain?" Is it a subjective or an objective standard?

2) Are "as is" clauses in adhesion or "boilerplate" contracts valid? Do these satisfy the "basis of the bargain" test?

3) What is the relationship between an "as is" defense and each of the following doctrines — "assumption of the risk," "contributory negligence," and "waiver?"

4) Does an "as is" clause extinguish a seller's statutory, "nondelegable duty" under a commercial or residential lease?

5) What is the connection between an "as is" clause and a "merger clause?" Consider the facts in *Oliver v. Ortiz*, 2008 WL 3166326, *2 (Tex.App.-Austin 2008):

> At closing, appellees paid appellants $180,000 in cash. The parties executed a "Commercial Lease" whereby appellees agreed to lease the store premises from appellees in exchange for monthly rent payments of approximately $1,500 for 157 months — $220,000 total— with the right to purchase the property at an amortized price. Appellees were also provided a "Bill of Sale" for the "Transferred Properties," defined as "Entire Inventory consisting of foodstuffs, perishable items, dry-goods, non-alcoholic beverages and all other items for resale o[n] the premises as of the date hereof." Of relevance to this appeal is the following provision of the Bill of Sale:
>
> WITH THE EXCEPTION OF THE WARRANTIES OF TITLE, INCLUDING THE WARRANTY THAT NO LIENS EXIST ON THE TRANSFERRED PROPERTIES EXCEPT AS RECITED, SELLER [the Olivers] HAS MADE NO AFFIRMATION OF FACT OR PROMISE RELATING TO THE TRANSFERRED PROPERTIES THAT HAS BECOME ANY BASIS OF THE BARGAIN, AND FURTHER, SELLER HAS MADE NO AFFIRMATION OF FACT OR PROMISE RELATING TO THE TRANSFERRED PROPERTIES THAT WOULD CONFORM TO ANY SUCH AFFIRMATION OR PROMISE. SELLER DISCLAIMS ANY WARRANTY OF FITNESS FOR ANY PARTICULAR PURPOSE WHATEVER WITH RESPECT TO THE TRANSFERRED PROPERTIES. THE TRANSFERRED PROPERTIES ARE SOLD ON AN "AS IS" BASIS.

Also pertinent are the following provisions of the Commercial Lease:

> 8. CONDITION OF PREMISES. Tenant [appellees] has EXAMINED AND ACCEPTS the leased premises and personal property in the present AS IS condition as suitable for the purposes for which the same are leased.
>
> * * *
>
> 33. PRIOR AGREEMENTS SUPERCEDED. This AGREEMENT constitutes the sole and only agreement of the parties to this lease and SUPERSEDES ANY PRIOR UNDERSTANDINGS OR WRITTEN OR ORAL AGREEMENTS between the parties respecting the subject matter of the lease. (The Merger Clause)

Appellees began operating the store. Within a week or two, according to appellees, they ascertained that store revenues were not close to what they contended appellants had led them to believe ("Fraudulent Representation").

E. *Mitigation-of-Damages and Duty-to-Settle Defenses*

The mitigation-of-damages doctrine requires an injured party to exercise reasonable care and to try to minimize his damages, if reasonable efforts will reduce the party's expenses. See *Cotten v. Weatherford Bancshares, Inc*., 187 S.W.3d 687, 708 (Tex. App.-Fort Worth 2006, pet. denied). Thus proof that an injured party failed to mitigate his damages is an affirmative defense. And that finding allows a defendant to reduce the amount of money that she has to pay once her liability has been established. *Austin Hill Country Realty, Inc. v. Palisades Plaza, Inc.,* 948 S.W.2d 293, 299-300 (Tex. 1997)

To be sure, on a number of occasions, the Texas Supreme Court has embraced defendants' arguments that aggrieved plaintiffs did not mitigate or try to mitigate their losses. For example, in *Moulton v. Alamo Ambulance Serv., Inc.,* 14 S.W.2d 444, 449 (Tex.1967), the injured party did not treat his injuries as a reasonable prudent person would have. Finding that the plaintiff did not behave like persons who experience "same or similar circumstances," the court reduced the defendant's liability. Also, in *Austin Hill Country Realty,* the Supreme Court of Texas embraced the defendant's defense and declared that "a landlord has a duty to make reasonable efforts to mitigate damages when [a] tenant breaches the lease and abandons the property, unless the commercial landlord and tenant contract otherwise." 948 S.W.2d at 300.

However, under Texas common law, an injured party has no duty to mitigate his losses by settling the lawsuit in a timely manner and receiving less money than the jury has awarded. On the other hand, the common law imposes a duty on liability insurers to settle claims when it is reasonably prudent to do so after third-party victims file claims and lawsuits against policyholders. This latter common-law duty is called the *Stowers* doctrine. See *G.A. Stowers Furniture Co. v. Am. Indem. Co*., 15 S.W.2d 544, 548 (Tex. 1929)

Before courts will impose a duty to settle on an insurer, an insured must establish: 1) the insured purchased third-party insurance to cover the victim's personal and property losses; 2) the third-party victim demanded a settlement within the financial limits under the policy; and 3) the third party offered reasonable settlement terms "that an ordinarily prudent insurer would accept it, considering the likelihood and degree of the insured's potential exposure to an excess judgment." *Am. Physicians Ins. Exch. v. Garcia*, 876 S.W.2d 842, 849 (Tex.1994). When these conditions are present and an insurer's negligent failure to settle a third-party claim produces an excess judgment against the insured, the insurer is liable. More specifically, under the *Stowers* doctrine, the liability insurer is liable for the entire amount of the judgment against its insured, including that part of the judgment that exceeds the policy limits. *G.A. Stowers Furniture Co.*, 15 S.W.2d at 548.

Arguably, the *Stowers doctrine* is a mitigation-of-damages doctrine. Stated simply, the rule forces a liability insurer to exercise prudence and settle a third-party lawsuit—on behalf of its insured—when there is a strong likelihood the insured will have to pay a judgment exceeding the amount the insurer promised to pay under the insurance contract. Now, assume that a DTPA defendant raises the following affirmative defense: The aggrieved consumer should not recover, because she failed to mitigate her damages by refusing to accept a reasonable and timely settlement. May the defendant successfully defend itself and reduce the amount of its financial exposure using that argument? Does the DTPA impose a statutory duty on an insurer to settle a claim or lawsuit on behalf of an insured consumer? This section will address these questions.

Pinson v. Red Arrow Freight Lines, Inc.
801 S.W.2d 14
(Tex.App.-Austin 1990)

Appellant Ron Pinson complains of the judgment of the district court of Bell County rendered after a jury trial. By its judgment, the district court ordered that Pinson recover $8,916.66 from appellee Red Arrow Freight Lines, Inc. for its violation of the Deceptive Trade Practices Act. Pursuant to the answers of the jury, the district court further rendered judgment that Pinson recover no attorney's fees.

Pinson and Red Arrow entered into an agreement by which Pinson would serve as Red Arrow's agent, or terminal manager, for its shipping business in Bell and Milam Counties. Pinson claimed, among other things, that Red Arrow promised him the exclusive business of several clients in that service area and that, once he had established his operation, neither Red Arrow nor any of its subsidiaries would venture into those two counties without compensating him. Pinson asserted further that he was guaranteed a minimum level of income from this operation when, in fact, it was a money-losing venture. Pinson alleged that Red Arrow's failure to carry out these promises violated the DTPA and was a producing cause of his losses.

The jury determined that Red Arrow's actions were a producing cause of Pinson's damages. On the other hand, the jury answered that Pinson failed to mitigate his damages and, that had he taken steps to mitigate, his losses would have been completely avoided.

Red Arrow moved for judgment that Pinson take nothing. Red Arrow grounded its motion upon the jury's answers to the questions concerning Pinson's failure to mitigate. The district court overruled Red Arrow's motion for judgment.

As the appeal reaches this Court, Pinson claims error by the court in failing to render judgment awarding him attorney's fees and Red Arrow asserts by cross-point that the court erred in rendering judgment for Pinson in light of the jury's determinations on the mitigation questions. We have concluded that Red Arrow's cross-point is dispositive of the appeal.

The question for resolution is whether a consumer under the DTPA owes a duty to mitigate his damages and, if he does, what are the consequences if the duty is breached.

In a DTPA suit, the prevailing plaintiff is entitled to "actual damages." Tex. Bus. and Com.Code § 17.50(b)(1) (1987). "Actual damages" are defined as those damages recoverable at common law. *W.O. Bankston Nissan v. Walters,* 754 S.W.2d 127, 128 (Tex.1988); *Brown v. American Transfer and Storage Co.,* 601 S.W.2d 931, 939 (Tex.1980)

The common law recognizes a duty on the part of an injured party to mitigate his damages.. Accordingly, we conclude that a claimant under the DTPA, likewise, owes a duty to minimize his losses.

When an injured party fails to comply with the duty to mitigate damages, recovery is not permitted as to that part of damages that could have been avoided or was incurred as a result of the failure to mitigate. The burden of proof with respect to whether the plaintiff failed to mitigate and the extent to which his failure to mitigate caused or increased the damages, is upon the party who caused the loss.

In the instant appeal, the jury determined that Pinson failed to mitigate his damages and that, had he done so, he would have suffered no loss. Accordingly, Pinson was not entitled to a judgment for damages. We sustain Red Arrow's cross-point.

The judgment is reversed and judgment is here rendered that Pinson take nothing.

DTPA § 17.5052 — Offers of Settlement

(a) A person who receives notice under Section 17.505 may tender an offer of settlement at any time during the period beginning on the date the notice is received and ending on the 60th day after that date.

(b) If a mediation under Section 17.5051 is not conducted, the person may tender an offer of settlement at any time during the period beginning on the date an original answer is filed and ending on the 90th day after that date.

(c) If a mediation under Section 17.5051 is conducted, a person against whom a claim under this subchapter is pending may tender an offer of settlement during the period beginning on the day after the date that the mediation ends and ending on the 20th day after that date.

(d) An offer of settlement tendered by a person against whom a claim under this subchapter is pending must include an offer to pay the following amounts of money, separately stated:

(1) an amount of money or other consideration, reduced to its cash value, as settlement of the consumer's claim for damages; and

(2) an amount of money to compensate the consumer for the consumer's reasonable and necessary attorneys' fees incurred as of the date of the offer.

(e) Unless both parts of an offer of settlement required under Subsection (d) are accepted by the consumer not later than the 30th day after the date the offer is made, the offer is rejected.

(f) A settlement offer tendered by a person against whom a claim under this subchapter is pending that complies with this section and that has been rejected by the consumer may be filed with the court with an affidavit certifying its rejection.

(g) If the court finds that the amount tendered in the settlement offer for damages under Subsection (d)(1) is the same as, substantially the same as, or more than the damages found by the trier of fact, the consumer may not recover as damages any amount in excess of the lesser of:

(1) the amount of damages tendered in the settlement offer; or

(2) the amount of damages found by the trier of fact.

(h) If the court makes the finding described by Subsection (g), the court shall determine reasonable and necessary attorneys' fees to compensate the consumer for attorneys' fees incurred before the date and time of the rejected settlement offer. If the court finds that the amount tendered in the settlement offer to compensate the consumer for attorneys' fees under Subsection (d)(2) is the same as, substantially the same as, or more than the amount of reasonable and necessary attorneys' fees incurred by the consumer as of the date of the offer, the consumer may not recover attorneys' fees greater than the amount of fees tendered in the settlement offer.

(i) If the court finds that the offering party could not perform the offer at the time the offer was made or that the offering party substantially misrepresented the cash value of the offer, Subsections (g) and (h) do not apply.

(j) If Subsection (g) does not apply, the court shall award as damages the amount of economic damages and damages for mental anguish found by the trier of fact, subject to Sections 17.50 and 17.501. If Subsection (h) does not apply, the court shall award attorneys' fees as provided by Section 17.50(d).

(k) An offer of settlement is not an admission of engaging in an unlawful act or practice or liability under this subchapter. Except as otherwise provided by this section, an offer or a rejection of an offer may not be offered in evidence at trial for any purpose.

Gunn Infiniti, Inc. v. O'Byrne
996 S.W.2d 854
(Tex. 1999)

We are called upon to decide whether various offers made to a consumer before he sent a DTPA notice letter and filed suit entitled the seller to a jury instruction or question on mitigation of damages. We conclude that in a DTPA case, a defendant's offer that attempts to ameliorate an injury caused by its conduct may raise a fact question on an affirmative defense of mitigation if the offer did not require the plaintiff to release its claims. Because the offers in this case were offers of settlement that implicitly required the plaintiff to relinquish his claims, the seller was not entitled to a jury question on mitigation. However, we agree with the seller that there is no evidence to support the award of mental anguish damages. Accordingly, we reverse the judgment of the court of appeals and remand this case to that court for further proceedings consistent with this opinion.

I

Donald O'Byrne, a resident of Shreveport, Louisiana, was in the market for a black-with-tan-interior five-speed manual transmission 1993 Infiniti G-20. After he failed to find this particular car in Louisiana, O'Byrne called several Infiniti dealerships in Texas. As a part of his Texas search, he contacted Gunn Infiniti, Inc. in San Antonio. A sales representative at Gunn searched the dealership's inventory and found a car that fit O'Byrne's desires in the body shop where it was being repainted. The Gunn employee told O'Byrne that the dealership had the car he sought. O'Byrne asked the sales representative if the car had ever been damaged, and she told him, falsely, that it had not and that it was brand new.

O'Byrne booked a one-way flight to San Antonio to purchase the car. At the dealership, O'Byrne again asked if the car had been damaged, and the sales representative again told him that it had not, knowing that it had suffered some slight damage. The sales representative also told O'Byrne that the car had an air bag, and a sticker under the hood of the car indicated that the car was equipped with an air bag. But it was not. The original hood of the car had been replaced with the hood of a later model that did have an air bag.

One week after purchasing the car, O'Byrne noticed that the paint on the front of the car was over sprayed and rough. He also suspected that the hood had been removed because the bolts and hinges had been reworked and painted. O'Byrne immediately called Gunn Infiniti. After initial denials, the sales representative eventually admitted that the car had been damaged, repaired, and repainted.

Gunn Infiniti then attempted to find an exact replacement but was unable to locate one because the model year for that car had ended. Gunn Infiniti thereafter made a number of offers to O'Byrne. It offered to refund the purchase price along with any transportation costs O'Byrne had incurred. O'Byrne rejected that offer. Then, Gunn Infiniti offered to replace the damaged car with another one that was the same model but a different color and to pay $1,000. O'Byrne rejected that offer because he wanted a black Infiniti. Next, Gunn Infiniti offered to replace O'Byrne's car with a 1993-and-a-half year model and charge him the dealer invoice price for the additional equipment that was standard on the newer model. Apparently, the 1993 Infiniti G-20 did not come with an air bag or a sun roof, but these additions, among others, were standard on the 1993-and-a-half model. O'Byrne rejected that offer because he did not want to pay for the additional equipment.

Finally, Gunn Infiniti offered to have the vehicle shipped to San Antonio and to repaint it for free. O'Byrne wanted Gunn Infiniti to pay for having the car repainted in Shreveport and submitted an estimate. Gunn Infiniti refused that proposal because it thought the estimate was too high. Several months later, O'Byrne attempted to accept the previous offer of a full refund plus expenses, but Gunn Infiniti said that the offer was no longer available because O'Byrne had put several thousand miles on the car.

O'Byrne sued Gunn Infiniti, alleging fraud and violations of the Texas Deceptive Trade Practices-Consumer Protection Act (DTPA). At trial, Gunn Infiniti tendered a jury question on the issue of mitigation of damages, but the trial court refused to include the question in the jury charge. The jury returned a verdict for O'Byrne, finding that Gunn Infiniti had violated the DTPA, had engaged in knowing conduct under the DTPA, and had committed fraud. The jury awarded O'Byrne $10,500 in benefit-of-the-bargain damages, $11,000 in mental anguish damages, $50,000 in exemplary or additional DTPA damages, and attorney's fees. The trial court rendered judgment for O'Byrne based on the DTPA findings, adding $2,000 to the actual damages as the DTPA required at the time, for a total of $73,500 in actual and additional damages. Gunn Infiniti appealed on the grounds that, among other things, the trial court failed to submit a question on the issue of mitigation of damages and that there was legally insufficient evidence to support an award of mental anguish damages. The court of appeals affirmed.

We first consider Gunn Infiniti's argument that it is entitled to a new trial because of the trial court's failure to submit the issue of mitigation to the jury.

II

As an initial matter, O'Byrne contends that the settlement-offer provisions of the DTPA foreclose the application of common-law mitigation principles. We disagree. Nothing in the DTPA evidences a legislative intent to withdraw mitigation of damages as an affirmative defense, even when a defendant alleges that the consumer failed to mitigate by failing to accept the defendant's offer to mitigate. Nor does the concept of mitigation inherently conflict with the DTPA.

The DTPA causes of action in this case are governed by the Act as it existed before the 1995 amendments. Former section 17.505 contained procedures under which a defendant could potentially limit the damages recovered by a plaintiff who rejected a settlement offer. Those procedures were largely reenacted in what is now section 17.5052 of the DTPA. Tex. Bus. & Com. Code § 17.5052. However, because there are some differences in the language used in the current statute and that used in its predecessor, we will refer only to former section 17.505.

The settlement-offer mechanism of former section 17.505 and the common-law doctrine of mitigation have some principles in common, but they nevertheless embody distinct concepts. The DTPA settlement-offer provisions of former section 17.505 were designed to limit the total amount of damages that a consumer could recover. They were not designed to mitigate damages that a consumer might otherwise suffer. *See* former Tex. Bus. & Com. Code § 17.505(d). A seller who committed a deceptive act or engaged in deceptive trade practices could attempt to avoid the punitive provisions of the DTPA, even after demand was made or suit was filed, by making a settlement offer that would compensate the consumer for actual damages. Under former section 17.505, the consumer's actual damages are to be determined by the trier of fact without reference to the settlement offer.

Under mitigation principles, the long-standing law of this state requires a claimant to mitigate damages if it can do so with "'trifling expense or with reasonable exertions.'" *Great Am. Ins. Co. v. North Austin Mun. Util. Dist. No. 1,* 908 S.W.2d 415, 426 (Tex. 1995), quoting *Walker v. Salt Flat Water Co.,* 96 S.W.2d 231, 232 (Tex. 1936). The duty to mitigate often is not dependent on an offer from the wrongdoer. And a consumer may have the opportunity to mitigate his or her damages immediately after the deceptive act or practice occurred, well before any DTPA notice letter is sent or suit is filed.

Nothing in the DTPA suggests that the Legislature intended to abrogate this aspect of the common law. Nor does the DTPA suggest that a defendant should be discouraged from offering to mitigate damages before a consumer sends a DTPA notice letter or files suit. A defendant may see the error of its ways promptly after the deceptive or unconscionable act occurred and seek to forestall all or at least some of the damages suffered by a consumer. Requiring a plaintiff to mitigate when a reasonably prudent person would do so is not at odds with the settlement mechanism contained in the DTPA.

Other differences between a DTPA settlement offer and the common-law duty to mitigate are the applicable time periods and whether a jury as opposed to a court determines the effect of a defendant's offer. But, here again, these differences do not result in a conflict or even tension between the DTPA and the common-law duty to mitigate. Under former section 17.505, a defendant such as Gunn Infiniti could make a settlement offer to a plaintiff only within defined periods after the plaintiff sent written notice or filed suit. *See* former Tex. Bus. & Com. Code § 17.505(c). If the plaintiff rejected the settlement offer, the defendant could file it with the trial court along with an affidavit confirming the rejection. *See id.* § 17.505(d). After trial, if the court found that the amount offered was the same as or substantially the same as the actual damages found by the trier of fact, then the plaintiff's recovery was limited to the lesser of the settlement offer or the actual damages found at trial. The settlement offer was not admissible as evidence in a jury trial.

We cannot agree with O'Byrne that the DTPA settlement-offer provisions supplant any common-law duty to mitigate if a defendant offers to alleviate some or all of a consumer's damages. Nor can we divine any reason for exempting DTPA damage claims from a duty to mitigate. Although the issue has never been squarely addressed by this Court, we observed in *Arthur Andersen & Co. v. Perry Equipment Corp.,* 945 S.W.2d 812 (Tex.1997), that "a [DTPA] plaintiff's recovery of damages [can be] limited . . . by the defendant's evidence of the plaintiff's failure to reasonably mitigate losses." *Id.* at 817. While that observation was not central to our holding, we note that some courts of appeals have considered the issue and have reasoned that, because the "actual damages" available under the DTPA before its amendment in 1995 were those available at common law, the "duty to mitigate" or the "doctrine of avoidable consequence" applies to the DTPA. We likewise hold that a plaintiff in a DTPA case has the same duty to mitigate damages as in other cases.

We turn to Gunn Infiniti's contention that the offers it made to O'Byrne entitled it to an instruction or jury question regarding mitigation.

III

Gunn Infiniti contends that the offers it made to O'Byrne raise a fact question on whether he failed to mitigate his damages, particularly his mental anguish damages. Gunn takes the position that none of its offers required O'Byrne to release his claims but that even if they had done so, a jury should be permitted to decide whether O'Byrne failed to mitigate.

The duty to mitigate has not generally included a duty that the claimant relinquishes its right to have its claims heard and resolved by a court. In breach of contract cases, it is well-settled that a plaintiff is not required to accept offers from the breaching party if they are "conditioned on surrender by the injured party of his claim for breach."

We recognize that when there is a claim for ongoing mental anguish damages, a claimant may actually increase his or her damages by rejecting a settlement offer that would put an end to the dispute. Gunn Infiniti insists that is the case here. At trial, O'Byrne sought mental anguish damages for the three years intervening between his purchase of the car and the date of trial. O'Byrne testified that his anguish was continuing and worsened over time because the car was a thorn in his side and because he was sickened each time that he saw or drove it. Gunn Infiniti counters that it offered to remove this thorn by taking the car back and refunding the purchase price, replacing the car with a red one, or repainting the car that O'Byrne bought. Gunn points out that the mental anguish damages continued to mount after these offers were rejected and then, at trial, the $50,000 in additional damages awarded by the trial court under former section 17.50(b)(1) of the DTPA were partially based on the alleged mental anguish.

The answer to Gunn Infiniti's argument is that each of its offers would raise a fact question for the jury on mitigation if the offers were indeed unconditional offers to mitigate damages rather than offers of settlement. If O'Byrne could have accepted any one of Gunn Infiniti's offers and still could have pursued claims at trial, then the jury could weigh all the evidence and reach a decision on mitigation. But foreclosing a plaintiff from pursuing suit is not mitigation. If a defendant is truly offering to mitigate, the offer cannot implicitly or explicitly seek a release of the plaintiff's claims. It must be an unconditional offer to mitigate.

We also note that whether an offer raises a fact question regarding mitigation does not turn, as the court of appeals indicated, on whether the offer would afford full relief to the plaintiff. In some circumstances, a defendant may offer to mitigate some but not all of a plaintiff's damages. For instance, if the car that O'Byrne purchased had also been defective and would not run, and if Gunn Infiniti had offered to loan him a replacement car for a period of time, this would be evidence of mitigation of some but not all damages. Or, in an example more similar to the facts of this case, if Gunn Infiniti had made an offer to mitigate, rather than to settle, by offering to replace the black G-20 with another car and if O'Byrne had accepted that offer, O'Byrne could still sue for consequential damages. Such damages might include his airfare to San Antonio, any mental anguish damages that might be legally recoverable, any uncompensated direct damages if the car that Gunn substituted had a value less than the value that the original car would have had if it had been as represented, and additional damages offered by the DTPA.

It would be problematic from a practical standpoint if a defendant's right to a question or instruction on mitigation turned on whether a settlement offer would have fully compensated the plaintiff. At the time when a trial court must decide whether to submit a mitigation question or instruction, there has not been a determination by the factfinder of the amount necessary to make the plaintiff whole. Therefore, it would be impossible in many cases for a court to determine if the settlement offer equaled or exceeded the plaintiff's damages.

In sum, we hold that when a defendant seeks a question or instruction regarding mitigation based on its own offer to a claimant, the defendant is entitled to that question or instruction only if the offer was clearly one for mitigation rather than settlement. We next consider whether any of Gunn Infiniti's offers to O'Byrne were of this nature.

IV

At various times, Gunn Infiniti made four offers to O'Byrne. Gunn's sales manager confirmed in his testimony that all four offers were attempts to "settle with Mr. O'Byrne." O'Byrne similarly testified that each of these offers were offers to settle with him and that in some instances, he made counteroffers that were rejected by Gunn Infiniti. Gunn argues that the use of the words "settle" or "settlement" cannot be taken literally and that there is a fact question about whether any of its offers were for mitigation rather than for settlement purposes.

While the word "settle" can mean "different things in different connections," it has a distinct connotation in the context of a dispute. When parties agree to settle their differences, this is commonly understood as fully resolving those differences. . . . Gunn Infiniti's offers implicitly if not explicitly required O'Byrne to release his claims. The trial court did not err in refusing to submit an instruction or question on mitigation, and retrial of the DTPA issue is not in order.

Perry Homes v. Alwattari
33 S.W.3d 376
(Tex.App.-Fort Worth 2000)

In this case we must decide once again whether the limitations on damages and defenses to liability provided to contractors in the Residential Construction Liability Act (RCLA) — Tex. Prop.Code Ann. §§ 27.001-.007 — apply to a homeowner's suit against a contractor for damages caused by a construction defect, when the contractor fails to make a reasonable written offer of settlement. We hold that the limitations on damages and defenses to liability do not apply in such a situation. We further hold that appellees' Deceptive Trade Practices Act (DTPA) — Tex.Bus. & Com.Code Ann. §§ 17.41-.63 — claim is not preempted by the RCLA under the facts of this case. We modify the trial court's judgment to delete the award to appellees for costs of repairs under the DTPA. We affirm the remainder of the judgment, as modified.

I. BACKGROUND FACTS

Appellees Aziz and Hajer Alwattari bought a new home in Arlington, Texas, constructed by appellant Perry Homes. The Alwattaris signed an earnest money contract in December 1991 to buy the house for $199,500. Prior to closing in January 1992, the Alwattaris received a warranty from Home Owners Warranty Corporation. In late 1992, the Alwattaris noticed hairline cracks in the walls and expansion joints of the house and contacted Perry Homes. Perry Homes sent David Redd to inspect the property and take elevation measurements. Redd reported to Perry Homes that there had been some shifting in the foundation.

In 1994, the Alwattaris were replacing the damaged flooring in their kitchen, when they noticed a crack in the foundation. Upon further inspection, Redd found additional settlement under the foundation. On August 31, 1994, Mr. Alwattari sent a letter to Perry Homes' warranty department and asked what remedial actions should be taken. Perry Homes sent Bill Ford to the house to investigate the Alwattaris' concerns. Based on Ford's findings, Perry Homes began performing cosmetic repairs to the house, which were needed due to the shifting of the foundation, and informed the Alwattaris that the "process will take 2-3 months." The Alwattaris continued to discover cracks in their walls and kitchen floor.

On December 7, 1995, the Alwattaris, through their lawyer, sent a letter to Perry Homes demanding that Perry Homes pay for an engineering report, the cost of any necessary repairs, temporary housing for the Alwattaris during the repairs, the reduction in the house's market value, and the Alwattaris' attorneys' fees. Less than a week later, the Alwattaris sued Perry Homes for breach of contract, violations of the DTPA, negligence, and gross negligence. On January 10, 1996, Perry Homes had a structural engineer inspect the Alwattaris' house. Based on the engineer's findings, Perry Homes responded to the Alwattaris' demand letter on January 23 with the following written offer of settlement:

Foundation Complaint. With regard to the foundation movement, twenty (20) piers will be installed starting at the northwest corner of the house continuing along the east side of the house and two-thirds (⅔) of the way along the south side of the house. The concrete piers will be twelve (12) inches in diameter with a twenty-four (24) inch underream. The concrete piers will be installed to approximately ten (10) feet below the surface. The total cost for piering approximately will be $7,000.00. At the time the piers are installed, any hairline crack in the foundation one thirty-second (1/32) of an inch in width or larger will be filled in with epoxy.

Perry Homes will pay sixty percent (60%), i.e. $4,200.00, of the total cost of installing the piers by way of a joint check payable to the Alwattaris and the independent contractor hired to perform the installation. The Alwattaris will pay the other forty percent (40%), i.e. $2,800.00, of the total cost of installing the piers. The Alwattaris will submit a proper claim regarding the foundation repair to Home Owners Warranty Corporation (HOW) in accordance with the terms of their Home Owners Warranty Program. Perry Homes will receive a copy of all documents sent to and received from HOW regarding the Alwattari's claim. If the claim is accepted, Perry Holmes will not be required to reimburse the Alwattaris for the $2,800.00 paid by them towards installation of the piers. It is Perry Homes' ... understanding that HOW is paying forty percent (40%) on all accepted claims. Therefore, the coverage provided by HOW will cover the additional $2,800.00 required to install the piers. If, however, the claim is rejected, Perry Homes will reimburse the Alwattaris for their $2,800.00 contribution.

Cosmetic Complaints. Three (3) months after the piers have been installed, Perry Homes or an independent professional engineer will reinspect the house and will, within one (1) month of the reinspection, repair all cosmetic items related to any foundation movement or the foundation repair process.

Attorneys' Fees. Because suit was filed before Perry Homes was sent a formal demand letter, Perry Homes is unwilling to pay the $1,500.00 demanded by you. In order to resolve this matter, Perry Homes will pay the Alwattaris $750.00 for attorneys' fees.

After receiving this offer, the Alwattaris began settlement negotiations with Perry Homes. Sometime later, they hired their own engineer, Gary McHale, to inspect the house. McHale determined that the Alwattaris' foundation was not performing adequately. A year later, McHale returned and determined that the foundation remained unchanged and had not settled any further.

In May 1997, the Alwattaris demanded that Perry Homes repair the foundation without requiring the Alwattaris to execute a release of their claims. Perry Homes then hired a foundation repair company to make approximately $10,000 worth of repairs. Perry Homes paid for the entire cost of the repairs. By the following month, Perry Homes had completed all of the repairs the Alwattaris demanded in accordance with McHale's report.

On July 21, 1997, McHale sent a letter to the Alwattaris stating that the structural repairs had been completed and that "the foundation repairs appear to have been properly completed." Perry Homes began making further cosmetic repairs in September 1997 and had substantially completed them at the time of trial in December 1997.

* * *

III. The Verdict and Judgment

The jury found that Perry Homes did not make a reasonable written offer of settlement and, therefore, did not answer the special questions related to the damage elements for the Alwattaris' RCLA claim. In answering the special questions on the Alwattaris' other submitted claims, however, the jury found that Perry Homes was negligent and that it had violated the DTPA by acting unconscionably, by breaching the warranty of good workmanship, and by engaging in such conduct knowingly.

The jury awarded the Alwattaris $1,557.39 in actual expenses, $10,000 for the diminution in fair market value of their home in its repaired condition, $5,000 for Perry Homes' knowing conduct, and $35,000 in attorneys' fees. Based on the Alwattaris' election to recover on the DTPA findings, the trial court doubled the first $1,000 of actual damages based on the jury's knowing conduct finding and rendered judgment awarding the Alwattaris total damages in the amount of $18,557.39 and $35,000 in attorneys' fees.

IV. Summary of Issues on Appeal

Perry Homes asserts that the Alwattaris are precluded from recovery under the DTPA because the preemptive provision of the RCLA applies to their construction defect claim. Specifically, Perry Homes contends that it made a reasonable written settlement offer as a matter of law and that the Alwattaris should take nothing on their RCLA claim because the Alwattaris unreasonably rejected its offer and presented no evidence to support recovery of the reasonable cost of repairs necessary to cure the defect. Perry Homes attacks other parts of the judgment and jury verdict, including multiple issues asserting that the trial court's judgment should be reversed because the jury's DTPA findings are not supported by the evidence.

Relying on our decision in *O'Donnell v. Roger Bullivant of Texas, Inc.,* 940 S.W.2d 411 (Tex. App.-Fort Worth 1997, writ denied) (op. on reh'g), four *amici curiae* argue that the RCLA applies to the Alwattaris' claims, even if Perry Homes did not make a reasonable written settlement offer, and that the effect of Perry Homes' failure to make a reasonable offer is that the limitation on the amount of damages provided for in subsection 27.004(i) does not apply. *Amici* argue, however, that under the controlling precedent of *O'Donnell,* the limitations on the types of damages provided for in subsection 27.004(h) apply to the Alwattaris' claims.

The Alwattaris also cite *O'Donnell* as authority for the opposite proposition that the RCLA's preemptive provisions do not apply, because the jury correctly found that Perry Homes failed to make a reasonable written settlement offer. They contend that the jury's DTPA verdict is supported by the evidence and that the judgment of the trial court should be affirmed.

V. The RCLA

The RCLA applies to "any action to recover damages resulting from a construction defect, except a claim for personal injury, survival, or wrongful death or for damage to goods." Tex. Prop. Code Ann. § 27.002(a). In enacting the RCLA, the legislature specifically provided that the RCLA would prevail "[t]o the extent of conflict between this chapter and any other law, including the Deceptive Trade Practices-Consumer Protection Act." Thus, a claim that exists solely by virtue of alleged construction defects falls exclusively within the RCLA. A homeowner, however, may bring other claims that do not conflict with the remedial purpose of the RCLA. *Bruce v. Jim Walters Homes, Inc.*, 943 S.W.2d 121, 123-24 (Tex.App.-San Antonio 1997, writ denied) (holding RCLA does not preempt common law fraud claims).

Under the RCLA, a homeowner who complains of a construction defect must give the contractor written notice of the claim. Tex. Prop.Code Ann. § 27.004(a). The contractor then has 45 days to make a written offer to settle the claim. *Id.* § 27.004(b). If a homeowner unreasonably rejects a contractor's written offer of settlement or refuses to permit the contractor a reasonable opportunity to repair the defect, the homeowner's total recovery is limited to the reasonable cost of the repairs that are necessary to cure the construction defect, plus the amount of reasonable and necessary attorneys' fees and costs incurred before the o0ffer was rejected or considered rejected. *Id.* § 27.004(f). Otherwise, the RCLA limits the homeowner's recovery to the following damages proximately caused by the construction defect:

(1) the reasonable cost of repairs necessary to cure any construction defect that the contractor failed to cure;
(2) the reasonable expenses of temporary housing reasonably necessary during the repair period;
(3) the reduction in market value, if any, to the extent the reduction is due to a structural failure; and;
(4) reasonable and necessary attorney's fees. *Id.* § 27.004(h).

Under subsection 27.004(i), however, the total damages that a homeowner may recover against a contractor may not exceed the purchase price of the residence. The limitations on damages and defenses to liability provided for in section 27.004 do not apply if the contractor fails to make a reasonable written settlement offer or otherwise cure the defect in the manner prescribed by the RCLA. Specifically, subsection 27.004(g) provides:

> If a contractor fails to make a reasonable offer under this section, or fails to make a reasonable attempt to complete the repairs specified in an accepted offer made under this section, or fails to complete, in a good and workmanlike manner, the repairs specified in an accepted offer made under this section, the limitations on damages and defenses to liability provided for in this section shall not apply. Id. § 27.004(g)

VI. Perry Homes' Settlement Offer

We first address Perry Homes' contention that it made a reasonable written offer of settlement to the Alwattaris as a matter of law within 45 days after receiving the December 7, 1995 written notice of the Alwattaris' complaints. As noted above, if Perry Homes made a reasonable settlement offer as a matter of law, it is entitled to the benefit of the limitations on damages and defenses to liability provided for in section 27.004.

A "matter-of-law" point is used when there is an adverse finding on an issue that the appellant had the burden of proving and the issue is conclusively established by the evidence. *Sterner v. Marathon Oil Co.*, 767 S.W.2d 686, 690 (Tex.1989). In reviewing a matter-of-law point, we first examine the record for evidence that supports the adverse finding while ignoring all evidence to the contrary. *Victoria Bank & Trust Co. v. Brady,* 811 S.W.2d 931, 940 (Tex.1991). If no evidence supports the adverse finding, we then examine the entire record to determine whether the evidence conclusively establishes all vital facts in support of the proposition as a matter of law. Id. If the issue is established conclusively by the evidence, the point must be sustained.

The evidence shows that the Alwattaris purchased their house in 1992. Less than one year later, the house began to show signs of structural damage due to shifting in the foundation. The damage, which included cracks in the foundation, the walls, and the floors, worsened over the next four years. Although Perry Homes knew of these problems, it only volunteered to perform cosmetic repairs until it received the Alwattaris' demand letter in January 1996.

In response to the Alwattaris' demand, Perry Homes offered to perform structural repairs to the foundation, but required the Alwattaris to pay 40% of the cost of the repairs out of their own pocket with a promise of future reimbursement, conditioned on whether their claim was paid by their homeowner's warranty. Perry Homes also conditioned its offer on the Alwattaris' executing a full release of their claims. We hold this is some evidence to support the jury's finding that Perry Homes' settlement offer was unreasonable. We must now determine the effect of this finding on the Alwattaris' RCLA action.

VII. *O'Donnell v. Roger Bullivant of Texas, Inc.*

We first addressed the resulting effect of a contractor's failure to make a reasonable settlement offer on a homeowner's RCLA action in *O'Donnell.* In that case, the homeowners sued their contractor for faulty foundation repairs to their home. The O'Donnells asserted causes of action for negligence, gross negligence, product liability, breach of warranty, breach of contract, and violations of the DTPA.

* * *

After first concluding that the defect was a "construction defect" as defined by the RCLA, we held the RCLA did, indeed, apply to the O'Donnells' claims. We further held that Bullivant's settlement offer was unreasonable as a matter of law, and that, under the "clear and unambiguous" language of subsections 27.004(f), (g), (h), and (i), the effect of the unreasonable settlement offer was that the limitation on the amount of damages provided for in subsection 27.004(i) did not apply. We, therefore, sustained, in part, the O'Donnells' point complaining of the trial court's application of the RCLA to their case, reversed the trial court's summary judgment limiting the O'Donnells' recovery to the amount of the purchase price of their home, and remanded the case to the trial court for further proceedings consistent with our opinion.

The language of section 27.004 is no less clear and unambiguous today than when we decided *O'Donnell*. However, we erred in *O'Donnell* by construing the language of subsection 27.004(g) to mean that only the limitation on the amount of damages provided for in subsection 27.004(i) does not apply when the contractor fails to make a reasonable settlement offer. Instead, subsection 27.004(g) obviously encompasses all "limitations on damages and defenses to liability provided for in this section"-both the limitation on the amount of damages provided for in subsection 27.004(i) and the limitation on the types of damages provided for in subsection 27.004(h).

We, therefore, hold that, under subsection 27.004(g), the effect of a contractor's failure to make a reasonable settlement offer is that the contractor loses the benefit of all limitations on damages and defenses to liability provided for in section 27.004, including both the limitation of subsection 27.004(h) on the types of damages recoverable by a homeowner and the limitation of subsection 27.004(i) on the amount of damages recoverable by a homeowner. We overrule *O'Donnell* to the limited extent that it may be interpreted as holding, either expressly or impliedly, that the only limitation on damages that does not apply when a contractor fails to make a reasonable settlement offer is the limitation on the amount of damages provided for in subsection 27.004(i).

Because the jury in this case failed to find that Perry Homes' written settlement offer was reasonable, the limitations on the types and amounts of damages and the defenses to liability that would otherwise be available to Perry Homes under section 27.004 of the RCLA do not apply, and, therefore, there is no conflict with the DTPA. Accordingly, the Alwattaris' DTPA cause of action is not preempted.

* * *

IX. Conclusion

We hold that because Perry Homes' settlement offer was unreasonable, the limitations on the types and amounts of damages and the defenses to liability that are available to a contractor under section 27.004 of the RCLA do not apply; thus, the Alwattaris' cause of action under the DTPA is not preempted by the RCLA.

We further hold that there is sufficient evidence to support the Alwattaris' recovery under the DTPA for Perry Homes' unconscionable conduct and that diminution in fair market value after repairs is a proper measure of damages under the DTPA. However, we modify the judgment to delete the award of $1,557.39 for costs of repairs, plus the prejudgment interest awarded on that amount, because there is no evidence that the amount of $1,557.39 is reasonable. The remainder of the judgment is affirmed, as modified. Tex. R. App. P. 43.2(b).

F. Merger Doctrine and Parol Evidence Rule

Consider the following presentation, which briefly outlines Texas's law regarding the parol evidence rule and the merger doctrine. Note especially the interrelationship between the two doctrines. Then, read the Texas Supreme Court's decisions appearing in this section and determine whether the doctrine of merger and the parol evidence rule apply under the DTPA.

Suggestions for Avoiding Parol Evidence Problems —Merger Clauses
49 Texas Practice, Contract Law § 8.9
David R. Dow and Craig Smyser

Because parol evidence is not admissible if a contract is fully integrated, the most important task for a lawyer drafting a contract is to indicate unmistakably whether it is fully integrated. The device used to indicate that the contract is fully integrated is the so-called merger clause. A typical merger clause states:

> This contract contains the entire agreement between (or among) the parties. There are no promises, understandings, agreements, representations, or warranties between (or among) the parties other than those specified within this writing.

Although a merger clause will not bar the introduction of all extrinsic evidence, it is the single most useful device for warding off in advance parol evidence difficulties.

At times courts suggest that there is a legal presumption that prior oral or written agreements merge into the final written agreement, even in the absence of a merger clause, but this reasoning is faulty. For one thing, parol evidence would be required to show the antecedent oral agreements that presumably merged into the final written expression. In any case, this so-called presumption is rarely invoked, and the more prudent manner for contract drafters to proceed is to include an express merger clause.

Weitzel v. Barnes
691 S.W.2d 598
(Tex. 1985)

This Deceptive Trade Practices-Consumer Protection Act case presents three major issues. First, does the parol evidence rule prevent proof of an oral representation as to the quality of goods when a written contract of sale gives the buyer the right to inspect those goods before purchase? Second, must a consumer show that the seller was motivated by trickery, artifice, or device, in making the representation as to the quality of the goods? Third, before a consumer can recover, is it necessary that he plead and prove that he relied upon such representation? Incidental to these three questions is whether a consumer is obligated to plead specifically the DTPA section he contends was violated; whether corporate agents may be individually liable under the DTPA; and whether error as to the reasonableness and necessity of repair bills was preserved.

Dennis and Lori Weitzel signed a contract on February 8, 1983, to purchase a remodeled home from Barnes/Segraves Development Company. The written contract of purchase gave the Weitzels the right to inspect, among other things, the plumbing and air conditioning systems in the house. If the Weitzels were dissatisfied with the systems, they were entitled to reject the contract; force Barnes/Segraves to make repairs up to $1,000; or, consummate the purchase and make all repairs in excess of $1,000 themselves. The Weitzels did not inspect the house but alleged that they were induced to accept it because of oral Barnes/Segraves' representations that the plumbing and air conditioning complied with Fort Worth's code specifications. When the Weitzels found the equipment did not function properly, they brought suit for damages under the DTPA.

A trial to the court resulted in findings that the representations were made and that the systems did not comply with code standards. The judge also found the Weitzels' actual damages to be $1,116 and after trebling the first $1,000, rendered judgment for them for $3,116, together with $750 in attorney's fees. Concluding that each of the first three questions posed above must be answered affirmatively, the court of appeals reversed the judgment and rendered that the Weitzels take nothing. 678 S.W.2d 747 (Tex.App.1984). We reverse the judgment of the court of appeals and affirm the judgment of the trial court.

Although the court of appeals found for Barnes/Segraves on three separate grounds, Barnes/Segraves' only argument before this court is that if we reinstate the judgment for the Weitzels, we will do violence to all written contracts which provide that the purchaser takes "as is." Moreover, Barnes/Segraves concedes that common law contractual requirements are not applicable and proof of intent to misrepresent is not necessary. Nevertheless, we are required to address the bases of the court of appeals' holding.

While several other courts of appeals have also addressed the question of the admissibility of oral representations in a DTPA case when a written contract exists, this court has never written on that precise subject. Generally speaking, each of the other intermediate courts has held that the parol evidence rule was not applicable because purchasers were not seeking to change or contradict the terms of the contract but were relying upon deceptive oral representations as the basis of their suit. Tex.Bus. & Com.Code Ann. § 17.43 provides that the remedies under the DTPA are cumulative and in addition to other remedies; section 17.44 of the act provides that the act shall be liberally construed to protect consumers from deceptive business practices. Following such broad guidelines, we conclude that oral representations are not only admissible but can serve as the basis of a DTPA action. There was no effort on the part of the Weitzels to show a breach of contract by Barnes/Segraves. The oral misrepresentations, which were made both before and after the execution of the agreement, constitute the basis of this cause of action, so traditional contractual notions do not apply.

Relying upon language in *Town North National Bank v. Broaddus,* 569 S.W.2d 489, 494 (Tex.1978), the court of appeals held that absent trickery, artifice, or device on the part of Barnes/Segraves, the Weitzels, having waived their inspection rights, were bound by the express terms of the contract. *Town North* was not a DTPA case. "Trickery," "artifice," and "device" are but synonyms for intent to deceive or misrepresent. The Weitzels' claim in this case is simply that Barnes/Segraves represented to them that certain goods were of a particular standard, when in fact they were not. Such representation is deemed to be a deceptive act under the provisions of Tex. Bus. & Com.Code Ann. § 17.46(b)(7). We said in *Smith v. Baldwin,* 611 S.W.2d 611 (Tex.1980), that "[s]ubdivision (7) contains no requirement of proof of intent." *Id.* at 616. We hold that such provision likewise makes no requirement of proof of trickery, artifice, or device.

Similarly, the court of appeals has erred by reading into the DTPA a requirement of proof of reliance on the misrepresentation before a consumer can recover. We first note that Barnes/Segraves assigned no error in the court of appeals in respect to reliance. Therefore, any error has been waived. But, as the court of appeals chose to write on the necessity of reliance on a misrepresentation as a prerequisite to recovery, we are obliged to address the subject. We disapprove of the dicta in the court of appeals' opinion. Relief for consumers is contained within the provisions of Tex. Bus. & Com.Code Ann. § 17.50.

Subsection (a) thereof provides that a consumer may maintain an action, among other things, when there is proof of a deceptive act or practice under § 17.46(b) which is a producing cause of the consumer's actual damages. The operative words for our purposes are "producing cause." This provision of the act was added by amendments enacted by the legislature in 1979. It should be noted that the bill containing the amendments, as originally introduced, provided in § 17.50(a) that a consumer could maintain an action if he had sustained actual damages as a result of reliance on any of certain enumerated acts. In the process of passing the bill into law, that language was changed, and "producing cause," not "reliance," became the ultimate standard. Following the same principle utilized by us in *Big H Auto Auction, Inc. v. Saenz,* 665 S.W.2d 756 (Tex.1984), we conclude that the legislature specifically rejected reliance as an element of recovery.

As to the matter of pleadings, while it is true that the Weitzels did not allege any specific provision of the DTPA as having been violated, their pleadings unquestionably comport with § 17.46(b)(7). They alleged in paragraph IV of their original petition that Barnes/Segraves had represented to them that equipment and systems in the home were within Fort Worth code specifications, when in truth the representations were false, misleading and deceptive in that the air conditioner and water heater did not meet Fort Worth code specifications. Such pleading is all that is necessary. Moreover, we note Barnes/Segraves filed no special exceptions requesting the Weitzels to elaborate their pleadings. If there were a pleading defect, it would be properly attacked by special exceptions.

We are not unsympathetic with the argument made by Barnes/Segraves that the Weitzels should have no cause of action if they agreed to take the house "as is," subject to their right of inspection, which they failed to make. While it is conceivable that in certain situations silence could amount to a misrepresentation, had Barnes/Segraves elected to remain silent as to the quality of the relevant systems, the outcome of this case would have been different. That, however, is not our situation. In this instance, Barnes/Segraves affirmatively represented that the systems had qualities which they did not actually possess. Even under a contract allowing inspection, an affirmative misrepresentation is actionable under the DTPA.

Barnes/Segraves urged two additional points of error before the court of appeals, which were not addressed by that court. Because of our disposition of the case, it becomes necessary for us to consider those two points of error. The first point of error is that Michael Barnes and Patrick Segraves should not be liable in their individual capacities. We have examined the record and it contains evidence as to statements of both men upon which the trial judge could have relied in concluding that they each made oral misrepresentations. The trial judge so concluded in his findings of facts. While it is true that in *Light v. Wilson,* 663 S.W.2d 813 (Tex.1983), we exonerated a corporate agent from individual liability in a DTPA case, we did so on the basis that "[t]here is no finding of fact that Light, individually, violated the Deceptive Trade Practices Act." *Id.* at 814. Implicit in our holding in that case is that there can be individual liability on the part of a corporate agent for misrepresentations made by him.

The second complaint before the court of appeals that we find necessary to discuss is that there was no evidence as to the reasonableness and necessity of the cost of repair to bring the house up to code specifications. There was no objection made as to reasonableness and necessity when the trial judge admitted into evidence plaintiff's exhibits 1, 9 and 10, reflecting cost of repairs adding up to $1,116. Error, if any, in admitting those exhibits into evidence has been waived by failure to make a proper objection.

The judgment of the court of appeals is reversed and the judgment of the trial court is affirmed.

Alvarado v. Bolton
749 S.W.2d 47
(Tex. 1988)

Petitioner's motion for rehearing is granted and the court's opinion and judgment of November 25, 1987 are withdrawn and the following is substituted.

This suit for reformation of deeds and for damages under the Deceptive Trade Practices Act involves the issue of whether the doctrine of merger applies in a suit under the Act based on breach of an express warranty. After a jury trial, the district court rendered judgment for Alvarado reforming the deeds, awarding actual damages for the value of the oil production; trebling actual damages and awarding attorney's fees under the DTPA. The court of appeals reversed the judgment of the trial court and rendered a take-nothing judgment against Alvarado predicated on the holding that the doctrine of merger applied. We hold that the doctrine of merger is not applicable, reverse the judgment of the court of appeals and remand this cause to that court.

In 1973, Bolton, as general partner in a limited partnership, and others purchased fifty acres of land. In the deeds conveying the land, Bolton received title to one-half of the oil, gas and other minerals. Bolton, as trustee, then subdivided a portion of the land into twenty-six tracts and conveyed certain tracts to Alvarado and other buyers. Each earnest money contract involved in the conveyances to Alvarado and others contained the clause that Bolton agreed to deliver a general warranty deed and convey the property free and clear of all encumbrances except those named. Some of the contracts were silent regarding Bolton's outstanding one-half mineral interest and some stated that the conveyance was subject to Bolton's one-half mineral interest. However, the warranty deeds by which title was conveyed to the plaintiffs specifically reserved one-half of the mineral interest to Bolton, grantor, and were "made subject to all outstanding mineral interests of record in Fort Bend County" for the other one-half of the minerals.

After oil was discovered on the land, plaintiffs learned of Bolton's reservation of mineral interests and brought suit against Bolton for reformation of the deeds and for damages under the DTPA.

The jury found that: (1) David R. Bolton, Trustee, intended by the earnest money contracts to sell the minerals he owned; (2) David R. Bolton, Trustee, breached an express warranty in his earnest money contracts by reserving minerals in the deeds; and (3) the reservation of minerals by David R. Bolton, Trustee, in the deeds to the plaintiffs was a producing cause of economic loss to the plaintiffs. These findings support the judgment for Alvarado under the DTPA.

The doctrine of merger is stated in *Baker v. Baker,* 207 S.W.2d 244 (Tex.Civ.App.-San Antonio 1947, writ ref'd n.r.e.):

When a deed is delivered and accepted as performance of a contract to convey, the contract is merged in the deed. Though the terms of the deed may vary from those contained in the contract, still the deed must be looked to alone to determine the rights of the parties. *Id.* at 249, *quoting* 2 Devlin, Law of Deeds § 850a.

We hold, however, that the doctrine of merger is not applicable in the present case. In 1980 we stated that "[t]he DTPA does not represent a codification of the common law" and a primary purpose of the Act was to provide consumers a cause of action for deceptive trade practices without the numerous defenses encountered in a common law fraud or breach of warranty suit. *Smith v. Baldwin,* 611 S.W.2d 611, 616 (Tex.1980). Whether described as a rule of evidence or as a substantive defense, the doctrine of merger was used here as a substantive defense. However, it is not necessary to resolve that issue as we have previously held that under the broad guidelines of the DTPA, the parol evidence rule will not prevent admissibility of oral misrepresentations which may also serve as the basis of a DTPA action. *Weitzel v. Barnes,* 691 S.W.2d 598, 600 (Tex.1985).

In the instant case, the jury found that statements made in the earnest money contracts created a warranty which was later breached when the deeds reserved Bolton's mineral interest. The merger doctrine prevents the admission of any warranties made in the prior earnest money contracts which are contradicted in the deed. The parol evidence rule operates identically. Thus, we hold that the doctrine of merger may not be applied to defeat a cause of action under the DTPA for breach of an express warranty made in an earnest money contract and breached by deed.

In his remaining point of error, Alvarado complained that "the court of appeals erred in failing to address [his] fifth counter-point and cross-point, and in failing to render judgment for attorney's fees in accordance with appellees' pleadings and uncontroverted evidence." Since the court of appeals based its disposition on the doctrine of merger, it failed to address Alvarado's concern and Bolton's remaining points of error. . . .

We, therefore, reverse the judgment of the court of appeals and remand this cause to that court for consideration of those remaining points and disposition in accordance with this opinion.

G. Statute-of-Frauds Defense

A contract for the sale of goods valued at more than $500 is subject to the statute of frauds. Tex. Bus. & Com.Code Ann. § 2.201(a). Where a contract contains a mixture of sales and services, Section 2.201 applies if the sale of goods is the "dominant factor" or "essence" of the transaction. *See Cont'l Casing Corp. v. Siderca Corp.*, 38 S.W.3d 782, 787 (Tex. App.-Houston [14th Dist.] 2001, no pet.); *Westech Eng'g, Inc. v. Clearwater Constructors, Inc.*, 835 S.W.2d 190, 197 (Tex. App.-Austin 1992, no writ). But, the relevant question is clear: Does the statute of frauds apply to DTPA actions?

Of course, the statute of frauds itself does not mention the DTPA. But the DTPA covers transactions whose values are worth $500,000 or less. Also, to qualify as a "consumer" under the DTPA, a person does not have to produce a written contract that shows a "contractual relationship" between a buyer and seller. Again, one only needs to show that he has a "relationship to a transaction" to qualify as a consumer and to secure standing to commence a DTPA action. *Flenniken v. Longview Bank & Trust Co.*, 661 S.W.2d 705, 707 (Tex. 1983). And those transactions may involve promises. However, the statute of frauds clearly requires "a writing" before a court will enforce certain contracts or promises. This section discusses whether a DTPA defendant may successfully defend himself by raising the statute-of-frauds defense.

TEXAS STATUTE OF FRAUDS
TEX. BUS. & COM. CODE ANN. § 26.01
PROMISE OR AGREEMENT MUST BE IN WRITING

(a) A promise or agreement described in Subsection (b) of this section is not enforceable unless the promise or agreement, or a memorandum of it, is
  (1) in writing; and
  (2) signed by the person to be charged with the promise or agreement or by someone lawfully authorized to sign for him.

(b) Subsection (a) of this section applies to:
  (1) a promise by an executor or administrator to answer out of his own estate for any debt or damage due from his testator or intestate;

(2) a promise by one person to answer for the debt, default, or miscarriage of another person;
(3) an agreement made on consideration of marriage or on consideration of nonmarital conjugal cohabitation;
(4) a contract for the sale of real estate;
(5) a lease of real estate for a term longer than one year;
(6) an agreement which is not to be performed within one year from the date of making the agreement;
(7) a promise or agreement to pay a commission for the sale or purchase of:
 (A) an oil or gas mining lease;
 (B) an oil or gas royalty;
 (C) minerals; or
 (D) a mineral interest; and
(8) an agreement, promise, contract, or warranty of cure relating to medical care or results thereof made by a physician or health care provider as defined in Section 74.001, Civil Practice and Remedies Code. This section shall not apply to pharmacists.

Moritz v. Bueche
980 S.W.2d 849
(Tex.App.-San Antonio, 1998)

Nature of the Case

Appellants, who are fourteen former students of the now-defunct San Antonio School of Law (Students), appeal an order granting summary judgment in favor of appellee, Clifford Bueche (Bueche).The motion was brought, in part, under rule 166a(i) of the Texas Rules of Civil Procedure. We hold that the Students pointed out evidence in their response that raised a genuine issue of material fact on the elements of their claims challenged in the summary judgment motion. We reverse the trial court's judgment.

Facts and Procedural History

In 1993, the Students enrolled in the newly formed San Antonio School of Law, allegedly managed by Ken Bueche and his wife, Joan. Clifford Bueche is Ken Bueche's father. According to their pleadings, the Students were told at enrollment that the school would qualify them to take the Texas Bar Examination and that, within a year, the school would be qualified to award a juris doctor (J.D.) degree. The Students charge that Ken, Joan, and Bueche represented that law books had or would be purchased, that the Bueche family would erect a building to house classrooms, and that professional faculty and a full-time dean would be hired. Initially, the Students raised negligence, gross negligence, estoppel, and breach of contract claims, as well as DTPA and fraud claims. The case was eventually narrowed to the DTPA and fraud causes of action.

In his Second Amended Original Answer, Bueche made a general denial of all claims against him and raised several affirmative defenses: failure of consideration, statute of frauds, and the statute of limitations on punitive damages. Bueche also filed a motion for summary judgment, arguing that the Students failed to establish that Bueche had made any misrepresentations regarding the management or financing of the school. Bueche also argued that the Students had not established their status as consumers under the DTPA. Finally, Bueche asserted that the statute of frauds barred the Students' claims. In support of this motion, Bueche filed an affidavit denying any connection to the school other than a natural interest in his son's business.

The Students filed a joint response. Attached to the response were the affidavits of four of the Students, Jay Moritz, Ronald Bruner, Lauro Montalvo, and Simon Rubinsky. Each affidavit stated that Bueche made representations regarding the financing of the school, the purchasing of books, and/or the management of the school in general.

The trial court granted Bueche's motion for summary judgment, and the Students appeal in one point of error, arguing that genuine issues of material fact remain.

Standard of Review

We must initially resolve a dispute regarding the proper standard of review to be applied in this appeal. Bueche argues that the summary judgment should be reviewed under the standards governing the new no-evidence summary judgment rule. *See* Tex.R. Civ. P. 166a(i). The Students contend that the relevant portion of Bueche's summary judgment motion was based on the traditional summary judgment rules, and the judgment should be reviewed accordingly. *See* Tex. R. Civ. P. 166a(a), (b).

The motion for summary judgment is divided into several parts. Parts one and two provide a statement of the facts of the case and a description of the evidence provided in support of the motion. Part two concludes with a reference to the standard to be applied in a traditional summary judgment motion, stating: "All of said Summary Judgment evidence shows that there is no genuine issue as to any material fact and Movants are entitled to Summary Judgment as a matter of law and that Plaintiffs take nothing by their action."

Part three is entitled "Specific Grounds for Summary Judgment." This part addressed only the claims of common law fraud and DTPA violations. In this part, Bueche argued that the Students "failed to establish the necessary elements" of these claims. With regard to the fraud claim, Bueche asserted that the Students failed to offer any evidence that Bueche made a material misrepresentation. With regard to the DTPA claim, Bueche asserted that the Students failed to establish that they were consumers. Finally, Bueche asserted that any purported promise was not in writing and was unenforceable under the statute of frauds.

Part four of the motion for summary judgment is entitled, "Summary Judgment Pursuant to Rule 166a(i)." In this part, Bueche argued that no evidence supported Moritz's claims of *negligence, gross negligence, estoppel, breach of contract, and fraudulent conveyance.* This portion of the motion does not deal with the fraud and DTPA claims.

The Students argue that, because of the bifurcated nature of the summary judgment motion, the motion as to the DTPA and fraud claims could not have been granted under 166a(i) and must be reviewed as a traditional summary judgment. The implication of this argument is that the new Rule 166a(i) must be specified as the basis of summary judgment. There is merit to demanding such specificity since the trial court should be informed as to the nature of the movant's burden when deciding a motion for summary judgment. Bueche confused this issue by reciting the traditional summary judgment standard in one section and including a specific section exclusively referring to Rule 166a(i). However, since Bueche argued that the Students failed to establish a specific element of their fraud and DTPA claims, we believe the motion should be construed as a motion based on the absence of evidence to support an essential element of these claims. Since the statute of frauds is an affirmative defense, we review that issue under our traditional summary judgment standard.

Under traditional summary judgment standards, a party moving for summary judgment has the burden of establishing as a matter of law that no genuine issue of material fact exists as to one or more essential element of the plaintiff's cause of action or, if the motion is based on an affirmative defense, that the defense is established as a matter of law. *Casso v. Brand,* 776 S.W.2d 551, 556 (Tex. 1989); *Nixon v. Mr. Property Management Co.,* 690 S.W.2d 546, 548-49 (Tex. 1985). If the defendant meets this burden, the plaintiff must then raise a genuine issue of material fact on that element or must produce evidence raising a genuine issue of material fact in avoidance of the affirmative defense.

On reviewing a summary judgment, an appellate court accepts as true all evidence supporting the non-movant. *Nixon,* 690 S.W.2d at 549. All inferences are indulged in favor of the non-movant and all doubts are resolved in his favor. *Id.* Where, as here, the trial court does not state the grounds for granting the motion, and several grounds are provided, the reviewing court must determine if any of the grounds would support the judgment. *Rogers v. Ricane Enters., Inc.,* 772 S.W.2d 76, 79 (Tex. 1989)

We apply the same legal sufficiency standard in reviewing a no-evidence summary judgment as we apply in reviewing a directed verdict. A no-evidence summary judgment is improperly granted if the respondent brings forth more than a scintilla of probative evidence to raise a genuine issue of material fact. *Moore,* at 269; Tex. R. Civ. P. 166a(i). Less than a scintilla of evidence exists when the evidence is "so weak as to do no more than create a mere surmise or suspicion" of a fact. *Kindred v. Con/Chem, Inc.,* 650 S.W.2d 61, 63 (Tex. 1983). More than a scintilla of evidence exists when the evidence "rises to a level that would enable reasonable and fair-minded people to differ in their conclusions." *Havner,* 953 S.W.2d at 711.

Discussion

DTPA

Bueche's summary judgment motion also contended that the Students failed to establish the requisite elements of their DTPA claim. *See* Tex. Bus. & Com. Code Ann. § 17.46(b)(2), (3), (5), (7), (9), (23), and § 17.50(a)(1), (2), (3). Those elements are: (1) that the plaintiff is a consumer; (2) that the act was a producing cause of actual damages; and (3) that the act was prohibited by section 17.50(a)(1-4) of the Texas Business and Commerce Code. Bueche argued that the Students could not be consumers vis-vis him, because his son owned and operated the school and sold the services of the school. He stated there was no allegation that he authorized any statements made by his son. Bueche argued that any representation by his son reflected nothing more than Bueche's intent to *donate* money to the school. According to Bueche, a donation is not considered a purchase for purposes of the DTPA.

A consumer under the DTPA is one who "sought or acquired by purchase or lease." *See* Tex. Bus. & Com. Code Ann. § 17.45(4). To come within this definition, the plaintiff must have sought or acquired goods or services by purchase or lease, and those goods and services must be the basis of the complaint. *Cameron v. Terrell & Garrett, Inc.,* 618 S.W.2d 535, 539 (Tex.1981). A gratuitous act is not a purchased good or service under the Act.

While here, too, Bueche met his summary judgment burden by asserting that the Students failed to establish their status as consumers, an essential element of their DTPA claim, we find that the four affidavits filed in response to Bueche's motion raise issues of fact that should be determined by a jury. The affiants assert that Bueche's business, Elegant Marble Imports, was used for registration purposes. At least one of the affiants states that he mailed his tuition checks to that business. Another states that Bueche was personally grateful for the affiant's enrolling in the school. These statements raise a fact issue about whether the Students were consumers of services offered by Bueche.

The case cited by Bueche to support his claims that he was doing no more than *donating* money to the school is inapposite to this case. *See Nabours,* 673 S.W.2d at 362. In *Nabours,* the court of appeals determined that the appellee was not a consumer within the meaning of the DTPA because he had not paid consideration to the appellant. *Id.* at 362. Instead, the appellee had merely asked the appellant for consent to purchase a home, and that consent was gratuitous. *Id.*

In this case, the Students argue that registration and at least some payment of tuition was accomplished through Bueche's business. Whether Bueche gratuitously donated money to his son's enterprise is not dispositive of our inquiry into whether the Students were consumers; clearly they were. The Students need not be in contractual privity with Bueche in order to be consumers. *See Flenniken v. Longview Bank & Trust Co.,* 661 S.W.2d 705, 707 (Tex.1983); *Inglish v. Union State Bank,* 911 S.W.2d 829, 834 (Tex.App.-Corpus Christi 1995), *rev'd on other grounds,* 945 S.W.2d 810 (Tex.1997); *Allied Towing Serv. v. Mitchell,* 833 S.W.2d 577, 581 (Tex.App.-Dallas 1992, no writ).

Consumer status under the DTPA is defined by the plaintiff's relationship to the goods or services, not by his relationship to his opponent. *Mitchell,* 833 S.W.2d at 582. It is enough that the defendant have a relationship to the transaction and enjoy the benefits of that transaction. *Inglish,* 911 S.W.2d at 834. While the Students have not conclusively proven that Bueche has done so, the evidence that some payments were sent to Bueche's business, that he personally thanked students for enrolling in the school, and that he assumed a management position in his son's absence pointed out evidence that raised a fact issue on this element of their DTPA claim.

Statute of Frauds

Bueche argues that summary judgment was appropriate because the Students' claims are barred by the statute of frauds. *See* Tex. Bus. & Com.Code Ann. § 26.01(b)(2). Since statute of frauds is an affirmative defense, Tex. R. Civ. P. 94, Bueche retains the burden of conclusively establishing all the elements of the affirmative defense as a matter of law such that there is no genuine issue of material fact. We review whether the summary judgment was properly granted based on the statute of frauds under the traditional summary judgment standard.

According to Bueche, his alleged promise to help support the school financially amounted to a "promise to answer for the debt, default, or miscarriage of another person" and, as such, is not enforceable if not in writing. *See* Tex. Bus. & Com.Code Ann. § 26.01(b)(2) (Vernon 1987). We disagree for several reasons.

Initially, we note that, in its present posture, this is not a suit to enforce a contract. Instead, this suit is brought under theories of common law fraud and DTPA violations. This court has held that a DTPA claim is statutory, not contractual. *Webb v. International Trucking Co., Inc.,* 909 S.W.2d 220, 228 (Tex.App.-San Antonio 1995, no writ). In *Webb,* we held that such claims cannot be barred by the statute of frauds. *Id.* Other courts have recognized that, in some cases, DTPA claims may be so barred. *See Rodriguez v. Klein,* 960 S.W.2d 179, 183 (Tex.App.-Corpus Christi 1997, no writ); *Keriotis v. Lombardo Rental Trust,* 607 S.W.2d 44, 46 (Tex.Civ.App.-Beaumont 1980, writ ref'd n.r.e.). To determine whether the statute of frauds could bar these and common law fraud claims, those courts look at the relationship of the alleged promise to the purpose of the statute of frauds and the nature of the damages sought. *Keriotis,* 607 S.W.2d at 46 (DTPA claims); *Leach v. Conoco, Inc.,* 892 S.W.2d 954, 960 (Tex.App.-Houston [1st Dist.] 1995, writ dism'd w.o.j.) (fraud claims). Applying this analysis, we conclude the claims are not barred.

The purpose of the statute of frauds is to safeguard the integrity of contracts and to prevent fraud and perjury when those contracts are brought into court. *See Davis v. Crockett,* 398 S.W.2d 302, 305 (Tex.Civ.App.-Dallas 1965, no writ). Damages are sought pursuant to a breach of contract claim and amount to the benefit of the bargain. *Leach,* 892 S.W.2d at 960. The Students here do not seek the benefit of their bargain, or what they would have obtained had any promise been performed. Their final petition seeks return of their tuition, fees, time, and income; damages for mental anguish (not recoverable in a contract action); and attorneys fees. In addition, they sought exemplary damages. We do not believe that this suit can be properly characterized as a suit to enforce an agreement. *See U.S. v. Henderson,* 19 F.3d 917, 922 (5th Cir.1994) (statute of frauds cannot be used to facilitate execution of fraud); *Inman v. Wallace,* 558 S.W.2d 554, 556 (Tex.Civ. App.-Waco 1977, no writ) (statute of frauds does not apply where claim is not based upon oral promises or agreement but upon defendant's fraud in making the promise).

Even if the statute should apply to these claims, we do not construe the Students' allegations to be that Bueche served as a guarantor of his son's debts. As we read the allegations and the affidavits filed in support of the Students' summary judgment response, the Students claim that Bueche was a *participant* in the founding, financing, and management of the school. *See Keith v. Woodul,* 616 S.W.2d 375, 377 (Tex.Civ.App.-Texarkana 1981, no writ) (where promisor's leading purpose is to serve some interest of his own, his promise to accept the primary responsibility for the debt of another does not fall within the statute of frauds and is enforceable, even if oral). The Students do not characterize Bueche's promises as promises made to his son to guarantee his debt. Instead, the promises are to the Students-that the school would have books, facilities, financial support, and a future. We find that the statute of frauds is inapplicable to this case.

Conclusion

The affidavits attached to the Students' response to Bueche's motion for summary judgment pointed out evidence that raised genuine issues of material fact on the elements of the Students' fraud and DTPA claims that were challenged in the motion. We reverse the trial court's judgment and remand the cause for trial.

Smith v. Elliott
68 S.W.3d 844
(Tex. App.-El Paso 2002)

This appeal involves the application of the statute of frauds in an action against a physician for misrepresentation. Sherrie Smith appeals a directed verdict in favor of defendant, Theresa M. Elliott, M.D., on Smith's action brought under the Deceptive Trade Practices Act (DTPA), Tex. Bus. & Com.Code Ann. § 17.46(b)(23). We affirm.

Facts

Sherrie Smith consulted Dr. Theresa Elliott about breast reduction surgery. Smith sought the procedure because she was having back problems and wanted to improve her appearance.

Smith testified at trial that she was hesitant to undergo the procedure because she was worried about possible negative results. Elliott assured her, however, that the results would be favorable. Smith testified that Elliott told her that her breasts would "look good" and that she would be very pleased with the results; she might have scarring but such scarring would be "fine-line." Elliott showed her before and after photos of similar surgeries she had performed that showed such positive results. Smith had the surgery, but the results were not as expected. Her breasts and her nipples were different sizes and she had very noticeable scarring.

Smith brought suit against Elliott under various theories, including misrepresentation under the DTPA. Elliott affirmatively pleaded the defense of statute of frauds.

At trial, Smith presented two witnesses: herself and Pat Cole, her stepmother. After Smith rested, Elliott brought a motion for directed verdict on the ground that the statute of frauds barred Smith's claims. Smith seemingly abandoned some of her claims, maintaining that she was only pursuing the misrepresentation cause of action at trial. She argued, "And what-we're not claiming that there's a breach of contract where services weren't provided as were contracted for. Our cause of action is that there was deception, there was misrepresentation for the purpose of inducing a person, an ignorant consumer, to act to that person's detriment."

The trial court ruled against Smith and entered final judgment for Elliott on the basis of the statute of frauds. In its judgment, the trial court stated that it "rendered judgment as a matter of law in favor of the Defendant for the reason that Plaintiff failed to introduce any evidence in writing, signed by Dr. Elliott, relating to medical care or results thereof." Smith appeals. Her sole point of error complains that the directed verdict was error because evidence of a writing is not required in a claim for misrepresentation.

Standard of Review

A directed verdict for defendant is appropriate where plaintiff fails to present evidence raising a fact issue essential to plaintiff's right of recovery or where the evidence conclusively establishes a defense to the plaintiff's cause of action. *Prudential Ins. Co. of America v. Fin. Review Servs., Inc.,* 29 S.W.3d 74, 77 (Tex. 2000). In reviewing the grant of a directed verdict, we must consider all of the evidence in the light most favorable to the party against whom the verdict was instructed and disregard all evidence and inferences to the contrary. *Szczepanik v. First S. Trust Co.,* 883 S.W.2d 648, 649 (Tex.1994). Where there is conflicting evidence of probative value on any theory of recovery, an instructed verdict is improper and we must remand the case for jury determination of the issue. *Id.*

The DTPA, the MLIIA, the Statute of Frauds, and *Sorokolit*

The issue here is whether a DTPA plaintiff alleging misrepresentation, as Smith did, must show that the defendant doctor or health care provider made those representations in a signed writing where the defendant has properly raised the affirmative defense of the statute of frauds, as Elliott did. In answering this question, we look primarily to three sources: the MLIIA section 12.01(a); the Texas Supreme Court case of *Sorokolit v. Rhodes,* 889 S.W.2d 239, 243 n. 5 (Tex.1994); and the Statute of Frauds, Tex. Bus. & Com. Code Ann. § 26.01.

Section 12.01(a) of the Medical Liability and Insurance Improvement Act prohibits DTPA actions against physicians or health care providers for damages for personal injury or death caused by the physician's negligence. Tex. Rev. Civ. Stat. Ann. art. 4590i, § 12.01(a)

Despite the restrictions of the MLIIA, DTPA actions against physicians and health care providers are not categorically prohibited. In *Sorokolit v. Rhodes,* 889 S.W.2d 239 (Tex.1994), the Texas Supreme Court held that MLIIA, while precluding DTPA suits against physicians based in negligence, does not prohibit DTPA suits based upon breach of express warranty or misrepresentation in cases where a physician guaranteed a particular result. *Id.* at 242-43. *Sorokolit* involved facts very similar to those here: plaintiff alleged that Dr. Sorokolit told her to choose a photograph of a nude model from a magazine, and promised that he would make her breasts look like those in the photo she selected. The results were not as guaranteed, and Rhodes sued Sorokolit for malpractice, breach of implied and express warranties under the DTPA, and knowing misrepresentation under the DTPA. Rhodes later dropped her malpractice claim. *Id.* at 240.

At issue here is footnote five in *Sorokolit's* majority opinion, which cautions:

> Our conclusion that section 12.01(a) does not prevent suit under the DTPA for claims not based on medical malpractice does not suggest that such a suit will succeed either procedurally or on the merits. For example, under Texas common law, a physician is not presumed to warrant a cure or a particular result, but a physician may enter into such an agreement. Concerns that a physician's reassurances may be mistaken for a guarantee may properly lead courts to hesitate in concluding that such a contract was created or that a guarantee was offered. *In addition, we note the possible application of the statute of frauds in such cases when properly raised by a defendant as an affirmative defense.*

In criticizing *Sorokolit's* majority opinion, moreover, Justice Cornyn maintained that:

> [T]he court has construed section 12.01 to allow a DTPA cause of action that is, in turn, barred by a 1977 amendment to the statute of frauds, another part of the same comprehensive statutory plan [which included the MLIIA]. Besides being misleading — to Ms. Rhodes and other litigants who will rely on the court's apparent recognition of a cause of action, only to find it barred by the statute of frauds — this construction violates our own mandate that 'in ascertaining the intent of the Legislature, all laws bearing on the same subject are to be considered and given effect.' *Id.* at 245 (Cornyn, J., dissenting).

The statute of frauds states:

> (a) A promise or agreement described in Subsection (b) of this section is not enforceable unless the promise or agreement, or a memorandum of it, is
> (1) in writing; and
> (2) signed by the person to be charged with the promise or agreement or by someone lawfully authorized to sign for him.
>
> (b) Subsection (a) of this section applies to: . . .
> (8) an agreement, promise, contract, or warranty of cure relating to medical care or results thereof made by a physician or health care provider as defined in Section 1.03, Medical Liability and Insurance Improvement Act of Texas. This section shall not apply to pharmacists. Tex. Bus. & Com. Code Ann. § 26.01.

It seems clear to this Court, reading the statutes and *Sorokolit* together, that where a defendant physician in a DTPA case raises the affirmative defense of statute of frauds and plaintiff fails to prove a writing, signed by defendant, which contains the representation or promise relied upon, the DTPA claim fails. Nevertheless, here plaintiff Smith attempts to create a distinction between breach of warranty actions, arising in contract, and misrepresentation actions, arising in tort. In so doing, she relies upon the older case of *Weitzel v. Barnes,* 691 S.W.2d 598, 600 (Tex.1985).

It is true that *Weitzel* states "oral representations are not only admissible but can serve as the basis of a DTPA action." *Weitzel,* 691 S.W.2d at 600. We do not agree, however, that in cases involving a physician or health care provider it creates a statute of frauds exception in misrepresentation cases. We conclude this for two reasons.

First, *Weitzel* was decided in 1985, nine years before *Sorokolit.* Thus, Smith's argument that *Weitzel* refines the language of the later case is backward: if anything, *Sorokolit* refines and creates an exception to the broader holding of *Weitzel.* Second, and in a similar vein, *Sorokolit* deals specifically with cases involving physicians and health care providers. *Sorokolit,* 889 S.W.2d at 240. In contrast, *Weitzel* enunciates a broad principle of DTPA law in a case dealing with representations that a home complied with the city building code, a more traditional field for misrepresentation claims. *Weitzel,* 691 S.W.2d at 599. *Sorokolit* addresses only actions involving a particular class of defendants, deemed by the legislature to need a comprehensive and specifically designed statutory scheme. *Sorokolit,* 889 S.W.2d at 245 (Cornyn, J. dissenting). The statute of frauds has a section specifically addressing representations by physicians and health care providers; there is no such protection for sellers of remodeled homes or DTPA defendants generally. Tex. Bus. & Com. Code Ann. § 26.01. We therefore conclude *Weitzel* does not create an exception to the more specific situation addressed in the statute of frauds section relied upon by Elliott.

Finally, we note that Smith's allegations in this case were that Elliott made false, misleading or deceptive representations and knowingly failed to disclose information that induced her to agree to surgery, specifically that her breasts would look good, that she would be very pleased with the results, and she would have only fine-line scarring. In a written Disclosure and Consent to Medical and Surgical Procedures, however, Smith acknowledged in writing that the breast reduction procedure involved risks of infection, scars, skin loss, and numb nipples. This signed writing contradicts the verbal representations Smith claims the doctor made to her. In these circumstances, the statute of fraud's requirement that a physician's representation be in writing to be actionable seems eminently fair. We overrule Smith's sole point of error.

Conclusion

We affirm the trial court's judgment.

Part II

Consumer Litigation and Insurance Defense Under Uniform Insurance Acts and Common Law

Chapter Eight: Insurance Regulation and the McCarran-Ferguson Act

Very likely, national and international commerce would stop altogether or proceed at a very slow crawl if corporations, small businesses, government entities, various institutions, and consumers generally could not purchase insurance. Thus, insurers and insurance contracts are ubiquitous. Insureds—private attorneys general—have the primary responsibility to enforce insurance contracts and to make certain that insurers honor their contractual obligations. On the other hand, both state and federal agencies regulate the "business of insurance" as well as the "business of insurers." Those agencies' primary responsibility is to ensure that insurance services comply with certain minimum standards. But even more important, regulators must ensure that unconscionable or invalid standardized insurance contracts never reach consumers.

Part II of this casebook begins by discussing the evolution of state and federal agencies' respective powers to regulate the "business of insurance." To be sure, whether a state or the federal government has supreme power to regulate the business of insurance generates a considerable amount of litigation. And that is significant, since the Supreme Court began addressing and purportedly "resolved" the controversy more than 140 years ago in *Paul v. Virginia,* 75 U.S. [8 Wall.] (1869). However, about half of the chapters in Part II outline insureds' burden when suing insurers in Texas courts and in federal district courts. The remaining chapters discuss insurance defense. More specifically, those chapters outline the various affirmative defenses that insurers employ to defeat insureds' efforts to collect proceeds under first- and third-party insurance contracts.

A. Federal Insurance Statutes and the "Business of Insurance"

Federal Courts and the Regulation of the Insurance Industry: An Empirical and Historical Analysis of Courts' Ineffectual Attempts to Harmonize Federal Antitrust, Arbitration, and Insolvency Statutes with the McCarran-Ferguson Act—1941-1993

43 Cath. U. L. Rev. 399 (1994)

Willy E. Rice

Nearly 125 years ago, the United States Supreme Court in *Paul v. Virginia*[1] adopted the view that state commissioners and agencies are primarily responsible for regulating the insurance industry. Since *Paul,* state insurance commissions have had to resolve a variety of insurance-related conflicts and problems. Congress, however, has intervened only once to correct a problem insurers described as a national crisis.

Seventy-six years after *Paul,* the Supreme Court ruled in *United States v. South-Eastern Underwriters Ass'n,*[2] that a transaction between an insurer and a policyholder from different states constitutes interstate commerce and is therefore subject to federal antitrust laws and regulations. *South-Eastern Underwriters* effectively overruled *Paul* and created major turbulence within the insurance industry.

* * *

Many insurers viewed the Supreme Court's decision in *United States v. South-Eastern Underwriters Ass'n* as an assault on states' authority to regulate the business of insurance within state boundaries. Therefore, Congress enacted the McCarran-Ferguson Act—15 U.S.C. §§ 1011-1015—to calm the anxieties of local and national carriers. The Act allocates regulatory power to state insurance commissions and, under some limited conditions, to the Federal Trade Commission. But a careful examination also reveals that the Act *does not* allocate any regulatory authority to federal courts. Yet, since the Act's enactment, the Supreme Court as well as lower federal courts have willingly or unwittingly accepted or seized opportunities to regulate significant portions of the nation's insurance industry. The exercise of such unwarranted judicial power has produced conflicting rules for both national insurers and consumers.

The language of the McCarran-Ferguson Act is less clear regarding two other important matters. First, whether state insurance regulations and enforcement proceedings must be merely adequate or genuinely effective, before intervention of some federal agency, is not easily discernible. This silence has generated some expected confusion among lower federal courts. For example, the United States Courts of Appeals for the Third, Fifth, Sixth and Ninth Circuits have held that only reasonable or sufficient state regulatory schemes are required to avert federal control of insurance

1 75 U.S. (8 Wall.) 168, 183-86 (1869) (noting that insurance contracts were "local transactions . . . governed by . . . local law" and that the business of insurance was not commerce under the Commerce Clause of the U.S. Constitution, and holding that Congress had no authority to regulate the insurance industry).

2 322 U.S. 533, 561-62 (1944)

activities. Courts in the Second and District of Columbia Circuits, however, have suggested that they would require active and effective state regulation of the business of insurance before preventing federal intervention.

Second, the McCarran-Ferguson Act allocates power to the Federal Trade Commission. But does the Act grant regulatory authority to other federal agencies? Under the Act, such agencies are neither encouraged to regulate nor prevented from regulating national or regional insurance companies. Nevertheless, in recent years, the Departments of Defense, Health & Human Services, Housing & Urban Development, Justice, and Treasury adopted the position that the Act does not prevent those federal agencies from regulating the insurance industry within and across state boundaries. The Securities and Exchange Commission and the Equal Employment Opportunity Commission also embrace this perspective.

The McCarran–Ferguson Act
59 Stat. 33 (1945)
As amended 15 U.S.C.A. §§ 1011–1015

§ 1011 — Declaration of policy

Congress declares that the continued regulation and taxation by the several States of the business of insurance is in the public interest, and that silence on the part of the Congress shall not be construed to impose any barrier to the regulation or taxation of such business by the several States.

§ 1012 — Regulation by State law; Federal law relating specifically to insurance; Applicability of certain Federal laws after June 30, 1948

(a) The business of insurance, and every person engaged therein, shall be subject to the laws of the several States which relate to the regulation or taxation of such business.

(b) No Act of Congress shall be construed to invalidate, impair, or supersede any law enacted by any State for the purpose of regulating the business of insurance, or which imposes a fee or tax upon such business, unless such Act specifically relates to the business of insurance: Provided,

That after June 30, 1948, the Act of July 2, 1890, as amended, known as the Sherman Act, and the Act of October 15, 1914, as amended, known as the Clayton Act, and the Act of September 26, 1914, known as the Federal Trade Commission Act, as amended, shall be applicable to the business of insurance to the extent that such business is not regulated by State law.

§ 1014 — Applicability of National Labor Relations Act and Fair Labor Standards Act of 1938

Nothing contained in this chapter shall be construed to affect in any manner the application to the business of insurance of the Act of July 5, 1935, as amended, known as the National Labor Relations Act, or the Act of June 25, 1938, as amended, known as the Fair Labor Standards Act of 1938, or the Act of June 5, 1920, known as the Merchant Marine Act, 1920

TEXAS INSURANCE CODE, § 31.002
DUTIES OF THE INSURANCE COMMISSIONER
"REGULATE THE BUSINESS OF INSURANCE"

In addition to the other duties required of the Texas Department of Insurance, the department shall:

(1) regulate the business of insurance in this state;
(2) administer the workers' compensation system of this state as provided by Title 5, Labor Code ; and
(3) ensure that this code and other laws regarding insurance and insurance companies are executed.

B. Insurance Regulation and the "Business of Insurance"

A careful reading of Tex. Ins. Code § 31.002 reveals that the Texas insurance commissioner may regulate the "business of insurance" and employ other laws to regulate *insurance companies' activities*. The distinction is important, because various entities sale or try to sale insurance and insurance-related services and those entities are not insurance companies. Clearly the insurance commissioner may regulate insurance companies. On the other hand, whether a commissioner may regulate all persons who "pitch" any insurance-related services is highly controversial.

The source of this controversy originates in the Tex. Ins. Code § 101.001. In pertinent part, that section outlines Texas's policy about and the purpose of insurance regulations:

STATE POLICY AND PURPOSE — UNAUTHORIZED INSURANCE

(a) It is a state concern that many residents of this state hold insurance policies issued by persons or insurers who are not authorized to do insurance business in this state and who are not qualified as eligible surplus lines insurers under Chapter 981. These residents face often insurmountable obstacles in asserting legal rights under the policies in foreign forums under unfamiliar laws and rules of practice.

(b) It is the policy of this state to protect residents against acts by a person or insurer who is not authorized to do insurance business in this state by:

(1) maintaining fair and honest insurance markets;

(2) protecting the premium tax revenues of this state;

(3) protecting authorized persons and insurers, who are subject to strict regulation, from unfair competition by unauthorized persons and insurers; and

(4) protecting against evasion of the insurance regulatory laws of this state.

(c) The purpose of this chapter is to subject certain insurers and persons to the jurisdiction of:

(1) the commissioner and proceedings before the commissioner; and

(2) the courts of this state in suits by or on behalf of the state or an insured or beneficiary under an insurance contract.

(d) It is also a concern that this state [does]not become a safe harbor for persons or insurers engaged in the unauthorized business of insurance in this state, regardless of whether the insureds or other persons affected by the unauthorized business of insurance are residents of this state.

Of course, the prevailing rule is extremely simple: If persons engage in the "business of insurance," the insurance commissioner may regulate the business and many of those persons' corporate activities, unless a federal statute preempts the application of Texas law. However, to reiterate, determining what comprises the "business of insurance" in Texas is an ongoing challenge for Texas state courts as well as for the Fifth Circuit Court of Appeals and federal district courts within Texas.

Ramirez v. Inter-Continental Hotels
890 F.2d 760
(5th Cir. 1989)

Plaintiff Peter Ramirez, Jr., filed suit in Texas state court, asserting various contract, tort, and statutory causes of action against his former employer, Inter-Continental Hotels (Inter-Continental), and its insurance carrier, The Travelers Insurance Company (Travelers). Defendants removed the case to federal district court, basing jurisdiction upon the Employee Retirement Income Security Act of 1974 (ERISA), 29 U.S.C. §§ 1001-1461, and, in the alternative, upon diversity of citizenship. Following removal, the district court concluded that Ramirez's state law causes of action were preempted by ERISA and dismissed the case, *sua sponte,* for failure to state a claim upon which relief could be granted. We affirm in part, vacate in part, and remand.

I. Background and Procedural History

Ramirez worked for several years as a restaurant manager for Inter-Continental and received, as part of his compensation, insurance coverage under an employee group medical plan issued by Travelers. Neither party disputes that the group medical plan was an employee benefit plan within the meaning of ERISA.

ERISA § 3(1), 29 U.S.C. § 1002(1), comprehensively defines an "employee welfare benefit plan" as "any plan, fund, or program which was . . . established or maintained by an employer or by an employee organization, or by both, maintained for the purpose of providing for its participants or their beneficiaries, through the purchase of insurance or otherwise, . . . medical, surgical, or hospital care or benefits in the event of sickness, accident, disability, death or unemployment...."

According to Ramirez, a prolonged illness which began in the spring of 1986 required him to incur various medical and hospitalization expenses. Unable to persuade Inter-Continental and Travelers to reimburse him, Ramirez filed suit in state court, seeking to recover the benefits he believed were due to him under the employee group medical plan. His complaint sought both compensatory and punitive damages and alleged breach of contract, breach of fiduciary duty, negligence, and violations of the Texas Insurance Code and the Texas Deceptive Trade Practices Act.

Following removal, Ramirez sought a remand, arguing that the well-pleaded complaint rule precluded removal based solely upon ERISA preemption, which was merely a federal defense to his state law causes of action, and that defendants' allegations of diversity were defective. Specifically, Ramirez argued that the diversity pleading was insufficient in that 1) it alleged only that Ramirez was a resident, rather than a citizen, of Texas; 2) it failed to allege that diversity existed both at the time of the commencement of the action and at the time the petition for removal was filed; and 3) it failed to allege the citizenship or place of incorporation of Travelers.

Concluding that ERISA creates federal question jurisdiction over suits to recover benefits from an ERISA plan, the district court denied the motion to remand. The district court also found the diversity issue to be "effectively mooted" and denied defendants' motion to amend the technical defects in their diversity pleading.

Inter-Continental and Travelers then moved for summary judgment on the ground that Ramirez's state law claims were preempted by ERISA. Agreeing with defendants' view of preemption, the district court denied the summary judgment motion and instead dismissed Ramirez's complaint for failure to state a claim upon which relief could be granted. At Ramirez's request, the district court later modified its order to provide that the dismissal was without prejudice.

II. Jurisdiction

On appeal, Ramirez renews his challenge to federal jurisdiction. He points out that his complaint raised only state law claims and argues that the well-pleaded complaint rule of *Louisville & Nashville Ry. v. Mottley,* 211 U.S. 149 (1908), precluded removal on the basis of ERISA preemption, which is merely a federal defense. We find this argument to be without merit in light of *Metropolitan Life Ins. Co. v. Taylor,* 481 U.S. 58 (1987).

As Ramirez concedes, this lawsuit is essentially one to recover benefits from an ERISA plan. As such, it comes within the scope of ERISA's civil enforcement provision, § 502(a)(1)(B), 29 U.S.C. § 1132(a)(1)(B), which allows "a civil action ... [to] be brought by a participant or beneficiary . . . to recover benefits due to him under the terms of the plan, or to clarify his rights to future benefits under the terms of the plan."

In *Metropolitan Life,* the Supreme Court held that any suit within the scope of § 502(a)(1)(B), even "though it purports to raise only state law claims, is necessarily federal in character by virtue of the clearly manifested intent of Congress. It, therefore, "arise[s] under the laws . . . of the United States," 28 U.S.C. § 1331, and is removable to federal court by the defendants, 28 U.S.C. § 1441(b). *Id.* at 67. That is to say, ERISA's "civil enforcement provisions operate to 'recharacterize' . . . [state law claims for ERISA benefits] into actions arising under federal law." *Degan v. Ford Motor Co.,* 869 F.2d 889, 893 (5th Cir.1989). Hence, we conclude that removal was properly granted under 28 U.S.C. § 1441(b), and, like the district court, we find it unnecessary to determine whether diversity of citizenship provides an alternate basis of subject matter jurisdiction.

III. ERISA Preemption

There can be no dispute that Ramirez's efforts to collect his medical benefits "relate to an employee benefit plan" and thus come within the scope of ERISA's express preemption provision § 514(a), 29 U.S.C. § 1144(a), which declares that ERISA "supersede[s] any and all state laws insofar as they may now or hereafter relate to any employee benefit plan. . . ." As the Supreme Court explained in two recent decisions, "[t]he phrase 'relate to' . . . [must be] given its broad common-sense meaning, such that a state law 'relates to' a benefit plan, 'in the normal sense of the phrase, if it has a connection with or reference to such a plan.' " *Metropolitan Life Ins. Co. v. Massachusetts,* 471 U.S. 724, 739 (1985), quoting *Shaw v. Delta Air Lines, Inc.,* 463 U.S. 85, 97 (1983)

Ramirez contends, however, that the dismissal of his suit was improper because Tex. Ins. Code Ann. art. 21.21 § 16 (section 16) — upon which he bases his right to recovery— is rescued from preemption as a statute that "regulate[s] insurance" within the meaning of the ERISA savings clause, § 514(b)(2)(A), 29 U.S.C. § 1144(b)(2)(A). Finding this question to be squarely controlled by *Pilot Life Ins. Co. v. Dedeaux,* 481 U.S. 41 (1987), we disagree.

In *Pilot Life,* the Supreme Court considered at length and rejected the plaintiff's argument that the Mississippi common law of bad faith, which had enabled many an aggrieved policyholder to recover exemplary damages for improper insurance claims handling, regulated insurance within the meaning of the ERISA savings clause. Relying upon case law interpreting the phrase "business of insurance" in the McCarran-Ferguson Act, 15 U.S.C. § 1012(a), the Court explained that a law regulates insurance when 1) it is specifically directed at the insurance industry; 2) it transfers or spreads policyholder risk; and 3) it affects an integral part of the policy relationship between insurer and insured. *Id.* at 48-49, citing *Union Labor Life Ins. Co. v. Pireno,* 458 U.S. 119, 129

(1982). Ramirez contends that section 16 meets all three criteria and is thus distinguishable from the Mississippi law held preempted in *Pilot Life.*

Section 16 furnishes a private right of action and allows treble damages and attorneys' fees to persons injured by certain enumerated "unfair methods of competition and unfair and deceptive acts or practices in the business of insurance . . . " Although the statute is contained within the Texas Insurance Code and therefore by its terms is directed specifically at the insurance industry, it also incorporates wholesale the Texas Deceptive Trade Practices Act, Tex. Bus. & Com.Code Ann. § 17.46, a law of general application, and provides a remedy for violations of that law by an insurance company.

Whether section 16 satisfies the first prong of the test enunciated in *Pilot Life* is thus a close question, but the statute plainly fails to satisfy the second and third prongs. Section 16 does not transfer or spread policyholder risk, and, like the Mississippi law of bad faith, it "does not define the terms of the relationship between the insurer and the insured; it declares only that, whatever terms have been agreed upon in the insurance contract, a breach of that contract" may in some cases entitle the policyholder to exemplary damages. *Pilot Life,* 481 U.S. at 51. At most, therefore, section 16 satisfies one of the three criteria used to interpret the phrase "regulates insurance" in the ERISA savings clause.

Even if section 16, by virtue of its location within the Texas Insurance Code, bears a closer relationship to the regulation of insurance than does the Mississippi law of bad faith, this lawsuit is in one vital respect indistinguishable from *Pilot Life.* Ramirez, like the plaintiff in *Pilot Life,* seeks to recover, under a state law cause of action, remedies unavailable to him under ERISA. To interpret the savings clause as authorizing such inconsistent state remedies would be to defeat Congressional intent by destroying the exclusivity of ERISA's civil enforcement provisions. As the Court explained in *Pilot Life*:

> [T]he detailed provisions of 502(a) set forth a comprehensive civil enforcement scheme that represents a careful balancing of the need for prompt and fair claims settlement procedures against the public interest in encouraging the formation of employee benefit plans. The policy choices reflected in the inclusion of certain remedies and the exclusion of others would be completely undermined if ERISA-plan participants and beneficiaries were free to obtain remedies under state law that Congress rejected in ERISA. *Id.* at 54.

In sum, *Pilot Life* requires us to conclude that ERISA preempts section 16-based claims to recover benefits from an ERISA plan. We thus join three of our sister circuits and numerous district courts in holding that ERISA preempts state statutes that provide a private right of action for the improper handling of insurance claims.

IV. Conclusion

Because Ramirez's state law causes of action are preempted by ERISA, we conclude that the district court properly dismissed his complaint for failure to state a claim upon which relief could be granted. However, we agree with the defendants that the dismissal order should be reformed in order to clarify that it operates as a decision on the merits of Ramirez's state law claims. We therefore vacate that part of the order making the dismissal without prejudice and remand with instructions to enter the order with prejudice and to grant Ramirez leave to amend his complaint to state a cause of action under ERISA.

Crown Life Insurance Company v. Casteel
22 S.W.3d 378
(Tex. 2000)

We overrule Casteel's Motion for Rehearing and grant in part Crown Life's Motion for Rehearing. We withdraw our opinion dated July 1, 1999, and substitute the following.

William E. Casteel sold insurance policies as an independent agent of Crown Life Insurance Company. One of the policies sold by Casteel led to a lawsuit by policyholders against Casteel and Crown. In that lawsuit, Casteel filed a cross-claim against Crown. In this appeal from that lawsuit, we consider several issues: 1) whether Casteel, who alleges that he has been injured by the unfair and deceptive practices of Crown, has standing to sue Crown under Article 21.21 of the Texas Insurance Code; 2) whether that standing extends to Article 21.21 claims that allow recovery for Deceptive Trade Practices Act violations; and 3) whether the inclusion of invalid theories of liability submitted to the jury in a single broad-form question constitutes harmful error.

We hold that Casteel does have standing to sue Crown under Article 21.21; but Casteel does not have standing under Article 21.21 to allege DTPA-based claims that require consumer status by their terms. We also hold that submitting invalid theories of liability in a single broad-form jury question is harmful error when it cannot be determined whether the jury based its verdict on one or more of the invalid theories. We affirm in part, reverse and render judgment in part, vacate in part, and reverse and remand in part the judgment of the court of appeals.

I

Between 1986 and 1989, Casteel sold Modified Vanishing Premium (MVP) policies as an agent for Crown. The MVP policies provided that substantial premiums be paid over a short period of time, after which the premiums would "vanish" and the policy would carry itself through fruition by the reinvestment of policy dividends. Crown provided Casteel with information about how the policies worked, and Casteel provided biographical information on prospective clients to Crown. Crown then produced illustrations tailored to the proposed insureds, which Casteel presented as part of his sales packages. Many of Casteel's clients who purchased MVP policies were friends from his church.

Casteel's clients began complaining about the MVP policies in 1990. The premiums had not vanished as Casteel had represented and, in some cases, never would. In the case of Randall and Sandra Ferguson, Casteel sold an MVP policy that would pay $5,000,000 to the survivor in the event that one of them died. Based on Crown's projections, Casteel had initially informed them that the premiums would total approximately $91,520 before vanishing, but the Fergusons later discovered that the premiums would never vanish and could total as much as $800,000. The Fergusons sued Casteel and Crown alleging DTPA, Article 21.21, and common-law causes of action.

Casteel filed a cross-claim against Crown alleging violations of Article 21.21, which included claims based on DTPA provisions incorporated in Article 21.21. Casteel also brought common-law claims for negligence, gross negligence, breach of fiduciary duty, breach of a duty of good faith and fair dealing, fraud, and constructive fraud. Crown moved for summary judgment on Casteel's claims, and the trial court granted partial summary judgment in Crown's favor on the common-law causes of action. Casteel's Article 21.21 claims, including those based on the DTPA, proceeded to trial with the Fergusons' claims.

With regard to the Fergusons' claims, the jury found that both Crown and Casteel had engaged in unfair or deceptive acts or practices that were a producing cause of damages to the Fergusons. The jury found that Crown had committed the alleged wrongful acts knowingly and was ninety-nine percent responsible for the Fergusons' damages, while Casteel, who was found not to have acted knowingly, bore only one percent of the responsibility. On Casteel's claims against Crown, the jury found that Crown had knowingly engaged in false, misleading, unfair, or deceptive acts or practices that were a producing cause of damages to Casteel. The jury awarded Casteel $400,000 for past lost income, $1,000,000 for future lost income, $6,000,000 for past mental anguish, and $100,000 for future mental anguish. Additionally, the jury awarded Casteel attorney's fees in the amount of forty percent of his recovery.

Following trial, Crown and the Fergusons settled. Under the settlement terms, the Fergusons assigned their rights against Casteel to Crown, so that Crown now stands in place of the Fergusons for purposes of this appeal. Crown moved for judgment notwithstanding the verdict on Casteel's claims. The trial court rendered judgment that Casteel take nothing against Crown, holding that Casteel was neither a "person" as defined under Article 21.21, nor a "consumer" under the DTPA, and therefore lacked standing to bring suit under those statutes. The court dismissed the Fergusons' claims against Crown with prejudice due to their settlement. The court rendered judgment on the verdict with respect to the Fergusons' claims against Casteel, holding Casteel individually liable for the Fergusons' actual damages, attorney's fees, and prejudgment interest in the amount of $1,366,983.

The court of appeals held that Casteel was a "person" with standing to sue Crown under Article 21.21, but that Casteel did not have standing to sue under the incorporated DTPA provisions because he was not a "consumer." The court of appeals reversed and rendered judgment in favor of Casteel in the amount of $1,400,000 for lost past and future income. The court held, however, that Casteel was not entitled to the $6,100,000 in mental anguish damages awarded by the jury because there was legally insufficient evidence to support the award. In addition, the court remanded the case to the trial court for further proceedings on the issues of settlement credit application, calculation of prejudgment interest, and attorney's fees. The rest of the judgment, including partial summary judgment in favor of Crown on Casteel's common-law claims, was affirmed.

II

Crown initially challenges Casteel's recovery under Article 21.21 of the Insurance Code. At the time that Casteel's claims against Crown arose, Article 21.21, section 16(a) provided:

> Any person who has sustained actual damages as a result of another's engaging in an act or practice declared in Section 4 of this Article . . . to be unfair methods of competition or unfair or deceptive acts or practices in the business of insurance or in any practice defined by Section 17.46 of the Business & Commerce Code, as amended, as an unlawful deceptive trade practice may maintain an action against the person or persons engaging in such acts or practices.

Thus, to assert a cause of action under Article 21.21, Casteel must be (1) a "person," as defined by Article 21.21, section 2(a), and (2) injured by another's acts or practices declared to be unfair or deceptive by either (a) Article 21.21, section 4, or (b) DTPA section 17.46. Id.; see Allstate Ins. Co. v. Watson, 876 S.W.2d 145, 147 (Tex.1994). Casteel alleged that he was injured by Crown's "unfair or deceptive acts or practices" defined by Article 21.21, section 4, and by certain deceptive trade practices prohibited by DTPA section 17.46(b), as those claims are incorporated within Article 21.21. We must initially determine whether Casteel, as an insurance agent, is a "person" with standing to sue Crown under Article 21.21. Additionally, we consider whether Casteel must also be a "consumer" to have standing to recover under Article 21.21 for incorporated DTPA violations.

a. Standing for Claims Arising under Article 21.21

Crown challenges the court of appeals' holding that Casteel, as Crown's agent, is a "person" with standing to sue under Article 21.21, section 16(a). Crown argues that the court of appeals erred by relying too heavily on the plain language of Article 21.21 and too little on the Insurance Code's purpose. Crown acknowledges that the statute's plain language grants a cause of action to "any person" injured by another's deceptive acts or practices in the business of insurance, and that "person" is defined broadly as " any individual, corporation, association, partnership, ... and any other legal entity engaged in the business of insurance, including agents, brokers, adjusters and life insurance counselors." Tex. Ins. Code art. 21.21, § 2(a) (emphasis added).

Despite this language, Crown argues that standing is limited to "persons relying on sales practices when buying policies, and the insureds and beneficiaries under those policies — not the agents selling policies." This, Crown asserts, is because Article 21.21 has two specific, discrete purposes: (1) to protect insurance companies and their agents from "unfair methods of competition," and (2) to protect the public from "unfair or deceptive acts or practices." Crown argues that "agents" were included in the section 2(a) definition of "person" only to provide them a cause of action under section 16(a) for "unfair methods of competition," but not for other "unfair and deceptive acts or practices," such as alleged by Casteel. See Tex. Ins. Code art. 21.21, § 16(a).

The primary rule in statutory interpretation is that a court must give effect to legislative intent. Tex. Gov't Code § 312.005. *See also Union Bankers Ins. Co. v. Shelton*, 889 S.W.2d 278, 280 (Tex.1994). When determining legislative intent, we look to the language of the statute, as well as its legislative history, the objective sought, and the consequences that would flow from alternate constructions. The Legislature explicitly declared its intent in passing Article 21.21:

> The purpose of this Act is to regulate trade practices in the business of insurance . . . by defining, or providing for the determination of, all such practices in this state which constitute unfair methods of competition or unfair or deceptive acts or practices and by prohibiting the trade practices so defined or determined.

The Legislature further admonished that Article 21.21 "shall be liberally construed and applied to promote its underlying purposes."

We do not glean from this stated purpose, nor any other language in the statute, a legislative intent to protect agents only from unfair competition. Rather, it is consistent with the Legislature's express objective to regulate all insurance trade practices to conclude that an insurance agent is a "person" with standing to sue an insurance company when the agent is damaged by company practices that violate Article 21.21. Crown's construction would allow an insurer to deceive its agent with impunity, despite knowing that the misinformation would eventually reach the public. The legislative intent does not support Crown's position.

* * *

In sum, we hold that an insurance agent is a "person," as defined under Article 21.21, section 2(a), for purposes of determining standing under Article 21.21, section 16(a). Thus, when an agent meets the other required elements for a cause of action under Article 21.21, section 16(a)-sustaining actual damages caused by another's engaging in an act or practice declared unfair or deceptive-the agent has standing to bring that claim. This result is required by both the plain language of the statute and its legislative intent.

* * *

Dallas Fire Insurance Company v. Texas Contractors Surety and Casualty Agency
159 S.W.3d 895
(Tex. 2004)

Article 21.21 of the Insurance Code provides a private cause of action for unfair or deceptive acts or practices in the business of insurance. Tex. Ins. Code art. 21.21, § 16(a). In *Great American Insurance Co. v. North Austin Utility District No. 1,* we held that suretyship was not included in the scope of this provision. 908 S.W.2d 415, 424 (Tex.1995). The court of appeals here interpreted that holding to apply only to suits between sureties and their bondholders, and thus affirmed a judgment under article 21.21 in a suit between a surety and its sales agents. Because our previous opinion excluded the business of suretyship rather than the particular parties involved, we hold the court of appeals' opinion conflicts with ours, and reverse the court of appeals' judgment and render judgment that respondents take nothing.

In December 1993, Texas Contractors Surety and Casualty Agency (TCSCA) signed an Agency-Company Agreement to issue surety, performance, and bid bonds on behalf of Dallas Fire Insurance Company. For each surety bond TCSCA sold, Dallas Fire agreed to pay a straight commission, plus a contingency profit commission based on premiums collected adjusted by a loss ratio reflecting losses and expenses.

For the years 1994 and 1995, Dallas Fire calculated the contingency commission using only *direct* expenses (such as legal and consulting fees) incurred in handling bond claims, and paid respondents on that basis. But for 1996, Dallas Fire calculated the contingency commission to reflect its own *indirect* expenses (such as salaries, rent, and other overhead) as well, thus denying respondents any contingency commission. Dallas Fire also recalculated the contingency commission for previous years, and demanded reimbursement on that basis.

TCSCA filed suit, and Young intervened for breach of his separate agreement incorporating similar terms. Both respondents alleged breach of the Agency-Company Agreement and deceptive acts in violation of article 21.21. *See* Tex. Ins. Code, art. 21.21, § 16(a) (defining deceptive acts to include violations of Texas Business & Commerce Code section 17.46(b)); Tex. Bus. & Com. Code 17.46(b)(12) (defining deceptive acts to include representing that an agreement confers or involves rights, remedies, or obligations which it does not have or involve, or which are prohibited by law). The jury found for Dallas Fire on the breach of contract question, but for respondents under article 21.21, and awarded $56,641.02 in damages to TCSCA and $82,641.02 to Young.

Dallas Fire asserts that respondents have no article 21.21 claim because *Great American* excludes the business of suretyship from the "business of insurance" under that article, and the parties' relationship consisted of nothing else. As this was the only basis for respondents' recovery, Dallas Fire asserts we must reverse and render judgment against them. We agree.

As we have previously noted, the Insurance Code is somewhat different from Texas's other statutory codifications in that it is not a formal, unified Code containing uniform definitions. *Great Am.,* 908 S.W.2d at 424. Thus, "the business of insurance" has meant different things in different sections of the Code. For example, at all times applicable here, suretyship was expressly *included* in the "doing an insurance business" in former article 1.14-1— (current version at Tex. Ins. Code § 101.051), but expressly excluded in article 21.55, section 5(a)(4).

While acknowledging our holding in *Great American* that the "business of insurance" in article 21.21 does not include suretyship, the court of appeals read that case narrowly to apply only to disputes between a surety and its obligee. It is true that we pointed out particular difficulties that would arise in the surety-obligee relationship if article 21.21 applied. But we also noted that the suretyship business predated the insurance business "by thousands of years" and had different characteristics. *Id.* at 424 (noting that insurance involves spreading risks with no right of indemnity, while suretyship involves risk of initial payment with full right of indemnity).

More important, our holding in *Great American* was not limited to *parts* of the business of suretyship:

> Given the unique character, rights, and obligations of suretyship, and the complexities that would result by the imposition of liability under 21.21, we cannot conclude that the Legislature intended to include suretyship in the definition of the business of insurance under article 21.21. Absent a clear legislative directive, we conclude that suretyship, as historically understood in the insurance and suretyship fields, does not constitute the business of insurance under article 21.21.

This holding leaves no room for applying article 21.21 to parts of the surety business.

The court of appeals also relied on evidence that Dallas Fire's primary line of business (though not through TCSCA) was commercial liability insurance, that its surety bonds were "insurance products" for the purpose of licensing under article 21.02, and that TCSCA sold surety bonds through agents licensed by the Texas Department of Insurance. But as already noted, the business of insurance is defined differently in different sections of the Insurance Code, and all that is involved here is a commission dispute involving the sale of surety bonds. *See Ins. Co. of N. Am. v. Morris,* 981 S.W.2d 667, 672 (Tex.1998) (holding surety bonds to be insurance products for purposes of article 21.02, though not for article 21.21). Here, TCSCA's claims arose in the business of suretyship, not the business of insurance.

Respondents contend that in *Crown Life Insurance Co. v. Casteel,* we extended the reach of article 21.21 beyond claims between an insured and insurer. 22 S.W.3d 378, 385 (Tex. 2000). But *Casteel* involved a claim against a life insurance carrier and its agent based on inaccurate language and illustrations contained in life insurance policies sold by Crown's agent, William Casteel. Thus, *Casteel* clearly involved the "business of insurance" and not the business of suretyship, which is implicated in this case.

By limiting the scope of article 21.21 to the business of insurance, the Legislature intended it to apply to a species of economic enterprise, not to particular contracts on a piecemeal basis. Accordingly, without hearing oral argument, we grant the petition for review, reverse the judgment of the court of appeals and render judgment that respondents take nothing.

NOTES & QUESTIONS

1) Again, the Supreme Court defined "business of insurance" in *Union Labor Life Ins. Co. v. Pireno,* 458 U.S. 119, 129 (1982). Yet, in *Crown Life Insurance Company* and *Dallas Fire Insurance Company,* the Texas Supreme Court never cited *Pireno*. Was the Texas Supreme Court's failure to cite the Supreme Court's *Pireno* decision intentional or simply an oversight?

2) Since the Texas Supreme Court did not embrace *Pireno*'s definition, how did the Supreme Court of Texas define the "business of insurance" in *Crown Life Insurance Company* and in *Dallas Fire Insurance Company*? In *Pireno*, the Supreme Court identified three criteria. How many did the Texas Supreme Court identify?

3. So, what is the test for identifying the "business of insurance" in Texas? Consider the decision in the following case:

Watson v. Allstate Insurance Company, 828 S.W.2d 423
(Court of Appeals of Texas C--Fort Worth, 1991)

Automobile accident victim brought suit directly against other driver's insurer as third-party beneficiary of policy. The 17th District Court, Tarrant County, Fred Davis, J., struck victim's pleadings and granted insurer summary judgment on certain causes of action. Accident victim appealed. The Court of Appeals, Hill, J., held that: (1) third-party beneficiary may not bring suit against insurer for breach of duty of good faith and fair dealing; . . . and (4) regardless of whether federal or state Insurance Code definition of "business of insurance" was used, insurer's handling of accident victim's claim constituted "business of insurance" for purposes of such claim.

* * *

A claim brought under Article 21.21 must be related to the *"business of insurance"* because Section 1(a) of Article 21.21 states that the purpose of the act is to regulate trade practices in the *business of insurance* in accordance with the intent of Congress as expressed in the McCarran Ferguson Act, ch. 20, 59 Stat. 33 (1945) . . . . We also agree with Allstate's contention that federal law is controlling in the interpretation of what constitutes the "*business of insurance." See Fry v. John Hancock Mutual Life Insurance Co.*, 355 F.Supp. 1151, 1153 (N.D.Tex.1973).

In determining whether the practice sought to be regulated constitutes the "*business of insurance,*" we must consider the following three criteria:

> 1) whether the practice being considered has the effect of *transferring or spreading a policyholder's risk*; 2) whether the practice is an integral part of the policy relationship between the insurer or insure; and 3) whether the practice is limited to entities within the insurance industry. *See, Union Labor Life Insurance Co. v. Pireno,* 458 U.S. 119 (1982).

We hold that an insurance company's practices in the settlement of its claims arising from the policy between itself and its insured meets all three of these criteria and constitutes the business of insurance.

4 ERISA and the federal preemption doctrine are powerful. They can undermine state insurance commissioners' ability to regulate health maintenance organizations' activities and employee benefits. In fact, this area of law has generated a lot of controversy. To help understand the conflict, consider the following synopsis of a long, complicated and heavily litigated lawsuit:

Corporate Health Insurance, Inc. v. Texas Department of Insurance
215 F.3d 526 (5th Cir. 2000)

This suit is a preemption challenge to Texas's Senate Bill 386 ♦ [Codified at Tex. Civ. Prac. & Rem. Code § 88.001 *et seq*.; Tex. Ins. Code: Art. 20A.09(e) (formerly (a)(3)); Art. 20A.12(a) & (b); Art. 20A.12A; Art. 21.58A §§ 6(b) and (c); Art. 21.58A § 6A; Art. 21.58A §§ 8(f) & 21.58C.] . . . Through that legislation, Texas asserted its police power to protect its citizens in regulating the new field of managed health care three ways.

First, it created *a statutory cause of action* against managed care entities that *fail to meet an ordinary care standard* for health care treatment decisions. The "liability" section of the bill stated:

> A health insurance carrier, health maintenance organization, or other managed care entity for a health care plan has the *duty to exercise ordinary care* when making health care treatment decisions and *is liable* for *damages* for *harm* to an insured or enrollee proximately caused by its failure (breach) to exercise such ordinary care. Tex. Civ. Prac. & Rem. Code Ann. § 88.002(a) (1999).

Second, it established *procedures for the independent review of health care determinations* to decide whether they were *appropriate and medically necessary* (the "independent review" provisions). Finally, it *protected physicians from HMO-imposed indemnity clauses* and from retaliation by health maintenance organizations (HMO) for advocating medically necessary care for their patients.

The plaintiffs -- Corporate Health Insurance, Inc., Aetna Health Plans of Texas, Inc., Aetna Plans of North Texas, Inc. and Aetna Life Insurance Company -- *are not ERISA plans*. Aetna Health Plans of Texas is an HMO licensed by the State of Texas that contracts with more than 2,900 independent health care providers and 39 hospitals. Aetna Life Insurance Company sells various health insurance products to employers, including programs available through a preferred provider organization (PPO).

* * *

Senate Bill 386 became effective on May 22, 1997. Aetna promptly filed suit in the United States District Court, claiming that the Act was preempted by ERISA's general preemption clause, *section 514, which preempts "any and all state laws insofar as they . . . relate to any employee benefit plan*" [29 U.S.C. § 1144(a)] and by the Federal Employees Health Benefit Act (FEHBA). [5 U.S.C. § 8901 et seq.].

* * *

Texas and the federal government urge that the preempted independent review provisions are saved under ERISA's savings clause for laws regulating insurance. 29 U.S.C. § 1144(b)(2)(A) (1999). The Supreme Court has interpreted the clause as designed to preserve Congress's reservation of the business of insurance to the states under the McCarran-Ferguson Act. *See Metropolitan Life Ins. v. Massachusetts,* 471 U.S. 724, 744 n. 21, (1985).

In determining whether the clause applies, the Supreme Court considers whether the rule regulates insurance as a commonsense matter, looking as well to the three McCarran-Ferguson factors as "guideposts" 1) whether the practice has the effect of transferring or spreading the policyholder's risk; 2) whether it is an integral part of the policy relationship between the insured and the insurer; and 3) whether the practice is limited to entities in the insurance industry. *See, UNUM Life Ins. Co. v. Ward*, 119 S.Ct. 1380, 1386 (1999). The law need not satisfy each of these tests. *See Ward*, 119 S.Ct. at 1389.

Our analysis does not end here, however, because even if the provisions would otherwise be saved, they may nonetheless be preempted if they conflict with a substantive provision of ERISA. In *Pilot Life v. Dedeaux,* 481 U.S. 41, 52 (1987), the Supreme Court held that our understanding of the saving clause must be informed by the legislative intent concerning [ERISA's] civil enforcement provisions. . . . [Therefore], the independent review provisions DO NOT create a cause of action for the denial of benefits.

FIFTH CIRCUIT'S THREE HOLDINGS

Holding A — Articles 20A.12A, 21.58A, § 6 (c), and 21.58A, § 6A allow appeals to "outside" state administrative utilization review agents-- *after adverse determinations by managed care entities*. We sever them from the remainder of the Texas Insurance Code and hold them preempted.

[REVERSED: *Rush Prudential HMO, Inc. v. Moran,* 122 S. Ct. 2151, 2170-2171 (2002) -- an employee benefit plan decision].

Holding B — We conclude that the liability provisions of the Texas statute, and the independent review provisions -- *insofar as they are merely a prerequisite to the filing of suit*-- are not preempted . . . under ERISA nor FEHBA because they *allow suit only for health services actually delivered,* not for coverage disputes.

Holding C — The anti-indemnity and anti-retaliation provisions are not preempted; they too address traditional state concerns regarding the quality of health care.

Chapter Nine:
The Formation, Construction and Interpretation of Insurance Contracts

Briefly put, traditional rules of contract construction govern the formation and enforcement of insurance contracts. If unconscionable, fraudulent, coerced, criminal, or immoral conduct contributed to the formation of an insurance agreement, the contract is invalid and void from its inception. Also, if an insured commences a breach-of-contract action against an insurer and expects to prevail in a court of law, the insured must establish a *prima facie* case. More specifically, the insured must prove 1) the existence of a valid insurance contract; 2) consideration; 3) a material breach of the insurance contract; and 4) that the breach was the cause in fact and proximate cause of the insured's injury and damages.

In most instances, determining whether a valid insurance contract exists is not an issue. The reason is not complicated. After insurers agree to insure applicants or applicants' property, insurance companies typically issue standardized insurance contracts. In truth, they are standardized adhesion contracts because the insured consumers rarely negotiate the terms and conditions appearing in those "boilerplate" forms. On the other hand, whether applicants are covered under "temporary" insurance contracts—after they complete applications, pay the first premiums and receive conditional binders or receipts from insurance agents—is frequently litigated in all states.

Do conditional binders or receipts always create valid contracts? May insurance agents modify or alter the terms in conditional binders? Do conditional binders create temporary insurance? Are insurers liable if agents misrepresent the terms in conditional receipts? Do insurers have affirmative defenses under Texas Insurance Code and the common law? This chapter addresses these questions and other issues involving the formation of valid insurance contracts because Tex. Ins. Code, § 549.001(2) reads: "'Insurance binder' means a contract that provides insurance coverage pending the issuance of an original insurance policy that will be issued on or before the 30th day after the date the insurance binder is issued."

A. *Conditional Binders and Temporary Insurance*

United Founders Life Insurance Company v. Carey
363 S.W.2d 236
(Tex. 1963)

This is a suit upon an alleged contract of life insurance, based upon an application to United Founders Life Insurance Company for life insurance and a "binding receipt" issued by such company, as distinguished from a suit upon a life insurance policy. The applicant, Billy Gene Bruce, died before any insurance policy was issued. Trial was to a jury and on the jury's verdict judgment was entered for respondent Glynda Bruce Carey, the surviving but remarried wife of the deceased applicant. The Court of Civil Appeals has affirmed that judgment.

On July 27, 1958, the applicant, Billy Gene Bruce, who was then an insurance salesman for the petitioner insurance company, applied to it in writing for life insurance on himself as a standard risk for $25,000, naming his wife, the respondent here, as his beneficiary. This application provided that the company would incur no liability until the application had been received, approved, and a policy issued and delivered while applicant was in good health, but had the further proviso, "However, if the full first premium specified in the application on the policy applied for is paid on the date of this application and receipt bearing the same serial number as this application is issued to the applicant, then the liability of the company shall be as stated in the receipt."

The premium mentioned was paid by the applicant and petitioner issued a receipt therefor containing this provision:

> The insurance under the policy for which application is made shall be effective on date of this receipt or the date of completion of the medical examination (if required) whichever is the later date, if in the opinion of the authorized Officers of the Company at its Home Office in Oklahoma City, Oklahoma, the Proposed Insured is insurable and acceptable for insurance under its rules and practices on the plan of insurance, for the amount of insurance and at the premium rate set in the application, exclusive of any amendments in the space for "Home Office Additions or Correction."

The trial court submitted the following issue to the jury, which answered it as indicated:

> "Do you find from a preponderance of the evidence that prior to Billy Gene Bruce's death in the opinion of the proper official of United Founders Life Insurance Company Billy Gene Bruce was insurable and acceptable for insurance under its rules and practices on the plan of insurance, for the amount of insurance, and at the premium rate set in his application for life insurance? Answer yes or no."
>
> Answer: "Yes."

The petitioner complains that there was no evidence to support the answer given by the jury to this issue. On this point we reverse the judgments of the Court of Civil Appeals and the trial court, but in the interest of justice we remand the cause for a new trial.

In May or June of 1958 Mr. Bruce, the applicant, began employment as an agent of petitioner insurance company for the purpose of selling life insurance. His immediate supervisor, the general agent in San Angelo for petitioner company, was Mr. Gerald Stewart. As such agent and salesman Mr. Bruce attended the company school in Oklahoma City shortly after the beginning of his employment to familiarize himself with life insurance and the sale of life insurance, and with the rules and practices of his own company. These practice, with which Mr. Bruce became familiar at this school and through his own selling efforts, included the necessity and requirement by petitioner for "reinsurance" in every case where application was made to petitioner for insurance in excess of $5,000.

By such procedure when an application for insurance in excess of $5,000 was received by petitioner, the company secured through its agent a medical examiner's report and a credit or inspection report. Petitioner company submitted these items, together with the application, and its own application for reinsurance, to its reinsurer, Republic National Life Insurance Company, for the latter's underwriting action, its consideration, and for either approval or refusal of the application for reinsurance. In every application for more than $5,000 it was the practice of petitioner to always rely on its reinsurer, Republic National Life Insurance Company, to pass upon the insurability and acceptability of the applicant before any determination was made by petitioner. In forming its opinion petitioner invariably followed the recommendation of Republic on such matters.

As was the usual procedure, petitioner submitted the application, the credit report and the medical examiner's report of Bruce to Republic on September 5, 1958. Bruce's application and medical report were never submitted to petitioner's medical director, because the coverage requested exceeded $5,000 and the application was considered as a reinsurance matter.

On September 8, 1958, Republic wired petitioner's underwriting department that the application of Mr. Bruce was approved as a standard risk subject to "statement of any doctor consulted within past five years regarding nervous disorder." An interoffice memorandum of September 9, 1958, advised petitioner's general agent, Gerald Stewart, that regarding the insured "it will be necessary that we have a statement from any doctor you have consulted during the past five years regarding nervous disorder before we can complete the processing of this application for life insurance." A report in response to this memorandum was made by Dr. Valton Sessums on September 29, 1958, and was received by petitioner on October 1, 1958. This report, among other facts, revealed that the doctor had viewed electrocardiograms of Bruce which showed his heart condition to be normal.

On October 6, 1958, petitioner's chief underwriter advised its general agent that the report from Dr. Sessums had been received and forwarded to its reinsurance company on October 1, and that she had on October 6 received a wire from the reinsurer requesting a review of the electrocardiograms made by Dr. Sessums, and that a loan of them from Dr. Sessums had been requested.

On October 16 petitioner's underwriter by interoffice memorandum to Bruce requested a follow-up on the last request made to Dr. Sessums. On October 18 Bruce was critically injured in an automobile accident, and died from such injuries on October 23.

On October 21 Dr. Sessums wrote to petitioner, advising it that the electrocardiograms were not made in his office, but were made by two physicians in Odessa, Texas, and a physician from Ballinger, Texas. This letter was received by petitioner on the date that Bruce died.

By letter dated November 18, 1958, from William D. Curlee, assistant secretary and treasurer of United Founders Life Insurance Company, to respondent, liability was denied, the letter saying in part:

> "The policy applied for was not issued and never became effective because, upon medical grounds, it was determined that Mr. Bruce was not insurable and acceptable under the company's rules and practices on the plan of insurance for the amount and at the premium rate set in the application."

On the question of whether or not an opinion had been formed as to the insurability or acceptability of Billy Gene Bruce at the time of his death, we have the testimony of Mrs. Helen Smith, chief underwriter and only officer authorized to pass upon the question of insurability and acceptability of an applicant, and also of Mr. Brunswick, the secretary of the reinsurance department of Republic National Life Insurance Company, the officer who passed on reinsurance matters for that company.

* * *

We think this evidence shows not only that the proper officer of the petitioner company had not formed any opinion as to the insurability and acceptability of Billy Gene Bruce before his death, but that up until that time they were diligently investigating his medical history in a good faith attempt to reach an opinion. We likewise are of the opinion that there is no evidence that any opinion was formed after the death of Billy Gene Bruce that he was insurable and acceptable. In fact, the letter quoted from above affirmatively states that it had been determined that he was not acceptable and insurable. But the letter does not foreclose the matter if the receipt delivered to Bruce was intended to provide him with temporary insurance from the date of his medical examination. If it was so intended, the opinion that he was not insurable and acceptable must have been a good faith opinion.

The crucial question, then, is whether the parties intended that the receipt should provide temporary insurance from the date of the medical examination until final action of petitioner in issuing or refusing to issue a policy of insurance. Whether a receipt of the general nature of that issued to Bruce affords temporary insurance has been the subject of considerable controversy and contrariety of opinion.

* * *

However, a careful analysis of the receipt convinces us that it was the intention of the parties to provide Bruce with temporary insurance from the date of completion of his medical examination if in the opinion of the proper officer he was insurable and acceptable, as provided in the receipt, on that date.

The receipt is obviously ambiguous, and the rule is well settled that ambiguities in insurance contracts are to be construed against the insurer. One thing we may say with certainty is that the receipt is intended to provide temporary insurance for some period of time. That conclusion necessarily follows from the express provision of the receipt that the insurance is to be effective upon completion of the medical examination if in the opinion of the authorized officers the applicant is insurable and acceptable rather than upon acceptance of the application or upon issuance or delivery of a policy. The opinion must be formed before the application is approved and a policy issued. There is no way of knowing how long in advance of approval of the application or issuance of a policy the requisite opinion will be formed, whether thirty minutes or three months, but in no event is the applicant to be without insurance until the application is accepted and the policy is issued. Petitioner seems to agree, for if it were otherwise liability could have been defeated by rejecting the application because of the applicant's death.

Assuming, then, that the receipt does provide temporary insurance for some period of time, we are confronted with the question of when it becomes effective. It is on this question that the receipt is particularly ambiguous. It provides that the insurance is to be effective on the date of the "receipt or the date of completion of medical examination (if required) whichever is the later date." What is meant by completion of medical examination? Does it mean completion of the medical examination by the doctor to whom the applicant is referred? Or does it mean completion of that examination and any further investigation the insurer decides to make of an applicant's medical history? Resolving the doubt against petitioner, we think it means the former.

Provision that the temporary insurance is to become effective if in the opinion of the authorized officers the applicant "is" insurable and acceptable would indicate that the temporary insurance is not to become effective until those officers have completed such investigation of the applicant's medical history as they deem necessary to the formation of a good faith opinion of insurability and acceptability. But the receipt does not speak of investigation; it speaks only of examination. A medical examination imports a physical examination as distinguished from a medical history investigation. Moreover, the receipt fixes the effective date of the temporary insurance as the date of completion of medical examination if required. We think the meaning of the words 'if required' in the context in which they are used is 'if required of the applicant.' this strengthens the view that the words 'medical examination' refer to a physical examination.

There is yet another reason for our construction. The formation of an opinion is purely a subjective process. No one but the officer to whom the decision is entrusted can know when an opinion is reached. It is unreasonable to suppose that it is intended, once an opinion of insurability and acceptability is announced, that the date of the effectiveness of the insurance should be so uncertain. Surely it is intended to fix a definite date, ascertainable by the applicant as well as the insurer, as the date for effectiveness of the insurance.

* * *

We thus conclude that the receipt issued to Bruce did provide for temporary insurance and that the insurance was to be effective on the date of completion of his physical examination if in the opinion of the authorized officers of petitioner he was on that date insurable and acceptable according to the terms of the receipt. We have stated that the formation of an opinion by the proper officers of petitioner of Bruce's insurability and acceptability was a condition precedent to the existence of temporary insurance. They could not defeat his right to temporary insurance by arbitrarily refusing to proceed to the formation of an opinion after his death.

We have also stated that an opinion that he was not insurable and acceptable could not be reached arbitrarily because of his death but that it must have been reached in good faith. Petitioner was certainly entitled to make any reasonable investigation as a basis for reaching a good faith opinion. The testimony set out above indicates that petitioner was in the course of making such an investigation when Bruce died, but that it promptly discontinued its investigation and thereafter wrote that it had been determined, on medical grounds, that Bruce was not insurable and acceptable. Inasmuch as the case is to be remanded for retrial, it may be well to indicate our views of the issues to be tried if supported by present or amended pleadings.

The burden is on respondents to prove that the temporary insurance provided by the receipt was in force when Bruce died. They must thus prove that in the opinion of the proper officers of petitioner Bruce was insurable and acceptable on the date of completion of his medical examination. They are confronted with the letter from petitioner stating that it had determined that Bruce was not insurable and acceptable. If respondents are to prevail they must obtain a fact finding that the determination was not made in good faith.

In addition, they must obtain a fact finding from a preponderance of the evidence that a reasonably prudent and careful authorized officer of petitioner company, acting in good faith, would, on the evidence available, find that Bruce was on the date of the completion of his medical examination insurable and acceptable for insurance under petitioner's rules and practices on the plan of insurance, for the amount of insurance and at the premium rate set in his application for life insurance. An answer to this issue should be required only if it is found that the actual determination made by petitioner was not made in good faith. It this issue is raised and reached on retrial it will likely be determined from evidence of the actual condition of Bruce's health on the date of his medical examination. . . . The judgments of the Court of Civil Appeals and the trial court are reversed and the cause is remanded to the trial court.

Southern County Mutual Insurance Company v. First Bank and Trust of Groves
750 S.W.2d 170
(Tex. 1988)

This is a suit to recover on a temporary insurance policy, commonly known as a binder of insurance. First Bank and Trust of Groves, Texas, as a loss payee on an insurance binder, sued Southern

County Mutual Insurance Company, R.O. Williams, Jr., R.O. Williams, Jr., *d/b/a* Colonial Surplus Underwriters Agency, R.O. Williams Co., Inc., Norman Edwards, Norman Edwards *d/b/a* Colonial Surplus Underwriters Agency, and Colonial Surplus Underwriters Agency. The Bank sued on alternate theories: 1) that Southern County Mutual was liable pursuant to an insurance binder in effect on the date of loss, or, if Southern County Mutual was not liable, 2) that R.O. Williams and the other five defendants were strictly liable for violations of the Texas Insurance Code. Trial was to the jury which answered all issues against the Bank. The court of appeals reversed and rendered against all of the defendants. We affirm in part and reverse in part.

In 1980, Melvin Kraehnke purchased a new White Auto Car tractor for use as a dump truck. Kraehnke had the tractor insured with State Farm Insurance. The Bank, which financed the purchase, obtained a security interest in any insurance proceeds issued under Kraehnke's tractor coverage. In May of 1982, Kraehnke converted his tractor into an 18-wheeler. State Farm informed Kraehnke that it would not insure a "single-shot" 18-wheeler.

On May 27, 1982, Kraehnke telephoned Charles Tuttle, an agent with the uncontested authority to issue binding insurance, who worked for R.O. Williams Company, regarding the possibility of procuring insurance on his 18-wheeler. Tuttle then checked with the underwriters at R.O. Williams Company to see if an admitted insurance company in Texas would insure a single unit 18-wheeler. Tuttle learned that no Texas companies would write such coverage.

Tuttle then contacted Norman Edwards at Colonial Surplus Underwriters Agency, a surplus lines agency which places coverage with insurance companies not licensed in Texas, to see if there was any surplus insurance available for Kraehnke's tractor. Edwards quoted a rate for the coverage and told Tuttle that the surplus lines carrier would be Southern County Mutual.

Tuttle called Kraehnke and told him the coverage price. Kraehnke agreed to the quoted price, inasmuch as his primary concern was the cost of the coverage as opposed to which company would provide the coverage. That same day, Kraehnke went to Tuttle's office to secure coverage with Southern County Mutual. Tuttle gave Kraehnke a typed binder which provided coverage on the 18-wheeler from May 27, 1982, to June 27, 1982. The binder reflected 1) Kraehnke as the insured, 2) Southern County Mutual as the insurer, 3) Colonial as the insurance agency, and 4) the Bank as loss payee. In exchange for the binder, Kraehnke gave Tuttle approximately $900, which was the quoted first premium.

Some two to three days later, Edwards telephoned Tuttle and told him that he had made a mistake in quoting the price of the policy and that Southern County would not write Kraehnke's coverage for the price Edwards had previously given Tuttle. However, Edwards informed Tuttle that he could secure insurance at the quoted price through Amherst Insurance Company. Tuttle, without notifying Kraehnke, authorized a substitution of insurance companies from Southern County Mutual to Amherst. Tuttle never relayed this information to Kraehnke. In fact, sometime during the week before June 27, 1982, Kraehnke called Tuttle inquiring about receiving his payment book and policy. During this conversation, Tuttle failed to mention the substitution of carriers.

On or about June 29, 1982, R.O. Williams Company executed an extension binder which was in effect from June 27, 1982, until July 27, 1982. Due to a clerical error, the extension binder listed the insurance company as Southern County Mutual instead of Amherst.

On July 2, 1982, Kraehnke's 18-wheeler was totally destroyed in a collision. Four days later, Kraehnke called R.O. Williams Company and provided information for the proof of loss. It was at this time that the personnel at R.O. Williams discovered the clerical error on the extension binder. Thereafter, the proof of loss was sent to Amherst. Kraehnke first learned that Amherst, and not Southern County Mutual, was his insurance company when an Amherst adjuster telephoned him in order to prepare the proof of loss. Amherst approved Kraehnke's claim and authorized payment.

On September 24, 1982, the Insurance Commissioner of Pennsylvania entered a Suspension Order against Amherst which prohibited the payment of any claims by Amherst without prior written consent of the Insurance Commissioner. Thereafter, on November 10, 1982, the Commonwealth Court of Pennsylvania issued an order declaring Amherst Insurance Company insolvent. Amherst's charter was dissolved and the Insurance Commissioner was appointed as liquidator.

In November of 1984, the Bank filed suit against Southern County Mutual alleging that Southern County Mutual was liable on the extension binder which was in effect on July 2, 1982, when Kraehnke's 18-wheeler was destroyed. In the alternative, if no Southern County Mutual binder was found to be in effect on the date of loss, the Bank alleged that R.O. Williams, Jr. and the five other defendants were strictly liable for violating portions of the Texas Insurance Code pertaining to surplus lines coverage. Southern County Mutual filed a cross-action against R.O. Williams, Jr. and the others seeking "indemnity and contribution" in the event that the jury found Southern County Mutual was liable on the extension binder.

The case was submitted to the jury on twenty issues, each of which the jury answered against the Bank. The jury did, however, find that the difference in the tractor's market value before and after the collision was $36,000. The trial judge overruled the Bank's Motion for Judgment Notwithstanding the Verdict, and on March 5, 1986, signed the final judgment ordering that the Bank take nothing in its suit against Southern County Mutual, R.O. Williams, Jr. and the other five defendants.

On appeal, the court of appeals, with one justice dissenting, reversed the judgment of the trial court and rendered judgment against all defendants. The court found that as a matter of law, the extension binder, listing Southern County Mutual as the insurance company, was "legally in full force and effect" on the date of the loss. Further, the court of appeals found that R.O. Williams, Jr. and the other defendants were strictly liable to the Bank for violating various sections of the Texas Insurance Code. In accordance with its holdings as to liability, the court of appeals held that the Bank was to recover $35,000 (the $36,000 market value of the tractor less the $1,000 deductible in the binder) from Southern County Mutual and $35,000 from R.O. Williams, Jr. and the others. We affirm the court's judgment as to Southern County Mutual but reverse that portion of the judgment imposing liability against R.O. Williams, Jr. and the five other defendants for violations of the Insurance Code.

When Kraehnke left Tuttle's office on May 27, 1982, he had a valid insurance binder with Southern County Mutual. The only action which remained was for R.O. Williams Company to forward Kraehnke a copy of his insurance policy. Therefore, any subsequent changes in insurance companies would have required approval either by Kraehnke or his authorized agent. As stated earlier, the first time Kraehnke learned that Amherst was his new insurance company was when an Amherst adjuster contacted him concerning his proof of loss. Obviously, Kraehnke never authorized a substitution of insurance companies. Therefore, the question then becomes whether Tuttle, as Kraehnke's agent, had the authority to order Edwards to cancel the binder with Southern County Mutual and obtain coverage with Amherst. Southern County Mutual argues that Tuttle had such authority. We disagree.

The crux of Southern County Mutual's argument is that Tuttle, as Kraehnke's agent, had the authority to substitute insurance companies. Thus, Southern County Mutual had the burden of pleading and proving this agency relationship. *Buchoz v. Klein,* 184 S.W.2d 271, 271 (Tex. 1944). The Bank was entitled to fair and adequate notice that Southern County Mutual was going to rely upon an agency theory at trial. *Murray v. O & A Express, Inc.,* 630 S.W.2d 633, 636 (Tex. 1982).

Southern County Mutual failed to plead that Tuttle was acting as an agent for Kraehnke. In fact, Southern County Mutual first suggested that Tuttle was Kraehnke's agent in its Motion for Directed Verdict. Southern County Mutual thus failed to carry its burden on its theory that Tuttle had the authority to substitute insurance companies without first obtaining Kraehnke's authorization to do so.

In addition to this procedural misstep, this court's holding in *Shaller v. Commercial Standard Fire Ins. Co.*, 158 Tex. 143, 309 S.W.2d 59 (Tex. 1958), also leads to the conclusion, on the merits, that Tuttle had not attained the status of Kraehnke's agent with the authority to cancel the binder with Southern County Mutual and bind Kraehnke with Amherst. In *Shaller*, one of the issues presented was whether an insurance recording agent, who was employed solely to procure insurance, could act as the insured's agent for the purpose of accepting cancellation of an insurance policy. In holding that such an agency relationship did not exist, we stated that it is settled law that one who authorizes another to procure insurance for him does not thereby constitute such person his agent to receive notice of cancellation or for the purpose of agreeing to a proposed cancellation of the policy. 309 S.W.2d at 64

In the case before us, Kraehnke contacted Tuttle for the sole purpose of acquiring insurance on his 18-wheeler. Such a limited solicitation by Kraehnke cannot serve as the basis for establishing a broad agency relationship between Kraehnke and Tuttle.

We therefore conclude that, as a matter of law, a valid Southern County Mutual Insurance binder was in effect on July 2, 1982. Accordingly, we affirm that portion of the court of appeals judgment that 1) Kraehnke had a valid binder with Southern County Mutual and 2) Southern County Mutual was liable to the Bank, as loss payee on Kraehnke's policy, for $35,000.

In both its pleadings and court of appeals brief, the Bank sought relief on two alternative theories. First, the Bank claimed that Southern County Mutual was liable because a valid Southern County

Mutual binder was in force on the date of the accident. Alternatively, if no binder was in effect, the Bank claimed that R.O. Williams, Jr. and the other defendants were strictly liable because they had violated selected provisions of the Insurance Code. By framing its grounds of recovery in this manner, the Bank was, in effect, stating that the existence of a Southern County Mutual binder precluded any imposition of strict liability under the Insurance Code. For if Southern County Mutual was liable to the Bank, this meant that R.O. Williams, Jr. and the other defendants had satisfied the Insurance Code requirements that govern the placement of surplus line insurance companies in Texas.

The court of appeals, however, did not view the situation in this manner. After establishing Southern County Mutual's liability under its binder with Kraehnke, the court nevertheless immersed itself into a lengthy discussion of how R.O. Williams, Jr. and the others were strictly liable to the Bank for violating certain provisions of the Insurance Code. Not only did this unnecessary finding of strict liability go further than any relief the Bank requested, it also resulted in an erroneous double recovery for the Bank.

* * *

The Bank's pleadings set forth alternative grounds of recovery. The court of appeals, however, rendered a judgment based upon both grounds of recovery pleaded. Not only does this judgment grant an impermissible double recovery to the Bank, it fails to conform to the Bank's pleadings. We therefore reverse that portion of the court of appeals judgment which finds the other defendants strictly liable and grants the Bank recovery against these individuals. The resulting judgment will correctly reflect Southern County Mutual's liability to the Bank.

* * *

In conclusion, we affirm that portion of the court of appeals judgment stating that a valid Southern County Mutual binder was in effect at the time of Kraehnke's loss. Further, we reverse that portion of the court of appeals judgment which granted the Bank an erroneous double recovery against these individuals.

NOTES & QUESTIONS

1) In *Carey,* the Texas Supreme Court stated that "Bruce's insurability and acceptability [created] a condition precedent to the existence of temporary insurance." Does that mean a condition precedent must be satisfied before there can be a formation of a valid temporary insurance "contract?" Or does the binding receipt create the "valid contract?"

2) Before parties can consummate a "valid contract," several elements must be established: a) an offer; b) acceptance of the offer; c) a meeting of the minds; d) proof that each party consented to the terms; e) execution of the contract; f) delivery of the contract; g) proof of mutual intent to be

bound under the contract; and h) mutual promises. See *Copeland v. Alsobrook,* 3 S.W.3d 598, 604 (Tex. App. Ct. — San Antonio, 1999).

3) Did the conditional insurance binders in *Carey* and in *Southern County* satisfy all of the necessary elements—those outlined in *Copeland*—to form a "valid" temporary or permanent contract?

4) Tex. Ins. Code § 705.103 reads: "Except as otherwise provided by this code, a life insurance policy must be accompanied by a copy of (1) the policy application; and (2) any questions and answers given in connection with the application." Tex. Ins. Code § 1101.003 states: "A life insurance policy must provide that the policy or the policy and the application for the policy constitute the entire contract between the parties." Do those sections contradict the Texas Supreme Court's temporary-contract rulings in *Carey* and *Southern County*?

B. Agents' Duties, Representations, Personal Liability and Vicarious Liability

Texas Insurance Code identifies a variety of insurance "agents," describes their respective obligations, reports the extent of agents' common-law and statutory liabilities, and outlines the scope of each agent's authority to bind an insurance company. The most outstanding sections in the Texas Insurance Code appear below.

TEX. INS. CODE § 550.001(a) —SOLICITATION OR COLLECTION OF CERTAIN PAYMENTS

An insurer or an insurer's agent or sponsoring organization may not solicit or collect, in connection with an application for insurance or the issuance of a policy, a payment other than: 1) a premium; 2) a tax; 3) a finance charge; 4) a policy fee; 5) an agent fee; 6) a service fee, including a charge for costs described by Section 4005.003; 7) an inspection fee; or 8) membership dues in a sponsoring organization.

‡

TEX. INS. CODE § 4001.051 — ACTS CONSTITUTING ACTING AS AGENT

(a) This section applies regardless of whether an insurer is incorporated under the laws of this state or another state or a foreign government.

(b) Regardless of whether the act is done at the request of or by the employment of an insurer, broker, or other person, a person is the agent of the insurer for which the act is done or risk is taken for purposes of the liabilities, duties, requirements, and penalties provided by this title, Chapter 21, or a provision listed in Section 4001.009 if the person:

(1) solicits insurance on behalf of the insurer;

(2) receives or transmits other than on the person's own behalf an application for insurance or an insurance policy to or from the insurer;

(3) advertises or otherwise gives notice that the person will receive or transmit an application for insurance or an insurance policy;

(4) receives or transmits an insurance policy of the insurer;

(5) examines or inspects a risk;

(6) receives, collects, or transmits an insurance premium;

(7) makes or forwards a diagram of a building;

(8) takes any other action in the making or consummation of an insurance contract for or with the insurer other than on the person's own behalf; or

(9) examines into, adjusts, or aids in adjusting a loss for or on behalf of the insurer.

(c) This section does not authorize an agent to orally, in writing, or otherwise alter or waive a term or condition of an insurance policy or an application for an insurance policy.

‡

Tex. Ins. Code § 4001.052. Solicitor of Application for Insurance —Agent of Insurer

(a) A person who solicits an application for life, accident, or health insurance or property or casualty insurance is considered the agent of the insurer issuing a policy on the application and not the agent of the insured in any controversy between the insurer and the insured, the insured's beneficiary, or the insured's dependents.

(b) The agent may not alter or waive a term or condition of the application or policy.

‡

Tex. Ins. Code § 4001.053 — Personal Liability for Acting As Agent

A person who takes an action listed in Section 4001.051 for or on behalf of an insurer before the insurer complies with the requirements of the laws of this state is personally liable to the holder of any insurance policy with respect to which the action was taken for any loss covered by the insurance policy. See pg. 40: Agents liability under DTPA

‡

Tex. Ins. Code § 4053.001(3) — Definition of a "Managing General Agent"

Stands in shoes of H/Q

"Managing general agent" means a person, firm, or corporation that has supervisory responsibility for the local agency and field operations of an insurer in this state or that is authorized by an insurer to accept or process on the insurer's behalf insurance policies produced and sold by other agents.

‡

Tex. Ins. Code § 4053.101 — Powers and Duties of Managing General Agents

A managing general agent acting for an insurer may (1) receive and pass on daily reports and monthly accounts; (2) receive and be responsible for agency balances; (3) handle the adjustment of losses; or (4) appoint or direct general property and casualty agents and personal lines property and casualty agents in this state.

International Security Life Insurance Company v. Finck
496 S.W.2d 544
(Tex. 1973)

The motion for rehearing is granted. The original and dissenting opinions and the judgment of the Court of November 22, 1972 are withdrawn and set aside, and this opinion is substituted as the opinion of the Court.

Suit was brought by C. F. Finck against International Security Life Insurance Company to recover indemnities for medical and hospital expenses under a policy of hospitalization insurance issued by the defendant below, statutory penalty and attorney fees, and for actual and exemplary damages for deceit in connection with the issuance of the policy. The trial court entered judgment for the plaintiff on a jury verdict for actual and exemplary damages and attorney fees. The court of civil appeals reformed the judgment by reducing the recovery of actual damages and affirmed. We reverse and remand.

Mrs. Finck, substituted as plaintiff after Mr. Finck's death on July 7, 1970, alleged the policy in question was issued pursuant to an application presented by David Cochrell, stipulated to be a soliciting agent for International Security Life Insurance Company and acting within the scope of his employment. Mrs. Finck testified the agent represented the policy "covered everything that medicare didn't cover"; and that the company always paid their claims promptly. The Fincks were not familiar with the insurer here, but they wanted a hospitalization policy and would have purchased another policy if they had not bought this one. When the policy was received in the mail by the Fincks, Mr. Finck did not read it, but Mrs. Finck read "a part of it." She noticed "there was a whole lot of difference in there from what he (Cochrell) was representing it." She did not notice the provision in the policy that it could be returned in ten days and the premium would be returned. She testified they intended to keep the policy. Mr. Finck was hospitalized some eleven months later. The claim was denied on the ground the illness had its origin prior to the effective date of the policy.

The petitioner first challenges the award of exemplary damages on dual grounds of the insured's waiver of any representation of the soliciting agent and the absence of any evidence of knowledge, authorization or ratification of the alleged wrongful acts of the agent by the insured. In response to the special issues submitted, the jury found: (2A) The insured's agent represented the policy would pay for everything medicare did not pay; (2B) that such representation was false; (2C) that the insureds relied upon the truth of such representation in purchasing the policy; (2D) that such representations were a material inducement in purchasing the policy; (3A) that, International Security Life, petitioner, had the reputation of refusing to pay legitimate claims; (3B) that such reputation was concealed by petitioner and its agents; (3C) such concealment was material inducement in purchasing the policy.

During the trial the parties stipulated Cochrell was a soliciting agent for the petitioners and was acting in the scope of his employment at all times material to this cause. It is the settled law of this State that a soliciting agent of an insurance company has no power or authority to make a contract on behalf of the company or to waive the terms of the policy. *Southland Life Ins. Co. v. Statler,* 163 S.W.2d 623, 630 (Tex. 1942)

So far as this record reflects the agent had no authority other than to solicit applications for hospitalization insurance and forward same to the home office for acceptance or rejection. Under this record the alleged representations were beyond Cochrell's authority to make. *Southland Life Ins. Co. v. Statler, supra* and *Indianapolis Life Ins. Co. v. Powell*, 127 S.W.2d 172 (Tex. 1939).

The insured claimed exemplary damages on account of the false and fraudulent representations of the policy coverage alleged to have been made by the insured's soliciting agent. It is the rule in Texas that a principal is liable for exemplary or punitive damages because of wrongful acts of his agent only if there is shown some misconduct on the part of the principal in connection with the agent's wrong, such as authorizing the agent's wrongful acts, or subsequent ratification of those acts. *Fisher v. Carrousel Motor Hotel,* 424 S.W.2d 627 (Tex.1967).

There is no evidence in this record tending to show the insurer authorized or had any knowledge of the agent's alleged false and fraudulent representations. Nor is there any evidence the insurer subsequently ratified these false and fraudulent representations. There is ample evidence the petitioner had a widespread reputation of refusing to pay legitimate claims, but there is no evidence respondent knew of this reputation at the time of making their application for the insurance. In fact, the Fincks had not known of petitioner prior to the visit of petitioner's agent. There is no evidence whatever that the insurer's reputation was concealed from the respondents. This record forms no basis for the assessment of actual or exemplary damages.

* * *

The judgments of the courts below awarding respondents actual and exemplary damages are reversed and rendered. The judgment of the trial court awarding recovery under the insurance policy, plus penalty and interest is affirmed. . . .

Royal Globe Insurance Company v. Bar Consultants, Incorporated
577 S.W.2d 688
(Tex. 1979)

This is a deceptive trade practice case. The principal in question presented on this appeal is whether a misrepresentation about coverage afforded by a policy of insurance, made by the insurance company's local recording agent, is a deceptive trade practice under Texas statutes for which the insurance company as principal is liable for treble damages.

Petitioner Royal Globe Insurance Company, defendant in the trial court, is appealing from a judgment obtained by Plaintiff and Respondent, Bar Consultants, Inc., for violation of the Deceptive Trade Practices Act (DTPA), Tex. Bus. & Com. Code Ann. § 17.46 *et seq.* and Article 21.21 of the Texas Insurance Code. The Court of Civil Appeals affirmed. We affirm, but on different grounds.

Bar Consultants, Inc. operated a bar near the campus of The University of Texas known as "The Bucket." The president of Bar Consultants, Inc. — John Barber — testified that he purchased a policy of insurance from Tully Embrey, an agent of Royal Globe, sometime prior to September 1975. The one-year policy was renewed on September 4, 1974 and again on September 4, 1975. Each contained identical terms which included a vandalism and malicious mischief endorsement. Barber testified that before the first policy was written, he had a lengthy discussion with Embrey about the problem of vandalism at which time Embrey assured him that he was "totally covered" from losses caused by vandalism. His testimony was uncontradicted.

The policy in question is a Texas Standard Policy covering fire and extended coverage. An endorsement attached includes coverage for vandalism and malicious mischief. The insurance memorandum says that the property covered is "(o)n the contents in the . . . building," giving the address of "The Bucket." The term "contents" is defined in the policy.

On January 31, 1974, during the policy year 1973-74, Royal Globe paid a vandalism claim filed by Bar Consultants. The description of the damage on the proof of loss form was "Vandals inflicted damage in the bathroom area for which insured is liable under lease contract."

On the night of March 5, 1976, the men's rest room at The Bucket sustained extensive damage. The main sewer line was stopped up by one or more plastic cups; the flush valve part of the urinal had been torn away. The stoppage in the main sewer line caused the facilities in both men's and women's rest rooms to overflow. The partitions between the commodes were torn down, water was nearly an inch deep on the floor of the rest room and out into the hall. The acoustical ceiling had been torn down, as had the light fixtures. In addition, the floor tiles came loose and the carpet was ruined. The trial court found that the damage was caused by vandalism or malicious mischief and that it cost $1,735.15 to repair.

The day following the damage Barber called Embrey's office. Embrey was not in, but his secretary, after a discussion with Barber, told Barber to "go ahead; have the work done. You're covered under the policy." Later Barber talked with Embrey who told him the same thing. Subsequently, Royal Globe refused the claim, and Bar Consultants filed this suit against Embrey and Royal Globe.

Bar Consultants alleged that the damages were covered by its policy and asked for actual damages plus a penalty of 12% interest and attorney's fees, or in the alternative for actual and exemplary damages because of the fraudulent misrepresentations of the agent, and in the further alternative for treble damages, attorney's fees and return of premiums because, if in fact the policy did not cover such damage, then such representations and policy terms were false, deceptive and misleading, in violation of Article 21.21, Section 4(1), Texas Insurance Code, and Section 17.46(a)(12) of the DTPA.

The trial court found that under Article 21.02 and under the facts and circumstances of this case Tully Embrey was "at all times an agent" for Royal Globe; that Embrey, as Royal Globe's agent, represented to Bar Consultants that the policy covered all damages caused by vandalism, including the damage in question; and that the policy did not cover the damage in question. The trial court awarded Bar Consultants a judgment for $5,205.45, as treble the cost of repairs, plus $1,991.00 attorney's fees against Royal Globe. The Court of Civil Appeals affirmed, holding that Embrey's statement on the day after the loss of March 5 that the loss was "covered" under the policy, when in fact it was not, was a violation of both Article 21.21 of the Insurance Code and Section 17.46 of the Deceptive Trade Practices Act.

In order to determine what is a deceptive trade practice or act, as that term applies to a local recording agent for an insurance company, it is necessary to look at the definition of such act or practice given by the legislature. Section 16 of Article 21.21 declares that a cause of action for treble the actual damages may be brought by:

> Any person who has been injured by another's engaging in any of the practices (1) declared in Section 4 of this Article or (2) in rules or regulations lawfully adopted by the Board under this Article to be unfair methods of competition and unfair and deceptive acts or practices in the business of insurance or (3) in any practice defined by Section 17.46 of the Business and Commerce Code, as amended, as an unlawful deceptive trade practice . . . ."

* * *

Royal Globe by its first point of error contends that there is no evidence that its agent Embrey had authority to make statements and representations that were binding upon Royal Globe. Having determined what activity is prohibited, it is necessary to examine Embrey's legal relationship with Royal Globe and to determine the extent to which Royal Globe is responsible in law for his actions in misrepresenting policy coverage.

It is clear from the record before us that Tully Embrey was the local recording agent of Royal Globe as that term is defined in Article 21.14, Section 2: "... a person or firm engaged in soliciting and writing insurance, being authorized by an insurance company ... to solicit business and write, sign, execute and deliver policies of insurance, and to bind companies on insurance risks . . . ."

Embrey issued the policy in question from the "Tully Embrey Insurance Agency"; he signed the policy for Royal Globe as its agent and Royal Globe has not denied his authority to do so. In describing the circumstances of a local recording agent's authority, this Court said in *Shaller v. Commercial Standard Insurance Co*., 309 S.W.2d 59, 63 (Tex. 1958):

> "The purpose of the statute was to vest local recording agents with authority co-extensive with that of the company insofar as writing insurance is concerned and to remove all questions of the local agent's actual or apparent authority from the field of cavil or dispute. . . ."

The trial court found that Embrey was Royal Globe's agent under the provisions of Article 21.02, which says:

> "Any person who solicits insurance on behalf of any insurance company, whether incorporated under the laws of this or any other state or foreign government, or who takes or transmits other than for himself any application for insurance or any policy of insurance to or from such company, or who advertises or otherwise gives notice that he will receive or transmit the same, or who shall receive or deliver a policy of insurance of any such company, or who shall examine or inspect any risk, or receive, or collect, or transmit any premium of insurance, or make or forward any diagram of any building or buildings, or do or perform any other act or thing in the making or consummating of any contract of insurance for or with any such insurance company other than for himself, or who shall examine into, or adjust, or aid in adjusting, any loss for or on behalf of any such insurance company, whether any of such acts shall be done at the instance or request, or by the employment of such insurance company, or of, or by, any broker or other person, shall be held to be the agent of the company for which the act is done, or the risk is taken, as far as relates to all the liabilities, duties, requirements and penalties set forth in this chapter. . . ."

* * *

Royal Globe cites Hart*ford Fire Insurance Company v. Walker,* 61 S.W. 711 (Tex. 1901), in which this Court held that the predecessor of Article 21.02 did not confer any power or authority to contract beyond what the law and the terms of his appointment already gave him. Not only was this case decided before Article 21.21 was enacted, but it and others cited by Royal Globe deal with the authority of a soliciting agent, which is clearly much more limited than the authority of a local recording agent authorized to sign and execute insurance policies. *International Security Life Ins. Co. v. Finck,* 496 S.W.2d 544 (Tex.1973). In *Home Ins. Co. of N.Y. v. Roberts*, 100 S.W.2d 91 (Tex. Comm. App.1937, opinion adopted), we held that a recording agent could orally waive a policy provision despite a policy provision to the contrary. The one case cited by Royal Globe which dealt with local recording agents, State Farm Mutual *Automobile Ins. Co. v. Matlock,* 462 S.W.2d 277 (Tex.1970), concerned representations made after the loss occurred.

More importantly, none of the cases cited by Royal Globe involved questions of deceptive acts or practices defined by the statutes here invoked; all involved the questions of contractual liability. *Hartford Fire Insurance Company v. Walker, supra*; *State Farm Mutual Automobile Ins. Co. v. Matlock, supra*; *International Security Life Ins. Co. v. Finck, supra*.

We are not to be understood as holding that the statutory authority granted an agent under Article 21.02 authorizes that agent to misrepresent policy coverage and bind the company to terms contrary to those of the written policy; that question was decided by us in *International Security Life Ins. Co. v. Finck, supra*. However, an insurance company that authorizes an agent to sell its policies may not escape liability for the misrepresentations made by that agent which violate Article 21.21 or Section 17.46 merely by establishing that the agent had no actual authority to make any such misrepresentation.

Neither Article 21.21 nor Section 17.46(b)(12) require either expressly or by implication that an agent have actual authority before an insurance company can be found to have vicariously committed a deceptive act or practice. Section 1 of the regulations of the Board of Insurance impliedly negates such a requirement when they include acts "whether done directly or indirectly, and irrespective of whether the person is acting as insurer, principal, agent, employer or employee, or in other capacity or connection with such insurer."

To require actual authority would emasculate both Article 21.21 and Section 17.46 and provide a violator with an easily manufactured defense. It would only be necessary for a corporate principal to deny that an agent had actual authority to perform an act, even though a reasonably prudent man, using diligence and discretion in view of the insurance company's conduct, would naturally suppose the agent possessed such authority.

There is even stronger evidence of legislative intent that the absence of actual authority of an agent is not a defense to a violation of Section 17.46 when the agent is clothed with apparent authority to do the act or make the representation. Section 17.46(c)(2) provides that in construing actions brought under the Act, the legislative intent is that "the courts to the extent possible will be guided by Subsection (b) of this section and the interpretations given by the federal courts to Section 5(a)(1) of the Federal Trade Commission Act."

Numerous federal decisions made applicable to this case by Section 17.46(c), hold that lack of actual authority is not a defense if the agent is acting within the apparent scope of his authority, and not even instructions not to mislead nor diligence in preventing the misrepresentations will exculpate the corporate principal.

Embrey as a local recording agent for Royal Globe, had statutory authority under Article 21.02 and Article 21.14(2) to sell insurance policies for the company and by necessary implication to represent the coverage afforded by such policies to the consumer. If his representations were false as the trial court here found, under the explicit language of Section 16, Article 21.21 and Section 17.46(b)(12) of the DTPA, his actions constituted a deceptive act or practice for which his principal is accountable.

Though it may be harsh to hold a principal liable for the deceptive acts of his agents where he does not authorize or have knowledge that they occurred, such result is clearly called for by the legislature's enactment of the DTPA. *Woods v. Littleton*, 554 S.W.2d 662, 669-71 (Tex.1977). The rationale behind this agency principle is expressed by Justice Learned Hand when he wrote: "since the principal has selected the agent to act in a venture in which the principal is interested, it is fair, as between him and a third person, to impose upon him the risk that the agent may exceed his instructions."

By its next point of error, Royal Globe argues that Bar Consultants has presented no evidence that it was "injured" or suffered damages as a result of Embrey's representations. We agree with Petitioner's contention with regard to the post-loss representation of coverage made on March 6, but hold that there is evidence that Bar Consultants was "adversely affected" and "injured" when it relied on the misrepresentations of coverage made by Embrey at the time of the initial policy in 1973 and impliedly made each time the policy was renewed. The injury to Bar Consultants was that it believed it was covered by a policy of insurance from any loss caused by vandalism when it was not so covered. Bar Consultants' damage was the reasonable and necessary cost of repairs made necessary by the vandalism. That belief was made even more logical and reasonable by the knowledge that, prior to renewing the policy, Royal Globe paid a claim for the same type damage to the bathroom area without questioning coverage, thus giving credence to the agent's previous misrepresentations.

Accordingly, the representations made by agent Embrey at the time the policy was sold in September 1973 and impliedly made to Bar Consultants upon each renewal do furnish a basis for deceptive act or practice liability of Royal Globe, and there is evidence to support the trial court's findings in this regard.

We disagree with the Court of Civil Appeals' holding that the representations made by Tully Embrey and his secretary after the loss had occurred constituted a deceptive trade act or practice. In the first place, Embrey was in the business of selling insurance, not the business of adjusting claims, and his post-loss statement that "you're covered" under the policy was not within his actual or apparent authority. Secondly, there is no evidence that Bar Consultants, Inc. took any action based on the post-loss representation to its injury or damage. The evidence was clear that Bar Consultants, Inc. would have repaired the damages to the rest rooms regardless of the post-loss representation in order to open for business immediately, whether or not the loss was covered by insurance. Since Bar Consultants was going to have the damage repaired anyway, it could not have been "injured" or "adversely affected" by the post-loss representation. We agree with Petitioner Royal Globe that the Court of Civil Appeals was in error in holding that Bar Consultants relied on the post-loss representation of Embrey in a way that caused Bar Consultants any actual damages.

The judgment of the Court of Civil Appeals is affirmed.

NOTES & QUESTIONS

1) For sure, the DTPA is a statute. However, as discussed in Part I of this casebook, DTPA causes of action are tort-based rather than contract-based actions. And among tort-based actions, one finds negligence-based and intentional torts. In *Royal Globe*, the Texas Supreme Court stated: "[The] question presented on this appeal is whether [the insurance company's local recording agent's] misrepresentation about coverage . . . is a deceptive trade practice." Are all "deceptive trade practices" intentional? Are all "misrepresentations" intentional?

2) *Employer's Vicarious Liability for Intentional Torts of Employee:* An employer is not liable for an employee's intentional torts. *See Viking v. Circle K Convenience Stores, Inc.,* 742 S.W.2d 732, 734 (Tex. App.-Houston [1st Dist.] 1987, writ denied). However, under the doctrine of respondeat superior, an employer may be liable for an employee's intentional act if the employee's act 1) falls within the scope of his general authority; 2) is in furtherance of the employer's business; and 3) is for the accomplishment of the object for which the employee was hired. See *Robertson Tank Lines, Inc. v. Van Cleave,* 468 S.W.2d 354, 357 (Tex. 1971). The Restatement (Second) of Torts § 909 (1965) states that a principal is liable for punitive damages only if the principal authorized or ratified the act, was reckless in employing or retaining the agent, or the agent was employed in a managerial capacity and was acting in the scope of employment.

3) Did the *Royal Globe* court discuss whether the local recording agent's conduct was intentional or negligent? Does the distinction matter under the agency principles and the doctrine of respondeat superior, since the agent was a recording rather than a soliciting agent?

4) Generally, an employer is not vicariously liable for an employee's intentional conduct. Is an insurer liable for a soliciting agent's intentional misrepresentation since a soliciting agent cannot bind an insurer or exceed the scope of the agent's authority? Consider the facts and holding in the next case.

Celtic Life Insurance Company v. Coats
885 S.W.2d 96
(Tex. 1994)

We grant John D. Coats' motion for rehearing and withdraw our prior opinion and judgment. The following is now the opinion of the Court.

This case presents three issues relating to an insurance company's liability for its agent's representations: first, whether the company's liability depends on its authorization of misrepresentations; second, whether reliance on the representations is an element of recovery; and third, whether the insured's damages should be trebled when the misrepresentations were not committed "knowingly." The court of appeals affirmed the trial court's judgment on a jury verdict against the insurer. We likewise affirm, but modify the court of appeals' judgment by deleting the award of trebled damages.

I.

Kenneth Harrell, a duly-appointed agent for Celtic Life Insurance Co., visited Aloha Pools in September 1984 and met with its owner, John Coats, to discuss health insurance for Aloha's employees and their families. Coats stated that he wanted a policy providing benefits for psychiatric care that would be equal to or better than the $20,000 coverage provided by his current policy. Coats explained that he needed such coverage because his oldest son had previously required psychiatric care, and he was concerned that his younger son might require similar care. Harrell responded that he understood Coats' needs fully, having experienced similar financial difficulties in providing psychiatric care for his own son.

Harrell subsequently proposed that Coats purchase a specific policy written by Celtic— a policy that provided a maximum lifetime hospitalization benefit of $1 million. Harrell did not point out that psychiatric benefits under the policy were limited to $10,000.

Coats asked his business manager, Paula Englemann, to review Celtic's brochure and discuss the matter further with Harrell. Englemann noticed the $10,000 limit on benefits for psychiatric care, and questioned Harrell about its meaning. Harrell assured her that the $10,000 limit applied only to out-patient psychiatric care. Based on that representation, Englemann recommended to Coats that he purchase the Celtic policy, and Coats agreed.

In January of 1985, Kenneth Harrell obtained enrollment cards, filled out an application, and collected an initial premium in order to obtain Celtic coverage for Aloha's employees. He then forwarded the enrollment cards, the application, and the premium check to Celtic. Celtic then sent an insurance policy to Harrell, who delivered it to Coats.

During the following August, Coats' son was admitted to Shoal Creek Hospital for psychiatric care. Coats filed a claim for his son's treatment; but despite Harrell's continued assurances that the in-hospital psychiatric treatment was covered by the $1 million hospitalization limit, Celtic paid only $10,000 of the $27,000 in medical expenses.

Coats filed this suit seeking relief under article 21.21 of the Texas Insurance Code and the Texas Deceptive Trade Practices—Consumer Protection Act (DTPA), Tex. Bus. & Com. Code § 17.41-.63. After hearing the evidence, the jury made the following findings:

(1) Harrell made misrepresentations concerning the terms, benefits, provisions, or conditions of the insurance policy such as to be a producing cause of damages to Coats, but he did not do so knowingly;

(2) Harrell had authority to explain, on Celtic's behalf, the benefits of the insurance policy; and

(3) Harrell did not have the authority of Celtic to make representations concerning the insurance policy's terms, benefits, provisions, or conditions which were outside the scope of the written document.

The jury also found that $17,000 would fairly and reasonably compensate Coats for his damages. The trial court rendered judgment on the verdict in favor of Coats, and the court of appeals affirmed.

II.

Celtic argues that it should not be held responsible for Harrell's representations for two reasons: first, Harrell was a mere soliciting agent, and as such lacked authority to bind Celtic; and second, the jury's answer to the third question — which was submitted over Coats' objection-establishes that Harrell was acting outside of his authority as Celtic's agent. We reject both arguments.

In the contexts of life, health, and accident insurance, the Texas Insurance Code makes no distinction between recording agents and soliciting agents. *See May v. United Serv. Ass'n of America,* 844 S.W.2d 666, 669 n. 8 (Tex.1992) (discussing Tex. Ins. Code art. 21.14, § 20). Rather, agents are defined generally: section 21.02 of the Code lists various acts performed in the ordinary course of providing insurance,[1] and states that any person who performs these acts "shall be held to be the agent of the company for which the act is done, or the risk is taken, as far as relates to all liabilities, duties, requirements and penalties set forth in this chapter."

There is no dispute that Harrell performed, on Celtic's behalf, at least some of the acts listed in section 21.02. Thus, under that provision, Harrell was clearly Celtic's agent.

An insurance company is generally liable for any misconduct by an agent that is within the actual or apparent scope of the agent's authority. *See, e.g., Royal Globe Ins. Co. v. Bar Consultants,* 577 S.W.2d 688, 693-94 (Tex.1979). This rule is based on notions of fairness: "since the principal has selected the agent to act in a venture in which the principal is interested, it is fair, as between him and a third person, to impose upon him the risk that the agent may exceed his instructions." *Royal Globe,* 577 S.W.2d at 694 (quoting *Standard Distributors v. FTC,* 211 F.2d 7, 15 (2d Cir.1954) (Hand, J.)).

In the present case, the jury was asked whether Harrell had authority to explain, on Celtic's behalf, the benefits of the insurance policy. The instructions accompanying this question explained that "authority" of an insurance agent can be actual or apparent; and in defining apparent authority, the instructions explained, among other things, that "[a]n insurance company may so clothe the agent with signs or indications of authority so as to lead a reasonably prudent person to believe that the agent actually has such authority." The jury answered the question affirmatively.

1 The acts listed include, among other things, soliciting insurance on behalf of an insurance company; transmitting an application or policy to or from the insurance company; receiving, collecting or transmitting an insurance premium; and adjusting a loss on behalf of an insurance company.

Celtic does not contend that Harrell's representations were so absurd that no reasonable person could have believed Harrell was acting within the scope of his authority. Nor does Celtic assert any other challenge to the jury's finding that Coats had authority to explain the policy. Thus, under common-law rules of agency, Celtic is liable for the representations Harrell made in explaining the policy.

Celtic's liability is not affected by the finding that Harrell lacked authority to make representations outside the scope of the written document. In determining a principal's vicarious liability, the proper question is not whether the principal authorized the specific wrongful act; if that were the case, principals would seldom be liable for their agents' misconduct. Rather, the proper inquiry is whether the agent was acting within the scope of the agency relationship at the time of committing the act. The misrepresentation in the present case was made in the course of explaining the terms of the policy-a task the jury specifically found to be within the scope of Harrell's authority. Thus, Celtic cannot escape liability on the basis that it did not authorize particular representations concerning the policy.

III.

Celtic asserts that Harrell is not entitled to recover under the DTPA because there has been no showing that Coats relied on Harrell's representations. The trial court refused Celtic's requested issue on reliance after Coats objected on the basis of *Weitzel v. Barnes,* 691 S.W.2d 598 (Tex.1985).

In *Weitzel,* we determined that the legislature had specifically rejected reliance as an element of recovery under the DTPA. 691 S.W.2d at 600. The legislature chose, instead, to allow recovery when there is proof of a deceptive act or practice that is a "producing cause" of the consumer's actual damages. *Id.* (discussing Tex. Bus. & Com. Code § 17.50(a)).

In the present case, the trial court submitted a question asking whether Harrell made any misrepresentations that were a "producing cause of damages" to Coats. This question, we hold, fairly presented the issue of producing cause to the jury. We decline Celtic's invitation to overrule *Weitzel.*

IV.

Finally, Celtic argues that the trebling of actual damages was erroneous in view of the jury's finding that Harrell's misrepresentations were not made "knowingly." Celtic points out that since 1979, the DTPA has required that conduct be committed knowingly before damages may be trebled. Tex. Bus. & Com.Code § 17.50(b)(1). Additionally, by amendment effective April 4, 1985, article 21.21 of the Texas Insurance Code has included a similar requirement of knowing conduct before damages may be trebled. Tex. Ins. Code art. 21.21 § 16(b)(1). Celtic argues that Coats' cause of action did not accrue until August 1985, when his benefits were denied, so that knowing conduct is required for trebling of damages under either article 21.21 or the DTPA.

We agree. A cause of action generally accrues at the time when facts come into existence that authorize a claimant to seek a judicial remedy. *Murray v. San Jacinto Agency, Inc.,* 800 S.W.2d

826, 828 (Tex.1990); *Robinson v. Weaver,* 550 S.W.2d 18, 19 (Tex.1977). In *Murray,* we held that a first-party bad faith claim against an insurer generally accrues on the date the insurer denies coverage. Likewise, in the present case, we hold that Coats' claim under article 21.21 accrued on the date that Celtic first denied coverage for his son's psychiatric care. Accordingly, Coats' claim is governed by the 1985 amendment to article 21.21. *See* Act of March 19, 1985, 69th Leg., R.S., ch. 22, § 4, 1985 Tex.Gen.Laws 395, 396 ("This Act applies to a cause of action that accrues on or after the effective date of this Act."). Because the DTPA contained a "knowingly" requirement at all times relevant to this case, we need not determine the accrual date of Coats' DTPA claim. Under either statute, the jury's finding that Harrell did not act knowingly bars an award of trebled damages.

* * *

We conclude that Celtic is responsible for its agent's misrepresentations. We modify the court of appeals' judgment to reflect an award of only actual damages, rather than trebled damages; and because attorney's fees were awarded on a percentage basis, we also modify the award of attorney's fees. In all other respects, the judgment of the court of appeals is affirmed.

C. Declaratory Judgments and *Theories of Contract Construction and Interpretation*

Insurance Contracts and Judicial Decisions Over Whether Insurers Must Defend Insureds Who Violate Constitutional And Civil Rights: An Historical And Empirical Review of Federal and State Court Declaratory Judgments 1900-2000

35 Tort & Ins. L.J. 995 (2000)

Willy E. Rice

Declaratory Relief & The Interpretation of Contracts

[C]ourts . . . employ one of the following principles to determine rights and duties [under all types of contracts]:

(1) Traditional Rules of Contract Construction [Four-Corner Doctrine] — *See, e.g., Thompson v. Continental Ins. Co.*, 351 S.E.2d 904 (S.C. Ct. App. 1986) (an insurance policy is simply a contract between the insurer and the insured; therefore, it is subject to general rules of contract construction); *Yarborough v. Phoenix Mut. Life Ins. Co.*, 225 S.E.2d 344, 348-49 (S.C. 1976) (the "contract must be read as a whole, giving appropriate weight to all provisions").

(2) The Doctrine of Plain Meaning — *See, e.g., Dora Township v. Indiana Ins. Co.*, 400 N.E.2d 921 (Ill. App. Ct. 1980) ("An insurance policy [must] be read as any other contract, that is, according to the plain and ordinary meaning of its terms. In order to

ascertain the intent of the parties, the court should not examine the policy in a vacuum but should look to the circumstance surrounding the issuance of the policy, such as the situation of the parties and the purpose for which the policy was obtained.").

(3) The Doctrine of Ambiguity or the *Contra Proferentem* Doctrine — *See Gaunt v. John Hancock Mut. Life Ins. Co.*, 160 F.2d 599, 602 (2d Cir. 1947) ("[T]he canon *contra proferentum* is more rigorously applied in insurance than in other contracts, in recognition of the difference between the parties in their acquaintance with the subject matter") and *Steigler v. Insurance Co. of N. Am.*, 384 A.2d 398, 400 (Del. Super. Ct.1978) (concluding that to the extent that ambiguity does exist, "the doctrine of *contra proferentum* [sic] requires . . . the language of an insurance contract be construed most strongly against the insurance company that drafted it");

(4) The Doctrine of Adhesion — *See, e.g.*, *Broadwell Realty Services, Inc. v. Fidelity & Casualty Co. of New York*, 528 A.2d 76, 80 (N.J. Super. Ct. App. Div. 1987) ("[O]ur Supreme Court has stated that while insurance policies are contractual in nature, they are not ordinary agreements but 'contracts of adhesion between parties who are not equally situated.' It has been said that '[c]ourts apply the adhesion doctrine because of the unequal bargaining power of the parties.' Insurance contracts have thus been described as 'unipartite in character.' Such contracts 'are prepared by the company's experts, [people] learned in the law of insurance,' and therefore it is not unfair that the insurer 'bear the burden of any resulting confusion.' These circumstances long ago fathered the principle that doubts as to the existence or extent of coverage must generally be resolved in favor of the insured."); and

(5) The Doctrine of Reasonable Expectation — *See, St. Paul Mercury Insurance Co. v. Corbett*, 630 A.2d 28, 30 (Pa. Super. Ct. 1993) ("This court has held that the proper focus regarding issues of coverage under insurance contracts is the reasonable expectations of the insured. In determining the reasonable expectations of the insured, courts must examine the totality of the insurance transaction involved. However, while reasonable expectations of the insured are the focal points in interpreting the contract language of insurance policies, an insured may not complain that his or her reasonable expectations were frustrated by policy limitations which are clear and unambiguous. Like every other contract, the goal of interpreting an insurance contract is to ascertain the intent of the parties.").

Courts may use one or a combination of these doctrines to resolve a single controversy under . . . contract[s].

TEXAS UNIFORM DECLARATORY JUDGMENTS ACT — TEX. CIV. PRAC. & REM.CODE ANN. § 37.002(b) states: "This chapter is remedial; its purpose is to settle and to afford relief from uncertainty and insecurity with respect to rights, status, and other legal relations; and it is to be liberally construed and administered."

In *Bonham State Bank v. Beadle*, 907 S.W.2d 465, 467 (Tex.1995), the Texas Supreme Court stressed that a declaratory judgment is appropriate only if there is a justiciable controversy and the declaration sought will resolve the controversy. And before a dispute can qualify as "a justiciable controversy," there must be evidence of "a real and substantial controversy involving genuine conflict of tangible interests and not merely a theoretical dispute."

Furthermore, The Act does not confer jurisdiction on a trial court. Instead, it simply allows a party to commence a declaratory judgment trial where a court already exercise jurisdiction over a controversy. *State v. Morales*, 869 S.W.2d 941, 947 (Tex.1994).

A declaratory-judgment trial is an action in equity. Therefore, a petitioner does not have to prove a *prima facie case* as required in a court of law. Still, there are some common elements that a petitioner must establish before a court of equity will award declaratory relief. Those elements are 1) proof that an actual controversy exists, 2) proof that controversy involves questions or doubts about the parties' respective rights and duties under a statute or a contract, and 3) proof that a declaratory judgment will terminate the controversy. If a petitioner also wants attorney's fees, she must establish why such fees would be equitable and just.

Frequently, both insurance consumers and insurers petition Texas courts and federal district courts for declaratory relief. And as the following cases in this section illustrate, insurers and insureds' respective likelihood of prevailing in declaratory-judgment trials depends on whether courts apply the adhesion doctrine, the four-corner doctrine or a combination of the five theories of contract construction and interpretation.

Transport Insurance Company v. Standard Oil Company of Texas
337 S.W.2d 284
(Tex. 1960)

This suit in its inception was one for a declaratory judgment filed by the respondent, Standard Oil Company of Texas, against the petitioner, Transport Insurance Company, and Lawrence W. Annis, Jr. Annis was later dismissed from the suit. For convenience, the petitioner will hereinafter be referred to as 'Transport' and the respondent as 'Standard'. Standard sought a declaration by the court that Transport was obligated to defend a previous suit brought by Annis against Standard. In that prior suit Annis sued Standard for personal injuries alleged to have been sustained because of the negligence of Standard. The accident occurred in April 1957. At that time, Annis was employed as a driver for The Transport Company of Texas, hereinafter referred to as 'employer'. On April 11, 1957, Annis went upon the premises of Standard with a 1956 Diamond T tractor, propelling a large four-compartment tank trailer, for the purpose of receiving a load of Diesel fuel. Briefly, it was alleged that Annis drove the truck to the loading rack, and, while the fourth compartment was being filled with fuel, an explosion was caused or occurred which blew or expanded itself though the opening of the compartment injuring Annis.

At the time of the accident, Transport had in force a comprehensive general automobile policy covering the "employer" as its named assured. Standard alleged in its petition that:

> "[Transport agreed to] defend any suit and to pay on behalf of the insured all sums which the insured should become legally obligated to pay as damages because of bodily injury arising out of the use of said truck, and agreed that the use of said truck includes the loading and unloading thereof. Further, by said policy, Defendant Insurance Company agreed that any person using said vehicle with permission of The Transport Company of Texas was an insured, and, on the occasion in question, Plaintiff Standard was using said vehicle, by its agents and employees, in loading same, with permission of The Transport Company of Texas, so that Plaintiff Standard was an insured within the meaning of the policy and was entitled to its benefits of said policy in defense of the suit brought by Defendant Annis."

Transport refused to accept liability on the ground that its policy expressly excluded coverage of a claim by an employee (Annis) of the insured employer.

Standard and Transport each filed a motion for summary judgment based on the petition in the Annis suit, the Transport policy on the truck, and the Fireman's Fund Indemnity policy on Standard. These motions for summary judgment were heard together by the trial court without a jury. By agreement of the parties, the petition in the Annis suit and the two above mentioned policies were considered by the court in passing on such motions.

Standard's motion for summary judgment presented the contention that the petition and the terms of each of the policies, together with the affidavit of H. S. Armstrong, which was attached to the motion, show that there was no genuine issue as to any material fact and that Standard was entitled to a summary judgment, because:

(1) the loading of the truck belonging to Transport employer in the manner described in Annis' petition constituted a permissive use of said truck by Standard, and that under the terms of Transport's policy, use of an automobile includes the loading and unloading thereof.

(2) Annis was an employee of Transport employer, but was "not an employee of the additional insured Standard Oil Company of Texas," and because, the "Transport Insurance Company policy specifically providing that 'the term insured is used severally and not collectively', so that the suit by said Annis is not a suit by 'an employee of the insured (Standard Oil) arising out of and in the course of his, employment by the insured (Standard Oil),' and is not an obligation for which the insured (Standard Oil) or any carrier as (its) insurer may be held liable under any workmen's compensation . . . law . . . or under any similar law."

(3) the truck was being loaded and was not being serviced at a service station, and "Standard Oil Company of Texas was not operating a 'service station' in any sense of the term, on the occasion in question," and

(4) Standard had no other insurance against the loss alleged in the suit by Annis, because "the truck in question was nonowned as to it and its policy with Fireman's Fund Insurance Company provides that the coverage of the Fireman's Fund policy would be excess coverage as to nonowned vehicles."

It was for these specifically alleged reasons that Standard claimed that Transport was obligated to defend the Annis suit and was obligated to pay on behalf of Standard all sums which Standard should become legally obligated to pay as damages in the Annis suit to the extent of the limits of liability of said policy.

Transport alleged several grounds for summary judgment. However, the only ground pertinent to our decision is the one that its policy specifically excluded any obligation for which the insured or any carrier as its insurer may be held liable under any workmen's compensation law, and also excluded coverage for bodily injury to any employee of the insured arising out of and in the course of his employment by the insured.

The trial court rendered judgment overruling Standard's motion for summary judgment and sustained Transport's motion.

* * *

Obviously, the trial court's action in sustaining Transport's motion for summary judgment was based solely on its interpretation of the exclusionary clauses. . . . Standard's single point on appeal to the Court of Civil Appeals was that the trial court erred in 'holding Standard Oil Company not an additional insured under Transport's policy because of the "employee exclusion" in said policy, where Standard as a permissive user in loading to truck at the time of the accident, was an additional insured under the policy, and Annis was not an employee of the insured against whom the claim was made (Standard).

Standard in its brief stated that the precise question presented by such point was "whether the 'employee exclusion' in a standardized automobile liability policy prevents a coverage where the claimant is an employee of the named insured, but is not an employee of the additional insured (Standard) against whom the claim is brought." Standard's position on this question was and is that since Standard was an insured under Transport's policy, and there was no employer-employee relationship between Standard and Annis, the (f) and (g) exclusionary clauses do not apply as to Standard.

The Court of Civil Appeals in its judgment of reversal and rendition for Standard held that Standard, as an "omnibus insured" was entitled to be protected by the automobile liability insurance policy of Transport issued to Transport Company of Texas, and that the exclusion clauses (f) and (g) applied only to an employee of the insured against whom the claim was made, and hence did not exclude Standard from coverage of a claim against it by an employee of the named insured.

Transport contends that its policy issued to the Transport Company of Texas (employer of Annis) is plain and unambiguous and admits of but one construction. Transport's position is that there is no coverage if Annis was an employee of any one of the insureds. It bases its contention primarily on the definition of the word "insured," and exclusion clauses (f) and (g) as contained in the policy. Transport takes the position that there is no coverage since its is admitted that Annis was an employee of Transport Company of Texas.

The parties appear to be in agreement in this court that the policy is unambiguous. The Court of Civil Appeals used language in its opinion which seems to indicate that it held with Standard partly at least on the theory that the policy was ambiguous. In connection with its holding that Standard was entitled to the protection of the automobile liability policy by the Transport Company, the court said "Language of an insurance policy which is susceptible of more than one construction should be interpreted strictly against the insurer, and liberally in favor of the insured." We agree that the language of the policy is unambiguous. Since the language is plain and unambiguous there is no occasion for construction, and the language must be given its plain meaning. The rule of liberal construction in favor of the insured applies only when the contract is ambiguous and susceptible of more than one interpretation.

The exact question involved is one of first impression in this jurisdiction. There is a split of authority in other jurisdictions, but the weight of authority is that if the injured party is the employee of any person who is insured under the policy, the employee exclusion is applicable although he may not have been an employee of the person committing the tort. The cases which support Transport's contention follow the weight of authority and apply the language of the policy as written.

The "severability of interests" clause contained in the two standardized policies presently involved was added to all standardized policies in 1955. . . . The addition of the 'severability of interests' clause does not indicate that the drafters of the policy form by the addition of such clause intended that the word "insured" means only the person claiming coverage. We cannot adopt Standard's theory that by severing the interests in the case at bar, Standard is an insured under the "omnibus clause" contained in the policy; the basis for Standard's contention being that the 'severability of interests' clause warrants the addition after the word "insured" the words "the insured who is asking for a defense," or "the insured against whom the claim is made." The cases cited in support of this theory were cases where the exclusionary clauses contained in the policies were not specific and clear.

* * *

We have concluded that the "severability of interests" clause in the present policy cannot alter the holdings in the cases relied upon by Transport. It is uncontroverted that the workmen's compensation insurance carrier of Transport Company of Texas was held liable under the Texas Workmen's Compensation Act for the injuries sustained by Annis. It follows that Standard's theory by adding the words "against whom the claim is made" coverage was not excluded must be rejected, even though the policy contains the "severability of interests" clause, supra. Exclusion (g) of the policy issued by Transport to Transport Company of Texas clearly says that the policy does not cover "bodily injury to . . . any employee of the insured." Exclusion (f) of the policy in equally as plain language, says that the policy does not apply under bodily injury liability to "any obligation for which the insured or any carrier as his insurer may be held liable under any workmen's compensation . . . law."

In the policy involved here there is no ambiguity in the exclusion clauses and no inconsistency is shown between the exclusionary clauses and the 'severability of interests' clause in the policy. The clear and unambiguous terms of the policy leads us to hold that no employee of the named insured engaged in the named insured's business can recover on the named insured's policy against anyone included as an additional insured.

* * *

In summation, since Annis was an employee of Transport Company of Texas, an insured under Transport's policy, and was injured in the course of such employment, and since exclusions (f) and (g) in plain and unequivocal language provide that the policy affords no coverage against the claim of an employee of the insured, and since the words 'against whom the claim was made' are not to be added to the contract, the judgment of the trial court in favor of Transport should be affirmed.

The judgment of the Court of Civil Appeals is reversed and that of the trial court is affirmed.

Ramsay v. Maryland American General Insurance Company
533 S.W.2d 344
(Tex. 1976)

The question on this appeal is whether the term "commercial automobile" as used in an exclusionary clause of an insurance policy applies to a Navy-owned pickup truck being operated by a Navy civilian employee in the course of his employment on Navy housing units.

In a suit by Rotha Ramsay, widow of Scott Ramsay, against Maryland American General Insurance Company to recover death benefits under a policy which named her Navy-employed husband as the insured, the trial court rendered a summary judgment for the plaintiff. A divided court of civil appeals reversed and rendered for the insurance company defendant, holding that Ramsay's accidental death occurred while he was engaged in duties incident to the operation of a "commercial automobile," and that this excluded his death from coverage under the policy. The plaintiff insisted that the term "commercial automobile" in the policy exclusion did not apply to the Navy-owned vehicle being operated by her deceased husband solely for governmental and military purposes, or in the alternative that the term was so uncertain and ambiguous that she should recover under the rule of law which resolves such ambiguities in favor of the insured. We agree with plaintiff's alternative argument and reverse the judgment of the court of civil appeals and affirm the judgment of the trial court.

The facts are undisputed. They are fully and accurately detailed in the majority and dissenting opinions of the court of civil appeals, from which we borrow freely, and sometimes verbatim, in our summary of the facts and nature of the case.

On June 26, 1973, Scott Ramsay, while driving a pickup truck which was owned by the United States Navy, collided with an automobile on a public highway in Bee County. He sustained serious injury in the accident and died the same day. At the time Ramsay was a civil service employee of the United States Navy at Chase Field Naval Air Station in Bee County. He was classified as an air-conditioning mechanic. On the day of the accident he and Rosendo Gonzales, a co-worker, left Chase Field in the pickup truck and proceeded to Capehart, a government-owned housing project for Navy personnel stationed at Chase Field. There they installed a compressor on an air-conditioning unit in one of the houses. When the accident occurred they were returning to Chase Field to pick up another compressor, which was also to be installed on an air-conditioning unit at Capehart.

The pickup was used solely for transporting Navy crews, tools, equipment and supplies (pertaining to air-conditioning and heating installation, repairs and maintenance) from Chase Field to Capehart, and for work at Capehart. It was a one-half ton vehicle, and had a utility bed with cabinets on each side which contained parts, tools, equipment and supplies used to service and work on refrigeration, air-conditioning and heating units. It was licensed by the United States Navy. Ramsay had a federal driver's license, and his use of the truck at the time of the accident was solely in connection with his governmental employment.

The main policy in this case is a "Family Combination Automobile Policy" with liability coverages relating to damages arising out of the ownership and use of the Ramsays' personal automobiles. Attached to the policy was an endorsement (157P), entitled "Automobile Death Indemnity, Total Disability and Specific Disability Benefits," which, among other provisions, insured Ramsay for $10,000 in the event he was killed in an accident and his death occurred "directly and independently of all other causes from bodily injury caused by accident and sustained by the insured while in or upon, or while entering into or alighting from, or through being struck by, an automobile . . ." The endorsement contained the following exclusion:

> "This insurance does not apply . . . to bodily injury or death sustained in the course of his occupation by any person while engaged (1) in duties incident to the operation, loading or unloading of, or as an assistant on, a public or livery conveyance or commercial automobile, or (2) in duties incident to the repair or servicing of automobiles . . .."

The term "automobile" is defined in the endorsement as "a land motor vehicle, trailer, or semi-trailer not operated on rails or crawler-treads," and thus clearly includes a pickup truck. The controlling term, "commercial automobile" is not defined in the main policy or the endorsement. As heretofore indicated, the sole question presented in this appeal relates to whether the United States Navy-owned pickup is a 'commercial automobile' within the meaning of the above quoted exclusion. With no definition in the policy, we must first determine whether the term has a readily ascertainable meaning in the plain, ordinary and popular sense of the words themselves. When terms of an insurance policy are unambiguous, they are to be given their plain, ordinary and generally accepted meaning unless the instrument itself shows that the terms have been used in a technical or different sense. *Guardian Life Insurance Company of America v. Scott*, 405 S.W.2d 64 (Tex.1966); *Western Reserve Life Ins. Co. v. Meadows*, 261 S.W.2d 554 (Tex. 1953)

Both parties argue that the term "commercial automobile" has a plain and generally accepted meaning, but they are at opposite poles as to what that meaning is. Neither has presented a Texas case that bears directly on the question, and we have found none. Neither have we been cited to any cases from other jurisdictions which apply the term as used in this policy exclusion to military or federally owned and operated vehicles. Some cases from other states have analogies helpful to the contentions of both parties, but none are directly in point.

The plaintiff, Mrs. Ramsay, resorts to the aid of dictionaries, as courts often do in seeking plain, ordinary and generally accepted meanings of undefined terms in insurance policies. Plaintiff insists that dictionary definitions of commerce, commercial, and commercial vehicles, relate to private transactions and transportation, and none mention "government," "military," or enterprises and operations conducted by governmental or military agencies. Webster's Third New International Dictionary (unabridged, 1971) is cited for the following definition of commercial: "of, in, or relating to commerce . . . from the point of view of profit; having profit as the primary aim . . . ."

* * *

Mrs. Ramsay argues, and all members of the court of civil appeals agreed, that the Navy was not engaged in business or commerce or operating for a profit. She contends that under the plain meaning of "commercial" the Navy pickup was not a vehicle owned or used at the time of the accident for any commercial enterprise or purpose; that it was Navy-owned, federally licensed, and driven by her husband as a full-time Navy civilian employee with a federal driver's license; and that neither the deceased nor the vehicle could be considered functioning instrumentalities of commerce or working in the general stream of commerce, because Ramsay worked and the pickup was used exclusively for a nonprofit organization of the United States Government. She insists that the deceased could not and did not receive commercial calls from private persons to do similar repair work, and neither could he nor did he use the Navy vehicle for any commercial venture. So, Mrs. Ramsay's plain meaning of the words 'commercial automobile' would exclude the government-owned Navy vehicle while used solely for Navy work. She argues that an average person would not consider the Navy pickup as a 'commercial' vehicle while it was being used exclusively for non-profit governmental activities.

On the other hand, Maryland American General Insurance Company argues that the plain and ordinarily accepted meaning of the term applies to any type of vehicle which is used for performing commercial type services and that "the United States Government is undoubtedly the largest commercial enterprise in the world." It contends that ownership is not important; that use is controlling; that the Navy vehicle was equipped and used in a proprietary commercial enterprise run by the government in competition with private enterprise; that Ramsay was a civilian rather than a military employee, engaged in business and commerce for himself in that he was earning a living through payment for his services; and that the use of the vehicle by Ramsay was of the same nature as would be employed by a private person or company in the repair of air conditioning equipment.

The majority of the court of civil appeals held Ramsay "was engaged in a commercial activity for profit," that his occupation was "commercial in nature, scope and fact." It held that the term "commercial automobile" is not an ambiguous term, because it has a meaning readily ascertainable in the plain, ordinary and popular sense of the words used.

* * *

We have concluded that both parties have offered reasonable, although conflicting, interpretations of the meaning of "commercial automobile" as applied to the facts and circumstances of this case. The term is not ambiguous when applied to a truck or automobile in actual use by a private individual or company for profit, but uncertainty and ambiguity arise when the term is applied to a Navy-owned truck used exclusively for non-profit activities of the United States Government. It is a settled rule that policies of insurance will be interpreted and construed liberally in favor of the insured and strictly against the insurer, and especially so when dealing with exceptions and words of limitation. *Providence Washington Ins. Co. v. Proffitt*, 239 S.W.2d 379 (Tex. 1951). When the language of a policy is susceptible of more than one reasonable construction, the courts will apply the construction which favors the insured and permits recovery. *Continental Cas. Co. v. Warren,* 254 S.W.2d 762 (Tex.1953); *Lloyd's Casualty Insurer v. McCrary*, 229 S.W.2d 605 (Tex.1950); *United Service Automobile Ass'n v. Miles*, 161 S.W.2d 1048 (Tex. 1942). Under this well settled rule of law, we are compelled to affirm the trial court's judgment in favor of Mrs. Ramsay.

Accordingly, the judgment of the court of civil appeals is reversed and the judgment of the trial court is affirmed.

Kulubis v. Texas Farm Bureau Underwriters Insurance Company
706 S.W.2d 953
(Tex. 1986)

This is a suit on a fire insurance policy. Betty Kulubis sued Texas Farm Bureau Underwriters Insurance Company for the proceeds of a policy after her estranged husband intentionally burned the couple's mobile home. The trial court rendered judgment for Texas Farm and the court of appeals, with one justice dissenting, affirmed that judgment. We reverse the judgment of the court of appeals and render judgment for Betty Kulubis.

Betty and John Kulubis were married in 1971. Her parents subsequently gave them a mobile home upon which they purchased a homeowners insurance policy from Texas Farm. Both Betty and John were named insureds in the policy. In 1982, Betty filed suit for divorce. After being served with the divorce citation, John set fire to the mobile home, destroying it and all of the personal property inside. He then unsuccessfully attempted suicide. It is uncontroverted that Betty had no knowledge of nor did she participate in the destruction of the mobile home.

The court of appeals denied recovery to Betty based upon *Jones v. Fidelity & Guaranty Insurance Co.,* 250 S.W.2d 281 (Tex.Civ.App.-Waco 1952, writ ref'd). Betty asks us to reconsider the holding in *Jones* inasmuch as a majority of the states that have addressed the issue have abandoned that rule and now permit recovery under the facts of this case.

The *Jones* decision was based upon a holding that co-insureds under an insurance policy covering jointly owned property acquire joint rights and obligations under the policy. Therefore, the illegal acts of one of the co-insureds prevent recovery by the other co-insured. At the time this court adopted the *Jones* rule it was the traditional rule in the United States. The *Jones* court cited *Monaghan v. Agricultural Fire Insurance Co.,* 53 Mich. 238, 18 N.W. 797 (1884); *Kosior v. Continental Insurance Co.,* 299 Mass. 601, 13 N.E.2d 423 (1938); *Bowers Co. v. London Assurance Corp.,* 90 Pa.Super. 121 (1926); and *Bellman v. Home Insurance Co.,* 178 Wis. 349, 189 N.W. 1028 (1922).

In 1942, the New Hampshire Supreme Court first permitted recovery by a co-insured in Betty Kulubis' position. *Hoyt v. New Hampshire Fire Insurance Co.,* 29 A.2d 121, 92 N.H. 242 (1942). That court reasoned that the proper test to be applied was what a reasonable person would have understood the fire insurance policy to mean. The court then held that an innocent victim of a co-insured's illegal act in destroying the jointly owned property would reasonably expect to be covered by the policy.

Between 1974 and 1985, sixteen other states adopted the test set out in *Hoyt.* We note that of the four jurisdictions relied on in *Jones,* two of them have adopted the test in *Hoyt,* and a third, Pennsylvania, has questioned the rule.

We will examine the reasoning supporting the *Jones* decision along with the reasoning of those jurisdictions which have rejected the *Jones* rule to determine if this court will continue to follow *Jones.* As stated above, the basis of *Jones* was that fraudulent losses are generally excepted from coverage of fire insurance contracts upon the grounds of public policy and morals. *Jones* at 281-82. Put another way, public policy dictates that a wrongdoer should not benefit from his wrongdoing. This led the court to hold that a joint owner who illegally destroys property could not benefit from his illegal act and, because his co-owner/co-insured was mutually obligated under the policy, the innocent victim of the illegal destruction was also barred from recovery. *Id.* at 282.

The reasoning adopted by the states that follow the *Hoyt* rule is also based on public policy. In *Morgan v. Cincinnati Insurance Co.,* 411 Mich. 267, 307 N.W.2d 53 (1981), the Michigan Supreme Court, in overruling *Monaghan,* held that public policy requires that an innocent co-insured be permitted to recover based upon the insured's reasonable expectations. The Wisconsin Supreme Court in *Hedtcke v. Sentry Insurance Co.,* 109 Wis.2d 461, 326 N.W.2d 727 (1982), in overruling *Bellman,* also followed the policy of not punishing the innocent victim for the wrongs of another.

Other policy considerations we must consider are: (1) prevention of fraud upon the insurance company; (2) prevention of unjust enrichment by the insurance company; and (3) refusal to impute the criminal acts of the wrongdoer to an innocent victim.

We hold the more enlightened reasoning dictates that the illegal destruction of jointly owned property by one co-insured shall not bar recovery under an insurance policy by an innocent co-insured. A trial court is uniquely situated to make the determination of the co-insured's innocence, and, unless there is a finding of lack of innocence, the co-insured shall be permitted to recover.

We hold that this test will best protect the insurance company from fraud while assuring that the insurance company will not be unjustly enriched. It will also permit an innocent victim whose property has been destroyed to collect under an insurance policy for a loss reasonably expected to be covered. This test also avoids the imputation of criminal action to an innocent victim.

Texas courts are faced with an additional problem in this situation because we are a community property state. It is not necessary for us to address that particular problem at this time inasmuch as the mobile home in question was a gift to Betty and John and as such an undivided one-half interest was the separate property of each of them. We are not to be understood as holding that an innocent spouse is barred from recovering under an insurance policy covering community property. We do not have that fact situation before us and therefore do not address the problem of how to compensate the innocent spouse and yet not permit benefit to the wrongdoing spouse. That problem will be addressed when and if it is presented to us.

In this case, Betty Kulubis was the owner of a one-half interest in the mobile home and the personal property which was destroyed by her husband. She is therefore entitled to recover one-half of the stipulated amount of the loss of $21,000 plus prejudgment and post-judgment interest as well as attorney's fees as found by the trial court.

The judgment of the court of appeals is reversed and judgment is rendered for Betty Kulubis.

Forbau v. Aetna Life Insurance Company
876 S.W.2d 132
(Tex. 1994)

Petitioner's motion for rehearing is overruled. We withdraw our opinion of May 5, 1993, and substitute the following opinion in its place.

In this case we are called upon to determine whether the insurance policy at issue created a vested right in unlimited lifetime benefits, or restricted benefits to the recovery of medical expenses incurred while the policy was in effect. The trial court rendered judgment on a jury's verdict in favor of Petitioner, Edwadine Forbau, as next friend of Amy Miller. The court of appeals reversed the trial court's judgment, holding that under the unambiguous terms of the policy, Petitioner's recovery was limited to those medical expenses incurred while Aetna's policy was in effect. 808 S.W.2d 664. We agree that Aetna's policy is unambiguous and does not afford the coverage claimed by Petitioner. We thus affirm the judgment of the court of appeals.

I.

In March of 1983 fourteen-year old Amy Miller suffered serious, permanent, and disabling injuries as a result of a motor vehicle accident. At the time, Amy's father, Mike Miller, was insured under an Aetna group insurance policy (Group Policy) issued to Affiliated Foods, Inc., a cooperative of grocery stores of which his employer, E Triple M, Inc., was a member. Miller's premiums and those of his dependents, including Amy's, were paid by E Triple M. Miller was eligible as an "individual" under the plan, defined as an "employee of any store owner who is a participant under this plan;" Amy was eligible for dependent coverage as an "individual's unmarried child under nineteen years of age." Group Policy at 1500, 1550.

After Amy's accident, Aetna paid her medical expenses as incurred until April 30, 1985, when Affiliated terminated the group contract with Aetna. Aetna continued to pay benefits until May 1, 1986, under the policy's one-year extension of benefits clause. After that date, Petitioner submitted claims to Safeco Life Insurance Company as Aetna's successor insurer for Affiliated's members. A dispute eventually arose between Petitioner and Safeco, which resulted in a lawsuit and settlement.

After settling with Safeco, Petitioner filed this lawsuit against Aetna, alleging breach of contract and of fiduciary duty, and violations of the Texas Deceptive Trade Practices-Consumer Protection Act and the Insurance Code. Only the breach of contract claims were submitted to the jury. In accordance with the jury's verdict, the trial court awarded Amy $238,000 in past damages, $2.5 million in future damages, and $500,000 in attorneys' fees.

II.

Interpretation of insurance contracts in Texas is governed by the same rules as interpretation of other contracts. *Upshaw v. Trinity Cos.,* 842 S.W.2d 631, 633 (Tex.1992); *Western Reserve Life Ins. Co. v. Meadows,* 152 Tex. 559, 261 S.W.2d 554, 557 (1953).

When construing a contract, the court's primary concern is to give effect to the written expression of the parties' intent. *Ideal Lease Serv., Inc. v. Amoco Prod. Co.,* 662 S.W.2d 951, 953 (Tex.1983); *R & P Enterprises v. LaGuarta, Gavrel & Kirk,* 596 S.W.2d 517, 518 (Tex.1980). This court is bound to read all parts of a contract together to ascertain the agreement of the parties. *See Royal Indem. Co. v. Marshall,* 388 S.W.2d 176, 180 (Tex.1965); *Pan Am. Life Ins. Co. v. Andrews,* 161 Tex. 391, 340 S.W.2d 787 (1960). The contract must be considered as a whole. *Reilly v. Rangers Management, Inc.,* 727 S.W.2d 527, 529 (Tex.1987); *Coker v. Coker,* 650 S.W.2d 391, 393 (Tex.1983).

Moreover, each part of the contract should be given effect. *See Barnett v. Aetna Life Ins. Co.,* 723 S.W.2d 663, 666 (Tex.1987). For example, when a contract provision makes a general statement of coverage, and another provision specifically states the time limit for such coverage, the more specific provision will control. This is but an application of our long-established rule that "[n]o one phrase, sentence, or section [of a contract] should be isolated from its setting and considered apart from the other provisions." *Guardian Trust Co. v. Bauereisen,* 132 Tex. 396, 121 S.W.2d 579, 583 (1938).

III.

The operative language in this policy states that Aetna will pay for "covered medical expenses *incurred during a calendar year for treatment of a covered family member.*" Group Policy at 6210 (emphasis added). Under the contract, Aetna is obligated only to a covered family member, that is, a covered individual or dependent. A person ceases to be a covered individual when the policy has been discontinued or the individual is no longer employed by the policy's sponsor. When this occurs, dependent coverage also terminates.

The policy also states that "[t]his policy does not provide insurance for any of the following: Charges incurred while he is not a covered family member." Under the unambiguous language of the contract, Aetna's obligation to pay benefits under the contract terminated upon the discontinuance of Affiliated's policy, unless some other provision of the policy extended coverage. As the contract contains such a provision, which extended Petitioner's benefits for one additional year, she was entitled to the additional benefits Aetna paid for this time period only. Under basic tenets of contract law, these provisions must be read together with the other sections of the contract to comprehensively address the rights and obligations of all parties to the insurance contract.

Petitioner urges that the policy afforded her a right to receive payment for all future medical services related to any accident occurring during the policy period. That interpretation is based on the following clause: "If any benefit ceases to apply to an individual or a dependent, coverage for that benefit will cease immediately but without prejudice to any rights under the benefit established by this person while the coverage was in force." Group Policy at 1850.

Petitioner further urges that even if this clause does not explicitly provide her with coverage, it at least creates an ambiguity which must be interpreted in favor of coverage. However, not every difference in the interpretation of a contract or an insurance policy amounts to an ambiguity. Both the insured and the insurer are likely to take conflicting views of coverage, but neither conflicting expectations nor disputation is sufficient to *create* an ambiguity. The "without prejudice" clause by its own terms preserves the right to benefits "established ... while the coverage was in force." It does not create new rights or benefits beyond those afforded by the other provisions of the policy. And it is undisputed that Aetna paid the benefits to which Petitioner was entitled-payment of charges incurred while she was a covered dependent and for the one-year extension.

Accordingly, we affirm the judgment of the court of appeals.

Balandran v. Safeco Insurance Company of America
972 S.W.2d 738
(Tex. 1998)

This case comes to us on a certified question from the United States Court of Appeals for the Fifth Circuit. The issue certified is whether the 1991 Texas Standard Homeowner's Policy-Form B covers damage to the insured's dwelling from foundation movement caused by an underground plumbing leak. We hold that the policy provides this coverage.

I

Safeco Insurance Company of America insured the home of Joe and Dolores Balandran. The form of the policy was the 1991 Texas Standard Homeowner's Policy-Form B. In September 1993, the Balandrans filed a claim against Safeco for damage to their home caused by an underground plumbing leak. The leak caused the soil to expand, damaging the home's foundation as well as its interior and exterior finishes. When Safeco denied the claim, the Balandrans sued the company in state district court. Safeco removed the case to federal court on diversity jurisdiction.

At trial, the jury found that the structural damage was caused by the plumbing leak and awarded the Balandrans $66,500. Safeco, however, moved for judgment as a matter of law, contending that the Balandrans' policy excluded this structural damage regardless of the underlying cause. The trial court granted this motion, rendering a take-nothing judgment for Safeco.

The Balandrans appealed to the Fifth Circuit Court of Appeals. While their appeal was pending, a separate Fifth Circuit panel considered this issue, holding that an identical policy did not provide coverage for foundation damage from a plumbing leak. Subsequently, however, the Texas Commissioner of Insurance issued a bulletin vigorously disagreeing with the *Sharp* decision. In light of these developments, the panel hearing the Balandrans' appeal certified to us the controlling question regarding policy coverage.

II

The Balandrans' policy provides two types of coverage. "Coverage A" insures the dwelling itself, while "Coverage B" insures personal property. Coverage A provides the following protection: We insure against all risks of physical loss to the [dwelling] unless the loss is excluded in Section I Exclusions. The exclusion relevant to this case is 1(h), which provides:

> We do not cover loss under Coverage A (Dwelling) caused by settling, cracking, bulging, shrinkage, or expansion of foundations, walls, floors, ceilings, roof structures, walks, drives, curbs, fences, retaining walls or swimming pools.
>
> We do cover ensuing loss caused by collapse of building or any part of the building, water damage or breakage of glass which is part of the building if the loss would otherwise be covered under this policy.

Safeco argues that the damage to the Balandrans' home clearly falls under this exclusion.

The Balandrans apparently concede that, if the exclusion applies, it excludes their claim. However, they present three arguments about why the exclusion does not apply. First, they contend that language in Coverage B (the personal property section of the policy) creates an exception to exclusion 1(h) when the structural damage results from a plumbing leak. Second, they argue that exclusion 1(h) does not apply to structural damage resulting from an underlying cause-in this case a plumbing leak-which itself is not an excluded peril under the policy. Finally, the Balandrans argue that the last sentence of exclusion 1(h) (the "ensuing loss" provision) creates an exception to exclusion 1(h) under the present circumstances. Because we conclude that the Balandrans are entitled to prevail on their first argument, we do not reach the other two.

III

A

Unlike Coverage A, which insures the dwelling against "all risks," Coverage B insures personal property only against twelve enumerated perils. The ninth of these twelve perils is: Accidental Discharge, Leakage or Overflow of Water or Steam from within a plumbing, heating or air conditioning system or household appliance.

A loss resulting from this peril includes the cost of tearing out and replacing any part of the building necessary to repair or replace the system or appliance. But this does not include loss to the system or appliance from which the water or steam escaped.

* * *

Safeco, relying on the structure of the policy, argues that the exclusion repeal provision applies only to personal property losses resulting from a plumbing leak. Because Coverage B deals with personal property coverage, Safeco contends that the exclusion repeal provision should be similarly limited. Safeco argues that we may not construe this sentence without considering its context within the policy. *See State Farm Life Ins. Co. v. Beaston,* 907 S.W.2d 430, 433 (Tex.1995) ("[C] ourts must be particularly wary of isolating from its surroundings or considering apart from other provisions a single phrase, sentence, or section of a contract.").

As we have already noted, one Fifth Circuit panel has adopted Safeco's approach. *See Sharp v. State Farm Fire & Cas. Ins. Co.,* 115 F.3d 1258 (5th Cir.1997). Under identical facts, the court held that the damage to the dwelling was excluded under exclusion 1(h), and that the exclusion repeal provision applied only to personal property losses . . . .

B

Several rules of construction guide our consideration of this issue. First, insurance contracts are subject to the same rules of construction as other contracts. *See Beaston,* 907 S.W.2d at 433; *National Union Fire Ins. Co. v. CBI Indus.,* 907 S.W.2d 517, 520 (Tex.1995); *Forbau v. Aetna*

Life Ins. Co., 876 S.W.2d 132, 133 (Tex.1994). Our primary goal, therefore, is to give effect to the written expression of the parties' intent. *See Beaston,* 907 S.W.2d at 433; *Forbau,* 876 S.W.2d at 133. We must read all parts of the contract together, *see Beaston,* 907 S.W.2d at 433, striving to give meaning to every sentence, clause, and word to avoid rendering any portion inoperative. *See United Serv. Auto. Ass'n v. Miles,* 139 Tex. 138, 161 S.W.2d 1048, 1050 (1942). While parol evidence of the parties' intent is not admissible to create an ambiguity, *see National Union,* 907 S.W.2d at 520, the contract may be read in light of the surrounding circumstances to determine whether an ambiguity exists. *See Columbia Gas Transmission Corp. v. New Ulm Gas, Ltd.,* 940 S.W.2d 587, 589 (Tex.1996); *National Union,* 907 S.W.2d at 520.

If, after applying these rules, a contract is subject to two or more reasonable interpretations, it is ambiguous. *See National Union,* 907 S.W.2d at 520. Where an ambiguity involves an exclusionary provision of an insurance policy, we "must adopt the construction ... urged by the insured as long as that construction is not unreasonable, even if the construction urged by the insurer appears to be more reasonable or a more accurate reflection of the parties' intent." *National Union Fire Ins. Co. v. Hudson Energy Co.,* 811 S.W.2d 552, 555 (Tex.1991); *see also Glover v. National Ins. Underwriters,* 545 S.W.2d 755, 761 (Tex.1977).

Applying these rules, we conclude that the exclusion repeal provision is subject to two reasonable interpretations, and is therefore ambiguous. We are mindful of the Fifth Circuit's reasoning in *Sharp,* and we agree that it reflects one reasonable interpretation of the policy language. However, the Balandrans' interpretation is also reasonable.

* * *

Accordingly, we hold that exclusion 1(h) in the 1991 Texas Standard Homeowner's Policy-Form B does not apply to loss caused by the accidental discharge, leakage or overflow of water or steam from within a plumbing, heating or air conditioning system or household appliance.

NOTES & QUESTIONS

1) The "Doctrine of Reasonable Expectation" and Its Origin in Early English Law

Master v. Fuller
30 English Reports 464 (1792)

> [An] agreement by wife without knowledge of husband to pay additional rent out of her separate property good.
>
> Fuller let a house to Master at the rent of £20 per annum. After the death of Mrs. Master her husband filed the bill, charging that . . . a secret agreement between Fuller and [his wife was consummated and that] she had paid him, 18 per annum

more in respect of the house out of her separate property, which was not discovered till after her death[.] [He prayed] that the Defendant should refund what he had received in respect of it, and deliver up the agreement. There was no charge of imposition upon the wife.

Argument for the Plaintiff. It was insisted, that this was a fraud on the husband; for though he had no power over this property, yet he might rely (reliance) upon it so far as to have a reasonable expectation of the benefit of it, if he behaved well to his wife; and if he had known of this agreement, perhaps he would not have taken the lease. It was compared to the case of marriage brokerage, &c. where the security, if founded upon fraud against a third person, is void, even though there can be no injury to the person who comes to complain of it. . . . *Redman v. Redman* and *Gale v. Lindo*, I Vern. 348, 475, and *Neville v. Wilkenson,* 2 Bro. C. C. 543, were cited.

The bill was dismissed with costs without hearing the Defendant. (Plaintiff lost). As to the absolute power of a married woman over her separate property, see *Fettiplace v. Gorges*, 1 Ves. jun. 46.)

2) In *Ramsey*, the Texas Supreme Court seems to suggest that a "reasonable interpretation" of the meaning of "commercial automobile" is proper in light of the facts and circumstances of a case. Is that test—"facts and circumstances"—a proper standard for determining whether the terms in a contract are ambiguous?

3) Should a "reasonable interpretation" of a contract clause be viewed from the perspective of the proverbial "reasonable and objective person," from the "subjective perspective" of a single individual, or from a court's subjective perspective?

Chapter Ten:
First-Party Insurance Contracts

In *Lamar Homes, Inc. v. Mid-Continent Casualty Company,* 242 S.W.3d 1, 17-18 (Tex. 2007), the Texas Supreme Court correctly observed: "A first-party insurance policy is typically payable only to the insured or a named beneficiary for losses personal to the insured." Notable examples are marine, property, theft, fire, life, accident, and health insurance contracts as well as key provisions under homeowners' and automobile policies.

Actually, the bulk of modern-day first-party insurance contracts evolved from "ancient" British marine insurance contracts, which, insured against "all risks" or "all physical loss" unless a "specified risk" was excluded. The following "all-risk" clause is an example of the types of clauses that appeared in marine insurance policies:

> Touching the adventures and perils which we, the said underwriters, are contented to bear and take upon us, they are of the seas, men of war, fire, lightning, earthquake, enemies, pirates, rovers, assailing thieves, jettisons, letters of mart and counter-mart, surprisals, takings at sea, arrests, restraints and detainments of all kings, princes and peoples, of what nation, condition or quality so ever, barratry of the masters and mariners and of all other like perils, losses and misfortunes that have or shall come to the hurt, detriment or damage of the said vessel, etc., or any part thereof; excepting, however, such of the foregoing perils as may be excluded by provisions elsewhere in the policy or by endorsement.[1]

Some examples of "named perils" or "specific perils" policies are life, fire, and flood insurance contracts. However, under both "all-risk" and "specified-risk" first-party insurance contracts, the insured has the initial burden of proving that a "covered peril" or a "peril insured against" caused a loss — a tangible or an intangible property loss, or a loss of the insured's life. Later, the burden shifts to the insurer to establish that an excluded peril(s) was the "efficient proximate cause" of the loss.

1 *See e.g., Ferrara & DiMercurio, Inc.. v. St. Paul Mercury Ins. Co.*, 169 F.3d 43, 48 n.6 (1st Cir. 1999)

Again, tangible property insurance, as well as other forms of first-party insurance evolved out of marine insurance. Therefore, this chapter begins with a discussion of the latter and focuses on some of the substantive and procedural barriers that insureds and insurers must overcome before either can prevail in courts of equity and law.

TEXAS INSURANCE CODE § 862.051
INSURANCE COVERAGE PROVIDED BY FIRE AND MARINE INSURANCE COMPANIES
KINDS OF INSURANCE AUTHORIZED

On filing notice of its intent with the department, an insurance company engaged in the business of insurance in this state under an appropriate certificate of authority may:

(1) insure houses, buildings, and other property against loss or damage by fire;
(2) insure goods, merchandise, and other property in the course of transportation by land or water, or vessels afloat, regardless of their location;
(3) insure motor vehicles, whether stationary or being operated under the motor vehicle's own power, against loss or damage by fire, lightning, windstorm, hailstorm, tornado, cyclone, explosion, transportation by land or water, theft, and collision;
(4) lend money on bottomry or respondentia;
(5) obtain insurance against:
  (A) any loss or risk the company has incurred in the course of its business; and
  (B) any loss or risk on an interest that the company has in property because of a loan it has made on bottomry or respondentia; and
(6) take any action proper to promote an activity described by this section.

A. *Marine Insurance*

Wilburn Boat Company v. Fireman's Fund Insurance Company
348 U.S. 310 (1955)

This case raises questions concerning the power of States to regulate the terms and conditions of marine insurance contracts.

Glenn, Frank and Henry Wilburn, merchants in Denison, Texas, bought a small houseboat to use for commercial carriage of passengers on nearby Lake Texoma, an artificial inland lake between Texas and Oklahoma. The respondent Firemen's Fund Insurance Company insured the boat against loss from fire and other perils. While moored on the lake the boat was destroyed by fire. Following respondent's refusal to pay for the loss, this suit was brought in a Texas state court by the Wilburns and by their wholly owned corporation, The Wilburn Boat Company to which the boat's legal title had been transferred.

After removal of the case to the United States District Court because of diversity, respondent answered, admitting issuance of the policy, payment of premiums and destruction of the boat. Liability was denied, however, because of alleged breaches of printed policy terms or "warranties," providing that, without written consent of the company, the boat could not be sold, transferred, assigned, pledged, hired or chartered, and must be used solely for private pleasure purposes. The case was submitted on stipulated facts supplemented by oral testimony. Contending that the evidence showed the policy contract to have been made and delivered in Texas, petitioners urged that all questions concerning alleged policy breaches were controlled by Texas law.

If Texas law does govern, the policy provision against pledging may be wholly invalid. Furthermore, no breach by the insured of the provisions of a fire insurance policy is a defense to any suit under Texas law unless the breach contributes to the loss. See, Vernon's Rev.Civ.Stat.1936, Art. 4930: "No breach or violation by the insured of any warranty, condition or provision of any fire insurance policy contract of insurance, or application therefor, upon personal property, shall render void the policy or contract, or constitute a defense to a suit for loss thereon, unless such breach or violation contributed to bring about the destruction of the property." Tex. Insurance Code, art. 6.14.

Without finding whether the policy had been made and delivered in Texas, the court refused to give that State's law any effect at all, holding that since a marine policy is a maritime contract, federal admiralty law-not state law-governed. The court went on to hold that there is an established admiralty rule which requires literal fulfillment of every policy warranty so that any breach bars recovery, even though a loss would have happened had the warranty been carried out to the letter. Finding that the Wilburns had breached policy provisions against transfer, pledge and use of the boat, the District Court entered judgment for the insurance company. Approving the District Court's actions in all respects, the Court of Appeals affirmed, saying that "It is the settled doctrine that a marine contract of insurance is 'derived from', is 'governed by,' and is a 'part of' the general maritime law of the world." Importance of the questions involved prompted us to grant certiorari.

Since the insurance policy here sued on is a maritime contract the Admiralty Clause of the Constitution brings it within federal jurisdiction. But it does not follow, as the courts below seemed to think, that every term in every maritime contract can only be controlled by some federally defined admiralty rule. In the field of maritime contracts as in that of maritime torts, the National Government has left much regulatory power in the States. As later discussed in more detail, this state regulatory power, exercised with federal consent or acquiescence, has always been particularly broad in relation to insurance companies and the contracts they make.

Congress has not taken over the regulation of marine insurance contracts and has not dealt with the effect of marine insurance warranties at all; hence there is no possible question here of conflict between state law and any federal statute. But this does not answer the questions presented, since in the absence of controlling Acts of Congress this Court has fashioned a large part of the existing rules that govern admiralty. And States can no more override such judicial rules validly fashioned than they can override Acts of Congress. Consequently the crucial questions in this case narrow down to these: (1) Is there a judicially established federal admiralty rule governing these warranties? (2) If not, should we fashion one?

The only decision of the Court relied on by the Court of Appeals to support its holding that there is an established admiralty rule requiring strict fulfillment of marine insurance warranties was *Imperial Fire Insurance Co. v. Coos County*, 151 U.S. 452. There, because of a breach of warranty, an insurance company was relieved of liability for loss of a court-house by fire, and this Court said it was immaterial whether the breach contributed to the loss. But no question of marine insurance was remotely involved nor was there any reliance on a marine insurance rule. Writing its own "general commercial law," as was the custom in diversity cases prior to *Erie R. Co. v. Tompkins*, 304 U.S. 64, this Court in the *Coos County* case simply followed a general doctrine commonly applied to warranties in all types of insurance.

A mere cursory examination of the cases, state and federal, will disclose that through the years this common-law doctrine, when accepted, has been treated not as an admiralty rule but as a general warranty rule applicable to many types of contracts including marine and other insurance. There are very few federal cases on marine insurance in which the strict breach of warranty rule has even been considered. . . . This Court did say in one marine insurance case that warranties "must be strictly and literally performed." *Hazard's Administrator v. New England Marine Ins. Co.*, 8 Pet. 557, 580, 8 L.Ed. 1043. But there is not the slightest indication that this statement referred to a federal admiralty rule and the Court in fact expressly followed and applied Massachusetts law to decide another question in that very case.

Whatever the origin of the 'literal performance' rule may be, we think it plain that it has not been judicially established as part of the body of federal admiralty law in this country. Therefore, the scope and validity of the policy provisions here involved and the consequences of breaching them can only be determined by state law unless we are now prepared to fashion controlling federal rules.

The whole judicial and legislative history of insurance regulation in the United States warns us against the judicial creation of admiralty rules to govern marine policy terms and warranties. The control of all types of insurance companies and contracts has been primarily a state function since the States came into being. In 1869, this Court held in *Paul v. Virginia,* 8 Wall. 168, 19 L.Ed. 357, that States possessed regulatory power over the insurance business and strongly indicated that the National Government did not have that power. Three years later, it was first authoritatively decided in *New England Mutual Marine Insurance Co. v. Dunham*, *supra*, that federal courts could exercise "jurisdiction" over marine insurance contracts.

In 1894, years after the *Dunham* holding, this Court applied the doctrine of *Paul v. Virginia* and held that States could regulate marine insurance the same as any other insurance. *Hooper v. People of State of California*, 155 U.S. 648. Later, the power of States to regulate marine insurance was reaffirmed in *Nutting v. Commonwealth of Massachusetts*, 183 U.S. 553. This constitutional doctrine carrying implications of exclusive state power to regulate all types of insurance contracts remained until 1944 when this Court decided *United States v. Southeastern Underwriters Ass'n,* 322 U.S. 533. Thus it is clear that at least until 1944 this Court has always treated marine insurance contracts, like all others, as subject to state control. The vast amount of insurance litigation in state courts throughout our history also bears witness that until recently state legislatures and state courts have treated marine insurance as controlled by state law to the same extent as all other insurance.

* * *

Not only courts, but Congress, insurance companies, and those insured have all acted on the assumption that States can regulate marine insurance. In the Merchant Marine Act of 1920, Congress recognized that marine insurance companies were operating under state laws. Then, following a three-year study of marine insurance, Congress in 1922 passed a law regulating all types of insurance in the District of Columbia. This enactment generally referred to as the District of Columbia Model Marine Insurance Act, had the backing of insurance companies generally and was hailed as a model which it was hoped States would copy. Because of a provision in the bill as offered relating to "policy forms and conditions,' the bill was first criticized by the national association of shipowners but was later approved after the criticized provision was removed. Hearings on the bill make it plain that shipowners and marine insurance companies recognized that marine insurance was then, and would continue to be, regulated by the States.

* * *

The hearings on the McCarran Act reveal the complexities and difficulties of an attempt to unify insurance law on a nationwide basis, even by Congress. Courts would find such a task far more difficult. Congress in passing laws is not limited to the narrow factual situation of a particular controversy as courts are in deciding lawsuits. And Congress could replace the presently functioning State regulations of marine insurance by one comprehensive Act. Courts, however, could only do it piece-meal, on a case-by-case basis. Such a creeping approach would result in leaving marine insurance largely unregulated for years to come.

In this very case, should we attempt to fashion an admiralty rule governing policy provisions, we would at once be faced with the difficulty of determining what should be the consequences of breaches. We could adopt the old common-law doctrine of forfeiting all right of recovery in the absence of strict and literal performance of warranties, but that is a harsh rule. Most States, deeming the old rule a breeder of wrong and injustice, have abandoned it in whole or in part. But that has left open the question of what kind of new rule could be substituted that would be fair both to insurance companies and policy holders. Out of their abundant broad experience in regulating the insurance business, some state legislatures have adopted one kind of new rule and some another. Some States for example have denied companies the right to forfeit policies in the absence of an insured's bad faith or fraud.

Other States have thought this kind of rule inadequate to stamp out forfeiture practices deemed evil. The result, as this Court has pointed out, has been state statutes like that of Texas which "go to the root of the evil" and forbid forfeiture for an insured's breach of policy terms unless the breach actually contributes to bring about the loss insured against. Thus there are a number of other possible rules from which this Court could fashion one for admiralty. But such a choice involves varied policy considerations and is obviously one which Congress is peculiarly suited to make. And we decline to undertake the task.

Under our present system of diverse state regulations, which is as old as the Union, the insurance business has become one of the great enterprises of the Nation. Congress has been exceedingly cautious about disturbing this system, even as to marine insurance where congressional power is undoubted. We, like Congress, leave the regulation of marine insurance where it has been — with the States.

The judgments of the Court of Appeals and the District Court are reversed and the cause is remanded to the District Court for a trial under appropriate state law. It is so ordered. Judgments reversed and cause remanded to District Court with directions.

Hull & Company Incorporated v. Chandler
889 S.W.2d 513
(Tex. App. -Houston [14th Dist.] 1994)

This is a bad faith insurance case. Appellee, R. Chandler (Chandler) sued appellants, The Various Underwriters at Lloyds on Certificate No. 90CQ 311719286 (Underwriters) and Hull & Company, Inc. (Hull), a wholesale insurance broker, alleging that they violated Texas law in denying Chandler's claim on a $400,000 marine insurance policy which covered Chandler's yacht, the ONE FINE DAY (the yacht). The yacht partially sank in calm harbor in Roatan, Honduras. A jury returned a verdict against Underwriters for breach of the common law duty of good faith and fair dealing, and against Underwriters and Hull for violation of the Insurance Code and the DTPA.

Chandler elected to recover against Underwriters under the common law and against both appellants under the Insurance Code. In accordance with the jury's verdict and Chandler's election, the trial court rendered judgment holding appellants liable to Chandler for nearly $8 million in damages. Underwriters and Hull, raising eighteen and fourteen points of error, respectively, bring this appeal from that judgment. Chandler also perfected a cross-appeal claiming that the trial court erred in refusing to disregard the jury's finding of actual damages and in refusing to assess prejudgment interest on treble damages and attorney's fees. We reverse and remand.

In 1987, Chandler, an Arizona resident, invested $400,000 in the purchase and refurbishing of the ONE FINE DAY, a 1960 era wooden yacht (the yacht). Before the purchase, Chandler sought insurance on the yacht through his agent, Gallagher Braniff, Inc. (Gallagher Braniff), located in Houston, Texas. Through Hull, a Florida corporation located in Fort Lauderdale, Chandler obtained a $400,000 named perils policy from Underwriters, an insurance syndicate located in London, England. That policy insured the yacht for losses up to $400,000 resulting from certain perils specifically enumerated in the policy. Chandler renewed the policy yearly and the policy was in effect at the time of the loss at issue.

On April 3, 1991, the yacht partially sank while unmanned and anchored in a calm harbor in Roatan, Honduras. The yacht captain, Phillip Richards, reported the sinking that same day to Gallagher Braniff in Texas, who in turn notified Hull in Florida by telephone and fax dated April 3rd. The initial notice of loss listed the probable amount of the entire loss as $400,000. Once notified of Chandler's claim, Underwriters immediately hired a surveyor, Edwin Geary, to investigate the partial sinking. Geary arrived in Roatan three days after the yacht sank. Geary inspected the yacht, interviewed Captain Richards, and prepared a written report. In his report, Geary concluded that the partial sinking of the yacht "was a direct result of rot and deterioration of the port and starboard stern tubes and wear and tear of the port and starboard packing glands."

In a letter dated April 30, 1991, Underwriters' agent, Hull, informed Chandler that "based on information provided to date," Underwriters did "not find evidence of a claim for loss or damage due to an insured peril." Hull also informed Chandler that Underwriters' investigation was continuing and that Underwriters reserved the right to deny coverage if that investigation "fail [ed] to reveal information which would indicate coverage exists." Hull also invited Chandler to provide any information to Underwriters that would indicate the existence of coverage. Chandler never provided such information. Chandler contends that he did not do so because appellants failed to provide him with a copy of Geary's report. Appellants on the other hand contend that it was unnecessary to provide a copy of the report because the information contained therein was relayed by telephone to Chandler's attorney.

In any event, both Chandler and Underwriters hired attorneys to provide a legal opinion regarding coverage. Needless to say, Underwriters' attorney disagreed with Chandler's attorney on the issue of whether the loss was covered by the policy. Relying on Geary's report and the opinion of its attorney, Underwriters denied Chandler's claim on September 3, 1991, five months after the loss.

In late June 1991, only three months after the loss, Chandler, then a Florida resident, brought suit against appellants for breach of contract, breach of the common law duty of good faith and fair dealing, and unfair and deceptive acts and practices under Tex. Ins. Code Ann. art. 21.21 and Tex. Bus. & Com. Code Ann. §§ 17.50, 17.46 Chandler alleged that his yacht deteriorated beyond repair as a result of appellants' conduct. Chandler claimed that he was entitled to the replacement and salvage costs of the yacht as actual damages, plus exemplary and treble damages and attorney's fees.

Before trial, the court made two crucial rulings. First, the court ruled that Chandler's loss was covered by the policy. Second, the court ruled that Texas law, not Florida law, applied to this lawsuit. The trial began on July 14, 1993. Two weeks later, the jury returned a verdict in favor of Chandler on most of the liability issues. The jury found that Chandler incurred actual damages of $1.2 million and $71,236.00, which were the reasonable and necessary costs to replace and salvage the yacht, respectively. The jury also found that Underwriters were grossly negligent and that appellants' acted knowingly, thereby entitling Chandler to recover exemplary damages under the common law and treble damages by statute, respectively. Finally, the jury awarded trial and appellate attorney's fees to Chandler as a percentage of his recovery. As we stated, Chandler elected to recover against Underwriters for breach of the duty of good faith and fair dealing and against both appellants for violation of the Insurance Code.

* * *

The court ordered that Chandler recover $2,053,481.40 from Underwriters and Hull, joint and severally. The court also ordered that Chandler recover $2,542,472.00 from Hull, individually, and $3,300,000.00 in exemplary damages from Underwriters. The court further ordered that Chandler recover $63,561.00 in appellate attorney's fees, plus post-judgment interest and costs. The damages totaled nearly $8 million. After filing additional post-judgment motions, the parties perfected an appeal from this judgment.

The parties agree that before we review the other points of error, we must first address the issue of what law applies.

In Underwriters' points of error sixteen through eighteen and in Hull's points of error twelve through fourteen, they complain about the application of Texas law to this dispute. Appellants initially contend that federal maritime law preempts the application of any state law on bad faith. Alternatively, appellants contend that if state law applies, federal maritime and Texas choice-of-law principles mandate application of Florida law to this dispute and that application of Texas law violated their constitutional rights under the Due Process Clause of the Fourteenth Amendment and the Full Faith and Credit Clause.

Like the coverage issue, the trial court resolved the dispute over the applicable law before the beginning of trial. . . . On appeal, appellants essentially contend that the trial court erred in granting Chandler's motion to apply Texas law.

* * *

In the instant case, the trial court determined the applicable law before trial by written order after giving due consideration to the parties' motions. Appellants argue that they properly invoked federal maritime law in their Answer to Plaintiff's Third Amended Original Petition and that both parties invoked federal maritime law on summary judgment regarding the coverage issue. Appellants' motion for partial summary judgment on choice-of-law also states that "... defendants do not waive the issue raised as to whether the Texas Deceptive Trade Practices Act and/or Texas Insurance Code can apply to this contract of marine insurance." Maritime law, although properly invoked, can be waived. *See De La Lastra,* 852 S.W.2d at 919. Notwithstanding the disclaimer urged in appellants' motion for partial summary judgment, at the time the choice-of-law dispute was before the trial court, appellants did not argue that federal maritime law preempted Chandler's bad faith claim under state law. Rather, appellants argued only that Florida law applied instead of Texas law. Preemption arguments which affect choice-of-law are waivable. *Id.* at 919-20. Accordingly, appellants waived any argument that federal maritime law preempts application of state law.

However, even if appellants had preserved error, we would hold that federal maritime law does not preempt Chandler's claims. The regulation of marine insurance is, in most instances, properly left with the states. *Wilburn Boat Co. v. Fireman's Fund Ins.,* 348 U.S. 310, 321, (1955)). Following the direction of the Court in *Wilburn Boat,* the Fifth Circuit has ruled that interpretation of a contract of marine insurance is-in the absence of any specific and controlling rule-to be determined by reference to appropriate state law. Thus, state law governs the interpretation of marine insurance policies unless an available federal rule controls the disputed issue.

* * *

Having determined that state law is controlling, the only remaining question is whether the trial court applied the proper state law under a choice-of-law analysis. That question is one of law and therefore, subject to *de novo* review. *See In the Matter of Humphreys,* 880 S.W.2d 402, 404 (Tex.1994) and *Duncan v. Cessna Aircraft Co.,* 665 S.W.2d 414, 421 (Tex.1984). In the instant case, the parties confined their choice-of-law dispute to a choice between Texas or Florida law.

* * *

In the instant case, Florida, has the most significant relationship to the issue in dispute. Acting on Chandler's behalf, Gallagher Braniff applied for coverage in Florida with Hull, a Florida corporation. Gallagher Braniff's account executive, Mark Jones, went to Florida to place the policy. The insurance contract was therefore formed in Florida and issued in Florida. The policy was delivered unconditionally to Chandler and his agent and thus, is deemed to have been made in Florida. The yacht, while covered for voyages in a variety of geographic areas, was berthed in Florida at the time it was insured. Notice of the claim occurred when Gallagher Braniff notified Underwriters' agent in Florida, not when Captain Richards notified Chandler's agent in Texas. At the time of the loss, Chandler maintained residence in both Arizona and Florida. At the time suit was filed and at the time of trial, Chandler lived in Florida.

The Texas contacts are that Chandler's agent, Gallagher Braniff, is located in Texas and Underwriters' agent, Hull, has a subsidiary with two offices located in Texas. These contacts do not significantly relate to the issue in dispute nor implicate state interests so as to justify application of Texas law. While Texas has an interest in protecting its *residents* from acts of bad faith or unfair claim settlement practices committed by insurers doing business in the state, that interest is not implicated here. No Texas defendant, injured party, or property is involved. The insured, Chandler, is a Florida resident seeking damages for alleged bad faith and/or unfair claim settlement practices by a British insurance syndicate and a Florida insurance broker under an insurance policy issued in Florida. Undoubtedly, Florida has an interest in protecting its residents from alleged bad faith or unfair insurance trade practices by a foreign insurance syndicate acting through a Florida broker under a policy issued in Florida.

The fact that Underwriters' agent had a subsidiary that did business in Texas or that Chandler's agent was located in Texas is inconsequential. As courts have stated, it is not the number of contacts with a particular state that is determinative, but the qualitative nature of the particular contacts insofar as they implicate important state policies underlying the particular substantive issue. Here, Hull's subsidiary had absolutely no connection to this dispute. Although Chandler suggests that the Houston office of the Hull subsidiary played a role in handling his claim, the record reflects otherwise.

* * *

Hence, we sustain Underwriters' seventeenth point of error and Hull's twelfth point of error complaining about the trial court's application of Texas law instead of Florida law. In light of our disposition, it is unnecessary for us to address appellants' remaining points of error or Chandler's cross-points. Accordingly, we reverse the judgment of the trial court and remand to the trial court for proceedings consistent with this opinion.

NOTES & QUESTIONS

1) In *Chandler*, the court reported that "certain perils [were] specifically enumerated in the policy." Of course, the court did not identify or discuss those perils since the court decided that Florida's law rather than the law of Texas controlled. But the court clearly stated: "The yacht, while *covered for voyages in a variety of geographic areas,* was berthed in Florida at the time it was insured."

2) May the "risk of an entire voyage" be a "covered peril" or a "peril insured against" under a marine insurance contract?

3) Does the geographic location of a property loss matter under a marine insurance contract? See *Marine Fire Ins. Co. v. Burnett*, 29 Tex. 433, 1867 WL 4543 ,*6 (Tex. 1867) ("[The court submitted to the jury] the question of fact [about] the seaworthiness of the *Betty Powell*. ... The court charged the jury, 'that if the steamboat was not approved by the company or their inspect[or], or that she was not seaworthy, not sufficiently officered and manned for the voyage, and that the loss resulted or occurred by reason of such insufficiency, then find for the defendant.")

4) "Coverage" under a marine or property insurance contract has a distinct and less-than-commonsensical meaning. Consider the discussion in the following case:

Garvey v. State Farm Fire & Casualty Company
770 P.2d 704 (Cal. 1989)

The Distinction Between Liability and Property Insurance

As we will demonstrate, the decision of the Court of Appeal, in applying the . . . concurrent causation analysis to property damage cases, like other recent insurance cases involving all-risk homeowner's policies, failed to differentiate between property loss coverage under a first-party policy and tort liability coverage under a third-party policy of insurance. First- and third-party coverage is today typically provided in a single policy, and under both types of coverage, once the insured shows that an event falls within the scope of basic coverage under the policy, the burden is on the insurer to prove a claim is specifically excluded. Moreover, exclusionary clauses are interpreted narrowly, whereas clauses identifying coverage are interpreted broadly. The scope of coverage and the operation of the exclusion clauses, however, are different in the separate policy portions and should be treated as such. As one commentator has recently stated:

"Liability and corresponding coverage under a third-party insurance policy must be carefully distinguished from the coverage analysis applied in a first-party property contract. Property insurance, unlike liability insurance, is unconcerned with establishing negligence or otherwise assessing tort liability."[2]

For these reasons it is important to separate the causation analysis necessary in a first-party property loss case from that which must be undertaken in a third-party tort liability case. The following quotation summarizes the distinction that must be drawn: "Property insurance . . . is an agreement, a contract, in which the insurer agrees to indemnify the insured in the event that the insured property suffers a covered loss. Coverage, in turn, is commonly provided by reference to causation, e.g., 'loss caused by. . .' certain enumerated perils. The term 'perils' in traditional property insurance parlance refers to fortuitous, active, physical forces such as lightning, wind, and explosion, which bring about the loss. Thus, the 'cause' of loss in the context of a property insurance contract is totally different from that in a liability policy. This distinction is critical to the resolution of losses involving multiple causes. Frequently property losses occur which involve more than one peril that might be considered legally significant. If one of the causes (perils) arguably falls within the coverage grant—commonly either because it is specifically insured (as in a named peril policy) or not specifically excepted or excluded (as in an "all risks" policy)—disputes over coverage can arise. The task becomes one of identifying the most important cause of the loss and attributing the loss to that cause."

On the other hand, the right to coverage in the third-party liability insurance context draws on traditional tort concepts of fault, proximate cause and duty. This liability analysis differs substantially from the coverage analysis in the property insurance context, which draws on the relationship between perils that are either covered or excluded in the contract. In liability insurance, by insuring for personal liability, and agreeing to cover the insured for his . . . negligence, the insurer agrees to cover the insured for a broader spectrum of risks.

5) What is "concurrent causation?" If a covered peril is the "efficient proximate cause" of a loss under a property insurance contract, does Texas law recognize the possibility of a second, competing "efficient proximate cause?" Answers might appear in the next immediate case.

---

2 Michael E. Bragg, *Concurrent Causation and the Art of Policy Drafting: New Perils for Property Insurers* 20 Forum 385, 386 (1985)

Travelers Indemnity Company v. McKillip
469 S.W.2d 160
(Tex.1971)

Respondents, Troy L. McKillip and wife brought this action against the Travelers Indemnity Co. to recover for damages to their poultry house under the terms of a policy of insurance issued by that Company. After a trial to a jury, respondents were awarded a recovery for $7,450. This judgment was affirmed by the Court of Civil Appeals. We reverse the judgments of the courts below, and remand the cause for a new trial.

The insureds were the owners of a turkey farm in Eastland County, which included two sheet metal buildings and a wooden building used as conditioning houses for breeder turkeys. The one damaged building was of steel truss type construction, 408 feet long by 40 feet wide. The other two buildings, located some distance from the damaged building, were undamaged. The second building was essentially of the same construction as the damaged building and was some fifty feet shorter. The third building was of wooden construction.

There was testimony of "a tremendous wind" on the McKillip farm on November 2, 1968. According to the insured's testimony the wind took an "obvious path" across his property and struck the turkey barn alleged to have suffered the damage. There is no contention the wind struck or damaged the other two turkey barns located on the same property. Following this windstorm no inspection was made of the building involved here, and by the insured's own testimony no apparent damage was detected. It is undisputed the wind twisted the insured's television antenna fixed to his home, disrupted the telephone service, broke large tree limbs and bent some steel posts around their yard enclosure. The wind also broke a large electric wire connecting two of these buildings. On November 8, 1968, six days later, a four or five inch snow fell on the McKillip farm and the one building collapsed.

The jury found (1) the turkey barn was damaged by a windstorm on November 2, 1968, (2) that such windstorm was the dominant efficient cause of the collapse of the building, although, other causes may have contributed thereto, (3) the fair market value of the building immediately prior to the windstorm was $11,400, (4) the fair market value of the building immediately after the windstorm was $2,000, (5) the fair market value of the building immediately after it collapsed on November 8, 1968, was $2,000, (6) the reasonable and necessary cost to repair or replace the building after the windstorm was $7,500, (7) that the reasonable and necessary cost to repair or replace the building after its collapse November 8, 1968, was $7,500, (8) that the damage was directly caused by windstorm, (9) the damage was not caused solely by weight of the snow. Judgment was rendered on the verdict for the respondents in the amount of $7,450.

The policy purchased by Mr. and Mrs. McKillip from Travelers insured them against "direct loss resulting from any of the perils[:] . . . "Extended Coverage . . . Windstorm, Hurricane, Hail, Explosion, Riot, Civil Commotion, Smoke, Aircraft and Land Vehicles." Under "Specific Coverage Condition," appears the following exclusionary clause: "conditions applicable only to Windstorm, Hurricane, and Hail: Unless specifically named hereon this company shall not be liable for loss to metal smokestacks . . . nor (b) by snowstorm. . . .

The insurance company pleaded the specific exclusion of loss by snowstorm set out in the policy. This pleaded exclusion thus raised the issue of coverage. The insureds had the burden to prove that their loss was not attributable to the pleaded excluded hazard. *Sherman v. Provident American Ins. Co.*, 421 S.W.2d 652 (Tex.1967), and, *Hardware Dealers Mut. Insurance Co. v. Berglund*, 393 S.W.2d 309 (Tex.1962)

Travelers having plead the exclusion under the policy of loss by snowstorm, the insureds were obligated to introduce evidence to prove and secure jury findings that the damage was caused solely by the windstorm, an insured peril; or segregating the damage caused by the insured peril from that caused by the snowstorm, an excluded peril. This construction of the exclusionary clause is well settled in Texas

The case was submitted to the jury and judgment rendered in the trial court upon the theory that if the windstorm was the dominant efficient cause of the building's collapse, although other causes may have contributed to the loss, the insurer was liable. This theory of submission was approved by the Court of Civil Appeals upon the authority of *Fidelity Southern Fire Ins. Co. v. Crow*, 390 S.W.2d 788 (Tex.Civ.App. writ ref'd n.r.e.). The court quoted with approval the following rule of law announced in Crow:

> "[T]he rule in Texas is to the effect that where a loss occurs under a standard fire, windstorm and extended coverage policy within the coverage of the policy, and such loss is contributed to by an excluded risk of the policy, the plaintiff may, nevertheless, recover if plaintiff proves that the dominant efficient cause of the loss is the covered risk."

* * *

We conclude the construction placed upon the exclusionary clause of the insured's policy by the trial court and the Court of Civil Appeals in the present case was improper. Such construction is contrary to the well settled rule of construction established in *Coyle v. Palatine Ins. Co., supra*, and uniformly followed by this Court. *Hardware Dealers Mut. Ins. Co. v. Berglund, supra; Paulson v. Fire Ins. Exchange, supra*; *United States Fidelity and Guaranty Co. v. Morgan,* 399 S.W.2d 537 (Tex.1966).

In the present case we think the evidence will support a finding that a portion of plaintiff's loss was the result of the weight of the snowstorm, an excluded peril. The testimony of Charles W. Parish, a structural engineer, demonstrates this. In view of the pleading of the exclusionary clause and the evidence, the trial court erred in refusing to submit the defendant's requested special issue inquiring whether damage to plaintiff's building was caused by a combination of the wind and the weight of the snow, and if so, the percentage or the proportionate part of the damage caused by the snow. Doctrine of concurrent causation.

The general theory of segregating the damages caused by the wind and excluded peril was set forth in the submission of the damage issues. The jury was asked to determine the market value of the building immediately prior to and after the windstorm; and its value after the building collapsed on November 8; and the cost of repairs or replacement of the building immediately after the windstorm, and the same inquiry immediately after its collapse six days later. The jury found the reduced market value was the same after the windstorm and the snowstorm; and the cost of repair or replacement after both occurrences was the same.

The evidence is undisputed that a windstorm took an "obvious path" across the insured's property and struck the turkey barn on November 2, 1968. The structure remained standing after the wind, and sustained no apparent damage. No inspection was made of the barn until it collapsed six days later following the snowstorm. It is the position of the insured that the legal effect of these findings is that the damages were wholly attributable to the windstorm. Assuming this to be a correct contention, the question then is whether the evidence, viewed most favorably in support of the verdict, will support the jury findings that the damage to the insured's barn was caused solely by the insured peril of windstorm, and that none of it was caused by the snow.

There was no evidence relating to the direct effect of the wind on the damaged building, nor did anyone attempt to estimate the damage caused by wind action independent of all other causes. There is a complete absence of evidence concerning the fair market value of the building immediately after the windstorm; or of the cost to repair or replace it immediately after the windstorm. Evidence of costs of repairs was related solely to the building's condition after the snowstorm and collapse. It is essential that the insured produce evidence which will afford a reasonable basis for estimating the amount of damage or the proportionate part of damage caused by a risk covered by the insurance policy. The insured has failed to do so.

The judgments of the courts below are reversed and the cause remanded to the district court for a new trial.

NOTES & QUESTIONS

1) Asserting that a "covered peril" was the efficient proximate cause of a property loss is an affirmative defense; the insurer has the burden to prove it. Who has the burden of proving that an excluded peril was the efficient proximate cause of a loss?

2) Who has the burden of proving "concurrent causation"—the insured or the insurer?

All Saints Catholic Church v. United National Insurance Company
257 S.W.3d 800
(Tex. App. -Dallas 2008)

All Saints Catholic Church and the Roman Catholic Diocese of Dallas (collectively, All Saints) sued United National Insurance Company (United National) to recover its costs to replace a roof under an insurance policy covering property damage. All parties moved for summary judgment. The trial court granted United National's motion and denied All Saints' motion. All Saints appeals, claiming the trial court erred in granting United National's motion and in denying their own motion.

All Saints' four issues can be summarized into two contentions: (1) the doctrine of concurrent causation does not apply and that they are entitled to the total cost of replacement of the roof under the policy; and (2) the proper measure of the cost of replacement is that which would put the entire roof in a condition equal to its condition when new. For the reasons set forth below, we affirm the trial court's judgment.

BACKGROUND

United National issued a commercial insurance policy to All Saints covering its property for the period of July 1, 2002 to July 1, 2003. Under the policy, hail was a covered peril, but wear and tear as well as latent defects were excluded. All Saints' roof was made with Hardi-Slate tiles, which allegedly absorb excessive moisture and rot, break, deteriorate, or otherwise fail when installed and incorporated on buildings and structures. Hardi-Slate tiles also allegedly suffer from delamination (separating into layers) or deconsolidating (crumbling or disintegrating).

On April 5, 2003, a hailstorm caused damage to portions of All Saints' roof. Because of the prematurely-aged Hardi-Slate tiles, the hail damaged tiles could not be "spot" repaired; the non-hail damaged tiles could not withstand the repairs without breaking. Thus, the entire roof needed to be replaced to prevent it from leaking.

United National paid All Saints $83,816, the amount necessary to replace only those tiles damaged by hail. All Saints chose to replace the roof with less expensive materials for $99,560. All Saints brought suit to recover the total cost for replacement of the Hardi-Slate roofing tiles, estimated between $159,600 and $196,875. All Saints and United National filed cross-motions for summary judgment and stipulated several facts. The trial court granted United National's motion, and denied All Saints'.

STANDARD OF REVIEW AND APPLICABLE LAW

The standards for reviewing summary judgments are well established, and we follow them in reviewing this appeal. *See Nixon v. Mr. Prop. Mgmt. Co.,* 690 S.W.2d 546, 548-49 (Tex.1985) (summary judgment standards of review). When both parties move for summary judgment, each party bears the burden of establishing that it is entitled to judgment as a matter of law. *City of Garland v. Dallas Morning News,* 22 S.W.3d 351, 356 (Tex.2000). When the trial court grants one motion and denies the other, we review the summary judgment evidence presented by both parties and determine all questions presented. *Id.* The reviewing court should render the judgment that the trial court should have rendered or reverse and remand if neither party has met its summary judgment burden. *Id.; Al's Formal Wear of Houston, Inc. v. Sun,* 869 S.W.2d 442, 444 (Tex.App.-Houston [1st Dist.] 1993, writ denied).

Under the doctrine of concurrent causation, where covered and non-covered perils combine to create a loss, the insured is entitled to recover only that portion of the damage caused solely by the covered peril. *Travelers Indemnity Co. v. McKillip,* 469 S.W.2d 160, 163 (Tex.1971); *Wallis v. United Servs. Auto. Ass'n,* 2 S.W.3d 300, 302-03 (Tex.App.-San Antonio 1999, pet. denied). The doctrine of concurrent causation is not an affirmative defense or an avoidance issue; rather, it is a rule embodying the basic principle that insureds are not entitled to recover under their insurance policies unless they prove their damage is covered by the policy. The burden is on the insured to prove coverage.

DISCUSSION

The policy states that United National will indemnify All Saints for loss or damage based on the lesser of the cost to repair, rebuild or replace the damaged property in a condition equal to, but not superior to, or more expensive, than its condition when new. The policy covers damage caused by hail, but not damage caused by wear and tear or by latent defects in the roofing materials.

All Saints contend that the doctrine of concurrent causation does not apply and that United National is bound by the policy to replace the entire roof. All Saints argues that even though the Hardi-Slate tiles were prematurely-aged, the roof functioned properly before the hailstorm. After the hailstorm, the roof no longer functioned; it no longer kept the rain out. Thus, the damage was not caused by the aged, defective Hardi-Slate tiles, but by the hailstorm alone. Because the only way to repair the roof is to replace it, All Saints argues that under the policy United National must pay the cost to replace the roof in a condition equal to when it was new.

All Saints further argues that United National is seeking a deduction from the cost of repair for betterment because the undamaged tiles must be replaced, which Texas law does not allow. In support of this contention, All Saints relies on *Great Texas County Mutual Insurance Co. v. Lewis,* 979 S.W.2d 72 (Tex.App.-Austin 1998, no writ). There, the insured sustained covered damage to his car engine from an accident. The engine had 110,000 miles on it, 75% of its useful life. *Id.* at 73-74. The insurance company paid the cost of replacement minus a charge for betterment, because the insured would get a windfall receiving a new engine to replace the old one. *Id.* The policy required repairs or replacement to be of like kind and quality. *Id.* at 73. The court held this language permitted, but did not require, the engine to be the exact same age or in the exact same condition; rather, the words "repair" or "replace" mean restoration to a condition substantially the same as that existing before the damage was sustained. *Id.* at 74. All Saints argues that the language of its policy, to repair or replace the roof in a condition equal to when it was new, is stronger than the language in *Lewis;* therefore, the roof should be restored to at least a condition substantially the same as that existing before the damage was sustained, and that condition is one of a functioning roof that keeps the rain out.

We reject All Saints' arguments. The policy obligates United National to indemnify All Saints-not for the costs of a roof-but for the cost to repair, rebuild or replace damaged property, including property damaged by hail and excluding property damaged by wear and tear and latent defects. The hailstorm damaged some of the tiles in All Saints' roof, but not all of them. As All Saints argued below and here, the remaining tiles were "functioning properly" after the hailstorm. Under the policy, United National is obligated to indemnify All Saints for the cost of repairing, rebuilding, or replacing the tiles damaged by the hailstorm-and those tiles only. Any other tiles constituting "damaged property" under the policy were not reduced to that condition by the hailstorm, but by wear and tear and the nature of the Hardi-Slate tiles. Although the hailstorm brought their condition to the forefront, it does not change the fact that these tiles were not damaged by a covered peril. *See Wallis,* 2 S.W.3d at 303 (insurer not liable for damage caused by non-covered perils).

To the extent All Saints insists on treating the roof as a single, integrated unit, we conclude the doctrine of concurrent causation does apply. Part of the loss of the roof resulted from a covered peril-the hailstorm, while part of the loss resulted from non-covered perils-wear and tear and latent defects. Thus, covered and non-covered perils combined to cause the loss of the roof, and the insured is entitled to recover only that portion of the damage caused solely by the covered peril. *See McKillip,* 469 S.W.2d at 163 (holding insured only entitled to proven damage from covered peril, wind; not non-covered peril, snow); *U.S. Fire Ins. Co. v. Matchoolian,* 583 S.W.2d 692, 693-94 (Tex.Civ.App.-Houston [14th Dist.] 1979, writ ref'd n.r.e.) (holding insured only entitled to proven damage from covered peril, wind; not non-covered peril, rain). Thus All Saints is not entitled to recover the cost of replacement of the non-hail damaged tiles.

Moreover, All Saints' reliance on *Lewis* is misplaced. There the insured was being denied a new engine in replacement of an old one damaged by one covered peril. Here, United National did not deny All Saints new tiles of the same quality to replace those damaged by the covered peril, hail; it only denied the cost of new tiles to replace those damaged by the non-covered perils of wear and tear or latent defects. Thus, United National did not seek or obtain an improper deduction for betterment.

All Saints is entitled only to the amount necessary to repair the hail-damaged tiles. It has already received this from United National in the amount of $83,816. Thus, we conclude the trial court properly granted summary judgment in favor of United National. We resolve All Saints' issues against it. We affirm the trial court's judgment.

NOTES & QUESTIONS

1) Does the doctrine of concurrent causation allow a trier of fact to assess whether only two variables—an excluded peril and a covered peril—or multiple factors produced a loss?

2) In *Allison v. Fire Ins. Exchange,* 98 S.W.3d 227, 258-259 (Tex. App.-Austin 2002), the appellate court presented a more complete statement of settled law:

> The doctrine of concurrent causation is not an affirmative defense or an avoidance issue; rather, it is a rule embodying the basic principle that insureds are not entitled to recover under their insurance policies unless they prove that their damage is covered by the policy. Thus, an insured may only recover for the amount of damage caused solely by the covered peril. The burden is on the insured to prove coverage. The insured must therefore present some evidence upon which the jury can allocate the damages attributable to the covered peril. Because allocation is central to the claim for coverage, an insured's failure to carry the burden of proof on allocation is fatal to the claim. The insured must attempt to segregate the loss caused by the covered peril from the loss caused by the excluded peril.

3) Which is correct? Insureds must "prove that their *damage is covered* by the policy," or property insurers must prove that a "covered peril" is not the efficient proximate cause of a *loss*?

4) Consider this assertion: "There is no coverage under the property insurance contract because there is no evidence that a covered peril produced the loss." Is this an affirmative defense?

B. Tangible and Intangible Property Insurance

Even a cursory survey of property insurance cases reveals that insured residential and commercial property owners are surprised to learn that their insurance contract does not "cover" their losses. Most insureds know that "property insurance" is designed to protect tangible, personal property—cash, coins, precious metals, commodities, goods and other movable chattels. Of course, real property—permanent structures and fixtures—is "tangible" and may be insured against a variety of perils. But many ordinary and savvy consumers do not know an important fact: Their property insurance contract might have an exception clause that excludes "coverage" for some of their personal and/or real property.

There is more. Among insured residential and commercial property owners, there is another prevailing belief: A homeowners' or business insurance contract usually covers or insures all "intangible" property against "all risks" or "specific risks" listed in the insurance contract. "Loss profits," "business interruptions," "loss of financial assets from mysterious disappearances," "economic losses," "loss of professional income," "loss of use" and "diminution of value": these are classic examples of "intangible" property losses.

Whether courts or juries will order property insurers to pay or reimburse homeowners and businesses for their tangible and intangible losses depends on a number of factors and consideration. The next batch of cases outlines and discusses some of the issues that influence insureds' and property insurers' likelihood of overcoming substantive and procedural barriers and winning in courts of law and equity.

Fiess v. State Farm Lloyds
202 S.W.3d 744
(Tex. 2006)

The question in this case is not whether insurers should provide mold coverage in Texas, a public policy question beyond our jurisdiction as a court. The question instead is whether the language in an insurance policy provides such coverage — no more and no less.

The rules for construing insurance policies have been around for a long time, long before this dispute arose. Those rules require us to construe a policy according to what it says, not what regulators or individual insurers thought it said. Ambiguities in the plain language must be settled in favor of consumers, but they must appear in the policy itself — we cannot create ambiguities from previous policies, an agency's interpretation, or a "mold crisis."

The policy here provides that it does not cover "loss caused by mold." While other parts of the policy sometimes make it difficult to decipher, we cannot hold that mold damage is covered when the policy expressly says it is not. Accordingly, we answer the Fifth Circuit's certified question "No."

I. "We do not cover loss caused by mold"

This case comes to us on a certified question from the United States Court of Appeals for the Fifth Circuit, which asks us:

> Does the ensuing loss provision contained in Section I-Exclusions, part 1(f) of the Homeowners Form B (HO-B) insurance policy as prescribed by the Texas Department of Insurance effective July 8, 1992 (Revised January 1, 1996), when read in conjunction with the remainder of the policy, provide coverage for mold contamination caused by water damage that is otherwise covered by the policy?

The policy provision in question provides as follows:

> We do not cover loss caused by . . . (1) wear and tear, deterioration or loss caused by any quality in property that causes it to damage or destroy itself, (2) rust, rot, mold or other fungi, (3) dampness of atmosphere, extremes of temperature,(4) contamination,(5) rats, mice, termites, moths or other insects.
>
> We do cover ensuing loss caused by collapse of the building or any part of the building, water damage, or breakage of glass which is part of the building if the loss would otherwise be covered under this policy.

The rules for construing this provision are well settled. If a policy provision has only one reasonable interpretation, it is unambiguous and we must construe it as a matter of law. If exclusion has more than one reasonable interpretation, we must construe it in favor of the insured as long as that construction is not unreasonable. A policy provision is not ambiguous merely because different parties or different courts have interpreted it differently.

As with any other contract, the parties' intent is governed by what they said, not by what they *intended* to say but did not. Moreover, in cases like this involving a standard form policy mandated by a state regulatory agency, we have held for more than 100 years that the actual intent of the parties is not what counts (as they did not write it), but the ordinary, everyday meaning of the words to the general public.

In this case, it is hard to find any ambiguity in the ordinary meaning of "We do not cover loss caused by mold." While the ensuing-loss clause that follows may be difficult to parse (a matter discussed below), few ordinary people would imagine that it changes the meaning of the first sentence to read "We *do too* cover loss caused by mold."

* * *

We must of course consider an insurance policy in its entirety. But in doing so, we cannot overlook the obvious — that the policy provision here begins by stating unambiguously, "We do not cover loss caused by mold."

II. "We do cover ensuing loss caused by water damage ..."

The Fiess's argue that we must disregard how this policy provision starts ("We do not cover loss caused by mold") because of how it ends ("We do cover ensuing loss caused by water damage"). We disagree; it has again long been the rule that we must read all parts of a policy together, giving meaning to every sentence, clause, and word to avoid rendering any portion inoperative.

In *Lambros v. Standard Fire Insurance Co.,* 530 S.W.2d 138 (Tex.Civ.App.-San Antonio 1975, writ ref'd), homeowners alleged underground water cracked the slab of their home. Like the policy here, their policy excluded losses due to cracked foundations, but also stated that this exclusion "shall not apply to ensuing loss caused by . . . water damage." Justice Cadena writing for the Fourth Court of Civil Appeals found that the only reasonable construction of this clause was that it applied when an excluded risk was followed by an intervening occurrence that in turn caused an ensuing loss:

> To "ensue" means "to follow as a consequence or in chronological succession; to result, as an ensuing conclusion or effect." An "ensuing loss," then, is a loss which follows as a consequence of some preceding event or circumstance.... If we give to the language of the exception its ordinary meaning, we must conclude that an ensuing loss caused by water damage is a loss caused by water damage where the water damage itself is the result of a preceding cause. What is the preceding cause which gives to the exception the effect of taking the ensuing loss out of the reach of

> exception k [the foundation exception]? Again, the plain language of the exception compels the conclusion that the water damage must be a consequence, i.e., follow from or be the result of the types of damage enumerated in exception k. "Ensuing loss caused by water damage" refers to water damage which is the *result,* rather than the *cause,* of "settling, cracking, ... of foundations ..."

This Court refused the application for writ of error, thus giving the *Lambros* opinion the same force and effect as one of our own.

The part of the ensuing-loss clause at issue in *Lambros* is indistinguishable from the part at issue here. The Department of Insurance asserts that the *Lambros* policy covered fewer water risks and the homeowners' claim did not involve mold. But the relevant ensuing-loss language has changed in no material respect; that *Lambros* involved a different house, different homeowners, and a different insurer does not make it distinguishable. If *Lambros* is still the law, then this clause too applies only to losses caused by an intervening cause (like water damage) that in turn follow from an exclusion listed in paragraph 1(f).

The Fiesses and the Department make several arguments for construing ensuing-loss clauses differently, but all would require reversing *Lambros.* That of course is not out of the question; our opinions are not like the law of the Medes and the Persians-unalterable once written. But we are bound to consider the principles of stare decisis before taking such a step.

Stare decisis has its greatest force in cases construing statutes, partly because our errors may be corrected by statutory amendments. Although *Lambros* did not construe a statute, it was the next thing to it-a mandatory policy form promulgated by a state agency that private parties could not alter. If our policy interpretation in *Lambros* was wrong, it is strange that insurance regulators did nothing to change the policy for a quarter century. Accordingly, we decline the invitation to overrule it.

* * *

Finally, a "yes" answer to the certified question today would give ensuing-loss clauses in Texas a different meaning from what they have in most other American jurisdictions. These clauses are common in all-risk policies, and while rarely identical they share more similarities than differences. Accordingly, we should strive for uniformity in construing them. But the Fiess's argument that an ensuing-loss clause can make an excluded loss reappear as a covered loss has been rejected by courts in Alabama, Arizona, California, Florida, Illinois, Massachusetts, Minnesota, New York, North Carolina, New Hampshire, Ohio, Pennsylvania, Vermont, Washington, and Wisconsin. There would have to be something very peculiar about the Texas ensuing-loss clause for its results to be so very different from similar clauses used everywhere else.

V. Conclusion

Courts adhere to prior precedents for reasons of efficiency, fairness, and legitimacy. For more than a century this Court has held that in construing insurance policies "where the language is plain and unambiguous, courts must enforce the contract as made by the parties, and cannot make a new contract for them, nor change that which they have made under the guise of construction." If the political branches of Texas government decide that mold should be covered in Texas insurance policies, they have tools at their disposal to do so; Texas courts must stick to what those policies say, and cannot adopt a different rule when a "crisis" arises.

Accordingly, for the reasons and to the extent stated in this opinion, we answer the certified question "No."

NOTES & QUESTIONS

1) Since property can be either tangible or intangible, may insurers insure all forms of property against "all risks" or "specified risks?"

2) May an insurer insure law students against the risk of making "failing grades?" Would such property insurance create a "moral hazard?"

3) May a property insurer insure an international drug dealer's "illicit activities" and "goods" against "all risks?" May pirates secure marine insurance to insure their "treasures in the name of the King" against the risks associated with "long-distance voyages?"

4) If property and marine insurers insure slave ships against the "perils of the sea," may the owners of the slave ships collect insurance proceeds when a loss occurs on the high seas? See *Brown v. Smith,* 1 Dow PC 349, 351-355, 3 Eng. Rep. 725, 726-728 (1813) ("This was a question of insurance on the ship and cargo of *The Friendship*, employed in a voyage to Africa in the slave-trade . . .. [I]n Barbados . . .she was boarded and taken possession of by a ship of war. . .. The Government Agent at Barbados took charge of the ship and, [disposed] . . . the whole of the cargo and stores . . . . The ship was sold accordingly." Lord Chancellor Eldon, sitting on the Court of Chancery held: "Under the particular circumstances of this case, . . . the Assureds were entitled to abandon [the ship altogether and collect the insurance proceeds.]").

5) May the owners of slave ships collect insurance proceeds when their servants intentionally destroy human cargo on the high seas? See *Gregson v. Gilbert,* 3 Douglas 232, 232-234, 99 Eng. Rep. 629 (1783) (On September 6, 1791, Captain Luke Collingswood of the *Zong* loaded the slave ship at Saint Thomas on the African Coast and headed for Jamaica. Four hundred seventeen slaves were onboard. Nearing the end of the voyage, the captain discovered that fresh water was running out. In addition, the outbreak of a disease compounded the situation. The captain had to do something. Concluding that the sick slaves were going to die anyway and wanting to reduce the owners' losses, the captain decided to throw unhealthy slaves overboard. Initially, fifty-four Africans were chained together and thrown overboard. Two days later, the captain drowned seventy-eight additional slaves. By the time the *Zong* reached its destination in the Caribbean,

132 persons had been murdered." The English court did not permit the insured to collect under the insurance contract, which was legally sound)

6) May insurers insure business owners against perils associated with an inventory of goods? What if those goods "mysteriously disappeared?" Is the insurer still liable?

7) What is a "mysterious disappearance?" Does theft qualify as a "mysterious disappearance?"

Mancha v. St. Paul Fire & Marine Insurance Company
474 S.W.2d 563
(Tex. Civ. App. 1971)

This is a suit on a homeowner's insurance policy for the recovery of the value of a ring alleged to have mysteriously disappeared. The trial court granted the insurance company's motion for summary judgment and entered judgment that the insured take nothing. The insured appeals.

Joe Mancha, the insured, alleged that he purchased a homeowner's insurance policy from Jesse Trevino Insurance Agency, who wrote the policy in question with The St. Paul Fire & Marine Insurance Company, the appellee herein. The policy was issued on May 20, 1969. Prior to that time, the insured submitted a list of jewelry to the insurance agent (appraised by a jeweler) and requested complete insurance coverage on the jewelry in question. The insured plead that the agent agreed to insure the jewelry and did in fact tell the insured that the jewelry was covered by insurance.

On or about June 2, 1969, the appellant lost his Masonic diamond ring, valued by the appraiser at $4,000.00. The agency informed the insured that he had no specific insurance on the jewelry as scheduled personal property. The agent denied that he told the insured that the jewelry was covered. He contended that he was unable to get the jewelry insured as requested.

The agent had, however, issued a homeowner's policy. This policy provided for coverage of unscheduled personal property, including jewelry, in the amount of $500.00. The insurance company denied the insured's claim under this policy, contending that as a matter of law the ring was not lost under such conditions that would permit recovery under the homeowner's policy.

The trial court severed the insured's suit against the agent for failure to write the specific insurance policy in question, from the cause of action against the insurance company on the homeowner's policy. The trial court then granted the insurance company's motion for summary judgment that the insured take nothing. The insured has appealed.

The insurer contends that the only possible way that the ring could have been covered under the homeowner's policy is under the terms of "Coverage B — Unscheduled Personal Property." The policy provides that unscheduled personal property is insured against loss by "theft, larceny, burglary, robbery, or attempts thereat, and Mysterious disappearance." The appellant takes the floater position that the ring in question did in fact disappear under such circumstances that coverage under the "mysterious disappearance" provisions of the insurance policy in question would apply. Appellee insurance company answers this contention by arguing that the term "mysterious disappearance" as used in the homeowner's policy does not mean that the policy in question is an all risk policy. Finally, appellee says that under the undisputed facts in this case, the plaintiff is not entitled to recovery because as a matter of law the loss of the ring was not a mysterious disappearance.

The insurance company points out that the insured's own testimony establishes (as a matter of law) that the ring slipped off of his finger, went down the drain while he was washing dishes, and therefore, this fact does not make the disappearance of the ring mysterious. Therefore, the insurer reasons that the insured's loss is not covered by the terms of the policy.

The insurance company selects certain statements made by the insured from his deposition to substantiate this contention. In his deposition the insured testified in part as follows:

> Q: All right. In other words, nobody robbed you of this ring or took it away from you?
> A: No, sir.
>
> Q: And nobody stole it, as far as you know?
> A: Neither that.
>
> Q: And you were working around the kitchen, washing dishes, your hands were wet and perhaps soapy —
> A: Yes, sir.
>
> Q: — and you know from your experience in the past that Sometimes rings come off when your hand gets slick and wet?
> A: Yes, sir.
>
> Q: And the Probabilities are that is what happened to this ring?
> A: Yes, sir.
>
> Q: And it could have washed down the sink and went off in the plumbing?
> A: Yes, sir.
>
> Q: Probably?
> A: Yes.
>
> Q: That is your opinion of what happened to it?
> A: I don't know of any other way.

We agree that this testimony, standing alone, would probably have supported a verdict of a jury that the ring in question did not disappear mysteriously. But this selected testimony evidencing uncertainty such as 'sometimes', 'probabilities', 'could have', 'probably', 'your opinion', 'I don't know', does not conclusively determine that the ring was lost under such circumstances that the insured knew for certain how it disappeared.

Rule 166-A, Texas Rules of Civil Procedure, provides that summary judgments shall be rendered if it is shown that there is no genuine issue as to any material fact and that the moving party is entitled to judgment as a matter of law. The burden of proof is on the movant. All doubts as to the existence of a genuine issue as to a material fact are resolved against him. The evidence must be viewed in a light most favorable to the party opposing the motion and all conflicts in the evidence are disregarded. The evidence which tends to support the position of the party opposing the motion is accepted as true. *Gibbs v. General Motors Corp.*, 450 S.W.2d 827 (Tex.1970); *Great American Reserve Insurance Co. v. San Antonio Pl. Sup. Co.*, 391 S.W.2d 41 (Tex.1965)

The selected testimony quoted by the insurance company to substantiate their position is taken out of context. Considering all of the testimony, the honest uncertain admission is weakened by other testimony in the record. The insured was a Latin American, educated in Mexico, who used a Spanish interpreter in the taking of the deposition. He stated that he opened his cafe business every morning at 5:00 a.m. and started working in the kitchen until the waitresses arrived. He said that about an hour or two after he had been working in the kitchen on the morning in question, he noticed that his ring had disappeared.

He stated "It came out or dropped out" . . . "I wasn't aware in which way." He stated that it was on his hand when he first came to work. He started washing dishes and working around in the kitchen. An hour or so later he noticed that it was not on his hand. He was not aware of how it came off of his hand. He admitted from his experience in the past, that sometimes rings come off when your hand gets wet and slick. He was then asked this question: "And the probabilities are that is what happened to this ring." Answer "Yes, sir." Q. "And it could have washed down the sink and went off in the plumbing?" Answer: "Yes, sir." He related that the first thing he did, when he noticed his ring was not on his finger, was to start looking for it, trying to locate where it was. He contacted the insurance agent and told him that he had lost it. The agent said he would report the loss to the company.

The insurance company admits that under coverage B of the insurance policy unscheduled personal property that is owned, worn or used by the insured, is insured against lost by theft . . . and against mysterious disappearance. An article is lost when the owner has lost the possession or custody of it. It is a condition where he is ignorant of its whereabouts and it cannot be recovered by ordinary diligent search. There is no contention made by the insurance company that the insured has intentionally concealed or deposited the ring in a secret place. The insured did not throw the ring away. He did not hide it; he did not give it away; he did not destroy it; nor did he actually know that the ring went down the drain. This latter fact may be implied by the insured's action in looking for it and trying to locate it. He "wasn't aware of how it came off." It is admitted that the ring is no longer in existence.

The insurance policy does not define the term "mysterious disappearance." However, the term has been defined in one case determined in Texas and in other cases in other jurisdictions. *Johnson v.*

General Accident, Fire & Life Assurance Corp., 454 S.W.2d 837 (Tex. Civ. App.-Waco 1970). The Waco Court wrote about the loss of a watch that was covered by the "mysterious disappearance clause" in a homeowner's policy. The watch was lost while the insured was shopping during a one hour interval and the insured had not seen the watch since then. The Waco Court said:

> We have found no Texas cases defining "mysterious disappearance," but there are cases from other jurisdictions which do this. The Supreme Court of North Carolina in *Davis v. St. Paul Mercury and Indemnity Co.*, 40 S.E.2d 609 (N.C. 1946) defined "mysterious disappearance" as "any disappearance or loss under unknown, puzzling or baffling circumstances which arouse wonder, curiosity, or speculation, or circumstances which are difficult to understand or explain. A mysterious disappearance is a disappearance under circumstances which excite, and at the same time baffle, wonder or curiosity."

The court reversed and rendered judgment for the plaintiff and against the insured.

This same definition is quoted and followed in the following cases (citations omitted). In each of the . . . cited cases, the ascertainment of what constituted "mysterious disappearance" was determined by the courts as a question of fact. Viewing the evidence as we must in a summary judgment case, we hold that the insured's loss of his Masonic ring was not as a matter of law excluded under the provisions of the policy in question. This is a fact issue that must be determined by a jury.

The case is, therefore, reversed and the cause remanded for trial.

Betco Scaffolds Company, Inc. v. Houston United Casualty Insurance Company
29 S.W.3d 341
(Tex. App. -Houston [14th Dist.] 2000)

Appellant's motion for rehearing en banc is overruled, the opinion issued in this case on August 12, 1999, is withdrawn, and the following majority and dissenting opinions are issued in its place.

In this insurance coverage case, Betco Scaffolds Company, Inc. (Betco) appeals a summary judgment entered in favor of Houston United Casualty Insurance Company (Houston United) on the grounds that: 1) coverage of Betco's claim is not barred by: (a) the "inventory exclusion" provision of the policy; or (b) Betco's failure to fully comply with the policy's sworn proof of loss provision; 2) Houston United acted in bad faith with regard to the spoliation of Betco's claim files and by not investigating Betco's claim; 3) a private cause of action exists for violation of Board Order 27085; and 4) Houston United did not have a reasonable basis to deny the claim. Because we conclude that coverage of Betco's claim is barred by the inventory exclusion provision of the policy, we affirm.

Background

Houston United issued Betco an insurance policy (the "policy") insuring against theft, among other things. On June 13 and July 3 of 1995, Betco allegedly suffered two burglaries on its property (the "June and July losses"). Betco promptly reported these losses to the local police but did not report them to Houston United until after a further shortage was discovered in Betco's annual September 30 physical inventory (the "September shortage"). Houston United denied Betco's claim for coverage of the September shortage on the grounds that: (a) Betco did not file a sworn proof of loss within ninety-one days of the dates of the June and July losses as provided in the "proof of loss" provision of the policy; and (b) the September shortage fell within the "inventory exclusion" provision of the policy because Betco discovered it upon taking inventory.

Betco thereafter sued Houston United for breach of contract, breach of the duty of good faith and fair dealing, deceptive trade practices, and violations of the Texas Insurance Code. Houston United moved for summary judgment against the contractual claims on the grounds that coverage was precluded by the proof of loss and inventory exclusion provisions of the policy. Houston United moved for summary judgment against the extra-contractual claims on the grounds that: 1) it had a reasonable basis to deny Betco's claim; 2) the extra-contractual claims were barred by the lack of a contractual claim; 3) the dispute over the claim was bona fide as a matter of law; 4) there is no private right of action for violation of Board Order 27085; and 5) Houston United did not violate the Texas Deceptive Trade Practices Act (DTPA) or Texas Insurance Code. The trial court entered two orders granting take nothing summary judgments against Betco's contractual and extra-contractual liability claims, respectively, without stating the grounds upon which either order was granted.

Inventory Exclusion Provision

The first of Betco's four points of error argues that its contractual claims were not barred by the inventory exclusion provision of the policy (the "inventory exclusion provision") which states "This policy does not insure against ... [l]oss or shortage disclosed upon taking inventory." Betco contends that such a provision excludes only a "paper" loss, i.e., a loss reflected solely on the insured's books, such as from a record-keeping error, but does not exclude an actual shortage of goods that is discovered upon taking a physical inventory. Betco further asserts that a construction of the provision favoring the insured must be adopted because the provision is susceptible to more than one reasonable interpretation.

Insurance contracts are interpreted according to the rules of contract construction. *See Kelley-Coppedge, Inc. v. Highlands Ins. Co.*, 980 S.W.2d 462, 464 (Tex.1998). In construing contracts, our primary concern is to ascertain the true intent of the parties as expressed in the instrument. We give effect to all contract provisions so that none will be rendered meaningless.

Where a policy exclusion is ambiguous, a court must adopt the construction urged by the insured as long as it is not unreasonable, even if the interpretation urged by the insurer appears to be a more reasonable or accurate reflection of the parties' intent. See *Balandran v. Safeco Ins. Co.*, 972 S.W.2d 738, 741 (Tex.1998). Importantly, however, an ambiguity does not arise merely because the parties advance conflicting interpretations, but only where the language of the policy is subject to two or more reasonable interpretations. Whether a contract is ambiguous is a question of law for the court to decide by looking at the contract as a whole in light of the circumstances present when the contract was entered.

Betco argues that its interpretation is necessarily a reasonable one because at least one court from another jurisdiction has adopted it. On the contrary, insurance policy provisions are not susceptible to more than one reasonable interpretation, and thus ambiguous, merely because other jurisdictions have reached differing conclusions about similar provisions. *See Grain Dealers Mut. Ins. Co. v. McKee*, 943 S.W.2d 455, 459 (Tex.1997). Rather, although "[o]pinions from other states about insurance policy interpretation can be persuasive, . . . ambiguity is for this Court to decide." Therefore, with due consideration of the reasoning of decisions from other jurisdictions, we must reach our own determination as to whether Betco's interpretation is reasonable.

The parties have cited and we have found no Texas court opinion interpreting the effect of a similar provision. Even decisions from other jurisdictions have rarely specifically construed "disclosed on taking inventory" language.[3] Of those which have, at least two have merely enforced the exclusion according to its plain meaning without much analysis.[4] A third case, and that upon which Betco primarily relies, reached the opposite result because the court felt that such an exclusion was unfair and unreasonable:

> In order to affirm the judgment below it is necessary to construe the exceptive clause of the policy to mean that no loss is covered if it is first discovered upon taking inventory, no matter what proof may be subsequently brought to light showing the loss to be clearly within the risks for which the policy was written. We feel that such a construction would be unrealistic. It does not seem reasonable to us that business men would enter into an agreement to insure against a loss discovered in

---

3 Many cases from other jurisdictions have dealt with exclusions pertaining to unexplained or mysterious losses of property disclosed on taking inventory, but have been decided based on the "unexplained or mysterious" language or other considerations rather than the "disclosed on taking inventory" language. *See, e.g., McCormick & Co. v. Empire Ins. Group*, 690 F.Supp. 1212, 1213 (S.D.N.Y.1988) (holding that exclusion in warehouseman's policy for unexplained loss, mysterious disappearance, or loss disclosed upon taking inventory did not apply to loss by warehouse of materials stored there on bailment); *Van Dutch Prods. Corp. v. Zurich Ins. Co.*, 413 N.Y.S.2d 8, 9 (N.Y.App.Div.1979) (finding a loss not to be unexplained or mysterious where there was evidence of theft); *Balogh v. Jewelers Mut. Ins. Co.*, 167 F. Supp. 763, 769-70 (S.D.Fla.1958) (holding that mysterious disappearance exclusion did not apply because insurer did not establish that cause of loss was a mysterious disappearance); see also *Dunlop Tire & Rubber Corp. v. Fidelity & Deposit Co.*, 479 F.2d 1243, 1248 (2d Cir.1973) (holding that provision excluding loss, the proof of which, either as to its existence or amount, was dependent upon an inventory computation, was applicable where claimant could not show with evidence other than the inventory computation that a loss was sustained due to employee dishonesty).

4 *See Jones v. Employers Mut. Cas. Co.*, 432 N.W.2d 535, 540 (Neb.1988) (holding loss to be excluded because it was discovered as a discrepancy between the inventory records and physical inventory); *Blue Stripe, Inc. v. United States Fidelity & Guar. Co.*, 167, 360 S.E.2d 140, 141 (N.C. App. 1987) (holding loss to be excluded because it was discovered upon taking regular monthly inventory of stock).

> one way and not insure against the same loss if it should be discovered in another way. We are, therefore, unable to accept this interpretation of the words under the circumstances of this case.
>
> On the other hand, it would be both reasonable and fair for an insurer to except itself from a loss or shortage reflected solely on the insured's books and not substantiated by any independent external proof-a mere theoretical inventory loss. Such an interpretation is compatible with the other provisions of the exceptive clause which excludes "unexplained loss or mysterious disappearance."

By contrast, Texas "courts cannot make new contracts between the parties, but must enforce the contracts as written." *Royal Indem. Co. v. Marshall*, 388 S.W.2d 176, 181 (Tex.1965).

In this case, relevant provisions of the policy provide:

> 3. This policy insures against all risks of direct physical loss of or damage to the insured property from any external cause, except as hereinafter excluded.
>
> 4. This policy does not insure against . . . (b) Loss or shortage disclosed upon taking inventory. . . .

Paragraph 3 establishes the overall scope of the policy to insure only against actual physical losses from external causes. In theory, a loss or shortage disclosed upon taking inventory can be the result of a variety of causes, such as: 1) errors not discovered in previous inventories; 2) errors or fraud in recording incoming and/or outgoing inventory; (3) errors or fraud in counting the current inventory; 4) theft by employees; or 5) theft by outsiders. Obviously, not all of these possibilities involve an actual physical loss, one resulting from an external cause, or both.

* * *

Based on what we perceive to be the overall intent of the policy and the plain meaning and rationale of the inventory exclusion clause, we conclude that this provision expressly allocates to the insured the risk of a loss or shortage which comes to the attention of the insured solely by reason of taking a regularly scheduled, i.e., periodic, physical inventory. We recognize that a regularly scheduled inventory could coincide with the investigation of a casualty in such a way that the inventory is intended by the insured as a means to quantify the loss. In that event, the inventory exclusion provision would not exclude the loss because the loss would not have been disclosed upon taking inventory.

The summary judgment evidence in this case established that Betco had completed its investigation of the two burglaries, unequivocally reported the amount stolen to police, and decided without qualification that the magnitude of the losses did not exceed the deductible and thus warrant filing an insurance claim. There is no evidence that Betco was continuing to investigate the loss, held any doubt as to the accuracy of its initial estimates of the losses, or was expecting to use the September 30 inventory in any way to measure the losses from the burglaries. It was only when a considerable inventory shortage was disclosed by its annual physical inventory that Betco sought to attribute any greater loss to the burglaries. This is precisely the type of situation which we believe the inventory exclusion provision was intended to avoid. The summary judgment evidence thus established that Betco's September shortage was disclosed upon taking inventory.

* * *

Regardless whether we agree with the rationale of such a provision or like the result it produces in a particular case, we are bound to enforce it as it is written, not to nullify it. *See Royal Indem. Co.*, 388 S.W.2d at 181 ("Courts cannot make new contracts between the parties, but must enforce the contracts as written.") Because Betco's interpretation of the inventory exclusion provision is not a reasonable interpretation, its first point of error fails to demonstrate that the trial court erred in granting summary judgment against Betco's contractual claims and is overruled.

* * *

NOTES & QUESTIONS

1) If "a loss from a fire" is a "covered peril" but "a mysterious disappearance" is not a "peril insured against" under a policy, does an insurer have to pay if a homeowner's watch "mysteriously disappeared" in the fire?

2) If an insurer does not pay or settle a fire-related claim before the insurer fully investigates a property loss, is the insurer's lack of movement prima facie evidence of "bad faith?" Again, what is the test for "bad faith?"

3) Assume a property insurer acts in "bad faith." Is that insurer liable for "punitive damages?"

State Farm Fire & Casualty Company. v. Simmons
963 S.W.2d 42
(Tex.1998)

The two principal issues in this cause are whether legally sufficient evidence supports a jury's finding that an insurer breached its duty of good faith and fair dealing and whether there is some evidence to support a punitive damages award. The court of appeals answered each question affirmatively. We reverse the punitive damages award, but render judgment awarding the Simmonses enhanced damages under the DTPA. We affirm the court of appeals' judgment in all other respects.

I. Background

James and Cynthia Simmons purchased their first home in 1983, financed by a Veterans Administration loan. The house was located on a large lot in a semi-rural part of Montgomery County. After buying the house, the Simmonses bought a homeowner's insurance policy from State Farm Fire & Casualty Insurance.

In the year and a half after the Simmonses and their two young children moved into the house, they substantially improved the property. They installed a driveway and sidewalk, remodeled the bathroom, improved the home's water well, and, for safety's sake, moved a butane fuel tank farther from the house. To indulge his "love for hogs," James constructed a hog pen with the hope of eventually purchasing some stock. He also built a dining room table for his wife and beds for each of his children, as well as a mantel and a number of picture frames.

In the first year after the Simmonses bought the house, James, a construction supervisor, experienced some down-time from work. Consequently, the Simmonses missed several monthly mortgage payments. As a result, in January 1985, to make up for the missed payments, the Simmonses worked out a repayment schedule with the VA that allowed them to make weekly payments of $185 in lieu of their monthly mortgage obligation of $603. Thereafter, most of the weekly payments the Simmonses made were for $190 or $200. They made their last weekly payment in late April 1985.

In the same month the Simmonses worked out their repayment schedule, someone burglarized their home. Several items, including a television, silverware, a shotgun, and the children's piggy banks, were stolen. Although the burglary occurred during the day, none of the Simmonses' neighbors saw anything amiss. The burglars apparently entered the house through one of two doors at the back of the house. After the burglary, James followed the tracks of a wheelbarrow through the woods abutting the Simmonses' house to the nearby home of eighteen- or nineteen-year-old Tim Mattix. There, James confronted Mattix and another youth, James Wooddell, about the burglary. James Simmons called the police, but the police made no arrest at that time. Mattix later confessed to the police that he had committed the burglary in company with James and Charles Wooddell. State Farm paid the Simmonses $7,069 for their claim within a few weeks of the burglary.

After James's confrontation with Mattix and Wooddell, the Simmonses experienced a spate of vandalism: their telephone line was tapped into, eggs were smashed in their mailbox, and their dog died under circumstances that caused James, who had studied animal husbandry at Prairie View A & M University, to suspect that someone had poisoned the dog. Within a couple of weeks of the burglary, Cynthia returned home one day to find that someone had again entered the house, although nothing appeared to have been stolen at that time.

On Sunday, June 2, 1985, sometime between 1:30 and 2:00 a.m., the Simmonses, along with James's mother, left the house to take the children to Cynthia's aunt's home in rural Louisiana for the summer. They planned to return that evening so that James could be at work the next day. The Simmonses locked all of the doors and windows before they departed. A short time after the family left, Irene Lawrence, who was delivering newspapers, noticed smoke emanating from the Simmonses' house. Within a few minutes, Lawrence reported the fire. Firefighters responded to the fire, but to no avail. When the Simmonses returned late Sunday afternoon, they found their home totally destroyed.

The Simmonses reported the loss to their State Farm agent the next day. The claim was immediately tagged as "suspicious" because of the relatively recent theft claim. State Farm soon referred the claim to an adjuster in what later came to be known as State Farm's Special Investigation Unit. Four months later, in October, State Farm denied the claim.

Thirteen months later, the Simmonses sued State Farm. State Farm asserted arson as an affirmative defense. The jury found that the Simmonses had not burned their home, thus establishing coverage under the policy. State Farm does not contest that finding in this Court. The jury also found that State Farm had breached its duty of good faith and fair dealing in handling the Simmonses' claim and knowingly violated the Deceptive Trade Practice-Consumer Protection Act. Finally, the jury found that State Farm acted with conscious indifference in determining whether there was a reasonable basis to deny the Simmonses' claim. Based upon those findings, the district court rendered judgment for the Simmonses for $275,000 in actual damages and $2 million in punitive damages. The court of appeals affirmed that judgment.

II. Bad faith

State Farm contends that the finding that State Farm breached its duty of good faith and fair dealing is not supported by legally sufficient evidence. We disagree.

This Court recently clarified the standard for recovery in bad faith cases. In *Universe Life Insurance Company v. Giles,* we held that an insurer breaches its duty of good faith and fair dealing by denying a claim when the insurer's liability has become reasonably clear. 950 S.W.2d 48, 56 (Tex.1997). Evidence establishing only a bona fide coverage dispute does not demonstrate bad faith. *State Farm Lloyds v. Nicolau,* 951 S.W.2d 444, 448 (Tex.1997); *Transportation Ins. Co. v. Moriel,* 879 S.W.2d 10, 17 (Tex.1994). But an insurer cannot insulate itself from bad faith liability by investigating a claim in a manner calculated to construct a pretextual basis for denial. *See Nicolau,* 951 S.W.2d at 448; *National Union Fire Ins. Co. v. Dominguez,* 873 S.W.2d 373, 376 (Tex.1994); *Lyons v. Millers Cas. Ins. Co.,* 866 S.W.2d 597, 601 (Tex.1993).

As State Farm conceded at oral argument, whether an insurer has breached its duty of good faith and fair dealing is a fact issue. In determining whether the evidence is legally sufficient to support a bad faith judgment, we resolve all conflicts in the evidence and draw all inferences in favor of the jury's findings. *Id.* at 51. Viewing the evidence in this case in the light most favorable to the judgment, the evidence is legally sufficient that State Farm breached its duty of good faith and fair dealing by denying the Simmonses' claim based upon a biased investigation intended to construct a pretextual basis for denial. An insurance company's obligation to investigate is obviously not unlimited. The scope of the appropriate investigation will vary with the claim's nature and value and the complexity of the factual issues involved. Here, however, the testimony of State Farm's own experts, as well as its own internal documents, established the deficiencies in the company's review of the Simmonses' claim.

A.

The Simmonses produced evidence from which the jury could logically infer that State Farm did not make a good-faith effort to objectively investigate the Simmonses' claim, but instead engaged in an outcome-oriented investigation designed to place the Simmonses at the center of an "arson triangle."[5] The Simmonses' fire loss claim was immediately deemed "suspicious" because of the earlier theft claim. In fact, by the time State Farm denied the fire claim, the legitimacy of the earlier burglary claim was unquestionable. The police had returned a shotgun taken in the burglary to the Simmonses, which James turned over to State Farm because the company had paid for it in settling the burglary claim.

Further, there was evidence that State Farm's investigation was not reasonable because State Farm failed to investigate the possibility that other potential suspects might have started the fire. At trial, Mike Hvasta, State Farm's adjuster, testified that revenge and spite are some of the more common motivations for arson. The Montgomery County fire marshal also testified that spite and revenge were the leading motivations for arson fires in the county in 1985. In their statements to State Farm, the Simmonses had identified five people who may have had grudges against them, including Mattix and the Wooddells. Yet, there is evidence that State Farm never attempted to locate or contact any of these potential suspects, even though Hvasta's preliminary combined fire report listed locating them as an unfinished item of investigation.

State Farm's explanation for its failure to attempt to contact Mattix and the Wooddells was contradictory. At trial, Hvasta first testified that he did not contact them because he could not locate them. When confronted with his deposition testimony, however, he conceded that his explanation at that time was that he felt that it was "not important" to do so. He also acknowledged that he never learned during his investigation that Mattix, who lived just down the road from the Simmonses, had confessed to burglarizing the Simmonses' home and been released from jail only two weeks before the fire. In fact, the evidence established that State Farm was unaware of that fact until some four years after it closed its investigation of the Simmonses' claim. In light of Hvasta's combined fire report, his testimony that spite and revenge are frequent motives for arson, and his testimony that "it was important for [him] to do everything [he] could to get information with regard to th[e] claim before [he] made a final decision," the jury could logically conclude that State Farm's investigation was biased and unreasonable.

The testimony about the burglars by State Farm's claims supervisor, Joe Tabor, provided further evidence from which the jury could infer that State Farm conducted its investigation in a manner designed, not to discover the objective facts, but only to defeat coverage. While Tabor agreed that an insurer should look at the motives of others besides its insureds, he testified that State Farm did not pursue Mattix because of the physical evidence; *i.e.,* the house was locked and there was no evidence of forced entry. Yet State Farm's own report on the fire's cause and origin concluded that "no evidence of forced entry could be established due to the heavy damage throughout the

5 Arson is an affirmative defense to an insurance claim for a loss resulting from a fire. The "arson triangle" refers to a means of establishing that defense by offering circumstantial evidence that the insured had a motive and the opportunity to set a fire and that the fire had an incendiary origin.

area." Tabor also testified that State Farm had eliminated Mattix as a suspect because "Mattix had confessed to the burglary and certainly had no grievance at this point against the Simmons." The jury may well have rejected this entire explanation as inherently incredible.

B.

Additional evidence suggested that State Farm did not objectively investigate the Simmonses' claim. Hvasta and Tabor described the common indicators of insurance fraud by arson. These include: 1) a recently purchased policy or a recently increased policy; 2) a policy that significantly exceeds the insured property's value; 3) efforts by the insured to sell the property or other concrete indications that the insured intended to move; 4) prior fire losses; 5) a strong alibi for the insured; 6) unusual money problems, such as high medical bills or legal fees; 7) the removal of furniture or personal items before the fire; or, 8) a "huge [financial] burden" resulting from the strain of meeting everyday expenses. The evidence was undisputed that none of the first six criteria were met.

As to the seventh criterion, State Farm attempted to show that the Simmonses had removed their clothing from the house before the fire. However, other evidence put that fact issue in dispute. Cynthia Simmons testified that, although she had packed most of the children's summer clothes for the trip, the Simmonses left behind the children's winter clothes and clothing that they had outgrown. In addition, Hvasta's claim activity log noted that the Simmonses' master bedroom closet did contain clothing and shoes. There was also evidence that the Simmonses lost irreplaceable personal items in the fire, including James's track awards and the family Bible.

Finally, as to the eighth criterion, the jury heard evidence that the Simmonses' financial situation was no different from what they were accustomed to over the course of their marriage. Although James had experienced some down time from work at about the time the Simmonses first missed some of their monthly mortgage payments, that situation had improved by the time of the fire. The evidence also showed that State Farm had concluded, based upon conversations with the Veterans Administration that the Simmonses' monthly mortgage obligation was $1,343 per month. But, in reality, the Simmonses were only obliged to make $185 weekly payments in lieu of their $603 monthly mortgage payment. State Farm's figure thus overstated the amount the Simmonses were required to pay by more than $540 a month. State Farm also was under the erroneous impression that the Simmonses had not made any mortgage payments since January 1985. Coupled with evidence of the inadequacies in State Farm's investigation, this evidence tends to support an inference that State Farm denied the claim in bad faith.

C.

State Farm's primary contention at trial was that it properly denied the Simmonses' claim because the company reasonably believed that the Simmonses had a strong financial motive to burn their home. The claims committee report that formed the basis for State Farm's denial of the Simmonses' claim stated that "the motive for this fire was to relieve the financial burden of the mortgage." And Tabor reiterated at trial that "the motive was certainly to get out from under the mortgage." But the evidence at trial called into question the reasonableness and credibility of State Farm's reliance on that motive.

The evidence was undisputed that the Simmonses' mortgage obligation exceeded the policy limits on their homeowners insurance by several thousand dollars. If the Simmonses had actually burned their house, they would have been left with no home and a deficiency owed to their mortgage lender. This fact may have suggested to the jury, in light of the other evidence, that State Farm's fundamental premise about the Simmonses' motivation was so lacking in credibility as to imply bad faith.

D.

At trial, Hvasta, State Farm's adjuster, described an insurer's investigative responsibilities in some detail. He testified that policyholders reasonably expect insurers to thoroughly and adequately investigate claims, to disclose material facts, and to give policyholders the benefit of the doubt. He further testified that an adjuster should approach a policyholder to help resolve apparent conflicts. However, in this case, both of the Simmonses testified that State Farm never revealed that it believed there was a discrepancy between the information the Simmonses had provided about their mortgage obligation and the information State Farm had obtained from other sources. Based upon Hvasta's description of an insurer's obligations, the jury could have inferred that a reasonable insurer would have approached its insureds to resolve apparently conflicting information and would have eventually concluded that the insureds lacked a sufficient motive to commit arson.

State Farm attempts to minimize the importance of its misunderstanding of the Simmonses' mortgage obligations, as it did at trial, by pointing to other evidence that the Simmonses were under some financial strain, even with a lower monthly mortgage obligation. This contention is inconsistent with Tabor's testimony that the claims committee report, which assumed a $1,343 obligation in calculating the Simmonses' expenses, was the basis upon which State Farm made its decision. Viewing the evidence in the light most favorable to the judgment, the jury could reasonably have concluded that this was nothing more than *post hoc* rationalization on State Farm's part.

Before this Court, State Farm argues that the deficiencies in its investigation do not support liability because the Simmonses have not identified any particular step that would have made State Farm's liability reasonably clear. In essence, State Farm takes the position that the Simmonses' bad faith claim must fail because they did not prove that someone else burned their home. But it is the insurer that has the duty to reasonably investigate a claim, not the insured. *See Giles,* 950 S.W.2d at 51. To adopt State Farm's position would simply turn that duty on its head. Under the investigation standards State Farm's own experts identified, there was more than a scintilla of evidence that State Farm's investigation was materially deficient. We hold that the evidence is legally sufficient that State Farm breached its duty of good faith and fair dealing.

III. Punitive damages

The trial court awarded the Simmonses punitive damages of $2 million based upon the jury's finding that State Farm acted with conscious indifference in denying the Simmonses' claim. State Farm asserts that the evidence in the record is legally insufficient to support an award of punitive damages. We agree.

In *Moriel,* we clarified the requirements for the imposition of punitive damages in a bad faith case. A plaintiff may not recover punitive damages merely because the insurer has breached its duty of good faith and fair dealing. *Moriel,* 879 S.W.2d at 18. Instead, "[o]nly when accompanied by malicious, intentional, fraudulent, or grossly negligent conduct does bad faith justify punitive damages." *Id.* Accordingly, the Simmonses were required to introduce evidence showing that State Farm "was actually aware that its action would probably result in extraordinary harm not ordinarily associated with breach of contract or bad faith denial of a claim— such as death, grievous physical injury, or financial ruin." *Id.* at 24.

The Simmonses rely primarily upon the fact that State Farm never paid the lienholder on their property, the VA, in arguing that the punitive damages in this case were awarded in compliance with *Moriel* — that is, State Farm was actually aware that its denial of the claim was likely to result in the Simmonses' financial ruin. In conjunction with the deficiencies in State Farm's investigation outlined above, the Simmonses argue, State Farm's failure to pay the VA establishes that State Farm's conduct was "guided by an evil mind," justifying punitive damages. *See Moriel,* 879 S.W.2d at 18.

The evidence is undisputed, however, that State Farm contacted the VA and agreed to pay it the policy limits of $47,000 in exchange for an assignment of the VA's lien. Sam Bernardino, the responsible VA loan officer, testified that the VA had actually intended to accept the policy limits and convey the property to State Farm, after foreclosing on the property in order to establish the deficiency between the policy limits and accrued interest. This transaction was never completed, though, because the VA "failed to monitor; and [the property] went under [the VA's] property management section, and it was just sold."

In light of State Farm's undisputed efforts to settle with the VA, we cannot conclude that State Farm was actually aware that its actions were likely to result in financial ruin to the Simmonses. Thus, we hold that the evidence is legally insufficient to support the punitive damages award in this case.

IV. DTPA liability

The jury also found that State Farm had knowingly violated the DTPA, and that the violation was a producing cause of damages to the Simmonses. However, the Simmonses elected to recover on their common-law bad faith claim. Because we hold that the evidence is legally insufficient to support a punitive damages award, the Simmonses are entitled to additional damages under the DTPA. Before this Court, State Farm argues that the evidence is legally insufficient to support liability under the DTPA because it did not violate its duty of good faith and fair dealing in denying the Simmonses' claim; as a result, State Farm asserts, any DTPA violations could not have been the producing cause of any damage to the Simmonses. Because we hold that the evidence is legally sufficient to support common-law liability, we need not consider this issue.

V. Conclusion

In summary, we hold that there is some evidence to support the jury's finding that State Farm breached its duty of good faith and fair dealing. We further hold that the evidence is legally insufficient to support the punitive damages award in this case. Accordingly, we affirm the judgment of the court of appeals in part, reverse it in part, and render judgment for additional damages for the Simmonses in accordance with the jury's finding that State Farm knowingly violated the DTPA.

NOTES & QUESTIONS

1) Under fire insurance contracts, property insurers promise to indemnify when a fire—the "peril insured against"—causes a loss. Is a "friendly fire" a "covered peril" under a fire insurance policy?

2) Does a "hostile fire" qualify as a "covered peril?" What are "hostile" and "friendly" fires?

3) Does a property insurer act in "bad faith" when the insurer requires the insured to prove that a "hostile fire" caused a loss?

4) Are "hostile fires" intentional acts? Can "hostile" and "friendly" fires be the concurrent, efficient proximate causes of a destroyed forest? If so, will the insurer be totally or proportionately liable for the damages?

Reliance Insurance Company v. Naman
6 S.W.2d 743
(Tex. 1928)

This cause is before us upon the following certificate from the Tenth District.

This suit was filed by appellee against appellant to recover damages to certain jewelry caused by fire. It was alleged that said jewelry was insured under a policy issued by appellant to appellee, and while said policy was in full force and effect said jewelry was damaged by fire, and that appellant was legally liable for such damage. The appellant answered that the fire which damaged said jewelry was not such a fire as was contemplated by the policy, and that there was no liability for said loss of damage by fire, for the reason that a servant of the assured placed the jewelry, together with inflammable substances, in a furnace located in the assured's residence, and that a fire which was purposely built in said furnace caused the loss and damage to said jewelry; that said furnace was constructed for containing fires therein built; that the fire which damaged the jewelry was contained solely within said furnace; and that such damage was not one covered by the policy of insurance.

The case was tried before the court without a jury upon an agreed statement of facts. The court rendered judgment against appellant for $2,584.15; the same being the agreed damage to said jewelry, together with 6 per cent interest on same from June 3, 1926. Appellant duly perfected its appeal to this court, and said cause has been submitted to this court and is now under consideration.

The question herein involved is one of law only, and is a question of very great importance in the law of insurance, and the members of this court are very much in doubt as to how said question of law should be decided. The material parts of the agreed statement on which the cause was tried in the trial court are as follows:

> On January 19, 1926, the wife of appellee placed the jewelry which was ordinarily used by her in a paper hat box in a clothes closet of said dwelling house described in said policy; that in said box there was some tissue paper; that the purpose of appellee's wife in placing said jewelry in said hat box was for safe-keeping as a hiding place against burglars; that said jewelry remained in said hat box, with the intention of appellee's wife of using the same from time to time, until January 23, 1926,
>
> [On that] date one of the servants employed in said dwelling house by appellee, while cleaning house, discovered the hat box in question, and, not knowing it contained the jewelry in question or anything else of value, but thinking the same contained only waste matter, handed said hat box to another servant who worked in the house, and directed her to throw it in the furnace in the basement as trash, and the servant who took said box, believing that it contained only waste paper or trash, threw it, with all of its contents, including said jewelry, into said furnace of said dwelling house; that said furnace was used in heating said dwelling, and at the time said box was thrown into said furnace it contained sufficient fire to ignite and did ignite and destroy said box and damage the jewelry contained in said box to the amount of $2,500.
>
> [At] the time said box was thrown into said furnace neither of said servants knew that it contained said jewelry, or anything else of value; that the fire in the furnace, in its usual place and of a usual volume for heating purposes, damaged said articles while in said furnace in the sum of $2,500; that at the time of said damage said jewelry was covered by the policy sued upon. Notice of said loss was duly given, and appellant denied liability on June 3, 1926. In the trial court, as above stated, appellee recovered $2,500, the agreed damage to said jewelry, together with 6 per cent interest on same to June 3, 1926, the date on which appellant denied liability, making a total of $2,584.15.

The cause is presented to this court upon one proposition as follows:

> Where a servant of the assured under a policy of fire insurance inadvertently placed jewelry in a furnace fire for heating the residence of the assured, and said jewelry was destroyed or damaged by a fire wholly confined to such furnace, such damage was due to a friendly fire, for which the insurance company is not liable.

This proposition of law was the only one urged in the trial in the court below. The court overruled the same, and rendered judgment for appellee. This is the only question involved in this case. There is only one case in the United States that we have found or that is cited by either side that is at all similar in its facts, to wit, the case of *Weiner v. St. Paul Fire & Marine Ins. Co.,* 124 Misc. Rep. 153, 207 N. Y. S. 279. However, we think this case was poorly considered and of little value as authority, and we think is distinguishable from the case before this court. The only other case, which we think is nearer in point in its facts, is a French decision copied in 23 Irish Law Times & Solicitors' Journal, March 30, 1889, p. 169, styled *Countess Fitz-James v. The Union Fire Insurance Company of Paris*. Both of those cases are referred to in the briefs of both parties and copied in full in appellant's brief.

Many cases are cited both by appellee and appellant, but none similar to the case at bar. The policy made the basis of this suit insured appellee "against all direct loss or damage by fire," with certain specified exceptions, but none of said exceptions cover the circumstances under which this fire occurred.

We refer to and make a part of this certificate the agreed statement of facts, which includes the policy on which the suit was based. By reason of the importance of the question of law involved, and because of the grave doubt among the members of this court as to how said question should be decided, we certify to the Supreme Court for its determination upon the agreed statement accompanying this certificate, the following question: First Question. Did the trial court err in holding that the appellant was liable for the damage to said jewelry?

The policy having insured the appellee "against all direct loss or damage by fire," it becomes important to determine whether or not the loss in this case has been sustained by "fire" within the meaning of that contract. It is uniformly held that the loss must be by a hostile fire; that is, one which becomes uncontrollable or breaks out from where it was intended to be, and becomes a hostile element. And such fire must be the proximate cause of the loss.

The case of *Weiner v. St. Paul, etc., Co., supra*, is more nearly like this case than any to which we have been cited or have found. There the plaintiff's wife, for the purpose of safe-keeping, placed her jewelry in a velvet handbag, and deposited it in the stove of the household. While the jewelry was in the stove she inadvertently caused a fire to be made in the stove, and the jewelry was damaged. In holding there was no liability, the Supreme Court of New York (a trial court in that state) said:

> "We are of the opinion that the decision below was correct. Of course, mere negligence would not bar recovery, nor would willful incendiarism by someone

> other than the assured, and without his consent. Upon principle and authority, recovery may be had for loss caused by the spread of fire, or the result of heat, from a stove or fireplace. We are not required to pass upon what may, possibly, be the difficult question whether recovery could be had for the loss of something that fell, or was blown, into a stove or fireplace. We are of the opinion, however, that, as matter of common sense and human experience, it must be held that, unless a fire policy expressly includes such a cause, the parties to the policy cannot be said to have contemplated a loss by flame or heat wholly confined to a stove used by the assured as a stove, where, as here, the property destroyed was placed in the stove, regardless of how or why it was so placed."

Countess Fitz-James v. Union, etc., Co., cited in the certificate, holds to the contrary, but its reasoning does not commend the decision to us, and it is not in line with the overwhelming weight of the authorities.

Where the fire which occasions the damage is confined to the usual and ordinary place, such as the range, grate, or furnace, it is usually denominated a friendly fire, and as such not a fugitive one within the contemplation of the contract of insurance. For it is of course contemplated always that the owner will have fire in these places.

Where a loss does come within the contract, the recovery is not dependent upon consumption, or even actual ignition, for a direct loss may otherwise result. The damage may be caused by smoke and soot, by heat, by water, by fall of building, by explosion, by theft as a result of the fire or by any other method directly due to the fire.

The contract of insurance contemplates that the insurer will pay to the insured the damages for all direct loss proximately caused by fire within the meaning of the policy. A friendly fire is not within the undertaking of the insurance company at all. If it were, the company would be liable, as in a case of unfriendly fire, for all direct loss or damage, irrespective of destruction or of actual ignition, and the fact that in this case there was an actual consumption of the insured property is of no importance in determining the liability of the insurance company.

If the fire in the furnace was such a fire as the company insured against, then it would be liable for any direct loss or damage therefrom, and it would follow the insured could recover his damage for loss occasioned by the cracking of the plaster in the furnace basement from the heat of the furnace, for the cracking of the paper on the walls from the heat of the grate, and for damage to the decoration and draperies through smoke and soot from the furnace or chimney place, and even for the replacement of furnace, grate, and range oven when burned out, for those clearly would be losses directly due to the respective fires.

Those are not extreme illustrations, but liability in each instance would follow if the fire in this case be held to be within the policy. In the sense in which the word "fire" is used in the policy, there has been no fire so long as it is kept within the proper and accustomed place. In common parlance one has not had "a fire" so long as it has only burned in the place where it was intended to burn, and the sense in which that word is used in common parlance accurately indicates the sense in which it is employed in a fire insurance policy.

The point is made by appellee that there are numerous exceptions to the liability of the insurance company printed in the policy, and the argument follows that this loss not falling within one of the exceptions is therefore within the contract. This by no means follows. In the very nature of an exception it is something taken out of the instrument, whether statute, grant, or contract, and is of a kind dealt with in the contract. Where the matter being considered is not within the contemplation of the parties to the contract in the first place, there is no need of an exception, and, since as we think the fire in this case was without the contract of insurance, the failure to except it cannot bring it within.

We recommend that the question certified be answered in the affirmative.

Cureton, C. J. The opinion of the Commission of Appeals answering the certified question is adopted and ordered certified.

NOTES & QUESTIONS

1) Does a fire insurer have a duty to pay where evidence strongly suggests that a "mysteriously friendly fire" was the efficient proximate cause of a destroyed home?

2) If a "deviant spouse" intentionally "torches community property," may the "innocent spouse" collect proceeds under a fire insurance contract?

Texas Insurance Code § 2002.003
Fire Insurance and Allied Lines
Including Residential Property Insurance
Coverages for Spouses and Former Spouses

A homeowner's insurance policy or fire insurance policy promulgated under Article 5.35 or filed and in effect as provided by Subchapter B, Chapter 2301, may not be delivered, issued for delivery, or renewed in this state unless the policy contains the following language:

> "It is understood and agreed that this policy, subject to all other terms and conditions contained in this policy, when covering residential community property, as defined by state law, shall remain in full force and effect as to the interest of each spouse covered, irrespective of divorce or change of ownership between the spouses unless excluded by endorsement attached to this policy until the expiration of the policy or until canceled in accordance with the terms and conditions of this policy."

Texas Farmers Insurance Company v. Murphy
996 S.W.2d 873
(Tex. 1999)

The question posed is whether an innocent spouse can recover insurance proceeds when the other co-insured spouse has intentionally destroyed the covered community property. The court of appeals based its affirmative answer on the fact that the spouses partitioned the community before the trial began. We affirm the court of appeals' judgment, but for different reasons: 1) the policy contractually entitles the co-insured spouse to recover, absent defenses not preserved in this case, and 2) the public policy defenses presented in this case do not overcome the co-insured's contractual right of recovery.

I

On September 23, 1993, Robert Murphy obtained a binder on a standard homeowners insurance policy covering his and his wife Daisy Murphy's home and contents. On September 30, 1993, the Murphys' home burned down. Robert sought reimbursement under the policy. Texas Farmers Insurance Company investigated the claim and concluded that Robert intentionally caused the fire.

On February 19, 1994, Farmers filed suit seeking a declaratory judgment of nonliability under the insurance policy. Farmers alleged that public policy prohibits arsonists from recovering for their losses. Farmers further alleged that Robert misstated and willfully concealed material facts, vitiating coverage under the insurance policy's concealment clause. Robert counterclaimed for breach of contract and violations of the Texas Insurance Code. In December 1995, Daisy intervened and filed her own claim for the policy benefits.

Meanwhile, Daisy filed for divorce, and on March 8, 1996, she and Robert executed a partition agreement to divide their community interests in any proceeds from the policy. Robert and Daisy's divorce became final on October 11, 1996.

The trial was held March 12-14, 1996. The court submitted a jury charge asking whether Robert caused the fire and whether Daisy had prior knowledge of or participated in the arson. Farmers did not submit or request questions asking whether Robert or Daisy intentionally misrepresented or concealed any material facts. The jury found that Robert burned down the home but that Daisy was innocent of prior knowledge of or complicity in the arson. On October 17, 1996, the trial court, notwithstanding the jury's innocent-spouse finding, rendered a take-nothing judgment against both Robert and Daisy.

The court of appeals reversed the take-nothing judgment against Daisy and rendered judgment that she take half of the amount the jury awarded for the Murphys' loss. In its petition for review, Farmers argues that both the policy language and public policy prohibit Daisy's recovery.

II

Until 1986, the deliberate destruction of jointly-owned property by one co-insured barred recovery by other co-insureds, even when they were innocent and the policy did not expressly bar such recovery. In *Kulubis v. Texas Farm Bureau Underwriters Insurance Co.,* 706 S.W.2d 953 (Tex.1986), we reexamined that rule. Betty Kulubis sued to recover homeowner's policy benefits covering a mobile home that her husband intentionally destroyed in a fit of rage after she served him a divorce citation. Citing public policy and Betty's "reasonable expectations," we held that she was entitled to recover her share of the insurance proceeds.

In *Kulubis*, we indicated "that the proper test to be applied was what a reasonable person would have understood the fire insurance policy to mean." In support of that test, we cited several out-of-state cases that construed the terms of homeowners policies to allow recovery by innocent co-insureds of those who had deliberately destroyed their jointly-owned property. The paramount question in those cases was whether the contract terms supported such a recovery. Although the *Kulubis* opinion did not cite any policy provisions, the same paramount question was implicit in our analysis there. And *Kulubis's* implicit answer was yes. Indeed, our review of the *Kulubis* record confirms that the policy did not explicitly bar Betty's recovery. In short, based on the policy terms, Betty would have reasonably understood the policy to provide such coverage.

In *Kulubis*, we also held that public policy supported Betty's right to recover her share of the insurance proceeds. Barring her recovery would have unjustly enriched Texas Farm by freeing it of its contractual obligation to her. Moreover, denying Betty any recovery despite her contractual right to it would have imputed her estranged husband's criminal wrongdoing to her, the target and victim of his outrage. On the other hand, allowing Betty, a completely innocent spouse, to recover did not work a fraud on the insurance company. Moreover, because she had a separate, rather than a community interest in her mobile home, her recovery did not directly benefit her husband.

Although in *Kulubis* we stated that in general, "the illegal destruction of jointly owned property by one co-insured shall not bar recovery under an insurance policy by an innocent co-insured," we expressly did not decide whether the principle applied to community property. The question we reserved presents a more difficult public policy dilemma. Fire insurance proceeds generally take the place of the destroyed property. If the destroyed property is community property, any proceeds will become community property in which the culpable spouse will necessarily have an interest unless there is a divorce or partition agreement.

Here, of course, we have a partition agreement. Any insurance benefits Daisy receives will now become her separate property. But this does not make the issue of recovery as simple as the one *Kulubis* addressed. In *Kulubis,* the spouses' interests in the insured property were separate from the outset. The innocent spouse could recover even without a partition or divorce. Here, to condition recovery under a policy covering community property on a post-arson partition or divorce in order to deny a benefit to the culpable spouse raises three difficult issues.

First, should courts craft a rule that may encourage partition or divorce? Second, by what date must the spouses partition or divorce-before the incident occurs, the claim is made, the insurer denies coverage, the start of trial, or the final judgment? Third, can any rule be crafted to allow innocent spouses to recover and ensure that the culpable spouse never benefits? If spouses partition or divorce but still live together or share their resources, the culpable spouse can still indirectly benefit. Not surprisingly, several post- *Kulubis* cases have struggled with these issues.

The Fifth Circuit decided *Norman v. State Farm Fire & Casualty Co.* 804 F.2d 1365 (5th Cir.1986), shortly after the *Kulubis* decision. The jury found that Mr. Norman intentionally burned down his community-owned home. The Fifth Circuit held that because Mr. Norman would benefit from Mrs. Norman's recovery, public policy barred Mrs. Norman from recovering under the policy, even if she was innocent. Of *Kulubis* 's various public policy considerations, that a wrongdoer not benefit from his wrongdoing was, in the Fifth Circuit's judgment, "by far the dominant one." The court warned that a rule permitting recovery whenever an insurance company could not prove both spouses' complicity would encourage collusion and threaten public safety.

In this case, the court of appeals . . . reasoned that because Daisy and Robert executed a partition agreement before trial separating their interests in any insurance proceeds, the situation mirrored Kulubis, in which the culpable spouse had no right to recover. Echoing *Kulubis's* public policy considerations, the court held that "[r]ecovery by Daisy Murphy will not cause a fraud on Farmers; will ensure that Farmers will not be unjustly enriched to Daisy Murphy's detriment; and will ensure that her reasonable expectations, as an innocent co-insured, will be met."

III

The foregoing cases share a common shortcoming. They all focus on conflicting public policy considerations without first evaluating the contract language. Although Kulubis may not make it clear, a court should not decide the question of public policy without first determining the contractual rights of the parties under the policy. Indeed, the principal case *Kulubis* cited states that whether an innocent co-insured can recover is a question of construction. And as another case considering this issue has held, "an insured may not complain that his or her reasonable expectations were frustrated by policy limitations which are clear and unambiguous." Therefore, we examine whether Daisy can recover under the contract's terms.

The parties agree that Robert's binder was for the 1991 Texas Standard Homeowners-Form B. The form was promulgated by the Texas Board of Insurance. Subject to the policy limits and some enumerated exclusions, the policy insures fire damage losses to an insured's home and its contents. The policy defines an "insured" as the named insured and any residents of the named insured's household who are relatives or who are less than twenty-one years old and in the care of the named insured. Farmers does not challenge Daisy's standing as an insured under the policy.

Initially, we note that unlike some homeowners policies, the Texas Standard Homeowners Policy-Form B does not include a clause barring or limiting recovery for losses intentionally caused by an insured. Section II of the policy excludes personal liability coverage for "bodily injury or property damages which is caused intentionally by or at the direction of the insured," but no similar exclusion applies to the insured's own property losses.

The policy, however, does include a condition to bar coverage for all insureds if any one of them commits a fraud or intentionally conceals or misrepresents a material fact:

> CONCEALMENT OR FRAUD. This policy is void as to you and any other insured, if you or any other insured under this policy has intentionally concealed or misrepresented any material fact or circumstance, made false statements or committed fraud relating to this insurance, whether before or after a loss.

Farmers claims that Robert triggered this exclusionary condition by making a claim on the policy after intentionally burning his house down. Farmers further asserts that this condition unambiguously bars recovery not only by Robert, but also Daisy.

In Texas, insurance contract interpretation is governed by general contract interpretation rules. Our goal is to give effect to the written expression of the parties' intent, viewing the contract in its entirety, consistent with applicable rules of law. A plaintiff seeking recovery under an insurance policy, however, must prove only those provisions that allow recovery. If there are any contractual provisions that could limit or bar recovery, it is incumbent on the insurer to plead and prove them. Although we generally "striv[e] to give meaning to every sentence, clause, and word to avoid rendering any portion inoperative," an insurer who does not plead or prove any applicable exclusionary provision waives the effect of that provision.

Farmers's assertion of fraud was an affirmative defense to its liability under the contract. Thus, Farmers had the burden to plead, prove, and secure findings to sustain this defensive plea of fraud.

Although Farmers plead the concealment-clause defense, it did not obtain any jury findings on it. Indeed, Farmers made no further mention of this defense before the trial court or the court of appeals. In its motion for judgment and to disregard certain jury findings, Farmers asserted that its arson defense "is not based upon or dependent upon a policy provision, but rather has its foundation in the public policy of preventing a litigant from benefiting from his own wrongful act." In sum, Farmers' challenge to Daisy's right of recovery was predicated entirely on public policy grounds alone.

Farmers has attempted to revive its concealment-clause defense in its brief and oral arguments before this Court. For the first time since it filed the lawsuit, it argues that the concealment clause—and not just public policy — bars Daisy's recovery. It argues that as a matter of law, Robert's filing of a claim on property that he had deliberately destroyed was a fraud — with or without proof or findings of misrepresentation, concealment, or reliance. We decline to consider this contention because Farmers affirmatively refused to make it at either trial or on appeal until now. Farmers abandoned and waived any defense to liability under the concealment clause.

Because Farmers did not preserve its concealment-clause defense, we treat the clause as if it was of no effect. Accordingly, we conclude that Daisy is contractually entitled to recover the amount of her interest in the policy at the time of the loss — which, as the court of appeals held, is fifty percent of the losses that the jury found the house and its contents had sustained.

IV

We next consider whether, notwithstanding Daisy's contract rights, public policy forbids Daisy's recovery because the policy covered community property. This Court has articulated a public policy that a wrongdoer should not be rewarded for wrongdoing. To prevent an arsonist from having a community interest in any recovery, Texas courts have generally conditioned an innocent spouse's recovery on whether and when the community interests in the insurance policy have been severed.

Farmers argues that innocent spouses should not recover even if there is an after-the-fact partition. It contends that such a rule would encourage spouses to enter into sham partition agreements, after which the wrongdoing spouse might still benefit from the insurance proceeds. In the alternative, it argues that recovery should be barred if on the dates the claim was made and denied the arsonist would have had an interest in the insurance proceeds as community property.

Daisy responds that it would be arbitrary to deny recovery even when the culpable spouse would receive no benefit. It would also be unfair to require an innocent spouse to obtain a partition or divorce before the claim was filed or denied. First, it assumes the innocent spouse knows that the other spouse committed arson and can obtain an equitable partition before the insurance company denies the claim. Second, it encourages an innocent spouse whose home burns down to hastily partition or divorce, even though a jury may later acquit the suspected spouse of any alleged wrongdoing. Daisy contends that if recovery must be conditioned on partition or divorce, she should have until the time of judgment to obtain a severance of the community estate.

In our view, a rule conditioning an innocent spouse's recovery on partition or divorce is neither practical nor satisfactory. Partition agreements require the consent of both spouses. The culpable spouse could still benefit by demanding, in exchange for his or her consent, a greater share of the remaining community estate. Or he or she could refuse to partition at all, leaving the innocent spouse with a choice between divorce and forfeiture. And an innocent spouse who wants a divorce might not be able to obtain it in time to protect her or his interest in any recovery. On the other hand, an innocent spouse who is committed to the marriage might enter into a partition agreement as a mere formality, fully intending to share any recovery with the culpable spouse. In short, a rule requiring partition may not effectively protect the innocent spouse's share or prevent the culpable spouse from benefitting. Additionally, it may have the unintended consequence of encouraging divorce.

It is not the courts' business to superintend what innocent co-insureds may do with any insurance proceeds they are contractually entitled to recover. Nor, under these circumstances, is it the courts' province to regulate an innocent spouse's marital relationship with the culpable spouse. The preferable rule is to allow innocent spouses to recover according to their contracts, regardless of partition or divorce.

We reaffirm our longstanding public policy preventing an arsonist from benefitting from fraud by denying recovery of his or her own one-half interest in the claim against the insurer. We conclude, however, that such public policy does not overcome an innocent spouse's contractual right to recover her or his one-half interest in the policy benefits.

The dissent raises the theoretical possibility that in the future, if the innocent spouse does not obtain a partition or divorce, and if the insurance carrier fails to prove any contractual defenses to recovery, the culpable spouse will still benefit through his or her one-half community interest in the innocent spouse's one-half recovery. But Robert does not benefit here; the partition agreement divested him of any interest in Daisy's recovery. And in the future, insurance carriers can take steps to prevent any recovery from occurring. Farmers has acknowledged that it believes the 1991 Homeowners Policy-Form B already provides insurance carriers with a contractual defense to coverage.

Our opinion today should mitigate any confusion Kulubis caused about the availability of contractual defenses. The law, moreover, allows insurance carriers to use forms adopted by a national organization of insurance carriers, provided they are filed and approved by the Insurance Commissioner. Such a form could include an intentional loss provision that voids coverage to all insureds if any insured intentionally destroys the covered property, provided, of course, the commissioner approves the provision as consonant with public policy.

Based upon the Texas Homeowners Policy-Form B terms that Daisy successfully pleaded and proved, Daisy is entitled to recover her share of the policy benefits. Farmers did not prove any policy exceptions or exclusions limiting or barring her recovery. We hold that Farmers' public policy defenses do not defeat Daisy's contractual right to recover. Accordingly, we affirm the court of appeals' judgment that she recover one half of the amount the jury awarded for the Murphys' losses.

* * *

NOTES & QUESTIONS

1) May "innocent" or "deviant" businesspersons insure their "illegal" or "corrupt" businesses against "the peril of business interruption?"

2) Assume that a "mysterious fire" erupts and partially destroys a Wal-Mart store and "interrupts" the business activities for two months. Must the property insurer reimburse Wal-Mart for "business interruption" losses and expenses?

3) What is the test for determining "business interruption"? How long must an "interruption" last before a property insurer becomes liable?

4) Are insurers only liable for "one long continuous business interruption," or, must insurers reimburse insureds for "intermittent or recurring business interruptions?"

5) Does a property insurer have a duty to pay a claim if only an "excluded peril" causes "business interruption?"

Quality Oilfield Products, Inc. v. Michigan Mutual Insurance Company
971 S.W.2d 635
(Tex. App.-Houston [14th Dist.] 1998)

The dispositive issue in this case is whether a "work slowdown" triggers coverage under a business interruption endorsement of a commercial insurance policy. We find it does not and affirm the judgment of the trial court.

Appellant, Quality Oilfield Products, Inc. (Quality), is a manufacturer of oilfield equipment used for drilling and production. In March, 1992, Quality's workplace was burglarized and engineering drawings, computer media disks, and design information used by Quality to process orders were stolen. Immediately after the burglary, Quality filed a claim for business interruption losses under an insurance policy issued by appellee, Michigan Mutual Insurance Company (Michigan). Quality claimed the items stolen were the nerve center of its operations and caused an interruption of its normal business activity. Michigan denied coverage stating Quality did not suspend operations as required by the policy.

Michigan, subsequently, sought a declaratory judgment that "Michigan has no obligation to compensate its insured, Quality, for losses arising from an alleged 'slow down' in Quality's business due to the theft of certain floppy disks and engineering drawings on or about March 15, 1992." Quality filed a counterclaim for recovery under the policy and bad faith in handling the claim. Quality and Michigan filed competing motions for summary judgment, both contending that the unambiguous language of the policy supported their respective positions on the issue of coverage as a matter of law. The trial court granted summary judgment in favor of Michigan and denied Quality's motion. This appeal followed. In two points of error, Quality contends the trial court erred in granting Michigan's motion for summary judgment and denying its partial motion for summary judgment.

The following standard for reviewing a motion for summary judgment is well-established: 1) the movant must show that no genuine issue of material fact exists and that it is entitled to summary judgment as a matter of law; 2) in deciding whether there is a disputed material fact issue precluding summary judgment, evidence favorable to the nonmovant will be taken as true; and 3) every reasonable inference must be resolved in the nonmovant's favor. *See Science Spectrum, Inc. v. Martinez,* 941 S.W.2d 910, 911 (Tex.1997) (citing *Nixon v. Mr. Property Management Co.,* 690 S.W.2d 546, 548-49 (Tex.1985)). When both parties file competing motions for summary judgment and one is granted and the other denied, we will determine all issues presented, including the order denying the losing party's motion. *Jones v. Strauss,* 745 S.W.2d 898, 900 (Tex.1988). Where, as here, the summary judgment order does not specify the grounds upon which summary judgment was granted, we will affirm the judgment if any of the theories advanced in the motion is meritorious. *State Farm Fire & Casualty Co. v. S.S.,* 858 S.W.2d 374, 380 (Tex.1993).

In its first point of error, Quality contends the trial court erred in granting Michigan's motion because the unambiguous language of the policy invokes coverage. Business interruption coverage under

Quality's policy provided for "loss resulting directly from the necessary interruption of business caused by damage to or destruction of real or personal property . . ." The provision does not define the term "interruption of business." Consequently, we must determine whether "interruption of business" is an unambiguous term meaning "suspension of operations" as Michigan claims, or includes a "work slowdown" as Quality alleges. Before making such a determination, we note that an intent to exclude coverage must be expressed in clear and unambiguous language. *See National Union Fire Ins. Co. v. Hudson Energy Co.,* 811 S.W.2d 552, 555 (Tex.1991).

An insurance contract is ambiguous when it is susceptible to more than one interpretation, each of which is fair and reasonable. A determination of whether an ambiguity exists in an insurance policy is a question of law for the court, decided by examining the contract as a whole in light of the circumstances present when the contract was formed. *Coker v. Coker,* 650 S.W.2d 391, 393-94 (Tex.1983). However, courts should not strain to find an ambiguity, if, in doing so, they defeat the probable intentions of the parties, even though the insured may suffer an apparent harsh result as a consequence. *See Glover v. National Ins. Underwriters,* 545 S.W.2d 755, 761 (Tex.1977).

Quality contends "interruption of business" does not mean *total* cessation, shutdown, or stoppage of business and cites to *Lexington Ins. Co. v. Island Recreational Dev. Corp.,* 706 S.W.2d 754 (Tex.App.-Beaumont 1986, writ ref'd n.r.e.). In *Lexington,* the court determined the insured was entitled to business interruption coverage for losses sustained from a storm while its restaurant remained opened for business. Quality argues the *Lexington* holding supports its proposition that total cessation is unnecessary. We disagree. In *Lexington,* the insured closed its restaurant for several months and the issue before the court was the duration of the business interruption, i.e., whether the insured could recover after the restaurant reopened until the previous level of operation was returned. The court held the terms of the policy were such as to allow recovery for the period the restaurant was rebuilding its business. Therefore, business interruption coverage was triggered when the insured suspended its operations and ceased business for a period of time. Because the precise issue of whether "interruption of business" is invoked by a work slowdown is one of first impression in our jurisdiction, we must turn to other jurisdictions and persuasive authority for guidance.

Other courts which have addressed whether similar language in a business interruption insurance clause requires an actual suspension of operations have found that it does. *See, e.g., Ramada Inn Ramogreen, Inc. v. Travelers Indem. Co. of America,* 835 F.2d 812, 814 (11th Cir.1988) (holding an insured could not recover under business interruption clause for decline in occupancy of a hotel which remained open following a fire in the restaurant); *National Children's Expositions Corp. v. Anchor Ins. Co.,* 279 F.2d 428, 431 (2d Cir.1960) (holding no partial business interruption loss because an insured's building was open during entire period when an unprecedented snow storm reduced attendance at an exposition); *Royal Indem. Ins. Co. v. Mikob Properties, Inc.,* 940 F.Supp. 155, 159 (S.D.Tex.1996) (holding under Texas law, business interruption insurance would not cover loss of income from adjacent buildings which were adversely affected by a fire because the insured never suspended operations on the adjacent buildings); *Keetch v. Mutual of Enumclaw Ins. Co.,* 212, 831 P.2d 784, 787 (Wash. 1992) (holding an insured could not recover under business interruption insurance when volcanic ash caused damage to motel and quality of service was reduced, but motel never ceased operations).

Quality, however, argues a finding that business interruption coverage is triggered only when an insured *totally* ceases operations would encourage policyholders to unnecessarily shutdown business and not mitigate damages. Quality relies on a Third Circuit opinion that held an insured was entitled to business interruption coverage when a fire destroyed its building, and the insured continued to do business at an alternate site. *See American Medical Imaging v. St. Paul Fire & Marine Ins. Co.*, 949 F.2d 690, 695 (3d Cir.1991). In *American,* the court found the insured would not have any motivation to mitigate losses if the business interruption insurance would not cover such an incident.

American, however, is distinguishable from this case. First, the policy language was different in *American* because it provided coverage for "losses from the necessary or potential suspension" of the insured's operations. Thus, the policy language was more expansive and covered losses that may potentially suspend an insured's operations. Second, coverage was invoked under the "necessary suspension" language in the policy because the insured totally suspended its operations for a brief period. Therefore, *American* does not support Quality's argument that it would not have to completely suspend operations in order to trigger business interruption coverage under its policy.

Michigan contends that a review of the entire policy supports their interpretation of "necessary interruption of business." A mitigation clause in Quality's policy requires the insured to mitigate damages by a "complete or partial resumption of operation of the property." Hence, Michigan argues, an interpretation of the policy which requires something less than a total suspension of business would render the mitigation clause meaningless. In other words, there could be no "resumption" if the insured never stopped doing business. The court in *Keetch* also found support for their holding from a similar mitigation provision. "By requiring the insured to mitigate the loss and resume operations as soon as practicable, the endorsement implies that a business interruption loss has forced the insured to cease business operations." .

Quality also argues many of the cases Michigan cites are distinguishable because the courts ultimately denied coverage based upon a lack of causation. While this may be true, in reaching their decisions the courts looked to whether the property or buildings covered by the policy were able to remain open despite the loss incurred. Thus, we find this distinction is irrelevant to the central issue presented in this case, that is, whether the insured must actually suspend operations to invoke business interruption coverage.

It is worth noting that the purpose of a business interruption policy is to indemnify the insured for loss caused by the interruption of a going business due to the destruction of the building, plant or parts thereof. This type of insurance is called use and occupancy insurance and is defined as indemnification for any loss sustained by the insured because of his inability to continue to use the premises or his inability to keep the premises occupied by a tenant. *Id.* at § 1:113. For example, in *Ramada Inn,* the issue was whether a hotel could recover for business interruption insurance when a fire destroyed part of the hotel, and the entire hotel experienced loss of income from a reduction in customers. The court held recovery for business interruption insurance is intended when the loss is due to an *inability to use the premises* where the damage occurs, and declined to cover income losses incurred from the portion of the hotel that remained open. *See id.* at 814 (emphasis added).

Likewise, the United States District Court in Houston found that under Texas law, business interruption insurance would not cover loss of income from adjacent buildings which were adversely affected by a fire. *Royal,* 940 F.Supp. at 159. The court concluded the insured could not recover under business interruption coverage "[e]ven if the character of the apartment complex was adversely impacted by the fire, [and] there was no "necessary suspension of operations or tenancy...." Similarly, Quality is claiming loss of income for a theft which adversely impacted their production, but it remained opened and continued to do business. In fact, Quality continued to operate at a rate of eighty percent of its previous level of capacity immediately after the theft.

In sum, after considering the policy as a whole and persuasive authority from other jurisdictions, we find that "interruption of business" is an unambiguous term meaning "cessation or suspension of business." Therefore, Quality was not entitled to business interruption coverage for the work slowdown it experienced, and we find the trial court did not err in granting Michigan's motion for summary judgment. Quality's first point of error is overruled.

In its second point of error, Quality argues the trial court erred in refusing to consider employee affidavits attached to its response to Michigan's motion for summary judgment. Quality contends this evidence would have created a fact issue concerning the intention of the parties and Quality's interpretation of business interruption. Only where a contract is first determined to be ambiguous may the courts consider the parties' interpretation and admit extraneous evidence to determine the true meaning of the instrument. *National Union Fire Ins. Co. v. CBI,* 907 S.W.2d 517, 520 (Tex.1995). Since we have determined the policy language is unambiguous, the trial court did not err in refusing to admit the affidavits in Quality's response. We overrule point of error two.

The judgment of the trial court is affirmed.

Lloyd's of London

Very likely, most consumers and businesspeople have heard of or know something about Lloyd's of London. The underwriters at Lloyd's have a long history of insuring businesses and property owners against all types of perils. It is fairly renowned that those London underwriters insure movie stars' various bodily parts as well as singers' voices against certain risks. However, it is less well-known that Lloyd's underwriters insured slave traffickers' ships, human cargo and voyages during the Transatlantic Slave Trade. Here is some additional information about that very old institution.

Fifth Circuit Survey June 2002–May 2003 Survey Article
Insurance Decisions—A Survey and An Empirical Analysis
35 Tex. Tech Law Rev. 947 (2004)
Willy E. Rice

At the outset, it is important to establish that Lloyd's of London, the Corporation of Lloyd's, and the Society of Lloyd's are labels for the same entity. The entity is more than three hundred years old.

Lloyd's provides office space and administrative assistance for insurance underwriters. However, Lloyd's does not underwrite insurance; instead, it serves as a market for Names—individual and corporate underwriters that insure all types of tangible and intangible interests worldwide through various syndicates. They also sell reinsurance contracts—Treaties of Reinsurance—to other insurers worldwide.

The Council of Lloyd's controls Lloyd's administrative functions. The Council also develops regulations or bylaws for the syndicates and Names. One regulation requires Names to become members of Lloyd's before they can participate in the insurance market. Also, Names "must pass a means test to ensure their ability to meet their underwriting obligations." But more important, they must appear in person before a representative of the Council in London and swear that they accept exposure to unlimited personal liability for the privilege to underwrite insurance in the Lloyd's market.

To be sure, the massive toxic-tort litigation and exposure during the late 1980s and earlier 1990s severely tested the Names' willingness and ability to honor various contractual agreements and to cover a colossal number of claims. Quite simply, an unacceptable number of Names miserably failed the test. Many underwriters could not cover billions of dollars in losses, thereby threatening the very existence of Lloyd's of London.

‡

Commercial Terrorism" from the Transatlantic Slave Trade to the World Trade Center Disaster: Are Insurance Companies and Judges "Aiders And Abettors" of Terror?—A Critical Analysis of American and British Court" Declaratory and Equitable Actions, 1654-2002
6 The Scholar: St. Mary's L. Rev. on Minority Issues 1 (2003)
Willy E. Rice

[I]n England, Lloyd's of London, the well-known financial institution opened its doors in 1688, at the peak of the African slave trade. "Lloyd's of London . . . is still . . . the largest meeting place for underwriters and shippers to transact marine insurance business. In 1906, the British Parliament enacted the Marine Insurance Act [which] continues to influence marine insurance policy wordings and conditions."

* * *

To be sure, a variety of insurers—including merchant underwriters, insurance companies and the esteemed subscribers at the prestigious Lloyd's of London—owned plantations, or had substantial shares or other interests in those institutions.

To illustrate, consider the conduct of John Julius Angerstein the purported "founder" of the "new" Lloyd's of London. Angerstein was perhaps the most savvy, highly regarded and extremely adept underwriter at Lloyd's. For years, he underwrote the maritime activities for a variety of merchants, including slave traders, but that "man of such integrity," also effected, sanctioned, and financed directly the enslavement and terrorization of African slaves. Put simply, Angerstein along with other underwriters at Lloyd's owned a significant share of a large plantation in Grenada. He made a fortune as an underwriter and a slave owner, a level of wealth that caused substantial intra-familial conflicts and a major legal battle after his death.

C. *Automobile Insurance*

The State Board of Insurance is now known as the Texas Department of Insurance, which is composed of the Commissioner of Insurance and other officers and employees. See Tex. Ins. Code Ann. arts. 31.003 and 31.007. The legislature requires the State Board of Insurance to promulgate standard and uniform insurance policies for those who write insurance in Texas for private passenger automobiles. In pertinent part, Tex. Ins. Code Ann. art. 5.06 reads:

Policy Forms and Endorsements

> (1) The Board shall adopt a policy form and endorsements for each type of motor vehicle insurance subject to this subchapter. The coverage provided by a policy form adopted under this subsection is the minimum coverage that may be provided under an insurance policy for that type of insurance in this State. Each policy form must provide the coverages mandated under Articles 5.06-1 and 5.06-3 of this code, except that the coverages may be rejected by the named insured as provided by those articles.
>
> (2) Except as provided by Subsections (3) and (4) of this article, an insurer may only use a form adopted by the Board under this section in writing motor vehicle insurance delivered, issued for delivery, or renewed in this State. A contract or agreement not written into the application and policy is void and of no effect and in violation of the provisions of this subchapter, and is sufficient cause for revocation of license of such insurer to write automobile insurance within this State.
>
> (3) The Board may approve the use of a policy form adopted by a national organization of insurance companies, or similar organization, if the form, with any endorsement to the form required and approved by the Board, provides coverage equivalent to the coverage provided by the form adopted by the Board under Subsection (1) of this section.
>
> (4) An insurer may use an endorsement to the policy form adopted or approved by the Board under this article if the endorsement is approved by the Board.

"Personal injury protection," "no-fault coverage," "underinsured-motorist losses," "uninsured-motorist losses," "collision," "comprehensive liability," "residential liability," and "accident" claims: these issues have generated a considerable amount of litigation. And given the ever increasing popularity of automobiles, trucks, and sports utility vehicles, disgruntled insurance consumers and their insurers are likely to generate even more conflicts and lawsuits. To be sure, space does not allow a discussion of these important issues. But here, three issues demand our careful consideration: 1) whether automobile insurers have a contractual, common-law, or statutory duty to pay or settle "diminished value" claims; 2) whether appraisal clauses in standardized automobile contracts are enforceable; and 3) whether automobile insurers have a duty to pay insurance proceeds when unauthorized drivers operate insureds' automobiles and cause property damage and bodily injuries.

American Manufacturers Mutual Insurance Company v. Schaefer
124 S.W.3d 154
(Tex. 2003)

In this case, we must decide whether the Texas Standard Personal Auto Policy obligates an insurer to compensate a policyholder for a vehicle's diminished market value when the car has been damaged but adequately repaired. We hold that it does not, and accordingly reverse the court of appeals' judgment.

I

Gary Schaefer purchased a standard automobile insurance policy from American Manufacturers Mutual Insurance Company (AMM). Part D of the policy, entitled "Coverage for Damage to Your Auto," provides that AMM will pay for "direct and accidental loss to your covered auto . . . ." The payment obligation is subject to a contractual limitation of liability that reads, in pertinent part, as follows:

> LIMIT OF LIABILITY: Our limit of liability for loss will be the lesser of the: 1) Actual cash value of the stolen or damaged property; or 2) Amount necessary to repair or replace the property with other of like kind and quality; or 3) Amount stated in the Declarations of this policy.

...ted to pay ... or decrease ... n value

The policy also provides for the method of paying the loss: PAYMENT OF LOSS — We may pay for loss in money or repair or replace the damaged or stolen property.

In October 1995, Schaefer's vehicle was involved in an accident. It was inspected by an AMM adjuster, and the insurance company elected to repair the vehicle. Schaefer does not dispute the quality or adequacy of the repairs. Instead, he maintains that its value decreased $2,600 due to market perceptions that a damaged and subsequently repaired vehicle is worth less than one that has never been damaged. Schaefer claims that the policy obligates AMM to compensate him for that diminished value.

Schaefer filed this class action against AMM and several other insurance companies that issue policies containing the same standard language. He claims that AMM's refusal to compensate him for his vehicle's diminished market value violated the Texas Insurance Code and breached the insurance contract. Before any class was certified, Schaefer filed a motion for partial summary judgment arguing that AMM was liable for his vehicle's diminished value as a matter of law. AMM responded and filed a cross-motion for summary judgment on the same issue. The trial court granted AMM's motion and denied Schaefer's.

The court of appeals reversed the trial court's summary judgment in AMM's favor holding that Schaefer could seek diminished-value damages under the policy and that the jury should determine if the repairs did or could restore the vehicle to "substantially the same condition and value" it had prior to the accident. The court expressly declined to follow a recent decision from the Fourteenth Court of Appeals, Carlton v. Trinity Universal Ins. Co., 32 S.W.3d 454 (Tex.App.-Houston [14th Dist.] 2000, pet. denied), which held that the same policy language did not obligate an insurer to pay diminished-value damages for a vehicle that was adequately repaired. Two other courts of appeals have also declined to follow Carlton. Courts in other states have similarly split over this issue. We granted AMM's petition to resolve the conflict among our courts of appeals.

II

We interpret insurance policies in Texas according to the rules of contract construction. If policy language is worded so that it can be given a definite or certain legal meaning, it is not ambiguous and we construe it as a matter of law. Whether a contract is ambiguous is itself a question of law. An ambiguity does not arise simply because the parties offer conflicting interpretations. Id. at 465; see also *Grain Dealers Mut. Ins. Co. v. McKee*, 943 S.W.2d 455, 458 (Tex.1997). An ambiguity exists only if the contract language is susceptible to two or more reasonable interpretations. When construing the policy's language, we must give effect to all contractual provisions so that none will be rendered meaningless.

The parties dispute whether the policy language obligates AMM to pay Schaefer for the diminished value of his fully repaired vehicle. Schaefer argues that a vehicle's diminished market value is a "direct or accidental loss" that AMM is required to compensate under the policy's insuring provision. Schaefer contends that construing the policy otherwise frustrates its underlying purpose to fully indemnify the insured. Citing as authority a number of cases from Texas and other jurisdictions, Schaefer contends that the policy language requiring AMM to pay the amount necessary "to repair or replace" with "other of like kind and quality" contemplates the payment of diminished value. AMM's payment obligation is further evidenced, Schaefer claims, by the policy's failure to expressly exclude diminished value from coverage under the policy's "Exclusions" section.

While Schaefer focuses on the "loss" language of the policy's insuring provision, AMM emphasizes the limitation of liability and payment provisions. AMM does not dispute that the term "loss" could encompass diminished value, but contends that the insuring language must be construed in light of the "Limit of Liability" section, which limits the insurer's liability to the lesser of the vehicle's actual cash value or the amount necessary to repair or replace it. According to AMM, the term "repair or replace" does not encompass any concept of "value." Like Schaefer, AMM cites cases from Texas and other jurisdictions that support its position. AMM also urges our consideration of the Texas Department of Insurance's interpretation of the policy language as not obligating an insurer to pay for a fully repaired vehicle's diminished value. See Tex. Dep't of Ins. Commissioner's

Bulletin, No. B-0027-00 (Apr. 6, 2002) ("[A]n insurer is not obligated to pay a first party claimant for diminished value when an automobile is completely repaired to its pre-damage condition. The language of the insurance policy does not require payment for, or refer to, diminished value.").

III

We agree with AMM that the policy's plain language, when read in context, giving effect to all contractual provisions, is unambiguous and does not require payment for diminished value when a vehicle has been fully and adequately repaired. While a vehicle's diminished value may be a "direct loss" under the policy's insuring provision, AMM's obligation to compensate the insured for that loss is circumscribed by the policy's "Limit of Liability" section. That section states, in pertinent part, that AMM's liability for loss is limited to the damaged vehicle's "actual cash value" or the amount needed "to repair or replace" the vehicle, whichever is less. We must give the policy language its ordinary and generally accepted meaning unless the policy shows that the words used are intended to impart a technical or different meaning. *Sec. Mut. Cas. Co. v. Johnson*, 584 S.W.2d 703, 704 (Tex.1979).

The concept of "repair" with regard to a vehicle connotes something tangible, like removing dents or fixing parts. See Black's Law Dictionary 1298 (6th ed.1990) (defining "repair" as "to mend, remedy, restore, renovate; to restore to a sound or good state after decay, injury, dilapidation or partial destruction"). We do not believe that the ordinary or generally accepted meaning of the word "repair" connotes compensating for the market's perception that a damaged but fully and adequately repaired vehicle has an intrinsic value less than that of a never-damaged car. To expand the ordinary meaning of "repair" to include an intangible, diminished-value element would be "ignoring the policy['s] language or giving the contract['s] text a meaning never intended."

A number of other state courts interpreting similar or identical policy language have expressly relied on the definition of "repair" articulated in Carlton. The plain meaning of AMM's obligation under the policy's "Limit of Liability" section, paragraph 2, is to restore the vehicle, either through repair or replacement, to the same physical and operating condition it was in before the damage occurred.

In addition to applying the plain meaning of the policy's language, we must also read the policy as a whole, giving effect to each provision. Interpreting the policy's "repair or replace" language to include diminished value, as Schaefer urges, would render other provisions of the policy meaningless. The policy provides that the insured is entitled to "the lesser of" actual cash value or the amount necessary to repair or replace the vehicle. To incorporate diminished value into the "repair or replace" provision would render the "lesser of" language meaningless. The insurer's obligation to compensate the loss would be cumulative-repair or replace and pay diminished value-in effect insuring the vehicle's "actual cash value" in every instance and undermining the insurer's right under the policy to choose a course of action.

It may be true, as Schaefer contends, that in some instances-say, when a very expensive car is damaged — an insurer will spend less money if it elects to repair and pay diminished value damages rather than declare the car a total loss and pay its actual cash value. But requiring an insurer, who elects repair, to additionally pay cash for the market's diminished perception incorporates an intangible value element into the repair provision that simply does not appear in the policy's language.

Inserting the concept of diminished value into the repair provision would similarly render the policy's "Payment of Loss" section meaningless. Under this section of the policy, the insurer has an option to pay the insured in "money or repair or replace[ment]." Including diminished value in the concept of repair would force an insurer that chooses to compensate a loss by exercising the repair option to also pay money, ignoring the clause's disjunctive language.

Schaefer also points to modifying language in paragraph two of the policy's Limitation of Liability provision, which refers to the "[a]mount necessary to repair or replace the property with other of like kind and quality." He contends that the phrase "of like kind and quality" modifies both "repair" and "replace," and obligates the insurer to compensate for a damaged vehicle's pre-accident value because the word "quality" encompasses the concept of value. But whether or not intrinsic value generally inheres in the word "quality," and assuming without deciding that the phrase "of like kind and quality" modifies both "repair" and "replace," we must look to the ordinary meaning of the words that are modified.

We have said that the words "repair" and "replace," with regard to a vehicle, connote something tangible, like removing dents, fixing parts, or replacing the vehicle with a comparable substitute. Thus, if an insurer elects to repair a vehicle and must replace parts in doing so, it must use parts "of like kind and quality." Likewise, if an insurer elects to replace the vehicle, it must do so with a vehicle "of like kind and quality." Schaefer's interpretation strains the policy's plain terms.

Schaefer also contends that the policy covers diminished-value damages because they are not expressly excluded in the policy's "Exclusions" section. But an exclusion's purpose is to remove from coverage an item that would otherwise have been included. *Liberty Mut. Ins. Co. v. Am. Employers Ins. Co.*, 556 S.W.2d 242, 245 (Tex.1977). Absence of an exclusion cannot confer coverage. Because the policy's language does not obligate AMM to pay for the diminished value of a car that has been fully and adequately repaired, the failure to include diminished-value damages in the policy's Exclusion section is immaterial.

Schaefer agrees that his claim is governed by the contract language, but contends that the court of appeals correctly interpreted the policy. However, the court of appeals did not perform a thorough analysis of the policy.

* * *

Schaefer claims, and the court of appeals agreed, that our decision in *Superior Pontiac Co. v. Queen Insurance Co.*, 434 S.W.2d 340 (Tex.1968), supports his interpretation of the policy. We disagree. In *Superior*, the insurer refused to return the repaired vehicle to its insured unless she agreed to accept the car as repaired and sign a release. The insured refused to sign the release and disputed the adequacy of the repairs. The vehicle was never returned to the insured or replaced with another of like kind and quality. Although there were jury findings from which the car's diminished value could have been calculated, we held that under the circumstances the insured was entitled to recover the vehicle's actual cash value before it was damaged. *Superior* does not support Schaefer's claim that the policy language requires an insurer to pay for diminished market value in addition to the cost of repair or replacement.

* * *

We note that diminished value claims have taken different forms. They have arisen when repairs are incomplete or faulty, or when the insurer elects to repair when declaring a total loss is the better option. Neither is the case here. AMM elected to repair the damaged vehicle, and Schaefer does not contend that the repairs were faulty, incomplete or inadequate. If he did, then the insurer might be liable for breaching its obligations under the policy's terms. But Schaefer would still only be entitled to the remedies outlined in the policy, which do not include compensation for a fully repaired vehicle's diminished market value. We acknowledge that Schaefer's repaired vehicle may command a smaller sum in the market than a like vehicle that has never been damaged, and that awarding Schaefer diminished value in addition to repair would go further to make him whole. But we may neither rewrite the parties' contract nor add to its language. *See Royal Indem. Co. v. Marshall*, 388 S.W.2d 176, 181 (Tex.1965).

IV

Schaefer's standard automobile insurance policy does not obligate AMM to compensate Schaefer for his fully repaired vehicle's diminished market value. Accordingly, we reverse the judgment of the court of appeals and render judgment in favor of AMM.

NOTES & QUESTIONS

1) What is the correct measure of "diminished value," "loss of value," or "loss in value" for vehicles?

2) Here are some competing measures: a) "Diminished value is the difference between the pre-loss value of an insured auto and its value after having been fully and properly repaired"; b) "Diminished value is the fair market value of an insured auto and the vehicle's fair market values after it has been fully and properly repaired"; and c) "Diminished value is the difference between the fair market value of an insured auto—immediately before an accident—and its "Blue Book value" after it has been fully and properly repaired." Which measure is fairer?

3) Again, automobile insurance contracts are generally "first-party, property insurance contracts." Therefore, "diminished value," "loss of value" and "loss in value" are "covered perils" or "perils insured against" under those contracts.

4) But note: It is common for car owners and operators to injure third parties and destroy third parties' property. Therefore, the State of Texas requires all motor-vehicle operators to establish their financial responsibility by purchasing liability insurance for the benefit of third-party victims. As a consequence, auto insurance policies have both first- and third-party "coverage" provisions. Regarding the latter, the Tex. Transp. Code Ann. § 601.051reads:

REQUIREMENT OF FINANCIAL RESPONSIBILITY

> A person may not operate a motor vehicle in this state unless financial responsibility is established for that vehicle through . . . (1) a motor vehicle liability insurance policy that complies with Subchapter D; (2) a surety bond filed under Section 601.121; (3) a deposit under Section 601.122; (4) a deposit under Section 601.123; or (5) self-insurance under Section 601.124.

In re Allstate County Mutual Insurance Company
85 S.W.3d 193
(Tex. 2002)

The trial court in this case determined that an appraisal provision in a personal automobile insurance policy promulgated by the Texas Department of Insurance is an agreement to arbitrate, and as such, the agreement is unenforceable because it is against public policy. Thus, the trial court refused to enforce the clause. But this provision concerns an appraisal, not arbitration, and is not unenforceable for the reason the trial court gave. Because the trial court abused its discretion and relators have no adequate remedy on appeal, we conditionally grant the writ of mandamus.

I

Plaintiff Terri Shields's car was stolen, and plaintiffs Renita Washington's and Lucilia Hernandez's vehicles were involved in accidents. Their insurance companies, Allstate, Farmers, and Progressive, respectively, determined that the vehicles were total losses and engaged CCC Information Services, Inc., to determine the values of the totaled cars. Plaintiffs allege that the insurance companies directed CCC to fraudulently generate low values for the totaled vehicles, that CCC intentionally undervalued their vehicles, and that the insurance companies thereby offered plaintiffs less than the full values for their vehicles. Washington and Hernandez accepted the insurance companies' offers. Shields has not yet received any compensation under her policy.

The plaintiffs allege that the insurance companies misrepresented their coverage by representing that actual cash value would be paid under the policies, when in fact CCC's and the insurance companies' conduct resulted in inaccurate, unreliable, and biased valuations, and payment of less than full value. Under the plaintiffs' theory, the insurance companies systematically undervalue vehicles, knowing that because of the costly appraisal process the insureds are unlikely to challenge the valuations. Based on these allegations, they pleaded fraud and fraudulent concealment, Texas

Deceptive Trade Practices Act and Texas Insurance Code violations, breach of the duty of good faith and fair dealing, breach of contract, and civil conspiracy.

The plaintiffs' insurance policies contain an appraisal clause, which may be invoked by either party, for determining a vehicle's value if the insurer and the insured disagree. Each party hires its own appraiser. If the two appraisers cannot agree on the value, they select an additional appraiser as an umpire, or a district judge will appoint one if the appraisers cannot agree on an umpire. A decision signed by two of the appraisers is binding as to the vehicle's value.

After plaintiffs filed suit, the insurance companies answered and then filed a plea in abatement and motion to invoke appraisal. The trial court denied the motion, finding that the appraisal provision, when considered as an arbitration agreement, was unenforceable. The defendants unsuccessfully sought mandamus relief from the court of appeals. They then petitioned this Court for mandamus relief.

II

The trial court's conclusion that the appraisal provision was an arbitration agreement and unenforceable was error. This Court distinguished between appraisal and arbitration clauses over a hundred years ago. In *Scottish Union & National Insurance Co. v. Clancy,* we concluded that while arbitration determines the rights and liabilities of the parties, appraisal merely "binds the parties to have the extent or amount of the loss determined in a particular way." We held that appraisal clauses are enforceable. Texas courts have continued to recognize this distinction, as has the United States Court of Appeals for the Fifth Circuit. And Texas courts have enforced appraisal clauses since that decision.

III

"[A] clear failure by the trial court to analyze or apply the law correctly will constitute an abuse of discretion" subject to correction by writ of mandamus when the relator has no adequate remedy by appeal. We hold that the trial court abused its discretion by determining that the appraisal clause in the plaintiffs' policies was an arbitration clause and unenforceable. But before issuing mandamus, we must determine whether relator has an adequate appellate remedy.

In an analogous situation, we have held that denial of discovery "going to the heart of a party's case may render the appellate remedy inadequate." As to the plaintiffs' breach of contract claim, the parties have agreed in the contracts' appraisal clause to the method by which to determine whether a breach has occurred. That is, if the appraisal determines that the vehicle's full value is what the insurance company offered, there would be no breach of contract. Accordingly, at a minimum, denying the appraisals will vitiate the defendants' ability to defend the breach of contract claim. Because the appraisals go to the heart of the plaintiffs' breach of contract claim, we need not decide here the significance of the appraisals to each of the remaining claims.

In *Walker v. Packer,* this Court reaffirmed the principle that "an appeal will not be an adequate remedy where the party's ability to present a viable claim or defense at trial is vitiated or severely compromised by the trial court's discovery error." A refusal to enforce the appraisal process here will prevent the defendants from obtaining the independent valuations that could counter at least the plaintiffs' breach of contract claim. We conclude that the failure to order the appraisals will vitiate or severely compromise the defendants' defenses to those claims.

IV

The parties in this case contracted for an appraisal if they disagreed about the damaged property's value. Texas courts have distinguished between appraisal and arbitration for over a hundred years. And they have enforced appraisal provisions over that same length of time. Under Texas law, the trial court's conclusion that the appraisal clause was one for arbitration and unenforceable was an error of law, constituting an abuse of discretion. That abuse of discretion denies the development of proof going to the heart of a party's case and cannot be remedied by appeal. Accordingly, we conditionally grant mandamus relief.

While the trial court's denial of the motion to invoke appraisal was error, the failure to grant the motion to abate is not subject to mandamus. In any event, the proceedings need not be abated while the appraisal goes forward. While the trial court has no discretion to deny the appraisal, the court does have some discretion as to the timing of the appraisal. We trust that the trial court will comply with this opinion; the writ will issue only if it fails to do so.

NOTES & QUESTIONS

1) This language appears in an auto insurance contract: "If we and you do not agree on the amount of loss, either may demand an appraisal of the loss." Does that "demand-an-appraisal" clause require the insurer and insured to settle, arbitrate, or litigate the issue? Does that clause clearly or unequivocally exclude one's request to arbitrate? Does it require the parties to arbitrate?

2) Assume that an appraiser determines that an insurance company's settlement offer was less than the vehicle's full value after an accident. What *prima facie* evidence must the insured present to establish that the insurer breached the insurance contract?

3) Again, most appraisal provisions allow either the insured or insurer to demand an appraisal. Each party may secure independent appraisal reports that contain very different estimates. That can lead to a "Battle of the Appraisal Reports." If a battle ensues, which estimate report controls?

4) Must an arbitration hearing convene to resolve a "Battle of the Appraisal Reports?" Did the *In re Allstate* Texas Supreme Court adequately address that very real "arbitration" issue?

Old American County Mutual Fire Insurance Company v. Renfrow
130 S.W.3d 70
(Tex. 2004)

This is a declaratory judgment action to determine coverage under the "omnibus clause"of a commercial auto liability policy that insured an employer and "anyone else while using with your [that is, the employer's] permission a covered auto." The principal issue is whether an employee had implied permission to use a company truck at the time of an accident so as to be covered by the policy. The trial court held as a matter of law that the employee was covered, but the court of appeals reversed and remanded for a resolution of subsisting fact issues. We hold that the employee, as a matter of law, materially deviated from any use he was permitted to make of the truck and therefore was not covered by the company policy.

In early 1999, Michael Renfrow worked for CD Consulting & Operating Co., an oil field services business located in Bridgeport, Texas, a town of about 4,000 at that time, northwest of Fort Worth. One Friday evening about 7 p.m., Renfrow returned from working at a well site near Justin, some thirty miles west of Bridgeport, finished his paperwork, and left CD Consulting's office for the day. Although Renfrow's personal truck was parked at the office, Bobby Campbell, CD Consulting's owner, let Renfrow take a company truck home, which was about half a mile away. Campbell would later testify that this was because Renfrow was due back at the well site at 6:00 a.m. the next day, and it was company policy to let an employee take a company truck home overnight when he had to be at a well site early the next morning. It is not entirely clear whether Renfrow knew of any such policy, and that Friday night he and Campbell did not specifically discuss what he could or could not do with the company truck. But Renfrow freely admits that he knew as a rule employees were not allowed to use company vehicles for personal business, this despite the fact that he was in the habit of driving a company truck to the home of his foreman, Jimmy Joe Stinnett, several nights a week to drink beer. Stinnett also lived in Bridgeport, not far from Renfrow.

Renfrow often drove a company truck to visit Mili Jo Roberts, too, and that is where he went when he left the office on the Friday night in question. Roberts lived in Bridgeport about a mile from CD Consulting's office. Sometime during the evening, Renfrow and Roberts decided to go to Saginaw, a suburb of Fort Worth, about forty miles away. Renfrow would later testify repeatedly and consistently that he knew he did not have permission to take the company truck to Roberts' home, let alone to Saginaw. Renfrow and Roberts were returning about 12:45 a.m. when the truck left the highway and hit an embankment. Roberts was killed and Renfrow was injured. Renfrow was later indicted by a Wise County grand jury for intoxication manslaughter.

Roberts' beneficiaries sued Renfrow and CD Consulting for wrongful death. The jury found Renfrow negligent and grossly negligent, but did not find CD Consulting directly or vicariously liable. The trial court rendered judgment against Renfrow, and he did not appeal.

Old American, CD Consulting's insurer, sued for a declaration that Renfrow was not covered by its policy because he lacked permission to drive the company truck to Saginaw on personal business. The Roberts beneficiaries counterclaimed for payment of their judgment against Renfrow. Both sides moved for summary judgment, and the trial court granted the beneficiaries' motion and denied

Old American's. The court of appeals reversed and remanded, concluding that while Renfrow unquestionably did not have express permission to take the company truck to Saginaw, evidence of whether he had implied permission was in dispute, thus precluding summary judgment for either side.

The Roberts beneficiaries argue, and the court of appeals agreed, that Renfrow's frequent use of a company truck to go to his foreman's and Roberts' homes was some evidence that he had implied permission to take the truck on personal business. But, there is no evidence to suggest that Renfrow ever used a company vehicle on personal business outside Bridgeport or had implied permission to do so.

The rule in Texas, stated in *Coronado v. Employers' National Insurance Co.*, is that a person may deviate from the permitted usage of an insured vehicle and still be covered under an omnibus provision if the use is not a material or gross violation of the terms of the initial permission. Under this rule, the court must determine in each instance-taking into account the extent of deviation in actual distance or time, the purposes for which the vehicle was given, and other factors-whether the deviation was "minor" or "material."

A deviation can be material as a matter of law, as it was in *Coronado.* In that case, one Sotelo, an employee of an oil well service business, was taking three of his crew members home late one afternoon in a company pickup when they decided to go to a bar about three or four miles out of their way. There they stayed for three or four hours before adjourning to another bar not far away. They left the second bar "sometime after midnight, apparently many beers after leaving the company yard" and were involved in an accident. A jury found that Sotelo was using the company pickup within the scope of his employer's permission, but the trial court set the finding aside, and the court of appeals affirmed. We agreed, holding that the eight hour deviation engaged in by Sotelo was so gross as to be a material deviation as a matter of law. The use of the vehicle at the time of the accident was so far outside the scope of the permission granted Sotelo for use of the vehicle that we cannot say that a fact issue is raised that his employer had impliedly consented to this use.

Similarly, in *Royal Indemnity Co. v. H.E. Abbott & Sons, Inc.*, 399 S.W.2d 343 (Tex.1966), Herring, a ranch owner, provided two pickups for his employee, Landers, to use on the ranch. On several occasions, however, Herring and Landers had taken personal trips off the ranch in one of the pickups, and Landers had sometimes driven off the premises to pick up Herring's children at a school bus stop about five miles away. One evening, however, Landers drove a little over thirty miles to San Angelo on a personal errand and had an accident shortly after he arrived. A jury found that Landers was using the truck with Herring's permission, but we held that the evidence shows neither a relationship nor a prior course of conduct from which implied permission might fairly be inferred. Landers . . . had never driven one of the vehicles off the ranch except when specifically instructed to do so, and had never used any of them for a personal errand.

His employer had always driven him to town whenever he wanted to go, and had no reason to believe that he intended or might need to use one of the vehicles on the evening of the accident. In view of these undisputed facts, the limited privileges Landers was allowed in the Herring house, his occasional pleasure trips with Herring, the availability of the vehicles, his use of the same on the ranch, Herring's inquiry about his driver's license, and the absence of any prior instruction not to take the vehicles off the ranch, afford no basis for concluding that Landers had implied permission to use the truck for a trip to San Angelo on a personal mission. We hold that there is no evidence to support a finding that the vehicle was being operated with the implied permission of the named insured.

Likewise, we think Renfrow's trip to Saginaw was, as a matter of law, a material deviation from any implied permission he may have had to use the vehicle in Bridgeport. Renfrow's trip was a diversion similar to the employees' trips in *Coronado* or *Royal Indemnity,* and it was at least as far outside the scope of any permitted use.

The Roberts beneficiaries complain that the trial court erred by excluding from the summary judgment evidence Renfrow's late-filed affidavit, which states in full:

> My name is Michael D. Renfrow. I am over the age of 18 years, and am competent to make this affidavit. I had permission to take the vehicle on the day in question. Any statement made to the contrary, whether taken at the time of trial or otherwise, is taken out of context or incorrect or otherwise is a mistake.

Assuming the affidavit should not have been excluded, the error was harmless. No one disputes that Renfrow had express permission to take the vehicle to his home, and we have assumed he had implied permission to take it to Roberts' home. The affidavit does not suggest that he had permission to take it as far away as Saginaw. The affidavit adds nothing.

Accordingly, we grant Old American's petition for review and without hearing oral argument, reverse the court of appeals' judgment and render judgment for Old American.

NOTES & QUESTIONS

1) Assume that a teenager—who is not a permissive user—operates insured's SUV and partially destroys the vehicle. However, the insured releases the minor from all liability. Must the insurer pay the insured's settlement demand?

2) Assume that a thief—who is not a permissive user—operates insured's SUV and partially damages the vehicle. The thief is injured and sues the insured for third-party damages. Must the insurer pay the third-party claim and/or defend the insured in a third-party lawsuit?

3) Assume that an insured employs a truck driver. The driver has no authority to operate the employer's family car. However, after the employer's son was injured, the trucker drives the child to a local hospital. After leaving the hospital, the truck driver has an accident in the family car.

Must the employer's auto insurer reimburse the employer for paying the truck driver's medical bills?

4) What is the legal standard for determining whether an individual is a "permissive" user, a driver or an operator of a vehicle? Is it a subjective test or an objective test?

D. Flood Insurance

The Court of Appeals for the Fifth Circuit:
A Legal Analysis and Statistical Review of 2005-2006 Insurance Decisions
39 Tex. Tech Law Rev. 843, 869-879 (2007)
Willy E. Rice

WHETHER THE NATIONAL INSURANCE FLOOD ACT PREEMPTS INSURED FLOOD VICTIMS' COMMENCING STATE LAW ACTIONS AGAINST PROPERTY INSURERS IN TEXAS COURTS

Although some insurers sell flood insurance in the United States' private markets, the price of that product is nearly prohibitive for the average homeowner. Therefore, among other reasons, Congress enacted the National Flood Insurance Act of 1968 (NFIA). The Act established the National Flood Insurance Program (NFIP) and FEMA, an agency of the Department of Homeland Security, administers the program. The NFIP has two components: a flood insurance program and a unified national plan for flood management.

In 1977, the Secretary of the Department of Housing and Urban Development (HUD) gave the primary responsibility for operating the NFIP to FEMA. To achieve the intended goals, FEMA enacted regulations and created the Standard Flood Insurance Policy (SFIP). The agency also encouraged private insurers — so-called "Write Your Own" (WYO) insurers — to market and sell the flood insurance contracts. More significant, WYO insurers sell the SFIP contracts in their own names.

In addition, WYO insurers are responsible for adjusting, settling, paying, and defending all claims arising under SFIP contracts. FEMA's regulations, however, establish the rates and premiums for SFIP contracts. Also, given that the NFIP is a federally-administered program, funds from the federal treasury support the program. But again, FEMA developed the SFIP contracts and WYO insurers cannot waive or modify those terms. Today, consumers purchase nearly all residential flood insurance under the NFIP.

Against that background, consider the brief reported facts in *Wright v. Allstate Insurance Co.*, 415 F.3d 384 (5th Cir. 2005). Dr. Thomas Wright lived in Houston, Texas. To insure his residential property, Wright purchased a SFIP insurance contract from Allstate Insurance Company-a WYO flood insurer. After Tropical Storm Allison struck Houston in 2001, a flood damaged Wright's home; therefore, he filed a SFIP claim. Allstate's claims adjuster, Jack Gardner of Pilot Catastrophe

Services, visited Wright and inspected his flood-damaged home. Gardner determined that Wright lost $125,840.23. Wright, however, hired his own certified public insurance adjuster and received a different estimate, $233,497.59. Although Wright and Allstate's representatives continued to squabble about the "true" value of the property loss, they were unable to settle the dispute amicably.

Under FEMA regulations, insureds must file a proof-of-loss form (POL) with a WYO insurer before receiving proceeds under a SFIP insurance contract. Wright, however, refused to sign a proper POL outlining Gardner's estimate. Instead, Wright submitted a POL form, in which the phrase "to be determined" appeared where the cost of repairs, cash value, depreciation, and net amount claimed should have appeared. Ultimately, Allstate rejected Wright's claim, citing the insured's failure to cooperate the terms of the flood-insurance contract and failure to file a proper and timely POL.

Wright commenced a lawsuit against Allstate in the District Court for the Southern District of Texas. The disgruntled insured raised several Texas common law actions, sounding in contract and in tort: breach of contract, fraud, and negligent misrepresentation. Wright also filed a statutory action, under the Texas Insurance Code and the Deceptive Trade Practices Act. In addition, the law in Texas is clear: Every insurance contract has a [common law duty] of good faith and fair dealing. Therefore, Wright claimed that Allstate breached that common law duty of good faith and fair dealing. But, in Wright's complaint, this claim or allegation appeared as if it were a cause of action-one containing specific elements and requiring proof of a prima facie case. As discussed more fully below, however, neither the district court nor the Fifth Circuit appreciated this important point; and consequently, their analyses were less than ideal.

The District Court for the Southern District of Texas dismissed every cause of action and claim, except the cause of action for breach of contract. The district court found that federal law preempts the tort-related state law actions. To defend itself against Wright's breach-of-contract action, Allstate argued that Wright failed to file a proper and timely POL claim. But the district court held that Allstate was equitably estopped from asserting that defense. The district court awarded only $24,029, plus court costs and attorneys' fees, after Wright failed to prove that the flood caused all of his damages. Both parties appealed.

Allstate raised two arguments before the Fifth Circuit. The insurer asserted that federal district courts may not apply the doctrine of equitable estoppel against a WYO insurer in light of the present facts and that Wright did not prove the elements of equitable estoppel. . . . [T]he Fifth Circuit embraced Allstate's arguments. The appellate court stated: "Here . . . we find the doctrine of equitable estoppel inapplicable. The Supreme Court has made clear that 'judicial use of the equitable doctrine of estoppel cannot grant respondent a money remedy that Congress has not authorized.'"

Therefore, in reversing the district court's finding in favor of Dr. Wright the Fifth Circuit concluded:

> [When] federal funds are implicated, the person seeking those funds is obligated to familiarize himself with the legal requirements for receipt of such funds. . . . Under these circumstances, and in light of our previous case law, we hold that the district

court erred in estopping Allstate from asserting Wright failure to file an adequate POL as a basis for denying his claim.

On appeal, Wright argued that federal law did not preempt his state law tort actions and that the allegation that Allstate breached the implied covenant of good faith and fair dealing. Thus, the insured asserted that the district court's ruling was erroneous and that the district judge reached that allegedly incorrect conclusion. . . . But, the Fifth Circuit stated that the district court's [ruling] incorrect.

* * *

A clear majority of jurisdictions have embraced this common law rule: Every contract— including insurance contracts— contains an implied covenant of good faith and fair dealing. And when there is an alleged breach of that covenant, the insured or insurer may commence a lawsuit that sounds either in tort, contract, or both. . . Also, on several occasions, the Texas Supreme Court ruled and reaffirmed its ruling that an insurer's breach of [a common law duty] of good faith and fair dealing allows the insured to commence a cause of action that sounds in tort. On other occasions, the Supreme Court of Texas has allowed insureds to commence a contract-based cause of action against insurers when the latter allegedly breached the [common law duty] of good faith and fair dealing. . . .

Therefore, whether a breach arises from a duty of good faith and fair dealing or from a breach of an implied covenant of good faith and fair dealing, the states in the Fifth Circuit allow complaining parties to commence a cause of action sounding in contract. In *Wright* . . . the court did not address this critical issue. Consequently, the Fifth Circuit's procedural rulings against the homeowners were arguably unfair. But more important, a failure to thoroughly review this issue and the accompanying rules seriously undermined the quality of the analyses. . . .

Hardware Dealers Mutual Insurance Company v. Berglund
393 S.W.2d 309
(Tex. 1965)

This is a Hurricane Carla case. Petitioner, Hardware Dealers Mutual Insurance Company, issued two insurance policies to respondents, Clifford L. Berglund and his wife, Robbie Mae Berglund; one contained both an "all risks" clause and a "named peril" clause, while the second policy contained a "named peril" clause only. The "named peril" clause covered direct losses by "windstorm, hurricane, hail," etc. On September 11, 1961, as a result of the storms, high winds and waters accompanying the hurricane, much of respondents' property was destroyed. Suit was brought upon the policies mentioned and after trial to a jury, respondents were awarded a recovery for $1,820.00 which represented the only items of damage which were not related to the excluded hazards named in the policies. This judgment was reversed by the Court of Civil Appeals and the case remanded for another trial. We reverse the judgment of the Court of Civil Appeals and affirm the judgment of the trial court.

The paramount question before us relates to the construction of the contracts between the parties. However, there is one procedural matter raised which we think is settled by cases decided prior to 1941. . . The insurance company pleaded that the damage sustained by respondents was not covered by the policies because the causes of such damage were expressly excluded from the insurance coverage of the contracts.

One of the policies contains an "all risks" coverage clause relating to a beach house located in the Bayou Vista Addition to Hitchcock, Texas. Respondents . . . that when a recovery is sought under an "all risks" policy, and the plaintiff proves that property described in the policy has been lost or damaged, the burden shifts to the insurer to show that the loss arose from a cause which is excluded from the policy coverage. In other words, when an "all risks" policy is sued upon, the plea of loss by an excluded risk is treated as being similar to a plea of confession and avoidance.

* * *

In *Pelican Ins. Co. v. Troy Co-op. Ass'n,* 77 Tex. 225, 13 S.W. 980 (1890) it was held that the party suing upon an insurance policy has the burden of proving that the insurance policy covered the loss and hence it was incumbent upon him to prove that the loss was not excluded from the insurance coverage. This Court said: The provisions of the policy above noticed are exceptions to the general liability assumed by appellant (the insurer), and the petition should have averred that the fire did not occur from one of the excepted causes. This was necessary to show a cause of action . . . ."

The use of an "all risks" clause in stating the "general liability" of the company calls for no change of the rule set forth. If it be necessary for a plaintiff to aver that the loss did not occur from one of the excepted causes, in order to state a cause of action, it would be necessary for him to prove the same in order to recover.

The rule of the *Pelican* case insofar as pleading is concerned was modified in 1941 by the adoption of Rule 94 as a part of the Texas Rules of Civil Procedure. The rule provides that when a suit is brought upon a policy "which insures against certain general hazards, but contains other provisions limiting such general liability, the party suing on such contract shall never be required to allege that the loss was not due to a risk or cause coming within any of the exceptions specified in the contract, nor shall the insurer be allowed to raise such issue unless it shall specifically allege that the loss was due to a risk or cause coming within a particular exception to the general liability; provided that nothing herein shall be construed to change the burden of proof on such issue as it now exists."

Here the insurance company pleaded specific exclusions which were set forth in the policy and thus raised issues of contract coverage. The burden of producing evidence to demonstrate that their losses were not attributable to the pleaded excluded hazards rested upon respondents. *Shaver v. National Title & Abstract Co.,* 361 S.W.2d 867 (Tex. 1962); *T. I. M. E., Inc. v. Maryland Casualty Co.*, 300 S.W.2d 68 (Tex. 1957). As the matter is specifically covered by Texas decisions and our Rules of Civil Procedure, cases based upon the practice rules of other jurisdictions have little or no application here.

One of the policies sued upon covers a beach house and certain unscheduled personal property. Insofar as the beach house was concerned, the contract insured Mr. and Mrs. Berglund against loss from "all risks of physical loss except as otherwise excluded." This policy also covered certain unscheduled personal property and insured Mr. and Mrs. Berglund against loss from certain named perils, including among others, "Windstorm, Hurricane and Hail."

A second policy covered a boathouse and under the heading, "Extended Coverage," insured Mr. and Mrs. Berglund against loss from, "Windstorm, Hurricane, Hail, Explosion, Riot, Civil Commotion, Smoke, Aircraft and Land Vehicles."

The first policy contains the following exclusion (which was pleaded by the company) viz.: "D. Loss caused by or resulting from . . . Flood, surface water, waves, tidal water or tidal wave, overflow of streams or of other bodies of water, or spray from any of the foregoing, all whether driven by wind or not . . . ."

The second policy contains a similar exclusion (which was pleaded by the company) viz.: "Unless specifically named herein, this Company shall not be liable for loss . . . caused by . . . tidal wave, high water, or overflow, whether driven by wind or not . . . .

The parties stipulated that: "The amount of damage to the dwelling (the beach house) in question was $6,000 and the applicable amount of deductible is $100. The amount of damage to the contents in question was $2,400. The amount of damage to the boathouse in question was $450 and the amount of deductible is $100."

The trial court submitted the case to the jury upon issues inquiring as to the percentage of loss relating to each item which was occasioned by specifically excluded perils. As to the percentage of damage which was caused by or resulted from 'flood, surface water, waves, tidal water or tidal wave, or spray from the foregoing, whether driven by wind or not,' the jury found 70 per cent as to the beach house, 95 per cent as to the unscheduled personal property and 100 per cent as to the boathouse. Judgment was accordingly rendered for 30 per cent of $6,000, less $100, plus $120, making a total of $1,820.00.

* * *

We have heretofore set out the wording of the insuring and excluding clauses of such policies. The "named peril" insuring clauses expressly cover direct losses resulting from "windstorm, hurricane, hail" etc. As direct losses from hurricanes are not in so many words excluded from the "all risks" clause contained in the policy covering the beach house, such losses are within the comprehension of the "all risks" provision, subject to the exclusion clauses of the contract.

* * *

It is apparent that the insurance coverage of the contract would be substantially broadened if respondents' theory of construction be accepted. In essence it would mean that all hurricane damage, whether caused by wind or water, or by a combination of both would be covered by the policies provided a hurricane is the dominant or proximate cause of the destruction or loss of the property described in the insurance policy; whereas, under the theory adopted by the trial court the insurance coverage would extend to wind damage unmixed with water damage occasioned by the hurricane. *Cf. McDonald v. New York Central Mutual Fire Ins. Co.*, 380 S.W.2d 545 (Tex. 1964)

In support of their position, respondents assert that a West Indian or Gulf Hurricane is a phenomenon in which high winds are invariably accompanied by heavy rains and high water; that the insuring clauses of the policies purport to cover hurricane damage, and that an interpretation of the water exclusion clause so as to exclude water damage caused by a hurricane would create an ambiguity and invoke the rule that insurance contracts should in cases of doubt or ambiguity be construed favorably to the insured. This is the argument that was accepted by the Court of Civil Appeals and while it is persuasive, there are considerations which compel its rejection.

* * *

In *Mitchell's Inc. v. Friedman,* 303 S.W.2d 775 (Tex. 1957), it was asserted that an indemnity contract should be construed favorably to the indemnitor. This Court said: "In determining the rights and liabilities of the parties, therefore, their intention will first be ascertained by rules of construction applicable to contracts generally. At this point neither party is favored over the other simply because their agreement is one of indemnity."

We believe the rule stated is applicable here. No ambiguity or uncertainty arises from the words used in the contract. In order to say that water damage accompanying a hurricane is not excepted from the policy it would be necessary to give the words of the exception — high water and overflow, etc. — a different meaning when used with an insuring clause covering losses from "tornado, windstorm, and cyclone" than they would have when used with an "all risks" type of insuring clause or one covering losses from 'windstorms, hurricane, hail,' etc. In our opinion this cannot be accomplished unless we refuse to give to words their ordinary accepted meaning and disregard the interpretation of phrases in standard insurance use which have been considered in prior opinions of this Court. The language used in the policies "must be construed according to the evident intent of the parties, to be derived from the words used, the subject-matter to which they relate, and the matters naturally or usually incident thereto," and it is only when "the words admit of two constructions, that one will be adopted most favorable to the insured." *Brown v. Palatine Insurance Company,* 35 S.W. 1060 (Tex. 1896)

* * *

For the reasons hereinabove set forth the judgment of the Court of Civil Appeals is reversed and that of the trial court affirmed.

NOTES & QUESTIONS

1) In *Hardware Dealers*, the following phrase appears: "the dominant or proximate cause of the destruction or loss of the property." Under tort principles, may the phrases "dominant cause" and "proximate cause" be used interchangeably?

2) "Proximate cause" appears regularly in property insurance cases as well as in contract-based and tort-based cases. In the latter cases, "proximate cause" is "legal cause" and it concerns "foreseeability." "Proximate cause" has a very different meaning in property-insurance cases.

3) In *Garvey v. State Farm Fire & Casualty Company*, 770 P.2d 704, 707 (Ca. 1989), the California Supreme Court presents a discussion of a covered peril's "efficient proximate cause" of a property loss:

THE EFFICIENT PROXIMATE CAUSE STANDARD

Our courts have long struggled to enunciate principles that determine whether coverage exists when excluded and covered perils interact to cause a loss. Initially, the courts attempted to reconcile section 530 (which provides for coverage when a peril insured against was the "proximate cause" of loss) with section 532 (which provides, that "If a peril is specifically excepted in a contract of insurance, and there is a loss which would not have occurred but for such peril, such loss is thereby excepted [from coverage] even though the immediate cause of the loss was a peril which was not excepted").

In our 1963 *Sabella* decision, supra, 377 P.2d 889, we faced a difficult property loss coverage question arising after a building contractor constructed a house on uncompacted fill and negligently installed a sewer line; negligent installation was a covered peril. Eventually, the sewer line ruptured causing water to saturate the ground surrounding the insureds' house, resulting in subsidence, an excluded peril.

* * *

Thus, *Sabella* held that: " '[I]n determining whether a loss is within an exception in a policy, where there is a concurrence of different causes, the efficient cause — the one that sets others in motion — is the cause to which the loss is to be attributed, though the other causes may follow it, and operate more immediately in producing the disaster," quoting from Couch on Insurance § 1466 (1930) . . . . Furthermore, in characterizing the "but for" clause of section 532 as referring to the efficient proximate cause of the loss, we impliedly recognized that coverage would not exist if the covered risk was simply a *remote* cause of the loss, or if an excluded risk was the efficient proximate (meaning predominant) cause of the loss.

On the other hand, the fact that an excluded risk contributed to the loss would not preclude coverage if such a risk was a remote cause of the loss. . . . The Court of Appeal here replaced the *Sabella* term "efficient proximate cause" with the term "moving cause." *Sabella* defined "efficient proximate cause" alternatively as the "one that sets others in motion" and as "the predominating or moving efficient cause." We use the term "efficient proximate cause" (meaning predominating cause) when referring to the *Sabella* analysis because we believe the phrase "moving cause" can be misconstrued to deny coverage erroneously, particularly when it is understood literally to mean the "triggering" cause.

E. Health Insurance

Persons may purchase health insurance under an individual contract, or they may receive health coverage under an employer's group health plan. Under the former, the individual should know more or less the "covered perils"—various illnesses, disabilities, and treatment. Those items should be fairly apparent in the insured's individual, health-insurance contract. On the other hand, persons who are members of a group plan do not receive a contract. Only the health insurer and the employer have a copy of the "master health policy." Members receive a "subscriber's certificate." It is not a contract, although it outlines generally the types of "covered risks"—illnesses and injuries—that the employer has insured each employee against.

Health insurers must clearly outline the types of risks that insureds have insured against. Consider,

TEXAS ADMINISTRATIVE CODE, § 3.3090
TEXAS DEPARTMENT OF INSURANCE
MINIMUM STANDARDS AND BENEFITS AND READABILITY FOR INDIVIDUAL ACCIDENT AND HEALTH INSURANCE POLICIES

OUTLINE OF COVERAGE GENERALLY

(a) In order to facilitate public understanding of coverages and to provide full and fair disclosure in the sale of individual accident and sickness insurance policies, no such policy may be delivered or issued for delivery in this state unless an appropriate outline of coverage, as prescribed in these sections is delivered.

(1) in the case of a direct response insurance product, the outline of coverage shall be delivered with the policy; and

(2) in all other cases, the outline of coverage shall be delivered to the applicant at the time application is made and acknowledgment of receipt or certificate of delivery of such outline of coverage is provided to the insurer. The insurer may secure acknowledgment of delivery of the outline

of coverage by an acknowledgment receipt attached to or made a part of the application; or by a certificate of delivery signed by the insured.

(b) In the event that a policy is issued on a basis other than that applied for which would require revision of the outline of coverage, a substitute, properly describing the policy, must be delivered with the policy and contain the following statement, in no less than 14-point type, at the top of the page: "NOTICE: READ THIS OUTLINE OF COVERAGE CAREFULLY." It is not the same as the outline of coverage given to you upon application because you have not been issued the coverage for which you first applied.

Without a doubt, uncertainty about the types and extent of medical coverage under an individual health-insurance contract or a "subscriber's pamphlet" generates a lot of conflicts and litigation between insureds and insurers. Clearly, the statute above attempts to reduce the likelihood of such conflicts and lawsuits. But there are many requirements and forms. Insureds have notice requirements; and health insurers must satisfy a number of requirements—those that govern the format, content, and readability of "coverage" outlines.

In addition, there are prescribed forms that must clearly outline the contours of basic hospital coverage, basic coverage for surgeries, hospital confinement and indemnity coverage, major medical coverage, coverage for disability income, accident-only coverage, specified disease or accident coverage, limited benefit coverage, and supplemental coverage.

This chapter discusses just a tiny fraction of the types of claims that applicants and insureds file against health insurers in Texas.

May v. United Services Association of America
844 S.W.2d 666
(Tex.1992)

This case involves the scope of an insurance agent's common-law duty to a customer in rendering advice about and procuring a policy for health insurance. The plaintiffs asserted only common-law causes of action, making no claim under the Texas Deceptive Trade Practices-Consumer Protection Act, Tex.Bus. & Com.Code §§ 17.41 *et seq.* or any other statute. While the jury found favorably for the plaintiffs on a claim of the agent's negligence, it failed to find for the plaintiffs as to misrepresentation. On this verdict, the trial court rendered judgment for the plaintiffs, but the court of appeals reversed. We affirm the judgment of the court of appeals because there is no evidence in the record before us that the agent breached the duty to use reasonable care, skill and diligence in procuring insurance in any way that proximately caused harm to the petitioners.

Facts

To reverse the judgment of the court of appeals, the petitioners, Daryl and Faith May, must demonstrate that some evidence in the record supports the verdict in their favor. The evidence most favorable to the Mays is that, because health insurance was not provided by Daryl's employer, they decided to take out a health insurance policy shortly after their marriage in December of 1982. Daryl's mother, Alice May, worked next door to Preston Insurance Agency, Inc. (Preston), from which Daryl had previously purchased automobile insurance. As a favor, Alice told Faith that she would find out what health insurance policies Preston offered. Alice visited Preston and spoke with one of the agents there, Rex Wiley. When she returned, she gave Faith a brochure describing the "Double Eagle" group policy.[6]

The Double Eagle policy was underwritten by Continental Bankers of the South (Continental) and could be purchased by members of the United Services Association of America (United). The Double Eagle policy featured relatively low premiums and deductibles, but its termination provision allowed the underwriter to cancel the entire group at any time. The policy also contained a deferral provision that permitted the underwriter to defer coverage on group members or covered dependents who were hospitalized or totally disabled at the time coverage began.

On March 16, 1983, Faith May visited the Preston Agency herself and spoke with Wiley about the Double Eagle policy. Wiley explained the basic provisions of the policy to her, though he did not tell her that Continental had only received a "C" rating from the A.M. Best Company, nor that Preston sold other coverages, including an individual health policy from Reserve Life.

In a prior marriage, Faith May had lost an infant child. Because the Mays were planning to have children of their own, they were interested in maternity and dependent health coverage. They told Wiley that they were concerned about covering medical expenses associated with pregnancy and childbirth. Wiley added a handwritten maternity rider to the policy. The Mays then joined the United group for a fifteen dollar membership fee and purchased the Double Eagle policy. Their coverage began on April 1, 1983.

In mid-1984, the Mays received notice that Continental had terminated the entire United group, and that another underwriter, Hermitage Insurance Company ("Hermitage"), had agreed to underwrite a plan with identical Double Eagle plan benefits for all United members previously insured by Continental. Faith May was pregnant at the time. Upon learning of the change in underwriters, she telephoned Wiley to determine what effect the change would have on the Mays' coverage. Wiley told her that Hermitage would continue to cover them on the same terms as Continental. Jared May was born on August 1, 1984, with congenital heart and lung disorders that required immediate medical attention. Hermitage covered his medical expenses under the policy.

6 In order to be eligible for the Double Eagle plan, an individual had to be a member of an approved Association (such as the United group), actively working full-time, under the age of 65, and not confined in a hospital or custodial care facility. The United membership application required the applicant to indicate whether the applicant or any member of his family had ever suffered from any of a variety of medical problems including stroke, heart attack, high blood pressure, diabetes, cancer, ulcer, disorders of the back, bones, kidneys, liver, lungs, eyes or nervous system, alcoholism or other problems.

In July 1985, however, Hermitage also terminated the United group. Keystone Life Insurance Company (Keystone) then voluntarily assumed the group. Keystone, however, classified Jared May as a totally disabled dependent and, asserting the deferral provision of the policy, refused to cover any of his medical expenses. Pursuant to the terms of the policy, Hermitage covered Jared May for ninety days after termination, until September 30, 1985. Thereafter, however, Jared May was without insurance coverage until he died in November of 1987.

On January 27, 1987, the Mays filed suit against Preston, United, Keystone, and Hermitage seeking actual damages for unpaid medical bills and mental anguish, punitive damages and interest. Their causes of action against Keystone and Hermitage were severed because both companies were involved in receivership proceedings. Against United and Preston, the Mays alleged a number of common law causes of action, including misrepresentation and negligence. Although the jury failed to find misrepresentation, it did find that the negligence of both United and Preston proximately caused the Mays' injuries, assessing their percentages of causation at 60% and 40%, respectively. The jury awarded $140,000 in damages for unpaid medical expenses and $40,000 in exemplary damages against Preston and United each. The jury awarded no damages for mental anguish. As the jury failed to find gross negligence against either defendant, the trial court rendered judgment against Preston and United jointly and severally for $140,000 plus interest and costs.

Only Preston appealed. The court of appeals, holding that there was no evidence of a negligent act by Preston that was a proximate cause of the loss of the Mays' coverage, reversed the trial court's judgment as to Preston's liability and rendered judgment that the Mays take nothing.

The questions submitted to the jury in this case did not require the jury to specify a particular negligent act by Preston.. Therefore, we must reverse the judgment of the court of appeals and render judgment on the jury verdict if there is any evidence that any of Preston's alleged failures constituted negligence and proximately caused the Mays' loss.

The Mays went to trial on a pleading alleging negligence in three particulars: 1) Preston was "negligent in placing the coverage of the Mays with [Hermitage and/or Keystone] in that it exposed them to the possibility of having no coverage on their minor child," as Preston "knew or should have known, of the danger of placing Plaintiffs in such a plan where the shifting of the insurance coverage could subject them to just exactly this type of catastrophic event;" 2) Preston was negligent "in placing the coverage of the Mays with [Hermitage and/or Keystone] in that [Preston] failed to investigate the financial solvency of the other Defendants to insure that the Plaintiffs would have insurance with a solvent company;" and (3) Preston was "negligent in placing the coverage with a near insolvent or potentially insolvent insurance company." We will address the first theory separately from the latter two.

Negligence in Selecting the Double Eagle Policy

The first theory charges that Preston was negligent in failing to procure for the Mays the type of policy that they requested or that would insure them against the risk they identified as important in their conversation with Wiley. It is established in Texas that an insurance agent who undertakes to procure insurance for another owes a duty to a client to use reasonable diligence in attempting to place the requested insurance and to inform the client promptly if unable to do so.

In *Burroughs v. Bunch,* 210 S.W.2d 211 (Tex.Civ.App.-El Paso 1948, writ ref'd), an agent was held liable for fire damage to a house being built by his customer when the agent, after agreeing to have a builder's risk policy issued on the house, failed to notify the customer that he had not procured such a policy. *Id.* at 214. Similarly, in *Scott v. Conner,* 403 S.W.2d 453 (Tex.Civ.App.-Beaumont 1966, no writ), an agent was held liable for fire damage after his customer requested a new policy to replace one cancelled by the insurer, and the agent neither procured such a replacement policy nor alerted the customer to this failure by returning the unearned portion of the premium from the original policy. *Id.* at 458.

Although some Texas courts have used the term "insurance broker" in this sense, the broker/agent distinction is not found in the Texas Insurance Code. Although the Code does distinguish in some contexts between local recording agents and soliciting agents, Tex.Ins.Code art. 21.14, this categorization does not apply to agents selling life, health and accident insurance, Tex.Ins.Code art. 21.14 § 20. Because this case involves only the sale of a health insurance policy, we do not address the differing duties imposed on Texas local recording agents and soliciting agents.

Liability was imposed in the *Burroughs* and *Scott* cases because the agent induced the plaintiff to rely on his performance of the undertaking to procure insurance, and the plaintiff reasonably, but to his detriment, assumed that he was insured against the risk that caused his loss. Unlike the plaintiffs in the *Burroughs* and *Scott* cases, however, the Mays were not misled into believing that a policy in their name existed. Moreover, they were not led wrongly to believe that their policy provided protection against a particular risk that was in fact excluded from the policy's coverage.

We need not decide whether . . . a relationship of entrustment existed in this case, because the Mays do not contend that Wiley failed to disclose any limitation in the Double Eagle policy's coverage.

The Mays failed to obtain favorable jury findings as to misrepresentation, and Faith May acknowledged at trial that Wiley told her of the termination provision allowing an underwriter to cancel coverage for the entire group. Rather, the Mays' first negligence claim directly challenges Wiley's professional judgment in recommending the Double Eagle policy to Alice May and in allowing Daryl and Faith May to purchase it. We have found no Texas cases addressing a similar claim, and few from any jurisdiction.

Several other courts have imposed liability where the client, though not misled in any way about his or her coverage, was misled about how that coverage compared to other policies. Although they have followed different approaches, these courts, departing from the theory of *Burroughs, Scott,* and *Rainey-Mapes,* have allowed the possibility of liability against an agent for negligent procurement based not on the customer's reliance on the existence or scope of coverage, but simply on the agent's failure to perform his duties with sufficient skill.

In the case before us, Faith May testified that in seeking health insurance from Preston, she told Wiley that she had previously lost a child and wanted to make sure that any policy she purchased for herself and her husband "would cover my pregnancy and any testing that I may need to have, and then any child and any problems that he may have or any testing that a child would have at birth." She also told Wiley that she and her husband "would like to have an insurance policy that we could afford, but we wanted to be guaranteed that it was a good policy." In response to this request, Wiley procured for them the Double Eagle policy with the maternity rider. This policy, according to his testimony, achieved lower rates and lower deductibles by its group structure and by excluding persons who could not answer the health questions affirmatively.

The shortcoming of the Double Eagle policy, as events developed for the Mays, was the interaction of the termination and the deferral provisions. The deferral provision became applicable anew for all insured individuals when there was a change of underwriters. Thus, hospitalized or disabled individuals whose medical care was covered because they became disabled at a time when they were already covered under the policy, or because they were born to individuals who were covered under the policy, faced the risk that they would lose coverage if the current underwriter dropped the entire group and a new underwriter took over.

The Mays contend that the procurement of a policy with this limitation in response to their request was negligent. Like the *Jones* plaintiffs, however, they base their claim solely on a limitation of coverage about which they were fully apprised, and do not identify a particular negligent failure by Wiley. The Mays claim that Wiley was negligent because he should have known of the risk posed to them by the potential shifting of the underwriters, but they offer no evidence as to why this risk was unjustified for them in particular, or why Wiley should have prevented them from assuming it.

Their claim does not rest on the theory that, with greater familiarity with or attention to the details of the Mays' situation, Wiley would have realized the policy was inappropriate. Under their theory, any of the seventy to eighty customers for whom Wiley also procured Double Eagle policies would have equally valid negligence claims against Wiley for any uncovered losses. *Jones* well captures the infeasibility of such a cause of action grounded solely on the failure to obtain complete insurance protection: if a breach of due care can be proved without a more concrete showing than a subsequent failure of coverage, agents would be rendered "blanket insurers."

Unquestionably, Wiley could have done a better job by ascertaining whether the Mays would have preferred to pay a higher premium for a nongroup policy without a comparable termination provision. However under the facts of this case, we do not believe that this failure constitutes any evidence of negligence. There is no testimony that Faith May ever asked to see different policies or even expressed any dissatisfaction with the Double Eagle. Unlike the *Sobotor* customer, whose request for the "best available" policy implies a comparison to obtain the most complete coverage and makes the agent's failure to advise of policies with higher limits a material nondisclosure, the Mays conveyed no such wish to Wiley.

Therefore, we hold that there is no evidence to support the Mays' first negligence theory.

Negligence in Failing to Investigate the Underwriters

The Mays' second and third theories allege that Preston was negligent in placing the coverage because Wiley either failed to investigate, or failed to adequately investigate, the financial solvency of Hermitage and Keystone, or if he did discover the financial condition of the underwriters, he was negligent for nonetheless placing the Mays' coverage with them.

At the time Wiley placed the coverage in 1983, Hermitage and Keystone were not yet in the picture; the underwriter was Continental. It is therefore difficult to see how any negligence by Wiley in investigating Hermitage or Keystone could be relevant to the earlier decision to place the Mays in the United group and procure the Double Eagle policy. Even reading their complaint in the most generous light possible-that is, construing it to allege negligence by Wiley in failing to withdraw the Mays from the Double Eagle plan when Hermitage or Keystone took over because he did not investigate those companies-we cannot discern a viable claim under the facts of this case.

Although at trial and in the Mays' brief to this Court much is made of the facts that Hermitage had a "C" rating from A.M. Best and that Hermitage and Keystone eventually ended up in receivership, there is no showing of how the financial condition of any of these companies contributed to the Mays' loss. No claims under the policy went unpaid because of the insolvency of any underwriter. Hermitage did not go into receivership in Texas until twenty-one months after it had cancelled the United group, and Faith May testified at trial that as far as she knew all claims she made while Hermitage was the underwriter were paid. The receiver for Hermitage was granted a directed verdict on this basis.

There is no evidence (or any allegation) that Keystone's decision to exclude Jared from coverage under the deferral provision was a consequence of a weak or precarious financial condition. The only potentially meritorious claim of harm the Mays could make is that Hermitage's decision to drop the United group — which exposed Jared to the possibility of being excluded under the deferral provision by Hermitage's successor — was prompted by its poor financial condition. There is, however, no testimony in the record to support this theory.

Consequently, we hold there is no evidence that either any failure by Wiley to discover Hermitage or Keystone's financial condition, or any decision to place coverage with them notwithstanding their financial weakness, proximately caused harm to the Mays.

Because there is no evidence to support the jury's finding as to any of the three theories alleged in the Mays' complaint, the judgment of the court of appeals was proper. We affirm.

NOTES & QUESTIONS

1) In *May*, what was the source of the supposed duty that the agent allegedly breached?

2) In *May*, the jury concluded that "the negligence of both United and Preston proximately caused the Mays' injuries, assessing their percentages of causation at 60% and 40%, respectively." What were the Mays' injuries?

3) In *May*, the Texas Supreme Court observed: "The first theory charges that Preston was negligent in failing to procure for the Mays the type of policy that they requested or that would insure them against the risk they identified as important in their conversation with Wiley." What was the risk or risks that the Mays wanted to insure against?

4) Did the Mays want to insure against "all medical risks?" Did they want to insure against "specific" or "specified" risks?

Balderama v. Western Casualty Life Insurance Company
825 S.W.2d 432
(Tex. 1991)

Article 3.70-2(E) of the Texas Insurance Code prohibits issuance of an accident and sickness insurance policy in this state which covers newborn children but limits or excludes that coverage for a period of time or for congenital defects. At issue in this case is whether insurance documents issued to John and Dolores Balderama, some covering their newborn children and some not, must be construed as a single policy and thus in violation of article 3.70-2(E). The district court concluded that the documents constituted two separate policies, and the court of appeals agreed. We disagree, and reverse and remand this case to the district court for further proceedings.

Through an agent, the Balderamas applied for insurance to Western Casualty Life Insurance Co. Using Western's application form for "Accident/Health and Life" insurance, the agent listed the Balderamas and their three children by name in the column provided for that purpose. Filling in the blanks, he showed the "Policy Form" as "CMH-2", the "Aggregate Amount" as "$100,000", the "Deductible Amount" as "$500.00", and "Endorsement Form(s)" as "OP-ACC-DD" with the number "500" written below. The "Total Premium Paid for All Members for one month" was shown as "$156.70", which was indicated elsewhere on the form to be the sum of $138.30 and $18.40. With this and other information filled out, the application form was sent to Western.

Western received and accepted the application, and returned an envelope containing four documents to the Balderamas. One was a copy of the application, now endorsed as approved, and adding a "Policy No." of "45085". The other three documents were entitled "Catastrophic Medical Hospital Policy" (Form CMH-2), "Accident Policy" (Form OP-ACC-DD), and "Endorsement" (Form EN.ACC.2).

The "Hospital Policy" specifies that it insures the applicant named in the "Policy Schedule", that is John Balderama, and "all other dependent members of [his] family, if any, named in the application". It does not cover newborn children. The "Policy Schedule", like the other pages of the "Hospital Policy", is marked "Form CMH-2". It lists the "policy number" as "45085", the "aggregate amount for each injury or sickness" as "$100,000", the "deductible" as "$500", and the "initial premium" as $156.70.

The "Accident Policy", a separate document, covers accidental injury to a limit of $500. It has no policy number but bears the printed form designation, OP-ACC-DD, listed in the application as "Endorsement Form(s)". It refers to but does not include a policy schedule naming the insured persons, but identifies them by reference to the application. It also provides:

> However, in regard to any child born to the insured, such coverage is effective from the moment of birth and is not subject to any evidence of insurability or acceptance of such newborn child and will pay for congenital defects in such newborn child.

The other document in the envelope, entitled "Endorsement", contains no insuring clause but adds accidental injury, death and dismemberment coverage in same aggregate amounts as in the "Accident Policy". Like the "Hospital Policy", the document bears the policy number "45085."

A year after receiving these documents, the Balderamas had another child, Jessica, who from birth suffered serious health problems. The Balderamas presented Western with a claim for Jessica's medical expenses, which Western denied, asserting in relevant part that Jessica was not covered because she was not named in the application. The Balderamas then sued, alleging causes of action for breach of contract, negligence, breach of the duty of good faith and fair dealing, and violations of the Deceptive Trade Practices Consumer Protection Act and the Texas Insurance Code.

The district court, sitting without a jury, tried separately the issue of whether Jessica was insured by Western. The court found that Western issued two separate policies to the Balderamas-the "Hospital Policy" with its "Endorsement", and the "Accident Policy"; that only the "Accident Policy" provided newborn coverage; and that its newborn clause did not apply to the "Hospital Policy." In accordance with its findings, the district court rendered judgment adverse to the Balderamas on their contract claim and severed it from their remaining claims. In the court of appeals, and now to us, the Balderamas complain of the merits of the district court's decision, and Western complains that the district court abused its discretion in severing the judgment on the contract claim from the other causes of action.

The Balderamas contend that Western's insurance documents comprise a single policy. They argue that the newborn clause in the "Accident Policy" applies not only to the coverage provided by that document but also to the coverage provided by the "Hospital Policy". Alternatively, they argue that if Western's single policy does not cover Jessica to the same extent as the Balderamas' other children, the policy violates article 3.70-2(E) of the Insurance Code. Western contends that its documents constitute two policies, as found by the district court. Alternatively, Western argues that even if the documents are held to be one policy, they are one policy providing separate coverages; that the newborn clause applies only to the coverage provided by the "Accident Policy"; and that both policies are therefore legal.

We conclude that Western issued a single policy. While the two purported "policies" contain separate insuring clauses, definitions and provisions, and do not refer to each other, the "Accident

Policy" cannot stand on its own. It lacks a "Policy Schedule" to which it refers. It has no policy number or any other separate designation. The application completed by Western's agent indicates the "Accident Policy" form to be an endorsement. Western accepted and approved that application. Western assigned the Balderamas a single policy number and charged them a single monthly premium. Western chose the form of the documents, and delivered those documents to the Balderamas as a set. Taken as a whole, Western's documents constitute a catastrophic medical hospital policy with endorsements for accident coverage. At best, whether Western's documents constitute a single policy is an ambiguity which, in these circumstances, must as a matter of law be resolved against Western, and in favor of coverage. *Barnett v. Aetna Life Insurance Co.,* 723 S.W.2d 663 (Tex. 1987)

As a single policy of insurance, the documents here afford coverage to newborn infants only to the extent provided in the "Accident Policy", that is, $500 accidental injury coverage. Far more extensive coverage is provided to the Balderamas' other children named in the application. A regulation of the State Board of Insurance promulgated in connection with article 3.70-2(E) of the Insurance Code explains:

> If the policy provides accident and sickness coverage for newborn children, such coverage shall be at least as comprehensive as the coverage provided under the policy for other children for loss as a result of an accident or sickness. 28 Tex. Admin. Code § 3.3403(c); *see also* §§ 3.3401-.3402; *cf.* Tex.Ins.Code art. 3.70-1(E).

Because Western issued the Balderamas a policy in violation of Texas law, Western must cover Jessica's medical expenses to the same extent as its policy covers the other Balderama children. *See Unigard Sec. Ins. Co. v. Schaefer,* 572 S.W.2d 303 (Tex.1978).

Accordingly, we reverse the judgment of the court of appeals and remand this cause to the district court for further proceedings consistent with this opinion.

NOTES & QUESTIONS

1) The of Acts 2003, 78th Leg., ch. 1274, § 26(a)(1) repealed Arts. 3.70-1 to 3.70-3B of the Texas Insurance Code. The effective date was April 1, 2005. Repealed Article 3.70-2(E) may be found at Tex. Ins. Code § 1367.003. It reads: CERTAIN LIMITATIONS ON COVERAGE FOR NEWBORN CHILDREN PROHIBITED A health benefit plan that provides maternity benefits or accident and health coverage for additional newborn children may not be issued in this state if the plan excludes or limits: (1) initial coverage of a newborn child for a period of time; or (2) coverage for congenital defects of a newborn child.

2) Repealed Art. 3.70-1 listed the purpose, definitions, the scope, rules and regulations, standards for policy provisions, an outline of coverage, preexisting conditions and administrative

procedures for accident and sickness insurance. Currently, repealed Art. 3.70-1 may be found in scattered sections: Tex. Ins. Code §§1201.101 to 1201.154.

3) Traditionally, pre-existing conditions have not been a major source of concern for health insurers when they decide to sell group insurance to employers who employ large groups of workers. On the other hand, when an individual enters the market to purchase "affordable" health insurance, a pre-existing medical condition is a major concern for the insurer. Why?

4) Tex. Ins. Code §§1201.151 states the following about preexisting conditions: PROHIBITION OF DEFENSE. Except as provided by this subchapter, an individual accident and health insurance policy may not include a provision that permits a defense based on a preexisting condition.

5) However, the pre-existing clauses in §1201.152 of the Tex. Ins. Code create some additional requirements for the insurer, while creating an exception. They read:

COVERAGE UNDER SIMPLIFIED APPLICATION FORM

> (a) Notwithstanding Clause (b) of the provision required by Section 1201.208(a), an individual accident and health insurance policy must cover any loss that occurs after 12 months from a preexisting condition if the insurer uses a simplified application form that does not include a question concerning the applicant's health history or medical treatment history.
>
> (b) This section applies regardless of whether the simplified application form includes a question regarding the applicant's health at the time of application.
>
> (c) This section does not require an insurer to cover a loss from a condition that the policy specifically excludes from coverage.

6) What is the test for determining whether a person's ailment is a "preexisting" condition? Is it a medical or legal standard?

Provident American Insurance Company v. Castaneda
988 S.W.2d 189
(Tex. 1998)

Denise Castañeda seeks damages from Provident American Insurance Company for alleged violations of the Insurance Code and the Deceptive Trade Practices Act arising out of the denial of her claim for benefits under a health insurance policy and the manner in which her claim was handled. Because the evidence is legally insufficient to support the jury's verdict, we reverse and render judgment that Castañeda take nothing.

I

Denise Castañeda's father, Guillermo Castañeda, Sr., applied for medical insurance with Provident American Insurance Company in May 1991. He sought a policy that would cover the entire family including his daughter Denise, who was twenty-one years old at the time, her sister, and their brother Guillermo, Jr. During the application process, Guillermo Castañeda, Sr. failed to disclose that just two days before he applied for the policy, Guillermo, Jr. had received medical attention from a physician for jaundice, anemia, and suspected hepatitis. Denise had received medical treatment for jaundice and hepatitis several years prior to the date her father applied for health insurance.

Provident American issued a policy to the family effective June 17, 1991. The policy contained two limitations that are relevant here: (1) it did not cover expenses resulting from a sickness that "manifests" within thirty days of the policy's effective date; and (2) it excluded diseases or disorders of certain internal organs, including the gallbladder, unless the loss occurred more than six months after the policy's effective date.

Less than thirty days after the issuance of the policy, the family learned that Denise's uncle had been diagnosed with hemolytic spherocytosis (HS), a hereditary condition that causes misshapen blood cells. The spleen destroys these cells, which causes the sufferer to exhibit anemia, jaundice, and, in 90% of the cases, gallstones. The treatment for this condition is to remove the spleen and, if gallstones are present, the gallbladder. Because the disease is hereditary, it was suggested that the Castañedas be tested for HS. Denise and Guillermo, Jr. had exhibited yellow skin all of their lives, and on July 20, 1991, the third day after the thirty-day period expired, they were taken to a physician who diagnosed them that same day with HS and referred them to a blood specialist. They saw the hematologist two days later, and he concurred in the HS diagnosis. Two weeks later, Denise and Guillermo, Jr. each had their spleen and gallbladder surgically removed.

The Castañedas submitted claims to Provident American, which were denied. Provident American first asserted the six-month policy exclusion for disorders of the gallbladder but later denied the claims on the basis that HS had manifested within thirty days of the policy's effective date.

Denise Castañeda sued Provident American, alleging violations of the DTPA and of article 21.21 of the Texas Insurance Code, and Guillermo Castañeda, Sr. sued on behalf of Guillermo, Jr. The two suits were consolidated, but Guillermo Castañeda, Sr. later nonsuited his claims. Denise Castañeda proceeded to trial, and the district court submitted three liability questions based on article 21.21 of the Insurance Code and on the DTPA. The jury answered "yes" to each and found that Provident American had engaged in knowing conduct. The jury awarded $50,000 for Denise Castañeda's loss of credit reputation and loss of benefits, collectively, but found no mental anguish damages. The jury also awarded reasonable attorney's fees of 33% of Castañeda's recovery. The trial court rendered judgment on the verdict, trebling the damages and adding a twelve percent penalty on the lost benefits.

The court of appeals affirmed, except as to the twelve percent penalty. Regarding other points of error, the court of appeals concluded that the trial court had erroneously submitted at least one subpart of the first liability question (subpart A) but held that this error was harmless because two other subparts (J and H) were properly submitted and supported by legally and factually sufficient evidence. The court of appeals also held that the evidence was sufficient to support the award of $50,000 for loss of credit reputation and loss of benefits.

Provident American filed an application for writ of error with this Court, which we granted. Because there is no evidence to support a finding of liability based on any of the theories submitted to the jury, we do not reach the question of whether a trial court's judgment may be affirmed if a liability question includes a theory that is not legally cognizable but other viable theories are included within the same question. Likewise, we do not reach Provident American's complaint that attorney's fees were improperly based on a percentage of the recovery, an issue that we addressed in *Arthur Andersen & Co. v. Perry Equipment Corp.* 945 S.W.2d 812, 818-19 (Tex.1997) (holding that a plaintiff must ask the jury to award attorney's fees in a specific dollar amount in a DTPA case).

II

We begin our review with the first question submitted to the jury. The numerous subparts of Question 1 can be distilled into three categories: 1) whether Provident American denied the claim without a reasonable basis or after its liability had become reasonably clear, 2) whether there was a misrepresentation about the policy, and 3) whether Provident American engaged in unfair claims settlement practices. We first consider whether there was any evidence to support a finding that Provident American denied Castañeda's claim without a reasonable basis or after its liability had become reasonably clear.

III

The trial court submitted two instructions to the jury regarding Provident American's denial of the claim. Subpart J of Question 1 was based on article 21.21-2, section 2(b)(4) and defined an unfair or deceptive act or practice as including: "[n]ot attempting in good faith to effectuate a prompt, fair, and equitable settlement of a claim when liability has become reasonably clear." Subpart G of Question 1 was a hybrid theory that defined an unfair or deceptive act or practice as including: "[d] enying a claim or delaying payment on a claim without a reasonable basis or failing to determine whether there is any reasonable basis for the denial or delay." This instruction embodied the pre-Giles common-law definition of bad faith, but the jury issue included producing cause, which is the causation element for an article 21.21 claim. However, the parties agree that only statutory claims were tried and that no common-law bad faith claim was submitted. Provident American did not urge the trial court to exclude subpart G from the definitions of an "[u]nfair or deceptive act or practice" and contends only that there is no evidence to support a jury finding based on this definition. Our no-evidence review of subpart G is governed by our pre- Giles decisions because this instruction was couched in the same terms as the pre- Giles definition of common-law bad faith. Thus, our decisions in *Lyons v. Millers Casualty Insurance Co.*, 866 S.W.2d 597 (Tex.1993), and *National Union Fire Insurance Co. v. Dominguez,* 873 S.W.2d 373 (Tex.1994)guide us in reviewing the record to see if there is any evidence that would support a jury finding based on subpart G.

To determine whether there is any evidence to support a jury finding under Subpart G or J, we must first identify the potential bases Provident American had for denying Castañeda's claim. Then we must determine whether there is any evidence that no reasonable insurer could have denied payment of her claim and whether there is any evidence that liability had become reasonably clear.

A

At varying times, Provident American gave varying reasons for denying Denise Castañeda's claim, but all were grounded in a common nucleus of facts. Provident American cited a policy provision that excluded coverage for a sickness or disorder involving the gallbladder unless the loss occurred more than six months after the date the policy went into effect. Provident American also relied on policy provisions that limited coverage to an illness or disease that first manifested more than thirty days after the policy went into effect. At least one Provident American employee thought that the claim also could have been denied based on the pre-existing condition provision of the policy, although that clause was never invoked. We conclude that, considering all the facts in existence at the time of the denial, there is no evidence that there was no reasonable basis for Provident American's denial of Castaneda's claim (subpart G) or that liability had become reasonably clear (subpart J).

We first consider denial based on manifestation of HS prior to the end of the thirty-day period. The parties dispute when Castañeda's illness manifested. Castañeda argues that there is some evidence that her hereditary illness first manifested after the thirty-day period, and Provident American contends that it manifested before the end of the thirty-day period. However, even if Castañeda were correct, evidence of coverage, standing alone, would not constitute evidence of bad faith denial. In *State Farm Lloyds v. Nicolau*, 951 S.W.2d 444, 448 (Tex.1997), we reconfirmed what we held in *Transportation Insurance Co. v. Moriel*, 879 S.W.2d 10, 17 (Tex.1994), *National Union Fire Insurance Co. v. Dominguez*, 873 S.W.2d at 376-77 and other cases, which is that evidence showing only a bona fide coverage dispute does not demonstrate that there was no reasonable basis for denying a claim. By the same token, evidence of a coverage dispute is not evidence that liability under the policy had become reasonably clear.

We held in Dominguez that one physician's opinion that the plaintiff's condition was work-related did not raise a fact issue of whether there was no reasonable basis for denial of a claim because the insurer was entitled to rely on the opinion of other medical professionals who had diagnosed the condition as a degenerative disease. Likewise, in *Lyons v. Millers Cas. Ins. Co.,* 866 S.W.2d 597, 600-01 (Tex.1993), we held that the jury was entitled to resolve a conflict in the evidence about whether a windstorm had damaged a home but that evidence related to contractual coverage was not evidence of bad faith unless there was also evidence that the information on which the insurance company relied in denying the claim was unreliable or not objectively prepared. Thus, when medical evidence is conflicting, liability is not reasonably clear, and it cannot be said that the insurer had no reasonable basis for denying the claim unless the medical evidence on which the insurer based its denial is unreliable and the insurer knew or should have known that to be the case.

In *State Farm Lloyds v. Nicolau*, 951 S.W.2d 444, 448 (Tex.1997), this Court concluded that there was evidence of no reasonable basis to deny the claim because the carrier had either relied on an expert's report that the carrier knew "was not objectively prepared" or because "the insurer's reliance on the report was unreasonable." By contrast, there is no evidence in this case that any of the information on which Provident American ultimately relied in denying coverage was "not objectively prepared" or that reliance on the information was unreasonable. The medical records revealed that just three days after the thirty-day waiting period expired, Denise Castañeda saw a physician and was diagnosed with a hereditary blood disorder. Two weeks later, she underwent surgery to remove her spleen as treatment for this condition. During surgery it was confirmed that her disorder had caused gallstones, and her gallbladder was also removed.

The undisputed evidence showed that Denise Castañeda and her brother had exhibited symptoms even before their father applied for the policy. Castañeda's father wrote to Provident American, providing facts that supported a conclusion that the disease had manifested before the end of the thirty-day period and that there was no coverage.

* * *

In order for subpart G to support a verdict, Castañeda was required to come forward with some evidence that no reasonable insurer could have believed that HS had manifested before the end of the thirty-day period (an objective prong of the "no reasonable basis" definition of bad faith) and that Provident American knew or should have known that it had no reasonable basis for denying the claim based on the thirty-day waiting period (the second prong). In order for subpart J to support a verdict, Castaneda was required to come forward with some evidence that liability was reasonably clear. She did not meet her burden.

The jury's failure to find that HS first manifested prior to July 17, 1991 is not dispositive of the issue of liability under the DTPA or the Insurance Code, which are extra-contractual claims. Provident American requested a defensive issue in an effort to establish that there was no coverage under the contract of insurance. But even if the jury's negative answer to this issue amounted to a finding of contractual coverage, coverage is not the equivalent of and cannot be the only evidence of bad faith. In Lyons, the jury found that the insured's loss was covered by the policy, but we explained that "bad faith focuses not on whether the claim was valid, but on the reasonableness of the insurer's conduct in rejecting the claim." There is no evidence that Provident American had no reasonable basis for concluding that HS had first manifested in Denise Castañeda prior to the end of the thirty-day period.

Provident American was not required to appeal the jury's failure to find that HS had manifested before the end of the thirty-day period because Castañeda never sought and did not receive any contractual relief. The only theories of liability at issue in the trial court were extra-contractual ones.

We express no opinion regarding the dissent's extended discussion of whether there was contractual coverage and the meaning of "manifest" as used in Castañeda's policy. We note only that there is considerable authority that "manifest" does not necessarily mean manifest to the insured.

B

Castañeda contends that Provident American is liable on an independent ground because one of the reasons it gave for denying coverage was the policy's exclusion of gallbladder disorders during the first six months that the policy was in effect. After Provident American initially had denied coverage on that basis, one of Castañeda's physicians advised that the gallbladder surgery was secondary to HS. At least some individuals within Provident American's organization thereafter concluded that the gallbladder exclusion did not apply. The claim was then denied based on the thirty-day provision discussed above, and the thirty-day provision was cited as the reason for denial when Provident American subsequently responded to an inquiry from the Department of Insurance. However, many months after the claim had been denied because of the thirty-day provision, one of Denise Castañeda's physicians called Provident American to inquire once again why the claim had not been paid and was told that it was because of the six-month exclusion regarding the gallbladder. The president of Provident American also maintained at trial that the claim was not payable because of the gallbladder exclusion and the thirty-day provision.

We assume, but need not decide for purposes of our analysis, that the removal of Castañeda's gallbladder did not fall within policy exclusions. We thus assume that the gallbladder exclusion was not a valid basis for denying coverage. But not every erroneous denial of a claim subjects an insurer to liability, as we confirmed once again in *Republic Insurance Co. v. Stoker*, 903 S.W.2d 338, 340 (Tex.1995) (stating that as long as the insurer has a reasonable basis to deny or delay payment of the claim, even if that basis is erroneous, the insurer is not liable for bad faith) (citing Lyons, 866 S.W.2d at 600). *See* also *Aranda v. Insurance Co. of N. Am.*, 748 S.W.2d 210, 213 (Tex.1988) (stating that carriers "will not be subject to liability for an erroneous denial of a claim" unless there was no reasonable basis for denial).

There is no evidence in this record that no reasonable insurance company would have denied coverage in light of other facts.

* * *

Castañeda and the dissent contend that because Provident American gave different reasons for denying the claim at different times, there is some evidence that the denial was pretextual, citing *State Farm Lloyds v. Nicolau,* 951 S.W.2d 444, 448-50 (Tex.1997), and *State Farm Fire & Cas. Co. v. Simmons*, 963 S.W.2d 42, 45-47 (Tex.1998). In *Nicolau*, the Court concluded that there was some evidence that the carrier knew that the expert report on which it relied was of questionable validity. In *Simmons*, the Court concluded that there was evidence that the investigation was biased and outcome-oriented because there was evidence that the carrier knowingly and repeatedly ignored evidence that the insureds did not burn down their home and that they had no motive for arson. Our use of the term "pretextual" in *Nicolau* and *Simmons* did not mean that an insured is relieved from its burden of offering evidence that liability had become reasonably clear or that there was no reasonable basis for denying the claim.

We did not redefine the common-law tort of bad faith or the legal sufficiency standard of review for article 21.21 cases to include a mechanism by which a factfinder could conclude that the denial was pretextual even though there was a reasonable basis for denying the claim. The use of the concept "pretextual" was another way of saying that there must be some evidence that there was no reasonable basis for denying the claim or that liability was reasonably clear. Here, there is no evidence that Provident American ignored information that would lead a reasonable person to conclude that liability under the policy was reasonably clear or that there was no reasonable basis to deny the claim.

* * *

V

Denise Castañeda contends that by pre-approving her surgery, Provident American represented that her condition was covered, and that when Provident American thereafter failed to pay her claim, this amounted to a violation of the Insurance Code and the DTPA. The pre-approval in this case was not a representation that is actionable under the Insurance Code or the DTPA. Nor is there any evidence that Castañeda relied on the pre-approval to her detriment.

At the time Provident American authorized surgery, it had not been given material facts that were in the possession of the Castañedas and the physicians who treated Denise Castañeda. Provident American did not know that Denise Castañeda had exhibited symptoms and had been treated for jaundice and hepatitis long before her father applied for the policy. Nor did it know that the hereditary disease HS had been diagnosed in another family member within the thirty-day waiting period or that Denise Castañeda's brother, Guillermo, Jr., also an insured, had been treated for jaundice, suspected hepatitis, and anemia just two days before their father met with Provident American to apply for this policy.

Under these circumstances, Provident American's pre-authorization at most amounted to an uninformed conclusion on its part, based on what it knew from the insured and the insured's physicians, that Castañeda's blood disorder was a covered sickness, namely, that HS had not manifested prior to the end of the thirty-day waiting period or was not otherwise excluded. The pre-approval does not constitute a false, misleading, or deceptive act; a misrepresentation of the terms of an insurance policy; or an assertion with respect to insurance that was untrue.

Castañeda's position, if accepted, would impose strict liability on carriers that are not given pertinent facts before a procedure is pre-approved and who later learn that they have a good faith, reasonable basis for denying coverage. We do not hold today that pre-approval of medical procedures can never constitute an actionable representation under article 21.21 or the DTPA. And we are not called upon to consider any other theory of liability. We hold only that the pre-approval given in this case does not subject Provident American to liability under the DTPA or article 21.21 because neither the insureds nor their physicians imparted key facts before the pre-approval was given.

Provident American also contends and we agree that there is no evidence that Castañeda relied on the pre-approval to her detriment. There is no evidence that but for the pre-approval, Castañeda would not have had the surgery. The evidence at trial was that removal of the spleen is the only known cure for HS. Castañeda never offered any evidence that she would have foregone the surgery if her insurer had not pre-approved it. This case is similar to the situation presented in *Royal Globe Insurance Co. v. Bar Consultants, Inc.*, 577 S.W.2d 688, 690-91 (Tex.1979) in which a bar was damaged by vandals. The insured called the insurer the next morning and was told that the loss was covered and to go ahead and have the damage repaired.

The policy in fact expressly excluded loss caused by vandalism. We held that no detriment was shown from reliance on the insurer's post-loss representation of coverage because the bar's owner conceded that he would have made the repairs even if there were no coverage. The representation of coverage by Provident American, like the representation in Royal Globe, will not support the judgment in this case because there is no evidence of reliance by the Castañedas.

VI

Two other liability issues were submitted. Question 3 inquired if Provident American had engaged in unconscionable conduct as defined in former DTPA section 17.45(5). Castañeda argues that the same evidence that she contends supports findings of liability under Question 1 is also evidence of unconscionability. But none of the evidence regarding the manner in which Provident American handled the claim nor the reasons for its denial of the claim amount to evidence that Provident American took "advantage of the lack of knowledge, ability, experience, or capacity" of Castañeda to a grossly unfair degree or that its conduct resulted in a "gross disparity between value received and consideration paid," which were the definitions of unconscionability in Question 3.

The only additional argument Castañeda makes regarding unconscionability is that her father paid the specified premium for this policy but that the policy was valueless because her claim was denied. Of course, if the policy did cover her claim, she was entitled to recover policy benefits, and the policy was not "valueless." If the policy did not cover this claim, it was still not valueless because it covered a myriad of other illnesses Castañeda could have contracted while the policy was in effect. Likewise, there is no evidence to support the findings under Question 4, which inquired if Provident American had made representations that goods or services had characteristics they did not have or were of a particular quality, or that an agreement conferred rights that it did not contain.

In sum, there is no support in the evidence for any of the extra-contractual claims on which Denise Castañeda obtained findings. Castañeda did not plead and did not obtain a determination from the trial court that Provident American was liable for breach of the insurance contract. Accordingly, there is no basis on which Castañeda may recover based on this record.

* * *

Because the judgment against Provident American is not supported by legally sufficient evidence, the judgment of the court of appeals is reversed, and judgment is rendered that Castañeda take nothing.

NOTES & QUESTIONS

1) Clearly, health insurers may discriminate based on a person's preexisting medical condition. When may an insurer discriminate without being liable?

2) What is the Health Insurance Portability and Accountability Act (HIPAA)?

3) Consider the following information that appears in *Texas Health Ins. Risk Pool v. Southwest Service Life Ins. Co.* 272 S.W.3d 797, 799 (Tex. App.-Austin 2008):

> Tex. Ins.Code Ann. §§ 1506.251, .253 provides that the Texas Health Insurance Risk Pool (Pool)] may levy annual and interim assessments on health insurers to cover operating expenses. . . . The legislature created the Pool in 1989 for the purpose of providing access to health insurance coverage to otherwise uninsurable Texans. See Act of May 27, 1989, 71st Leg., R.S., ch. 1094, 1989 Tex. Gen. Laws 4477. However, the Pool was not funded for operation at that time and remained dormant for several years.
>
> In 1996, Congress enacted the Health Insurance Portability and Accountability Act (HIPAA), which, among other things, set new federal minimum standards for insurers offering insurance policies to individuals, prohibiting these insurers from 1) declining coverage, 2) limiting coverage, 3) charging a higher premium, or 4) imposing preexisting condition limitations on certain qualifying applicants. See 42 U.S.C. § 300gg-41(a).
>
> HIPAA allowed states to opt out of enforcing these minimum standards by implementing an acceptable state-run alternative mechanism, such as a qualifying high-risk pool. See id. § 300gg-44(a)(1)(D)(ii) (West 2003). In response to HIPAA, the Texas Legislature funded the Pool for operation and brought it into compliance to serve as a state-run alternative mechanism. See Act of May 10, 1997, 75th Leg., R.S., ch. 837, 1997 Tex. Gen. Laws 2679. The legislature decided that the Pool's funding would be derived in part from interim and annual assessments on health insurance companies doing business in Texas. See Tex. Ins.Code Ann. §§ 1506.251, .253.

F. *Life and Accidental-Death Insurance*

If one were to ask a retired 91-year-old West Texas rancher whether death is a risk or peril that he would consider insuring against, the gentleman would probably say: "At my age death is not a risk, it is a certainty." Yet, the elderly, along with young working parents, are significantly more likely to purchase life insurance.

To be sure, death is inevitable. And arguably, in our Western culture, it is a peril that most people try to avoid as long as possible. Therefore, "just like a good neighbor," property and casualty insurers enrich themselves and their investors by selling life insurance to cover expenses associated with a definite event. Insurers sell two types of life insurance contracts: "term-life" and "whole-life" agreements. Term life insurance is the less expensive of the two. Put simply, under term-life insurance contracts, insurers promise to pay a fixed benefit to a primary or contingent beneficiary if death occurs within a fixed period of time. In addition, term-life insurance is the inferior of the two: It does not have a cash-value provision that would allow the insured to build wealth during the life of the contract.

On the other hand, a standardized, whole-life insurance contract has more "attractive" features: a fixed death benefit that the insurer may not contest if the policy has been enforced for two years, a cash-value provision that promises to pay a fixed interest rate, a loan provision, and a provision that promises to pay "fixed scheduled payments" for a certain period of time or after the death of the insured. Additionally, whole-life insurance appears in two forms: "participating" and "nonparticipating." Briefly put, when insurance consumers pay premiums, insurers invest those funds. Therefore, under a "participating whole-life insurance contract," the owners of the contract may receive dividends. Historically, insurers promise to pay dividends, after the contract's second anniversary and for as long as the insured lives.

There is more. If one were to read antiquated phrases in wordy life insurance contracts, one might see the following sentence: "This is a non-participating whole-life insurance policy with an accidental-death provision, covering the life of the insured." Although "accidental death benefits" is just another name for "double indemnity," consumers are probably more familiar with the latter. If the owner of a life insurance contract is willing to pay extra premiums, an insurer will add an indemnity clause or endorsement to the contract. Generally, that provision promises to pay the owner or a beneficiary a sum that doubles the face value of the life insurance contract.

Generally, to be eligible for whole-life insurance, an applicant must be free of any "major preexisting" medical problem. And to receive double indemnity, a beneficiary must prove that an "accident" was the efficient proximate cause of the insured's death. Determining whether a deceased insured had a "preexisting" condition and whether an "accident" caused the death has generated an appreciable amount of litigation in Texas. Therefore, we begin the legal discussion of life insurance contracts by examining whether a pre-existing medical condition precludes recovery under various first-party insurance contracts.

Mutual Benefit Health and Accident Association v. Hudman
398 S.W.2d 110
(Tex. 1965)

The question presented is whether Mary Louise Hudman, the beneficiary of an accident policy which limited coverage to death from accidental injury 'independently of other causes,' may recover under the policy when the insured's death resulted from the combined effects of the injury and a pre-existing disease. She obtained a judgment in a case tried before the court without a jury and the intermediate court affirmed. We reverse those judgments and render judgment that the beneficiary take nothing.

Paul Hudman, a fifty-four year old pharmacist, was the insured under an accident policy issued by Mutual Benefit Health & Accident Association which limited recovery for accidental death by these two clauses:

> The applicable benefit amount shown below will be paid to the beneficiary named in the policy . . . if covered injuries result in your death, independently of other causes, within 90 days after the date of the accident.
>
> Covered injuries' mean accidental bodily injuries which you receive while you are driving or riding in any private passenger automobile.

Hudman worked on his farm outside of San Angelo during the afternoon of April 28, 1963. The evidence supports the trial court's findings that he died in his pickup truck of ventricular fibrillation after he had worked hard on a hot day that was marked by extreme fluctuations in humidity. One of the medical witnesses testified that Hudman's 'continued exertion of driving the pickup, after the extremely hard labor of the day, contributed to the onset of fibrillation.' Prior to his death he was in apparently good health and had never had a diagnosis of or treatment for heart trouble. The trial court also found that arteriosclerosis of Hudman's coronary artery was a predisposing condition and not a proximate cause of his death, and that of itself, the condition would not have caused Hudman's death.

All of the evidence shows that Hudman died from the effects of two concurring causes. The cause of death was proved by three medical experts, one called by the plaintiff and two by the defendant. Their testimony is in agreement that death resulted from fibrillation of Hudman's heart and the evidence shows that Hudman's overexertion and his diseased heart concurrently caused the fibrillation. The Court of Civil Appeals found from the facts that "(t)here is no question but that the diseased condition of Mr. Hudman's heart contributed to his death." We shall briefly summarize the testimony.

Dr. Lloyd R. Hershberger testified about an autopsy he performed in the presence of two other doctors and the attorneys for the parties. His report described the anterior descending branch of the left coronary. It stated that "2 cm. below its origin, it becomes quite narrow and is reduced to a slit-like opening . . . . I would estimate that the diameter of the channel is about one-eighth of that which is normal. This descending branch then returns to a more normal diameter as it is examined distal to this narrowing, but about 4 cm. distal to the origin, we again find a second area of extreme narrowing. This area shows eccentric thickening of the blood vessel wall with a very narrow lumen that I would again estimate at about one-eighth the normal diameter." He testified that Hudman's heart disease was very significant and a contributing cause of the death. He said that the primary cause of death was 'a combination of pre-existing heart disease and the physical exercise performed the day of his death.' When questioned more specifically, he said that both causes were primary; neither was remote. He considered the two causes of death equal.

Dr. John L. Goforth was not present at the autopsy but testified as an expert about it. He said that a person with the kind of heart Hudman had, doing the heavy labor to which he was not accustomed and working on the hot humid day, overtaxed the function of his heart. He said that Hudman, in the absence of heart disease, probably would not have died by reason of the exertion. He expressed the opinion that one with the degree of Hudman's arteriosclerosis is in imminently serious trouble and the disease was alone sufficient cause for sudden death.

Dr. P. O. B. Montgomery, who was present at the autopsy, testified: "In my opinion, his death was caused by ventricular fibrillation, and the cause of the ventricular fibrillation was the unusual amount of work that he did under the emotional pressure that he did it, on a day when the temperature was unseasonably hot, and the humidity showed an extraordinary variation. These factors, coupled with his coronary arteriosclerosis disease, caused his heart to fibrillate, and this was the immediate cause of his death." He said that the decreased blood supply caused by the narrowing of the artery in and of itself would not have caused the death, but he also said that the decreased blood supply and the increased demand for blood by reason of the exertion "and the impinging of these two things caused his heart to fibrillate." He said that the physical stress and the disease combined to cause Hudman's death.

Plaintiff, Mary Louise Hudman, argues that there is evidence that heart disease did not cause the death because an immediate heart massage would have restored the rhythm of the heart, that twenty-five to thirty per cent of all males have equally advanced arteriosclerosis as that of Hudman at his age, and the disease was dormant and only a predisposing condition. From this, she reasons that there was evidence to support the finding, that overexertion caused the fibrillation, which caused death. This, however, is not what the doctors unanimously testified. They said that it was overexertion and disease that caused fibrillation. It took two things to produce the fibrillating process which produced death. Overexertion or disease alone, they said, did not produce the fibrillation.

Plaintiff, Mary Louise Hudman, failed to prove an accidental bodily injury, "independently of other causes." This limitation upon the cause of death cannot be ignored, because it was the basis of the agreement. *Pan American Life Ins. Co. v. Andrews,* 340 S.W.2d 787, 790 (Tex. 1960); *United American Ins. Co. v. Selby*, 338 S.W.2d 160, 164 (Tex. 1960). Plaintiff's argument is that the phrase means the same as mere proximate cause which can be a concurring cause. While it is true that the cause must be proximate rather than remote, the real question is whether the beneficiary must prove the accidental injury was a proximate cause or the sole proximate cause. "Independently" means "solely," "only," [or] "standing alone."

The logical meaning of the policy terms limits the coverage to accidental bodily injuries which are the sole cause of death. We are dealing with death under an accident policy. It obligated the insurer to pay " . . . if covered injuries (accidental bodily injuries) result in your death, independently of other causes." The coverage is for accidental bodily injuries. The term "other causes" would mean non-accidental causes. The policy does not purport to cover non-accidental bodily injuries such as Hudman's heart disease. A reasonable construction of the accident policy is that it covered accident-caused injuries rather than non-accident-caused injuries.

We reach the same result when we look at the whole phrase "independently of other causes." The phrase does not mean that the insurer agreed to provide coverage for a death which results from accidental bodily injuries though "dependent upon other causes." Logically this is what the beneficiary here argues. Her argument would compel the result that overexertion (the accidental bodily injury), though dependent upon heart disease (the other cause) was yet "independent of other causes." The idea that one factor is independently a cause leaves no room for the idea that it yet may be dependently caused. An independent cause does not mean that it is a joint, contributing or concurring cause.

All of the evidence shows that two causes proximately concurred to produce death and the policy limited its coverage to one cause, accidental bodily injury. It solves nothing when applying a sole-cause test, to resort to a but-for test . . . When we have two concurring factors which produce death, one within and the other without the policy coverage, results under such a test would depend upon the factor to which the test is applied. It is a true statement that Hudman's death would not have occurred but for his overexertion, the bodily injury and accidental cause. It is also true that his death would not have occurred but for the pre-existing heart disease, the non-accidental cause.

If we apply the but-for test to the accidental bodily injury, we can say that the death would not have occurred but for the overexertion and the plaintiff would win. When we apply the same test to the other concurring cause, the non-accidental heart disease, we get an opposite result. This is so because the death would not have occurred but for the non-accidental heart disease, and the plaintiff would lose. It took both causes to produce death and but for both, death would probably not have occurred. We conclude that by definition of the policy terms and by logic, the policy coverage was limited to accidental bodily injuries which must be the sole cause of death.

The decisional law of Texas is in accord with these principles. We must put aside as irrelevant those cases which construe policies which provide coverage upon proof of mere proximate cause. Those are cases which do not have a limiting clause such as "independently of other causes." *Pledger v. Business Men's Accident Ass'n,* 228 S.W. 110, 113 (Tex.Com.App.1921). Nor are we concerned with precedents which discuss the other and different requirement found in many policies that the injury result from "external, violent and accidental means." *Pan American Life Ins. Co. v. Andrews*, 340 S.W.2d 787 (Tex. 1960)

Continental Casualty Co. v. Fountain, 257 S.W.2d 338 (Tex. Civ. App.1953, writ ref.), discussed an accident policy which limited coverage to bodily injury "which is the sole cause of the loss which is effected solely through accidental means . . . . ." The word "sole" was not disregarded. The Court held that the plaintiff failed as a matter of law to discharge her burden that death resulted solely from accidental means and not from cancer. In *Robinson v. Aetna Life Ins. Co., 276 S.W. 900* (Tex.Com.App.1925), the policy insured against loss "resulting directly and independently of all other causes from bodily injury effected solely through external, violent, and accidental means."

Plaintiff contended that the insured died from a fall on his head but the defendant claimed that death resulted from apoplexy. In affirming the right of defendant to an issue inquiring whether apoplexy caused or contributed directly to the death, the Court held: ". . . the burden was upon the plaintiff to show that the death of Charles W. Robinson resulted directly and independently of all other causes from bodily injuries effected solely thorough external, violent, and accidental means. If apoplexy caused or contributed directly to cause the death, the plaintiff could not recover, and a finding to that effect was therefore most material to the defense."

* * *

The result we reach in this case is compelled by the terms of the policy and the evidence of all the physicians. We do not hold that every preexisting frailty or enfeeblement of the human body which co-exists with an accidental injury will defeat recovery under such policies as Hudman's. To do so would defeat recovery in most instances because mere senescence makes all flesh heir to infirmity and weakness. Policies are, to use Cordozo's phrase, issued to those who are neither "an Apollo nor Hercules." *Silverstein v. Metropolitan Life Ins. Co.*, 171 N.E. 914 (N.Y. 1930). Recovery is not defeated when a preexisting condition or disorder is so remote in the scale of causation, so dormant and insubstantial, or so temporary and transient that it does not materially contribute to the death or injury. In most cases, the competent evidence of qualified persons separates the real causes of death or injury from mere conditions or at least raises issues for the determination by the fact finder.

* * *

It is our conclusion that the beneficiary failed to prove that death was the result solely of Hudman's overexertion, because all of the evidence shows that preexisting serious heart disease and overexertion concurred to cause the fibrillation of Hudman's heart and in turn, his death. Therefore, we reverse the judgments of the courts below and render judgment that the plaintiff take nothing.

Republic National Life Insurance Company v. Heyward
536 S.W.2d 549
(Tex 1976)

Velma L. Heyward was the named beneficiary of a group life insurance policy issued by Republic National Life Insurance Company and insuring the life of her husband, Bennie T. Heyward. She brought this suit to recover benefits under an accidental death rider to the policy. At the close of plaintiff's evidence the trial court instructed a verdict for Republic. The Court of Civil Appeals has reversed and remanded. We affirmed the judgment of the Court of Civil Appeals.

The pertinent provisions of the accidental death rider are as follows:

> If a person, while insured under this Section of the Group Policy, sustains an injury effected solely through external, violent and accidental means and as a result thereof, directly and independently of all other causes, suffers a loss specified below within ninety days following the date of such injury, the Company, subject to all provisions of the Group Policy, will pay (a) the Principal Sum for loss of life; . . . Benefits shall not be payable for any loss to which a contributing cause is (e) participation in or as the result of the commission of a felonious act.

The evidence introduced by plaintiff reveals that Bennie Heyward died on September 23, 1973, from multiple gunshot wounds. The Medical Examiner's Report shows that there were five gunshot wounds in his body, two entering from the front and three from the back; in addition, there were multiple lacerations on his head and back made by a sharp object, possibly a knife. One 357 magnum bullet was recovered. The Medical Examiner's Report concluded that the manner of death was homicide. The Medical Examiner testified that in his opinion insured was intentionally shot by another.

Plaintiff's proof showed that at the time of his death Bennie Heyward was an employee of the City of San Antonio and was covered by the above Group Policy with the accidental death rider. Republic paid the basic $3,000.00 life insurance benefits to plaintiff, but refused to pay the additional $12,000.00 under the accidental death provisions.

Portions of the depositions of James Edda Anderson and Oscar M. Anderson were introduced into evidence. They both testified that they lived at 311 Vine Street (the place where insured's death occurred, according to the death certificate), but they refused to answer any other questions on the ground that their answers might tend to incriminate them.

Antone Dykes, an ordained minister, testified that he was acquainted with insured, and that his reputation for being a law-abiding citizen and a peaceful person was good.

Based on the above evidence the trial court directed a verdict for the insurance company. Republic contends that the directed verdict was proper because plaintiff failed to produce any evidence that Bennie Hayward died from injuries "effected solely through . . . accidental means," and alternatively because there was no evidence that 'a contributing cause' of death was not "participation in or as the result of the commission of a felonious act."

I.

The first issue presented by Republic's points of error is: does the above evidence, construed most favorably to plaintiff, raise a question of fact as to whether Bennie Heyward's death was accidental under the terms of the policy? Republic admits that the policy in question was in force at the time of insured's death. Republic also admits that plaintiff's evidence raised a fact issue as to whether insured's injuries were effected solely through violent and external means as those terms were used in the policy. Republic denies, however, that insured's injuries were "effected solely through

. . . accidental means." No definition of the term "accidental means" is provided by the policy. Republic contends that, under the Texas cases defining similar provisions, a death is not effected solely through accidental means if it results from injuries intentionally inflicted by another.

In *Releford v. Reserve Life Insurance Co.,* 276 S.W.2d 517 (Tex. 1955), insured died from injuries intentionally inflicted by his wife. Insured's policy provided indemnity against loss of life 'resulting from accidental bodily injuries.' Reversing the Court of Civil Appeals' judgment for the insurance company, this Court held that the court below had applied the wrong test to determine liability under the policy. The Per Curiam opinion states, at page 518:

> In reaching its conclusion the Court (of Civil Appeals) seems to have given controlling weight to its finding that "viewed from the standpoint of Velma Releford' the deceased was making an unlawful assault upon her and she was acting 'in her own self-defense." As stated in . . . (*Hutcherson v. Sovereign Camp, W.O.W.*, 112 Tex. 551, 251 S.W. 491 (1923), the test of whether the killing is accidental within the terms of an insurance policy is not to be determined from the viewpoint of the one who does the killing, but rather from the viewpoint of the insured. If from his viewpoint his conduct was such that he should have anticipated that in all reasonable probability his wife would kill him, his death was not accidental; if from his viewpoint his conduct was not such as to cause him reasonably to believe that she would probably kill him, then his death was accidental. This was the jury question under the facts in this case.

This test (referred to below as the *Hutcherson* test) has been consistently followed in Texas to determine whether death intentionally caused by another is accidental within the meaning of an insurance policy. *Seaboard Life Insurance Co. v. Murphy*, 132 S.W.2d 393 (Tex. 1939).Under the *Hutcherson* test, Bennie Heyward's death might be accidental even though it resulted from injuries intentionally inflicted by another.

Republic contends, however, that the *Hutcherson* test does not apply where the policy covers death "by accidental means" rather than "accidental death." Republic cites numerous Texas cases which distinguish between coverage for accidental death and coverage for death by accidental means; Republic argues that under these authorities, where death results from the actions of another person, the death is not by accidental means unless the actor did not intend to inflict the fatal injuries. We disagree.

First, Republic cites no Texas authority, nor have we found any, for the proposition that injuries are not effected through accidental means merely because the assailant intentionally inflicted them. To the contrary, several Texas courts have applied the Hutcherson test to situations similar to the case at hand under very similar policy provisions. In *Texas Prudential Insurance Co. v. Turner,* 127 S.W.2d 563 (Tex.Civ.App.-Beaumont 1939, writ dism'd), insured died from gunshot wounds received in an affray. Insured's life insurance policy obligated insurer to pay double indemnity if insured's death resulted from bodily injury sustained "solely through external, violent and accidental means." The Court of Civil Appeals, applying the *Hutcherson* test, held that insured's death was not sustained through accidental means because insured, "by his conduct on the occasion in question, provoked the difficulty with Garrett under conditions which would have led a reasonably prudent man to believe that Garrett would shoot him if he continued the assault."

In *Life & Casualty Insurance Co. v. Martinez*, 299 S.W.2d 181 (Tex.Civ.App.-San Antonio 1957, no writ), the insured was shot by a police officer while fleeing from the officer. The court reversed and remanded for a new trial a judgment for the beneficiaries of insured's accident insurance policy, on the ground that the trial court did not apply the correct test to determine whether the insured's death was accidental. The policy in question covered death "from violent, external and accidental means." Citing Releford, supra, the court stated that the determination of whether the death was by accidental means must be determined from the viewpoint of the insured, and that the evidence presented a question of fact "whether insured, from his viewpoint, should have anticipated that in all reasonable probability the policeman would kill him if he did not stop."

Although *Praetorian Mutual Life Insurance Co. v. Humphrys*, 484 S.W.2d 413 (Tex.Civ.App.-Fort Worth 1972, writ ref'd, n.r.e.) has some language to the contrary, we believe that the result in that case is supportable on other grounds. In *Humphrys*, the insured was killed by a burglar when he unexpectedly came upon the burglar in his home. Insured's policy covered death by accidental means, but it also excluded coverage when death resulted from injuries intentionally inflicted by another person. This exclusionary provision, which is not present in Mr. Heyward's policy, clearly excluded Mr. Humphrys' death from coverage.

While the above cases are not controlling, they do indicate that a distinction between "accidental death" and "death by accidental means" has not been recognized where insured has died from injuries intentionally inflicted by another. In both "accidental death" and "accidental means" policies, the test applied has been the *Hutcherson* test: whether, from the viewpoint of the insured, he should have reasonably anticipated that his conduct would probably bring about his own death.

Several other jurisdictions which recognize a distinction between "accidental death" and "death by accidental means" also apply the *Hutcherson* test, or a similar rule, where the insured has died at the hands of another. In fact, the *Hutcherson* test appears to be accepted by almost all jurisdictions to determine whether a homicide was accidental within the meaning of an insurance policy.

More important, however, we believe that a real distinction between the terms "accidental death" or "accidental injury" and "death by accidental means" is no longer recognized in Texas. The purported distinction between these terms originated in *United States Mutual Accident Ass'n v. Barry*, 131 U.S. 100 (1889). The Supreme Court in *Barry* affirmed the trial court's judgment that internal injuries suffered by an insured when he jumped from a platform were injuries "effected through external, violent and accidental means." The Court gave the following definition of "accidental means":

> (I)f a result is such as follows from ordinary means, voluntarily employed, in a not unusual or unexpected way, it cannot be called a result effected by accidental means; but that if, in the act which precedes the injury, something unforeseen, unexpected, unusual, occurs which produces the injury, then the injury has resulted through accidental means. 131 U.S. at 121

Numerous Texas cases, following the reasoning of the Supreme Court in *Barry*, have recognized a distinction between "accidental death" and "death by accidental means." In *Bryant v. Continental Casualty Co.*, 182 S.W. 673 (Tex. 1916), this Court held that death from sunstroke was death by accidental means within the meaning of the insurance policy. Citing *Barry*, we stated, at 182 S.W. 675-676:

> The word "means" is employed in the policy in the sense of "cause"; the phrase, "due to accidental means," is one of qualification; and the purpose of its use in the ordinary accident policy is to limit the liability of the insurer to injuries effected by an accidental cause, as distinguished from those which are merely accidental in their result. . . . In the numerous adjudicated cases upon the subject, therefore, it is determined that whereby the terms of the contract the risk insured against is an injury effected by "accidental means," the element of accident must consist in that which produces the injury, rather than the mere fact that an injury occurs.

This Court again recognized a distinction in International *Travelers' Ass'n v. Francis,* 23 S.W.2d 282, 284-285 (Tex.1930). There we held that death from an infection resulting from the pulling of a wisdom tooth was caused solely and exclusively by "external, violent and accidental means" within the meaning of the policy. This Court there quoted with approval from Cooley's Briefs on Insurance (2d ed.) Vol. 6, p. 5234, as follows:

> Whether or not the means is accidental is determined by the character of its effects. Accidental means are those which produce effects which are not their natural and probable consequences. The natural consequence of means used is the consequence which ordinarily follows from its use — the result which may be reasonably anticipated from its use, and which ought to be expected. The probable consequence of the use of a given means is the consequence which is more likely to follow from its use than it is to fail to follow. An effect which is the natural and probable consequence of an act or course of action is not an accident, nor is it produced by accidental means. It is either the result of actual design, or it falls under the maxim that every man must be held to intend the natural and probable consequence of his deeds. On the other hand, an effect which is not the natural or probable consequence of the means which produced it, an effect which does not ordinarily follow and cannot be reasonably anticipated from the use of such means, an effect which the actor did not intend to produce and which he cannot be charged with the design of producing, is produced by accidental means. It is produced by means which was neither designed nor calculated to cause it. Such an effect is not the result of design, cannot be reasonably anticipated, is unexpected, and is produced by an unusual combination of fortuitous circumstances; in other words, it is produced by accidental means.

Another leading Texas case is *Hanna v. Rio Grande National Life Ins. Co.*, 181 S.W.2d 908 (Tex. Civ.App.-Dallas 1944, writ ref'd). In *Hanna*, insured died from an overdose of sulfanilamide. Insured's policy provided for payment of double indemnity in event of death from bodily injury sustained solely through external, violent and accidental means. In her suit the beneficiary alleged that the overdose of the drug was by mistake, and alternatively that because of unknown elements in both the drug and the system of the insured, a fatal reaction to the drug ensued, causing insured's death. The trial court granted defendant's motion for judgment on the pleading, holding as a matter of law that the petition did not state a cause of action. The Court of Civil Appeals reversed and remanded for trial. The court recognized that:

> Many jurisdictions hold that if the means which cause an injury are voluntarily employed in the usual and intended way, the resulting injury, even though it be entirely unusual, unexpected and unforeseen, is not produced by accidental means; in short, that the means, as well as the result, must be accidental; (citations omitted). Other State authorities, however, apply to the term an interpretation of somewhat broader scope. It is stated in 1 C.J., p. 427, viz.: "Where the effect is not the natural and probable consequence of the means which produce it — an effect which does not ordinarily follow and cannot be reasonably anticipated from the use of the means, or an effect which the actor did not intend to produce, and which he cannot be charged with a design of producing — it is produced by accidental means."At least since *International Travelers' Ass'n v. Francis*, 119 Tex. 1, 23 S.W.2d 282, 284, our Supreme Court has been committed to the latter or more liberal rule."

This test has become the accepted test in Texas for determining whether an injury or death resulted from accidental means.

* * *

The attempted distinction between accidental results and accidental means will plunge this branch of the law into a Serbonian Bog. 'Probably it is true to say that in the strictest sense and dealing with the region of physical nature there is no such thing as an accident.' (Citations omitted) On the other hand, the average man is convinced that there is, and so certainly is the man who takes out a policy of accident insurance. It is his reading of the policy that is to be accepted as our guide, with the help of the established rule that ambiguities and uncertainties are to be resolved against the company. The proposed distinction will not survive the application of that test.

Texas courts have waded through Justice Cardozo's Serbonian bog, and we are now convinced that the terms "accidental death" and "death by accidental means," as those terms are used in insurance policies, must be regarded as legally synonymous unless there is a definition in the insurance contract itself which requires a different construction. These terms in an insurance contract should be given their ordinary and popular meaning according to the understanding of the average man; the court's guide should not be the technical meaning of the words used, but rather the intention of the parties as inferred from the contract as a whole.

A fine distinction between means and results would never occur to an average policyholder, and the insurer should not be able to escape liability by resort to such a technical definition. If the insurer wishes to distinguish between accidental results and injuries caused by accidental means, he should do so expressly, so as to give the policyholder clear notice of any limitations of liability which the insurer wishes to impose by use of the latter term. We therefore hold that injuries are "accidental" and within the coverage of an insurance policy — whether the policy speaks in terms of "accidental injuries" or "injuries effected through accidental means" — if, from the viewpoint of the insured, the injuries are not the natural and probable consequence of the action or occurrence which produced the injury; or in other words, if the injury could not reasonably be anticipated by insured, or would not ordinarily follow from the action or occurrence which caused the injury.

Applying this rule to the facts of the present case, it necessarily follows that, where an insured's injuries are caused by the intentional acts of another, the injuries are nevertheless accidental within the terms of an insurance policy covering death by "accidental means" if from the insured's viewpoint his conduct was not such as to cause him to reasonably believe that it would result in his injury. We believe that a person insured against injury effected through accidental means would consider himself insured against such a casualty, since the very purpose of such insurance is to provide indemnity against any fortuitous, unexpected, or undersigned injury. If a policyholder is struck by a car, can it be reasonably said that the means of injury are any less accidental, as regards the purpose of his accident policy, because the driver of the vehicle intended to injure him? We think not. In either case the purpose of the policy is the same — to insure against such an unexpected and unusual occurrence.

II.

* * *

The burden of proof was upon plaintiff to prove that insured died from injuries "effected solely through external, violent and accidental means" in order to recover under the policy. *International Travelers' Ass'n v. Marshall,* 114 S.W.2d 851 (Tex.1938). Plaintiff contends that her evidence showing death by violent and external means raises a presumption that death was by accidental means, and that this presumption raises an issue of fact whether the death was accidental, at least until defendant introduces evidence to the contrary. Republic does not deny that plaintiff has produced some evidence that insured's death was by violent and external means, but Republic does deny that this evidence raises a fact issue as to whether insured's death was accidental.

We have held that evidence of death by violent and external means raises a presumption that insured did not commit suicide. *Combined American Insurance Co. v. Blanton,* 163 Tex. 225, 353 S.W.2d 847 (1962). This presumption does not constitute evidence in itself or shift the burden of proof; it merely raises an issue of fact as to whether insured's death was not by his own hand. The presumption "disappears" when evidence to the contrary is introduced. *Prudential Insurance Co. of America v. Krayer,* 366 S.W.2d 779 (Tex.1963)

A presumption of accidental death from evidence of death by violent and external means has been recognized by some Texas courts — even where the evidence conclusively showed that the cause of death was not suicide.

* * *

[There is no evidence in the case before us that insured provoked his assailant or that he was the aggressor in the incident which resulted in his death. Unless some evidence to the contrary is produced, we think it is reasonable to presume that insured did not act in such a way that he should have reasonably known his actions would probably result in his death. The law assumes that one's natural instinct is to avoid injury and preserve his own life. We therefore hold that plaintiff's evidence raised an issue of fact whether insured's death was accidental. * * *

The judgment of the Court of Civil Appeals is affirmed.

NOTES & QUESTIONS

1) "Accidental injuries" and "injuries effected through accidental means"—Are these terms that a jury could easily understand?

2) The court in *Heyward* insisted that "[a] fine distinction between *means* and *results* would never occur to an average policyholder." Is this true? Would the average beneficiary or juror appreciate the fine distinction between *cause* and *effect*?

3) Why would a double-indemnity insurer require a beneficiary to prove that the deceased insured lost his life "solely through external, violent and accidental means"?

4) Again, to collect double-indemnity proceeds, the beneficiary must prove that the insured died from injuries "effected solely through external, violent and accidental means." How would a beneficiary overcome this legal burden?

Chapter Eleven: Third-Party Insurance Contracts

Once more, given the incredible amount of confusion among many jurists as well as consumers, it is important to restate the differences between third-party liability insurance and first-party property insurance. In *Warrilow v. Norrell,* 791 S.W.2d 515, 527-528 (Tex.App.-Corpus Christi, 1989), the Court of Appeals presents an excellent synopsis:

The Distinction Between Liability and Property Insurance

> Warrilow fails to differentiate between property loss coverage under a first-party insurance policy, typically an all-risk homeowner's policy, and tort liability coverage under a third-party insurance policy. . . . This distinction is critical. . . . Property insurance, unlike liability insurance, is unconcerned with establishing negligence or otherwise assessing tort liability. Coverage in a property policy is commonly provided by reference to causation, such as "loss caused by ..." certain enumerated forces. It is precisely these physical forces that bring about the loss.
>
> * * *
>
> Conversely, in the third-party liability insurance context, the right to coverage is established by traditional tort concepts of fault, proximate cause, and duty. By insuring for personal liability and agreeing to cover the insured for his own negligence, the insurer agrees to cover the insured for a broader spectrum of risks. Thus, the focus is on the insured's legal obligation to pay for an injury or damage arising out of a certain occurrence, and coverage should extend to an insured risk, negligence, which constitutes a concurrent proximate cause of the injury. By finding coverage for an injury resulting from the insured's negligence, the reasonable expectations of the parties to the insurance contract are not frustrated.

There is more. Both liability and indemnity insurance contracts are called third-party insurance. However, insurers' contractual rights and obligations under liability and indemnity contracts are quite different. Typically, liability insurance agreements contain right-to-settle and duty-to-defend clauses. The former requires an insurer to make a good faith effort to settle a third-party claim, and the latter requires a liability insurer to provide an adequate legal defense if a third-party victim sues the insured.

On the other hand, indemnity insurance contracts have a duty-to-pay, a duty-to-indemnify or a duty-to-reimburse clause. Quite simply, under these insurance agreements, a liability insurer promises to pay various amounts of money after the insured settles a lawsuit or the insured pays to defend itself.

Finally, consumers purchase liability insurance for the ultimate benefit of third-party victims or complainants.[1] Actually, in most jurisdictions, states have enacted compulsory liability-insurance statutes, which require automobile owners/drivers to purchase a minimum level of insurance for the benefit of third-party victims. However, there is a large variety of liability insurance. As a consequence, third-party liability contracts are ubiquitous. All sorts of corporations, partnerships, small-to-large businesses, organizations, institutions, homeowners and government entities purchase liability insurance routinely.

Of course, an inordinate amount of litigation occurs each year over whether liability insurers must settle third-party claims, defend insureds against third-party lawsuits or indemnify insureds for the latter's out-of-pocket expenditures. This chapter highlights and presents a discussion of the most salient procedural and substantive issues that appear in these conflicts.

A. *Liability Insurance and Insurer's Duty to Settle Third-Party Claims*

1) Injury to Third-Party Complainants' Persons

G.A. Stowers Furniture Company v. American Indemnity Company
15 S.W.2d 544
(Tex. Com. App. 1929)

This case involves issues that are questions of first impression in this court, and are so important to the jurisprudence of this state that we deem it advisable to make a very full and complete statement of the issues involved.

---

1 *See, e.g., In the Matter of the Estate of Martin Cohen*, No. 1996 WL 264651, at *2 (Del. Ch. 1996) ("A contract of insurance is a third-party beneficiary contract, that is, a contract between the contracting parties for the benefit of a third-party who does not participate in the making of the contract and who assumes no obligations under the contract."); *Southern Guaranty Ins. Co. v. Preferred Risk Mut. Ins. Co.*, 359 S.E.2d 665 (Ga. 1987) (stressing that compulsory liability insurance coverage is required not only for the benefit of the insured, but also to ensure compensation for innocent victims of negligent motorists); *Flattery v. Gregory*, 489 N.E.2d 1257, 1260-61 (Mass. 1986) (holding that injured highway travelers are third-party beneficiaries of automobile liability insurance); *Shingleton v. Bussey*, 223 So. 2d 713, 715 (Fla. 1969) (concluding that a direct cause of action inures to a third-party beneficiary against insurer in motor vehicle liability insurance coverage as matter of public policy); and, *Evans v. Grange Mut. Cas. Co.*, 230 N.E.2d 751, 753 (Ohio 1964) (ruling that a liability insurance policy is actually a contract for the direct benefit of the aggrieved third-party as well as for the protection of the negligent party).

This suit was originally filed by the G. A. Stowers Furniture Company, plaintiff in error, hereinafter styled plaintiff, against American Indemnity Company, defendant in error, hereinafter styled defendant, for $14,103.15, together with interest, and for cause of action the petition states, in substance:

That defendant was a private corporation in the city of Galveston, and was engaged during the years 1919 and 1920 in the business of writing and issuing insurance policies and bonds to indemnify the assured against loss by reason of liability imposed by law upon the assured for injuries on account of bodily injuries, etc., and that the said indemnity company issued to said Stowers Furniture Company a policy of insurance for the sum of $5,000 which proposed to indemnify the said furniture company against loss by reason of injuries accidentally suffered by any person or persons if such loss or damage so sustained was by reason of the said furniture company's ownership of the automobiles described in said policy.

It was further charged that defendant, indemnity company, agreed in said policy, and had reserved the right, to defend any suit in the name and behalf of said named assured for such damage or loss sustained if same was by reason of said plaintiff's ownership.

It was further provided that the furniture company should immediately, in the case of an accident, give notice to defendant, indemnity company, at Galveston and should forward to said indemnity company any summons or other process served upon them, and, when requested by said company, the assured should aid in effecting settlement, etc.

It was further stipulated in said policy that the assured, meaning said furniture company, should not voluntarily assume any liability, settle any claim or expense, except at its own cost, and should not engage in any negotiations of such settlement or legal proceedings without the consent of said insurance company, and the said insurance company reserved the right to settle any and all claims or suits brought against the plaintiff.

It was further alleged that the premiums were all paid on said policy, and the same was valid and subsisting and in full force and effect that said policy had been mislaid, and that proof would be offered of its contents.

It was further charged in said petition that on the 23d day of January, 1920, a truck belonging to said furniture company, and covered by said policy of insurance, which was hauling and delivering furniture and being operated by one of the said furniture company's servants, and was being driven on Austin street in the city of Houston, Tex., at about the hour of 7 p. m., came in contact with a wagon standing on the side of Austin street and was thereby disabled and so crippled that said servant could no longer operate it, and that it was left by the servant of said furniture company, without a light and without any one to watch it, and that shortly thereafter Miss Mamie Bichon, who was an employee in a drug store, left for her home at about 8:30 p. m. and was driven by Jamail in a Ford coupé very rapidly along said street, and came in collision with said truck; that the coupé was turned over, and that she was very seriously injured; and that about the 3d day of March, 1920, the said Miss Bichon brought suit for damages against said Stowers Furniture Company for $20,000.

It was further charged that defendant herein took charge of the defense of said suit for this plaintiff in accordance with the terms of said policy.

It was further charged that defendant herein employed counsel and proceeded to trial in said cause of Miss Bichon against the plaintiff, furniture company, and that, after hearing the evidence and the charge of the court, the jury returned a verdict for Miss Bichon for the sum of $12,207 besides cost; that there was an appeal by the defendant herein from said judgment; that the same was affirmed; and that this plaintiff paid to Miss Bichon the sum of $14,107.15, including interest and costs of court.

It was further charged that during the pendency of this suit, and before the trial, Miss Bichon offered to accept $4,000 in full settlement for the damages due her; that defendant herein refused to pay more than $2,500, although its policy bound it to pay $5,000; that the defendant herein knew that the case which Miss Bichon had against this plaintiff was a very dangerous one, and that she was likely to get a judgment for far more than $5,000, and that a person of ordinary prudence would have settled said cause for said sum of $4,000; that defendant admitted that said offer of settlement was a good one and should be accepted; that it willfully and negligently refused to make such settlement, knowing at the time it did so that it was jeopardizing the interests of this plaintiff in a very large amount; that, in refusing to make such settlement, it did not act in good faith, and it did not act like a prudent person would have done under like circumstances; and that by reason of such conduct of said indemnity company the furniture company had been compelled to pay the said sum of more than $14,000.

The material portion of the defendant's answer as shown in the opinion of the Court of Civil Appeals, is as follows:

> That after the happening of the said accident made the basis of this suit the defendant investigated it, and after suit was filed and after citation was forwarded to it by plaintiff herein, it made defense of said suit and defended it through all the courts. That under the terms and provisions of said contract it was to have control of the defense of said suit and no settlement was to be made without its consent, it having the option of settling or defending the suit as it might deem best, and it was under no duty to settle said suit, and it elected to and did defend the said suit. That after making investigation in reference to said accident and the extent of the injuries suffered by Mamie Bichon, this defendant reached the conclusion that the facts of the accident were of such nature that it could and did reasonably suppose that judgment would ultimately result in a verdict for the defendant, and that the injuries suffered by Mamie Bichon as a result of the accident were not of a permanent nature or of such seriousness as to justify a settlement of this case for $4,000.
>
> * * *
>
> For further and special answer herein, defendant says that by the terms of said contract of indemnity its liability was limited, as hereinbefore alleged, to $5,000, with interest thereon at 6 per cent. from the date of the judgment to the

affirmance thereof. This defendant says that it has already carried out the terms and provisions of said contract except the payment of $5,000 and interest thereon, which immediately upon the affirmance of this case by the Supreme Court was tendered to the plaintiff herein and plaintiff was notified that defendant was ready and willing to pay the same, but was notified by the plaintiff that plaintiff would not release this defendant from liability, which it was entitled to be released from if it complied with its contract, and stated it was useless to tender the actual money because plaintiff would not accept it; that this defendant has always been ready and willing to pay the limit of its liability, to wit, $5,000, with interest at 6 per cent. until plaintiff's notice it would not be accepted, and is now ready and willing to pay the same, which amount next above mentioned represents principal of $5,000 interest thereon to the date of the notification that tender would not be effective, together with court costs, which are also tendered, which notification to the plaintiff and the understanding that a complete release from liability would not be effected was within ten days of the affirmance of said case by the Supreme Court.

The policy mentioned in the petition contains, among others, the following provision:

American Indemnity Company
Home Office
Galveston, Texas

In consideration of the premium of this Policy, as expressed in Statement 5, and of the other statements which are set forth in the Schedule of Statements herein made, and which the Assured warrants to be true by the acceptance of this Policy, and also subject to the conditions of this Policy as hereinafter set forth:

Does hereby agree . . . To indemnify the Assured named and described in Statement 1 of the Schedule of Statements forming part hereof . . . "Against loss by reason of the liability imposed by law upon the Assured for damages on account of bodily injuries, including death at any time resulting therefrom, accidentally suffered or alleged to have been suffered while this Policy is in force by any person or persons except employees of the Assured while engaged in operating, riding in or on, or caring for automobiles covered hereby.

And in addition the company agrees:

(A) To defend in the name and on behalf of the Assured any suits even if groundless, brought against the Assured to recover damages on account of such happenings as are provided for by the terms of the preceding paragraphs.

(B) To pay irrespective of the limits of liability expressed in Condition 8 (Limits) hereof, all costs taxed against the Assured in any legal proceeding defended by the Company, all interest accruing after entry of judgment upon such part thereof as shall not be in excess of said liability and the expense incurred by the Assured for such immediate medical or surgical relief as is imperative at the time of the accident, together with all the expense incurred by the Company growing out of the investigation of such an accident, the adjustment of any claim or the defense of any suit resulting therefrom.

The policy further provides:

> This policy does not cover Injuries and/or Death, or Loss, Damage and/or Expense . . . Assumed by the Assured under any Contract or Agreement, oral or written.

The policy further provides:

> "The Company's Liability is Limited . . . Under Clause One (Liability) regardless of the number of Assured involved, the Company's liability for the loss from an accident resulting in bodily injuries to or in/death of one person is limited to five thousand dollars ($5,000.00), and, subject to the same limit for each person, the Company's total liability for loss from any one accident resulting in bodily injuries to or in the death of more than one person is limited to ten thousand dollars ($10,000.00).

The policy further provides:

> "No action shall lie against the Company to recover for any loss, Damage and/or Expense, under this Policy, unless it shall be brought by the Assured for Loss, Damage and/or Expense actually sustained and paid by him in money in satisfaction of a judgment after trial of the issue, and no such action shall lie to recover under any other agreement of the Company herein contained unless brought by the Assured himself to recover money actually expended by him. In no event shall any such action lie unless brought within ninety days after the right of action accrues, as herein provided.
>
> The Assured shall upon the occurrence of an accident give immediate written notice thereof to the Company's Home Office, at Galveston, Texas, or its Agent duly authorized by law to receive the same, with the fullest information obtainable. He shall give like notice with full particulars of any claim made on account of such accident. If, thereafter, any suit is brought against the Assured he shall immediately forward to the Company, every summons or other process served upon him. The Assured, when requested by the Company, shall aid in effecting settlements, securing evidence, the attendance of witnesses and in prosecuting appeals. The Assured shall not voluntarily assume any liability, settle any claim or incur any expense, except at his own cost, or interfere in any negotiation for settlement or legal proceeding without the consent of the Company previously given in writing. The Company reserves the right to settle any such claim or suit brought against the Assured."

At the close of the testimony in the district court, the trial court withdrew the case from the jury, and entered judgment for the defendant. This judgment was, on appeal, affirmed by the Court of Civil Appeals.

The case is now before this court on writ of error granted on application of the plaintiff.

We are of the opinion that the plaintiff's petition states a cause of action against the defendant for the amount sued for, and that the evidence in the case raised an issue of fact to be submitted to the jury by the trial court under proper instructions.

The Court of Civil Appeals, in passing on the issues of this case holds: "We do not think the indemnity company was, by the terms of the policy, under any obligation to do more than faithfully defend the suit. As before stated, it had not agreed to settle the suit, but had reserved the right to do so. It had the unquestioned right to defend the suit to the end that it might not be called upon to pay a judgment which might be rendered in favor of Miss Bichon."

As stated in the beginning, the matters involved in this litigation are of first impression in this state, and the holding of the Court of Civil Appeals is in the main supported by the authorities cited by that court.

We, however, are of the opinion that the Court of Civil Appeals was in error in the above holding, and that the better and sounder authorities, and those more in harmony with the spirit of our laws, support a contrary rule. *Douglas v. United States Fidelity & Guaranty Co.,* 81 N. H. 371 (1924)

As shown by the above-quoted provisions of the policy, the indemnity company had the right to take complete and exclusive control of the suit against the assured, and the assured was absolutely prohibited from making any settlement, except at his own expense, or to interfere in any negotiations for settlement or legal proceeding without the consent of the company; the company reserved the right to settle any such claim or suit brought against the assured. Certainly, where an insurance company makes such a contract; it, by the very terms of the contract, assumed the responsibility to act as the exclusive and absolute agent of the assured in all matters pertaining to the questions in litigation, and, as such agent, it ought to be held to that degree of care and diligence which an ordinarily prudent person would exercise in the management of his own business; and if an ordinarily prudent person, in the exercise of ordinary care, as viewed from the standpoint of the assured, would have settled the case, and failed or refused to do so, then the agent, which in this case is the indemnity company, should respond in damages.

It is true that the policy is for $5,000, so far as this accident is concerned, but when the liability arose against plaintiff the indemnity company was in duty bound to exercise ordinary care to protect the interest of the assured up to the amount of the policy, for the reason that it had contracted to act as his agent, and assumed full and absolute control over the litigation arising out of the accident covered by the policy. The provisions of the policy giving the indemnity company absolute and complete control of the litigation, as a matter of law, carried with it a corresponding duty and obligation, on the part of the indemnity company, to exercise that degree of care that a person of ordinary care and prudence would exercise under the same or similar circumstances, and a failure to exercise such care and prudence would be negligence on the part of the indemnity company.

It is the duty of the court to give effect to all the provisions of the policy, and it would certainly be a very harsh rule to say that the indemnity company, in a case such as this, owed no duty whatever to the insured further than the face of the policy, regardless of whether it was negligent in discharging its duties as the sole and exclusive agent of the assured, in full and complete control. Such exclusive authority to act in a case of this kind does not necessarily carry with it the right to act arbitrarily.

In the *Douglas Case, supra*, the Supreme Court of New Hampshire lays down the law, which we think applies to the issues of the case at bar, as follows:

> The fundamental question is, Does or does not the insurer owe to the insured a duty in the matter of a settlement? If it does not owe such a duty, it is not liable either for a failure to act or for the manner of action. It may refrain from completing a settlement for any reason, however essentially dishonest, and still there would be no liability. If, as the cases roundly state, it has an exclusive and absolute option, no one can question its motives for the exercise or nonexercise of the privilege. No case has gone that far. All acknowledge a liability for fraudulent conduct, or lack of good faith, in refusing to settle. But they are silent as to any reasoning which would sustain such liability and at the same time deny responsibility for negligent conduct.
>
> The whole question of insurance against loss may be laid out of the case, and still the defendant would be accountable for negligence. It has contracted to take charge of the defense of this claim. That contract created a relation out of which grew the duty to use care when action was taken. The insurer entered upon the conduct of the affair in question. It had and exercised authority over the matter in every respect, even to negotiating for a settlement. It is difficult to see upon what ground it could escape responsibility when its negligence resulted in damage to the party it had contracted to serve
>
> Denial of agency upon the part of the insurer is put upon the ground that, if there were such a relation the insurer would be bound to consider the interests of the insured, when in conflict with its own. It is then said that, when there is such conflict, the insurer may consult its own interests solely. Therefore, it is concluded, there can be no agency.
>
> This reasoning seems to imply that one party cannot be the agent of the other party. But the law is plainly otherwise. The parties may make that sort of an agreement if they see fit. The result of such a compact is not to leave the promissor free to act as though he had made no promise. On the contrary, his conduct will be subject to closer scrutiny than that of the ordinary agent, because of his adverse interest. The fact that here the insurer stood to lose but a part of the claim, and that as to

> the balance of the chances of loss growing out of mismanagement of the defense were upon the insured, is an added reason for holding the defendant to the use of reasonable care in the exercise of its exclusive control over the negotiations. Where one acts as agent under such circumstances, he is bound to give the rights of his principal at least as great consideration as he does his own. The insurer cannot betray the trust it has undertaken nor be relieved from the usual rule that in such a case an agent must serve as he has promised to serve.

* * *

In our opinion the other authorities above cited sustain the rule announced by us, and, while there are authorities holding the contrary rule, we are constrained to believe that the correct rule under the provisions of this policy is that the indemnity company is held to that degree of care and diligence which a man of ordinary care and prudence would exercise in the management of his own business.

The Court of Civil Appeals holds that the trial court did not err in refusing to permit Miss Bichon and others, all witnesses for plaintiff, to testify as to the serious nature of her injuries. We think this holding is error. Further, we are of the opinion that the serious nature of Miss Bichon's injuries and all the facts and circumstances surrounding her injury, are material as bearing on the question of negligence on the part of the indemnity company in failing and refusing to make the settlement.

Of course knowledge on the part of the indemnity company is also an issue. The facts and circumstances surrounding the original injury, and the extent of same, would not raise the issue of negligence on the part of the indemnity company unless it had knowledge thereof, or by the exercise of ordinary care could have had such knowledge.

We think, further, that the testimony offered by plaintiff, to the effect that it was a rule of the indemnity company never to make a settlement for more than one-half the amount of the policy, should have been admitted as bearing on the issue of negligence on the part of the indemnity company.

What we have said disposes of all the assignments.

We recommend that the judgments of the Court of Civil Appeals and of the district court be both reversed and the cause remanded to the district court for a new trial.

NOTES & QUESTIONS

1) Necessarily, when deciding to settle a third-party claim, an insurer will consider its own interest, investors' interests and the insured's interest. Whose interest is paramount?

2) In *Stowers*, the court observed that the insurer "had not agreed to settle the suit, but had reserved the right to do so." What is a reservation of right? Under Texas law, will a liability insurer be "penalized" for failing to send reservation-of-rights letters to its insureds?

3) Does a liability insurer have a contractual duty to settle third-party claims and lawsuits?

4) In *Stowers*, the Texas Supreme Court stated that the insurer must "make a good faith effort to settle a third-party claim." What is the source of that duty?

Arnold v. National County Mutual Fire Insurance Company
725 S.W.2d 165
(Tex. 1987)

Glen Arnold appeals from a summary judgment granted defendant National County Mutual Insurance Company. The court of appeals, in an unpublished opinion, affirmed the trial court's judgment on the grounds that Arnold's common law and statutory causes of action, if valid, were barred by limitations. We reverse that part of the judgment denying the common law cause of action and remand the cause to the trial court.

This is a suit on an insurance contract. In June 1974, Arnold was severely injured when the motorcycle he was operating was struck by a car driven by an uninsured motorist. Arnold was insured by NCM under a policy that included "uninsured motorist" protection with a limit of $10,000. Arnold made timely demand for payments up to the limit and an independent insurance adjusting firm recommended, within six months following the date of the accident, that NCM pay the entire policy limit to Arnold. NCM refused to pay although it is not clear when it specifically denied the claim.

Arnold sued both the uninsured motorist and the insurance company in late June 1974. In December 1977, Arnold obtained a judgment against both defendants for approximately $17,975. NCM then paid Arnold the $10,000 policy limit. Arnold filed this suit on December 27, 1978, alleging various statutory causes of action and a common law cause of action for NCM's breach of its duty of good faith and fair dealing in its handling of his claim. The trial court granted summary judgment in favor of NCM on all of Arnold's causes of action.

Summary judgment evidence shows that NCM based its decision to deny the claim on the advice of its agent, who was the attorney handling the file. Even though the uninsured motorist admitted that the collision was his fault, NCM refused to negotiate a settlement. In his deposition the attorney handling the file admitted that he was inexperienced in insurance matters and based his recommendation on his perception that a jury would be prejudiced against motorcyclists, that Arnold was driving too fast under the existing conditions and that Arnold was intoxicated. The summary judgment evidence relied on by Arnold also showed that the defenses of speed and intoxication proffered by the attorney were very weak at best and ultimately intoxication was not pleaded. NCM failed to investigate the facts supporting the attorney's contentions. An issue of fact was raised as to NCM's reasonableness in failing to settle the claim and forcing Arnold to trial.

In order to decide if the court of appeals erred in upholding the summary judgment on limitations grounds, we must first resolve those points of error directed to the underlying causes of action.

Statutory Causes of Action

The court of appeals did not err in upholding the trial court's rendition of summary judgment on Arnold's causes of action under the Deceptive Trade Practices Act (DTPA) and articles 21.21 and 21.21-2 of the Texas Insurance Code. His causes of action under the Texas Insurance Code, both independently and as pleaded through the DTPA, are barred by article 17.22 of the Texas Insurance Code which exempted county mutual insurance companies from articles 21.21 and 21.21-2 at the time this suit was brought. *Jewell v. Mobile County Mutual Insurance Company,* 566 S.W.2d 295 (Tex.1978)

Arnold also pleaded that NCM violated § 17.46(a) and (b)(5) and (12) of the DTPA "by representing that the policy would pay uninsured motorist benefits when certain prerequisites were fulfilled and when, in fact, no payment of those benefits was made after complete compliance by Plaintiff of the prerequisites until judgment after jury verdict." Arnold did not plead and there is no summary judgment evidence that NCM made any misrepresentations. Even if Arnold had stated a cause of action for misrepresentation, it was barred by limitations.

Common Law Cause of Action — Duty of Good Faith And Fair Dealing

Arnold raises the issue of whether there is a duty on the part of insurers to deal fairly and in good faith with their insureds. We hold that such a duty of good faith and fair dealing exists.

While this court has declined to impose an implied *covenant* of good faith and fair dealing in every contract, we have recognized that a duty of good faith and fair dealing may arise as a result of a special relationship between the parties governed or created by a contract. *Manges v. Guerra,* 673 S.W.2d 180, 183 (Tex.1984); *See, English v. Fischer,* 660 S.W.2d 521, 524 (Tex.1983) (Spears, J., concurring).

In the insurance context a special relationship arises out of the parties' unequal bargaining power and the nature of insurance contracts which would allow unscrupulous insurers to take advantage of their insureds' misfortunes in bargaining for settlement or resolution of claims. In addition, without such a cause of action insurers can arbitrarily deny coverage and delay payment of a claim with no more penalty than interest on the amount owed. An insurance company has exclusive control over the evaluation, processing and denial of claims. For these reasons a duty is imposed that "[An] indemnity company is held to that degree of care and diligence which a man of ordinary care and prudence would exercise in the management of his own business." *G.A. Stowers Furniture Company v. American Indemnity Company,* 15 S.W.2d 544, 548 (Tex. Comm'n App.1929, holding approved).

A cause of action for breach of the duty of good faith and fair dealing is stated when it is alleged that there is no reasonable basis for denial of a claim or delay in payment or a failure on the part of the insurer to determine whether there is any reasonable basis for the denial or delay. Arnold pleaded and produced sufficient summary judgment proof to raise an issue of material fact that NCM had no reasonable basis for its refusal to pay his uninsured motorist claim and with actual knowledge of that, forced him to a trial on the accident before it would pay the claim.

Exemplary Damages

Arnold further complains that the trial court erred in granting summary judgment by ruling that he was not entitled to recover exemplary damages and mental anguish damages. It is clear from the record that the summary judgment does not specifically address the issue of damages and, of course, in the absence of a viable cause of action there would not be a damage recovery. However, we would point out that exemplary damages and mental anguish damages are recoverable for a breach of the duty of good faith and fair dealing under the same principles allowing recovery of those damages in other tort actions. *See, e.g., Trenholm v. Ratcliff,* 646 S.W.2d 927 (Tex.1983) and authorities cited therein; *Clements v. Withers,* 437 S.W.2d 818 (Tex.1969); *Ware v. Paxton,* 359 S.W.2d 897 (Tex.1962); *Bennett v. Howard,* 141 Tex. 101, 170 S.W.2d 709 (1943).

* * *

The judgment of the court of appeals denying Arnold's statutory causes of action is affirmed. We reverse that part of the judgment denying the common law cause of action and remand the cause to the trial court for further proceedings consistent with this opinion.

NOTES & QUESTIONS

1) Assume an insurer has an absolute right to settle a third-party claim. Must an insured always secure the insurer's consent before the insured settles or attempts to settle a claim?

2) What are the legal consequences of an insured's settling a third-party claim or lawsuit without securing the insurer's consent?

3) If an insured settles a claim without the insurer's consent, does the insured have a contractual or statutory duty to protect the insurance company's interest during the settlement negotiations with the third-party victim?

Ford v. State Farm Mutual Automobile Insurance Company
550 S.W.2d 663
(Tex. 1977)

This is a suit to recover under the uninsured motorist provisions of a Texas standard automobile policy issued by State Farm Mutual Automobile Insurance Company. The principal question is whether State Farm's unconditional denial of liability constituted a waiver of its right to consent before its insured subsequently settled with another insurance carrier.

The trial court, hearing the case without a jury, rendered judgment for the insured. The Court of Civil Appeals reversed and rendered. We reverse the judgment of the Court of Civil Appeals and affirm that of the trial court.

On October 18, 1969, Mrs. Joan Elizabeth Ford was a passenger in an automobile driven by Mrs. Shirley Harvey when the Harvey automobile was in a collision with a vehicle driven by Jeffrey Whitten. The collision resulted in Joan Ford's death and damages in excess of $20,000. Mrs. Ford was survived by her husband, Robert W. Ford, Jr., and their three children. Jeffrey Whitten, whose negligence caused the collision, was an uninsured motorist.

At the time of the collision, the Harvey automobile was covered by a policy of automobile liability insurance issued by Gulf Insurance Company, with a standard, uninsured motorist clause coverage of bodily injury limits for one person in the amount of $10,000. At the same time, Ford also had an automobile liability policy with State Farm containing the same standard uninsured motorist coverage.

On July 21, 1970, suit was filed by Robert W. Ford, Jr., individually and as guardian of his three minor children, against State Farm and Gulf Insurance for recovery under the uninsured motorist provisions of each policy, in the total sum of $20,000. Plaintiffs plead the existence and coverage of both policies. Separate answers were filed for State Farm and Gulf by different members of the same law firm. Gulf had indicated a willingness to settle for the $10,000 limit of its policy. Before consummation, the parents of Mrs. Ford filed a conflicting claim, and Gulf interpleaded them in its answer of July 29, 1970.

On October 23, 1970, State Farm filed its original answer generally denying any liability. Thereafter, on April 16, 1971, plaintiff amended his petition to claim a total of $30,000 against the two insurance companies. On April 20, 1971, State Farm filed its first amended answer with pleas in bar "to Plaintiff's action in its entirety." One of these pleas alleged that plaintiff's action was barred by the policy's "OTHER INSURANCE" clause inasmuch as Mrs. Ford was riding in a car which was covered by the uninsured motorist provisions of a Gulf Insurance Company policy. It alleged that the Gulf policy was applicable and available to plaintiff, and that State Farm was in no event liable to pay anything under its policy.

In the meantime, on June 29, 1971, an interlocutory judgment was entered dismissing the interpleader suit against Mrs. Ford's parents and in favor of plaintiff against Gulf for its policy limit in the amount of $10,000, without prejudice to plaintiff's cause of action against the remaining defendant, State Farm. Contemporaneously, plaintiff and Gulf entered a release-trust agreement by which Gulf, and only Gulf, was released from claims growing out of the accident and authorizing Gulf, at its sole expense, to proceed in the name of plaintiff against the person or organization responsible for the operation of the uninsured automobile at the time of the accident.

This agreement contained the usual subrogation and trust provisions authorized by Article 5.06-1(3) of the Texas Insurance Code, which reads in part as follows:

> In the event of payment to any person under the coverage required by this Section and subject to the terms and conditions of such coverage, the insurer making such payment shall, to the extent thereof, be entitled to the proceeds of any settlement or judgment resulting from the exercise of any rights of recovery of such person against any person or organization legally responsible for the bodily injury, sickness or disease, or death for which such payment is made, ...

The remaining cause as to State Farm was severed on July 26, 1971, and on November 9, 1972, State Farm filed its second amended answer in which it set up as an additional defense the allegation that plaintiff's claim was barred because of the settlement with Gulf Insurance without the written consent of State Farm. It specifically plead an exclusionary clause in its policy relating to Part IV (the uninsured motorist provisions), which reads as follows:

> Exclusions. This policy does not apply under Part IV . . . to bodily injury to an insured with respect to which such insured, his legal representative or any person entitled to payment under this coverage shall, without written consent of the company, make any settlement with any person or organization who may be legally liable therefor.

It was stipulated that State Farm "had denied liability to the plaintiffs as evidenced by, among other things, the Original Answer . . . and had refused to pay any money damages prior to the entering of the interlocutory judgment made between Robert William Ford, Jr., and Gulf Insurance Company . . . ." It was also stipulated that prior to the settlement with Gulf, "Plaintiffs or their representatives made no request or demand" upon State Farm to consent to the settlement.

Robert W. Ford, Jr., died on November 19, 1973. His mother, Mrs. Margaret Ford, was substituted as plaintiff in the capacity as guardian of Ford's three minor children. The trial court heard evidence and stipulations on October 14, 1974, received briefs, and kept the case under consideration until July 29, 1975. On that date it rendered judgment that plaintiff recover against State Farm the sum of $10,000 on behalf of the children.

* * *

We granted this writ on petitioner's (plaintiff's) point which alleged error of the Court of Civil Appeals in failing to sustain the waiver counterpoint.

Plaintiff-petitioner also asserts that the exclusionary provision of the policy is wholly invalid because it deprives the insured of the statutory protection of Article 5.06-1 of the Insurance

Code. Although there is a trend in other jurisdictions toward narrow construction or voiding such clauses as unreasonable restrictions on mandatory uninsured motorist coverage, Texas courts have consistently upheld the validity of the provision as a means of protecting the insurer's subrogation rights against the uninsured motorist or any other person legally responsible for the insured's injuries.

The question of whether the insurer waives the consent provision by prior unconditional denial of liability is one of first impression for Texas courts. . . .Those jurisdictions which have examined the issue agree that such denial of liability prior to the insured's settlement with a third party constitutes a waiver of the consent clause.

* * *

[T]he cases cited above are in accord with principles of Texas contract law. State Farm's contract was to pay up to its policy limits "all sums which the insured or his legal representative shall be legally entitled to recover as damages from the owner or operator of an uninsured automobile because of bodily injury . . . including death . . . caused by accident and arising out of the . . . use of such uninsured automobile . . . ." Awaiting payment, the policy provides how State Farm may determine by agreement, arbitration, or judicial process any issues affecting the claimant's entitlement to payment.

State Farm neither paid nor pursued any of its affirmative steps for determination of what, if anything, it was due to pay plaintiff. Instead, it unconditionally denied all liability under the policy. This intentional conduct was inconsistent with claiming the right under the policy to consent before its insured settled with a third party. Such conduct constituted a waiver of that right. "Waiver has been frequently defined as an intentional relinquishment of a known right or intentional conduct inconsistent with claiming it." *Massachusetts Bonding & Ins. Co. v. Orkin Exterminating Co.,* 416 S.W.2d 396, 401 (Tex.1967); *Womack v. Allstate Insurance Company*, 296 S.W.2d 233, 236 (Tex. 1956); *Niagara Ins. Co. v. Lee*, 11 S.W. 1024 (Tex 1889

If State Farm had been correct in unconditionally denying coverage and liability, it would have lost nothing by plaintiff's settlement with Gulf. Since State Farm was incorrect in its denial, it has lost only the inconsistent right to assert the exclusionary consent clause as a grounds for forfeiture of plaintiff's entire coverage. It has not lost its right of subrogation. See Art. 5.06-1(3), Texas Insurance Code. When it pays the amount adjudged to plaintiff by the trial court, State Farm will still have its right to institute proceedings in the name of plaintiff against the uninsured motorist or any other person responsible for the accident. It is true that State Farm will have to share subrogation rights with Gulf Insurance which may, by reason of the earlier settlement, have a call on the first $10,000 recovered by plaintiff from any person responsible for the accident. The relative status of the subrogation rights of the two companies, as between themselves, is a question which is not now before us, and we express no opinion thereon.

The judgment of the Court of Civil Appeals is reversed and the judgment of the trial court is affirmed.

NOTES & QUESTIONS

1) Assume that a liability insurer must negotiate and settle a third-party claim in good faith. Who represents the insured's interest in those negotiations? Must an insurer hire an attorney to represent the insurance company's interest and hire a different attorney to represent the insured's interests?

2) During settlement negotiations, are the insurer's and insured's interests identical?

3) What must an insurer do to satisfy its burden to settle third-party claims and lawsuits in good faith?

Ranger County Mutual Insurance Company v. Guin
723 S.W.2d 656
(Tex. 1987)

This case concerns the liability of an insurance company for negligence in the handling of a claim against its insured. Pursuant to a jury verdict the trial court rendered judgment for the plaintiff insureds. The insurer appealed and the court of appeals affirmed the judgment of the trial court. We affirm the judgment of the court of appeals.

Billy Wayne Peden, as owner of a dump truck, was the named insured under an insurance policy issued by Ranger County Mutual Insurance Company. The policy limits were \$10,000/\$20,000/\$10,000. John Wesley Guin, as an independent contractor, operated the truck to haul for various entities including Peden's employer, Texas Bitulithic Company. Guin, while hauling sand for G. & G. Construction Company, was involved in a collision with a truck owned by Eagle Trucking Company and operated by Robert Fitch. The Peden truck struck the Eagle truck broadside causing Fitch to incur serious injuries including a broken neck and a broken leg. Guin was also injured in the collision. Property damage to the Eagle truck and resulting consequential damages were in excess of \$37,000.

Peden and Guin filed suit against Fitch and Eagle Trucking Company for property damage to Peden's truck and personal injury damage incurred by Guin. Fitch and Eagle Trucking Company cross-claimed for personal injury damages to Fitch and property damages to Eagle's truck. Fitch and Eagle later included Texas Bitulithic Company and G. & G. Construction Company as third-party defendants.

The jury found Guin's negligence to be 100% of the cause of the collision. They assessed actual damages to Fitch in the amount of \$216,232.25 and property damages to Eagle in the amount of \$47,000.

Claiming that Ranger could have settled this claim within the policy limits, Peden and Guin subsequently brought this suit against Ranger under the "Stowers Doctrine." Based upon a jury verdict, the trial court rendered a judgment of $175,000 actual damages and $50,000 punitive damages for Peden and a like amount for Guin, for a total judgment of $450,000.

The dispositive issues before us are: 1) whether the basis for a "*Stowers* Doctrine" suit is limited to the insurer's refusal to settle in response to an unconditional offer to settle all claims against the insured within the policy limits and 2) whether there was legally sufficient evidence to support the jury verdict. The trial court submitted the case to the jury based upon the following Special Issue:

> Special Issue No. 1
>
> Do you find from a preponderance of the evidence that the Defendant, Ranger County Mutual Insurance Company, was negligent in the manner in which it handled the claim and lawsuit asserted against its insureds, Billy Wayne Peden and John Wesley Guin? Answer: "We do" or "We do not."
>
> Answer: "We do."
>
> "Negligence" as used in this special issue means the failure to exercise that degree of care and diligence which an ordinarily prudent person would exercise in the management of his own business. If an ordinarily prudent person in the exercise of ordinary care, as viewed from the standpoint of the insured, would have settled the case, but the defendant failed or refused to do so, then the defendant is negligent. The duty to settle implies the duty to negotiate.
>
> You are instructed that the Defendant, Ranger County Mutual Insurance Company, by the nature of its insurance contract with its insureds, Billy Wayne Peden and John Wesley Guin, assumed the responsibility to act as the exclusive and absolute agent of the insured in all matters pertaining to the questions in litigation and, as such agent, the Defendant is held to that degree of care and diligence which an ordinary prudent person would exercise in the management of his own business.
>
> You are further instructed that when an insurance company hires an attorney, pursuant to an insurance contract, to represent an insured in litigation, then that attorney is deemed, under the law, to be the sub-agent of the insurance company. As such, the insurance company is as responsible to the insured for the conduct of the sub-agent with reference to the litigation as the insurance company is for its own conduct. Therefore, the insurance company is liable to the insured for damages caused to the insured, if any, by the negligence, if any, of the sub-agent in conducting the affairs of the insured with reference to the litigation.
>
> Where an insurance company acts as the agent of its insureds in the defense of a claim for monetary damages, it is bound under the law to give the rights of its insureds at least as great consideration as it does its own.

> You are further instructed that under the law of Texas, an insurance carrier is required to exercise ordinary care in considering whether an offer of settlement should be accepted and whether it should offer the liability limits of its insurance policy but it is not necessarily a failure to exercise ordinary care merely because its decision proves to be wrong by reason of a jury verdict; in other words, the duty to exercise ordinary care leaves room for an error in judgment, without negligence necessarily resulting therefrom.

Ranger, in multiple points of error, contends that a "*Stowers* Doctrine" case can be based only upon an insurer's failure to settle a claim against the insured when the claimant offers to settle within the policy limits and fully release the insured from all liability. As authority for this position, Ranger relies on *G.A. Stowers Furniture Co. v. American Indemnity Co.,* 15 S.W.2d 544 (Tex. Comm'n App.1929, holding approved). Peden and Guin also rely on *Stowers* as authority for their contention that an insurer is liable to the insured for negligent handling of the claim.

The insurance policy in *Stowers* contained provisions very similar to the Ranger policy in this case. It gave the insurer the right to take complete and exclusive control of the investigation, negotiation and defense of the claim. The policy limited the insurer's duty to a defense of the insured and payment of any judgment up to the policy limits.

We held in *Stowers* that an insurer which, under the terms of its policy, assumes control of a claim, investigates the claim and hires an attorney to defend the insured, becomes the agent of the insured and the attorney becomes the sub-agent of the insured. We further held in *Stowers* that an insurer is held to that degree of care and diligence which an ordinary prudent person would exercise in the management of his own business. If an insurer refuses an offer of settlement when it appears that an ordinary prudent person in the insured's situation would have settled, the insurer may be held liable for damages. *Stowers,* 15 S.W.2d at 547.

When Ranger undertook to defend Peden and Guin, it became their agent. Ranger hired attorney Otto Ritter to represent Peden and Guin, so Mr. Ritter became their sub-agent. Any negligence on the part of either Ranger or Mr. Ritter would support a suit by Peden and Guin for damages. An insurer's duty to its insured is not limited to the narrow boundaries contended by Ranger, rather it extends to the full range of the agency relationship. In this case, that includes investigation, preparation for defense of the lawsuit, trial of the case and reasonable attempts to settle.

There is no contention that Ranger was negligent in investigation or trial of the Fitch/Eagle lawsuit. Peden and Guin contend that Ranger failed to advise them of any settlement offer, and failed to offer its policy limits despite its awareness that the liability factors were adverse and there was a probability that the jury verdict would exceed policy limits.

There is evidence from Ranger's employees in charge of this claim file that their attorney was given no authority to settle the property damage claim in excess of $37,000 even though their limit was only $10,000 and there was a high probability that they would lose on the liability issue. There is evidence to support the contention that Ranger authorized its attorney to offer only the $10,000 personal injury limits of its policy, and nothing for property damage, when it was aware of the very serious injuries incurred by Fitch, that the liability factors favored Fitch and that a jury verdict would very likely exceed the policy limits. Mr. Ritter testified that he did offer the policy limits before judgment. His testimony was corroborated by two lawyers in his law firm. His testimony was contradicted by Peden, Guin, their wives, and the two lawyers representing them. This presented a fact question which the jury found adverse to Ranger.

Eagle and Fitch made the following offer to settle during trial:

> We hereby offer to settle the claim of Robert Fitch for personal injuries against Bill Peden and G. & G. Construction and agree not to collect any judgment against Johnny Guinn (sic) for the total settlement sum of $19,500.00. We further offer to settle on the same terms and basis for $19,500.00 for property damage to the Eagle Trucking Company vehicle. This will finally settle the claim of Robert Fitch together with the Workmen (sic) Compensation carrier's subrogation claim and Eagle Trucking's property damage claim. The above offer is based on your representation that the insurance policies involved have limits of 10/20/10. If limits are otherwise, we offer to settle for such limits less $500.00. We will settle with either defendant separately for one-half of the above offer.

Ranger contends this settlement offer of Fitch and Eagle was conditional in that it offered only to release Peden and not to collect any judgment against Guin. The court of appeals held this to be an unconditional offer to settle. We need not reach that point. The evidence was contradictory as to whether Mr. Ritter advised Peden and Guin of the offer or explained it to them. His failure to do so would support a finding of negligence. The jury found negligence, which was the controlling issue. The finding was supported by the evidence, so the question of an unconditional offer was merely evidentiary.

Mr. Ritter, although hired by Ranger, also represented Peden in his claim for property damage and Guin in his claim for personal injury against Fitch and Eagle. There is evidence that he refused to offer the $10,000 personal injury limit to Fitch unless Eagle agreed to pay Peden and Guin something on their claim. The jury was entitled to consider that evidence in making their determination of Ranger's negligence. There is ample evidence to support the jury verdict of negligence.

Ranger further contends that the instructions accompanying Special Issue No. 1 were inadequate in that they did not outline the legal criteria for handling claims and lawsuits. This contention is erroneous. The instructions given by the trial court properly explained the basis upon which the jury could find negligence in a case of this type. The instructions also properly limited the jury to the evidence before them and cited the pertinent law. The conduct of an ordinary prudent person in the exercise of ordinary care does not require further definition.

Ranger contends that at most it merely breached its contract and there is no basis for an award of exemplary damages. A negligent breach of an agency relationship constitutes an independent tort for which an action for damages will lie. This point of law has been well-settled since this Court's holding in *Williams v. O'Daniels,* 35 Tex. 542 (1871).

In reviewing Ranger's no evidence points attacking the jury's finding of gross negligence, we are guided by our opinion in *Burk Royalty Co. v. Walls,* 616 S.W.2d 911 (Tex.1981). We look to evidence of the mental state of the defendant to determine if there was a conscious disregard of the rights of the injured party. The testimony of Ranger's claim personnel and its claim file, as set out in detail in the court of appeals opinion, is some evidence of the requisite mental state of Ranger to support exemplary damages. We have carefully re-examined all of Ranger's points of error and find none of them to be valid.

The judgment of the court of appeals is affirmed.

NOTES & QUESTIONS

1) If an insured settles a third-party claim or lawsuit in good faith, must the insured secure a full release from the third-party victim?

2) What is a release? Must there be consideration to enforce a release? Are rights transferred between parties under a release agreement?

3) What are the prerequisites for a "valid" release?

4) What is the relationship between a settlement and a release?

5) Following a successful settlement of a third-party claim, may an insurer recoup its settlement expense if a court declares that the contract did not cover the third-party claim?

Trinity Universal Insurance Company v. Bleeker
966 S.W.2d 489
(Tex. 1998)

This case concerns Ronnie Dale Bleeker's claim for damages from Trinity Universal Insurance Company (Trinity) under the *Stowers* doctrine and the Deceptive Trade Practices Act (DTPA). Bleeker alleges that Trinity is liable because it did not settle third-party claims against him, thereby exposing him to a judgment in excess of his policy limits. Because we hold that the third party did not offer to release Bleeker fully, we reverse the court of appeals' judgment on these two issues and render judgment that Bleeker take nothing.

I. FACTS

Tragically, on July 14, 1990, Bleeker was drunk and chose to drive on Interstate Highway 35 in Williamson County. He veered off the highway and struck a pickup truck that was stopped on the shoulder. Fourteen members of the Villarreal and Ochoa families were in the truck. Filiberto Villarreal was killed, and the others suffered serious or life-threatening injuries.

Bleeker carried Southern County insurance for the minimum legal amount of $40,000 per accident. Trinity reinsured and handled claims for Southern County. Hospital bills alone exceeded $40,000 by July 18, 1990. It is not disputed that Brackenridge Hospital in Austin filed liens for more than that amount with the Williamson County clerk of court by August 1, 1990. In March 1991, attorney Albert Villegas informed Trinity that he represented five of the Villarreals and extended several oral offers to settle.

In April, Villegas wrote to Trinity, demanding that Trinity pay the $40,000 policy limit into the Hidalgo County court registry for distribution to his five clients and the other nine claimants. The letter did not explicitly offer to release any potential claims against Bleeker, but it did threaten a lawsuit if Trinity did not meet the demand and also stated that "[y]ou are aware of the *Stowers* doctrine...." Assuming that an offer to release Bleeker can be inferred from such a letter, the release nevertheless could not have covered the nine claimants whom Villegas did not then represent. Furthermore, none of Villegas' settlement offers included or even mentioned the hospital liens. Trinity refused to pay the policy limits into the court registry without a full release for Bleeker.

Villegas later came to represent all fourteen claimants, never made another settlement offer, and sued Bleeker on behalf of the fourteen claimants. Villegas obtained a trial court judgment of approximately $11.5 million. Bleeker then assigned any claim that he might have against Trinity to the fourteen claimants, and they brought this action in his name. Following a jury trial, the trial court rendered judgment against Trinity under the DTPA and the Insurance Code, for breach of a common-law duty of good faith and fair dealing, and for negligently failing to settle under the *Stowers* doctrine. The trial court awarded actual damages of approximately $13 million, trebled under the DTPA to approximately $38.5 million, plus attorneys' fees of approximately $38.5 million. The court of appeals reversed and rendered judgment for Trinity on all claims except the million *Stowers* award, which it affirmed, and one DTPA claim for unconscionable conduct that the trial court had refused to submit to the jury, which it remanded for a new trial.

II. THE *STOWERS* CLAIM

Trinity first argues that the court of appeals erred because it did not render judgment for Trinity on the *Stowers* claim. We agree.

Under the doctrine established in *G.A. Stowers Furniture Co. v. American Indemnity Co.,* an insured can sue his insurer for negligently failing to settle a third party's claim against the insured. *See* 15 S.W.2d 544, 547 (Tex. Comm'n App.1929, holding approved). As a threshold matter, "a settlement demand must propose to release the insured fully in exchange for a stated sum of money." *Texas Farmers Ins. Co. v. Soriano,* 881 S.W.2d 312, 314 (Tex.1994); *accord American Physicians Ins.*

Exch. v. Garcia, 876 S.W.2d 842, 848-49 (Tex.1994). Assuming without deciding that Villegas's letter was in fact a settlement offer, and further assuming that a *Stowers* demand may be made on behalf of only some of the total pool of potential plaintiffs, Villegas did not meet the requirement that he offer to release those claims *fully. See Soriano,* 881 S.W.2d at 314-15.

Here, Trinity never had a *Stowers* duty to settle because Villegas never offered a full release even of his five clients' claims. When a hospital lien exists, a release is not valid unless:

(1) the hospital's charges were paid in full before the execution and delivery of the release;
(2) the hospital's charges were paid before the execution and delivery of the release to the extent of any full and true consideration paid to the injured individual by or on behalf of the other parties to the release; or
(3) the hospital is a party to the release.

TEX. PROP.CODE § 55.007(a)

Villegas made one written and several oral offers to settle. None of the offers included the hospital liens. In fact, when Villegas contacted the hospitals, they refused to release their liens. Any implied release that Villegas offered to Trinity was not a full one under section 55.007(a). Consequently, he could not have fully settled the case, even for his initial five clients. Accordingly, Bleeker cannot prove his *Stowers* case.

III. THE DTPA

Trinity also argues that the court of appeals erred in remanding for a trial on whether Trinity violated the DTPA's prohibition of unconscionable conduct. *See* TEX. BUS. & COM.CODE § 17.50(a)(3). Again, we agree.

Bleeker claims that Trinity's failure to inform either Bleeker or his attorney of Villegas's letter and oral settlement offers was unconscionable conduct under the DTPA. Bleeker cannot recover on such a claim unless he proves that Trinity's actions were a "producing cause" of Bleeker's damages. *Id.* § 17.50(a); *Doe v. Boys Clubs of Greater Dallas, Inc.,* 907 S.W.2d 472, 481 (Tex.1995). A "producing cause" is an act that is a substantial factor that brings about injury and without which the injury would not have occurred.

Trinity claims that its failure to inform Bleeker and Bleeker's attorney of Villegas's letter and oral offers was not a producing cause of damage to Bleeker because Bleeker produced no evidence that either he or his attorney would have been inclined to meet Villegas's demand. We agree with the court of appeals' conclusion:

> There is no evidence that Bleeker would have wanted to accept the settlement offer if he had been informed of it, and therefore no causal connection between appellants' failure to inform him of the settlement offer and the excess judgment entered against Bleeker. We sustain appellants' point of error pertaining to the legal

insufficiency of the evidence to support appellee's claim under the DTPA for failure to inform the insured of settlement offers.

In the foregoing quotation, the court of appeals was analyzing Bleeker's "failure to inform" claim under the DTPA, not his unconscionability claim. Yet both claims depend on only one allegation: that Trinity failed to inform Bleeker and his attorney of Villegas's letter. Consequently, both claims fail due to lack of evidence. Because there is no evidence of producing cause, we need not consider Trinity's assertion that Bleeker cannot state a DTPA claim based on Trinity's handling of a third-party settlement demand.

IV. CONCLUSION

We reverse those parts of the court of appeals' judgment affirming the *Stowers* judgment and remanding for trial on the DTPA unconscionability claim. We affirm the court of appeals' judgment in all other respects and render judgment that Bleeker take nothing.

NOTES & QUESTIONS

1) What is a settlement? Must there be consideration to enforce a settlement? Are rights transferred between parties under a settlement agreement?

2) What are the prerequisites for a "valid" settlement?

3) Following a successful settlement of a third-party claim, may an insurer recoup its settlement expenses if a court declares that the insurance contract did not cover the third-party claim?

TACC Government Risk Management Pool v. Matagorda County
52 S.W.3d 128
(Tex. 2000)

In this case, we decide whether the Texas Association of Counties County Government Risk Management Pool (TAC) may obtain reimbursement from its insured, Matagorda County, for an amount that TAC paid to settle a claim that was later determined to be excluded from coverage. The trial court ruled that TAC was entitled to reimbursement, but the court of appeals reversed. Because TAC established neither an implied-in-fact nor an implied-in-law right to reimbursement, we affirm the court of appeals' judgment.

I

Since the late 1980s, TAC has provided law-enforcement-liability insurance to Matagorda County. Because Matagorda County's jail fell out of compliance with the minimum requirements of the Texas Commission on Jail Standards, in 1991 TAC began including an endorsement to its policy excluding coverage for any claim "arising out of jail."

In 1993, inmates armed with razor blades physically and sexually assaulted three other prisoners (collectively "the *Coseboon* plaintiffs"). The *Coseboon* plaintiffs sued Matagorda County and its sheriff, Keith Kilgore (collectively "the County"), both of whom demanded that TAC defend and indemnify them under the law-enforcement-liability insurance policy. TAC initially denied coverage because of the jail exclusion. But after negotiations with the County, TAC agreed to pay the defense costs of the counsel that the County had retained to represent it in the *Coseboon* suit, subject to a reservation of rights to continue to deny coverage. Also, TAC filed this suit seeking a declaratory judgment that the claims were not covered. The County asserted that the claims were covered, and filed several counterclaims against TAC.

In 1995, the *Coseboon* plaintiffs offered to settle their lawsuit for $300,000. This demand was within the policy limits. The County's lawyer advised TAC that the proposed settlement was reasonable and prudent, given the facts and circumstances of the case. The Matagorda county judge, the chief administrative officer for the County, was advised of the proposed settlement and the County was asked to fund the settlement. The County, however, continued to insist that the claim was covered, and advised TAC that it would not contribute to the settlement.

TAC then issued a second reservation-of-rights letter to the County, this time reserving its rights to continue to deny coverage and to seek reimbursement of the settlement funds from the County if the declaratory-judgment action established that the *Coseboon* suit was not covered. The letter stated:

> 1) We have advised you of ongoing settlement discussions with Coseboon's counsel;
>
> 2) You have chosen not to contribute to the funding of the settlement;
>
> 3) Jim Ludlum, your counsel, agrees with [TAC] that a $300,000 settlement of the *Coseboon* matter is not only *not* unreasonable, but prudent given the facts and circumstances [ ];
>
> 4) [TAC is not] waiving any of its rights to pursue full recovery of this settlement amount from the County ... in the declaratory judgment action;
>
> 5) The funding of this settlement by [TAC and its reinsurers] is based solely upon the recognition of the exposure inherent in the *Coseboon* litigation and their desire to avoid having this opportunity to settle fall through, possibly resulting in a jury verdict far in excess of the $300,000 settlement;

6) This funding should not be construed by anyone as a voluntary payment and is specifically made without prejudice to the rights of [TAC] to recover up to the entire amount as determined in [the declaratory-judgment action.]

The letter concluded:

> If you have any question that the intent of [TAC] is anything other than funding settlement of the Cosboon [sic] matter and proceeding with the declaratory judgment action to recover the full amount of the funding, please advise me immediately.

The County did not respond to the letter.

The insurance agreement between the County and TAC allowed TAC to settle any claim at its own discretion, and without the County's consent. TAC settled the *Coseboon* litigation for $300,000, and the *Coseboon* plaintiffs dismissed their lawsuit. The settlement agreement released the County and its employees from any and all claims, and released any claims against TAC. The County did not object to the settlement. After the settlement, TAC amended its declaratory-judgment action to request reimbursement of the settlement funds. The County stipulated that it "does not dispute the reasonableness of TAC's settlement of the *Coseboon* litigation."

The case proceeded to trial on the coverage dispute. The trial court ruled that the jail exclusion was not ambiguous, and a jury resolved the remaining issues in TAC's favor. The trial court rendered a declaratory judgment for TAC and awarded recovery of its $300,000 settlement payment, together with interest, attorneys' fees, and costs. The court of appeals concluded that no equitable remedy allowed TAC to recover the settlement funds, and that there was no indication that the County agreed either to be bound by the settlement or to reimburse TAC. Accordingly, the court of appeals reversed and rendered judgment that TAC take nothing.

II

Whether an insurer may seek reimbursement from its insured for settlement funds paid under a reservation of rights upon an adjudication of noncoverage is an issue of first impression for this Court. We begin by examining the insurance contract between the parties. It is undisputed that the insurance policy that defines the parties' rights and obligations does not provide TAC a right of reimbursement; TAC first asserted such a right in its reservation-of-rights letter. It is similarly undisputed that the County did not otherwise expressly agree to reimburse TAC for the *Coseboon* settlement. We must decide whether the County's consent to reimburse TAC may be implied from this record, or whether the circumstances presented warrant imposing, in law, an equitable reimbursement obligation. We consider first the implied-consent issue.

A

Implied Consent to Reimburse

TAC contends that the County's silence in response to its reservation-of-rights letter, together with the County's stipulation acknowledging no dispute as to the settlement's reasonableness, establishes an implied-in-fact contractual obligation for the County to provide reimbursement. For a number of reasons, we disagree.

First, a unilateral reservation-of-rights letter cannot create rights not contained in the insurance policy. *See Shoshone First Bank v. Pac. Employers Ins. Co.,* 2 P.3d 510, 515-16 (Wyo.2000) (rejecting the notion that the insurer could base a right to recover defense costs on a reservation letter and stating "we will not permit the contract to be amended or altered by a reservation of rights letter."). The insurance policy at issue allows TAC to settle a case against its insured without the insured's consent. It would have been a simple matter for TAC to also state in the policy that it could seek reimbursement for those settlement funds if it is later determined that the policy does not provide coverage. If TAC had done so, its reservation letter would in fact be reserving contractual rights. But TAC's "reservation" letter was simply a unilateral offer to append a reimbursement provision to the insurance contract. That provision is binding only if the County accepted it.

TAC contends that the County implicitly agreed to reimburse the settlement funds by not responding to TAC's reservation-of-rights letter. But as a general rule, "silence and inaction will not be construed as an assent to an offer," and none of the narrow exceptions to this general rule apply in this case. TAC cites our decision in *Preston Farm & Ranch Supply, Inc. v. Bio-Zyme Enters.,* 625 S.W.2d 295, 298 (Tex.1981), for the proposition that an insured's silence may suffice to show that it consented to reimburse the insurer. But our decision in *Preston Farm* did not turn on one party's failure to respond to a unilateral offer. Instead, it rested on a continuing course of conduct between two merchants[.]

* * *

There is a difference between an insurer's reservation of its right to disclaim coverage, which occurred here, and an agreement by the insured that he will reimburse the insurer for any reasonable settlement, which did not occur here. An insurer's reservation of rights is the notification to the insured that the insurer will defend the insured, but that the insurer is not waiving any defenses it may have under the policy, and it protects an insurer from a subsequent attack on its coverage position on waiver or estoppel grounds. If this became common practice, the insurance industry might extract coercive arrangements from their insureds. . . ." Thus, the County's silence in response to TAC's reservation-of-rights letter cannot support an implied agreement to reimburse settlement costs.

Moreover, a meeting of the minds is an essential element of an implied-in-fact contract. *See Haws & Garrett Gen. Contractors, Inc. v. Gorbett Bros. Welding Co.,* 480 S.W.2d 607, 609 (Tex.1972). Yet TAC's own evidence demonstrates that there was no meeting of the minds between the County and TAC regarding reimbursement. TAC's letter advising the County that it intended to settle the

Coseboon case specifically acknowledged that "the County was 'looking to [TAC] to settle the *Coseboon* litigation *without a contribution from Matagorda County,*' " and further noted that the County had "chosen not to contribute to the funding of the settlement." (Emphasis added). The record demonstrates that the County consistently contested TAC's coverage position and insisted that TAC pay under the policy.

TAC relies upon the County's failure to dispute the settlement's reasonableness to support a reimbursement right. But the mere fact that the County did not dispute the settlement's reasonableness does not imply that it agreed to reimburse TAC should TAC decide to accept the settlement and then later prevail on its coverage defense.

We hold that the County's agreement to reimburse TAC for funds paid to settle the *Coseboon* suit cannot be implied from this record. We now consider whether the circumstances presented will support imposing upon the County an equitable reimbursement obligation.

B

Equitable Rights to Reimbursement

TAC argues that we should apply the doctrine of equitable subrogation to support its reimbursement claim. Typically, an insurer paying a claim under a policy is equitably subrogated to any claim the insured may have against a third party responsible for the insured's injury. In *Medina v. Herrera,* we considered whether the election-of-remedies doctrine, which bars the pursuit of remedies that are so inconsistent as to result in manifest injustice, barred an injured worker's tort suit against his employer when the worker had recovered workers' compensation benefits. 927 S.W.2d at 600. The worker contended that no double recovery would result if he were allowed to pursue his tort claims because the employer's compensation carrier could recoup the benefits it had paid via a subrogation action. We concluded that manifest injustice would result if the compensation carrier were equitably subrogated to its insured, in part because the carrier would be required to, in effect, sue its own policyholder.

As the court of appeals recognized, allowing an insurer to unilaterally settle claims and then step into the shoes of the claimant could potentially foster conflict and distrust in the relationship between an insurer and its insured. Allowing subrogation of an insurer against its insured has been widely rejected in this context. Accordingly, we hold that TAC is not entitled to reimbursement on an equitable subrogation theory.

Finally, TAC argues that it is entitled to recover under the intertwined quasi-contractual theories of quantum meruit and unjust enrichment. We agree with the court of appeals that these equitable theories do not apply in the circumstances presented.

* * *

III

TAC contends that denying a reimbursement right places insurers faced with a reasonable settlement offer within policy limits in an untenable position. We recognize that, however the issue is resolved, either insurers or insureds will face a difficult choice when coverage is questioned. But an insurer in such a situation that cannot obtain the insured's consent may, among other options, seek prompt resolution of the coverage dispute in a declaratory judgment action, a step we have encouraged insurers in TAC's position to take. *See State Farm Fire & Cas. Co. v. Gandy,* 925 S.W.2d 696, 714 (Tex.1996); *see also Farmers Texas County Mut. Ins. Co. v. Griffin,* 955 S.W.2d 81, 84 (Tex.1997) (holding that insurer's duty to indemnify is justiciable before insured's liability is decided in an underlying suit when the insurer has no duty to defend and the same reasons that negate the duty to defend negate any possibility that insurer will ever have a duty to indemnify). In *Gandy,* we required insurers either to accept coverage or make a good-faith effort to resolve coverage before resolving the underlying claim. TAC's position undermines *Gandy* by reducing insurers' incentive to seek early resolution of coverage disputes.

Requiring the insurer, rather than the insured, to choose a course of action is appropriate because the insurer is in the business of analyzing and allocating risk and is in the best position to assess the viability of its coverage dispute. *Gonzalez v. Mission Am. Ins. Co.,* 795 S.W.2d 734, 737 (Tex.1990) (observing that, if a policy provision is vague or ambiguous, the fault lies with the insurer as the policy's drafter). On balance, insurers are better positioned to handle this risk, either by drafting policies to specifically provide for reimbursement or by accounting for the possibility that they may occasionally pay uncovered claims in their rate structure.

IV

Conclusion

We hold that the County's consent to reimburse TAC's settlement costs cannot be implied from this record, and no equitable remedy will support a right of reimbursement under the circumstances presented. Accordingly, we affirm the court of appeals' judgment.

NOTES & QUESTIONS

1) Is the decision in *Matagorda* sound? Did the *Matagorda* court overlook an important issue? Does the decision encourage one's "unjust enrichment?"

2) Consider the Texas Supreme Court's decision in *Excess Underwriters At Lloyds of London And Certain Companies vs. Frank's Casing Crew & Rental Tools, Inc.,*—S.W.3d—, 2005 WL 1252321 (Tex.) — which was issued three years after *Matagorda*:

[At *3] — In *Texas Ass'n of Counties County Government Risk Management Pool v. Matagorda County,* 52 S.W.3d 128 (Tex. 2000), the insurer had the unilateral right to settle claims against the insured without the insured's consent.

[Matagorda County precluded reimbursement to an insurer of settlement payments made to resolve claims that are *later found not to be covered,* and allowed reimbursement to be sought by the insurer "*only if* it obtains the insured's *clear and unequivocal* consent to the settlement and the insurer's right to seek reimbursement." *Id.* at 135]

[At *3]— One of the chief concerns expressed by the Court in *Matagorda County* was that when an insurer has the unilateral right to settle, an insurer could accept a settlement that the insured considered out of the insured's financial reach, and the insured could be required to reimburse the insurer for that amount. "[T]he insured is forced to choose between rejecting a settlement within policy limits or accepting a possible financial obligation to pay an amount that may be beyond its means, at a time when the insured is most vulnerable." The facts of the case before us today lead us to conclude that this concern is ameliorated if not eliminated in at least two circumstances:

1) when an insured has demanded that its insurer accept a settlement offer that is within policy limits, or
2) when an insured *expressly agrees* that the settlement offer should be accepted.

In these situations, the insurer has a right to be reimbursed if it has timely asserted *its reservation of rights, notified the insured it intends to seek reimbursement,* and *paid to settle claims that were not covered.*

[At *3]— The insured in this case, Frank's Casing, *specifically demanded* that the excess underwriters accept and fund ARCO's settlement offer. Even *when a claim is covered, an insurer has no duty to accept a settlement offer within policy limits unless "an ordinarily prudent person, in the exercise of ordinary care, as viewed from the standpoint of the assured, would have."*

[At *4]— Requiring *an insured to reimburse its insurer for settlement payments* — if it is later determined there was no coverage— *does not prejudice the insured.* The insured's substantial exposure to a judgment against it greater than the settlement amount has been eliminated, at its insistence, and by its own admission the settlement amount was reasonable.

The insured is in the same, or at least no worse, position than it would have been in if there had been no policy. . . . The insurer should be entitled to settle with the injured party for an amount *the insured has agreed is reasonable* and *to seek recoupment from the insured* if the claims against it were not covered. From the insured's point of view, *it is in precisely the same position it would have been in absent any insurance policy*, except that the insurer is now the insured's creditor rather than the injured third party.

[At *6]— To the extent *Matagorda County* indicated that the *only* circumstance under which an insurer may obtain reimbursement from an insured for settlement payments when there is no coverage is *when there is an express agreement that there is a right to seek reimbursement*, we clarify that there are additional circumstances that will give rise to a right of reimbursement. Those include the circumstances in the case presently before us.

[At *7]— JUSTICE HECHT, CONCURRING

I join fully in the Court's opinion and write separately only to say that while I agree distinctions can be found between this case and *Texas Association of Counties County Government Risk Management Pool v. Matagorda County* in *fact those distinctions are immaterial*, and the rule in *Matagorda County* cannot survive today's decision for the reasons *Matagorda County* was *wrongly decided.*

The *question in both cases* is this: [Whether] a liability insurer [may] accept a reasonable offer within policy limits to settle a claim for which coverage is disputed and — if the claim is later determined not to have been covered —obtain reimbursement from the insured.

In the present case, we answer "yes"; in *Matagorda County,* the Court said "no". The Court sees two distinctions in the cases. In the present case, the insured 1) *had the right to consent to any settlement* and 2) *demanded that the insurer accept the claimant's settlement* offer. Neither of these things was true in *Matagorda County,* but neither distinction matters to the decision in either case.

The *insured's right to consent to settlement does not matter because neither case is about a settlement forced on an insured.* The insureds in both cases *wanted* the insurer to settle. The insured in *Matagorda County* "advised [the insurer] that the proposed settlement was reasonable and prudent, given the facts and circumstances of the case."

[At *8]— Since the present case cannot be distinguished from *Matagorda County* on any ground that matters, this case effectively overrules *Matagorda County,* as it should. "[A]n insurer has no duty to settle a claim that is not covered under its policy."

In both the present case and *Matagorda County,* the insurer ultimately prevailed on its arguments of no coverage. Yet the insurer in *Matagorda County* paid $300,000, and the insurer in the present case paid over $7 million, hoping for reimbursement, rather than take the chance that they were wrong about coverage. When insurers are forced to pay doubtful claims, the premiums paid by policyholders who have purchased coverage must be used to satisfy claims against policyholders who have not purchased coverage.

The rule in *Matagorda County* thus allows a non-covered policyholder to extort payments not only from the insurer but from the insurer's other policyholders. The result in *Matagorda County* was especially egregious because it fell on the public: in effect, the Court allowed the Matagorda County Commissioners' Court to force the innocent and unknowing taxpayers of the risk pool's other member counties to pay for damages the members had not agreed to cover.

3) Assume a liability insurer does not settle a third party's property-damage claim. Is that *prima facie* evidence of "bad faith?"

4) Assume an insurer breaches Texas's common-law duty of good faith and fair dealing. Is that breach conclusive evidence of "bad faith?"

5) Again, liability insurers do not have to secure their insureds' consent. Insurers have "absolute" discretion whether to settle third-party, property-damage claims. Assume that insureds destroyed or partially destroyed third parties' property and the insurers' failure to settle is *prima facie* evidence of "bad faith." May insureds assign their first-party "bad faith" claims against their insurers to the aggrieving third-party property owners?

2) Damage to Third-Party Complainants' Tangible Property

Republic Insurance Company v. Stoker
903 S.W.2d 338
(Tex. 1995)

This case presents the question whether an insurer breaches its duty of good faith and fair dealing to its insured if it denies a claim for an invalid reason when there was at the time a valid reason for denial. The trial court granted summary judgment against the insureds on their policy claim holding that there was no coverage, but rendered judgment on the jury verdict for the insureds on their extra-contractual claims. The court of appeals affirmed, concluding that a finding of no liability on the policy action does not, as a matter of law, defeat an insured's extra-contractual claim. The court rested its decision on *Viles v. Security Nat'l Ins. Co.,* 788 S.W.2d 566 (Tex.1990). Because the court of appeals misapprehends *Viles,* we reverse the judgment of the court of appeals and render judgment that the Stokers take nothing.

This case arises out of a multiple car accident in which the Stokers' automobile struck the rear end of another vehicle. It is undisputed that an unidentified pickup truck dropped a load of furniture on the highway, causing a chain reaction collision. Also, it is undisputed that this truck was not struck by any of the vehicles involved in the collision. The Stokers had no collision insurance and, therefore, submitted a claim to recover under their uninsured/underinsured vehicle coverage with Republic.

Republic hired Southwest to investigate the Stokers' claim. Southwest recommended that the uninsured motorist claim be denied because it concluded that Mrs. Stoker, who was the driver, was more than fifty percent at fault in causing the accident. A Republic senior claims examiner confirmed Southwest's decision. Mrs. Stoker acknowledged at the trial of her bad faith claim that fault is an issue in recovering under the uninsured motorist coverage.

The Stokers' policy provided uninsured motorist coverage for damages caused by an unidentified hit and run vehicle only if the vehicle hit the insureds' car. The language of the policy is in accord with the requirements of the Insurance Code regarding uninsured motorist coverage. Tex. Ins. Code art. 5.06-1(2)(d) (in order to recover under uninsured motorist coverage "actual physical contact must have occurred."). Republic initially did not rely on the lack of physical contact with the pickup as a reason for denying the Stokers' claim.

Following Republic's denial of the uninsured motorist claim, the Stokers sued for breach of the insurance contract, breach of the duty of good faith and fair dealing, and violations of the Deceptive Trade Practices Act and article 21.21 of the Insurance Code. The Stokers predicated all their allegations against Republic and Southwest on the fact that the companies gave an invalid reason for denial of the Stokers' claim — Mrs. Stoker's alleged fault. Republic and Southwest responded with a motion for summary judgment, asserting that because there was no physical contact there was no coverage under the policy, and consequently, the Stokers had no contractual and extra-contractual claims as a matter of law.

The trial court granted summary judgment on the contract issue. However, it submitted the balance of the case to a jury that found that Republic and Southwest had breached their duty of good faith and fair dealing and violated the DTPA and article 21.21 of the Insurance Code. The statutory violations were premised solely on the Stokers' bad faith claim. The trial court rendered judgment for the Stokers on the verdict. The court of appeals affirmed both the summary judgment on the policy claim and the judgment for extra-contractual damages.

The Stokers have not perfected an appeal to this Court of that portion of the court of appeals' judgment affirming summary judgment on their policy claim. We therefore take it as established that the uninsured/underinsured motorist coverage in the Stokers' policy does not cover their claim. Additionally, Southwest does not contend here that because it was merely Republic's agent, it owed the Stokers no duty of good faith and fair dealing. *See Natividad v. Alexsis, Inc.,* 875 S.W.2d 695 (Tex.1994). Nor do the Stokers contend that they were damaged by any delay in the processing of their claim by Republic. Therefore, the only issue we address is whether the defendants are liable to the Stokers for denying their claim for an incorrect reason — the accident was mostly Mrs. Stoker's fault — when there was a correct reason for denial which the defendants did not give the Stokers — the incident was not covered by the policy. We note that the issue of Mrs. Stoker's fault has never been resolved by a jury, but for purposes of this opinion we will assume that Republic was incorrect in its evaluation of Mrs. Stoker's fault.

An insurer has a duty to deal fairly and in good faith with its insured in the processing and payment of claims. *Arnold v. National County Mut. Fire Ins. Co.,* 725 S.W.2d 165, 167 (Tex.1987). A breach of the duty of good faith and fair dealing is established when: (1) there is an absence of a reasonable basis for denying or delaying payment of benefits under the policy and (2) the carrier knew or should have known that there was not a reasonable basis for denying the claim or delaying payment of the claim. *Aranda v. Insurance Co. of N. Am.,* 748 S.W.2d 210, 213 (Tex.1988). "The first element of this test requires an objective determination of whether a reasonable insurer under similar circumstances would have delayed or denied the claimant's benefits." *Id.* This assures that a carrier "will not be subject to liability for an erroneous denial of a claim," *id.,* as long as a reasonable basis for denial of the claim exists. *Lyons v. Millers Casualty Ins. Co. of Texas,* 866 S.W.2d 597, 600 (Tex.1993)

In affirming the trial court's judgment, the court of appeals cited to our decision in *Viles,* 788 S.W.2d 566. *Viles,* however, does not support affirmance. In *Viles,* the insurers investigated and denied the claim based on the ground that the property damage claimed to be covered actually predated coverage. The insurer denied the claim before the Viles submitted a proof of loss and before their time for doing so had expired. After the claim was denied, the Viles did not submit a proof of loss because it would have been futile to do so. At trial, the evidence established, contrary to the insurers' position, that the damage existing before coverage had already been repaired. Thus, the claim was improperly denied. Nevertheless, the insurers attempted to justify denial of the claim based on the Viles' failure to file a timely proof of loss. *Id.* We rejected this argument stating: "The record shows ... that the insurance companies denied the Viles' claim before the proof of loss form was due. Hence, the failure to file that form ... could not have been a basis for denial."

We stated in *Viles:* "Whether there is a reasonable basis for denial [of a claim] must be judged by the facts before the insurer at the time the claim was denied." This statement, does not support the Stokers' claim in this case. Unlike the situation in *Viles,* the Stokers' accident was never covered by their policy because there was no collision with the pickup truck. The facts compelling denial of the Stokers' claim were in existence at the time of the denial. Republic and Southwest's reliance on a different, perhaps erroneous, reason for denying coverage is not dispositive. What is dispositive is whether, based upon the facts existing at the time of the denial, a reasonable insurer would have denied the claim.

An argument has been made that because a policy claim is independent of a bad faith claim, an insured may recover for a bad faith denial of a claim even if the claim is not covered by the policy. We accept the premise of the argument — that a policy claim is independent of a bad faith claim. *Transportation Ins. Co. v. Moriel,* 879 S.W.2d 10, 17 (Tex.1994). The asserted conclusion, however, does not necessarily follow. Several cases have been cited to us as support for this conclusion, but none of the cases cited holds an insurer liable for denying a claim not covered by the policy. As we have noted, one element of a bad faith claim is an absence of a reasonable basis for denying or delaying payment of benefits. *Arnold,* 725 S.W.2d at 167; *Aranda,* 748 S.W.2d at 213; *Viles,* 788 S.W.2d at 568. Republic did not fail to determine whether there was a reasonable basis for denying the Stokers' claim; its decision was timely, it simply made the right decision for the wrong reason.

It is further argued that the Stokers should have been entitled to rely on Republic's reason for denying their claim in deciding whether to file suit. The Stokers were no more persuaded by the coverage language than they were by Republic's statement to them that Mrs. Stoker was mostly to blame for the accident. They vigorously contested both reasons for denial of their claim. The Stokers cannot preclude Republic from relying on a reason for denying their claim that existed at the time, even if it was not the reason Republic gave.

As a general rule there can be no claim for bad faith when an insurer has promptly denied a claim that is in fact not covered.

* * *

The Stokers' claim fails because, as a matter of law, they cannot meet the first prong of the *Aranda* test. As all the Stokers' causes of action are predicated on their bad faith allegation, they are not entitled to recover against defendants. Accordingly, the judgment of the court of appeals in favor of the Stokers is reversed, and judgment is rendered that the Stokers take nothing.

NOTES & QUESTIONS

1) Again, Texas requires the operators of motor vehicles to prove that they have secured automobile insurance for third parties. Texas Motor Vehicle Safety Responsibility Act Tex. Transp. Code Ann. § 601.072 reads in pertinent part:

> (a) Effective April 1, 2008, the minimum amounts of motor vehicle liability insurance coverage required to establish financial responsibility under this chapter are:
>
> (1) $25,000 for bodily injury to or death of one person in one accident;
>
> (2) $50,000 for bodily injury to or death of two or more persons in one accident, subject to the amount provided by Subdivision (1) for bodily injury to or death of one of the persons; and
>
> (3) $25,000 for damage to or destruction of property of others in one accident.
>
> (b) The coverage required under this section may exclude, with respect to one accident:
>
> (1) the first $250 of liability for bodily injury to or death of one person;

(2) the first $500 of liability for bodily injury to or death of two or more persons, subject to the amount provided by Subdivision (1) for bodily injury to or death of one of the persons; and

(3) the first $250 of liability for property damage to or destruction of property of others.

2) Effective January 1, 2011, the minimum amounts of motor vehicle liability insurance coverage required to establish financial responsibility under this chapter are: (1) $30,000 for bodily injury to or death of one person in one accident; (2) $60,000 for bodily injury to or death of two or more persons in one accident, subject to the amount provided by Subdivision (1) for bodily injury to or death of one of the persons; and (3) $25,000 for damage to or destruction of property of others in one accident.

INSURANCE BAD-FAITH LITIGATION IN A NUTSHELL

Judicial Bias, the Insurance Industry and Consumer Protection: An Empirical Analysis of State Supreme Courts' Bad-Faith, Breach-of-Contract, Breach-of-Covenant-of-Good-Faith, and Excess-Judgment Decisions, 1900–1991
41 CATH. U. L. REV. 325 (1992)
Willy E. Rice

As early as 1872, the United States Supreme Court accepted the view that an insurance contract is an agreement to pay money. State courts, however, disagree on the type and amount of award an insured must receive when an insurer breaches that agreement. Much of this conflict stems from state supreme courts' adoption of competing theories of recovery.

History reveals that many state supreme courts adopted the principles outlined in the well-known 1854 English contract case, *Hadley v. Baxendale*, to settle disputes between insureds and insurers. State courts viewed insurance policies as another form of contract and, therefore, construed such policies according to strict principles of contract interpretation. Consequently, when deciding whether to compensate an aggrieved policyholder, courts examined the express terms of the contract. If a breach had occurred, the insured was entitled to receive only limited damages, plus interest. Further, the insured could not recover damages for mental distress, medical expenses or inconvenience; courts considered such compensation to be outside the contemplation of the parties when they consummated the insurance contract.

Gradually, some state supreme courts recognized that an unwavering adherence to strict principles of contract law would be unjust. Thus, they applied another principle of contract law that an implied covenant of good faith and fair dealing exist in every insurance contract. In 1882 the Court of Appeals of Kentucky embraced this principle in *Germania Insurance Co. v. Rudwig & Co.* Thirty-two years later, in *Brassil v. Maryland Casualty Co.*, the New York Court of Appeals stressed that an insured's rights "go deeper than the mere surface of the contract," because a contractual obligation of good faith underlies all written agreements including insurance policies. Moreover, the *Brassil* court held that insurers have an obligation of good faith to carry out both the express and implied terms of an insurance contract.

Perhaps, more than any other factor, the inconsistent application of the implied good faith principle explains why so many insurance-law litigants believe that "judicial bias" permeates state supreme courts. Under the principle of good faith and fair dealing, both disgruntled policyholders and third parties may recover financial rewards for a number of violations, including a breach of the express terms of the insurance policy. Nonetheless, both the amount and the types of damages recoverable under an implied covenant of good faith seriously divide state supreme courts. Some supreme tribunals allow both first-party and third-party plaintiffs to recover extensive consequential and punitive damages. Others restrict the amount of recoverable damages to the value specified in the policy-limits clause of the insurance contract.

In addition, another conflict arises—one more serious than the amount-of-recovery controversy: Jurisdictions differ in their treatment of a breach of the implied covenant of good faith and fair dealing in [an] insurance context. Some jurisdictions characterize the cause of action as merely a breach of contract; others characterize the cause of action as a tort in third-party cases but not in first-party cases[.] [S]till others characterize the cause of action as a tort in both first-party and third-party cases.

Moreover, another rule further complicates this morass: under either a contract or in independent-tort-of-bad-faith action, the insured may obtain consequential damages for economic loss and emotional distress and, when appropriate, punitive damages.

[A] careful analysis of first-party and third-party decisions reveals even deeper divisions among state supreme courts that recognize the tort of bad faith as an independent cause of action. For example, in suits involving first-party insurance, courts have reached conflicting results over whether damages should be awarded where insurers allegedly failed to process, investigate, defend, bargain, settle or pay a claim. Moreover, in third-party insurance actions, a major controversy exists over the proper test for assessing whether an insurer is liable for a judgment in excess of the policy limits. Some supreme courts apply the doctrine of good faith and fair dealing when the complainant is a policyholder or an excess insurer. Other courts apply the doctrine of subrogation when the aggrieved party is an excess insurer. Arguably, the inconsistent application of bad-faith rules among first-party and third-party litigants contributes to the impression that state supreme courts unwittingly discriminate against consumers or in favor of the insurance industry.

* * *

[W]hile some state supreme courts allow insureds to sue insurance companies in tort for bad faith, others do not. But among those tribunals which recognize an independent tort action for bad faith, significant confusion exists over whether an insurer's duty to act responsibly is implied in fact or implied in law. Stated differently, state supreme courts are seriously divided over whether the duty to satisfy the reasonable expectations of the insured evolves from the insurance contract, from the contractual relationship between the parties, or from some other body of law.

Much of this confusion stems from state supreme courts' use of imprecise language when deciding bad-faith causes of actions. Cases holding that an insurer's duty to act stems from the terms of the insurance contract support this observation. For example, Kentucky's highest court concluded that the "rule of good faith and fair dealing … form[s] a part of every insurance contract." Conversely, the Arizona Supreme Court held that "the duty to … act is imminent in the contract." To further complicate matters, the Supreme Court of Colorado decided that "the basis for liability in tort … is grounded upon the special nature of the insurance contract." Nonetheless, that court, along with several other supreme tribunals, maintained that the duty to act arises from a contractual relationship rather than from the contract.

Furthermore, an Oklahoma Supreme Court's decision illustrates another unnecessarily complicated bad-faith holding. Accepting the general notion that an insurer has a duty to deal fairly and in good faith with its insured, the Supreme Court of Oklahoma, unlike other supreme courts, maintained: "There must be either a contractual or [a] statutory relationship between the insurer and the party asserting the bad faith claim before the duty arises."

While the Supreme Court of Kansas has refused to recognize an independent tort of bad faith, it has held that "only contractual damages are available for a breach of an insurance contract." That ruling, however, is bothersome, because it only exacerbates the confusion surrounding bad-faith litigation. Thus, in Kansas, an insurance company's duty to deal fairly and in good faith evolves from a state-imposed statutory relationship rather than from a contractual relationship.

Finally, some courts have ruled that an insurer is a trustee; therefore, a quasi-fiduciary relationship exists between an insurance company and a policyholder. Specifically, Colorado, Florida, New Jersey and Wisconsin Supreme Courts have ruled that "an insurance company stands in a position similar to that of a fiduciary," particularly when handling third-party claims brought against the insured. In *Farmers Group, Inc. v. Trimble*, the Supreme Court of Colorado held that insurance contract forms the basis of the quasi-fiduciary relationship.

Conflict Over the Standard for Determining a Bad-Faith Breach of Duty

In addition to the implied-in-law and implied-in-fact controversy, the standard for establishing an independent tort of bad faith is unclear. Is it an intent standard or a negligence standard? This issue confuses state supreme courts. Consequently, the results of these courts differ. Some courts that subscribe to the intent standard adopt an "objective" test. To maintain a bad-faith claim under that test, the insured must demonstrate that the insurer did not have a reasonable basis for denying coverage. The insured must also show "defendant's knowledge or reckless disregard … for denying the claim." This "objective standard" has been frequently labeled the "fairly-debatable" intent test and several states within the First, Seventh, Ninth and Tenth Circuits have adopted it.

Other supreme courts within the Fifth and Eleventh Circuits also embrace an "objective" intent standard. In those jurisdictions, however, the measure is called the "arguably-debatable" standard.

Under this latter version, an aggrieved policyholder must go beyond a mere showing of nonpayment of a claim. He also must prove that the insurance company intentionally refused to pay the claim. Finally, the policyholder must show that the insurance company lacked a "reasonably-legitimate" or "arguably-debatable" reason for the refusal.

These competing intent standards are complex and provide little guidance for insurers, first-party complainants or triers of fact. A well-reasoned dissenting opinion in *Vincent v. Blue Cross-Blue Shield* illustrates the current confusion. There, Justices Embry asked:

> What is the test for the tort of bad faith? . . . In California 'the ultimate test of liability in . . . first-party cases is whether the refusal to pay policy benefits is unreasonable. . . .' [T]he Wisconsin Supreme Court held the tort of bad faith to be an intentional one, but based its test . . . on the lack of a reasonable basis for denial of a claim. . . . Similarly, in Ohio an insured may recover upon proof that the insurer had no intention of paying the claim, but such intention may be demonstrated by the lack of reasonable basis for denial. . . . [But according to the tests of these other courts,] [w]hat a reasonable insurer would do or not do is a negligence test.

Although Justice Embry would reject the use of the negligence standard, his last comment illuminates that negligence standard. But as the Supreme Court of Montana observed, a clear distinction between a cause of action for negligence and for bad faith does not exist. In fact, the Montana court pointed out that while differences between bad faith and negligence tests exist, in practice courts have merged the two tests. More important, a careful comparison of the intent and negligence standards, within the context of a bad-faith action, shows little difference between the two measures. Under either test, a complainant must prove that an insurer's action or inaction was unreasonable.

Arguably, no significant difference exists between a negligence and an intent standard in the context of first-party suits. Citing the limited amount of evidence presented thus far, bad-faith litigants could reasonably conclude that state supreme courts are biased. In first-party situations, justices must articulate more precise and intelligible decisions in this area of law. By outlining definitive standards, state supreme courts would help counter the widespread impression that state courts are politically motivated. A delineation of objective standards would also counter the perception that state supreme courts are more concerned about obtaining a particular result than about consistently applying legal principles.

B. *Liability Insurer's Duty to Indemnify or Reimburse*

Insurance Contracts and Judicial Discord over Whether Liability Insurers Must Defend Insureds' Allegedly Intentional and Immoral Conduct: A Historical and Empirical Review of Federal and State Courts' Declaratory Judgments 1900–1997

47 Am. U. L. Rev. 1131 (1998)

Willy E. Rice

In most instances, insurance consumers purchase third-party insurance to help pay third-party victims' claims in the event of a loss of property, bodily injuries, or death. But some consumers purchase third-party insurance contracts, for example, automobile and homeowners' policies to help pay their own personal expenses when they experience property damage or bodily injuries. More significantly, third-party insurance falls into two very broad categories: liability contracts and indemnity contracts.

Liability contracts have several common features: (1) a coverage clause that outlines the types of risks the insurer is willing to assume; (2) a broad exclusion provision that highlights various types of risks or behaviors that the insurance company is unwilling to assume; (3) a narrower "intentional acts" provision stating that injuries or acts "expected or intended" from the insured's perspective are excluded; (4) a right-to-settle clause that gives the insurer the exclusive right to settle all third-party claims filed against the insured; (5) a duty-to-defend provision that compels the company to hire legal counsel for the insured and pay defense costs; and (6) a duty-to-pay clause that outlines the conditions under which the insurer will pay once liability has been established.

A major purpose of liability insurance is to help shield the insured from having to pay damages to a third-party victim. In addition, "[u]nder a liability policy ... the insurer's obligation to pay arises as soon as the insured incurs liability for [a] loss ..."

Under an indemnity contract, however, the insurer is only required to make whole the insured after he has sustained an actual loss after the insured has paid or been compelled to make a payment to a third-party claimant. In comparison, an insurer incurs an obligation to the insured whereupon the insured has paid, or is obligated to pay, a third-party claimant. Although both liability and indemnity insurance contracts exclude coverage for malicious, dishonest, and fraudulent conduct and for claims involving libel or slander, indemnity agreements generally do not contain a duty-to-defend provision. Therefore, with indemnity agreements, control of the legal defense resides exclusively with the policyholder and with the legal counsel chosen to defend the policyholder against the third-party allegations

Insurers sell several types of so-called indemnity contracts: Professional indemnity plans, hospital indemnity insurance, workers compensation indemnity plans, excess employers indemnity policies, and industrial indemnity insurance. Directors' and officers' policies ("D&O"), however, appear to be the most widely distributed and well-known type of indemnity contracts.

Southern Title Guaranty Company, Inc. v. Prendergast
494 S.W.2d 154
(Tex. 1973)

This is a suit on a title insurance policy by the insured, Vincent Prendergast and wife, against the insurer, Southern Title Guaranty Company. Prendergast bought 22 acres of Harris County land for $10,233 in 1964. His owner's policy in that amount was issued by Southern Title Guaranty Company on February 17, 1964. In July of 1965 Prendergast entered into a contract to sell the 22 acres for $25,000. The prospective purchaser objected to the title on the ground that an undivided one-tenth outstanding interest was owned by Theresa Krug Matlage. Prendergast called upon Southern Title Guaranty Company to purchase the Matlage interest for him, but this was not done and the sale of 22 acres for $25,000 was lost. Prendergast then sued to recover the damages to which he was entitled under his title policy.

There have been two trials and appeals in the case. The first trial was terminated by a directed verdict in favor of the insurance company, the ground therefor being Prendergast's failure to prove a title defect. . . .The Court of Civil Appeals held that Prendergast had made his proof of the prior ownership of a one-tenth interest by Theresa Matlage and that he would be entitled to recover in the event the company could not prove divestment of the Matlage interest to the benefit of the title acquired by Prendergast. It was also held that the assertion of the claim adverse to Prendergast warranted his suit for breach of the insurance contract even though the adverse claimant had not obtained a judgment validating the claim and was not interfering with Prendergast's possession of the land.

The second trial resulted in a verdict and judgment in favor of Prendergast and then an appeal which has again turned the case back for new trial. That appeal now reaches us with questions of the computation of damages, but first we deal with those questions treated by the first opinion of the Court of Civil Appeals. We agree with that holding and find no evidence in the second trial that would preclude Prendergast's recovery.

There is the question of whether the insured may sue on the policy merely because of the failure of his title. The insurance company insists that eviction should be a prerequisite to this suit, as it is to a suit for breach of a covenant of warranty. *See, Rancho Bonito Land & Live-Stock Co. v. North,* 45 S.W. 994 (Tex. 1898). It bases this argument upon the following language of the policy:

> (Said Company) shall, at its own cost, defend said assured in every suit or proceeding on any claim against or right to said land, or any part thereof, adverse to the title hereby guaranteed, provided the party or parties entitled to such defense shall, within a reasonable time after the commencement of such suit or proceeding and in ample time for defense therein, give said Company written notice of the pendency of the suit or proceeding, and authority to defend, and said Company shall not be liable until such adverse interest, claim, or right shall have been held valid by a court of last resort to which either litigant may apply. . . .

It follows that the insurance company is allowed the opportunity to complete its defense of a suit brought by an adverse claimant before being forced to pay the insured, but it does not follow that the company's covenant is limited to protection against an adverse claimant who moves to evict the insured. By the terms of the policy the company does more than agree to warrant and defend the insured against anyone claiming adverse title.

The policy contract begins by saying in emphatic type: "The Southern Title Guaranty Co., Inc. . . . Does hereby guarantee to Vincent Prendergast and wife, Leola Prendergast . . . that they have good and indefeasible title to the following described real property . . . ." This is the basic assurance of the contract, and a failure of that guarantee gives rise to a cause of action for damages. It would be a substantial reduction of that assurance to make the insured bear his detriment until the owner of the superior title is found and sued to judgment; the policy will not be given that effect in the absence of language more explicit than the provision advanced by the company and quoted above.

The insurance company also insists that Prendergast has not proved the existence of an outstanding one-tenth interest in the property. If Theodore and Emilie Krug owned this property in community, when Emilie Krug died her daughter Theresa Krug Matlage inherited a one-tenth interest therein. Prendergast acquired the interests of the other children of Theodore and Emilie Krug, but not that of Theresa Krug Matlage. It is established that Theodore Krug acquired the property in 1904 while he was married to Emilie. It is the presumption that the property was acquired as community. *Wilson v. Wilson,* 201 S.W.2d 226 (Tex. 1947). There are suggestions that Theodore Krug may have acquired the land as his separate property and that the brother of Theresa Krug Matlage may have perfected a limitation title by adverse use and occupancy, but there is no evidence to warrant finding the suggestions to be fact. It follows that Prendergast has made his case of the outstanding interest.

In the second trial a jury verdict was obtained, the findings being that-in July of 1965 when the resale was lost — the value of full fee title to the 22 acres was $25,000 while the value of the land with an outstanding one-tenth interest was only $10,200. The difference between these two figures being thought to be Prendergast's damages, the trial court rendered judgment for the amount of the policy limit, $10,233. This judgment has been reversed by the Court of Civil Appeals because its effect would be to give to the insured the benefit of his 1965 bargain rather than to indemnify him for the failure of the title guaranteed on the date of the policy. We agree that the trial court judgment was erroneous, but we disagree with the opinion of the Court of Civil Appeals in two respects which will become significant when the trial court reaches the case once more.

Our first disagreement is with respect to the effect of the proportionate payment provision of the policy. It provides that if there is established an outstanding interest in "less than the whole of the property, then the liability of the Company shall be only such part of the whole liability limited above as shall bear the same ratio to the whole liability that the adverse interest, claim, or right established may bear to the whole property, such ratio to be based on respective values determinable as of the date of this policy." The application of this provision is not limited to the situation where outstanding title to a physically identifiable segment of the acreage is established. It applies in all cases where there is a loss of title 'for less than the whole of the property'-meaning anything less than the title and acreage insured. It simply means that the parties deal with the insured property on the assumption that its value is equal to the amount of the policy, and this assumption is to be applied whether the insured loses part or all of what the policy insures.

Thus, the amount recoverable on the policy bears the same ratio to the policy amount as the value of the outstanding interest bears to the value of the full insured title. The formula may be stated: the liability of the insurance company (X) is to the whole liability or policy limit (A) as the value of the outstanding interest (B) is to the value of the whole property without an outstanding interest (C), or X/A=B/C. *Lawyers Title Ins. Corp. v. McKee*, 354 S.W.2d 401 (Tex. Civ .App., 1962, no writ). Under the express terms of Prendergast's policy, the values of B and C are determined as of the date of the policy.

If the amount of the policy is the same as the value of what is insured, the assumption of the policy is correct and the recoverable loss is the value of the outstanding interest. This Value may or may not bear the same fractional relationship to the totel Value as the undivided interest or portion of the land area (lost to the insured) bears to the whole title and property. A one-tenth interest in land might carry an added bargaining weight and be worth more than one-tenth of what the market would allow to the whole. *Humble Oil and Refining Co. v. Kishi,* 291 S.W. 538 (Tex.Com. App.1927).

If the market value of the whole property and the policy amount differ, the ratio of the quoted provision must be applied. This avoids any advantage to insurer or to insured. To illustrate, suppose the jury were to find the values for the 22 acres as of the date of the policy to been as follows: $25,000 for the whole, $4,800 for the one-tenth, and $20,200 for the land with an outstanding one-tenth interest. The approach of the trial court would be to consider the loss to be $4,800. The approach of the Court of Civil Appeals would be to allow recovery of the actual loss: 'the difference between what they paid for the land and what it was worth at the date of their purchase with its defective title.' 478 S.W.2d 806. This would allow no recovery, because they paid less for the land ($10,233) than it was worth with its defective title ($20,200). If the policy provision is applied and the ratio of $4,800 to $25,000 is used, the recovery would be 19.2% Of $10,233 or $1,964.74.

In holding that this proportionate reduction clause applies to any defect in the insured ownership, whether it be because of a partial interest or because of an interest in partial acreage, we overrule Shaver v. National Title & Abstract Co., 361 S.W.2d 867 (Tex.1962), to the extent of the inconsistency.

A final question, perhaps a determinative one, is presented by the attempt of the insurance company to introduce into evidence a quitclaim deed from the executor of the estate of Theresa Krug Matlage, which deed is said to cure any defect in Prendergast's title. The trial court refused to admit the deed, and this ruling was upheld by the Court of Civil Appeals under the authority of *Shaver v. National Title & Abstract Co.,* supra. However, *Shaver* is distinguishable upon this point as the release discussed there was not offered at the trial and only appeared in support of a motion to dismiss the cause when pending before the Supreme Court. It was held that the release did not make the case moot. Whether to admit a deed which cures the defect and mitigates the loss of damages of the insured is another question.

Title insurance is a contract of indemnity and the insured is limited to recovery for actual damages sustained. The insurer should be allowed a reasonable opportunity to clear the title insured. In *Stewart Title Guaranty v. Lunt Land Corp.*, 347 S.W.2d 584 (Tex. 1961) it was said that the insured should "notify the title company of a prospective sale of the property so they could mitigate an impending loss under their policy by negotiating with the gas company for a removal of the pipe line or the purchase of its easement rights."

The Court of Civil Appeals has written that the "procurement of the quit-claim deed under the facts of this case, as a matter of law, was not a reasonable exercise of any right to cure the defect as an alternative to their duty to pay damages for their breach of the contract of guaranty." Southern Title Guaranty Company filed no suit to cure this defect because Prendergast did not request that action, and during the first trial and appeal the company expressed its willingness to prosecute such a suit. After that appeal and after the death of the adverse claimant, the company was finally successful in purchasing the quitclaim deed which it contends resolves the matter. We hold that it should not be precluded from making that proof and mitigating the damages owed to Prendergast. If upon a new trial it appears that the defect in Prendergast's title is cured, his damages will be no more than nominal.

The judgment of the Court of Civil Appeals is affirmed. The cause is remanded to the trial court for further proceedings consistent with this opinion.

NOTES & QUESTIONS

1) Does the action or cause in *Pendergast* sound in equity or in law? What was the action in *Pendergast*?

2) Of course, Pendergast is a duty-to-indemnify case. But a title insurer may be liable for a failure to indemnify the insured as well as for violating the DTPA. Consider the Texas Supreme Court's analysis and ruling in *Chicago Title Ins. Co. v. McDaniel,* 875 S.W.2d 310, 310-311 (Tex. 1994):

> [T]he McDaniels received notice from the bankruptcy trustee of Couch Mortgage that their property was subject to a preexisting lien that had been properly filed and recorded . . . . The McDaniels abandoned the property . . . Three months later, a federal bankruptcy court ruled that the McDaniels' purchase money lien on the property was superior to the preexisting lien.
>
> The Mc5Daniels brought this suit . . . , seeking damages under the DTPA based on Chicago Title's representations. . . . Chicago Title secured the release of the preexisting lien. Chicago Title asserts that it has discharged its obligations under the title insurance policy, and that it cannot be liable under the DTPA because it has

made no representations regarding the status of the title to the McDaniels' property. We agree.

A title insurance policy is a contract of indemnity. *Southern Title Guar. Co. v. Prendergast,* 494 S.W.2d 154, 158 (Tex.1973). In other words, the only duty imposed by a title insurance policy is the duty to indemnify the insured against losses caused by defects in title. Thus, Chicago Title's issuance of a policy did not constitute a representation regarding the status of the property's title; rather, it constituted an agreement to indemnify the McDaniels against losses caused by any defects.

A title insurer may be held liable under the DTPA for an affirmative representation that is the producing cause of damages to the insured. *First Title Co. v. Garrett,* 860 S.W.2d 74 (Tex.1993). In the present case, however, there is no allegation of any such affirmative representation. Nor is there any allegation that Chicago Title breached its duty under the contract, or that it may be liable to the McDaniels in any other respect apart from the DTPA. Accordingly, because there is no genuine issue of fact regarding the representations made in the title insurance policy, a majority of this Court grants Chicago Title's application for writ of error and, without hearing oral argument, reverses the judgment of the court of appeals and renders judgment for Chicago Title.

3) Under directors' and officers' (D & O) liability insurance contracts, does an insurer promise to indemnify all officers and directors individually or jointly?

4) Under directors' and officers' (D & O) liability insurance agreements, does the duty-to-reimburse clause require an insurer to reimburse all monies that the directors and officers spent to settle a lawsuit?

Medical Care America, Inc. v. National Union Fire Insurance Company of Pittsburgh, Pennsylvania
341 F.3d 415 (5th Cir. 2003)

Following a precipitous decline in stock value, shareholders sued (among others) the director and officers of a Texas corporation formed through merger. After the suit settled, the corporation sued its insurer for coverage under its directors and officers liability policy. At issue was whether the policy covered the directors and officers' post-merger wrongful acts that were the same as or related to their pre-merger wrongful acts. A jury concluded that there was no coverage. The corporation now appeals the district court's pretrial grant of partial summary judgment, its rulings on three motions for judgment as a matter of law at the close of the evidence, and its judgment on the verdict. We AFFIRM.

I - A

In the Summer of 1992, Medical Care International, Inc. (MCI) and Critical Care America (CCA) announced that they would merge to become wholly owned subsidiaries of a new company, Medical Care America, Inc. (Medical Care). The companies issued statements trumpeting expectations for Medical Care's increased earnings. On August 3, 1992, they filed a joint proxy-prospectus with the Securities and Exchange Commission (SEC) and sent copies of the filing to their shareholders. The merger became final on September 9, 1992, at which time the directors of MCI and CCA became the directors of Medical Care.

In anticipation of the merger, Medical Care's risk management director, Theresa Major-Gable, consulted Larry Waldie, an insurance broker employed by Marsh & McLennan, Inc. (Marsh), about purchasing directors and officers (D&O) liability insurance for Medical Care "going forward" from the date of the merger. In conjunction with this consultation, Medical Care appointed Marsh its exclusive agent of record. Acting on Medical Care's behalf, Waldie solicited quotes from several insurance companies, including National Union Fire Insurance Company (National Union).

Major-Gable subsequently instructed Waldie to bind National Union's quote. On September 4, 1992, National Union sent Waldie a letter that represented a temporary conditional binder outlining its agreement to provide Medical Care with $10 million worth of D&O coverage from September 9, 1992, to September 9, 1993. The temporary conditional binder conditioned coverage on National Union's receipt, review, and acceptance of certain information from Medical Care, including a completed application. It explained that the policy would be issued with ten endorsements, including one for "prior acts as of September 9, 1992." Waldie summarized the temporary conditional binder in a separate binder (Binder) he sent to Major-Gable on September 15, 1992. The Binder indicated that the policy would exclude "all prior acts prior to policy inception date." On September 28, 1992, Medical Care satisfied the conditions of the temporary conditional binder.

I - B

The pre-merger expectations for Medical Care proved overly optimistic, and on September 25, 1992, the new company announced flat earnings. The announcement caused share value to plummet over 50% in one day, at which point the New York Stock Exchange suspended trading of Medical Care stock. In response, at least 15 shareholder class action lawsuits were filed against Medical Care, CCA, MCI, and the directors and officers. The lawsuits were consolidated into a single action in the United States District Court for the Northern District of Texas. The consolidated suit alleged violations of §§ 10(b)and 20(a) of the Securities Exchange Act of 1934 and of SEC Rule 10b-5.The complaint alleged that the defendants made misrepresentations and failed to make necessary disclosures in public statements and filings.

On January 30, 1993, National Union issued the D&O liability policy that Medical Care had applied for the previous September. Endorsement # 7 of the policy provided:

> In consideration of the premium charged, it is hereby understood and agreed that this policy only provides coverage for Loss arising from claims for alleged Wrongful

> Acts occurring on or after September 9, 1992 and prior to the end of the Policy Period and otherwise covered by this policy. Loss(es) arising out of the same or related Wrongful Act(s) shall be deemed to arise from the first such same or related Wrongful Act.

By letter dated January 27, 1993, National Union denied coverage for the claims asserted in the class action based on the related acts language of the second sentence of Endorsement # 7. On March 9, 1993, the class action plaintiffs filed an amended complaint. National Union restated its denial of coverage by letter dated May 21, 1993, repeating its reliance on Endorsement # 7.

The shareholder suit was settled in principle pursuant to court-ordered mediation for $60 million and the full release of all claims asserted against the defendants. Medical Care advised National Union of the settlement, asking it to reconsider its denial of coverage and to participate in the settlement, which had not yet been funded or approved by the court. National Union reiterated its previous position. After the district court approved the settlement, the $60 million was paid to the class action plaintiffs and the claims against Medical Care, MCI, CCA, and their respective officers and directors were released.

In February 1995, the defendants entered into an agreement that allocated responsibility for the $60 million settlement among five of the six defendants. Under that agreement, Medical Care owed a contribution to the settlement but its directors and officers, who were separate defendants in the shareholder suit, did not. The agreement allocated sums . . . as follows: MCI, $10 million; the directors of MCI, $10 million; CCA, $10 million; the directors of CCA, $10 million; Medical Care, $10 million; and the directors of Medical Care, $10 million.

I - C

Medical Care filed the present lawsuit in November 1996 after National Union denied coverage under the D&O policy. It stated claims for breach of contract, breach of the duty of good faith and fair dealing, and violations of the Tex. Ins. Code art. 21.21.

The district court granted in part and denied in part the parties' competing motions for summary judgment. Of relevance to this appeal, the court ruled for Medical Care in holding that "the binder agreements are the controlling contracts of insurance at issue in this case"; ruled against Medical Care in finding that there was a triable issue as to whether National Union was estopped from relying on the related acts exclusion; and ruled for National Union in dismissing with prejudice Medical Care's extracontractual claims.

Medical Care's remaining claim for breach of contract was tried to a jury. At the close of the evidence, both parties filed motions for judgment as a matter of law ("JMOL"). The court denied Medical Care's motion *in toto*. Of relevance here, it held that Medical Care had not shown that it was due coverage as a matter of law. The court granted National Union's motion in part, ruling that the insurance contract included a "related acts" exclusion and that National Union was not equitably estopped from relying on that "related acts" exclusion. The jury returned a take-nothing verdict for Medical Care, finding that Medical Care proved that its directors and officers had incurred loss arising from the shareholders' claims about their alleged wrongful acts occurring on or after September 9, 1992, and that Medical Care had indemnified its directors and officers for such loss. The jury found, however, that National Union proved that all the directors' and officers' wrongful acts occurring after September 9, 1992, were the same as or related to wrongful acts occurring prior to September 9, 1992.

After the court denied its motion for a new trial and its renewed motion for JMOL, Medical Care appealed.

* * *

III - A

The parties agree that under Texas law an insurance binder provides coverage according to the terms and provisions of the ordinary form of the contemplated policy. *Ranger County Mut. Ins. Co. v. Chrysler Credit Corp.*, 501 S.W.2d 295, 298 (Tex.1973) ("As long as a binder is in effect, the insured may look to the form of the contemplated policy for coverage, duration, cancellation, and other terms").

In this case, the Binder expressly states that the policy would exclude coverage of "all prior acts prior to policy inception date," but it is silent as to coverage of subsequent acts that are related to the prior acts. At issue is whether the ordinary form of prior acts endorsement used in D&O policies contains language excluding coverage of subsequent related acts. At the close of evidence, the district court granted a partial JMOL for National Union on this issue, finding as a matter of law that Endorsement # 7, the prior acts endorsement containing related acts language that was used in the policy issued to Medical Care in January 1993, "was the standard form normally or ordinarily issued by National Union" in its D&O liability policies. The consequence of this ruling under Maxey and Ranger County was to make the related acts exclusion a term of the Binder. We agree that National Union met its burden under Rule 50(a) and that JMOL was appropriate on this issue.

Two disinterested witnesses testified that National Union's standard practice, like that of the industry, was to use related acts language in prior acts endorsements. Lawrence Waldie, the insurance broker who served as Medical Care's agent, testified that Endorsement # 7 was in a form that was the "customary and normal form of a prior acts endorsement issued by National Union" and other carriers writing D&O policies under similar circumstances. . . . Anthony Codding testified similarly. Codding, a former assistant division manager of National Union's D&O division, was involved in underwriting between 5000 and 8000 D&O policies at National Union. He testified that in his experience National Union had never used a prior acts endorsement that did not include related acts language.

* * *

In addition to Waldie and Codding, Elliot Rothman appeared on behalf of National Union as an expert witness in the area of D&O liability insurance. Rothman testified that the standard industry practice was to include related acts language in prior acts endorsements.

Medical Care offered no evidence to contradict the testimony of Waldie, Codding, or Rothman. Instead, it argued that the lone endorsement form that did not contain related acts language and the testimony that all D&O policies were different and subject to negotiation created a triable issue about the scope of coverage under the Binder. But neither piece of evidence supports a reasonable inference that the customary and standard form of D&O liability insurance issued by National Union did not contain related acts language. There is no evidence that National Union ever used the lone endorsement form that does not contain related acts language. And there is no evidence that National Union ever issued a D&O policy with a prior acts endorsement that did not contain related acts language. Indeed, Codding testified that he could not recall a single instance when a broker or client negotiated the related acts language out of a prior acts endorsement.

After carefully reviewing the record, we conclude that the evidence and inferences point so strongly and overwhelmingly in favor of a finding that National Union's standard prior acts endorsement normally or ordinarily used in its D&O liability policies contained related acts language that JMOL in National Union's favor is warranted.

III - B

Medical Care asserts that National Union was equitably estopped from relying on the related acts language to deny coverage. Under Texas law, a plaintiff relying on the doctrine of equitable estoppel must show: (1) a false representation or concealment of material facts; (2) made with knowledge, actual or constructive, of those facts; (3) with the intention that it should be acted on; (4) to a party without knowledge or means of obtaining knowledge of the facts; (5) who detrimentally relies on the representations. *Johnson & Higgins v. Kenneco Energy*, 962 S.W.2d 507, 515-16 (Tex.1998), citing *Schroeder v. Texas Iron Works, Inc.*, 813 S.W.2d 483, 489 (Tex.1991). "The burden of proving an estoppel and the essential elements thereof is on the party asserting it and the failure to prove any one or more of the elements is fatal." *Barfield v. Howard M. Smith Co. of Amarillo*, 426 S.W.2d 834, 838 (Tex.1968)

At the close of evidence, the district court granted a partial JMOL for National Union on the applicability of equitable estoppel to the case. The court concluded that Medical Care had presented legally insufficient evidence to establish the first or fourth elements. Because no facts or inferences support a finding of those two elements, we agree that JMOL for National Union was appropriate as to this issue.

Medical Care asserts that National Union concealed the true scope of the prior acts endorsement by omitting from its binder any reference to related acts. As we discussed above, the uncontroverted evidence shows that the Binder indicated that the policy would include a prior acts endorsement; that a prior acts endorsement used in the context of a D&O policy would normally and ordinarily be understood to contain related acts language; and that National Union's standard prior acts endorsement normally and ordinarily contained related acts language. There is no positive evidence that National Union misrepresented or concealed coverage terms. Because the evidence points so strongly and overwhelmingly in favor of National Union, we conclude that a jury could not reasonably infer that National Union had anything to conceal, intended to conceal anything, or in fact concealed anything from Medical Care. Because Medical Care failed to establish the first element of equitable estoppel, summary judgment was appropriate.

Furthermore, under Texas law, "[a] party claiming an estoppel must have used due diligence to ascertain the truth of the matters upon which he relies in acting to his detriment." There is no evidence that Medical Care or any of its representatives made any inquiry of Marsh or National Union as to either the scope or effect of the prior acts endorsement. Nor is there evidence that Medical Care lacked the means to make such an inquiry or was somehow prevented from doing so. On the contrary, Waldie testified that he encouraged Major-Gable to contact him with questions about the Binder. In short, our review of the record reveals that it cannot reasonably be inferred that Medical Care used due diligence to ascertain the scope or effect of the prior acts endorsement or that Medical Care lacked the means of obtaining knowledge of the extent of the prior acts exclusion. Thus, Medical Care also failed to establish the fourth element of equitable estoppel, further demonstrating that summary judgment was warranted.

* * *

On appeal, Medical Care does not directly challenge the sufficiency of the evidence supporting the verdict. Instead, it presents a legal argument for indemnification coverage. Its argument, however, rests on faulty premises. First, it is not true, as Medical Care contends, that the coverage issue must be resolved by looking at the allegations of the underlying shareholders suit. Under well-established Texas law, an insurer's duty to defend its insured is determined by considering the allegations in the underlying litigation in the light of the policy provisions. *Heyden Newport Chem. Corp. v. Southern Gen. Ins. Co.*, 387 S.W.2d 22, 24 (Tex.1965). But National Union had no duty to defend Medical Care by express provision of the policy.

Instead we must look to the rule governing an insurer's duty to indemnify its insured. Under Texas law, this duty depends on the actual facts of the underlying litigation.

Second, Medical Care argues that indemnification coverage is required based on a selective reading of the policy. Because the policy defines "Loss" to mean "settlements," it argues that there must be coverage of settlements arising from claims of alleged wrongdoing. But its reading fails to account for the limitations on the definition of "Loss" imposed by Endorsement # 7, which clearly provides that not all loss is covered. In particular, the prior acts endorsement expressly excludes loss arising from wrongful acts related to prior wrongful acts predating the coverage period: [T]his policy only provides coverage for Loss arising from claims for alleged Wrongful Acts occurring on or after September 9, 1992. . . . Loss(es) arising out of the same or related Wrongful Act(s) shall be deemed to arise from the first such same or related Wrongful Act.

By its very terms, therefore, the policy does not cover settlements arising from claims of alleged wrongdoing that is the same as or related to alleged wrongdoing occurring before September 9, 1992.

* * *

With regard to the common law claim, the parties dispute whether National Union owed a duty of good faith under the circumstances. Under Texas law, an insurer owes a duty of good faith in handling its insured's own claim of loss. *Arnold v. National County Mut. Fire Ins. Co.,* 725 S.W.2d 165, 167 (Tex.1987) This duty arises from the special relationship that exists between the insurer and its insured. An insured, however, has no claim for bad faith premised on the insurer's investigation or defense of a claim brought against it by a third party. *See Maryland Ins. Co. v. Head Indus. Coatings and Servs., Inc.*, 938 S.W.2d 27, 27-28 (Tex.1996). This is because "an insured is fully protected against his insurer's refusal to defend or mishandling of a third-party claim by his contractual and *Stowers* rights," which give rise to causes of action sounding in contract and negligence. Under *G.A. Stowers Furniture Co. v. American Indem. Co*., 15 S.W.2d 544 (Tex. Comm'n App.1929), an insurer must use ordinary care in considering an offer of settlement.

In this case, Medical Care does not allege that National Union acted in bad faith in investigating or defending the shareholders' claims of loss. Indeed, it admits that National Union had no duty to defend the shareholder suit. Medical Care alleges instead that National Union acted in bad faith in handling its own claim of loss (i.e., reimbursement of its indemnification of the $10 million allocated to its directors and officers following the settlement of the shareholder suit). Its allegation concerns the relationship between it and National Union-not between National Union and the shareholders. Thus, we will treat Medical Care's claim as a first-party claim to which the duty of good faith applies.

"[A]n insurer breaches its duty of good faith and fair dealing by denying a claim when the insurer's liability has become reasonably clear." *State Farm Fire & Cas. Co. v. Simmons*, 963 S.W.2d 42, 44 (Tex.1998)."Evidence that shows only a bona fide coverage dispute does not rise to the level of bad faith." Thus, "[a]s a general rule there can be no claim for bad faith when an insurer promptly denied a claim that is in fact not covered." *Republic Ins. Co. v. Stoker,* 903 S.W.2d 338, 341 (Tex.1995).

Here, the evidence overwhelmingly shows that there was a bona fide coverage dispute, which National Union subsequently won. In the absence of coverage, summary judgment for National Union was appropriate as to Medical Care's bad faith claim.

* * *

For the foregoing reasons, we AFFIRM the judgment.

C. Liability Insurer's Duty to Defend Insureds against Third-Party Claims

1. The Origin of the Duty-to-Defend Doctrine in Texas

Quite simply, duty-to-defend doctrines vary considerably across states. State supreme courts have not crafted and accepted a universal rule. Some jurisdictions embrace and apply the so-called "complaint-potentiality rule," which requires a liability insurer to defend an insured if the insurance contract "may potentially" cover the third-party victim's claims. Other courts have adopted the "complaint-analysis-of-facts" rule, which requires insurers to examine the facts in the third-party complaint to determine if the policy covers the allegations. And there are several other doctrines.

Texas, however, and most jurisdictions require liability insurers to examine the third-party complaint and the insurance agreement to determine whether a legal defense is warranted. This rule is often called "the allegation of the complaint doctrine." In Texas, it is called "eight corners doctrine." The cases appearing below highlight some of the major duty-to-defend issues that consumers and insurers present to judges and juries in Texas's courts.

Heyden Newport Chemical Corporation v. Southern General Insurance Company
387 S.W.2d 22
(Tex. 1965)

This is a suit between petitioners, Heyden Newport Chemical Corporation and its insurer, The Insurance Company of North America, against Southern General Insurance Company, the respondent, to recover the cost of defending a prior suit under the omnibus clause of Southern General's policy. In the prior suit Heyden Newport Chemical Corporation, Newport Industries Division, hereinafter referred to as "Newport Industries," was named as a defendant along with Raymond Pickering and Arthur Marks in an action brought to recover damages for the death of Sam Traylor.

The defendant, Raymond Pickering, carried an automobile liability insurance policy with the Southern General Insurance Company, hereinafter referred to as "Southern General." Newport Industries demanded that Southern General furnish it a defense in such prior suit, claiming to be an additional insured under the omnibus provision of the policy covering Pickering. Southern General furnished Pickering and Marks a defense but refused to defend Newport Industries. Newport Industries had a policy of insurance with The Insurance Company of North America, who furnished this defense and joined Newport Industries in the present suit as a plaintiff. A jury being waived, the trial court after hearing evidence granted judgment for Southern General. The Court of Civil Appeals has affirmed. We reverse the judgments of the Court of Civil Appeals and the trial court and remand with instructions.

The allegations in the prior suit were in part as follows:

II

> Defendant, Newport Industries, is a turpentine refining business along with other related items. The raw materials from which said turpentine and other items are refined are old pine stumps that are full of resin and are sometimes referred to as "rich" and "littered" stumps. The principal source or supply of said raw materials or stumps is from the pine woods of Louisiana and East Texas. The stumps are purchased from lumber companies, dynamited and removed from the ground with bulldozers, loaded by men onto trucks, and hauled to Newport Industries by means of trucks.
>
> At all material times herein, Defendant, Raymond Pickering was an agent for Newport Industries, and his job was to purchase said stumps in the field, and get the said stumps to Newport Industries at Oakdale, Louisiana. Defendant Raymond Pickering was the owner of many trucks, which were used to haul said stumps and had employees to load and haul said stumps. Defendant Arthur Marks job was to drive a truck into the forest, load it with stumps, and haul the stumps to Newport Industries in Oakdale, Louisiana.

IV.

> Heretofore, to-wit: On or about the 16th day of February, 1961, at about 6:30 A.M., Sam Traylor, a husband and father of plaintiffs was wrongfully killed when a motor vehicle driven by defendant Arthur Marks, who was then and there in the course of his employment with defendant Raymond Pickering, collided with his pickup truck on Highway #63, approximately Seven (7) miles east of Jasper, Texas. The said collision, made the basis of this suit, was brought about by one or more of the negligent acts on the part of the said Arthur Marks as hereinafter set out with particularity . . . At the time of said collision made the basis of this suit, the driver of the vehicle, Arthur Marks, was within the scope of his employment with defendant Raymond Pickering, and at the time of said collision under the exclusive direction of defendant Raymond Pickering.

The policy of insurance contained the following provisions:

> I. Coverage A — Bodily Injury Liability: To pay on behalf of the insured all sums which the insured shall become legally obligated to pay as damages because of bodily injury, sickness or disease, including death at any time resulting therefrom, sustained by any person, caused by accident and arising out of the ownership, maintenance or use of the automobile. . . .
>
> II. Defense, Settlement, Supplementary Payments: With respect to such insurance as is afforded by this policy for bodily injury liability and for property damage

liability, the company shall: (a) defend any suit against the insured alleging such injury, sickness, disease or destruction and seeking damages on account thereof, even if such suit is groundless, false or fraudulent;

* * *

III. Definition of Insured: (a) With respect to the insurance for bodily injury liability and for property damage liability the unqualified word "insured" includes the named insured and, if the named insured is an individual, his spouse if a resident of the same household, and also includes any person while using the automobile and any person or organization legally responsible for the use thereof, provided the actual use of the automobile is by the named insured or such spouse or with the permission of either. . . .

The petitioners contend that Newport Industries was entitled to be defended under respondent's policy by reason of the fact that the allegations in the prior suit say in effect that Pickering was an agent of Newport Industries at all material times, and that therefore Newport Industries was legally responsible for the use of the automobile involved in the collision causing the death of Sam Traylor. After the allegations were made Newport Industries advised the respondent, Pickering's insurer, that Pickering was not in fact an agent of Newport Industries at any relevant time. It was on the sole ground that Pickering was not an agent of Newport Industries and time of the collision that Southern General for the use of the automobile at the time of the collision that Southern General refused to defend the lawsuit against Newport Industries. It contends that no duty to defend the lawsuit arose under the policy until a legal determination had been made and that the one demanding a defense be shown to be legally responsible for the use of the automobile in question.

In upholding the contention of respondent the Court of Civil Appeals has held in effect that in determining liability under the defense clause of the policy the court must look further than the terms of the policy and allegations of the suit against petitioner. It must actually determine the question of legal responsibility. We do not agree.

We think that in determining the duty of a liability insurance company to defend a lawsuit the allegations of the complainant should be considered in the light of the policy provisions without reference to the truth or falsity of such allegations and without reference to what the parties know or believe the true facts to be, or without reference to a legal determination thereof. By refusing a writ outright this court has determined this to be so in *Maryland Casualty Co. v. Moritz*, 138 S.W.2d 1095 (Tex. Civ. App., 1940, wherein the Court of Civil Appeals held that:

In the instant case, the issue involved depends not upon ultimate liability, established after trial on the merits, of the insurer for the damages sustained; but upon the provision of the policy wherein the insurer bound itself to defend any suit against the insured alleging damages within the terms of the policy even though such suit may have been groundless, false or fraudulent. In such instance, in testing the liability of the insurer to defend, the proof is not material. Liability depends upon the allegations of the plaintiff's petition.

* * *

> As above stated, we are not here concerned with what the proof showed upon the trial of that damage suit. The issue of appellant's liability to pay whatever judgment was rendered, and whether such judgment came within the terms of coverages A and B of its policy, is not the question here presented. The only issue before us is whether the allegations above quoted, if taken as true, were sufficient to state a cause of action against Moritz coming within the terms of the policy. If so, it was the duty of appellant, under its policy, to defend the suit. We construe these allegations as broad enough to do so; and think that the trial court properly so held. The judgment will therefore be affirmed.

The case of *Travelers Insurance Company v. Newsom*, 352 S.W.2d 888 (Tex. Civ. App. 1962, refused n. r. e.), follows the *Moritz* case and reviews a number of out of state authorities which agree with the holding in the *Moritz* case. The Court of Civil Appeals takes cognizance of these two cases, but seeks to distinguish them from its holding on the ground that in those cases the named insureds were seeking relief, whereas here it is a party claiming to be covered as an additional insured. We cannot see that the policy makes any distinction between the named insured and the additional insured under the omnibus clause.

Paragraph I of the policy set out in part above describes the contingencies of liability covered by the policy. Paragraph III describes and defines who are insured with respect to the coverage described in Paragraph I. The insurer does not pay because one is alleged to be legally responsible but because one has been adjudicated to be legally responsible. The coverage in Paragraph II is entirely different from the coverage in Paragraph I. No legal determination of ultimate liability is required before the insurer becomes obligated to defend the suit. That paragraph has reference to a suit seeking to recover damages that are covered in Paragraph I. It starts off "With respect to such insurance (coverage under Paragraph I) as is afforded by this policy . . . the company shall: (a) defend any suit against the insured . . ." The word "insured" used here means the same parties that are covered in Paragraph I because this paragraph is speaking with respect to that coverage.

The coverage in Paragraph II does not depend on what the facts are or what might finally be determined to be the facts. It depends only on what the facts are alleged to be. To put it simply, Paragraph I protects all parties described in Paragraph III from payment of damages they may be found legally obligated to pay under Paragraph I. Paragraph II protects the same parties against the expense of any suit seeking damages under Paragraph I.

Respondent says that even if the Court of Civil Appeals be wrong in holding the Moritz case is not controlling here, the trial court's judgment should be affirmed on other grounds not passed on by the Court of Civil Appeals. It is contended that the plaintiff's petition in the prior suit did not allege a cause of action against Newport Industries in that it did not specifically say that Pickering, the alleged agent of Newport Industries, was using or owned the truck involved or that at the place and time of the collision Pickering or his alleged employee Arthur Marks was in the course of his employment or agency with Newport Industries. Further, the petition did not allege facts which could make Newport Industries legally responsible for the use of the truck in question.

We have set out above in full Paragraphs II and IV of said plaintiff's petition in the prior suit which contain the pertinent pleadings in question. While they are not as complete as they should be, they do allege that Pickering was at all material times an agent of Newport Industries and his job was to procure and get pine stumps to Newport's place of business; for this purpose he had many trucks and had employees to load and haul said stumps to Newport Industries; Arthur Marks was such an employee and at the time and place of the fatal collision he was driving a truck in the course of his employment for Pickering. We think these pleadings are sufficient to permit proof on a trial that Marks was hauling stumps to Newport Industries in a truck belonging to Pickering at the time of the collision. Since this is the very work Pickering was to do for Newport, we think such alleged facts are sufficient to support a holding that Newport was responsible for the use of the truck involved and would be an additional insured under the omnibus clause.

While we have said above that the court is limited to a consideration of the allegations and the insurance policy in determining an insurer's duty to defend, we wish to point out that in considering such allegations a liberal interpretation of their meaning should be indulged. It is stated in the comprehensive annotation in 50 A.L.R.2d 458, at 504:

> Where the complaint does not state facts sufficient to clearly bring the case within or without the coverage, the general rule is that the insurer is obligated to defend if there is, potentially, a case under the complaint within the coverage of the policy. Stated differently, in case of doubt as to whether or not the allegations of a complaint against the insured state a cause of action within the coverage of a liability policy sufficient to compel the insurer to defend the action, such doubt will be resolved in insured's favor.

Respondent contends further that respondent is not liable in any event because the trial court found that the truck involved was not covered by the policy of insurance here sued on. It is true the trial court made such finding, but it was made in the face of an admission by respondent in reply to requests for admissions under Rule 169, Texas Rules Civ. Proc., that the truck in question was covered by its policy on Pickering. Such finding does not have support in the evidence and will not support the judgment.

The policy introduced in evidence by both petitioner and respondent was a Southern General policy insuring Raymond Pickering at all material times on some 98 trucks and other automobiles. Although no witness testified specifically that this was the policy in question, under all the facts and circumstances we think reasonable minds could not differ as to the conclusion that it was the same policy.

Other cross points raised by respondent do not merit discussion and we overrule them.

We reverse the judgment of the Court of Civil Appeals and the trial court and remand the cause to the trial court for entry of judgment in accordance with this opinion.

NOTES & QUESTIONS

1) How long must an insurer provide a legal defense for its insured? Is it indefinite?

2) Must insurers select the "best" insurance defense firms to defend insureds? Must an insurer also pay insured's "retained attorneys?"

3) When must the insurer pay the insurance defense firm? May insurers wait until all litigation ends before paying defense bills, attorneys, court costs, and other fees? If the insurer waits until the case reaches "finality," it that evidence of the insurer's "bad faith?"

2. Duty to Defend After Insureds Cause Third-Party "Bodily Injuries"

GuideOne Elite Insurance Company v. Fielder Road Baptist Church
197 S.W.3d 305
(Tex. 2006)

In this declaratory judgment action, we are asked to create an exception to the complaint-allegation or eight-corners rule. The eight-corners rule provides that when [a third party sues] the insured . . . , the liability insurer is to determine its duty to defend solely from terms of the policy and the pleadings of the third-party claimant. Resort to evidence outside the four corners of these two documents is generally prohibited.

The trial court, relying on evidence extrinsic to the policy and pleadings, declared that the insurer had no duty to defend the underlying claim against its insured. The court of appeals, however, reversed, concluding that because the circumstances of the case presented no reason to create an exception to the eight-corners rule, the trial court had erred in using extrinsic evidence to defeat the insurer's duty to defend. We agree and, accordingly, affirm the court of appeals' judgment.

I.

GuideOne Elite Insurance Company issued a commercial general liability insurance policy to Fielder Road Baptist Church, effective March 31, 1993. The policy included the following liability coverage for sexual misconduct:

> We agree to cover your legal liability for damages because of bodily injury, excluding any sickness or disease, to any person arising out of sexual misconduct which occurs during the policy period. We shall have the right and duty to investigate any claim ... and to defend any suit brought against you seeking damages, even if the

allegations of the suit are groundless, false or fraudulent, and we may make any settlement we deem expedient.

The policy expired on March 31, 1994. On June 6, 2001, Jane Doe filed a sexual misconduct lawsuit against the Church and Charles Patrick Evans. In her pleadings, Jane Doe alleged that "[a]t all times material herein from 1992 to 1994, Evans was employed as an associate youth minister and was under Fielder Road's direct supervision and control when he sexually exploited and abused Plaintiff." The Church demanded that GuideOne defend it in the lawsuit and indemnify it for any judgment or settlement. GuideOne agreed to defend, but questioned coverage under the policy and reserved its rights to determine that issue at a later time.

A few months later, GuideOne filed this declaratory judgment action seeking the policy's construction and a declaration that GuideOne had no duty to defend or indemnify the Church in the underlying sexual misconduct lawsuit. In this action, GuideOne sought discovery of Evans' church employment history. The Church objected, asserting that GuideOne's duty to defend should be determined from the pleadings and the insurance policy, without resort to extrinsic evidence. The trial court, however, declined to block the discovery request, and the Church thereafter advised GuideOne that Evans ceased working for it on December 15, 1992, before the GuideOne policy took effect.

After both parties filed motions for summary judgment, the trial court granted GuideOne's motion, denied the Church's, and rendered judgment declaring that GuideOne had no duty to defend the Church in the underlying sexual misconduct case. The court of appeals, however, reversed the summary judgment, concluding that the trial court had erred in considering extrinsic evidence to defeat GuideOne's duty to defend its insured. The court of appeals further concluded that Jane Doe's allegations were sufficient to invoke that duty, remanding the case to the trial court for a hearing only on costs and attorney's fees. GuideOne petitioned this Court for review.

II.

GuideOne argues that it had no duty to defend the Church against the underlying claim of sexual misconduct because Evans left his job as a youth minister before the policy's effective date. Because Jane Doe's allegations against the Church involved Evans' conduct while a youth minister, GuideOne suggests, that extrinsic evidence of when that relationship ended establishes no coverage existed for Evans' acts during the policy period. Recognizing the eight-corners rule as an impediment to its argument, however, GuideOne contends a number of reasons support its proposition that extrinsic evidence regarding Evans' employment status be considered as an exception to the rule.

First, GuideOne argues that an exception should apply because the extrinsic evidence here was primarily relevant to the issue of coverage, rather than the merits of the plaintiff's underlying claim. Alternatively, GuideOne argues that extrinsic evidence is needed to supplement the plaintiff's allegations because those allegations alone are insufficient to determine coverage or the duty to defend. Finally, GuideOne submits that should the Court conclude that the employment evidence is relevant both to coverage and liability, an exception to the eight-corners rule should nevertheless be recognized for this type of "mixed" or "overlapping" extrinsic evidence.

Under the eight-corners or complaint-allegation rule, an insurer's duty to defend is determined by the third-party plaintiff's pleadings, considered in light of the policy provisions, without regard to the truth or falsity of those allegations. *Argonaut Sw. Ins. Co. v. Maupin,* 500 S.W.2d 633, 635 (Tex.1973); *Heyden Newport Chem. Corp. v. S. Gen. Ins. Co.,* 387 S.W.2d 22, 24 (Tex.1965). The rule takes its name from the fact that only two documents are ordinarily relevant to the determination of the duty to defend: the policy and the pleadings of the third-party claimant. *King v. Dallas Fire Ins. Co.,* 85 S.W.3d 185, 187 (Tex.2002). Facts outside the pleadings, even those easily ascertained, are ordinarily not material to the determination and allegations against the insured are liberally construed in favor of coverage. *Nat'l Union Fire Ins. Co. v. Merchants Fast Motor Lines, Inc.,* 939 S.W.2d 139, 141 (Tex.1997).

Although this Court has never expressly recognized an exception to the eight-corners rule, other courts have. Generally, these courts have drawn a very narrow exception, permitting the use of extrinsic evidence only when relevant to an independent and discrete coverage issue, not touching on the merits of the underlying third-party claim.

* * *

GuideOne relies on extrinsic evidence that is relevant both to coverage and the merits and thus does not fit the above exception to the rule. Hence, GuideOne argues that we should broaden the exception to include this type of "mixed" or "overlapping" extrinsic evidence. But very little support exists for this position. . .

* * *

Those courts that have recognized an exception to the eight-corners rule have done so under limited circumstances involving pure coverage questions. For example, in *International Service Insurance Co. v. Boll,* 392 S.W.2d 158, 160 (Tex.Civ.App.-Houston 1965, writ ref'd n.r.e.), the insurer refused to defend its insured in an auto-collision case because of a policy endorsement that excluded coverage for "any claim arising from accidents which occur while any automobile is being operated by Roy Hamilton Boll." The plaintiff's petition alleged that the insured's son was driving the insured's car when the accident occurred, but did not otherwise identify the driver. After resolving the third-party claim, the insured sued his insurer to recover his defense costs. During this subsequent litigation, the parties stipulated that the insured's only son, Roy Hamilton Boll, was driving the insured vehicle. The court of appeals concluded that the stipulation established the accident had not been covered and that the insurer had no duty to defend.

The extrinsic evidence in *Boll,* however, went strictly to the coverage issue. It did not contradict any allegation in the third-party claimant's pleadings material to the merits of that underlying claim. In contrast, the extrinsic evidence here concerning Evans' employment directly contradicts the plaintiff's allegations that the Church employed Evans during the relevant coverage period, an allegation material, at least in part, to the merits of the third-party claim. Under the eight-corners rule, the allegation's truth was not a matter for debate in a declaratory judgment action between insurer and insured.

Moreover, were we to recognize the exception urged here, we would by necessity conflate the insurer's defense and indemnity duties without regard for the policy's express terms. Although these duties are created by contract, they are rarely coextensive. *See Utica Nat'l Ins. Co. of Texas v. Am. Indem. Co.,* 141 S.W.3d 198, 203 (Tex.2004) (observing that duty to defend and duty to indemnify are distinct and separate); *Whatley v. City of Dallas,* 758 S.W.2d 301, 304 (Tex.App.-Dallas 1988, writ denied) (duty to defend is defined by the terms of the contract). The policy here obligated GuideOne to indemnify the Church in the event of a meritorious claim for sexual misconduct, but with respect to the duty to defend, the contract provided that GuideOne should "defend any suit brought against [the insured] seeking damages, even if the allegations of the suit are groundless, false or fraudulent ...."

The policy thus defined the duty to defend more broadly than the duty to indemnify. This is often the case in this type of liability policy and is, in fact, the circumstances assumed to exist under the eight-corners rule. Because the respective duties differ in scope, they are invoked under different circumstances. *Trinity Universal Ins. Co. v. Cowan,* 945 S.W.2d 819, 821-22 (Tex.1997). A plaintiff's factual allegations that potentially support a covered claim is all that is needed to invoke the insurer's duty to defend; whereas, the facts actually established in the underlying suit control the duty to indemnify.

Jane Doe alleged that Evans sexually assaulted her during the policy period and was a youth minister at the Church at the time. As the court of appeals observed, the allegations were sufficient to trigger GuideOne's duty to defend.

GuideOne contends that it should not have to defend because it *knows* that Evans was not in fact an employee of the Church during this period, but the duty to defend does not turn on the truth or falsity of the plaintiff's allegations. One amicus argues, however, that it should because ignoring the truth invites fraudulent and even collusive pleadings. The amicus further suggests that we should adopt a true-facts exception to the eight-corners rule to prevent the rule's recurring use as a tool for fraud. But the record before us does not suggest collusion or the existence of a pervasive problem in Texas with fraudulent allegations designed solely to create a duty to defend.

Under the present policy, GuideOne agreed to defend the Church against allegations of sexual misconduct potentially within coverage, even if the plaintiff's allegations were false or fraudulent. Therefore if GuideOne knows these allegations to be untrue, its duty is to establish such facts in defense of its insured, rather than as an adversary in a declaratory judgment action. *Heyden Newport Chemical Corp.,* 387 S.W.2d at 25 (observing that the duty to defend coverage protects policyholders against the expense of suits seeking damages). Application of the eight-corners rule here thus conforms with the parties contract, and accordingly we agree with the court of appeals that the circumstances of this case present no basis for an exception to that rule.

III.

GuideOne also argues that Doe's pleadings failed to invoke its duty to defend because her allegations did not sufficiently describe her bodily injury. The policy defined "bodily injury" to mean "bodily injury, sickness or disease sustained by a person, including death resulting from any of these at any time." GuideOne maintains it had no duty to defend because Doe's pleadings sought damages for emotional and psychological injuries rather than "bodily injury."

The court of appeals disagreed, noting that Doe's allegations of sexual assault, abuse, molestation and violation were sufficient. Because the policy attributed no technical or special meaning to the term "bodily injury," the court applied its ordinary and generally accepted meaning, concluding that bodily injury is commonly understood to be a consequence of sexual assault and abuse. We agree.

Finally, GuideOne complains that the court of appeals erred in remanding the case to the trial court for determination of costs and attorneys' fees because Doe did not herself file a declaratory judgment action and did not pray for attorneys' fees in the proceedings below. Contrary to GuideOne's argument, however, the Church asked in its second amended motion for summary judgment that the court not only grant its motion, but also conduct a hearing and award it attorneys' fees.

The Declaratory Judgments Act provides that in any proceeding under the Act "the court may award costs and reasonable and necessary attorney's fees as are equitable and just." Tex. Civ. Prac. & Rem. Code § 37.009. The reasonable and necessary requirements are questions of fact to be determined by the factfinder; the equitable and just requirements are questions of law for the trial court to decide. *Bocquet v. Herring,* 972 S.W.2d 19, 21 (Tex.1998). The court of appeals therefore did not err in remanding the issue of attorneys' fees and costs to the trial court.

* * *

Finding no error in the court of appeals' judgment, we affirm.

NOTES & QUESTIONS

1) Fairly often, third-party victims' complaints have multiple claims and theories of recovery. Some are covered and some are excluded under the insureds' liability polices. If a third party files a mixed-claims suit against the insured, does the insurer still have to defend the insured?

2) What "triggers" a liability insurer's duty to defend when a third party files a personal injury lawsuit against the insured?

3) What "triggers" a liability insurer's duty to defend when a third party files a property damage claim against the insured?

3. Duty to Defend After Insureds Destroy Third Parties' Property

Don's Building Supply, Inc. v. OneBeacon Insurance Company
267 S.W.3d 20
(Tex. 2008)

This insurance-coverage dispute presents two certified questions from the United States Court of Appeals for the Fifth Circuit. The Fifth Circuit asks generally when property damage "occurs" under Texas law for purposes of an occurrence-based commercial general liability insurance policy, a question this Court has never answered. More specifically, is an insurer's duty to defend triggered where damage is alleged to have occurred during the policy period but was inherently undiscoverable until after the policy expired? As to this policy, which focuses on when damage comes to pass, not when damage comes to light, we answer "yes" — the insurer's duty is triggered under Texas law; the key date is when injury happens, not when someone happens upon it.

I. Background

The relevant facts are set out in the Fifth Circuit's opinion certifying the questions to us. Don's Building Supply, Inc. (DBS) sells and distributes a synthetic stucco product known as an Exterior Insulation and Finish System (EIFS). This siding system was installed on various homes from December 1, 1993 to December 1, 1996, during which DBS was covered by comprehensive general liability (CGL) policies issued by Potomac Insurance Company of Illinois and assigned to OneBeacon Insurance Company (OneBeacon). From 2003 to 2005, various Texas homeowners filed state-court lawsuits against DBS, alleging the EIFS was defective and not weather-tight, thus allowing moisture to seep into wall cavities behind the siding and causing wood rot and other damages. The homeowners argue these injuries "actually began to occur on the occasion of the first penetration of moisture behind" the EIFS, which they say was "within six months to one year after the application of the EIFS." The alleged result of this ongoing moisture exposure was extensive damage to the homes, reduced property values, and the need to retrofit or replace the EIFS.

In their suits alleging negligence, fraud, and violations of the Texas Deceptive Trade Practices Act, the homeowners seek to avoid the statutes of limitations for their various claims by pleading the discovery rule, arguing the home damage was "hidden from view" by the siding's undamaged exterior and "not discoverable or readily apparent to someone looking at that surface until after the policy period ended."

OneBeacon initially provided a defense to DBS but then filed a declaratory judgment action in federal district court seeking a ruling that it had no duty to defend and indemnify under the CGL policies. The court agreed with OneBeacon that the duty does not arise until the damage becomes identifiable. DBS appealed to the Fifth Circuit, which certified the coverage trigger-date questions to us.

II. Discussion

A. First Certified Question

The Fifth Circuit first asks: When not specified by the relevant policy, what is the proper rule under Texas law for determining the time at which property damage occurs for purposes of an occurrence-based commercial general liability insurance policy?

We construe insurance policies according to the same rules of construction that apply to contracts generally. Effectuating the parties' expressed intent is our primary concern. If an insurance contract uses unambiguous language, we must enforce it as written. If, however, a contract is susceptible to more than one reasonable interpretation, we will resolve any ambiguity in favor of coverage. Policy terms are given their ordinary and commonly understood meaning unless the policy itself shows the parties intended a different, technical meaning. "No one phrase, sentence, or section [of the policy] should be isolated from its setting and considered apart from the other provisions." In addition, "we must give the policy's words their plain meaning, without inserting additional provisions into the contract."

With these principles in mind, we turn to the relevant policy language. The first page provides a one-year policy period with designated start and end dates. The policy provides "bodily injury" and "property damage" coverage as follows:

> We will pay those sums that the insured becomes legally obligated to pay as damages because of "bodily injury" or "property damage" to which this insurance applies. We will have the right and duty to defend any "suit" seeking those damages.

The policy further provides: This insurance applies to "bodily injury" and "property damage" only if . . . (1) The "bodily injury" or "property damage" is caused by an "occurrence" that takes place in the "coverage territory;" and (2) The "bodily injury" or "property damage" occurs during the policy period.

The policy defines an "occurrence" as "an accident, including continuous or repeated exposure to substantially the same general harmful conditions." We recently noted, in construing the same CGL language, that "[a]n accident is generally understood to be a fortuitous, unexpected, and unintended event." *Lamar Homes, Inc. v. Mid-Continent Cas. Co.*, 242 S.W.3d 1, 8 (Tex.2007). The policy's requirement that property damage be caused by an "occurrence" limits coverage in at least two respects. First, because the occurrence must be an "accident," coverage for intentional torts is excluded. Second, because a single occurrence can be "an accident" and consist of "continuous or repeated exposure to substantially the same general harmful conditions," the definition of occurrence serves to limit the number of occurrences an insured can claim for what the policy deems to be a single accident. This limitation is sometimes important because the dollar limits of the policy include an aggregate limit and also a lower dollar limit per occurrence.

The policy covering December 1993 to December 1994, for example, has a $1 million aggregate limit and a $500,000 limit per occurrence. The policy defines "property damage" to mean:

> a. Physical injury to tangible property, including all resulting loss of use of that property. All such loss of use shall be deemed to occur at the time of the physical injury that caused it; or
>
> b. Loss of use of tangible property that is not physically injured. All such loss shall be deemed to occur at the time of the "occurrence" that caused it.

Considering these provisions together and reading them for their plain meaning, we hold that property damage under this policy occurred when actual physical damage to the property occurred. The policy says as much, defining property damage as "[p]hysical injury to tangible property," and explicitly stating that coverage is available if and only if "'property damage' occurs during the policy period." So in this case, property damage occurred when a home that is the subject of an underlying suit suffered wood rot or other physical damage. The date that the physical damage is or could have been discovered is irrelevant under the policy.

We recognize, however, the existence of caselaw discussing when the duty to defend is "triggered" under occurrence-based and other policies.

* * *

Many courts agree with the analysis we adopt today, sometimes called the "actual injury" or "injury-in-fact" approach, that the insurer must defend any claim of physical property damage that occurred during the policy term. Other courts, including several Texas appellate courts, have followed a "manifestation rule" that imposes a duty to defend only if the property damage became evident or discoverable during the policy term. The manifestation approach takes different forms, with some courts having the rule turn on when the damage is actually discovered, and others looking to when the damage could have been discovered.

Even those courts favoring the latter manifestation trigger appear to take differing views of how easily discoverable the damage or injury must be. We also note that decisions sometimes cited as following the manifestation rule, and which indeed use a form of the word "manifest" in their analysis, do not actually follow the manifestation rule as opposed to the actual-injury rule, because they were not concerned with latent damage where these two rules diverge. Instead, these cases merely hold that the time of the injury or damage, as opposed to the time of the alleged negligent conduct that caused the injury, is the triggering event under the policy. These cases, when carefully reviewed, may actually be more aligned with the actual-injury rule than with the manifestation rule, and appear to use a form of the verb "manifests" merely as a synonym for "results in" or "leads to," rather than drawing a distinction between the actual occurrence of damage and the later discovery or obviousness of damage.

Other courts, including two Texas courts of appeals, follow an "exposure rule" that finds coverage if the plaintiff is exposed to whatever agent ultimately results in personal injury or property damage during the policy period. Again, what some courts call the "exposure rule" may actually be what others would call the injury-in-fact rule.

Still other courts adopt other approaches, including multiple trigger rules, and a rule that looks to the date of the alleged negligent conduct rather than the date of the actual injury to the claimant. In cases involving continuous losses, California follows a manifestation rule for first-party property insurance claims (such as claims under a homeowners' policy) but a continuous-injury rule for liability insurance policies (such as claims under CGL policies). A related if not overlapping body of law, which we do not explore today, addresses when coverage is triggered on bodily injury claims under CGL and other policies.

* * *

As for the manifestation rule, the rule urged by OneBeacon and followed by most Texas cases to date, the policy before us simply makes no provision for it. The policy in straightforward wording provides coverage if the property damage "occurs during the policy period," and further provides that property damage means "[p]hysical injury to tangible property." Whatever practical advantages a manifestation rule would offer to the insured or the insurer, the controlling policy language does not provide that the insurer's duty is triggered only when the injury manifests itself during the policy term, or that coverage is limited to claims where the damage was discovered or discoverable during the policy period.

Similarly, the policy's language does not support adoption of an exposure rule, at least not where there is "physical injury to tangible property" as alleged in this case. Again, the policy provides coverage if the "'property damage' occurs during the policy period." The policy does not state that coverage is available if property is, during the policy period, exposed to a process, event, or substance that later results in bodily injury or physical injury to tangible property.

We therefore decline to recognize a manifestation rule or exposure rule for the property damage claims alleged under this policy. This policy links coverage to damage, not damage detection. Engrafting a manifestation rule to limit coverage — by conditioning coverage on the observations of a third-party claimant — would blur the distinction between this occurrence-based policy and a claims-made policy. If the manifestation rule offers advantages of ease of application or proof for the insurer or insured, insurance companies might consider adopting policies where coverage depends on manifestation of damage, and seeking approval of such policies by Texas insurance regulators. We note, however, that the manifestation rule does not eliminate the need to address sometimes nettlesome fact issues. In fact, the actual-injury rule may well make claims more predictable insofar as one type of manifestation trigger turns not on when the claimant actually identified the damage but rather on when the damage was capable of identification.

Pinpointing the moment of injury retrospectively is sometimes difficult, but we cannot exalt ease of proof or administrative convenience over faithfulness to the policy language; our confined task is to review the contract, not revise it. Our prevailing concern is not one of policy but of law, and we must honor the parties' chosen language-covering third-party claims if damage to the claimant's property occurred during the policy period. The policy asks when damage happened, not whether it was manifest, patent, visible, apparent, obvious, perceptible, discovered, discoverable, capable of detection, or anything similar. Occurred means when damage occurred, not when discovery occurred. In this case, property damage occurred when the home in question suffered wood rot or some other form of physical damage.

Looking to the date of actual injury, besides being consistent with the policy terms, is also consistent with scholarly authority. To quote one leading insurance law treatise, "the time of the occurrence of the accident within an indemnity policy is generally not considered to be the time the wrongful act was committed but the time when the complaining party was actually damaged."

* * *

Finally, we stress that we do not attempt to fashion a universally applicable "rule" for determining when an insurer's duty to defend a claim is triggered under an insurance policy, as such determinations should be driven by the contract language-language that obviously may vary from policy to policy.

B. Second Certified Question

The Fifth Circuit next asks: Under the rule identified in the answer to the first question, have the pleadings in lawsuits against an insured alleged that property damage occurred within the policy period of an occurrence-based commercial general liability insurance policy, such that the insurer's duty to defend and indemnify the insured is triggered, when the pleadings allege that actual damage was continuing and progressing during the policy period, but remained undiscoverable and not readily apparent for purposes of the discovery rule until after the policy period ended because the internal damage was hidden from view by an undamaged exterior surface?

As to the duty to defend, we answer this question "yes." Under the "eight corners" rule of Texas insurance law, the insurer's defense duty turns on the policy's terms and the plaintiff's allegations. The duty is triggered if the plaintiff alleges facts that would give rise to any claim against the insured that is covered by the policy.

The OneBeacon policy itself imposes a duty to defend without regard to the merits of the underlying claim against the insured; it imposes on the insurer "a duty to defend any" suit seeking damages for "bodily injury" or "property damages" covered by the policy, regardless of whether the plaintiff in the underlying action has a legally meritorious claim. By purchasing the policy, DBS acquired a contractual right to a defense against both meritorious and nonmeritorious claims for property damage. *See Argonaut Sw. Ins. Co. v. Maupin*, 500 S.W.2d 633, 635 (Tex.1973) ("The ... duty to defend is determined by the allegations of the petition ... without reference to the truth or falsity of such allegations.")

Based on our answer to the first certified question, the insurer's duty to defend DBS depends on whether the homeowners' pleadings allege property damage that occurred during the policy term. Under the actual-injury rule applicable to this policy, a plaintiff's claim against DBS that any amount of physical injury to tangible property occurred during the policy period and was caused by DBS's allegedly defective product triggers OneBeacon's duty to defend. This duty is not diminished because the property damage was undiscoverable or not readily apparent or "manifest," until after the policy period ended. Nor does it depend on whether DBS has a valid limitations defense. The parties could have conditioned coverage on identifiability, but the contract imposes no such limitation.

Today's decision rests upon the specific language of these parties' CGL policies regarding property damage in the construction-defect context, and it is directed only to the specific questions posed by the Fifth Circuit. We intend no position as to whether plaintiffs' claims in the underlying suits are meritorious.

Pine Oak Builders, Inc. v. Great American Lloyds Insurance Company
279 S.W.3d 650
(Tex. 2009)

Upon being sued by five different homeowners alleging various construction defects, Pine Oak Builders, Inc. made written demand on its insurers, including Great American Lloyds Insurance Co., for a defense. When the insurers denied any duty to defend, Pine Oak sued for breach of the insurers' defense obligations. This coverage dispute revisits issues addressed in three of our recent cases, which decide some matters in Pine Oak's favor and some in Great American's favor.

I. Background

Great American issued occurrence-based commercial general liability (CGL) policies to Pine Oak, a homebuilder, covering April 1993 to April 2001. Another insurer, Mid-Continent Casualty Co., issued CGL policies covering April 2001 to April 2003. Between February 2002 and March 2003, five homeowners sued Pine Oak, alleging their homes suffered water damage because of defective construction. Four of the suits alleged improper installation of a synthetic stucco product known as an Exterior Insulation and Finish System (EIFS). The other suit, the Glass suit, alleged water damage due to improper design and construction of columns and a balcony.

The insurers denied Pine Oak's request for a defense in the homeowner suits, prompting Pine Oak to file this suit. The insurers in turn sought a declaratory judgment that they had no obligation to defend or indemnify Pine Oak. Both sides sought summary judgment — Pine Oak arguing its right to a defense and damages, and Great American arguing the policies did not cover the claims in the underlying suits. The trial court granted summary judgment for the insurers on all issues.

The court of appeals affirmed the summary judgment for Mid-Continent because of an EIFS exclusion found in Mid-Continent's policies, and Pine Oak does not appeal this ruling. As for Great American, the court affirmed the summary judgment relating to the Glass suit, reasoning that it only alleged defective work by Pine Oak that was excluded under the policies' "your work" exclusion. However, the court concluded Great American had a duty to defend the four other homeowner suits, though Pine Oak could not recover statutory damages under the Prompt Payment of Claims statute —Tex. Ins. Code §§ 542.051-.061 (previously codified as Tex. Ins. Code art. 21.55) — for Great American's failure to defend the suits. We granted the parties' cross-petitions.

II. Discussion

A. *Lamar Homes* — Whether Faulty Workmanship Claims Are Covered and Whether Insurance Code Article 21.55 Applies

Great American urges us to hold that Pine Oak's faulty-workmanship claims do not allege "property damage" caused by an "occurrence" under the terms of the policies. This argument is foreclosed by *Lamar Homes, Inc. v. Mid-Continent Casualty Co.,* 242 S.W.3d 1, 4-5, 16 (Tex. 2007), where we held that a claim of faulty workmanship against a homebuilder was a claim for property damage caused by an occurrence under a CGL policy. The relevant policy language in the Great American policies is identical to the policy language we construed in *Lamar Homes.*

Pine Oak asks us to reverse the court of appeals' holding that the Prompt Payment of Claims statute does not apply to an insurer's breach of its duty to defend under a liability policy. We agree, as *Lamar Homes* again controls, making clear the statute does apply to such situations.

B. *Don's Building Supply*— What Triggers Coverage Under an Occurrence-Based CGL Policy?

The underlying suits concern homes built in 1996 and 1997. Great American's policies, consecutive one-year policies, cover the period from April 5, 1993 to April 5, 2001. On the question of whether Great American's policies were triggered under facts alleged in the underlying suits, the court of appeals followed the "exposure rule" for determining whether a property-damage claim is covered under an occurrence-based CGL policy. Great American urges us to adopt the "manifestation rule" for deciding whether a property-damage claim is covered. We rejected both of these rules in *Don's Building Supply, Inc. v. OneBeacon Insurance Co.,* 267 S.W.3d 20 (Tex. 2008), another case involving insurance coverage of EIFS claims.

We adopted instead the actual-injury rule, under which property damage occurs during the policy period if "actual physical damage to the property occurred" during the policy period. As we explained in that case, "the key date is when injury happens, not when someone happens upon it"— that is, the focus should be on "when damage comes to pass, not when damage comes to light." he policy language construed in *Don's Building Supply* is identical to the relevant language in Great American's policies. So property damage occurred under the Great American policies "when a home that is the subject of an underlying suit suffered wood rot or other physical damage." On remand, the trial court should apply the actual-injury rule to any remaining disputes about whether the property-damage claims fall within the terms of the Great American policies.

C. *GuideOne Elite* —Extrinsic Evidence and the Eight-Corner Rule

The final issue is whether evidence extrinsic to the eight corners of the policy and the underlying lawsuit may be used to establish the insurer's duty to defend. Exclusion " *l* " of the CGL policy removes coverage for property damage to the insured's completed work. This exclusion contains an exception "if the damaged work or the work out of which the damage arises was performed on your behalf by a subcontractor." As *Lamar Homes* explained, coverage therefore depends in part on whether the alleged defective work was performed by Pine Oak or a subcontractor. *See Lamar Homes, Inc. v. Mid-Continent Cas. Co.,* 242 S.W.3d 1, 11 (Tex.2007)

In four of the underlying suits against Pine Oak, the petitions expressly alleged defective work by one or more subcontractors. In the Glass case, the petition contains no allegations of defective work by a subcontractor. The petition asserted causes of action for breach of contract and warranty, violation of the Residential Construction Liability Act, Tex. Prop.Code §§ 27.001-.007, and negligence, based on Pine Oak's alleged failure to perform its work in a good and workmanlike manner and a failure to make requested repairs.

In this coverage suit, Pine Oak submitted evidence that the defective work alleged in the Glass case was performed by subcontractors. Based on this extrinsic evidence, Pine Oak contends Great American had a duty to defend Pine Oak in the Glass case.

Under the eight-corners rule, the duty to defend is determined by the claims alleged in the petition and the coverage provided in the policy. *See Nat'l Union Fire Ins. Co. of Pittsburgh, PA, v. Merchs. Fast Motor Lines, Inc.,* 939 S.W.2d 139, 141 (Tex.1997); *Heyden Newport Chem. Corp. v. S. Gen. Ins. Co.,* 387 S.W.2d 22, 26 (Tex.1965). "If a petition does not allege facts within the scope of coverage, an insurer is not legally required to defend a suit against its insured." *Nat'l Union,* 939 S.W.2d at 141.

In *GuideOne Elite Insurance Co. v. Fielder Road Baptist Church,* 197 S.W.3d 305, 307 (Tex. 2006) —issued six days before the court of appeals' decision in this case, the plaintiff in an underlying suit alleged that an employee of the insured had sexually abused her. The insurer brought a declaratory judgment action to determine coverage. The underlying third-party petition alleged that the abuse occurred from 1992 to 1994. The insurer sought to introduce extrinsic evidence that the employee ceased working for the insured on December 15, 1992, before the insurance policy took effect. We stated:

> Although this Court has never expressly recognized an exception to the eight-corners rule, other courts have. Generally, these courts have drawn a very narrow exception, permitting the use of extrinsic evidence only when relevant to an independent and discrete coverage issue, not touching on the merits of the underlying third-party claim.

Without recognizing an exception to the eight-corners rule, we held that any such exception would not extend to evidence that was relevant to both insurance coverage and the factual merits of the case as alleged by the third-party plaintiff. We further reasoned that the extrinsic evidence here concerning Evans' employment directly contradicts the plaintiff's allegations that the Church employed Evans during the relevant coverage period, an allegation material, at least in part, to the merits of the third-party claim. Under the eight-corners rule, the allegation's truth was not a matter for debate in a declaratory judgment action between insurer and insured.

The extrinsic fact Pine Oak seeks to introduce in this coverage action contradicts the facts alleged in the Glass suit. The petition in the Glass suit alleges that Pine Oak agreed to construct the plaintiffs' house, that Pine Oak alone "constructed columns that provided inadequate support," "failed to properly seal seams," "negligently attempted to correct" a problem with the balcony, failed "to perform the work in a good and workmanlike manner," and failed "to make the repairs described above." These claims of faulty workmanship by Pine Oak are excluded from coverage under the "your work" exclusion. Faulty workmanship by a subcontractor that might fall under the subcontractor exception to the "your work" exclusion is not mentioned in the petition. "If the petition only alleges facts excluded by the policy, the insurer is not required to defend." *Fid. & Guar. Ins. Underwriters, Inc. v. McManus,* 633 S.W.2d 787, 788 (Tex.1982).

Pine Oak urges that the references in the Glass petition to Pine Oak as the culpable party can be read as either Pine Oak or one of its subcontractors. Unlike the petitions in the other four suits, the petition in the Glass case does not accuse any subcontractor-a separate legal entity-of defective work or other legally actionable conduct, nor does it allege that Pine Oak is liable under any theory for the conduct or work of a subcontractor. It does not allege negligent supervision of a subcontractor or any other third party. It alleges that Pine Oak alone is liable for its own actionable conduct. "We will not read facts into the pleadings. . . . Nor will we look outside the pleadings, or imagine factual scenarios which might trigger coverage." *Nat'l Union Fire Ins. Co. of Pittsburgh, PA, v. Merchs. Fast Motor Lines, Inc.,* 939S.W.2d 139, 142 (Tex.1997). Instead, "an insurer is entitled to rely solely on the factual allegations contained in the petition in conjunction with the terms of the policy to determine whether it has a duty to defend." *Trinity Universal Ins. Co. v. Cowan,* 945 S.W.2d 819, 829 (Tex.1997)

Pine Oak views *GuideOne Elite* as distinguishable because in that case the insurer was attempting to introduce extrinsic evidence to *limit* its duty to defend, whereas here Pine Oak, the insured, offered extrinsic evidence to *trigger* the duty to defend. This distinction is not legally significant.

In deciding the duty to defend, the court should not consider extrinsic evidence from either the insurer or the insured that contradicts the allegations of the underlying petition. The duty to defend depends on the language of the policy setting out the contractual agreement between insurer and insured. A defense of third-party claims provided by the insurer is a valuable benefit granted to the insured by the policy, separate from the duty to indemnify. But the insurer's duty to defend is limited to those claims actually asserted in an underlying suit.

Great American's policy provides that it shall "have the right and duty to defend any 'suit' seeking" damages for bodily injury or property damage covered by the policy. "Suit" is defined as "a civil proceeding in which damages because of [property damage or other injuries] to which this insurance applies are alleged." The policy imposes no duty to defend a claim that might have been alleged but was not, or a claim that more closely tracks the true factual circumstances surrounding the third-party claimant's injuries but which, for whatever reason, has not been asserted. To hold otherwise would impose a duty on the insurer that is not found in the language of the policy. Such a construction would subject an insurer to common-law and statutory liability for failing to defend the insured against a third-party claim that has not been alleged, despite policy language limiting the duty to defend to claims that have been alleged.

Such a construction would also "conflate the insurer's defense and indemnity duties," since the duty to defend turns on the "factual allegations that potentially support a covered claim," while "the facts actually established in the underlying suit control the duty to indemnify." *GuideOne Elite Ins. Co. v. Fielder Rd. Baptist Church,* 197 S.W.3d 305, 310 (Tex. 2006)

The duty to defend protects the insured by requiring a legal defense to allegations without regard to whether they are true, but it does not extend to allegations, true or false, that have not been made. *See Heyden Newport Chem. Corp.*, 387 S.W.2d at 24 ("We think that in determining the duty of a liability insurance company to defend a lawsuit the allegations of the complainant should be considered in the light of the policy provisions without reference to the truth or falsity of such allegations and without reference to what the parties know or believe the true facts to be, or without reference to a legal determination thereof.").

Great American's duty to defend was not triggered by the Glass petition in the record before us.

III. Conclusion

We affirm in part and reverse in part the court of appeals' judgment, and remand the case to the trial court for further proceedings consistent with this opinion.

NOTES & QUESTIONS

1) Again, what is an "occurrence-based" Comprehensive General Liability (CGL) insurance contract? And what is a claims-made CGL policy? See *American Physicians Ins. Exch. v. Garcia,* 876 S.W.2d 842, 853-54 n. 21 (Tex.1994) (noting that language in policies defining an "occurrence" or a "claim occurrence" as an accident "including continuous or repeated exposure to substantially the same general conditions" or a "series of acts or occurrences arising out of one event" is intended to limit the number of claims the insured can make for what the policy deems a single occurrence).

2) "Exposure Rule," "Manifestation Rule," and "Actual-Injury Rule"— Courts have employed these to determine whether a property-damage claim is covered under an occurrence-based liability insurance contract. What are the major differences among these three doctrines?

3) When large manufacturers, chemical companies, oil and gas companies, and other large industrials pollute the environment accidently, they reasonably expect comprehensive general liability insurers to settle class-action or third-party victims' mass-tort claims. After all, the doctrines

of strict products liability and absolute liability acknowledge that third-party property losses might occur—when companies engage in ultra-hazardous or dangerous enterprises. To be sure, insurers know these rules extremely well. In fact, many liability insurers employ these doctrines to help sell liability insurance contracts. Yet, insurers balk and refuse to defend mass-tort claims. Is that evidence of bad faith? Should insurers have a mandatory duty to defend insured against mass-tort claims?

E & L Chipping Co., Inc. v. Hanover Insurance Company
962 S.W.2d 272
(Tex. App.-Beaumont 1998)

This appeal from the granting of summary judgments in favor of St. Paul Insurance Company and Hanover Insurance Companies raises several important issues concerning insurance law and the scope of environmental insurance coverage under Texas law.

Appellants (collectively referred to as E & L) are a lumber company (E & L Chipping Co., Inc.) and its owners (the Lowerys). Appellees are three insurance companies: St. Paul Insurance Company (St. Pau") and The Hanover Insurance Company and Hanover Lloyd's Insurance Company (collectively referred to as Hanover).

E & L sued the insurance companies on breach of contract grounds for their refusal to defend E & L in four underlying lawsuits. The underlying lawsuits arose from allegations that, in spraying water on a fire on their property, appellants caused a run-off of contaminated water into a nearby stream, thereby also contaminating lakes and a spring of landowners located downstream. In addition to the breach of contract allegations, E & L also pleaded extra-contractual causes of action — fraud, misrepresentation, negligence, breach of the duty of good faith and fair dealing, and violations of the Texas Deceptive Trade Practices Act and Art. 21.21 of the Texas Insurance Code. The extra-contractual causes of action, all of which arose out of the refusal by the insurance companies to defend E & L in the underlying suits, are dependent upon the existence of a duty to defend for their viability.

St. Paul and Hanover, both insurers of E & L, denied coverage and refused to tender a defense. E & L claims it was forced to incur over $500,000 in legal expenses in the underlying lawsuits, which E & L successfully defended.

Both St. Paul and Hanover filed motions for summary judgment which were granted by the trial judge without specifying the grounds for his ruling. St. Paul's motion for summary judgment was based on the following grounds: 1) the underlying lawsuits were not "accidents" during St. Paul's policy period; 2) the underlying claims were "known losses" or "losses in progress" prior to the inception of St. Paul's policy; and 3) E & L failed to disclose the known claims to St. Paul when E & L applied for the St. Paul policy. Hanover's motion for summary judgment claimed (1) E & L failed to tender to Hanover the *Collie, Lane,* and *Bailey* lawsuits for a defense and, as a result,

Hanover had no duty to defend; and 2) the policy's "pollution exclusion" precluded coverage for claims alleged in the *Miller* lawsuit.

"When an insurer is faced with the dilemma of whether to defend or refuse to defend a proffered claim, it has four options: 1) completely decline to assume the insured's defense; 2) seek a declaratory judgment as to its obligations and rights; 3) defend under a reservation of rights or a non-waiver agreement; and 4) assume the insured's unqualified defense. As noted above, both St. Paul and Hanover chose the first option.

An insurer's duty to defend and duty to indemnify are distinct and separate duties. *Trinity Universal Ins. Co. v. Cowan,* 945 S.W.2d 819, 821-22 (Tex.1997). Thus, an insurer may have a duty to defend, but no duty to indemnify. *See Farmers Texas County Mut. Ins. Co. v. Griffin,* 955 S.W.2d 81, 82 (Tex.1997). The duty to defend is, therefore, broader than the duty to indemnify. In the instant case, the issue before us is the duty to defend; since E & L successfully defended the underlying suits, there is no duty on the part of the insurers to indemnify.

A duty to defend is determined solely by the allegations in the underlying pleadings and the language of the insurance policy. *Nat'l Union Fire Ins. Co. of Pittsburgh, Pa. v. Merchants Fast Motor Lines, Inc.,* 939 S.W.2d 139, 141 (Tex.1997). Whether an insurance carrier owes a duty to defend under an insurance policy is a question of law which the appellate court reviews de novo. If the underlying petition does not allege facts within the scope of coverage, an insurer is not legally required to defend a suit against its insured. . This is sometimes referred to as the "eight corners" rule. *Id.* When applying the eight corners rule, we give the allegations in the petition a liberal interpretation. "[I]n case of doubt as to whether or not the allegations of a complaint against the insured state a cause of action within the coverage of a liability policy sufficient to compel the insurer to defend the action, such doubt will be resolved in the insured's favor." *Heyden Newport Chem. Corp. v. Southern Gen. Ins. Co.,* 387 S.W.2d 22, 26 (Tex.1965).

In reviewing the underlying pleadings, the court must focus on the factual allegations that show the origin of the damages rather than on the legal theories alleged. We do not consider the veracity of the allegations in the underlying pleadings, read facts into the pleadings, or look outside the pleadings to determine if facts within coverage could have been pled.

St. Paul's Duty to Defend

The St. Paul policy on which E & L was insured is Commercial General Liability Policy (hereafter "the policy"), issued pursuant to application for such insurance dated January 9, 1989. As noted above, the scope of our review in determining the duty to defend is the language of the insurance policy itself, as well as the facts alleged in the underlying pleadings.

We look first at the facts alleged in the *Miller, Collie, Lane,* and *Bailey* lawsuits. Each petition alleges that a fire occurred in a wood chip pile on E & L's property around October 24, 1988, and that E & L attempted to extinguish the fire by spraying large quantities of water on it. The landowners, in the underlying suits, further contend that contaminated water from the wood chip pile ultimately ran onto their properties downstream and polluted lakes (*Miller, Collie,* and

Bailey suits) and a spring (*Lane* suit). Miller and Lane contend the run-off also contaminated the underground water system. The contamination, as alleged by the four petitioners, was ongoing at the time each landowner filed suit and had continued unabated from the October 1988 date. The St. Paul policy period was February 1, 1989, to February 1, 1990. The individual suits were filed on the following dates: *Miller*-November 22, 1989; *Lane*-February 9, 1990; *Collie*-March 27, 1990; *Bailey*-December 28, 1990.

Having reviewed the facts alleged in the underlying suits, we look now at the language of the insurance contract. St. Paul's policy covers "property damage" occurring during the policy period. The policy does not require that an occurrence take place during the policy period. What the policy does provide is that the property damage must be caused by an occurrence, which the policy defines as "an accident, including continuous or repeated exposure to substantially the same general harmful conditions."

As defined by the policy, "property damage" means: "a. [p]hysical injury to tangible property, including all resulting loss of use of that property; or b. [l]oss of use of tangible property that is not physically injured." The policy specifically states that St. Paul has a duty to defend "any suit seeking those damages." In other words, if a suit against the insured factually alleges property damage occurring during the policy period and resulting from an accident, St. Paul must defend its insured in that suit, unless a policy exclusion applies.

On the face of the pleadings, it is apparent the fire itself occurred prior to the inception of the policy and is clearly outside the policy period. We cannot determine from the underlying pleadings when the spraying of the water on the wood chip pile commenced or when it ended. The pleadings also do not state when the fire was extinguished or when the run-off or contamination ended. However, the petitions do clearly state that the property damage from the resulting run-off had been continuous since the date of the fire and, indeed, was continuing at the very time the underlying suits were filed. According to the policy, property damage must occur during the policy period; on the face of the pleadings, at least some of the property damage did so. In looking at the "eight corners" of the insurance policy and the underlying pleadings, it is apparent the facts pleaded are within the scope of the policy period.

* * *

Based on the facts alleged in the four suits in question, we do not perceive the alleged damage, which resulted from E & L's attempt to extinguish a fire caused by "spontaneous combustion," can in any way be viewed as "expected or intended" by the insured. The mere fact that E & L intended to engage in the conduct (i.e., spray water on the wood chip pile) that gave rise to the alleged injury (contamination of landowners' water downstream) does not mean there was no "accident" or "occurrence." As the Texas Supreme Court explained in *Cowan,* this interpretation would render insurance coverage illusory for many of the things for which insureds commonly purchase insurance. The facts, as pleaded in the underlying suits, evidence an "accident" or "occurrence" and do not fall within the "expected and intended" exclusion of the policy.

St. Paul further contends that the underlying claims were "known losses" or "losses in progress" prior to the inception of St. Paul's policy and are not covered by the policy. Both doctrines involve a knowledge of a loss which has already occurred or a loss in progress before the inception of the policy. In seeking to determine the applicability of those doctrines to the instant case, we turn once again to the eight corners rule. In so doing, we restrict our review to the insurance policy and the underlying pleadings, and again point out that the facts, as pleaded, evidence property damage occurring during the policy period as required by the policy.

The third ground upon which St. Paul bases its motion for summary judgment is E & L's alleged misrepresentation in the insurance application wherein E & L failed to list any claims regarding the fire water run-off. As a condition precedent to the insurer's liability under the policy, the insured's representations and statements in the declaration page must have been complete and accurate. In determining the duty to defend, as opposed to the duty to indemnify, we do not go outside the eight corners of the underlying pleadings and the insurance policy. Even if we could do so, we would reach the same conclusion — namely that there is no evidence of E & L's intent to deceive St. Paul with any of its representations. *See Union Bankers Ins. Co. v. Shelton,* 889 S.W.2d 278 (Tex.1994).

Construing the allegations in the underlying petitions liberally, as we are required to do under the standard of review in "duty to defend" cases, we find St. Paul did not establish as a matter of law that the facts alleged in the underlying suits were not within the scope of the coverage of the policy. The trial court erred in granting summary judgment for St. Paul. Appellants' point of error one is sustained.

Hanover's Duty to Defend

The Hanover policy contains the following "absolute pollution exclusion": f. (1) "Bodily injury" or "property damage" arising out of the actual, alleged or threatened discharge, dispersal, release or escape of pollutants: Pollutants means any solid, liquid, gaseous or thermal irritant or contaminant, including smoke, vapor, soot, fumes, acids, alkalis, chemicals and waste. Waste includes materials to be recycled, reconditioned or reclaimed.

MILLER SUIT

The *Miller* petition stated the lawsuit became necessary because E & L "released contaminated water from its premises into the Magnus Branch in Tyler County Texas which has flowed downstream into Lake Electra." Ms. Miller alleged that "fire water runoff containing various hazardous and toxic substances was allowed to run unimpeded into Magnus Branch and thereafter came to rest on plaintiff's [Miller's] property, Electra Lake, among other places" as the result of E & L's attempt to extinguish a fire in the firewood chip pile located on E & L's premises. The *Miller* petition also alleged that a tank constructed to trap fire water was improperly built, resulting in "contaminated waters seeping into the underground water system thereby further contaminating plaintiff's water system." Included in the petition's assertions of negligence are allegations that E & L (1) had discharged contaminated firewater into her lake; (2) had discharged stored contaminated water from a decking pond on E & L's property into the water system, thereby damaging plaintiff's lake; and (3) was responsible for contamination by seepage of ground water from its operations.

Elsewhere in the pleading, Ms. Miller alleged that E & L Lumber Company had violated provisions of the Texas Water Code pertaining to the discharge of waste. Among the damages Ms. Miller sought to recover were loss of use and enjoyment of the property as a result of "offensive odor and possible toxic contamination," reduced market value of the property, and the cost of "drainage, dredging and clean up of said lake." Ms. Miller also alleged E & L "allowed fire water and other contaminated waters to be discharged into the Manges [sic] Branch as well as seep into the ground water which feeds Manges [sic] Branch and other lakes and streams thereby contaminating same."

* * *

In *National Union Fire Ins. Co. v. CBI Industries, Inc.*, 907 S.W.2d 517 (Tex.1995), the Texas Supreme Court followed the great weight of authority in other jurisdictions that have found the absolute pollution exclusion to be unambiguous:

Courts usually strive for uniformity in construing insurance provisions, especially where, as here, the contract provisions at issue are identical across the jurisdictions. Most courts which have examined the same or substantially similar absolute pollution exclusions have concluded that they are clear and unambiguous. (footnote omitted) "This pollution exclusion is just what it purports to be-absolute ...". We agree. The language in this pollution exclusion is clear and susceptible of only one possible interpretation in this case.

* * *

Thus, we sustain appellants' first point of error as to the granting of the summary judgment of St. Paul; we reverse and remand for trial. We overrule appellant's second point of error and affirm the summary judgment granted in favor of Hanover.

Affirmed in part; reversed and remanded in part.

INSURANCE DUTY-TO-DEFEND LITIGATION IN A NUTSHELL

Insurance Contracts and Judicial Discord over Whether Liability Insurers Must Defend Insureds' Allegedly Intentional and Immoral Conduct: A Historical and Empirical Review of Federal and State Courts' Declaratory Judgments 1900–1997
47 AM. U. L. REV. 1131 (1998)
Willy E. Rice

GENERAL RULES—THE ORIGIN OF THE LIABILITY INSURER'S DUTY TO DEFEND

Many large liability insurers sell the same insurance contract in every state. Moreover, each liability contract contains a duty-to-defend statement or clause. But determining whether and when liability carriers must defend insureds in the respective states is not easily discernible. Consider, for example, a fairly common occurrence. Each year, State Farm Insurance Co. sells thousands of homeowners' contracts in every state of the union. A third-party victim from each state accuses a homeowner of either sexual molestation, wrongful death, or spousal abuse. Fifty homeowners approach State Farm and ask for a legal defense. Should the insurer review the liability contract to determine whether it should commence a legal defense? Should the company examine the third-party complaint to find the answer? Or should the company file a declaratory judgment action? Sadly, but for good reasons, too many insurers elect to do the latter.

Simply put, there is no universal rule. More disturbing from both the insureds' and the national insurers' perspectives, state supreme courts have adopted a wide variety of conflicting and overlapping tests to help determine whether the insurer must defend based on the liability. For example, the Iowa Supreme Court and the Supreme Court of Pennsylvania have embraced the so-called "complaint-potentiality rule": The duty to defend arises only where the third-party victim's complaint suggests "potential liability" or when the complaint may "potentially come within" policy coverage. The Arizona Supreme Court and three other courts, however, have chosen the "complaint-analysis of facts" rule: Generally, insurers must examine the facts outlined in the third-party complaint—rather than the third-party victims' allegations—to determine whether a defense is required.

At least thirteen state supreme courts instruct liability insurers to review their insurance policies rather than the third-party complaints. But within this group, there are many tests. For instance, the Supreme Courts of Michigan, Nevada, and Oklahoma have embraced the "policy-obligation rule," which requires the insurer to defend when the policy language clearly requires a defense.

In contrast, the New Mexico and South Dakota Supreme Courts have fashioned the "arguably within policy rule": Liability companies are required to defend when known, but unpleaded facts, bring a third-party claim arguably within the scope of the policy's coverage provision. The Wisconsin and Idaho Supreme Courts have established a somewhat similar test—the "fairly debatable rule." It states that the duty to defend may or may not arise if there is doubt about the likelihood of recovery under the policy.

Five state supreme courts have adopted a position that may be described as the "policy-potentiality rule." For example, thirty-two years ago, the California Supreme Court outlined the test in *Gray v. Zurich Insurance Co.* The court stated: "[T]he duty to defend should be fixed by the facts which the insurer learns from the complaint, the insured, or other sources. An insurer, therefore, bears a duty to defend its insured whenever it ascertains facts which give rise to the potential of liability under the policy." The Arkansas Supreme Court announced a closely related doctrine. It held that "the duty to defend arises where there is a possibility that the injury or damage may fall within the policy coverage."

Of course, the majority of state supreme courts compel liability insurers to examine the third-party victim's complaint as well as the insurance contract to determine whether a duty to defend exists. In Texas, the doctrine is known as the "eight corners rule": This rule requires the trier of fact to examine ... the allegations in the complaint and the insurance policy [to] determin[e] whether a duty to defend exists. The duty to defend is not affected by facts ascertained before suit … [or during] the process of litigation, or by the ultimate outcome of the suit.

In Florida, Illinois, Minnesota, New York, Ohio, Washington, and several other jurisdictions, the doctrine is termed the "allegation of the complaint rule." Perhaps the Supreme Court of Massachusetts has stated the rule most intelligibly: "the initial duty of a liability insurer to defend third-party actions against the insured is decided by matching the third-party complaint with the policy provisions … [I]f the allegations of the complaint … reasonably [fall under the coverage provisions], the insurer must undertake the defense."

An Analysis of Specific Factors Triggering Liability Insurers' Obligation to Defend

Even if insurers know they must examine either the contract, complaint, or both documents to determine whether a defense is necessary, there is still another conflict-generating question: What specific act, incident, or behavior triggers the duty? Put another way: assuming an insurer knows a defense is required, does the insurer have discretion to commence the representation at will? Or may the insured compel the insurer to start the legal representation immediately, on a specific date, or upon occurrence of a specific event? Without doubt, this is a serious issue, because the majority of state supreme courts embrace the rule that liability insurers have the exclusive right to organize, commence, and control the legal defense.

Although they have recognized insurers' right to control a defense, state and federal courts still have adopted some very broad, conflicting, and less-than-intelligible instructions that dictate when insurers should start spending money to protect insureds' interests. For example, a few courts have employed the "exposure rule" and held that the duty to defend is triggered when the initial exposure to an injury-causing condition takes place. Conversely, some courts have applied the "manifestation rule," which suggests that where manifestation of an injury is delayed, coverage or the duty to defend is not triggered until third-party injuries or property damages become known to the victims.

Some additional tribunals have embraced the "injury-in-fact rule." This rule states that coverage is triggered when actual property damage or a personal injury first occurs. Still, other federal and state courts have adopted the so-called "multiple" or "triple-trigger" approach, which requires coverage under policies during a period of continuing exposure and manifestation.

Of course, there is more confusion. Some courts ignore these rules altogether and conclude that the duty to defend is triggered: (1) "when there is a 'suit,' [although] … standard policies often fail to define 'suit" '; (2) when insureds exhibit "coincidental involvement in the underlying accidents"; (3) when "a suit … allege[s] an injury"; (4) "when a complaint is filed against the insured"; and (5) "when the injury takes place." Clearly, these various rules are onerous and are sources of much conflict. However, there is one rule that is superior to the former and is fairly easy to follow: liability insurers must commence a legal defense when they first discover, learn, or receive information indicating that insureds have injured a third party.

Chapter Twelve: Insurers' Common-Law and Statutory Defenses

Article 554.002 of the Texas Insurance Code is fairly clear:

BURDEN OF PROOF AND PLEADING

> In a suit to recover under an insurance or health maintenance organization contract, the insurer or health maintenance organization has the burden of proof as to any avoidance or affirmative defense that the Texas Rules of Civil Procedure require to be affirmatively pleaded. Language of exclusion in the contract or an exception to coverage claimed by the insurer or health maintenance organization constitutes an avoidance or an affirmative defense. [Formerly Art. 21.28, repealed]

There should be little debate about who qualifies as an "insurer" under Art. 554.002, because Art. 554.001 states:

> This chapter applies to each insurer or health maintenance organization engaged in the business of insurance or the business of a health maintenance organization in this state, regardless of form and however organized, including: (1) a stock life, health, or accident insurance company; (2) a mutual life, health, or accident insurance company; (3) a stock fire or casualty insurance company; (4) a mutual fire or casualty insurance company; (5) a Mexican casualty insurance company; (6) a Lloyd's plan; (7) a reciprocal or interinsurance exchange; (8) a fraternal benefit society; (9) a title insurance company; (10) an attorney's title insurance company; (11) a stipulated premium company; (12) a nonprofit legal services corporation; (13) a statewide mutual assessment company; (14) a local mutual aid association; (15) a local mutual burial association; (16) an association exempt under Section 887.102; (17) a nonprofit hospital, medical, or dental service corporation, including a corporation subject to Chapter 842; (18) a county mutual insurance company; (19) a farm mutual insurance company; and (20) an insurer or health maintenance organization engaged in the business of insurance or the business of a health maintenance organization in this state that does not hold a

> certificate of authority issued by the department or is not otherwise authorized to engage in business in this state.

Perhaps, more than any other defendants, insurers have two large arsenals of defenses to help increase their likelihood of success in courts of law and equity. First, common-law contract principles govern the formation and enforcement of insurance contracts. And when insureds assert that insurers breached those agreements, insurers may defend themselves successfully by employing a variety of common-law defenses in a court of law. In particular, insurers may argue: 1) the insureds breached various conditions precedent and subsequent in the insurance contract; 2) the insureds breached various express and implied warranties in the contract; 3) the insureds failed to establish that the insurers' alleged breach was material and the proximate cause of the insureds' damages; 4) the insureds failed to mitigate damages; 5) the insureds failed to commence an action within the statute-of-limitations period; and 6) the insured failed to pay consideration (premiums).

In addition, insurers have an arsenal of insurance-specific defenses. For example, insurers have successfully defended their interests by proving that: 1) the insured had "no insurable interest;" 2) the insured assigned the insurance contract without the insurer's consent; 3) there was no coverage under the insurance contract; 4) an excluded peril was the efficient proximate cause of a loss; 5) the insured misrepresented a loss; 6) the insured failed to disclose a fact on an application; 7) there was no temporary coverage or insurance; 8) the insured failed to report a loss as soon as practicable; 9) the insured's inaction or negligence prejudiced the insurer's interests; 10) the insured breached a warranty in the application; 11) the insured breached a warranty in the insurance contract; and 12) the insurance contract excluded insured's loss.

Arguably, insurers are more successful when they raise the so-called insurance-specific defenses than when they present traditional common-law defenses. If that assertion is true, the reason is not very complicated. Many of the insurance-specific defenses—concealment, misrepresentation, nondisclosure, breach of warranty and breach of condition—evolved from the doctrine of *uberrimae fidei* ("utmost good faith"). In *Stipcich v. Metropolitan Life Ins. Co.*, 277 U.S. 311,316-317 (1927), the Supreme Court concluded:

> Insurance policies are traditionally contracts *uberrimae fidei* and a failure by the insured to *disclose* conditions affecting the risk, of which he is aware, makes the contract voidable at the insurer's option. Concededly, the modern practice of requiring the applicant for life insurance to answer questions prepared by the insurer has relaxed this rule to some extent, since information not asked for is presumably deemed immaterial.
>
> But the reason for the rule still obtains, and with added force, as to changes *materially affecting the risk* which come to the knowledge of the insured after the application and before delivery of the policy. For even the most unsophisticated person must know that, in answering the questionnaire and submitting it to the insurer, he is furnishing the data on the basis of which the company will decide whether, by issuing a policy, it wishes to insure him.

> If, while the company deliberates, he discovers facts which make portions of his application no longer true, the most elementary spirit of fair dealing would seem to require him to make a full disclosure. If he fails to do so the company may, despite its acceptance of the application, decline to issue a policy, or, if a policy has been issued, it has a valid defense to a suit upon it.

"Utmost good faith" is a well-known marine-insurance principle. The Ninth Circuit's discussion in *New Hampshire Ins. Co. v. C'Est Moi, Inc.*, 519 F.3d 937 (9th Cir. 2008) partially explains why concealment, misrepresentation, breach of warranty, breach of condition and nondisclosure have been some of the most litigated and successful affirmative defenses. In *C'Est Moi,* the Ninth Circuit stated:

> *Uberrimae fidei* is a "longstanding federal maritime doctrine" that "applies to marine insurance contracts." *Uberrimae fidei* "imposes a duty of utmost good faith," so "an applicant for a marine insurance policy is bound to reveal every fact within his knowledge that is material to the risk," If an insured fails to do so, the insurer may rescind the policy, even if the material misrepresentation wasn't intentional.
>
> * * *
>
> *Uberrimae fidei* is a well-entrenched doctrine that protects not merely the insurer but also the integrity of the risk pool; only "an unambiguous statement" in the policy, purporting to supersede the doctrine in express terms, would be sufficient to accomplish that purpose.

Without doubt, Texas courts have embraced the doctrine of "utmost good faith" and the law of marine insurance. To illustrate, consider the Fifth Circuit's analysis in *Fireman's Fund Ins. Co. v. Wilburn Boat Co.,* 300 F.2d 631, 646-647 (5th Cir. 1962), *abrogated on other grounds by* 927 F.2d 882 (5th Cir 1991):

> Nothing is better established in the law of marine insurance than that a mistake or commission material to a marine risk, whether it be wilful or accidental, or result from mistake, negligence or voluntary ignorance, avoids the policy. And the same rule obtains, even though the insured did not suppose the fact to the material.
>
> * * *
>
> "Concealment," in the law of marine insurance, is the failure to disclose any material fact or circumstance in relation to the subject matter of the contract which may increase the liability to loss, or affect the risk or obligation assumed, and which is, in fact or law, within, or ought to be without, the knowledge of one party, and of which the other party has no actual or presumptive knowledge. In the case of marine insurance the insured must disclose all facts material to the risk, and in default of such duty the contract may be avoided by the insurer.

In other words, an applicant for marine insurance must state all material facts which are known to him and unknown to the insurer. It has been said that the insured is bound to communicate every material fact within his knowledge not known or presumed to be known to the underwriter, whether inquired for or not; and that a failure in either particular, although it may arise from mistake, accident, or forgetfulness, is attended with the rigorous consequences that the policy never attaches and is void, for the reason that the risk assumed is not the one intended to be assumed by the parties.

Although we have found no Texas case expressly applying this rule, there is no indication that the Texas courts have departed from this firmly established principle of marine insurance.

More comprehensive discussions of insurance-specific and traditional affirmative defenses appear in this chapter.

A. "Insured Misrepresented, Failed to Disclose and Concealed Information"

1. "Insured's Misrepresentation Defeats Coverage"

The Texas Insurance Code has five (5) statutes that allow insurers to defend themselves by proving that insureds misrepresented information in an insurance application. Three of the statutes are fairly long. The language in one statute is very general — covering misrepresentations in any insurance application. The language in the remaining two statutes is specific — covering misrepresentations in life, health and accident insurance applications. Arguably, the words and phrases in the "no-misrepresentation" statutes are redundant — stating essentially the same prohibitions, provisos and exceptions.

However, after a careful review, it becomes readily apparent that an insurer may successfully invoke the statutory misrepresentation defense only if the insurer establishes that the insured's misrepresentation was "material." But there is one overriding question: What must the misrepresentation materially affect? Briefly put, the statutes give different answers. For example, under Tex. Ins. Code § 705.003(b)(2), an insurer may use the misrepresentation defense successfully if the insurer can prove that the insured "misrepresented a fact material to the question of the insurer's liability." In its entirety, Tex. Ins. Code § 705.003 reads:

POLICY PROVISION: MISREPRESENTATION IN PROOF OF LOSS OR DEATH

(a) An insurance policy provision that states that a misrepresentation, including a false statement, made in a proof of loss or death makes the policy void or voidable: (1) has no effect; and (2) is not a defense in a suit brought on the policy.

(b) Subsection (a) does not apply if it is shown at trial that the misrepresentation: (1) was fraudulently made; (2) misrepresented a fact material to the question of the insurer's liability under the policy; and (3) misled the insurer and caused the insurer to waive or lose a valid defense to the policy.

[Repealed Art 21.19 has been codified under Tex. Ins. Code §§ 705.001, 705.002 and 705.003]

On the other hand, under Tex. Ins. Code § 705.004(b)(1)(2), an insurer may employ the misrepresentation defense effectively if the insurer proves that "the matter misrepresented was material to the risk" or "contributed to the event on which the policy became due and payable." In its entirety, Tex. Ins. Code § 705.004 states:

POLICY PROVISION: MISREPRESENTATION IN POLICY APPLICATION

(a) An insurance policy provision that states that false statements made in the application for the policy or in the policy make the policy void or voidable: (1) has no effect; and (2) is not a defense in a suit brought on the policy.

(b) Subsection (a) does not apply if it is shown at trial that the matter misrepresented: (1) was material to the risk; or (2) contributed to the contingency or event on which the policy became due and payable.

(c) It is a question of fact whether a misrepresentation made in the application for the policy or in the policy itself was material to the risk or contributed to the contingency or event on which the policy became due and payable.

Union Bankers Insurance Company v. Shelton
889 S.W.2d 278
(Tex. 1994)

This case requires that we determine (1) whether an insured's intent to deceive must be proved in order for an insurance company to successfully raise a defense of misrepresentation to a breach of contract action in connection with the cancellation of an individual health insurance policy within two years of the date of its issuance when the cancellation is based upon the insured's misrepresentation in the application for insurance; and (2) whether a cause of action for breach of the duty of good faith and fair dealing exists when an insurer cancels an insurance policy without a reasonable basis. We conclude that (1) an insured's intent to deceive is required for an insurer to cancel an individual health insurance policy within two years of the date of its issuance on the grounds of a misrepresentation in the application and (2) the duty of good faith and fair dealing extends to an insurer's cancellation of a policy.

Thomas and Ann Shelton sued Union Bankers Insurance Company ("Union Bankers") and its agent Donny Stone (Stone) after Union Bankers cancelled Mr. Shelton's health insurance policy on the basis of an alleged misrepresentation in his application. Among other things, the Sheltons alleged that Union Bankers breached the contract and the duty of good faith and fair dealing by improperly cancelling the policy. The trial court rendered a take-nothing judgment in favor of Union Bankers and Stone. The court of appeals reversed and remanded the case to the trial court for a new trial concerning the duty of good faith and fair dealing. For the reasons explained herein, we affirm the judgment of the court of appeals.

I.

In April 1988, Mr. Shelton applied to Union Bankers for a health insurance policy. Mr. Shelton completed the application form with Stone's assistance. In response to certain medical history questions, Mr. Shelton indicated that he had never been treated for, and had no indications of, any disorders of the skeletal or muscular systems. Union Bankers issued a health policy to Mr. Shelton on April 9, 1988.

In November 1988, seven months after the policy was issued, Mr. Shelton underwent total hip replacement surgery to correct necrosis in his left hip joint. Shortly thereafter, the Sheltons filed a claim for benefits under the Union Bankers policy. Union Bankers concluded that the necrosis was an undisclosed pre-existing condition, notified Mr. Shelton that it was denying the claim, and requested that Mr. Shelton execute a rider specifically excluding hip disorders. When he refused to sign the rider, Union Bankers refunded all premiums and cancelled the policy on the ground that the failure to disclose the hip condition was a material misrepresentation in the application for insurance.

The Sheltons sued Union Bankers and Stone, alleging breach of contract, violations of the Deceptive Trade Practices Act and Texas Insurance Code, and breach of the duty of good faith and fair dealing. The jury answered all questions against the Sheltons, except that the jury failed to find that Mr. Shelton intended to deceive Union Bankers when he made the misrepresentation. Based on the jury's verdict, the trial court rendered a take-nothing judgment in favor of Union Bankers and Stone. The court of appeals reversed, holding that because the jury failed to find that Mr. Shelton intended to deceive Union Bankers by misrepresenting his condition, Union Bankers breached the contract as a matter of law when it cancelled the insurance policy. The court of appeals remanded the case to the trial court for a new trial concerning whether Union Bankers breached the duty of good faith and fair dealing in connection with its cancellation of Mr. Shelton's policy.

II.

Union Bankers contends that the jury's failure to find that Mr. Shelton intended to deceive Union Bankers is irrelevant because article 3.70-3(A)(2)(a) of the Texas Insurance Code implies that an insurer may cancel a health insurance policy within two years from the date of its issuance on the basis of an insured's innocent misrepresentation in the application for insurance. We disagree. Article 3.70-3(A) sets forth minimum standards for provisions that must be contained in each accident and sickness policy delivered or issued for delivery to any person in this state. *See* Tex. Ins. Code Ann. art. 3.70-3(A). Among the required provisions contained in the policy issued to Mr. Shelton, is the following clause:

> Time Limit on Certain Defenses: (a) After two years from the date of issue of this policy no misstatements, except fraudulent misstatements, made by the applicant in the application for such policy shall be used to void the policy or to deny a claim for loss incurred or disability (as defined in the policy) commencing after the expiration of such two-year period.
>
> (The foregoing policy provision shall not be so construed as to affect any legal requirement for avoidance of a policy or denial of a claim during such initial two-year period, nor to limit the application of Section 3(B), (1), (2), (3), (4), and (5) in the event of misstatement with respect to age or occupation or other insurance.)

The primary rule in statutory interpretation is that a court must look to the intent of the legislature and must construe the statute so as to give effect to that intent. *Monsanto Co. v. Cornerstones Mun. Util. Dist.,* 865 S.W.2d 937, 939 (Tex.1993); *Knight v. International Harvester Credit Corp.,* 627 S.W.2d 382, 384 (Tex.1982). When determining legislative intent, the courts may look to the language of the statute, legislative history, the nature and object to be obtained, and the consequences that would follow from alternate constructions. *Sharp v. House of Lloyd, Inc.,* 815 S.W.2d 245, 249 (Tex.1991) (considering the nature and object of the act and the consequences of alternate constructions).

* * *

The phrase "except fraudulent misstatements" represents the "prime feature of compromise in the time limit provisions," functioning to distinguish section 3(A)(2)(a) from the incontestability provisions traditionally contained in life insurance policies, which provide that the policy is not contestable after two years for any reason.

It appears that the Commissioners did not intend for section 3(A)(2)(a) to apply to an insurer's right to void its policy or deny a claim during the initial period.

* * *

Thus, construing article 3.70-3(A)(2)(a) to imply that an insurer may cancel a health insurance policy within two years from the date of its issuance on the basis of an innocent misrepresentation conflicts with the apparent intent of the Commissioners and the Texas legislature as expressed in the additional provision concerning the avoidance of a policy or denial of a claim during the initial two-year period.

We hold that article 3.70-3(A)(2)(a) was not intended to affect the determination of whether an intent to deceive must be proved to cancel a health insurance policy within two years of the date of its issuance when the cancellation is based on the insured's misrepresentation in the application for insurance. Thus, we must examine both the relevant statutes and the common law to determine whether the insurer must prove the insured's intent to deceive in order to successfully raise a defense of misrepresentation to a breach of insurance contract action.

III.

By statute, a misrepresentation in an application for any type of insurance must be material in order to avoid the policy. The proposition that an insured's intent to deceive is likewise required is well established in the common law of this state. The rule was first announced by this court in a personal property fire insurance case, *Lion Fire Insurance Co. v. Starr,* 12 S.W. 45, 46 (Tex.1888), and more recently in several life insurance policy cases. *Mayes v. Massachusetts Mut. Life Ins. Co.,* 608 S.W.2d 612, 616 (Tex.1980); *Allen v. American Nat'l Ins. Co.,* 380 S.W.2d 604, 607-08 (Tex.1964); *Clark v. National Life & Accident Ins. Co.,* 145 Tex. 575, 200 S.W.2d 820, 822-23 (1947). In *Mayes,* we stated:

> It is now settled law in this state that these five elements must be pled and proved before the insurer may avoid a policy because of the misrepresentation of the insured: (1) the making of the representation; (2) the falsity of the representation; (3) reliance thereon by the insurer; (4) the intent to deceive on the part of the insured in making the same; and (5) the materiality of the representation.

All of the cases cited by the court of appeals and Mr. Shelton properly stand for the proposition that, in Texas, an insured's intent to deceive must be shown in order for an insurance company to successfully raise a defense of misrepresentation on the basis of a false statement made by the insured in the application for any type of insurance.

We hold, therefore, that an intent to deceive must be proved to cancel a health insurance policy within two years of the date of its issuance when the cancellation is based on the insured's misrepresentation in the application for insurance. Because the jury failed to find that Mr. Shelton intended to deceive United Bankers when he misrepresented his physical condition, we affirm the judgment of the court of appeals in so far as it holds that, as a matter of law, Union Bankers breached the insurance contract when it improperly cancelled the policy based on the misrepresentation.

* * *

B.

Because the jury failed to find that Union Bankers breached the contract when it canceled the policy, it did not reach the issue of bad faith in connection with the cancellation. Because we hold as a matter of law that Union Bankers breached the insurance contract when it canceled the policy, this cause must be remanded for a new trial concerning the breach of the duty of good faith and fair dealing issue.

Union Bankers argues that remand is improper because there is no evidence of bad faith in connection its cancellation of Mr. Shelton's policy. We disagree. There is some evidence in the record to support Mr. Shelton's assertions that Union Bankers' initial correspondence concerning the claim stated that the information omitted from the application was "probably an oversight," and that Union Bankers failed to discuss the application, condition, or claim with Mr. Shelton before making its final determination. In addition, the policy itself states in offset print on the first page:

IMPORTANT NOTICE ABOUT STATEMENTS IN THE APPLICATION

> Please read the copy of the application which is a part of this policy. Check to see if any medical history has been left out. Write Us if any information shown isn't right or complete. We issued this policy on the basis that the answers to all questions are right and complete. Any wrong or left out statements could cause an otherwise valid claim to be denied.

This notice contains no indication that a wrong statement might result in an attempted exclusion of coverage for certain medical conditions or cancellation of the entire policy, it may even indicate to the contrary. We hold that this evidence constitutes some evidence of bad faith in connection with the cancellation of the policy, and requires the remand of this cause to the trial court for a new trial.

For the reasons explained herein, we affirm the judgment of the court of appeals.

NOTES & QUESTIONS

1) Tex. Ins. Code § 705.005 reads:

NOTICE TO INSURED OF MISREPRESENTATIONS

(a) This section applies to any suit brought on an insurance policy issued or contracted for after June 29, 1903.

(b) A defendant may use as a defense a misrepresentation made in the application for or in obtaining an insurance policy only if the defendant shows at trial that before the 91st day after the date the defendant discovered the falsity of the representation, the defendant gave notice that the defendant refused to be bound by the policy: (1) to the insured, if living; or (2) to the owners or beneficiaries of the insurance policy, if the insured was deceased.

(c) This section does not: (1) make available as a defense an immaterial misrepresentation; or (2) affect the provisions of Section 705.004.

2) Tex. Ins. Code § 3.70-3(A) has been repealed. It has been recodified as Tex. Ins. Code § 1201.208(a) and reads:

POLICY PROVISION: INCONTESTABILITY

Except as provided by Subsection (c), an individual accident and health insurance policy must contain the following provision:

> Time Limit on Certain Defenses: (a) After the second anniversary of the date this policy is issued, a misstatement, other than a fraudulent misstatement, made by the applicant in the application for the policy may not be used to void the policy or to deny a claim for loss incurred or disability (as defined in the policy) beginning after that anniversary.

3) What is the test for determining "materiality" or "material to the risk?"

Bankers Standard Life Insurance Company v. Atwood
205 S.W.2d 74
(Tex. Civ. App. 1947)

Mrs. Atwood, joined pro forma by her husband, sued the Company (Bankers Standard Life Insurance Company) upon a policy of insurance in which she was beneficiary, written by the Company on March 20, 1943, upon the life of her then husband, Fred P. Martin, who died November 3, 1943, of "Malignancy of the Stomach." The judgment upon a special issue verdict was in favor of Mrs. Atwood and the Company has appealed.

The pertinent defense relied upon by the company was predicated upon a false statement in the application of Mr. Martin, in the following question and answer: "Do you have or have you ever had . . . any of the following diseases or ailments: . . . Asthma *No* . . . ." The contentions of Company (under appropriate pleadings) were: (1) the applicant warranted the truth of the statement and its falsity (shown conclusively) rendered the policy void as a matter of law; (2) the statement was fraudulently made, was material to the risk and relied upon by the Company, and therefore the policy was void.

Upon the first contention: The Company was a "Mutual Assessment Life Insurance Company". . . . as to which the general insurance laws do not apply. And it is asserted upon authority of *Casstevens v. Texas etc. Ins. Co.*, 155 S.W.2d 916, 918 (Tex. 194), that Art. 4859f, §§ 1-20, contains no provision "that a misrepresentation, in order to avoid a policy, must be material to the risk." This statement in that opinion was evidently inadvertently made, as § 11 of the Act contains this language in reference to applications for policies written by such companies: "no representation therein shall constitute a defense unless same shall be shown to be material to the risk."

We have examined the application for writ of error, from which it appears that a holding of the Court of Civil Appeals in substantial language as that of the Supreme Court, above, was not challenged, which readily accounts for the above quotation from Sec. 11 being overlooked. This particular holding, however, was not essential to the decision. Regardless thereof the court held that the warranty provisions in the application (the same as those here) were modified by certain provisions of the by-laws of the insurer, the court saying: 'It does not follow, however, that since the insurance statutes concerning warranties and misrepresentations do not apply to mutual aid companies, such companies are inhibited, in the absence of statutory regulation upon the subject, from voluntarily incorporating in their insurance contracts qualifying provisions which have the effect of converting such warranties into representations merely.'

Paragraph XII of the policy here contains the following: "All statements contained in the application for this policy shall, in the absence of fraud, be deemed representations and not warranties."

Independently therefore of the above provision of Sec. 11 of Art. 4859f, the burden rested upon the company to show (and, where not shown by conclusive evidence, to obtain a jury finding) each of the following factual elements: (1) reliance upon the truth of the statement by the insurer; (2) intent of insured to deceive insurer in making the same; and (3) "the materiality thereof, that is, was it material to the risk or the fact represented contributed to the loss in maturing the policy."

The issues submitted which have bearing upon the questions urged in the appeal were Nos. 9, 10 and 11, which, with the answers thereto, were:

> No. 9 found that the fact that Martin had suffered from asthma prior to March 16, 1943, was, under the policy in issue, not material to the risk.
>
> No. 10 inquired whether Martin, at the time he signed the application, intended to deceive the Company in regard to the fact that he had theretofore suffered from asthma. The jury was instructed to answer this issue only in case they answered No. 9 "'Yes"; otherwise they "need not answer it." They answered No. 9 "No" and did not answer No. 10.
>
> No. 11 found in issuing the policy the Company "relied upon the statement that Fred P. Martin had never suffered from asthma."

The Company urges five points of error in support of its appeal.

The first point is to the effect that the policy was void, as a matter of law, by reason of the false statement in the application that assured had never suffered from asthma, irrespective of whether it was material to the risk. This point is overruled for the reasons already stated.

Points 2 and 3 challenge the sufficiency of the evidence as a matter of law to support the answer to special issue No. 9.

Point 4 asserts that the jury in answering issue No. 9 disregarded the court's definition of "material to the risk."

Point 5 urges that the answers to issues Nos. 9 and 11 are conflicting.

The only evidence upon the issue whether the pre-existence of asthma was material to the risk was that of the Vice-President-General Manager of the Company to the effect that he relied upon the statement in the application; that had he known that insured had been suffering from recurrent attacks of asthma over a period of years prior to the application the Company would not have issued the policy, "unless the applicant would accept a rider waiving any liability to the Company in the event of death directly or indirectly as a result of it, and it is only doubtful that they would do it then"; that "asthma or anyone suffering with asthma in any form is not considered an insurable risk"; and "that the Company would consider that asthma was material to the risk."

It is well settled in this jurisdiction that the question of materiality to the risk is a fact question to be determined by the jury. The jury was warranted in disregarding this evidence, though uncontradicted, as the witness was interested.

Unless we could hold that the evidence as a matter of law showed that the false statement was material to the risk, there is no basis for the contention that the jury disregarded the court's definition of "materiality to the risk." We, therefore, overrule point 4.

Nor do we think there is any necessary conflict between the answers to issues 9 and 11. Materiality to the risk and reliance upon the truth of a statement in the application are clearly two separate and distinct facts. The Company could rely upon the truth of an immaterial as well as a material statement. The jury may well have believed the vice-president's testimony that the Company relied upon the truth of the statement, and yet may not have believed that the burden resting upon the Company had been met to establish the materiality of the statement.

But, independently of the last two above holdings, there is another ground upon which the judgment must be sustained. Under the quoted provision of paragraph XII of the policy the statements in the application (in the absence of fraud) were "representations and not warranties." As above shown, one of the essential elements of fraud is the intent to deceive, and that in order to avoid a policy on the ground of misrepresentation of a material fact, it is incumbent upon the insurer to show (and obtain a jury finding thereon), not only that the statement was false, known to be false, material to the risk, and relied upon by the insurer, but that it was "made wilfully and with the intention of inducing the insurer to issue him the policy."

There was no objection to the court's charge as submitted, and the issue of intent to deceive (No. 10) was submitted conditionally only upon an affirmative answer to No. 9. In not answering issue No. 10 the jury literally followed the court's instruction not to do so in case of a negative answer to No. 9. Manifestly the Company acquiesced in this conditional submission of No. 10, and waived a jury finding thereon upon the jury's affirmative answer to No. 9.

* * *

It is contended, however, that the evidence conclusively shows a fraudulent intent — that is, an intent to deceive. We do not so hold. The evidence upon that issue will support findings in substance as follows: Martin had in previous years suffered from asthma, which was of a "seasonal, allergic" character. In August 1937 he had a severe attack, but by October of that year he was doing fine and never thereafter had a severe attack. During the two or three years prior to the application he did not have "any asthma at all — practically none," and when the policy was applied for he was in the best of health and free of asthma.

The name and address of his family physician were given in the application, and this physician testified upon the trial. In the application Martin stated that in the preceding two years he had had a "physical examination for employment." This examination was made under the United States Civil Service Commission at Austin on August 31, 1942, and in it Martin stated that he had "Seasonal allergy-Asthma." Upon this application for employment he was accepted and worked at Randolph Field as a machinist until late in the summer of 1943. The examining physician stated that in his opinion Martin was capable of performing duties of "Arduous-Moderate" physical exertion.

This evidence, we think, clearly sufficient to support a finding that the misstatement as to asthma was not made with intention to deceive the Company.

The trial court's judgment is affirmed.

NOTES & QUESTIONS

1) Tex. Ins. Code § 705.051 states:

IMMATERIAL MISREPRESENTATION IN LIFE, ACCIDENT,
OR HEALTH INSURANCE APPLICATION

A misrepresentation in an application for a life, accident, or health insurance policy does not defeat recovery under the policy unless the misrepresentation: (1) is of a material fact; and (2) affects the risks assumed.

2) Tex. Ins. Code § 705.104 reads:

MISREPRESENTATION IN APPLICATION FOR LIFE INSURANCE

A defense based on a misrepresentation in the application for, or in obtaining, a life insurance policy on the life of a person in or residing in this state is not valid or enforceable in a suit brought on the policy on or after the second anniversary of the date of issuance of the policy if premiums due on the policy during the two years have been paid to and received by the insurer, unless:

(1) the insurer has notified the insured of the insurer's intention to rescind the policy because of the misrepresentation; or

(2) it is shown at the trial that the misrepresentation was: (A) material to the risk; and (B) intentionally made.

2. "Insured's Nondisclosure Defeats Coverage"

Mayes v. Massachusetts Mutual Life Insurance Company
608 S.W.2d 612
(Tex. 1980)

Massachusetts Mutual Life Insurance Company brought this suit to rescind three policies of insurance on the life of Albert W. Mayes, deceased, because Mayes did not disclose to the insurer that certain answers in his applications which were correct when made had become false by the time the policies were delivered. Petitioner, who was the named beneficiary in the policies, counterclaimed for the proceeds of the policies together with penalty, interest and attorney's fees. The trial court rendered judgment for petitioner on the jury verdict. The court of civil appeals reversed the judgment of the trial court and remanded the cause with instructions to limit recovery to return of the premiums. We reverse the judgment of the court of civil appeals and remand the cause to that court for consideration of respondent's factual insufficiency point over which we have no jurisdiction.

On May 6, 1976, Albert Mayes signed and delivered to an agent of insurer Part 1 of two applications for life insurance. These applications had been filled out by the agent and his secretary from information secured from a previous policy issued to Mayes through this agent. The applications are identical except for the amount of insurance requested by each application. On page three of each application is the following paragraph:

> SIGNATURE SECTION — MUST BE COMPLETED IN ALL CASES
>
> To the best of my (our) knowledge and belief, all answers and statements contained herein are full, complete and true and were correctly recorded before this application was signed; and it is agreed that:
>
> (a) if the first premium on the insurance herein applied for has been paid to the Company's agent in exchange for the Company's Conditional Receipt signed by said agent, the Company shall be liable only under and pursuant to the terms and conditions set forth in said receipt;
>
> (b) if the first premium on the insurance herein applied for has not been paid, the Company shall incur no liability under this application unless and until the application has been completed and approved and the policy has been issued and delivered to the owner designated therein and the first premium specified in the policy has been paid during the lifetime of each person proposed for insurance and then only if at the time of said delivery and payment all answers and statements contained in Parts 1 and 2 of this application and any amendments thereof and supplements thereto are then full, complete and true to the best of my (our) knowledge and belief as though given at the time of said delivery and payment;

> (c) no agent of the Company has authority to make, alter or modify the terms of this application or of any policy issued hereon or to waive any of the Company's rights or requirements or to extend the time for the payment of premiums, and
>
> (d) acceptance of any policy issued on this application will constitute ratification of any correction or amendment of the application made by the Company as shown in the Amendment of Application attached to the policy, provided, however, that any such correction or amendment of application relating to amount, classification, plan or additional benefits shall be agreed to in writing.

> If this application is also signed by a purchaser, such purchaser ratifies the representations, declarations, statements, answers and agreements contained in Parts 1 and 2 of this application and any amendments of and supplements to this application, and agrees to be bound thereby.

Both applications required a physical examination of this forty-year-old prospect and the information relative to this examination is contained in Part 2 of the applications. Although Part 2 was filled out by Dr. Rattan, the insurer's medical examiner, it contains a number of answers to medical history questions propounded to the insured by the doctor on May 27, 1976 when the physical examination was had. Question 4 inquired as to whether the insured within the past five years: (A) had been treated by a physician; (B) had been treated or observed in a hospital; or (C) had undergone an electrocardiogram.

Only question 4A was answered in the affirmative and the explanation given related only to a 1974 physical examination which Mayes had undergone in connection with a prior policy issued by Massachusetts Mutual. Questions 5A and 6A inquired if he had been treated for or had any known indication of any disorder of the heart or if he had experienced any pain, pressure or discomfort in the chest. Both of these questions were answered in the negative.

Part 2 of the applications were referred to the home office of insurer and, because the first examination showed an elevated blood pressure, the medical examiner was directed to make a recheck of the blood pressure. This reexamination was made by Dr. Rattan on July 14, 1976. At this time, the medical examiner determined, at the request of the insurer, that the proposed insured had not had any recent medical or dietary treatment for hypertension. The policies were issued to Mayes at a higher premium because of the elevated blood pressure. The policies were delivered to Mayes by the agent on August 17, 1976 after Mayes agreed to the higher premium.

On June 29, 1976, Mayes attempted to drink cold water while having a cup of coffee. He was unable to swallow the water and felt a pain in his chest. Mayes' next door neighbor, who was a general practitioner, was called; pursuant to this doctor's advice, Mayes went to the hospital so that Dr. Schilling, a specialist in internal medicine, might examine him. Mayes was kept in the hospital overnight by Dr. Schilling while a number of tests were made. Dr. Schilling was unable to arrive at a definite diagnosis, but concluded that the chest pain was probably the result of esophagitis, which is an inflammation of the esophagus. Dr. Schilling advised Mayes that he did not think Mayes had heart disease, but that he could not exclude that possibility. Mrs. Mayes testified she understood that the problem in Mayes' chest related to the esophagus.

Dr. Schilling next saw Mayes on July 28, 1976 at the doctor's office. Mayes complained of two more episodes of chest pain under circumstances similar to the initial episode. He was given a stress electrocardiogram to see if heart disease was involved. Again the doctor was unable to pin down the cause of the chest pain. Dr. Schilling advised Mayes of his high blood pressure and told him certain things to do to correct it. Mayes was advised that he was overweight and smoked too much. The doctor did not diagnose heart disease, but said again that he could not rule it out. He did not see Mayes again professionally. Mayes died suddenly on July 25, 1977 from a heart attack of some undetermined variety.

The verdict was substantially as follows:

> 1. That the condition of Mayes' health changed between May 27, 1976 and the date the policies of insurance were delivered to him, August 17, 1976, to the extent that his answers to Questions 4A, 4B, 4C, 5A, and 6A became untrue.
>
> 2. That on the date the policies were delivered to him, Mayes knew that the condition of his health had changed to the extent that the answers to these questions had become untrue.
>
> 3. That Mayes failed to disclose to Massachusetts Mutual that the condition of his health had changed after he applied for the policies to the extent that his answers to these questions had become untrue.
>
> 4. That the failure of Mayes to disclose that the condition of his health had changed to the extent that the answers to these five questions became untrue WAS NOT for the purpose of inducing Massachusetts Mutual to issue the policies in question.
>
> 5. That the answers as actually given by Mayes to these five questions were material.
>
> 6. That Massachusetts Mutual relied on the answers actually given by Mayes to these questions when issuing the policies.
>
> 7. A reasonable fee for services rendered by Mrs. Mayes' attorney in this case is $7,500.00.

The trial court overruled insurer's motion for judgment on the verdict or, in the alternative, *judgment non obstante veredicto* and rendered judgment on the verdict for the beneficiary, Mrs. Mayes. In doing so, the trial court apparently considered the insured's answers to the questions in Part 2 of the applications as representations. The trial court followed those authorities which hold that an insurer cannot avoid liability on the ground of misrepresentation by the insured unless there is a finding that the insured intended to procure issuance of the policy by representations known to be false. *See Washington v. Reliable Life Ins. Co.,* 581 S.W.2d 153 (Tex.1979); *Allen v. American National Insurance Company*, 380 S.W.2d 604 (Tex.1964); *Clark v. National Life & Accident Ins. Co.*, 200 S.W.2d 820 (Tex. 1947).

The court of civil appeals disagreed and held that the Signature Section quoted above was in the nature of a condition precedent and that the insurer's liability depended on whether the insured knew and believed that the statements in his applications were still true at the time of delivery of the policy. Since they were not true in certain material respects, the court of civil appeals followed those authorities which have given controlling effect to contractual provisions that a policy shall not become effective unless delivered when the insured is in good health. *See Lincoln Income Life Insurance Company v. Mayberry*, 347 S.W.2d 598 (Tex. 1961); *Texas Prudential Insurance Company v. Dillard*, 307 S.W.2d 242 (Tex.1957); *Great Nat. Life Ins. Co. v. Hulme*, 136 S.W.2d 602 (Tex. 1940)

It must be recognized at the outset that the policies in question do not contain a "good health" contractual provision. Therefore, the basic question before us is whether the requirement in the Signature Section of Part 1 of the applications that the answers in the application be true and correct at the time of delivery of the policy should be considered as a condition precedent or as a representation. We believe that this requirement is in the nature of a representation and should be controlled by the law applicable to a misrepresentation.

It is now settled law that if the answers to the questions in the application were untrue at the time they were given, the untrue answers constituted misrepresentations. There is no logical reason to give the failure to correct these same answers at a later time any greater significance than we give to answers which were originally untrue. In fact, there would be a greater chance that an insured was acting in good faith when he failed to report a change of condition than he would be in his originally making an untrue answer.

Furthermore, the insurer knows the length of delay between the completion of the application and the issuance of the policy. If this period was significant, the insurer could easily ensure that the answers were still correct at the time of issuance of the policy either by putting a good health provision in the application or by requiring a supplemental statement of health. Here the insurer's medical doctor made a limited second physical examination of insured shortly before the policies were delivered. It is hard to understand why inquiry was not routinely made by the doctor at that time regarding the insured's recent health. The agent personally delivered the policies to the insured and persuaded the insured to accept the policies with the increased premium. It is not contended that the insured made a false statement to the doctor or the agent.

Under these circumstances we hold that insured's failure to advise the insurer of the changes in his prior answers were misrepresentations. It is now settled law in this state that these five elements must be pled and proved before the insurer may avoid a policy because of the misrepresentation of the insured: 1) the making of the representation; 2) the falsity of the representation; 3) reliance thereon by the insurer; (4) the intent to deceive on the part of the insured in making same; and 5) the materiality of the representation.

Here, although the jury found that these misrepresentations were material to the risk and were relied on by the insurer, the insurer failed to establish the legal defense of misrepresentation because it failed to secure a jury finding of intentional deception.

Insurer urges by a cross-point that the insured violated his duty to disclose material changes in his health that had occurred subsequent to the date of his applications but prior to delivery of the policies and, therefore, that the policies never came into existence. In support of this proposition, it relies largely on the case of *Stipcich v. Metropolitan Life Ins. Co.,* 277 U.S. 311 (1927), wherein it was said:

> Insurance policies are traditionally contracts uberrimae fidei and a failure by the insured to disclose conditions affecting the risk, of which he is aware, makes the contract voidable at the insurer's option.
>
> Concededly, the modern practice of requiring the applicant for life insurance to answer questions prepared by the insurer has relaxed this rule to some extent, since information not asked for is presumably deemed immaterial....
>
> But the reason for the rule still obtains, and with added force, as to changes materially affecting the risk which come to the knowledge of the insured after the application and before delivery of the policy. For even the most unsophisticated person must know that in answering the questionnaire and submitting it to the insurer he is furnishing the data on the basis of which the company will decide whether, by issuing a policy, it wishes to insure him. If, while the company deliberates, he discovers facts which make portions of his application no longer true, the most elementary spirit of fair dealing would seem to require him to make a full disclosure. If he fails to do so the company may, despite its acceptance of the application, decline to issue a policy . . . or if a policy has been issued, it has a valid defense to a suit upon it.

Under the controlling Texas authorities cited earlier, the *Stipcich* rule has no application to a misrepresentation by the insured in the application for a policy. Since the failure of the insured here to correct his answers resulted in a misrepresentation, the *Stipcich* holding does not control this case under Texas law.

Insurer also urges by a cross-point that the evidence established as a matter of law that the insured's failure to disclose that certain answers in his application had become untrue was for the purpose of inducing the insured to issue the policies in question. Insured does not question that it had the burden of proof on this issue. We therefore must determine this question based on a "no evidence" review of the record.

We recognize the rule that when, as here, an application for insurance is attached to and made a part of the policy and is accepted and retained by the insured, the insured is conclusively presumed to have knowledge of its contents and to have ratified any false statements therein. *Odom v. Insurance Company of State of Penn.*, 455 S.W.2d 195 (Tex.1970). Nevertheless, the circumstances present in this case are of some significance on the question of fraud.

The Signature Section is contained only in Part 1 of the application. Mayes signed that part of the applications on May 6. They remained in the possession of the insurer until the policies were delivered on August 17. The answers around which the lawsuit revolves are contained in Part 2 of the applications which related to the physical examination given Mayes on May 27. It is understandable that Mayes would be unaware of the requirement in the Signature Section to correct his answers, at least until after he received the policies.

Mayes had reason to believe that the chest pains were insignificant. The doctor who examined him after those episodes so advised him. In fact, Mayes did not find it necessary to even consult with a doctor during the year before his fatal heart attack. There is no evidence that he had any physical difficulty of any type during that year. In May of 1977 he converted a substantial part of the term policy in question into permanent insurance. We cannot say from this record that fraudulent intent was established as a matter of law.

Insurer also urged in the court of civil appeals that the evidence is factually insufficient to support the jury finding that Mayes' failure to disclose changes in his health was not for the purpose of inducing insurer to issue the policies. Inasmuch as this factual insufficiency point is within the exclusive jurisdiction of the court of civil appeals, we remand the cause to that court for determination of that point. *Custom Leasing, Inc. v. Texas Bank & Tr. Co. of Dallas*, 491 S.W.2d 869 (Tex.1973).

The judgment of the court of civil appeals is reversed and the cause is remanded to that court for further proceedings not inconsistent with this opinion.

NOTES & QUESTIONS

1) Initially, the court in *Mayes* basically described the central question this way: whether the insurer had a duty to pay proceeds given that the insured failed to *disclose* certain information about his health. However, later in the opinion, the Texas Supreme Court stated: "We believe [this inquiry] should be controlled by the law applicable to a *misrepresentation*." Why? Are these words and phrases synonymous: "a failure to disclose a fact," "a misrepresentation of a fact," "nondisclosure," and "misrepresentation?"

2) Under the law of marine insurance, the doctrine of "utmost good faith" requires an insured to disclose all facts that an insurer must know or ought to know. And if the insured does not disclose, the insurer has no contractual duty to indemnify. Yet in *Mayes,* the Texas Supreme Court refused to apply the doctrine of "utmost good faith." Why?

3) Consider this statement which appears in *Mayes*: "[T]he basic question before us is whether the requirement ... that the answers in the application be true and correct at the time of delivery of the policy should be considered as a *condition precedent* or as a *representation*." Assume that an applicant has a duty to disclose certain facts on an insurance application. May that duty to

disclose be both a condition precedent and a condition subsequent? Was Mayes's failure to disclose conclusive evidence that he breached a condition subsequent in the application?

3. "Insured's Concealment Defeats Coverage"

Georgia Home Insurance Company v. Golden
91 S.W.2d 695
(Tex. Com. App. 1936)

The certificate of the Court of Civil Appeals is lengthy, and we will state only the material facts.

On February 27, 1932, appellee, I. J. Golden, sold to one M. R. Billings certain furniture and retained a mortgage lien thereon to secure the purchase price. At the time of the sale Billings agreed to obtain a policy of fire insurance on the furniture containing a mortgage clause providing that in the event of loss by fire the insurance should be payable to Golden as his interest might be. On March 7, 1932, Billings obtained a policy from appellant, Georgia Home Insurance Company, covering the furniture. Two days later the building in which the furniture was located was burned and the furniture was destroyed.

Shortly thereafter, the insurance company refunded to Billings the premium on which he had paid and Billings executed a release. Among other things, this release recited that in obtaining the policy Billings had withheld from the company certain information, which, if known by the company at the time, would have caused the company not to issue the policy. Billings testified on trial of the case that at the time he took out the insurance he knew that there existed a conspiracy to burn the building and the furniture; that he had been told by one Crabtree that he (Crabtree) would see that the house and furniture were burned; that the main reason he had for taking out the policy was because he thought the furniture was going to be burned. He did not advise the insurance company before the issuance of the policy or before the date of the fire that the house would likely be burned. It is undisputed that appellee, Golden, had no information of any conspiracy to burn the property or of the fraud on the part of Billings in securing the policy.

The policy of insurance contained provisions which made it void because of the fraud practiced by Billings in obtaining same. It contained what is known as the "Loss Payable Clause," and also what is known as the "Standard Mortgage Clause," or "Union Mortgage Clause." However, under the section in the policy which provided for an election between these two clauses, it was stated that the "Loss Payable Clause" was to govern. . . .

The Court of Civil Appeals has certified to the Supreme Court two questions as follows:

1) Did the act of fraud perpetrated before the policy was issued, by M. R. Billings in concealing the existence of the conspiracy to burn the furniture

after it was insured, invalidate the insurance of the appellee, who was the mortgagee?

2) Was the knowledge of the fraud and conspiracy possessed by M. R. Billings, whom appellee had required to secure a policy of fire insurance on the furniture as additional security for his debt, imputable to the appellee, who was the mortgagee?

In the case of *Hamburg-Bremen Fire Insurance Company v. Ruddell*, 37 Tex.Civ.App. 30, 82 S.W. 826, it was held that a policy stipulating that same would be void in case of fraud upon the part of the insured in obtaining same, and containing a clause to the effect that the loss, if any, should be payable to the mortgagee as his interest might be, was void both as to the mortgagee and mortgagor. That opinion seems to be in accord with the general rule recognized in many states where there is no statute governing the matter. That decision would probably control here, but for the fact that the matter is governed by article ~~4931~~ 862.055 of the Revised Statutes of 1925. This article is as follows:

> The interest of a mortgagee or trustee under any fire insurance contract hereafter issued covering any property situated in this State shall not be invalidated by any act or neglect of the mortgagor or owner of said described property or the happening of any condition beyond his control, and any stipulation in any contract in conflict herewith shall be null and void.

This article became a part of the contract of insurance as a matter of law and controlled the inconsistent provisions of the policy. Thus, by virtue of the statute, the "Union Mortgage Clause" automatically became a part of the policy in question and superseded the "Loss Payable Clause."

While it has frequently been held that under the statute a policy of insurance is not void as to the mortgagee for acts of the mortgagor subsequent to the issuance of the policy, even though made void by such acts as to the mortgagor, yet we do not find that our courts have had occasion to determine whether or not under the statute a policy would be void as to the mortgage on account of fraud by the mortgagor in procuring the policy. However, practically the unanimous weight of authority in other jurisdictions is to the effect that when a policy of insurance contains a clause to the effect that the insurance shall not be invalidated by any act or neglect of the mortgagor or owner, whether expressly written into the policy or incorporated therein by virtue of law, the mortgagee, in case of loss, is protected against any act or neglect of the mortgagor of which the mortgagee is ignorant, whether prior or subsequent to the issuance of the policy.

This rule is based on the ground that such a clause constitutes an independent contract between the insurer and the mortgagee covering the mortgagee's insurable interest, and not merely the property, and is affected only by acts of the mortgagee himself. The leading American case is that of *Syndicate Insurance Company v. Bohn* (C.C.A.) 65 F. 165, 177, 27 L.R.A. 614, opinion by Judge Sanborn. Discussing policies containing the "Union Mortgage Clause," the substance of which is incorporated into our statute, the court said:

> When this mortgage clause was attached to the policies in suit, it had been introduced and generally adopted by insurance companies and mortgagees to secure indemnity to the latter. The purpose of its introduction and adoption had been to protect that indemnity against every act and neglect of the mortgagors, whether prior or subsequent to the issue of the mortgage indemnity clause. Ten years before, the highest judicial tribunal of the state of New York had declared that a mortgage clause which contained these provisions accomplished that purpose, and every court whose attention had been called to the question had approved that decision. Under these circumstances, the mortgagee and the insurance companies in these cases selected a mortgage clause that contained these identical provisions, and made it their contract. The inference is irresistible that they intended to, and that they did thereby, agree that no act or neglect of the mortgagors, unknown to the mortgagee, whether prior or subsequent to the date of this contract, should avoid it.

As this clause had by almost unanimous judicial decision been so construed for years prior to the adoption of what is now article 4931, we are convinced that the Legislature intended to give it this meaning.

Both questions propounded by the Court of Civil Appeals are answered in the negative.

Opinion adopted by the Supreme Court.

NOTES & QUESTIONS

1) If a mortgagor and a mortgagee have insurable interests in property, may those interests be based on fraud? If contracts are based on fraud, are they valid and enforceable? Was the insurance contract in *Golden* based on fraud?

2) Are these words and phrases synonymous: "fraud," "concealment," "fraudulent concealment" and "conspiracy?" In *Golden*, would the result be different if the insurer had invoked the doctrine of "utmost good faith?"

B. *"Insured Breached a Warranty"*

1. "Insured breached a warranty in an application"

Equitable Life Assurance Society v. Hazlewood
12 S.W. 621
(Tex. 1889)

[Henry C. Hazlewood completed an application for life insurance. In 1887, Equitable Life Assurance Society — appellant— issued a $15,000 policy. Henry C. Hazlewood was both the owner of and the insured under the policy. The primary beneficiary was Robert R. Hazlewood. The contingent beneficiary was another brother. The insured died in March, 1888, He was about 28-years-old. The beneficiary filed a claim with the insurer. Equitable refused to pay, asserting that the insured had breached a warranty in the life-insurance application. The beneficiary sued.]

Appellee, beginning with the year 1881, and between that time and the date of the application for the insurance, had advanced to the said Henry C. Various sums of money, amounting to about $1,200, . . . which . . Henry acknowledged an indebtedness. On the back of the application for the insurance, and just above the signatures of both of said Hazlewoods, is a printed agreement in the following words: "It is hereby agreed that all the foregoing statements and answers, as well as those made, or to be made, to the society's medical examiner, are warranted to be true, and are offered to the society as a consideration of the contract."

In the body of, and on the back of, the application, and above said signatures, there are a number of questions and answers relating to the risk. Attached to the application is another paper, styled, "Medical Examiner's Report," at the beginning of which appears the signature of Henry Clay Hazlewood and at the end of it the name of the medical examiner. Between the two signatures there appear a great number and variety of questions and answers, relating to the history of the said Henry and of his ancestors, and collateral kindred, and to his physique, system, general health record, habits, and environment. The answers are usually 'Yes" or "No," and, from the space allowed for them in the form used it is evident that they are required to be monosyllabic. Some of the answers are evidently made by the medical examiner, and some by the subject of the examination.

* * *

All answers were written down by the medical examiner. The policy sets out on its face that it is issued "in consideration of the application, and of each statement made therein." Among the provisions of the policy is one reading: "If any statement made in the application for this policy be in any respect untrue, this policy shall be void.'"The application sets out on its face: "I certify that I am temperate in my habits, and am, to the best of my knowledge and belief, in sound physical condition, and a satisfactory subject for life assurance." This was signed by the insured, and indorsed by the beneficiary.

Under the general health record, the question was asked in the written and printed medical examination which was sent forward to the company in New York: "(13) Any history of serious illness, injury, or infirmity, etc.?" to which the insured answered, "No." "(16 *b*) When, and for what, has medical advice been sought within the last three years?" to which the insured answered, "Nothing." The medical examiner of defendant testified that he asked both of the above questions, and the assured answered them as recorded, and made no other statements under those heads.

* * *

In the written examination the question was asked: "(6) Any history of mental derangement?" to which the applicant answered, "No." In the medical examination is the printed question to the applicant: "(8 *a*) Ever spat blood, or any history of chronic hoarseness or cough, or of asthma, or shortness of breath?" To which the insured answered, "No."

The controverted questions as to breaches of warranty raised by the pleadings, referred to in the evidence, and discussed in the brief of appellant's counsel, are thus stated in the brief:

> The applicant covenants in writing, and warrants, that to the best of his knowledge and belief he is in sound physical condition. He warrants that he has not sought medical advice for anything within the last three years. He warrants that there has been no mental derangement. He warrants that there is no application pending for other insurance. He warrants that there has been no severe illness, coughs, or other ailments, etc.

It is contended that the court erred in refusing to give the following charge at the request of defendant:

> If the jury believe from the evidence that Henry Clay Hazlewood, in the application for the policy of assurance, warranted that all the statements in such application, and all the statements and answers made to the society's medical examiner, true, and that such application was made a part of the policy, and it was therein provided that if any statement in such application was in any respect untrue, the said policy should be void, then I charge you that all three of such instruments, taken together, constitute the contract between the parties, and a warranty on the part of the assured that all the statements and answers to the medical examiner were true[.]
>
> [A]nd, if you further believe from the evidence that the said Henry Clay Hazlewood, in his medical examination, in answer to the printed questions propounded by the society, had his answers to said questions put down in writing by the medical examiner opposite said questions, after said Hazlewood had signed said medical examination, and that after said answers were put down he read over and examined the same, and assented thereto, and the same was sent forward with the application, as the basis of the policy, and the same was issued by defendant upon the reliance of the truth of such answers, then, if you find from the evidence that said written answers in said medical examination were in any respect untrue, you will find for the defendant.

And also:

> In refusing to grant the defendant's motion for a new trial in this, that it was clearly proved that the contract was embraced in the application, the answers of the assured to the medical examiner, and the policy, taken together, and they constitute a warranty that the statements therein made were true, when the facts fully show that they were not true, that at the time of the application the assured was not in sound physical condition, but was in bad health, and misled defendant and its officers by his statements regarding his condition.

The doctrine contended for by appellant, that a warranty must be strictly complied with, is fully maintained by the authorities quoted in his brief.

Doctrine of utmost good faith

* * *

While the doctrine of warranty will be strictly applied, it should be as strictly limited to the precise undertaking of the party making it. If, beyond requiring that the insured should warrant the truth of all answers given by him, the company intended, as it had the right to do, that he should also warrant that his answers should be correctly written down and reported, and that he would warrant them, not only as given by himself, but as written down, the agreement could have been made to so express, and it ought to have been done.

* * *

In view of the fact that plaintiff's contention was that the insured gave true answers to the questions, which were incorrectly written down and reported by the medical examiner, and that the insured did not read the answers, or sign the paper containing them, which there was evidence tending to support, we think the charge was incorrect in this particular. The signature of the insured, being at the beginning of the examination instead of at its close, seems to us to have been required to be placed there as one means of identifying him as the person who had made the application, rather than for the purpose of binding him, as a party, for the truth of the contents of the paper.

* * *

We deem it sufficient to say that we do not think this character of issue was presented by the pleadings or the charge of the court, and the record before us suggests that the evidence upon it would have been thoroughly conflicting, and amply sufficient to support a verdict in favor of plaintiff.

NOTES & QUESTIONS

1) Why is it legally significant that the insurer's agent—the medical examiner — secured answers from the applicant and transferred those responses to paper?

2) Did the applicant sign the application? What is the legal significance of one's signing a legal document? Does a life insurance application qualify as a legal document?

3) What is the test for determining whether "yes" and "no" answers on an insurance application are "warranties," "covenants," "promises," or simply representations?

4) What is the test for determining whether "true" warranties, covenants and conditions are "material," and, thus enforceable?

5) Tex. Ins. Code § 1101.007 reads: "A life insurance policy must provide that, in the absence of fraud, a statement made by an insured is considered a representation and not a warranty."

2. "Insured breached a warranty in a the fire insurance contract"

Lane v. Travelers Indemnity Company
391 S.W.2d 399
(Tex. 1965)

Petitioner Lane sued The Travelers Indemnity Company, respondent, on a fire insurance policy and to recover part of the premium which had been paid. The case was submitted to a jury on a number of special issues. Following return of the jury's verdict the trial court rendered judgment that the plaintiff takes nothing. The Court of Civil Appeals modified the judgment to the extent of decreeing recovery by the plaintiff of the total premium paid for the policy, and affirmed the judgment as thus modified. We reverse the judgments of the courts below and remand the case to the trial court with directions to render judgment for plaintiff Lane.

The only question for decision is whether statements in a Texas Standard Fire Insurance Policy descriptive of the property are warranties. We hold they are not. There were other issues between the parties in the trial court but they have gone out of the case.

Lane purchased the contract of fire insurance on a house situated nine miles southwest of Linden, Texas. Lane was not the owner of the property, but he had an insurable interest in it as a lienholder. A printed Texas standard fire insurance policy form was used in preparing the contract. In the section of the form titled "DESCRIPTION OF PROPERTY" are blank lines for showing number of stories, type of roof, construction, location and occupancy. The words "Dwelling-Tenant" were written on the line over "occupancy." The house was a dwelling and it was occupied as such at all relevant times, but it was not occupied by a tenant; it was occupied by its owners, Mr. and Mrs. Floyd McGowen. It was destroyed by fire some five and one-half months after the contract was purchased. Lane sued for the amount of his debt which was less than the amount of insurance.

In answer to a special issue the jury found that "Plaintiff warranted in the insurance contract that the property insured was to be occupied as a dwelling-tenant." The question submitted by the issue is one of law and not of fact, and the Court of Civil Appeals properly so treated it. However, we disagree with the Court of Civil Appeals' conclusion that the statement of occupancy was a contractual warranty and that the falsity of the statement relieves the respondent insurer of liability.

The basis on which the Court of Civil Appeals affirmed the trial court's judgment denying recovery on the policy is difficult to determine from its opinion. That court held that the statement in the policy that the dwelling was occupied by a tenant was a "contractual warranty," and yet it did not hold that a breach of the warranty voided the policy. Instead, the court seems to have used another policy provision as a basis for denying recovery. The policy provision used by the court is one of several appearing under the heading "BASIC CONDITIONS," and is titled "CONDITIONS SUSPENDING OR RESTRICTING INSURANCE." It reads:

> Unless otherwise provided in writing added hereto, this Company shall not be liable for loss occurring (a, b, and c applicable only to Coverage F-Fire): (a) while the hazard is increased by any means within the knowledge and control of the insured, provided such increase in hazard in not usual and incidental to the occupancy as hereon described; or (b) while a described building, whether intended for occupancy by owner or tenant, is vacant beyond a period of thirty consecutive days; or (c) as a result of explosion or riot, unless fire ensue, and in that event for loss by fire only; or (d) following a change in ownership of the insured property; or (e) while any other stipulation or condition of this policy is being violated.

But if the basis of the Court of Civil Appeals' judgment is somewhat unclear, the position of respondent Travelers is not. Travelers' position is that the statement was a warranty; that the truth of the matter warranted was a condition precedent to validity of the contract; and that the policy never became effective.

If the quoted provision of the policy is intended to relieve an insurer of liability because of mere misrepresentations, without proof and findings of materiality, it runs afoul of Art, 21.16, Vernon's Texas Insurance Code, which provides:

> Any provision in any contract or policy of insurance issued or contracted for in this State which provides that the answers or statements made in the application for such contract or in the contract of insurance, if not true or false, shall render the contract or policy void or voidable, shall be of no effect, and shall not constitute any defense to any suit brought upon such contract, unless it be shown upon the trial thereof that the matter or thing misrepresented was material to the risk or

> actually contributed to the contingency or event on which said policy became due and payable, and whether it was material and so contributed in any case shall be a question of fact to be determined by the court or jury trying such case.

The stricture of the statute is applicable whether the exonerating policy provision be that the contract "shall be void" or only that the insurer "shall not be liable." It follows that Travelers was not entitled to be relieved of liability in this case unless the statement that the dwelling was occupied by a tenant was a warranty.

Travelers argues that the statement cannot be a representation and it must, therefore, be a warranty. A semblance of support for the argument is found in *Doyle v. Great Southern Life Ins. Co.*, Tex. Civ.App., 126 S.W.2d 735, 737 (1939), affirmed 136 Tex. 377, 151 S.W.2d 197 (1941), in which Couch on Insurance, 1st Edition, is quoted as defining a representation as "an oral or written statement which precedes the contract of insurance and is no part thereof, unless it be otherwise stipulated, . . . and relates to the facts necessary to enable the underwriter to form his judgment whether he will accept the risk, and at what premium." But Couch qualifies the quoted statement in s 35:9, 2d Ed., as follows:

> By the basic definition, the representation is not a part of the contract of insurance and therefore is not a term of the contract. This, however, does not preclude the inclusion or repetition within the policy itself of the representations. Such statements will be given effect only as representations and not as warranties when it is expressly stipulated that they are merely representations, or if it appears from the contract read as a whole that they were so intended."

Moreover, Art. 21.16, quoted above, contains a clear recognition that a statement "in the contract of insurance" may be nothing more than a representation the falsity of which must be shown to have been material to the risk or to have contributed to the event on which the policy became payable before an insurer is relieved of liability.

The word "warranty" as related to contracts of insurance has been variously defined. Respondent adopts a definition taken from Texas Jurisprudence and quoted in *Trinity Universal Ins. Co. v. Winter*, 67 S.W.2d 926, 928 (Tex.Civ.App. 1934, writ dismissed), as follows:

> [G]enerally speaking, warranties are statements, stipulations, or conditions which form a part of the contract, whereby the insured contracts as to the existence of certain facts, circumstances, or conditions, the literal truth as to which is essential to the validity of the contract.

A definition given by Couch is substantially in accord. Petitioner adopts a definition found in the opinion of this Court in *Phoenix Assur. Co. v. Munger Imp. Cotton-Mach. Mfg. Co.*, 49 S.W. 222, 225 (Tex.1898), as follows:

> A warranty in an insurance contract is a statement made therein by the assured, which is susceptible of no construction other than that the parties mutually intended that the policy should not be binding unless such statement be literally true.

There is no real or substantial difference between the two definitions. Both embrace the central idea that for a statement in a policy to constitute a warranty, the parties must have intended that the policy stand or fall on the literal truth or the falsity of the statement. In addition to that idea, the second definition incorporates the rule that in determining whether a particular statement is a warranty or only a representation, the entire policy will be considered and construed to prevent a forfeiture. The rule is a well recognized one.

We adopt the view that statements in a policy of insurance may be representations, and we conclude that statements in a Texas Standard Fire Insurance Policy descriptive of the property are representations and not warranties. Normally, statements descriptive of the property will be made orally by the applicant to the agent of the insurer before they are placed in the policy. At this stage of contractual negotiations they are clearly representations. Their purpose is to enable the agent to form a just estimate of the risk, and to determine whether to accept or reject it and what premium will be charged if it is accepted.

When included in the policy, these statements have none of the indicia usually associated with a warranty. There is no express declaration in the policy that they are warranties. There is no provision that the policy is to be effective only if the statements are true. There is no provision that the policy shall be void if the statements are untrue. To hold that statements of this character are warranties could lead to absurd results. For example, an insurer could escape liability if a statement of occupancy was "Storage-Explosives" when in fact the property was occupied by the insured and his family as their unencumbered dwelling. Another descriptive statement in the instant policy is that the insured property is of frame construction with a composition roof. If the statement is a warranty, the insurer could escape liability by proving that the house was constructed of brick and had a sheet metal roof, even though with the actual type of construction and roof the risk was less and the premium much lower. It would be unreasonable to conclude that parties to a fire insurance contract intend its provisions to lead to such absurd results.

Moreover, another provision under the "BASIC CONDITIONS" part of the policy expressly states the circumstances under which the policy shall be void. The provision is titled "Concealment, fraud" and reads:

> This entire policy shall be void if, whether before or after a loss, the insured has wilfully concealed or misrepresented any material fact or circumstance concerning this insurance, or the subject thereof, or the interest of the insured therein, or in case of any fraud or false swearing by the insured relating thereto.

The provision is the only one in the policy defining conditions which render the policy void. By the provision, a Texas Standard Fire Insurance Policy is void only if material facts or circumstances concerning the insurance or the subject of the insurance are wilfully concealed or falsely represented. The policy provisions are inconsistent if statements describing the property are held to be warranties and their falsity voids the policy without reference to their materiality. By holding the statements to be representations to which Art. 21.16 is applicable, the two provisions are made consistent and harmonious.

No useful purpose would be served by a lengthy review of the many Texas decisions dealing with warranties and representations.

* * *

The judgments of the Court of Civil Appeals and the trial court are reversed and the cause is remanded to the trial court with directions to render judgment in accord with this opinion for the plaintiff for such sum as may be due.

NOTES & QUESTIONS

1) Again, Tex. Ins. Code § 21.16 has been repealed. The new codification may be found at Tex. Ins. Code §§ 705.003 and 705.004.

2) In *Lane,* the court states: "The only question for decision is whether statements in a Texas Standard Fire Insurance Policy descriptive of the property are *warranties*." Yet, "Travelers' position [was] that the statement was a warranty; that the truth of the matter *warranted* was a *condition precedent* to validity of the contract; and that the policy never became effective." What is the test for distinguishing *warranties* from *conditions* precedent and subsequent?

3) The *Lane* court stated: "There is no express declaration in the policy that [these statements] are warranties." If that conclusion is correct, describe the court's methodology for concluding that the statements were not warranties. Is that test readily apparent in *Lane*?

C. *"Insured Breached a Condition"*

Conditions appear in all types of contracts, including claims-made, occurrence-based, health, life, property and liability insurance contracts. Put simply, a condition precedent is a stipulation. In an insurance contract, it typically requires an insured to perform some act before receiving a benefit under the policy. Sometimes conditions precedent require certain events to occur before an insurer pays various proceeds or satisfies other contractual obligations. In *Hohenberg Bros. Co. v. George E. Gibbons & Co.*, 537 S.W.2d 1, 3 (Tex. 1976), the Texas Supreme Court stated:

> A condition precedent may be either a condition to the formation of a contract or to an obligation to perform an existing agreement. Conditions may, therefore, relate either to the formation of contracts or to liability under them. Conditions precedent to an obligation to perform are those acts or events, which occur subsequently to the making of a contract, that must occur before there is a right to immediate performance and before there is a breach of contractual duty.

Some notable conditions precedent in insurance contracts are the requirements that an insured must 1) give a notice of loss to the insurer; 2) file a proof of loss in a timely manner; 3) report certain losses to proper authorities; 4) file a lawsuit within a specified time; and 4) forward legal documents, third-party complaints and demand letters to a liability insurer in a timely manner.

Conditions subsequent appear in contracts, too. Under insurance contracts, conditions subsequent require certain acts or events after coverage has been established. Or stated slightly differently, conditions subsequent impose obligations on an insured once the contract has been formed and the insured has paid the premiums. Generally, an insurer may successfully defend itself by showing that the insured failed to behave in a certain manner to maintain coverage. For example, under a commercial fire insurance contract, Dell Computer Company might have a duty to submit monthly inventory reports to the insurer. Assume that a fire completely destroys the inventory in a Dell's warehouse. If Dell "forgot" to file each report, the insurer probably would not have to pay for the lost inventory. The insurer's arguing that Dell breached the condition subsequent to coverage would be a sound defense.

However, determining whether a statement is a condition or simply a representation generates much conflict and interest. The Texas Supreme Court has defined a representation as an oral or written statement that precedes a contract of insurance. In addition, a representation is not part of the contract; it only enables an underwriter to decide whether to accept a risk for a certain premium. *Lane v. Travelers Indemnity Co.,* 391 S.W.2d 399, 401 (Tex.1965).

On the other hand, in *Criswell v. European Crossroads Shopping Center, Ltd.,* 792 S.W.2d 945, 948 (Tex.1990), the Supreme Court of Texas presented the following test to determine whether a statement is a condition precedent:

[T]o determine whether a condition precedent exists, the intention of the parties must be ascertained; and that can be done only by looking at the entire contract. In order to make performance specifically conditional, a term such as "if," "provided that," "on condition that," or some similar phrase of conditional language must normally be included. If no such language is used, the terms will be construed as a covenant in order to prevent a forfeiture. While there is no requirement that such phrases be utilized, their absence is probative of the parties' intention that a promise be made, rather than a condition imposed.

As you read the breach-of-condition cases in this section, try to determine if the Texas Supreme Court employed the *Criswell* test or some other standard to decide whether certain statements in the insurance contracts were enforceable conditions precedent, covenants, or merely representations.

1. "The notice requirement is a condition precedent and not a covenant"

PAJ, Inc. v. The Hanover Insurance Company
243 S.W.3d 630
(Tex. 2008)

[The majority of facts in this case appear in the "Breach of Notice" section. Here, it is sufficient to know that PAJ, Inc. — a jewelry manufacturer and distributor — purchased a commercial general liability insurance contract from Hanover. The policy required PAJ to notify Hanover "as soon as practicable" when a third party presented a claim or sued PAJ. Yurman Designs, Inc. sued PAJ for copyright infringement. PAJ did not notify Hanover of the suit until four to six months after the litigation commenced. The parties dispute whether the policy's prompt-notice requirement was a condition precedent or merely a covenant.

Hanover cited *Hohenberg Bros. Co. v. George E. Gibbons & Co.,* 537 S.W.2d 1, 3 (Tex.1976) and argued that the language in the policy created a condition precedent — the failure of which defeats coverage regardless of whether the insurer was prejudiced. Conversely, PAJ cited *Centex Corp. v. Dalton,* 840 S.W.2d 952, 956 (Tex.1992) and argued that the prompt-notice language was a covenant —the breach of which excuses an insurer's performance only if the breach is "material." The Texas Supreme Court embraced PAJ's argument, concluding that only a material breach of the timely notice provision could excuse Hanover's performance under the policy. Also while the majority in PAJ refused to discuss whether the language in the insurance contract was covenant, the dissenting justices performed that analysis and severely criticized the majority. First, consider what the majority said about the *condition versus covenant issue*.]

III.

Hanover pins its analysis on our decision in *Members Mutual Insurance Co. v. Cutaia,* 476 S.W.2d 278 (Tex.1972), and that is where we will begin. The policy at issue in *Cutaia* required the insured to forward any suit papers immediately to the insurer and provided that "no action shall lie against the [insurer] unless, *as a condition precedent thereto,* there shall have been full compliance with all of the terms of this policy. The insured failed to forward the suit papers to his insurer until five months after the occurrence in question.

Stipulating that it had suffered no harm, the insurer denied liability, contending a condition precedent to coverage had not been met. We agreed that the insured's failure to timely comply with the policy's forwarding condition precluded the insurer's liability whether or not prejudice resulted. But we emphasized "the apparent injustice which results in this particular case," and deferred consideration of the issue to the State Board of Insurance or the Legislature.

* * *

Two decades after Board Order 23080 became effective, we decided *Hernandez*. . . .Without distinguishing between covenants and conditions or classifying the exclusion as one or the other, we concluded that the insured's breach of the settlement-without-consent provision was immaterial and thus the insurer could not avoid liability under the policy. Notably, we recognized that "[m] ost other jurisdictions presented with this issue have likewise imposed a prejudice requirement, primarily on public policy grounds."

* * *

The dissent today attempts to distinguish *Hernandez* by characterizing the settlement-without-consent clause at issue in that case as a covenant rather than a condition, even though in *Hernandez* we made no distinction between the two. They arrive at that conclusion only through reasoning, backwards, that because we required a showing of prejudice in *Hernandez,* the policy language at issue must have been a covenant.

* * *

The dissent's construction would have the absurd consequence that identical policy language creates a condition precedent as to one type of coverage (advertising injury) but a covenant as to the other (bodily injury and property damage). We have said unequivocally that "when a condition would impose an absurd or impossible result, the agreement will be interpreted as creating a covenant rather than a condition." *Criswell v. European Crossroads Shopping Ctr., Ltd.,* 792 S.W.2d 945, 948 (Tex.1990)

Moreover, we question the dissent's fundamental premise that the timely notice provision before us creates a condition precedent rather than a covenant. The policy language in *Cutaia* specifically provided that "no action shall lie against the company unless, *as a condition precedent thereto,* the insured shall have fully complied with all the terms of this policy." The "as a condition precedent" language was deleted from the standard CGL policy following our decision in *Cutaia,* and it does not appear in PAJ's policy.

* * *

Dissenting Opinion of Justice Willett, Joined By Justices Hecht, Wainwright and Johnson

I respectfully dissent. I would follow *Members Mutual Insurance Co. v. Cutaia,* 476 S.W.2d 278, 279 (Tex.1972) and hold that a policy's unambiguous notice-of-suit language— a condition precedent to coverage — constitutes a defense to liability and must be enforced as written, unless positive law dictates otherwise. Because positive law does not dictate otherwise, I would affirm the court of appeals.

I. Discussion

PAJ argues that under *Hernandez v. Gulf Group Lloyds,* 875 S.W.2d 691 (Tex.1994) and *Harwell v. State Farm Mutual Automobile Insurance Co.,* 896 S.W.2d 170 (Tex.1995) the policy's notice provisions are covenants, not conditions precedent to coverage[.] [T]herefore Hanover must demonstrate prejudice before denying coverage for untimely notice. I disagree. Settled Texas precedent construes notice provisions as conditions precedent that impose no prejudice requirement, unless the policy's literal text, a statute, or an agency directive demands it.

A. The Timely Notice Provision Is a Condition Precedent, Not a Covenant

The parties dispute whether the policy's prompt-notice language constitutes a condition precedent (as Hanover argues), the failure of which defeats coverage, *Klein v. Century Lloyds,* 154 Tex. 160, 275 S.W.2d 95, 96 (1955), or a covenant (as PAJ argues), the breach of which, if immaterial, does not defeat coverage. *See Hernandez,* 875 S.W.2d at 692. PAJ concedes that "[f]or years, Texas courts have held that timely notice of suit provisions in liability insurance policies [are] conditions to coverage" and that a "long line of Texas cases hold[s] that the notice requirements of policies similar to the Policies [in this case] are conditions precedent to liability," but contends that those cases involved "*materially different*" policy language.

This Court has indeed repeatedly described insurance policy notice provisions as conditions precedent to coverage. In 1972, we held in *Cutaia* that when a notice provision requiring the immediate forwarding of suit papers is breached, "liability on the claim [was] discharged, and harm (or lack of it) resulting from the breach [is] immaterial." The policy in *Cutaia* provided that "'no action shall lie against the company unless, as a condition precedent thereto, the insured shall have fully complied with all the terms of this policy,' " including the notice requirement in issue.

PAJ insists the notice requirement in Hanover's CGL policy is necessarily a covenant because it omits the "as a condition precedent thereto" clause present in the *Cutaia* policy. I disagree. "Magic words" are not controlling; labeling something a "condition precedent" does not make it so, and the absence of such a label does not make it not so. Whether a notice provision constitutes a condition precedent turns on what the provision actually does, its nature and purpose, not merely on what it is called or because it appears under a heading, as here, that includes the word "Conditions." "A condition precedent may be either a condition to the formation of a contract or to an obligation to perform an existing agreement." *Hohenberg Bros. Co. v. George E. Gibbons & Co.,* 537 S.W.2d 1, 3 (Tex.1976)

A condition precedent to an obligation to perform is an act or event that "must occur before there is a right to immediate performance and before there is a breach of contractual duty"; failure to comply with such a condition forfeits coverage and releases the insurer from any duty to defend or indemnify. By contrast, a covenant is "an agreement to act or refrain from acting in a certain way," and only a material breach will forfeit coverage. *Hernandez v. Gulf Group Lloyds,* 875 S.W.2d 691, 692-93 (Tex.1994). While no mantra or magic words are necessary, an intent to create a condition precedent is sometimes indicated by the use of conditional terms such as "if," "provided that," "on condition that," or some similar limiting phrase that conditions performance. *Criswell v. European Crossroads Shopping Ctr., Ltd.,* 792 S.W.2d 945, 948 (Tex.1990). As the Court has explained, such terms "usually connote an intent for a condition rather than a promise."

The notice provision at issue is a condition precedent, as coverage is expressly conditioned on compliance with the notice requirement. Section IV of the policy, entitled "Commercial General Liability Conditions," contains a list of "Duties In The Event Of Occurrence, Offense, Claim Or Suit," one of which states: "If a claim is made or 'suit' is brought against any insured, you must . . . . [n]otify us as soon as practicable." Section IV also specifies that "[n]o person or organization has a right under this Coverage Part . . . to sue us on this Coverage Part *unless all of its terms have been fully complied with.*" The prompt-notice requirement, expressly identified in the policy as a condition and, more importantly, providing that no suit may take place absent full compliance, is plainly a condition that precedes the insurer's obligations to perform under the policy.

PAJ's reliance on *Hernandez* is misplaced. *Hernandez* involved an insured's breach of a settlement-without-consent exclusion in an automobile policy, which said that the insurance did not apply to "bodily injury or property damage with respect to which the insured ... shall, without written consent of the company, make any settlement with any person or organization who may be legally liable therefor." Rather than treat the exclusion as a condition precedent, the Court viewed it as a covenant, an ordinary contractual obligation, the performance of which was excused only if the breach were material. As such, we found it "unenforceable absent a showing by the insurer that it has been prejudiced by an insured's failure to obtain consent before settling." The Court recognized a prejudice requirement in *Hernandez* consistent with the basic contract law principle that one party's breach of a covenant must be material in order to excuse performance by the other party.

Hernandez's materiality-of-breach analysis is inapposite here because PAJ did not breach a covenant. Rather, it failed to comply with a condition precedent, a strict requirement that precedes any obligation on the part of Hanover under the policy. As noted above, and as PAJ concedes, the Court has long and consistently treated notice requirements as conditions precedent to coverage rather than covenants. Such treatment flows naturally from the fact that performance of an obligation to defend or indemnify cannot ordinarily be expected of an insurer until it first receives notice of a claim's existence.

Breach of a settlement-without-consent exclusion, on the other hand, might occur long after the insurer has learned of a suit and assumed its duty to defend. Hence, I agree with the court of appeals in this case in recognizing "a significant difference between a policy condition (performance of which is necessary to trigger any obligation for coverage) and a policy exclusion (which operates only after the obligation for coverage is in place)."

Further, treating every breach of a settlement-without-consent clause as automatically ending the insurer's obligations not only makes little sense from a timing standpoint but also disserves the interests of both parties to the insurance contract. It is easy to conceive of instances where a resourceful insured succeeds through its own efforts in obtaining a favorable third-party settlement that the insurer is only too happy to fund. Considering the prejudice, if any, to the insurer of a breach of the consent requirement is therefore warranted. On the other hand, it is hard to conceive of an instance where a failure to give notice of a suit or claim at the outset of litigation would ever operate to the insurer's benefit. In short, *Hernandez* is distinguishable.

* * *

NOTES & QUESTIONS

1) Was it important for the *PAJ* court to determine whether the insured breached a condition precedent—prompt notice requirement—or a covenant? Breach of covenant and breach of condition: aren't they both effective affirmative defenses?

2) What was the conflict in *PAJ*: "no coverage," "breach of a condition precedent before coverage," breach of a condition precedent before securing a right to a legal defense," or a "breach of a promise/covenant to notify promptly?"

2. "Insured breached a condition precedent in a homeowner's insurance contract"

Perrotta v. Farmers Insurance Exchange
47 S.W.3d 569
(Tex.App.-Houston [1st Dist.] 2001)

This is an appeal from a summary judgment, disposing of complaints regarding the denial of an insurance claim, rendered in favor of appellee, Farmers Insurance Exchange. Appellant, Raymond J. Perrotta, complains the trial court erred in (1) granting Farmers's motion for summary judgment on his contractual and extra-contractual claims; and (2) denying his motion for continuance in order to conduct discovery prior to consideration of the motion for summary judgment. We affirm.

Background and Procedural History

This case arises from an insurer's denial of a theft loss claim filed by the insured under a homeowner's insurance policy. Perrotta, the insured, purchased homeowner's insurance from Farmers, the insurer, in 1993, and he maintained a policy with Farmers up to and including the date of the alleged theft. The insurance policy covered the premises and the contents of Perrotta's residence.

In September 1996, Perrotta discovered several boxes of personal property missing from his residence. He reported the theft to the police, and an officer came out to his residence. In October, Perrotta filed a loss claim with the Pickett Agency, which forwarded it to the appropriate Farmers claims office. Mike Stevens, an adjuster for Farmers, came out to Perrotta's residence and met with him. They constructed a loss worksheet listing the items stolen, and Stevens took a recorded statement from Perrotta. Stevens reviewed a proof of loss form with Perrotta and requested that he fill it out and return it to Farmers. Stevens also asked Perrotta to complete an authorization form so that Farmers could obtain information confirming Perrotta's financial status.

Perrotta mailed the requested proof of loss to Farmers in November. Farmers took exception to the proof of loss, contending that it did not specify the amount claimed and did not have a notary seal. Farmers subsequently sent Perrotta a new proof of loss to fill out, along with another authorization form, but Farmers never received the completed forms back from Perrotta.

Farmers asked Perrotta to appear at an Examination Under Oath (EUO) on December 2, 1996, and to bring certain documents with him to the EUO. Perrotta attended the EUO and provided the attorney conducting the EUO with nine photographs depicting some of the items Perrotta alleged to have been stolen. Perrotta did not provide Farmers with any receipts or other documents evidencing his ownership of the stolen items, and he never signed and returned the transcription of the EUO to Farmers.

Several follow-up letters were forwarded by Farmers to Perrotta renewing their requests for information and asking him to sign and return the EUO. Farmers ultimately denied Perrotta's loss claim in July 1997, on the following grounds: 1) Perrotta either intentionally caused the alleged theft or no such theft occurred; 2) fraud and/or false swearing in the proof of loss, EUO, and presentation of his claim; and 3) lack of cooperation as required by the policy in that Perrotta had failed to provide Farmers with certain items it had requested since the EUO.

In February 1999, Perrotta filed suit against Farmers, Paul Antonucci, Jerry Pickett, and Pickett Insurance Agency claiming: damages for breach of contract; violations of the Texas Insurance Code and Texas Deceptive Trade Practices Act; breach of the common law duty of good faith and fair dealing; gross negligence; libel; slander; and defamation.

Farmers answered with a general denial; it pleaded further, and in the alternative, that Perrotta failed to conform to the insurance policy conditions and violated the policy's concealment provision.

On September 24, 1999, Farmers filed a motion for summary judgment. Farmers asserted summary judgment was proper on the contractual claims because: (1) Perrotta committed fraud in applying for the insurance; (2) Perrotta breached the policy by refusing to comply with the terms and conditions of the policy; and (3) Perrotta violated the concealment provision of the policy. Farmers contended summary judgment was proper on the extra-contractual claims because: liability was never reasonably clear; Farmers had a reasonable basis to deny the claim; and there was no evidence of any extra-contractual violation nor of independent damages related to such claims.

Perrotta replied by filing a motion for continuance requesting additional time for discovery along with a response to Farmers's summary judgment motion. In his response, Perrotta asserted: summary judgment on Farmers's defense of misrepresentation on the policy application is not proper; he had fully cooperated and satisfied all conditions of the insurance policy; Farmers failed to establish he had committed fraud or intended to deceive Farmers in violation of the policy's concealment clause; and the extra-contractual claims concerning Farmers's conduct involved a fact issue to be decided by the trier of fact.

The trial court denied Perrotta's motion for continuance and rendered summary judgment for Farmers.

* * *

In his first point of error, Perrotta contends the trial court erred by rendering summary judgment for Farmers on both his contractual and extra-contractual claims. We will first consider the judgment rendered on the contractual claims.

A. Breach of Contract

In its motion for summary judgment, Farmers claimed that Perrotta breached several conditions of the insurance policy. Specifically, Farmers alleged Perrotta never signed and returned the transcription of his EUO as required by the policy.

Other terms and conditions Farmers claimed that Perrotta breached were: refusing to provide any documents establishing his ownership of the items he claimed to have lost; refusing to provide copies of financial statements confirming his claims of wealth; refusing to provide identities and locations of individuals to corroborate his claims of ownership of the stolen items; never providing any written notice of the facts of the loss; providing a deficient proof of loss in that it was incomplete and did not have a notary seal; not providing locations of storage facilities where he claims to have stored items; refusing to provide names and addresses of persons from whom some of the stolen items were purchased; and not completing the supplemental loss form from the Constable's office. Farmers claims these breaches denied Farmers the right it had under the insurance policy to expect Perrotta's cooperation in the investigation of his claim.

The policy contains a "Conditions" section enumerating the insured's "Duties After Loss." One of these enumerated duties is that the insured must "submit to [EUO] and sign and swear to it" in case of a loss to covered property. Additionally, the policy has an "Agreement" provision, which explicitly provides that Farmers "will provide the insurance described in this policy in return for the premium and compliance with all applicable provisions of this policy."

Insurance policy provisions requiring the insured to submit to an EUO are valid. *See Philadelphia Underwriters' Agency of Fire Ins. Ass'n v. Driggers*, 238 S.W. 633, 635 (Tex. 1922) (holding that failure or refusal to submit to EUO after loss suspends insured's right of recovery). When the language of the insurance policy is unambiguous, it is the court's duty to give the words used their plain meaning. Here, the policy unambiguously required the insured, Perrotta, to submit to an EUO and sign and swear to it.

Perrotta relies on *Century Ins. Co. v. Hogan*, 135 S.W.2d 224 (Tex.Civ.App.-Austin 1939, no writ) for the proposition that his failure to sign and return the EUO was not a material breach of the policy. *Hogan*, however, is distinguishable. In that case, the insured provided a reason for not signing the EUO: the notary was unable to take down everything the insured said because he talked too fast. Additionally, the court held that, because the insurer had not "directed attention" to the insured's failure to sign the EUO, further compliance was waived. In this case, Farmers made several requests that Perrotta sign and return the EUO. Unlike in *Hogan*, Perrotta never provided a reason for not signing and returning the EUO, and Farmers never waived further compliance with the EUO provision of the policy.

Farmers included the affidavit of Mike Stevens, an adjuster for Farmers, in its summary judgment motion. In the affidavit, Stevens states that Perrotta "never signed and returned [the EUO] as requested and as required by [the] policy." Perrotta did not present any summary judgment evidence controverting Farmers's claim that he did not sign and return the original EUO. Perrotta's own affidavit, included in his response to the summary judgment, does not claim that he ever signed or returned the EUO to Farmers. As such, Farmers's summary judgment proof established as a matter of law that Perrotta did not comply with the EUO provision of the policy, and Perrotta presented no evidence to create a fact issue about his noncompliance.

A clear reading of the policy, coupled with the summary judgment proof presented, shows that Perrotta breached a term of the policy. Perrotta's own breach of the policy precludes him from maintaining suit for breach of contract. *See Gulf Pipe Line Co. v. Nearen*, 138 S.W.2d 1065, 1068 (Tex. 1940) (holding a party to a contract who is himself in default cannot maintain a suit for its breach. Because we find Perrotta breached the terms of the insurance policy, we affirm summary judgment for Farmers on the contractual claims.

* * *

Conclusion

We affirm the summary judgment of the trial court.

NOTES & QUESTIONS

1) What was the insurer's affirmative defense in *Perrotta*: breach of a condition precedent, breach of contract or breach of a condition subsequent?

2) In *Perrotta*, the insurer claimed that the insured did not cooperate, because he failed to submit certain items that the insurer requested. Perrotta did not provide certain items or did not disclose certain information. He: 1) refused to provide copies of financial statements confirming his wealth; 2) refused to provide the identities and locations of individuals to corroborate his claims of ownership the stolen items; and, 3) refused to provide names and addresses of persons from whom some of the stolen items were purchased. Were those items and information "material?" Did Farmers' prove "materiality?"

3) In *Perrotta*, the insurer petitioned the court for summary relief, asserting in part that Perrotta intentionally caused the alleged theft or that no such theft occurred. What was the insurer's summary judgment evidence?

3. "Insured breached a condition precedent in a health-insurance contract"

American National Insurance Company v. Lawson
127 S.W.2d 294
(Tex.Comm.App.1939, opinion adopted)

The certificate by the Honorable Court of Civil Appeals, Second District, discloses that appellee was named as beneficiary in a policy of life insurance issued by appellant upon the life of his wife, Ethel Lawson. The suit is upon that policy. It was issued on September 10, 1934, for the sum of $240. Insured died on March 7, 1936, and the question of whether . . . the defense hereinafter to be considered would be available to appellant after two years from the date of the issuance of the policy . . . . The answer setting up the defense was filed in July, 1936. At the time the policy was issued insured was afflicted with pulmonary tuberculosis and had been so afflicted for an unknown period of time prior to that date. She first learned of her affliction on September 20, 1934. The sole and immediate cause of her death was pulmonary tuberculosis. The policy contained this provision: ". . . provided however, that no obligation is assumed by the Company prior to the date hereof nor unless on said date the Insured is alive and in sound health."

The question certified is as follows: "Should the stipulation in the policy sued on to the effect that no obligation is assumed by the company unless the insured be in sound health at the date of the policy, be construed as a condition precedent to the policy becoming effective in its entirety in the first instance or merely as an attempted limitation of the obligation of the insurer to pay the face value of the policy upon the death of the insured after the contract of insurance should become effective?"

From the tentative opinion of the Court of Civil Appeals accompanying the certificate it is made to appear that the doubt and uncertainty in the mind of that Court which prompted it to certify this case to this Court was brought about by its construction of the opinion of this Court in *Atlanta Life Insurance Company v. Cormier,* 126 Tex. 179, 85 S.W.2d 1045. The tentative opinion cites and discusses a number of cases which hold that provisions in policies of life insurance substantially the same as that quoted above are valid and may be invoked as defenses to suits upon such policies. The question was squarely before the Court in *Wright v. Federal Life Insurance Company*, 248 S.W. 325 (Tex. Com. App.), and it was held that such a stipulation is valid and enforceable. That decision has not been departed from, but has been followed. . . .

The rule is well stated in [a case] . . . from which we quote as follows: "It is now well settled in this state that a stipulation in a life insurance policy that such policy shall not take effect unless the insured is in sound health at the date the policy is delivered is, unless restrained by some statute, valid and enforceable, and it is immaterial whether the insured knew of his condition in that respect or not. His good faith in believing that he was in sound health at the time the policy was delivered will not authorize a recovery if in fact at the time of the delivery of the policy he was suffering from an ailment of a substantial nature which continued and ultimately caused his death.

The decision in *Atlanta Life Insurance Company v. Cormier, supra*, was upon a certified question; the certificate disclosing that the defense pleaded was the following provision of the policy: "No death benefit shall be payable hereunder when death is the result of immorality, or a disease contracted prior to the date hereof, or of resisting the legal execution of law, or legal authority by the insured, or when death is the result of suicide, it being understood and agreed to that death resulting from these causes, or any one of them, is not a risk undertaken or assumed under this policy of insurance."

In connection with our consideration of the case now before us we have consulted the record in that case and find that there was a provision in the policy there sued upon similar to the one involved in the instant case, but our decision was based upon a certificate which did not disclose that such provision was pleaded as a defense. On the contrary, it disclosed that the defense pleaded was the provision next above quoted. The question certified in that case was whether or not the insurance company could defend upon the ground that the cause of the death of the insured was a risk not insured against. Our holding was not that parties could not make a valid stipulation like that here involved, but that a provision adding exceptions to those enumerated in the statute was void. In that case the question of the validity of the policy at its inception was not involved, but rather the question of the validity of a provision adding exceptions to those enumerated in the statute and thereby excluding risks which otherwise would be insured against. We did not in that case overrule, modify or declare an exception to the rule announced in the *Wright* case, *supra*, and the other cases following it.

We answer the question certified as follows:

> The stipulation in the policy sued on to the effect that no obligation is assumed by the company unless the insured be in sound health at the date of the policy, should be construed as a condition precedent to the policy's becoming effective.

Opinion adopted by the Supreme Court.

NOTES & QUESTIONS

---

1) How did the court reach its conclusion in *Lawson*? Did the court employ any of the five doctrines of contract construction and interpretation?

2) Consider the following dates in *Lawson*: The insurer delivered the life insurance contract to the insured on September 10, 1934 for $240. She discovered her illness on September 20, 1934. She died on March 7, 1936. Could the beneficiary argue successfully that the insurer impliedly waived the "sound health" condition in light of those facts and others?

3) The *Lawson* court tells us: "At the time the policy was issued, insured was afflicted with pulmonary tuberculosis and *had been so afflicted for an unknown period of time prior to that date*." Assume the insurer knew she was not in "sound health" and continued to accept the insured's premium. Is that evidence sufficient for the beneficiary to raise an equitable estoppel argument?

D. "No Contract" and "No Coverage"

To be sure, the terms "contract" and "coverage" have traditional, commonsensical definitions when they appear in insurance law principles and theories of recovery. However, in light of the considerable variation among the types of insurance services that insurance companies provide, the Texas Legislature, courts and insurers have also defined these terms—"contract" and "coverage" —in ways that are less reasonable or foreign to ordinary consumers. For example, when an insurer mails a life-insurance, automobile or health-insurance policy to a new customer, it is reasonable for that consumer to conclude: Standing alone, this policy comprises the "entire insurance contract."

However, there are other, less-than-commonsensical definitions of a "contract" and "coverage." Consider the variability among the following provisions which appear in the Texas Insurance and Transportation Codes:

1) Tex. Ins. Code § 841.303 — "Each policy of insurance issued or delivered in this state by any life insurance company engaged in business in this state constitutes the *entire contract* between the parties, *except that if the application is made a part of the contract, the policy and the application constitute the entire contract.*

2) Tex. Ins. Code § 1101.003 — "A life insurance policy must provide that the policy *or* the policy and the application for the policy constitute the *entire contract* between the parties";

3) Tex. Ins. Code § 1201.001 — "In this chapter, (1) 'Accident and health insurance policy' includes any policy or contract that provides insurance against loss resulting from: (A) accidental bodily injury; (B) accidental death; or (C) sickness. (2) 'Policy' means the *entire contract* between an insurer and an insured and *includes riders, endorsements, and the application, if attached*;

4) Tex. Ins. Code § 1201.207 — "An individual accident and health insurance policy must contain the following provision: 'ENTIRE CONTRACT; CHANGES: This policy, *including the endorsements and the attached papers, if any, constitutes the entire contract of insurance.* A change in this policy is not valid until the change is approved by an executive officer of the insurer and unless the approval is endorsed on or attached to the policy. An agent does not have authority to change this policy or to waive any of its provisions.'"; and,

5) Texas Motor Vehicle Safety Responsibility Act, Tex. Trans. Code § 601.073 (f) — "The policy, any written application for the policy, and any rider or endorsement that *does not conflict with this chapter constitute the entire contract* between the parties." (Emphasis added)

Furthermore, assuming that an "entire insurance contract" exists, determining whether that "entire contract" provides "coverage" for the insured's losses, injuries or damages becomes the next challenge. Fairly often, it is a big challenge for the insureds and trier of facts, and the reason is not overly complicated. As discussed in earlier chapters, "coverage" is defined very differently under property and liability insurance contracts. However, once the appropriate definition of "coverage" has been isolated, both property and liability insurers may defend themselves successfully by asserting that the insurance contracts did not cover the insureds' losses, allegations or damages. Of course, there are exceptions to this general rule.

1. "No Coverage Under a Disability Insurance Contract"

Great American Reserve Insurance Company v. Laney
498 S.W.2d 674
(Tex. 1973)

The question presented by this appeal is whether plaintiff, Sam Milton Laney, proved his right to recover for a confining sickness which was defined in a policy with Great American Reserve Insurance Company as one which "shall totally and continuously disable and necessarily confine the Insured continuously within doors . . . ." The trial court, without a jury, rendered judgment for Laney. The court of civil appeals affirmed. Great American contends that proof of facts to establish a confining sickness was a condition precedent to Mr. Laney's right to recover for total disability and that, as a matter of law, the proof showed that Laney was not continuously confined within doors. We agree and accordingly reverse the judgments of the court below and render judgment that plaintiff Laney takes nothing.

On June 19, 1962, Great American issued its policy which entitled Mr. Laney to $400.00 per month until he reached age sixty-five, upon proof of a confining sickness. Another provision of the policy entitled him to the same amount of money per month but for no more than twenty-four consecutive months if his sickness was a non-confining one. These two relevant policy provisions are:

(Confining Sickness)

> ARTICLE II. Section 1. If such sickness shall totally and continuously disable and necessarily confine the Insured continuously within doors and shall require the personal care and regular attendance of a legally qualified physician or surgeon, the Company will pay, beginning after the number of days excepted in the schedule, the monthly indemnity specified in the schedule and continuing as long as the Insured remains so disabled and so confined up to the Insured's attained age of sixty-five, or a period of twenty-four months whichever period is greater.

(Non-Confining Sickness)

> Section 2. Or, if such sickness shall totally and continuously disable the Insured, but shall not necessarily continuously confine the Insured within doors, and shall require the personal care and regular attendance of a legally qualified physician or surgeon, the Company will pay, beginning after the number of days excepted in the schedule, the monthly indemnity specified in the schedule, and continuing as long as the Insured remains so disabled, not to exceed twenty-four consecutive months for any period of sickness.

Mr. Laney claims that the provisions of the 1952 policy have the meaning that court decisions at that time attributed to them. The state of the law construing the confinement provisions, he says, was expressed by the 1927 decision in *Federal Surety Co. v. Waite,* 297 S.W. 312 (Tex.Civ.App. 1927, writ dism'd). The court ruled in that case that the phrase, "strictly and continuously confined indoors," was only an expression of what, from an evidentiary point of view, would establish total disability. The court in *Waite* rejected the argument that the phrase stated a condition precedent to the insured's right to recover for total disability for the greater period of time than that allowed for disability which was a non-confining illness.

It was not until eight years after the issuance of the policy, that the Supreme Court disapproved the *Waite* decision as well as other similar decisions by courts of civil appeals, none of which had the approval of the Supreme Court. *United American Insurance Company v. Selby*, 338 S.W.2d 160, 163-164 (Tex.1960). *Selby* held that the policy provision which described a confining illness, such as the one we have in this case, was a condition precedent to the insured's right to recover and was not merely a statement of what evidence would show total disability. Mr. Laney argues that he possessed vested contractual rights in the policy and that the *Selby* decision by the Supreme Court did not retroactively defeat those rights.

It is not necessary that we decide whether the *Waite* rule became a part of the 1952 policy. In our opinion, Mr. Laney has not brought himself within the provisions of either the *Selby* rule or the more liberal *Waite* rule. His own testimony conclusively shows that his sickness, during the period of time here involved, was a non-confining rather than a confining sickness as defined in the policy. It thus fell under section 2 rather than section 1. On May 18, 1955, Mr. Laney suffered a heart attack. Great American commenced paying him $400.00 each month and continued those payments until May 22, 1962. Mr. Laney then filed this suit. He seeks damages in the amount of $400.00 for each month from May 22, 1962, up to February 11, 1968, when he became sixty-five years of age.

Mr. Laney was an active businessman and citizen at the time he first became ill. He operated the Sam Laney Tire Company and also the Sam Laney Motors in Denton, but he has not managed the business or participated in its operation since his heart attack. In the fall of 1955, following his attack in May, he began driving a car equipped with power steering and power brakes. From that time to the time of trial, according to Mr. Laney, each day he would drive by his business, pick up his mail and visit for five or ten minutes and leave. A few times he tried walking to the business from his home but he gave that up because it was too tiring. In the summer of 1956, he went with his wife and son to an automobile show in New Orleans. That was a two-day trip, and he did none of the driving. In 1958, he made two trips to visit his mother in Longview, and he did part of the driving. He would occasionally drive the family maid to and from work. He testified that he regularly drove his ten-year-old son to school.

Mr. Laney's wife passed away in 1963. He and his young son then began driving to some restaurant each evening to eat. He did his own shopping. After his wife died, he would pick up the maid every Wednesday and later drive her home. In October, 1963, he went with one of his sons to Arkansas to see the Arkansas-Texas football game. Later that same month he drove to Dallas to see the

Texas-SMU game, and in November of 1963 he drove to Austin to see the Texas-TCU game. He said he went to Dallas a number of times to see his wife while she was in the hospital.

He testified that in 1965 he was still driving his son to school each day. He attended Sunday morning church services rather regularly. In January of 1965, Mr. Laney commenced calling on a lady, and he visited her in her home three or four evenings a week. They were married in June of that year. In September of 1965, Mr. and Mrs. Laney drove from Denton to the State of Washington on an extended pleasure trip. They would drive from two to three hundred miles each day, and they shared the driving duties. They returned through San Francisco where they took a bus tour of the city. They spent one night in Las Vegas where they saw a show in the evening. They then visited the Grand Canyon. In 1966, he and his wife drove to Tennessee. In 1967, he and his wife drove to Biloxi, Mississippi, to a family reunion.

By way of generalization, he said, "I have been confined more or less indoors . . . the greater part of the time." He said at one point in his testimony that he would average being in the house twenty hours and out of the house four hours over a twenty-four hour time span. He said that his physician encouraged him to walk and to take trips or at least consented to the trips.

Mr. Laney's absences from the house were for business and personal reasons. They were regular and extensive rather than occasional and therapeutic in nature. To hold that he was nevertheless necessarily confined continuously within doors as pleaded by plaintiff requires us to disregard section 2 of the policy and its definition of a non-confining sickness. We hold that the proof conclusively shows that Mr. Laney's sickness during the time for which he sues, was a non-confining sickness rather than a confining sickness.

The judgments of the courts below are reversed and judgment is rendered that plaintiff take nothing.

NOTES & QUESTIONS

---

1) In *Laney*, the insurer argued that "a confining sickness was a condition precedent to Mr. Laney's right to recover for total disability." What was "covered" under the policy: "total disability," "a sickness" or a "confining sickness?" Did the Supreme Court of Texas clearly state what was covered?

2) In *Laney*, the policy is a disability insurance contract. Therefore, one should ask: Did the policy state unambiguously that a "confining sickness" was a condition precedent before the insurer would pay for the insured's "total disability?"

---

2. "No Coverage Under an Aviation Liability Insurance Contract"

Glover v. National Insurance Underwriters
545 S.W.2d 755
(Tex. 1977)

The question in this case is whether the pilot of an airplane which crashed and killed all aboard was "properly rated for the flight" within the meaning of an aviation liability insurance policy. The trial court held that he was and entered judgment for the petitioners. The court of civil appeals, with one justice dissenting, reversed the judgment of the trial court and rendered judgment for the insurer. We reverse the judgment of the court of civil appeals and affirm that of the trial court.

The crash in question occurred on the Mexican border near Quemado, Texas, north of Eagle Pass, on December 9, 1972. The pilot of the airplane was William O. Rogers, and he was accompanied by two passengers on the flight, Burlon E. Glover and Ray Eugene Rives. All were killed.

The petitioners, herein referred to as the plaintiffs, are the wives and children of the deceased passengers. They brought an action against the estate of the pilot, Rogers, and against the Bill Rogers Trucking Company for the wrongful deaths of Glover and Rives. National Insurance Underwriters, herein called National, had prior to the crash issued a liability insurance policy to the owner of the airplane, the Bill Rogers Trucking Company. National refused to defend the wrongful death suit and denied liability under the policy it had issued to the trucking company. The parties to that suit then entered into an agreement that National would institute this suit, a declaratory judgment action, to determine its liability to the estate of Rogers under the insurance policy. The agreement provided that if National were found to be liable, then it would pay to the plaintiffs the policy limits in full settlement of their cause of action against the estate. On the other hand, if National were found not to be liable under the policy, then the plaintiffs agreed that they would dismiss their wrongful death action and make no further effort to recover for the deaths of the passengers.

Pursuant to the agreement, National brought this declaratory judgment action against the people we here call "the plaintiffs." The parties filed a document of stipulated facts in the trial court and submitted the cause to that court for determination. The trial court found as a matter of law that the insurance policy afforded coverage, and it ordered National to pay the plaintiffs the policy limits. The court of civil appeals reversed and rendered judgment for

The insurance policy was attached as an exhibit to the stipulated facts. Under Part I of this policy, National agreed to pay all sums which the insured would become legally obligated to pay as damages because of bodily injury or death, sustained by any person, including occupants. Under "Exclusions Applicable to Part I," however, the policy contained a provisions commonly known as a "Pilot Warranty Clause." This clause provided that coverage under Part I would Not apply "to any aircraft, while in flight, . . . whenever the pilot operating the aircraft is not qualified in accordance with the requirements specified in Item 6 . . .."

Item 6 of the declarations provided in part:

> PILOTS: This policy applies when the aircraft is in flight . . . (only when being operated by Rogers) . . . while holding an F.A.A. pilot certificate and ratings at least equal to those described below, with a currently effective Medical Certificate, and while properly rated for the flight and the aircraft . . . .

National's contention is that the pilot of the airplane, Rogers, was not "properly rated for the flight." It is therefore argued that the pilot clause operated to suspend National's liability under the policy. The plaintiffs, on the other hand, argue that Rogers was "properly rated for the flight" and that National is therefore liable under its contract of insurance.

The case was tried upon an "Agreed Statement of Facts" and five attached exhibits. The agreed statement recites that the passengers, Glover and Rives, were business acquaintances of Rogers, and the three men were en route from Odessa to Eagle Pass on a fishing trip when the crash occurred. The site of the crash was between Del Rio and Eagle Pass, about 30 miles southeast of Del Rio and 204 miles southeast of Odessa. The airplane was a single engine Piper aircraft. Rogers had a private pilot's license to operate a single engine land aircraft, but he did not have an instrument flight rating.

* * *

The weather reports and weather forecasts recited in the agreed statement were apparently taken from a National Transportation Safety Board (N.T.S.B.) report that was attached as an exhibit to the agreed statement. This report summarized an N.T.S.B. investigation that was conducted after the crash, and the accuracy of the material in that report was stipulated to by the parties. Included in the report was a statement by the Air Traffic Control (A.T.S.) Specialist who briefed Rogers on the weather conditions on the morning of the flight. The Specialist's statement contained the following:

> At 1355 GMT (Greenwich Mean Time), the pilot of N7714P (Rogers) called by telephone and requested an outlook for a proposed VFR flight from Ector County Airport, Odessa, Texas to Eagle Pass, Texas. His proposed departure time was "in the next three or four hours."
>
> I gave the pilot of N7714P all the information available to me at the time which was pertinent to his proposed flight. Source material used for the briefing included surface reports from SA29 091300, MAF FT amendment 09111, and GSW FA 091240 with emphasis on pertinent AIRMET information it contained. The pilot then indicated that he intended to delay departure.

* * *

It was stipulated for the purposes of this action that the pilot, Rogers, was negligent in each of the particulars set out in the plaintiffs' petition in the wrongful death suit. They there alleged that Rogers was negligent:

(a) In operating the airplane under conditions which required an instrument pilot rating;

(b) In failing to communicate with the various ground communication stations in the Del Rio, Eagle Pass area to ascertain the weather conditions existing in that area;

(c) In operating the airplane at an altitude which was dangerously low to the surface;

(d) In failing to return to Odessa or other alternate airports where the VFR weather existed: (and)

(e) In flying into an area wherein the weather was such that IFR Flight Rules existed with full knowledge of the existing inclement weather conditions."

We agree with the parties that the only question to be here decided is whether Rogers was "properly rated for the flight" within the meaning of the pilot warranty clause. In order to construe properly that clause, a review of the regulations which govern aviation is necessary.

The Federal Aviation Act of 1958, 49 U.S.C. Sections 1301 *et seq.*, gives the Administrator of the Federal Aviation Administration the authority to prescribe reasonable rules and regulations to govern, among other things, airmen and the operation of aircraft in the United States. The regulations promulgated by the Administrator are codified in 14 C.F.R. Sections 1-399 and shall hereafter be referred to as the FARs (Federal Aviation Regulations).

* * *

The question here is: Was the pilot "properly rated for the flight" that ended in his death and the deaths of his passengers? The answer to this question requires an analysis of the pilot warranty clause, and its applicability to the stipulated facts of this case. In view of the Federal Aviation Regulations, which define "ratings" and prescribe the rules for aircraft operation, we believe that our inquiry should be directed to the meaning of the term 'the flight' in the pilot clause. Once it is determined what "the flight" was that Rogers and his passengers undertook on December 9, 1972, then whether he was "properly rated" for it may be ascertained by reference to the relevant FARs.

In making our inquiry, we are mindful of the rules of construction set forth in *Continental Casualty Co. v. Warren*, 254 S.W.2d 762 (Tex. 1953). That case stated the rule to be that exceptions and rules of limitation will be strictly construed against the insurer. Further, we must adopt the construction of an exclusionary clause urged by the insured as long as that construction is not itself unreasonable, even if the construction urged by the insurer appears to be more reasonable or a more accurate reflection of the parties' intent. *See also Insurance Co. of North America v. Cash*, 475 S.W.2d 912 (Tex.1972).

On the other hand, we recognize that these rules of construction will be applied only when the language of the policy is such that it may reasonably be given one of several constructions. In other words, the plain language of an insurance policy, like that of any other contract, will be given effect when the parties' intent may be discerned from that language. But when the language of an insurance contract is ambiguous — that is, subject to two or more reasonable interpretations, then that construction which affords coverage will be the one adopted.

We have concluded that the pilot clause here . . . is ambiguous. One possible construction of the clause finds support in the dissenting opinion in the court of civil appeals below . . . . Under this construction, "the flight" of an aircraft could be viewed as being either a visual flight or an instrument flight, depending on the conduct of the pilot in operating the airplane. If the pilot used only his instruments to maintain the proper attitude, altitude, velocity, navigational course, and other positions of the craft, then "the flight" would be an instrument flight. If, however, the pilot used his instruments only partially, and used his vision to maintain, for example, the proper attitude of the aircraft, then "the flight" would be a visual one.

* * *

The remaining question is whether the flight of the Rogers aircraft in this case was a VFR flight, for which the pilot was properly rated, or an IFR flight, for which he was not. The answer to this question depends on at what point in time the status of the flight should be determined. We have concluded, . . . that the flight should be characterized as of its inception. The weather conditions existing at the beginning of the flight should thus be looked to in determining whether the flight is a VFR or an IFR flight. National argues that the knowledge of the pilot of the weather conditions along his flight path and at his destination should also be considered in characterizing the flight. It argues that if the pilot takes off in VFR weather with knowledge that IFR conditions exist at his destination, then the flight is an IFR flight for which the non-instrument rated pilot is not properly rated.

* * *

The plaintiffs, on the other hand, vigorously contend that it was not stipulated that Rogers knowingly flew into IFR conditions and that the court of civil appeals was erroneous in so concluding. The plaintiffs also argue that the weather forecasts which Rogers received on the morning of the flight show that he fully expected to encounter VFR conditions at Eagle Pass that day.

We are not inclined to consider as controlling the pilot's knowledge of weather conditions along his flight path or at his destination in characterizing a flight as an IFR or VFR flight. Our reluctance arises from our belief that very few pilots actually know when they take off what weather conditions they will encounter over two hours later. When a pilot begins a flight, he has an expectation of what weather conditions will exist later on during the flight; and this expectation is necessarily based upon his knowledge of the weather conditions existing when he takes off and the forecasts as to how those conditions will change by the time he gets to his destination.

* * *

We therefore conclude that the flight on which Rogers and his passengers embarked was a VFR flight, and Rogers was properly rated to fly it. The pilot warranty clause did not operate to exclude coverage and National is liable under the insurance policy.

Our holding may seem harsh to the insurer because we have held this insurance policy applicable even though it is undisputed that the non-instrument rated pilot was flying in IFR conditions when the crash occurred. We note that our construction of this pilot clause was necessary, however, only because National chose to phrase the insurance policy in the ambiguous manner heretofore discussed. Language was available to, and known to, National which would have clearly and plainly excluded from coverage a non-instrument rated pilot who operated his aircraft in IFR weather conditions..

The judgment of the court of civil appeals is reversed and that of the trial court is affirmed.

NOTES & QUESTIONS

1) In *Glover*, the Texas Supreme Court reports that the only question is whether the pilot — who died in a crashed airplane—was "properly rated for the flight" within the meaning of an aviation liability insurance policy. The court discussed several doctrines of contract construction and interpretation—ambiguity doctrine, four-corners doctrine and the doctrine of plain meaning. Did the court employ one or several of these doctrines to reach its conclusion?

2) In *Glover*, "[t]he trial court found as a matter of law that the insurance policy afforded *coverage*"; and the Supreme Court of Texas stated: "Inquiries into the reasonableness of a person's actions might best be ignored in determining the *coverage* of an insurance policy." Yet, the Texas Supreme Court highlighted the following language which appeared in the aviation liability insurance contract:

> "*EXCLUSIONS* APPLICABLE TO PART I" . . . . The policy contained a provision commonly known as a "Pilot *Warranty* Clause." This clause provided that *coverage* under Part I would not apply "to any aircraft, while in flight . . . whenever the pilot operating the aircraft is not qualified in accordance with the requirements . . . ." (emphasis added).

"Exclusions," "warranty" and "coverage" — Each appears in that clause. And the Texas Supreme Court discussed each. So here is the question: Is *Glover* a "coverage case," an "exclusion case" or a "breach-of-warranty case"?

3) Did the pilot breach a warranty under the aviation liability insurance contract? Did the insurance contract exclude the pilot's "stipulated" negligence?

4) How does a court determine whether a clause in a property or liability insurance contract is a coverage, exclusion, or warranty clause?

---

3. "No Coverage Under a Commercial General Liability Insurance Contract"

Zurich American Insurance Company v. Nokia, Inc.
268 S.W.3d 487
(Tex. 2008)

A wireless telephone manufacturer, sued in a number of putative class actions alleging that radiation emitted by the phones caused biological injury, turned to its insurers, who had agreed to defend claims seeking damages because of bodily injury. After initially providing a defense, the insurers later sought a declaration that they had no duty to do so. Because we conclude that most of the underlying suits seek damages because of bodily injury, we modify the court of appeals' judgment and, as modified, affirm.

I. Factual and Procedural Background

Nokia, Incorporated, a Texas corporation, is the world's largest manufacturer of wireless telephone handsets. Nokia and other wireless telephone manufacturers were sued in a number of putative class action cases filed in various courts across the country. The consumer-plaintiffs in those cases alleged that radio frequency radiation (RFR) from wireless phones causes "biological injury."

Nokia tendered the defense of one of these cases to Zurich American Insurance Company, from which it had purchased several commercial general liability (CGL) insurance policies covering the years 1985-89 and 1995-2000. Zurich agreed to defend Nokia but reserved its right to later contest its obligation to defend or indemnify. Nokia's other insurers, National Union Fire Insurance Company and Federal Insurance Company, followed suit.

Seeking to resolve the coverage issue, Zurich sued Nokia, National Union, and Federal in Dallas County and sought a declaration that Zurich had no duty to defend or indemnify Nokia and that Zurich was not responsible for defense or indemnity payments made by National Union or Federal. Zurich also sought contribution and subrogation against all defendants. National Union and Federal cross-claimed against Nokia asserting, among other things, that they had no duty to defend or indemnify Nokia.

* * *

The trial court granted Zurich's amended motion for summary judgment and signed a judgment declaring, in pertinent part, that Zurich, National Union, and Federal had no duty to defend or indemnify Nokia in the MDL cases or in Dahlgren. The court ordered that Nokia take nothing on its counterclaims for declaratory relief regarding the duty to defend, breach of contract, failure to make prompt payment, breach of the duty of good faith and fair dealing, and for violation of article 21.21 of the Texas Insurance Code. The trial court severed the adjudicated claims, and Nokia appealed.

The court of appeals reversed as to the MDL cases, holding that, because (1) the complaints alleged claims for "bodily injury" and sought "damages because of bodily injury"; and (2) the "business risk" exclusions did not apply, the insurers had a duty to defend Nokia. As to Dahlgren, in which the plaintiffs had explicitly disclaimed personal injuries and sought only economic and related equitable relief, the court of appeals affirmed the trial court's judgment and held that the insurers had no duty to defend Nokia. Finally, the court of appeals held that, in light of its determination that the insurers had a duty to defend the MDL cases, the trial court's ruling that there was no duty to indemnify Nokia in those cases was premature. Thus, the court of appeals reversed and remanded that portion of the trial court's judgment.

The insurers petitioned this Court for review, arguing that they had no duty to defend the MDL cases, as the complaints did not state claims for bodily injury or seek damages because of bodily injury. We granted the petitions for review.

II. Duty to Defend

In exchange for premiums paid, CGL insurers typically promise to defend and indemnify their insureds for covered risks. "[T]he duty to defend is distinct from, and broader than, the duty to indemnify."

An insurer must defend its insured if a plaintiff's factual allegations potentially support a covered claim, while the facts actually established in the underlying suit determine whether the insurer must indemnify its insured. *GuideOne Elite Ins. Co. v. Fielder Rd. Baptist Church,* 197 S.W.3d 305, 310 (Tex.2006). Thus, an insurer may have a duty to defend but, eventually, no obligation to indemnify. *Farmers Tex. County Mut. Ins. Co. v. Griffin*, 955 S.W.2d 81, 82 (Tex.1997).

In determining a duty to defend, we follow the eight-corners rule, also known as the complaint-allegation rule: "an insurer's duty to defend is determined by the third-party plaintiff's pleadings, considered in light of the policy provisions, without regard to the truth or falsity of those allegations." Thus, "[e]ven if the allegations are groundless, false, or fraudulent the insurer is obligated to defend." We resolve all doubts regarding the duty to defend in favor of the duty, *King v. Dallas Fire Ins. Co.*, 85 S.W.3d 185, 187 (Tex.2002), and we construe the pleadings liberally,

Nat'l Union Fire Ins. Co. v. Merchs. Fast Motor Lines, Inc., 939 S.W.2d 139, 141 (Tex.1997). "Where the complaint does not state facts sufficient to clearly bring the case within or without the coverage, the general rule is that the insurer is obligated to defend if there is, potentially, a case under the complaint within the coverage of the policy." *Heyden Newport Chem. Corp. v. S. Gen. Ins. Co.*, 387 S.W.2d 22, 26 (Tex.1965).

The duty to defend is not affected by facts ascertained before suit, developed in the course of litigation, or by the ultimate outcome of the suit. *Trinity Universal Ins. Co. v. Cowan*, 945 S.W.2d 819, 829 (Tex.1997). If a complaint potentially includes a covered claim, the insurer must defend the entire suit.

III. The Policies and the Pleadings

A

Bodily Injury

With this in mind, we turn to the policy language at issue here. The policies covered "all sums which [Nokia] shall become legally obligated to pay as damages because of . . . bodily injury" caused by an occurrence during the policy period. Some of the Zurich policies define bodily injury, some do not. Of those that do, bodily injury is defined as "bodily injury, sickness or disease sustained by a person, including death resulting from any of these at any time." But this circular definition is not helpful in answering the question before us: have the MML cases alleged bodily injury?

None of the complaints use the term "bodily injury"; all are phrased in terms of "biological injury" or "biological effects." Thus, we must determine whether biological injuries or effects qualify as bodily injury. We have held that purely emotional injuries are not "bodily injuries," *Trinity Universal Ins. Co. v. Cowan*, 945 S.W.2d 819, 823 (Tex.1997), and the insurers urge that this rule precludes relief here. But we also concluded that "'bodily injury'. . . unambiguously requires an injury to the physical structure of the human body," and the MDL cases certainly allege that.

Each of the original and amended MDL complaints contains allegations that essentially mirror those set forth in the Gilliam amended complaint:

> This class action seeks damages and declaratory relief on behalf of plaintiff and a class of persons who purchased or leased wireless handheld telephones (WHHPs) . . . . Through a common and uniform course of conduct, the defendants have manufactured, supplied, promoted, sold, leased and provided wireless service for WHHPs when they knew or should have known that their products generate and emit radio frequency radiation (RFR) that causes an adverse cellular reaction and/or cellular dysfunction ("biological injury") through its adverse health effects on: calcium and ion distribution across the cell membrane; melatonin production; neurological function; DNA single and double strand breaks and chromosome damage; enzyme activities; cell stress and gene transcription; and the permeability

> of the blood brain barrier (hereinafter collectively described as the "health risk" and/or the "biological effects").
>
> Through a common and uniform course of conduct, the defendants, acting individually and collectively, failed to adequately disclose to the consuming public the fact that WHHPs emit RFR that causes biological injury and a risk to the users' health. The purpose of this action is to hold accountable and to obtain maximum legal and equitable relief from those corporations and entities that are responsible for producing and placing into the stream of commerce WHHPs which create a health risk to users by causing biological injury.

The lengthy complaints assert that the named plaintiffs were exposed to RFR from their phones and thus were subjected to "RFR's biological effects and the risk to human health arising therefrom" and then discuss numerous studies linking RFR to adverse health consequences, including changes in the brain, headaches, heating behind the ear, sleep problems, and production of high levels of "heat shock proteins." In addition, the Gimpelson and Pinney original complaints assert that the plaintiffs "sustained biological injuries," and all of the amended complaints allege that the plaintiffs "sustained repeated biological injuries and/or harm" and "did incur biological injury and/or harm as a result of using Defendants WHHPs."

The court of appeals, relying on dictionary definitions and similar cases from other jurisdictions, concluded that injury at the cellular level was sufficient to allege a bodily injury under the policies at issue here.

* * *

[W]e conclude that the biological injuries alleged by the plaintiffs potentially state a claim for bodily injuries under the policies, much like the subclinical injuries alleged by plaintiffs who have been exposed to asbestos. We, of course, express no opinion on the merits of the underlying claims.

* * *

V. Exclusions

Those exclusions do not, however, preclude a duty to defend in the remaining cases. The relevant exclusions apply to "property damage to your product," "property damage ... arising out of a defect, deficiency, inadequacy or dangerous condition in 'your product,'" and damages related to a product recall. We agree with the court of appeals, which held that these exclusions did not excuse the duty to defend: "[t]he underlying actions did not contain allegations of property damage to the cell phones or to 'impaired property' (defined as 'tangible property, other than your product or your work') or damages for the recall of the cell phones."

Our holding is in accord with other cases that have discussed the issue.

* * *

VI. Conclusion

As the Fourth Circuit concluded, the "plaintiffs are seeking remedies designed to eliminate already existing bodily injuries. While their claims may lack merit, we are unable to state with certainty that they do not seek 'damages because of bodily injury.' " Neither can we.

NOTES & QUESTIONS

1) In *Nokia*, the Supreme Court of Texas cited and reaffirmed settled law: "An insurer must defend its insured if a [third-party] plaintiff's factual allegations potentially support a covered claim." Thus, one should ask: What is the central issue or question in *Nokia*—whether the third-party claims were "covered" under the liability insurance contract or whether the insurer had a duty to defend the insured?

2) To repeat, the Texas Supreme Court in *Glover* discussed several doctrines of contract construction and interpretation—ambiguity doctrine, four-corners doctrine and the doctrine of plain meaning. Which doctrine did the Texas Supreme Court employ in *Nokia*, to reach its conclusion? Is there any discussion of these doctrines in *Nokia*? If not, why not?

3) In *Nokia*, the court reported: "The policies covered 'all sums which [Nokia] shall become legally obligated to pay as damages because of … bodily injury' caused by an occurrence during the policy period." In its analysis, the Texas Supreme Court discussed "damages" and "bodily injury." But the court did not discuss "an occurrence." What is a "covered occurrence" or "an occurrence?"

E. *"Insured Has No Insurable Interest"*

Lucena v. Craufurd
3 Bosanquet & Puller (N. R.) 75
127 Eng. Rep 630 (1806)
In the House of Lords

This was a writ of error, brought to revise the judgments of the Courts of King's Bench and Exchequer-chamber, given for the Defendants in error upon a bill of exceptions

* * *

The Plaintiff in error having assigned the same errors as in the Exchequer Chamber, prayed that the judgment of that Court might be reversed, [b]ecause a policy of insurance being both in form and in substance a contract of indemnity, the party who claims the benefit of indemnification under it must show that a loss has been sustained by him upon the subject insured, and for that purpose must necessarily prove that he had at the time some right of property in that subject susceptible of loss or damnification.

* * *

Graham, B. answered in the affirmative as to all the ships, and argued in substance as follows. The subject of the present insurance being the ships and goods themselves, and not any profit or commission expected to arise from the sale, management, or disposition of them, the arguments which are founded upon the uncertainty of such interests may be laid out of the question. There can be no doubt that the ships and goods were insurable. But the question is: Whether the commissioners had a sufficient interest in those ships to authorize them to effect the insurance?

The peculiar circumstances which attended the property insured are stated in the declaration; the act of parliament and commission are referred to; the seizure of the ships at sea for the purpose and to the intent of their being sent to this country and put into the possession of the commissioners is stated, and that the Plaintiffs effected the policy on those ships by name, not naming themselves individually as making the insurance, but as commissioners for the sale of Dutch property. It is with reference to these premises they aver, that they as such commissioners were interested, and that the insurance was made for their use and benefit as commissioners. The nature of their connexion with the property insured appears from the previous part of the declaration. They claimed no beneficial interest in it: they were merely consignees, agents, or trustees for others; and to make the whole declaration consistent, the averment must be taken to import, what the words will fairly admit, that the insurance was made for the benefit of those, for whose benefit the Plaintiffs were authorized by the act of parliament and commission to manage the property as consignees; that is, in the present instance for the king.

* * *

The operation of the act and commission was to constitute the commissioners parliamentary trustees or consignees of the property; and vested in them an insurable interest for the benefit of those who might ultimately be entitled. To such persons, whoever they might be, the Plaintiffs having insured in their character of commissioners, would be accountable for the produce of the insurance, as much as for the sale of the property itself if it had arrived. It was their duty to provide for the security of the property till the event should happen which would enable them to take possession; and in insuring they only followed the provisions of the act of parliament, and the commission founded upon it. The Dutch owners knowing nothing of the situation of the property could make no insurance.

But if the commissioners were trustees, they were authorized to act respecting the property as if it was their own, for the manifest benefit of the cestuy que trust. If the commissioners had been ordered by the crown to insure, there can be no doubt that it would have been their duty to have obeyed; and whether they had any directions is a matter of private trust, not now to be inquired into. The insurance being for the benefit of those ultimately entitled, the approbation of the crown may be presumed. It is not necessary to consider whether if a mere strangers were to insure a ship, and such insurance were afterwards to be ratified by the owner, it would be valid. But there does not appear to be any rule of law to prevent it. It is not against the 19 Geo. 2.

The insurance would be made by such person bona fide as agent for the owner, and if ratified why should it not, like any other contract, be binding on the parties? If this be so with respect to a private individual having no connexion with the property, . . . [then] the insurance by these commissioners must be good. Though a consignee be usually appointed by bill of lading, it is not necessary to invest a person with that character.

* * *

Where there is an *expectancy* coupled with a present existing title, there is an insurable interest.

It is argued that the title of the commissioners was *contingent*, because the ships which were the subject of their authority might never arrive. But although it was matter of *contingency* whether any ships would arrive upon which this *right* could operate, the *right* itself was not *contingent*.

Antecedent to the arrival of any ships, the commissioners were *invested with a right* to take into their *possession* all ships of the description mentioned in the act of parliament which should arrive: and it might as well be insisted that the power of justices of the peace, or of the judges of assize, who act under a commission from the crown, was *contingent*, because no felony might be committed which could be the subject of their jurisdiction.

The interest of the commissioners was very different from that of a prize agent, where the *title* to its *profits* arises from meritorious services to be performed at the end of the voyage; and from that of the next of kin of a lunatic, who at the end of the voyage would have no interest whatever, and who eventually may never have any interest, because the lunatic may survive him.

* * *

Chambre, J. To constitute an interest, such as that which in the declaration is averred to *be vested* in the Plaintiffs as commissioners under the act, I presume it must be necessary to show that the ships and goods at the time of the sailing, or at least before or at the times of the losses, had become *the objects of the Plaintiff's commission.* If they were not the objects of their commission, I have no conception in what way they could have an interest in them as commissioners. The duties of their office were confined to Dutch property that was actually in the kingdom, and provisionally detained there under the king's authority. No matter who brings it in.

They have nothing to do as commissioners with consignments from abroad, nor was there any consignment in fact made to them. They have been called statutable consignees. If that phrase means anything, it must mean that the statute had consigned these particular ships to the commissioners; but look at the statute, and we find nothing more than that it authorizes a commission under which whatever property of a certain description arrives, it will, if they continue commissioners, fall within their care and management officially to prevent its perishing.

[The majority in the House of Lords held for the commissioners].

NOTES & QUESTIONS

1) The complete version of the decision in *Lucena* is extremely long. It presents multiple questions of law and fact that involve Admiralty Law as well as Insurance Law. In addition, the decision contains a lot of old English terms making it difficult to follow in part. Still, the general facts and the insurable-interest question are not difficult to understand. First, the controversy in *Lucena* erupted after a foreign ship was seized. An act of Parliament gave the royal commissioners the power to seize certain ships and cargo if those vessels entered the United Kingdom's territories during a war. "On the 16th of March 1795, an act passed for the further protection of the property voluntarily brought in, and on the 22nd of May, the 35 Geo. 3, c. 80 (being the act referred to in the question), passed. The subject of this latter act, and the commission to the Plaintiffs, was the Dutch property which was or should be seized and detained in pursuance of the instructions of the 9th of February. The instructions are to bring into British ports all Dutch vessels." 2 Bosanquet & Puller (N.R.), at 284

Customarily the commissioners would insure the ships and cargo under marine insurance agreements. And underwriters at Lloyd's of London would usually insure a fraction of a ship, its voyage, or the cargo. In *Lucena,* several ships and cargo were lost during the voyage between the port of seizure and the destination in a British port. Thus, the legal question in *Lucena* was whether the commissioners had an insurable interest in the ships, cargo, and loss profits. Ultimately, the commissioners prevailed. They were the "owners" of the seized goods, even though the losses occurred before the commissioners took "possession" of the seized goods and ships. Expected "loss profits" are intangible property, and the ships and cargo are tangible property. After much deliberation, the court found that the commissioners had an insurable interest in both the tangible and intangible property.

2) According to 3 VANCE ON INSURANCE 161, an insured has an "insurable interest" when the insured has:

a) legal title to the property insured—whether vested or contingent, defeasible or indefeasible;

b) equitable title, regardless of its character or the manner in which it was acquired;

c) a qualified property or possessory right in the subject of the insurance, such as a bailee;

d) a mere possession or a right of possession; and,

e) neither possession of the property, nor any other legal interest in it, but stands in such relation with respect to it that he may suffer from its destruction, loss of a legal right dependent upon its continued existence.

And the rule in *Lucena* is worth stressing: "Where there is an *expectancy* coupled with a present existing title, there is an insurable interest."

3) Statutory definition of an "Insurable Interest"— Tex. Ins. Code § 2210.201 reads: "In this subchapter, 'insurable interest' includes any lawful and substantial economic interest in the safety or preservation of property from loss, destruction, or pecuniary damage."

4) Again, it is worth asking: May consumers insure all properties and interest in property against "loss, destruction, or pecuniary damage?"

Leggio v. Millers National Insurance Company
398 S.W.2d 607
(Tex. Civ. App. 1966)

Appellant J. M. Leggio brought this suit against appellees, Millers National Insurance Co., Commercial Union Insurance Co. of New York, Agricultural Insurance Company and Security Insurance Company of New Haven, upon four separate fire insurance policies issued by each of the appellees in the sum and amount of $5,000.00, insuring a building owned by appellant and situated in the City of Dallas. Appellant's pleadings allege that on October 31st, 1963, the said building was destroyed by fire resulting in a total loss. Appellees denied liability on the policies, alleging that the appellant had no insurable interest in the building at the time of the fire and further alleged that even though he did have insurable interest, he suffered no pecuniary loss because his tenant later constructed a building of equal value on the premises.

Typ

Trial was before a jury and in response to the five Special Issues submitted by the court, the jury found that: (1) the fire caused a total loss of the building in question; (2) the reasonably cash market value of the building in question immediately before the fire was $17,500.00; (3) appellant J. M. Leggio had an insurable interest in the building; (4) the building in question was not vacant for a period of more than 30 days immediately preceding the fire; (5) the removal by J. M. Leggio of the front door, wood paneling, flooring, light fixtures and other items, if any, from the building before the fire did not materially increase the hazard of fire.

Upon motion of the appellees, the trial court granted a judgment notwithstanding the verdict denying appellant, J. M. Leggio, any recovery upon the policies of fire insurance. Appellant has perfected this appeal, contending that the jury's verdict was supported by the evidence and the trial court therefore had no authority to grant judgment non obstante.

The record reveals that on July 15, 1963, Leggio leased the building to Anthony's, Inc. to be used as a restaurant. The company made considerable improvements in the building such as installing lighting fixtures, paneling the walls, installing new floor decking, replacing the front door and installing other equipment ordinarily found in a rather exclusive cafe. Shortly before the fire, Anthony's, Inc. went out of business and assigned the lease to Hughes-Peters who subsequently assigned it to Miracle Ford Company.

Section 14 of the lease provided that in the event the building should be totally destroyed by fire or damaged to such an extent that repairs could not be completed within 120 days the lease would terminate, but if not so damaged and repairs could be completed within 120 days, the landlord was obligated to rebuild or repair the same in substantially the same condition as existed prior to the fire.

Section 27(B) granted the lessee the following option:

> Tenant shall have the right to tear down and remove the existing structures provided he replaces the same with equal or better structures, submits to landlord for approval written and specifications for the new structures, 30 days prior to the removal of existing structures, and when new structures are completed to pay all ad valorem taxes to all taxing authorities thereafter. Any new structures placed upon the demised premises shall become the property of landlord.

Section 27(D) provides:

> Notwithstanding other provisions of this lease regarding damage and repairs to the property, landlord shall not be required to expend more than $20,000.00 in repairing or rebuilding the improvements that might be damaged by fire, tornado or other casualty but tenant may make such additional contribution to repairs as he wishes and may carry insurance to cover such additional repairs.

Appellees take the position that the evidence shows as a matter of law that appellant Leggio had no insurable interest at the time of the fire because Miracle Motor Company had theretofore exercised their option to demolish the building and replace the same with a new building and that appellant had accepted and approved such plan.

The argument advanced by the appellees is that after the option was exercised and approved by Leggio, the building was of no further use to him and therefore he could not expect any pecuniary benefit or advantage by its preservation and continued existence. In effect, they contend that he had disposed of the building and therefore could have no insurable interest, hence the court correctly denied any recovery for a total loss of the building. In any event, appellees contend that under the undisputed evidence, Leggio suffered no pecuniary loss because Miracle Ford Company rebuilt other structures on the property in excess of the amount of insurance and thus for this additional reason, they contend the trial court correctly denied appellant any recovery.

Upon the question of insurable interests, the Supreme Court of this state in *Smith v. Eagle Star Insurance Co.*, 370 S.W.2d 448 (Tex. 1963), adopted the following quotation contained in 29 Am. Jur. 781, Insurance, Sec. 438: "The principle may be stated generally that anyone has an insurable interest in property who derives a benefit from its existence or would suffer loss from its destruction."

Upon the question of whether or not an insured has sustained a pecuniary loss, the Supreme Court of this state in *Paramount Fire Insurance Company v. Aetna Casualty & Surety Company*, 353 S.W.2d 841 (Tex. 1962), has adopted the rule that there is no pecuniary loss when the loss has been made good out of a related transaction, holding as follows:

> The court looks to the substance of the whole transaction rather than to seek a metaphysical hypothesis upon which to justify a loss that is no loss. This is not a case where a stranger to the transaction, out of charity, or for other reasons, might make good the loss . . . . The loss has been made good out of a related transaction . . . .

It may be conceded that the foregoing cases form the basis of the defenses asserted by appellees.

Before applying these legal principles, however, we must first determine the primary question of whether or not at the time of the fire, the lessee had exercised its option to demolish and rebuild in accordance with the terms of the lease as set forth in Paragraph 27(B) and whether the lessor had accepted and approved the exercise of the option.

If the option was effectively exercised and accepted before the fire, appellant would no longer have any pecuniary interest in the continued existence of the building and would thus have no insurable interest. If, on the other hand, the option was not exercised and accepted before the fire, appellant would have continued to have an insurable interest because of his pecuniary interest in the building and the lease contract and there would be no related transaction. The inquiry therefore involves questions of fact.

In 13 Tex. Jur.2d, page 161-2, Sec. 37, it is said:

> An option is merely an offer that binds the optionee or holder of the option to do nothing; he may or may not accept the offer, as he chooses, within the time specified. Until it is accepted, an option is not, in legal effect, a completed contract. However, when accepted within the time limited and in the manner specified, an option becomes a completed contract that is binding on both parties.

In Vratis v. Baxter, 315 S.W.2d 331, 337 (Tex. Civ. App. 1958), the court held:

> The acceptance of an option, to be effectual, must be unqualified, absolute, unconditional, unequivocal, unambiguous, positive, without reservation, and according to the terms or conditions of the option. Substantial compliance with the terms of the option is held not sufficient to constitute an acceptance; to be effectual, the acceptance must be identical with the offer, or, at least, there must be no substantial variation between them. An acceptance of an option must be such a compliance with the conditions as to bind both parties, and if it fails to do so it binds neither.

By granting a judgment notwithstanding the verdict of the jury, the trial court ruled, in effect, that as a matter of law appellant had no insurable interest at the time of the fire, or if he did have, he suffered no pecuniary loss because of a related transaction. We find ourselves unable to agree with the conclusion for the following reasons.

It is fundamental that a reviewing court, in passing upon a contention that there is no evidence to sustain a jury's finding, whether raised by a "no evidence" point or by a motion for judgment notwithstanding the verdict or by a motion for instructed verdict, must view the evidence in a light most favorable to the appellant, indulging every legitimate conclusion favorable to him, and disregard all evidence adverse to the appellant.

Viewed in a light most favorable to appellant, we think the testimony shows that while both parties to the lease contemplated that the option would be exercised and had actually made some preparation for the demolition of the building prior to the fire, yet they had not gone far enough to reach a definite agreement.

In our search of the record we have been unable to find any evidence that either Miracle Ford or any of the previous lessees ever complied with the provisions of Section 27(B) of the lease. This section specifically provides that the existing building was not to be torn down until lessee "submits to landlord for approval written plans and specifications for the new structures, 30 days prior to the removal of existing structures . . . . "

Richard L. Blosser, president of Miracle Ford, testified that at the time of the fire the building was still in use and although he gave the appellant and his family permission to remove various items from the building and was contemplating building a new building, demolition had not commenced. Nowhere in his testimony does he state that he delivered written plans and specifications of a new building to appellant which were approved by him.

Subsequent to the fire, he testified that Miracle Motor Company constructed on the premises a building at a cost of $12,500.00, together with appurtenances at a cost of five to six thousand dollars and also another metal building at a cost of ten to twelve thousand dollars. Nowhere, however, did he testify that these improvements were constructed in accordance with plans and specifications approved by the appellant prior to the fire. There is nothing in his testimony showing that Miracle Motor Company ever called upon appellant to rebuild or repair in accordance with the lease contract.

Appellant testified that at various times he had given each of the tenants his consent to proceed with the construction of another building; however, we find nothing in his testimony indicating that he was ever furnished any written plans and specifications of the proposed building or that he ever approved such. At one point in his testimony he did admit that "with the construction of the new building, they had submitted some plans and a sketch," however, he did not admit that he ever approved same, nor does his testimony show whether the "plans and sketch" were submitted before the fire or whether they were submitted after the fire just prior to the time Miracle Motor made their improvements. The "plans and sketch" were never produced in the trial court and are therefore not before us. Appellant also testified that the improvements made by Miracle Motor Company consisted of only a sales office containing 400 square feet which was not of like value to the building destroyed.

At most, we think the evidence will only raise an issue of fact upon the question of whether or not the option was exercised and accepted, and would not be sufficient to establish the question as a matter of law. The trial court, however, failed to submit any issues inquiring of any of the facts and circumstances in connection with the exercise or acceptance of the option.

Both the question of insurable interest and the question of whether appellant's loss was made good by a related transaction were legal defenses raised by appellees' pleadings. The basis of these defenses must turn upon the facts and circumstances surrounding the alleged exercise and acceptance of the option.

It is without dispute that at the time the policies were issued appellant had an insurable interest. If the facts and circumstances had changed in the meantime, the insurance companies had the burden of proving facts showing a lack of insurable interest..

In order to establish their defense, appellees had the burden of requesting the submission of issues inquiring of the status of the fact situation created by the appellant and his lessee at the time of the fire. This the appellees failed to do and therefore waived the submission of these issues forming the basis of the alleged defense. The defenses, not having been conclusively established, must be deemed to have been waived. Rule 279, Texas Rules of Civil Procedure.

We do not overlook the fact that in response to Special Issue No. 3 the jury found that appellant had an insurable interest; however, since the question propounded to the jury was a legal question, we think the court was authorized to consider the finding as immaterial.

There being ample evidence to support the jury's finding that the building was a "total loss" and appellees having failed to sustain their burden of obtaining jury findings establishing their defenses, the cause must be reversed and rendered in favor of appellant J. M. Leggio.

Reversed and rendered.

NOTES & QUESTIONS

1) Does a bona fide purchaser have an insurable interest in stolen goods? Consider the court's ruling in *State Farm Mutual Automobile Insurance Company v. Kelly*, 945 S.W.2d 905, 909-910 (Tex. App. Ct. -Austin 1997):

> In this case, the plaintiff was a bona fide purchaser of a stolen car who had received a title and listed the car under his policy. . . . [T]he insurer had a duty to clearly express coverage limitations in the policy, the court found the language of the policy implied that coverage would be granted in every case of damage to, or loss of, the vehicle except by collision, which was the only explicit exclusion. [There is a] longstanding Texas precedent that ownership is not required for an insurable interest in this state. Additionally, Texas courts have held that property loss occurs when the injury or damage is manifested. Mr. Kelly's loss only became evident at the time his car was confiscated, not when he received bad title.

2) Although bona fide purchasers generally have an insurable interest in stolen property, some persons may not have such an interest in stolen goods. In *Ludeau v. Phoenix Insurance Company,* 204 S.W.2d 1008, 1009 (Tex. Civ. App. 1947), the court agreed that a man's conditional gift of a diamond engagement ring to his fiancée only conferred title to the fiancée. However, someone stole the ring from the fiancée. The ring was insured against theft under an "all-risk" property insurance contract. The man submitted a claim to the insurer, which was denied. The man sued. the court ruled in favor of the insurer, concluding that, even though a conditional transfer of title occurred, the man had no insurable interest in the ring.

3) Do mortgagors and mortgagees retain an insurable interest in a residential or commercial property after an assignee or optionee takes possession of the property?

4) A mortgagee has an insurable interest in a mortgaged property which is entirely separate and distinct from a mortgagor's interests. See *American General Ins. Co. v. Sessions*, 331 S.W.2d 812, 814 (Tex. Civ. App.-Austin 1960, no writ); *National Reserve Ins. Co. v. McCrory*, 160 S.W.2d 972, 974 (Tex. Civ. App.-Amarillo 1942, no writ). See also *Reynolds v. Allstate Ins. Co.*, 629 F.2d 1111, 1114 (5th Cir.1980) (applying Texas law, the Fifth Circuit concluded that a mortgagor's insurable interest was not extinguished because an attempted foreclosure was void).

St. Paul Fire & Marine Insurance Company v. Daughtry
699 S.W.2d 321
(Tex.App. – San Antonio [4th Dist.] 1985)

This is an appeal from a judgment, based on a jury verdict, granting recovery on a fire insurance policy for the loss of a house.

The house in question was situated on acreage owned by Morton Southwest, a land developer. Morton Southwest had other plans for the acreage and wanted the house removed. Matt Martinez, vice president of Morton Southwest, offered the house to a house mover named Jim Dye, provided he could remove it by December 31, 1982. Martinez also gave appellee a letter which permitted him to move the house after January 1, 1983, in the event that Dye failed to exercise his option. Before Dye's option expired, on December 17, 1982, appellee applied for a "builder's risk" policy on the house, and appellant's agent issued a binder on the policy. A fire of unknown origin destroyed the house on December 21, 1982, and the appellant refused to pay the proceeds of the policy on the grounds that appellee did not have an insurable interest in the property.

In its first two points of error, appellant asserts (1) that the evidence is legally and factually insufficient to support the jury findings, and (2) that the court should have granted its motion to modify the judgment because appellee had, as a matter of law, no insurable interest in the house.

The standard of review for a legal sufficiency question was established in *Garza v. Alviar*, 395 S.W.2d 821 (Tex.1965). We apply this standard and we will consider only the probative evidence and inferences that may properly be drawn therefrom which support the judgment.

The facts which support the jury's findings in this case may be summarized as follows: Appellee was in the business of moving houses; he owned lots onto which he planned to move houses; he made a few investigative trips to the property to estimate the value of the house and the cost of moving it; he obtained permission to move it if Dye chose not to do so; he agreed to remove the foundation and debris; he insured the house; the house burned down.

The primary issue on appeal is whether appellee had an insurable interest in the property. The Texas Supreme Court has held that neither legal nor equitable title to property is required to establish an insurable interest. *Smith v. Eagle Star Insurance Co.*, 370 S.W.2d 448 (Tex.1963). What is required, however, is that the insured either derive a pecuniary benefit from the continued existence of the property or suffer a pecuniary loss from its destruction.

In *Smith,* the court held that the insured had an insurable interest in the house that burned because she suffered a pecuniary loss because of the destruction, even though the house was situated on land owned by the State. The court reasoned that since Smith had enjoyed the "undisturbed use of the house long prior to and at the time the policy was written, and at the time the loss occurred," the fire caused Smith a loss of such use. Unlike Smith, appellee had never come into possession, and had no prior period of use on which to base a claim of pecuniary loss. Smith had made a sizeable investment in the property. Appellee had paid nothing for the house, for permits to move it, for the services of those who assisted in its evaluation, or for the insurance.

Because appellee failed to produce evidence that he had ever possessed the house, that he had ever had any use of the house, or that he had expended any funds, labor, or any substantial amount of time preparing to move the house, we hold that he sustained no loss as a result of the destruction of the house.

We must next decide whether appellee would derive a pecuniary benefit from the continued existence of the house. To determine that, we must first examine the nature of appellee's interest in the property. Appellee claims no right to possession at the time of the fire on December 21, 1982. His only right to the property is derived from a letter of permission to move the house after January 1, 1983. The letter, signed only by Martinez on behalf of Morton Southwest, obligates appellee to remove the foundation and debris if and when appellee moved the house; it does not obligate appellee to move the house. Appellee paid nothing for the letter of permission which was revocable and was contingent upon Dye's not exercising his prior option to move the house.

Although the *Smith* court stated that a person who would derive a pecuniary benefit from the continued existence of the insured property has an insurable interest in it, that case was decided on the premise that a person who sustains a loss from the destruction of property has an insurable interest in it. Because the court held Smith's loss, not her benefit, was the basis of the decision, *Smith* is not pertinent to the discussion of whether appellee would derive a pecuniary benefit from the continued existence of the property.

No Texas court has yet determined whether a person would derive a pecuniary benefit from the continued existence of property to which someone else has a superior right of possession. The following cases from other jurisdictions have held that there is no insurable interest in such a situation: *Hane v. Hallock Farmers Mutual Insurance Co.,* 258 N.W.2d 779 (Minn.1977) (A non-binding option to repurchase property did not create an insurable interest.); *Allstate Insurance Co. v. Thompson*, 164 Ga. App. 508, 297 S.E.2d 520, 522 (1982) (An ex-husband's option to repurchase ex-wife's one-half interest in a house did not create an insurable interest, the court holding, "An option to purchase land does not, before acceptance, vest in the holder of the option any interest, legal or equitable, in the land itself."); *Christ Gospel Temple v. Liberty Mutual Insurance Co*., 273 Pa.Super. 302, 417 A.2d 660, 663 (1979) (The insured's only legal interest in the property was an option to repurchase in the event that the property was used for purposes other than church services. The court held that the insured "had a mere possibility of the expectancy that it might exercise its option to repurchase upon the happening of a contingency," and "this does not amount to an insurable interest.").

Because appellee suffered no pecuniary loss from the destruction of the property, and because he would derive no pecuniary benefit from the continued existence of the house until Dye's option period expired, we hold that appellee had, as a matter of law, no insurable interest.

In view of our holding that appellee has, as a matter of law, no insurable interest, it is unnecessary to reach appellant's other points of error.

We reverse and render judgment that appellee take nothing.

NOTES & QUESTIONS

1) INSURABLE INTEREST OF A BENEFICIARY—Tex. Ins. Code § 1103.002 reads in pertinent part: "A beneficiary … who is designated in a life insurance policy has an insurable interest for the face amount of the policy and is entitled to collect that amount."

2) INSURABLE INTEREST OF BENEFICIARY, OWNER, TRANSFEREE, OR ASSIGNEE—Tex. Ins. Code § 1103.053 reads in pertinent part:

> (a) Except as provided by Subsection (b), a beneficiary or owner of a life insurance policy who is designated in accordance with this subchapter or an entity to which a life insurance policy or an interest, benefit, right, or title in a life insurance policy is transferred or assigned . . . has . . . an insurable interest in the life of the individual who is insured under the policy.
>
> (b) An individual, partnership, association, corporation, or other legal entity that is directly or indirectly engaged in the business of burying the dead does not directly or indirectly have an insurable interest in the life of an individual unless the interest is established under other applicable statutory law or under common law.

3) Does one have an "insurable interest" in one's own life? Consider the language in Tex. Ins. Code § 1103.054: "An individual of legal age may … (1) apply for a policy insuring the individual's life; and (2) designate in writing in the application for the policy any individual, partnership, association, corporation, or other legal entity as … (A) a beneficiary of the policy; (B) an absolute or partial owner of the policy; or (C) both a beneficiary and an absolute or partial owner of the policy."

Equitable Life Assurance Society v. Hazlewood
12 S.W. 621
(Tex. 1889)

[Henry C. Hazlewood completed an application for life insurance. In 1887, Equitable Life Assurance Society — appellant— issued a $15,000 policy. Henry C. Hazlewood was both the owner of and the insured under the policy. The primary beneficiary was Robert R. Hazlewood. The contingent beneficiary was another brother. The insured died in March, 1888, He was about 28-years-old. The beneficiary filed a claim with the insurer. Equitable refused to pay, asserting that the insured had no insurable interest when he purchased the life insurance contract. The beneficiary sued.]

* * *

The defendant alleged in its answer that the insurance was taken out by plaintiff as a speculative and wagering policy. It was proved that plaintiff loaned to the insured the money with which he paid the required premium. The corporation's agent through whom the insurance was effected was permitted to testify to the negotiations preceding the application, tending to show that both the plaintiff and the insured were urged by the agent of the corporation to apply for the insurance; that the premium was paid by the insured; and that he first thought of making the minor children of the plaintiff the beneficiaries of the policy, but he finally concluded not to do so, because, in the event of his own marriage and desire to change the beneficiary to one more nearly connected with himself, it would be easier accomplished if his brother was the beneficiary than it would be if his minor children were the beneficiaries.

The application for insurance contains the following questions and answers: "Is any negotiation for other insurance now pending or contemplated?" to which the insured answered, in writing, "No." "Has a policy ever been applied for which was not thereafter issued, or which, if issued, was modified in amount, kind, or rates? If yes, for what company, and when?" to which the insured answered, in writing, "No." There was conflicting evidence as to whether the insured had not applied for membership in an order known as the "Legion of Honor."

Plaintiff was permitted to prove, by the agent of the corporation by whom the application was secured, that pending negotiations between him and the insured, and before the insured made answer to said questions, he (the insured) asked him (the agent) "what was meant by that, — if it referred to assessment companies or mutual companies." Witness explained that it did not; and the insured then said he had made application to the Legion of Honor for assurance, whereupon witness told him that the Legion of Honor was a mutual company, and was not regarded as a life insurance company, and he was instructed by the general agent of defendant not to consider them as assurance companies. We think the evidence was properly admitted in each instance.

On the issue as to whether it was a wagering policy, the statements made by the witness were pertinent, and have no tendency to control any written evidence or the contract. Nor can we see any impropriety in permitting the agent of the corporation to give the subject of the insurance information about facts proper for him to know. Lodges that furnish insurance to their members may also perform other important functions, and a rejection of an applicant by one of them would not necessarily be predicated upon his unfitness for insurance. It may be a rule of the defendant company not to treat such societies as coming within the meaning of the question, and, if it is, we are not able to perceive any sufficient reason why the fact that the statement was made may not be proved. Outside of the evidence objected to, the record fails to show that the insured in fact ever made an application for such membership, or that he was ever rejected.

It is contended that the plaintiff had no insurable interest in his brother's life, wherefore the cause of action sued upon was a wagering contract, and void, as against public policy. The rule is stated generally . . . that "no person can procure a valid insurance upon a life, unless he has an interest in such life." The Supreme Court of the United States — in the case of *Insurance Co. v. Schaefer,* 94 U. S. 460 (1876) — says:

> It is generally agreed that mere wager policies, that is, policies in which the insured party has no interest whatever in the matter insured, but only an interest in its loss or destruction, are void, as against public policy. . . . It is well settled that a man has an insurable interest in his own life, and in that of his wife and children; a woman, in the life of her husband; and the creditor, in the life of his debtor. Indeed, it may be said generally that any reasonable expectation of pecuniary benefit or advantage from the continued life of another creates an insurable interest in such life; and there is no doubt that a man may effect an insurance on his own life for the benefit of a relative or friend . . . . The essential thing is that the policy shall be obtained in good faith, and not for the purpose of speculating upon the hazard of a life in which the assured has no interest.

* * *

The doctrine is well settled by the weight of authority that a person not having an insurable interest in the life of another cannot take and hold by an assignment a policy upon the life of such other person, and that a creditor can only take and hold such a policy, by assignment, to an extent sufficient to secure his debt. . . .It is contended by appellee that every person has an insurable interest in his own life, and that when he is the actor he may take out an unlimited amount of insurance upon his own life, and make it payable to whoever he may please, as beneficiary, without regard to such person's having an insurable interest in his life.

In Bliss on Life Insurance, it is said:

> A person has undoubtedly an insurable interest in his own life, and that interest supports a policy whether he makes the loss payable to himself, his executors, or his assigns, or to a nominee or appointee named in the policy. Nor is a policy obtained by one on his own life, for the benefit of another, which latter advances the premium, necessarily void. The question is whether the policy was in fact intended to be what it purports to be, or whether the form was adopted as a cover for a mere wager. If the plaintiff and the insured confederate together to procure a policy for the plaintiff's benefit, when he is not, and does not expect to be, a creditor of the

> insured, and with a view of having the policy assigned to him without consideration, the policy is void.

The only distinction we can see in any case between the assignment of a policy taken by a person on his own life to one having no insurable interest, and the designating such person, without insurable interest, in the original transaction as the beneficiary, is that the insurer may not know of the assignment, but would necessarily be aware of the designation in the policy. So far as the question of public policy is concerned, we can see no substantial distinction between the two proceedings; and, if one is invalid, it seems to us the other ought to be held equally so.

An assignment of a valid policy to one having no insurable interest in the life of the insured does not invalidate the policy. The assignee may collect and apply the proceeds, if he is a creditor, to the extinguishment of his own debt, and such sums as he may have disbursed for the purpose of keeping the policy alive; and the surplus may be collected for the benefit of the heirs of the person whose life was insured. We see no reason why the same rule may not be applied to a person designated in the policy as the beneficiary, treating him, when he has no insurable interest, as an assignee, appointee, or trustee, to receive the proceeds for whoever may be lawfully entitled to enjoy them. The insurer will then be required to pay the sum it has promised to pay, and the money cannot be appropriated by anybody not having a legitimate right to it.

The exact degree of relationship that must exist between two persons to give one an insurable interest in the life of the other, on account of the relationship alone, we have not found to be clearly defined. Brothers and sisters seem to be on the dividing line. Whether that degree of relationship can be included, has been disputed. . . . To what extent a creditor may insure the life of his debtor is not announced when it is decided that he can only appropriate of such insurance an amount sufficient to pay his debt and interest. He must be allowed to provide for a sum sufficient, when collected, to cover his demand, and such disbursements as may be required to keep the policy in force, with accrued interest. The sum required for the purpose may very many times exceed the debt. It would be an extreme case in which a court would be justified in saying that the amount secured was too great.

When the insurance is obtained by a person on his own life, and made payable originally, or by assignment, to another, having none, or only a limited insurable interest in his life, as the surplus, after the payment of the charges, will go to the party whose life is insured, we see no reason for limiting the amount for which the insurance may be taken out. When the insurance is not contracted for by the person whose life is insured, but by a creditor, in his own name, so that there is no party to the contract except himself and the insurer, it becomes immaterial what amount may be contracted for, as no more will be collected than will be ultimately sufficient to discharge his debt and disbursements on the policy, including interest upon both.

We find no error in the proceedings, and the judgment is affirmed.

NOTES & QUESTIONS

1) May a minor—a 15-year-old—and Wal-Mart form an exclusive-dealings contract? Would that contract be enforceable in Texas? May a 14-year-old boy in Texas and New York Metropolitan Life Insurance Company form an insurance contract? Would that life insurance contract be enforceable in a Texas court?

2) INSURANCE AND MINORS' AUTHORITY TO CONTRACT—Tex. Ins. Code § 1104.003 (a) reads in relevant part: "[A] minor 14 years of age or older who is without a guardian of the estate of the minor may … (1) contract for or otherwise acquire a life, term, or endowment insurance policy or an annuity contract, including: (A) applying for the policy or contract; and (B) making agreements with respect to the policy or contract or a right, privilege, or benefit under the policy or contract; (2) exercise all rights and powers in regard to the policy or contract in the same manner as an adult; and (3) surrender an interest in the policy or contract and give a discharge for a benefit paid under the policy or contract."

3) Do minors have an insurable interest in the lives of their parents, stepparents, and stepbrothers? Do minors have an insurable interest in the lives of their friends and/or strangers? §-1104 §.002 Ins code

4) MINORS AND INSURABLE INTERESTS: Tex. Ins. Code § 1104.003 (b) reads in pertinent part: "An insurance policy acquired by a minor … must: (1) be owned by the minor; and (2) insure the life of … (A) the minor; (B) a spouse, child, parent, grandparent, or sibling of the minor; or (C) another in whose life the minor has an insurable interest.

5) Does allowing minors to be the owners and beneficiaries under life insurance contracts create a "moral hazard?" When comparing the propensities of minors and adults, which group is more likely to murder insureds to collect life-insurance proceeds?

6) If you had to devise a scheme to decrease beneficiaries' likelihood of murdering insureds to collect insurance money, what would be your strategy?

F. "Primary or Contingent Beneficiary Is Disqualified"

Crawford v. Coleman
726 S.W.2d 9
(Tex. 1987)

This is an insurance disqualification case involving the distribution of proceeds of life insurance policies. The trial court disqualified the primary beneficiary under the policy and awarded the proceeds to the contingent beneficiaries. The court of appeals affirmed. We reverse that part of the court of appeals judgment awarding proceeds to one of the contingent beneficiaries and render judgment for Phynies and Flora Crawford.

On May 14, 1979, Sandra Shoaf was stabbed to death by her husband, Cornelius Shoaf. Sandra's life was insured under four insurance policies, each designating Cornelius as the primary beneficiary. The trial court disqualified Cornelius from receiving Sandra's death benefits because the jury found that Cornelius willfully caused Sandra's death. The contingent beneficiaries under the policies are Sandra's parents, Phynies and Flora Crawford (the Crawfords) and Sandra's stepson, Cornell. Cornell is Cornelius's son by a prior marriage. Martha Coleman is Cornell's mother.

After disqualifying Cornelius, the trial court awarded the proceeds of two of the four policies to the Crawfords as the contingent beneficiaries under those policies. Those proceeds awarded to the Crawfords are not a part of this appeal. The trial court also awarded the proceeds of the remaining two policies — Equitable Life Insurance Society of the United States policy and Metropolitan Life Insurance Company policy — to Cornell Shoaf as the contingent beneficiary.

The court of appeals affirmed the trial court's judgment. The Crawfords dispute the award of the benefits of these two policies to Cornell.

The Equitable policy named Cornelius Shoaf as the "insured," and Sandra as the "insured spouse" under a family plan of insurance included in the policy. The preprinted language of the policy provides that the "beneficiary" of the insured spouse is "the insured, if living; if not living, the surviving children of the insured."

The Metropolitan policy was obtained by Cornelius Shoaf through his employment with the State of Texas as authorized by the Texas Employees Uniform Group Insurance Beneficiary Act, Tex. Ins.Code Ann. art. 3.50-2. Sandra's life was insured under this policy at Cornelius's option. The preprinted beneficiary designations in this policy awarded proceeds at the insured's death to the insured's beneficiary, then to the insured's spouse, then to the insured's children, and then to the insured's parents.

It is undisputed that the distribution of these policy proceeds is governed by Tex.Ins.Code Ann. § 21.23 (Vernon 1981). Section 21.23 states:

> The interest of a beneficiary in a life insurance policy or contract heretofore or hereinafter issued shall be forfeited when the beneficiary is the principal or an accomplice in willfully bringing about the death of the insured. When such is the case, the nearest relative of the insured shall receive said insurance.

In construing § 21.23, this court has said that insurance proceeds are distributed to the nearest relative of the insured only "if *all* of the beneficiaries, primary and contingent, are disqualified from receiving such proceeds." *Deveroex v. Nelson,* 529 S.W.2d 510, 513 (Tex.1975). In *Deveroex,* the primary beneficiary murdered the insured. We construed § 21.23 as directing distribution of the proceeds to the insured's adoptive son who was a designated beneficiary under the policy rather than awarding the proceeds to the adopted son and the insured's natural son who was not designated as a beneficiary.

The Crawfords argue that the proceeds of the Equitable policy and the Metropolitan policy covering Sandra's life are distributable to them because they are Sandra's "nearest relative" upon Cornelius's disqualification. The Crawfords read *Deveroex* as directing proceeds to the contingent beneficiary only when the contingent beneficiary is expressly named and is an object of the deceased insured's obvious intent. Cornell argues that he should receive the proceeds because he is the contingent beneficiary under these policies, and distribution to the nearest relative is not triggered until all beneficiaries are disqualified. We agree that the Crawfords should receive the proceeds on Sandra's life, but for reasons different than those offered by the Crawfords.

It is undisputed that Cornelius has forfeited any interest in the proceeds because he willfully brought about Sandra's death. Tex. Ins. Code Ann. § 21.23. Sandra is the "insured" under § 21.23. Affidavits signed by the Crawfords indicate they are Sandra's nearest relatives.

In *Deveroex,* we reasoned that distributing insurance proceeds to the nearest relative only if all beneficiaries were disqualified effectuated both the obvious intent of the insured and the legislature's objective to deny proceeds to the individual responsible for the insured's death. Upon review, we find our reasoning no longer persuasive.

As Justice Daniel stated in his dissent, our holding was contrary to the plain words of the statute. *Deveroex,* 529 S.W.2d at 514 (Daniel, J., dissenting). Justice Daniel correctly reasoned that § 21.23 contains a specific provision for payment of insurance proceeds when a beneficiary willfully causes the death of the insured. The specific provision directs payment of proceeds to the nearest relative. The fact that the legislature chose to withhold proceeds from the beneficiary/killer does not mean that the legislature intended that the nearest relative would succeed to the proceeds only upon the disqualification of all beneficiaries. Moreover, § 21.23 is "as much a part of the insured's contract as if it has been incorporated in the policy. *Camden Fire Ins. Ass'n v. Harold E. Clayton & Co.,* 6 S.W.2d 1029 (Tex. 1928). The rights of parties to contract with respect to insurance are limited by state laws which are a part of every contract."

Id. at 514 (Daniel, J., dissenting)

Our reasoning that the *Deveroex* distribution scheme effectuates the obvious intent of the deceased is also incorrect. In *Deveroex,* we said the insured's "obvious intent" was evidenced by the designation of the contingent beneficiary. When a beneficiary willfully causes the death of the insured, however, we are confronted with a situation where reasonable people would not form an intent regarding the distribution of the proceeds. We may safely presume that neither Sandra, Cornelius, the Crawfords, nor Cornell envisioned the circumstances of Sandra's death when the policies were obtained.

It is clear that the legislature has deliberately chosen to direct the manner in which the benefits are awarded. The practice, as dictated by *Deveroex,* of beginning our inquiry under the statute, moving into the policy once a beneficiary is disqualified, and then moving back under the statute once we determine no qualified beneficiaries are present, is inconsistent with the explicit language of § 21.23. Instead, by following the language the legislature employed, the inquiry begins, proceeds, and ends under § 21.23. We, therefore, overrule our interpretation of § 21.23 in *Deveroex v. Nelson,* 529 S.W.2d 510 (Tex.1975), and hold that when any beneficiary under a life insurance policy willfully causes the death of the insured, the policy proceeds are distributed to the nearest relative of the insured.

We recognize that other jurisdictions have reached a different result on somewhat similar statutes and facts. Moreover, we are aware that Cornell was in no way involved in Sandra's death. Today's opinion is not to be read as implying that Cornell falls under the corruption of blood doctrine. Rather, our holding recognizes the specific direction of § 21.23 that when a beneficiary willfully brings about the death of the insured, the proceeds succeed to the insured's nearest relative.

Accordingly, we reverse the judgment of the court of appeals and render judgment that Phynies and Flora Crawford are entitled to the proceeds from Equitable Life Insurance policy . . . and Metropolitan Life Insurance Company policy . . . as the nearest relative of Sandra Crawford Coleman.

NOTES & QUESTIONS

1) FORFEITURE OF BENEFICIARY'S RIGHTS: Tex. Ins. Code § 1103.151 reads: "A beneficiary of a life insurance policy or contract forfeits the beneficiary's interest in the policy or contract if the beneficiary is a principal or an accomplice in wilfully bringing about the death of the insured."

2) PAYMENT OF PROCEEDS TO CONTINGENT BENEFICIARY OR TO RELATIVE: Tex. Ins. Code § 1103.152 states:

> (a) Except as provided by Subsection (b), if a beneficiary of a life insurance policy or contract forfeits an interest in the policy or contract under Section 1103.151, a contingent beneficiary named by the insured in the policy or contract is entitled to receive the proceeds of the policy or contract.
>
> (b) A contingent beneficiary is not entitled to receive the proceeds of a life insurance policy or contract if the contingent beneficiary forfeits an interest in the policy or contract under Section 1103.151.
>
> (c) If there is not a contingent beneficiary entitled to receive the proceeds of a life insurance policy or contract under Subsection (a), the nearest relative of the insured is entitled to receive those proceeds.

3) Tex. Ins. Code Ann. § 21.23 has been repealed. Currently, those sections are codified as Tex. Ins. Code § 1103.151 and Tex. Ins. Code § 1103.152.

4) Can you think of ways that an insurer might unintentionally waive the "no insurable interest," "disqualification," and "forfeiture" defenses?

5) Note: Both insurers and insureds may employ the doctrines of waiver and equitable estoppel as "defenses."

6) Assume that a beneficiary has no insurable interest in a sibling's life or that a tenant has no insurable interest in her destroyed apartment. May a court estop the insurers from asserting the "no insurable interest" defense?

G. *Doctrines of Waiver and Equitable Estoppel*

Republic Insurance Company v. Silverton Elevators, Inc.
493 S.W.2d 748
(Tex. 1973)

This suit was brought by Respondents, Silverton Elevators, Inc. and Carl L. Tidwell, against Petitioner, Republic Insurance Company, to recover under a Texas Standard Fire Policy issued to Silverton Elevators by Republic covering a residential dwelling and household goods contained therein. In a non-jury trial, Silverton was awarded $3,000 'for the use and benefit' of Carl L. Tidwell for the loss of the household goods. The Court of Civil Appeals affirmed. We affirm.

Carl L. Tidwell was at all times material to this controversy, an officer, director and the general manager of Silverton Elevators, Inc. Silverton owned and furnished to Tidwell a house near its elevators, together with the insurance on the house and on Tidwell's household goods, as part of his compensation as general manager. Since 1964, Republic's local agent had issued and renewed insurance policies in the name of Silverton covering the dwelling and its household goods. It is undisputed that the local agent, who had authority to issue the policies and receive the premiums, knew that the household goods belonged to Tidwell and that Silverton was carrying the insurance for the benefit of Tidwell. On April 17, 1970, a tornado destroyed the house and the household goods.

On the date of the tornado there was in effect a Texas Standard Fire Policy with Extended Coverage on Dwelling & Household Goods in the sum of $10,000 issued by Republic to Silverton for the period of April 20, 1969 to April 20, 1972, insuring against loss from windstorm the specifically described "occupied dwelling" for $7,000 and "household goods . . . while in the described building" for $3,000.00. It is undisputed that Silverton paid the $227.00 premium, and the local agent admitted that at the time he issued the policy he knew the facts heretofore mentioned with respect to actual ownership of the insured property. He testified that he wrote the policy to cover

Tidwell's household goods located in the dwelling which Tidwell and his family occupied; that he knew Silverton was carrying the policy on the household goods for the benefit of Tidwell; that when he issued the policy he did not think it made any difference that it was in the name of Silverton because "they were paying the premium"; and that he told Tidwell that the policy covered his household goods both before and after the tornado.

Republic acknowledged coverage on the house and paid Silverton $7,000 for its damage, but it denied any liability to Silverton or Tidwell on the household goods. Thereupon, Silverton and Tidwell brought this suit against Republic claiming coverage to the limit of the policy ($3,000) on the household goods owned by Tidwell. Republic defended on the grounds that Silverton had no ownership and therefore no insurable interest in the household goods and that the policy as written was limited by its terms to household goods owned by Silverton Elevators, Inc., the named insured.

Silverton and Tidwell's pleadings asserted that they both had insurable interests; that the insurance was purchased by Silverton and extended to Tidwell as part of his compensation as manager and as "a legal representative of Silverton Elevators, Inc."; and that when Republic issued its policy and accepted premiums with full knowledge of the true ownership and relations between Silverton and Tidwell, it waived the right to complain about any lack of ownership or insurable interest of the named insured and was estopped from denying coverage on behalf of Tidwell. As heretofore indicated, the trial court awarded Silverton Elevators $3,000 "for the use and benefit of Carl L. Tidwell."

Since the policy refers to and clearly purports to cover the household goods located in the specifically described dwelling, we agree with the Court of Civil Appeals that the knowledge of Tidwell's ownership of the household goods by Republic's local agent had his actions with respect thereto were imputed to and binding upon Republic. Issuance of the policy and collection of the premiums with such knowledge operates as a waiver of any requirement that the named insured own or possess a beneficial interest in the insured property. *National Fire Ins. Co. of Hartford v. Carter*, 257 S.W. 531 (Tex.Comm'n App.1924); *Continental Ins. Co. v. Cummings,* 98 Tex. 115, 81 S.W. 705 (Tex. 1904); *Wagner v. Westchester Fire Ins. Co.*, 50 S.W. 569 (Tex. 1899); *Liverpool and London and Globe Insurance Company v. Ende*, 65 Tex. 118 (1885);

In the above cases, the named insureds were not the owners or sole owners of the insured properties. In each case, the true owner was known to the insurance agent and was allowed direct recovery, or recovery for his benefit, on the grounds that the insurance company had waived warranties of sole ownership or lack of insurable interest. There is no conflict between the above cases and those which hold that waiver and estoppel cannot operate to bring within the terms of a policy liabilities or benefits which were expressly excepted therefrom, such as liability from injuries due to gunshot wounds in *Washington Nat. Ins. Co. v. Craddock*, 130 Tex. 251, 109 S.W.2d 165 (Tex. 1937); as in *Great American Reserve Ins. Co. v. Mitchell*, 335 S.W.2d 707 (Tex.Civ.App.1960, writ ref.).

The latter cases recognize that waiver and estoppel may operate to avoid forfeiture of coverage and benefits stated in the policy, but not to add specifically excluded risks or to enlarge the benefits or risks therein set forth. In the present case, plaintiffs seek to recover only on the risk assumed by Republic under the terms of the written policy. Republic's policy insured against the destruction of precisely the same household goods identified in its policy and for which it collected its premiums. There is no evidence that its risk was enlarged because the household goods were owned by Tidwell rather than Silverton.

Although it is undisputed that Tidwell rather than Silverton owned the household goods in the dwelling when the policy was issued and when the property was destroyed and that they were the household goods intended to be insured, Republic contends that the description, and thus the coverage, was limited by the written policy to household goods owned by Silverton. The effect is to say that the policy covered only non-existent household goods; that even though Republic wrote a $3,000.00 policy on household goods located in the described dwelling, there was never in fact any coverage on anybody's household goods.

This is inconsistent not only with the undisputed intention of its own agent but with the provisions of the policy as written. The household goods were referred to on the face of the policy as being located in the dwelling specifically described in the policy. There was no misdescription of the location of the property by the agent as .... Their location and identity were definitely and correctly stated. Page 1 bears a typed designation of the insured property as "Dwelling & Household Goods." Other relevant portions read as follows:

> Republic Insurance Company ... In Consideration of the stipulations and conditions herein or added hereto which are made a part of this policy, and of the premiums provided does insure Silverton Elevators, Inc. and legal representatives ... against direct loss resulting from any of the perils (listed below) which HAVE a premium inserted opposite thereto and only on the property described and located as provided hereon.

Next, under "Coverage" is listed in Column 4, TOTAL INSURANCE, the sum of $10,000.00, and in Column 6 the separate premiums for Fire and Lightning and Extended Coverage, totaling $227.00. Thereafter, under DESCRIPTION OF PROPERTY is 'Item 1, $7000.00 — On the ONE story, COMPOSITION type of roof, ASBESTOS SIDING, building, LOCATION . . . SILVERTON, Texas 79257, Lot 7, 8 & 9, Block 143 — OCCUPIED DWELLING," and "Item 2, $30000.00 — HOUSEHOLD GOODS . . . Unless otherwise provided, Insurance on personal property shall cover only while in the described building.' Under the above DESCRIPTION OF PROPERTY heading, in small type are the words: "See definitions of Building, Household Goods, Stock, Furniture, Fixtures, and, or Machinery, and Contents."

None of the typed or printed words on the face of the policy limit or restrict the coverage or description of household goods to those owned by Silverton Elevators, Inc., unless, as contended by Republic, the reference to and terms of the small-type printed definition on page 2 have that effect. It reads: "Household Goods: Insurance on household goods shall include all personal property, usual to a residence, of the insured and his family."

* * *

Republic's argument to the contrary ignores the purpose served by definitions in a Texas Standard Fire Policy, the terms of which were promulgated by the State Board of Insurance under Articles 5.35 and 5.36 Texas Insurance Code. Insurance companies are prohibited from departing from the provisions of these approved terms. *Commercial Union Assurance Co. v. Preston*, 282 S.W. 563 (Tex. 1926). Descriptive words of coverage, including location and description of the property, terms of coverage, and amount of premium for each coverage, are to be typed in on the face of the policy (page 1) as was done by Republic's agent on the policy before us.

* * *

We have found no instance in which a Texas court has held that a definition in the Texas Standard Fire Policy limits or restricts either the coverage or the description of the property as contained on the face of the policy. Perhaps this is due to the well settled rule that the words "include," "including," and "shall include" are generally employed as terms of enlargement rather than limitation or restriction. We hold that the words "shall include" as used in this definition are terms of enlargement rather than limitation, and the definition does not have the effect of restricting the coverage or description of the property as set forth on the face of the policy.

* * *

Even though the provision does not speak of "named insured," and for all practical purposes Tidwell was the "insured" because the policy as to household goods was written for his benefit, there are other more compelling reasons why this provision is inapplicable to the personal property involved in this case. Clearly, the entire clause refers to loss on "building items," their value at the time of loss less depreciation, repair, replacement and reconstruction, etc. None of the language refers to personal property.

* * *

The above clause has been a part of the Texas Standard Fire Policy form prescribed by the Insurance Commission since 1943. Since then we have found no case involving a claim of an actual owner for whose benefit a policy was taken out with full knowledge by the insurance company of the true ownership, in which this clause has been applied to deny recovery by or on behalf of the true owner.

* * *

Whether applicable to personal property or not, we hold that the portion of the clause relating to limitation of liability to "the interest of the insured" falls within the category of ownership provisions which may be waived; the insurer may be estopped from denying liability to the true owner on policies issued in the names of third parties covering the risks on identified property with full knowledge by the company that the property is actually owned by the one for whose benefit the policy was written or maintained. *National Fire Ins. Co. of Hartford v. Carter et al.*, 257 S.W. 531 (Tex.Comm'n App. 1924, jdgmt. adopted); *Scott et al v. Law Union & Rock Ins. Co.*, 12 S.W.2d 147 (Tex.Comm'n App.1929, jdgmt adopted); *Maryland Casualty Co. et al v. Palestine Fashions, Inc. et al.*, 402 S.W.2d 883 (Tex.1966).

Republic insists that reformation of the policy is the only proper remedy, if any, for recovery by Silverton on behalf of Tidwell, because of failure of the written policy to identify the household goods as belonging to Tidwell. We disagree. As heretofore indicated, under the undisputed facts, the household goods described in the policy belonged to Tidwell and were insured by Silverton for his benefit in a policy drawn by Republic's agent for such purpose, with assurances from the agent that it would cover Tidwell's furniture. If this was a mistake, it was made by Republic's agent, and it was mutual, because Tidwell and Silverton took the agent's word that it expressed the true agreement.

With this evidence being fully developed in the present record, there is no reason to require another trial for reformation of the written policy. It has been held that even without a plea for reformation, when the facts show the true agreement intended and a mutual mistake, or mistake of the agent, in preparing the written policy, the agreement intended will be enforced without going through the formal proceedings of reformation.

Silverton and Tidwell made every proof in this case that would entitle recovery on the policy as written. Under the above cited authorities, the trial court and Court of Civil Appeals have properly held that Silverton is entitled to recover for the benefit of Tidwell on the written policy without seeking a reformation thereof.

Accordingly, the judgments of the lower courts are affirmed.

NOTES & QUESTIONS

1) What are the doctrines of waiver and equitable estoppel? Consider the court's explanation in *Salloum Foods & Liquor, Inc. v. Parliament Ins. Co.*, 69 Ill.App.3d 422, 388 N.E.2d 23, 27-28 (1979):

An insurance company can waive the limitation provision of an insurance contract, or, by its conduct, become estopped from invoking the provision as a defense to an action on the policy.

In the context of insurance law, and especially with regard to limitation provisions in insurance policies, the terms "waiver" and "estoppel" have often been used without careful distinction, and thereby abused and confused.

This doctrinal confusion, epitomized by the frequently echoed phrase "waiver by estoppel" is so deeply rooted some courts have suggested that the term waiver, as applied in Illinois to insurance cases, is simply another name for estoppel.

Notwithstanding the confusion already engendered by many of these cases, it is elementary that waiver and estoppel are two separate and distinct doctrines. The fact that these doctrines are closely akin and often may coexist does not mean they are identical in connotation.

Waiver encompasses either an express or an implied voluntary and intentional relinquishment of a known and existing right. Waiver is essentially unilateral in character, focusing only upon the acts and conduct of the insurer. Prejudice to, or detrimental reliance by the insured is not required..

Equitable estoppel, on the other hand, generally is based upon an insurance carrier's conduct and/or representations which mislead an insured to his detriment. Thus, if an insurance carrier's investigation and/or negotiation of a policy claim reasonably induces within the insured a false sense of security namely, that the claim will be settled without suit and the insured, in reliance thereon, foregoes filing suit during the policy's limitation period, the insurance carrier is estopped from later raising the limitation provision as a defense to an action on the policy.

It is not necessary that the insurer intentionally mislead or deceive the insured, or even intend by its conduct to induce delay. All that is necessary is that the insured reasonably relies on the insurer's representations or conduct in forbearing suit.

2) What is the major distinction between an implied-in-law waiver and equitable estoppel? Both are equitable doctrines. How does one "prove" each? What are the tests?

3) What is the chief difference between an "incontestability clause" in an insurance contract and waiver?

4) May an incontestability clause and the doctrines of waiver and equitable estoppel expand coverage or change the meaning of terms in an insurance contract?

Minnesota Mutual Life Insurance Company v. Morse
487 S.W.2d 317
(Tex 1972)

Ethel C. Morse brought this suit to collect insurance benefits due under group life policies which protected her husband, James K. Morse. The dispute is over the amount of those benefits and the effect of provisions of incontestability. The trial court held the insurance company liable for the full amount sought, and the court of civil appeals affirmed. Holding the incontestability provisions to be inapplicable, we reverse.

James K. Morse was an employee of the Red River Ordnance Depot until the time of his retirement by reason of total and permanent disability on October 29, 1962. He continued thereafter as a member of the Red River Employees Federal Credit Union. The Minnesota Mutual Life Insurance Company provided group life insurance coverage for members of the Credit Union under two master policies issued on September 1, 1963. Under policy no. 4666-W Minnesota Mutual provided insurance in an amount equal to the member's savings account at the time of death. Under policy no. 4666-G it agreed to pay a sum equal to a member's loan balance with the Credit Union at the time of the member's death. The premiums, based on total deposits and loan balances, were paid monthly by the Credit Union as a benefit to its members.

At the time of his retirement on November 29, 1962, James K. Morse had a deposit balance of $700 and a loan balance of $341. The loan balance was paid at that time by a prior insurer. On the date of the issuance of Minnesota Mutual policies on September 1, 1963, Morse had a deposit balance of $737.31, and he owed no loan indebtedness to the Credit Union. At the time of his death on November 17, 1967, Morse's deposit balance was $5,000 and his loan account balance was $2,003.08. Ethel C. Morse, the widow and sole beneficiary under the will of James K. Morse, seeks payment by the insurance company of a sum equal to the full deposit and loan balances as of the date of her husband's death. Minnesota Mutual contends that it owes the smaller deposit balance and a premium return of $117.72. Under the lower court judgments, Ethel Morse has recovered the full amount plus penalty and attorney fees.

The amount of premiums paid and the amount of life insurance on the Credit Union members changes from month to month under these policies. Policy 4666-W, covering deposit accounts, provides that it "is issued for a term period of one month" and "may be renewed for further consecutive monthly periods by timely payment of the premium."

On September 1, 1963 when Minnesota Mutual first issued its policies, James K. Morse had no loan balance and there was no amount of insurance on his life as of that date under policy 4666-G. The terms of policy 4666-W provide for the full coverage of the deposit balance of each member as of the date of issuance (with some reduction because of the member's age): "INSURABLE BALANCE. The Insurable Balance in the Member's total ledger balance, up to a maximum of $5,000, for which a premium has been paid or is payable during the time this policy is in force . . . ."

As of the date of issuance every member of the Credit Union enjoyed this coverage irrespective of employment or disability. To this extent we agree with the construction of the policy made by the court of civil appeals. This is not a construction reached because of the effect of the incontestability clause; it is reached under the policy terms which do not otherwise limit coverage. As of September 1, 1963 the amount of coverage of James K. Morse under policy 4666-W was $737.31. No withdrawals were made by Morse and the coverage to this extent, at least, continued until his death. The problem is with the subsequent increases in his savings account as well as the subsequent loans.

Policy no. 4666-W contains this provision:

> INCREASES IN AMOUNT OF INSURANCE. Except when evidence of insurability is required, increases in Amounts of Insurance because of an increase in the Member's ledger balance shall be the date of the increase provided the Member is physically able to perform the usual duties of his livelihood; if not, the increase shall become effective on the first day following the ledger increase that he is physically able to perform the usual duties of his livelihood.

Policy No. 4666-G contains a similar provision:

> All members under age 70 who become indebted to the Credit Union subsequent to the date of issue of this policy, and who are physically able to perform, or within a reasonable time may be expected to resume, the usual duties of their livelihood, shall become eligible for insurance on the date of their indebtedness.

This case was tried under an agreed statement of facts by which it was agreed that James K. Morse was neither able to perform, nor expected to resume, the usual duties of his livelihood at any time after October 29, 1962. However, it has been held that Minnesota Mutual is liable to the extent of the deposits and loans made subsequent to the original issuance of these policies because the incontestability clauses in those policies bar the company from raising the disability defense.

The incontestability clause in policy no. 4666-W states: "This policy shall be incontestable two years from its date of issue." Policy no. 4666-G provides: "The validity of the policy shall not be contested, except for nonpayment of premiums, after it has been in force for two years from its date of issue . . .." All premiums, computed on the increased balances, have been paid on these policies up to the date of Morse's death. Both policies had been in effect for more than two years when he died in 1967. Petitioner did not contest coverage of the deceased prior to his death.

The purpose of incontestability clauses in insurance policies . . . is to protect the insured from a contest as to the validity of the policy after the expiration of the set period. *Kansas Life Ins. Co. v. First Bank of Truscott*, 78 S.W.2d 584 (Tex. 1935); *American Nat. Ins. Co. v. Tabor*, 230 S.W. 397 (Tex.1921). The incontestability clause should not be applied to change the meaning of the terms of the policy or to enlarge its coverage. Whatever might have been the effect of the incontestability provisions if the policies issued by Minnesota Mutual had excluded coverage at the time of their issuance for any member of the Credit Union then disabled that is not the question before us. The original policy coverage here was clearly valid.

The question is how the subsequent deposits and loans affect the amount of that coverage. The incontestability clauses speak of the validity of the Policy from its Date of issue and do not purport to limit or extend amounts of insurance. Under the express terms of the policies, withdrawals or decreases in the accounts of the members would correspondingly reduce the amount of the insurance coverage. That coverage would also be increased by deposits or new loans, but only if or when the member was physically able to perform the usual duties of his livelihood. Since James K. Morse was disabled at the times when his accounts were increased, no increase resulted in the amount of his insurance coverage.

The court of civil appeals held that by acceptance of the premiums computed on the full balances of these accounts of James K. Morse up to the date of his death, Minnesota Mutual has waived any defense relative to the disability of Morse and is now estopped to deny coverage to the full extent of the balances as of the death of Morse. Whereas waiver and estoppel may operate to avoid forfeiture of a policy and may prevent an insurance company from avoiding payment because of the failure on the part of the insured to comply with some requirement of the policy, waiver and estoppel cannot enlarge the risks covered by a policy and cannot be used to create a new and different contract with respect to the risk covered and the insurance extended.

Under the agreed facts of this case, Minnesota Mutual Life Insurance Company owed at the time of the death of James K. Morse no more than $737.14 and the return of excessive premiums. The judgments below are reversed; the case is remanded to the trial court for entry of judgment in accordance with this opinion.

NOTES & QUESTIONS

1) LIFE INSURANCE & INCONTESTABILITY PROVISION: Tex. Ins. Code § 884.354 (c) states: "A life insurance policy must provide that a policy in force for two years becomes incontestable, except for nonpayment of premiums, on the second anniversary of the date of issuance, if the insured does not die before that date."

2) INSURANCE CERTIFICATES, APPLICATION FORMS AND INCONTESTABILITY Provisions: Tex. Ins. Code § 887.251 reads in pertinent part:

> (a) An insurance certificate issued by an association must include:
>
> > (1) any condition of the certificate, including any portion of the bylaws of the association that affects the insurance rights of the parties in any material way; and

(2) a statement that the certificate is issued subject to:

(A) the association's constitution and bylaws; and

(B) any amendments to the constitution and bylaws approved by the commissioner.

(b) An insurance certificate must provide that a certificate in force for two years becomes incontestable, except for nonpayment of dues or assessments, on the second anniversary of the date of issuance, if the insured does not die before that date.

(c) An insurance certificate issued by an association or an application for the certificate may not contain language or be in a form that misleads the certificate holder or applicant about the kind of insurance provided under the certificate.

3) In *Morse*, Ethel sued the insurer to collect benefits under some group life insurance contracts. Did she have access to the master group insurance contract or a copy? What is a "master group insurance contract"? What is the relationship between a master group policy and an insurance certificate? Does an incontestability clause appear in both a master group insurance contract and in an insurance certificate?

4) Which are superior: the terms in a "group master policy" or the terms in a "certificate"? Certificates are also called "subscriber's agreements" and employees or members' "benefits handbooks." In *Romano v. New England Mutual Life Insurance Company*, 362 S.E.2d 334, 335-340 (W.Va. 1987), the Supreme Court of West Virginia provides some insight:

> In this appeal from a summary judgment, we consider whether the trial court erred in holding as a matter of law that a condition contained in the master policy of a group insurance plan was binding upon an insured. The master policy was not made available to the insured prior to his death, and the condition in question was inconsistent with promotional materials prepared by the insurer and relied upon by the insured.
>
> * * *
>
> The narrow question we address is whether the distribution of promotional materials by New England to Mr. Romano, upon which he relied in obtaining the insurance, will bar New England from asserting contrary provisions in the master policy.
>
> * * *
>
> It is useful to begin our analysis with a review of the relevant principles of insurance law. Group insurance has been defined as the coverage of several individual persons under one comprehensive insurance policy. Though typically group insurance

involves the employees of a single employer, it has been increasingly utilized among persons with other types of shared interests.

While group insureds are not policyholders and usually do not enjoy privity of contract with the insurer, it is recognized that they are beneficiaries of the insurance contract and may sue directly to enforce its provisions. Thus, ordinarily, the general rules which govern all contracts of insurance are held to apply as well to group contracts.

* * *

A number of courts have applied the doctrines of estoppel and waiver to prevent an insurer from invoking conditions or exclusions in a master policy where contrary information has been provided to and relied upon by the insured. . . . Where an insurer does not timely issue a certificate as required, it may be estopped to deny coverage based upon any such policy provisions. . . . This rule is bottomed on the recognition that insureds will ordinarily be privy to and rely upon the certificate rather than the master policy.

* * *

In *Lewis v. Continental Life & Accident Co.,* 461 P.2d 243 (Idaho 1969), an insurer under a group life policy provided to prospective insureds an "easy read" promotional handbook. The handbook stated that if the insured became totally disabled prior to age sixty, his insurance under the plan would continue without the payment of premiums. It also said that proof of disability would be required from the insured "from time to time." Upon the death of the insured, the insurer denied coverage based upon a more restrictive proof requirement contained in the master policy. The Idaho Supreme Court held, based upon the "composition and distribution" of the handbook, that the insurer was estopped to invoke the contrary master policy provisions.

The court commented:

"[The] handbook explained coverage under the program in clear, informal and easily read English. It was expected that employees would read and rely upon this booklet. And the company did or at least should have known that if an employee wished to determine what his coverage was he would turn to this pamphlet before the hard to decipher certificate of insurance or the master policy. . . ."

* * *

Other courts, applying a variant analysis, have held that representations contained in promotional materials must be looked to so as to construe the policy in accordance with the insured's reasonable expectations. *E.g., Sparks v. Republic National Life Ins. Co.,* 647 P.2d 1127, (Ariz. 1982). . . .

We approve of both the *Lewis* and *Sparks* decisions. They represent a growing trend in the law to give binding effect to sales and promotional materials provided to insureds by the insurer. We recognize, as have other jurisdictions, that lay insureds rely upon such materials as an authoritative summary of the requirements for eligibility and the coverages provided under the insurance plan.

Where a conflict exists between a master policy and other informational resources prepared and distributed at the insurer's behest, courts have not hesitated to hold that insureds are not bound by more restrictive provisions in the policy.

We, therefore, conclude that where an insurer provides sales or promotional materials to an insured under a group insurance policy, which the insurer knows or should know will be relied upon by the insured, any conflict between such materials and the master policy will be resolved in favor of the insured.

H. "Exclusion Clause Bars Insured's Claim"

1. "Business Liability Insurance Provision Excludes Claim"

Allstate Insurance Company v. Hallman
159 S.W.3d 640
(Tex. 2005)

In this case we must determine whether, under a homeowner's insurance policy's terms, an insurer has a duty to defend and indemnify an insured's potential liability for damages resulting from limestone mining operations conducted on the insured's property. Neighboring property owners sued Ruth Hallman (Hallman) for damages related to limestone mining on her property. Hallman sought coverage under her homeowner's insurance policy (the policy) with Allstate Insurance Company (Allstate), requesting that Allstate defend and indemnify her in the lawsuit.

Allstate and Hallman both sought a declaratory judgment to determine whether the policy covered the underlying litigation. The trial court granted summary judgment in Allstate's favor. The court of appeals reversed the trial court's judgment and remanded for further proceedings, holding that Allstate had a duty to defend and indemnify Hallman in the limestone mining litigation. Because we conclude that damages to third parties caused by commercial limestone mining conducted on an insured's property fall within the policy's business-pursuits exclusion, we reverse the court of appeals' judgment and render judgment for Allstate.

I

Background

In 1995, Hallman leased property she owns in rural Kaufman County to Norton Crushing, Inc. (Norton) for limestone mining. In 1996, neighboring landowners sued Hallman, Norton, and all subcontractors involved in the mining project, alleging that the blasting from the mining damaged their property and their health. Hallman filed a claim under the policy requesting defense and indemnification. Allstate agreed to defend Hallman under a reservation of rights but filed this declaratory judgment action seeking a determination that Hallman's claim was not covered under the policy's terms. Hallman counterclaimed seeking a declaration that Allstate had a duty to defend and indemnify her in the underlying litigation. Both parties sought attorney's fees.

Allstate moved for summary judgment, arguing that the injuries and damages relating to the limestone mining did not constitute an "occurrence" as required for coverage under the policy, and alternatively, that the mining operations were excepted from coverage under the policy's business pursuits exclusion. Hallman moved for partial summary judgment, asserting that she was entitled to a defense because her neighbors' allegations constituted an "occurrence" as defined in the policy. The trial court granted Allstate's motion, denied Hallman's, and denied both parties' requests for attorney's fees. The court of appeals reversed, concluding that the policy covered Hallman's claim because: 1) the mining damages constituted an "occurrence," and 2) the business pursuits exclusion did not apply. The court of appeals remanded the attorney's fees issue to the trial court for further proceedings. We granted Allstate's petition for review to determine whether the policy covers potential liability for damages from commercial limestone mining.

During oral argument before this Court, the parties announced that the underlying lawsuit between Hallman and her neighbors had recently concluded with a jury verdict in Hallman's favor. Allstate provided Hallman with a defense throughout the trial and does not intend to seek reimbursement for the defense costs.

II

Mootness

As a preliminary matter, we must consider whether the conclusion of the underlying litigation renders this case moot. The main issue here is whether Allstate has a duty to defend and indemnify Hallman in the mining litigation. Allstate, however, has already provided the requested defense, for which it will not seek reimbursement. Additionally, because Hallman was not found liable at trial, there is nothing for Allstate to indemnify. Nevertheless, both parties maintain that a justiciable controversy remains because Hallman continues to seek an award of attorney's fees for expenses incurred in defending against Allstate's declaratory judgment action and in pursuing her own declaratory relief.

We agree with the parties that this case is not moot. A case becomes moot if a controversy ceases to exist or the parties lack a legally cognizable interest in the outcome. *Bd. of Adjustment of San Antonio v. Wende,* 92 S.W.3d 424, 427 (Tex.2002). In *Camarena v. Texas Employment Commission,* 754 S.W.2d 149, 151 (Tex.1988), we held that a dispute over attorneys fees is a live controversy. In that declaratory judgment action, farm workers sued to challenge the constitutionality of the Texas Unemployment Compensation Act's (TUCA) agricultural exemption. The trial court held that the act was unconstitutional but found that sovereign immunity barred the farm workers' request for attorney's fees.

Four months later, the Legislature amended the TUCA, rectifying the offending provision. Consequently, the trial court modified its judgment, holding that the amended act was constitutional and enjoining the former act's enforcement. The Texas Employment Commission appealed, arguing that the amendment rendered the case moot. The farm workers cross-appealed, contesting the denial of attorney's fees. The court of appeals held that the case was moot and that attorney's fees were barred by sovereign immunity. We disagreed, holding:

> Clearly, a controversy exists between the farm workers and TEC. The "live" issue in controversy is whether or not the farm workers have a legally cognizable interest in recovering their attorney's fees and costs. The fact that the Legislature wisely undertook action to bring the farm workers within the scope of TUCA does not moot or void the workers' interest in obtaining attorneys fees and costs for the successful disposition of their claim. Contrary to the court of appeals' suggestion, the attorney's fees issue need not be severed in order to be considered; it is an integral part of the farm workers' claim and as such breathes life into the appeal. Due to the existence of the "live" issue of attorney's fees and costs, we hold that the suit was not moot.

Similarly, Hallman's remaining interest in obtaining attorney's fees "breathes life" into this appeal and prevents it from being moot. The parties correctly point out that in order to resolve the attorney's fees dispute, we must first determine whether Allstate had a duty to defend and indemnify under the policy. In a declaratory judgment proceeding, the trial court has the discretion to award "equitable and just" attorney's fees. Tex. Civ. Prac. & Rem.Code § 37.009. Here, the trial court, having found against Hallman on the coverage issue, also denied her request for attorney's fees. Because the court of appeals found that Hallman prevailed on the coverage issue, it remanded the attorney's fees question to the trial court.

Our decision in this case will resolve whether Allstate had a duty to defend. The controversy is live because an affirmative answer would necessitate a remand to the trial court to consider whether an award of attorney's fees is appropriate in light of the changed status of prevailing parties. Accordingly, we will address the merits of this coverage dispute.

III

Discussion

To determine an insurer's duty to defend, we look at the allegations in the pleadings and the insurance policy's language. *Nat'l Union Fire Ins. Co. of Pittsburgh, Pa. v. Merchs. Fast Motor Lines, Inc.,* 939 S.W.2d 139, 141 (Tex.1997); *Heyden Newport Chem. Corp. v. S. Gen. Ins. Co.,* 387 S.W.2d 22, 24 (Tex.1965). If the pleadings do not allege facts within the scope of the policy's coverage, an insurer does not have a duty to defend. *Am. Physicians Ins. Exch. v. Garcia,* 876 S.W.2d 842, 848 (Tex.1994). However, in the event of an ambiguity, we construe the pleadings liberally, resolving any doubt in favor of coverage.

Under the terms of the policy, Allstate has a duty to defend Hallman against a suit alleging damages caused by an "occurrence." However, the policy specifically excludes from coverage: "bodily injury or property damage arising out of or in connection with a business engaged in by an insured. But this exclusion does not apply to activities which are ordinarily incidental to non-business pursuits." "Business" is defined as "includ[ing] trade, profession or occupation." Allstate argues that Hallman's claim is barred from coverage under this business pursuits exclusion.

Although the business pursuits exclusion is a fairly common provision of insurance policies, we have never directly addressed its application. We have, however, addressed the "activities incidental to non-business pursuits" exception to the exclusion. *See State Farm Fire & Cas. Co. v. Reed,* 873 S.W.2d 698, 698-701 (Tex. 1993). The parties and the court of appeals relied on the standard set forth by the San Antonio Court of Appeals in *United Services Automobile Ass'n v. Pennington,* 810 S.W.2d 777, 778-80 (Tex.App.-San Antonio 1991, writ denied), a case involving a business pursuits exclusion provision substantially identical to the one here. The *Pennington* court, after reviewing the dictionary definitions of "trade," "profession," and "occupation," as well as case law from other jurisdictions, defined the "business pursuits" inquiry as involving two elements: "(1) continuity or regularity of the activity, and (2) a profit motive, usually as a means of livelihood, gainful employment, earning a living, procuring subsistence or financial gain, a commercial transaction or engagement." Regarding the second element, the court further noted: "The profit need not be realized-the issue is the expectation or anticipation for profit in the future-since often business ventures result in a loss."

Most jurisdictions follow similar versions of this two-part inquiry when construing business pursuits exclusions. A few jurisdictions, however, limit the exclusion's application to those activities that constitute an insured's principal occupation. Because the policy's definition of business — "including trade, profession or occupation" — encompasses more than an insured's primary occupation, we conclude that the majority approach more accurately describes the exclusion's parameters. Accordingly, we adopt the two-part standard articulated in *Pennington* for determining whether a claim is excluded from coverage under the business pursuits exclusion.

Applying the *Pennington* standard, the court of appeals concluded that the underlying petition did not allege continuity of activity because Hallman entered into only one lease agreement, which was executed nearly ten years ago. The court further noted the petition's failure to allege that Hallman leased her property as a means of livelihood, or earning a living, or that her principal business was leasing property. Based on these conclusions, the court of appeals held that the business pursuits exclusion did not apply to Hallman's claim.

We disagree. By narrowly limiting its focus to Hallman's initial execution of the lease, the court of appeals misconstrued the nature of commercial leasing activity. The pleadings establish that the mining activity conducted on Hallman's property pursuant to the lease began in 1995, was ongoing at the time the plaintiffs initiated their suit in 1996, and remained ongoing at the time the plaintiffs filed their sixth amended petition in 2001. Although Hallman executed only one lease, until that lease expires, she is perpetually engaged in the continuous act of leasing her property to the mining company. Thus, the limestone mining lease meets the continuity requirement of the business pursuits exclusion.

Next, we consider whether profit was Hallman's motivation for leasing her property. The court of appeals, noting that courts are limited to the language in the pleadings and the policy when determining an insurer's duty to defend, concluded that the lease failed to meet the profit motive requirement. Admittedly, the pleadings do not contain any reference to Hallman's pecuniary interest in the lease, nor do they expound on her motive for leasing her property. However, we conclude that, in this circumstance, a profit motive can be inferred from the nature of the activity. One generally does not allow limestone mining with dynamite blasting to occur on his or her property without some expectation of remuneration or monetary gain.

Furthermore, as numerous courts have recognized, the purpose of the business pursuits exclusion is to lower homeowners insurance premiums by removing coverage for activities that are not typically associated with the operation and maintenance of one's home. Commercial limestone mining is not an activity typically associated with owning and maintaining a home. Thus, the limestone mining lease at issue here is exactly the type of commercial enterprise that the business pursuits provision was designed to exclude.

We hold that Hallman's lease to Norton constituted a business pursuit and therefore the allegations in the underlying litigation are excluded from coverage under the policy.

IV

Conclusion

Therefore, even if the allegations in the underlying lawsuit state an "occurrence," — a question we do not reach — we nevertheless conclude that the business pursuits exclusion applies and bars coverage. Because the trial court reached the same conclusion and denied Hallman's request for fees, there is no need to remand this case to the trial court for a determination of Hallman's request for attorney's fees. Accordingly, we reverse the court of appeals' judgment and render judgment for Allstate.

NOTES & QUESTIONS

1) The Texas Supreme Court has repeatedly reminded lower courts to apply one of several doctrines to interpret clauses in insurance contracts. Again those doctrines are: the adhesion doctrine, the ambiguity doctrine, the reasonable-expectation doctrine, the four-corners doctrine, and the doctrine of plain meaning. Which doctrine(s) did the Texas Supreme Court apply in *Hallman* to interpret the terms in the business-pursuits exclusion clause?

2) In *Hallman*, the central question is whether the homeowner's insurer had a duty to defend the insured who was potentially liable for damages. Did the Texas Supreme Court apply the "eight-corners" doctrines to decide that question?

3) In *Hallman*, the Texas Supreme Court stated: "[C]ourts are limited to the language in the pleadings and the policy when determining an insurer's duty to defend. ... Admittedly, the pleadings do not contain any reference to Hallman's pecuniary interest in the lease ... [or to] her motive for leasing her property. However, we conclude that, in this circumstance, a profit motive can be inferred from the nature of the activity." Does that conclusion—which is based on an inference rather than facts in a pleading—undermine settled law in Texas?

2. "Automobile Insurance Exclusion Clause Bars Insured's Claim"

National County Mutual Fire Insurance Company v. Johnson
879 S.W.2d 1
(Tex.1993)

This cause involves the validity of a family-member exclusion in a Texas automobile liability policy. Randall Johnson filed a declaratory judgment to determine his rights under an automobile policy containing a family member exclusion. The issuer of the policy, National County Mutual Fire Insurance Company (National County), counterclaimed. The trial court held [that] the family member exclusion [was] invalid. The court of appeals affirmed. For the reasons explained herein, we affirm the judgment of the court of appeals.

While driving his truck, Johnson collided with another automobile. Johnson's wife, a passenger in the truck, was injured in the collision and later brought suit against her husband seeking compensation for her injuries. Johnson requested that National County unconditionally defend him in the suit and National County refused. Instead, National County contended that the family-member exclusion in the policy precluded coverage for the claim . . . and offered to defend Johnson subject to a reservation of its rights to deny coverage and payment of any judgment rendered against him.

Johnson filed a declaratory judgment to determine his rights under the policy and National County filed a counterclaim for declaratory relief asking the court to determine the validity of family member exclusion. The exclusion is known as "Endorsement 575" and provides "We do not provide Liability Coverage for you or any family member for bodily injury to you or any family member."

The trial court rendered judgment for Johnson holding the family member exclusion [was] invalid and [concluding that] National County [was] liable for Johnson's defense and coverage under the policy. The trial court [concluded that] the family member exclusion 1) conflicts with the Texas Motor Vehicle Safety Responsibility Act, 2) has no rational justification supporting its adoption by the State Board of Insurance, 3) contravenes the public policy of the state and, 4) fails to serve the interests of the people of Texas. The court of appeals affirmed the trial court's decision holding that the family member exclusion violated the Safety Responsibility Act's mandate requiring liability insurance for "all sums which the insured shall become legally obligated to pay."

I.

National County argues that the family member exclusion is a valid exclusion which is consistent with the public policy underlying the Texas Motor Vehicle Safety Responsibility Act. We disagree.

The Texas Motor Vehicle Safety Responsibility Act (the Act) originated in 1951 and was enacted for the benefit of "all citizens of this state." Amendments to the Act in 1982 effectively mandate automobile liability insurance by requiring "[p]roof of ability to respond in damages for liability, on account of accidents . . . arising out of the ownership, maintenance or use of a motor vehicle." In addition, the statute requires that no motor vehicle may be operated in this State unless a policy of automobile liability insurance in at least the minimum amounts to provide evidence of financial responsibility under this Act is in effect to insure against potential losses which may arise out of the operation of the vehicle. This section of the Act makes it clear that the legislature's purpose in amending the Act was to protect claimants from losses by requiring all drivers to be responsible for damages arising out of their use of an automobile.

This court has recognized that the public policy behind the Texas Motor Vehicle Safety Responsibility Act is to protect all potential claimants from damages resulting from automobile accidents.

There is no question in our minds that the compulsory insurance requirement of the Texas motor vehicle safety law implies that all potential claimants for damages resulting from automobile accidents are intended as beneficiaries of the statutorily required automobile liability coverage. *Dairyland County Mut. Ins. v. Childress*, 650 S.W.2d 770, 775 (Tex.1983).

We must consider whether the family-member exclusion is consistent with the legislative purpose of ensuring that every motor vehicle is covered by an automobile liability policy that will protect all claimants against losses which arise out of the operation of the vehicle. We hold that it is not.

"When the Legislature specifies a particular extent of insurance coverage any attempt to void or narrow such coverage is improper and ineffective." *Unigard Security Ins. Co. v. Schaefer*, 572

S.W.2d 303, 307 (Tex.1978). Actions by the State Board of Insurance must be consistent with, and in furtherance of, expressed statutory purposes. If the Board approves a clause which conflicts with the statute, the Board's approval is ineffective. *American Liberty Ins. Co. v. Ranzau*, 481 S.W.2d 793, 797 (Tex.1972); *Railroad Comm'n v. Lone Star Gas Co.*, 844 S.W.2d 679 (Tex.1992); *Gerst v. Oak Cliff Savings & Loan Ass'n*, 432 S.W.2d 702, 706 (Tex.1968) (the provisions of an agency's rules must be in harmony with the general provisions of the Act involved).

Here, the Board's approval of the family-member exclusion results in a situation in which a claimant for damages resulting from an automobile accident is not allowed to recover damages under an automobile liability insurance policy that the legislature statutorily requires to protect such claimants from losses. The exclusion prevents a specific class of innocent victims, those persons related to and living with the negligent driver, from receiving financial protection under an insurance policy. Such a result is clearly contrary to the express legislative mandate. See, *Whitworth v. Bynum*, 699 S.W.2d 194, 197 (Tex.1985) ("We refuse to indulge in the assumption that close relatives will prevaricate so as to promote a spurious lawsuit"). The Board's action in approving a family-member exclusion providing for such scenarios is inconsistent with the statutory purpose of the Act, and thus their approval of the exclusion is ineffective.

The majority of jurisdictions with mandatory insurance laws hold family member exclusions invalid because they are contrary to public policy. . . . We join those jurisdictions which reason that because the family-member exclusion violates public policy, the provision is completely void.

The family member exclusion makes drivers uninsured for claims against them by their own family members, despite the statutorily mandated requirement that all drivers carry liability insurance to "to respond in damages for liability on account of accidents" and "ensure against potential losses which may arise out of the operation of the vehicle." Thus, we hold that the family member exclusion is completely void because it conflicts with the Texas Motor Vehicle Safety-Responsibility Act as well as with the public policy underlying the Act. Accordingly, we affirm the judgment of the court of appeals.

NOTES & QUESTIONS

1) In *Johnson*, who was the plaintiff and what type of action did the plaintiff file in the trial court? What did the plaintiff want the court to declare? Did the court make a declaration?

2) In *Johnson*, the Texas Supreme Court abrogated the family-member exclusion clause. The court stated: "The question in this case is whether the family member exclusion is inconsistent with the stated policy in the statute that there be financial responsibility for the operation of a motor vehicle." Is that policy stated in the statute? Did the plaintiff ask the trial court to "abrogate" the family-member exclusion clause?

3) In *Johnson*, Justice Enoch wrote an arguably powerful and intelligent dissenting opinion. He wrote: "In this case there is no constitutional challenge … [to the Insurance Board's authority to] promulgate a family-member exclusion for automobile liability insurance policies." Is that correct? Again, why did the plaintiff in *Johnson* file the lawsuit: to interpret rights under the exclusion clause or to attack the constitutionality of the exclusion clause?

4) Does the majority's holding in *Johnson* apply to all family-member exclusion clauses in automobile and vehicle liability insurance contracts?

---

3. "Automobile Policy Excludes Family Member's Uninsured Vehicle"

Armendariz v. Progressive County Mutual Insurance Company
112 S.W.3d 736
(Tex.App.-Houston [14 Dist.] 2003)

Appellants, Alejandro and Alma Armendariz, appeal from cross-motions for summary judgment granted in favor of Progressive County Mutual Insurance Company, appellee. In two issues, they contend that Progressive owed Alma the duty to defend and indemnify her in a wrongful death lawsuit filed by Alma's mother. Finding that Progressive's insurance policy does not obligate it to defend or indemnify Alma, we affirm the trial court's judgment.

Background

The Progressive automobile insurance policy in this case covered two cars, one owned by Alejandro and the other owned by his sister, Alma. Alejandro was the named insured on the policy. Additionally, Alejandro's parents, who lived with him, and Alma were named as "listed drivers" on the policy. When Alejandro first purchased insurance from Progressive, the policy also covered his parents' van. However, Alejandro deleted the van from the policy because his parents wanted to sell it. Four months later, while driving her parents' then uninsured van, Alma accidently backed over and killed her father. Alma's mother then sued Alma for the father's wrongful death.

Contending that the van was not a covered auto and Alma was not an insured, Progressive filed a declaratory judgment action to determine whether it owed a duty to defend and indemnify Alma in the underlying wrongful death suit. It sought summary judgment based on exclusionary language in the policy as follows:

> We do not provide liability coverage for the ownership, maintenance, or use of any vehicle other than your covered auto which is owned by a family member or furnished or available for the regular use of any family member.

The Armendarizes filed a cross-motion for summary judgment. The trial court granted summary judgment to Progressive and denied the Armendarizes' motion. In two issues, the Armendarizes appeal the trial court's denial of their summary judgment motion and the summary judgment granted to Progressive.

* * *

Analysis

The Armendarizes contend that the exclusion at issue violates public policy and the Texas Motor Vehicle Safety Responsibility Act. There are two pertinent portions of the Progressive policy in this case. The first is the exclusion at issue:

> We do not provide Liability Coverage for the ownership, maintenance or use of. . . Any vehicle, other than your covered auto, which is . . . a) owned by any family member, or b) furnished or available for the regular use of any family member. . . . However, this exclusion does not apply to [the insured's] maintenance or use of any vehicle which is . . . owned by a family member.

The second pertinent portion of the policy is the definition of "family member" — "a person who is a resident of [the insured's] household and related to [the insured] by blood, marriage or adoption." In this case, Alejandro's parents, who lived with him, owned the van. Further, the van was no longer a covered auto under the policy. Lastly, Alma was not an insured under the Progressive policy, but merely a listed driver for the two covered autos. Because Alma caused the accident while driving her father's uninsured van, the exclusion, if valid, precludes liability coverage.

The Armendarizes argue that Alma was clearly a "covered person" in the Progressive policy, although she was not the named insured. However, even if she were a covered person, the exclusion would still preclude liability coverage because the uninsured van belonged to a family member.

The Armendarizes argue that the exclusion in this case is akin to the invalid "family member exclusion." *See Nat'l County Mut. Fire Ins. Co. v. Johnson,* 879 S.W.2d 1, 5 (Tex.1993).

> The family member exclusion, also called Endorsement 575, reads, "We do not provide Liability Coverage for you or any family member for bodily injury to you or any family member." The family member exclusion is invalid because it conflicts with Texas's public policy to ensure "that every motor vehicle is covered by an automobile policy that will protect all claimants against losses which arise out of the operation of the vehicle." The family member exclusion runs afoul of this purpose because it makes otherwise-insured drivers uninsured for claims against them by innocent family members. (Paraphrasing the court's decision in *Johnson*)

Thus, the Armendarizes analogize that the exclusion in this case precludes coverage simply because a family member was the victim of Alma's accident.

However, there was no liability coverage here because the family member's vehicle was uninsured, not because a family member was the injured claimant. Even if an unrelated third party had been struck by the van, the exclusion would still apply because the van was owned by a family member but was uninsured. Several courts have considered similar "owned-but-uninsured" exclusions, and, in each case, the exclusion has been found valid. The reasoning for this line of cases is succinctly set forth in *Holyfield v. Members Mut. Ins. Co.,* 566 S.W.2d 28, 29 (Tex.Civ.App.-Dallas 1978), *writ ref'd n.r.e.,* 572 S.W.2d 672 (Tex.1978) (per curiam) (PIP).

In *Holyfield,* the insured argued that an owned-but-unscheduled-vehicle exclusion restricted the breadth of coverage required by Texas statute. The court disagreed, reasoning that "[a]n insurer is entitled to accurately reflect in the policy the risks being insured and to charge premiums based upon those risks." The Armendarizes' contention would permit an insured and family members, who own more than one vehicle, to obtain insurance and pay premiums "based solely on the risk attendant to one vehicle, and thereby render the insurer liable for injuries sustained in or because of other vehicles owned" by them.

The summary judgment evidence bolsters this reasoning: it reflects that when Alejandro deleted the van's coverage, he received a $361.00 decrease in the cost of the policy. Simply, "the public policy of this state . . . does not require that a person be allowed to insure and pay premiums based solely on the risks attendant to one vehicle, and then recover from the insurer for injuries sustained in or because of a different, unscheduled vehicle owned by the insured or a family member."

Our decision in this case is consistent with the interpretation of owned-but-uninsured exclusionary language in other states.

Accordingly, we hold that Alma was not entitled to liability coverage under the Progressive policy for an accident occurring while she drove an unscheduled van owned by the named insured's family member. Because the trial court correctly granted Progressive's motion for summary judgment and denied the Armendarizes' motion, we affirm the trial court's judgment.

NOTES & QUESTIONS

1) In *Johnson*, the family-member exclusion clause reads:

> "We do not provide liability coverage for you or any family member for bodily injury to you or any family member."

And in *Armendariz*, the family-member exclusion states:

> "We do not provide liability coverage for the ownership, maintenance, or use of any vehicle other than your covered auto which is owned by a family member or furnished or available for the regular use of any family member.."

Can the two exclusion clauses be harmonized? Does one exclude "property losses" and the other excludes "personal injuries"?

2) What would be the ordinary, reasonable consumer's understanding and definition of "use" as that term appears in the *Armendariz* exclusion clause?

3) May a reasonable interpretation of the phrase, "available for the regular use of any family" in the *Armendariz* exclusion clause bar "bodily injury to you or any family member," which appears in the *Johnson* case?

I. "Insured Breached the Notice Requirement"

"Claims-made policy" and "occurrence policy": These terms appear in cases throughout this text. Put briefly, they are names for various types of property and liability insurance contracts. Typically, an occurrence-based policy covers all claims *based on an event occurring during the policy period*, regardless of whether the claim or occurrence is brought to the attention of the insured or made known to the insurer during the policy period. See *Am. Physicians Ins. Exch. v. Garcia*, 876 S.W.2d 842, 844 n. 4 (Tex.1994). In contrast, a claims-made policy covers *only claims made during the policy period* for injuries or occurrences within a coverage period. *Garcia*, 876 S.W.2d at 844 n. 3.

From an insurer's perspective, the differences between a claims-made and an occurrence-based insurance contract are stark and significant in many ways. In particular, the notice-of-loss requirements and their respective effects are vastly different under the two types of insurance contracts. For example, "the notice requirements in claims-made policies allow the insurer to 'close its books' on a policy at its expiration and thus to 'attain a level of predictability unattainable under standard occurrence policies.'" See *F.D.I.C. v. Mijalis*, 15 F.3d 1314, 1330 (5th Cir. 1994), quoting *Burns v. Int'l Ins. Co.*, 709 F.Supp. 187, 191 (N.D.Cal.1989), aff'd, 929 F.2d 1422 (9th Cir. 1991).

In addition, some claims-made or claims-made-and-reported policies require insureds to report claim within the policy period *and* within a specific number of days after a loss. However, most occurrence-based and claims-made insurance contracts require insureds to notify the insurers "promptly" or "as soon as practicable" to keep from "prejudicing the insurers' interests" in the wake of a property loss or personal injury.

Of course, whether insureds must always report a loss "as soon as practicable" has generated a considerable amount of interest and litigation in Texas. Also, some insureds do not notify their insurers promptly, as required under both claims-made and occurrence-based policies. Thus, whether that failure prejudices insurers' interests has generated an appreciable amount of controversy, too. In recent years, the Texas Supreme Court has issued a slew of notice-of-loss decisions. From the viewpoint of insurers and the defense bar, some decisions are more sound and reliable than others. Some of the most controversial notice-of-loss decisions and questions appear in this section.

1. "Insured's No-Consent Settlement Prejudiced Insurer's Interests"

Hernandez v. Gulf Group Lloyds
875 S.W.2d 691
(Tex.1994)

In this cause, we consider whether an insurer may deny an uninsured/underinsured motorist claim on the basis of a "settlement without consent" exclusion clause absent any showing that the settlement prejudiced the insurer. The trial court rendered judgment in favor of the insureds. The court of appeals reversed, reasoning that the insureds had violated their insurance contract by settling with the underinsured motorist without the insurer's consent. We hold that an insurer may escape liability on the basis of a settlement-without-consent exclusion only when the insurer is actually prejudiced by the insured's settlement with the tortfeasor.

This case was tried on the following stipulated facts. On November 21, 1987, Elizabeth Hernandez was killed when the car in which she was a passenger flipped over. The sole proximate cause of the accident was the negligence of the driver of the car, Charles McCullough, Jr. At the time of the accident, McCullough was nineteen years old and his only asset was a $25,000 liability policy with State Farm Mutual Automobile Insurance Company. Elizabeth Hernandez was covered by her parents' insurance policy with Gulf Group Lloyds. That policy included uninsured/underinsured motorist coverage in the amount of $100,000. The damages suffered by Elizabeth Hernandez and her parents exceeded $125,000.

Six weeks after the accident, the Hernandezes, without the consent of Gulf, entered into a settlement with McCullough for the limits of McCullough's State Farm policy. On March 30, 1990, the Hernandezes sought to recover from Gulf under the underinsured motorist coverage. Gulf denied coverage based upon the Hernandezes' failure to obtain its consent before settling with McCullough.

The insurance contract between the Hernandezes and Gulf Group Lloyds contained the following settlement-without-consent clause:

> This insurance does not apply . . . a) to bodily injury or property damage with respect to which the insured, his legal representative or any person entitled to payment under this insurance shall, without written consent of the company, make any settlement with any person or organization who may be legally liable therefor[.]

After a bench trial, the trial court rendered judgment for the Hernandezes in the amount of $100,000 (the amount of the underinsured motorist policy), plus pre-judgment interest, post-judgment interest, and attorney's fees. In its conclusions of law, the trial court stated that Gulf had suffered no material prejudice because of the Hernandezes' failure to comply with the settlement-without-consent exclusion, and that invocation of the exclusion would deprive the Hernandezes of protection required by the Texas Uninsured/Underinsured Motorist Statute, Tex. Ins. Code Ann. art. 5.06-1. The court of appeals disagreed with the latter conclusion, and thus reversed the trial court's judgment and rendered a take-nothing judgment against the Hernandezes.

The Hernandezes do not dispute the validity of settlement-without-consent exclusions. *See Guaranty County Mut. Ins. Co. v. Kline,* 845 S.W.2d 810 (Tex.1992). They argue, however, that such an exclusion is unenforceable absent a showing by the insurer that it has been prejudiced by an insured's failure to obtain consent before settling with an uninsured or underinsured motorist. We agree.

Insurance policies are contracts, and as such are subject to rules applicable to contracts generally. *See Barnett v. Aetna Life Ins. Co.,* 723 S.W.2d 663, 665 (Tex.1987); *First Texas Prudential Ins. Co. v. Ryan,* 82 S.W.2d 635, 637 (Tex. 1935). A fundamental principle of contract law is that when one party to a contract commits a material breach of that contract, the other party is discharged or excused from any obligation to perform. *See Jack v. State,* 694 S.W.2d 391, 398-99 (Tex.App.-San Antonio 1985, writ ref'd n.r.e.) (citing *Mead v. Johnson Group, Inc.,* 615 S.W.2d 685, 689 (Tex.1981)).

In determining the materiality of a breach, courts will consider, among other things, the extent to which the nonbreaching party will be deprived of the benefit that it could have reasonably anticipated from full performance.[1] The less the non-breaching party is deprived of the expected benefit, the less material the breach.

In the context of an underinsured motorist claim, there may be instances when an insured's settlement without the insurer's consent prevents the insurer from receiving the anticipated benefit from the insurance contract; specifically, the settlement may extinguish a valuable subrogation right. *Cf. Liberty Mut. Ins. Co. v. Cruz,* (Tex.1994) (insured's failure to provide notice of suit prejudiced insurer as a matter of law). In other instances, however, the insurer may not be deprived of the contract's expected benefit, because any extinguished subrogation right has no value. In the latter situation — where the insurer is not prejudiced by the settlement — the insured's breach is not material.

---

1 The other factors courts consider in determining the materiality of a breach are: (i) the extent to which the injured party can be adequately compensated for the part of that benefit of which he will be deprived; (ii) the extent to which the party failing to perform or to offer to perform will suffer forfeiture; (iii) the likelihood that the party failing to perform or to offer to perform will cure his failure, taking account of all the circumstances including any reasonable assurances; (iv) the extent to which the behavior of the party failing to perform or to offer to perform comports with standards of good faith and fair dealing. RESTATEMENT (SECOND) OF CONTRACTS § 241 (1981).

We conclude, therefore, that an insurer who is not prejudiced by an insured's settlement may not deny coverage under an uninsured/underinsured motorist policy that contains a settlement-without-consent clause.

Applying this materiality principle to the facts of this case, we conclude that the Hernandezes' failure to obtain Gulf's consent before settling with McCullough was not a material breach. Gulf stipulated that it knew of no case in which it has refused its consent to settle a claim when an underinsured driver has tendered the full limits of his or her policy. The parties stipulated that McCullough had no assets other than the $25,000 State Farm policy, and that he did not believe his financial situation would change in the foreseeable future; and Gulf further stipulated that it "has not incurred any financial losses . . . with regard to its subrogation rights by the failure of the [Hernandezes] to obtain [its] consent before settling with McCullough and releasing him from all liability." Gulf, therefore, remains in the same position it would have occupied had the Hernandezes complied with the settlement-without-consent clause. Since Gulf has not been prejudiced by the Hernandezes' breach, the breach is not material, and Gulf therefore is not excused from its obligation to perform under the contract.

Because the stipulated facts establish as a matter of law that Gulf was not prejudiced by the Hernandezes' settlement with McCullough, Gulf may not escape liability by invoking the settlement-without-consent exclusion. We therefore reverse the judgment of the court of appeals and affirm the trial court's judgment in favor of the Hernandezes.

NOTES & QUESTIONS

1) Again, insurers have the absolute right to settle third-party suits. However, in *Hernandez*, the Texas Supreme Court concluded that the insurer's interests were not prejudiced when the insured did not notify Gulf or secure the insurer's consent. Did the Texas Supreme Court clearly outline the parameters of the "prejudice" test that it applied in *Hernandez*?

2) What is the test for determining "prejudice"? Is it a "subjective" standard or an "objective" standard?

3) Do you see any problems that the *Hernandez* court overlooked or did not anticipate?

2. "Insured Breached Notice Requirement Under an Occurrence Policy"

PAJ, Inc. v. The Hanover Insurance Company
243 S.W.3d 630
(Tex. 2008)

In this case, we must decide whether an insured's failure to timely notify its insurer of a claim defeats coverage under the policy if the insurer was not prejudiced by the delay. We hold, as we did in *Hernandez v. Gulf Group Lloyds,* that an immaterial breach does not deprive the insurer of the benefit of the bargain and thus cannot relieve the insurer of the contractual coverage obligation. Accordingly, we reverse the court of appeals' judgment, render judgment that the insurer could not deny coverage because of untimely notice, and remand the remaining issues to the trial court.

I.

PAJ, Inc., a jewelry manufacturer and distributor, purchased a commercial general liability (CGL) policy from Hanover Insurance Company that covered, among other things, liability for advertising injury. The policy required PAJ to notify Hanover of any claim or suit brought against PAJ "as soon as practicable." In 1998, Yurman Designs, Inc. demanded that PAJ cease marketing a particular jewelry line, and a month later sued PAJ for copyright infringement. Initially unaware that the CGL policy covered the dispute, PAJ did not notify Hanover of the suit until four to six months after litigation commenced.

PAJ brought this suit against Hanover seeking a declaration that Hanover was contractually obligated to defend and indemnify PAJ in the copyright suit, and asserting several extracontractual claims. The parties stipulated that PAJ failed to notify Hanover of the Yurman claim "as soon as practicable" and that Hanover was not prejudiced by the untimely notice. Both parties moved for summary judgment on the notice issue based on these undisputed facts. The trial court granted Hanover's motion and denied PAJ's, holding that Hanover was not required to demonstrate prejudice to avoid coverage under the policy. The court of appeals affirmed. We granted PAJ's petition for review to determine the effect on coverage when an insured fails to timely notify its insurer of a claim but the insurer suffers no harm as a result.

II.

The Hanover policies issued to PAJ provide coverage for "advertising injury," which the policy defines to include injury arising out of copyright infringement. The policy contains a prompt-notice provision that requires PAJ to notify Hanover of an occurrence or an offense that may result in a claim "as soon as practicable." The parties dispute whether the policy's prompt-notice requirement constitutes a condition precedent or merely a covenant. Hanover contends the policy language creates a condition precedent, the failure of which defeats coverage under the policy irrespective of prejudice to the insurer. *See Hohenberg Bros. Co. v. George E. Gibbons & Co.,* 537 S.W.2d 1, 3 (Tex.1976).

PAJ, on the other hand, contends the prompt-notice language creates a covenant, the breach of which excuses performance only if the breach is "material." *See Centex Corp. v. Dalton,* 840 S.W.2d 952, 956 (Tex.1992). PAJ further asserts that even if the policy language creates a condition precedent to coverage, Texas law nonetheless requires an insurer to demonstrate prejudice before it may avoid coverage based on untimely notice. We agree with PAJ that only a material breach of the timely notice provision will excuse Hanover's performance under the policy.

III.

Hanover pins its analysis on our decision in *Members Mutual Insurance Co. v. Cutaia,* 476 S.W.2d 278 (Tex.1972), and that is where we will begin. The policy at issue in *Cutaia* required the insured to forward any suit papers immediately to the insurer and provided that "no action shall lie against the [insurer] unless, *as a condition precedent thereto,* there shall have been full compliance with all of the terms of this policy. The insured failed to forward the suit papers to his insurer until five months after the occurrence in question.

Stipulating that it had suffered no harm, the insurer denied liability, contending a condition precedent to coverage had not been met. We agreed that the insured's failure to timely comply with the policy's forwarding condition precluded the insurer's liability whether or not prejudice resulted. But we emphasized "the apparent injustice which results in this particular case," and deferred consideration of the issue to the State Board of Insurance or the Legislature. *Id.*

The State Board of Insurance responded the very next year by issuing Board Order 23080, which requires a mandatory endorsement to all Texas CGL policies that precludes forfeiture of coverage for an insured's failure to comply with notice or forwarding conditions unless the insurer is prejudiced thereby. The endorsement provides:

> As respects bodily injury liability coverage and property damage liability coverage, unless the company is prejudiced by the insured's failure to comply with the requirement, any provision of this policy requiring the insured to give notice of action, occurrence or loss, or requiring the insured to forward demands, notices, summons or other legal process, shall not bar liability under this policy.

It is important to note that, at the time the State Board of Insurance created this endorsement, there was no standard coverage for advertising injury.

Two decades after Board Order 23080 became effective, we decided *Hernandez.* There, the insured sought recovery under the uninsured/underinsured motorist provision of an automobile policy. The insurer denied liability because the insured had settled the underlying claim without the insurer's consent in violation of the policy's "settlement without consent" exclusion. Applying "fundamental principle[s] of contract law," we held that when one party to a contract commits a material breach, the other party's performance is excused. In determining the materiality of a breach, we said, courts must consider, among other things, "the extent to which the nonbreaching party will be deprived of the benefit that it could have reasonably anticipated from full performance."

Without distinguishing between covenants and conditions or classifying the exclusion as one or the other, we concluded that the insured's breach of the settlement-without-consent provision was immaterial and thus the insurer could not avoid liability under the policy. Notably, we recognized that "[m]ost other jurisdictions presented with this issue have likewise imposed a prejudice requirement, primarily on public policy grounds."

* * *

The dissent today attempts to distinguish *Hernandez* by characterizing the settlement-without-consent clause at issue in that case as a covenant rather than a condition, even though in *Hernandez* we made no distinction between the two. They arrive at that conclusion only through reasoning, backwards, that because we required a showing of prejudice in *Hernandez,* the policy language at issue must have been a covenant. In truth, the policy language we construed in *Hernandez* is indistinguishable from that presented here. As under PAJ's policy, the language before the Court in *Hernandez* provided:

> This insurance *does not apply:* a) to bodily injury or property damage with respect to which the insured, ... without written consent of the company, makes any settlement with any person ... who may be legally liable therefor.

The dissenting justice in *Hernandez,* like the dissenting justices today, saw this language as rather clearly indicating a condition to coverage. ("[T]his case is not about a breach of contract. This case is about coverage."). Nevertheless, we made no distinction between the two in deciding that the insurer had to show prejudice before it could avoid its coverage obligation.

The fact that *Hernandez* involved a policy exclusion rather than a policy provision does not supply a valid ground for distinguishing its application here. Exclusions and conditions are in effect two sides of the same coin; exclusions avoid coverage *if* the insured does something, and conditions avoid coverage *unless* an insured does something. The dissent's construction would have the absurd consequence that identical policy language creates a condition precedent as to one type of coverage (advertising injury) but a covenant as to the other (bodily injury and property damage). We have said unequivocally that "when a condition would impose an absurd or impossible result, the agreement will be interpreted as creating a covenant rather than a condition." *Criswell v. European Crossroads Shopping Ctr., Ltd.,* 792 S.W.2d 945, 948 (Tex.1990).

Moreover, we question the dissent's fundamental premise that the timely notice provision before us creates a condition precedent rather than a covenant. The policy language in *Cutaia* specifically provided that "no action shall lie against the company unless, *as a condition precedent thereto,* the insured shall have fully complied with all the terms of this policy." The "as a condition precedent" language was deleted from the standard CGL policy following our decision in *Cutaia,* and it does not appear in PAJ's policy.

* * *

In addition, the timely notice provision was not an essential part of the bargained-for exchange under PAJ's occurrence-based policy. The Fifth Circuit, applying Texas insurance law, aptly describes the critical distinction between "occurrence" polices and "claims-made" policies as follows:

> In the case of an "occurrence" policy, any notice requirement is subsidiary to the event that triggers coverage. Courts have not permitted insurance companies to deny coverage on the basis of untimely notice under an "occurrence" policy unless the company shows actual prejudice from the delay.

Matador Petroleum Corp. v. St. Paul Surplus Lines Ins. Co., 174 F.3d 653, 658 (5th Cir.1999) The dissent, by focusing on the type of coverage rather than the type of *policy,* entirely disregards this important distinction.

Finally, and perhaps most disturbingly, the dissent's analysis of the policy language would impose draconian consequences for even *de minimis* deviations from the duties the policy places on insureds. The policy in this case requires, in the same section at issue, not only notice of suit "as soon as practicable," but also that PAJ "immediately send . . . copies of any demands, summonses or legal papers." Thus, under the dissent's construction, an insured's failure to promptly forward a deposition notice or a certificate of conference would work a forfeiture of coverage, even when the insurer is not at all harmed. This is precisely the result that Board Order 23080 attempted to avoid and we rejected in *Hernandez.*

* * *

We hold that an insured's failure to timely notify its insurer of a claim or suit does not defeat coverage if the insurer was not prejudiced by the delay. Accordingly, we reverse the court of appeals' judgment, render judgment that the insurer could not deny coverage because of untimely notice, and remand the remaining issues to the trial court.

NOTES & QUESTIONS

1) Breach of a settlement-without-consent exclusion, breach of a condition precedent, breach of a covenant, and breach of a prompt notice requirement: What are the distinguishing characteristics of each breach?

2) In *PAJ,* the insured—PAJ—argued that under *Hernandez v. Gulf Group Lloyd's* and *Harwell v. State Farm Mutual Automobile Insurance Co.,* the policy's notice provisions are covenants rather than "conditions precedent to coverage." Therefore, Hanover had to demonstrate prejudice before denying coverage for untimely notice. Do you agree?

3) Why would an insurer want an insured to give notice of a loss "as soon as practicable" under an occurrence-based insurance contract? Are there real and serious disadvantages for an insurer if an insured does not give prompt notice under an occurrence policy?

3. "The Additional Insured Failed to Notify Promptly"

National Union Fire Insurance Company of Pittsburgh, Pa., v. Crocker
246 S.W.3d 603
(Tex. 2008)

This insurance-coverage case comes to us on certified questions from the United States Court of Appeals for the Fifth Circuit. The principal issue is whether an insurer has a duty to notify an additional insured of available liability coverage. On the facts presented, we conclude that Texas law imposes no such extra-contractual duty. We further hold that an insurer's actual knowledge that an additional insured has been served with process does not establish as a matter of law that the insurer has not been prejudiced by the additional insured's failure to notify the insurer of the receipt of process.

I. Background

Beatrice Crocker was a resident of Redwood Springs Nursing Home, which is owned by Emeritus Corporation. She filed suit in state court against Emeritus and Richard Morris, a nursing home employee, seeking compensation for injuries suffered when she was hit by a door swung open by Morris. Crocker's claims against Emeritus were covered by a commercial general liability policy issued by National Union Fire Insurance Company of Pittsburgh, because Morris was acting within the course and scope of his. The policy provides:

You or your means the individual, partnership, or corporation designated as Named Insured in Item 1 of the Declarations, including any present or former employee . . . solely while acting in his or her capacity as such.

When the accident occurred, he qualified as an additional insured under the policy. National Union defended Emeritus, the named insured, but did not defend Morris even though the claims against him were covered by the policy and National Union knew he was a named defendant that had been served. As the Fifth Circuit points out, "Morris was not aware of the terms and conditions of the Emeritus policy [and] did not know that he was an additional insured under the policy." National Union did not inform Morris that he was an insured, nor did it offer to defend him.

Morris was served, but he "did not forward the suit papers to National Union or otherwise inform it that he had been sued, and did not request a defense from either National Union or Emeritus." Morris never answered the suit and did not appear at trial. National Union attempted to contact Morris about Crocker's claims, both before and after Crocker filed her lawsuit, but to no avail-the certified mail was returned, and the repeated phone messages were not returned. Morris spoke privately with Crocker's attorney at a deposition, but Morris refused to speak in private with Emeritus's counsel.

After the evidence was presented, the state trial court granted Crocker's motion to sever the claims against Morris. The claims against Emeritus were submitted to the jury, which returned a take-nothing verdict, finding that Emeritus, acting "by and through its agents acting within the course and scope of their employment," including Morris, was not negligent. A few days later, however, the trial court entered a $1 million default judgment against Morris on the severed claims.

Crocker sued National Union to collect the judgment, asserting she was a third-party beneficiary to the policy. National Union removed the case to federal court, and both parties moved for summary judgment. National Union argued that Morris never triggered the duty to defend because he failed to forward the suit papers or otherwise notify National Union that he had been sued and he did not ask National Union to provide a defense. The policy provides:

> Before coverage will apply, you must notify us as soon as possible of an occurrence or offense which may result in a claim or suit against you. Notice should include: How, when and where the occurrence or offense took place; Names and addresses of any witnesses and injured people; Nature and location of any injury or damage.
>
> Before coverage will apply, you must notify us in writing of any claim or suit against you as soon as possible. You must: immediately record the specifics of the claim and the date you received it; send us copies of all demands, suit papers or other legal documents you receive, as soon as possible.

National Union contends that, because Morris failed to comply with the notice provisions, he did not invoke coverage or the right to a defense under the policy, meaning that Crocker, who now purports to stand in Morris's shoes, cannot collect under the policy either.

Crocker responds that even though Morris did not comply with the notice-of-suit provision, National Union had actual knowledge of Crocker's suit, and hence was not prejudiced by Morris's failure to forward the suit papers. Crocker contends that National Union's actual knowledge of the suit coupled with its failure to notify Morris that he was covered amounted to a breach of its duty to defend Morris, thus making National Union liable to Crocker for the full $1 million default judgment.

The federal district court agreed with Crocker, concluding that Texas law required National Union to show prejudice in order to establish a notice-based policy defense. The court also found that National Union breached a duty to defend Morris by failing to notify Morris that it would defend him. Therefore, the court granted summary judgment in favor of Crocker and awarded her $1 million. National Union appealed to the Fifth Circuit, which certified three questions to us.

II. Discussion

A. First Certified Question

The Fifth Circuit first asks:

> Where an additional insured does not and cannot be presumed to know of coverage under an insurer's liability policy, does an insurer —that has knowledge that a suit implicating policy coverage has been filed against its additional insured — have a duty to inform the additional insured of the available coverage?

We answer the question, no. Insurance policies are written contracts, and, as with other contracts, we interpret and enforce them according to settled rules of construction. *Am. Mfrs. Mut. Ins. Co. v. Schaefer,* 124 S.W.3d 154, 157 (Tex.2003). Most importantly, we must give the policy's words their plain meaning, *Puckett v. U.S. Fire Ins.* Co., 678 S.W.2d 936, 938 (Tex.1984) — without inserting additional provisions into the contract. *See Fortis Benefits v. Cantu,* 234 S.W.3d 642, 649 (Tex.2007).

Our 1978 decision in *Weaver v. Hartford Accident & Indemnity Co.* 570 S.W.2d 367 (Tex.1978) governs today's case. In *Weaver,* we held that an insurer was not liable to an additional insured's judgment creditor when the additional insured failed to notify the insurer that he had been served with process, even though the insurer knew about the suit, and the additional insured knew nothing about the policy. Weaver sued Hartford, an insurer, to recover under an automobile liability policy on the basis of a default judgment obtained against an additional insured. Hartford had issued the policy naming J.C. Thomas Enterprises as the insured. The policy defined "insured" to include any person using a vehicle owned by Thomas Enterprises with its permission. One of Thomas Enterprises's employees, while driving a company vehicle, had an accident with Weaver.

Weaver sued the employee and later added Thomas Enterprises as a co-defendant. Thomas Enterprises notified its insurer of the suit, and an answer was filed on its behalf, denying that the employee had permission to use the vehicle. During the insurer's investigation of the accident, the employee told the insurer that he did not have permission to use the vehicle at the time of the accident. He also acknowledged that he never notified Hartford of the lawsuit, filed an answer, or had an answer filed on his behalf. Weaver nonsuited Thomas Enterprises and was granted a default judgment against the employee.

After winning the judgment, Weaver sued Hartford to collect under the policy as a third-party beneficiary, alleging that Thomas Enterprises gave its employee permission to drive the vehicle. Despite the employee's previous statement that he did not have permission to drive the vehicle, the jury found that he was an additional insured. The policy provided that an insured's failure to forward suit papers to Hartford relieved it of any liability to an injured third party, but the trial court entered judgment in favor of Weaver.

On appeal, we held that the liability insurer had no duty to volunteer to defend the additional insured We noted that one purpose served by the insured's obligation to forward suit papers "is to enable the insurer to control the litigation and interpose a defense." We emphasized, however, that "a more basic purpose is to advise the insurer that an insured has been served with process and that the insurer is expected to timely file an answer." Under *Weaver,* an insurer's knowledge that a suit has been filed against an additional insured does not satisfy this "more basic purpose" or require the insurer to "gratuitously subject[ ] itself to liability." The insured's ignorance of any rights or obligations under the policy did not affect our analysis in that case. Put simply, there is no duty to provide a defense absent a request for coverage.

The similarities between this case and *Weaver* abound. First, both Morris and the employee in *Weaver* were additional insureds under the liability policies at issue. Second, the injured party in each case sued both the named insured and the additional insured but did not recover anything from the named insured. Third, both additional insureds failed to forward suit papers to the insurers, so neither was defended by the insurer. Fourth, both additional insureds lacked knowledge of the existence of the employers' liability policies and the notice-of-suit provisions. Fifth, both insurers argued that they had no duty to inform the additional insured of the possibility of coverage. While in *Weaver* we did not directly address the additional insured's ignorance of the policy, we nevertheless held that the insurer had no duty to inject itself gratuitously into a lawsuit by defending an additional insured who had not requested a defense and who failed to comply with the policy's forwarding conditions.

We unanimously reaffirmed this holding several years later in *Harwell v. State Farm Mutual Automobile Insurance Co.,* 896 S.W.2d 170, 172, 174 (Tex.1995) where we said that the insurer did not have to "gratuitously subject[ ] itself to liability," until Harwell, the administrator of the estate of an additional insured, fulfilled her duty to notify the insurer of service of the suit against her. We confirmed that *Weaver* remained the governing law and reaffirmed that "[o]ne of the purposes of a notice of suit provision in an insurance policy is to notify the insurer that the insured has been served with process and that the insurer is expected to defend the suit."

Both *Weaver* and *Harwell* turn on the recognition that notice and delivery-of-suit-papers provisions in insurance policies serve two essential purposes: (1) they facilitate a timely and effective defense of the claim against the insured, and more fundamentally, (2) they trigger the insurer's duty to defend by notifying the insurer that a defense is expected. Mere awareness of a claim or suit does not impose a duty on the insurer to defend under the policy; there is no unilateral duty to act unless and until the additional insured first *requests* a defense-a threshold duty that the insured fulfills under the policy by notifying the insurer that the insured has been served with process and the insurer is expected to answer on its behalf.

In both cases, we declined to subject the insurer to liability for failing to perform " 'the sentry duty of tracking back and forth to the court house to keep a check on if or when ... [the insured] may be served with process.' " Of course, an insurer that is aware an additional insured has been sued may, and perhaps should, choose to inform the insured that a defense is available; in this case, had National Union done so, a judgment against Morris and years of subsequent litigation would have been avoided. But an insurer that has not been notified that a defense is expected bears no extra-contractual duty to provide notice that a defense is available to an additional insured who has not requested one. The answer to the first certified question is, therefore, no.

B. Third Certified Question

* * *

The Fifth Circuit's third certified question asks us:

> Does proof of an insurer's actual knowledge of service of process in a suit against its additional insured, when such knowledge is obtained in sufficient time to provide a defense for the insured, establish as a matter of law the absence of prejudice to the insurer from the additional insured's failure to comply with the notice-of-suit provisions of the policy?

We also answer this question, no.

National Union was obviously prejudiced in the sense that it was exposed to a $1 million judgment. The question, however, is not whether National Union suffered exposure to a financial risk, but whether it should be estopped to deny coverage because it was aware that Morris had been sued and served and had ample time to defend him. The answer must be "no" based on the discussion above — National Union had no duty to notify Morris of coverage and no duty to defend Morris until Morris notified National Union that he had been served with process and expected National Union to answer on his behalf. "Because [National Union] was not under a duty to defend the suit against its insured when [it received notice of the claim], it is not estopped from asserting [the insured's] breach of the policy as a bar to its liability." Absent a threshold duty to defend, there can be no liability to Morris, or to Crocker derivatively.

Recently, in *PAJ, Inc. v. Hanover Insurance Co.*, 243 S.W.3d 630 (Tex.2007), we held that tardy notice of a covered claim will not defeat coverage unless the insurer was actually prejudiced by the delay. The issue in *PAJ* was whether a named insured's untimely compliance with the notice-of-suit provision is excused if the delay inflicts no prejudice on the insurer. There are fundamental differences, however, between *PAJ* and today's case: in *PAJ*, the named insured made a request for coverage under the policy, albeit several months after "as soon as [was] practicable." In the pending case, however, the additional insured's notice was not merely late; it was wholly lacking. PAJ's notice was tardy; Morris's was nonexistent.

More importantly, as we have said, the requirement that an additional insured provide notice that it has been served with process is driven by a purpose distinct from the purpose underlying the requirement for notice of a claim or occurrence. Notice of service of process lets the insurer know that the insured is subject to default and expects the insurer to interpose a defense. An insurer cannot necessarily assume that an additional insured who has been served but has not given notice to the insurer is looking to the insurer to provide a defense. Potential insureds, for a variety of reasons, might well opt against seeking a defense from an insurer.

For example, an additional insured may opt against invoking coverage because it wants to hire its own counsel and control its own defense. Indeed, Emeritus's counsel believed that Morris had done just that in this case. Counsel for Emeritus testified that he had asked Morris before his deposition if he could speak to him and Morris "refused on the basis that he was waiting for a call from his attorney. [Emeritus's counsel] assumed that [Morris] had an attorney and did not want to talk to [Emeritus's counsel] on that basis."

As explained above, despite its actual knowledge of a covered suit against and service of process on Morris, National Union did not incur a duty to inform Morris of available coverage or his entitlement to a defense or to sua sponte provide one without any indication from Morris, either explicit or implicit, that he wanted or expected to be defended. Neither TDI's 1973 endorsement, nor our recent decision in *PAJ,* nor any other changes to Texas law since *Weaver* alter that conclusion.

III. Conclusion

Insurers owe no duty to provide an unsought, uninvited, unrequested, unsolicited defense. Consistent with our decision in *Weaver,* we decline to impose an extra-contractual duty on liability insurers that would force them to keep track of potential litigants who may or may not be additional insureds, may or may not be entitled to coverage, and may or may not expect a defense to a claim.

Accordingly, because insurers need not provide coverage to additional insureds who never seek it, National Union had no duty either to inform Morris of available coverage or to voluntarily undertake a defense for him, and its actual knowledge did not establish lack of prejudice as a matter of law.

NOTES & QUESTIONS

1) Is the *Crocker* decision harsh from the perspective of an insured that was not a party to the contract negotiation or bargained-for exchange?

2) Could the "unaware" insured in Crocker argue successfully that the insurer waived the prompt-notice requirement? What is the evidence?

3) Is there sufficient evidence in the Record to allow the "unaware" insured to raise an equitable estoppel argument as well as a no-prejudice argument?

4. "Insured Breached Notice Requirement Under an Claims-Made Policy"

Ulico Casualty Company v. Allied Pilots Association
262 S.W.3d 773
(Tex. 2008)

In this case we consider whether an insurer's contractual coverage under a claims-made policy can be expanded by the doctrines of waiver and estoppel to cover a risk not otherwise within the policy coverage: a suit against the insured that was not reported until after the policy expired. We hold that if an insurer's actions prejudice its insured, the insurer may be estopped from denying benefits that would be payable under its policy as if the risk had been covered, but the doctrines of waiver and estoppel cannot be used to re-write the contract of insurance and provide contractual coverage for risks not insured.

I. Background

Ulico Casualty Company issued a claims-made liability policy to the Allied Pilots Association (APA). The policy specified that it was effective from August 25, 1998 through August 25, 1999 and provided coverage, as relevant to this matter, for "all Loss which such Insured shall become legally obligated to pay on account of any claim made against the Insured during the Policy Period or, if exercised, during the Extended Reporting Period, for a Wrongful Act committed, attempted, or allegedly committed or attempted by such Insured before or during the Policy Period, and reported to [Ulico] ... during the Policy Period or the Extended Reporting Period, if elected."

The policy defined "loss" to include defense costs. The policy required . . . as a condition precedent to APA's rights under the policy, APA "[to give Ulico] written notice during the Policy Period or the Extended Reporting Period, if elected, of any claim made against [APA] for a Wrongful Act."

* * *

APA paid premiums for and Ulico issued two written endorsements, each amending the policy and providing for an extension of the Policy Period. The endorsements first changed the policy period from August 25, 1998 to September 25, 1999, and then to October 25, 1999. On October 4, 1999, twenty-one days before the amended policy period expired, APA was served with a suit styled *Allen v. American Airlines, Inc.* APA forwarded the *Allen* suit papers to its insurance broker and to the law firm of James & Hoffman, its regular outside litigation counsel. James & Hoffman undertook defense of APA. Ulico was not notified of the suit until APA's agent forwarded notice of the suit on November 5, 1999.

In December 1999, Ulico's claims analyst, Sheila Bowers wrote [a letter to APA] which stated that pursuant to the reservation of rights letter of March 1, 2000, "Ulico has agreed to reimburse [APA] for reasonable and necessary defense expenses." In May 2001, the firm responded and enclosed its billings of approximately $635,000 for defending APA in the suit. At that point, the law firm had defended the suit and filed a motion for summary judgment on behalf of APA without any reports to or further contact with Ulico. Neither APA nor its defense firm had sought Ulico's approval for any actions or for authorization to incur expenses in defense of the lawsuit. The trial court granted summary judgment in APA's favor in September, and an appeal by the Allen plaintiffs was dismissed.

Ulico filed suit in November 2001 seeking a declaratory judgment [asserting that APA was not covered and that it did not have to pay] APA's defense costs. APA counterclaimed. At trial, a jury found . . . that Ulico 1) granted an [extended reporting period] during which APA reported the *Allen* suit, 2) agreed to pay the Allen defense costs separately and apart from the policy, 3) waived its right to assert that the policy did not cover the *Allen* defense costs, and 4) was estopped from asserting that the policy did not cover the *Allen* defense costs. The jury found damages of $308,235. On cross-motions for judgment notwithstanding the verdict, the trial court set aside the jury findings that Ulico granted an ERP, that Ulico agreed to pay defense costs separately from the policy, and of damages. The trial court entered judgment in favor of APA on the waiver and estoppel findings for $616,468.55.

Relying on what has come to be referred to as the *Wilkinson* exception, see *Farmers Texas County Mutual Insurance Co. v. Wilkinson*, 601 S.W.2d 520 (Tex.Civ.App.-Austin 1980, writ ref'd n.r.e.), the court of appeals affirmed on the basis of waiver and estoppel. It held that APA's recovery under its waiver and estoppel theories was effectively a recovery under the contract of insurance, thus APA was entitled to recover attorney's fees pursuant to Texas Civil Practice and Remedies Code section 38.001(8). The court remanded the case for a determination of the amount of attorney's fees.

Ulico asserts that the court of appeals erred in holding it had contractual coverage for the *Allen* suit based on either waiver or estoppel. Ulico notes that there was no evidence of promissory estoppel or reliance damages. See *Wheeler v. White,* 398 S.W.2d 93, 97 (Tex.1965). The jury charge did not contain questions as to such damages, and APA lodged no objections to the omission of those questions. APA urges that the trial court erred in disregarding the jury findings that Ulico granted an ERP during which APA gave written notice of the suit, and that Ulico agreed separately from the policy to pay defense costs for the Allen suit. Because its holding on the waiver and estoppel issues was dispositive, the court of appeals did not reach the issues APA urges.

We hold that Ulico's policy coverage was not expanded by either the doctrine of waiver or the doctrine of estoppel so as to bring the *Allen* claims within the policy coverage. We also hold that the trial court properly disregarded the jury findings that Ulico granted an ERP extending the policy period and that Ulico separately agreed to cover the *Allen* suit defense costs.

II. Discussion

When Ulico received notice of the *Allen* suit on November 5, 1999, it did not have a contract of insurance in force with APA. Its policy had terminated as of October 25, 1999. Ulico's liability to APA turns on whether Ulico's actions after it received notice of suit created obligations to APA.

* * *

B. Waiver and Estoppel

1. The Law

Proceeding to the merits of Ulico's complaints, we note that insurance policies are contracts. *Barnett v. Aetna Life Ins. Co.,* 723 S.W.2d 663, 665 (Tex.1987). As such, the rights and obligations arising from them and the rules used to construe them are those generally pertaining to contracts. See *Forbau v. Aetna Life Ins. Co.*, 876 S.W.2d 132, 133 (Tex.1994). If an insurance contract covers certain risks but the policy contains exclusions or limitations of coverage, when the insured makes a claim for loss from a covered risk, the insurer must assert any applicable exclusion or limitation to avoid liability.

But when a policy covers risks for a certain time period, the time of the event allegedly triggering coverage is a precondition to coverage and is not considered a defensive matter to be pleaded and proved by the insurer. The insurer has neither a "right" nor a burden to assert noncoverage of a risk or loss until the insured shows that the risk or loss is covered by the terms of the policy. Once the insured does so, then it becomes incumbent on the insurer — that is the insurer has the "right" — to assert any exclusions or limitations as affirmative defenses.

In the context of issues such as those presented by this case, the doctrines of waiver and estoppel are frequently referenced together, but they are different. Waiver is the intentional relinquishment of a right actually known, or intentional conduct inconsistent with claiming that right. *In re Gen. Elec. Capital Corp*., 203 S.W.3d 314, 316 (Tex.2006); *Jernigan v. Langley*, 111 S.W.3d 153, 156 (Tex.2003); *Bocanegra v. Aetna Life Ins. Co.*, 605 S.W.2d 848, 851 (Tex.1980). The elements of waiver include (1) an existing right, benefit, or advantage held by a party; (2) the party's actual knowledge of its existence; and (3) the party's actual intent to relinquish the right, or intentional conduct inconsistent with the right. *See Tenneco Inc. v. Enter. Prods. Co.*, 925 S.W.2d 640, 643 (Tex.1996)

Estoppel, on the other hand, generally prevents one party from misleading another to the other's detriment or to the misleading party's own benefit. *See, Johnson & Higgins of Tex., Inc. v. Kenneco Energy, Inc.*, 962 S.W.2d 507, 515-16 (Tex.1998) ("[T]he doctrine of equitable estoppel requires: 1) a false representation or concealment of material facts; 2) made with knowledge, actual or constructive, of those facts; 3) with the intention that it should be acted on; (4) to a party without knowledge or means of obtaining knowledge of the facts; 5) who detrimentally relies on the representations."); *Trammell Crow Co. No. 60 v. Harkinson*, 944 S.W.2d 631, 636 (Tex.1997)

("Promissory estoppel generally is a defensive doctrine in that it estops a promisor from denying the enforceability of [a] promise.").

2. Can the Doctrines Be Used to Rewrite the Policy?

This court addressed the question of whether the contractual coverage of an insurance policy can be expanded by waiver or estoppel over seventy years ago in *Washington National Insurance Co. v. Craddock*, 109 S.W.2d 165 (Tex. 1937). . . The issue and this Court's answer were straightforward: * * *

> The question presented is not whether the act of the insurance company in making payments would constitute a waiver of its right to forfeit the policy on account of some breach by the insured of its terms, but is whether a contractual liability may be created by a waiver. By its policy the insurance company did not assume any liability for the risk declared upon and no consideration moved to it after the accident for the assumption of such liability. The insured seeks to create that liability by invoking the doctrine of waiver. The doctrine cannot be made to serve that purpose.

* * *

Fifty years later, in *Texas Farmers Insurance Co. v. McGuire*, 744 S.W.2d 601 (Tex.1988), we considered whether estoppel could be applied to enlarge the coverage of a liability policy. . . . We [held] that the court of appeals erred in applying the estoppel rule . . . . The doctrine of estoppel cannot be used to create insurance coverage when none exists by the terms of the policy.

Waiver and estoppel may operate to avoid a forfeiture of a policy, but they have consistently been denied operative force to change, re-write and enlarge the risks covered by a policy. In other words, waiver and estoppel cannot create a new and different contract with respect to risks covered by the policy.

* * *

III. Conclusion

Jury questions three and four were immaterial and could not form the basis of a judgment against Ulico. The trial court correctly rendered judgment notwithstanding the verdict in favor of Ulico as to jury questions one and two. There is no basis for a judgment against Ulico and the judgment of the court of appeals must be reversed. Judgment is rendered that APA take nothing.

5. "Insured Failed to Notify Promptly Under a Claims-Made Policy"

Prodigy Communications Corporation v. Agricultural Excess & Surplus Insurance Company
288 S.W.3d 374
(Tex. 2009)

In *PAJ, Inc. v. The Hanover Insurance Co.*, 243 S.W.3d 630, 636-37 (Tex. 2008), we held that "an insured's failure to timely notify its insurer of a claim or suit does not defeat coverage if the insurer was not prejudiced by the delay." PAJ involved an occurrence-based commercial general liability (CGL) policy with a prompt-notice provision that required the insured to notify the insurer of "an occurrence or an offense that may result in a claim 'as soon as practicable.'"
Noting that "the timely notice provision was not an essential part of the bargained-for exchange under PAJ's occurrence-based policy," we held that PAJ's untimely notice did not defeat coverage in the absence of prejudice to the insurer.

Today, we decide whether PAJ's notice-prejudice rule applies to a claims-made policy when the notice provision requires that the insured, "as a condition precedent" to its rights under the policy, give notice of a claim to its insurer "as soon as practicable ..., but in no event later than ninety (90) days after the expiration of the Policy Period or Discovery Period." The parties dispute whether notice of the claim was given "as soon as practicable" but agree that the insured gave notice within the ninety-day cutoff period. The insurer also admits that it was not prejudiced by the delayed notice.

For the reasons explained below, we conclude that "notice as soon as practicable" was not an essential part of the bargained-for exchange under the claims-made policy at issue here. Following PAJ, we hold that, in the absence of prejudice to the insurer, the insured's alleged failure to comply with the provision does not defeat coverage. Because the court of appeals held otherwise, we reverse its judgment, render judgment that the insurer may not deny coverage based on the fact that notice was not given "as soon as practicable," and remand the remaining issues to the trial court.

I

Factual Background

Prodigy Communications merged with FlashNet Communications in May 2000. At the time of the merger, FlashNet was insured under a claims-made "Directors' and Officers' Liability Insurance Policy Including Company Reimbursement" issued by Agricultural Excess & Surplus Insurance Company (AESIC). In exchange for a $19,519 premium, the policy covered losses resulting from certain "claims first made" against FlashNet and its directors and officers during the policy period of March 16, 2000 to May 31, 2000. In anticipation of its merger with Prodigy, FlashNet purchased a 3-year "Discovery Period" which, in exchange for a $93,750 premium, extended coverage under the policy to any "claims first made" against the Insureds between May 31, 2000 and May 31, 2003.

The policy contained the following amended "notice of claim" provision:

> The [Insureds] shall, as a condition precedent to their rights under this Policy, give the Insurer notice, in writing, as soon as practicable of any Claim first made against the [Insureds] during the Policy Period, or Discovery Period (if applicable), but in no event later than ninety (90) days after the expiration of the Policy Period, or Discovery Period, and shall give the Insurer such information and cooperation as it may reasonably require.

On November 28, 2001, FlashNet was named as a defendant in a class-action securities lawsuit (commonly referred to as the "IPO litigation"). The underlying FlashNet lawsuit constituted a "Securities Claim first made against [FlashNet]" "during the ... Discovery Period" of the policy, as described in the insuring agreement added by Policy Endorsement 16." Prodigy was served with a copy of the complaint on June 20, 2002 and first notified AESIC of the FlashNet lawsuit in a letter dated June 6, 2003. Apparently assuming that AESIC was already aware of the underlying lawsuit, the June 6 letter requested AESIC's consent to a proposed settlement agreement of the claims brought against FlashNet, rather than purporting to provide the initial notice of the claim.

By letter dated June 18, 2003, AESIC denied coverage on the ground that the June 6 letter did not comply with the policy's notice requirements. In response, Prodigy provided AESIC with formal written notice of the claim on June 26, 2003. Along with this notice, Prodigy attached a letter asserting that notice was timely because it had been sent within ninety days of the expiration of the Discovery Period. Despite Prodigy's efforts, AESIC never retreated from its no coverage stance.

II

Procedural Background

Prodigy sued AESIC, seeking a declaration that Prodigy was contractually entitled to coverage. Prodigy also asserted several extra-contractual claims alleging, among other things, that AESIC violated certain Insurance Code provisions as an unauthorized surplus lines insurer and was thus liable to Prodigy for the full amount of coverage. AESIC moved for summary judgment arguing that Prodigy did not satisfy the policy's condition precedent that notice of a claim be given "as soon as practicable." Prodigy filed a cross-motion for summary judgment. The trial court denied Prodigy's motion and granted AESIC's motion in part, ruling that Prodigy failed to comply with the condition precedent of timely notice and that this failure "avoids coverage, with or without prejudice to AESIC." AESIC and Great American Insurance Company then moved for summary judgment on the remaining Insurance Code issues, and the trial court granted a final summary judgment in their favor.

The court of appeals affirmed, holding that: 1) Prodigy was required to give notice "as soon as practicable," even though the policy allowed notice within ninety days after the expiration of the discovery period; 2) notice given almost one year after the filing of the lawsuit against the insured was not "as soon as practicable" as a matter of law; 3) AESIC was not required to prove that it was prejudiced by Prodigy's late notice; and 4) Insurance Code provisions did not prevent AESIC from enforcing the policy's notice provision. Prodigy petitioned this court for review on the issues of late notice and Insurance Code violations.

III

Discussion

We must decide whether, under a claims-made policy, an insurer can deny coverage based on its insured's alleged failure to comply with a policy provision requiring that notice of a claim be given "as soon as practicable," when 1) notice of the claim was provided before the reporting deadline specified in the policy; and 2) the insurer was not prejudiced by the delay.

As noted earlier, we recently held in *PAJ*, that an "insured's failure to timely notify its insurer of a claim or suit does not defeat coverage if the insurer was not prejudiced by the delay." In reaching that conclusion, we followed our holding in *Hernandez* that "an immaterial breach does not deprive the insurer of the benefit of the bargain and thus cannot relieve the insurer of the contractual coverage obligation." Prodigy argues that, even assuming it breached the policy's requirement that notice of a claim must be given "as soon as practicable," under our holding in PAJ, that breach was immaterial and cannot defeat coverage given AESIC's admitted lack of prejudice. AESIC responds that our holding in *PAJ* does not control the outcome of this case for several reasons.

First, unlike the *PAJ* policy, this one states unambiguously that the insured's duty to give "notice, in writing, as soon as practicable" is a "condition precedent" to coverage. Importantly however, our holding in *PAJ* did not rest on the distinction between conditions and covenants. Instead, we followed our reasoning in *Hernandez,* where we applied "'fundamental principle[s] of contract law,' "to hold "that when one party to a contract commits a material breach, the other party's performance is excused." We noted that one consideration in determining the materiality of a breach is "'the extent to which the nonbreaching party will be deprived of the benefit that it could have reasonably anticipated from full performance.' Thus, while the Prodigy policy describes the notice provision as a "condition precedent," we must go further to determine whether prejudice is, or is not, required.

This brings us to AESIC's second reason for distinguishing this case from *PAJ.* Unlike the occurrence-based policy in *PAJ,* the policy at issue here is a "claims-made" policy. According to AESIC, timely notice is always inherent to, and an essential part of, the bargained-for exchange in a claims-made policy. In *PAJ*, we recognized a "critical distinction" between the role of notice in claims-made policies and the role of notice in occurrence policies and concluded that timely notice was not an essential part of the bargained-for exchange in *PAJ*'s occurrence-based policy. In reaching this conclusion, we were persuaded by the Fifth Circuit's explanation that " '[i]n the case of an "occurrence" policy, any notice requirement is subsidiary to the event that triggers coverage.'

To determine whether "notice as soon as practicable" is an essential part of the bargained-for exchange in the claims-made policy at issue here, it is helpful to review the basic distinctions between occurrence and claims-made policies and the different types of notice requirements associated with each.

As one treatise explains:

> D & O insurance policies today are invariably written on a "claims-made" basis, which means that the policy only covers those claims first asserted against the insured during the policy period. This limitation appears in the insuring clauses. This coverage differs from "occurrence" type coverage, written for most casualty insurance, which covers only claims arising out of occurrences happening within the policy period, regardless of when the claim is made.

Thus, the main difference between these two types of policies is that a "claims-made" policy provides unlimited retroactive coverage and no prospective coverage, while an "occurrence" policy provides unlimited prospective coverage and no retroactive coverage.

For the insurance company, the primary advantage of a claims-made policy "is the limitation of liability to claims asserted during the policy period." This allows insurers "to calculate risks and premiums with greater precision." Furthermore, "the elimination of exposure to claims filed after the policy expiration date enables liability insurance companies to issue the claims made policies at reduced premiums."

Both occurrence policies and claims-made policies tend to have a requirement that notice of a claim be given to the insurer promptly, or "as soon as practicable." Unlike occurrence policies, however, some claims-made policies (often called "claims-made-and-reported policies) have an additional requirement that the claim be reported to the insurer within the policy period or within a specific number of days thereafter.

As courts and commentators have recognized, the different kinds of notice requirements when found in a claims-made policy serve very different purposes.

In a claims-made policy, the requirement that notice be given to the insurer "as soon as practicable" serves to "maximiz[e] the insurer's opportunity to investigate, set reserves, and control or participate in negotiations with the third party asserting the claim against the insured." By contrast, the requirement that the claim be made during the policy period "is directed to the temporal boundaries of the policy's basic coverage terms.... [This type of notice] is not simply part of the insured's duty to cooperate, but defines the limits of the insurer's obligation, and if there is no timely notice, there is no coverage." Similarly, a notice provision requiring that a claim be reported to the insurer during the policy period or within a specific number of days thereafter "define [s] the scope of coverage by providing a certain date after which an insurer knows it is no longer liable under the policy." of the essence in determining whether coverage exists" in a claims-made policy).

The role of notice in claims-made policies has been described as follows:

> Claims made or discovery policies are essentially reporting policies. If the claim is reported to the insurer during the policy period, then the carrier is legally obligated to pay; if the claim is not reported during the policy period, no liability attaches. Claims made policies require notification to the insurer to be within a reasonable time. Critically, however, claims made policies require that that notice be given during the policy period itself.

Because the requirement that a claim be reported to the insurer during the policy period or within a specific number of days thereafter is considered essential to coverage under a claims-made-and-reported policy, most courts have found that an insurer need not demonstrate prejudice to deny coverage when an insured does not give notice of a claim within the policy's specified time frame.

* * *

In a claims-made policy, when an insured gives notice of a claim within the policy period or other specified reporting period, the insurer must show that the insured's noncompliance with the policy's "as soon as practicable" notice provision prejudiced the insurer before it may deny coverage. Here, it is undisputed that Prodigy gave notice of the FlashNet lawsuit before the ninety-day cutoff. Even assuming that Prodigy did not give notice "as soon as practicable," AESIC was not denied the benefit of the claims-made nature of its policy as it could not "close its books" on the policy until ninety days after the discovery period expired.

Accordingly, we conclude that Prodigy's obligation to provide AESIC with notice of a claim "as soon as practicable" was not a material part of the bargained-for exchange under this claims-made policy. As AESIC has admitted that it was not prejudiced by the delay in receiving notice, it could not deny coverage based on Prodigy's alleged failure to provide notice "as soon as practicable ."

IV

Conclusion

In a claims-made policy, when an insured notifies its insurer of a claim within the policy term or other reporting period that the policy specifies, the insured's failure to provide notice "as soon as practicable" will not defeat coverage in the absence of prejudice to the insurer. Accordingly, we reverse the court of appeals' judgment, render judgment that AESIC cannot deny coverage because of Prodigy's alleged failure to give notice "as soon as practicable," and remand the remaining issues to the trial court.

6. "Insured Gave Notice Within Policy Period But Not Promptly"

Financial Industries Corporation, v. Xl Specialty Insurance Company
285 S.W.3d 877
(Tex. 2009)

This case comes before us on a certified question from the United States Court of Appeals for the Fifth Circuit. Pursuant to Article V, section 3-c of the Texas Constitution and Texas Rule of Appellate Procedure 58.1, we answer the following question:

> Must an insurer show prejudice to deny payment on a claims-made policy, when the denial is based upon the insured's breach of the policy's prompt-notice provision, but the notice is nevertheless given within the policy's coverage period?

I

Background

XL Specialty Insurance Company (XL) issued a claims-made, management liability policy to Financial Industries Corporation (FIC) for the policy period of March 12, 2005 to March 12, 2006. In exchange for a $475,000 premium, XL agreed to pay on behalf of FIC losses resulting from certain claims-including securities claims — "first made" against FIC during the policy period. The policy's notice provision, found in section VI under the heading "GENERAL CONDITIONS," provided: "As a condition precedent to any right to payment under this Policy with respect to any Claim, the Insured shall give written notice to the Insurer of any Claim as soon as practicable after it is first made."

On June 5, 2005, two plaintiffs sued FIC in Texas state court for breach of contract and fraud. FIC notified XL seven months after the suit was filed, but within the policy's coverage period. XL and FIC stipulate that this notification breached the policy's prompt-notice provision but did not prejudice XL. XL subsequently sued FIC in federal district court, seeking a declaratory judgment that the policy did not cover FIC for the lawsuit; XL also sent FIC a letter denying coverage. The district court granted XL's summary judgment motion, holding that under Texas law, an insurer need not demonstrate prejudice from late notice to avoid coverage on a claims-made policy. FIC appealed.

II

> **Must an insurer show prejudice to deny payment on a claims-made policy, when the denial is based upon the insured's breach of the policy's prompt-notice provision, but the notice is nevertheless given within the policy's coverage period?**

In *Prodigy Communications Corp. v. Agricultural Excess & Surplus Insurance Co.,* decided today, we hold that, "[i]n a claims-made policy, when an insured notifies its insurer of a claim within the policy term or other reporting period that the policy specifies, the insured's failure to provide notice 'as soon as practicable' will not defeat coverage in the absence of prejudice to the insurer. *Prodigy* involved a claims-made policy with a notice provision requiring that the insured, "as a condition precedent" to its rights under the policy, give notice of a claim to its insurer "as soon as practicable ..., but in no event later than ninety (90) days after the expiration of the ... Discovery Period." Prodigy gave notice of its claim before the ninety-day reporting deadline, but the insurer denied the claim alleging that the notice was not given "as soon as practicable." The insurer admitted it was not prejudiced by the delayed notice.

Recognizing that, for the insurer, the inherent benefit of a claims-made policy is the insurer's ability "to 'close its books' on a policy at its expiration and thus to attain a level of predictability unattainable under standard occurrence policies," we concluded that Prodigy's alleged failure to give notice "as soon as soon as practicable" was immaterial because it did not interfere with this benefit.

XL's claims-made policy differs slightly from the *Prodigy* policy in that XL's policy requires only that notice of a claim be given "as soon as practicable" and does not contain a clear-cut reporting deadline. However, the same reasons for requiring the insurer to demonstrate prejudice apply: FIC gave notice of the claim within the policy's scope of coverage, i.e., before XL could "close its books" on the policy. Because XL was not denied the benefit of the claims-made nature of its policy, it could not deny coverage based on FIC's immaterial breach of the policy's prompt-notice provision. *See PAJ, Inc. v. The Hanover Ins. Co.,* 243 S.W.3d 630, 631 (Tex.2008) (holding that "an immaterial breach does not deprive the insurer of the benefit of the bargain and thus cannot relieve the insurer of the contractual coverage obligation"); *Hernandez v. Gulf Group Lloyds,* 875 S.W.2d 691, 693 (Tex.1994) ("In determining the materiality of a breach, courts will consider, among other things, the extent to which the nonbreaching party will be deprived of the benefit that it could have reasonably anticipated from full performance.").

III

Conclusion

For the reasons stated above and explained more fully in *Prodigy Communications Corp. v. Agricultural Excess & Surplus Insurance Co.,* we answer the certified question in the affirmative and hold that an insurer must show prejudice to deny payment on a claims-made policy, when the denial is based upon the insured's breach of the policy's prompt-notice provision, but the notice is given within the policy's coverage period.

NOTES & QUESTIONS

1) *Hernandez, PAJ, Crocker, Ulico, Prodigy* and *Xl Specialty*: In each of these cases, the question was whether the insured breached the prompt-notice requirement in either a claims-made or an occurrence-based insurance contract. Yet, in each case, the Texas Supreme Court spent a modest to a considerable amount of judicial resources discussing "a condition precedent." Why?

2) Does "a condition precedent to exercise a right to payment" have the same meaning as "a condition precedent to coverage?"

3) Assume that a prompt-notice requirement is a condition precedent. Is it "a condition precedent to insurance coverage" or "a condition precedent to exercise a right to payment?" Which is correct?

4) Once more, consider the decisions in *Hernandez, PAJ, Crocker, Ulico, Prodigy*, and *Xl Specialty.* Which court concluded that the prompt-notice requirement was "a condition precedent to insurance coverage"?

5) Is a notice requirement a condition precedent to coverage under an insurance contract or a condition subsequent to maintain coverage?

6) What is the major distinction between the no-prompt-notice defense and the statute-of-limitations defense? Is proof of "prejudice" required under both defenses? Is "prejudice" an aspect of both defenses?

J. "Statutes of Limitations Bars Insured's Action"

1. Whether the the two-year torts or four-year contracts limitations period control

Arnold v. National County Mutual Fire Insurance Company
725 S.W.2d 165 (Tex. 1987)

Glen Arnold appeals from a summary judgment granted defendant National County Mutual Insurance Company. The court of appeals, in an unpublished opinion, affirmed the trial court's judgment on the grounds that Arnold's common law and statutory causes of action, if valid, were barred by limitations. We reverse that part of the judgment denying the common law cause of action and remand the cause to the trial court.

This is a suit on an insurance contract. In June 1974, Arnold was severely injured when the motorcycle he was operating was struck by a car driven by an uninsured motorist. Arnold was insured by NCM under a policy that included "uninsured motorist" protection with a limit of $10,000. Arnold made timely demand for payments up to the limit and an independent insurance adjusting firm recommended, within six months following the date of the accident, that NCM pay the entire policy limit to Arnold. NCM refused to pay although it is not clear when it specifically denied the claim.

Arnold sued both the uninsured motorist and the insurance company in late June 1974. In December 1977, Arnold obtained a judgment against both defendants for approximately $17,975. NCM then paid Arnold the $10,000 policy limit. Arnold filed this suit on December 27, 1978, alleging various statutory causes of action and a common law cause of action for NCM's breach of its duty of good faith and fair dealing in its handling of his claim. The trial court granted summary judgment in favor of NCM on all of Arnold's causes of action.

Summary judgment evidence shows that NCM based its decision to deny the claim on the advice of its agent, who was the attorney handling the file. Even though the uninsured motorist admitted that the collision was his fault, NCM refused to negotiate a settlement. In his deposition the attorney handling the file admitted that he was inexperienced in insurance matters and based his recommendation on his perception that a jury would be prejudiced against motorcyclists, that Arnold was driving too fast under the existing conditions and that Arnold was intoxicated.

The summary judgment evidence relied on by Arnold also showed that the defenses of speed and intoxication proffered by the attorney were very weak at best and ultimately intoxication was not pleaded. NCM failed to investigate the facts supporting the attorney's contentions. An issue of fact was raised as to NCM's reasonableness in failing to settle the claim and forcing Arnold to trial.

In order to decide if the court of appeals erred in upholding the summary judgment on limitations grounds, we must first resolve those points of error directed to the underlying causes of action.

Statutory Causes of Action

The court of appeals did not err in upholding the trial court's rendition of summary judgment on Arnold's causes of action under the Deceptive Trade Practices Act (DTPA) and articles 21.21 and 21.21-2 of the Texas Insurance Code. His causes of action under the Texas Insurance Code, both independently and as pleaded through the DTPA, are barred by article 17.22 of the Texas Insurance Code which exempted county mutual insurance companies from articles 21.21 and 21.21-2 at the time this suit was brought. *Jewell v. Mobile County Mutual Insurance Company,* 566 S.W.2d 295 (Tex.1978)

Arnold also pleaded that NCM violated § 17.46(a) and (b)(5) and (12) of the DTPA "by representing that the policy would pay uninsured motorist benefits when certain prerequisites were fulfilled and when, in fact, no payment of those benefits was made after complete compliance by Plaintiff of the prerequisites until judgment after jury verdict." Arnold did not plead and there is no summary judgment evidence that NCM made any misrepresentations. Even if Arnold had stated a cause of action for misrepresentation, it was barred by limitations.

* * *

Limitations

The court of appeals held that all of Arnold's causes of action including his good faith and fair dealing claim were barred by both the two-year (tort) and four-year (contract) statutes of limitations. Tex. Rev. Civ. Stat. Ann. art. 5526 and art. 5527 (now Tex.Civ.Prac. & Rem.Code §§ 16.003 & 16.004). This was based on that court's reasoning that Arnold's rights were invaded at the time his claim was rejected.

Arnold argues that as in "*Stowers* " cases the statute of limitations should not begin to run until judgment in the underlying cause becomes final. *See Linkenhoger v. American Fidelity & Casualty Company, Inc.,* 152 Tex. 534, 260 S.W.2d 884 (1953).

We agree with the reasoning in *Linkenhoger* and hold that the statute of limitations does not begin to run on a good faith and fair dealing claim until the underlying insurance contract claims are finally resolved.[2] *See also Maryland American General Insurance Company v. Blackmon,* 639 S.W.2d 455 (Tex.1982).

Thus, Arnold's cause of action for breach of the duty of good faith and fair dealing is not barred by the applicable two-year statute of limitations governing actions for personal injury. Tex.Rev.Civ. Stat.Ann. art. 5526 (now Tex.Civ.Prac. & Rem.Code § 16.003).

* * *

The judgment of the court of appeals denying Arnold's statutory causes of action is affirmed. We reverse that part of the judgment denying the common law cause of action and remand the cause to the trial court for further proceedings consistent with this opinion.

---

2 This does not mean that a contract claim and a claim for breach of the duty of good faith and fair dealing may not be tried together when possible.

2. Whether "prejudice" is an aspect of a statute-of-limitations defense

Lexington Insurance Company v. Buckingham Gate, Ltd., Inc.
993 S.W.2d 185
(Tex. App. -Corpus Christi 1999)

Buckingham Gate, Ltd., Inc. sued its insurer, Lexington Insurance Company, for violations of the DTPA and article 21.21 of the Texas Insurance Code after it refused to pay a claim under an "all-risks" insurance policy. The jury answered special questions favorable to Buckingham, and the trial court rendered a judgment against Lexington for $1,703,825, plus $318,255 in prejudgment interest. Lexington brings eight issues for our consideration, and Buckingham brings three issues. We reverse and render.

Ferromet Resources, Inc. was a company that bought surplus-and-used stainless steel and sold it to steel mills in Europe and the Far East, shipping by sea. This required warehouses and a dock on the Houston Ship Channel. Larry Whyte, the head of Ferromet, formed Buckingham Gate, Ltd., Inc. for the purpose of buying the needed property. On December 31, 1987, Buckingham paid $2.6 million for approximately fourteen acres of land, which included two docks on the Houston Ship Channel. Buckingham leased one of the docks to Ferromet at $25,000 per month for five years and the other dock to Schroeder Marine. This suit centers solely on the Ferromet dock.

In the fall of 1988, several insurance brokers, including Adams & Porter, contacted Ferromet to sell it insurance. Scott Breimeister, Ferromet's vice-president and chief financial officer, asked these brokers to evaluate Ferromet's current insurance coverage and make a proposal. Adams & Porter advised Breimeister that they were experts in marine insurance and that they would evaluate his insurance needs. Breimeister explained to John Hilliard, an Adams & Porter insurance agent, the importance of the docks and that he wanted complete coverage for both docks.

Adams & Porter submitted Buckingham's insurance risk to the market. Lexington, through its underwriting arm, Southern Risk Specialists, Inc., (Southern Risk) sold an "all-risks" property insurance policy to Buckingham and Ferromet, the named insureds.

* * *

The original policy as issued excluded coverage of the docks, but Southern Risk corrected the problem by issuing a policy endorsement covering them. While the policy was in effect, Ferromet employees noticed a depression in the soil behind the dock. Sonny Flores, a civil engineer, inspected the dock and found that the bulkhead wall behind the dock had failed, the concrete beams and slabs between the abutment wall were damaged, and the dock on the downstream side had moved substantially. He encouraged Buckingham to replace the dock.

Buckingham gave Lexington its initial notice of the loss on February 7, 1990. The cause of the loss was stated as "freeze." However the policy did not cover the docks against loss caused by freezing or thawing.

* * *

I. Limitations

Lexington's first issue is whether the statute of limitations barred Buckingham's claims under the DTPA and article 21.21. An action under both of these statutes must be brought within two years of the accrual of the cause of action.

Buckingham filed suit against Lexington on March 11, 1992, but did not serve it until January 1993. Lexington argues that it first denied coverage of Buckingham's claim in its letter of April 30, 1990, and, therefore, Buckingham's DTPA and Insurance Code claims accrued, as a matter of law, at that time. Lexington points out that its denial of coverage became final on September 15, 1990.

The jury found that Buckingham used diligence after filing this suit to obtain service of citation on Lexington. It also found that Buckingham, in the exercise of reasonable diligence, should have discovered all of Lexington's false, misleading, or deceptive acts or practices by May 4, 1992.

Lexington's April 30 letter advised Buckingham that "Lexington has made a preliminary determination that coverage is not provided for the damages claimed under the policy. The insured should not consider this preliminary determination that coverage is not provided as a final determination, and Lexington will review any additional evidence which the insured believes supports its claim."

By a second letter dated August 9, 1990, Lexington's counsel advised Buckingham's counsel:

> [We] will again review this matter on September 10, 1990. If no further information has been received from you by that time, the determination that coverage is not provided for the damages claimed under the policy shall become final. If additional information is provided by September 10, 1990, such additional information will be taken into consideration in reaching a final determination on this claim. However, unless you are otherwise advised in writing by Lexington Insurance Company, its attorneys or adjusters, prior to September 15, 1990, the preliminary determination as stated in my April 30, 1990 letter is final.
>
> By letter dated September 5, 1990, Adams & Porter advised Lexington that the proximate cause of the loss was earth movement, which the policy covered. They urged Lexington to further investigate the claim and reconsider its position. However in its May 4, 1992, letter Lexington unequivocally and unconditionally rejected Buckingham's proof of loss.

A two-year limitations period governs causes of action under article 21.21 and the DTPA. Tex. Ins. Code Ann. § 21.21, § 16(d) and Tex. Bus. & Comm. Code Ann. § 17.565. The statute of limitations is an affirmative defense. Tex. R. Civ. P. 94. A defendant thus bears the initial burden to plead, prove, and secure findings to sustain the plea of limitations. *Woods v. William M. Mercer, Inc.*, 769 S.W.2d 515, 517 (Tex.1988).

A. Due Diligence for Service

If Buckingham's claims accrued on April 30, 1990, it timely filed suit within the two-year limitations period on March 11, 1992. The issue is whether the evidence supported the jury's finding that Buckingham used due diligence in serving Lexington nearly nine months after limitations expired.

The mere filing of suit will not toll the running of limitations unless due diligence is exercised in the issuance and service of citation. *Murray v. San Jacinto Agency, Inc.*, 800 S.W.2d 826, 830 (Tex.1990); *Rigo Mfg. Co. v. Thomas*, 458 S.W.2d 180, 182 (Tex.1970). When a plaintiff files a petition within the limitations period, but does not serve the defendant until after the statutory period has expired, the date of service relates back to the date of filing if the plaintiff exercised diligence in effecting service. *Gant v. DeLeon*, 786 S.W.2d 259, 260 (Tex.1990) (per curiam); *Zale Corp. v. Rosenbaum,* 520 S.W.2d 889, 890 (Tex.1975) (per curiam).

In *Gant*, the supreme court pointed out that Texas courts have consistently held that due diligence was lacking as a matter of law based on unexplained lapses of time between the date a claimant filed suit and the date of service.

When a defendant affirmatively pleads the defense of limitations, and when failure to timely serve the defendant is shown, the plaintiff has the burden to explain the delay. The duty to use diligence continues until the defendant is served. The diligence required to meet this test is that which an ordinary prudent person would use under the same circumstances. If no excuse is offered for a delay in procuring service of citation, or if lapse of time and the plaintiff's acts conclusively negate diligence, a lack of diligence will exist as a matter of law.

In the instant case, Buckingham's counsel, Brad Irelan, gave Lexington's counsel, Robert Wellenberger, a settlement brochure which contained information to substantiate Buckingham's claim. During trial of this case, Mr. Irelan gave two reasons why he did not serve Lexington immediately after filing suit in state court. First, his testimony showed that Mr. Wellenberger advised him not to proceed with service until Lexington had responded to the settlement offer. Second, on March 17, 1992, (six days after the plaintiffs filed suit) Ferromet's creditors placed it into involuntary bankruptcy. When Ferromet went into bankruptcy, Buckingham, as its wholly owned subsidiary, went into bankruptcy as well.

Once Ferromet went into bankruptcy Mr. Irelan claimed that he no longer had the authority to proceed with the suit. He testified that If he had gone forward with service, and Lexington or Adams & Porter wanted to take the deposition of either plaintiff, "I'd be out of luck because there was no one there on behalf of the companies anymore." By this time Larry Whyte, who was the head of Buckingham and Ferromet, had resigned and was no longer at the helm of either company. Mr. Irelan believed he needed the bankruptcy court's permission to go forward with the suit. Mr. Irelan said he was having problems with the bankruptcy court and trustee. By letter dated December 17, 1992, Ferromet's bankruptcy trustee sent Mr. Irelan $61 to cover the cost of service. Mr. Irelan testified that from that date he vigorously moved on the case. When counsel asked him if there was any lack of diligence in serving the defendants he said that he did everything as diligently as he possibly could.

Mr. Wellenberger did not recall any agreement with Buckingham about not having to serve Lexington.

Section 108(a) of the bankruptcy code tolls the running of limitations for two years from the time a party files bankruptcy.

Because Buckingham filed suit prior to expiration of limitations, Section 108(a) tolled the limitations period for two years from March 17, 1992, the date Ferromet filed bankruptcy. Thus Buckingham timely served Lexington in January 1993.

B. Accrual

A cause of action generally accrues, and the statute of limitations begins to run, when facts come into existence that authorize a party to seek a judicial remedy. *Johnson & Higgins of Texas, Inc. v. Kenneco Energy Inc.*, 962 S.W.2d 507, 514 (Tex.1998). Johnson & Higgins involved an insured's negligence claim against the insurer based upon a denial of coverage for loss of profits. The court held that the insured "sustained injury when coverage was denied and, therefore, limitations commenced on that date because all facts required for a cause of action existed at that time."

In its analysis the Johnson & Higgins court cited with approval *Celtic Life Ins. Co. v. Coats*, 885 S.W.2d 96 (Tex.1994) In *Celtic Life* the court held that a claim under article 21.21 accrued on the date the insurer "first denied coverage." In *Long* the court held that in the insurance context a cause of action under the DTPA accrues on the date that coverage is denied.

In *Murray*, the supreme court stated that when there is no outright denial of a claim the exact date of accrual of a cause of action becomes more difficult to ascertain and should be a question of fact to be determined on a case-by-case basis.

The jury found that Buckingham, in the exercise of reasonable diligence, should have discovered all of Lexington's false, misleading, or deceptive acts or practices by May 4, 1992. . . .
We analyze the several letters denying coverage as follows:

> (1) The April 30 letter did not constitute an outright denial of coverage under the policy; rather, the letter showed that Lexington had made only a preliminary determination that it would not cover the claim.

(2) The August 9 letter is not on its face an outright denial of coverage. It provided that unless Buckingham sent additional information by September 10, 1990, the initial denial of coverage would become final. It also provided that the preliminary determination announced in the April 30 letter would become final if Lexington, its attorneys, or adjusters, did not advise Buckingham in writing prior to September 15, 1990. Additional information concerning the claims was provided to Lexington prior to the deadline. Lexington did not show that Buckingham failed to meet the requirements stated in the August 9 letter. Thus, Lexington did not establish that Buckingham's cause of action accrued on either April 30, 1990, or September 15, 1990.

(3) The evidence showed that the injury-producing event occurred on May 4, 1992 when Lexington rejected the proof of loss. On that date facts came into existence that authorized Buckingham to seek a judicial remedy.

Accordingly the evidence supports the jury's finding that Buckingham should have discovered Lexington's deceptive acts or practices by May 4, 1992. Buckingham timely filed suit on March 11, 1992.

* * *

We reverse the judgment and render that Buckingham Gate, Ltd., Inc., take nothing by its suit against Lexington Insurance Company.

NOTES & QUESTIONS

1) Assume that an insurer raises the statute-of-limitations defense and asserts that the insured's "delay" prejudiced the insurer's interest. What is the test for establishing "prejudice"?

2) What type of evidence is required if the insurer raises the prejudice defense and desires to employ the limitations argument effectively? May the insurer use the same evidence that was used to establish prejudice when the insured failed to give a prompt notice of a loss?

K. *"Insured's Assignment of Claim Was Invalid"*

State Farm Fire and Casualty Company v. Gandy
925 S.W.2d 696
(Tex. 1996)

Julie Gandy sued her stepfather, Ted Pearce, for sexually abusing her as a child. State Farm Fire and Casualty Company, which at one time had issued Pearce a homeowner's policy, agreed to pay an attorney chosen by Pearce to defend him but reserved the right to deny coverage. While the case was pending, Pearce pleaded *nolo contendere* to criminal charges initiated by Gandy and was given a probated sentence of five years' imprisonment.

Without notice to State Farm, Pearce settled with Gandy by agreeing to a judgment in her favor of over $6 million and assigning her any claims he had against State Farm. In return, Gandy agreed never to try to collect the judgment from Pearce. Gandy, as Pearce's assignee, then sued State Farm to collect her agreed judgment under Pearce's policy and to recover damages for State Farm's alleged failure to defend Pearce properly.

The district court granted summary judgment for State Farm on Gandy's policy claim, holding that sexual abuse was intentional conduct not covered by the homeowner's policy and therefore State Farm never had a duty to defend Pearce. But since State Farm voluntarily undertook Pearce's defense, the court held that State Farm had a duty to conduct the defense properly. On a verdict that State Farm failed to do so, the court rendered judgment for Gandy. The court of appeals affirmed.

We hold that Pearce's assignment to Gandy violated public policy and therefore conveyed her nothing. Because she had no right to recover against State Farm except as Pearce's assignee, we reverse the judgment of the court of appeals and render judgment that Gandy take nothing.

I

Julie Gandy was eight years old when her mother, 32, who had been divorced from her father a little more than a year, married Ted Pearce, 49, and the three of them moved to Eustace, Texas. Pearce, who had ended his formal education in the ninth grade, owned and operated a service station in nearby Athens.

In December 1988, four months before her seventeenth birthday, Gandy told her mother that Pearce had been sexually abusing her at home and at the service station for three and one-half years. Gandy also gave a statement to the district attorney. Within a few weeks, Gandy's mother filed for divorce, and the Henderson County grand jury indicted Pearce for engaging in sexual intercourse with Gandy.

About two years later, in January 1991, Gandy sued her mother and Pearce in Dallas County, alleging that Pearce had negligently and intentionally abused her and that her mother had negligently failed to prevent it. Gandy claimed actual damages of not less than $1 million for mental anguish and medical expenses, and punitive damages from each defendant equal to four times actual damages.

Gandy later amended her pleadings to name as a defendant a physician Pearce had once sent her to for birth control pills.

Pearce took the papers served on him to attorney E. Ray Andrews, who was representing him in the still pending divorce and criminal cases, and Andrews agreed to represent him in Gandy's suit. Gandy's mother took her suit papers to attorney Melvin G. Bateman, who was representing her in the divorce case, and Bateman agreed to represent her.

Bateman notified State Farm, which had insured the Pearces' home beginning in September 1987 (but never the service station where some of the alleged abuse occurred), that the suit had been filed. State Farm immediately investigated Gandy's allegations and concluded that they might not be covered by its policy, but that it should nevertheless undertake the Pearces' defense. In such circumstances State Farm's procedure was to allow each insured to choose his or her own counsel. State Farm would pay both attorneys' fees. Bateman told State Farm that he would file an answer for Gandy's mother, and he did so. State Farm learned that Andrews had been representing Pearce and contacted him to inquire whether he intended to represent Pearce in Gandy's suit. Andrews advised State Farm that he represented Pearce in Gandy's suit and would file an answer on Pearce's behalf, which he did.

A month after Gandy filed suit, State Farm sent Pearce the following letter, with a copy to Andrews:

> Dear Mr. Pearce:
>
> There is a question as to whether this company is obligated to defend or indemnify you for claims arising out of the incident which is alleged to have occurred on or about March 17, 1983 at 312 West Corsicana, Athens, Texas [the address of Pearce's service station] and Highway 136 South, Eustace, Texas [the Pearces' home address].
>
> We wish to call your attention to the fact that we specifically reserve our rights to deny coverage to you for the following reasons: 1) There is a question as to whether there was a policy in force on the date of loss. This question is raised due to the fact that State Farm Insurance did not provide you with a Homeowner's policy until September 8, 1987 and this loss occurred sometime in the years 1983 through 1988; [and] 2) "Coverage D, Section 2 Liability: shall not apply to Bodily Injury or Property Damage caused intentionally by or at the direction of the insured." The lawsuit contains allegations of intentional acts.
>
> For these reasons, you are hereby notified that any action taken by State Farm Fire and Casualty Company or its authorized representative in investigating, negotiating, denying or defending claims arising out of such incident, shall not be considered a waiver of such policy defense or of any policy defense which may be involved in this case, nor shall such action waive any of your rights under the policy.

> If we do not hear from you to the contrary, we will assume that it is acceptable for us to continue to handle the case on these terms.
>
> State Farm sent an identical letter to Gandy's mother and her attorney. Neither of the Pearces and neither of their attorneys objected to the letter.

After Pearce received this letter he called State Farm's agent, who asked for an appointment to take his statement. Pearce said he would contact Andrews and call back. He did so on March 25, 1991, and agreed to meet with State Farm's agent three days later. When the agent met with Pearce to take his statement, Andrews was present. Pearce told the agent he absolutely denied all Gandy's allegations.

Pearce called State Farm again in June, and the agent told him she was sending a letter concerning State Farm's decision to defend him. That letter, sent to Andrews with a copy to Pearce, stated:

> Dear Mr. Andrews:
>
> Please be advised that State Farm has made the decision to defend Ted Pearce under a Reservation of Rights. The coverage questions we will continue to reserve are: 1) There is a question as to whether there was a policy in force on the date of the loss, and 2) "Coverage D, Section II Liability; shall not apply to bodily injury or property damage caused intentionally by or at the direction of the insured."
>
> Additionally, the insuring agreement states: "To pay on behalf of the insured all sums which the insured shall become legally obligated to pay as damages."
>
> To the extent that any attempt is made to impose liability on one spouse for the tort of the other, there may be no coverage.
>
> Also, please be advised State Farm will be filing a Declaratory Relief Action, asking the court to resolve the issues of coverage in this matter.
>
> If you have any questions with regards to the above, please feel free to contact [our claims representative].

Neither Pearce nor Attorney Andrews called State Farm in response to this letter.

* * *

[Shortly thereafter], Pearce pleaded *nolo contendere* to the criminal charges against him. He was sentenced to five years' imprisonment, with the sentence probated. [Later], Pearce signed an assignment of his claims against State Farm [to Gandy] that provided as follows:

> WHEREAS, in Cause No. 91-00426 in the 193rd Judicial District Court of Dallas County, Texas, Plaintiff Julie Kathleen Gandy has obtained a Judgment against Defendant Teddy Pearce, on January 16, 1992; and
>
> WHEREAS, Teddy Pearce had previously advised his insurer(s) that he had accepted citation in this case, and requested that they provide him with a defense; and
>
> WHEREAS, his insurer(s) have completely ignored Mr. Pearce's request for a defense and/or denied him a defense and denied coverage, resulting in the aforementioned Judgment; and
>
> WHEREAS, as a result of the failure to defend and denial of coverage, Teddy Pearce is the present owner of certain purported claims, causes of action, and choses in action against State Farm Insurance Company, and/or other insurance carriers that insured Mr. Pearce in connection with the events alleged in the Petitions filed in Cause No. 91-00426; and
>
> WHEREAS, Julie Kathleen Gandy is willing to execute and provide to Teddy Pearce a Covenant to Limit Execution on the Judgment, in return for this Assignment of Claims;
>
> NOW THEREFORE, Teddy Pearce does, for the consideration set forth herein and in return for the immediate execution of a Covenant to Limit Execution, and for other good and valuable consideration, hereby grant, sell, convey and assign to Julie Kathleen Gandy and her heirs and/or assigns, any and all claims that Teddy Pearce may have against State Farm Insurance Company, and/or other insurance carriers for breach of contract, negligence, breach of warranty, breach of fiduciary relationship, failure to defend, and any and all other statutory or common law claims, if any, of whatever nature, arising out of the acts and omissions of those parties as set forth herein.
>
> FURTHER, Teddy Pearce does, for the consideration set forth herein and in return for the immediate execution of a Covenant to Limit Execution, and for other good and valuable consideration, hereby grant, sell, convey and assign to Julie Kathleen Gandy and her heirs and/or assigns, any and all claims that Teddy Pearce may have against any party arising out of the suit and claims asserted by Gandy against him.

On the same day, Pearce and Gandy signed a covenant to limit execution that provided as follows:

> By this Agreement, made by and between Julie Kathleen Gandy (Gandy), on the one hand, and Teddy Pearce (Pearce), on the other hand, it is hereby agreed as follows:

It is hereby stipulated that certain claims or causes of Gandy against Pearce were the subject of that certain litigation entitled Julie Kathleen Gandy v. Teddy Pearce, Linda Pearce and Clifford Haynes, M.D., which litigation was Cause No. 91-00426 on the docket of the 193rd Judicial District Court of Dallas County, Texas. It is further expressly stipulated that Gandy proceeded against and took a Judgment against Pearce, said Judgment being dated January 16, 1992. Gandy expressly stipulates that said Judgment is subject to the following provisions concerning execution or abstract of Judgment:

For and in consideration of the sum of Ten Dollars ($10.00) and other good and valuable consideration, the receipt of which is hereby acknowledged, Gandy agrees and covenants that she, and/or anyone for her or on her behalf, will limit any levy or execution or any other process, including an issuance or filing of abstract of judgment, against any assets or property, of any kind or description, of Pearce. Any such levy, execution or other process will be limited to any and all claims or causes of action of whatever nature or kind which Pearce might have or possess against State Farm Insurance Company, or any other insurance company which should have, but failed to appear and defend him, or any insurance company that otherwise has provided coverage for any liability he might have by reason of the claims asserted against Pearce in the above-referenced litigation or by reason of the Judgment.

Gandy specifically is assigned and obtains the right, from the Judgment against Pearce, to proceed against State Farm Insurance Company, and/or any other insurer(s) for recovery, or other satisfaction, of Pearce's claims against State Farm Insurance Company or the other insurer(s) for damages arising out of the facts and circumstances described herein and in Cause No. 91-00426, styled *Julie Kathleen Gandy v. Teddy Pearce, Linda Pearce and Clifford Haynes*, M.D., in the 193rd Judicial District Court of Dallas County, Texas. Gandy further expressly obtains the right to proceed against those parties to the extent of all available insurance policies, including any that provided coverage to Pearce in connection with the matters alleged in the Petitions filed in Cause No. 91-00426, or that otherwise may provide coverage in connection with the insurer(s)' failure to defend Pearce, for breach of fiduciary duties, breach of contract, and any other statutory or common law remedies.

As further consideration . . . , Pearce herein assigns any and all causes of action he may have against any party arising out of the suit and claims asserted by Gandy against him, including, but not limited to, any and all causes of action which Pearce may have against State Farm Insurance Company, arising out of the facts and circumstances described in the pending litigation or otherwise.

By virtue of the assignment contained herein, Pearce has specifically assigned any and all causes of action he might have or have had against State Farm Insurance Company, including but not limited to, claims or causes of action for breach of fiduciary duty, bad faith, failure to defend, or any other claim for actual, statutory, common law, or punitive damages. Pearce also expressly waives and hereby assigns to Gandy herein any right he may have had to assert any attorney-client privilege regarding any of the facts, conversations, or communications Pearce had with any of the attorneys for State Farm Insurance Company and agrees to fully cooperate and testify fully and truthfully as to all factual matters giving rise to said assigned claims, on reasonable notice of such a need for his testimony. Gandy shall hereafter be vested with full ownership of all said claims and of any right to assert or waive any attorney-client privilege regarding said claims.

Pearce also expressly waives and hereby assigns to Gandy any right he may have had to assert any husband-wife communications privilege regarding any of the facts, conversations, or communications Pearce had with Linda Pearce or with any of the attorneys representing Linda Pearce. Gandy shall hereafter be vested with full ownership of all said claims and of any right to assert or waive any husband-wife communication privilege regarding said claims.

Gandy further agrees that, upon the ultimate resolution of the claims and causes of action assigned herein, whether by settlement, judgment or otherwise, she will deliver to Pearce a copy of the Judgment against him, endorsed by her "Paid In Full."

It is hereby stipulated by and between Gandy and Pearce that this agreement is merely a contract to limit the scope and extent of execution against Pearce, and is not a release.

This agreement shall be governed by, construed and enforced in accordance with the laws of the State of Texas, without reference to principles of choice or conflict of laws.

* * *

[T]he district court signed the following judgment:

FINAL AGREED JUDGMENT

Being advised by counsel for both Plaintiff, Julie Kathleen Gandy, and for Defendant, Teddy Pearce, that all controversies in this matter had been settled as between them, the Court received formal, oral stipulations, which are incorporated herein by reference, from counsel for those parties regarding the terms and conditions for an agreed judgment based upon the settlement between those parties. The Court was then requested by counsel for those parties to enter an agreed judgment in the stipulated format.

> The Court, having heard the stipulation of the parties, and having been informed by counsel for each of those parties that each agreed to those stipulations, and finding it in the interest of justice that judgment as requested be entered,
>
> IT IS THEREFORE ORDERED, ADJUDGED, AND DECREED that Plaintiff, Julie Kathleen Gandy, have and recover from Defendant, Teddy Pearce, her actual damages of $12,500.00 for each of the three hundred and twenty-five (325) or more events or occurrences of sexual abuse, for a total award of $4,062,500.00 in actual damages, together with pre-judgment interest of ten (10%) percent per annum from January 11, 1991, until the date of this judgment, and post-judgment interest at the rate of ten per cent (10%) per annum from the date of this judgment until paid in full, and all costs of court, for which let execution issue.
>
> IT IS FURTHER ORDERED that Plaintiff, Julie Kathleen Gandy, have and recover exemplary damages of and from Defendant, Teddy Pearce, of $2,000,000.00, together with post-judgment interest at the rate of ten per cent (10%) per annum from the date of this judgment until paid in full, for which let execution issue.
>
> This Court further finds that no fraud or collusion has occurred in the entry of this judgment or in the circumstances surrounding the same, and specifically finds that Plaintiff did enter into a Covenant to Limit Execution with Teddy Pearce, which Covenant is in all things proper and which Covenant Plaintiff and Teddy Pearce are entitled under the circumstances to enter into, but which does not in any way effect [sic] Teddy Pearce's legal liability to pay this judgment. All relief not granted is denied.

The signatures of Gandy's lawyer and of Pearce's lawyer, Pattison, follow the signature of the district judge. Gandy nonsuited her mother and the defendant physician, making the judgment final.

* * *

Gandy sued State Farm and Andrews in Harrison County, although Gandy and Pearce resided in Dallas County and Andrews resided in Henderson County. Gandy alleged that State Farm owed her the more than $6 million awarded her against Pearce. In addition, she claimed damages for State Farm's failure to defend Pearce and settle her claims against him. She alleged negligence, gross negligence, bad faith, breach of contract, and violations of the Deceptive Trade Practices-Consumer Protection Act, Tex. Bus. & Com. Code §§ 17.41-.63, and of Article 21.21, Section 16 of the Insurance Code. Gandy also alleged that Andrews was negligent in conducting Pearce's defense, and that Andrews was State Farm's agent.

Gandy and State Farm both moved for summary judgment on her claim against State Farm's policy. The district court granted summary judgment for State Farm, holding that it had no duty to defend Pearce in Gandy's suit against him because Gandy's allegations against Pearce were not covered by State Farm's policy. The court also held that State Farm was not obligated to indemnify

Pearce for the agreed judgment against him. But because State Farm had voluntarily undertaken to defend Pearce, the court held that State Farm should have done so properly and permitted Gandy to try her claim that State Farm mishandled Pearce's defense.

Gandy relied heavily on Pearce's testimony, although he steadfastly insisted, despite the agreed judgment, that he had never abused Gandy and that Gandy was a "liar." Pearce testified that he did not want Andrews to represent him in Gandy's suit but thought that Andrews was State Farm's choice. Although Gandy's mother and her attorneys had no misunderstanding in dealing with State Farm, Pearce testified that he never understood that State Farm would pay for an attorney of his choice. He testified that his limited education and experience made it impossible for him to secure competent counsel. Pearce stated that he called State Farm repeatedly to complain of Andrews, but that State Farm offered him no assistance. State Farm denies receiving any such calls and has no record of them.

Andrews also testified on Gandy's behalf. He stated that he represented Pearce in Gandy's suit out of friendship. Prior to trial, while Andrews was a defendant in the present case, he testified at his deposition that he represented Pearce in his divorce case and that he was qualified to represent Pearce in Gandy's lawsuit. A few minutes before Andrews testified at trial, Gandy nonsuited her claims against him. Andrews then testified, contrary to his deposition, that he had not represented Pearce in the divorce case and that he was not qualified to represent Pearce in Gandy's lawsuit.

* * *

The jury found that State Farm was negligent but not grossly negligent, and that it violated the DTPA, but not knowingly. The jury found that Gandy should recover $200,000 damages, and that a reasonable attorney fee was fifteen percent of the judgment. The district court rendered judgment on the verdict against State Farm for $200,000 actual damages plus prejudgment interest, $2,000 statutory penalty, fifteen percent of the total as attorney fees, postjudgment interest, and costs.

The court of appeals affirmed. It held that Pearce was a consumer as defined by the DTPA because he sought legal services from Attorney Andrews in a transaction in which State Farm was involved. The court also held that evidence that State Farm did not "explicitly set out the extent of its responsibility, its relationship with Andrews, or Pearce's options to select counsel of his own" was legally sufficient to support liability under the DTPA.

The appeals court held that while State Farm was not legally obligated to defend Pearce, it voluntarily undertook to do so and was obliged to use ordinary care in that undertaking. The court concluded that the same evidence that supported DTPA liability also supported liability for negligence. Regarding damages, the court held that there was some evidence of injury to Pearce's reputation, credit and ability to conduct his business.

The court also concluded, albeit reluctantly, that the agreed judgment was some evidence of Pearce's damages. The court was very critical of Pearce's settlement with Gandy:

> The amount of the judgment in a case like this, where a covenant not to execute is given contemporaneously with and as a part of a settlement and agreed judgment, cannot constitute damage to the judgment debtor. Allowing an assignee of the named judgment debtor in such a case to collect all or part of the judgment amount perpetrates a fraud on the court, because it bases the recovery on an untruth, i.e., that the judgment debtor may have to pay the judgment. See *Garcia v. American Physicians Ins. Exch.*, 812 S.W.2d 25 (Tex.App.-San Antonio 1991) (Peeples, J. dissenting), rev'd, 876 S.W.2d 842 (Tex.1994).
>
> Such a result should be against public policy, because it allows, as here, parties to take a sham 5 judgment by agreement, without any trial or evidence concerning the merits, and then collect all or a part of that judgment from a third party. Allowing recovery in such a case encourages fraud and collusion and corrupts the judicial process by basing the recovery on a fiction. It is true that there is no finding of fraud or collusion between Pearce and Gandy in this case, and it is also true that Gandy was undoubtedly injured by Pearce's actions. But the fact remains that the courts are being used to perpetrate and fund an untruth-that Pearce was damaged by the bare amount of the judgment.
>
> Despite our protestations noted above, it appears that our Supreme Court is of the opinion that, even when there is a covenant not to execute, the amount of the judgment can be evidence of some damage to the one who suffered the judgment. *American Physicians Ins. Exch. v. Garcia*, 876 S.W.2d 842. It is difficult to reconcile such a view with the Supreme Court's holding that "Mary Carter" agreements are against public policy because they "skew the trial process, mislead the jury, promote unethical collusion among nominal adversaries, and create the likelihood that a less culpable defendant will be hit with the full judgment." *Elbaor v. Smith*, 845 S.W.2d 240 (Tex.1992). To the extent that our Supreme Court would hold that the bare amount of the judgment constitutes damage in a case like this, we believe it is wrong, and we urge it to correct the matter when it has the opportunity. Until it does so, however, we defer to what we believe is the stated law and hold that the judgment here is some evidence of damage to Pearce, even though the judgment can never be collected from him, and is sufficient evidence to support the jury's finding.

For the reasons expressed by the court of appeals, State Farm argues that Pearce's assignment to Gandy should not be given effect. We agree, and we do not read our decision in *Garcia* to the contrary. In reaching this conclusion, we begin with a brief history of the law of alienability of choses in action, next consider certain exceptions in Texas to the general rule favoring alienability, and then explain why there must also be an exception for assignments like the one in this case. We conclude with an examination of the law in a few other jurisdictions.

II

Alienability of choses in action has its roots in equity, not law. At early common law, a chose in action could not be assigned. *Reef v. Mills Novelty Co.,* 89 S.W.2d 210, 211 (Tex. Com. App.1936) and *Galveston H. & S.A. R.R. v. Freeman,* 57 Tex. 156, 157-158 (1882).... Two principal bases have been suggested for the rule. One is that the rule precluded litigation like that already prohibited by champerty and maintenance. An early proponent of this explanation was the great Lord Coke, who declared "the aversion of the 'sages and founders of our law' to the 'multiplying of contentions and suits,'" quoting *Lampet's Case*, 77 Eng. Rep. 994, 997 (K.B.1613).

The second basis offered for the rule is that the common law regarded rights as personal. Expounding on this view, Holmes argued that rights at common law (and in most early legal systems) were perceived to be relational and situational — that is, determined by the identity of the particular individuals involved and their transaction or circumstances. A claim or cause of action was part of a right of redress that was personal to the holder by virtue of the injury suffered and thus incapable of transfer. To separate a cause of action from a particular plaintiff's right of redress was to risk unjust prosecution of claims. A right or obligation could not be enforced apart from its context without risking distortion.

As early as the fifteenth century the common-law rule against alienability of choses in action began to give way to the demand of commerce that assigned debts be enforceable. What law courts would not oblige, chancery courts would. For a long period of time, assignments of some debts conveyed equitable rights of enforcement but no legal rights. Two common-law principles provided a beachhead for incursion against the rule of inalienability. One was inheritance, which expanded to include not only property rights but rights of action. The other was attorney, the designation of a representative to act in one's stead.

In the thirteenth century only the king could appoint an attorney to conduct prospective litigation. Over time, the right to appoint an attorney for such purposes was extended to the king's subjects, but still the law resisted its use to validate assignments because "it was thought unduly to stimulate litigation, and therefore to fall within the statutory prohibition of maintenance, unless the power was executed for the benefit of a creditor of the transferor." Little by little, the common law's resistance to alienability of choses in action was weakening, and by the eighteenth century it had collapsed. The pressures against the rule of inalienability were commercial and thus affected only debts and other contract rights that were not personal to the owner and could survive to his estate upon his death. Causes of action *ex delicto* for personal torts did not survive the plaintiff's death and could not be assigned.

The only remnants of the rule against alienability of choses in action to survive passage of the common law to America were those pertaining to some torts. In Texas, the merger of law and equity allowed assigned rights to be enforced as fully as they would have been in chancery court. *See Cleveland v. Heidenheimer*, 46 S.W. 30, 31 (Tex. 1898). Only five days after the Congress of the Republic of Texas adopted the common law, it provided by statute for assignment of both negotiable and non-negotiable written instruments... But even contract rights not covered by the statute could be assigned. *Kelley v. Bluff Creek Oil Co.,* 309 S.W.2d 208, 212 (Tex. 1958); *Citizens State Bank v. O'Leary*, 167 S.W.2d 719, 721 (Tex. 1942)

In some jurisdictions the rule expanded to include claims *ex delicto* as well as *ex contractu*. An 1895 Texas statute provided that personal injury claims survived to the heirs and legal representatives of the injured party. On the theory that assignability of a chose in action depended on whether it survived the owner's death, personal injury claims thus became assignable in Texas. *See Beech Aircraft Corp. v. Jinkins*, 739 S.W.2d 19, 22 (Tex.1987). This is not true in every state.

Practicalities of the modern world have made free alienation of choses in action the general rule, but they have not entirely dispelled the common law's reservations to alienability, or displaced the role of equity or policy in shaping the rule. Even today, the general rule is that a contractual assignment may be "inoperative on grounds of public policy." The Restatement notes numerous limitations on alienation of choses in action. Id. ch. 15, introductory note. The increase in litigation caused by assignments, noted by Lord Coke, remains a matter of concern. So does the effect of alienability on the parties and circumstances in the original transaction or occurrence. As Holmes succinctly summarized, "[t]he history of early law everywhere shows that the difficulty of transferring a mere right was greatly felt when the situation of fact from which it sprung could not also be transferred. Analysis shows that the difficulty is real."

III

This Court has held an assignment of a chose in action invalid in at least four instances. Each is based on the historical reservations to such assignments, and each relates to the current case, so we examine them in some detail.

A

In *Zuniga v. Groce, Locke & Hebdon*, 878 S.W.2d 313 (Tex.App.-San Antonio 1994, writ ref'd), we considered "whether a client may assign his cause of action for legal malpractice arising out of litigation." . . . Noting that legal malpractice claims are not assignable in most jurisdictions, we observed:

> Most of the authorities disallowing assignment have reasoned that to allow assignability would make possible the commercial marketing of legal malpractice causes of action by strangers, which would demean the legal profession. This is a legitimate concern. We do not relish the thought of entrepreneurs purchasing the legal rights of clients against their attorneys as an ordinary business transaction in pursuit of profit.

We also noted most of these entrepreneurs were plaintiffs who had been suing the clients:

> Most legal malpractice assignments seem to be driven by forces other than the ordinary commercial market. In most of the reported cases, the motive for

assignment was the plaintiff's inability to collect a judgment from an insolvent, uninsured (or underinsured) defendant.

* * *

B

In *Elbaor v. Smith,* 845 S.W.2d 240 (Tex.1992), we held that Mary Carter agreements are void as against public policy. A Mary Carter agreement is any settlement arrangement between the plaintiff and some of the defendants in a case by which the settling defendants agree to pay the plaintiff a certain amount of money and to participate in the trial against the nonsettling defendants, and the plaintiff agrees to release the settling defendants from liability and, if the judgment against a nonsettling defendant is large enough, to repay the settlement amount. In effect, the plaintiff assigns the settling defendants part of plaintiff's claim against the nonsettling defendants.

We noted two principal objections to such arrangements. First, they tend to promote litigation rather than settle it. "Although the agreements do secure the partial settlement of a lawsuit, they nevertheless nearly always ensure a trial against the non-settling defendant." A Mary Carter agreement "creates a tremendous incentive for the settling defendant to ensure that the plaintiff succeeds in obtaining a sizable recovery, and thus motivates the defendant to assist greatly in the plaintiff's presentation of the case." I The settling defendants' interest in plaintiff's recovery drives the case to trial. Indeed, "Mary Carter agreements frequently make litigation inevitable, because they grant the settling defendant veto power over any proposed settlement between the plaintiff and any remaining defendant."

Second, Mary Carter agreements distort the trial against the nonsettling defendants.

* * *

We determined that Mary Carter agreements "present to the jury a sham of adversity between the plaintiff and [a settling defendant], while these parties are actually allied for the purpose of securing a substantial judgment for the plaintiff and, in some cases, exoneration for the settling defendant."

* * *

We concluded that the Mary Carter agreement was "an unwise and champertous device"

As a matter of public policy, this Court favors settlements, but we do not favor partial settlements that promote rather than discourage further litigation. And we do not favor settlement arrangements that skew the trial process, mislead the jury, promote unethical collusion among nominal adversaries, and create the likelihood that a less culpable defendant will be hit with the full judgment. The bottom line is that our public policy favoring fair trials outweighs our public policy favoring partial settlements.

This case typifies the kind of procedural and substantive damage Mary Carter agreements can inflict upon our adversarial system. Thus, we declare them void as violative of sound public policy.

C

In *International Proteins Corp. v. Ralston-Purina Co.*, 744 S.W.2d 932 (Tex.1988), we held that a tortfeasor cannot take an assignment of a plaintiff's claim as part of a settlement agreement with the plaintiff and prosecute that claim against a joint tortfeasor. In that case, the plaintiff sued IPC and Purina for products liability and negligence, alleging that they had sold him contaminated chicken feed. Purina settled with the plaintiff and as part of their agreement took an assignment of plaintiff's claim against IPC. Purina then prosecuted plaintiff's claim against IPC. The case was tried as if the plaintiff were present, although he did not appear at trial. We held that "[a]s a general rule a cause of action may be assigned, but it is contrary to public policy to permit a joint tortfeasor the right to purchase a cause of action from a plaintiff to whose injury the tortfeasor contributed."

We based our decision in part on *Beech Aircraft Corp. v. Jinkins*, 739 S.W.2d 19 (Tex.1987), in which we held that a tortfeasor cannot completely settle a plaintiff's claim against him, take an assignment of the plaintiff's claim, and continue to prosecute a claim for contribution against a joint tortfeasor. We determined that allowing such assignments would not promote settlements and would confuse juries.

We see no advantage in allowing defendants responsible for the plaintiff's injuries a right to, in effect, buy the plaintiff's claims and prosecute the other jointly responsible parties. It is not apparent that such settlements will result in any significant savings of time or resources. We can, however, envision that the settling defendant's unusual posture as surrogate plaintiff, co-defendant and cross-plaintiff will confuse a jury and possibly prejudice the remaining parties....

We are mindful of the general rule that a cause of action for damages for personal injuries may be sold or assigned. Our holding in the present case is an exception to this general rule. A settling defendant who is jointly responsible for personal injuries to a common plaintiff may not preserve contribution rights either by obtaining a complete release for all other parties allegedly responsible or by obtaining assignment of the plaintiff's entire claim.

In essence, we concluded that the assignments in these cases were invalid and conveyed no viable rights to the assignees. . . .

D

Finally, in *Trevino v. Turcotte*, 564 S.W.2d 682 (Tex.1978), we held an assignment of interests in an estate invalid.

* * *

IV

The common law's concerns about alienability of choses in action, voiced by Lord Coke and Holmes, echo in our own decisions. In widely different contexts we have invalidated assignments of choses in action that tend to increase and distort litigation. We have never upheld assignments in the face of those concerns. With these things in mind, we turn to the assignment in this case, and others like it.

A

First, Pearce's settlement with Gandy did not end the litigation, nor could there have been any reasonable contemplation that it would. Once Gandy attempted to enforce against State Farm a $6 million agreed judgment against Pearce for sexual abuse, the likelihood of a negotiated end to the litigation was virtually nil. Even after the district court held as a matter of law that State Farm's policy did not cover Gandy's claims, and that State Farm was never obliged to defend Pearce, the litigation forged on. Had the coverage issue been resolved early on in Gandy's litigation against Pearce, it is doubtful that Gandy would have proposed settlement with Pearce on the terms she did. An assignment of Pearce's actions against State Farm for mishandling Gandy's non-covered claim would have been of no value to Gandy.

The point of this settlement was not to end the litigation but to prolong it. Had it ended simply with a judgment against Pearce, Gandy would have had little hope of ever recovering anything at all, given Pearce's impecunious circumstances. Obviously, as Gandy's counsel freely testified, the entire purpose of the arrangement was to find a way to recover against State Farm.

Second, Pearce's settlement with Gandy greatly distorted the litigation that followed. In her suit against Pearce, Gandy alleged that he sexually abused her for three and one-half years. From the beginning she claimed to be entitled to recover at least $1 million actual damages, as well as punitive damages. Her sworn statements to the district attorney and her deposition testimony consistently assert a despicable, egregious pattern of sexual abuse by her stepfather over a number of years. Gandy testified that she suffered damages of $50,000 on each occasion. When Gandy's lawyer prepared an agreed judgment, he concluded that it was unrealistic to expect the district court to render judgment for an amount equal to $50,000 per occurrence — well over $15 million in actual damages alone.

His opinion as an experienced litigator in the area was that a finding of 325 separate incidents of abuse and actual damages of $12,500 per incident was "a fair evaluation of what the scope and extent of her injuries were." Had Gandy's lawyer remained of that opinion when this action against

State Farm was tried, there would have been no apparent injury to Pearce. If Pearce indeed got exactly what was coming to him in the agreed judgment, then he was not damaged by his alleged lack of competent counsel. The difference between the agreed judgment rendered against Pearce and the judgment that should have been rendered against him would be zero.

Instead, however, Gandy's position in this case is-as it must be for her to succeed-that Pearce would never have been found liable for so large an amount of damages had State Farm handled his defense properly. Even if her lawyer had testified that his "fair evaluation" of Gandy's damages was much higher than it would have been had Pearce had competent counsel, Gandy cannot avoid shifting positions. In her suit against Pearce, her incentive, fueled by belief in her cause, was to obtain as large a judgment as possible. In her suit as Pearce's assignee against State Farm, her incentive, driven by the economic realities of obtaining a judgment against a solvent defendant, is to argue that Pearce was not as liable as she earlier asserted. Inevitably, Gandy's settlement with Pearce forced her to take inconsistent positions if she was to have any hope of actually recovering anything.

Gandy was not the only party moved to alter positions. Pearce at first steadfastly denied that he abused Gandy, ever. Then, he pleaded nolo contendere to criminal abuse charges and agreed to a judgment reciting that he had abused Gandy 325 times in two years. He agreed to a judgment against himself for more than $6 million, knowing that it could not be rendered without his agreement. In the present case he returned to his prior position: he never abused Gandy. And he claims he would have been able to establish his total innocence if only State Farm had provided competent counsel to represent him. In Gandy's suit against him, Pearce opposed her as hard as he could. In Gandy's suit against State Farm, he agreed to cooperate with her.

Parties often take inconsistent positions in lawsuits. Generally the law permits this, but the situation here is different. Here the parties took positions that appeared contrary to their natural interests for no other reason than to obtain a judgment against State Farm. Gandy and Pearce arranged for an agreed judgment to be rendered without notice to State Farm, even though State Farm had contacted Pearce's attorneys repeatedly and had instructed them to send their fee statements for payment. Gandy and Pearce obviously attempted to take advantage of State Farm. The court of appeals did not exaggerate when it called Gandy's agreed judgment against Pearce "a sham", or when it stated that the judgment "perpetrates a fraud" and "an untruth". 880 S.W.2d at 138. The agreed judgment was an essential element of the settlement allowing Gandy to prosecute Pearce's claim against State Farm. Without the assignment and covenant not to execute, the agreed judgment would never have been rendered. In these circumstances, we have no hesitation in holding that the assignment was invalid.

B

Settlement arrangements like the one here are not unusual in cases in which plaintiffs' claims are arguably covered by defendants' insurance. They are also used in other contexts. We first discuss the cases involving insurance.

* * *

Balancing the various considerations we have mentioned, we hold that a defendant's assignment of his claims against his insurer to a plaintiff is invalid if (1) it is made prior to an adjudication of plaintiff's claim against defendant in a fully adversarial trial, (2) defendant's insurer has tendered a defense, and (3) either (a) defendant's insurer has accepted coverage, or (b) defendant's insurer has made a good faith effort to adjudicate coverage issues prior to the adjudication of plaintiff's claim. We do not address whether an assignment is also invalid if one or more of these elements is lacking. In no event, however, is a judgment for plaintiff against defendant, rendered without a fully adversarial trial, binding on defendant's insurer or admissible as evidence of damages in an action against defendant's insurer by plaintiff as defendant's assignee.

We believe this balancing of interests minimizes any hardship on an insured defendant. Determining an insurer's obligations before its insured incurs liability benefits both the insurer and the insured by removing that uncertainty. An insurer has ample disincentives to deny coverage or a defense without good reason: it will be liable for its own attorney fees in litigating the dispute and may be liable for the insured's attorney fees, a statutory penalty, and even bad faith damages. The significance of the disincentives to denying coverage and a defense without clear justification is apparent in this case. Although Pearce's sexual abuse of Gandy was clearly intentional conduct excluded from coverage under Pearce's homeowner's policy, State Farm nevertheless volunteered to pay for counsel to defend him and his wife against Gandy's claims. Pearce may have been confused about State Farm's offers to him, but there can be no question about what State Farm intended, given its defense of Gandy's mother.

* * *

C

The settlement arrangement we have examined has three elements: an assignment of a defendant insured's claims against his insurer, a covenant by the plaintiff to limit recovery from the defendant personally, and a judgment for plaintiff against defendant. Courts in other jurisdictions have considered the validity of each element as a component of the arrangement. In the present case we have focused on the validity of the assignment. Our decision follows from principles we articulated in prior cases regarding the validity of assignments of choses in action in other contexts, and from reservations that for centuries the common law has harbored about such assignments.

* * *

For the reasons explained, we reverse the judgment of the court of appeals and render judgment that plaintiff take nothing.

L. *"Insurer's Subrogation-of-Rights Claim Is Valid"*

Consider the language in Tex. Ins. Code § 1506.301. It reads:

TEXAS HEALTH INSURANCE RISK POOL
SUBROGATION TO RIGHTS AGAINST THIRD PARTY

> The pool . . . (1) is subrogated to the rights of an individual covered by the pool to recover against a third party costs for an injury or illness for which the third party is liable under contract, tort law, or other law that have been paid by the pool on behalf of the covered individual; and (2) may enforce that liability on behalf of the individual.

Now, consider the words and phrases in Tex. Ins. Code § 1952.155. In its entirety, that statute states:

PERSONAL INJURY PROTECTION COVERAGE
BENEFITS PAYABLE WITHOUT REGARD TO FAULT OR COLLATERAL SOURCE
EFFECT ON SUBROGATION

(a) The benefits under coverage required by this subchapter are payable without regard to: (1) the fault or nonfault of the named insured or recipient in causing or contributing to the accident; and (2) any collateral source of medical, hospital, or wage continuation benefits.

(b) Except as provided by Subsection (c), an insurer paying benefits under coverage required by this subchapter does not have a right of subrogation or claim against any other person or insurer to recover any benefits by reason of the alleged fault of the other person in causing or contributing to the accident.

(c) An insurer paying benefits pursuant to this subchapter, including a county mutual insurance company, shall have a right of subrogation and a claim against a person causing or contributing to the accident if, on the date of loss, financial responsibility as required by Chapter 601, Transportation Code, has not been established for a motor vehicle involved in the accident and operated by that person.

Arguably, sections 1506.301 and 1952.155(c) highlight and outline the circumstances or conditions under which insurers may exercise their right of subrogation. But conflicts between insureds and insurers as well as between insurers and others persist over insurers' equitable-subrogation claims and rights. Therefore, the cases in this section highlight some of those conflicts and issues as well as the methodology that courts have employed to resolve such controversies.

1. "Insurer's contract-based subrogation right trumps insured's right to be made whole"

Fortis Benefits v. Cantu
234 S.W.3d 642
(Tex. 2007)

The issue in this insurance subrogation case is whether the equitable "made whole" doctrine — the rule that an insurer is not entitled to subrogation of medical benefits unless the insured has been "made whole"— trumps an insurer's contract-based subrogation right.

After respondent Vanessa Cantu sued multiple parties for severe injuries she sustained in an auto accident, her medical insurer, petitioner Fortis Benefits, intervened, claiming a subrogation right under the policy. The various defendants settled with Cantu, and Fortis looked only to Cantu for its recovery. A divided court of appeals upheld a trial court finding that because Cantu's medical expenses exceeded the settlement amount plus the benefits Fortis had paid, Fortis's subrogation claim was barred by the equitable "made whole" doctrine. We hold that the "made whole" doctrine must yield to Fortis's right to contractual subrogation under the plain terms of the insurance policy.

I. Background

Cantu suffered severe injuries in a car wreck and later sued the driver of the vehicle in which she was riding, his employer, the vehicle seller, and the vehicle manufacturer (Ford). Fortis intervened and asserted contractual subrogation and reimbursement rights to recoup from Cantu's tort recovery the amount of medical benefits it had paid under the policy. At a pretrial conference, Fortis agreed with all parties on the record that Fortis was excused from participating in the pretrial and trial proceedings and that Fortis at the post-verdict phase would look only to Cantu to resolve its subrogation and reimbursement claims.

Cantu settled her claims with the defendants before trial for $1.445 million. Cantu and Fortis disputed what portion of the settlement proceeds, if any, should go to Fortis, and Cantu moved for summary judgment, arguing she had not been "made whole" by the settlement. Cantu's past medical expenses totaled $378,500 (of which Fortis claimed to have paid $247,534.14), and her summary judgment evidence included two "life care plans" estimating her future medical expenses at roughly $1.7 million and $5.3 million. She argued that her past and future medical expenses, exclusive of other amounts like pain and suffering, exceeded the amount of the settlement plus what Fortis had already paid. Cantu argued that the "made whole" doctrine precluded Fortis's contractual claims of subrogation and reimbursement. The trial court granted summary judgment in favor of Cantu, and a divided court of appeals affirmed.

II. Subrogation and the "Made Whole" Doctrine

This Court recognized the "made whole" doctrine twenty-seven years ago in *Ortiz v. Great Southern Fire & Casualty Insurance Co.* 597 S.W.2d 342 (Tex.1980). The Ortiz family had a fire insurance policy from Great Southern on their home, but not the contents. A fire caused damages of $4,000 to the home and $11,614 to personal property, and Great Southern paid $4,000 for home repairs. The Ortizes then sued Stacy-Mason, Inc., alleging that one of its employees negligently started the fire. Great Southern intervened, claiming a right of equitable subrogation. After the Ortizes settled with Stacy-Mason for $10,000, the trial court awarded, and the court of appeals affirmed, $4,000 of that settlement to Great Southern.

We reversed, holding, "An insurer is not entitled to subrogation if the insured's loss is in excess of the amounts recovered from the insurer and the third party causing the loss." We reasoned that one justification for equitable subrogation is to prevent the insured from receiving a double recovery, first from the insurer, then from the third party. We also recognized, however, that if the insured's total recovery is less than his or her losses, equity cuts the other way: "when 'either the insurer or the insured must to some extent go unpaid, the loss should be borne by the insurer for that is a risk the insured has paid it to assume.'" Because the settlement in *Ortiz* encompassed both covered and noncovered items, we remanded for a determination of how much of the $10,000 related to house damage.

Ortiz would govern if Fortis were merely asserting a claim for *equitable* subrogation. But Fortis is not citing principles of equity to recover its money; its policy with Cantu conferred on Fortis two separate *contractual* rights of recovery, one styled "subrogation" and one styled "reimbursement." The policy states:

> Subrogation Right. Upon payment of benefits, We will be subrogated to all rights of recovery a Covered Person may have against any person or organization. This includes but is not limited to recoveries against such third party, against any liability coverage for such third party or against automobile insurance in the event a claim is made under the uninsured or underinsured motorist coverages. Such right extends to the proceeds of any settlement or judgment; but is limited to the amount of benefits We have paid. You must 1) do nothing to prejudice any right of recovery; 2) execute and deliver any required instruments or papers; and 3) do whatever else is necessary to secure such rights.
>
> If We are precluded from exercising Our Subrogation Right, We may exercise Our Right of Reimbursement.
>
> Right of Reimbursement. If benefits are paid under this plan, and any Covered Person recovers against any person or organization by settlement, judgment or otherwise, We have a right to recover from that Covered Person an amount equal to the amount We have paid. This includes but is not limited to recoveries against such third party, against any liability coverage for such third party or against automobile insurance in the event a claim is made under the uninsured or underinsured motorist coverages.

Fortis argues that these provisions authorize recovery from Cantu's $1.445 million settlement with the defendants, and that neither provision is displaced by the "made whole" doctrine. We agree.

A. Equitable Subrogation v. Contractual Subrogation

Our *Ortiz* decision addressed the "made whole" doctrine in the context of equitable subrogation, but it did not discuss how the doctrine applies, if at all, to contractual subrogation. Other courts, however, have discussed whether the doctrine applies in the face of a contract that grants the insurer greater subrogation rights.

* * *

We do not disagree that equitable and contractual subrogation rest upon common principles, but contract rights generally arise from contract language; they do not derive their validity from principles of equity but directly from the parties' agreement. The policy declares the parties' rights and obligations, which are not generally supplanted by court-fashioned equitable rules that might apply, as a default gap-filler, in the absence of a valid contract. If subrogation arises independent of any contract, then an express subrogation agreement would be superfluous and serve only to acknowledge this preexisting right, a position we reject.

Contractual subrogation clauses express the parties' intent that reimbursement should be controlled by agreed contract terms rather than external rules imposed by the courts. The United States Supreme Court addressed this very point in a subrogation case decided shortly after we granted the instant case. In *Sereboff v. Mid Atlantic Medical Services, Inc.*, 547 U.S. 356, 126 S.Ct. 1869, 1872-73. (2006), the insurer Mid Atlantic was an ERISA plan fiduciary for the Sereboffs. When the Sereboffs were injured in an auto accident, Mid Atlantic paid the couple's expenses pursuant to the plan. When the Sereboffs settled the tort claims that arose from the accident, Mid Atlantic filed suit under ERISA to collect the medical expenses it had paid. Mid Atlantic sought reimbursement under an "Acts of Third Parties" provision in the plan.

The Sereboffs argued that the equitable defense of the "made whole" doctrine should apply, even though language in the plan document was to the contrary. The Court disagreed, comparing an action under the "Acts of Third Parties" provision to an action to enforce an equitable lien established by agreement. The Court refused to apply the "made whole" doctrine, deeming the Sereboffs' equitable defenses "beside the point" because Mid Atlantic's subrogation claims arose by written agreement.

* * *

The three varieties of subrogation — equitable, contractual, and statutory — represent three separate and distinct rights that, while related, are independent of each other. Independent, however, does not mean co-equal. We generally adhere to the maxim that "equity follows the law," which requires equitable doctrines to conform to contractual and statutory mandates, not the other way around. Where a valid contract prescribes particular remedies or imposes particular obligations, equity generally must yield unless the contract violates positive law or offends public policy.

This Court has "long recognized a strong public policy in favor of preserving the freedom of contract." *Lawrence v. CDB Servs., Inc.*, 44 S.W.3d 544, 553 (Tex.2001)(citing *Wood Motor Co. v. Nebel,* 150 Tex. 86, 238 S.W.2d 181, 185 (1951). And in *Texas Ass'n of Counties County Government Risk Management Pool v. Matagorda County,* 52 S.W.3d 128, 136 (Tex. 2000), we emphasized that insurers are well equipped to evaluate and reduce risk by, for example, "drafting policies to specifically provide for reimbursement." Fortis did exactly that, drafting two separate recovery provisions that replaced equitable rights with specific contractual rights. Neither subrogation nor reimbursement clauses violate Texas public policy. As we have stated, "'the State's public policy is reflected in its statutes,'" and Texas workers' compensation law specifically embraces an insurer's first-money right of subrogation, thus indicating no blanket legislative disfavor of such provisions. It is indeed difficult to declare something contrary to public policy when state law, both statutory and regulatory, actually suggests approval.

* * *

Given this insurance policy's plain language, we are loathe to judicially rewrite the parties' contract by engrafting extra-contractual standards that neither the Legislature nor the Texas Department of Insurance has thus far decided to promulgate. As we have said before, balancing dueling policy concerns is generally for non-judicial bodies, and it remains the "better policy for the contracts of insurance to be changed by the public body charged with their supervision, the State Board of Insurance, or by the Legislature, rather than for this Court" to contravene the express language of insurance contracts with equitable arguments. The contrary, however — replacing equitable protections with specific contract language — is not unknown in Texas law. Parties are thus free to negate the "made whole" doctrine contractually, and to do so before an event occurs that triggers medical benefits under the policy.

Leading insurance law treatises likewise recognize that specific policy terms can override equitable principles and that many jurisdictions, though not all, apply the "made whole" doctrine only in the absence of contrary reimbursement language in the contract. We agree with those courts holding that contract-based subrogation rights should be governed by the parties' express agreement and not invalidated by equitable considerations that might control by default in the absence of an agreement.

B. Subrogation Under Cantu's Insurance Contract With Fortis

We turn now to the specific language of the policy in issue, which defines the parties' rights and obligations. It contains a section called "Recovery," which includes a "Subrogation Right" provision and a separate (and broader) "Right of Reimbursement" provision. The former establishes a right of subrogation: "Upon payment of benefits, We [Fortis] will be subrogated to *all* rights of recovery a Covered Person [Cantu] may have against *any* person or organization." The provision continues: "Such right extends to the proceeds of *any* settlement or judgment; but is limited to the amount of benefits We have paid." Fortis thus retained an unfettered right to recover the proceeds from the settlement of the underlying suit, the only limitation being the *amount* of recovery — what Fortis had paid under the contract. Nowhere does this provision suggest that Cantu must first be "made whole" for Fortis to recover. This provision does not use the modifier "first money," but its meaning is not imprecise or ambiguous. The contract's specific language controls Fortis's right to subrogation, and the equitable defense of the "made whole" doctrine must give way.

Accordingly, we hold that Fortis is contractually entitled to recover from the $1.445 million settlement the total amount of benefits it paid to Cantu.

IV. Conclusion

The equitable "made whole" doctrine is inapplicable when the parties' agreed contract provides a clear and specific right of subrogation. Accordingly, while we affirm that part of the court of appeals' judgment regarding respondent Ford, we reverse and remand to the trial court for further proceedings consistent with this decision.

---

2. "Insurer owns insured's automobile under doctrine of subrogation"

Ysasaga v. Nationwide Mutual Insurance Company
2009 WL 471095
(Tex. App.-Dallas 2009)

This case arises out of a dispute over title to a vehicle following settlement of a claim for theft of the vehicle. After reporting that his vehicle had been stolen, Michael Ysasaga initiated an action against his insurer Nationwide Mutual Insurance Company (Nationwide) in Dallas County, Texas (the "Insurance Case"). The Insurance Case subsequently settled with payment to Ysasaga and a full release of all claims. Title to the vehicle was never formally transferred to Nationwide. After the settlement, the vehicle was recovered in Mexico and Nationwide took possession of it. Ysasaga then filed an action against Nationwide in Cameron County, Texas claiming the vehicle was his and demanding its return (the "Conversion Case"). Nationwide filed an action in Dallas County, Texas seeking a declaration that it owned the vehicle by virtue of payment of Ysasaga theft claim (the "Dec Action").

Following a successful venue challenge by Nationwide, the Conversion Case was transferred to Dallas County and consolidated with the Dec Action (the "Consolidated Case"). The trial court granted a traditional summary judgment in favor of Nationwide. Ysasaga and his wife Jill Ysasaga (together, "Ysasaga") now appeal the trial court's judgment in the Consolidated Case. In twelve issues that can be grouped in four main categories, Ysasaga contends: 1) the trial court had no jurisdiction to consider the Dec Action; 2) the consolidation of the Conversion Case and the Dec Action was improper; 3) the trial court erred in granting summary judgment; and (4) the Cameron County court erred in granting Nationwide's motion to transfer the Conversion Case to Dallas County. Concluding that appellant's arguments are without merit, we affirm the trial court's judgment.

I. BACKGROUND

On March 2, 2002, Ysasaga reported that his 2001 Chevrolet Corvette had been stolen in Dallas and filed an insurance claim with Nationwide. Ysasaga subsequently initiated the Insurance Case against Nationwide in Dallas County, Texas. In the Insurance Case, Ysasaga sought the recovery of damages arising out of the theft of the Corvette, including policy benefits and extra-contractual damages. Ysasaga claimed the Corvette was valued at $49, 200. On March 4, 2004, the parties entered into a settlement agreement. Pursuant to the settlement, Ysasaga signed a release of all claims "which arise out of the facts alleged and situation described in [the Insurance Case]." In consideration of the release, Nationwide paid Ysasaga $110,000. From these settlement proceeds, $34, 281.09 was paid to Ysasaga and First State Bank for the release of the lien on the vehicle and $75,718.91 was paid to Ysasaga and his attorneys. As provided in the release, the Insurance Case was dismissed. Despite the payment to Ysasaga and the release of the lien, title to the vehicle was never formally transferred to Nationwide.

In June 2005, the vehicle was recovered in Mexico. Nationwide informed Ysasaga of the vehicle's recovery and requested Ysasaga's endorsement of the certificate of title. In response, on August 9, 2005, Ysasaga initiated the Conversion Case in Cameron County and asserted Nationwide had converted the vehicle. Nationwide moved to transfer venue to Dallas County. On August 30, 2005, Nationwide initiated the Dec Action in Dallas County seeking a declaration that it owned the vehicle by virtue of having paid Ysasaga's theft claim. The Dec Action was abated on Ysasaga's plea because the Conversion Case had been filed first.

After a hearing, on October 3, 2006, the Cameron County court signed an order sustaining Nationwide's motion to transfer venue and directing that the Conversion Case be transferred to Dallas. Nationwide then moved for the Dallas court to lift the abatement of the Dec Action and to consolidate it with the Conversion Case. The motion was agreed to and granted by the court.

Following consolidation, Nationwide filed an amended motion for summary judgment. The motion asserted that the vehicle is the legal property of Nationwide pursuant to the settlement, payment of Ysasaga's theft claim, and payoff of the lien on the vehicle. Nationwide further argued that because it is the rightful owner of the vehicle, Ysasaga was not entitled to recover on his conversion claim. In response, Ysasaga filed a document entitled "Special Appearance, Collateral Attack on Transfer Order for Want of Jurisdiction, Motion to Transfer and Response to Nationwide's Motion for Summary Judgment." On June 19, 2007, the trial court granted Nationwide's amended motion for summary judgment declaring that Nationwide owned the vehicle and decreeing that Ysasaga take nothing on his claims against Nationwide. This appeal of the final judgment in the Consolidated Case followed.

II. DISCUSSION

* * *

With regard to declaratory relief, Ysasaga appears to argue the Dallas County court could not award declaratory relief because the Conversion Case was first filed in Cameron County. Again, this argument is premised on a faulty procedural assumption. The Conversion Case was not pending in Cameron County at the time the Dallas court awarded declaratory relief. Instead, the Conversion Case had been consolidated with the Dec Action and was part of the Consolidated Case in which the court awarded relief.

A declaratory judgment is a remedial action that determines the rights of the parties and affords relief from uncertainty with respect to rights, status, and legal relations. Tex. Civ. Prac. & Rem. Code Ann. § 37.002. Thus, "a court of record, within its jurisdiction has power to declare rights, status, and other legal relations whether or not further relief could be claimed." Tex. Civ. Prac. & Rem.Code Ann. § 37.003(a) A declaratory judgment is not available to settle legal disputes already pending before the court. *BHP Petroleum Co. v. Millard,* 800 S.W.2d 838, 841 (Tex.1990). This rule applies when a plaintiff's cause of action is mature and enforceable and the pending suit involves the same parties and the same issues involved in the declaratory judgment action.

Summary Judgment

In issues four, five, six, seven, and eight, Ysasaga argues the trial court erred in granting Nationwide's motion for traditional summary judgment. The standard for reviewing a traditional motion for summary judgment is well-established. *See Sysco Food Servs. v. Trapnell,* 890 S.W.2d 796, 800 (Tex.1994); *Nixon v. Mr. Prop. Mgmt. Co.,* 690 S.W.2d 546, 548-49 (Tex.1985). We review a summary judgment de novo to determine whether a party's right to prevail is established as a matter of law. *Dickey v. Club Corp.,* 12 S.W.3d 172, 175 (Tex.App.-Dallas 2000, pet. denied). A party moving for traditional summary judgment is charged with the burden to establish that there are no genuine issues of material fact and it is entitled to judgment as a matter of law. Tex.R. Civ. P. 166a(c); *M.D. Anderson Hosp. & Tumor Inst. v. Willrich,* 28 S.W.3d 22, 23 (Tex.2000) (per curium). A matter is conclusively established if ordinary minds could not differ as to the conclusion to be drawn from the evidence. *Triton Oil & Gas Corp. v. Marine Contractors & Supply, Inc.,* 644 S.W.2d 443, 446 (Tex.1982)

In its motion for summary judgment, Nationwide argued that it acquired Ysasaga's right to possession by paying Ysasaga's theft claim and compensating him for the loss of the vehicle. The right to possession was premised on the doctrines of contractual and equitable subrogation. Nationwide further argued that because it is the rightful owner of the vehicle, Ysasaga's conversion claim fails as a matter of law. The summary judgment evidence adduced by Nationwide included a copy of the insurance policy, the release, and an affidavit on attorney's fees. Nationwide's evidence also included a copy of Ysasaga's petition in the Insurance Case which declared the vehicle was valued at $49,200.

Ysasaga's evidence included his unsworn response to Nationwide's request for disclosure in the Insurance Case, his affidavit, and a trial report of a substantial jury verdict obtained by other counsel in an unrelated bad faith case. The trial court's judgment is silent as to whether the granting of the summary judgment was based on contractual or equitable subrogation. Accordingly, we will uphold the court's decision if it is correct under any theory advanced in the motion. *See Cincinnati Life Ins. Co. v. Cates,* 927 S.W.2d 623, 626 (Tex.1996)

A. The Effect of The Insurance Policy

In his fifth issue, Ysasaga contends the trial court erred by giving effect to the underlying insurance policy because the release extinguished all subrogation rights under the policy. Neither party claims the release is ambiguous. Therefore, we examine the release to ascertain the intent of the parties as expressed in the four corners of the document. Ysasaga directs our attention to the release generally, but fails to identify specific language to support his contention. Having reviewed the release in its entirety, we conclude there is no indication the parties intended that it replace the insurance contract. Instead, the release is a negotiated settlement of claims asserted in the Insurance Case that bars related future claims in exchange for monetary consideration.

The effect of the insurance policy is significant because it is through the policy that Nationwide obtained its ownership rights by application of the principle of subrogation. Nationwide's summary judgment was based on two types of subrogation-equitable and contractual. Contractual (or conventional) subrogation is created by an agreement or contract that grants the right in exchange for payment of a loss. Equitable (or legal) subrogation does not depend on contract but arises in every instance in which one person, not acting voluntarily, has paid a debt for which another was primarily liable and which in equity should have been paid by the latter. *See Mid-Continent Ins. Co. v. Liberty Mut. Ins. Co.,* 236 S.W.3d 765, 744 (Tex.2007). Contractual subrogation clauses express the parties' intent that reimbursement should be controlled by agreed contract terms rather than external rules imposed by the courts. *Fortis Benefits v. Cantu,* 234 S.W.2d 642, 647-48 (Tex.2007).

Here, the insurance policy provides a right of subrogation. The policy states:

> If we make a payment under this policy and the person to or for whom payment was made has a right to recover damages from another, we shall be subrogated to that right ...If we make a payment under this policy and the person to or for whom payment is made recovers damages from another, that person shall: 1) Hold in trust for us the proceeds of the recovery; and 2) Reimburse us to the extent of our payment.

The policy further provides that Nationwide's limit of liability for theft loss will be the lesser of the: 1) Actual cash value of the stolen or damaged property; 2) Amount necessary to repair or replace the property with other of like kind or quality; or 3) Amount stated in the declaration of the policy.

The policy also states that Nationwide has the option to either return the property to the insured or keep all or part of the property.

Nationwide's summary judgment evidence established that the value of the vehicle was $49,200 and Nationwide paid Ysasaga $110,000 in exchange for which Ysasaga fully released his claim for benefits under the policy. Based on the unambiguous language of the policy, we conclude Nationwide acquired Ysasaga's ownership rights in the vehicle when this payment was made.

A plaintiff in a conversion case must show ownership, possession or entitlement to possession of personal property. Once Nationwide established it was entitled to ownership of the vehicle, Ysasaga could not recover on his conversion claim as a matter of law.

Ysasaga also contends the trial court failed to recognize fact issues concerning whether he received full value for the vehicle. We construe this argument to suggest the trial court should have applied the "made-whole" doctrine. Under this principle, an insurer is not entitled to subrogation if the loss suffered by the insured is greater than the combined amount recovered from the insurer and the tortfeaser. In other words, the insurer's right of subrogation may not be exercised until the insured is made whole. The "made-whole" doctrine is a rule of equity.

However, these equitable considerations are not implicated when the right to subrogation arises by contract. When a contract provides for subrogation, the specific language of the contract controls and the equitable defense of the "made whole" doctrine must give way. This result is based on the principle that "contract-based subrogation rights should be governed by the parties' express agreement and not invalidated by equitable considerations that might control by default in the absence of an agreement." *Fortis,* 234 S.W.3d at 650.

We have determined Nationwide's right to subrogation was defined by the policy; therefore, equitable subrogation and the "made-whole" doctrine have no application here. Because there was no material fact issue concerning Nationwide's ownership of the vehicle arising from its contractual right to subrogation, the trial court did not err when it granted summary judgment. Ysasaga's fifth issue is overruled.

* * *

D. Equitable Subrogation

In his sixth issue, Ysasaga maintains the trial court erred because it shifted the summary judgment burden to the non-movant. Although Ysasaga fails to demonstrate how the burden allegedly shifted, the essence of his argument appears to be based on the court's alleged misapplication of the "made-whole" doctrine. As we have stated, the "made-whole" doctrine is only applicable in the context of equitable subrogation. *See Fortis,* 234 S.W.3d at 651.

In his eighth issue, Ysasaga complains that the trial court failed to apply the principles of equity when it applied the doctrine of equitable subrogation. We have concluded Nationwide was contractually entitled to ownership of the vehicle by virtue of having paid Ysasaga's theft claim, and the trial court did not err in its determination that Nationwide was entitled to judgment as a matter of law. Our resolution of these issues obviates the need to address the remaining issues pertaining to equitable subrogation. Ysasaga's sixth and eighth issues are overruled.

Having resolved all of Ysasaga's issues against him, we affirm the judgment of the trial court.

NOTES & QUESTIONS

1) In *Fortis*, the Texas Supreme reiterated: "This Court has 'long recognized a strong public policy in favor of preserving the freedom of contract." Was the contract in *Fortis* an "arms-length," freely negotiated contract?

2) Under the adhesion doctrine, Texas courts must construe the language in an adhesion contract in favor of the insured. Yet, in *Fortis*, the Supreme Court applied the plain-meaning doctrine to interpret the subrogation provision in favor of the insurer. Why? Was the contract in *Fortis* an adhesion contract?

3) In *Ysasaga,* the appeals court found the following: "*The policy also states that Nationwide has the option to either return the property to the insured or keep all or part of the property.*" How did Nationwide secure that option?

4) There are two ways to view an option. There are option contracts. Traditional rules of contract govern option contracts. In addition, an option is a right. However, before one secures an option, he must pay for it. There must be consideration. Otherwise, the alleged option is an unenforceable gift. Is there any evidence of an option contract or a fully negotiated option clause in *Ysasaga?* Is there any evidence that Nationwide paid a separate consideration for that right—for that option?

APPENDIX

Appendix

A. List of Relevant Texas Statutes & DTPA Tie-In Statutes

1. Business Opportunity Act — Tex. Bus. & Com. Code § 41.001 et seq.
2. Cancellation of Certain Consumer Transactions — Tex. Bus. & Com. Code §§ 39.001 - 39.009
3. Career Counseling Services Act — Tex. Occ. Code § 2502.001 et seq.
4. Certain Sales of Homestead — Tex. Prop. Code §41.001 et seq.
5. Credit Services Organizations — Tex. Fin. Code § 393.001 et seq.
6. Coastal Lands Management Act of 1973 — Tex. Nat. Res. Code § 33.001 et seq.
7. Consumer Credit Commissioner — Tex. Finance Code §§ 14.001 - 14.303
8. Contest and Giveaway Act — Tex. Bus. & Com. Code § 40.001 et seq.
9. Deceptive Trade Practices—"Current Version" — Tex. Bus. & Com. Code §§ 17.01 - 17.885
10. Deceptive Trade Practices Act— "Pre-1995 Version" — Tex. Bus. & Com. Code §§ 17.41 - 17.63
11. Disclosure to Purchaser of Property — Tex. Nat. Res. Code § 61.001 et seq.
12. Debt Collection Practices Act — Tex. Finance Code §§ 392.001 - 392.404
13. Fraud in Real Estate and Stock Transactions — Tex. Bus. & Com. Code § 27.01 - 27.02
14. Health Spa Act — Tex. Occ. Code § 702.001 et seq.
15. Health Spa Regulations — Tex. Administrative Code §§ 102.1 - 102.50
16. Home Improvement Contracts — Tex. Prop. Code § 41.001 et seq.
17. Home Solicitation Act — Tex. Bus. & Com. Code § 39.001 et seq.
18. Licensing of Speech-Language Pathologists & Audiologists — Tex. Occ. Code § 401.001 et seq.
19. Medical Liability, Arbitration Agreements — Tex. Civ. Prac. & Rem. Code § 39.001 et seq.
20. Personal Employment Services — Tex. Occ. Code § 2501.001 et seq.
21. Private Child Support Enforcement Agencies — Tex. Fin. Code § 396.001 et seq.
22. Prompt Payment of Insurance Claims — Tex. Ins. Code §§ 542.051 - 542.061
23. Regulation of Consumer Credit Reporting Agencies — Tex. Bus. & Com. Code, Chapter 20, §§ 542.001-542.014
24. Regulation of Invention Development — Tex. Rev. Civ. Stat. § 9020
25. Removal of Unauthorized Vehicles on Parking Facility or Public Roadway — Tex. Trans. Code § 684.001 et seq.
26. Rental-Purchase Agreements — Tex. Bus. & Com. Code § 35.71 et seq.

27. Representation of Attorney — Tex. Gov't Code § 406.001 et seq.
28. Residential Contractors' Liability Act — Tex. Property Code §§ 27.001 - 27.007
29. Residential Service Company Act — Tex. Occ. Code § 1303.001 et seq.
30. Sales of Certain Fuel Mixtures — Tex. Rev. Civ. Stat. § 8614
31. Self-Storage Facility Liens — Tex. Prop. Code § 59.001 et seq.
32. Talent Agencies Regulation Act — Tex. Occ. Code § 2105.001 et seq.
33. Texas Credit Title, Regulation of Interest, Loans, and Financial Transactions — Tex. Finance Code §§ 301.001 - 350.004
34. Texas Lemon Law — Tex. Occ. Code §§ 2301.204, 2301.601-.613
35. Texas Manufactured Housing Standards Act — Tex. Occ. Code § 1201.001 et seq.
36. Texas Membership Camping & Resort Act — Tex. Prop. Code § 222.001 et seq.
37. Texas Motor Vehicle Commission Code — Tex. Occ. Code §§2301.204, 2301.601 et seq.
38. Texas Residential Construction Commission Act — Tex. Property Code §§ 401.001 - 438.001
39. Texas Optometry Act — Tex. Occ. Code § 351.001 et seq.
40. Texas Timeshare Act — Tex. Prop. Code § 221.001 et seq.
41. Treatment Facilities Marketing Practices Act — Tex. Health & Safety Code § 164.001 et seq.
42. Unfair Methods of Competition and Unfair or Deceptive Acts or Practices — Tex. Ins. Code §§ 541.008 - 541.061
43. Unfair Claim Settlement Practices Act — Tex. Ins. Code §§ 542.001 - 542.014
44. Unfair Methods & Practices By Financial Institutions — Tex. Ins. Code §§ 556.001 - 556.154
45. Warranty Provisions — Tex. Bus. & Com. Code §§ 2.301 - 2.725

B. List of Pertinent Federal Statutes

1. Clayton Act — 15 U.S.C. § 18
2. Fair Credit Billing Act — 15 U.S.C. §§ 1666 - 1666j
3. Fair Debt Collection Practices Act — 15 U.S.C. §§ 1692 - 1692o
4. Federal Arbitration Act — 9 U.S.C. §§ 1 - 16
5. Federal Trade Commission Act — 15 U.S.C. § 45
6. Magnuson-Moss Warranty Act — 15 U.S.C. §§ 2301 - 2312
7. McCarran-Ferguson Act — 15 U.S.C. § 1011 et seq.
8. Sherman Act, § 1, 15 U.S.C.A. § 1

Acknowledgments

David A. Fischer and Robert H. Jerry, II, Excerpts from "Teaching Torts Without Insurance: A Second-Best Solution," 45 *St. Louis U. L.J.* 857, 2001, pp. 857–858, 894–896. Permission to reprint granted by the publisher.

Stephen E. McConnico, Excerpt from "Unresolved Problems In Texas Legal Malpractice Law," 36 *St. Mary's L.J.* 989, 2005, pp. 1018–1021. Permission to reprint granted by the publisher.

James W. Paulsen, Excerpts from "Lenders and the Texas DTPA: A Step Back From the Brink," 48 *Southern Methodist University Law Review* 487, 1995, pp. 490–493, 501–508.

Robert Carl Jones, Excerpts from "Consumer protection — Breach of Warranty — Merger Doctrine No Defense to Deceptive Trade Practices Suit for Breach of Express Warranty — Alvarado v. Bolton, 749 S.W. 2d47 (Tex. 1988)," 20 *St. Mary's L.J.* 689, 1989, pp. 695–696. Permission to reprint granted by the publisher.

David Dow and Craig Smyser, Excerpt from "Contract Law," *Interpretation of Contract*, § 8.9 (Vol. 49, Texas Practice Series). West/Thomson/Reuters Publishers, 2005–2008, p. 350. Permission to reprint granted by the publisher.

Willy E. Rice, Excerpts from "Federal Courts and the Regulation of the Insurance Industry: An Empirical and Historical Analysis of Courts' Ineffectual Attempts to Harmonize Federal Antitrust, Arbitration, and Insolvency Statutes with the McCarran-Ferguson Act — 1941–1993," 43 *Catholic University Law Review* 399, 1994, pp. 400–401, 411–413. Permission to reprint granted by the author.

Willy E. Rice, Excerpt from "Insurance Contracts and Judicial Decisions Over Whether Insurers Must Defend Insureds Who Violate Constitutional And Civil Rights: An Historical And Empirical Review of Federal and State Court Declaratory Judgments 1900–2000," 35 *Tort & Ins. L.J.* 995, 2000, pp. 1021–1022. Permission to reprint granted by the author.

Willy E. Rice, Excerpt from "Fifth Circuit Survey June 2002-May 2003 Survey Article Insurance Decisions — A Survey and An Empirical Analysis," 35 *Texas Tech Law Review* 947, 2004, pp. 1018–1019. Permission to reprint granted by the author.

Willy E. Rice, Excerpts from "Commercial Terrorism from the Transatlantic Slave Trade to the World Trade Center Disaster: Are Insurance Companies & Judges "Aiders And Abettors" of Terror? — A Critical Analysis of American and British Court" Declaratory And Equitable Actions, 1654–2002,"

6 *The Scholar: St. Mary's Law Review on Minority Issues* 1, 2003, pp. 51–52, 70–71. Permission to reprint granted by the author.

Willy E. Rice, Excerpt from "The Court of Appeals for the Fifth Circuit: A Legal Analysis and Statistical Review of 2005–2006 Insurance Decisions," 39 *Texas Tech Law Review* 843, 2007, pp. 869–879. Permission to reprint granted by the author.

Willy E. Rice, Excerpt from "Judicial Bias, The Insurance Industry and Consumer Protection: An Empirical Analysis of State Supreme Courts' Bad-Faith, Breach-of-Contract, Breach-of-Covenant-of-Good-Faith and Excess-Judgment Decisions, 1900–1991," 41 *Catholic University Law Review* 325, 1992, pp. 334–340. Permission to reprint granted by the author.

Willy E. Rice, Excerpt from "Insurance Contracts and Judicial Discord over Whether Liability Insurers Must Defend Insureds' Allegedly Intentional and Immoral Conduct: A Historical and Empirical Review of Federal and State Courts' Declaratory Judgments 1900–1997," 47 *American University Law Review* 1131, 1998, pp. 1145–1147. Permission to reprint granted by the author.

Willy E. Rice, "Insurance Contracts and Judicial Discord over Whether Liability Insurers Must Defend Insureds' Allegedly Intentional and Immoral Conduct: A Historical and Empirical Review of Federal and State Courts' Declaratory Judgments 1900–1997," 47 *American University Law Review* 1131, 1998, pp. 1149–1156. Permission to reprint granted by the author.

All cases reprinted from Westlaw with permission.

ISBN 978-1-60927-274-6
90000
9 781609 272746
SKU 80081-2